INTROD

Social

EDITION

Psychology

About the artist

TANA POWELL

Born in 1956 and educated in Toronto, Canada, Tana Powell has earned a reputation as an award winning illustrator. Her works are commission pieces, utilised in the editorial, advertising, packaging, corporate, educational and entertainment fields.

Although still a Canadian citizen, Tana Powell currently resides in San Francisco, California, and has lived along the California coastline for the last 23 years, residing in San Francisco, Berkeley, Santa Barbara and San Diego. Having travelled extensively throughout the globe Tana regularly spends time abroad each year and also co-pilots to her second home in Nevada, Lantana Ranch, where she spends much of her time developing the working ranch.

Tana freely moves and selects among several different media to express her art, utilising the chosen media as a means to communicate and meet the needs of her wide base of clients. Her art is influenced by her life, by the world of her own experiences. Her work has varied from art directing a news/art department for a large metropolitan newspaper in the East Bay, California, and design directing a city magazine in San Diego, California, to working as a corporate art consultant.

Educated at York University, Ontario, Canada, Tana Powell graduated with a Specialized Honors, Bachelor of Fine Art degree, specialising in the Visual Arts with a major in printmaking. After receiving her Specialized Honors BFA, Tana continued to further enhance her education, taking postgraduate classes at the University of California, Santa Barbara; the Ontario College of Art, Toronto, Canada, and the California College of Arts, California.

Tana Powell has worked as a designer, illustrator, art director, design director and art consultant. Having studied fine art painting for years, fine art being a passion, Tana has travelled full circle to ultimately return to painting as an illustrator.

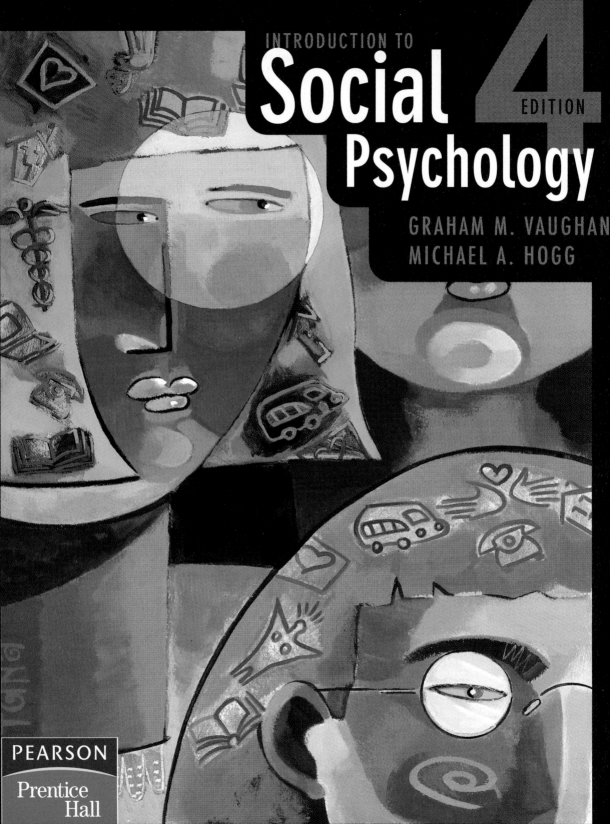

INTRODUCTION TO
Social
Psychology

4 EDITION

GRAHAM M. VAUGHAN
MICHAEL A. HOGG

PEARSON

Prentice
Hall

Pearson Education Australia
Unit 4, Level 2
14 Aquatic Drive
Frenchs Forest NSW 2086

www.pearsoned.com.au

Senior Acquisitions Editor: Nicole Meehan
Senior Project Editor: Carolyn Robson
Senior Editorial Coordinator: Jill Gillies
Copy Editor: Jo Rudd
Proofreader: Ron Buck
Permissions Coordinator: Louise Burke
Cover and internal design by designBITE
Cover painting © 1996 Tana Powell c/- theispot.com <www.theispot.com/artist/tpowell>
Typeset by Midland Typesetters, Maryborough, Vic.

Printed in China

1 2 3 4 5 09 08 07 06 05

National Library of Australia
Cataloguing-in-Publication Data

Vaughan, Graham M. (Graham Michael).
Introduction to social psychology.

    4th ed.
    Bibliography.
    Includes index.
    ISBN 1 74103 230 X.

    1. Social psychology. I. Hogg, Michael A. II. Title.

302

An imprint of Pearson Education Australia (a division of Pearson Australia Group Pty Ltd)

Contents

CHAPTER FIFTEEN
Language and communication 384

CHAPTER SIXTEEN
Culture 410

Preface

This is the fourth edition of our *Introduction to Social Psychology*. The original idea for an Australasian social psychology text was born at the annual conference of Australasian social psychologists in Ballarat, Victoria, in April 1991. We felt there was an urgent need for a comprehensive introductory social psychology text written specifically for universities in Australia and New Zealand—a text that captured the scope and detail of contemporary social psychology as an international enterprise, but at the same time dealt with the subject in a way that was relevant to university teaching and social psychology research in Australia and New Zealand.

The first edition was published early in 1995 and launched at a fine reception, sponsored by Prentice Hall Australia, in Hobart at the inaugural meeting of the Society of Australasian Social Psychologists. The first edition was enormously successful—not only did it receive an award for excellence in the tertiary educational publishing sector, but it was quickly adopted and widely used at universities in Australia and New Zealand. We felt vindicated.

Subsequent editions followed fast upon earlier editions—no sooner did one edition appear in bookshops than, it seemed, we were hard at work preparing the next. The second edition was published early in 1998 and publicly launched in Christchurch at the annual meeting of the Society of Australasian Social Psychologists. This edition was a relatively modest revision aimed primarily at improving layout and presentation, though the text and coverage were thoroughly updated, and we raised the profile of some applied topics in social psychology.

The third edition was published at the beginning of 2002 and launched in Adelaide at the annual meeting of the Society of Australasian Social Psychologists. It was shortlisted for an award for excellence in tertiary education publishing. The third edition represented a major revision to accommodate significant changes in the field since the first edition. The structure and approach remained the same but some chapters were dropped, some entirely rewritten, others amalgamated, and some entirely new chapters written. In addition, the text was updated and the layout and presentation significantly improved.

After the dramatic changes for the third edition, this fourth edition is a more modest revision aimed mainly at updating the field and improving on explication, pedagogy, and layout and presentation. Some sections are more heavily revised than others, there are some changed figures and features, and there are some new sections within chapters—but there are no dramatic changes in content. We sought feedback on the third edition from as many of our colleagues and graduate and undergraduate students as we could find who had used the text as teacher, tutor, or student. We are extremely grateful for this invaluable feedback—we see our text as a partnership between us as authors, and all those who use the book in various different capacities.

We are also indebted to our absolutely wonderful publishing team at Pearson Education in Sydney—in particular to our Senior Acquisitions Editor Nicole Meehan, Senior Editorial Coordinator Jill Gillies, Senior Project Editor Carolyn Robson, Supplements Editor Marji Backer, Copy Editor Jo Rudd and Proofreader Ron Buck. We were sustained and energised by their enthusiasm, good humour, encouragement and wisdom and kept on our toes by their timeline prompts, excellent editing and breathtaking efficiency.

Planning for this fourth edition was accomplished in Auckland in November 2002. Mike visited Graham for a few days, in absolutely stunning late-spring weather, and we did most of the planning sitting in cafés and restaurants around the edge of Auckland's beautiful harbour. The Americas' Cup was under way and we felt inspired by the lovely yachts racing around the harbour. Of course, inspirational planning is one thing—but, sadly, at some point real work needs to be done. The actual writing was done later in 2003 and early in 2004 when Mike was in Santa Barbara and Graham in Auckland.

Writing a big book like this is a courageous undertaking. There is a great deal of drama and even more hard slog. We'd like to thank all the people around us, our family, friends and colleagues, for their patience and understanding. Amanda Willetts and Ulrike Andres gave us great help with researching materials, and Peter Smith of Sussex University made excellent suggestions for sections of the text. A very special thanks goes to Jan Vaughan and to Alison.

HOW TO USE THIS BOOK

This fourth edition is an up-to-date and comprehensive coverage of social psychology as an international scientific enterprise. In recognition of the new higher education environment in which students need to pursue independent study to supplement formal classes, we provide a full, annotated list of further reading at the end of each chapter.

At the end of Chapter 1 we also advise on important primary and review sources for finding out more about specific topics in social psychology. The colour, format, *chapter topics*, *focus questions* and *links* sections at the beginning and end of each chapter have all been crafted with the student in mind (see the box 'Explanation of features within each chapter' over the page).

There is an invaluable companion to this text—a detailed study guide prepared by Katy White at Queensland University of Technology, which has also been completely rewritten. As well, there is an updated companion website for students to test their knowledge and to extend their reading via web links. For lecturers and teaching assistants, there is an instructor's manual full of good ideas for classes and assessment that can be obtained from Pearson Education.

As with the earlier editions, the book has a logical structure, with earlier chapters leading into later ones—however, it is not essential to read the book from beginning to end. The chapters are cross-referenced so that, with a few exceptions, chapters or groups of chapters can be read independently in almost any order.

Here are some tips about the sequence in which you read this book:

- Chapter 1 describes the structure of the book, why we decided to write it, and how it should be read—it is worthwhile reading the last section of Chapter 1 before starting later chapters. Chapter 1 also defines social psychology—its aims, methods and history.
- When exploring the topic of the self, read Chapter 4 and then culture's role in Chapter 16.
- In dealing with attitudes, read Chapter 5 before tackling Chapter 6.
- When you treat groups, read Chapter 8 before Chapter 9.
- In examining prejudice and discrimination between groups, read Chapter 10 before Chapter 11.

Some of this material in this book will benefit from a second reading—after you have studied other chapters and become familiar with the theories, topics and issues of social psychology.

The primary target of our book is the student, although we hope it may be of some help to the teacher, and even to the researcher, as well. We will be grateful to any of you who take the time to share your reactions with us.

Listed in the following table are the several domains or applied topics that have attracted the attention of social psychologists to a considerable degree in recent years. We have noted the chapters in this edition that are relevant to each domain. Sometimes, an application is by way of an example or a reference, but at times is an extended discussion, a text box or figure.

Graham Vaughan, Auckland
Michael Hogg, Brisbane
August 2004

APPLIED TOPICS	RELEVANT CHAPTERS
Gender and sex differences	1, 2, 3, 6, 7, 10, 12, 13, 14 and 15.
Health	3, 4, 5, 6, 9, 10, 11,12 and 14.
Social development	1, 3, 5, 9, 10, 11, 12, 13, 14 and 15.
Ethnicity	3, 4, 10 and 11.
Organisational	1, 7, 8, 9, 10, 11 and 12.
Mass media	2, 6 and 12.
Sport	1, 4, 8, 9 and 12.
Criminal justice	1, 2, 8, 9 and 12.

EXPLANATION OF FEATURES WITHIN EACH CHAPTER

This chapter discusses	This section lists the chapter's key issues.
Focus questions	These are either prompts or hypothetical scenarios relating to the chapter's content. They are also cross-referenced to specific portions of a chapter.
A classic in social psychology	These are studies or research programs that, in their time, helped define fields in social psychology.
Summary	The key issues are summed up at the end of each chapter.
Links	Selected issues in the left-hand column are connected to issues in other chapters, shown in the right-hand column. These links are not necessarily obvious.
Key terms	Important words are emboldened within each chapter. They are also listed in alphabetical order at the end of the chapter, and at the back of the book, in the glossary, with full definitions.
Further reading	There is a list of further reading relating to the content of the chapter, with a brief explanation of the relevance of each work.
Box	Boxed features within each chapter highlight critical issues, research findings and real life applications.

Features in this book

A classic in social psychology. These are studies or research programs that, in their time, helped define fields in social psychology.

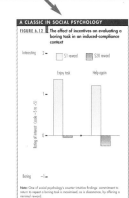

A CLASSIC IN SOCIAL PSYCHOLOGY

FIGURE 6.12 The effect of incentives on evaluating a boring task in an induced-compliance context

FIGURE 6.13 Degree of liking fried grasshoppers as food by military cadets in relation to the interpersonal style of an officer

A CLASSIC IN SOCIAL PSYCHOLOGY

BOX 6.4 To know grasshoppers is to love them

This chapter discusses. This section lists the chapter's key issues.

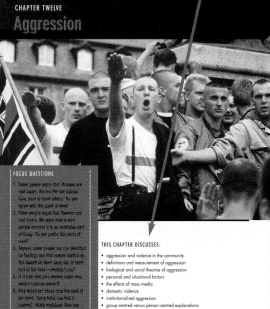

CHAPTER TWELVE

Aggression

FOCUS QUESTIONS

THIS CHAPTER DISCUSSES:

- aggression and violence in the community
- definitions and measurement of aggression
- biological and social theories of aggression
- personal and situational factors
- the effects of mass media
- domestic violence
- institutionalised aggression
- group-centred versus person-centred explanations
- reducing aggression at interpersonal and intergroup levels.

Focus questions. These are either prompts or hypothetical scenarios relating to the chapter's content. They are also cross-referenced to specific portions of a chapter.

Box. Boxed features within each chapter highlight critical issues, research findings and real life applications.

Companion website. An updated companion website tests students' knowledge and extends their reading via web links

Summary. The key issues are summed up at the end of each chapter.

Links. Selected issues in the left-hand column are connected to issues in other chapters, shown in the right-hand column. These links are not necessarily obvious.

Key terms. Important words are emboldened within each chapter. They are also listed in alphabetical order at the end of the chapter, and at the back of the book, in the glossary, with full definitions.

Further reading. There is a list of further reading relating to the content of the chapter, with a brief explanation of the relevance of each work.

About the authors

GRAHAM VAUGHAN, a Professor of Psychology, served as Head of the Department of Psychology for 12 years at the University of Auckland. He was a student at three New Zealand universities, completing a BA at Auckland, an MA at the University of Canterbury and a PhD at the Victoria University of Wellington. He was a Fulbright Fellow and visiting Assistant Professor at the University of Illinois at Champaign-Urbana in 1966; a Visiting Lecturer in 1973 and a Ford Foundation Fellow in 1975 at the University of Bristol; a visiting Associate Professor at Princeton University in 1981; a visiting Directeur d'Etudes at the Maison des Science de l'Homme, Paris, in 1981; and a visiting Senior Fellow at the National University of Singapore in 1988. In 1996 he was a visiting Professor at the University of Queensland and visiting Fellow at Churchill College, Cambridge.

He has served as Editor of the *New Zealand Journal of Psychology,* and on the Board of Editors of several other journals. He has been a reviewer for a number of international journals and for various research funding agencies in Australia, New Zealand and Hong Kong. His primary areas of interest in social psychology include attitudes and attitude development, group processes and intergroup relations, ethnic relations and identity, and the history of social psychology. A former President of the New Zealand Psychological Society, he was selected by the Society for a Golden Jubilee Special Award in 1997 and elected an Honorary Fellow in 2002. He was President of the Society of Australasian Social Psychologists during 1999–2001. He edited and contributed to a book, *Racial Issues in New Zealand* (1972), the first to deal with ethnic relations in that country. He is the author of numerous journal articles and book chapters. In 1995, he and Michael Hogg wrote the first edition of *Introduction to Social Psychology,* and second and third editions in 1998 and 2002. In the same years they published special European editions of the book.

MICHAEL HOGG is Professor of Social Psychology and an Australian Research Council Professorial Fellow at the University of Queensland. He is also a Fellow of the Academy of the Social Sciences in Australia, a Fellow of the Society for the Psychological Study of Social Issues, and an Honorary Visiting Professor at the University of California, Santa Barbara. He received his BSc from the University of Birmingham, and his PhD from the University of Bristol where he lectured for three years. In 1985 he took up a postdoctoral fellowship at Macquarie University and, in 1986, moved to a lectureship and then senior lectureship at Melbourne University. In 1991 he moved to the University of Queensland where he became Reader in 1992 and Professor in 1997. He has also held honorary visiting appointments at the University of California, Los Angeles (1990), the University of California, Santa Cruz (1994) and the City University Hong Kong (2001). From 1997 to 1998 he was seconded to Princeton University as Professor of Social Psychology, and from 2000 to 2002 he was Associate Dean, Research, for the Faculty of Social and Behavioural Sciences at the University of Queensland.

His research interests are intergroup relations, group processes, self-concept and social cognition, and he has been involved for almost 25 years in the development of the social identity approach in social psychology. In addition to publishing over 200 scientific books, chapters and articles, he is foundation editor with Dominic Abrams of the journal *Group Processes and Intergroup Relations* and has been, or currently is, an editorial board member of the *Journal of Personality and Social Psychology, Personality and Social Psychology Bulletin,* the *European Review of Social Psychology,* the *British Journal of Social Psychology, Group Dynamics: Theory, Research, and Practice,* and the *Asian Journal of Social Psychology.* He is also editor of the Sage series *Essential Texts in Social Psychology,* and has served as a guest editor for *Social Psychology Quarterly* and the *British Journal of Social Psychology.* Two of his books have become citation classics: *Rediscovering the Social Group: A Self-Categorization Theory* (1987) with John Turner and others, and *Social Identifications: A Social Psychology of Intergroup Relations and Group Processes* (1988) with Dominic Abrams. His most recent other books include *Blackwell Handbook of Social Psychology: Group Processes* (2001) with Scott Tindale; *Intergroup Relations: Essential Readings* (2001) with Dominic Abrams; *The Sage Handbook of Social Psychology* (2003) with Joel Cooper; and *Leadership and Power: Identity Processes in Groups and Organizations* (2004) with Daan van Knippenberg.

Introducing social psychology

THIS CHAPTER DISCUSSES:

- social psychology and its relation to other disciplines
- its use of both the scientific and other empirical methods
- using statistics in data analysis and the use of qualitative methods
- ethical issues for researchers
- differing theoretical approaches
- criticisms often levelled against social psychology
- the relevance of the history of the discipline
- social psychology in Australia and New Zealand.

FOCUS QUESTION

A man enters a café, greets with a kiss on each cheek a young woman waiting for him at a table, and sits opposite her. He orders them both an espresso and subsequently dominates the conversation about a recently released movie. How would a social psychologist go about explaining this rather ordinary event? How would we assess whether the explanation was correct?

What is social psychology?

Social psychology has been defined as 'the scientific investigation of how the thoughts, feelings and behaviours of individuals are influenced by the actual, imagined or implied presence of others' (e.g. Allport, 1935). But what does this mean? What do social psychologists actually do, how do they do it and what do they study?

Social psychologists are interested in explaining human behaviour, and generally do not study animals. Some general principles of social psychology may be applicable to animals, and research on animals may provide evidence for processes that generalise to people (e.g. social facilitation—see Chapter 8). Furthermore, certain principles of social behaviour may be general enough to apply to humans and, for instance, other primates (e.g. Hinde, 1982). As a rule, however, social psychologists believe that the study of animals does not take us very far in explaining human social behaviour, unless we are interested in its evolutionary origins (e.g. Buss & Kenrick, 1998).

Social psychologists study **behaviour** because behaviour can be observed and measured. However, behaviour refers not only to gross motor activities (such as running, kissing, jumping) but also to more subtle actions such as a raised eyebrow or a smile and, of course, to what we say and what we write. In this sense, behaviour is publicly verifiable. However, the meaning attached to behaviour is a matter of theoretical perspective, cultural background or personal interpretation.

Social psychologists are interested in behaviour, but they are also interested in feelings, thoughts, beliefs, attitudes, intentions and goals. These are not directly observable, but can, with varying degrees of certainty, be inferred from behaviour. Unobservable processes are important because they may directly influence overt behaviour—a crucial point in understanding, for example, the relationship between attitudes and behaviour (see Chapter 5). Unobservable processes are also the psychological dimension of social behaviour, as they occur within the human brain. However, social psychologists almost always want to go one step beyond relating social behaviour to underlying psychological processes. They often attempt to relate psychological aspects of social behaviour to even more fundamental cognitive processes and structures (see Chapter 2).

What makes social psychology *social* is that it deals with how people are affected by other people who are actually physically present (e.g. an audience—see Chapter 8) or who are imagined to be present (e.g. anticipating performing in front of an audience), or even whose presence is implied. This last influence is more complex and addresses the fundamentally social nature of our experiences as humans. For instance, we tend to think in words, and words derive from language and communication, which would not exist without social interaction (see Chapter 15). Thought, which is an internalised and private activity that can occur when we are alone, is clearly based on implied presence. As another example of implied presence, consider that most of us do not 'litter', even if no one is watching and there is no possibility of ever being caught. This is because people, through the agency of society, have constructed a powerful social convention or norm that proscribes such behaviour. Such a norm implies the presence of other people and 'determines' behaviour even in their absence (see Chapters 7 and 8).

Social psychology is a **science** because it uses the scientific method to construct and test theories. Just as physics has concepts such as electrons, quarks and spin to explain physical phenomena, social psychology has concepts such as dissonance, attitude, categorisation and identity to explain social psychological phenomena. The scientific method dictates that no **theory** is 'true' simply because it is logical and makes internal sense. On the contrary, the validity of a theory is based on its correspondence with fact. Social psychologists construct theories from **data** and/or previous theories and then conduct empirical research in which data are collected to test the theory (see below).

SOCIAL PSYCHOLOGY AND RELATED DISCIPLINES
Social psychology is poised at the crossroads of a number of related disciplines and subdisciplines (see Figure 1.1). It is a subdiscipline of general psychology and is, therefore, concerned with explaining human behaviour in terms of processes that occur within the human mind. It differs from individual psychology in that it seeks to explain *social* behaviour (as defined above). For example, a general psychologist might be interested in perceptual processes that are responsible for people overestimating the size of coins, but a social psychologist might focus on the fact that coins have value (a case of implied presence, because the value of something generally depends on what others think), and that perceived value might influence the judgment of size. A great deal of social psychology is actually concerned with face-to-face interaction between individuals or among members of groups, whereas general psychology focuses on people's reactions to stimuli, which do not have to be social (e.g. shapes, colours, sounds).

The boundary between individual and social psychology is often approached from both sides. For instance, having developed a comprehensive and highly influential theory of the individual human mind, Freud set out, in his 1921 book *Group Psychology and the Analysis of the Ego*, to develop a social psychology. Freudian, or psychodynamic, notions have left a significant mark

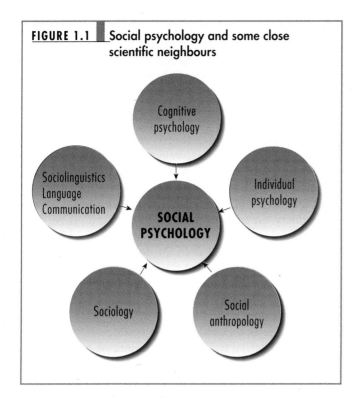

FIGURE 1.1 Social psychology and some close scientific neighbours

Just as the boundary between social and individual psychology has been approached from both sides, so has the boundary between social psychology and sociology. From the sociological side, for example, Marx's theory of cultural history and social change has been extended to incorporate a consideration of the role of individual psychology (Billig, 1976). From the social psychological side, intergroup perspectives on group and individual behaviour draw on sociological variables and concepts (Hogg & Abrams, 1988; see Chapter 11). Contemporary social psychology also abuts sociolinguistics and the study of language and communication (Giles & Coupland, 1991; see Chapter 15) and even literary criticism (Potter, Stringer, & Wetherell, 1984). It also feeds a variety of applied areas of psychology, such as sports psychology, health psychology and organisational psychology.

Social psychology's location at the intersection of different disciplines is part of its intellectual and practical appeal. However, it is also a cause of vigorous debate about what precisely constitutes social psychology as a distinct scientific discipline. If we lean too far towards individual cognitive processes, then perhaps we are pursuing individual psychology or cognitive psychology. If we lean too far towards the role of language, perhaps we are being scholars of language and communication. If we overemphasise the role of social structure in intergroup relations, then perhaps we are being sociologists. The issue of exactly what constitutes social psychology provides an important ongoing metatheoretical debate (i.e. a debate about what sorts of theories are appropriate for social psychology) that forms the background to social psychology (see below).

TOPICS OF SOCIAL PSYCHOLOGY

One way to define social psychology is by identifying what social psychologists study. This book is intended to be a comprehensive coverage of the principal phenomena that social psychologists study now and have studied in the past. As such, social psychology can be defined by the contents of this book and other books that present themselves as social psychology texts. A brief look at the contents of this book will give a flavour of the scope of social psychology. Social psychologists study an enormous range of topics, including conformity, persuasion, power, influence, obedience, prejudice, prejudice reduction, discrimination, stereotyping, bargaining, sexism and racism, small groups, social categories, intergroup relations, crowd behaviour, social conflict and harmony, social change, overcrowding, stress, the physical environment, decision-making, the jury, leadership, communication, language, speech, attitudes, impression formation, impression management, self-presentation, identity, emotion, attraction, friendship, the family, love, romance, sex, violence, aggression, altruism

on social psychology (Billig, 1976), in particular in the explanation of prejudice (see Chapter 10). Since the late 1970s social psychology has been influenced by cognitive psychology, in an attempt to employ its methods (e.g. reaction time) and its concepts (e.g. memory) to explain a wide range of social behaviours. In fact, what is now called social cognition (see Chapter 2) is in many ways the dominant force in contemporary social psychology (Augoustinos & Walker, 1995; Fiske & Taylor, 1991; Taylor, 1998) and surfaces in almost all areas of the discipline (Devine, Hamilton, & Ostrom, 1994).

In dealing, for example, with groups, social and cultural norms, language and intergroup behaviour, social psychology has links with sociology and social anthropology. In general, sociology focuses on how groups, organisations, social categories and societies are organised, how they function and how they change. The unit of analysis (i.e. the focus of research and theory) is the group as a whole rather than the individuals who compose the group. Social anthropology does much the same but, historically, has focused on 'exotic' societies (i.e. non-industrial tribal societies that exist or have existed largely in developing countries). Social psychology deals with many of the same phenomena but seeks to explain how individual human interaction and human cognition influence 'culture' and, in turn, are influenced by culture (M. H. Bond & Smith, 1996; Smith & Bond, 1998). The unit of analysis is the individual within the group. In reality, some forms of sociology (e.g. microsociology, psychological sociology, sociological psychology) are closely related to social psychology (e.g. Delamater, 2003).

Conformity: Norms govern the attitudes and behaviour of group members. These monks in Laos not only dress similarly but also share fundamental beliefs in common.

and prosocial behaviour (acts that are positively valued by society).

One problem with defining social psychology solely in terms of its topics is that this does not properly differentiate it from other disciplines. For example, intergroup relations is a focus not only of social psychology but also of political scientists and sociologists. The family is studied not only by social psychologists but also by clinical psychologists. What makes social psychology distinct is a combination of *what* it studies, *how* it studies it and what *level of explanation* is sought.

Methodological issues

SCIENTIFIC METHOD

Social psychology employs the scientific method to study social behaviour (Figure 1.2). Science is a *method* for studying nature, and it is the method—not the people who use it, the things they study, the facts they discover or the explanations they propose—that distinguishes science from other approaches to knowledge. In this respect the main difference between social psychology and, say, physics, chemistry or biology is that the former studies human social behaviour while the others study non-organic phenomena and chemical and biological processes.

Science involves the formulation of **hypotheses** (predictions) on the basis of prior knowledge, assumption, and casual or systematic observation. Hypotheses are formally stated speculations about what factor or factors may cause something to occur; they are stated in such a way that they can be empirically tested to see if they are true. For example, we might hypothesise that ballet dancers perform better in front of an audience than when alone: this hypothesis can be empirically tested by assessing performance alone and in front of an audience. Strictly speaking, empirical tests can falsify hypotheses (causing the investigator to reject the hypothesis, revise it, or test it in some other way) but not prove them (Popper, 1969). If a hypothesis is supported, it increases confidence in its accuracy and may allow us to generate more finely tuned hypotheses. For example, if we find that ballet dancers do indeed perform better in front of an audience, we might then go on to hypothesise that this effect occurs only when the dancers are already very well practised. An important feature of the scientific method is replication: this guards against the possibility that a finding is tied to the way in which a test was conducted; it also guards against fraud.

The alternative to science is dogma or rationalism, where understanding is based on authority—something is true ultimately because authorities (e.g. the ancient philosophers, the religious scriptures, charismatic leaders) say it is so. Valid knowledge is acquired by pure reason: that is, by learning well, and uncritically accepting, the pronouncements of authorities. Even though the scientific revolution, championed by such people as Copernicus, Galileo and Newton, occurred in the 16th and 17th centuries, dogma and rationalism still exist as influential alternative paths to knowledge.

As a science, social psychology has at its disposal an array of methods for conducting empirical tests of hypotheses. There are two broad types of method, *experimental* and *non-experimental*, and they each have advantages and limitations. The choice of an appropriate method is determined by a range of factors to do with the nature of the hypothesis under investigation, the resources available for doing the research (e.g. time, money, participants) and the ethics of the method. Confidence in the validity of a hypothesis is greatly enhanced if it has been supported a number of times by different research teams using different methods. Methodological pluralism helps to minimise the possibility that the finding is an artifact of a particular method, and replication by different research teams helps to avoid confirmation bias—a tendency for researchers to become personally involved in their own theories to such an extent that they lose a degree of objectivity in interpreting data (Greenwald & Pratkanis, 1988; Johnson & Eagly, 1989).

EXPERIMENTS

An experiment is a hypothesis test in which something is done in order to see its effect on something else. For

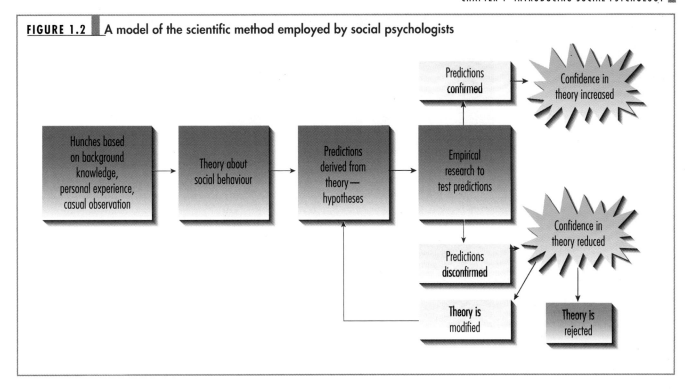

FIGURE 1.2 A model of the scientific method employed by social psychologists

example, if I hypothesise that my car guzzles excessive petrol because the tyres are not adequately inflated, then I can conduct an experiment. I can note petrol consumption over an average week, then I can increase the tyre pressure and again note petrol consumption over an average week. If consumption is reduced, then my hypothesis is supported. Casual experimentation is one of the most important and common ways in which people learn about their world—it is an extremely powerful method because it allows us to identify the causes of events and thus gain control over our destiny.

Not surprisingly, systematic experimentation is the most important research method in science. Experimentation involves *intervention* in the form of *manipulation* of one or more **independent variables,** and then measurement of the effect of the treatment (manipulation) on one or more focal **dependent variables.** In the example above, the independent variable is tyre inflation, which was manipulated to create two experimental conditions (lower versus higher pressure), and the dependent variable is petrol consumption, which was measured on refilling the tank at the end of the week. More generally, independent variables are dimensions that the researcher hypothesises will have an effect, and that can be varied (e.g. tyre pressure in the present example, and the presence or absence of an audience in the ballet-dancing example). Dependent variables are dimensions that the researcher hypothesises will vary as a consequence of varying the independent variable (petrol consumption or quality of the ballet dancer's performance). Variation in the dependent variable is

dependent on variation in the independent variable.

Social psychology is largely experimental, in that most social psychologists would prefer to test hypotheses experimentally if at all possible, and much of what we know about social behaviour is based on experiments. Indeed, two of the most prestigious scholarly societies for the scientific study of social psychology are (in the United States) the Society for Experimental Social Psychology and (in Europe) the European Association of Experimental Social Psychology.

A typical social psychology experiment might be designed to test the hypothesis that violent television programs increase aggression in young children. One way to do this would be to distribute 20 children randomly between two conditions in which they individually watch a violent or a non-violent program, and then monitor the degree of aggression expressed immediately afterwards by the children while they are at play. Random assignment of participants (in this case, children) reduces the chance of systematic differences between the participants in the two conditions. If there were any systematic differences, say, in age, sex or parental background, then any significant effects on aggression might be due to age, sex or background rather than to the violence of the TV program. That is, age, sex or parental background would be *confounded* with the independent variable. Likewise, the TV program viewed in each condition should be identical in all respects except the degree of violence. For instance, if the violent program also contained more action, then we would not know whether subsequent

Experiments: Laboratory experiments play a central role in social psychology. This autistic boy is being tested for social and emotional skills.

differences in aggression were due to the violence, the action or both. The circumstances surrounding the viewing of the two programs should also be identical. If the violent programs were viewed in a bright red room and the non-violent programs in a blue room, then any effects might be due to room colour, violence or both. It is crucially important in experiments to avoid **confounding**: the conditions must be identical in all respects except for those represented by the manipulated independent variable.

We must also be careful about how we measure effects—that is, the dependent measures that assess the dependent variable. In our example it would probably be inappropriate, because of the children's age, to administer a questionnaire measuring aggression. A better technique would be unobtrusive observation of behaviour, but then what would we code as 'aggression'? The criterion would have to be sensitive to changes: in other words, loud talk or violent assault with a weapon might be insensitive, as all children talk loudly when playing (there is a 'ceiling' effect), and virtually no children violently assault one another with a weapon while playing (there is a 'floor' effect). In addition, it would be a mistake for whoever records or codes the behaviour to know which experimental condition the child was in, as such knowledge might undermine objectivity. The coder(s) should know as little as possible about the experimental conditions and the research hypotheses.

The example used here is of a simple experiment that has only two levels of only one independent variable—called a one-factor design. Most social psychology experiments are more complicated than this. For instance, we might formulate a more textured hypothesis that aggression in young children is increased

by TV programs that contain *realistic* violence. To test this hypothesis, a two-factor design would be adopted. The two factors (independent variables) would be (a) the violence of the program (low versus high) and (b) the realism of the program (realistic versus fantasy). The participants would be randomly assigned across four experimental conditions in which they watched (a) a non-violent fantasy program, (b) a non-violent realistic program, (c) a violent fantasy program or (d) a violent realistic program. Finally, independent variables are not restricted to two levels. For instance, we might predict that aggression is increased by moderately violent programs, while extremely violent programs are so distasteful that aggression is actually suppressed. Our independent variable of program violence could now have three levels (low versus moderate versus extreme).

The laboratory experiment

The classic social psychology experiment is conducted in a **laboratory** so that as many potentially confounding variables as possible can be controlled. The aim is to isolate and manipulate a single aspect of a variable, an aspect that may not normally occur in isolation outside the laboratory. Laboratory experiments are intended to create artificial conditions. Although a social psychology laboratory may contain machines, wires and flashing lights, usually it is simply a room containing tables and chairs. For example, our ballet hypothesis could be tested in the laboratory by formalising the hypothesis to one in which we predict that someone performing a well-learned task performs the task more quickly in front of an audience. We could unobtrusively time individuals taking off their clothes and then putting them back on again (a well-learned task) either alone in a room or while being watched by two other people (an audience). We could compare these speeds with someone dressing up in unusual and difficult clothing (a poorly learned task). This method was actually used by Markus (1978) when she investigated the effect of an audience on task performance (see Chapter 8 for details).

Laboratory experiments allow us to establish cause–effect relationships among variables. However, laboratory experiments have a number of drawbacks. Because experimental conditions are artificial and highly controlled, laboratory findings cannot be directly generalised to the less 'pure' conditions that exist in the 'real' world outside the laboratory. However, laboratory findings address *theories* about human social behaviour, and on the basis of laboratory experimentation we can generalise these theories to apply to conditions other than those in the laboratory. Laboratory experiments are intentionally low on **external validity** or **mundane realism** (i.e. how similar the circumstances are to those usually encountered by participants in the real world) but should always be high on **internal validity** or **experimental realism** (i.e. the manipulations must be full of psychological impact and meaning for the participants) (Aronson, Ellsworth, Carlsmith, & Gonzales, 1990).

Laboratory experiments can be prone to a range of biases. There are **subject effects** that can cause participants' behaviour to be an artifact of the experiment rather than a spontaneous and natural response to a manipulation. Artifacts can be minimised by carefully avoiding **demand characteristics** (Orne, 1962) and *evaluation apprehension* and *social desirability* (Rosenberg, 1969). Demand characteristics are features of the experiment that seem to 'demand' a particular response: they give information about the hypothesis and thus inform helpful and compliant participants about how to react to confirm the hypothesis. Participants are thus no longer naive or *blind* regarding the experimental hypotheses. Participants in experiments are real people, and experiments are real social situations. Not surprisingly, participants may want to project the best possible image of themselves to the experimenter and other participants present. This can influence spontaneous reactions to manipulations in unpredictable ways. There are also **experimenter effects**. The experimenter is often aware of the hypotheses and may inadvertently give cues that cause participants to behave in a way that confirms the hypotheses. This can be minimised by a **double-blind** procedure, in which experimenters are unaware of which experimental condition they are running.

Since the 1960s, laboratory experiments have tended to rely on psychology undergraduates as participants (Sears, 1986). The reason is a pragmatic one—psychology undergraduates are readily available in large numbers. In almost all major universities there is a 'subject pool' scheme whereby psychology students act as experimental participants in exchange for course credits, or as a course requirement. Critics have often suggested that this overreliance on a particular type of participant may provide us with a somewhat distorted view of social behaviour—one that is not easily generalised to other sectors of the population. In their defence, experimental social psychologists point out that theories, not experimental findings, are generalised, and that replication and methodological pluralism will ensure that social psychology is about people, not just about psychology students.

The field experiment

Social psychology experiments can be conducted in more naturalistic settings outside the laboratory. For example, we could investigate the hypothesis that prolonged eye contact is uncomfortable and causes 'flight' by having an experimenter stand at traffic lights and either gaze intensely at the driver of a car stopped at the lights or gaze in the opposite direction. The dependent measure would be the speed at which the car sped away once the lights changed (Ellsworth, Carlsmith, & Henson, 1972; see Chapter 15). Field experiments have high external validity and, as participants are usually completely unaware that an experiment is taking place, are not reactive (i.e. no demand characteristics are present). However, there is less control over extraneous variables, random assignment is sometimes difficult, and it can be difficult to obtain accurate measurements or measurements of subjective feelings (generally, overt behaviour is all that can be measured).

NON-EXPERIMENTAL METHODS

Systematic experimentation tends to be the preferred method of science and, indeed, it is often equated with science. However, there are all sorts of circumstances where it is simply impossible to conduct an experiment to test a hypothesis. For instance, theories about planetary systems and galaxies can pose a real problem: we can't move planets around to see what happens! Likewise, social psychological theories about the relationship between biological sex and decision-making are not amenable to experimentation because we cannot experimentally manipulate biological sex and see what effects emerge. Social psychology also confronts ethical issues that can proscribe experimentation. For instance, hypotheses about the effects on self-esteem of being a victim of violent crime are not at all easily tested experimentally—we could not randomly assign participants to two conditions and then subject one group to a violent crime and see what happened!

Where experimentation is not possible or not appropriate, social psychologists have a range of non-experimental methods from which to choose. Because these methods do not involve the manipulation of independent variables against a background of random assignment to condition, it is almost impossible to draw reliable causal conclusions. For instance, we could compare the self-esteem of people who have been victims of violent crime with those who have not. Any differences could be attributed to violent crime, but could also be due to other uncontrolled differences between the two groups. We can only conclude that there is a **correlation** between self-esteem and being the victim of violent crime. There is no evidence that one causes the other (i.e. that being a victim lowers self-esteem, or that having lower self-esteem increases the likelihood of becoming a victim). Both could be correlated or co-occurring effects of some third variable, such as chronic unemployment, which independently lowers self-esteem and increases the probability of becoming a victim. In general, non-experimental methods involve the examination of correlation among naturally occurring variables and, as such, do not permit us to draw causal conclusions.

Archival research

Archival research is a non-experimental method that is useful for investigating large-scale, widely occurring phenomena that may be remote in time. The researcher assembles data collected by others, often for reasons unconnected with those of the researcher. For instance, Janis (1972) used an archival method to show that overly cohesive governmental decision-making groups may make poor decisions with disastrous consequences because they adopt poor decision-making procedures (called 'groupthink'; see Chapter 9). Janis constructed his theory on the basis of examination of biographical, autobiographical and media accounts of the decision-making procedures associated with, for example, the 1961 Bay of Pigs fiasco in which the United States tried to invade Cuba. Archival methods are often used to make comparisons between different cultures or nations regarding things such as suicide, mental health or child-rearing strategies. The archival method is not, of course, reactive, but can be unreliable because the researcher usually has no control over the primary data collection, which might be biased or unreliable in other ways (e.g. missing vital data). The researcher has to make do with whatever is there.

Case studies

The **case study** allows an in-depth analysis of a single case (either a person or a group) or a single event. Case studies often employ an array of data-collection and analysis techniques involving structured and open-ended interviews and questionnaires, and the observation of behaviour. Case studies are well suited to the examination of unusual or rare phenomena that could not be created in the laboratory (e.g. bizarre cults, mass murderers or disasters). Case studies are useful as a source of hypotheses, but findings may suffer from researcher or subject bias (the researcher is not blind to the hypothesis, there are demand characteristics and participants suffer evaluation apprehension) and findings may not easily be generalised to other cases or events.

Survey research

Another non-experimental method is data collection by *survey*. Surveys can involve structured interviews, in which the researcher asks the participants a number of carefully chosen questions and notes down the responses, or a questionnaire, in which participants write their own responses to written questions. In either case the questions can be open-ended (i.e. respondents can give as much or as little detail in their answers as they wish) or closed-ended (where there is a limited number of predetermined responses, such as circling a number on a nine-point scale). For instance, if we wanted to investigate Asian immigrants' experiences of prejudice in Australia or New Zealand, we could ask respondents a set of predetermined questions and summarise the thrust of their responses, or we could simply assign a numerical value. Alternatively, respondents could record their own responses by writing a paragraph or by circling numbers on scales in a questionnaire.

Surveys can be used to obtain a large amount of data from a large sample of participants, hence generalisation is often not a problem. However, it is a method that, like the case study, is subject to experimenter bias, subject bias and evaluation apprehension. Anonymous and confidential questionnaires may minimise experimenter bias, evaluation apprehension and some subject biases, but demand characteristics may remain, and poorly constructed questionnaires may obtain biased data due to 'response set' (i.e. the tendency for some respondents unthinkingly to agree with statements, or to choose mid-range responses or extreme responses).

Field studies

The final non-experimental method is the field study. We have already described the field experiment; the field study is essentially the same, but without any interventions or manipulations. Field studies involve the observation, recording and coding of behaviour as it occurs. Most often, the observer is non-intrusive by not participating in the behaviour, and 'invisible' by not having an effect on the ongoing behaviour. For instance, you could research the behaviour of students in the student refectory by concealing yourself in a corner and observing what goes on. Sometimes 'invisibility' is impossible and so the opposite strategy is used—the researcher becomes a full participant in the behaviour. For instance, it would be difficult to be an invisible observer of gang behaviour. Instead, you could study the behaviour of a street gang by becoming a full member of the gang and surreptitiously taking notes (e.g. Whyte, 1943; see Chapter 8). Field studies are excellent for investigating spontaneously occurring behaviour in its natural context, but are particularly prone to experimenter bias, lack of objectivity, poor generalisability, and distortions due to the impact of the researcher on the behaviour under investigation. Also, if you join a gang there is an element of personal danger!

DATA AND ANALYSIS

Research provides data that are analysed to draw conclusions about whether hypotheses are supported. The type of analysis undertaken depends on at least:

- *the type of data obtained*—for example, binary responses such as 'yes' versus 'no', continuous variables such as temperature or response-latency, defined positions on nine-point scales, rank ordering of choices, open-ended written responses (text);
- *the method used to obtain data*—for example, controlled experiment, open-ended interview, participant observation, archival search; and
- *the purposes of the research*—for example, to describe in depth a specific case, to establish differences between two groups of participants exposed to different treatments, to investigate the correlation between two or more naturally occurring variables.

Overwhelmingly, social psychological knowledge is based on statistical analysis of quantitative data. Data are obtained as, or are transformed into, numbers (i.e. quantities) and these numbers are then compared in various formalised ways (i.e. by **statistics**). For example, to decide whether women are friendlier interviewees than men, we could compare transcripts of interviews of both men and women. We could then code the transcripts to count how often participants made positive

Statistics: Social psychological data are often quantitative, requiring statistical analysis to find patterns that give meaning to the numbers.

remarks to the interviewer and compare the mean count for, say, 20 women with the mean for 20 men. In this case we would be interested in knowing whether the difference between men and women was 'on the whole' greater than the difference among men or among women. To do this, we could use a simple statistic called the *t*-test, which computes a single number, called the *t*-statistic, that is based on both the difference between the women's and men's mean friendliness scores and the amount of variability of scores within each sex. The larger the value of *t*, the larger the between-sex difference relative to within-sex differences. The decision about whether the difference between groups is psychologically significant depends on its **statistical significance**. Social psychologists accept the arbitrary convention that if the obtained value of *t* has less than a 1 in 20 probability of occurring simply by chance (e.g. if we randomly selected two lots of 20 people and compared their friendliness, less than 5 in 100 times would we obtain a value of *t* as great as or greater than that obtained in the study), then the obtained difference is statistically significant and there really is a difference in friendliness between male and female interviewees (see Figure 1.3).

The *t*-test is very simple. However, the principle underlying the *t*-test is the same as that underlying more sophisticated and complex statistical techniques used by social psychologists to test whether two or more groups differ significantly. The other major method of data analysis used by social psychologists is correlation, which assesses whether the co-occurrence of two or more variables is significant. Again, although the example below is simple, the underlying principle is the same for an array of correlational techniques.

To investigate the idea that rigid thinkers tend to hold more conservative attitudes (Rokeach, 1960; see Chapter 10), we could have 30 participants answer a questionnaire measuring cognitive rigidity (dogmatism—a rigid and inflexible set of attitudes) and attitudinal conservatism (e.g. endorsement and espousal of right-wing political and social policies). If we rank the 30 participants in order of increasing dogmatism and find that conservatism also increases, with the least dogmatic person being the least conservative and the most dogmatic the most conservative, then we can say that the two variables are positively correlated (see Figure 1.4, in which dots represent individual persons, positioned with respect to their scores on both dogmatism and conservatism scales). If we find that conservatism systematically decreases with increasing dogmatism, then we say the two variables are negatively correlated. If there seems to be no systematic relationship between the two variables, then they are uncorrelated—or there is zero correlation. A statistic can be calculated to represent correlation numerically: for instance, Pearson's

FIGURE 1.3 Distribution of friendliness scores for 20 male and 20 female interviewees: Using the *t*-statistic

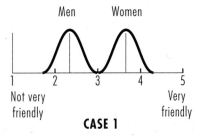

CASE 1

The *t*-statistic is relatively large because the difference between means is large and the variation within sex groups is small

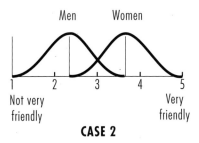

CASE 2

The *t*-statistic is relatively small because, although the difference between means is still large, the variation within sex groups is large

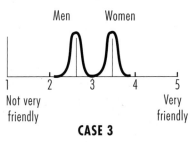

CASE 3

The *t*-statistic is large because, although the difference between means is smaller, the variation within sex groups is small

FIGURE 1.4 Correlation between dogmatism and conservatism for 30 respondents: Using Pearson's correlation coefficient

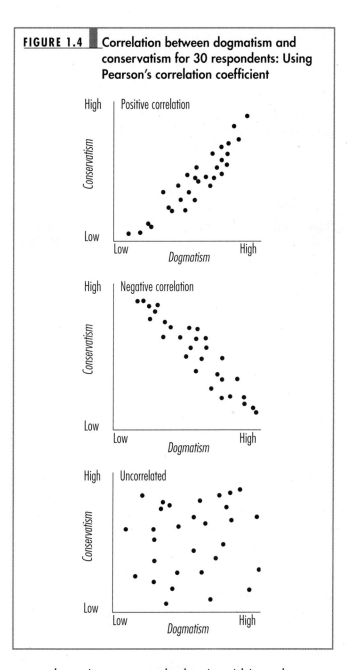

r-statistic varies from −1 for a perfect negative to +1 for a perfect positive correlation. Depending on, among other things, the number of persons, we can also know whether the correlation is statistically significant at the conventional 5% level.

Although statistical analysis of quantitative data is the bread and butter of social psychology, some social psychologists find that this method is unsuited to their purposes and prefer a more *qualitative* analysis. For example, analysis of people's explanations for unemployment or prejudice may sometimes benefit from a more discursive, non-quantitative analysis in which the researcher tries to unravel what is said in order to go beyond surface explanations and get to the heart of the underlying beliefs and reasons. One form of qualitative analysis is *discourse analysis* (e.g. Potter & Wetherell, 1987). Discourse analysis treats all 'data' as 'text'—that is, as a communicative event that is replete with multiple layers of meaning, but which can be interpreted only by considering the text in its wider social context. For example, discourse analysts believe that we should not take people's responses to attitude statements in questionnaires at face value and subject them to statistical analysis. They believe, instead, that we should interpret what is being communicated. This is made possible only by considering the response as a complex conjunction of social-communicative factors deriving from the immediate context and the wider sociohistorical context. Discourse analysis is, however, more than a research method; it is a systematic critique of 'conventional' methods and theories of social psychology (see below).

Research ethics

As researchers, social psychologists confront important ethical issues. For instance, is it ethical to expose experimental participants to a treatment that is embarrassing or has potential effects on their self-concept? If such research is important, what are the rights of the person, what are the ethical obligations of the researcher, and what guidelines are there for deciding? Although ethical considerations surface most often in experiments (e.g. Milgram's 1974 obedience studies; see Chapter 7), they can also confront non-experimental researchers. For example, is it ethical for a non-participant observer investigating crowd behaviour to refrain from interceding in a violent assault? To guide researchers, the American Psychological Association established, in 1972, a set of principles for ethical conduct in research involving humans, which was completely revised and updated in 2002 (American Psychological Association, 2002). Researchers design their studies with these guidelines in mind, and then obtain official approval from a university or departmental research ethics committee. There are five ethical principles that have received most attention: protection from harm, right to privacy, deception, informed consent and debriefing.

PHYSICAL WELFARE OF PARTICIPANTS
Clearly, it is unethical to expose people to physical *harm*. For example, the use of electric shocks that cause visible burning would be difficult to justify. However, in most cases it is also difficult to establish whether non-trivial harm is involved and, if so, what its magnitude is, and whether debriefing (see below) deals with it. For instance, telling experimental participants that they have done badly on a word-association task may have long-term effects on self-esteem, and could therefore be considered harmful. On the other hand, the effects may be so small and transitory as to be insignificant.

RESPECT FOR PRIVACY
Social psychological research often involves invasion of *privacy*. Participants can be asked intimate questions, can be observed without their knowledge, and can have their moods, perceptions and behaviours manipulated. It is sometimes difficult to decide whether the research topic justifies invasion of privacy. At other times it is more straightforward—for example, intimate questions about sexual practices are essential for research into behaviour that may put people at risk of contracting

HIV. Concern about privacy is usually satisfied by ensuring that data obtained from individuals are entirely *confidential*: that is, only the researcher knows who said or did what. Personal identification is removed from data (rendering them anonymous), research findings are reported as means for large groups of people, and data no longer useful are usually destroyed.

USE OF DECEPTION
Laboratory experiments, as we have seen, involve the manipulation of people's cognitions, feelings or behaviours in order to investigate the spontaneous, natural and non-reactive effect of independent variables. Because people need to be naive regarding hypotheses, experimenters often conceal the true purpose of the experiment. A degree of *deception* is often necessary. Between 50% and 75% of published experiments involve some degree of deception (Adair, Dushenko, & Lindsay, 1985; Gross & Fleming, 1982). Because the use of deception seems to imply 'trickery', 'deceit' and 'lying', it has attracted a great deal of criticism—as with Baumrind's (1964) attack on Milgram's (1963, 1974) obedience studies (see Chapter 7). Social psychologists have been challenged to abandon controlled experimental research (in preference to role-playing or simulations; e.g. Kelman, 1967) if they cannot do experiments without deception.

This is probably too extreme a request, as social psychological knowledge has been enriched enormously by classic experiments that have used deception (many such experiments are described in this book). Although some experiments have used an amount of deception that seems excessive, in practice the deception used in most social psychology experiments is trivial: for example, an experiment may be introduced as a study of group decision-making when in fact it is part of a program of research into prejudice and stereotyping. In addition, no one has yet shown any long-term negative consequences of the use of deception in social psychology experiments (Elms, 1982) and experimental participants themselves tend to be impressed, rather than upset or angered, by cleverly executed deceptions, and view deception as a necessary withholding of information or a necessary ruse (Christensen, 1988; Smith, 1983).

INFORMED CONSENT
One way to safeguard people's rights in experiments is to obtain their *informed consent* to participate. In principle, people should freely give their consent (preferably in writing) to participate on the basis of full information about what they are consenting to take part in, and must be entirely free to withdraw from the research whenever they wish. Researchers cannot lie or withhold information in order to induce people to participate, nor can they make it 'difficult' to say 'no' or to withdraw (i.e. via social pressure or by exercise of personal

or institutionalised power). In practice, however, terms such as 'full information' are difficult to define and, as we have just seen, experiments often require some deception in order that participants remain naive.

DEBRIEFING

Participants should be fully *debriefed* after taking part in an experiment. Debriefing is designed to make sure that people leave the laboratory with an increased respect for and understanding of social psychology. More specifically, debriefing involves a detailed explanation of the experiment and its broader theoretical and applied context. Any deceptions are explained and justified to the satisfaction of all participants, and care is taken to make sure that the effects of manipulations have been undone.

Social psychologists often conduct and report research into socially sensitive phenomena, or research that has implications for socially sensitive issues such as prejudice, discrimination, racism, sexism and ageism (see Chapters 10, 11 and 15). In these sorts of areas the researcher has to be especially careful that both the conducting and reporting of research is done in such a way that it is not biased by personal prejudices and is not open to public misinterpretation, distortion or misuse. For example, early research into sex differences in conformity found that women conformed more than men. This finding is, of course, supportive to the view that women are more dependent than men. Later research discovered that men and women conform equally, and that whether they conform or not depends largely on how much familiarity and confidence they have with the conformity task. Early research used tasks that were more familiar to men than women, and many researchers looked no further because the findings confirmed their assumptions (Chapters 7 and 10).

Theoretical issues

Social psychologists construct and test theories of human social behaviour. A social psychological theory is an integrated set of propositions that explains the causes of social behaviour, generally in terms of one or more social psychological processes. Theories rest on explicit assumptions about social behaviour and contain a number of defined concepts and formal statements about the relationship among concepts. Ideally, these relationships are causal ones that are attributed to the operation of social and/or psychological processes. Theories are framed in such a way that they generate hypotheses that can be tested empirically. Social psychological theories vary greatly in terms of their rigour, testability and generality (Shaw & Costanzo, 1982). Some theories are short-

Social identity: This police officer has a job on his hands. Some graffiti are the markers of individual taggers. Others symbolise group membership and social identity.

range minitheories that are tied to specific phenomena, others are much broader general theories that explain whole classes of behaviour—some even approach the status of 'grand theory' (such as evolutionary theory, Marxism, general relativity theory, psychodynamic theory) in that they furnish a general perspective on social psychology.

The social identity approach in social psychology (e.g. Hogg, 2003b; see Chapters 4 and 11) is a good example of a relatively general mid-range social psychological theory. It is an analysis of the behaviour of people in groups and how this relates to their self-conception as group members. The general approach integrates a number of compatible (sub)-theories that deal with and emphasise:

- intergroup relations and social change;
- motivational processes associated with group membership and group behaviour;
- social influence and conformity processes within groups;
- cognitive processes associated with self-conception and social perception.

These, and other associated, processes operate together to produce group behaviour, as distinct from interpersonal behaviour. This theory generates testable predictions about a range of group phenomena, including stereotyping, intergroup discrimination, social influence in groups, group cohesiveness, social change and even language and ethnicity.

THEORIES IN SOCIAL PSYCHOLOGY

Theories in social psychology can generally be clustered into types of theory, with different types of theory reflecting different *metatheories*. Just as a theory is a set of interrelated concepts and principles that explain a phenomenon, a **metatheory** is a set of interrelated concepts and principles about which theories or types of theory are appropriate. The adherents of some theories may extend their theories to account for almost the whole of human behaviour.

Here we list several major types of theories that have had an impact on social psychology.

Behaviourism

Behaviourist or learning perspectives derive from Pavlov's early work on conditioned reflexes and Skinner's work on operant conditioning. The **radical behaviourist** believes that behaviour can be explained and predicted in terms of reinforcement schedules—behaviours associated with positive outcomes or circumstances grow in strength and frequency. More popular with social psychologists, however, is the **neobehaviourist**, who believes that we need to invoke unobservable intervening constructs (e.g. beliefs, feelings, motives) to make sense of behaviour.

The behaviourist perspective in social psychology produces theories that emphasise the role of situational factors and reinforcement/learning in social behaviour. One example is the *reinforcement–affect model* of interpersonal attraction (e.g. Lott, 1961; Chapter 13): people grow to like the people they associate with positive experiences (e.g. we like people who praise us). Another more general example is *social exchange theory* (e.g. Kelley & Thibaut, 1978; Chapter 13): the course of social interactions depends on subjective evaluation of the rewards and costs involved. Social modelling is another broadly behaviourist perspective: we imitate behaviour that is reinforced in others, and thus our behaviour is shaped by vicarious learning (e.g. Bandura, 1977; Chapter 12). Finally, *drive theory* (Zajonc, 1965; Chapter 8) explains improvement and deterioration of task performance in front of an audience in terms of the strength of a learned response.

Cognitive psychology

Critics have argued that behaviourist theories exaggerate the degree to which people are passive recipients of external influences. **Cognitive theories** redress the balance by focusing on how people actively interpret and change their environment, through the agency of cognitive processes and cognitive representations. Cognitive theories have their origins in Koffka and Köhler's *Gestalt* psychology in Germany during the 1930s, and in many ways social psychology has always been cognitive in its perspective (Landman & Manis, 1983; Markus & Zajonc, 1985).

One of the earliest cognitive theories in social psychology was Lewin's (1951) field theory, which dealt with the way in which people's cognitive representations of features of the social environment produced motivational forces to behave in various ways. Lewin is generally considered the father of experimental social psychology.

In the 1950s and 1960s, cognitive consistency theories dominated social psychology (Abelson, Aronson, McGuire, Newcomb, Rosenberg, & Tannenbaum, 1968). These theories assumed that cognitions about ourselves, our behaviour and the world, which were contradictory or incompatible in other ways, produced an uncomfortable state of cognitive arousal that motivated people to resolve the cognitive conflict. This perspective has been used to explain attitude change (e.g. Aronson, 1984; Chapter 6).

In the 1970s attribution theories dominated social psychology. Attribution theories focus on the way in which people explain the causes of their own and other people's behaviours, and on the consequences of causal explanations (e.g. Hewstone, 1989; Chapter 3). Finally, since the late 1970s, social cognition has been the dominant perspective in social psychology. This perspective contains a number of theories dealing with the way in which cognitive processes (e.g. categorisation) and cognitive representations (e.g. schemas) are constructed and influence behaviour (e.g. Fiske & Taylor, 1991; Chapter 2).

Evolutionary social psychology

A recent theoretical development comes from a field now referred to as **evolutionary social psychology** (Buss, 1990, 1999; Buss & Kenrick, 1998; Simpson & Kenrick, 1997). Drawing on both 19th-century Darwinian theory and later work in sociobiology (e.g. Wilson, 1975, 1978), evolutionary social psychologists argue that many behavioural tendencies are grounded in the ancestral past of our species. For example, the survival of our forebears depended on avoiding predators and toxic plants, being attracted to mates with particular qualities, caring for the young, banding together into groups and helping others in distress. As these tendencies had survival value for the species, in time they became part of our genetic makeup. This biological perspective can be pushed to an extreme and used as a sovereign explanation for most, even all, behaviour. In contrast, social psychology also needs to account for the role of learning, subtle effects on behaviour of the social context, and for cultural variation in behaviour. Nevertheless, evolutionary social psychology has relevance for several major topics in this book—aggression (Chapter 12), interpersonal attraction (Chapter 13), prosocial behaviour (Chapter 14) and non-verbal and human spatial behaviour (Chapter 15).

Personality

Social psychologists have often tried to explain social behaviour in terms of enduring (sometimes innate) personality attributes. For instance, good leaders have charismatic personalities (Chapter 9), prejudice is expressed by people with prejudiced personalities

(Chapter 10) and people who overly conform have conformist personalities (Chapter 7). In general, social psychologists now consider personality to be at best a partial explanation, at worst an inadequate explanation, of social phenomena. There are at least two reasons for this:

1. There is actually very little evidence for stable personality traits. People behave in different ways at different times and in different contexts—they are influenced by situation and context.
2. If personality is defined as behavioural consistency across contexts, then rather than being an explanation of behaviour it is something to be explained: Why do some people resist social and contextual influences on behaviour? What is it about their interpretation of the context that causes them to behave in this way?

Personality theories can be contrasted with collectivist theories. Collectivist theories focus on the way in which people are socially constituted by their unique location in society: people behave as they do, not because of personality or individual predispositions but because they internally represent socially constructed group norms that influence behaviour in specific contexts. An early collectivist viewpoint was McDougall's (1920) theory of the 'group mind' (Chapter 11). In groups, people change the way they think, process information and act, so that group behaviour is quite different from interpersonal behaviour—a group mind appears to emerge.

More recently this idea has been elaborated by European social psychologists seeking a perspective on social behaviour that stresses the part played by the wider social context of intergroup relations in shaping behaviour (e.g. Tajfel, 1984). Of these, social identity theory is perhaps the most developed (e.g. Tajfel & Turner, 1979; Chapter 11). Its explanation of the behaviour of people in groups depends largely on an analysis of the social relations between groups. Collectivist theories adopt a 'top-down' approach, in which individual social behaviour can be explained only with reference to groups, intergroup relations and social forces. Individualistic theories, in contrast, are 'bottom-up': individual social behaviour is constructed from individual cognition or personality.

It is important to recognise that many social psychological theories contain elements of two or more different perspectives, and also that these and other perspectives often merely lend emphasis to different theories. Social psychological theories rarely make their underlying metatheory explicit.

THE 'CRISIS' IN SOCIAL PSYCHOLOGY

Social psychology occurs against a background of (often latent) metatheoretical differences. In many respects this is an intellectually appealing feature of the discipline.

From time to time these differences come to the fore and become the focus of intense public debate. The most recent occurrence was in the late 1960s and early 1970s, when social psychology appeared to many to have reached a crisis of confidence (e.g. Elms, 1975; Israel & Tajfel, 1972; Rosnow, 1981; Strickland, Aboud, & Gergen, 1976). There were two principal worries about social psychology:

1. It was overly *reductionist* (i.e. by explaining social behaviour mainly in terms of individual psychology it failed to address the essentially social nature of the human experience).
2. It was overly *positivistic* (i.e. it adhered to a model of science that was distorted, inappropriate and misleading).

REDUCTIONISM AND LEVELS OF EXPLANATION

Reductionism is the practice of explaining a phenomenon in terms of the language and concepts of a lower level of analysis. Society is explained in terms of groups, groups in terms of interpersonal processes, interpersonal processes in terms of intrapersonal cognitive mechanisms, cognition in terms of neuropsychology, neuropsychology in terms of biology, and so on. A problem of reductionist theorising is that it can leave unanswered the original question. For example, the act of putting an arm out of the car window to indicate an intention to turn can be explained in terms of muscle contraction, or nerve impulses, or understanding of and adherence to social conventions, and so on. If the **level of explanation** (or analysis) does not match the level of the question, then the question remains effectively unanswered. In researching interpersonal relations, to what extent does an explanation in terms of cognition really address interpersonal relations?

Although some reductionism may be necessary for theorising, too much is undesirable. Social psychology has been criticised for being inherently reductionist because it tries to explain social behaviour in terms of asocial intrapsychic cognitive and motivational processes (e.g. Moscovici, 1972; Pepitone, 1981; Sampson, 1977; Taylor & Brown, 1979). The problem is most acute when social psychologists try to explain group processes and intergroup relations. By tackling these phenomena exclusively in terms of personality, interpersonal relations or intrapsychic processes, social psychology essentially leaves some of its most important phenomena less than adequately explained—for example, prejudice, discrimination, stereotyping, conformity and group solidarity (Billig, 1976; Hogg & Abrams, 1988; Turner & Oakes, 1986).

Doise (1986; Lorenzi-Cioldi & Doise, 1990) has recently suggested that one way around this problem is to accept the existence of different levels of explanation but to make a special effort to construct theories that formally integrate (Doise uses the term 'articulate') concepts from different levels (see Box 1.1). This idea has been adopted to varying degrees by many social psychologists (see Tajfel, 1984). One of the most successful attempts is social identity theory (e.g. Tajfel & Turner, 1979) as we have noted (see Chapter 11), in which individual cognitive processes are articulated with large-scale social forces to explain group behaviour. Doise's ideas have also been employed to reinterpret group cohesiveness (Hogg, 1992) and attribution theories (Hewstone, 1989). Organisational psychologists have also advocated articulation of levels of explanation—though here the debate is less developed than in social psychology; the issue is one of *cross-level research* and very little has actually been done (Wilpert, 1995).

POSITIVISM

Positivism is the non-critical acceptance of scientific method as the only way to arrive at true knowledge. Positivism was introduced in the early 19th century by the French mathematician and philosopher Auguste Compte, and was extremely popular until the end of

---

BOX 1.1   **Levels of explanation in social psychology**

I INTRAPERSONAL

Analysis of psychological processes to do with individuals' organisation of their experience of the social environment (e.g. research on cognitive balance).

II INTERPERSONAL AND SITUATIONAL

Analysis of interindividual interaction within circumscribed situations. Social positional factors emanating from outside the situation are not considered. The object of study is the dynamics of relations established at a given moment by given individuals in a given situation (e.g. some attribution research, research using game matrices).

III POSITIONAL

Analysis of interindividual interaction in specific situations, but with the role of social position (e.g. status, identity) outside the situation taken into consideration (e.g. some research into power and social identity).

IV IDEOLOGICAL

Analysis of interindividual interaction that considers the role of general social beliefs, and of social relations between groups (e.g. some research into social identity, social representations and minority influence; studies considering the role of cultural norms and values).

Source: Hogg (1992: 62), based on Lorenzi-Cioldi and Doise (1990: 73) and Doise (1986: 10–16).

---

that century. The character Mr Gradgrind in Charles Dickens' 1854 novel *Hard Times* epitomises positivism: science as a religion.

Social psychology has been criticised for being positivistic (e.g. Gergen, 1973; Henriques, Holloway, Urwin, Venn, & Walkerdine, 1984; Potter, Stringer, & Wetherell, 1984; Shotter, 1984). It is argued that because social psychologists are ultimately studying themselves they cannot achieve the level of objectivity of, say, a chemist studying a compound or a geographer studying a landform. As complete objectivity is unattainable, scientific methods, particularly experimental ones, are simply not appropriate for social psychology. Social psychology can only masquerade as a science—it cannot be a true science. Critics argue that what social psychologists propose as fundamental causal mechanisms (e.g. categorisation, attribution, cognitive balance, self-concept) are only 'best-guess' concepts that explain some historically and culturally restricted data—data that are subject to unavoidable and intrinsic bias. Critics also feel that, by treating humans as objects or clusters of variables that can be experimentally manipulated, we are not only cutting ourselves off from a rich reservoir of subjective or introspective data—we are dehumanising people.

These criticisms have produced some quite radical alternatives to traditional social psychology. Examples include social constructionism (Gergen, 1973), humanistic psychology (Shotter, 1984), ethogenics (Harré, 1979), discourse analysis or discursive psychology (Edwards, 1997; Potter & Wetherell, 1987) and poststructuralist perspectives (Henriques, Holloway, Urwin, Venn, & Walkerdine, 1984). There are marked differences among these alternatives, but they share a broad emphasis on understanding people as whole human beings who are constructed historically and who try to make sense of themselves and their world. Research methods tend to emphasise in-depth subjective analysis (often called 'deconstruction') of the relatively spontaneous accounts people give of their thoughts, feelings and actions. Subjectivity is considered a virtue of, rather than an impediment to, good research.

Most social psychologists, however, respond to the problem of positivism in a less dramatic manner, which does not involve abandoning the scientific method. They deal instead with the pitfalls of positivism by being rigorous in the use of appropriate scientific methods of research and theorising (e.g. Campbell, 1957; Kruglanski, 1975; Turner, 1981a). Included in this is awareness of the need for **operational definitions** of social processes, such as aggression, altruism or leadership. Operationalism is a product of positivism, and refers to a plea that theoretical terms in science be defined in a manner that renders them susceptible to measurement. As scientists, we should be mindful of our own subjectivity, and should acknowledge and make explicit our biases. Our theories should be sensitive to the pitfalls of reductionism and, where appropriate, articulate different levels of analysis. We should also recognise that experimental participants are real people, who do not throw off their past history and become unidimensional 'variables' when they enter the laboratory. On the contrary, culture, history, socialisation and personal motives are all present in the laboratory—experiments are social situations (Tajfel, 1972a). Finally, attention should be paid to language, as that is perhaps the most important way in which people represent the world, think, plan action, and manipulate the world around them (Chapter 15). Language is also the epitome of a social variable: it is socially constructed and internalised to govern individual social cognition and behaviour.

Refer again to the focus question that opened this chapter. Your response will be coloured by the theory you adopt, the methods you choose and the kind of data analysis you employ in undertaking research.

Historical context

Social psychology, as we have described it, is not a static science. It has a history, and it is invaluable to consider a science in its proper historical context. Although ancient forms of social and political philosophy examined such questions as the nature–nurture controversy, the origins of society and the function of the state, it was mostly a speculative exercise devoid of fact-gathering (Hollander, 1967). An empirical approach to the study of social life did not appear until the latter part of the 19th century.

SOCIAL PSYCHOLOGY IN THE 19TH CENTURY
Anglo-European influences

An important precursor to the development of an independent discipline of social psychology was the work of a number of people in Germany known as the *folk psychologists*. In 1860 a journal devoted to **Völker-psychologie** was founded by Steinthal and Lazarus, and contained both theoretical and factual articles. Whereas general psychology (elaborated later by Wundt) dealt with the study of the mind, folk psychology, following the stimulus of the philosopher Hegel, dealt with the study of the collective mind. This concept was interpreted in conflicting ways by Steinthal and Lazarus to mean, at the same time, a societal way of thinking within the individual and a form of super-mentality that could enfold a whole group of people (Haines, 1980).

This idea, of a *group mind*, became a dominant way, in the 1890s and early 1900s, to account for social behaviour. An extreme example of it was found in the work of the French writer LeBon (1896/1908), in his account

of why crowds often behave badly—namely, because the behaviour of the individual becomes subject to the control of the group mind. Likewise, the English psychologist McDougall (1920) subscribed to the group mind explanation when he dealt with collective behaviour, devoting a whole book to the topic. Asch (1951) observed, much later, that the issue that such writers wanted to deal with has not gone away: that to understand the complexities of an individual's behaviour requires us to view the person in the context of group relations.

Early texts

At the turn of the century there were two texts dealing with social psychology, by Bunge (1903) and Orano (1901). Because they were not in English, they received scant attention in Britain and the United States. Even earlier, an American, Baldwin (1897), touched on the field of social psychology in a work that dealt mainly with the social and moral development of the child. A book by the French sociologist Tarde (1898) had definite implications for the kind of data and the level of explanation that social psychology should adopt. His view was a bottom-up approach and was offered in debate with Durkheim. Whereas Durkheim argued that the way people behave is determined by social laws that are set by society, Tarde proposed that a science of social behaviour must derive from laws that deal with the individual case. The way he conceived of social psychology is closer in flavour to most current American thinking than any of the other early texts (Clark, 1969).

The two early texts that caught the attention of the English-speaking world were by McDougall (1908) and the American sociologist Ross (1908). Neither looks much like a modern social psychology text, but we need to remember that living scientific disciplines continue to be redefined. The central topics of McDougall's book, for example, were the principal instincts, primary emotions, the nature of sentiments, moral conduct, volition, religious conceptions and the structure of character. Compare these with the chapter topics of the present textbook.

THE RISE OF EXPERIMENTATION

An influential textbook by Allport (1924) provided an agenda for social psychology that was quickly and enduringly followed by many teachers in psychology departments. Following the manifesto for psychology as a whole laid out by the behaviourist Watson (1913), Allport argued strongly that social psychology would flourish only if it became an experimental science. A little later, Murphy and Murphy (1931/1937) felt justified in producing a book entitled *Experimental Social Psychology*. Not all of the studies reviewed were actually experiments, but their intentions for the discipline were clear.

Although the earlier texts had not shown it, the

Competition and audience effect: Triplett found that cyclists ride faster when competing than when cycling alone. This triathlete has no rivals in sight, but his performance is socially facilitated by enthusiastic onlookers.

closing decade of the 19th century had set a scene in which social psychology would be inextricably entwined with the broader discipline of general psychology. As such, its subsequent development reflects the way in which psychology was defined and taught in university departments of psychology, particularly in the United States, which rapidly replaced Germany as the leading country for psychological research. Just as the psychological laboratory at Leipzig, founded by Wundt in 1879, had provided an experimental basis for psychology in Germany, so the laboratories set up at American universities did likewise. In the period 1890–1910 the growth of laboratories devoted to psychological research was rapid (Ruckmick, 1912). Thirty-one American universities established experimental facilities in those 20 years. The subject taught in these departments was clearly defined as an experimental science. In the United States, therefore, it is not surprising that social psychology should quite early on look towards the **experimental method** as a touchstone. By the time Allport produced his 1924 text, this trend was well established.

When was social psychology's first experiment?

This is a natural question to ask, but the answer is clouded. One of the oldest psychological laboratories was at Indiana University. It was here that Triplett (1898) conducted a study that some modern textbooks have listed as the first experiment in social psychology (e.g. Lippa, 1990; Penrod, 1983; Sears, Peplau, & Taylor, 1991) and quote as an experiment on social facilitation (e.g. Baron & Byrne, 1994; Brigham, 1991; Deaux & Wrightsman, 1988; see Chapter 8). Allport (1954) implied that what Wundt did in 1879 for experimental psychology Triplett did in 1898 for a scientific social psychology. Read Box 1.2 and judge for yourself whether you think this was a study in social psychology.

The search for a founding figure, or a first idea, is

not a new phenomenon in the history of science nor, indeed, in the history of civilisation. Sometimes it has the trappings of an origin myth. In the present case, there were studies earlier than 1898 that might just as easily be called the 'first' in social psychology (Burnham, 1910; Haines & Vaughan, 1979). Vaughan and Guerin (1997) point out that sports psychologists have claimed Triplett as one of their own. Certainly, his work dealt with competition rather than social facilitation.

LATER INFLUENCES

Social psychology's development after the early impact of **behaviourism** was redirected by a number of other important developments, some of which came from beyond mainstream psychology.

Attitude scaling

One of these developments was the arrival of several methods for constructing scales to measure attitudes (Bogardus, 1925; Likert, 1932; Thurstone, 1928), two of which were published in sociology journals, and are discussed in Chapter 5. The discipline of sociology has often thrown up approaches to social psychology that have been critical of an individual-behaviour level of analysis. Thomas and Znaniecki (1918), for example, defined social psychology as the scientific study of attitudes rather than of social behaviour.

Studies of the social group

Central to social psychology is an abiding interest in the structure and function of the social group (see Chapters 8, 9 and 11). Kurt Lewin, considered the 'father' of experimental social psychology, put much of his energy into the study of group processes (Marrow, 1969). For example, one of Lewin's imaginative studies was an experiment dealing with the effect of leadership style on small-group behaviour (Lewin, Lippitt, & White, 1939; see Chapter 9), and by 1945 he had founded a research centre (which still exists, now at the University of Michigan) devoted to the study of group dynamics.

Another important thread in research on the nature of the social group came from the field of industrial psychology. A famous study carried out in a factory setting showed that work productivity can be more heavily influenced by the psychological properties of the work group, and by the degree of interest management shows in its workers (Roethlisberger & Dickson, 1939), than by mere physical working conditions. A major outcome of research of this kind was to reinforce an approach to social psychology in which theory and application can develop together.

Famous textbooks

The 1930s marked several quite different themes, which had a striking impact on the continuing development of

BOX 1.2	Triplett (1898): A historic experiment

IT IS OFTEN CLAIMED THAT TRIPLETT'S STUDY WAS SOCIAL PSYCHOLOGY'S FIRST EXPERIMENT. HOWEVER, FURTHER CONSIDERATION SUGGESTS THAT IT HAD CLOSER LINKS TO PSYCHOPHYSIOLOGY AND SPORTS PSYCHOLOGY

Norman Triplett was a 37-year-old teacher when he returned to postgraduate studies at Indiana University to work on his masters thesis, published in 1898 as 'The dynamogenic factors in pacemaking and competition'. His supervisors were two experimental psychologists, Bryan and Bergström, and the laboratory (along with that at Clark University) was one of the best established settings in the country. His experiment is often referred to as a study in social facilitation (a topic discussed in Chapter 8) and classified by some textbook writers as the first social-psychological experiment ever conducted. Is this claim justified?

Triplett's interest had been stimulated by the popular knowledge that racing cyclists go faster when racing, or when being paced, than when riding alone. Cycling as an activity had increased enormously in popularity in the closing decade of the 19th century and was participated in both as a pastime and as a sport, with spectacular press coverage. Triplett listed a variety of possible explanations for the superior performance of cyclists who were racing or being paced:

- The pacer in front provided a suction that pulled the following rider along, helping to conserve energy; or else provided shelter from the wind.
- A 'brain worry' theory, popular at the time, predicted that solitary cyclists did poorly because they worried about whether they were going fast enough. This exhausted their brain and muscles, possibly because phosphoric acid was released, which numbed the brain and inhibited motor performance.
- Friends usually rode as pacers and no doubt encouraged the cyclists to keep up their spirits.
- In a race, a follower might be hypnotised by the wheels in front and so rode automatically, leaving more energy for a later, controlled burst.
- A dynamogenic theory, favoured by Triplett, proposed that the presence of another person racing aroused a 'competitive instinct'. The competitive instinct released 'nervous energy' (a concept fairly close to the modern idea of arousal). The sight of movement in another suggested a higher speed and inspired greater effort. Other racers released a level of nervous energy that an isolated rider cannot achieve alone. The energy of a movement was in proportion to the idea of that movement.

In the psychology of Triplett's day, it was thought that to perform a movement an 'idea' of that movement had to be present. This idea 'suggested' the action to be performed and the stronger the idea, the stronger the movement.

In the most famous of Triplett's experiments, he recorded the performance of 40 boys and girls aged from 8 to 17. They worked in two conditions, in pairs and alone. The apparatus consisted of two fishing reels, which turned silk bands around a drum. Each reel was connected by a loop of cord to a pulley located 2 metres away, and a small flag was attached to each cord. To complete one trial, a flag sewn to the silk band had to travel four times around the wheel.

The results showed that some children were slower in competition, some were faster in competition, and others were little affected. He interpreted the faster ones as showing the effects of both 'the arousal of their competitive instincts and the idea of a faster movement' (Triplett, 1898, p. 526). For those who were slower, he thought that they were overstimulated and 'going to pieces' (a nice modern turn of phrase!).

In expanding on the dynamogenic theory, his main interest was in the ideo-motor responses—that is, the effects of one competitor's bodily movements acting as a cue for the other competitor. It is interesting that essentially non-social cues are highlighted by Triplett to illustrate the idea of movement being used as a cue by his participants.

The leading American psychological journals in the decade after Triplett's study scarcely made reference to it. It was catalogued in general sources, but not under any headings with a 'social' connotation. In Baldwin's 1901 dictionary it was located under 'Will', but not under 'Individual and Social'. Likewise, in the 1899 volume of *L'Année Psychologique*, it was excluded from the section called 'Sociology', which in turn subsumed social psychology. Instead, it was listed under 'Movement and Volition' in a section with other papers that were mostly physiological or psychophysiological in nature.

What is clear is that Triplett himself cannot be considered a social psychologist. By adopting a revisionist view of history, the spirit of his experiment emerges as a precursor to the theme of social facilitation research.

Role transition: Marriage marks a significant role transition that carries with it changed expectations about how one will behave.

the discipline. Murchison (1935) produced the first handbook for the subject, a weighty tome that suggested this was a field to be taken seriously. A later, expanded edition of the Murphy and Murphy text (1931/1937) appeared which summarised the findings of more than 1000 studies, although it was used mainly as a reference work. Perhaps the most widely used textbook of this period was that by LaPiere and Farnsworth (1936). Klineberg (1940), also popular, featured contributions from cultural anthropology and emphasised the crucial role that culture plays in the way that an individual's personality develops. Just after World War II, a mainstream work by Krech and Crutchfield (1948) appeared which emphasised a phenomenological approach to social psychology—that is, an approach focusing on the way in which people actually experience the world and account for their experiences.

In the 1950s and the next two decades, the number of textbooks appearing on the bookshelves increased exponentially. Most have been published in the United States, with a heavy reliance on both American data and American theory.

Famous experiments

For different reasons, several experiments stand out over the years that have fascinated teachers and students alike. The following have had an impact beyond the immediate discipline—reaching out to the wider perspective of general psychology, and some further, to other disciplines. We will not go into detail about these studies here, as they are treated in later chapters.

Sherif (1935) conducted an experiment on *norm formation* that caught the attention of psychologists eager to pinpoint what could be 'social' about social psychology (Chapter 7). Asch (1951) demonstrated the stunning effect that *group pressure* can have in persuading an indi-

vidual to conform (Chapter 7). Sherif and Sherif (1953) looked at the role that competition for resources can have on intergroup conflict (Chapter 11). Festinger (1957) used his theory of *cognitive dissonance* to show that a smaller reward can induce more attitude change than a larger reward (Festinger & Carlsmith, 1959), a finding that annoyed the orthodox reinforcement theorists of the time (Chapters 5 and 6). Milgram's (1963) study of *destructive obedience* highlighted the dilemma faced by a person ordered by an authority figure to perform an immoral act, a study that was to take centre stage in a crisis period of questioning about the future of the experimental method in social psychology (Chapter 7).

Finally, Zimbardo (1971) set up a simulated prison in the basement of Stanford University's psychology department to study *deindividuation* and the reality and extremity of roles (Chapter 8). Recently, this study caught the imagination of a reality-TV oriented society—see the movie *The Experiment*, and a 2002 BBC TV series by social psychologists Alex Haslam and Stephen Reicher.

Famous programs

One way of viewing the network within which a discipline develops is to ask the question 'Who's who?' and then 'Who influenced whom?' Looked at in this way, the group-centred research of the charismatic Lewin (Marrow, 1969) had a remarkable impact on other social psychologists in the United States. One of his students was Leon Festinger, and one of Festinger's students was Stanley Schachter. Schachter's work on the cognitive labelling of emotion is a derivative of Festinger's notion of social comparison (i.e. the way individuals use other people as a basis for assessing their own thoughts, feelings and behaviours).

There have been other groups of researchers whose impact is more obvious by the nature of the concepts emerging from their programs. There were two influential groups whose research concerned questions posed by World War II. One studied the *authoritarian personality* (Adorno, Frenkel-Brunswik, Levinson, & Sanford, 1950). Stimulated by the possibility that the rise of German autocracy resided in the modal personality of the German people and was a product of the way they reared their children, the researchers embarked on an ambitious cross-cultural study of authoritarianism in the United States (Chapter 10). Another group studied how to change people's attitudes. The Yale *attitude change* program, led by Hovland, was designed to uncover the theory and techniques of propaganda (Hovland, Janis, & Kelley, 1953; see Chapter 6).

Later developments

Thibaut and Kelley (1959) developed an influential approach to the study of interpersonal relationships, based on an economic model of *social exchange*

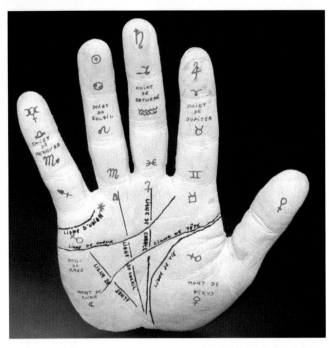

Attribution: People try to make sense of their lives in many different ways. We can try palmistry, or more mundanely examine the immediate causes of our experiences.

(Chapter 13), which continued to stimulate theories into the 1980s. Likewise, Deutsch (Deutsch & Krauss, 1960) applied exchange theory to open up the field of inter-personal bargaining to the psychologist. The remarkable contribution made by Lewin to the manner in which social psychology was to develop can again be seen: all these innovators (Thibaut, Kelley, Deutsch) were his students.

The modern period has been dominated by cognitive approaches. *Attribution theory* was set on its path by Jones (Jones & Davis, 1965), who focused attention on the ordinary person's ideas about causality (Chapter 3). Darley and Latané (1968) employed an innovative cognitive model to research *prosocial behaviour* by throwing light on the way in which people interpret an emergency and sometimes fail to help a victim (Chapter 14).

Following earlier work by Heider (1946) and Asch (1946) in a field loosely described as social perception, a major restructuring developed this avenue into modern *social cognition* (see Chapter 2). Several researchers made major contributions to this development, including Mischel (Cantor & Mischel, 1977), who dealt with the way that perceived behaviour traits can function as prototypes, and Nisbett and Ross (1980) who opened up the domain of cognitive heuristics (mental short-cuts in social thinking).

European contributions

It is ironic that the beginnings of social psychology and, indeed, psychology are to be found in Europe and yet now the field is largely dominated by American concepts,

journals and books. Much of this shift can be attributed to the devastating intellectual and material consequences of European fascism during the period 1930–45. However, as Europe has rebuilt itself there has been a steady reconstruction and renaissance of a distinct and vibrant European social psychology (Jaspars, 1980). It has its own scientific association, the European Association of Experimental Social Psychology, prestigious English-language periodicals (*European Journal of Social Psychology*, *European Review of Social Psychology* and *British Journal of Social Psychology*) and its own textbooks (e.g. Hewstone & Stroebe, 2001; Hogg & Vaughan, 2002). European social psychology places a greater emphasis than its American counterpart on the societal and intergroup context within which social behaviour takes place (e.g. Tajfel, 1984). It has made a significant international impact particularly on the study of group processes and intergroup behaviour (e.g. Hogg & Abrams, 1999; Moreland, Hogg, & Hains, 1994).

Historically, there are two figures who have particularly shaped European social psychology: Henri Tajfel and Serge Moscovici. Tajfel (1974), at the University of Bristol, initiated a major approach to the study of intergroup relations; his social identity theory took a look at the topic of intergroup relations, favouring an emphasis on the way in which a person's identity is defined in social terms by belonging to a group. It questioned Sherif's argument that an objective clash of interests was the necessary ingredient in intergroup conflict (Chapter 11). Moscovici (1961), at the Maison des Sciences de l'Homme in Paris, resuscitated an interest in the work of the 19th-century sociologist Durkheim, with his idea of collective representations (Chapter 3). In addition, he stimulated a major reinterpretation of the field of social conformity by demonstrating that minorities can sometimes turn around the view of a dominant majority group (Chapter 7).

THE JOURNALS

Traditional journals that were important up to the 1950s were the *Journal of Abnormal and Social Psychology* and the *Journal of Personality*. A sociological journal, *Sociometry*, also catered for social psychological work.

From the 1960s there was an increased demand for further outlets. This reflected the increase in the number of actively researching social psychologists around the world, and also the need for some regional representation. The patriarchal *Journal of Abnormal and Social Psychology* divided into two, one side devoted to abnormal psychology and the other titled the *Journal of Personality and Social Psychology* (founded in 1965). *Sociometry* was retitled *Social Psychology Quarterly* (1979) to reflect more accurately its major social psychological content.

Anglo-European interests were represented by the *British Journal of Social and Clinical Psychology* (1963) (which split in about 1980 to produce the *British Journal of Social Psychology* and the *British Journal of Clinical Psychology*) and the *European Journal of Social Psychology* (1971). Room for a second, American journal dedicated to experimental research was found for the *Journal of Experimental Social Psychology* (1965). Other journals devoted to the area include *Personality and Social Psychology Bulletin* (1975), *Journal of Applied Social Psychology* (1971) and *Social Cognition* (1982). In the last ten years there has been a growth of other key journals, including *Personality and Social Psychology Review*, *Group Processes and Intergroup Relations* and *Self and Identity*.

From the point of view of number of articles published there was, therefore, an explosion of interest in the subject during the decade bridging the 1960s and 1970s.

Social psychology in Australia and New Zealand

In Australia and New Zealand social psychology had its origins in British social psychology, and is now about equally influenced by Europe and the United States (Taft & Day, 1988). We are in the enviable position of being able to *choose* to integrate the best of American and European social psychology without any compulsion to adhere to the metatheoretical and ideological agendas of either. It is perhaps through this perspective that social psychology in Australia and New Zealand acquires a special character. However, with a combined population of a little under 25 million, we are naturally and quite rightly influenced by the social psychology of North America and Western Europe, where about 700 million people live. Perhaps because of this, our social psychology is more international than that to be found in the United States or Britain. Because Australia and New Zealand are recent immigrant countries that strive to practise multiculturalism, it is not surprising that issues to do with ethnicity, communication, language, culture, prejudice and intergroup relations are important areas of research (see Chapters 10, 11, 15 and 16). Another important area has arisen out of our progressive attitude towards HIV, smoking and sun protection: research into attitudes towards health-protective behaviours has a relatively high profile here.

Australian and New Zealand social psychologists are strongly represented on editorial boards of the top international journals, they publish widely and prolifically, and they pop up in disproportionate numbers at scientific conferences around the world. Most have had sabbatical, postdoctoral or doctoral experience at American or British universities. Some prominent social psychologists have moved here from the United States and from Britain, and some Australians and New Zealanders have left to make important contributions overseas. Many of the leading international scientific conferences for social psychologists have been hosted in Australia, and the annual Sydney Symposium on Social Psychology (SSSP), hosted by the University of New South Wales, has in a few short years become an important venue for leading scientists from around the world. In addition there is the annual Brisbane Symposium on Social Identity (BSSI), hosted by the University of Queensland, which has been running since 1992, and more recently a series of social psychology meetings in Melbourne, hosted by a group of Melbourne universities.

Many areas of research currently conducted here have a high international profile. There is vigorous research in fields such as social identity, person perception, affect and emotion, language and ethnicity, group decision-making, attitudes and values, studies of indigenous and migrant groups, interpersonal and intergroup communication, marital satisfaction, self-esteem and body image, and the social psychological aspects of AIDS and cancer. The list of topics continues to expand. While the longer established universities have served a major role in stimulating such work, the past decade or so has witnessed a distribution of talented people into newer tertiary settings. This is a healthy trend and augurs well for the future of social psychology in this part of the world.

Social psychology in Australia and New Zealand has been further invigorated by the establishment in 1995 of the Society of Australasian Social Psychologists (SASP), which has about 250 members. SASP is a formalisation and extension of the annual and peripatetic meeting of Australian social psychologists which began in 1972 at Flinders University in Adelaide (Feather, 1995). It is perhaps significant that 1995 witnessed the inaugural meeting, in Hong Kong, of the Asian Association of Social Psychology (AASP), in which prominent Australian and New Zealand social psychologists are now active office-holders. Close Asia–Pacific ties have developed between SASP and AASP. Indeed, in mid-2001 the SASP and AASP meetings were run together in Melbourne, with a number of overlapping and joint sessions. Finally, a report on psychological science in Australia, commissioned by the Australian government and prepared under the auspices of the Australian Academy of Science in 1996, identified social psychology as both an area of special strength and a priority area for further development (Commonwealth of Australia, 1996, p. 44).

About this book

We have written this introductory text, which is now in its fourth edition, because the burgeoning health and

vitality of Australian and New Zealand social psychology has cried out for it. As teachers of social psychology we had, until our first edition came out in 1995,
made do with a frustrating and unsatisfactory blend of
American and European texts. The American texts are
often simplified, and the European ones are idiosyncratic. Both tend to be culture-specific in terms of
content, style and perspective. Australian texts, of which
there have been very few, tended to lean towards the
European style, have been rather fragmented in coverage
or have, we feel, aimed too low.

Our aim has been to write an introduction to social
psychology for second-, third- and possibly fourth-year
university students of psychology. Its language caters for
intelligent adults. However, as it is an introduction, we
pay careful attention to sensitive use of specialist
language (i.e. scientific or social psychological jargon).
It is intended to be a comprehensive introduction to
mainstream social psychology and there are no intentional omissions. We cover classic and contemporary
theories and research, generally adopting a historical
perspective, as that most accurately reflects the unfold-
ing of scientific enquiry. The degree of detail and scope
of coverage is determined by the scope and intensity of
undergraduate social psychology courses in Australia
and New Zealand.

Because Australian and New Zealand social psychology is intrinsically less culture-specific than its North
American and European counterparts, we found it both
easy and appropriate to our own region to write what
we consider to be an international text. We have ironed
out many biases and have combined the most important
and enduring features of North American and European
social psychology. However, because we live in Australia
or New Zealand, not North America or Europe, we
have where appropriate taken examples from our own
historical, cultural and day-to-day experiences. For
instance, American texts rely on baseball, and European
texts on soccer, for sports examples; in Australia and
New Zealand our own football codes, cricket and
netball are more appropriate.

Many social psychology texts separate basic theory
and research from applied theory and research, generally by having 'applied' chapters at the end of the book
that typically focus on health, gender, organisations or
justice. Much like Kurt Lewin's view that there is nothing
so practical as a good theory, our philosophy is that basic
and applied research and theory are intertwined or best
treated as intertwined—they are naturally interdependent. Thus, applied topics are interwoven with basic
theory and research. Currently, some important areas of
application of social psychology include human development (e.g. Durkin, 1995), health (e.g. Stroebe &
Stroebe, 1995), gender (e.g. Basow, 1992), organisations
(e.g. Haslam, 2000), criminal justice (e.g. Stephenson,

1992) and culture (e.g. Smith & Bond, 1998; Moghaddam, Taylor, & Wright, 1993; Triandis, 1994). The topic
of culture has probably now become an integral part of
contemporary social psychology (see Chapter 16).

The book is structured so that Chapters 2 to 6 deal
with what goes on in people's heads—cognitive activities and cognitive representations. This includes discussion of attitudes and how they may change. Chapter
7 deals with the pivotal notion of social influence—how
people influence one another. Because an important class
of influence relies on being a member of a group, this
chapter flows logically into Chapters 8 and 9, which
deal with group processes. Chapters 10 and 11 broaden
the discussion of groups to consider what happens
between groups—prejudice, discrimination, conflict and
intergroup behaviour. That the nature of intergroup
behaviour involves so many instances of conflict invites
a discussion of human aggression, which is dealt with
in Chapter 12.

Lest we become disillusioned with our species,
Chapter 13 deals with interpersonal relations, including
attraction, friendship and love, and also with the topic
of breakdowns in relationships. Continuing the emphasis
on the more positive aspects of human behaviour,
Chapter 14 discusses how people can be altruistic and
can engage in selfless prosocial acts of kindness and
support. At the core of interpersonal interaction lies communication, of which spoken language is the richest form:
Chapter 15 deals with language and communication.
Chapter 16 recognises that social behaviour is anchored
in culture, and raises the question of how we can foster
indigenous psychologies and yet maintain a global view.

Each chapter is self-contained, though integrated into
the general logic of the entire text. There are plentiful
cross-references to other chapters, and at the end of each
chapter are references to further, more detailed coverage
of topics in the chapter. Many of the studies referred to
in this book can be found in the social psychology
journals that we have already noted in the historical
section. You are strongly encouraged to check new issues
of these publications to learn about the latest research.
Other articles that offer state-of-the-art summaries and
reviews of topics in social psychology appear in the
Annual Review of Psychology, *Psychological Bulletin*,
Psychological Review, *Advances in Experimental Social
Psychology*, *Personality and Social Psychology Review*
and *European Review of Social Psychology*.

For a very general introduction to social psychology,
see Hogg's (2000b) chapter in Pawlik and Rosenzweig's
International Handbook of Psychology. In contrast, the
most authoritative and detailed sources of information
about social psychology are undoubtably the current
handbooks of social psychology, of which there are
three: (1) Gilbert, Fiske and Lindzey's (1998) *Handbook
of Social Psychology*, currently in its fourth edition,

(2) Hogg and Cooper's (2003) *The Sage Handbook of Social Psychology* and (3) the four-volume *Blackwell Handbook of Social Psychology* of which each volume is a stand-alone book (*Intraindividual Processes* by Tesser & Schwartz, 2001; *Interpersonal Processes* by Fletcher & Clark, 2001; *Group Processes* by Hogg & Tindale, 2001; and *Intergroup Processes* by Brown & Gaertner, 2001).

A wonderful source of short definitions and slightly longer overviews of social psychological theories, topics, phenomena and findings is the 1996 paperback version of Manstead and Hewstone's *The Blackwell Encyclopedia of Social Psychology*. Finally, Hogg's (2003c) *Sage Benchmarks in Psychology: Social Psychology* is a four-volume edited and annotated collection of almost 80 benchmark research articles in social psychology—it contains many of the discipline's most impactful classic and contemporary works. The volumes are divided into sections with short introductions.

Summary

- Social psychology can be defined as the scientific investigation of how the thoughts, feelings and behaviours of individuals are influenced by the actual, imagined or implied presence of others. Although social psychology can also be described in terms of what it studies, it is probably more useful to describe it as a way of looking at human behaviour.
- Social psychology is a science. It employs the scientific method to study social behaviour. Although this involves a whole range of empirical methods to collect data to test hypotheses and construct theories, experimentation is usually the preferred method as it is the best way to reveal causal processes. Nevertheless, methods are matched to research questions, and methodological pluralism is highly valued.
- Social psychological data are usually transformed into numbers, which are analysed by a range of formal numerical procedures—that is, statistics. Statistics allow conclusions to be drawn about whether a research observation is a true effect or some chance event.
- Social psychology is enlivened by fierce and invigorating debates about the ethics of research methods, the appropriate research methods for an understanding of social behaviour, the validity and power of social psychology theories, and the type of theories that are properly *social* psychological.
- Although having origins in 19th-century German folk psychology and French crowd psychology, modern social psychology really began in America in the 1920s with the adoption of the experimental method. Enormous impetus was given to social psychology by Kurt Lewin in the 1940s and the discipline has grown exponentially ever since. Although the discipline is still dominated by America, European perspectives have had an increasing influence since the late 1960s.
- Initially influenced by Britain, social psychology in Australia and New Zealand is now relatively equally influenced by North American and Western European perspectives. Without any pressure to align ourselves ideologically or metatheoretically with either camp, we are free to integrate the best from both. Being immigrant countries Australia and New Zealand have a special interest in such issues as intergroup relations, prejudice, ethnicity, culture, language and communication.

LINKS

YOU HAVE READ ABOUT:	WHICH LINKS TO:
Relevance of the scientific method	using the scientific method to draw inferences from behaviour such as attitudes (5); and to seek out fundamental cognitive processes (2)
Levels of explanation	in relation to: attribution (interpersonal and intergroup) (3); aggression (12)
Research ethics	ethics and the psychological experiment (7)
Nature of theorising in social psychology	theories of prejudice (10); theories of aggression (12); theories of altruism (14)
Historic experiments	Yale studies of attitude change (6); Sherif's study of group norms and Asch's study of conformity (7)

continues

| Connections with sociology, anthropology, economics, linguistics | prejudice (10); intergroup relations (11); aggression (12); social exchange (13); altruism (14) |
| Importance of theory | attribution of motives (3); conflict between attitudes and behaviour (6); nature of leadership (9); origins of aggression (12) |

Key terms

archival research *(p. 8)*
behaviour *(p. 2)*
behaviourism *(p. 17)*
case study *(p. 8)*
cognitive theories *(p. 13)*
confounding *(p. 6)*
correlation *(p. 8)*
data *(p. 2)*
demand characteristics *(p. 7)*
dependent variables *(p. 5)*
double-blind *(p. 7)*
evolutionary social psychology *(p. 13)*

experimental method *(p. 17)*
experimental realism *(p. 7)*
experimenter effects *(p. 7)*
external validity *(p. 7)*
hypotheses *(p. 4)*
independent variables *(p. 5)*
internal validity *(p. 7)*
laboratory *(p. 6)*
level of explanation *(p. 14)*
metatheory *(p. 12)*
mundane realism *(p. 7)*
neo-behaviourist *(p. 13)*

operational definition *(p. 15)*
positivism *(p. 15)*
radical behaviourist *(p. 13)*
reductionism *(p. 14)*
science *(p. 2)*
social psychology *(p. 2)*
statistical significance *(p. 9)*
statistics *(p. 9)*
subject effects *(p. 7)*
t-test *(p. 9)*
theory *(p. 2)*
Völkerpsychologie (p. 16)

FURTHER READING

Allport, G. W. (1954a). The historical background of modern social psychology. In G. Lindzey (Ed.), *Handbook of social psychology* (Vol. 1, pp. 3–56). Reading, MA: Addison-Wesley. Traditional and often-cited account of the history of social psychology, covering the period up to the 1950s.

Aronson, E., Ellsworth, P. C., Carlsmith, J. M., & Gonzales, M. H. (1990). *Methods of research in social psychology* (2nd ed.). New York: McGraw-Hill. Detailed, well-written and now classic coverage of research methods in social psychology.

Ellsworth, P. C., & Gonzales, R. (2003). Questions and comparisons: Methods of research in social psychology. In M. A. Hogg & J. Cooper (Eds.), *The Sage handbook of social psychology* (pp. 24–42). London: Sage. Up-to-date, concise and readable overview of how to move from the research question to research itself in social psychology, and how to make choices about methods.

Farr, R. M. (1996). *The roots of modern social psychology: 1872–1954.* Oxford, UK: Blackwell. A very scholarly and provocative discussion of the intellectual roots of modern social psychology. Farr is a renowned historical commentator on the discipline.

Goethals, G. R. (2003). A century of social psychology: Individuals, ideas, and investigations. In M. A. Hogg & J. Cooper (Eds.), *The Sage handbook of social psychology* (pp. 3–23). London: Sage. A very readable, comprehensive and inclusive coverage of the history of social psychology.

Howell, D. C. (1997). *Statistical methods for psychology* (4th ed.). Boston, MA: Boston-Duxbury. Highly respected and often-used basic introduction to psychological statistics. With all the usual equations and formulae, it is also easy to read.

Jones, E. E. (1998). Major developments in five decades of social psychology. In D. T. Gilbert, S. T. Fiske, & G. Lindzey (Eds.), *The handbook of social psychology* (4th ed., Vol. 1, pp. 3–57). New York: McGraw-Hill. This treatment overlaps with and moves on from Allport's (1968) chapter, covering the period 1935–85. In addition to classical developments it covers the growth of such areas as social comparison, cognitive dissonance, attitude change, conformity, person perception and attribution.

Judd, C. M., McClelland, G. H., & Culhane, S. E. (1995). Data analysis: Continuing issues in the everyday analysis of psychological data. *Annual Review of Psychology, 46,* 433–465. Up-to-date, relatively readable and brief discussion of the main statistical problems confronted by psychologists designing studies and analysing data.

Rosnow, R. L., & Rosenthal, R. (1997). *People studying people: Artifacts and ethics in behavioural research.* New York: Freeman. An introduction to the major biases that can distort the validity of studying human behaviour, and a brief account of ethical issues.

Shaw, M. E., & Costanzo, P. R. (1982). *Theories of social psychology* (2nd ed.). New York: McGraw-Hill. Because the authors organise social psychological theories in terms of general types of theory, this is a good place to get a general overview of the types of theoretical orientations that inform specific social psychological theories.

Tabachnik, B. G., & Fidell, L. S. (1989). *Using multivariate statistics* (2nd ed.). New York: HarperCollins. The acknowledged 'bible' for doing, interpreting and reporting multivariate statistics in psychology.

Taylor, S. E. (1998). The social being in social psychology. In D. T. Gilbert, S. T. Fiske, & G. Lindzey (Eds.), *The handbook of social psychology* (4th ed., Vol. 1, pp. 58–95). New York: McGraw-Hill. A historical coverage of recent social psychology that takes a somewhat American social cognition perspective. Taylor is one of the leading figures of social psychology and one of the early champions of social cognition.

Social cognition and social thinking

THIS CHAPTER DISCUSSES:

- how we process social information: the nature of social cognition
- forming impressions of other people
- types of social schemas and the role of categorisation
- person memory
- how social inference is affected by biases and errors
- cognitive short-cuts or heuristics
- feelings and emotion.

FOCUS QUESTIONS

1. You have just been interviewed for a job. Mrs Jones in the human resources department has probably figured out that you are intelligent, sincere and helpful. However, you did not laugh readily at one of her jokes—she may suspect you don't have a sense of humour! How would she form an overall impression of you?
2. John's hair is multi-coloured and the colours change almost every month. Would others spot him immediately at a student–staff meeting in your psychology department? What about at a board meeting of your city's largest accountancy firm?
3. Aaron comes to mind rather differently for Julie and Rosa. Julie remembers him mostly when she thinks of the various lawyers that she knows. Rosa thinks about his quirky smile and his knowledge of top-selling novels. Why might their memories differ in these ways?

Social psychology and cognition

Social psychology is the science of human thought, feeling and behaviour as they are influenced by and have influence on other people. Within this broad definition (see Chapter 1), thought has always occupied a pivotal role: people think about their social world, and on the basis of thought they act in certain ways. Thought is very much the internal language and symbols we use. It is often conscious, or at least something we are or could be aware of. In contrast, cognition is largely automatic. We are unaware of it and only with difficulty notice it, let alone characterise it in language or shared symbols. Perhaps a useful way to think about cognition is as a computer program: it operates in the background, running all the functions of the computer that we are aware of.

Cognition and thought occur within the human mind. They are the mental activities that mediate between the world out there and what people subsequently do. Their operation can be inferred from what people say and do—from people's expressions, actions, writings and sayings. If we can understand cognition, we may gain some understanding of how and why people behave in the ways they do. **Social cognition** is a major approach in social psychology that focuses on the way in which cognition is affected by wider and more immediate social contexts and on how cognition affects our social behaviour.

During the 1980s there was an explosion of research on social cognition. According to Taylor (1998), during its heyday 85% of submissions to the *Journal of Personality and Social Psychology*, social psychology's flagship journal, were social cognition articles. Social cognition remains healthy and vibrant as a dominant perspective on the explanation of social behaviour (e.g. Gollwitzer & Bargh, 1996; Wyer, 1998). It has taught us much about how we process and store information about people, and how this affects the way we perceive and interact with people. It has also taught us new methods and techniques for conducting social psychological research—methods and techniques borrowed from cognitive psychology and then refined for social psychology. Social cognition has had an enormous impact on social psychology (Devine, Hamilton, & Ostrom, 1994).

A HISTORY OF COGNITION IN SOCIAL PSYCHOLOGY

Wundt (1897) was one of the founders of modern empirical psychology. He used self-observation and introspection to gain an understanding of cognition (people's subjective experience), which he believed to be the main purpose of psychology. This methodology became unpopular because it was not scientific. Data and theories were idiosyncratic and almost impossible to refute, because people could not use their own cognition as data to challenge someone else's theory of their own cognition.

Because psychologists felt that theories should be based on publicly observable and replicable data, there was a shift away from studying internal (cognitive) events towards external, publicly observable events. The ultimate expression of this change in emphasis was American **behaviourism** of the early 20th century (e.g. Skinner, 1963; Thorndike, 1940; Watson, 1930)—cognition became a dirty word in psychology for almost half a century. Behaviourists focused on overt behaviour (e.g. a scream) as a response to observable stimuli in the environment (e.g. a shark), based on past punishments and rewards for the behaviour (e.g. being rescued from the surf by a surf lifesaver).

By the 1960s psychologists began to take a fresh interest in cognition. This was partly because behaviourism seemed cumbersome and inadequate as an explanation of human language and communication (see Chomsky, 1959); some consideration of how people represent the world symbolically and how they manipulate such symbols was needed. Moreover, the world was becoming more and more dominated by the manipulation and transfer of information: information processing became an increasingly important focus for psychology (Broadbent, 1985; Wyer & Gruenfeld, 1995). This development continued with the computer revolution, which has encouraged and enabled psychologists to model or simulate highly complex human cognitive processes. The computer has also become a metaphor for the human mind, with computer software/programs standing in for cognition. Cognitive psychology, sometimes called cognitive science, has re-emerged as a legitimate scientific pursuit (e.g. Anderson, 1990; Neisser, 1967).

In contrast to general psychology, social psychology has almost always been strongly cognitive (Manis, 1977; Zajonc, 1980). This emphasis can be traced at least as far back as Lewin, who is often referred to as the father of experimental social psychology. Drawing on *gestalt* psychology, Lewin (1951) believed that social behaviour is most usefully understood as a function of people's perceptions of their world and of their manipulations of such perceptions. As such, cognition and thought are placed centre stage in social psychology. The cognitive emphasis in social psychology has had at least four guises (Jones, 1998; Taylor, 1998): cognitive consistency, naive scientist, cognitive miser and motivated tactician.

After World War II, in the 1940s and 1950s, an enormous amount of research was done on attitude change. This produced a number of theories sharing an assumption that people strive for **cognitive consistency**—that is, they are motivated to reduce perceived discrepancies among their various cognitions because such discrepancies are aversive (e.g. Abelson, Aronson, McGuire, Newcomb, Rosenberg, & Tannenbaum, 1968; Festinger, 1957; Heider, 1958; see Chapters 5 and 6). Consistency theories gradually lost popularity in the 1960s as evidence accumulated that people are in fact very tolerant of cognitive inconsistency.

In its place there arose in the early 1970s a **naive scientist** model that characterised people as having a need to attribute causes to behaviours and events in order to render the world a meaningful place in which to act. This model underpins the **attribution** theories of human behaviour that dominated social psychology in the 1970s (see Chapter 3). The naive scientist model assumes that people are basically rational in making scientific-like cause–effect analyses. They are, however, compromised by limited information and by various motivational factors (e.g. self-interest), allowing all sorts of errors and biases to creep in.

In the late 1970s it became clear that even in ideal circumstances people are not very careful scientists. Instead, it seems that they are limited in their capacity to process information and they take a number of cognitive short-cuts—that is, they are **cognitive misers** (Nisbett & Ross, 1980; Taylor, 1981). The various errors and biases associated with social thinking are not motivated departures from some ideal form of information processing, but are intrinsic to social thinking. Motivation has almost disappeared from the cognitive miser perspective. However, as this cognitive miser perspective has matured, the importance of motivation has again become evident (Gollwitzer & Bargh, 1996; Showers & Cantor, 1985)—the social thinker has become characterised as a **motivated tactician** (Fiske & Taylor, 1991, p. 13): 'a fully engaged thinker who has multiple cognitive strategies available and chooses among them based on goals, motives and needs. Sometimes the motivated tactician chooses wisely, in the interests of adaptability and accuracy, and sometimes . . . defensively, in the interests of speed or self-esteem'.

Forming impressions of other people

People spend a great deal of time thinking about other people. We form impressions of the people we meet, have described to us or encounter in the media. We communicate these impressions to others, and we use them as bases for deciding how we will feel and act. Impression formation and person perception are important aspects of social cognition (Schneider, Hastorf, & Ellsworth, 1979).

ASCH'S CONFIGURAL MODEL

According to Asch's (1946) **configural model**, in forming first impressions we latch onto certain pieces of information, called **central traits**, which have a disproportionate influence over the final impression. Other pieces of information, called **peripheral traits**, have much less influence. Central and peripheral traits are ones that are more or less intrinsically correlated with other traits, and therefore more or less useful in constructing an integrated impression of a person. Central traits influence the meanings of other traits and the perceived relationship among traits—that is, they are responsible for the integrated configuration of the impression.

To investigate this idea, Asch had students read one of two lists of seven adjectives describing a hypothetical person. The lists differed only slightly—one contained the word *warm* and the other the word *cold* (see Figure 2.1). Participants then evaluated the target person on a number of other bipolar evaluative dimensions, such as generous/ungenerous, happy/unhappy, reliable/unreliable. Asch found that participants exposed to the list containing *warm* generated a much more favourable impression of the target than did those exposed to the list containing the trait *cold* (see Figure 2.1). When the words *warm* and *cold* were replaced by *polite* and *blunt*, the difference in impression was far less marked. Asch argued that warm/cold is a central trait dimension that has more influence on impression formation than polite/blunt, which is a peripheral trait dimension.

Asch's experiment was replicated in a naturalistic setting by Kelley (1950), whose introduction of a guest lecturer to students ended with: 'People who know him consider him to be a rather *cold* (or very *warm*) person, *industrious*, *critical*, *practical* and *determined*'. The lecturer gave identical lectures to a number of classes, half of which received the *cold* and half the *warm* description. After the lecture, the students rated the lecturer on a number of dimensions. Those who received the *cold* trait rated the lecturer as more *unsociable*, *self-centred*, *unpopular*, *formal*, *irritable*, *humourless* and *ruthless*. They were also less likely to ask questions and to interact with the lecturer. This seems to support the *Gestalt* view that impressions are formed as integrated wholes based on central cues.

Critics, however, have wondered how we can decide what is a central trait. *Gestalt* theorists believe that the centrality of a trait rests on its intrinsic degree of correlation with other traits. Others have argued that centrality is a function of context (e.g. Wishner, 1960; Zanna & Hamilton, 1972): in Asch's experiment, warm/cold was central because it was distinct from the other trait dimensions and was semantically linked to the response dimensions. People tend to employ two main dimensions for evaluating other people: good/bad social, and good/bad intellectual (Rosenberg, Nelson,

A CLASSIC IN SOCIAL PSYCHOLOGY

FIGURE 2.1 | Impressions of a hypothetical person, based on central and peripheral traits

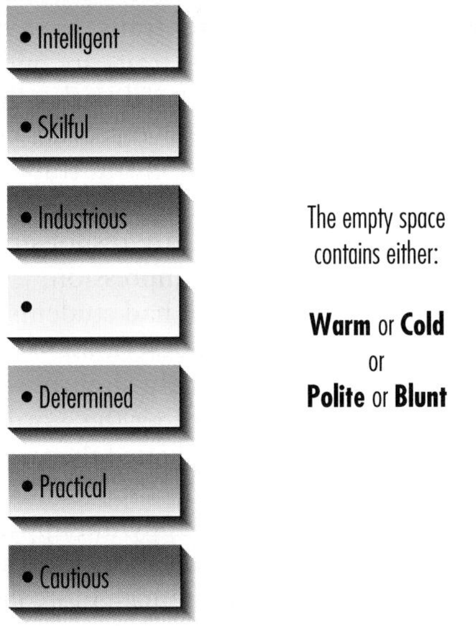

- Intelligent
- Skilful
- Industrious
- •
- Determined
- Practical
- Cautious

The empty space contains either:

Warm or **Cold**
or
Polite or **Blunt**

Percentage of subjects assigning additional traits as a function of the focal trait inserted:

Additional traits	Focal traits inserted in the list			
	Warm	Cold	Polite	Blunt
Generous	91	8	56	58
Wise	65	25	30	50
Happy	90	34	75	65
Good-natured	94	17	87	56
Reliable	94	99	95	100

Note: Asch (1946) presented participants with a 7-trait description of a hypothetical person in which either the word warm or cold, or polite or blunt appeared. The percentage of participants assigning other traits to the target was markedly affected when warm was replaced by cold, but not when polite was replaced by blunt.

Source: Based on Asch (1946).

& Vivekanathan, 1968). Warm/cold is clearly good/bad social, and so are the traits used to evaluate the impression (*generous, wise, happy, good-natured, reliable*). However, the other cue traits (*intelligent, skilful, industrious, determined, practical, cautious*) are clearly good/bad intellectual.

BIASES IN FORMING IMPRESSIONS
Primacy and recency

The order in which information about a person is presented can have profound effects on the subsequent impression. Asch (1946), in another experiment, used six traits to describe a hypothetical person. For half the participants, the person was described as *intelligent,*

industrious, impulsive, critical, stubborn, envious (i.e. positive traits first and negative traits last). The order of presentation was reversed for the other group of subjects. Asch found evidence for a **primacy** effect: the traits presented first disproportionately influenced the final impression, so that the person was evaluated more favourably when positive information was presented first than when negative information was presented first. Perhaps early information acts much like central cues, or perhaps people simply pay more attention to earlier information.

A **recency** effect can emerge where later information has more impact than earlier information. This might happen when you are distracted (e.g. overworked, bombarded with stimuli, tired) or when you have little motivation to attend to someone. Later, when you learn, for example, that you may have to work with this person, you may attend more carefully to cues. All other things being equal, however, primacy effects are more common (Jones & Goethals, 1972), with the clear implication that first impressions are indeed important.

Positivity and negativity

Research indicates that, in the absence of information to the contrary, people tend to assume the best of others and form a positive impression (Sears, 1983). However, if there is any negative information, this tends to attract our attention and assume a disproportionate importance in the subsequent impression—we are biased towards negativity (Fiske, 1980). Furthermore, once formed, a negative impression is much more difficult to change in the light of subsequent positive information than is a positive impression likely to change in the light of subsequent negative information (e.g. Hamilton & Zanna, 1974). We may be sensitive in this way to negative information because:

- it is unusual and distinctive (unusual, distinctive or extreme information attracts attention: Skowronski & Carlston, 1989); or
- it indirectly signifies potential danger, and so its detection has survival value for the individual and ultimately the species.

Personal constructs and implicit personality theories

Kelly (1955) has suggested that, even within a culture, individuals tend to develop their own idiosyncratic ways of characterising people. These **personal constructs** can, for simplicity, be treated as sets of bipolar dimensions. So, for example, I might consider *humour* as the single most important organising principle for forming impressions of people, while you might consider *intelligence* as more important. We have different personal construct systems and would be likely to form very different impressions of the same person. Personal constructs develop over time as adaptive forms of person perception, and so are resistant to change. We also tend to develop our own **implicit personality theories** (Schneider, 1973) or *philosophies of human nature* (Wrightsman, 1964). These are general principles about what sorts of characteristics go together to form certain types of personality: for instance, Rosenberg and Sedlak (1972) found that people assumed that intelligent people are also friendly but not self-centred. Implicit personality theories are widely shared within cultures, but differ between cultures (Markus, Kitayama, & Heiman, 1996). But, like personal constructs, they are resistant to change, and they can also be idiosyncratically based on personal experiences (Smith & Zárate, 1992).

Physical appearance

Although we would probably like to believe that we are much too sophisticated to be swayed in our impressions by mere physical appearance, research suggests that this is not true. Because people's appearance is often the first information we have about them, appearance is very influential in first impressions, and, as we have seen above, primacy effects are influential in enduring impressions (Park, 1986). This is not necessarily always a bad thing—according to Zebrowitz and Collins (1997), appearance-based impressions can be surprisingly accurate. One of the most immediate appearance-based judgments we make is whether we find someone physically attractive or not. Research confirms that we tend to assume that physically attractive people are 'good' (Dion, Berscheid, & Walster, 1972)—they are interesting, warm, outgoing, socially skilled, and have what the German poet Schiller (1882) called an 'interior beauty, a spiritual and moral beauty'. Physical attractiveness has a marked impact on affiliation, attraction and love (see Chapter 13).

It also has some problematic effects on people's careers. For example, in the United States, Knapp (1978) found that professional men over 1.88 m received 10% higher starting salaries than men under 1.83 m, and Heilman and Stopeck (1985) found that attractive male executives were considered more able than less attractive male executives. Heilman and Stopeck also found that this effect was reversed for female executives— apparently participants suspected that attractive female executives had been promoted because of their appearance, not their ability (see Chapter 10).

Stereotypes

Impressions of people are also strongly influenced by widely shared assumptions about the personalities, attitudes and behaviours of people based on group membership—for example, ethnicity, nationality, sex, race and class. These are **stereotypes** (discussed below, and in detail in Chapters 3, 10 and 11). One of the salient characteristics of people we first meet is their category membership (e.g. sex) and this tends to engage a stereotype-consistent impression. Haire and Grune (1950) found that people had little difficulty composing a paragraph describing a 'working man' from stereotype-consistent information, but enormous difficulty incorporating one piece of stereotype-inconsistent information— that the man was *intelligent*. Participants ignored the information, distorted it, took a very long time, or even promoted the man from worker to supervisor!

COGNITIVE ALGEBRA

Impression formation involves the integration of sequential pieces of information about a person (i.e. traits presented over time) into a complete image. The image is generally evaluative and so are the pieces of information themselves. Imagine being asked your impression of a person you met at a party. You might answer: 'He seemed very friendly and entertaining—all in all a nice person'. The main thing we learn from this is that you formed a positive/favourable impression. Impression formation is very much a matter of evaluation, not

Making an impression: He really wants this job and has been short-listed for an interview. Should he highlight ALL of his positive qualities or just the very best?

description. **Cognitive algebra** refers to an approach to the study of impression formation which focuses on how we assign positive and negative valence to attributes, and how we then combine these pluses and minuses into a general evaluation (Anderson, 1965, 1978, 1981).

There are three principal models of cognitive algebra: summation, averaging and weighted averaging.

Summation

Summation refers to a process where the overall impression is simply the cumulative sum of each piece of information. Say that we have a mental rating scale that goes from –3 (very negative) to +3 (very positive), and that we can assign values to specific traits such as *intelligent* (+2), *sincere* (+3) and *boring* (–1). If we met someone who had these characteristics, our overall impression would be the sum of the constituents: (+2+3–1) = +4 (see Table 2.1). If we now learned that the person was *humorous* (+1), our impression would improve to +5. It would improve to +6 if we then learned that the person was also *generous* (+1). Every bit of information counts, and to project a favourable impression you would be advised to present every facet of yourself that was positive, even marginally positive. In this example, you would be wise to conceal the fact that you were *boring*; your impression on others would now be (2+3+1+1) = +7.

Averaging

Averaging refers to a process where the overall impression is the cumulative average of each piece of information. So, from the example above, our initial impression would be: (+2+3–1)/3 = +1.33 (see Table 2.1). The additional information that the person was *humorous* (+1) would actually worsen the impression to +1.25: (+2+3–1+1)/4 = +1.25. It would worsen still further to +1.20 with the information that the person was *generous* (+1): (+2+3–1+1+1)/5 = +1.20. The implication is that, to project a favourable impression, you would be advised to present only your single very best facet. In this example, you would be wise to present yourself as sincere, and nothing else; your impression on others would now be +3.

Weighted averaging

Although research tends to favour the averaging model, it has some limitations. The valence of separate pieces of information may not be fixed, but may depend on the context of the impression formation task. Context may also influence the relative importance of pieces of information, and thus weight them in different ways in the impression. These considerations led to the development of a **weighted averaging** model. For example (see Table 2.1), if the target person was being assessed as a potential friend, we might assign relative weights to *intelligent*, *sincere* and *boring* of 2, 3 and 3. The weighted average would be +3.33: ((+2×2)+(+3×3)+(–1×3))/3= +3.33. If the person was being assessed as a potential politician, we might assign weights of 3, 2 and 0, to arrive at a weighted average of +4: ((+2×3)+(+3×2)+ (–1×0))/3 = +4.00. Table 2.1 shows how additional information with different weighting

---

TABLE 2.1 | Forming an impression by summation, averaging or weighted averaging

	SUMMATION	AVERAGING	WEIGHTED AVERAGING	
	All traits weighted 1	All traits weighted 1	Potential 'friend' weighting	Potential 'politician' weighting
Initial traits				
Intelligent (+2)			2	3
Sincere (+3)			3	2
Boring (–1)			3	0
Initial impression	+4.0	+1.33	+3.33	+4.00
Revised impression on learning that the person is also *humorous* (+1)	+5.0	+1.25	(weight = 1) +2.75	(weight = 0) +3.00
Final impression on learning that the person is also *generous* (+1)	+6.0	+1.20	(weight = 2) +2.60	(weight = 1) +2.60

might affect the overall impression. (Try using these models to answer the first focus question at the beginning of this chapter.)

Weights reflect the subjective importance of pieces of information in a particular impression formation context. They may be determined in a number of different ways. For instance, we have already seen that negative information may be weighted more heavily (e.g. Kanouse & Hanson, 1972). Earlier information may also be weighted more heavily (the primacy effect we discussed above). Paradoxically, we may now have come full circle to Asch's central traits: the weighted averaging model seems to allow for something like central traits, which are weighted more heavily in impression formation than other traits. With respect to central traits, the difference between Asch and the weighted averaging perspective is that for the latter they are simply more heavily weighted and salient information, while for Asch they actually influence the meaning of surrounding traits and reorganise the entire way we view the person. Asch's perspective retains the descriptive or qualitative aspect of traits and impressions, whereas cognitive algebra focuses only on quantitative aspects and suffers accordingly. More recent developments in social cognition have tended to supplant central traits with the more general concept of cognitive schema (Fiske & Taylor, 1991).

Social schemas and categories

A **schema** is a 'cognitive structure that represents knowledge about a concept or type of stimulus, including its attributes and the relations among those attributes' (Fiske & Taylor, 1991, p. 98). It is a set of interrelated cognitions (e.g. thoughts, beliefs, attitudes) that allows us quickly to make sense of a person, situation, event or place on the basis of limited information. Certain cues activate a schema. The schema then 'fills in' missing details.

For example, imagine you are visiting Paris. Most of us have a place schema about Paris, a rich repertoire of prior knowledge about what one does when in Paris—sauntering along boulevards, sitting in parks, sipping coffee at sidewalk cafés, browsing through bookshops or eating at restaurants. The reality of life in Paris is more diverse, yet this schema helps to interpret events and guide choices about how to behave. While in Paris you might visit a restaurant. Arrival at a restaurant might invoke a 'restaurant schema', which is a set of assumptions about what ought to occur (e.g. someone seats you, you study the menu, someone comes to take your order, you eat, talk and drink, you pay the bill, you leave); an event schema such as this is called a **script** (see

below). While at the restaurant, your waiter may have a rather unusual accent that identifies him as English and engages a whole set of assumptions about his attitudes and behaviours; a schema about a social group is a stereotype (Chapters 10, 11 and 15).

Once invoked, schemas (or schemata) facilitate top-down, conceptually driven or theory-driven processing, as opposed to bottom-up or data-driven processing (Rumelhart & Ortony, 1977)—we tend to fill in gaps with prior knowledge and preconceptions, rather than seek information gleaned directly from the immediate context. The concept of cognitive schema first emerged in Bartlett's (1932) early non-social memory research, which focused on the way memories are actively constructed and organised to facilitate understanding and behaviour. It also has a precedence in Asch's (1946) *configural model* of impression formation (discussed above), Heider's (1958) *balance theory* of person perception (see Chapters 3 and 5) and, ultimately, in *Gestalt* psychology (Brunswik, 1956; Koffka, 1935)—all are approaches in which simplified and holistic cognitive representations of the social world act as relatively enduring templates for the interpretation of stimuli and the planning of action.

The alternative to a schema approach is one in which perception is treated as an unfiltered, veridical representation of reality (e.g. Mill, 1869); impression formation is, as discussed above, the cognitive algebra of trait combination (e.g. Anderson, 1981); and memory is passively laid down through the repetitive association of stimuli (e.g. Ebbinghaus, 1885).

TYPES OF SCHEMAS

There are many types of schemas; however, they all influence the encoding (internalisation and interpretation) of new information, memory of old information and inferences about missing information. The most common schemas, some of which have been used as examples above, are person schemas, role schemas, event schemas or scripts, content-free schemas and self-schemas.

Person schemas

These are individualised knowledge structures about specific people. For example, you may have a person schema about your best friend (e.g. that she is kind and intelligent but tends to clam up in company and would rather frequent cafés than go bushwalking) or about a specific politician, a well-known author or a next-door neighbour.

Role schemas

These are knowledge structures about role occupants—for example, airline pilots (they fly the plane and should not be seen swigging whisky in the cabin) and doctors (although often complete strangers, they are allowed to ask personal questions and get you to undress). Although role schemas can quite properly apply to **roles** (i.e. types of function or behaviour in a group; see Chapter 8), they can sometimes be better understood as schemas about social groups; in this case, if such schemas are shared they are social stereotypes (Chapters 10 and 11).

Scripts

Schemas about events are generally called scripts (Abelson, 1981; Schank & Abelson, 1977). We have scripts for attending a lecture, going to the movies, having a party, giving a presentation or eating out at a restaurant. For example, people who often go to soccer matches might have a very clear script for what goes on both on and off the pitch. This makes the entire event meaningful. Imagine how you would fare if you had never been to a soccer match and had never heard of soccer (see Box 3.2 in Chapter 3, which describes one such scenario). The lack of relevant scripts can often be a major contributor to the feelings of disorientation, frustration and lack of efficacy encountered by sojourners in foreign cultures (e.g. new immigrants; see Chapter 16).

Content-free schemas

These do not contain rich information about a specific category, rather a limited number of rules for processing information. Content-free schemas might specify that if you like John and John likes Tom, then in order to maintain balance you should also like Tom (see balance theory; Heider, 1958, Chapter 6), or they might specify how to attribute a cause to someone's behaviour (e.g. Kelley's 1972a idea of causal schemata, discussed in Chapter 3).

Self-schemas

Finally, people have schemas about themselves. They represent and store information about themselves in a similar but more complex and varied way than information about others. Self-schemas form part of people's concept of who they are—the self-concept (they are discussed in Chapter 4, which deals with self and identity).

CATEGORIES AND PROTOTYPES

To apply schematic knowledge, you first need to be able to categorise a person, event or situation as fitting a particular schema. Based on principles first noted by the philosopher Wittgenstein (1953), cognitive psychologists now believe that categories are best described as collections of instances that have a **family resemblance** (e.g. Cantor & Mischel, 1977, 1979; Mervis & Rosch, 1981; Rosch, 1978). What is meant by this is that there is rarely a set of attributes that are necessary criteria for category membership; instead, instances are more or less

typical in terms of a range of attributes, with a most typical or *prototypical* instance representing the category. In general, however, as prototypes are abstracted or constructed from instances, no instances may actually fit the **prototype**—they vary in prototypicality.

Prototypes are cognitive representations of the category—standards against which family resemblance is assessed and category membership decided. As instances within a category are not identical but differ from one another to varying degrees, categories can be considered **fuzzy sets** centring around a prototype (see Box 2.1).

BOX 2.1 **Categories are fuzzy sets organised around prototypes**

Here is a short exercise to illustrate the nature of categories as fuzzy sets.

1. Consider the category 'university lecturer'. Whatever comes immediately to mind is your prototype of a university lecturer—most likely it will be a set of characteristics and images.
2. Keep this in mind, or write it down. You may find this rather more difficult than you imagined—prototypes can become frustratingly nebulous and imprecise when you try to document them.
3. Now, picture all the university lecturers you can think of. These will be lecturers who have taught you in large lecture halls or small classes, lecturers you have met after classes, in their offices, or lecturers just seen lurking around your psychology department. Also include lecturers you have read about in books and newspapers, or seen in movies or on television. These are all instances of the category 'university lecturer'.
4. Which of these instances is most prototypical? Do any fit the prototype perfectly, or are they all more or less prototypical? Which of these instances is least prototypical? Is any so non-prototypical that it has hardly any family resemblance to the rest? You should discover that there is an enormous range of prototypicality (the category is relatively diverse, a fuzzy set containing instances which have family resemblance) and that no instance fits the prototype exactly (the prototype is a cognitive construction).
5. Finally, compare your prototype to those of your classmates. You may find that many are similar, that your prototype is shared among students. Prototypes of social groups (e.g. lecturers) that are shared by members of a social group (e.g. students) can be considered social stereotypes.

Are prototypes accurate? Is this young woman a typical student? People have fuzzy prototypes of social categories that they use as the basis of more general impressions.

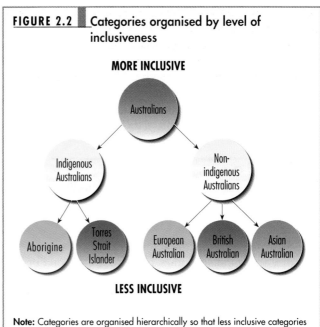

FIGURE 2.2 Categories organised by level of inclusiveness

Note: Categories are organised hierarchically so that less inclusive categories are nested beneath more inclusive categories.

Although prototypes are generally considered to represent the average category member, this is not necessarily always the case (Chaplin, John, & Goldberg, 1988). Under certain circumstances the prototype may be the ideal member (e.g. the ideal environmentalist) or an extreme member (the most anti-logging member of the category). These sorts of prototypes may prevail when social categories are in competition (e.g. environmentalists versus developers): this analysis is used in Chapter 7 to explain how people may conform to more extreme or polarised group norms (e.g. Wetherell, 1987).

The relationship between categories is thought to be hierarchical, with less inclusive categories nested beneath more inclusive categories (i.e. categories that include fewer members and fewer attributes are nested under categories that include more members and more attributes; see Figure 2.2). In general, people are more likely to rely on intermediate-level categories than on those that are very inclusive or very exclusive: these basic-level categories are neither too broad nor too narrow. For instance, we are more likely to identify something as a car than as a vehicle (too inclusive) or as an 'early-model Volvo station wagon' (too exclusive).

Basic-level categories are the default option but they may not be at all common in social perception, where contextual and motivational factors may dominate the choice of level of categorisation (Cantor & Kihlstrom, 1987; Hampson, John, & Goldberg, 1986; Turner, 1985).

In addition to representing categories in terms of abstractions from many instances (i.e. prototypes), people may represent them in terms of specific instances they have encountered (i.e. **exemplars**) (Smith & Zárate, 1992). To categorise new instances, people sometimes use exemplars rather than prototypes as the standard.

For instance, Brewer (1988) suggests that, as people become more familiar with a category, they shift from prototypical to exemplar representation, and Judd and Park (1988; Klein, Loftus, Trafton, & Fuhrman, 1992) suggest that people use both prototypes and exemplars to represent groups to which they belong, but only exemplars to represent outgroups. Social psychologists are still not certain about the conditions of use of prototypes versus exemplars (Fiske & Neuberg, 1990; Linville, Fischer, & Salovey, 1989; Park & Hastie, 1987), nor about the advisability of blurring the distinction between abstraction-based prototypes and instance-based exemplars in so-called 'blended' models of category representation (Hamilton & Sherman, 1994; Hilton & von Hippel, 1996).

A third way in which we can represent categories is as **associative networks** of affectively, causally or merely associatively linked attributes such as traits, beliefs or behaviours (e.g. Wyer & Carlston, 1994; see below).

Once a person, event or situation is categorised, a schema is invoked. Schemas and prototypes are similar and, indeed, are often used interchangeably. One way to distinguish them is in terms of their organisation. Prototypes, as just described, are relatively nebulous, unorganised fuzzy representations of a category; schemas are highly organised specifications of features and their interrelationships (Wyer & Gordon, 1984).

CATEGORISATION AND STEREOTYPING

Stereotypes are widely shared generalisations about members of a social group (Hilton & von Hippel, 1996; Leyens, Yzerbyt, & Schadron, 1994; Macrae, Stangor,

& Hewstone, 1996). They are usually highly simplified images, often derogatory when applied to outgroups, and they are often based on, or create, clearly visible differences between groups (e.g. in terms of physical appearance; Zebrowitz, 1996). Box 2.2 shows Australian students' stereotypes of some commonly mentioned and rather visible groups on campus in the early 1980s (Forgas, 1983, 1985a). Stereotypes and

stereotyping are central aspects of prejudice and discrimination (see Chapter 10) and of intergroup behaviour as a whole (see Chapter 11).

First described scientifically by Lippman (1922), stereotypes were treated as simplified mental images that act as templates to help interpret the huge diversity of the social world. Decades of research aimed at describing the content and form of stereotypes have produced a number of clear findings (Brigham, 1971; Hogg & Abrams, 1988; Katz & Braly, 1933; Oakes, Haslam, & Turner, 1994; Tajfel, 1978):

- People show an easy readiness to characterise vast human groups in terms of a few fairly crude common attributes.
- Stereotypes are slow to change.
- Stereotype change is generally in response to wider social, political or economic changes.
- Stereotypes are acquired at an early age, often before the child has any knowledge about the groups that are being stereotyped.
- Stereotypes become more pronounced and hostile when social tensions and conflict arise between groups, and then they are extremely difficult to modify.
- Stereotypes are not inaccurate or wrong; rather, they serve to make sense of particular intergroup relations.

Although stereotypes have usually been thought to be associated in some way or other with social categories (e.g. Allport, 1954b; Ehrlich, 1973), it was Tajfel (1957, 1959) who specified exactly how the process of categorisation might be responsible for stereotyping. Tajfel reasoned that, in making judgments on some focal dimension, people recruit any other peripheral dimension that might be of some assistance (see also Bruner & Goodman, 1947).

So, for example, if you had to judge the length of a series of lines (focal dimension), and you knew that all lines labelled A were bigger than all lines labelled B (peripheral dimension), then you might use these labels to help your judgment. Tajfel and Wilkes (1963) tested this idea. They had participants judge the length of a series of lines presented one at a time, a number of times and in varying order. There were three conditions: (a) the lines were randomly labelled A or B; (b) all the shorter lines were labelled A, and all the longer ones B; and (c) there were no labels. Participants appeared to use the information in the second condition to aid judgment, and tended to underestimate the average length of A-type lines and overestimate the average length of B-type lines.

The relevance of this experiment to social stereotyping becomes clear if, for example, you substitute intelligence for line length and Irish/non-Irish for the A/B labels. Because people might believe that intelligence and

---

BOX 2.2 **Outgroup stereotypes**

WOULD YOU RECOGNISE THESE 1980S STUDENTS' STEREOTYPES OF OTHER GROUPS ON CAMPUS?

- *Radicals*—scruffy appearance, often protesting, wear overalls or Indian clothes, hand out leaflets on library lawn, wear badges, organise marches, outspoken, noisy, usually leftist, live in communal accommodation, aggressive.
- *Engineers*—often in groups among themselves, chauvinistic, wear checked shirts and jeans, short hair, glasses, like beer, live at home with parents, poor social skills, arrogant, little concern for culture, carry calculators, uncouth behaviour, interested in football, go to pub frequently, play cards.
- *Radical feminists*—left-wing views, outspoken, often lesbian, usually unattractive looking, no bra, wear women's lib badges, sell feminist literature, aggressive, chip on the shoulder, wear overalls.
- *Surfies*—bleached blond hair, wear thongs and shorts, drive panel vans, go up the coast for holidays, have suntan all year round, dumb, very fit, sexist, use drugs.
- *Christians*—fairly innocuous, keen, thrifty, studious, clean, caring, narrow-minded, have 'Jesus loves you' stickers all over briefcase, fish signs over books, try to convince others about religion, go to Bible readings.
- *College types*—healthy country looks, clean-cut, good-natured, a bit dazed by it all, wear college sweaters, often get drunk, have a good time, go to college for lunch, spend holidays in the country, have college friends.
- *Mature-age students*—anxious, conscientious, housewifey females, sensibly dressed, orderly habits, keen, often talk at tutorials, stable, motherly, well-off, middle-aged, conservative.
- *Asian students*—neat, conscientious, wear glasses, ambitious, competitive, lonely, work hard, they stick together, unfriendly, never speak English when in groups, bright, conservative.

Source: Based on Forgas (1983, 1985a).

'Irishness' are correlated (i.e. a social stereotype exists), the categorisation of people as Irish or non-Irish produces a perceptual distortion on the focal dimension of intelligence: that is, categorisation produces stereotyping.

This, and a number of other experiments with physical and social stimuli (see Doise, 1978; Eiser, 1986; Eiser & Stroebe, 1972; McGarty & Penny, 1988; McGarty & Turner, 1992; Tajfel, 1981a; Taylor, Fiske, Etcoff, & Ruderman, 1978), uphold Tajfel's (1957, 1959) **accentuation principle**:

- The categorisation of stimuli produces a perceptual accentuation of intracategory similarities and intercategory differences on dimensions believed to be correlated with the categorisation.
- The accentuation effect is enhanced where the categorisation has importance, relevance or value to the participant.

The accentuation principle lies at the core of Tajfel's work on intergroup relations and group membership, which has fed into the subsequent development by Turner, at the Australian National University, and his associates of **social identity theory** and **self-categorisation theory** (e.g. Hogg, 2003b; Hogg & Abrams, 1988; Tajfel & Turner, 1979; Turner, 1982; Turner, Hogg, Oakes, Reicher & Wetherell, 1987); these theories are described in Chapter 11. Tajfel (1981a) felt, however, that while categorisation might explain the process of stereotyping as a context-dependent perceptual distortion of varying strength, it could not explain, for example, the origins of specific stereotypes about specific groups.

Stereotypes are not only consensual beliefs held by members of one group about members of another group, but are also more general *theories* (von Hippel, Sekaquaptewa, & Vargas, 1995) or social representations (Farr & Moscovici, 1984; Lorenzi-Cioldi & Clémence, 2001; see Chapters 3 and 5) of the attributes of other groups. To flesh out our understanding of stereotypes we may need to go beyond cognitive processes and once again incorporate an analysis of the content of specific stereotypes (Hamilton, Stroessner, & Driscoll, 1994) and an analysis of how stereotypes are formed, represented and used in language and communication (Maass & Arcuri, 1996). Tajfel believed that, to do this, both the social functions of stereotypes and the wider sociohistorical context of relations between groups would need to be considered (Tajfel, 1981a; see also Hogg & Abrams, 1988; Leyens, Yzerbyt, & Schadron, 1994; Oakes, Haslam, & Turner, 1993)—an idea pursued in Chapters 3 and 11.

Although stereotypes have inertia, they are not static. They are highly responsive to social context and socially structured individual motives. The idea that immediate or more enduring changes in social context (e.g. with

whom we compare ourselves and for what purpose) affect the content and expression of stereotypes has been explored by Penelope Oakes and her associates at the Australian National University (Oakes, Haslam, & Turner, 1994). Generally speaking, stereotypes will persist if they are readily accessible to us in memory (probably because we use them a great deal and they are self-conceptually important) and seem to make good sense of people's attitudes and behaviour (i.e. they neatly fit 'reality'). Changes in accessibility or fit will change the stereotype.

Motivation also plays an important role because stereotypical thinking serves multiple purposes (Hilton & von Hippel, 1996). In addition to helping with cognitive parsimony and the reduction of social uncertainty (Hogg, 2000a), stereotypes can clarify social roles (Eagly, 1995), power differentials (Fiske, 1993b) and intergroup conflicts (Robinson, Keltner, Ward, & Ross, 1995); they can justify the status quo (Jost & Banaji, 1994; Jost & Kramer, 2003) or contribute to a positive sense of ingroup identity (Hogg & Abrams, 1988).

Schema use and development

SCHEMA USE

People, situations and events possess so many features that it may not be immediately obvious which features will be used as a basis of categorisation and, consequently, which schemas will apply (see Figure 2.3). For instance, a person may be an Australian, female Aborigine from the state of Queensland, who is witty, well-read, not very sporty and works as an engineer. What determines which of these cues will be used as a basis of categorisation and schema use?

Because people tend to use basic-level categories that are neither too inclusive nor too exclusive (Mervis & Rosch, 1981; Rosch, 1978; see above), they initially access subtypes rather than superordinate or subordinate categories (e.g. career woman, not woman or female lawyer; Ashmore, 1981; Pettigrew, 1981) and they access social stereotypes and role schemas rather than trait schemas (e.g. politician, not intelligent). People are also more likely to use schemas that are cued by easily detected features, such as skin colour, dress or physical appearance (Brewer & Lui, 1989; Zebrowitz, 1996), or features that are contextually distinctive (e.g. a single man in a group of women). Accessible schemas, those that are habitually used or are salient in memory (Bargh, Lombardi, & Higgins, 1988; Bargh & Pratto, 1986; Wyer & Srull, 1981), and schemas that have a bearing on features that are important to us in that context, have a high probability of being invoked. So, for example, a racist (someone for whom race is important, salient in memory, and habitually used to process

Schemas: Social settings can invoke many schemas. These people are . . . footballers, females, young, British, Indian, English . . .? What schema is most salient here?

FIGURE 2.3 | Some major influences on commonly used schemas

Costs of being wrong
- Outcome dependency
- Accountability

Costs of being indecisive
- Anxiety and stress
- Performance pressure
- Communication goals

Individual differences
- Attributional complexity
- Uncertainty orientation
- Communication goals
- Need for cognition
- Cognition complexity
- Self-schemas
- Chronic accessibility

Commonly used schemas
- Subtypes
- Prototypes
- Roles
- Easily detected schemas
- Accessible schemas
- Self-referent schemas
- Mood-congruent schemas

Note: Some schemas are more commonly used than others, and their use is influenced by a range of individual and information-processing factors.

person information) would tend to use racial schemas more than someone who was not racist. Finally, people tend to cue mood-congruent schemas (Erber, 1991) and schemas that are based on earlier rather than later information (i.e. a primacy effect; see above).

These fairly automatic schema-cueing processes access schemas that are typically functional and accurate enough for immediate interactive purposes. They have *circumscribed accuracy* (Swann, 1984). Sometimes, however, people need to use more accurate schemas that correspond more closely to the data at hand, in which case there is a shift from theory-driven cognition towards data-driven cognition (Fiske, 1993a). If the costs of being wrong are increased, people are more attentive to data and may use more accurate schemas.

The costs of being wrong can become important where people's outcomes (i.e. rewards and punishments) depend on the actions or attitudes of others (Erber & Fiske, 1984; Neuberg & Fiske, 1987). Under these circumstances people probe for more information, attend more closely to data, particularly to schema-inconsistent information, and generally attend more carefully to other people. The costs of being wrong can also be important where people need to be more accountable— that is, to explain or justify their decisions or actions. Under these circumstances there is greater vigilance and attention to data, and generally more complex cogni-

tion that may improve accuracy (Tetlock & Boettger, 1989; Tetlock & Kim, 1987).

If the costs of being indecisive are high, people tend to make a quick decision or form a quick impression; indeed, any decision or impression, however inaccurate, may be preferable to no decision or impression, and so people rely heavily on schemas. Performance pressure (i.e. making a judgment or performing a task with insufficient time) can increase schema use. For example, in one study, time pressure caused men and women with conservative sex-role attitudes to discriminate against female job applicants, and women with more radical sex-role attitudes to discriminate against male applicants (Jamieson & Zanna, 1989).

Distraction and anxiety can also increase the subjective cost of indecisiveness and cause people to become more reliant on schematic processing (Wilder & Shapiro, 1989). When we have the task of communicating information to others (e.g. formal presentations), it often becomes more important to be well organised, decisive and clear and thus more important to rely on schemas (Higgins, 1981). This may particularly be the case when the communication is in a scientific mode rather than a narrative mode—that is, when we are communicating something technical rather than telling a story that requires rich description and characterisation (Zukier, 1986).

People can be aware that schematic processing is inaccurate, and in the case of schemas of social groups undesirable, because it involves stereotyping and prejudice. Consequently, people can actively avoid overreliance on schemas. Although this can have some success, it is often rather insignificant against the background of the processes described above (Ellis, Olson, & Zanna, 1983). There are, however, some general *individual differences* that may influence the degree and type of schema use.

- *Attributional complexity*—people vary in the complexity and number of their explanations of other people (Fletcher, Danilovics, Fernandez, Peterson, & Reeder, 1986).
- *Uncertainty orientation*—people vary in their interest in gaining information versus remaining uninformed but certain (Sorrentino & Roney, 1999).
- *Need for cognition*—people differ in how much they like to think deeply about things (Cacioppo & Petty, 1982).
- *Cognitive complexity*—people differ in the complexity of their cognitive processes and representations (Crockett, 1965).

People also differ in the sorts of schemas they have about themselves (Markus, 1977; see above). In general, components that are important in our self-schema are also important in the schematic perception of others (Markus, Smith, & Moreland, 1985). Individual differences in the chronic **accessibility** (i.e. frequent use, ease of remembering) of schemas can also quite obviously affect schema use for perceiving others. For instance, Battisch, Assor, Messe and Aronoff (1985) conducted a program of research showing that people differ in terms of their habitual orientations to others in social interaction (some being more dominant and controlling, some more dependent and reliant) and that this influences schematic processing.

Two types of schemas that have been relatively extensively researched, and on which people differ, are gender and political schemas. People tend to differ in terms of the traditional or conservative nature of their gender or sex-role schemas (Bem, 1981) and, among other things, this influences the extent to which they perceive others as being more or less masculine or feminine (see Chapter 10). Political schemas appear to rest on political expertise and knowledge and their use predicts rapid encoding, focused thought and relevant recall (Fiske, Lau, & Smith, 1990; Krosnick, 1990).

ACQUISITION, DEVELOPMENT AND CHANGE

We can acquire schemas second-hand: for example, you might have a lecturer schema based only on what you have been told about lecturers. In general, however, schemas are constructed, or at least modified, from encounters with category instances (e.g. exposure to individual lecturers in literature, the media or face to face). *Schema acquisition* and *development* involve a number of processes:

- Schemas become more *abstract*, less tied to concrete instances, as more instances are encountered (Park, 1986).
- Schemas become richer and more *complex* as more instances are encountered: greater experience with a particular person or event produces a more complex schema of that person or event (Linville, 1982).
- With increasing complexity, schemas also become more tightly *organised*: there are more and more complex links between schematic elements (McKiethen, Reitman, Rueter, & Hirtle, 1981).
- Increased organisation produces a more *compact* schema—one that resembles a single mental construct that can be activated in an all-or-nothing manner (Schul, 1983).
- Schemas become more *resilient*—they are better able to incorporate exceptions rather than disregard them because they might threaten the validity of the schema (Fiske & Neuberg, 1990).
- All other things being equal, this entire process should make schemas generally more *accurate*.

Schemas lend a sense of order, structure and coherence to a social world that would otherwise be highly complex and unpredictable. For this reason, there are strong pressures to maintain schemas (Crocker, Fiske, & Taylor, 1984). People are enormously resistant to schema-disconfirming information, which they generally disregard or reinterpret. For example, Ross, Lepper and Hubbard (1975) allowed participants to form impressions of a target individual on the basis of the information that the target made good decisions or poor decisions (getting 24 or 10 items correct out of a total of 25). Although participants were then told that the information was false, they maintained their impressions—predicting that on a subsequent task the target would get 19 or 14.5 items correct.

The perseverance of schemas has implications for courtroom practice. Lawyers often introduce inadmissible evidence. The judge then demands that the evidence be withdrawn and struck from the official trial record, and instructs the jury to disregard the evidence. But we know that an impression formed from inadmissible evidence will not vanish just because the judge has instructed jurors to disregard it (Thompson, Fong, & Rosenhan, 1981).

Schemas are also maintained by thought: people think a great deal about schemas, which effectively involves a process of cognitively mustering schema-consistent evidence (Millar & Tesser, 1986). People also protect their schemas by uncritically relying on their own earlier judgments—they construct justifications and rationalisations based on prior judgments, which are in turn based on even earlier judgments. The original basis of the schema is lost in the mists of time and is rarely unearthed, let alone critically re-examined (Schul & Burnstein, 1985).

The possession of relatively stable and unchanging schemas, even slightly inaccurate ones, provides us with significant information-processing advantages. Gross inaccuracy, however, will lead to schema change. For example, a schema that characterised wild lions as cuddly, good-natured and playful pets might, if you encountered one on foot in the wild, change rather dramatically—assuming that you survived the encounter!

Rothbart (1981) has suggested three processes of schema change:

1. **Bookkeeping**—there is a slow process of gradual change in response to new evidence.
2. **Conversion**—disconfirming information gradually accrues until something like a critical mass has been attained, at which point there is a sudden and massive change.
3. **Subtyping**—schemas change their configuration, in response to disconfirming instances, by the formation of subcategories.

Research tends to favour the subtyping model (Weber & Crocker, 1983; see Chapter 11 for a discussion of stereotype change). For example, a woman who believes that all men are instinctively violent might, through encountering many who are not, form a subtype of non-violent men to contrast with violent men.

Schema change may also depend on the extent to which schemas are *logically disconfirmable* or *practically disconfirmable* (Reeder & Brewer, 1979). Logically disconfirmable schemas are more easily changed by disconfirming evidence: if my schema of Paul is that he is *honest*, then evidence that he has cheated is very likely to change my schema (honest people do not cheat). Practically disconfirmable schemas are also more easily changed: they are ones for which the likelihood of encountering discrepant instances is relatively high—for example, *friendliness*, because it is often displayed in daily life (Rothbart & Park, 1986). There is less opportunity to display, for example, *cowardice*, and so a *cowardly* schema is less practically disconfirmable.

Social encoding

Social encoding refers to the process whereby external social stimuli are represented in the mind of the individual. There are several stages to this process (Bargh, 1984):

- *Preattentive analysis*—there is a general, automatic and non-conscious scanning of the environment.
- *Focal attention*—once noticed, stimuli are consciously identified and categorised.
- *Comprehension*—stimuli are given semantic meaning.
- *Elaborative reasoning*—the semantically represented stimulus is linked to other knowledge to allow for complex inferences.

Clearly, the process of social encoding depends heavily on what captures our attention.

SALIENCE

Attention-capturing stimuli are salient stimuli. In social cognition, **salience** refers to the property of a stimulus that makes it stand out relative to other stimuli in that context. Consider the second focus question. A single man is salient in an all-female group, but not salient in a sex-balanced group; a woman in the late stages of pregnancy is salient in most contexts except the obstetrician's clinic; and someone wearing a bright T-shirt is salient at a funeral but not on the beach. Salience is 'out there'—a property of the stimulus domain. People can be salient because:

- they are novel (single man, pregnant woman) or figural (bright T-shirt) in the immediate context (McArthur & Post, 1977);
- they are behaving in ways that do not fit prior expectations of them as individuals, as members of a particular social category or as people in general (Jones & McGillis, 1976); or
- they are important to your specific or more general goals, they dominate your visual field or you have been told to look out for them (Erber & Fiske, 1984; Taylor & Fiske, 1975; see Figure 2.4).

Standing out: Salient stimuli capture our attention. This woman is salient because she is in the minority. Will this make her more effective in this executive meeting?

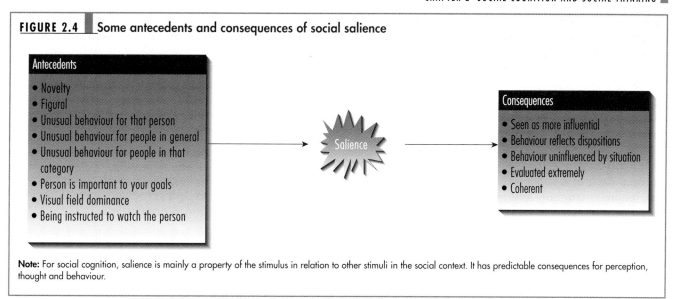

FIGURE 2.4 Some antecedents and consequences of social salience

Note: For social cognition, salience is mainly a property of the stimulus in relation to other stimuli in the social context. It has predictable consequences for perception, thought and behaviour.

Salient people attract attention and, relative to non-salient people, tend to be considered more influential in a group. They are also more personally responsible for their behaviour and less influenced by the situation, and are generally evaluated more extremely (McArthur, 1981; Taylor & Fiske, 1978; see Figure 2.4). Because we attend more to salient people, they dominate our thoughts and, consequently, increase the coherence (i.e. organisation and consistency) of our impressions. People do not necessarily recall more about salient people, but rather find it easier to access a coherent impression of the person. For example, imagine that you generally do not like very tall men. Suppose you go to a party where a particularly tall man stands out. You may feel very negative about him and, in trying to be coherent, also imagine that he talks a lot and dominates others. Although you won't necessarily recall much accurate information about his behaviour, you will have formed a fairly coherent impression of him as a person.

VIVIDNESS

While salience is a property of the stimulus in relation to other stimuli in a particular context, **vividness** is an intrinsic property of the stimulus itself. Vivid stimuli are ones that are:

- emotionally interesting (e.g. a violent crime);
- concrete and imagery-provoking (e.g. a gory and detailed description of a violent crime); or
- close to you in time and place (e.g. a violent crime committed yesterday in your street) (Nisbett & Ross, 1980).

Vivid stimuli ought to attract attention just like salient stimuli and ought, therefore, to have similar social cognitive effects. However, research has not confirmed this (Taylor & Thompson, 1982). When the presentation of information is vivid (e.g. through direct experience or colourful language accompanied by pictures or videos) rather than pallid, it may be more entertaining but it is not more persuasive. Apparent effects of vividness can often be attributed to other factors that co-occur with vividness. For example, vivid stimuli may convey more information, and thus it may be the information and not the vividness that influences social cognition.

ACCESSIBILITY

Attention is often directed not so much by stimulus properties 'out there' but by the accessibility, or ease of recall, of categories or schemas that we already have in our heads (Higgins, 1996). Accessible categories are readily and automatically subject to **priming** by features of the stimulus domain to make sense of the intrinsically ambiguous nature of social information. They are categories that we often use, have recently used, and they are consistent with current goals, needs and expectations (Bruner, 1957, 1958). For example, people who are very concerned about sex discrimination (i.e. it is an accessible category) may find that they see sexism almost everywhere: it is readily primed and used to interpret the social world. Some categories are chronically accessible; they are habitually primed in many contexts (Bargh, Lombardi, & Higgins, 1988), and this can have pervasive effects. Bargh and Tota (1988) suggest that depression may in part be attributed to chronic accessibility of negative self-schemas.

Research on accessibility exposes people to cues that prime particular categories. This is done in such a way that people do not consciously detect the cue–category link. Participants then interpret ambiguous behaviours (Higgins, Bargh, & Lombardi, 1985). Participants could be exposed to words such as *adventurous* or *reckless*, and then be asked to interpret behaviour such as 'shooting rapids in a canoe'. The interpretation of the behaviour would be different depending on the category primed by the cue word. For example, studies in the United States have shown that racial categories can be primed by words relating to African Americans: White participants so primed interpreted ambiguous behaviour as being more hostile and aggressive, which is consistent with racial stereotypes (Devine, 1989).

Once primed, a category tends to encode stimuli by assimilating them to the primed category—that is, interpreting them in a *category-consistent* manner. This is particularly true of ambiguous stimuli. However, when people become aware that a category has been primed, they often contrast stimuli to the category—that is, interpret them in a *category-incongruent* manner (Herr, Sherman, & Fazio, 1983; Martin, 1986). For example, gender is often an accessible category that is readily primed and used to interpret behaviour (Stangor, 1988); but if you knew that gender had been primed, you might make a special effort to interpret behaviour in a non-sexist way.

Person memory

Social behaviour depends very much on how we store information about other people—that is, on what we remember about other people (Fiske & Taylor, 1991; Martin & Clark, 1990; Ostrom, 1989b). Social psychological approaches to person memory draw on cognitive psychological theories of memory and adopt mainly what is called an associative network or *propositional* model of memory (e.g. Anderson, 1990). The general idea is that we store *propositions* (e.g. 'The student reads the book', 'The book is a social psychology text', 'The student has a ponytail') that consist of nodes or ideas (e.g. book, ponytail, student, reads) that are linked by relationships between ideas. The links are *associative* insofar as nodes are associated with other nodes (e.g. *student* and *ponytail*), but some associative links are stronger than others. Links become strengthened the more they are activated by cognitive rehearsal (e.g. recalling or thinking about the propositions), and the more different links there are to a specific idea (i.e. alternative retrieval routes) the more likely it is to be recalled.

Recall is a process in which nodes become activated and the activation spreads to other nodes along established associative links: for example, the node *student* activates the node *ponytail* because there is a strong associative link. Finally, a distinction is made between *long-term memory*, which is the vast store of information that can potentially be brought to mind, and *short-term memory* (or working memory), which is the much smaller amount of information that you actually have in consciousness, and is the focus of your attention, at a specific time.

This sort of memory model has been applied to person memory (Hastie, 1988; Srull & Wyer, 1989; Wyer & Carlston, 1994), with the important feature that information that is inconsistent with our general impression of someone is generally better recalled than impression-consistent information. This is because impression-inconsistent information attracts attention and generates more cognition and thought, thus strengthening linkages and retrieval routes. However, inconsistent information is not better recalled:

- if we already have a well-established impression (Fiske & Neuberg, 1990);
- if the inconsistency is purely descriptive and not evaluative (Wyer & Gordon, 1982);
- if we are making a complex judgment (Bodenhausen & Lichtenstein, 1987); or
- if we have time afterwards to think about our impression (Wyer & Martin, 1986).

CONTENTS OF PERSON MEMORY

Consider your best friend for a moment. No doubt, an enormous amount of detail comes to mind—her likes and dislikes, her attitudes, beliefs and values, her personality traits, the things she does, what she looks like, what she wears, or where she usually goes. This array of information varies in terms of how concrete and directly observable it is: it ranges from appearance, which is concrete and directly observable, through behaviour, to traits which are not directly observable but are based on inference (Park, 1986). Cutting across this continuum is a general tendency for people to cluster together features that are positive and desirable and, separately, those that are negative and undesirable.

Most person-memory research concerns *traits*. Traits are stored in the usual propositional form ('Mary is mean and nasty'), but are based on elaborate inferences from behaviours and situations. The inference process rests heavily on making causal attributions for people's behaviour (the subject matter of Chapter 3). The storage of trait information appears to be organised with respect to two continua: social desirability (e.g. *warm, pleasant, friendly*) and competence (e.g. *intelligent, industrious, efficient*; see Schneider, Hastorf, & Ellsworth, 1979). Trait memories can be quite abstract and can colour more concrete memories of behaviour and appearance.

Behaviour is usually perceived as purposeful action, and so memory for behaviour may be organised with respect to people's goals: the behaviour 'Angelo runs to catch the bus' is stored in terms of Angelo's goal to catch the bus. In this respect, behaviour, although more concrete and observable than traits, also involves some inference—inference of purpose (Hoffman, Mischel, & Mazze, 1981).

Memory for *appearance* is usually based on directly observable concrete information ('Winston has long blond hair and an aquiline nose') and is stored as an analog rather than a proposition. In other words, appearance is stored directly, like a picture in the mind that retains all the original spatial information, rather than as a deconstructed set of propositions that have symbolic meaning. Laboratory studies reveal that we are phenomenally accurate at remembering faces: we can often recall faces with 100% accuracy over very long periods of time (Freides, 1974). However, we tend to be less accurate at recognising the faces of people who are of a different race from our own (Malpass & Kravitz, 1969). One explanation of this effect is that we simply pay less attention to, or process more superficially, outgroup faces (Devine & Malpass, 1985). Indeed, superficial encoding undermines memory for faces in general, and one remedy for poor memory for faces is simply to pay greater attention (Wells & Turtle, 1988).

We are also remarkably inaccurate at remembering appearances in natural contexts where eyewitness testimony is required—for example, identifying or describing a stranger we saw commit a crime (Kassin, Ellsworth, & Smith, 1989; Loftus, 1979). This is probably because witnesses or victims often do not get a good, clear look at the offender: the offence may be frightening, unexpected, confusing and over quickly, and the offender may only be glimpsed through a dirty car window or may wear a mask or some other disguise. Eyewitness testimony, even if confidently given, should be treated with caution. However, its accuracy is more assured if certain conditions are met (Shapiro & Penrod, 1986; see Box 2.3).

ORGANISATION OF PERSON MEMORY

In general, we remember people as a cluster of information about their traits, behaviours and appearances. However, we can also store information about people in a very different way: we can cluster people under attributes or groups. Social memory, therefore, can be organised by *person* or by *group* (Pryor & Ostrom, 1981) (see Figure 2.5). In most settings the preferred mode of organisation is by person, probably because it produces richer and more accurate person memories that are more easily recalled (Sedikides & Ostrom, 1988). (Check the third focus question.) Organisation by person is particularly likely when people are significant to us because they are familiar, real people, with whom we expect to interact across many specific situations (Srull, 1983).

Organisation by group membership is likely in first encounters with strangers: the person is pigeonholed, described and stored in terms of stereotypic attributes of a salient social category (e.g. sex, age, ethnicity; see

| BOX 2.3 | Factors that improve the accuracy of eyewitness testimony |

Although often unreliable, here are ways that can make eyewitness testimony more accurate.

The witness:

- mentally goes back over the scene of the crime to reinstate additional cues;
- has already associated the person's face with other symbolic information;
- was exposed to the person's face for a long time;
- gave testimony a very short time after the crime;
- is habitually attentive to the external environment;
- generally forms vivid mental images.

The person:

- had a face that was not altered by disguise;
- looked dishonest.

Source: Based on Shapiro & Penrod (1986).

Chapter 10). Over time, the organisation may change to one based on the person (e.g. Duck, 1977). For example, your memory of a lecturer you have encountered only a few times lecturing on a topic you are not very interested in will most likely be organised in terms of the stereotypical properties of the social group 'lecturers'. If you should happen to get to know this person a little better, you might find that your memory gradually or suddenly becomes reorganised in terms of the lecturer as a distinct individual person.

There is an alternative perspective on the relationship between person-based and group-based person memory, and that is that they can coexist as essentially distinct forms of representation (Srull & Wyer, 1986; Wyer & Martin, 1986). These distinct forms of

Person memory: 'You were at the scene. So who did this while we weren't looking, then? Tell us exactly what you saw. Can you describe the perpetrator—in detail?'

FIGURE 2.5 Person memory organised by person or by group

PERSON
INFORMATION

Giovanna is a movie buff.
Ling is a swimmer.
David is a medical student.
Giovanna is a medical student.
David is a swimmer.

ORGANISED
BY PERSON

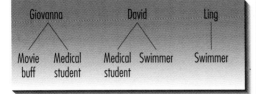

ORGANISED
BY GROUP

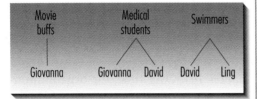

Note: We can organise information about people in two quite different ways. We can cluster attributes under individual people, or we can cluster people under attributes or groups.

Source: Based on Fiske & Taylor (1991).

USING PERSON MEMORY

Presumably, in making social judgments we draw on person memory. In fact, it appears that sometimes we do, but sometimes we do not. Hastie and Park (1986) have integrated the findings from a large number of studies to conclude that, by default, people tend to form impressions of people *on-line*—that is, they rely disproportionately on incoming data which is assimilated by schemas in order to produce an impression. There is little correlation between memory and judgment. It is more unusual for people to draw on memory and make *memory-based* judgments, but when they do there is a stronger correlation between memory and judgment. Whether people make on-line or memory-based judgments or impressions is influenced by the sorts of goals and purposes they bring to the interaction or to the judgment task.

The general principle is that recall of information about other people improves as the purpose of the interaction becomes more psychologically engaging and less superficial (Srull & Wyer, 1986, 1989; Wyer & Srull, 1986). Psychologically engaging interactions entail information processing at a deeper level that involves the elaboration of more complex and more varied links among elements, and consequently a more integrated memory (Greenwald & Pratkanis, 1984). Paradoxically, then, instructing someone to memorise another person (psychologically not very engaging) will be less effective than asking someone to form an impression, which in turn will be less effective than asking someone to empathise. Box 2.4 shows a number of goals and how they affect person memory.

representation may be associated with different sorts of identities that people may have, based either on interpersonal relationships or on group memberships. This idea is consistent with *social identity theory*, which is a theory of group behaviour as something quite distinct from interpersonal behaviour (e.g. Hogg & Abrams, 1988; Tajfel & Turner, 1979; Turner, 1982) (see Chapter 11).

Social inference

Social inference is, in many respects, the core of social cognition. It addresses the inferential processes (these

BOX 2.4	**Goals and their effects on person memory**
Goal	**Effect**
• Comprehension	Limited memory
• Memorising	Variable memory, organised in an ad-hoc manner, often by psychologically irrelevant categories
• Forming impressions	Good memory, organised by traits
• Empathising	Good memory, organised by goals
• Comparing to oneself	Excellent memory, organised by psychological categories (traits or goals)
• Anticipated interaction	Excellent, well-organised memory, type of organisation not yet clear
• Actual interaction	Variable memory, depending on concurrent goals

Note: People's information processing and social interactive goals affect their memory for people.

Source: Based on Fiske & Taylor (1991).

can be quite formal and abstract, or intuitive and concrete) we use to identify, sample and combine information to form impressions and make judgments. There appear to be two distinct ways in which we process social information. On the one hand we can automatically rely on general schemas or stereotypes in a top-down deductive fashion; on the other we can deliberatively rely on specific instances in a bottom-up inductive fashion. This distinction is a theme that runs through social cognition and surfaces in different guises.

We have already discussed in this chapter the distinction between Asch's configural model (where impressions are based on holistic images) and Anderson's cognitive algebra model (where impressions are based on integration of pieces of information). More recently, Brewer (1988, 1994) has proposed a dual-process model that contrasts relatively automatic category-based processing of social information with more deliberate and personalised attribute-based processing. Closely related is Fiske and Neuberg's (1990; Fiske & Dépret, 1996) continuum model, which makes a similar distinction between schema-based and data-based inferences. From research into attitudes come two other related distinctions (Eagly & Chaiken, 1993; see Chapter 6 for details). Petty and Cacioppo's (1986b) elaboration-likelihood model distinguishes between *central route processing* where people carefully and deliberately consider information, and *peripheral route processing* where people make rapid top-of-the-head decisions based on stereotypes, schemas and other cognitive short-cuts. Almost identical is Chaiken's (Bohner, Moskowitz, & Chaiken, 1995; Chaiken, Liberman, & Eagly, 1989) heuristic–systematic model: people process information carefully and systematically, or they rather automatically rely on cognitive heuristics.

Generally, social cognition researchers have studied inferential processes in comparison with ideal processes, called **normative models**, which produce the best possible inferences. Collectively, these normative models are known as **behavioural decision theory** (Einhorn & Hogarth, 1981). The intuitive strategies of social inference involve a range of biases and errors that produce suboptimal inferences—inferences that fall short of those dictated by the principles of behavioural decision theory (e.g. Fiske & Taylor, 1991; Nisbett & Ross, 1980).

DEPARTURES FROM NORMALITY
Gathering and sampling social information

The first stage in making an inference involves the gathering of data and the sampling of information from those data. In doing this, people tend to be overreliant on schemas. This can cause them to overlook information that is potentially useful, or to exaggerate the importance of information that is misleading. For example, members of selection committees believe they are objectively assessing candidates on the basis of information provided by the candidate. However, what often seems to happen is that person schemas are quickly, and often unconsciously, activated and used as the basis for candidate assessment. This reliance on person schemas is referred to as 'clinical judgment' and, although by no means all bad, it can produce suboptimal inferences and judgments (Dawes, Faust, & Meehl, 1989).

People can also be unduly influenced by extreme examples and small samples (small samples are rarely representative of larger populations: this is called the *law of large numbers*); and they can be inattentive to whether a sample is typical of its population or not and to biases in samples. For example, in Australia and New Zealand there is a great deal of media coverage of dangerous and criminal driving by male youths, leading to injury and death of innocent bystanders. From this, people tend to infer that male youths generally behave like this. However, this is based on a possibly biased source (most mass media present extreme, not ordinary, cases), which presents a small sample of atypical youths behaving in an extreme manner.

Regression

Individual cases or instances are often more extreme than the average of the population from which they are drawn: over a number of cases or instances there is a **regression** to the population mean. For example, a restaurant you have just visited for the first time may have been truly excellent, causing you to extol its virtues to all your friends. However, the next time you go it turns out to be mediocre. On the next visit, it is moderately good, and on the next fairly average. This is an example of regression. The restaurant is probably actually moderately good, but this would not become apparent from one visit—a number of visits would have to be made. The way to control for regression effects in forming impressions is to be conservative and cautious in making inferences from limited information (one or a few cases or instances). People tend, however, not to do this—they are generally ignorant of regression and do not control for it in forming impressions and making judgments (Kahneman & Tversky, 1973).

We can, however, be induced to make more conservative inferences if the initial information is made to seem less diagnostic by the presence of other information. For example, knowing that Hans shoots cats may generate an extreme and negative impression of him: shooting cats is relatively diagnostic of being a nasty person. However, if this piece of information is *diluted* (Nisbett, Zukier, & Lemley, 1981) by other information that he is a committed conservationist who writes poetry, collects antiques, drives an early-model Holden and cares for his infirm mother, the impression is likely to become less extreme, because the tendency to use the diagnosis 'he shoots cats' is weakened.

Base-rate information

Base-rate information is general information, usually factual and statistical, about an entire class of events. For instance, if we knew that only 5% of university lecturers gave truly awful lectures, or that only 7% of social security recipients preferred being on the dole to working, this would be base-rate information. Research shows that people chronically underuse this information in making inferences, particularly when more concrete anecdotal case studies exist (Bar-Hillel, 1980; Taylor & Thompson, 1982). So, on the basis of vivid and colourful media exposés of 'dull lecturers' or 'dole bludgers', people will tend to infer that these are stereotypical properties of the parent categories, even if they have the relevant base-rate information to hand.

The main reason that base-rate information is ignored is not so much that it is pallid and uninteresting in comparison with vivid individual instances, but that people often fail to see the relevance of base-rate information, relative to other information, to the inference task (Bar-Hillel, 1980). People increase their use of base-rate information when it is made clear that it is more relevant than other information (e.g. case studies) to the inferential task.

Covariation and illusory correlation

Judgments of covariation are judgments of how strongly two things are related. They are essential to social inference and form the very basis of schemas (schemas, as we saw above, are beliefs about the covariation of behaviours, attitudes or traits). To judge covariation accurately—for example, the relationship between hair colour and how much fun one has—we should consider the number of blondes having fun and not having fun, and the number of brunettes having fun and not having fun. The scientific method provides formal statistical procedures that we could use to assess covariation (Chapter 1). However, in making covariation judgments, people fall far short of normative expectations (Alloy & Tabachnik, 1984; Crocker, 1981). In general, this is because they are influenced by prior assumptions (i.e. schemas) and tend to search for or recognise only schema-consistent information: people are generally not interested in disconfirming their cherished schemas. So, in assessing the relationship between hair colour and fun, people may have available the social schema that 'blondes have more fun', and instances of blondes who have fun will come to mind much more readily than blondes who are having a miserable time or brunettes who are having a ball.

When people assume that a relationship exists between two variables, they tend to overestimate the

Departures from normality: If we rely too heavily on schemas, we may ignore interesting details, attend too closely to misleading information, or even worse!

degree of correlation or see a correlation where none actually exists. This phenomenon, called **illusory correlation**, was demonstrated by Chapman (1967). Chapman presented students with lists of paired words such as *lion/tiger, lion/eggs, bacon/eggs, blossoms/notebook* and *notebook/tiger*. The students then had to recall how often each word was paired with each other word. Although every word was paired an equal number of times with every other word, participants overestimated meaningful pairings (e.g. *bacon/eggs*) and distinctive pairings (e.g. *blossoms/notebook*—words that were much longer than all the other words in the list).

Chapman reasoned that there are two bases for illusory correlation: **associative meaning** (items are seen as belonging together because they 'ought' to, on the basis of prior expectations) and **paired distinctiveness** (items are thought to go together because they share some unusual feature).

Distinctiveness-based illusory correlation may help to explain stereotyping, particularly negative stereotypes of minority groups (Hamilton, 1979; Hamilton & Sherman, 1989; Mullen & Johnson, 1990; see Chapter 11). Hamilton and Gifford (1976) had students recall sets of positive and negative behaviours about two groups, A and B. The numbers and ratios of positive to negative behaviours were: for group A (the 'majority') 16:8 and for group B (the 'minority') 8:4—the negative statements were half as common as positive statements for both groups. The students erroneously recalled relatively more of the less-common negative statements about the less-common minority group B.

In real life, negative events are distinctive, as they are perceived to be more rare than positive events (Parducci, 1968); and minority groups are distinctive, as people have relatively few contacts with them. Thus, the conditions for distinctiveness-based illusory correlation are met. There is also evidence for an associative meaning basis to the negative stereotyping of minority groups: people have preconceptions that negative attributes go with minority groups (McArthur & Friedman, 1980).

Although illusory correlation may be involved in the formation and use of stereotypes, its role may be limited to conditions where people make memory-based rather than on-line judgments (McConnell, Sherman, & Hamilton, 1994)—after all, they have to remember distinctiveness or associative information in order to make illusory correlations.

More radically, and from a social identity perspective (Chapter 11), it can be argued that stereotypes are not 'illusory' at all. Rather, they are rational and even deliberate constructs that differentiate ingroups from outgroups in ways that evaluatively favour the ingroup (Leyens, Yzerbyt, & Schadron, 1994; McGarty, Haslam, Turner, & Oakes, 1993; Oakes, Haslam, & Turner, 1994). Stereotypical differences are real, and the process of stereotyping is one in which these differences are automatically (and strategically—for example, through rhetoric) accentuated as a consequence of categorising oneself as a member of one of the groups.

HEURISTICS

We have now seen how bad we are, by standards from behavioural decision theory, at making inferences. Perhaps the reason for this is that we have limited short-term memory available for on-line processing but enormous capacity for long-term memory. It pays, then, to store information schematically in long-term memory and call up schemas to aid inference. Social inference is thus likely to be heavily theory/schema-driven, with the consequence that it is biased towards conservative, schema-supportive inferential practices. Despite doing this, and being so poor at social inference, human beings seem to muddle through. Perhaps the process is adequate for most of our inferential needs most of the time, and we should study these 'adequate' rather than optimal processes in their own right.

With just this idea in mind, Tversky and Kahneman (1974; Kahneman & Tversky, 1973) detail the sorts of cognitive short-cuts, called **heuristics**, that people use to reduce complex problem-solving to simpler judgmental operations. There are three main heuristics that have been researched: (1) representativeness, (2) availability and (3) anchoring and adjustment. (See Box 2.5 for an example in which two of these heuristics may operate.)

Representativeness heuristic

In deciding how likely it is that a person or an event is an instance of one category or another, people often simply estimate the extent to which the instance represents or is similar to a typical or average member of the category. The **representativeness heuristic** is basically a relevancy judgment that disregards base-rate infor-

mation, sample size, quality of information and other normative principles. Nevertheless, it is fast and efficient and produces inferences that are accurate enough for our purposes most of the time. For example, consider the following information: 'Steve is very shy and withdrawn, invariably helpful, but with little interest in people or in the world of reality. A meek and tidy soul, he has a need for order and structure, and a passion for detail' (Tversky & Kahneman, 1974). The representativeness heuristic would very quickly lead to the inference that Steve is a librarian rather than, say, a farmer, surgeon or trapeze artist and, in general, that would probably be correct.

Availability heuristic

The **availability heuristic** is used to infer the frequency or likelihood of an event on the basis of how quickly instances or associations come to mind. Where instances are readily available, we tend to inflate frequencies. For example, exposure to many media reports of violent crime will make that information available and will tend to inflate our estimate of the overall frequency of violent crime. Similarly, in forming an impression of Paul, who has very short hair and tattoos, you might overestimate the likelihood that he will also be violent, because you have just seen the movie *Romper Stomper*.

Under many circumstances, availability is adequate as a basis for making inferences—after all, things that come to mind easily are probably fairly plentiful. Availability is, however, subject to bias, as it does not control for such factors as idiosyncratic exposure to unusual samples.

Anchoring and adjustment

In making inferences we often need a starting point—an anchor—from which, and with which, we can adjust subsequent inferences (e.g. Wyer, 1976). **Anchoring and adjustment** is a heuristic that ties inferences to initial standards. So, for example, inferences about other people are often anchored by beliefs about ourselves: we decide how intelligent, artistic or kind someone else is with reference to our own self-schema. Anchors can also come from the immediate context. For example, Greenberg, Williams and O'Brien (1986) found that participants in a mock jury study who were instructed to contemplate the harshest verdict first used this as an anchor from which only small adjustments were made. A relatively harsh verdict was rendered. Participants instructed to consider the most lenient verdict first likewise used this as an anchor, subsequently rendering a relatively lenient verdict.

IMPROVING SOCIAL INFERENCE

Social inference is not optimal. We are biased, we misrepresent people and events, and we make mistakes.

BOX 2.5 | **Why it won't happen to me . . . Underestimating risk of exposure to AIDS**

PEOPLE MAY UNDERESTIMATE THEIR RISK OF EXPOSURE TO AIDS BECAUSE THEY BASE ASSESSMENT TOO HEAVILY ON COGNITIVE HEURISTICS.

AIDS is one of the most devastating diseases to confront humanity and yet, ironically, it is transmitted most often by sexual intercourse, an 'act of love'. Small wonder it is difficult to control, particularly when we consider that people also have a strong feeling of personal invulnerability with respect to health matters (Weinstein, 1980, 1989). In recent years, health professionals in many countries have made strenuous attempts to encourage safe sex practices among those most at risk—the young, the unmarried and, given that unprotected anal intercourse is listed as a very high-risk behaviour, the gay community.

 People are not oblivious to these concerns, as Australian researchers Viney and Crooks (1992) have noted. Exposure to the media, and perhaps to their own network of acquaintances, has made gay males aware that people infected with the HIV virus or with full-blown AIDS report feelings of uncertainty, anxiety, guilt, depression, frustration, help-lessness and social isolation. One healthy gay male was moved to say: 'The panic is here. I know lots of people who worry about every bruise they get, who worry about a swollen lymph node, the night sweats, even a slight fever. Every gay man I know worries about AIDS—I mean profoundly worries' (cited in Rosser, 1991). Despite this, gay men often underestimate the risks they run. In a study of New Zealand gay and bisexual men, Rosser found that almost all respondents judged themselves personally to be less at risk than society in general.

 Richards (1991) suggests that underestimation of risk of exposure to HIV among homosexuals can be explained in terms of the availability heuristic (if it does not come to mind easily about oneself, then it cannot happen) and the representativeness heuristic (by use of stereotypical images, such as becoming clean by having a shower after sex). Richards divided a sample of 52 New Zealand gay men into two groups: those who reported low-risk behaviour (pro-tected sex, one partner) and those who reported high-risk behaviour (unprotected sex, multiple partners). They were asked for two judgments of risk perception: (1) absolute risk: 'Considering all the different factors that may contribute to AIDS, including your own past and present behaviour, what would you say are your chances of con-tracting HIV, the virus that causes AIDS?'—51% of the low-risk group, but 72% of the high-risk group, perceived only a low risk or less! (2) comparative risk: 'When you compare yourself with other "men who have sex with men", what would you say are your chances of contracting HIV, the virus that causes AIDS?'—70% of the low-risk group, but 87% of the high-risk group, perceived a lower than average risk! These results are a clear challenge to sex educators: how to break the cycle of high-risk behaviour leading to a low-risk mentality?

Many of these shortcomings, however, may be more apparent than real (Funder, 1987). Social cognition experiments may provide unnatural contexts, for which our inference processes are not well suited. Intuitive inference processes may actually be well-suited to everyday life. For example, on encountering a pit bull terrier in the street, it might be very adaptive to rely on availability (media coverage of attacks by pit bull terriers) and to flee automatically, rather than adopt more time-consuming normative procedures: what is an error in the laboratory may not be so in the field.

 Nevertheless, inferential errors can sometimes have serious consequences. Negative stereotyping of minority groups and suboptimal group decisions, for example, may be partly caused by inferential errors. In this case, there may be something to be gained by considering ways in which we can improve social inference. The basic principle is that social inference will improve to the extent that we become less reliant on intuitive infer-ential strategies. This may be achieved through formal education in scientific and rational thinking as well as

statistical techniques (Fong, Krantz, & Nisbett, 1986; Nisbett, Krantz, Jepson, & Fong, 1982).

Affect and emotion

Traditionally, social cognition has focused on thinking rather than feeling, but in recent years there has been an 'affective revolution' (Forgas & Smith, 2003). Research has focused on the way that feelings (affect, emotion, mood) influence and are influenced by social cognition. Different situations (funeral, party) evoke different emotions (sad, happy), but also the same situation (exam-ination) can evoke different emotions (anxiety, challenge) in different people (weak student, competent student).

 Research suggests that people process information about a situation and their own hopes, desires and abil-ities, and on the basis of these cognitive *appraisals* dif-ferent affective reactions and physiological responses follow (Blascovich & Mendes, 2000). Because affective response (emotion) is, fundamentally, a mode of action readiness tied to appraisals of harm and benefit, the appraisal process is continuous and largely automatic (see Box 2.6).

CONSEQUENCES OF AFFECT

Emotion and mood influence thought and action. Affect infuses into and therefore affects thinking, judgment and behaviour. Joseph Forgas, at the University of New South Wales, has developed an **affect–infusion model** to describe the effects of mood on social cognition (Forgas, 1994, 1995, 2002). The core prediction is that affect infusion occurs only where people process information in an open and constructive manner that involves active elaboration of stimulus details and information from memory.

According to Forgas, there are four distinct ways in which people can process information about one another:

1. direct access—they can directly access schemas or judgments stored in memory;

2. motivated processing—they can form a judgment on the basis of specific motivations to achieve a goal or to 'repair' an existing mood;

3. heuristic processing—they can rely on various cognitive short-cuts or heuristics;

4. substantive processing—they can deliberately and carefully construct a judgment from a variety of informational sources.

Current mood states do not influence judgments involving direct access or motivated processing, but they do affect judgments involving heuristic processing or substantive processing. In the latter cases, cognition is infused with affect such that social judgments reflect current mood, either indirectly (affect primes target judgment) or directly (affect acts as information about the target). For example, under heuristic processing mood may itself be a heuristic that determines response—being in a bad mood would produce a negative reaction to another person (i.e. mood congruence). Under substantive processing, the more we deliberate the greater the mood-congruence effect. This model fares well in predicting the effects of affect on social cognition.

Affect influences social memory and social judgment—for example, people tend to recall current mood-congruent information more readily than current mood-incongruent information, and judge others and themselves more positively when they themselves are in a positive mood. In line with the affect–infusion model, the effect of mood on self-perception is greater for peripheral than central aspects of self—peripheral aspects are less firmly ensconced and therefore require more elaboration and construction than central aspects (e.g. Sedikides, 1995). Stereotyping is also affected by mood. Being in a good mood can increase reliance on stereotypes when group membership is not very relevant (Forgas & Fiedler, 1996), but negative affect can encourage people to correct hastily made negative evaluations of outgroups (Monteith, 1993).

| BOX 2.6 | How we decide when to respond affectively |

According to Smith and Lazarus (1990) affective response rests on seven appraisals, which can be framed as questions that people ask themselves in particular situations. There are two sets of appraisal dimensions, primary and secondary, that are relevant to all emotions.

PRIMARY APPRAISALS

1. How relevant (important) is what is happening in this situation to my needs and goals?

2. Is this congruent (good) or incongruent (bad) with my needs or goals?

SECONDARY APPRAISALS

These appraisals relate to accountability and coping.

1. How responsible am I for what is happening in this situation?

2. How responsible is someone or something else?

3. Can I act on this situation to make or keep it more like what I want?

4. Can I handle and adjust to this situation however it might turn out?

5. Do I expect this situation to improve or to get worse?

Together, these seven appraisal dimensions produce a wide array of affective responses and emotions. For example, if something was important and bad, and caused by someone else, we would feel anger and be motivated to act towards the other person in a way that would fix the situation. If something was important and bad, but caused by ourselves, then we would feel shame or guilt and be motivated to make amends for the situation.

Where is the 'social' in social cognition?

Social psychology has always been concerned to describe the cognitive processes and structures that influence and are influenced by social behaviour, and there is no doubt that modern social cognition, which really only emerged in the late 1970s, has made enormous advances in this direction. However, critics wonder if social cognition has been *too* successful. It may have taken social psychology too far in the direction of cognitive psychology, and at the same time diverted attention from many of social psychology's traditional topics. There is a worry that there may not be any 'social' in social cognition (Augoustinos & Walker, 1995; Forgas, 1981; Kraut & Higgins, 1984; Markus & Zajonc, 1985; Moscovici, 1982; Zajonc, 1989).

Many of the postulated processes and structures seem to be little affected by social context and seem more accurately to represent *asocial* cognition operating on social stimuli (i.e. people). In this respect, critics have applied a label of **reductionism** to social cognition (see Chapter 1) and have increased their attempts to locate it in the social context of human interaction (Levine, Resnick, & Higgins, 1993; Nye & Bower, 1996; Wyer & Gruenfeld, 1995).

Two failures in research on social cognition have been identified:

1. to deal with language and communication, which are two fundamentally social variables (Kraut & Higgins, 1984; Markus & Zajonc, 1985); an exception is Maass and Arcuri's (1996) work on language and stereotyping (see Chapter 15);

2. to articulate cognitive processes with wider interpersonal, group and societal processes. Social identity and self-categorisation theory try to redress this problem by connecting cognitive and social processes (e.g. Hogg, Terry, & White, 1995; see Chapter 11). Recently, Nye and Bower (1996) have assembled research on small interactive groups that locate social cognition in its social interactive context. As well, Abrams and Hogg (1999) have assembled social cognition and social identity research in a way that sets out to integrate these two approaches.

Summary

- Social cognition refers to cognitive processes and structures that affect and are affected by social context. It is assumed that people have a limited capacity to process information and are cognitive misers who take all sorts of cognitive short-cuts; or they are motivated tacticians who choose, on the basis of their goals, motives and needs, among an array of cognitive strategies.
- The overall impressions we form of other people are dominated by stereotypes, unfavourable information, first impressions, and idiosyncratic personal constructs. Research suggests that, in forming impressions of other people, we weight components and then average them in complex ways; or certain components may influence the interpretation and meaning of all other components and dominate the resulting impression.
- Schemas are cognitive structures that represent knowledge about people, events, roles, the self and the general processing of information. Once invoked, schemas bias all aspects of information processing and inference in such a way that the schema remains unassailed.
- Categories are fuzzy sets of features organised around a prototype. They are hierarchically structured in terms of inclusiveness in such a way that less inclusive categories are subsets of broader, more inclusive categories. The process of categorisation accentuates perceived intracategory similarities and intercategory differences on dimensions that a person believes are correlated with the categorisation. This accentuation effect is the basis for stereotyping, but it requires articulation with a consideration of intergroup relations to provide a full explanation.

- In processing information about other people we tend to rely on schemas relating to subtypes, stereotypes, current moods, easily detected features, accessible categories and self-relevant information. However, people are less dependent on schemas when the cost of making a wrong inference is increased, when the cost of being indecisive is low, and when people are aware that schematic processing may be inaccurate.
- Schemas become more abstract, complex, organised, compact, resilient and accurate over time. They are hard to change but can be modified by schema-inconsistent information, mainly through the formation of subtypes.
- The encoding of information is heavily influenced by the salience of stimuli and by the cognitive accessibility of existing schemas.
- We tend to remember people mainly in terms of their traits, but also in terms of their behaviour and appearance. They can be stored as individual people or as category members.
- The processes we use to make inferences fall far short of ideal. Our schemas dominate us, we disregard regression effects and base-rate information and we perceive illusory correlations. We rely on cognitive short-cuts (heuristics) such as representativeness, availability, and anchoring and adjustment, rather than on more optimal information-processing techniques.
- Affect and emotion are cognitively underpinned by appraisals of accountability and our needs, goals and capacity to cope in a particular situation. In turn, affect influences social cognition—it infuses social cognition only where people process information in

an open and constructive manner that involves the active elaboration of stimulus details and information from memory.
- Social cognition has been criticised for being too cognitive and for not properly relating cognitive processes and structures to higher-level social processes, consequently failing to address many topics of central concern to social psychology.

LINKS

YOU HAVE READ ABOUT:	WHICH LINKS TO:
Social schemas, categories and stereotyping	cognitive activities and cognitive representations (3, 5, 6); stereotyping and prejudice (10); stereotyping and social identity theory (11)
Salience, vividness, accessibility	attitude accessibility (5)
Person memory	stereotyping and prejudice (10)
Social inference and heuristics	biases in attribution (3); heuristic–systematic model of attitude (5)

Key terms

accentuation principle *(p. 35)*
accessibility *(p. 37)*
affect–infusion model *(p. 47)*
anchoring and adjustment *(p. 45)*
associative meaning *(p. 44)*
associative network *(p. 33)*
attribution *(p. 27)*
availability heuristic *(p. 45)*
averaging *(p. 30)*
base-rate information *(p. 44)*
behavioural decision theory *(p. 43)*
behaviourism *(p. 26)*
bookkeeping *(p. 38)*
central traits *(p. 27)*
cognitive algebra *(p. 30)*
cognitive consistency *(p. 27)*
cognitive miser *(p. 27)*

configural model *(p. 27)*
conversion *(p. 38)*
exemplars *(p. 33)*
family resemblance *(p. 32)*
fuzzy sets *(p. 32)*
gestalt psychology *(p. 26)*
heuristics *(p. 45)*
illusory correlation *(p. 44)*
implicit personality theories *(p. 29)*
motivated tactician *(p. 27)*
naive scientist *(p. 27)*
normative models *(p. 43)*
paired distinctiveness *(p. 44)*
peripheral traits *(p. 27)*
personal constructs *(p. 28)*
primacy *(p. 28)*
priming *(p. 39)*

prototype *(p. 32)*
recency *(p. 28)*
reductionism *(p. 48)*
regression *(p. 43)*
representativeness heuristic *(p. 45)*
roles *(p. 32)*
salience *(p. 38)*
schema *(p. 31)*
script *(p. 31)*
self-categorisation theory *(p. 35)*
social cognition *(p. 26)*
social identity theory *(p. 35)*
stereotype *(p. 29)*
subtyping *(p. 38)*
summation *(p. 30)*
vividness *(p. 39)*
weighted averaging *(p. 30)*

FURTHER READING

Abrams, D., & Hogg, M. A. (Eds.). (1999). *Social identity and social cognition*. Oxford, UK: Blackwell. A large collection of chapters from leading social psychologists whose research contrasts or integrates basic social cognition and social identity processes in and between groups.

Augoustinos, M., & Walker, I. (1995). *Social cognition: An integrated introduction*. London: Sage. An introduction to social cognition from two leading Australian researchers. In addition to covering traditional topics, it places emphasis on the group context of social cognition and on the relationship between social cognition and discursive social psychology.

Devine, P. G., Hamilton, D. L., & Ostrom, T. M. (Eds.). (1994). *Social cognition: Impact on social psychology*. San Diego, CA: Academic Press. Leading experts discuss the impact that social cognition has had on a wide range of topics in social psychology.

Fiske, S. T., & Taylor, S. E. (1991). *Social cognition* (2nd ed.). New York: McGraw-Hill. This book remains the classic mainstream text on social cognition. It is comprehensive, detailed, and very well written.

Forgas, J. P., & Smith, C. A. (2003). Affect and emotion. In M. A. Hogg & J. Cooper (Eds.), *The Sage handbook of social psychology* (pp. 161–189). London: Sage. Comprehensive, up-to-date, and readable overview of what we know about the social cognitive antecedents and consequences of people's feelings.

Levine, J. M., Resnick, L. B., & Higgins, E. T. (1993). Social foundations of cognition. *Annual Review of Psychology, 44,* 585–612. A critical review of social cognition that focuses on the way in which cognition may be 'social' because it is shared.

Nye, J. L., & Bower, A. M. (Eds.). (1996). *What's social about social cognition?: Research on socially shared cognition in small groups.* Thousand Oaks, CA: Sage. Social cognition has tended to focus on the social thinker in isolation, neglecting the impact of social interaction on cognition. The book contains a diverse collection of chapters that challenge this approach from the perspective of research into groups.

Taylor, S. E. (1998). The social being in social psychology. In D. T. Gilbert, S. T. Fiske, & G. Lindzey (Eds.), *The handbook of social psychology* (4th ed., Vol. 1, pp. 58–95). New York: McGraw-Hill. An authoritative historical overview of social psychology, with a special emphasis on the development and role of social cognition.

Tesser, A., & Schwarz, N. (Eds.). (2001). *Blackwell handbook of social psychology: Intraindividual processes.* Oxford, UK: Blackwell. An up-to-date collection of 28 chapters by leading scholars on intraindividual processes. It includes many chapters covering social cognition topics.

Wyer, R. S. Jr., & Srull, T. K. (Eds.). (1994). *Handbook of social cognition* (2nd ed.). Hillsdale, NJ: Erlbaum. Comprehensive two-volume sourcebook of social cognition, with contributions from distinguished social cognition researchers.

Attribution and social knowledge

You have just arrived in a foreign country and find yourself becoming very irritated at the seemingly aloof and offhand manner in which people respond to your requests for directions to the hotel. Is their unfriendliness deliberate? Are you an intolerant person to have taken offence so readily, or does their behaviour simply confirm your expectations about people from that country? Do you really care? If you do, what factors would you take into account to explain their behaviour and your reactions? What might be the consequences of the explanation you arrive at?

THIS CHAPTER DISCUSSES:

- how people explain their own and others' behaviour
- major theories of causal attribution
- biases in attribution
- intergroup attributions
- social knowledge and societal attributions.

Social explanation

Human thought is greatly occupied with seeking, constructing and testing explanations of our experiences. We try to understand our world in order to render it sufficiently orderly and meaningful for adaptive action, and we tend to feel uncomfortable if we do not have such an understanding. So, for example, through life most of us gradually construct adequate explanations (i.e. theories) of why people behave in certain ways; in this respect, we are all 'naive' or lay psychologists. This is enormously useful because it allows us, with varying degrees of accuracy, to predict when someone will behave in a certain way; it also allows us to influence whether someone will behave in that way or not. Thus, we can gain some control over our destiny.

People construct explanations for both physical phenomena (e.g. earthquakes, the seasons) and human behaviour (e.g. anger, a particular attitude), and in general such explanations are *causal* explanations, in which specific conditions are attributed a causal role. Causal explanations are particularly powerful bases for prediction and control (Forsterling & Rudolph, 1988).

In this chapter we discuss how people make inferences about the causes of their own and other people's behaviours, and the antecedents and consequences of such inferences. Social psychological theories of causal inference are called *attribution theories* (Harvey & Weary, 1981; Hewstone, 1989; Kelley & Michela, 1980; Ross & Fletcher, 1985). There are six main theoretical emphases that make up the general body of **attribution** theory:

1. Heider's (1958) theory of naive psychology;
2. Jones and Davis's (1965) theory of correspondent inference;
3. Kelley's (1967) covariation model;
4. Schachter's (1964) theory of emotional lability;
5. Bem's (1967, 1972) theory of self-perception; and
6. Weiner's (1979, 1985) attributional theory.

Basic attribution processes

HEIDER'S THEORY OF NAIVE PSYCHOLOGY

Heider (1958) drew the attention of social psychologists to the importance of studying people's naive, or commonsense, psychological theories. He believed that these theories are important in their own right because they influence behaviour. For example, people who believe in astrology are likely to have different expectations and to act in different ways from those who do not. Heider believed that each person is a **naive psychologist** who

In search of the meaning of life: Religions are one expression of our most basic need to understand the world we live in.

intuitively constructs causal theories of human behaviour. And because such theories have the same form as systematic scientific social psychological theories, each person is actually a **naive** (or intuitive) **scientist**.

Heider based his ideas on three principles:

1. Because we generally feel that our own behaviour is motivated, we tend to look for the causes and reasons for other people's behaviour in order to discover their motives. The search for causes does seem to pervade human thought and, indeed, it can be difficult to explain or comment on something without using causal language. Heider and Simmel (1944) demonstrated this in an ingenious experiment in which people who were asked to describe the movement of abstract geometric figures described them as if they were humans with intentions to act in certain ways. Nowadays, we can see the same phenomenon in people's often highly emotional assigning of human motives to inanimate figures in video and computer games.

   The pervasive need that people have for causal explanation reveals itself perhaps most powerfully in the way that almost all societies construct an elaborate causal explanation for the origin and meaning of life—for example, religions.

2. Because we construct causal theories in order to be able to predict and control the environment, we tend to look for stable and enduring properties of the world about us. We try to discover the personality traits and enduring abilities in people or the stable properties of situations that cause behaviour.

3. In attributing causality to behaviour, we distinguish between personal factors (e.g. personality, ability) and environmental factors (e.g. situations, social pressure). The former are examples of an **internal** (or **dispositional**) **attribution** and the latter of an **external** (or **situational**) **attribution**. So, for example, it might be useful to know whether someone you meet at a party who seems aloof and distant *is* an aloof and distant person, or is acting in that way because she is not enjoying that particular party.

Heider believed that, because internal causes, or intentions, are hidden from us, we can only infer their presence if there are no clear external causes (however, as we see below, people tend to be biased in preferring internal to external attributions even in the face of evidence for external causality).

It seems that we readily tend to attribute behaviour to people's enduring and stable characteristics. Scherer (1978), for example, found that people made assumptions about the personality traits of complete strangers simply on the basis of hearing their voices (using cues such as pitch and tone) on the telephone.

Heider identified the major themes, and provided the insight that forms the blueprint for all subsequent, more formalised, theories of attribution.

JONES AND DAVIS'S THEORY OF CORRESPONDENT INFERENCE

Jones and Davis's (1965; Jones & McGillis, 1976) theory of **correspondent inference** explains how people infer that a person's behaviour corresponds to an underlying disposition or personality trait—how we infer, for example, that a friendly action is due to an underlying disposition to be friendly. People like to make correspondent inferences (attribute behaviours to underlying dispositions) because a dispositional cause is a stable one that renders people's behaviour predictable and thus increases our own sense of control over our world.

To make a correspondent inference, we draw on five sources of information, or cues (see Figure 3.1):

1. *Freely chosen* behaviour is more indicative of a disposition than behaviour that is clearly under the control of external threats, inducements or constraints.
2. Behaviour with effects that are relatively exclusive to that behaviour rather than other behaviours (i.e. behaviour with **non-common effects**) tells us more about dispositions. People assume that others are aware of non-common effects and that the specific behaviour was intentionally performed to produce the non-common effect. For example, suppose your friend Mary dates a man who seems no different from several other male prospects whom you know.

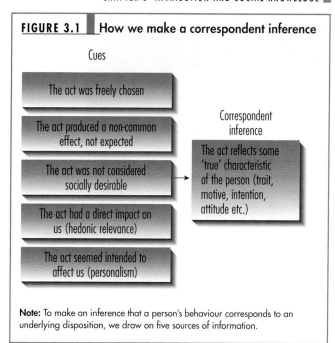

FIGURE 3.1 How we make a correspondent inference

Cues

- The act was freely chosen
- The act produced a non-common effect, not expected
- The act was not considered socially desirable
- The act had a direct impact on us (hedonic relevance)
- The act seemed intended to affect us (personalism)

Correspondent inference

- The act reflects some 'true' characteristic of the person (trait, motive, intention, attitude etc.)

Note: To make an inference that a person's behaviour corresponds to an underlying disposition, we draw on five sources of information.

You would have no basis for deciding how she made her choice. Then you discover that he is a Buddhist, as is Mary. Her behaviour now makes sense—it is unique and has to led to a non-common effect.
3. *Socially desirable* behaviour tells us little about a person's disposition because it is likely to be controlled by societal norms. However, socially undesirable behaviour is generally non-conforming and is thus a better basis for making a correspondent inference.
4. We make more confident correspondent inferences about others' behaviour when it has important consequences for ourselves—that is, behaviour that has **hedonic relevance**.
5. We make more confident correspondent inferences about others' behaviour when it appears to be directly intended to benefit or harm us—that is, behaviour that is high in **personalism**.

Experiments designed to test correspondent inference theory provide some support. Jones and Harris (1967) found that American students making attributions for speeches given by other students tended to make more correspondent inferences for freely chosen socially unpopular positions, such as freely choosing to make a speech in support of Fidel Castro.

In another experiment, Jones, Davis and Gergen (1961) found that participants made more correspondent inferences for out-of-role behaviours, such as friendly, outer-directed behaviour by someone who was applying for an astronaut job, in which the required attributes favour a quiet, reserved, inner-directed person.

Correspondent inference theory has some limitations and has declined in importance as an attribution theory

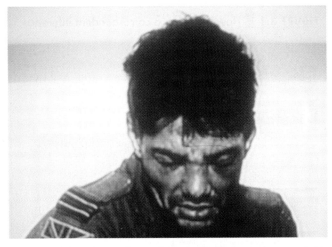

Free chosen behaviour? A confession obtained under duress is neither very reliable nor a good pointer to a prisoner's internal beliefs.

(Hewstone, 1989; Howard, 1985). For instance, the theory holds that correspondent inferences depend to a great extent on the attribution of intentionality, yet unintentional behaviours (e.g. careless behaviour) can be a strong basis for a correspondent inference (e.g. that the person is a careless person).

There is also a problem with the notion of non-common effects. While correspondent inference theory maintains that people assess the commonality of effects by comparing chosen and non-chosen actions, other research indicates that people simply do not attend to non-occurring behaviours and so would not be able to compute the commonality of effects accurately (Nisbett & Ross, 1980; Ross, 1977). More generally, although we may correct dispositional attributions in the light of situational factors, this is a rather deliberate process, whereas correspondent inferences themselves are relatively automatic (Gilbert, 1995).

KELLEY'S COVARIATION MODEL

The best-known attribution theory is Kelley's (1967, 1973) **covariation model**, according to which we explain multiple events on the basis that they occur together over time. Kelley believed that in trying to discover the causes of behaviour people act much like scientists. They try to identify what factors covary with the behaviour and then assign that factor a causal role. The procedure is similar to that embodied by the statistical technique of analysis of variance (ANOVA), and for this reason Kelley's model is often referred to as an ANOVA model. People use this covariation principle to decide whether to attribute a behaviour to internal dispositions (e.g. personality) or external environmental factors (e.g. social pressure).

In order to make this decision, people assess three classes of information associated with the co-occurrence of a certain action (e.g. laughter) by a specific person (e.g. Tom) with a potential cause (e.g. a comedian):

1. **Consistency information**—whether Tom always laughs at this comedian (high consistency) or only laughs at this comedian sometimes (low consistency);
2. **Distinctiveness information**—whether Tom laughs at everything (low distinctiveness) or only at the comedian (high distinctiveness);
3. **Consensus information**—whether everyone laughs at the comedian (high consensus) or only Tom laughs (low consensus).

Where consistency is low, people engage in **discounting**—they discount the potential cause and search for an alternative (see Figure 3.2). If Tom sometimes laughs and sometimes does not laugh at the comedian, then presumably the cause of the laughter is neither the comedian nor Tom, but some other factor—for example, whether or not Tom inhaled laughing gas before listening to the comedian, or whether or not the comedian told a funny joke (see McClure, 1998, for a review of the conditions in which discounting is most likely to occur). Where consistency is high and distinctiveness and consensus are also high, we can make an external attribution to the comedian (the cause of Tom's laughter was the comedian), but where distinctiveness and consensus are low we can make an internal attribution to Tom's personality (Tom laughed at the comedian because Tom is simply the sort of person who tends to laugh a lot).

McArthur (1972) tested Kelley's theory by having participants make internal or external attributions for a range of behaviours (e.g. 'Tom laughs at the comedian'), each accompanied by one of the eight possible configurations of high or low consistency, distinctiveness and consensus information. Although the

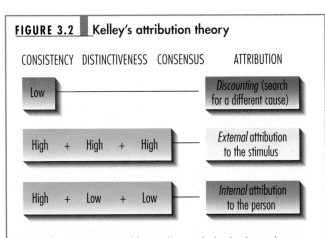

FIGURE 3.2 Kelley's attribution theory

CONSISTENCY DISTINCTIVENESS CONSENSUS ATTRIBUTION

Low ———————————————— *Discounting* (search for a different cause)

High + High + High ——— *External* attribution to the stimulus

High + Low + Low ——— *Internal* attribution to the person

Note: Kelley's covariation model states that people decide what attributions to make after considering the consistency, distinctiveness and consensus of a person's behaviour.

theory was generally supported (see review by Kassin, 1979), there was a tendency for people to underuse consensus information.

There are also some general issues worth considering:

- Just because people can use three sources of information, consistency, distinctiveness and consensus to attribute causality (the case in experimental tests of Kelley's model), this does not mean that in the normal course of events they do.
- There is evidence that people are actually poor at assessing covariation between events, even when they occur together over time (Alloy & Tabachnik, 1984).
- There is no guarantee that people are using the covariation principle—they may attribute causality to the most salient feature or to whatever causal agent appears to be similar to the effect (Nisbett & Ross, 1980).
- If people do attribute causality on the basis of covariance or correlation, then they are indeed being *naive* scientists (Hilton, 1988)—covariation is not causation (see Chapter 1).

Another drawback of the covariation model is that consistency, distinctiveness and consensus information require multiple observations. Sometimes, we have this information: we may know that Tom does indeed laugh often at almost anything (low distinctiveness) and that others do not find the comedian particularly amusing (low consensus). At other times we may have, at best, incomplete information or even no information from multiple observations. How do we attribute causality under these circumstances?

To deal with this, Kelley (1972a) introduced the notion of *causal schemata*—beliefs or preconceptions, built up from experience, about how certain kinds of causes interact to produce a specific effect. One such schema is that a particular effect requires at least two causes (called the 'multiple necessary cause' schema): for example, someone with a drink-driving record must have consumed a certain amount of alcohol and have been in control of a vehicle. Although the notion of causal schemata does have some empirical support (Kun & Weiner, 1973), and does help resolve attributional problems raised by the case of a single observation, it is by no means uncritically accepted (Fiedler, 1982).

Extensions of attribution theory

EMOTIONAL LABILITY

Schachter (1964, 1971; Schachter & Singer, 1962) has suggested the intriguing idea that emotions have two distinct components: a state of physiological *arousal* that does not differentiate between emotions, and *cognitions* that label the arousal and determine which emotion is experienced. Sometimes, cognitions may precede arousal (e.g. identifying a snake as a tiger snake will produce arousal that is experienced as fear); at other times a state of arousal may occur that prompts a search of the immediate environment for possible causes. (See Chapter 2 for more on affect and emotion.)

To test this idea that emotions may indeed be labile (i.e. changeable), Schachter and Singer (1962) conducted a now-classic experiment. Students were given an injection of either the drug epinephrine (adrenaline) or a placebo (salt water) to provide a control condition. Students with the drug were then allocated to one of three conditions: (1) they were correctly informed that the drug would cause symptoms of arousal (e.g. rapid breathing, increased heart rate); (2) they were given no explanation; or (3) they were misinformed that they might experience a slight headache and some dizziness. All participants then waited in a room with a confederate to fill out some paperwork. For half, the confederate behaved in a euphoric manner (engaging in silly antics and making paper aeroplanes), and for the other half in an angry manner (ripping up the papers and stomping around).

Schachter and Singer predicted that the 'drug-misinformed' participants would experience unexpected arousal and would search for a cause in their immediate environment. The behaviour of the confederate would act as a salient cue, encouraging participants in the 'euphoric' condition to feel euphoric and those in the 'angry' condition to feel angry. The emotions of the other two drug groups and the control group would be unaffected by the behaviour of the confederate: the control participants had experienced no arousal from the drug and the 'informed participants' already had an explanation for their arousal. The results of the experiment largely supported these predictions.

Perhaps the most significant implication of Schachter's work is its therapeutic application (Valins & Nisbett, 1972). If emotions depend on what cognitive label is assigned, through causal attribution to undifferentiated arousal, then it might, for example, be possible to transform depression into contentment simply by reattributing arousal. A paradigm has been devised to test this idea—called the *misattribution paradigm* (Valins, 1966). People who feel anxious and bad about themselves because they attribute arousal internally are encouraged to attribute arousal to external factors: for example, someone who is shy can be encouraged to attribute the arousal associated with meeting new people to ordinary environmental causes rather than to personality deficiencies, and thus no longer feel shy. A number of experiments have employed this type of intervention with some success (e.g. Olson, 1988; Storms & Nisbett, 1970; for critical reviews of clinical

applications of attribution theory, see Buchanan &
Seligman, 1995; Forsterling, 1988).

Initial enthusiasm for emotional lability and the
clinical application of misattribution has, however,
waned in the light of subsequent criticisms (Reisenzein,
1983):

• Emotions may be significantly less labile than was
originally thought (Maslach, 1979). Environmental
cues are not readily accepted as bases for inferring
emotions from unexplained arousal and, because
unexplained arousal is intrinsically unpleasant,
people have a propensity to assign it a negative label.
• The misattribution effect seems to be limited (Parkinson, 1985). It is largely restricted to laboratory investigations and is unreliable and short-lived. It is not
clear that the effect is mediated by an attribution
process, and in any case it is restricted to a limited
range of emotion-inducing stimuli.

SELF-PERCEPTION THEORY

One far-reaching implication of treating emotion as cognitively labelled arousal is that people may make more
general attributions for their *own* behaviour. This idea
has been elaborated by Bem (1967, 1972) in his **self-perception theory**. Self-perception theory is an account of
how people construct their self-concept, and so we
describe it in Chapter 4, which explores the nature of
self and identity.

WEINER'S ATTRIBUTIONAL THEORY

Attributional dimensions of task achievement are the
focus of another extension of attribution theory, by
Weiner (1979, 1985, 1986). Weiner was interested in
the causes and consequences of the sorts of attributions
made for people's success or failure on a task—for

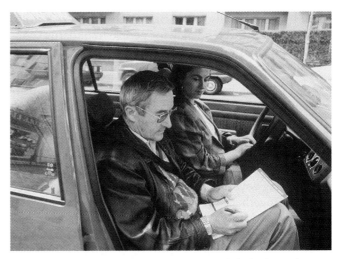

Performance attribution: Does this young Parisienne think she deserved to pass
the test? What might she take into account while she awaits the outcome?

example, success or failure in a social psychology examination. He believed that in making an achievement attribution we consider three performance dimensions:

1. *Locus*—Was the performance caused by the actor
(internal) or the situation (external)?
2. *Stability*—Was the internal or external cause a stable
or an unstable one?
3. *Controllability*—To what extent is future task performance under the actor's control?

These dimensions produce eight different types of
explanation for task performance (see Figure 3.3). For
example, failure in a social psychology examination
might be attributed to 'unusual hindrance from others'
(the top right-hand box in Figure 3.3) if the student was
intelligent (therefore, failure is external) but was disturbed by a nearby student sneezing from hayfever

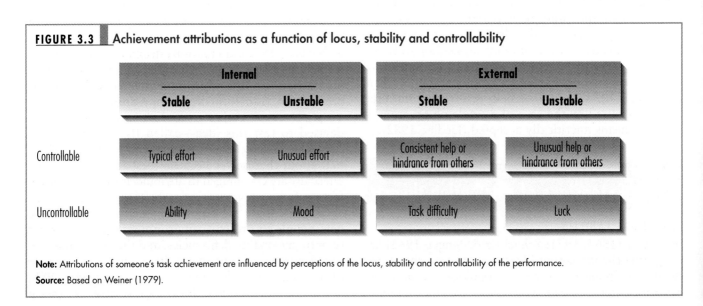

FIGURE 3.3 Achievement attributions as a function of locus, stability and controllability

	Internal		External	
	Stable	**Unstable**	**Stable**	**Unstable**
Controllable	Typical effort	Unusual effort	Consistent help or hindrance from others	Unusual help or hindrance from others
Uncontrollable	Ability	Mood	Task difficulty	Luck

Note: Attributions of someone's task achievement are influenced by perceptions of the locus, stability and controllability of the performance.
Source: Based on Weiner (1979).

(unstable and controllable, because in future examinations the sneezing student might not be present, and/or one could choose to sit in a place away from the sneezing student).

Weiner's model is a dynamic one, in that people first assess whether someone has succeeded or failed and accordingly experience positive or negative emotion. They then make a causal attribution for the performance, which produces more specific emotions (e.g. pride for doing well due to ability) and expectations that influence future performance.

Weiner's model is relatively well supported by experiments that provide participants with performance outcomes and locus, stability and controllability information, often under role-playing conditions (e.g. de Jong, Koomen, & Mellenbergh, 1988; Frieze & Weiner, 1971). However, critics have suggested that the controllability dimension may be less important than was first thought. They have also wondered to what extent people outside controlled laboratory conditions really analyse achievement in this way. More recently, Weiner (1995) has extended his model to place an emphasis on judgments of responsibility: on the basis of causal attributions people make judgments of responsibility and it is these latter judgments, not the causal attributions themselves, that influence affective experience and behavioural reactions.

Applications of attribution theory

The idea that people need to locate the cause of their own and others' behaviour in order to plan their own actions has, in some senses, revolutionised social psychology. We have already seen some ways in which this idea has been applied—for example, achievement attributions, and the reattribution of arousal as a therapeutic technique. In this section, we look at two further areas in which attribution ideas have been used: attributional styles and interpersonal relationships.

INDIVIDUAL DIFFERENCES AND ATTRIBUTIONAL STYLES
The investigation of enduring individual differences in the sorts of attributions people make, or their **attributional style**, has been championed by Rotter (1966), who believes that people differ regarding the amount of control they feel they have over the reinforcements and punishments they receive. *Internals* believe they have an enormous amount of personal control over their destiny—things happen because they make them happen. *Externals* are more fatalistic: they believe they have little control over what happens to them—things simply occur by chance, luck or the actions of powerful external agents.

Rotter devised a 29-item locus of control scale, which has been used to relate locus of control to a range of behaviours, including political beliefs, achievement behaviour, reactions to illness and the like. One problem with the scale is that it may not actually measure a single construct (i.e. a single personality dimension) but, rather, a number of relatively independent beliefs to do with control (Collins, 1974).

A number of other questionnaires have been devised to measure attributional styles—a tendency for individuals to make particular kinds of causal inferences, rather than others, across different situations and across time (Feather & Tiggerman, 1984; Metalsky & Abramson, 1981). Of these, the Attributional Style Questionnaire, or ASQ (Peterson, Semmel, von Baeyer, Abramson, Metalsky, & Seligman, 1982; Seligman, Abramson, Semmel, & von Baeyer, 1979), is perhaps the most widely known. It measures the sorts of explanations people give for aversive (i.e. unpleasant) events on three dimensions: internal/external, stable/unstable, global/specific. The global/specific dimension refers to the extent to which a cause has a wide or narrow range of effects—e.g. 'the economy' is a global explanation for someone being made redundant, whereas the closing of a specific company is a specific explanation. People who tend to view aversive events as being caused by internal, stable, global factors have a 'depressive attributional style' which may promote helplessness and depression and have adverse health consequences (Abramson, Seligman, & Teasdale, 1978; Abramson, Metalsky, & Alloy, 1989; Crocker, Alloy, & Kayne, 1988).

A more recent Attributional Complexity Scale, or ACS, has been devised by Fletcher, Danilovics, Fernandez, Peterson and Reeder (1986). The ACS measures individual differences in the complexity of the attributions people make for events.

The notion of attributional style as a personality trait is not without problems: for instance, the ASQ and the ACS provide only limited evidence of cross-situational individual differences in causal attribution (e.g. Cutrona, Russell, & Jones, 1985). Also not without problems is the important link between attributional style, learned helplessness and clinical depression. Although more than 100 studies involving about 15 000 participants confirm an average correlation of 0.30 between attributional style and depression (Sweeney, Anderson, & Bailey, 1986), this does not prove causation—it is a correlation in which one factor explains 9% of variance in the other.

More useful are diachronic studies, which show that attributional style measured at one time, predicts depressive symptoms at a later date (Nolen-Hoeksma, Girgus, & Seligman, 1992), but again causality is not established. Causality is difficult to establish because it is, of course, unethical to induce clinical depression in experimental settings. We are left with experimental evidence from studies of transitory mood, a pale analogue of depression. Is it justified to generalise from feelings about doing well or poorly on a trivial laboratory task to full-blown clinical depression?

INTERPERSONAL RELATIONSHIPS

Attributions assume great importance in interpersonal relationships (also see Chapter 13), particularly close interpersonal relationships (e.g. marriage and friendship), where attributions are *communicated* to fulfil a variety of functions—for instance, to explain, justify or excuse behaviour, as well as to attribute blame and instil guilt (Hilton, 1990).

Harvey (1987) suggests that interpersonal relationships go through three basic phases: formation, maintenance and dissolution (see also Moreland & Levine's, 1982, 1984, model of group socialisation in Chapter 7). Fincham (1985) explains that, during the formation stage, attributions reduce ambiguity and facilitate communication and an understanding of the relationship. In the maintenance phase, the need to make attributions decreases because stable personalities and relationships have been constructed. The dissolution phase is characterised by an increase in attributions in order to regain an understanding of the relationship.

A notable feature of many interpersonal relationships is attributional conflict (Horai, 1977), where partners proffer divergent causal interpretations of behaviours and disagree over what attributions to adopt. Often partners cannot even agree on a cause–effect sequence, one exclaiming, 'I withdraw because you nag', the other, 'I nag because you withdraw'. Attributional conflict has been shown, mainly from research in heterosexual couples, to be correlated strongly with relationship satisfaction (Kelley, 1979; Orvis, Kelley, & Butler, 1976; Sillars, 1981).

The main thrust of research has, however, focused on the role of attributions in marital satisfaction (e.g. Fincham & Bradbury, 1991; Fletcher & Thomas, 2000; Noller & Ruzzene, 1991). An important aim has been to distinguish between distressed and non-distressed spouses in order to provide therapy for dysfunctional marital relationships. Correlational studies (e.g. Fincham & O'Leary, 1983; Holtzworth-Munroe & Jacobson, 1985) reveal that happily married (or non-distressed) spouses tend to credit their partners for positive behaviours by citing internal, stable, global and controllable factors to explain them. Negative behaviours are explained away by ascribing them to causes viewed as external, unstable, specific and uncontrollable. Distressed couples behave in exactly the opposite way. It also appears that, while women tend fairly continually to engage in attributional thought about the relationship, men do so only when the relationship becomes dysfunctional. In this respect, and contrary to popular

Attributing blame: Couples sometimes cannot agree on what is cause and what is effect. For example, does nagging cause withdrawal or vice versa?

opinion, men may be the more diagnostic barometers of marital dysfunction.

Do attributional dynamics produce dysfunctional marital relationships, or do dysfunctional relationships distort the attributional dynamic? This important causal question has been looked at by Fincham and Bradbury (1987; see overview by Hewstone, 1989), who obtained responsibility attributions, causal attributions and marital satisfaction measures from 39 married couples on two occasions 10–12 months apart. Attributions made on the first occasion were found reliably to predict marital satisfaction 10–12 months later, but only for wives.

Another longitudinal study (though only over a 2-month period) by Fletcher at the University of Canterbury confirmed that attributions do have a causal impact on subsequent relationship satisfaction (Fletcher, Fincham, Cramer, & Heron, 1987). Subsequent, more extensive and better controlled longitudinal studies have replicated these findings for both husbands and wives (Fincham & Bradbury, 1993; Senchak & Leonard, 1993).

Biases in attribution

The attribution process is clearly subject to bias—it can be biased by personality, biased by interpersonal dynamics, biased to meet communication needs. We do not approach the task of attributing causes for behaviour in an entirely dispassionate, disinterested and objective manner, and the cognitive mechanisms that are responsible for attribution may themselves be subject to imperfections that render them suboptimal.

Accumulating evidence for attributional biases and 'errors' has occasioned a shift of perspective. Instead of viewing people as naive scientists or even statisticians (in which case, biases were considered largely a theoretical nuisance), we now think of people as **cognitive misers** (Taylor, 1981, 1998—see Chapter 2). People use cognitive short-cuts (called heuristics) to make attributions that, although not objectively correct all the time, are quite satisfactory and adaptive.

Biases are entirely adaptive characteristics of ordinary, everyday social perception (Fiske & Taylor, 1991; Nisbett & Ross, 1980; Ross, 1977). We now discuss some of the most important attributional biases.

THE FUNDAMENTAL ATTRIBUTION ERROR

The **fundamental attribution error** (sometimes referred to as the *correspondence bias*—e.g. Gilbert & Malone, 1995*)*, identified by Ross (1977), refers to a tendency for people to make dispositional attributions for others' behaviour, even when there are clear external/environmental causal contenders. For example, in the Jones and Harris (1967) study briefly mentioned earlier, participants read speeches about Fidel Castro, ostensibly written by fellow students, in order to infer the speech writers' attitudes to Castro. The speeches were either pro-Castro or anti-Castro and the writers had, ostensibly, either freely chosen to write the speech or been instructed to do so. Where there was a choice, participants not surprisingly reasoned that those who had written a pro-Castro speech were in favour of Castro, and those who had written an anti-Castro speech were against Castro—an internal, dispositional attribution was made (see Figure 3.4).

However, a dispositional attribution was also made even when the speech writers had been instructed to write the speech. Although there was overwhelming evidence for an exclusively external cause, participants seemed largely to overlook this information and prefer a dispositional explanation—the fundamental attribution error.

Other studies furnish additional empirical evidence for the fundamental attribution error (Jones, 1979; Nisbett & Ross, 1980). Indeed, the fundamental attribution error, or correspondence bias, has been repeatedly demonstrated both inside and outside the social psychology laboratory (Gilbert, 1998; Jones, 1990). The fundamental attribution error may also be responsible for a number of more general explanatory tendencies—for example, the tendency to attribute road accidents unduly to the driver rather than to the vehicle or the road conditions (Barjonet, 1980), and the tendency among some people to attribute poverty and unemployment to the person rather than to social conditions (see below).

Pettigrew (1979) has suggested that the fundamental attribution error may emerge in a slightly different form in intergroup contexts where groups are making attributions about ingroup and outgroup behaviour—this he calls the *ultimate attribution error* (see below).

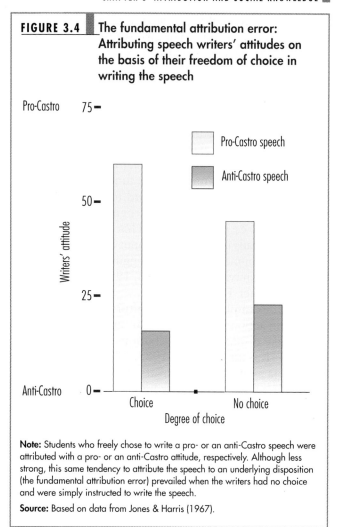

FIGURE 3.4 The fundamental attribution error: Attributing speech writers' attitudes on the basis of their freedom of choice in writing the speech

Note: Students who freely chose to write a pro- or an anti-Castro speech were attributed with a pro- or an anti-Castro attitude, respectively. Although less strong, this same tendency to attribute the speech to an underlying disposition (the fundamental attribution error) prevailed when the writers had no choice and were simply instructed to write the speech.

Source: Based on data from Jones & Harris (1967).

A number of explanations of the fundamental attribution error have been proposed:

- *Focus of attention.* The actor's behaviour attracts relatively more attention than the background: it is disproportionately salient in cognition, is effectively the figure against the situational background, and is thus overrepresented causally (Taylor & Fiske, 1978). Thus, the actor and the actor's behaviour form what Heider (1958) called a 'causal unit'. This explanation makes quite a lot of sense. Procedures designed to focus attention away from the actor and onto the situation have been shown to increase the tendency to make a situational rather than dispositional attribution (e.g. Rholes & Pryor, 1982).

  Again, when people really want to find out about a situation from a person's behaviour, they focus on the situation and are less likely to leap to a dispositional attribution—the fundamental attribution error is muted or reversed (e.g. Krull, 1993).
- *Differential forgetting.* Attribution requires the representation of causal information in memory. There

is some evidence that people tend to forget situational causes more readily than dispositional causes, thus producing a dispositional shift over time (e.g. Moore, Sherrod, Liu, & Underwood, 1979; Peterson, 1980).

Other studies show the opposite effect (e.g. Miller & Porter, 1980), and Funder (1982) has argued that the direction of shift depends on the focus of information processing and occurs immediately after attribution of the behaviour.

- *Cultural and developmental factors*. Attempts have been made to characterise the fundamental attribution error as an automatic and universal outcome of perceptual experience and cognitive activity (e.g. McArthur & Baron, 1983). This sort of approach, however, fails to take into account important cultural and developmental factors (Higgins & Bargh, 1987; Markus, Kitayama, & Heiman, 1996; see also below, and Chapter 16).

For example, in Western cultures, young children explain action in concrete situational terms and learn to make dispositional attributions only in late childhood (Kassin & Pryor, 1985; White, 1988). This process may not be universal—Miller (1984, further details below) reports that Indian Hindu children do not drift towards dispositional explanations but towards increasingly situational explanations. Perhaps these processes reflect different cultural norms for social explanation, or more basic differences between Western and non-Western conceptions of self—the autonomous and independent Western self and the interdependent non-Western self (Markus, Kitayama, & Heiman, 1996; see Chapters 4 and 16).

The fundamental attribution error is a relatively ubiquitous and socially valued feature of Western cultures (Beauvois & Dubois, 1988; Jellison & Green, 1981) but, although present, it is less dominant in non-Western cultures (Fletcher & Ward, 1988; Morris & Peng, 1994). Perhaps the fundamental attribution error is not quite as fundamental as first thought: instead, it may be, at least to some extent, a normative way of thinking (see discussion of norms in Chapters 7 and 8). It has been suggested (e.g. Gilbert, 1995; Gilbert & Malone, 1995) that the term 'fundamental attribution error' should perhaps be replaced by the less extreme and more accurate term *correspondence bias*.

- *Linguistic factors*. One final, interesting observation by Nisbett and Ross (1980) is that the English language is so constructed that it is usually relatively easy to describe an action and the actor in the same terms, and much more difficult to describe the situation in the same way: for example, we can talk about a kind or honest person and a kind or honest action, but not a kind or honest situation. The English language seems to facilitate dispositional explanations (Brown & Fish, 1983; Semin & Fiedler, 1991).

THE ACTOR–OBSERVER EFFECT

Imagine the last time a shop assistant was rude to you. You probably thought, 'What a rude person!'—in other words, you made an internal attribution to the shop assistant's enduring personality. In contrast, how did you explain the last time *you* snapped at someone? Probably not in terms of your personality, more likely in terms of external factors such as time pressures or stress. The **actor–observer effect** (or the self–other effect) is really an extension of the fundamental attribution error: it refers to the tendency for people to attribute others' behaviour internally to dispositional factors and their own behaviour externally to environmental factors (Jones & Nisbett, 1972). Twenty years of research has provided a great deal of support for this effect (Watson, 1982) and has produced some extensions and qualifications. For example, not only do we tend to attribute others' behaviour more dispositionally than our own, but we tend to consider their behaviour to be more stable and predictable than our own (Baxter & Goldberg, 1988).

The actor–observer effect can be influenced by a number of factors. People tend to make more dispositional attributions for socially desirable than socially undesirable behaviours irrespective of who the actor is (e.g. Taylor & Koivumaki, 1976), and there is a tendency for actors to be more dispositional than observers in attributing positive behaviours and more situational in attributing negative behaviours (e.g. Chen, Yates, & McGinnies, 1988).

The actor–observer effect can be overturned if the actor knows that his or her behaviour is dispositionally caused: for example, you may 'adopt' an injured possum in the full knowledge that you are a sucker for injured animals and you have often done this sort of thing in the past (Monson & Hesley, 1982). Finally, the actor–observer effect can be abolished or reversed if the actor is encouraged to take the role of the observer regarding the behaviour to be attributed, and the observer the role of the actor. Under these circumstances, the actor becomes more dispositional and the observer more situational (e.g. Frank & Gilovich, 1989).

There are two main explanations for the actor–observer effect:

1. *Perceptual focus*. This explanation is almost identical to the 'focus of attention' explanation for the fundamental attribution error (see above). For the observer, the actor and the actor's behaviour are figural against the background of the situation. An actor, however, cannot 'see' himself behaving, and so the background situation assumes the role of figure

against the background of self. The actor and the observer quite literally have different perspectives on the behaviour and thus explain it in different ways (Storms, 1973).

Perceptual salience does indeed seem to have an important role in causal explanation. For example, McArthur and Post (1977) found that observers tended to make more dispositional attributions for an actor's behaviour when the actor was strongly illuminated than when dimly illuminated.

2. *Informational differences.* Another reason why actors tend to make external attributions and observers internal ones is that actors have a wealth of information to draw on about how they have behaved in other circumstances. They may actually know that they behave in very different ways in different contexts, and thus quite accurately tend to see their behaviour as being under situational control.

Observers are not privy to this autobiographical information. They tend simply to see the actor behaving in a certain way in one context, or a limited range of contexts, and have no information about how the actor behaves in other contexts. It is therefore not an unreasonable assumption to make a dispositional attribution. This explanation, first suggested by Jones and Nisbett (1972), does have some empirical support (Eisen, 1979; White & Younger, 1988).

THE FALSE CONSENSUS EFFECT

Kelley (1972b) identified consensus information as being one of the three types of information that people used to make attributions about others' behaviour (see above). One of the first cracks in the naive scientist model of attribution was McArthur's (1972) discovery that attributors in fact underused or even ignored consensus information (Kassin, 1979).

Recently, it has become apparent that people do not ignore consensus information, but rather provide their own consensus information: they tend to see their own behaviour as typical and assume that under similar circumstances others would behave in the same way. Ross, Greene and House (1977) first demonstrated this **false consensus effect**. They asked students if they would agree to walk around campus for 30 minutes wearing a sandwich board carrying the slogan 'Eat at Joe's'. Those who agreed estimated that 62% of their peers would also have agreed, while those who refused estimated that 67% of their peers would also have refused.

There are well over 100 studies that bear testimony to the robust nature of the false consensus effect (Marks & Miller, 1987; Mullen, Atkins, Champion, Edwards, Hardy, Story, & Vanderklok, 1985).

The false consensus effect may have a number of causes (Marks & Miller, 1987; Wetzel & Walton, 1985).

The false consensus effect: This bungee jumper suddenly discovers a major attributional bias! A novice bungee jumper probably overestimates the percentage of others who would jump.

As people tend to seek out the company of similar others, they may simply encounter more people who are similar to them than different from them—thus experiencing inflated consensus. Another possibility is that our own opinions tend to be so salient that they displace consideration of alternatives and thus any comparison that might provide a more accurate estimate of consensus. A third possibility is that we subjectively justify the correctness of our opinions and actions by grounding them in an exaggerated consensus. This suggests the important possibility that false consensus is a mechanism for maintaining a stable perception of reality—reality grounded in consensus.

Research into factors influencing the false consensus effect suggests that the effect is stronger for important beliefs that we care a great deal about (e.g. Granberg, 1987) and for beliefs about which we are certain (e.g. Marks & Miller, 1985). External threat, positive qualities, perceived similarity of others and minority group status also inflate perceptions of consensus (e.g. Sanders & Mullen, 1983; Sherman, Presson, & Chassin, 1984; van der Pligt, 1984).

SELF-SERVING BIASES

There is a range of biases that are quite clearly self-serving, because they seem to protect or enhance self-evaluation (see Chapter 4). People tend to attribute internally and take credit for their successes (a self-enhancing bias) and attribute externally and deny responsibility for their failures (a self-protecting bias). This is a robust effect that has been found in many different cultures (Fletcher & Ward, 1988). Although initial explanations for success and failure may be relatively modest, dispositional attributions for success and situational attributions for failure become more pronounced with time (Burger, 1986).

In general, self-enhancing biases are more common than self-protecting biases (Miller & Ross, 1975), but this may be partly because people with low self-esteem tend not to protect themselves by attributing their failures externally; rather, they attribute them internally (Campbell & Fairey, 1985).

Self-serving biases are clearly ego-serving (Snyder, Stephan, & Rosenfield, 1978). However, Miller and Ross (1975) suggest that there may also be a cognitive component, particularly for the self-enhancing aspect. People generally expect to succeed and therefore accept responsibility for success. If they try hard to succeed they correlate success with their own effort, and they generally exaggerate the amount of control they have over successful performances. Together, these cognitive factors might encourage internal attribution of success. In general, however, it seems likely that both cognitive and motivational factors have a role (Anderson & Slusher, 1986; Tetlock & Levi, 1982), and that they are difficult to disentangle from one another (Tetlock & Manstead, 1985; Zuckerman, 1979).

Self-serving biases have a number of other ramifications. Self-presentational considerations may influence the degree to which people publicly take credit for success (modesty can often preclude self-enhancement) or deny responsibility for failure (the facts may make attempts at self-protection embarrassingly transparent) (e.g. Schlenker, Weingold, & Hallam, 1990). Riess, Rosenfield, Melburg and Tedeschi (1981) investigated this idea and found that self-presentational considerations weakened but did not abolish self-serving biases.

There is also evidence for an anticipatory self-serving bias, in which people who anticipate failure intentionally and publicly make external attributions before the event. Berglas (1987) has called this **self-handicapping** (see Box 3.1 and Figure 3.5).

Another self-serving attributional phenomenon is the attribution of responsibility (Weiner 1995), which is influenced by an **outcome bias** (Allison, Mackie, & Messick, 1996). People tend to attribute greater responsibility to someone who is involved in an accident with large rather than small consequences (Burger, 1981; Walster, 1966). For example, we would attribute greater responsibility to the captain of a tanker that spills millions of litres of oil than to the captain of a small

> ## BOX 3.1   Self-handicapping: Explaining away your failure
>
> Imagine that you are waiting to take an examination in a subject you find difficult and that you fully anticipate failing. You might well make sure that as many people as possible know that you have done no revision, are not really interested in the subject and have a dreadful hangover to boot. Your subsequent failure is thus externally attributed without it seeming that you are making excuses to explain away your failure. Berglas (1987) has called this self-handicapping.
>
> To investigate this phenomenon, Berglas and Jones (1978) had participants perform a problem-solving task where the problems were either solvable or not solvable. They were told that they had done very well, and before continuing with a second problem-solving task they were given the choice of taking either a drug called 'Actavil', which would ostensibly improve intellectual functioning and performance, or 'Pandocrin', which would have the opposite effect. As predicted, those participants who had succeeded on the solvable puzzles felt confident about their ability and so chose Actavil in order to improve further (see Figure 3.5). Those who had succeeded on the not-solvable puzzles attributed their performance externally to luck and chose Pandocrin in order to be able to explain away more easily the anticipated failure on the second task.
>
> **Source:** Based on data from Berglas & Jones (1978).

boat that spills only a few litres, though the degree of responsibility may actually be the same.

This effect may be part of a general tendency to cling to an **illusion of control** (Langer, 1975) by believing in a *just world* (Lerner, 1977). People like to believe that bad things happen to 'bad people' and good things to 'good people' (i.e. people get what they deserve) and that people have control over their outcomes. This pattern of attributions makes the world seem a controllable and secure place, in which we can determine our destiny.

The **belief in a just world** can result in a general pattern of attribution in which victims are deemed responsible for their misfortune—poverty, oppression, tragedy and injustice all happen because victims deserve it. Examples of the just-world hypothesis in action are the views that the unemployed are responsible for being out of work, that rape victims are responsible for the violence against them and that Australian Aborigines are responsible for their disadvantage. Another example is the belief, held by some people, that the six million Jewish victims of the Holocaust were responsible for their fate—that they deserved it (Davidowicz, 1975).

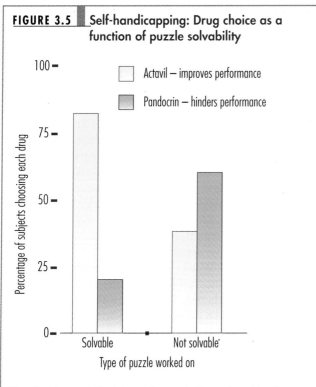

FIGURE 3.5 Self-handicapping: Drug choice as a function of puzzle solvability

Percentage of subjects choosing each drug

☐ Actavil – improves performace
▨ Pandocrin – hinders performance

Type of puzzle worked on

Note: Participants who had done well on a solvable puzzle could attribute their performace internally (e.g. to ability): anticipating an equally good performance on a second similar task, they chose a performance-enhancing drug, Actavil, rather than a performance-impairing drug, Pandocrin. Participants who had done well on a not solvable puzzle could only attribute their performance externally (e.g. to luck): with little prospect of an equivalent performance on the second task they chose the performance-impairing drug, as the self-handicapping option.

Source: Based on data from Berglas & Jones (1978).

The belief in a just world may also be responsible for self-blame. Victims of traumatic and violent events such as incest, debilitating illness, rape and other forms of violence can experience a strong and debilitating sense that the world is no longer stable, meaningful, controllable and just. One way to reinstate an illusion of control is by taking some responsibility for the event (Miller & Porter, 1983).

Intergroup attribution

Attribution theories are concerned mainly with how people make dispositional or situational attributions for their own and others' behaviour, and the sorts of biases that occur in this process. The perspective is very much tied to interpersonal relations: people as unique individuals make attributions for their own behaviour or the behaviour of other unique individuals. There is, however, another attributional context, intergroup relations, where individuals as group members make

Counter-stereotypical behaviour: Go Boris! Sometimes behaviour flies in the face of stereotypical expectations.

attributions for the behaviours of themselves as group members and others as either ingroup or outgroup members (Deschamps, 1983; Hewstone, 1989; Hewstone & Jaspars, 1982, 1984).

Examples of such **intergroup attributions** abound—such as the attribution of economic ills to minority outgroups (e.g. Asian immigrants in Australia, Eastern European immigrants in Britain) or the explanation of behaviours in terms of stereotypical properties of group membership (e.g. attributions for performance are consistent with the sex-stereotype; Deaux, 1984).

The first point that can be made about intergroup attributions is an extension of the self-serving bias described above. Intergroup attributions are characterised by **ethnocentrism**, or an ingroup-serving bias, in which socially desirable or positive behaviours by ingroup members and socially undesirable or negative behaviours by outgroup members are internally attributed to dispositions, and negative ingroup and positive outgroup behaviours are externally attributed to situational factors (Hewstone & Jaspars, 1982; Hewstone, 1989, 1990). This effect is more prevalent in Western than non-Western cultures (Fletcher & Ward, 1988).

It is common in team sports contexts, where the success of one's own team is attributed to internal stable abilities rather than effort, luck or task difficulty; this group-enhancing bias is stronger and more consistent than the corresponding group-protective bias (Mullen & Riordan, 1988; Miller & Ross, 1975).

Pettigrew (1979) has described a related bias, called the **ultimate attribution error**—an extension of Ross's (1977) fundamental attribution error to the domain of attributions for outgroup behaviours. Pettigrew argued that negative outgroup behaviours are dispositionally attributed, and positive outgroup behaviours are externally attributed or explained away in other ways that preserve our unfavourable outgroup image. The ultimate attribution error refers to attributions made for outgroup behaviours only, whereas broader intergroup perspectives focus on ingroup attributions as well.

One of the first studies of intergroup attributions was conducted by Taylor and Jaggi (1974) in Southern India, against a background of intergroup conflict between Hindus and Muslims. Hindu participants read vignettes describing Hindus or Muslims acting in a socially desirable way (e.g. offering shelter from the rain) or socially undesirable way (e.g. refusing shelter) towards them, and then chose one of a number of explanations for the behaviour. The results were as predicted in terms of intergroup bias. The Hindu participants made more internal attributions for socially undesirable acts when the vignettes described Hindus rather than Muslims.

Hewstone and Ward (1985) conducted a more complete and systematic follow-up, with Malays and Chinese in Malaysia and Singapore. Participants made internal or external attributions for desirable or undesirable behaviours described in vignettes as being performed by Malays or by Chinese. In Malaysia, Malays showed a clear ethnocentric attribution bias—they attributed a positive act by a Malay more to internal factors than a similar act by a Chinese, and a negative act by a Malay less to internal factors than a similar act by a Chinese (see Figure 3.6). The ingroup enhancement effect was much stronger than the outgroup derogation effect. The Chinese showed no ethnocentric bias—instead, they showed a tendency to make similar attributions to those made by Malays. In Singapore, the only significant effect was that Malays made internal attributions for positive acts by Malays.

Hewstone and Ward explain these findings in terms of the nature of intergroup relations in Malaysia and Singapore. In Malaysia, Malays are the clear majority group and Chinese an ethnic minority. Furthermore,

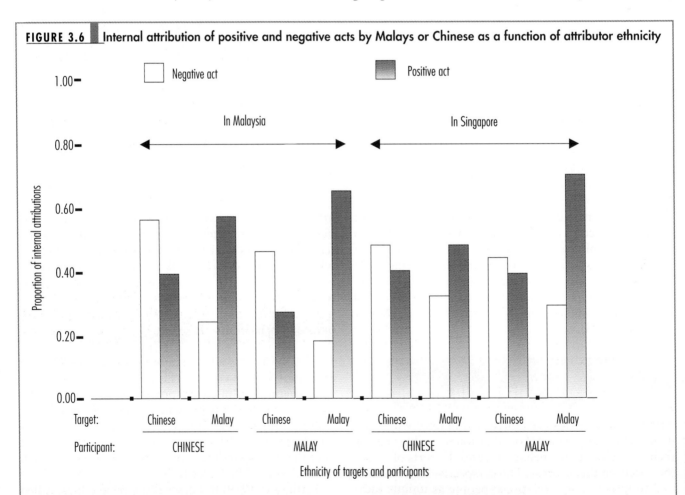

FIGURE 3.6 Internal attribution of positive and negative acts by Malays or Chinese as a function of attributor ethnicity

Note: Malays showed an ethnocentric attributional bias in which a positive act was more internally attributed to a Malay than a Chinese, and a negative act less internally attributed to a Malay than a Chinese: the differential effect was more pronounced in Malaysia, where Malays are the dominant group and Chinese the ethnic minority, than in Singapore. Chinese did not show an ethnocentric attribution bias.

Source: Based on data from Hewstone & Ward (1985).

relations between the two groups were tense and in relative conflict at the time, with Malaysia pursuing a policy of ethnic assimilation. Both Malays and Chinese generally shared an unfavourable **stereotype** of Chinese and a favourable stereotype of Malays. Singapore is ethnically more tolerant. The Chinese are in the majority, and ethnic stereotypes are markedly less pronounced.

The important implication of this analysis is that ethnocentric attribution is not a universal tendency that reflects cognitive processes in general; rather, it depends on intergroup dynamics in a sociohistorical context. The sorts of attributions that group members make about ingroup and outgroup behaviour are influenced by the nature of the relations between the groups.

This is consistent with Hewstone's (1989) argument that a full analysis of attribution, more accurately described as *social explanation*, requires careful articulation (i.e. theoretical integration or connection) of different **levels of explanation** (see Doise, 1986; also Chapter 1). In other words, we need to know how individual cognitive processes, interpersonal interactions, group membership dynamics and intergroup relations all affect, are affected by and are interrelated with one another.

Further evidence for ethnocentric intergroup attributions comes from studies of interracial attitudes in educational settings in the United States (Duncan, 1976; Stephan, 1977), from studies of interethnic relations between Israelis and Arabs (Rosenberg & Wolfsfeld, 1977) and between Hindus and Muslims in Bangladesh (Islam & Hewstone, 1993), and from studies of race, sex and social class-based attributions for success and failure (Deaux & Emswiller, 1974; Feather & Simon, 1975; Greenberg & Rosenfield, 1979; Hewstone, Jaspars, & Lalljee, 1982). These and other studies are reviewed by Hewstone (1989).

There are at least two processes that may explain ethnocentric intergroup attributions. The first is a cognitive one. Social categorisation generates expectations that are congruent with the category (Deaux, 1976), schemata (e.g. Fiske & Taylor, 1991), or group prototypes or stereotypes (e.g. Hogg & Abrams, 1988; Turner, 1985; Turner, Hogg, Oakes, Reicher, & Wetherell, 1987; see Chapter 11).

Research indicates that stereotype-consistent or expectancy-consistent behaviour is attributed to stable internal factors, whereas expectancy-inconsistent behaviour is attributed to unstable or situational factors (e.g. Bell, Wicklund, Manko, & Larkin, 1976; Rosenfield & Stephan, 1977). When people explain expectancy-confirming behaviour, they may simply rely on dispositions implied by a stereotype, without bothering to put cognitive effort into consideration of additional factors (Kulik, 1983; Pyszczynski & Greenberg, 1981).

The second process involved in intergroup attribu-

tions is the individual need to obtain group-membership-based self-esteem from intergroup comparisons. This process is described by **social identity theory** (Hogg & Abrams, 1988; Tajfel & Turner, 1979; Turner, 1982; see Chapter 11). Because people derive their social identity from the groups to which they belong (a description and evaluation of themselves in terms of the defining features of the group), they have a vested interest in maintaining or obtaining an ingroup profile that is relatively more positive than that of relevant outgroups. The ethnocentric attributional bias quite clearly fulfils this aim: it attributes internally good things about the ingroup and bad things about the outgroup, and attributes externally bad things about the ingroup and good things about the outgroup.

ATTRIBUTION AND STEREOTYPING

Attribution processes operating at the societal level in an intergroup context may well play an important role in shaping the profile and dominance of specific stereotypes. Tajfel (1981a) argued that stereotyping serves a number of adaptive functions for social groups as well as individuals (see also Chapter 2). Social groups may activate or accentuate existing stereotypes in order to attribute large-scale distressing events to the actions of specific outgroups—that is, scapegoats. For instance, during the 1930s in Germany the Jews were blamed for the economic crisis. It was convenient to activate the 'miserly Jew' stereotype to explain in simplistic terms the lack of money (there is no money because the Jews are hoarding it).

Stereotypes may also be elaborated to justify actions committed or planned against an outgroup. For instance, a group might develop a stereotype of an outgroup as dull-witted, simple, lazy and incompetent, in order to explain or justify the economic and social exploitation of that group.

Social knowledge and societal attributions

People do not wake up in the morning and causally reconstruct their world anew every day. In general, we rely on well-learned causal scripts (Abelson, 1981) and general **causal schemata** attached to situational, personality and group membership labels. We stop, think and make causal attributions only when events are unexpected or inconsistent with expectations (e.g. Hastie, 1984; Langer, 1978; Pyszczynski & Greenberg, 1981), when we are in a bad mood (Bohner, Bless, Schwarz, & Strack, 1988), when we feel a lack of control (Liu & Steele, 1986) or when attributions are occasioned by conversational goals—for example, when we want to offer an explanation or justification of behaviour to the person we are talking to (Hewstone & Antaki, 1988; Lalljee, 1981; Tetlock, 1983).

Usually, we rely on a wealth of acquired and richly textured cultural knowledge that automatically explains what is going on around us. This knowledge resides in cultural beliefs, social stereotypes, collective ideologies and social representations (see Box 3.2).

SOCIAL REPRESENTATIONS

One way in which cultural knowledge about the causes of things may be constructed and transmitted is described by Moscovici's theory of **social representations** (e.g. Farr & Moscovici, 1984; Lorenzi-Cioldi & Clémence, 2001; Moscovici, 1961, 1981, 1988; Purkhardt, 1995). (See Chapter 5 for a discussion of the relationship between social representations and attitudes.) Social representations are consensual under-

standings shared by group members. They emerge through everyday informal communication. They transform the unfamiliar and complex into the familiar and straightforward, and thus provide a commonsense framework for interpreting our experiences.

An individual or a specialist interest group derives a sophisticated, non-obvious, technical explanation of a commonplace phenomenon—e.g. explaining mental illness in terms of biological or social factors rather than spiritual forces. This attracts public attention and becomes widely shared and popularised (i.e. simplified, distorted and ritualised) through informal discussion among non-specialists. It is now a social representation—an accepted, unquestioned commonsense explanation that tends to oust alternatives and become an orthodoxy.

Moscovici's original formulation focused on the development of the theory of psychoanalysis, but it is just as applicable to other formal theories and phenomena that have been transformed to become part of popular consciousness—for example, evolutionary theory, relativity theory, dietary and health theories, Marxist economics and AIDS. Although the theory of social representations has been the subject of some criticism—often for the rather imprecise way in which it is formulated (e.g. Augoustinos & Innes, 1990)—it does, nonetheless, suggest a way in which ordinary social interaction in society constructs commonsense or 'naive' causal theories that are widely used to explain events (Heider, 1958).

One source of criticism is that it has always been difficult to analyse social representations quantitatively. Recently, some steps have been taken towards the development of appropriate quantitative techniques (Doise, Clémence, & Lorenzi-Cioldi, 1993). In general, however, a broad range of methodologies is used (Breakwell & Canter, 1993): for example, Jodelet's (1991) classic description of social representations of mental illness in the small French community of Ainay-le-Chateau employed questionnaires, interviews and ethnographic observation.

Social representations, like norms (see Chapters 7 and 8), tend to be grounded in groups and differ from group to group, such that intergroup behaviour can often revolve around a clash of social representations (Lorenzi-Cioldi & Clémence, 2001). For example, in Western countries attitudes and behaviours that promote healthy lifestyles are positively correlated with social status, and health promotion messages tend to emanate from middle-class professional groups (Salovey, Rothman, & Rodin, 1998). A social representations analysis suggests that these messages are relatively ineffective in promoting healthy lifestyles for non-middle-class people, because they are inconsistent with the wider representational framework of a good life for such people.

BOX 3.2	A very strange custom: The cultural context of causal attribution

Gün Semin tells a fictitious story about a Brazilian aborigine who visits Rio de Janeiro and then returns home to his tribe deep in the Amazonian rainforest to give an account of the visit (Semin, 1980, p. 292).

On particular days more people than all those you have seen in your whole lifetime roam to this huge place of worship, an open hut the size of which you will never imagine. They come, chanting, singing, with symbols of their gods, and once everybody is gathered the chanting drives away all alien spirits. Then, at the appointed time the priests arrive wearing colourful garments, and the chanting rises to war cries until three high priests, wearing black, arrive. All priests who were running around with sacred round objects leave them and at the order of the high priests begin the religious ceremony. Then, when the chief high priest gives a shrill sound from himself they all run after the single sacred round object that is left, only to kick it away when they get hold of it. Whenever the sacred object goes through one of the two doors and hits the sacred net the religious followers start to chant, piercing the heavens, and most of the priests embark on a most ecstatic orgy until the chief priest blows the whistle on them.

(Reprinted with permission from the *British Journal of Social and Clinical Psychology*.)

This is, of course, a description of a soccer match by someone who does not know the purpose or rules of the game. It illustrates an important point. For causal explanations to be meaningful they need to be part of a highly complex general interpretive framework that constitutes our socially acquired cultural knowledge.

RUMOUR

The process through which social representations are constructed has more than a passing resemblance to the way in which rumours develop and are communicated. One of the earliest studies of rumour was conducted by Allport and Postman (1945), who found that if experimental participants described a photographic slide to someone who had not seen the slide, and then this person described it to another person, and so on, only 30% of the original detail remained after five retellings.

Allport and Postman identified three processes associated with rumour transmission:

1. *Levelling*—the rumour very quickly becomes shorter, less detailed and less complex.
2. *Sharpening*—certain features of the rumour are selectively emphasised and exaggerated.
3. *Assimilation*—the rumour is distorted in line with people's pre-existing prejudices, partialities, interests and agendas.

More naturalistic studies have found rather less distortion as a consequence of rumour transmission (e.g. Caplow, 1947; Schachter & Burdeck, 1955).

Whether or not rumours are distorted, and even whether rumours are transmitted at all, seems to depend on the anxiety level of those who hear the rumour (Buckner, 1965; Rosnow, 1980). Uncertainty and ambiguity increase anxiety and stress, which leads people to seek out information with which to rationalise anxiety, which in turn enhances rumour transmission. Whether the ensuing rumour is distorted or becomes more precise depends on whether people approach the rumour with a critical or uncritical orientation (Buckner, 1965). In the former case the rumour becomes refined, while in the latter (which often accompanies a crisis) the rumour becomes distorted.

Rumours always have a source and, often, this source purposely elaborates the rumour for a specific reason—mostly to discredit individuals or groups. An organisation can spread a rumour about a competitor in order to undermine the competitor's market share (Shibutani, 1966), or a social group can spread a rumour to blame another group for widespread crises. A good example of this is the fabrication and promulgation of conspiracy theories (Graumann & Moscovici, 1987).

CONSPIRACY THEORIES

Conspiracy theories are elementary and exhaustive causal theories that attribute widespread natural and social calamities to the intentional and organised activities of certain social groups that are seen to form conspiratorial bodies set on ruining and then dominating the rest of humanity. The best-known conspiracy theory is the myth of the Jewish world conspiracy (Cohn, 1966) which surfaces periodically and often results in massive systematic persecution. Other conspiracy theories include the belief that immigrants are intentionally plotting to undermine the economy, that homosexuals are intentionally spreading HIV and that witches (in the Middle Ages), the CIA (more recently) and Al-Qaeda (most recently) are behind virtually every world event you care to mention (e.g. Cohn, 1975).

Conspiracy theories wax and wane in popularity. They were particularly popular from the mid-17th to the mid-18th century (Wood, 1982, p. 407):

Everywhere people sensed designs within designs, cabals within cabals; there were court conspiracies, backstairs conspiracies, ministerial conspiracies, factional conspiracies, aristocratic conspiracies, and by the last half of the eighteenth century even conspiracies of gigantic secret societies that cut across national boundaries and spanned the Atlantic.

The accomplished conspiracy theorist can, with consummate skill and breathtaking versatility, explain even the most arcane and puzzling events in terms of the devious schemes and inscrutable machinations of hidden conspirators.

Billig (1978) believes it is precisely this that can make conspiracy theories so attractive. They provide a causal explanation in terms of enduring dispositions that can explain a wide range of events, rather than complex situational factors that are less widely applicable. Furthermore, worrying events become controllable and easily remedied because they are caused by small groups of highly visible people rather than complex sociohistorical circumstances (Bains, 1983).

SOCIETAL ATTRIBUTIONS

The emphasis on attributions as social knowledge finds expression in research on the explanations people give for large-scale social phenomena. In general, this research furnishes evidence for the view that causal attributions for specific phenomena are located within and moulded by wider, socially constructed belief systems.

For example, research on explanations for poverty reveals that both the rich and the poor tend to explain poverty in terms of the behaviour of poor people rather than situationally (e.g. Feagin, 1972; Feather, 1974). This individualistic tendency is not so strong for people with a more left-wing or socialist ideology, or for people living in developing countries where poverty is widespread (Pandey, Sinha, Prakash, & Tripathi, 1982).

Explanations for wealth tend to depend on political affiliation. In Britain, Conservatives ascribe it to positive individual qualities of thrift and hard work, while Labour supporters attribute it to the negative individual quality of ruthless determination (Furnham, 1983). Not surprisingly, there are also cross-cultural differences—for example, the individualistic explanations so common in Hong Kong (Forgas, Morris, & Furnham, 1982; Furnham & Bond, 1986).

Similarly, the explanations given for unemployment are influenced by people's wider belief and value systems (Chapter 5). Feather, at Flinders University (1985), had Australian students give their explanations of unemployment on a number of statistically derived dimensions. They preferred societal over individualistic explanations: for example, defective government, social change and economic recession were seen as more valid causes of unemployment than lack of motivation and personal handicap (see also Feather & Barber, 1983; Feather & Davenport, 1981). Students who were politically more conservative tended to place less emphasis on societal explanations. This effect was confirmed in a second study reported by Feather (1985).

Studies conducted in Britain also reveal that societal explanations are more prominent than individualistic explanations, and that there is general agreement between employed and unemployed subjects (Furnham, 1982; Gaskell & Smith, 1985; Lewis, Snell, & Furnham, 1987).

Other research has focused on the explanations that people give for riots (social unrest, collective behaviour and riots are discussed in detail in Chapter 11). Riots are enormously complicated social phenomena in that there are both proximal and distal causes—a specific event or action might trigger the riot, but only because of the complex conjunction of wider conditions. For instance, the proximal cause of the 1992 Los Angeles riot may have been the acquittal of the police officers charged with the beating of Rodney King (see Box 11.1 in Chapter 11); however, this alone would have been unlikely to promote a riot without the background of racial unrest and socioeconomic distress in the United States.

As with explanations of poverty, wealth and unemployment, the sorts of explanations people give for a specific riot seem to be influenced by the person's sociopolitical perspective (e.g. Litton & Potter, 1985; Reicher, 1984, 2001; Reicher & Potter, 1985; Schmidt, 1972): more conservative members of the establishment tend to identify deviance, or personal or social pathology, while people with more liberal social attitudes tend to identify social circumstances.

For example, Schmidt (1972) analysed printed media explanations of the spate of riots that occurred in American cities in 1967. The explanations could be classified with respect to the three dimensions of:

1. legitimate–illegitimate
2. internal–external cause
3. institutional–environmental cause.

The first two dimensions were strongly correlated, with legitimate external causes (e.g. urban renewal

mistakes, slum conditions) going together and illegitimate internal causes (e.g. criminal intent, belief that violence works) going together. Media sources on the political right tended to identify illegitimate internal causes, whereas those classified as 'left–centre' (i.e. liberal) stressed legitimate external causes.

Finally, Sniderman, Hagen, Tetlock and Brady (1986) investigated the way in which people give explanations for racial inequality and have preferences for different government policies. They used a national sample of Whites in the United States (in 1972) and were interested in investigating the influence of level of education.

They found that less-educated Whites employed an 'affect-driven' reasoning process. They started with their (mainly negative) feelings about Blacks, then proceeded directly to advocate minimal government assistance. Having done this, they 'doubled back' to fill in the intervening link to justify their advocacy—namely, that Blacks were personally responsible for their own disadvantage. In contrast, more-educated Whites adopted a 'cognition-driven' reasoning process, in which they reasoned both forwards and backwards. Their policy recommendations were based on causal attributions for inequality, and in turn their causal attributions were influenced by their policy preference.

CULTURE'S CONTRIBUTION

It is increasingly clear that specific attributions or causal explanations can be fully understood only by taking into account the wider belief and value systems of individuals. We have already seen, for example, the influence of sociopolitical values, educational status, group membership and ethnicity; and cultural factors have cropped up throughout.

People from different cultures often make very different attributions, make attributions in different ways or approach the entire task of social explanation in

Culture and attribution: Is the puppet responsible for its own actions? Easterners are less likely than Westerners to make dispositional attributions about people— let alone puppets!

different ways (R. Bond & Smith, 1996; Markus, Kitayama, & Heiman, 1996; Smith & Bond, 1998; Triandis, 1976; Triandis, Vassiliou, Vassiliou, Tanaka, & Shanmugam, 1972). Consequently, the potential for cross-cultural interpersonal misunderstanding is enormous. For example, the Zande people of West Africa have a dual theory of causality, where common-sense proximal causes operate within the context of witchcraft as the distal cause (Evans-Pritchard, 1937; see Jahoda, 1979). For the Zande, an internal–external distinction would make little sense.

Another example: Lévy-Bruhl (1925) reported that the natives of Motumotu in New Guinea attributed a pleurisy epidemic to the presence of a specific missionary, his sheep, two goats and, finally, a portrait of Queen Victoria. Although initially quite bizarre, these sorts of attributions are easily explained as social representations: how much more bizarre are they than, for example, the 'string theories' that became popular in physics in the mid-1980s to construct a unified theory of the universe (see Hawking, 1988)? Consider the focus question in the light of what you have just read.

One area of cross-cultural attribution research is the fundamental attribution error (see above). We have seen that in Western cultures people have a tendency to make dispositional attributions for others' behaviours (Ross, 1977). There is also evidence that such dispositional attributions become more evident as children mature (e.g. Pevers & Secord, 1973).

In non-Western cultures, however, people are less inclined to make dispositional attributions (Carrithers, Collins, & Lukes, 1986; Morris & Peng, 1994). This is probably partly a reflection of the more pervasive and all-enveloping influence of social roles in more collectivist non-Western cultures (Fletcher & Ward, 1988; Jahoda, 1982), and partly a reflection of a more holistic world view that promotes context-dependent, occasion-bound thinking (Shweder & Bourne, 1982).

To investigate further the role of culture in dispositional attributions, Miller (1984) compared middle-class North Americans and Indian Hindus from each of four

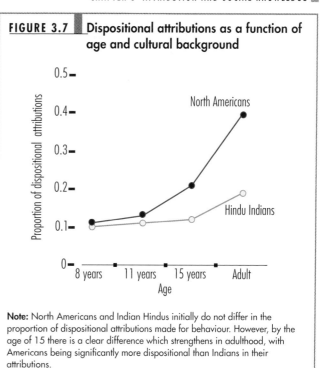

FIGURE 3.7 Dispositional attributions as a function of age and cultural background

Note: North Americans and Indian Hindus initially do not differ in the proportion of dispositional attributions made for behaviour. However, by the age of 15 there is a clear difference which strengthens in adulthood, with Americans being significantly more dispositional than Indians in their attributions.

Source: Based on data from Miller (1984).

age groups (adults, 15-, 11- and 8-year-olds). Participants narrated prosocial and antisocial behaviours and gave their own spontaneous explanations of the causes of these behaviours. Miller was able to code responses to identify the proportion of dispositional and contextual attributions that participants made. Among the youngest children there was little cross-cultural difference (see Figure 3.7). As age increased, however, the two groups diverged, mainly because the Americans increasingly came to adopt dispositional attributions. For context attributions the results were reversed.

The important lesson this study teaches us is that cultural factors have a significant impact on attribution and social explanation. We return to the role of culture and how humans function socially in Chapter 16.

Summary

- People are naive psychologists seeking to understand the causes of their own and other people's behaviour.
- Much like scientists, people take account of consensus, consistency and distinctiveness information in deciding whether to attribute behaviour internally to personality traits and dispositions, or externally to situational factors.

- The attributions we make can have a profound impact on our emotions, self-concept and relationships with others. There may be individual differences in propensities to make internal or external attributions.
- People are actually poor scientists when it comes to making attributions. They are biased in many

different ways, of which the most significant are a tendency to attribute others' behaviour dispositionally and their own behaviour externally, and a tendency to protect the self-concept by externally attributing their own failures and internally attributing their successes.

- Attributions for the behaviours of people as ingroup or outgroup members are ethnocentric and based on stereotypes. This bias is, however, affected by the real

or perceived nature of intergroup relations.

- Stereotypes may originate in a need for groups to attribute the cause of large-scale distressing events to outgroups which have (stereotypical) properties that are causally linked to the events.
- People resort to causal attributions only when there is no readily available social knowledge (e.g. scripts, causal schemata, social representations, cultural beliefs) to explain things automatically.

LINKS

YOU HAVE READ ABOUT:	WHICH LINKS TO:
Theories in attribution	theory in social psychology (1); the 'naive scientist' (2)
Interpersonal and intergroup attributions	levels of explanation (1)
Biases in attribution	heuristics in cognition (2)
Social knowledge and societal attributions	social representations (5)
Interpersonal relationships	maintaining relationships (13)
Culture and attribution	culture and the self (4); cultural variations in behaviour (16)

Key terms

actor–observer effect *(p. 60)*
attribution *(p. 52)*
attributional style *(p. 57)*
belief in a just world *(p. 62)*
causal schemata *(p. 65)*
cognitive miser *(p. 59)*
consensus information *(p. 54)*
consistency information *(p. 54)*
conspiracy theories *(p. 67)*
correspondent inference *(p. 53)*
covariation model *(p. 54)*
discounting *(p. 54)*

distinctiveness information *(p. 54)*
ethnocentrism *(p. 63)*
external (or situational) attribution *(p. 53)*
false consensus effect *(p. 61)*
fundamental attribution error *(p. 59)*
hedonic relevance *(p. 53)*
illusion of control *(p. 62)*
intergroup attributions *(p. 63)*
internal (or dispositional) attribution *(p. 53)*
level of explanation *(p. 65)*

naive psychologist (or scientist) *(p. 52)*
non-common effects *(p. 53)*
outcome bias *(p. 62)*
personalism *(p. 53)*
self-handicapping *(p. 62)*
self-perception theory *(p. 56)*
self-serving biases *(p. 62)*
social identity theory *(p. 65)*
social representations *(p. 66)*
stereotype *(p. 65)*
ultimate attribution error *(p. 63)*

FURTHER READING

Fiske, S. T., & Taylor, S. E. (1991). *Social cognition* (2nd ed.). New York: McGraw-Hill. Still the most authoritative and comprehensive coverage of social cognition, this book also provides excellent coverage of classic attribution theory and research. This is not surprising, given that attribution processes are social cognitive processes and that attribution theory was a forerunner of contemporary social cognition.

Fletcher, G., & Fincham, F. D. (Eds.). (1991). *Cognition in close*

relationships. Hillsdale, NJ: Erlbaum. A collection of leading scholars provides detailed chapters on attribution and other social-cognitive approaches to close relationships.

Hewstone, M. (1989). *Causal attribution: From cognitive processes to collective beliefs*. Oxford, UK: Blackwell. A comprehensive and detailed coverage of attribution theory and research, which also includes coverage of European perspectives that locate attribution processes in the context of society and intergroup relations.

McClure, J. (1991). *Explanations, accounts, and illusions: A critical analysis*. Cambridge, UK: Cambridge University Press. A critical, wide-ranging and eclectic discussion of attribution as social explanation.

Smith, E. R. (1994). Social cognition contributions to attribution theory and research. In P. G. Devine, D. L. Hamilton, & T. M. Ostrom (Eds.), *Social cognition: Impact on social psychology* (pp. 77–108). San Diego, CA: Academic Press. Recent and focused coverage of social cognitive dimensions of attribution processes.

Trope, Y., & Gaunt, R. (2003). Attribution and person perception. In M. A. Hogg, & J. Cooper (Eds.), *The Sage handbook of social psychology* (pp. 190–208). London: Sage. A recent, comprehensive and very readable overview of attribution research.

Weary, G., Stanley, M. A., & Harvey, J. H. (1989). *Attribution*. New York: Springer-Verlag. A discussion of applications of attribution theory and the operation of attribution processes in clinical settings and everyday life outside the laboratory.

CHAPTER FOUR

Self and identity

FOCUS QUESTIONS

1. Is it true that our identity is what distinguishes each of us as a unique human being, distinct from all other people?

2. There is a popular belief that low self-esteem leads people to be aggressive and antisocial and, therefore, that social institutions should do all they can to nourish high self-esteem, especially in children. Is it true that high self-esteem is a panacea for society's ills?

3. Alec was born in Scotland and raised in a traditional, middle-class way. He dearly wants to finish his degree, get a job in External Affairs and then travel. Ibrahim is from Nigeria. He thinks that the needs of his family, who are Muslim, are much more important to him than seeing the world. How could these two men think so differently?

THIS CHAPTER DISCUSSES:

- major theories of the self
- awareness of and knowledge about ourselves
- types of selves and identities, and the search for self-conceptual coherence
- social identity and personal identity
- motives influencing the search for self-knowledge
- why we pursue self-esteem
- how we present ourselves
- self, identity and culture.

Who are you?

Take a look in your wallet. You'll probably find any number of cards and pieces of paper that have your name on them, and perhaps a rather gruesome photograph of yourself. What happens when you meet someone socially? Very early in the piece you discover each other's name, and soon after that you establish things like their occupation, their attitudes and what they like to do. You also try to identify mutual acquaintances. In more formal contexts people sometimes display their identity through uniforms, name/role badges and business cards.

Social interaction, and social existence itself, depends on people knowing who they are and who others are. Identity and self-conception underpin everyday life: knowing who you are allows you to know what you should think and do, and knowing who others are allows you to predict what they think and what they do. Knowledge of identity regulates and structures human interaction; in turn, interactive and societal structures provide identities for us.

Many scholars have argued that it is reflexive thought—that is, the ability to think about ourselves thinking—that separates us from almost all other animals. Reflexive thought means that we can think about ourselves, about who we are, how we would like to be and how we would like others to see us—humans have a highly developed sense of self. Self and identity, then, are fundamental parts of being human. We should not be surprised that psychologists, particularly social psychologists, have always been intrigued by the self.

In this chapter we explore the self—where it comes from, what it looks like and how it influences thought and behaviour. Because self and identity are cognitive constructs that influence social interaction and perception, and are themselves influenced by society, the material in this chapter connects to virtually all other chapters in the book. In recent years there has been an explosive revival of research on the self (e.g. Banaji & Prentice, 1994; Sedikides & Brewer, 2001; Sedikides & Strube, 1997). A recent review reported 31 000 social psychological publications on the self over a two-decade period to the mid-1990s (Ashmore & Jussim, 1997).

Self and identity in historical context

The self is, historically, a relatively new idea. Baumeister (1987) paints a picture of medieval society in which social relations were fixed and stable, and legitimised in religious terms. People's lives and identity were tightly mapped out according to position in the social order—by visible ascribed attributes such as family membership, social rank, birth order and place of birth. In many ways, what you saw was what you got, and so the idea of a complex individual self lurking underneath it all was difficult to entertain and probably superfluous.

All this started to change in the 16th century and the change has gathered momentum ever since. Some of the forces for change included:

- *Secularisation*—the idea that fulfilment would occur in the afterlife was replaced by the idea that you should actively pursue fulfilment in this life.
- *Industrialisation*—people were increasingly seen as units of production who would move from place to place to work, and thus would have a portable personal identity that was not locked into static social structures such as the extended family.
- *Enlightenment*—people felt they could organise and construct different, better identities and lives for themselves by overthrowing orthodox value systems and oppressive regimes (e.g. the American and French revolutions of the late 18th century).
- *Psychoanalysis*—Freud's (e.g. 1921) theory of the human mind crystallised the notion that the self was unfathomable because it lurked in the gloomy depths of the unconscious.

Psychoanalysis has probably done most to problematise self and identity, because it attributes behaviour to complex dynamics that are hidden deep within a person's sense of who they are. In Chapter 3 (see also Chapter 5) we explore the theory of social representations—a theory that used psychoanalysis as an example of how a novel idea or analysis can entirely change the way that people think about their world (e.g. Moscovici, 1961; also see Lorenzi-Cioldi & Clémence, 2001). Together, these and other social, political and cultural changes caused people to think about self and identity as highly complex and problematic. Theories of self and identity propagated and flourished in this fertile soil.

PSYCHODYNAMIC SELF

Freud (e.g. 1921) believed that unsocialised and selfish libidinal impulses (the id) are repressed and kept in check by internalised societal norms (the super-ego) but that, from time to time and in strange and peculiar ways, repressed impulses surface. Freud's view of the self is one in which you can only truly know yourself, or indeed others, when special procedures, such as hypnosis or psychotherapy, are put in place to reveal repressed thoughts. Freud's ideas about self, identity and personality are far-reaching in social psychology—for example, Adorno, Frenkel-Brunswik, Levinson and Sanford's (1950) influential authoritarian personality theory of prejudice is a psychodynamic theory (see Chapter 10).

INDIVIDUAL VERSUS COLLECTIVE SELF

Freud, like many other psychologists, viewed the self as very personal and private—the apotheosis of individuality, something that uniquely describes an individual human being. When someone says 'I am . . .' they are describing what makes them different from all other human beings. But think about this for a moment. 'I am Australian', 'I am a social psychologist', 'I live in Brisbane'—these are all descriptions of my-*self*, but they are also descriptions of many other people's selves (there are 20 million Australians, and at last count almost 1.8 million people living in Brisbane). So the self can also be a shared or collective self—a 'we' or 'us'.

Social psychologists have argued long and hard for more than a century about whether the self is an individual or a collective phenomenon. The debate has created polarised camps, with advocates for the individual self and advocates for the collective self slogging it out in the literature. It is fair to say that the advocates for the individual self have tended to prevail. This is largely because social psychologists have considered groups to be made up of individuals who interact with one another, rather than individuals who have a collective sense of shared identity. Individuals interacting in aggregates make up the province of social psychology, whereas groups as collectives is the province of several other social sciences, such as sociology and political science (see Chapters 1 and 11).

This perspective is summed up by Floyd Allport's famous proclamation that 'There is no psychology of groups which is not essentially and entirely a psychology of individuals' (Allport, 1924, p. 4). This perspective on groups has made it difficult for the collective self to thrive as a research topic. However, in recent years the field has loosened up—as we shall see during the course of this chapter.

COLLECTIVE SELF

In the early days of social psychology there was little interest in the person as the unit of analysis (see Farr, 1996; Hogg & Williams, 2000). Wundt was the founder of psychology as an experimental science and he proposed (Wundt, 1916, p. 3) that social psychology was the study of:

. . . those mental products which are created by a community of human life and are, therefore, inexplicable in terms merely of individual consciousness since they presuppose the reciprocal action of many.

Wundt's social psychology dealt with collective phenomena, such as language, religion, customs and myth, that could not, according to Wundt, be understood in terms of the psychology of the isolated individual. Durkheim (1898), one of the founding fathers of sociology, was influenced by Wundt's interest in collective

life, but went one step further in maintaining that collective phenomena could not be explained in terms of individual psychology.

The view that the self draws its properties from groups is shared by many other early social psychologists—for example, early theorists of collective behaviour and the crowd (e.g. LeBon, 1908; Tarde, 1901; Trotter, 1919; see Chapter 11). Notably, McDougall, in his book *The Group Mind* (1920), argued that out of the interaction of individuals there arose a 'group mind' that had a reality and existence that was qualitatively distinct from the isolated individuals making up the group—there was a collective self that was grounded in group life.

Although phrased in rather old-fashioned language, this idea has a direct line of descent to subsequent experimental social psychological research which confirms that human interaction has emergent properties that endure and influence other people: for example, Sherif's (1936) research on how norms emerge from interaction and are internalised to influence behaviour, some of Asch's (1952) research on conformity to norms, and more recent research on the emergence of social representations out of social interaction (e.g. Farr & Moscovici, 1984; Lorenzi-Cioldi & Clémence, 2001; Chapters 3, 5, 7 and 8).

In recent years the notion of a collective self has been most fully elaborated by the social identity perspective (e.g. Hogg & Abrams, 1988; Tajfel & Turner, 1979; Hogg, 2003b). This is discussed later in this chapter and covered fully in Chapter 11.

SYMBOLIC INTERACTIONIST SELF

Another twist to the idea of the collective self is recognition that the self emerges and is shaped by social interaction. Early psychologists such as William James (1890) distinguished between self as stream of consciousness, 'I', and self as object of perception, 'me'. In this way reflexive knowledge is possible because the 'I' can be aware of the 'me', and people can know themselves. However, this is not to say that people's self-knowledge is particularly accurate. People tend to reconstruct who they are without being aware of doing it (Greenwald, 1980) and, in general, although people may be aware of who they are in terms of their attitudes and preferences, they are rather bad at knowing how they arrived at that knowledge (Nisbett & Wilson, 1977).

Nevertheless, people do have a sense of 'me' and, according to **symbolic interactionism**, the self arises out of human interaction (Mead, 1934; see also Blumer, 1969). Mead believed that human interaction is largely symbolic. When we interact with people it is mainly in terms of words and non-verbal cues that are rich with meaning because they are able to symbolise much more than is superficially available in the behaviour itself (see Chapter 15). Mead pointed out that society comes before the individual in the temporal sense. The self 'is essentially a social structure, and it arises in social experience' (Mead, 1934, p. 140). Self-conception, therefore, emerges from and is continually modified through interacting with people. This interaction involves symbols that must have shared meaning if they are to be effectively communicated.

Interacting with another involves taking that person's role in order to understand what the person is communicating. This means seeing oneself as a social object, 'me', rather than social subject, 'I'. Because others often see us as category representatives, the 'me' is probably more accurately seen as a collective 'me'—we might even think of it as an 'us'. Whole groups of people have consensual representations of the world and these are traded through symbolic interaction. To do this effectively we actually play the roles of everyone in our group and thus we see ourselves as others (ultimately society) do. In this way we construct a self-concept that reflects the society we live in; we are socially constituted.

Symbolic interactionism offers quite a sophisticated and complex model of self-conception. Nevertheless, it generates a very straightforward prediction. Because self-conception comes from seeing ourselves as others see us (the idea of the **looking-glass self**), there should be a strong correlation between how we rate ourselves and how others rate us. Shrauger and Schoeneman (1979) reviewed 62 relevant empirical studies to see whether this was true. What they found was that people did *not* tend to see themselves as others saw them, but instead saw themselves as they *thought* others saw them.

So, for example, Tice (1992) had participants provide information that indicated they were emotionally stable or emotionally responsive to different situations—in other words, this is how they thought others would see them. They provided this information under private conditions in which they believed no one was watching them or under public conditions in which they believed a graduate student was closely monitoring their behaviour—the latter condition would engage the looking-glass self. As predicted, subsequent descriptions of self were more radically altered under public conditions than under private conditions (see Figure 4.1).

One implication of the idea that people do not see themselves as others see them, but instead see themselves as they think others see them, is that we do not actually take the role of the other in constructing a sense of self. An alternative reading is that the communicative process in social interaction is noisy and inaccurate. It is influenced by a range of self-construal motivations (motives to view others, and be viewed by them, in particular ways) that conspire to construct an inaccurate image of others and what they think about us. People are generally unaware of what other people really think of them (Kenny & DePaulo, 1993).

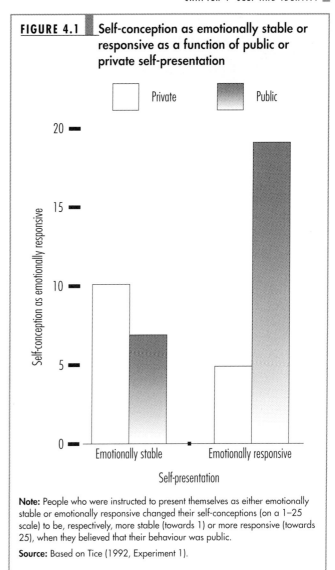

FIGURE 4.1 Self-conception as emotionally stable or responsive as a function of public or private self-presentation

Note: People who were instructed to present themselves as either emotionally stable or emotionally responsive changed their self-conceptions (on a 1–25 scale) to be, respectively, more stable (towards 1) or more responsive (towards 25), when they believed that their behaviour was public.

Source: Based on Tice (1992, Experiment 1).

As we discover below, self-conception is tightly associated with self-enhancement motives. For example, Taylor and Brown (1988) found that people normally overestimate their good points, overestimate their control over events and are unrealistically optimistic—Sedikides and Gregg (2003) call this the *self-enhancing triad*.

Self-awareness

People do not spend all their time thinking about the self. Self-awareness comes and goes for various reasons and has an array of consequences.

Duval and Wicklund (1972) believe that self-awareness is a state in which we are aware of ourselves as an object—much as we might be aware of a tree or

The looking-glass self: Mead thought that our self-concept derives from seeing ourselves as others see us. It is more likely based on how we *think* others see us.

distinguish between two types of self that you can be aware of: (1) the *private self*—your private thoughts, feelings and attitudes, (and) the *public self*—how other people see you, your public image. Private self-awareness produces behaviours aimed at matching your internalised standards, whereas public self-awareness is oriented towards presenting yourself to others in a positive light.

Being self-aware can be uncomfortable. We all feel self-conscious from time to time and are only too familiar with how it affects our behaviour—we feel anxious, we become tongue-tied or we make mistakes on tasks. We can even feel slightly paranoid (Fenigstein, 1984). However, being self-aware can be a terrific thing—particularly on those occasions when we have accomplished a great feat. Most of us would have watched the 2000 Sydney Olympics—and the swimmers Ian Thorpe, Grant Hackett and Inge de Bruijn certainly did not appear to be suffering any aversive consequences when receiving their gold medals.

Self-awareness can also make us feel good, when the standards against which we compare ourselves are not too exacting—for example, when we compare ourselves with standards derived from 'most other people' or from people who are less fortunate than ourselves (Taylor & Brown, 1988; Wills, 1981). Self-awareness can even improve introspection, intensify emotions, and improve performance of controlled effort-sensitive tasks that do not require undue skill (e.g. proofreading an essay you have written).

The reverse side of being objectively self-aware is being in a state of reduced objective self-awareness. Because elevated self-awareness can be stressful or aversive, people may try to avoid this state by consuming alcohol, or by even more extreme measures such as suicide (Baumeister, 1991). Reduced self-awareness has also been identified as a key component of **deindividuation**—'deindividuated persons are blocked from awareness of themselves as separate individuals and from monitoring their own behaviour' (Diener, 1980, p. 210), and therefore are able to behave in disinhibited, impulsive and anti-normative ways. Thus, reduced self-awareness may be implicated in crowd behaviour and other forms of social unrest (see Chapter 11 for a full discussion of crowd behaviour).

Self-knowledge

When people are self-aware, what are they aware of? What do we know about ourselves and how do we construct a sense of who we are? Self-knowledge is constructed in much the same way and through many of the same processes as we construct representations

another person. Thus, they speak of *objective self-awareness*. When you are objectively self-aware you make comparisons between how you actually are and how you would like to be—an ideal, a goal or some other standard. The outcome of this comparison is often a sense that you have shortcomings, and there are negative emotions associated with this recognition. People then try to overcome their shortcomings by bringing their self closer in line with ideal standards. This is sometimes difficult and people may give up trying, experience reduced motivation and feel even worse about themselves.

Objective self-awareness is generated by any circumstances that focus our attention on ourselves as an object—for example, being in front of an audience (Chapter 8) or catching sight of our image in a mirror. Indeed, a very popular method of raising self-awareness in laboratory studies is placing participants in front of a mirror.

Carver and Scheier (1981; Scheier & Carver, 1981) introduce a qualification to self-awareness theory. They of other people. Chapter 2, on social cognition and social thinking, and Chapter 3, on attribution and social knowledge, describe some of these general processes.

SELF-SCHEMAS

In Chapter 2 we see how information about other people is stored in the form of a **schema**. Research suggests that we store information about the self in a similar but more complex and varied way. Information about self is stored as separate context-specific nodes; different contexts activate different nodes and thus, effectively, different aspects of self (Breckler, Pratkanis, & McCann, 1991; Higgins, van Hook, & Dorfman, 1988).

People tend to have clear conceptions of themselves (i.e. self-schemas) on some dimensions but not others—they are schematic on some but aschematic on others. People are self-schematic on dimensions that are important to them, on which they think they are extreme and on which they are certain the opposite does not hold (Markus, 1977). For example, if you think you are athletic, and being athletic is important to you, then you are self-schematic on that dimension—it is part of your self-concept. If you don't consider yourself athletic and you don't really care much about being athletic or about

the attribute *athletic*, then you are aschematic on that dimension.

Most people have a complex self-concept, with a relatively large number of discrete self-schemas. Linville (1985, 1987; and see below) has suggested that this variety helps to buffer people from the negative impact of life events by making sure that there are always self-schemas from which they can derive a sense of satisfaction.

Showers (1992) has suggested that if our self-schemas are too highly compartmentalised there may be some disadvantages. Specifically, if some self-schemas are very negative and some are very positive, events may cause extreme mood swings according to whether **priming** of a positive or negative self-schema takes place. Evaluatively, more integrated self-schemas may be preferable.

So, for example, if James believes he is a wonderful cook but an awful musician, he has evaluatively compartmentalised self-schemas—contexts that prime one or the other self-schema will produce very positive or very negative moods. Contrast this with Sally, who believes she is a reasonably good cook and a fairly poor musician. She has self-schemas that are evaluatively more integrated—context effects on mood will be much less extreme.

Self-schemas influence information processing and behaviour in much the same way as schemas about other people (Markus & Sentis, 1982): self-schematic information is more readily noticed, is overrepresented in cognition and is associated with longer processing time.

Self-schemas do not only describe how we are. Markus and Nurius (1986) have suggested that we have an array of possible selves—future-oriented schemas of what we would like to become or what we fear we might become. For example, a graduate student may have future selves as a university lecturer or a singer in a rock-and-roll band.

Another perspective is offered by Higgins' (1987) **self-discrepancy theory**. Higgins suggests that we have three types of self-schemas:

1. *actual self*—how we currently are
2. *ideal self*—how we would like to be
3. *'ought' self*—how we think we should be.

The last two are 'self-guides'. Ideal self-guides are associated with promotional goals that we strive for, and 'ought' self-guides with prevention goals that we strive to avoid (Higgins, 1998). The same goal (e.g. prosperity) can be constructed as an ideal (strive to be prosperous) or an 'ought' (strive to avoid not being prosperous). Discrepancies between actual and ideal or 'ought' can motivate change to reduce the discrepancy. Failure to resolve the actual–ideal discrepancy produces dejection-related emotions (e.g. disappointment, dissatisfaction, sadness), whereas failure to resolve

An ideal self: This Marilyn Monroe look-alike has studied her idol well, though she seems unconcerned about the plaster on her leg!

the actual–ought discrepancy produces agitation-related emotions (e.g. anxiety, threat, fear).

One test of self-discrepancy theory, by Higgins, Bond, Klein and Strauman (1986), identified students who had either a low discrepancy between their actual and ideal and actual and 'ought' selves, or a high discrepancy. Four to six weeks later these students participated in an experiment in which a range of dejection and agitation emotions were measured both before and after a priming procedure in which their ideal or their 'ought' self was primed—the priming procedure involved focusing on and describing the relevant self and its discrepancy with their actual self.

Figure 4.2 shows the priming-induced change in emotion for high-discrepancy participants—low-discrepancy participants experienced insignificant change in either emotion in either priming condition.

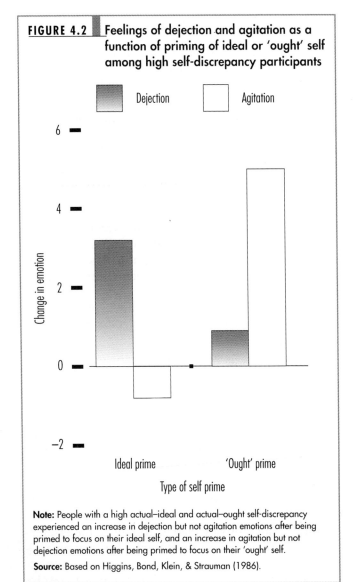

FIGURE 4.2 Feelings of dejection and agitation as a function of priming of ideal or 'ought' self among high self-discrepancy participants

Note: People with a high actual–ideal and actual–ought self-discrepancy experienced an increase in dejection but not agitation emotions after being primed to focus on their ideal self, and an increase in agitation but not dejection emotions after being primed to focus on their 'ought' self.

Source: Based on Higgins, Bond, Klein, & Strauman (1986).

INFERENCES FROM OUR BEHAVIOUR

One of the most obvious ways to learn about who you are is to examine your private thoughts and feelings about the world. Knowing what you think and feel about the world is a very good cue to the sort of person you are.

However, when these internal cues are weak we may make inferences about ourselves from what we do—our behaviour. This idea underpins Bem's **self-perception theory** (Bem, 1967, 1972). Bem argues that we make attributions not only for others' behaviour (see Chapter 3) but also for our own, and that there is no essential difference between self-attributions and other-attributions. Furthermore, just as we construct an impression of someone else's personality on the basis of being able to make internal dispositional attributions for their behaviour, we construct a concept of who we are—not by introspection but by being able to attribute our own behaviour internally.

So, for example, I know that I enjoy eating seafood because I often eat seafood of my own free will and in preference to other foods, and not everyone likes seafood—I am able to make an internal attribution for my behaviour.

Self-perception processes can also be based on simply imagining ourselves behaving in a particular way (Anderson & Godfrey, 1987). So, for example, van Gyn, Wenger and Gaul (1990) divided runners into two groups—one group practised strength training on exercise bikes, the other did not. Half of each group were instructed to imagine themselves sprint training, the others were not. Of course, the sweaty business of strength training improved subsequent performance, but remarkably those who imagined themselves sprint training did better than those who did not. The researchers concluded that imagery had affected self-conception, which in turn produced performance that was consistent with self-conception.

Self-attributions have important implications for motivation. The theory predicts that if someone is induced to perform a task either by enormous rewards or heavy penalties, task performance is attributed externally and thus motivation to perform is reduced. If there are minimal or no external factors to which performance can be attributed, we cannot easily avoid attributing performance internally to enjoyment or commitment, and so motivation increases. This has been called the **over-justification effect** (see Figure 4.3), for which there is now substantial evidence (Deci & Ryan, 1985).

For example, Lepper, Greene and Nisbett (1973) had nursery school children draw pictures with felt-tip pens. Some of the children simply drew of their own free will, while the rest were induced to draw with the promise of a reward, which they were subsequently given. A few days later, the children were unobtrusively observed

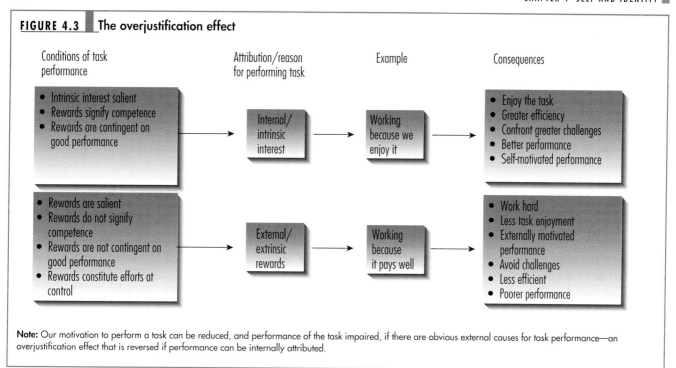

FIGURE 4.3 The overjustification effect

Note: Our motivation to perform a task can be reduced, and performance of the task impaired, if there are obvious external causes for task performance—an overjustification effect that is reversed if performance can be internally attributed.

playing; the children who had previously been rewarded for drawing spent half as much time drawing as did the other group. Those who had received no extrinsic reward seemed to have greater intrinsic interest in drawing.

In fact, there is evidence that the provision of external rewards for a previously intrinsically motivated task can actually reduce motivation and enjoyment and worsen performance of that task (e.g. Condry, 1977). An interesting paradox follows from this: antisocial behaviour might be controlled by *rewarding* people, rather than punishing them, for behaving antisocially!

SOCIAL COMPARISON AND SELF-KNOWLEDGE

Although we can learn about ourselves through introspection and self-perception, we can also learn about ourselves by comparing ourselves with other people. Indeed, Festinger (1954) developed **social comparison theory** to describe how people learn about themselves through comparisons with others (also see Suls & Wheeler, 2000; Wheeler, 1991). People need to be confident about the validity of their perceptions, attitudes, feelings and behaviours; and because there is rarely an objective measure of validity, people ground their cognitions, feelings and behaviours in those of other people. In particular, they seek out similar others to validate their perceptions and attitudes—which can, to some extent, be read as meaning that people anchor their attitudes and self-concept in the groups to which they feel they belong.

In the case of behaviours, people do not seek out similar others. Instead, they seek out people who

perform slightly worse than they do—they make downward social comparisons that deliver an evaluatively positive self-concept (Wills, 1981). Often, however, we cannot choose with whom we make comparisons—for example, in families younger siblings often have no option but to compare themselves with their more competent older brothers and sisters.

If we are constrained to make an upward comparison it can have quite deleterious effects on self-esteem (Wood, 1989). To avoid this, people can, according to Tesser's (1988) **self-evaluation maintenance model**, try to downplay their similarity to the other person or withdraw from their relationship with that person. An intriguing study along these lines was conducted by Medvec, Madley and Gilovich (1995). They coded the facial expressions of medal winners at the 1992 Olympic Games in Barcelona and found that the bronze medallists expressed noticeably more satisfaction than the silver medallists! Medvec and colleagues argued that silver medallists were constrained to make unfavourable upward comparisons with gold medallists, whereas bronze medallists could make self-enhancing downward comparisons with the rest of the field who received no medal at all.

Downward comparisons also occur between groups. Groups try to compare themselves with inferior groups, in order to feel that 'we' are better than 'they'. Indeed, intergroup relations are largely a struggle for evaluative superiority of our own group over relevant outgroups (see Hogg, 2000c; Turner, 1975). This in turn influences self-conception as a group member—social identity

(Tajfel & Turner, 1979). According to **self-categorisation theory** (Turner, Hogg, Oakes, Reicher, & Wetherell, 1987), an extension of social identity theory, the underlying process is one in which people who feel they belong to a group categorise themselves as group members and quite automatically internalise as a self-evaluation the attributes that describe the group—if the group is positive, the attributes are positive, and thus self is positive (see also Chapter 11).

Sports provide a wonderful context in which the outcome of this process can be seen. Few Australians will not have felt positive about Australia and being Australian when Cathy Freeman won the 400 metres at the 2000 Sydney Olympics. Cialdini and his associates referred to this phenomenon as 'basking in reflected glory' or **BIRGing** (Cialdini, Borden, Thorne, Walker, Freeman, & Sloan, 1976).

To illustrate the effect, they conducted experiments in which they raised or lowered self-esteem via feedback on a general knowledge test, and then student participants were seemingly incidentally asked about the outcome of a recent football game. Cialdini and associates found that participants who had had their self-esteem lowered tended to associate themselves with winning and not with losing teams—they tended to refer to the teams as 'we' in the former case and as 'they' in the latter.

Selves and identities

Most researchers now believe that it is probably inaccurate to characterise the self as a single undifferentiated entity. It is more accurate to think of the self-concept as containing a repertoire of relatively discrete and often quite varied identities, each with its own circumscribed bodies of self-knowledge (e.g. Gergen, 1971). These identities probably have their origins in the vast array of different social relationships that form, or have formed, the anchoring points for our lives—ranging from close personal relationships with friends and family, through relationships and roles defined by work groups and professions, to relationships defined by ethnicity, nationality and gender.

Research suggests that people differ in self-complexity (Linville, 1985; see above), with some people having a much more diverse and extensive set of selves than others—people with many independent aspects of self have higher self-complexity than people with only a few, relatively similar aspects of self.

TYPES OF SELVES AND IDENTITIES

Social identity theorists (see below) have argued that there are two broad classes of identity that define different types of selves:

1. **social identity**, which defines self in terms of group memberships;
2. **personal identity**, which defines self in terms of idiosyncratic personal relationships and traits (see Hogg & Abrams, 1988; Tajfel & Turner, 1979).

Brewer and Gardner (1996) distinguish between three forms of self: (1) the *individual self* (defined by personal traits that differentiate self from all others); (2) the *relational self* (defined by dyadic relationships that assimilate self to significant other persons); and (3) the *collective self* (defined by group membership that differentiates 'us' from 'them').

More recently, Brewer (2001) has proposed four types of identity: (1) *person-based social identities* emphasise the way in which group properties are internalised by individual group members as part of the self-concept; (2) *relational social identities* define self in relation to specific other people with whom one interacts in a group context—this corresponds to Brewer and Gardner's (1996) relational identity, and to Markus and

	IDENTITY ATTRIBUTES	RELATIONSHIP ATTRIBUTES
TABLE 4.1	Self and self-attributes as a function of social versus personal level of identity, and identity versus relationship types of attribute	
Social identity	*Collective self* Set of attributes shared with others and contrasted with a specific outgroup or with outgroups in general.	*Collective relational self* Set of attributes specifying the relationship between self as an ingroup member and specific others as ingroup or outgroup members.
Personal identity	*Individual self* Set of attributes unique to self and contrasted with specific other individuals or with other individuals in general.	*Individual relational self* Set of attributes specifying the relationship between self as a unique individual and others as individuals.

Social identity salience: Maasai warriors in Tanzania wear full tribal dress to proclaim their identity and distinguish themselves from other tribes.

Kitayama's (1991) 'interdependent self'; (3) *group-based social identities* are equivalent to social identity as defined above; and (4) *collective identities* refer to a process whereby group members do not just share self-defining attributes but also engage in social action to forge an image of what the group stands for and how it is represented and viewed by others.

(How would you use these views about types of selves to answer the first focus question?)

Table 4.1 shows one way in which different types of self and self-attributes could be classified according to level of identity (social versus personal) and type of attributes (identity-defining versus relationship-defining).

CONTEXTUAL SENSITIVITY OF SELF AND IDENTITY

Evidence for the existence of multiple selves comes from research where contextual factors are varied to discover that people describe themselves differently and may even behave quite differently in different situations. For example, Fazio, Effrein and Falender (1981) were able to get participants to describe themselves in very different ways, by asking them loaded questions that made them search through their stock of self-knowledge for information that presented self in a different light. Other researchers have found, time and time again, that experimental procedures that focus on group membership produce very different behaviours from procedures that focus on individuality and interpersonal relationships.

The classic paradigm, called the *minimal group paradigm* (e.g. Tajfel, 1970; see Diehl, 1990, Chapter 11), is one in which participants are identified as individuals or are explicitly categorised, randomly or by

some trivial criterion, as group members. When people are categorised they tend to be significantly more discriminatory and show an array of behaviours, attitudes and feelings that indicate a sense of belonging to the group and conformity to group norms. This is an extremely robust finding.

The idea that we may have many selves, and that contextual factors can bring different selves into play, has a number of ramifications. Social constructionists have suggested that the self is entirely situation-dependent. An extreme form of this position argues that we do not carry self-knowledge around in our heads as cognitive representations at all—rather that we construct disposable selves through talk (e.g. Potter & Wetherell, 1987; see discussion of discourse analysis in Chapter 15).

A less extreme version has been proposed by Oakes (e.g. Oakes, Haslam, & Reynolds, 1999), who does not emphasise the role of talk but still maintains that self-conception is highly context-dependent. A middle way is to argue that people do have cognitive representations of self that they carry in their heads as organising principles for perception, categorisation and action, but that these representations are ephemerally or enduringly mutated by situational factors (e.g. Abrams & Hogg, 2001).

IN SEARCH OF SELF-CONCEPTUAL COHERENCE

The notion that we may have many selves needs to be kept in perspective. Although we may have a diversity of relatively discrete selves, there needs to be a degree of self-conceptual integration and coherence that provides a continuing theme for our lives—an autobiography that weaves our various identities and selves together into a whole person. People who have highly fragmented selves (e.g. some people with schizophrenia, amnesia or Alzheimer's) find it extraordinarily difficult to function effectively.

People use many strategies to construct a coherent sense of self (Baumeister, 1998). One strategy is to restrict your life to a limited set of contexts—in which case, as selves are cued by context, you will protect yourself from self-conceptual clashes. Another strategy is to keep revising your integrative autobiography to accommodate new identities—like the societal practice of rewriting history to demonise or revere past leaders (Greenwald, 1980). A third strategy is to attribute changes in self to changing circumstances rather than fundamental changes in who we are—this reflects the actor–observer attribution effect, in which people are more inclined to attribute their own behaviours externally to situations and others' behaviour internally to their personality (Jones & Nisbett, 1972; see Chapter 3).

Finally, people can develop a self-schema (Markus, 1977; see above) that embodies a core set of attributes which, they feel, distinguishes them from all other people. People then tend disproportionately to recognise these attributes in all their other selves, and this provides a linkage that delivers a sense of a stable and unitary self (Cantor & Kihlstrom, 1987).

Social identity

Over the past 30 years, **social identity theory** has grown to be a major perspective and influence on how social psychologists conceptualise the relationship between social categories and the self-concept (see Hogg, 2003b; Hogg & Abrams, 1988, 2003). Because this perspective addresses a whole range of social psychological phenomena, aspects of social identity theory surface in some detail in almost all chapters of this book (see especially Chapter 11).

The social identity perspective has its origins in the work of Henri Tajfel on social categorisation, intergroup relations, social comparison, and prejudice and stereotyping (e.g. Tajfel, 1969, 1974; Tajfel & Turner, 1979), and in later theorising by John Turner and his associates on the role of self-categorisation in generating group behaviours associated with collective self-conception (Turner, Hogg, Oakes, Reicher, & Wetherell, 1987).

SOCIAL IDENTITY AND PERSONAL IDENTITY

As we have noted, social identity theorists have suggested that there are two broad classes of identity that define different types of selves: (1) *social identity*, which defines self in terms of group memberships; and (2) *personal identity*, which defines self in terms of idiosyncratic

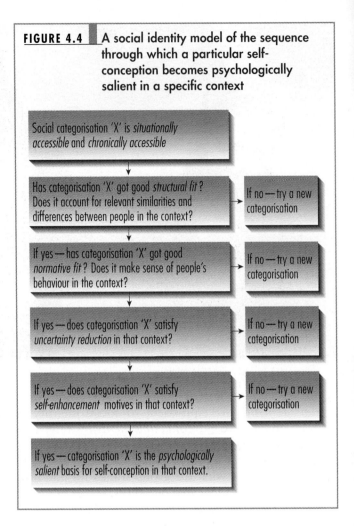

FIGURE 4.4 A social identity model of the sequence through which a particular self-conception becomes psychologically salient in a specific context

Social categorisation 'X' is *situationally accessible* and *chronically accessible*

↓

Has categorisation 'X' got good *structural fit*? Does it account for relevant similarities and differences between people in the context? → If no — try a new categorisation

↓

If yes — has categorisation 'X' got good *normative fit*? Does it make sense of people's behaviour in the context? → If no — try a new categorisation

↓

If yes — does categorisation 'X' satisfy *uncertainty reduction* in that context? → If no — try a new categorisation

↓

If yes — does categorisation 'X' satisfy *self-enhancement* motives in that context? → If no — try a new categorisation

↓

If yes — categorisation 'X' is the *psychologically salient* basis for self-conception in that context.

personal relationships and traits. Social identity is associated with group and intergroup behaviours—ethnocentrism, ingroup bias, group solidarity, intergroup discrimination, conformity, normative behaviour, stereotyping and prejudice. Personal identity is associated with positive and negative close interpersonal relationships and with idiosyncratic personal behaviours. We have as many social identities as there are groups that we feel we belong to, and as many personal identities as there are interpersonal relationships we are involved in and clusters of idiosyncratic attributes that we believe we possess.

PROCESSES OF SOCIAL IDENTITY SALIENCE

In any given situation our sense of self and associated perceptions, feelings, attitudes and behaviours hinges on whether social or personal identity, and which specific social or personal identity, is the psychologically salient basis of self-conception. The principle that governs social identity salience hinges on the process of social categorisation and on people's motivation to make sense of, and reduce uncertainty about, themselves and others and to feel relatively positive about themselves (e.g. Hogg, 2001b; Oakes, 1987; see Figure 4.4).

We use limited perceptual cues (what someone looks like, how they speak, what attitudes they express, how they behave) to categorise other people. Generally, we first 'try out' categorisations that are readily accessible to us because we often use them, they are important to us or, perhaps, they are glaringly obvious in the situation. The categorisation brings into play all the additional schematic information we have about the category. This information is cognitively stored as a **prototype** that describes and prescribes the attributes of the category, in the form of a fuzzy set, rather than a precise checklist, of attributes.

Category prototypes not only accentuate similarities within groups but also accentuate differences between groups—they obey what is called the **metacontrast principle**. As such, group prototypes usually do not identify average or typical members or attributes, but ideal members or attributes. If the categorisation fits, in the sense that it satisfactorily accounts for similarities and differences among people (called *structural fit*), and it makes good sense of why people are behaving in particular ways (called *normative fit*), then the categorisation becomes psychologically salient.

SOME CONSEQUENCES OF SOCIAL IDENTITY SALIENCE

When a categorisation becomes psychologically salient, people's perceptions of themselves and others become *depersonalised*. What this means is that people no longer consider themselves or others as unique multidimensional persons but as simple embodiments of the category prototype—they are viewed through the relatively narrow lens of a group membership that is defined by the specific ingroup or outgroup prototype.

In addition to the transformation of self-conception into social identity, people also think, feel, believe and behave in terms of the relevant prototype. The process produces the range of general behaviours we characteristically associate with people in groups and with the way groups treat each other, a theme that recurs throughout this book.

The actual nature of the behaviour depends on the specific content of the relevant prototype (what sort of person does the prototype describe?) and on people's beliefs about the nature of the relations between groups (Ellemers, 1993; Tajfel & Turner, 1979). This last point refers to the fact that, because groups define social identity and social identity defines our self-concept, then the evaluative implications of a specific group (the status, prestige and regard in which it is held) govern the esteem in which we are held by others. This may additionally affect the esteem in which we hold ourselves (Crocker & Major, 1994; see discussion of social stigma in Chapter 10).

Thus, people strive for membership in positive groups, or strive to protect or enhance the esteem of their existing group. If the group's social evaluation in a particular society is generally unfavourable you might try to leave the group entirely—however, this is often difficult because the psychological boundaries between groups can be effectively impermeable or impassable. For example, various migrant or indigenous groups in Australia may find it difficult to 'pass' as European Australian, because they simply do not look like European Australians or they are readily 'given away' by subtle cues in their accent. If 'passing' is not possible, people can try to make sure that the attributes that do define their group are positive ones, or they can focus attention on less prestigious groups in comparison with which they will look rather good.

Groups sometimes recognise that the entire basis on which their group is considered low-status is illegitimate and unfair. If this recognition is tied to practical strategies, then groups will compete directly with one another to gain the upper hand in the status stakes—a competition that can range from rhetoric and democratic process to terrorism and war.

Self-motives

Because selves and identities are such critical reference points for adaptive life, people are highly motivated to secure self-knowledge. Entire industries are based on this search for knowledge, ranging from relatively scientific personality tests to scientifically more questionable practices such as astrology and palmistry. People do not, however, go about this search in a dispassionate manner—they have preferences about the sort of information they want, and they can be dismayed when the quest turns up information that they didn't expect or didn't want to encounter.

Social psychologists have identified three classes of motive that may interact to influence self-construction and the search for self-knowledge: validity, consistency and favourability.

SELF-ASSESSMENT AND SELF-VERIFICATION

The first, somewhat obvious, motive is a simple desire to have accurate and valid information about oneself—there is a **self-assessment** motive (e.g. Trope, 1986). People strive to find out the truth about themselves regardless of how unfavourable or disappointing the truth may be. But people also like to engage in a quest for confirmation—they like to confirm what they already know about themselves and so they seek out self-consistent information through a **self-verification** process (e.g. Swann, 1987). So, for example, people who have a negative self-image will actually seek out negative information to confirm that image.

SELF-ENHANCEMENT

Above all else, people like to learn things about themselves that cast self in a favourable light. People seek new favourable knowledge about themselves as well as ways to revise pre-existing, but unfavourable, views of themselves. People are guided by a **self-enhancement** motive (e.g. Kunda, 1990). One manifestation of this motive is described by **self-affirmation theory** (Steele, 1988), which shows how people strive publicly to affirm positive aspects of who they are: this can be done blatantly by boasting, or more subtly through rationalisation or dropping hints. The urge to self-affirm is particularly strong when an aspect of one's self-esteem has been damaged. So, for example, if someone draws attention to the fact that you are a lousy artist, you might retort that that might be true, but that you are an excellent scientist.

Self-affirmation rests on people's need to maintain a global image of themselves as being competent, good, coherent, unitary, stable, capable of free choice, capable of controlling important outcomes and so on.

Steele (1975) reports a study in which Mormon women in Salt Lake City who were at home during the day were telephoned by a female researcher posing as a community member. She asked them if they would be willing to list everything in their kitchen to assist the development of a community food co-op—those who agreed would be called back the following week. Because community cooperation is a very strong ethic among Mormons, about 50% of women agreed to this large request.

In addition to this baseline condition, there were three other conditions in the study, which involved a previous call, two days earlier, by an entirely unrelated researcher posing as a pollster. In the course of the call, the pollster mentioned in passing that it was common knowledge that, as members of their community, (a) they were uncooperative with community projects (direct threat to a core component of their self-concept), or (b) they were unconcerned about driver safety and care (a threat to a relatively irrelevant component of their self-concept), or (c) they were cooperative with community projects (positive reinforcement of their self-concept).

Consistent with self-affirmation theory, *both* threats (i.e. (a) and (b)) greatly increased the probability that women would subsequently agree to help the food co-op—about 95% of women agreed to help. Among the women who had been given positive reinforcement of their self-concept (i.e. (c)), 65% agreed to help the co-op.

Which of these motives (self-assessment, self-verification, self-enhancement) are more fundamental and more likely to prevail in the pursuit of self-knowledge? Sedikides (1993) conducted a series of six experiments that pitted the three motives against one another. He used a self-reflection task, where participants can ask themselves more or less diagnostic questions about different aspects of self—the asking of more diagnostic questions indicates greater self-reflection. Self-reflection differs depending on what self-motive is operating:

- *Self-assessment*—greater self-reflection on peripheral aspects than on core aspects of self, irrespective of whether the aspect is desirable or undesirable, indicates a drive to find out more about self (people already have knowledge about their more central attributes).
- *Self-verification*—greater self-reflection on core than on peripheral aspects of self, irrespective of attribute valence, indicates a drive to confirm what is already known about self.
- *Self-enhancement*—greater self-reflection on positive than negative aspects of self, irrespective of attribute centrality, indicates a drive to learn positive things about self.

From the six experiments, Sedikides found that self-enhancement was strongest, with consistency (self-verification) a distant second and validity (self-assessment) an even more distant third. The desire to think well of ourselves reigns supreme—it dominates both the pursuit of accurate self-knowledge and the pursuit of information that confirms self-knowledge.

Because self-enhancement is so important, we have developed a formidable repertoire of strategies and techniques to pursue self-enhancement. People engage in elaborate self-deceptions to enhance or protect the positivity of their self-concepts (Baumeister, 1998). See Box 4.1 for examples of esteem-enhancing and esteem-protecting behaviours.

Self-esteem

Why are people so strongly motivated to think well of themselves—to self-enhance? That people do like to think well of themselves has enormous empirical support. Research suggests that people generally have a rosy sense of self—they see, or try to see, themselves through 'rose-tinted spectacles'. For example, people who are threatened or distracted have been shown to display what Paulhus and Levitt (1987) have called *automatic egotism*—a widely favourable self-image. Taylor and Brown (1988) conclude, from a review of research, that people normally overestimate their good points, overestimate their control over events and are unrealistically optimistic.

We have noted that these three tendencies have been referred to as the *self-enhancing triad* (Sedikides & Gregg, 2003). For example, Kruger and Dunning (1999)

Strategies and techniques that people use to enhance or protect the positivity of their self-concept

You may have noticed how people (perhaps you!) are sometimes inclined to boost themselves in the following ways:

- They take credit for their successes but deny blame for their failures (e.g. Zuckerman, 1979)—in the terminology of attribution theory, this is called the *self-serving attribution bias* (see Chapter 3).

- They forget failure feedback more readily than success or praise (e.g. Mischel, Ebbesen, & Zeiss, 1976).

- They accept praise uncritically, but receive criticism sceptically (e.g. Kunda, 1990).

- They try to dismiss interpersonal criticism as being motivated by prejudice (e.g. Crocker & Major, 1989).

- They perform a biased search of their self-knowledge to support a favourable self-image (e.g. Kunda & Sanitoso, 1989).

- They place a favourable spin on the meaning of ambiguous traits that define self (e.g. Dunning, Meyerowitz, & Holzberg, 1989).

- They persuade themselves that their flaws are widely shared human attributes, but that their qualities are rare and distinctive (e.g. Campbell, 1986).

Body image: Has this girl lost her appetite, or is she concerned about her weight?

found, in an American setting, that very low achievers (in the bottom 12% of grades) considered themselves to be relatively high achievers (in the top 38% of grades). You might also be interested in learning that your lecturers may be equally prone to positivity bias—Cross (1977) found that 94% of lecturers regarded their teaching ability as above average.

People who fail to exhibit these biases tend towards depression and certain other forms of mental illness (e.g. Tennen & Affleck, 1993). Thus, a self-conceptual positivity bias, based on positive illusions, is psychologically adaptive.

Box 4.2 describes some health aspects of self-esteem and self-conception.

However, a breathlessly inflated sense of how wonderful we are is not only nauseatingly gushy but also maladaptive, as it does not match reality. Having an accurate sense of self is important (Colvin & Block, 1994) but, as we have seen, less important than feeling good about ourselves. Generally, it seems that the self-conceptual positivity bias is small enough not to be a serious threat to self-conceptual accuracy (Baumeister, 1989) and that people suspend their self-illusions when

important decisions need to be made (Gollwitzer & Kinney, 1989). Nevertheless, a positive self-image and associated self-esteem is a significant goal for most people most of the time.

It is worth noting that the pursuit of **self-esteem** has some cross-cultural generality. For example, although Japanese society stresses communality and interconnectedness and engages in self-criticism, researchers argue that this is simply a different way of satisfying self-esteem—in Western countries, self-esteem is more directly addressed by overt self-enhancement (Kitayama, Markus, Matsumoto, & Norasakkunkit, 1997). According to Leary, Tambor, Terdal and Downs (1995), self-esteem is, as we see below, a reflection of successful social connectedness.

SELF-ESTEEM AND SOCIAL IDENTITY

As we have seen above (see also Chapters 10 and 11), self-esteem is closely associated with social identity—by identifying with a group, that group's prestige and status

---

BOX 4.2 **Threats to self-concept can damage your health: Ways of coping**

There are three major sources of threat to our self-concept and all can affect our sense of self-worth.

1. *Failures*—these can range from failing a test, through failing a job interview, to a marriage ending in divorce.
2. *Inconsistencies*—these can be unusual and unexpected positive or negative events that make us question the sort of person we are.
3. *Stressors*—these are sudden or enduring events that seem to exceed our capacity to cope; they can include bereavement, a sick child and overcommitment to work.

Self-conceptual threats not only arouse negative emotions that can lead to self-harm and suicide, but they also contribute to physical illness (Salovey, Rothman, & Rodin, 1998)—they affect our immune responses, nervous system activity and blood pressure. For example, Strauman, Lemieux and Coe (1993) found that, when people were reminded of significant self-discrepancies, the level of natural killer cell activity in their bloodstream decreased. These cells are important in defending the body against cancers and viral infections.

There are several ways in which people try to cope with self-conceptual threat.

- *Escape*—people may physically remove themselves from the threat situation. Duval and Wicklund (1972) found that people who had done poorly on an intelligence and creativity task, and then were asked to wait in another room that was equipped with a mirror and video camera (to heighten self-awareness), fled the scene much more quickly than participants who had done well on the task.
- *Denial*—people may take alcohol or other drugs, or engage in risky 'just for kicks' behaviour. This is not a particularly constructive coping mechanism since it can create additional health problems.
- *Downplay the threat*—this is a more constructive strategy, either by re-evaluating the aspect of self that has been threatened or by reaffirming other positive aspects of self (Steele, 1988). For example, Taylor (1983) found that breast cancer patients who were facing the possibility of death often expressed and reaffirmed what they felt were their most basic self-aspects—some quit dead-end jobs, others turned to writing and painting, and others reaffirmed important relationships.
- *Self-expression*—this is a very effective response to threat. Writing or talking about one's emotional and physical reactions to self-conceptual threat can be an extraordinarily useful coping mechanism. It reduces emotional heat, reduces headaches, muscle tension and pounding heart, and improves immune system functioning (Pennebaker, 1997). Most benefits come from communication that enhances understanding and self-insight.
- *Attack the threat*—people can directly confront threat by discrediting its basis ('This is an invalid test of my ability'), by denying personal responsibility for the threat ('The dog ate my essay'), by setting up excuses for failure before the event (on the way into an exam, announcing you have a terrible hangover—**self-handicapping** (Berglas, 1987; see Chapter 3) or by taking control of the problem directly, such as seeking professional help or addressing any valid causes of threat.

---

in society tends to attach to our self-concept. Thus, all things being equal, being identified as belonging to the group of obese people is less likely to mediate positive self-esteem than being identified as belonging to the group of 2000 Olympians (Crandall, 1994). There is, however, a general caveat: members of stigmatised social groups can generally be extremely creative in avoiding the self-esteem consequences of that group membership (Crocker & Major, 1989; Crocker, Major, & Steele, 1998; see Chapter 10).

In practice, and according to social comparison theory (see above, and also Chapter 11), there can be several outcomes when self-esteem interfaces with social identity; these depend on the perceived relative status of the outgroups with which our various membership groups are usually compared.

Take the example of Jesse Owens: he was the star athlete at the 1936 Berlin Olympics, the winner of four gold medals. As a member of the United States team he was triumphant, particularly being a Black American who defeated the best that Nazi Germany and its 'master race' had to offer. Adolf Hitler presided over these Games and fully expected White athletes to defeat Black athletes. Ironically, Jesse Owens was less happy on his return home, where he was just another member of an underprivileged Black minority.

Ethnic, and racial, identity is a significant source of social identity-mediated self-esteem. For example, studies in the United States, Australia and New Zealand have shown that members of ethnic minorities often report perceptions of lowered self-esteem when making inter-ethnic comparisons. However, these findings need to be treated with caution, as the conditions under which they occur are specific in at least two ways (see Chapter 10):

1. The **level of explanation** for self-esteem must be *intergroup* (e.g. question—'As an African American I feel good/bad'; answer—'very often, often, occasionally, seldom') rather than *personal* (e.g. question—'I often feel good/bad'; answer—'very often, often, occasionally, seldom'); see Cross (1987).
2. The status relationship between the ethnic minority and the majority must be distinctly unequal (Tajfel, 1978).

The seminal research dealing with ethnic identity was carried out in the United States in the 1930s and 1940s and was restricted to studies of African American and White American children (see Box 4.3). Later work extended the samples to include other non-White minorities such as American Indian, Chicano, Chinese and French Canadian (see review by Aboud, 1987), New Zealand Maori (e.g. Vaughan, 1978a), and Australian Aborigines (Pedersen & Dudgeon, 2003; Pedersen, Walker, & Glass, 1999). Consistently, children from non-White minorities showed clear outgroup preference and wished they were White themselves.

Nesdale (in press) at Griffith University has rightly pointed out that most studies of ethnic identity and attitudes in children use a methodology based on ethnic preference. So, they have not actually demonstrated ethnic prejudice coloured by dislike so much as ethnic *preference*.

Although preadolescent children from an ethnic minority might prefer to be members of the ethnic majority, this effect gradually declines with age (see Box 11.3 for a New Zealand example). It is probable that young, disadvantaged children experience a conflict between their actual and ideal selves (discussed above). As they grow older they have some options:

- avoid damaging intergroup comparisons (see Chapter 11);
- join other group members in a quest for equity with the majority group (again see Chapter 11);

BOX 4.3 Depressed self-esteem and ethnic minority status

Studies of children's ethnic identity have a long history in social psychology. Among the earliest were those carried out by two African Americans, Kenneth and Mamie Clark (1939a, 1939b, 1940). The Clarks showed young African American children pairs of Black and White dolls, probing for the children's ethnic identity and ethnic preference. Independently, Horowitz (1936, 1939) used a different method—sketches of Black and White people to test White children's awareness of differences between ethnic groups and attitudes towards Blacks. Mary Goodman (1946, 1952), who worked with the famous social psychologist Gordon Allport at Harvard University, studied ethnic awareness and attitudes among White and African American nursery school children in more detail. She extended the Clarks' method by including a doll play technique to allow the children to project attitudes towards their ethnic ingroup and outgroup.

These investigations used different samples in various American states, in slightly different time periods, and with an extensive range of tests. Their results consistently showed that, when making ethnic comparisons:

- White children preferred White children;
- African American children preferred White children;
- African American children had lower self-esteem.

Goodman referred to the main effect as 'White over Brown'. A wider recognition of the impact of these studies led to Kenneth Clark appearing as a witness in a landmark case in the United States Supreme Court—*Brown versus the Topeka Board of Education* (1954)—in which he testified that Black children's self-esteem was extensively damaged over time. Flowing from this case, the legal decision to outlaw school segregation was instrumental in helping to legitimise the civil rights movement in the United States (Goodman, 1964).

Despite later claims that the 'doll studies' were methodologically flawed (Hraba, 1972; Banks, 1976), an analysis of the trends in ethnic identity studies carried out in other countries pointed to at least two stable patterns (Vaughan, 1986):

1. Ethnic minorities that are disadvantaged (educationally, economically, politically) are typified by lowered self-esteem when intergroup comparisons are made.
2. Social change in the status relationship between ethnic groups leads to a significant improvement in minority pride and individuals' feelings of self-worth.

With respect to the second pattern, Hraba and Grant (1970) documented a phenomenon in African American children called 'Black is Beautiful', following the success of the American Black Power movement in the late 1960s. (A detailed discussion of the processes underlying social change is provided in Chapter 11, and a discussion of social stigma and self-esteem in Chapter 10.)

- identify ingroup characteristics that provide a sense of uniqueness and positivity, such as language (see Chapter 15).

INDIVIDUAL DIFFERENCES

We all know people who seem to hold themselves in very low regard and others who seem to have a staggeringly positive impression of themselves—do these differences reflect enduring and deep-seated differences in self-esteem? The main thrust of research on self-esteem as a trait is concerned with establishing individual differences in self-esteem and investigating the causes and consequences of these differences.

One view that has become somewhat entrenched, particularly in the United States, is that low self-esteem is responsible for a range of personal and social problems such as crime, delinquency, drug abuse, unwanted pregnancy and underachievement in school. This view has spawned a huge industry, and accompanying mantra, to boost individual self-esteem, particularly in child-rearing and school contexts. However, critics have argued that low self-esteem may be a product of the stressful and alienating conditions of modern industrial society, and that the self-esteem 'movement' is an exercise in rearranging deckchairs on the *Titanic* that merely produces selfish and narcissistic individuals.

So, what is the truth? First of all, research suggests that individual self-esteem tends to vary between moderate and very high, not between low and high: most people, as we discussed above, feel relatively positive about themselves, at least in the United States (Baumeister, Tice, & Hutton, 1989). Lower self-esteem scores have, however, been obtained from Japanese students studying in Japan or the United States (Kitayama, Markus, Matsumoto, & Norasakkunkit, 1997; see also Chapter 16).

Even if we focus on those people who have low self-esteem, there is little evidence that low self-esteem causes the social ills it is purported to cause. For example,

Baumeister, Smart and Boden (1996) searched the literature for evidence for the popular belief that low self-esteem causes violence (see also Chapter 12). They found quite the opposite. Violence was associated with high self-esteem and, more specifically, violence seems to erupt when individuals with high self-esteem have their rosy self-image threatened.

We should not, however, lump together all those with high self-esteem. Consistent with common sense, some people with high self-esteem are quietly self-confident and non-hostile, while others are arrogant, conceited and overly assertive (Kernis, Granneman, & Barclay, 1989). These latter individuals also feel 'special' and superior to others, and actually have relatively volatile self-esteem—they are narcissistic (Rhodewalt, Madrian, & Cheney, 1998). Colvin, Block and Funder (1995) found that it was this latter type of individual with high self-esteem who was likely to be maladjusted in terms of interpersonal problems.

Narcissistic individuals may also be more prone to aggression in response to an ego threat. Indeed, this seems to be true. Bushman and Baumeister (1998) conducted laboratory experiments to test Baumeister, Smart and Boden's (1996) threatened egotism model of the relationship between self-esteem and aggression. Participants were provoked by being given a bad evaluation (or not, in a control condition) of an essay they had written and were then given the opportunity to aggress against the person who had offended them. Self-esteem did not predict aggression, but narcissism did—narcissistic individuals were more aggressive towards people who had provoked and offended them.

Overall, research on the trait of self-esteem provides quite a clear picture of what people with high and low self-esteem are like (Baumeister, 1998; see Table 4.2). There seem to be two main underlying differences associated with the trait of self-esteem (Baumeister, Tice, & Hutton, 1989; Campbell, 1990): (1) self-concept confusion—those with high self-esteem have a more thorough, consistent and stable stock of self-knowledge

TABLE 4.2 Characteristics of people with high and low self-esteem	
HIGH SELF-ESTEEM	LOW SELF-ESTEEM
• persistent and resilient in the face of failure	• vulnerable to impact of everyday events
• emotionally and affectively stable	• wide swings in mood and affect
• less flexible and malleable	• flexible and malleable
• less easily persuaded and influenced	• easily persuaded and influenced
• no conflict between wanting and obtaining success and approval	• want success and approval but are sceptical of it
• react positively to a happy and successful life	• react negatively to a happy and successful life
• thorough, consistent and stable self-concept	• sketchy, inconsistent and unstable self-concept
• self-enhancement motivational orientation	• self-protective motivational orientation

Self-esteem: Positive self-esteem seems to have won out!

than people with low self-esteem; (2) motivational orientation—people with high self-esteem have a self-enhancing orientation in which they capitalise on their positive features and pursue success, while those with low self-esteem have a self-protective orientation in which they try to remedy their shortcomings and avoid failures and setbacks.

(Try to apply these findings to the second focus question.)

IN PURSUIT OF SELF-ESTEEM

Why do people pursue self-esteem? This may initially seem a silly question—the obvious answer is that having self-esteem makes you feel good. There is probably a grain of truth here, but on the other hand there are causality issues to be addressed: being in a good mood, however caused, may provide a rosy glow that distorts the esteem in which people hold themselves. So, rather than self-esteem producing happiness, feeling happy may inflate self-esteem.

One intriguing, and somewhat gloomy, reason given for why people pursue self-esteem is that they do so in order to overcome their fear of death. Greenberg, Pyszczynski and Solomon (1986; Greenberg, Solomon, & Pyszczynski, 1997; Solomon, Greenberg, & Pyszczynski, 1991) developed this idea in their **terror management theory**. They argue that knowledge of the inevitability of death is the most fundamental threat that people face and, therefore, it is the most powerful motivating factor in human existence. Self-esteem is part of a defence against that threat. Through high self-esteem, people can escape from the anxiety that would otherwise arise from continual contemplation of the inevitability of death—the drive for self-esteem is grounded in terror of death. High self-esteem makes

people feel good about themselves—they feel immortal, and positive and excited about life.

In support of this analysis, Greenberg and his colleagues conducted three experiments in which participants did or did not receive feedback about being successful and having a positive personality (manipulation of self-esteem) and then either watched a video about death or else anticipated painful electric shocks (Greenberg, Solomon, Pyszczynski, Rosenblatt, Burling, Lyon, Simon, & Pinel, 1992). They found that participants who had had their self-esteem raised had lower physiological arousal and reported less anxiety (see Figure 4.5).

Another reason why people pursue self-esteem is that self-esteem is a very good index, or internal monitor, of social acceptance and belonging. In this respect, self-esteem has been referred to as a 'sociometer'. Leary and

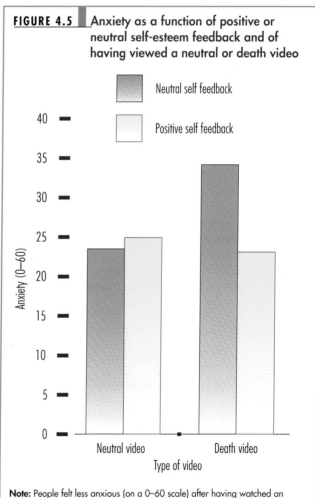

FIGURE 4.5 Anxiety as a function of positive or neutral self-esteem feedback and of having viewed a neutral or death video

Note: People felt less anxious (on a 0–60 scale) after having watched an explicit video about death if their self-esteem had previously been elevated through positive feedback than if their self-esteem had not previously been elevated.

Source: Based on data from Greenberg, Solomon, Pyszczynski, Rosenblatt, Burling, Lyon, Simon and Pinel (1992, Experiment 1).

his colleagues have shown that self-esteem is quite strongly correlated (at about 0.50) with reduced anxiety over social rejection and exclusion (e.g. Leary & Kowalski, 1995); and there is strong evidence that people are pervasively driven by a need to form relationships and to belong (e.g. Baumeister & Leary, 1995; see also Chapter 13 for discussion of the consequences of ostracism and social isolation). Leary feels that having high self-esteem does not mean that we have conquered the fear of death, but rather that we have conquered the threat of loneliness and social rejection.

Leary and colleagues conducted a series of five experiments to support their view (Leary, Tambor, Terdal, & Downs, 1995). They found that participants with high self-esteem reported greater inclusion in general, and in specific real social situations. They also found that social exclusion from a group for personal reasons depressed participants' self-esteem.

Before you proceed, try the questions in Table 4.3.

Self-presentation and impression management

Selves are constructed, modified and played out in interaction with other people. As the self that we project has consequences for how others react, we try to control the self we present; Goffman (1959) likens this process of **impression management** to the theatre, where people play roles in real life just as actors do on stage. Like used-car dealers we can put on an act and we can adapt our portrayal for different audiences. There is evidence from hundreds of studies that people behave differently in public than in private (Leary, 1995).

There are two general classes of motives for self-presentation: strategic and expressive. Research by Snyder (1974) on individual differences in **self-monitoring** suggests that high self-monitors adopt strategic self-presentation strategies because they typically shape their behaviours to project the impression they feel their audience or the situation demands, whereas low self-monitors adopt expressive self-presentation strategies because their behaviour is less responsive to changing contextual demands.

STRATEGIC SELF-PRESENTATION

Jones and Pittman (1982) identified five strategic motives: (1) self-promotion—an attempt to persuade others that you are competent; (2) ingratiation—an attempt to get others to like you; (3) intimidation—an attempt to get others to think you are dangerous; (4) exemplification—an attempt to get others to regard you as a morally respectable individual; and (5) supplication—an attempt to get others to take pity on you as helpless and needy. The behaviours that represent the operation of these motives are fairly obvious (see Chapter 6 on persuasion tactics). In fact, ingratiation and self-promotion service two of the most common goals of social interaction—to get people to like you, and to get people to think you are competent (Leary, 1995).

Research on ingratiation tends to show that ingratiation has little effect on observers' liking for you but a

---

TABLE 4.3 ■ **How do you interact with other people?**

The eight statements below, taken from Snyder (1974), deal with your personal reactions to a number of different situations. No two statements are exactly alike, so consider each statement carefully before answering. If a statement is TRUE or MOSTLY TRUE as applied to you, circle 'T' next to that number. If a statement is FALSE or MOSTLY FALSE as applied to you, circle 'F' next to that number.

T	F	1.	I guess I put on a show to impress or entertain people.
T	F	2.	In different situations and with different people, I often act like very different people.
T	F	3.	I can only argue for ideas that I really believe.
T	F	4.	I'm not always the person I appear to be.
T	F	5.	I may deceive people by being friendly when I really dislike them.
T	F	6.	At parties and social gatherings I do not attempt to do or say things that others will like.
T	F	7.	I would not change my opinions (or the way I do things) in order to please someone or win their favour.
T	F	8.	I can look anyone in the eye and tell a lie with a straight face (if for a right end).

Note: An explanation and scoring key is provided at the end of this chapter.

big effect on the target—flattery can be hard to resist (Gordon, 1996; see also Box 4.4).

EXPRESSIVE SELF-PRESENTATION

Strategic **self-presentation** is focused on manipulating others' perceptions of you. Expressive motives for self-presentation involve people trying to demonstrate and gain validation for their self-concept through their actions—the focus is more on themselves than on others (Schlenker, 1980)—but people do tend to seek out and interact or form relationships with others who are likely to validate who they are. The expressive motive for self-presentation is a strong one, because a particular identity or self-concept is relatively worthless unless it is recognised and validated by others: it is of little use to me if I think I am a genius but no one else does. Identity requires validation for it to persist and serve a useful function.

For example, research by Emler and Reicher (1995) shows that delinquent behaviour among boys is almost always performed publicly, or in forms that can be publicly verified, because its primary function is identity validation—validation of possessing a delinquent reputation. There is little point in being a closet delinquent.

Identity on display: Young urban teens need to validate their developing identities, and they often do this by 'hanging out' together.

BOX 4.4	Tips on how to present yourself so that others like you

The key to getting people to like you through strategic self-presentation is to be relatively subtle so that it does not look too obviously like ingratiation. According to Jones (1990), there are four principal strategies you should adopt:

1. Try to agree with people's opinions (similarity enhances attraction—see Chapter 13), but make it credible (a) by balancing agreement on important issues with disagreement on trivial issues, and (b) by balancing forceful agreement with weak disagreement.

2. Be selectively modest (a) by making fun of your standing on unimportant issues, and (b) by putting yourself down in areas that do not matter very much.

3. Try to avoid appearing too desperate for others' approval. Try to get others to do the strategic self-presentation for you and, if it is left up to you, use the strategy sparingly and do not use it under conditions where it would be expected.

4. Basking in reflected glory really does work. Make casual references to your connections with winners, and only make links with losers when such links cannot be turned against you.

Source: Based on Jones (1990).

Other research confirms that people prefer social situations that allow them to act in ways that are consistent with their self-concept (e.g. Snyder & Gangestad, 1982), and prefer partners who agree with their own self-image (Swann, Hixon, & de la Ronde, 1992).

Social validation of expressed behaviour also seems to be implicated in self-concept change. For example, Tice (1992) conducted a series of experiments in which she asked participants to act as if they were emotionally stable, or emotionally volatile. Half the participants performed the behaviour very publicly, and half very privately. They all then completed ratings of what they believed their 'true self' was like.

Tice found that only publicly performed behaviours were internalised as descriptors of the self-concept. It appears that what is important in self-concept change is that other people perceive you in a particular way—it is not enough for you internally to perceive the self in a particular way (Schlenker, Dlugolecki, & Doherty, 1994).

The self-conceptual consequences of public behaviour have additional support from a program of research by Snyder (1984; see Chapter 10, Figure 10.10). Participant observers were led to believe that a target stranger they were about to meet was an extravert. Snyder then monitored what happened. The participants' expectation constrained the target's behaviour to be extravert, which of course confirmed the expectation and strengthened the constraint, and subsequently led the target to believe that she really was extravert.

Cultural differences in self and identity

Interdependent self: A young Korean girl conceals her identity from a stranger. Westerners reveal more about themselves to people whom they do not know.

We discuss social psychological aspects of culture and cultural differences fully in Chapter 16. With respect to self and identity, there is one major finding. Western cultures such as Australia, the United States and Western Europe tend to be individualistic, whereas most other cultures such as those found in Asia, South America and Africa tend to be collectivist (Triandis, 1989; also see Oyserman, Coon, & Kemmelmeier, 2002). The anthropologist Geertz (1975, p. 48) puts it beautifully:

The Western conception of the person as a bounded, unique, more or less integrated, motivational and cognitive universe, a dynamic centre of awareness, emotion, judgement, and action organized into a distinctive whole and set contrastively both against other such wholes and against a social and natural background is, however incorrigible it may seem to us, a rather peculiar idea within the context of the world's cultures.

Markus and Kitayama (1991) describe how people in individualistic cultures tend to have an independent self, whereas people in collectivist cultures have an interdependent self. Although in both cases people seek a coherent sense of who they are, the independent self is grounded in a view of self as autonomous, separate from other people, and revealed through a person's inner thoughts and feelings. The interdependent self is grounded in the person's connection to and relationships with other people. It is expressed through roles and relationships:

TABLE 4.4 | **Differences between independent and interdependent selves**

	INDEPENDENT SELF	INTERDEPENDENT SELF
Self-definition	• Unique, autonomous individual, separate from context, represented in terms of internal traits, feelings, thoughts and abilities.	• Connected with others, imbedded in social context, represented in terms of roles and relationships.
Self-structure	• Unitary and stable, constant across situations and relationships.	• Fluid and variable, changing across situations and relationships.
Self-activities	• Being unique and self-expressive, acting true to your internal beliefs and feelings, being direct and self-assertive, promoting your own goals and your difference from others.	• Belonging, fitting in, acting appropriately to roles and group norms, being indirect and non-confrontational, promoting group goals and group harmony.

Source: Based on Markus & Kitayama (1991).

Self . . . is defined by a person's surrounding relations, which often are derived from kinship networks and supported by cultural values such as filial piety, loyalty, dignity, and integrity. (Gao, 1996, p. 83)

Table 4.4 shows the ways in which independent and interdependent selves differ. (Now try to answer the third focus question.) We return to this cultural difference in the self in Chapter 16 (in particular, see Table 16.2).

From a recent conceptual review of the cultural context of self-conception, Vignoles, Chryssochoou and Breakwell (2000) conclude that the need to have a distinctive and integrated sense of self is probably universal; however, individual distinctiveness means something quite different in individualist and collectivist cultures. In one it is the isolated and bounded self that gains meaning from separateness, whereas in the other it is the relational self that gains meaning from its relations with others.

Consistent with our historical analysis of conceptions of self at the beginning of this chapter, the most plausible account of the origins of individualist and collectivist cultures, and associated independent and interdependent self-conception, is probably in terms of economic activity. Western cultures have developed over the past two or three hundred years in the shadow of an economic system based on labour mobility. People are units of production who are expected to move from places of low labour demand to places of high demand—they are expected to organise their lives, their relationships and their self-concept around mobility and transient relationships.

Independence, separateness and uniqueness have become more important than connectedness and the long-term maintenance of enduring relationships—these values have become ensconced as key features of Western culture. Self-conception reflects cultural norms that codify economic activity.

Summary

- The modern Western idea of the self has gradually crystallised over the past 200 years as a consequence of a number of social and ideological forces, including secularisation, industrialisation, enlightenment and psychoanalysis. As a very recent science, social psychology has tended to view the self as the essence of individuality.
- In reality there are many different forms of self and identity. The three most important are probably the collective self (self defined in terms of attributes shared with ingroup members and distinct from outgroup members), the individual self (self defined in terms of attributes that make one unique relative to other people) and the relational self (self defined in terms of relationships with specific other people).
- People experience different selves in different contexts, and yet also feel that they have a coherent self-concept that integrates or interrelates all these selves.
- People are not continually consciously aware of themselves. Self-awareness is sometimes very uncomfortable and other times very uplifting—it depends on what aspect of self we are aware of and on the relative favourability of that aspect.
- Self-knowledge is stored as schemas. We have many self-schemas, and they vary in terms of how clear they are. In particular, we have schemas about our actual self, our ideal self and our 'ought' self. We often compare our actual self with our ideal and 'ought' selves: an actual–ideal self-discrepancy makes us feel dejected, whereas an actual–'ought' self-discrepancy makes us feel anxious.
- People construct a concept of self in a number of different ways in addition to introspection. They can observe what they say and what they do, and if there are no external reasons for behaving in that way they assume the behaviour reflects their true self. People can compare themselves with others to get a sense of who they are: they ground their attitudes in comparisons with similar others but their behaviours in comparisons with slightly less well-off others. The collective self is also based on downward comparisons, but with outgroup others.
- Collective self is associated with group memberships, intergroup relations and the range of specific and general behaviours we associate with people in groups.
- Self-conception is underpinned by three major motives: self-assessment (to discover what sort of person you really are); self-verification (to confirm what sort of person you are); and self-enhancement (to discover what a wonderful person you are). People are overwhelmingly motivated by self-enhancement, with self-verification a distant second and self-assessment bringing up the rear. This is probably because self-enhancement services self-esteem, and self-esteem is a key feature of self-conception.

- Some people have generally higher self-esteem than others. People with high self-esteem have a clear and stable sense of self, and a self-enhancement orientation; people with low self-esteem have a less clear self-concept and a self-protective orientation.
- People pursue self-esteem for many reasons—probably mainly because it is a good internal index of social integration, acceptance and belonging. It may indicate that one has successfully overcome loneliness and social rejection. To protect or enhance self-esteem, people carefully manage the impression they project: they can do this strategically (manipulating others' images of self) or expressively (behaving in ways that project a positive image of self).
- Individualist Western cultures emphasise the independent self, whereas other (collectivist) cultures emphasise the interdependent self (self defined in terms of one's relations and roles relative to other people).

LINKS

YOU HAVE READ ABOUT:	WHICH LINKS TO:
Self-schemas	schemas (2); attribution (3)
Self-perception theory	self-attribution (3); cognitive dissonance (6)
Self-evaluation and social identity	social identity and group membership (11)
Self-awareness	deindividuation (11, 12)
Collective self	group membership and identity (11); collectivism (16)
Self-concept and positivity	self-serving bias (3)
Ethnic identity and self-esteem	social identity and intergroup relations (11)
Strategic self-presentation	techniques for persuading others (6)
Independent and interdependent selves	individualism and collectivism (16)

Key terms

BIRGing *(p. 80)*
deindividuation *(p. 76)*
impression management *(p. 90)*
level of explanation *(p. 87)*
looking-glass self *(p. 75)*
metacontrast principle *(p. 83)*
overjustification effect *(p. 78)*
personal identity *(p. 80)*
priming *(p. 77)*
prototype *(p. 83)*
schema *(p. 77)*
self-affirmation theory *(p. 84)*
self-assessment *(p. 83)*
self-categorisation theory *(p. 80)*

self-discrepancy theory *(p. 77)*
self-enhancement *(p. 84)*
self-esteem *(p. 85)*
self-evaluation maintenance model *(p. 79)*
self-handicapping *(p. 86)*
self-monitoring *(p. 90)*
self-perception theory *(p. 78)*
self-presentation *(p. 91)*
self-verification *(p. 83)*
social comparison theory *(p. 79)*
social identity *(p. 80)*
social identity theory *(p. 82)*
symbolic interactionism *(p. 74)*
terror management theory *(p. 89)*

Key to Table 4.3
The items in Table 4.3 are examples from Snyder's (1974) Self-Monitoring Scale. Use the key below to score yourself. According to Snyder, a high score suggests a more 'chameleon' character, a person who is careful to create an impression that suits the audience. A low score characterises people who focus on just expressing themselves, regardless of the audience.
Key: A maximum score on self-monitoring is gained as follows: 1 T, 2 T, 3 F, 4 T, 5 T, 6 F, 7 F, 8 T

FURTHER READING

Abrams, D., & Hogg, M. A. (2001). Collective identity: Group membership and self-conception. In M. A. Hogg & R. S. Tindale (Eds.), *Blackwell handbook of social psychology: Group processes* (pp. 425–460). Oxford, UK: Blackwell. Detailed discussion and overview of the relationship between the self-concept and group membership, with an emphasis on the collective self and social identity.

Baumeister, R. F. (Ed.). (1993). *Self-esteem: The puzzle of low self-regard*. New York: Plenum. An edited collection of chapters from most of the leading researchers of self-esteem, each describing and overviewing their research program and general conclusions.

Baumeister, R. F. (1998). The self. In D. T. Gilbert, S. T. Fiske, & G. Lindzey (Eds.), *Handbook of social psychology* (4th ed., Vol. 1, pp. 680–740). New York: McGraw-Hill. Comprehensive and detailed review of the social psychology of the self, by one of social psychology's leading self researchers— the 'handbook' is one of the most authoritative references in social psychology.

Baumeister, R. F. (Ed.). (1999). *The self in social psychology*. Philadelphia, PA: Psychology Press. A detailed overview of theory and research on self and identity, organised around reprints of a set of 23 key and classic publications on the self. There is an integrative introductory chapter and short introductory pieces to each set of readings. This is an excellent resource for the study of self and identity.

Leary, M. R., & Tangney, J. P. (2003). *Handbook of self and identity*. New York: Guilford. A comprehensive and completely up-to-date selection of chapters from leading scholars of self and identity.

Sedikides, C., & Gregg, A. P. (2003). Portraits of the self. In M. A. Hogg & J. Cooper (Eds.), *The Sage handbook of social psychology* (pp. 110–138). London: Sage. A comprehensive and up-to-date overview of research and theory on self and identity. Sedikides is one of the world's leading self researchers.

Attitudes

FOCUS QUESTIONS

1. Just how meaningful is the term 'attitude'? An animal lover says an attitude is the body posture a hunting dog assumes when indicating the presence of a prey. A sports coach says that a certain team player has an 'attitude problem', which presumably is something to do with the player's state of mind. Is the term worth keeping in our psychological dictionary if it has several other everyday meanings?

2. Citizens often say that polling people's attitudes (or opinions) is a waste of public money and that polls do not predict elections—or anything else, for that matter—very well. Is there any useful link between attitudes and behaviour?

3. There is only one way to find out what people's attitudes are: just ask them. True or false?

THIS CHAPTER DISCUSSES:

- contemporary and historical views of 'attitude'
- models of attitude structure
- the functions of attitudes
- cognitive theories of attitudes and behaviour
- the theory of reasoned action
- attitude formation: behavioural and cognitive approaches
- values, ideology and social representations
- measuring attitudes: attitude scales, physiological and behavioural measures.

Structure and function of attitudes

BACKGROUND

The term 'attitude' has now become part of our commonsense language. Many years ago, the social psychologist Gordon Allport referred to **attitude** as social psychology's most indispensable concept. In the *Handbook of Social Psychology*, an influential treatise on the discipline at that time, he wrote (1935, p. 798):

The concept of attitudes is probably the most distinctive and indispensable concept in contemporary American social psychology. No other term appears more frequently in the experimental and theoretical literature.

Looking at the context in which Allport was writing, his view is not surprising. Others, such as Thomas and Znaniecki (1918) and Watson (1930), had previously defined the whole of social psychology as the scientific study of attitudes! As we shall see, the early 1930s also brought the tangible results of questionnaire-based scales, which could be used to measure attitudes. According to Allport (1935, p. 810), an attitude is:

. . . a mental and neural state of readiness, organised through experience, exerting a directive or dynamic influence upon the individual's response to all objects and situations with which it is related.

Allport was not to know that such a fashionable concept would become the centre of much controversy in the decades ahead. In time, a radical behavioural view would emerge to argue that an attitude is a figment that a person might construct to explain a behaviour that has already occurred.

In looking at broad historical trends in how attitudes have been treated by social psychologists, McGuire (1986) distinguished three phases of burgeoning attention, punctuated by a waning interest between them:

1. a concentration on fairly static issues of attitude measurement and how these related to behaviour (1920s and 30s);
2. a focus on the dynamics of change in an individual's attitudes (1950s and 60s);
3. a swing towards unravelling the structure and function of systems of attitudes (1980s and 90s).

The word 'attitude' is derived from the Latin *aptus*, which means 'fit and ready for action'. This ancient meaning refers to something that is directly observable, such as a boxer in a boxing ring. Today, however, attitude researchers view 'attitude' as a construct which, although not directly observable, precedes behaviour and guides our choices and decisions for action.

Attitude research in psychology and the social sciences has generated enormous interest and many hundreds of studies covering almost every conceivable topic about which attitudes might be expressed. During the 1960s and 1970s, research and theorising on attitudes entered a period of pessimism and decline. To some extent, this was a reaction to concern about the apparent lack of relationship between attitudes as measured and behaviours as recorded.

During the 1980s, however, attitudes again became a centre of attention for social psychologists, stimulated considerably by modern cognitive psychology (see reviews by Tesser & Shaffer, 1990, and Olson & Zanna, 1993). This resurgence included applications from experimental research that focused on how information is processed and how memory works, and the effects of these on attitude formation and change (Lieberman, 2000; Murphy, Monahan, & Zajonc, 1995; Murphy & Zajonc, 1993).

In Chapters 5 and 6 we take the view that attitudes are basic to and pervasive in human life. In doing this, we will not take McGuire's evolutionary sequence too literally, as the three foci he refers to have always been, and continue to be, of interest to social psychologists. Without the concept of attitude, we would have difficulty in construing and reacting to events, in trying to make decisions, and in making sense of our relationships with people in everyday life. Attitudes continue to fascinate researchers and remain a key, if controversial, part of social psychology.

HOW MANY COMPONENTS?

Constructing models of the components that make up an attitude has long been a source of fascination to social psychologists. Over the years this has led to major differences between theorists, even with respect to such an apparently simple question as how many crucial components are actually required in the construction of an attitude.

One component

Thurstone preferred a **one-component attitude model**, defining an attitude as 'the affect for or against a psychological object' (1931, p. 261). A later influential text dealing with techniques for constructing attitude scales reiterated this view: an attitude is 'the degree of positive or negative affect associated with some psychological object' (Edwards, 1957, p. 2). How simple can you get—do you like the object or not? Such a straightforward view becomes more complex when we examine how Thurstone went about measuring an object using an early form of attitude scale. Thurstone actually believed that the concept of attitude was holistic, and that an attitude object had many possible attributes and elements (Ostrom, 1989a). The centrality of affect, however, was the dominant feature of Thurstone's approach, and is the basis of a more sophisticated sociocognitive model put forward by Pratkanis and Greenwald (1989), to which we return later.

Two components

Another approach, with its origins in Allport's theory, favoured a **two-component attitude model**. From this perspective an attitude is a state of mental readiness, or an implicit predisposition, that has a generalising and consistent influence on evaluative (judgmental) responses. It is something inside of us that influences our decisions about what is good or bad, desirable or undesirable. An attitude is therefore a private event that is externally unobservable, and whose existence we can only infer. We might do this by examining our own mental processes introspectively. As we see later, we might also make inferences by examining the ways in which we behave, speak or act. You cannot see, touch or physically examine an attitude; it is a hypothetical construct. According to Petty and Cacioppo (1986b), this leads to a definition of attitudes as 'lasting, general evaluations of people (including oneself), objects, or issues'.

Three components

Yet a third view is the **three-component attitude model**, which is an approach to the definition of attitude from an ancient philosophical paradigm (McGuire, 1989, p. 40):

The trichotomy of human experience into thought, feeling, and action, although not logically compelling, is so pervasive in Indo-European thought (being found in Hellenic, Zoroastrian, and Hindu philosophy) as to suggest that it corresponds to something basic in our way of conceptualisation, perhaps . . . reflecting the three evolutionary layers of the brain: cerebral cortex, limbic system, and old brain.

The three-component model of attitude was particularly popular in the 1960s, following the work of Rosenberg and Hovland (1960) and Krech, Crutchfield and Ballachey (1962). It was also reflected in the later work of Himmelfarb and Eagly (1974). Himmelfarb and Eagly described an attitude as a relatively enduring organisation of beliefs, feelings and behavioural tendencies towards socially significant objects, groups, events or symbols. Note that this definition not only included the three components but also emphasised that:

- Attitudes are relatively permanent—that is, they persist across time and situations. A transitory feeling is not an attitude.
- Attitudes are limited to socially significant events or objects.
- Attitudes are generalisable and involve at least some degree of abstraction. If you drop a book on your toe and find that it hurts, this is not a sufficient basis

for forming an attitude, because it is a single event in one place and at one time. But if the experience makes you dislike books or libraries, or clumsiness in general, then that dislike is an attitude.

Each attitude, then, is made up of a cluster of feelings, likes and dislikes, behavioural intentions, thoughts and ideas. Other theorists who have favoured the three-component model include Breckler (1984) and Ostrom (1968).

Despite the appeal of the 'trinity', this model presents a problem by prejudging a link between attitude and behaviour (Zanna & Rempel, 1988), itself a thorny issue and of sufficient complexity to be dealt with in more detail in Chapter 6. It is enough to say here that most modern definitions of attitude involve both belief and feeling structures, and are much concerned with how, if each can indeed be measured, the resulting data will help to predict the future acts of an individual. (Based on what you have read so far, try to answer the first focus question.)

FUNCTION OF ATTITUDES

If attitudes have a structure, they must have a function as well. The approaches we have considered so far make at least an implicit assumption of purpose. Some writers have been more explicit. Katz (1960), for example, proposed that there are various kinds of attitudes, each serving different functions, such as:

- knowledge
- instrumentality (means to an end or goal)
- ego-defence (protecting our self-esteem)
- value-expressiveness (allowing people to display those values that uniquely identify and define them).

According to Smith, Bruner and White (1956), an attitude saves energy, as we do not have to figure out 'from scratch' how we should relate to the object or situation in question. We can note a parallel here between the utility of stereotypes (Chapter 2) and the function of attitudes. Smith, Bruner and White's proposition is that an attitude enables a person to maximise the probability of having positive experiences while minimising the aversive ones.

Fazio (1989) later argued that the main function of any kind of attitude is a utilitarian one: that of object appraisal. This should hold regardless of whether the attitude has a positive or negative valence—that is, whether our feelings about the object are good or bad. Merely possessing an attitude is useful because of the orientation towards the object that it provides for the person. For example, holding the attitude that snakes are dangerous, while not always correct, serves as a useful cognitive structure for those of us who are unable to differentiate between safe and deadly varieties. However, for an attitude truly to fulfil this function it must be accessible. We develop this aspect of Fazio's thinking about attitude function when we deal with the link between attitude and behaviour.

COGNITIVE CONSISTENCY

In the late 1950s and 1960s several theories of attitude structure were developed that emphasised the role of **cognition** above all else. These became known as **cognitive consistency theories**. The best known of these was probably cognitive dissonance theory and, because of its importance in dealing with the connection between attitude and behaviour, we return to it in Chapter 6. Another early example was balance theory, which is dealt with below.

As well as specifying that beliefs are the building blocks from which an attitude is structured, such theories have focused on the inconsistencies that can arise among some of the beliefs that an individual might hold. These theories may differ in the terminology used to define consistency and inconsistency in cognitive structures, but they all share the important assumption that an attitude structure built on beliefs that are in disagreement (inconsistent) is subjectively aversive. Two thoughts are said to be inconsistent if one seems to contradict the other and if such a state of mind is bothersome. This disharmony is known as *dissonance*. Such an approach to attitude structure goes on to argue that people will be motivated to change one or more contradictory beliefs so that the set as a whole is in harmony. The outcome of this is restoration of consistency.

For instance, in the 1980s in Australia and New Zealand, some citizens who considered themselves to be socialist found it difficult to support a Labor government, as it was perceived to have turned away from wholeheartedly supporting workers.

Balance theory

The cognitive consistency theory with the clearest implications for attitude structure is **balance theory**, which was derived from the work of Heider (1946) and then extended by Cartwright and Harary (1956). Heider's ideas were grounded in the *Gestalt* school, a psychological approach to perception popular in Germany in the early 20th century and extended by Heider to the field of interpersonal relations. The general approach is field-theoretical, meaning that perceptions of people, objects and events make up a person's cognitive field.

Balance theory focuses on the P-O-X unit of the individual's cognitive field. Imagine a triad consisting of three elements: a person (P), another person (O) and an attitude, object or topic (X). Such a triad is said to be consistent if it is balanced, and balance is assessed by counting the number and types of relationships among the elements. For instance, P liking X is a positive (+) relationship; O disliking X is negative (–) and P disliking

O is negative (–). Altogether, there are eight possible combinations of relationships between two people and an attitude object, four of which are balanced and four unbalanced. These are shown in Figure 5.1.

A triad is balanced if there is an odd number of positive relationships, which may occur in a variety of ways. If P likes O, O likes X and P likes X, then the triad is balanced. From P's point of view, balance theory acts as a divining rod in predicting interpersonal relationships: if P likes the object X, then any compatible other, O, should feel the same way. Likewise, if P already likes O, then O will be expected to evaluate object X in a fashion similar to P. By contrast, if P likes O, O likes X and P dislikes X, then the relationship is unbalanced. As we have noted, the principle of consistency that underlies balance theory means that, in unbalanced triads, people may feel tense and be motivated to restore balance (Jordan, 1953). Heider proposed that balance is restored in whichever manner requires the least effort. So, in the last example, P could decide not to like O or to change his/her opinion about X, depending on which required the least effort.

On the whole, research has shown that unbalanced structures are more unstable and more unpleasant than balanced structures. There are several additional factors that influence how stable and pleasant a structure is. Everything else being equal, most people prefer to agree with each other. Furthermore, the theory predicts that we assume others will like what we like, in the absence of contradictory information.

As well as preferring balanced structures, most people seek out structures in which P and O agree rather than disagree in their evaluations of the third element in the structure (Zajonc, 1968). Despite this, people do not always seek to resolve inconsistency. They sometimes organise their attitudes and beliefs so that elements are isolated from each other and are quite resistant to change (Abelson, 1968). For example, if P likes opera and O doesn't, and if P and O like each other, P may decide to isolate the element of opera from the triad by listening to opera when O is not present.

Overall, research on balance theory and related issues has been extensive, and mostly supportive. At about the same time, other researchers developed cognitive dissonance theory (Festinger, 1957; see Chapter 6), which is now better known than balance theory.

COGNITION AND EVALUATION

We note above that some have argued that a single component is the essence of an attitude. In the 1930s Thurstone saw affect as the cornerstone of an attitude. By the 1950s, Osgood (discussed later) stressed a central process of evaluation as the essence of an attitude.

Pratkanis and Greenwald gave impetus to this emphasis in their **sociocognitive model**, defining an

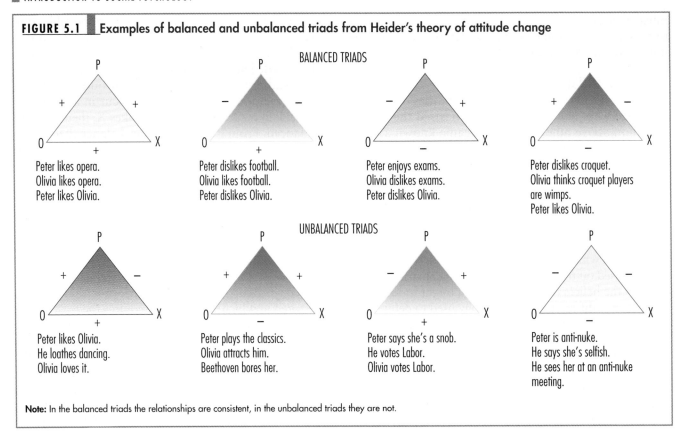

FIGURE 5.1 Examples of balanced and unbalanced triads from Heider's theory of attitude change

BALANCED TRIADS

Peter likes opera.
Olivia likes opera.
Peter likes Olivia.

Peter dislikes football.
Olivia likes football.
Peter dislikes Olivia.

Peter enjoys exams.
Olivia dislikes exams.
Peter dislikes Olivia.

Peter dislikes croquet.
Olivia thinks croquet players
are wimps.
Peter likes Olivia.

UNBALANCED TRIADS

Peter likes Olivia.
He loathes dancing.
Olivia loves it.

Peter plays the classics.
Olivia attracts him.
Beethoven bores her.

Peter says she's a snob.
He votes Labor.
Olivia votes Labor.

Peter is anti-nuke.
He says she's selfish.
He sees her at an anti-nuke
meeting.

Note: In the balanced triads the relationships are consistent, in the unbalanced triads they are not.

attitude as 'a person's evaluation of an object of thought' (1989, p. 247). However, they complicate this simple picture by drawing on theoretical developments (e.g. Wyer & Srull, 1984) in the field of social cognition, an area we deal with in Chapter 2. The attitude object (see Figure 5.2) is represented in memory by:

- an object label and the rules for applying that label;
- an evaluative summary of that object; and
- a knowledge structure supporting that evaluation.

For example, the attitude object we know as a 'shark' may be represented in memory as: a really big fish with very sharp teeth (*label*); that lives in the sea and eats other fish and sometimes people (*rules*); is frightening and best avoided while swimming or surfing (*evaluative summary*); and a well-documented threat to our physical wellbeing, through both science and fiction (*knowledge structure*). However, despite the use of the term 'cognitive', Pratkanis and Greenwald highlighted an evaluative component.

We can also note that several recent theories of racist attitudes have proposed a fundamental evaluative component: a deep-seated emotional antipathy towards racial outgroups (Hilton & von Hippel, 1996; see also Chapter 10). In the wider literature, various terms have been used almost interchangeably in denoting this component, such as 'affect', 'evaluation', 'emotion' and

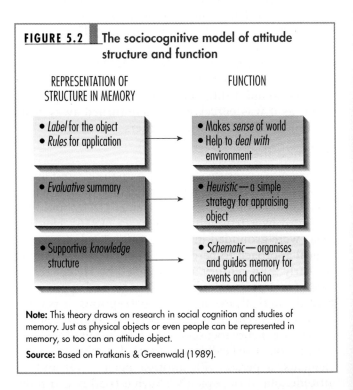

FIGURE 5.2 The sociocognitive model of attitude structure and function

REPRESENTATION OF STRUCTURE IN MEMORY

- *Label* for the object
- *Rules* for application

- *Evaluative* summary

- Supportive *knowledge* structure

FUNCTION

- Makes *sense* of world
- Help to *deal with* environment

- *Heuristic* — a simple strategy for appraising object

- *Schematic* — organises and guides memory for events and action

Note: This theory draws on research in social cognition and studies of memory. Just as physical objects or even people can be represented in memory, so too can an attitude object.

Source: Based on Pratkanis & Greenwald (1989).

'feeling', pointing to the need for the terminology to be tidied up and standardised. Breckler and Wiggins (1989a, 1989b), for example, distinguished between affect and evaluation—the former referring to an emotional reaction to an attitude object, the latter to particular kinds of thoughts, beliefs and judgments about the object.

DECISION-MAKING AND ATTITUDES
Do we perform cognitive algebra?

Information-processing approaches to attitudes emphasise how complex it is to acquire knowledge and to form and change our attitudes. According to Anderson's (1971, 1980) **information integration theory**, most of our attitudes are constructed in response to information we receive about attitude objects. People function as sophisticated problem-solvers and as vigilant evaluators of new information. How we receive and combine this information provides the basis for attitude structure. For example, the salience of some items and the order in which they are received become important determinants of the way in which they are processed. As new information arrives, people evaluate it and combine it with existing information stored in memory. For example, a warning from health authorities that a certain brand of food may cause serious illness will probably lead people to re-evaluate their attitude towards that product, and subsequently change their behaviour by not eating it again.

In Anderson's approach, people acquire and re-evaluate attitudes by a type of cognitive algebra, which involves 'mentally' averaging the values attached to discrete bits of information that are collated and stored in memory about an attitude object. Ordinary people habitually use such mathematics: for example, if you considered a friend to be shy, energetic and compassionate, your overall attitude would be an average of the evaluative meanings you attach to those traits. There would be a different average for another friend who was outgoing, energetic and charismatic. (See Chapter 2 for details of how cognitive averaging operates.)

Construals and attitudes

A recent perspective challenges classical attitude theory. Devine (1989) has suggested that people's attitudes are underpinned by implicit and automatic judgments of which they are unaware. Devine calls these **construals** and argues that, because they are automatic and unconscious, people are less influenced by *social desirability bias* (i.e. how others might judge their response) and construals are therefore a more reliable measure of a person's 'true' attitudes.

But what can we buy with a construal approach to attitudes? According to Schwarz (2000), a construal model of attitude should, among other things, help us better understand the relationship between people's attitudes and their behaviour (see below). Others are more cautious. For example, implicit measures (construals)

may be as dependent on context as explicit measures (attitudes), but in different ways (Glaser & Banaji, 1999). Implicit measures correlate only weakly with both explicit self-reports and overt behaviour (Hilton & Karpinski, 2000), and correlations between implicit and explicit measures of intergroup attitudes are generally low (Dovidio, Kawakami, & Beach, 2001). In considering recent developments in attitude theory, van der Plight and de Vries (2000) proposed a decision-making strategy continuum that ranges from intuition at one end to controlled information processing (e.g. Anderson, 1971) at the other.

Dispute over the best way to characterise attitudes continues and shows little sign of being definitively resolved. Is an attitude a directive and organised state of readiness (Allport), an outcome of algebraic calculation (Anderson) or a temporary construal (Devine)?

Can attitudes predict behaviour?

Why study attitudes, especially if scientists cannot agree about how best to define them? One answer is that attitudes may be useful for predicting what people will do: if we change people's attitudes we might be able to change their behaviour. But not so fast—even though the assumption that behaviour might correspond to attitudes seems reasonable, a number of social scientists have questioned this view.

In New Zealand, for instance, Stacey found only a small positive correlation between attitudes and self-reported alcohol consumption (Gregson & Stacey, 1981). Furthermore, there was no evidence of any benefits in focusing on attitude change rather than on economic incentives to control alcohol use (e.g. avoiding fines, increasing taxes). Some critics have seen this as a crunch question for social psychology. If attitude is a crucial concept, and yet its measures cannot relate to what people actually do, then the entire enterprise of studying attitudes looks shaky. It is interesting that an early study of ethnic attitudes by LaPiere (1934) revealed a glaring inconsistency between what people do and what they say (see Box 5.1; see also Chapter 10).

Following LaPiere's provocative study, dozens of researchers used more sophisticated methods to study the attitude–behaviour relationship. Many obtained relatively low correspondence between questionnaire measures of attitudes and measures of overt behaviour. After reviewing this research, Wicker (1969) concluded that the correlation between attitudes and behaviours is seldom as high as 0.30 (which, when squared, indicates that only 9% of the variability in a behaviour is accounted for by an attitude). Wicker, in fact, found that the average correlation between attitudes and behaviour

BOX 5.1   Do attitudes really predict behaviour?

The sociologist LaPiere (1934) was interested in the difference between prejudiced attitudes towards Chinese in general and discriminatory behaviours towards a Chinese couple in particular. In the early 1930s anti-Asian prejudice was known to be quite strong among Americans. LaPiere embarked on a 10 000-mile sightseeing tour of the United States, accompanied by two young Chinese friends. They visited 66 hotels, caravan parks and tourist homes and were served in 184 restaurants. As they went from place to place, LaPiere was concerned that his friends might not be accepted but, as it turned out, they were refused service only once.

Six months after their trip, LaPiere sent a questionnaire to all the places visited, asking, 'Will you accept members of the Chinese race as guests in your establishment?' Of the 81 restaurants and 47 hotels that replied, 92% said that they would *not* accept Chinese customers! Only 1% said they would accept them and the remainder checked 'Uncertain, depends on circumstances'. These written replies from the erstwhile hosts directly contradicted the way they had actually behaved.

This study was not, of course, scientifically designed—perhaps the people who responded to the letters were not those who dealt face-to-face with the Chinese couple; they may have responded differently in writing if they had been told that the couple was educated and well dressed; attitudes may have changed in the six months between the two measures. Nevertheless, the problem that LaPiere had unearthed provided an early challenge to the validity of the concept of attitude.

was only 0.15. This view was seized on during the 1970s as prime evidence that the attitude concept is worthless, as it has little predictive power. (Abelson, 1972). However, attitudes are still being researched (see Fazio & Olson, 2003) and the field commands two chapters of this book.

What emerged later was that attitudes and overt behaviour are not related in a one-to-one fashion. There are conditions that promote or disrupt the correspondence between an attitude and a behaviour—for example, attitude–behaviour consistency can vary according to whether:

- an attitude is more rather than less accessible (Doll & Ajzen, 1992—see below);
- an attitude is expressed publicly, say in a group, or privately, such as when responding to a questionnaire (Smith & Stasson, 2000);
- an individual's identification with a relevant ingroup is high or low (Smith & Stasson, 2000).

Not all classes of social behaviour can be accurately predicted from verbally expressed attitudes. We look now at some theoretical developments that cast new light on the difficulties of forming a direct equation between attitudes and behaviour.

BELIEFS, INTENTIONS AND BEHAVIOUR

According to Fishbein (1967a, 1967b, 1971), the basic ingredient of an attitude is affect, a position that follows Thurstone's (1931) early definition. However, a score based entirely on a unidimensional, bipolar evaluative scale (such as good/bad) does not predict reliably how a person will later behave. To do so depends on accounting for the interaction between attitudes, beliefs and behavioural intentions, and the connections of all these with subsequent actions.

In this equation we need to establish both how strong and how valuable an individual's beliefs are: some beliefs will carry more weight than others in relation to the final act. For example, the strength or weakness of an individual's religious convictions may be pivotal in their decision-making processes regarding moral behaviours. Without this information, trying to predict an outcome for a given individual must be a hit-or-miss affair.

Consider the example in Table 5.1. A young, heterosexually active man might believe, strongly or not, that certain things are true about two forms of contraception, the pill and the condom. *Belief strength* (or expectancy) has a probability estimate ranging from 0 to 1 regarding the truth; for example, he may hold a very strong belief (0.90) that the pill is a most reliable method of birth control. Reliability of a contraceptive is a 'good' thing, so his *evaluation* (or value) of the pill is +2, say, on a 5-point scale ranging from +2 to −2. These components interact, producing a final rating of

Attitudes and behaviour: Predicting election outcomes from people's attitudes can be surprisingly unreliable. One notable failure was an incorrect prediction of the 1993 Australian federal election.

+1.80. (We can note here that Fishbein's view incorporates the idea that people can perform cognitive algebra; see also Chapter 2.)

Next, the young man might be fairly sure (0.70) that the condom is less reliable (–1), a rating of –0.70. Likewise, he thinks that using a condom is potentially embarrassing in a sexual encounter. His further belief that using a condom has no known side effects is not sufficient to offset the effects of the other two beliefs. Check the hypothetical algebra in Table 5.1. Consequently, the young man's intention to use a condom, should he possess one, may be quite low (perhaps he hopes that the women who cross his path use the pill!). Only by having all this information could we be fairly confident about predicting his future behaviour.

This approach to prediction also offers a method of measurement, the expectancy-value technique (to which we return in a later section). In subsequent work with his colleague Ajzen, Fishbein developed the *theory of reasoned action* to link beliefs to intentions to behaviour (we return to this model later). Fishbein and Ajzen's work was a major step forward in understanding issues that had previously complicated the overall relationship between attitudes and behaviours. Predictions can be clarified when the inherent links are brought to the surface. Furthermore, behavioural predictions can be much improved if the measures of attitudes are specific rather than general.

Specific attitudes

Ajzen and Fishbein's view is that the success of any attempt to predict the way in which we behave is determined by asking us whether we would perform a given act or series of acts. The key lies in using questions that are quite specific rather than ones that deal with generalities.

Ajzen and Fishbein argued that much previous attitude research had suffered from either trying to predict specific behaviours from general attitudes or vice versa, so that low correlations were to be expected. This is, in essence, what LaPiere did. An example of a specific attitude predicting a specific behaviour would be that attitudes towards a psychology test should predict the extent to which students study for that test. In contrast, an example of a general attitude predicting a general class of behaviours would be attitudes towards psychology as a whole, predicting fairly well the tendency to engage in behaviours generally relevant to learning more about psychology, such as reading magazine articles. How interested you are in psychology generally is not likely to be predictive of how well you prepare for a specific psychology exam.

In a two-year longitudinal study by Davidson and Jacard (1979), women's attitudes towards birth control were measured at different levels of specificity and used as predictors of their actual use of the contraceptive pill. The measures, ranging from very general to very specific, were correlated with actual pill use (correlations in parentheses): 'Attitude towards birth control' (0.08), 'Attitude towards birth control pills' (0.32), 'Attitude towards using birth control pills' (0.53) and 'Attitude towards using birth control pills during the next two years' (0.57). Thus, this last measure was the variable most highly correlated with actual use of the contraceptive pill, and indicates quite clearly that the closer the question was to the actual behaviour, the more accurately the behaviour was predicted. (See Kraus (1995) for a **meta-analysis** of attitudes as predictors of behaviour.)

General attitudes

Fishbein and Ajzen (1975) also argued that we can predict behaviour from attitudes at a more general level. To do so, however, requires that a **multiple-act criterion** be established. This is a general behavioural index based on an average or combination of various specific behaviours. General attitudes usually predict multiple-act

---

TABLE 5.1 A young man's hypothetical attitude towards contraceptive use: The strength and value of his beliefs

Attribute	MAN'S BELIEF ABOUT WOMAN USING PILL			MAN'S BELIEF ABOUT MAN USING CONDOM		
	Strength of belief	Value of belief	Result	Strength of belief	Value of obelief	Result
Reliability	0.90	× +2	= +1.80	0.70	× –1	= –0.70
Embarrassment	1.00	× +2	= +2.00	0.80	× –2	= –1.60
Side effects	0.10	× –1	= –0.10	1.00	× +2	= +2.00
Outcome			= +3.70			= –0.30

Note: The strength of a belief in this example is the probability (from 0 to 1) that a person thinks that it is true. The value of a belief is an evaluation on a bipolar scale (in this case, ranging from +2 to –2).

criteria much better than they predict single acts because single acts are usually affected by many factors: for example, the specific behaviour of participating in a paper-recycling program on a given day is a function of any number of factors, even the weather. Yet such a person may claim to be 'environmentally conscious'—a general attitude. While environmental attitudes are no doubt one determinant of this behaviour, they are not the only determinant and perhaps not even the major determinant.

Reasoned action

The ideas outlined so far were brought together in a general model dealing with the links between attitude and behaviour—the **theory of reasoned action** (TRA) (Ajzen & Fishbein, 1980; Fishbein & Ajzen, 1974). The model comprised three broad processes of beliefs, intention and action, and included the following components:

- subjective norm—a product of what the individual perceives to be others' beliefs. Significant others provide a guide about 'what is the proper thing to do';
- attitude towards the behaviour—a product of the individual's beliefs about the target behaviour, and also of how these beliefs are evaluated (refer back to the cognitive algebra in Table 5.1). Note that this is an attitude towards behaviour (such as taking a birth control pill in Davidson and Jacard's study), not towards the object (such as the pill itself);
- behavioural intention—an internal declaration to act;
- behaviour—the action performed.

Usually, an action will be performed if: (a) the person's attitude is favourable; (b) the social norm is also favourable; and (c) the level of perceived behavioural control is high (discussed below in relation to the role of volition). In early tests of the theory, Fishbein and Coombs (1974) and Fishbein and Feldman (1963) gave participants a series of statements about the attributes of various attitude objects—for example, political candidates. The participants estimated *expectancies*—that is, how likely it was that the object (candidate) possessed the various attributes—as well as giving the attributes a *value*. These expectancies and values were then used to predict the participants' feelings towards the attitude object, assessed by asking the participants how much they liked or disliked that object.

The correlation between the scores and the participants' feelings was high, pointing to some promise for the model.

Other research reported that voting intentions:

- correlated 0.80 with how people voted in the 1976 American presidential election (Fishbein, Ajzen, & Hinkle, 1980);

- correlated 0.89 with how they voted in a referendum on nuclear power (Fishbein, Bowman, Thomas, Jacard, & Ajzen, 1980).

Planned behaviour: The role of volition

The theory of reasoned action emphasises not only the rationality of human behaviour but also the belief that the target action is under the person's conscious control: for example, 'I know I can stop smoking if I really want to'. However, some actions are less under people's control than others. Consequently, the basic model was extended by Ajzen (1989) to emphasise the role of volition. Perceived behavioural control is the extent to which the person believes it is easy or difficult to perform an act. The process of coming to such a decision can include consideration of past experiences, as well as present obstacles that the person may envisage.

Ajzen and Madden (1986), for example, found that students, not surprisingly, want to achieve A-grades in their courses: A-grades are highly valued by the students (attitude) and they are the grades that their family and friends want them to score (subjective norm). However, any prediction of actually scoring an A will be faulty

Planned behaviour: The promotion of a health practice, such as breast self-examination, requires that a woman believes that she knows what to do and what to look for.

unless the students' perceptions of their own abilities are taken into account. Ajzen has argued that perceived behavioural control can act either on the behavioural intention or directly on the behaviour itself. He referred to this modified model as the **theory of planned behaviour** (TPB). The two theories are not in conflict. The concepts and the way in which they are linked in each theory are shown in Figure 5.3.

In one study, Beck and Ajzen (1991) started with students' self-reports of the extent to which they had been dishonest in the past. The behaviours sampled included exam cheating, shoplifting, and telling lies to avoid completing written assignments—actions that were quite often reported. They found that measuring the perception of control that students thought they had over these actions improved the accuracy of prediction of future actions and, to some extent, the actual carrying out of the act. This was most successful in the case of cheating, which may well be planned in a more deliberate way than shoplifting or lying.

In another study, Madden, Ellen and Ajzen (1992) measured students' perceptions of control in relation to nine behaviours. These ranged from 'getting a good night's sleep' (quite hard to control) to 'taking vitamin supplements' (quite easy to control). The results were calculated to compare predictive power by squaring the correlation coefficient between each of the two predictors (sleep and vitamins) and each of the outcomes (intentions and actions). Perceived control improved the

prediction accuracy for both intentions and actions. This improvement was substantially effective in predicting the action itself. These effects are evident in the steep gradient of the two lower lines in Figure 5.4.

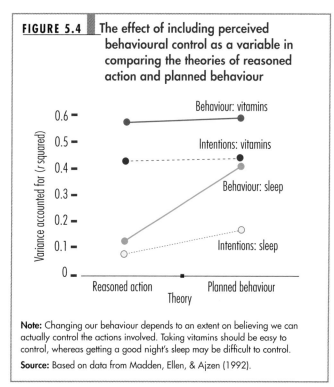

FIGURE 5.4 The effect of including perceived behavioural control as a variable in comparing the theories of reasoned action and planned behaviour

Note: Changing our behaviour depends to an extent on believing we can actually control the actions involved. Taking vitamins should be easy to control, whereas getting a good night's sleep may be difficult to control.

Source: Based on data from Madden, Ellen, & Ajzen (1992).

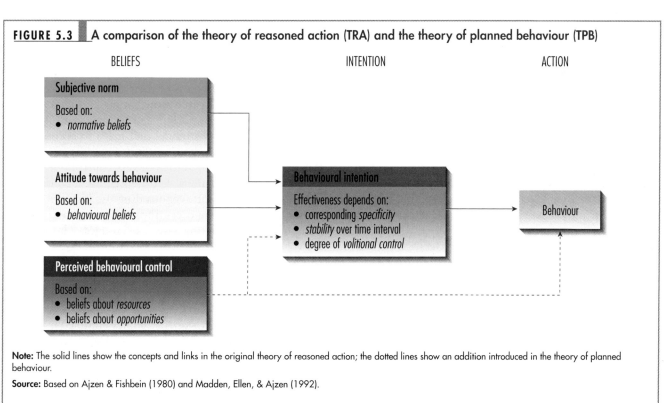

FIGURE 5.3 A comparison of the theory of reasoned action (TRA) and the theory of planned behaviour (TPB)

Note: The solid lines show the concepts and links in the original theory of reasoned action; the dotted lines show an addition introduced in the theory of planned behaviour.

Source: Based on Ajzen & Fishbein (1980) and Madden, Ellen, & Ajzen (1992).

Research in Australia has applied features of both models in understanding people's attitudes towards their health. Terry and her colleagues at the University of Queensland (Terry, Gallois, & McCamish, 1993) have shown how Fishbein and Ajzen's concepts can be applied to the study of safe-sex behaviour as a response to the threat of contracting HIV (see Box 5.2). Specifically, the target behaviours include monogamous relationships, non-penetrative sex and the use of condoms. All the variables shown in Figure 5.3 can be applied in this setting.

The particular variable of perceived behavioural control probably needs to be accounted for—the scenario envisages being with a sex partner, where neither individual may be fully confident of controlling the wishes of the other person. A practical question that may need to be examined, for example, is the degree of control a woman might perceive she has about whether a condom will be used in her next sexual encounter. (See Sheeran and Taylor (1999) for a meta-analysis of studies predicting condom use from people's declared intentions.)

In extensive research in the United Kingdom, Parker, Manstead and Stradling (1995) applied TPB to the study of driver behaviour. Their concern was the predictability of intention to commit driving violations. Nearly 600 British drivers were interviewed and questioned about their attitudes and intentions regarding three driving scenarios: cutting in, reckless weaving, and overtaking on the inside lane on a motorway (illegal in the UK). Questionnaires assessed what drivers believed would be their reaction in each situation (belief-based measure).

Results found that adding the belief-based measure to TRA, to become TPB, significantly enhanced the predictive value of the former, in that significant correlations were found between participants' perceived control over their driving behaviours and their attitudes to committing each of the three driving violations.

In critically evaluating both TRA and TPB, Manstead and Parker (1995) argued that the inclusion of 'perceived behavioural control' in TPB is an improvement on the original theory. At the same time, they point to problems of measurement in TPB research and conclude that there is scope for development of the model.

In contrast to both TRA and TPB models, some researchers have suggested that other variables may play a role in determining action, such as people's moral

BOX 5.2   Reasoned action, planned behaviour and safe sex

TRA AND TPB ARE THEORIES THAT HAVE PROVED USEFUL IN UNDERSTANDING AND PROMOTING RESPONSIBLE SEX BEHAVIOUR

More and more, social psychologists have turned their attention to promoting health practices such as avoiding the abuse of alcohol, tobacco and other substances; promoting dental hygiene; vaccinating against infectious diseases; participating in cervical smear tests; and using sun-screen products (see also Chapter 6).

Another sphere of application has been the promotion of contraceptive practices to avoid unwanted pregnancies. In recent years, health professionals have shown intense concern about the spread of HIV and the deadly spectre of AIDS. (We noted in Chapter 2 that some people tend to underestimate the riskiness of their sexual practices.)

In this context, social psychologists have mounted a concerted program of research aimed at promoting condom use, safe sex and monogamous relationships. Several researchers have explicitly recognised Fishbein and Ajzen's (Fishbein & Ajzen, 1974; Ajzen & Fishbein, 1980) theory of reasoned action as a model that helps to account for variability in people's willingness to practise safe sex (see Terry, Gallois, & McCamish, 1993). One feature of this work has been to focus on establishing the degree to which people feel they can actually exert control over their health. A woman with this sense of control is more likely to wear a seat belt, examine her breasts, use a contraceptive, have sex in an exclusive relationship, and discuss her partner's sexual and intravenous drug use history.

Apart from a sense of control, other factors such as perceptions of condom proposers (those who initiate condom use), as well as expectations and experience of safe sex, are implicated in initiating safe sex (Hodges, Klaaren, & Wheatley, 2000). Coupled with these factors, the cultural dimension should also be considered in the gender and sexuality equation, especially in a multicultural society. For example, Conley, Collins and Garcia (2000) found that Chinese Americans reacted more negatively than European Americans to the female condom proposer. Furthermore, Japanese Americans perceived the female condom proposer to be less sexually attractive than did the Chinese or European Americans (see also Chapter 16).

A problem with practising safe sex with one's partner is that it is not a behaviour that comes completely under one individual's volitional control, whereas going for a jog usually is. The theory of reasoned action, together with its extension, the theory of planned behaviour (see Figure 5.3), provides a framework for psychologists and other health professionals to target particular variables that have the potential to encourage safe sex, as well as other health behaviour.

values (Gorsuch & Ortbergh, 1983; Pagel & Davidson, 1984; Schwartz, 1977). For example, if someone wanted to find out whether we would donate money to charity, they would do well to find out whether acting charitably is a priority in our lives. Despite these suggestions, Madden, Ellen and Ajzen (1992) have argued that there is little evidence to show that additional variables improve prediction. Both TRA and TPB models, as well as other related psychological theories such as **protection motivation theory** (PMT), are increasingly applied to account for how protective health behaviours can be initiated and maintained and how risky behaviours can be avoided (see Box 5.3 and Figure 5.5).

Issues to which these models have been applied include HIV prevention (Smith & Stasson, 2000), condom use and safer-sex behaviour (Sheeran & Taylor, 1999; Boldero, Sanitioso, & Brain, 1999), alcohol consumption (Conner, Warren, Close, & Sparks, 1999) and smoking (Godin, Valois, Lepage, & Desharnais, 1992). However, the models are not restricted to the health

domain. For example, Fox-Cardamone, Hinkle and Hogue (2000) used TPB to examine anti-nuclear behaviour. Anti-nuclear attitudes emerged as significant predictors of either anti-nuclear intentions or behaviours. All three theories share the idea that motivation towards protection results from a perceived threat and the desire to avoid potential negative outcomes (Floyd, Prentice-Dunn, & Rogers, 2000).

A reservation that can be applied to both TRA and TPB is their assumption that attitudes are rational and that socially significant behaviours are intentional, reasoned and planned. This may not always be true. (How would you apply the theories covered above to answer the second focus question?)

ATTITUDE ACCESSIBILITY

We have noted that many models of attitude feature a cognitive component. Beliefs are seen as the building blocks of the more general concept of attitude. Even other modern approaches that stress an evaluative

---

BOX 5.3   Can we protect ourselves against major diseases?

Cardiovascular disease and cancer were the leading causes of death in the early 1990s, according to American health statistics, a trend that is current in most affluent Western countries. It is already known that preventive behaviour for both diseases includes routine medical examinations, regular blood pressure readings, exercising aerobically for at least 20 minutes three times per week, eating a well-balanced diet that is low in salt and fat, maintaining a healthy weight level and choosing not to smoke. A major challenge to health psychologists is to find a robust model of health promotion, particularly of the prevention of these major killer diseases.

According to Floyd, Prentice-Dunn and Rogers (2000), protection motivation theory has emerged as such a model. The model was developed initially to explain the effects of fear appeals on maladaptive health attitudes and behaviour (Rogers, 1975, cited in Floyd, Prentice-Dunn, & Rogers, 2000) and was derived from Fishbein's theories of expectancy–value and reasoned action (also covered in this chapter). Other components built into protection motivation theory included the effects of intrinsic and extrinsic reward (related to social learning theory) and Bandura's (1986, 1992) concept of **self-efficacy**.

From their meta-analysis of research based on 65 studies and more than 20 health issues, Floyd and his colleagues argue that adaptive intentions and behaviour are facilitated by:

- an increase in the perceived severity of a health threat;
- the vulnerability of the individual to that threat;
- the perceived effectiveness of taking protective action;
- self-efficacy.

In considering why Joe, for example, might either continue to smoke or quit, protection motivation theory includes two mediating cognitive processes:

1. *Threat appraisal*—smoking has intrinsic rewards (e.g. taste in mouth, nicotine effect) and extrinsic rewards (e.g. his friends think it's cool). These are weighed up against the extent to which Joe thinks there is a severe risk to his health (e.g. after reading the latest brochure in his doctor's waiting room) and that he is vulnerable (e.g. because a close relative who smoked died of lung cancer).
2. *Coping appraisal*—Joe takes into account the factors of response efficacy (whether nicotine replacement therapy might work) and self-efficacy (whether he thinks he can adhere to the regime).

The trade-off when Joe compares his appraisals of threat and coping determines his level of protection motivation and whether he decides to quit smoking (see Figure 5.5).

FIGURE 5.5 | Mediating cognitive processes in protection motivation theory

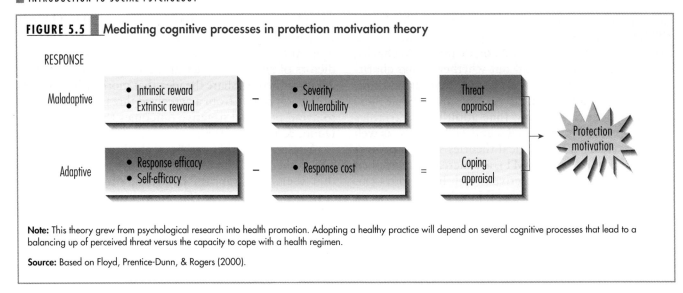

Note: This theory grew from psychological research into health promotion. Adopting a healthy practice will depend on several cognitive processes that lead to a balancing up of perceived threat versus the capacity to cope with a health regimen.

Source: Based on Floyd, Prentice-Dunn, & Rogers (2000).

component agree on one matter: attitudes are represented in memory (Olson & Zanna, 1993).

Accessible attitudes are those that can be recalled from memory more easily and are expressed more quickly (Eagly & Chaiken, 1998). They can exert a strong influence on behaviour (Fazio, 1986) and are associated with improved attitude–behaviour consistency (Doll & Ajzen, 1992). They are also more stable, more selective in judging relevant information and more resistant to change (Fazio, 1995). There is some interesting evidence that affective evaluations are faster than cognitive evaluations, suggesting that they are more accessible in memory (Verplanker, Hofstee, & Janssen, 1998).

Most studies of attitude accessibility have focused on highly accessible attitudes, drawing from Fazio's (1995) model of attitudes as evaluative associations with the object in memory. The rationale behind Fazio's model is that the degree to which an attitude is 'handy', or functional and useful for the individual, depends on the extent of automatic activation of the attitude from memory. Simultaneously, the likelihood of automatic activation depends on the strength of the object-evaluation association (Bargh, Chaiken, Govender, & Pratto, 1992). Thus, the idea is that strong object-evaluation associations are truly functional, for example, in facilitating decision-making.

Although the theoretical conceptualisation is intuitively appealing and supported by some research (e.g. Fazio, Ledbetter, & Towles-Schwen, 2000), there is also some evidence that implicit measures (as object-evaluation associations) correlate weakly with explicit self-reports (Hilton & Karpinski, 2000).

In addition to facilitating decision-making, accessible attitudes orient visual attention and categorisation processes in useful ways (Roskos-Ewoldsen & Fazio, 1992; Smith, Fazio, & Cejka, 1996) and free up resources for coping with the stresses an individual is experiencing (Fazio & Powell, 1997). To demonstrate the orienting effect of accessible attitudes on categorisation, Smith, Fazio and Cejka (1996) showed that, when choosing from a number of possible categories to describe an object, people were more likely to select one that was more accessible. For example, when statements dealing with dairy products had been rehearsed, yoghurt was more likely to cue as a *dairy product*. However, if attitudes toward health food had been experimentally enhanced—and therefore made more accessible in memory—yoghurt was more likely to cue as a *health food* (Eagly & Chaiken, 1998).

Fazio's studies confirmed earlier findings that perceptions of stimuli will probably be biased in the direction of an individual's attitude (Lambert, Solomon, & Watson, 1949; Zanna, 1993). However, he has gone further to demonstrate that costs are associated with highly accessible attitudes. We have noted that accessible attitudes remain stable over time. However, Fazio, Ledbetter and Towles-Schwen (2000) have shown that if the object of an attitude changes, then accessible attitudes to that object may become dysfunctional for the individual. Accessibility can actually produce insensitivity to change. Consequently, an individual who feels negatively about a particular attitude object may not be able to detect whether the object has changed for the better, or perhaps for the worse (see Box 5.4).

ATTITUDE STRENGTH

Strong attitudes come to mind more readily and exert more influence over behaviour than weak attitudes. Fazio argued that attitudes are evaluative associations with objects, which makes his approach a one-component model. Associations can vary in strength from (a) 'no link' (i.e. a non-attitude) to (b) a weak link to (c) a strong link. Only an association that is strong allows the **automatic activation** of an attitude (Fazio,

BOX 5.4 Accessible attitudes can be costly

There may be costs associated with more accessible attitudes. Fazio and his colleagues (Fazio, Ledbetter, & Towles-Schwen, 2000) tested this idea using computer-based morphing. The experimental manipulation involved modifying the facial features of human images by morphing. The dependent variable was detection of change to a human image by the participants.

Fazio conducted several experiments using participants whose attitudes were highly accessible (HA) or less accessible (LA). HA attitudes were induced through rehearsal using a 'morph' or a modified human image. HA participants took longer to reach the same level of accuracy as LA participants in detecting a change in the original unmodified image. They also had a higher error rate when required to respond quickly to brief stimulus exposures. These effects were restricted to morphs closely resembling the original and thus likely to automatically activate an attitude associated with the original. Therefore, HA participants had an initial tendency to judge the stimulus as unchanged, a process called *perceptual assimilation*.

This shows that stimulus perception is biased in the direction of an individual's attitudes, although with sufficient time and motivation they can overcome this bias. Without time-consuming effort, HA participants made more errors. Finally, even when change was detected by these participants, it was still biased: they were less likely to perceive the morph as sufficiently different from the original, but they were more likely to perceive it as a different photo of the same image than as a different human image altogether.

Sanbonmatsu, Powell, & Kardes, 1986; Fazio, Blascovich, & Driscoll, 1992; Fazio, 1995; Fazio & Powell, 1997; see Figure 5.6).

Direct experience of an object and having a vested interest in it (i.e. something with a strong effect on your life) make the attitude more accessible and increase its effect on behaviour. For example, we can assume that people who have had a nuclear reactor built in their neighbourhood will have stronger and more clearly defined attitudes regarding the safety of nuclear reactors. As a result, such people's behaviour may be motivated by their attitudes—they may be more involved in protests or more likely to move house.

As another example, consider the attitudes that people might hold towards doctor-assisted suicide. Haddock, Rothman, Reber and Schwarz (1999) pointed to the impact of subjective experiences on reports of the certainty, intensity and importance of people's attitudes to this form of dying. As subjective experience with the issue increased, the corresponding attitude about doctor-assisted suicide became stronger (i.e. more certain, intense and important).

The more often you think about an attitude, the more likely it is to resurface and influence your behaviour, leading to easier decision-making (Fazio, Blascovich, & Driscoll, 1992). Powell and Fazio (1984) were able to increase attitude accessibility simply by asking participants on six different occasions what their attitude was, as opposed to asking them only once.

Accessing general attitudes can affect behaviour in specific situations. If the general attitude is never accessed, it cannot affect behaviour. Therefore, the activation step of Fazio's model is critical, as only activated attitudes can guide subsequent information processing

Attitude strength: If your home had been bulldozed how do you think you would feel?

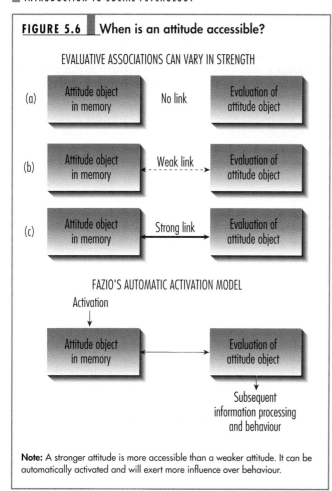

FIGURE 5.6 ▌ When is an attitude accessible?

EVALUATIVE ASSOCIATIONS CAN VARY IN STRENGTH

(a) Attitude object in memory — No link — Evaluation of attitude object

(b) Attitude object in memory — Weak link → Evaluation of attitude object

(c) Attitude object in memory ↔ Strong link → Evaluation of attitude object

FAZIO'S AUTOMATIC ACTIVATION MODEL

Activation

Attitude object in memory → Evaluation of attitude object → Subsequent information processing and behaviour

Note: A stronger attitude is more accessible than a weaker attitude. It can be automatically activated and will exert more influence over behaviour.

and behaviour. Think of a sports coach **priming** a team by asking the question 'Who's going to win?', demanding a shouted response of 'We are!' and repeating this scenario a number of times before the game begins.

Direct experience

In addition to its strength, the accessibility of an attitude is a function of direct experience with the attitude object. Attitudes formed through actually experiencing the attitude object show more consistent relationships to behaviour than those formed less directly (Regan & Fazio, 1977; Doll & Ajzen, 1992). For example, a student's attitude towards psychology experiments is more likely to predict future participation if that student has participated in several already than if she has only read about them (Fazio & Zanna, 1978). Another example: your attitude towards UFOs is far less likely to predict your actual behaviour, should you ever encounter one (!), than your attitude towards lecturers is likely to predict your lecture-room behaviour. Likewise, it would be nice to think that those people who had been caught driving with excess blood alcohol levels would be less likely to drink and drive in the future. Unfortunately, this is not always the case.

Therefore, although the 'direct experience' variable appeals as a factor of importance, establishing its actual effectiveness is a difficult task. We consider the role of direct experience again in the context of attitude formation.

Apart from attitude accessibility and direct experience with the attitude object, issues such as attitude salience, ambivalence, consistency between affect and cognition, how extreme one's position is, affective intensity, certainty, importance, latitudes of rejection (tolerance of outlying opinion) and non-commitment are common themes in recent attitudinal research under the general topic of 'attitude strength'.

Not surprisingly, Krosnick, Boninger, Chuang, Berent and Carnot (1993) postulated that attitude strength may in fact consist of many related constructs rather than a single one. They confirmed this using a complex statistical method (multitrait-multimethod confirmatory factor analysis) to show that, although some dimensions of attitude strength are strongly related, most are not.

MODERATOR VARIABLES

Despite the difficulties of predicting single acts from general attitudes, many researchers persevere in the task, typically adding moderator variables to the attitude–behaviour equation. A **moderator variable** qualifies an otherwise simple research hypothesis, with the aim of improving prediction. Such variables include the situation, personality, habit, sense of control and direct experience. It appears that a moderating effect may also originate from the functions of attitudes. Maio and Olson (1994) found that the attitude–behaviour link was stronger for people with value-expressive attitudes (where the function is to express one's central values and self-concept) than for those with utilitarian attitudes (where the function is to maximise rewards and minimise punishments).

Ironically, moderator variables may turn out to be more powerful predictors of an action than the more general, underlying attitude. We consider two cases below.

Situational variables

Aspects of the situation, or context, can cause people to act inconsistently with their attitudes (Calder & Ross, 1973). Furthermore, it appears that weak attitudes are more susceptible to context (Lavine, Huff, Wagner, & Sweeney, 1998). A situational variable that has been widely studied is the social norm. For instance, if university students expect each other to dress in jeans and casual clothes, these expectations are a norm for proper student attire.

Norms have always been considered important in attitude–behaviour relations, but they have generally been separated from attitudes: attitudes are in here (private, internalised cognitive constructs), while norms are out there (public, external pressures representing cumulative expectations of others).

Deborah Terry and her associates at the University of Queensland have challenged both this view of norms and the separation of norms from attitudes. They suggest instead that attitudes are more likely to express themselves as behaviours if the attitudes (and associated behaviour) are normative properties of a social group with which people identify (Terry & Hogg, 1996; 2001; Terry, Hogg, & Duck, 1999; Terry, Hogg, & White, 2000).

Terry and colleagues draw on social identity theory (see Chapter 11) as a basis for their research. They argue that, in circumstances where membership of a particular social group becomes salient as a basis of self-definition, the attitudes and behaviours defining membership (i.e. the group norms) come to govern our own behaviour. Attitudes express themselves as behaviour if they are normative and when group membership is salient.

To test this idea, Terry and Hogg (1996) conducted two longitudinal questionnaire studies of students' intentions to take regular exercise and to protect themselves from the sun. These intentions were stronger among participants who identified strongly with a student peer group that they judged was guided by such norms (Figure 5.7).

Personality variables

There is a fundamental conflict between explanations that favour situational variables when contrasted with personality variables—a conflict that extends well beyond the field of attitude research (Ross & Nisbett, 1991). Mischel (1968), for example, argued that situational characteristics were more reliable predictors of behaviours than were personality traits (see also the low correlations reported between personality measures and leadership in Chapter 9).

Yet Bem and Allen (1974) and Vaughan (1977) have shown that people who were consistent in their *answers* on a personality scale were more likely to be consistent in their *behaviour* across a variety of relevant situations than were people who gave variable answers. For example, a high scorer on an extraversion–introversion scale would be more likely to behave in an extraverted manner, and be a low scorer in an introverted manner, across different social settings. On the other hand, those who were variable (mid-range scorers) in their answers on the scale would not behave consistently.

It has also been proposed that people's *habits* and their *degree of control* over the behaviour in question must be considered (Langer, 1975; Petty & Cacioppo, 1981; Triandis, 1980). Triandis (1977) proposed a model similar to Fishbein and Ajzen's, including a habit factor that reflected the number of times a particular

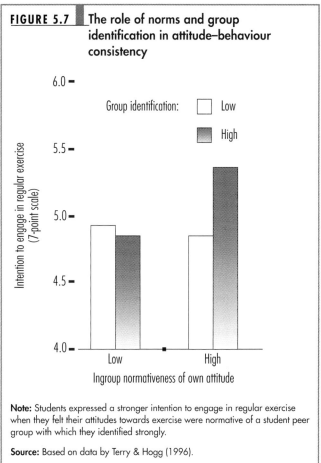

FIGURE 5.7 The role of norms and group identification in attitude–behaviour consistency

Note: Students expressed a stronger intention to engage in regular exercise when they felt their attitudes towards exercise were normative of a student peer group with which they identified strongly.

Source: Based on data by Terry & Hogg (1996).

action had been performed by the person in the past. Habits are behaviours that are automatic in certain situations and occur without thinking. Smoking, for instance, is habitual for many people and is often due partly to a physiological and/or psychological dependency. Thus, the behaviour of smokers may bear little relationship to their attitudes towards cigarettes. In an American national survey, 72% of smokers agreed that smoking was one of the causes of lung cancer, and 71% agreed that 'cigarette smoking causes disease and death' (Oskamp, 1984). Likewise, some people living in post-apartheid South Africa may have difficulty adopting new racial attitudes, despite logical and legal arguments, due to habits formed over many years.

Therefore, habit is an important variable to be taken into account when considering attitudes and may confound the otherwise simple relationship between attitudes and behaviours, especially in terms of cognitive dissonance theory (discussed in Chapter 6).

Mood as a moderator variable may be considered both a situational and a personality variable. Smith and Stasson (2000) at Flinders University, in Adelaide, examined the effects of trial-induced mood on jurors' processing and decision-making. They found that being sad did not affect a juror's judgment, despite an increase in irrelevant thought. However, angry jurors actually reported more irrelevant thoughts, detected fewer inconsistencies in the witness's testimony and judged the defendant more harshly.

Other moderator variables important to consider in the attitude–behaviour equation are *cognitive biases*, such as the self–other discrepancy (see also Chapter 4). Paglia and Room (1999) examined people's expectancies regarding drinking alcohol and their policy attitudes towards the control of alcohol availability. They found that support for alcohol control is determined partly by what people expect from drinking, both their own and others' drinking. However, the results also show a distinct self–other discrepancy, where people are more likely to expect alcohol to have a greater effect on others than on themselves. Furthermore, the self–other discrepancy bias was shown to be the strongest predictor of favouring tighter alcohol controls.

This study is a useful insight into the structure of public opinion on alcohol policy.

Forming attitudes

We have noted that attitudes are learned rather than innate. The learning of attitudes is an integral part of the socialisation process (Fishbein & Ajzen, 1975; McGuire, 1969; Oskamp, 1977) and may occur through direct experiences or vicariously through interactions with others, or be a product of cognitive processes. Social psychologists have generally confined their work to understanding the basic psychological processes that underlie **attitude formation** rather than exploring how particular classes of attitudes develop. The study of these processes most often involves laboratory experiments, rather than survey research or public opinion findings.

BEHAVIOURAL APPROACHES
Effects of direct experience

Many of the attitudes people hold are the products of direct experience with attitude objects. People encounter an attitude object and have a positive or negative experience which, at least partly, shapes their attitude towards that object (e.g. having a negative attitude towards dogs in general after being bitten by one as a child). Traumatic or frightening experiences can be important in the formation of attitudes (Oskamp, 1977; Sargant, 1957). Several explanations of the effect of personal experiences on attitude formation have been offered: mere exposure, classical conditioning, operant conditioning, social learning theory and self-perception theory.

Fazio and Zanna (1981) found that the attitudes of students forced to live in makeshift quarters during a campus housing shortage were more predictive of their subsequent behaviour concerning the housing shortage than the attitudes of students who lacked such direct experience.

Fishbein and Ajzen (1975) have proposed that direct experience can affect attitudes towards an object by providing people with information about the attributes of a particular attitude object. According to the expectancy-value model of attitude structure (see below), this information leads to beliefs that will influence how much people like or dislike the attitude object. Direct experiences that are especially negative or traumatic make certain beliefs more salient than others. For example, if your first visit to the dentist is painful, you may conclude that dentists hurt people.

If you attend rallies or meetings to ban mineral exploration in forest reserves, you might conclude that you are anti-mining, but one component of your attitude might have changed since the first rally: you might feel even more strongly opposed to mining. This is what Zajonc (1968) termed the **mere exposure effect**. He proposed that mere exposure to an object (the number of times one has encountered it) affects our evaluation of that object. Most people are probably aware of this effect. The first time you hear a new song on the radio, for instance, you may find you neither strongly like nor dislike it. Repetition is likely to strengthen your response in one direction or the other. Repeated exposure does, however, have diminishing returns. In a meta-analysis of the exposure effect, Bornstein (1989) found that increased liking for photos of people levelled off after about ten exposures.

Mere exposure has most impact when we lack information about an issue. This is a reason why standing MPs, for example, often have an advantage over other candidates in an election, as their names are probably more familiar. Consider the importance of experience in attitude formation and subsequent behaviour in the context of politics. Would you want a minister of education who had no experience of being a tertiary student making policy decisions regarding your education?

Classical conditioning

Through repeated association, a formerly neutral stimulus can elicit a reaction that was previously elicited only by another stimulus. For example, children may initially be indifferent to politics, but later vote as young adults for a party after years of exposure to a parent who has been an enthusiastic supporter—a classically conditioned response has become the basis of a subsequent political attitude. Some have suggested that classical conditioning underlies the formation of a wide variety of attitudes (Staats & Staats, 1957; Zanna, Kiesler, & Pilkonis, 1970).

Classical conditioning: Pleasant surroundings put us in a good mood which we associate with the people present, increasing our liking for them.

Classical conditioning can be a particularly powerful and insidious form of attitude learning. Janis, Kaye and Kirschner (1965) demonstrated the power of contextual stimuli by reinforcing some participants with soft drinks while they were reading a persuasive message. Those given soft drinks were more persuaded by what they read than those who were not. Galizio and Hendrick (1972) arranged for their participants to listen to pleasant guitar music as an accompaniment to persuasive messages presented in the form of folk songs. The songs proved more persuasive when accompanied by guitar music than without.

The reasonable interpretation of these experiments is that the positive feelings associated with the soft drinks or with guitar music became associated, via classical conditioning, with the persuasive messages.

Instrumental conditioning

In this form of learning, responses that yield positive outcomes or eliminate negative ones are strengthened. Behaviours that are followed by positive consequences are reinforced and are more likely to be repeated than behaviours that are followed by negative consequences. Parents use verbal reinforcers in an attempt to encourage acceptable behaviour in their children. Playing quietly and cooperatively with others, for example, is a social behaviour that can win praise. Fighting might lead to the withholding of a reinforcer or even to the introduction of a punishment, such as scolding. Instrumental learning can be accelerated or slowed by the frequency, temporal spacing and magnitude of the reinforcement (Kimble, 1961). By rewarding and punishing their children, parents can shape their attitudes on many issues, such as their religious or political beliefs and practices.

Even in adulthood, attitudes may continue to be shaped by verbal reinforcers. Insko (1965) showed that students' responses to an attitude survey had been influenced by an apparently unrelated telephone conversation, which took place a week earlier, in which particular opinions were 'rewarded' by the interviewer responding with the reinforcer 'good'.

Both forms of conditioning (classical and instrumental) emphasise the role of direct reinforcers in the acquisition and maintenance of behaviour in general. The relevance to the topic of attitudes depends on defining an attitude as a class of behaviour. This becomes a relatively straightforward matter if an attitude is operationalised as an *evaluative response*. Such a view has been argued by Osgood, Suci and Tannenbaum (1957) and by Fishbein (1967a).

Observational learning

Other social psychologists view attitude formation as a social learning process, one that does not depend on direct reinforcers. Bandura (1973) and others have studied social learning and concentrated on a process of **modelling** (see also Chapters 12 and 14), where one person's behaviour is modelled on another's. Modelling is learning by observation: individuals learn new responses, not by directly experiencing positive or negative outcomes but by observing the outcomes of others' responses. Having a successful working mother, for instance, is likely to influence the future career and lifestyle choices of a daughter. Likewise, racial attitudes can be instilled in otherwise naive children if the models are significant adults in their lives. This can be seen in the case of children who use racial slurs and insults, and claim to hate a certain racial group, but who are unable correctly to define the group or to show any factual knowledge regarding its members (Allport, 1954b; see also Chapter 11).

Observational learning: Young children model their social attitudes and values on significant adults, particularly their parents.

COGNITIVE DEVELOPMENT

Other social psychologists prefer to think of attitude formation in terms of cognitive development. Cognitive consistency theories (e.g. balance, cognitive dissonance; see Chapter 6) allow us to view attitude acquisition as an elaborative exercise of building connections (balanced or consonant) between more and more elements (e.g. beliefs). As the number of related elements increases, it is more likely that a generalised concept—an attitude—is being formed. Similarly, information integration theory can handle attitude learning as a case in which more and more items of information about an attitude object have been processed (say, by averaging their weights).

A difference between cognitive and behavioural approaches is the relative weight that each gives to internal events versus principles of reinforcement. Since the 1970s there has been a trend in social psychology to favour a cognitive perspective, as we noted in Chapters 2 and 3. Despite this, we should not ignore certain advantages of behavioural approaches: traditionally, they have been linked to the study of learning and often deal directly with developmental data (generated from studies of animals or children).

For this reason, learning theories continue to be of interest to social psychologists in relation to the topic of attitude acquisition.

One interesting approach with both a behavioural and a perceptual flavour is Bem's (1972) **self-perception theory** (see Chapter 4 for details). Bem proposed that people acquire knowledge about what kind of person they are by examining their own behaviour and asking, 'Why did I do that?' It follows that many attitudes can be acquired in this way. A person may engage in a behaviour for reasons that are not obvious and then determine their attitude from the most readily available cause. For example, if you often go for long walks, you may conclude that 'I must like them, as I'm always doing that'.

Bem's theory suggests that people act, and form attitudes, without much deliberate thinking.

SOURCES OF LEARNING

Parents

An important source of your attitudes are the actions of other people around you. For the child, parents are a powerful influence and all the kinds of learning mentioned above (classical conditioning, instrumental conditioning, observational learning) are involved. However, Connell (1972) reported that, although the correlation between the *specific* attitudes of parents and their children towards a given issue is generally positive, it is also weak. When measuring attitudes towards *broad* issues, the relationship is stronger.

Jennings and Niemi (1968) found a 0.60 correlation between high school children's preferences for a particular political party and their parents' choices, and a correlation of 0.88 between parents' and children's choices of religion. Of course, such correlations may be limited by oppositional conduct, which is a common feature in adolescent development. Many high school students deliberately adopt, or appear to adopt, attitudes that are inconsistent with their parents', purely to be contrary.

Mass media

The media, particularly television, are also major influences on the learning of attitudes. For example, MacKay and Covell (1997) reported a relationship between viewing sexual images of women in advertisements and holding attitudes supportive of sexual aggression (see also Chapter 12). Although the impact of television on adults is not clear-cut (Barney, 1973; Oskamp, 1984), there is little question that it plays an important part in attitude formation in children. Goldberg and Gorn (1974) argued that mass communication is most influential when attitudes are not strongly held, as in young children. A study by Chaffee, Jackson-Beeck, Durall and Wilson (1977) showed that, before age seven, American children get most of their political information from television; this affected their views on politics and on political institutions (Atkin, 1977; Rubin, 1978).

The impact of commercials on children's attitudes has also been investigated. Atkin (1980) found that children who were heavy watchers of television were twice as likely as light watchers to believe that sugar-coated candies and cereals were good for them. In the same study, it was found that two-thirds of a group of children who saw a circus strong man eat a cereal believed it would make them strong too! These findings are of particular concern in the light of recent murders committed by children and carried out in ways similar to those portrayed in certain movies.

Concepts related to attitudes

VALUES

We have generally concentrated on attitudes as a relatively high-level concept involving affect as a central dimension. We have also noted that some theorists argue that beliefs constitute an additional dimension. If we accept this view, an attitude could be conceptualised as a set of integrated beliefs with an affective loading. From such an approach springs a further level of analysis and another term—**values**.

There was an early emphasis on the global concept of values in a psychological test (Allport & Vernon,

1931) designed to measure the relative importance to a person of six broad classes of value orientation:

1. *theoretical*—an interest in problem-solving, and the basis of how things work;
2. *economic*—an interest in economic matters, finance and money affairs generally;
3. *aesthetic*—an interest in the arts, theatre, music, architecture;
4. *social*—a general concern for one's fellows, a social welfare orientation;
5. *political*—an interest in political structures and power arrangements;
6. *religious*—a general concern with theology, the after-life and morals.

Later, Rokeach (1973) suggested that values should be conceived less in terms of interests or activities and more as preferred end-states (goals). He distinguished between terminal values (e.g. equality and freedom) and instrumental values (e.g. honesty and ambition). A terminal value, such as equality, could have significant effects on the way someone might feel about racial issues, which is just what Rokeach found. From this viewpoint, a value is a higher-order concept having broad control over an individual's more specific attitudes.

Australian research dealing with values as a higher-order concept has suggested that they can have strong links with more specific attitudes. Measuring values can help to predict people's attitudes: to the unemployed, according to Heaven (1990) at Wollongong University; and to beliefs in a just world, according to Feather (1991) at Flinders University.

Feather's extensive research (Feather, 1994) has suggested that values have the following properties:

- They are general beliefs about desirable behaviour and goals.
- Unlike wants and needs, they involve goodness and badness and have an 'oughtness' quality about them.
- They both transcend attitudes and influence the form these attitudes take.
- They provide standards for evaluating actions, justifying opinions and conduct, planning behaviour, deciding between different alternatives, engaging in social influence and presenting self to others.
- They are organised into hierarchies for any given person and their relative importance may alter across the life span.
- Value systems vary across individuals, groups and cultures.

In a series of studies, Feather (1989, 1993a, 1993b) focused on a common penchant to cut high achievers down to size—called, in Australia, the **'tall poppy' syndrome**. He found that attitudes towards 'tall poppies' can be accounted for by one or more values. The effect is stronger among people motivated by equalitarianism (equality of opportunity and social position) and right-wing authoritarianism (conventionalism) than among people motivated by achievement (success, ambition) and social power (recognition).

Work of this kind is not in conflict with that of Fishbein and Ajzen, as the controlling function played by values is being applied to global attitudes rather than to a specific attitude and a related behaviour.

IDEOLOGY

The terms **ideology** and value intersect. It connotes an integrated and widely shared system of beliefs, usually with a social or political reference, that serves an explanatory function (Thompson, 1990). Most familiar to us are the religious and sociopolitical ideologies that serve as rallying points for many of the world's most intransigent intergroup conflicts (see Chapters 10 and 11).

Tetlock (1989) has proposed that terminal values, such as those described by Rokeach, underlie all kinds of *political ideology*. For example, Machiavellianism as an ideology, named after Machiavelli (a 16th-century Florentine diplomat, considered by some to be the first social scientist), is the notion that craft and deceit are justified in pursuing and maintaining power in the political world (Saucier, 2000). Ideologies can vary as a function of two characteristics:

1. They may assign different priorities to particular values: traditionally, we might expect liberals and conservatives to rank 'individual freedom' and 'national security' in opposite ways.
2. Some ideologies are pluralistic and others are monistic. A pluralistic ideology can tolerate a conflict of values—for example, neoliberalism as a pluralistic ideology refers to emphasising economic growth, but also to being concerned with social justice. A monistic ideology will be quite intolerant of conflict, seeing issues in starkly simplistic terms (see the discussion of authoritarianism in Chapter 10). An example of a monistic ideology is Manicheism, or the notion that the world is divided between good and evil principles.

Billig (1991) has suggested that a good deal of our everyday thinking arises from what he calls ideological dilemmas. Teachers, for example, face the dilemma of being an authority and yet trying to encourage equality between teacher and student. When conflict between values takes place, it can cause a clash of attitudes between groups. For example, Katz and Haas (1988) reported that racial attitudes in a community can become polarised when values such as communalism and individualism clash.

SOCIAL REPRESENTATIONS

A somewhat different perspective on attitudes is proposed by researchers who work in a **social representations** tradition. In Chapter 3 we describe social representations in detail: first introduced by Moscovici (1961) and based on earlier work by the French sociologist Emile Durkheim (1912/1995) on 'collective representations', social representations refers to the way that people elaborate, through social interaction, simplified and shared understandings of often quite challenging phenomena (see also Farr & Moscovici, 1984; Lorenzi-Cioldi & Clémence, 2001; Moscovici, 1981, 1988; Purkhardt, 1995).

From an attitudinal perspective, the important point is that specific attitudes are framed by, and embedded within, wider representational structures that are in turn grounded in social groups. In this sense, attitudes are socially constructed and tend to reflect the society or groups in which people live their lives.

This type of perspective on attitudes reflects a much broader 'top-down' perspective on social behaviour that is a hallmark of European social psychology (see Chapter 1). It prompted the American social psychologist William McGuire (1986) to observe that 'the two movements serve mutually supplementary uses', in that the European concept of collective representations highlights how *alike* group members are, while the American individualist tradition shows how *different* they are (see also Tajfel, 1972a).

If social representations are cognitive structures that are shared within groups, we might expect agreement between members to increase with age. This idea was tested by Augoustinos (1991). Augoustinos, at the University of Adelaide, compared the images that high school and university students had of 12 groups in Australian society, representing four categories: socioeconomic status, ethnicity, politics and gender. Using a *multidimensional scaling* procedure (discussed later), Augoustinos isolated dimensions that allowed the 12 groups to be compared. Figure 5.8 shows two sets of results, one for younger students (13–14 years old) and one for older students (third year at university). For the younger group, the vertical dimension was identified as 'wealth, power and success', but the horizontal dimension was more difficult to describe. For the older group, Augoustinos identified the vertical dimension as socioeconomic status, whereas the horizontal dimension was possibly male–female.

This study is a good example of social representations research and indicates that the images a community has of its own constituent groups can become clearer as a function of age (see Box 5.5).

Social representations may influence the evaluative tone of attitudes 'nested' within them. For example, Moliner and Tafani (1997) have shown how attitudes

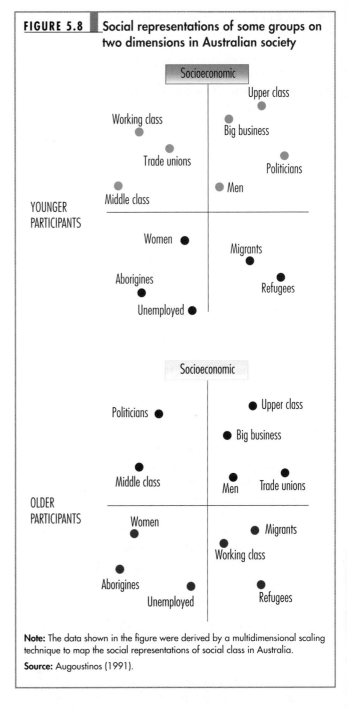

FIGURE 5.8 Social representations of some groups on two dimensions in Australian society

Note: The data shown in the figure were derived by a multidimensional scaling technique to map the social representations of social class in Australia.

Source: Augoustinos (1991).

towards objects are based on the evaluative components of the representation of those objects, and that a change in attitudes towards an object may be accompanied by changes in the evaluative dimension of its representation. Other recent research, much of it Australasian, on the relationship between social representations and attitudes has been quite broad-ranging, focusing on Internet addiction (Hansen, 2000), organ donation (Moloney & Walker, 2000), psychologists' representation of mental illness (Correia, 2000) and the representation of history, authority and legitimising myths (Liu, 2000).

Use of a multidimensional scale to map social representations in Australia

The concept of social representations was applied by Augoustinos (1991) of the University of Adelaide in a study of 12 societal groups in Australia. Her participants were students at either school or university. The students made judgments about these groups that were chosen as representative cases of socioeconomic status, ethnicity, decision-makers and gender. Examples of each of these in order were 'working class', 'migrants', 'politicians' and 'women'. The judgments were made on 17 scales similar to the semantic differential, such as ACTIVE–PASSIVE, WISE–FOOLISH, RICH–POOR, WORK HARD–LAZY.

Augoustinos used a *multidimensional scaling* analysis to uncover dimensions that the students found useful in classifying the twelve groups. The data in Figure 5.8 are sets of responses chosen from the younger (13–14 years old) and older (third-year university) students.

The graphs are two-dimensional plots that show how the 12 groups were placed relative to each other. The vertical dimension was statistically more salient for the students. It also had a stronger impact on the older sample: whereas it accounted for 26% of the variance in judgments for the younger students, the figure rose to 61% for the older students. The dimension was interpreted by Augoustinos as socioeconomic status. She was not able to give a clear meaning to the horizontal dimension.

The age effect, which can be seen by comparing the upper and lower graphs, suggests that it takes years for young people to reflect a social representation of a concept of social class in a way that may be widely held in an adult community. The group 'working class' drops well down on this dimension for the older students, who also see a widening gap in status between 'men' and 'women'

Measuring attitudes

Measuring an attitude is not an easy task as attitudes cannot be observed directly: how can we measure something that is in a person's mind? The usual solution is to ask people. Researchers rely heavily on this strategy and often use attitude questionnaires or scales.

Because the study of attitudes has been an active part of social psychology for a long time, a well-developed technology exists for measuring attitudes. Several different paper-and-pencil tests have been developed, and four techniques have been refined and used extensively:

1. Thurstone's method of equal-appearing intervals
2. Likert's method of summated ratings
3. Guttman's scalogram
4. Osgood's semantic differential.

We shall see that techniques of attitude measurement assume different things about the nature of the test items that are used or the data that are collected, and about the kind of information these provide about a person's attitudes. They also have assumptions in common:

- Attitudes can be measured by a quantitative technique, so that each person's opinion can be represented by a numerical score.
- A particular test item, or other behaviour indicating an attitude, has the same meaning for all respondents, so that a given response is scored identically for everyone making it.

Such assumptions may not always be justified and implicit assumptions should always be treated warily.

In a typical attitude questionnaire, respondents are asked to indicate whether they agree or disagree with each of a series of belief statements about an attitude object. A key question, dealt with below, is how these statements are selected. Occasionally, attitudes are measured by a single question that asks people to make a positive or negative evaluation about a specific topic.

Consider the example of a seven-point **self-rating scale** in Figure 5.9. The respondent checks one of the points on the scale. The scales do not always have seven points: five, six or even 100 points have been used. Sometimes only the endpoints are labelled and the rest are blank. The advantage of such a scale is simplicity. The disadvantage is possible oversimplification of complex issues. Although such a question directly assesses evaluation of an attitude object, the use of a single question to measure an attitude is not usually favoured. The reason for employing a larger set of items is that responses to any one question are often affected by irrelevant factors (such as the wording of the question), which can create errors. If responses are averaged or summed across a number of questions, a more valid measure is obtained because the error associated with individual items tends to cancel out across a number of items.

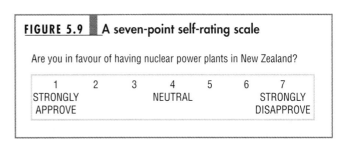

FIGURE 5.9 | **A seven-point self-rating scale**

Are you in favour of having nuclear power plants in New Zealand?

1	2	3	4	5	6	7
STRONGLY APPROVE			NEUTRAL			STRONGLY DISAPPROVE

The final statements included in an attitude questionnaire are thus carefully selected. Ideally, each represents a different and independent view about the object and covers both favourable and unfavourable attitudes, so that the nature of the response to one item should not affect the response to another item. There are several systems for choosing appropriate statements, and each is known as an attitude-scaling method.

THURSTONE'S METHOD OF EQUAL-APPEARING INTERVALS

The first formal technique for measuring an attitude was developed by Thurstone (1928) in his study of attitudes towards religion. The scale, derived from psychophysics, introduced precise measurement into an area of research where it had never been used before. Like other attitude theorists, Thurstone viewed attitudes as statements lying along an evaluative continuum ranging from favourable to unfavourable. Furthermore, these statements could be ordered so that there appeared to be an equal distance between adjacent statements on the continuum. Because of this assumption, judgments could be made about the degree of discrepancy among different people's attitudes. Thurstone also assumed that the statements were uncorrelated and that each statement had a position independent of the others: that is, acceptance of one statement did not necessarily imply acceptance of any others.

As originally designed, a **Thurstone scale** is made up of 22 independent statements about a particular issue. Each statement has a numerical scale value determined by its average judged position on the continuum, and people's attitudes on the issue are measured by asking them to check those statements with which they agree. Each person's score is the mean scale value of the items they check. Figure 5.10 is a shortened version of this type of scale. (In practice, the scale values would not be shown. The participant could choose any number of the statements with which to agree.)

The hallmark of a Thurstone scale is that the intervals between the statements are approximately equal, a property that derives from the method of construction. The features involved in constructing this kind of scale are these.

- A large number of statements of opinion about an issue are formulated. Any whose meanings are confusing or ambiguous are discarded.
- The remaining statements are sorted into 11 categories by a group of judges who are, in practice, a group of up to 100 participants drawn from the same population as the final participants whose attitudes are later to be measured.
- The 11 categories are steps on an equal-intervals scale ranging from 'favourable' through 'neutral' to 'unfavourable' with respect to the attitude object.

FIGURE 5.10 ■ Scale value of items on an 11-point Thurstone equal-intervals scale

How favourable	Value on 11-point scale	Item
Least	1.3	Practising contraception should be punishable by law.
	3.6	Contraception is morally wrong in spite of possible benefits.
Neutral	5.4	Contraception has both advantages and disadvantages.
	7.6	Contraception is a legitimate health measure.
	9.6	Contraception is the only solution to many of our social problems.
Most	10.3	We should not only allow but enforce limitation on family size.

THURSTONE SCALE — Attitude towards contraception

- The task for the judges is to determine to what degree agreement with each item would reflect a favourable, neutral or unfavourable (from 1 to 11) attitude towards the issue.
- This judgment should be made without regard to the judges' own attitude.
- By tabulating the ratings of the judges, it is possible to calculate the numerical scale position (the average) of each statement, as well as the extent to which the judges agreed on its placement (its range).
- The statements selected for the final scale are those that have high interjudge agreement and fall at relatively equal intervals along the continuum. There are 22 items, two per scale position, in the final scale.
- Other people's attitudes towards the issue are derived from their responses to this final set of items. If the scale is statistically reliable, we would expect a person to agree with only two or three items out of 22. The average of the scale values for these endorsed items would reflect that person's position on the 11-point scale.
- If a sufficient number of reliable items is available, it would be possible to make up two 22-item questionnaires as forms A and B, which might, for example, be used as before and after measures in a study of attitude change.

LIKERT'S METHOD OF SUMMATED RATINGS

One of the practical drawbacks of the Thurstone scale is that its construction is very tedious and time-consuming. To cope with this problem, Likert (1932) developed a different technique that produces a

Using a rating scale: Students' ratings of their lecturers' performance are often based on Likert scales. One might worry here about the independence of their responses!

reasonably reliable attitude scale with relative ease. A series of attitude statements is presented and respondents indicate how much they agree or disagree with each statement, using a five-point scale, with the points usually labelled 'strongly agree', 'agree', 'undecided', 'disagree', 'strongly disagree'. Look at the example in Figure 5.11.

When a number of these statements is used, a person's score is summed across the statements and the resulting total used as an index of the person's attitude. When developing a **Likert scale**, researchers find that not all questions will correlate equally with the total: some will be more accurate measures of the attitude than others. Those that do not correlate highly with the total are dropped and the ones that are left are summed as an index of a person's attitude. Any ambiguous items, or items that do not differentiate between people with differing attitudes, are dropped.

If possible, items are selected so that, for 50% of the items, 'agree' represents a positive attitude and for 50%

of the items 'agree' represents a negative attitude. The scoring of the latter set of items is reflected (i.e. 5 becomes 1, 4 becomes 2, etc.) before the item scores are summed. This procedure permits control of an **acquiescent response set**—that is, a confounding of a highly positive attitude score with a tendency simply to agree with a series of statements.

Likert assumed that each statement used in the scale is a linear function of the same attitude dimension. This assumption is the basis for the operation of adding up a person's individual scores (or summating the ratings) to obtain a final score. A further implication is that the items in a scale must be highly correlated with a common attribute and thus with each other, as opposed to Thurstone's distinct and independent items. Likert did not assume equal intervals between scale values. For example, it is quite possible that the difference between 'agree' and 'strongly agree' is much larger than the difference between 'agree' and 'undecided'. This means a Likert scale can provide information on the ordering of people's attitudes on a continuum, but is unable to indicate how close or far apart different attitudes might be.

Likert's method of scale construction is similar to Thurstone's in the initial collecting and editing of a variety of opinion statements. The remaining statements are then rated by a sample group of participants on the five-point response scale in terms of their own opinions about the statements. This is in contrast to the Thurstone scale approach, where the ratings are made by trained judges and based, not on personal opinions, but on some relatively objective evaluation of where the statements fall on a continuum.

The Likert scale is composed of those items that best differentiate between sample participants with the highest and lowest total scores (see Ballard, 1973; Gregson & Stacey, 1980; and Surgenor, 1985, for some Australasian examples of the use of a Likert-type scale).

FIGURE 5.11 | Items on a five-point Likert summated ratings scale

LIKERT SCALE

What are your opinions of the following statements? Your answer is correct if it expresses your real opinion. This is not a test and you are not to be graded. DO NOT OMIT ANY ITEM. Place a tick in one of the five boxes that represents your own ideas about each statement.

Item	Strongly agree	Agree	Undecided	Disagree	Strongly disagree
Farming is a great occupation.	❏	❏	❏	❏	❏
Farm work is drudgery.	❏	❏	❏	❏	❏
To be a farmer for the rest of my life would be terrible.	❏	❏	❏	❏	❏
A farm is a wonderful place to live.	❏	❏	❏	❏	❏
The independence of farm life appeals to me.	❏	❏	❏	❏	❏
Living on a farm sounds too much like hard work.	❏	❏	❏	❏	❏

In contrast to a Thurstone scale, a Likert scale is usually more statistically reliable (see Table 5.2 on page 121) and is also less time-consuming to construct. Unlike the Thurstone scale, it is not intended to access an absolute range of attitude scores (determined by judges); instead, the range reflects directly the attitudes of the participants who constitute the sample.

GUTTMAN'S SCALOGRAM METHOD

A **Guttman scale** (or scalogram) is based on the assumption that a single, unidimensional trait can be measured by a set of statements that are ordered along a continuum of difficulty of acceptance. The statements range from those that are easy for most people to accept to those that few people could endorse. Such scale items are cumulative, as the acceptance of one item implies that the person accepts all those of lesser magnitude. To the extent that all this is true, we can predict a person's attitude towards other statements on the basis of knowing the most difficult item they will accept (see the example in Figure 5.12).

To obtain a scale that represented a single dimension, Guttman (1944) presented sample participants with an initial set of items and recorded the extent to which they responded to the items with specified answer patterns. These patterns, which are referred to as *scale types*, follow a certain step-like order. The participant may accept none of the items in the set (score 0), accept item A only (score = 1), accept items A and B only (score = 2), accept items A, B and C only (score = 3) and so on. If the participant gives a non-scale response pattern (e.g. accepts item C only and not those of lesser magnitude), then either (a) the participant has made an error or (b) the items used do not scale in a cumulative fashion.

By analysing the numbers of response errors made, Guttman determined *scalability*—that is, the degree to which the initial set of items reflects a unidimensional attribute. **Unidimensionality**, then, refers to the extent to which the items being used are scalable, or cumulative. The final scale is obtained by eliminating poor items and retesting sample participants until a scalable set of items has been developed. People's attitudes are then measured by having them check all the statements they find acceptable.

To provide an estimate of how scalable a set of items is, Guttman developed the coefficient of *reproducibility*. If there are n items to which a person could respond 'yes' or 'no', then there are 2^n possible response patterns and, of these, only $n + 1$ should occur if the set is perfectly scalable. Response patterns of the non-scale type should be low in practice. Such errors detract from the perfection of the scale—that is, they reduce reproducibility: Rep = 1 − (total errors/total responses).

It is almost impossible to develop a perfect unidimensional scale. This usually indicates that people respond on multiple dimensions rather than on a single one.

You may be wondering which is the best scale of the traditional forms that we have considered. There is no simple answer. In statistical terms, scales focus on different properties of the dimension on which the items are located. They also differ somewhat in statistical reliability—which is the property of a measuring instrument to reproduce the same score for a person on different occasions—and, importantly for the researcher, in ease of construction. According to Shaw (1966), no scale actually achieves equal intervals—not even the Thurstone scale, which was designed to fulfil this very purpose. Nor do any of them have a zero point. A comparison of their qualities is shown in Table 5.2.

There is also some evidence that judges' own attitudes can influence the way in which they rate the extremity of items (Edwards, 1957; Eiser & Stroebe, 1972).

OSGOOD'S SEMANTIC DIFFERENTIAL

In contrast to approaches where respondents indicate agreement with opinion statements, Osgood studied attitudes by focusing on the meaning that people give to a word or concept. Underlying this technique is the assumption of a hypothetical semantic space of an unknown number of dimensions, in which the meaning of any word or concept can be represented as a particular point. The **semantic differential** method of attitude measurement was developed from research on the connotative meanings of words.

The *connotative meaning* is the meaning a word suggests apart from the thing it explicitly denotes or names. For example, studies of the connotative meanings of words consistently show that one of the major dimensions involves evaluation, the goodness or

---

FIGURE 5.12 | Items on a Guttman cumulative scale

GUTTMAN SCALE
Attitude towards mixed-ethnic housing

How acceptable	Statement
Least	Generally speaking, people should be able to live anywhere they want.
	Real estate agencies should not discriminate against minority groups.
	The local council should actively support the idea of open housing.
	There should be a local review board that would pass on cases of extreme discrimination in housing.
Most	There should be laws to enforce mixed-ethnic housing.

TABLE 5.2 | Thurstone, Likert and Guttman scales compared

CHARACTERISTICS	THURSTONE	LIKERT	GUTTMAN
Ease of construction	Moderately easy	Easy	Difficult
Item content	Must refer directly to attitude object	Need not refer directly to attitude object	Usually must refer directly to attitude object
Ease of scoring	Moderately easy	Moderately easy	Very easy
Score interpretation	Independent of total distribution of scores	Dependent on total distribution of scores	Relatively independent of total distribution of scores
Respondent's reaction	Neutral to moderately negative	Neutral to moderately negative	Negative
Reliability			
Two-forms	0.60–0.85	0.72–0.94	—
Split-half	0.52–0.89	0.78–0.92	—
Reproducibility	0.82–0.88	0.79–0.90	0.85–0.95
Validity	Not clearly established	Not clearly established	Not clearly established
Unidimensionality	No	Approximate	Yes
Equality of units	No	No	No
Neutral point	Yes	No	No

Source: Shaw (1966).

badness implied by the word (Osgood, Suci, & Tannenbaum, 1957). The word 'friend' tends to be thought of as good and the word 'enemy' as bad. According to Osgood, this evaluative dimension corresponds to our definition of an attitude. The procedure is to have people judge a particular concept on a set of semantic scales. The idea or topic to be rated is listed at the top of a page and underneath are several seven-point scales that have words at each end. These scales are defined by verbal opposites with a neutral midpoint. In the example in Figure 5.13, the meanings that people attach to the

concept of 'nuclear power' are measured by their ratings of the concept on a set of semantic scales.

Respondents check the space on the scale that indicates their feeling about the topic. Several pairs of words dealing with evaluations are used; some common ones include good/bad, nice/awful, pleasant/unpleasant, fair/unfair, valuable/worthless. An analysis of the ratings collected by this method may reveal the particular dimensions that people use to qualify their experience, the types of concepts that are regarded as similar or different in meaning, and the intensity of the meaning given to a particular concept.

Osgood's own research pointed to three major dimensions that people use in judging concepts: evaluative (e.g. good/bad), potency (e.g. strong/weak) and activity (e.g. active/passive).

The main advantage of this approach is that a researcher does not have to construct questions for each attitude being studied. When several pairs of words are used, the resulting attitude score is generally reliable. A disadvantage is that the measure can be too simple. Furthermore, although this method can provide a lot of information about a concept, it is not exactly clear how

FIGURE 5.13 | Rating the concept of 'nuclear power' on a seven-point semantic differential scale

SEMANTIC DIFFERENTIAL SCALE
Nuclear power

```
GOOD    — — — — — — —   BAD
STRONG  — — — — — — —   WEAK
FAST    — — — — — — —   SLOW
```

the concept's meaning for a person is related to the opinion statements they make regarding it.

Some research uses variations on the original scales developed by Osgood. The study by Augoustinos (1991) discussed earlier in this chapter compared a variety of groups in Australian society on scales such as active/passive, wise/foolish, independent/dependent, rich/poor, work hard/lazy. She used a multidimensional scaling procedure (see below) to delineate dimensions, based on data generated from these scales, on which the 12 groups could be plotted (refer back to Figure 5.8).

FISHBEIN'S EXPECTANCY-VALUE TECHNIQUE

We noted earlier that Fishbein and Ajzen (1974) argued that there is a better attitude–behaviour fit if an evaluative component of the attitude is incorporated with a belief component. Fishbein went on to propose a technique of measurement called the **expectancy-value model**, in which each contributing belief underlying an attitude domain is weighted by the strength of its relationship to the attitude object. We note the main elements of this technique in an earlier section (refer back to Figure 5.3). Another example is given in Figure 5.14.

Despite some criticisms (see Eagly & Chaiken, 1993), Fishbein's technique has had considerable impact in a variety of behavioural settings. These include marketing and consumer research (Assael, 1981), politics (Bowman & Fishbein, 1978), family planning (Vinokur-Kaplan, 1978), classroom attendance (Fredericks & Dossett, 1983), seatbelt wearing (Budd, North, & Spencer, 1984), preventing HIV infection (Terry, Gallois, & McCamish, 1993) and even predicting how mothers will feed their infants (Manstead, Proffitt, & Smart, 1983).

THE USE OF ATTITUDE SCALES TODAY

Combinations of the Likert scale and the semantic differential have been used successfully to deal with quite complex evaluations. For example, voters can be asked to evaluate various issues using a semantic differential scale. Then, using a Likert scale, they can be asked how they think each candidate stands on particular issues. Combining the two measures enables us to predict for whom they will vote (Ajzen & Fishbein, 1980).

The Likert scale has also contributed significantly to many modern questionnaires that start from the premise that there will be more than one underlying dimension in the attitude domain being measured. Powerful statistical computer programs have greatly increased the likelihood that researchers will choose from a variety of multivariate statistical methods, such as factor analysis, to analyse psychological data.

Whereas Likert tested for unidimensionality in a fairly simple way by calculating item–total score correlations, factor analysis starts from a correlation matrix based on correlations between all pairs of items making up the questionnaire scale. It is then possible to estimate whether a single general factor (or dimension), or more than one factor, is required to explain the variance in the respondents' pattern of responses to the questionnaire. An example of this might be if attitudes towards your country's possession of nuclear weapons in turn involved your reactions to war, to nuclear contamination, to relationships with other countries and so on. Each of these might be measured on a different dimension, so that the questionnaire could well consist of several subscales (see Oppenheim, 1992). In the process of extracting factors, decreasing amounts of variance are accounted for: that is, successive factors (dimensions) have weaker explanatory power.

Sometimes, factor analysis unearths substructures underlying a set of items that can be both interesting and subtle. In the development of a scale designed to measure 'sexism towards women', Glick and Fiske (1996) found evidence of two underlying subscales—'hostile sexism' and 'benevolent sexism'—pointing to a covert ambivalence in their participants.

Another multivariate procedure is multidimensional scaling analysis. In the study by Augoustinos (1991), 12 groups were compared two at a time on 17 bipolar scales. These data were then analysed using a computer program to yield several orthogonal dimensions, which successively accounted for decreasing amounts of variance in the data. Augoustinos found that the vertical and horizontal dimensions for her younger participants accounted for 59% and 23% of variance, and for her

FIGURE 5.14 Items on a Fishbein expectancy-value scale

FISHBEIN SCALE
Attitude towards politicians

Instruction: Rate your degree of *belief* in each of the following statements by indicating the probabilty that it is true, on a scale for which:

0 = not at all true
10 = certainly true

Instruction: Rate your *evaluation* of each of the following attributes on a scale for which:

−10 = extremely undesirable
0 = neutral
+10 = extremely desirable

Politicians are:
—Untrustworthy
—Honest
—Devious
—Intelligent

—Untrustworthy
—Honest
—Devious
—Intelligent

Source: Fishbein & Ajzen (1975).

older participants 72% and 28%, respectively (refer back to Figure 5.8).

PHYSIOLOGICAL MEASURES

A variety of physiological measures has been used to assess attitudes. These include skin resistance (Rankin & Campbell, 1955), heart rate, heart cycle (Westie & DeFleur, 1959) and pupil dilation (Hess, 1965). A person's attitude is usually inferred by comparing a physiological reading (such as heartbeat) taken in the presence of a neutral object, such as a loaf of bread, with a reading taken in the presence of the attitude object, such as an attractive person. The larger the difference between the responses to the two objects, the more intense the participant's attitude is assumed to be.

Physiological measures have one big advantage over self-report measures: people may not realise that their attitudes are being assessed and, even if they do, they may not be able to alter their responses. This is the premise behind using a polygraph or lie detector in criminal investigations.

There are drawbacks. Most physiological measures are sensitive to variables other than attitudes (Cacioppo & Petty, 1981). Skin resistance can change in the presence of novel or incongruous stimuli that may have nothing to do with the attitude being assessed. Similarly, heart rate is sensitive to task requirements. Problem-solving tasks raise heart rate, while vigilance tasks (such as watching a VDU screen) usually lower it. Another problem is that physiological measures provide only limited information about attitudes. They can indicate intensity of feeling but not direction—that is, two people who feel equally strongly about an issue, but are totally opposed, cannot be distinguished.

However, one physiological measure is regarded as very useful in distinguishing the kinds of attitudes people have. It is based on Charles Darwin's suggestion that different facial expressions are used to convey different emotions (see Chapter 15).

Cacioppo and his colleagues (Cacioppo & Petty, 1979; Cacioppo & Tassinary, 1990) linked measures of facial muscle movements to underlying attitudes. Cacioppo and Petty reasoned that people who agreed with a speech they were listening to would display facial movements different from those of people who disagreed with the speech. To test this, they recorded the movements of specific facial muscles before and during a speech that advocated a conservative or a liberal view—either stricter or more lenient university regulations regarding alcohol or visiting hours. Before the speech, movements of the muscles showed one pattern if students agreed with the topic and a different pattern if they disagreed. The differences in the patterns became more pronounced when the students actually listened to the speeches. Thus, facial muscle

movements provide a useful way of distinguishing people with favourable attitudes on a topic from those with unfavourable attitudes.

This approach does not indicate the intensity of an attitude present: no single physiological measure assesses both attitude position and strength together, something that is possible with self-report measures.

MEASURES OF OVERT BEHAVIOUR

Yet another way to measure attitudes is to watch what people do, as their behaviours can be an indication of their attitudes. This technique is reliable only when people do not realise that their behaviour is being observed. Several such **unobtrusive measures** for assessing positive attitudes have been developed. Webb, Campbell, Schwartz and Sechrest (1969) suggested that we might infer attitudes from physical traces and archival records. For example, in a museum the noseprints on a display case could be counted to determine how popular a particular display is, and the height of the noseprints could indicate the ages of the most interested viewers! Similarly, public records can also provide information about attitudes, and archival information can be used to examine whether significant historical events influence relevant attitudes.

Changes in attitudes about sex roles over time could be investigated by examining the roles of male and female characters in children's books. If attitudes have changed, male and female characters may be differently represented in recent books than in books published 20 years ago. Library withdrawals also provide archival data: are people reading more fiction or more non-fiction than in the past? Webb and colleagues (Webb, Campbell, Schwartz, & Sechrest, 1969) described an investigation that found that withdrawals of fiction, but not non-fiction, books dropped after the introduction of television. Library withdrawals can also be used to gauge the effect of the mass media. If a book or play receives a favourable radio review, is it likely to be more popular than if it receives an unfavourable review? Nowadays, DVD/video rental companies' records of rental statistics may identify trends in viewing preferences.

Non-verbal behaviour can also serve as an attitude measure. For example, people who like each other tend to sit closer together. Thus, if strangers in a waiting room sit far apart from members of other groups, maybe we can infer some underlying prejudice?

Interpersonal distance can also measure fear. Webb and his colleagues described a study in which adults told ghost stories to young children seated in a circle. The size of the circle of children grew smaller with each successive scary story.

(A social distance scale developed by Bogardus in 1925 was an early attempt to assess attitudes towards different social and ethnic groups. It was based on the distance people felt comfortable with between themselves and others, as measured by a scale on the floor: a willingness to be more socially intimate with members of a given group would be indicated by the respondent moving closer to a target person.)

However, Webb and colleagues (Webb, Campbell, Schwartz, & Sechrest, 1969) concluded that these unobtrusive measures were not as good as self-report. The value of unobtrusive measures lies in the fact that their limitations are different from those of standard measures, so that, when both types are used together, and correlate, a researcher can be more confident of the validity of the results.

The major problem with unobtrusive measures is deciding which behaviour reflects an underlying attitude. The ideal behaviour would be one that was affected only by the person's evaluation of an issue and not by any irrelevant variables, which is unlikely in real life. It may be that behaviour in isolation is not a good measure of attitude. A person's attitude may determine behaviour the first time a particular action is performed, but with repetition the behaviour becomes a habit and is less likely to be dependent on the relevant attitude (Triandis, 1980). For example, a person might believe that drug-taking will enhance acceptance by peers, but after taking the drugs a physiological dependence might govern subsequent behaviour, irrespective of the initial attitude. These problems can usually be overcome if the overt behaviour is measured under conditions that enhance the salience, or obviousness, of an attitude.

PROBLEMS AND SOLUTIONS IN MEASURING ATTITUDES

Whenever attitude researchers question participants, there is the possibility that participants will be reluctant to reveal their true feelings. This is especially so when a person's attitude (e.g. holding racist views) runs counter to a prevailing norm (e.g. equity towards all groups). Researchers have devised several techniques to overcome such problems. However, these techniques have sometimes raised questions about research ethics, especially if participants do not know their attitudes are being measured.

An example of this is the **bogus pipeline technique** (Jones & Sigall, 1971), which involves convincing participants that they cannot hide their true attitudes. Participants are connected to a machine resembling a lie detector and are told that the machine can measure both the strength and direction of a person's emotional responses, thus revealing their true attitudes and implying that there is no point in lying. Several studies have shown that participants are indeed convinced by the bogus pipeline and are less likely to conceal socially undesirable attitudes when the technique is used. Examples of what people will reveal include racial prejudice (Allen, 1975; Quigley-Fernandez & Tedeschi, 1978); and

drinking in excess, snorting cocaine and having frequent oral sex (Tourangeau, Smith, & Rasinski, 1997).

Using the bogus pipeline might be unethical: it deceives participants and invades the privacy of those who are fooled by it. To justify its use, the researchers would probably need to demonstrate that the scientific benefits of the research outweighed the possible ethical costs (see Chapter 1 for a discussion of research ethics).

In making comparisons across attitude studies, there are two further problems:

1. a fundamental lack of agreement about the definition of attitudes; and
2. the lack of common methods for measurement.

Even when there is agreement about how an attitude might be defined and then measured, the ways in which data are then treated can vary markedly from one investigation to another. To illustrate, consider some of the ways that studies of attitude change (see Chapter 6) have operationalised (defined and measured) 'change'. Suppose that we have measured people's attitudes before and after an intervention and then want to know how much change has occurred. The following measures of change have been employed:

- percentage of participants showing any positive change at all;
- percentage of participants showing 'large', 'moderate', 'small' or 'no' change (categories arbitrarily defined);
- net percentage change (positive minus negative changes);
- any of the above for an arbitrarily determined combination of opinion items;
- absolute mean scale distance changed;
- distance changed relative to amount of change possible; and
- scale distance change weighted (corrected) for the subjective distance between scale points (i.e. two units' movement across neutral is 'worth more' than two units within one side of the scale).

If you are dubious about how valid it is to compare findings across a group of studies, join our team!

Rating scales have varied in the number of scale points (from 4 to 100), in the presence or absence and in the number of verbal labels at various points, and in their arrangement horizontally (across the page) or vertically (up and down the page). Attitudes have been measured by scale ratings of verbal statements (agree/disagree, true/false, like/dislike, etc.), of objects (good/bad, desirable/undesirable), of other people (like/dislike) and of self (degree of esteem, confidence). They have been measured by ratings of acceptance and rejection of individual opinion statements (latitudes of acceptance/rejection), by choices or rankings of alter-

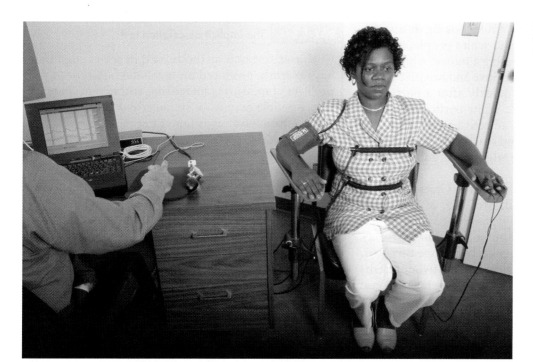

The bogus pipeline technique: Although this apparatus is not really working, she believes that it will detect lies.

natives, perceived instrumental value of items or actions, ratings of mood, ratings of intention, willingness to endorse an action or product, and likelihood of future behaviour.

Behavioural (non-questionnaire) measures of attitude have similarly spanned a huge variety. Verbal reports (about smoking, serving certain foods, dental hygiene practices) have been used, as well as observations of actual compliance with recommendations (taking an X-ray, getting tetanus shots, agreeing with group norms, etc.). Time measures (decision time, time spent listening to supportive information, etc.), physiological measures (galvanic skin response to indicate reactions of an ethnically prejudiced person to stimuli associated with a certain ethnic group) and learning measures (recall of stimuli) have all been conceived of as attitude indicators.

There are many others that rely on unobtrusive observational methods (a count of empty beer and whisky bottles in garbage cans as indicators of attitudes towards alcohol in a given neighbourhood, chemists' records of which doctors prescribe new drugs). More recently, discourse analysis and the analysis of non-verbal communication (see Chapter 15) have also been explored.

Other procedures and considerations, such as attitude-congruent facilitation effects and linguistic intergroup bias, are discussed in Chapter 10 (see also Box 5.6; check this box, and the next section, and look again at the third focus question).

You may now appreciate that the measurement of attitudes is a research area with its share of challenges.

MEASURES OF COVERT ATTITUDES

In recent decades social psychologists have trialled a variety of less obtrusive measures of attitude—ones that are free of any tendency to make socially desirable responses (Crosby, Bromley, & Saxe, 1980; Devine, 1989).

The search for more covert techniques continues. Here are three:

1. *Bias in language use* An instance comes from the field of linguistic research by Maass and her colleagues (Franco & Maass, 1996; Maass, Salvi, Arcuri, & Semin, 1989). Maass has revealed that there are positive ingroup and negative outgroup biases in the way that language is used. People are more likely to talk in abstract than concrete terms about an outgroup's undesirable characteristics, and vice versa for desirable characteristics. Consequently, the ratio of abstract to concrete language usage, in relation to desirable versus undesirable characteristics, could be used as an index of prejudiced attitudes towards a particular group. Other techniques have involved the detailed analysis of discourse to reveal hidden attitudes (van Dijk, 1987, 1993; see Chapter 15) and a similar analysis of non-verbal communication (Burgoon, Buller, & Woodall, 1989; see Chapter 15).

2. *Attitude priming* Fazio and his colleagues (Fazio, Sanbonmatsu, Powell, & Kardes 1986; Fazio, Jackson, Dunton, & Williams, 1995) have used priming to explore how we make a judgment more quickly when an underlying attitude is congruent

with a 'correct' response. While looking at a series of photographs of black and white people, participants had to decide by pressing a button whether an adjective (from a series of positive and negative adjectives) that followed very quickly after a particular image was 'good' or 'bad'. White participants were slower in rating a positive adjective as good when it followed a black image, and black participants were slower in rating a positive adjective as good when it followed a white image.

3. *Implicit Association Test* Similarly, Greenwald and his colleagues (Greenwald, McGhee, & Schwartz, 1998; see Kihlstrom, 2004) developed the **implicit association test** (IAT) using a computer display coupled with responses via a keyboard (see Box 5.6). They aimed to reveal underlying negative interethnic attitudes, for example, by comparing the response latencies of American Japanese with American Koreans. The Japanese responded more quickly when a Japanese name was paired with a pleasant word, and the Koreans did the same when a Korean name was paired with a pleasant word.

CONCLUDING THOUGHTS ON ATTITUDE MEASUREMENT

Attitudes have been treated as comprising three components: cognitive, affective and behavioural. However, what is traditionally done in attitude research is to present a set of belief or cognitive statements in a communication, and then to measure only changes in affect. Even more curious and alarming is that the areas of psychological scaling (psychometrics) and attitude change have largely ignored each other. Few of the hundreds of studies performed on attitude change make use of the scaling techniques developed by Thurstone, Likert, Guttman, Osgood and others. It is equally rare for those interested in measurement and scaling procedures to be interested in applied, empirical research on attitude change (Osgood's use of the semantic differential being a notable exception).

Having seen the great variety of measures (and operational definitions) employed for attitudes, we should not be surprised that findings in this area often conflict. Some investigators using attitude scales do so on the basis of ease of measurement, or intuition. The area of attitude measurement needs to be treated with caution,

---

BOX 5.6 — The implicit association test

Cognitive research methods used in social cognition have recently produced an ingenious solution to the problem of measuring underlying attitudes in contexts where people may want to conceal what they really think—the implicit association test (IAT) (Greenwald, McGhee, & Schwartz, 1998).

Based on the ideas that attitudes are associative mental networks and that associations are stronger if the attitude exists than if it doesn't, it follows that people will more quickly link concepts that are related than those that are not. So, if you dislike property developers, you will more quickly respond 'yes' to the word 'nasty' and 'no' to the word 'nice' than if you do not have a negative attitude to developers. The IAT has participants press different keys on a keyboard or button box to match concepts (e.g. Aborigine, lazy). What happens is that, where an attitude exists, the reaction is much faster when the concepts share a response key than when they do not.

The IAT has become remarkably popular in recent years as a technique for measuring prejudice in liberal Western societies like the United States (see Chapter 10). It appears to be internally consistent and well correlated with, and often superior to, other measures of prejudice and implicit attitudes (Cunningham, Preacher & Banaji, 2001; Greenwald, Banaji, Rudman, Farnham, Nosek, & Mellott, 2002). It can even measure newly emergent negative attitudes to very minimally defined laboratory groups (Ashburn-Nardo, Voils, & Monteith, 2001).

---

and it is easy to see why some researchers wanted to abandon the attempt during the 1960s and early 1970s.

Finally, we must remember that the failure to detect a certain attitude does not imply that it does not exist; our choice of method may limit our capacity to unearth it. Further, an attitude may 're-emerge' after a period of time. Consider the very public expressions of racism in recent years by some Australian political figures. Has an attitude re-emerged that was more prevalent in years gone by, or is it an overt expression of a commonly held attitude that runs counter to the usually expressed norm of equality? Chapter 10 confronts some of these issues.

Summary

- Attitudes have been a major interest of social psychologists since the early days of the field. They have also been described as the most important concept in social psychology.

- Theories dealing with attitude structure generally agree that attitudes are lasting general evaluations of socially significant objects (including people and issues). Some theories also emphasise that attitudes are relatively enduring organisations of beliefs and behavioural tendencies towards social objects.

- Attitude structure has been studied mostly from a cognitive viewpoint. Heider's balance theory stimulated interest in the phenomenon that people strive to be internally consistent in their beliefs.
- The link between attitudes and behaviour has been a source of controversy. The apparently poor predictive power of attitude measures led to a loss of confidence in the concept itself. Fishbein argued that attitudes can indeed predict behaviour. However, if the prediction concerns a specific act, the measure of attitude must also be specific.
- Fishbein and Ajzen's theory of reasoned action included the need for relating a specific act to a measure of the intention to perform that act. Other variables that can affect the predicted behaviour are norms provided by other people, and the extent to which the individual has control over the act.
- A strong attitude, according to Fazio, has a powerful evaluative association with the attitude object. This

makes it more accessible in memory and more likely to be activated and the related behaviour performed. A more accessible attitude can also involve a cost; high accessibility can lead to insensitivity to change in the attitude object.

- Attitudes are learned. They can be formed by means of direct experience, conditioning, observational learning, and by drawing inferences from our own behaviour (self-perception).
- A value is a higher-order concept, which can play a guiding and organising role in relation to attitudes. Ideology and social representations are other related concepts.
- Measuring attitudes is both important and difficult. Traditional techniques include Thurstone's method of equal-appearing intervals, Likert's method of summated ratings, Guttman's scalogram and Osgood's semantic differential. A more recent method is Fishbein's expectancy-value scale.
- Physiological and overt behavioural measures are further indirect attitude measurement techniques.

LINKS

YOU HAVE READ ABOUT:	WHICH LINKS TO:
Structure and function of attitudes	cognitive activities and cognitive representations (2, 3, 4)
How attitudes are linked to behaviour	how prejudice is linked to discrimination (10, 11)
Forming attitudes	modelling and aggression (12), modelling and prosocial behaviour (14)
Social representations	discourse and social representations (15)
Physiological measures of attitude	facial expressions of emotion (15)

Key terms

acquiescent response set (p. 119)
attitude (p. 97)
attitude formation (p. 112)
automatic activation (p. 108)
balance theory (p. 99)
bogus pipeline technique (p. 124)
cognition (p. 99)
cognitive consistency theories (p. 99)
construal (p. 101)
expectancy-value model (p. 122)

Guttman scale (p. 120)
ideology (p. 115)
implicit association test (p. 126)
information integration theory (p. 101)
information processing (p. 101)
Likert scale (p. 119)
mere exposure effect (p. 112)
meta-analysis (p. 103)
modelling (p. 113)
moderator variable (p. 110)
multiple-act criterion (p. 103)

norms (p. 110)
one-component attitude model (p. 97)
priming (p. 110)
protection motivation theory (p. 107)
self-efficacy (p. 107)
self-perception theory (p. 114)
self-rating scale (p. 117)
semantic differential (p. 120)
social representations (p. 116)
sociocognitive model (p. 99)
'tall poppy' syndrome (p. 115)

FURTHER READING

Belch, G. E., & Belch, M. A. (2004). *Advertising and promotion: An integrated marketing communications perspective* (6th ed.). New York: McGraw-Hill/Irwin. Advertising principles developed over several decades have drawn heavily on major attitude theories formulated by social psychologists. This textbook details this interface and gives many examples of applied attitude research.

Eagly, A. H., & Chaiken, S. (1993). *The psychology of attitudes.* San Diego, CA: Harcourt Brace Jovanovich. A comprehensive and detailed review of attitude theory and research—probably already a classic—which rode the crest of the upsurge in attitude research in the 1980s.

Eagly, A. H., & Chaiken, S. (1998). Attitude structure and function. In D. T. Gilbert, S. T. Fiske, & G. Lindzey (Eds.), *The handbook of social psychology* (4th ed., Vol. 1, pp. 269–322). Boston, MA: McGraw-Hill. An up-to-date coverage of attitude components and dimensions, beliefs, ideology, attitude strength, memory and links with behaviour.

Fazio, R. H., & Olson, M. A. (2003). Attitudes: Foundations, functions, and consequences. In M. A. Hogg & J. Cooper (Eds.), *The Sage handbook of social psychology* (pp. 139–160). London: Sage. An up-to-date, comprehensive and readable overview of attitude theory and research.

Oppenheim, A. N. (1992). *Questionnaire design, interviewing and attitude measurement* (2nd ed.). London: Pinter. A well-illustrated and comprehensive guide to using survey methods, interviewing, sampling and other social research techniques. It incorporates easy-to-follow and field-relevant examples and is an invaluable companion to the practitioner.

Oskamp, S. (1991). *Attitudes and opinions* (2nd ed.). Sydney: Prentice Hall. A broad coverage of research and concerns about attitudes and opinion. Written in an interesting and readable manner, it presents a historical perspective, relevant theory and fairly recent research.

Robinson, J. P., Shaver, P. R., & Wrightsman, L. S. (Eds.) (1991). *Measures of personality and social psychological attitudes.* New York: Academic Press. A comprehensive source book of scales commonly used in social psychology and the study of personality.

Schwarz, N. (1996). Survey research: collecting data by asking questions. In G. R. Semin & K. Fiedler (Eds.), *Applied social psychology* (pp. 65–90). London: Sage. A brief but useful bird's-eye view of questionnaire design, with examples.

Terry, D. J., & Hogg, M. A. (Eds.). (2000). *Attitudes, behaviour, and social context: The role of norms and group membership.* Mahwah, NJ: Erlbaum. The chapters are contributed by leading scholars on the role of group norms and other social contextual factors in the relationship between attitudes and behaviour. The consideration of norms, group membership and social identity processes is a growing new direction for attitude research.

CHAPTER SIX

Persuasion and attitude change

THIS CHAPTER DISCUSSES:

- the persuasion process: communicator, message and audience
- current models of persuasion: elaboration likelihood and heuristic–systematic processing
- tactics for enhancing compliance
- the theory of cognitive dissonance and its research paradigms
- resistance to persuasion.

FOCUS QUESTIONS

1. Angeline offers you $500 for your prized mountain bike, which you think is a fair price. After checking her bank balance, she reduces the offer to $450, saying that's all she can afford. Could such a tactic work?

2. You have just joined the army. Along with other cadets you listen to an amazing talk by an officer skilled in the use of survival techniques in difficult combat conditions. Among other things, he asks you to eat some fried grasshoppers. 'Try to imagine this is the real thing! You know, you might have to do this to save your life one day,' he says. Despite your first reaction, you go ahead and eat them. Would you end up liking these critters more if the officer's style of presentation was warm and friendly or cold and distant?

Attitudes, arguments and behaviour

In Chapter 5 we saw that attitudes do not readily predict behaviour, and that the attitude–behaviour relationship can be so weak that some researchers have, in frustration, even suggested abandoning the attitude concept entirely.

In this chapter we focus on how attitudes can change over time, concentrating our attention on what kind of interventions might bring about such change and the nature of the processes involved. By the time we have finished, we trust you will conclude that much of the reservation about the usefulness of the concept of attitude is misdirected. In particular, we hope to show that discrepancies between attitudes and behaviour, rather than being an embarrassment to attitude theory, engage crucial processes through which **attitude change** can occur.

Given the many hundreds of studies that have dealt with the topic of changing attitudes, and the variety of perspectives that have been taken in interpreting the findings, we concentrate on two general approaches that have guided the development of explanation.

The first is an orientation that concentrates on using arguments to convince people that a change of mind, and perhaps of behaviour, is needed. Research in this area has concentrated on the nature of the message— that is, the persuasive communication that will be effective—and considers a large number of variables that may determine what will do the trick in trying to change another person's mind. Obvious areas of application relate to political propaganda and advertising. Not surprisingly, these contexts have provided impelling needs for both basic and applied research and have stimulated many studies over recent decades.

The second orientation focuses on the active participation of the person. By engaging people in carrying out certain activities, we may have it in mind to change their underlying attitudes. This path to attitude change is a particular focus of **cognitive dissonance**, one of the consistency theories of attitude referred to in Chapter 5. The first orientation starts from the premise that you reason with people to change how they think and act, but the second orientation eliminates reasoning. Simply persuade others to act differently, even if you have to use trickery; later they may come to *think* differently (i.e. change their attitude) and should then continue acting the way you want.

Persuasive communication

The receptive powers of the masses are very restricted, and their understanding is feeble. On the other hand,

Persuading the masses: Hitler felt that the content of an effective public message needed to be simple. Slogans were a key ingredient of Nazi propaganda.

they quickly forget. Such being the case, all effective propaganda must be confined to a few bare essentials and those must be expressed as far as possible in stereotyped formulas. These slogans should be persistently repeated until the very last individual has come to grasp the idea that has been put forward. If this principle be forgotten and if an attempt be made to be abstract and general, the propaganda will turn out ineffective; for the public will not be able to digest or retain what is offered to them in this way. Therefore, the greater the scope of the message that has to be presented, the more necessary it is for the propaganda to discover that plan of action which is psychologically the most efficient.

Hitler, *Mein Kampf*, 1933

Research dealing with the relationship between **persuasive communication** and attitude change is most closely associated with advertising. According to Schwerin and Newell (1981, p. 7), behavioural change 'obviously cannot occur without [attitude change] having taken place'. For a long time, social psychologists have been interested in the nature of successful versus unsuccessful persuasion. Yet, despite the large part persuasive messages play in influencing human social behaviour, only in the past 30 or so years have social scientists studied what makes persuasive messages effective.

Systematic investigation began towards the end of World War II. Carl Hovland was employed by the United States War Department to investigate research questions arising from the extensive use of wartime propaganda (e.g. by Adolph Hitler and the Nazi Party; see the quotation above). After the war, Hovland continued this work at Yale University, in what was the first coordinated research program dealing with the social psychology of persuasion. Research funding was again politically motivated. This time it was the United States' concern with the perceived threat felt during the 'Cold War' period with the Soviet Union, and the 'wish to justify its ways to the classes and win the hearts and minds of the masses' (McGuire, 1986, p. 99). The main features of this pioneering work were outlined in the research team's book, *Communication and Persuasion* (Hovland, Janis, & Kelley, 1953). They suggested that

the key to understanding why people would attend to, understand, remember and accept a persuasive message was to study the characteristics of the person presenting the message, the contents of the message, and the characteristics of the receiver of the message.

The general model of the Yale approach, shown in Figure 6.1, is still employed as the basis of contemporary *communications theory* in marketing and advertising (see Belch & Belch, 2004).

Hovland, Janis and Kelley asked, 'Who says what to whom and with what effect?', and studied three variables in the context within which persuasion takes place:

1. the communicator, or the source (who);
2. the communication, or message (what);
3. the audience (to whom).

Hovland and his colleagues identified at least three distinct steps in the persuasion process: attention, comprehension and acceptance. This research program spanned nearly three decades and produced a vast amount of data. Box 6.1 is a summary of the main findings.

Not all the findings based on the early Yale research program have lasted. Baumeister and Covington (1985)

A CLASSIC IN SOCIAL PSYCHOLOGY

FIGURE 6.1 The Yale approach to communication and persuasion

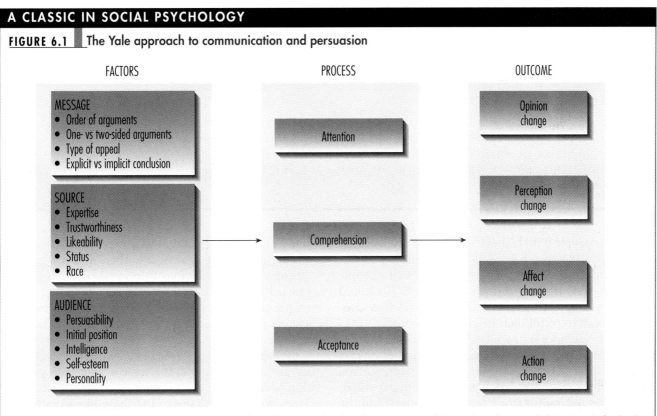

Note: In this classic research, various message, source and audience factors were found to affect the extent to which people can be persuaded. See Box 6.1 for details of such message factors.

Source: Based on Janis & Hovland (1959).

BOX 6.1   Characteristics of a communication likely to lead to attitude change

Finding	Factor
• Experts are more persuasive than non-experts (Hovland & Weiss, 1952). The same arguments carry more weight when delivered by someone who presumably knows all the facts.	Communicator
• Popular and attractive communicators are more effective than unpopular or unattractive ones (Kiesler & Kiesler, 1969).	Communicator
• People who speak rapidly are more persuasive than people who speak slowly (Miller, Maruyama, Beaber, & Valone, 1976). One reason is that rapid speech conveys the impression that the speaker knows what she is talking about.	Communicator
• We are more easily persuaded if we think the message is not deliberately intended to persuade or manipulate us (Walster & Festinger, 1962).	Message
• Persuasion can be enhanced by messages that arouse fear in the audience (Leventhal, Singer, & Jones, 1965). To persuade people to stop smoking, for instance, it may be useful to create a fear of dying from lung cancer by showing a cancerous lung to smokers. You have seen this approach in television adverts designed to reduce the road toll or promote safety in the workplace.	Message
• Persuasion can be enhanced by using evaluatively biased language, but these effects depend on the amount of cognitive effort. [Evaluatively biased language refers to using evaluatively biased terms in judging an attitudinal issue.] (van Schie, Martijn, & van der Pligt, 1994).	Message
• People with low self-esteem are persuaded more easily than people with high self-esteem (Janis, 1954).	Audience
• People are sometimes more susceptible to persuasion when they are distracted than when paying full attention, at least when the message is simple (Allyn & Festinger, 1961).	Audience
• When persuasion is tough—that is, when the audience is hostile—it is more effective to present both sides of the issue than just one side (Hovland, Lumsdaine, & Sheffield, 1949).	Message and audience
• A message is less persuasive when given in a powerless linguistic style (frequent hedges, tag questions and hesitations) than in a powerful linguistic style (absence of the mentioned features). The speaker and the arguments are perceived more negatively with a powerless linguistic style (Holtgraves & Lasky, 1999). See Chapter 15 for a discussion of linguistic style.	Communicator and message

found that people with high self-esteem are just as easily persuaded as those with low self-esteem, but they do not want to admit it. When persuasion does occur, people may even deny it. Bem and McConnell (1970) found that when people do succumb to persuasion they conveniently fail to recall their original opinion.

Most contemporary social psychologists see the persuasion process as a series of steps. They do not always agree on what the important steps in this sequence are, but do agree that the audience has at least to pay attention to the communicator's message, understand the contents and think about what was said (Eagly & Chaiken, 1984). The audience's thoughts are critical in this process (Petty & Cacioppo, 1981): the message will ultimately be accepted if it activates favourable ideas, whereas the communication will be rejected if the recipients argue strongly against it in their minds.

People are not oblivious to persuasion attempts. We can hardly avoid commercial advertising, public education programs and political propaganda. Interestingly, most people consider that they are less likely to be influenced than others by advertisements. This has been called the **third-person effect** ('You and I are not influenced, but they are'). For example, if we see a mundane product being advertised by using attractive models in an exotic setting, we assume that we (and those like us) are wiser than others to the tricks of the advertising industry, whereas we are really just as susceptible.

Julie Duck and her associates at the University of Queensland have conducted a series of studies of the third-person effect, demonstrating its application to political advertising and AIDS advertising (Duck, 1998; Duck, Hogg, & Terry, 1995, 1998; Duck, Terry, & Hogg, 1995, 1998).

In the next three sections, we look at each of the three links in the persuasion chain: the communicator, the message and the audience. It must be stressed that in any given context all three are operative. Some of the studies noted below do indeed deal with more than one of these three variables at a time, and they often interact: for example, we note that whether an argument should present a one-sided or a two-sided case can depend on how intelligent the audience is considered to be.

THE COMMUNICATOR

The Yale communication program showed early on that there is a group of variables relating to characteristics of the source (communicator) that can have significant effects on the acceptability of a message to an audience. A good level of expertise, good physical looks and extensive interpersonal and verbal skills will make a communicator more effective. Triandis (1971) has argued that a communicator who is an expert with knowledge, ability and skill demands more of our respect. Furthermore, there are people with whom we are familiar, or to whom we feel close and to whom we are attracted. Such people are able to exert more influence on us than others. There are others who have power and can therefore exert some control over the kinds of reinforcements we might receive.

In all these cases, such sources of influence are likely to have the best chance of persuading us to change our attitudes and behaviour.

Source credibility

The communicator variable affects the acceptability of persuasive messages. Other source characteristics playing a part in whether recipients will accept or reject a persuasive message include attractiveness, likeability and similarity. *Attractiveness* was shown to be effective in the 1980s, when the American actor Bill Cosby was used extensively in television commercials advertising everything from home computers to frozen ice-cream, while pop stars Michael Jackson and Tina Turner advertised soft drinks. The assumption of these advertising campaigns is that attractive, popular and likeable spokespersons are persuasive and thus are instrumental in enhancing consumer demand for a product. Attitude research generally supports this logic (Chaiken, 1979, 1983).

With regard to *similarity*, as people tend to like those who are similar to them, sources who are similar to a recipient should be more persuasive than sources who are dissimilar: for example, a member of your peer group should be more persuasive than a stranger. However, it is not quite this simple (Petty & Cacioppo, 1981). When the issue concerns a matter of taste or judgment (e.g. who was Australia's greatest tennis player of all time?), similar sources are better accepted than dissimilar sources. However, when the issue concerns a matter of fact (e.g. which German athlete won the greatest number of gold medals at the Olympic Games?), dissimilar sources are accepted more readily (Goethals & Nelson, 1973).

We have already noted that no one communication variable can be treated in total isolation, and that what

Source credibility: This is not a job for you! It takes a top professional coach to advise players at Real Madrid about their game plan.

'works' in the persuasion process is an interaction of three categories of variables ('communication language' terms are given in parentheses):

1. The **source** (sender)—from whom does the communication come?
2. The **message** (signal)—what medium is used, and what kinds of arguments are involved?
3. The **audience** (receiver)—who is the target?

Many experiments have focused on a single variable; others look at two variables, one from each of two categories. An example of the latter kind was a study by Bochner at the University of New South Wales (Bochner & Insko, 1966), which dealt with source *credibility* in combination with the discrepancy between the opinion of the target and that of the source. With respect to credibility, Bochner expected that an audience would pay more attention to the opinion of the communicator who was thought to be more believable. He predicted that there is more room for attitude change when the target's opinion is more discrepant from that of the source.

Bochner's participants were students who were initially asked how much sleep was required to maintain their health. Most said eight hours. They were then exposed to two sources of opinion that varied in expertise and therefore credibility. One was a Nobel Prize-winning physiologist with expertise in sleep research (higher credibility), the other a YMCA instructor (lower credibility). Discrepancy was manipulated in terms of the amount of variation between student opinion and that of the source. If the source said that five hours was enough, the discrepancy was three hours with respect to the typical view of eight hours: the pressure to shift should be higher than if the discrepancy was only one hour. However, what would happen if the source said two hours was sufficient? Look at the results in Figure 6.2.

In terms of the discrepancy variable, more opinion change occurred at moderate levels of difference between the students and the source. It seems that extreme discrepancy is not a good tactic in influencing a target. The audience will resist if the difference is too great and may look for ways of discrediting the communicator ('They don't know what they are talking about!'). However, this effect interacted with the variable of credibility. It was the expert who could induce the greatest amount of change and this took place when discrepancy was marked. In Bochner and Insko's study, the change was maximal when the highly credible source advocated one hour of sleep and students had suggested eight hours, a discrepancy of seven hours.

THE MESSAGE

Several message variables have been intensively investigated for their relative power in inducing attitude change. When, for example, would we choose to present

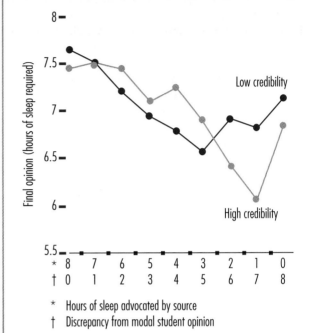

FIGURE 6.2 The effect of communicator credibility and position discrepancy on opinion change

Final opinion (hours of sleep required)

* Hours of sleep advocated by source
† Discrepancy from modal student opinion

Note: As a position adopted in a message becomes increasingly discrepant from what most people would accept, a more credible communicator becomes very effective in inducing opinion change.

Source: Based on data from Bochner & Insko (1966).

both sides of an argument rather than just our own? This variable reacts strongly according to characteristics of the audience. If the audience is against the argument but is also rated as fairly intelligent, it is more effective to present both sides. It is better to present only one side, however, if the audience is already on side and rather less intelligent (Lumsdaine & Janis, 1953; McGinnies, 1966).

Comparative advertising, in which a rival product is presented as inferior to a target product, is a common instance of using two-sided messages. When a consumer is not very motivated to buy the target product, comparative advertising can work (Pechmann & Esteban, 1994). An attentive and interested consumer is likely to process message information quite carefully, whereas comparative advertising is simply geared to making a product appear better. (How messages are handled in terms of dual-processing models of attitude change is dealt with below.)

Refer back to Box 6.1 for other examples of message variables that have been studied.

Effects of repetition

In the advertising industry, it is a maxim that a message needs to be repeated often in order to be both understood and recalled. It would be tempting to infer that advertising agencies wish to increase their profits by recommending to their client that frequent exposure of a message increases its effectiveness. If we believe the advertising industry, however, this is not a major motive. According to Ray (1988), the main goal is to strive for repetition minimisation—that is, to have the maximum impact with the minimum exposures and therefore the most cost-effective expenditure. It seems that television advertising exposure reinforces preferences more than it motivates brand choices; and that the optimum rate is two to three times per week (Tellis, 1987).

In general, the issue of message repetition invites a look at the way in which information is processed and at how memory works. We see below that two recent models of attitude change that examine the process of message reception adopt a cognitive approach of this kind. Somewhat more startling is a finding by Arkes, Boehm and Xu (1991) that simple repetition of a statement makes it seem truer! Repeated exposure to an object clearly increases familiarity with that object. Repetition of a name can make that name seem famous (Jacoby, Kelly, Brown, & Jasechko, 1989).

(Note also that an increase in familiarity between people can increase interpersonal liking: see Chapter 13.)

Another variable that has received intensive study, because of the way in which it has been used by the media to induce people to obey the law or care for their health, is the use of fear.

Does fear work?

Fear-arousing messages may enhance persuasion—but how fearful can a message become and still be effective? Many agencies in our community persist with forms of advertising that are intended to frighten us into complying with their advice or admonitions. Health workers may visit the local school to give the children a talk about how 'Smoking is dangerous to your health'. To drive the point home, they might show the children pictures of a diseased lung. Television advertising may remind you that 'If you drink, don't drive', and perhaps try to reinforce this message with graphic scenes of carnage on the roads. In the late 1980s there was a now famous advertisement associating the Grim Reaper with unsafe sexual practices and the likelihood of contracting HIV. Does this work? The answer is a mixed one.

In an early study by Janis and Feshbach (1953), participants were encouraged to take better care of their teeth in three different contexts. In a low-fear condition, they were told of the painful outcomes of diseased teeth and gums, and suggestions were made about how to maintain good oral health. In a moderate-fear condition, the warning about oral disease was more explicit. In a high-fear condition, they were told that the disease could spread to other parts of their body and very

unpleasant visual slides were used showing decayed teeth and diseased gums. The participants reported on their current dental habits and were followed up again after one week.

Janis and Feshbach found an inverse relationship between degree of (presumed) fear arousal and change in dental hygiene practices. The low-fear participants were taking the best care of their teeth after one week, followed by the moderate-fear group and then by the high-fear group.

Leventhal, Watts and Pagano (1967) reported a contradictory result in a study of how a fearful communication might aid in persuading people to stop smoking. The participants were volunteers who wanted to give up their habit. In a moderate-fear condition the participants listened to a talk with charts used as illustrations to show the link between death from lung cancer and the rate at which cigarettes were used. In a high-fear condition, they also saw a graphic film about an operation on a patient affected by lung cancer. Their results pointed to a greater willingness to stop smoking among people in the high-fear condition.

How do we explain the discrepancy between these results? Both Janis (1967) and McGuire (1969) suggested that an inverted U-curve hypothesis might be applied to conflicting results (see Figure 6.3). McGuire's analysis distinguishes two parameters that could control the way we respond to a persuasive message, one involving comprehension and the other involving the degree to which we yield to change. The more we can understand what is being presented to us, and can conceive of ways to put this into effect, the more likely we are to go along with a particular message.

In the case of the role of fear as a variable, when it is at a very low level an audience may be little motivated

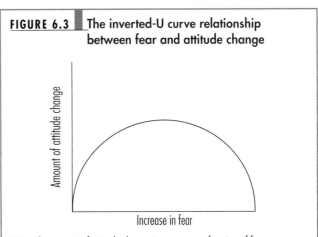

FIGURE 6.3 The inverted-U curve relationship between fear and attitude change

Amount of attitude change

Increase in fear

Note: The amount of attitude change increases as a function of fear up to a medium level of arousal. At high levels of fear, however, there is a fall-off in attitude change. This could be due to lack of attention to the stimulus, or to the disruptive effects of intense emotion, or both.

to attend to the message. As the fear content increases, so does arousal, interest and attention to what is going on. However, a very frightening way of presenting an idea may arouse so much anxiety, even to a state of panic, that we become distracted and miss some of the factual content of the message. What we don't know is whether the high-fear condition in the Janis and Feshbach study aroused more fear than the one in the Leventhal, Watts and Pagano study. If it did, then a curvilinear fit might be appropriate for the data. Therefore, there may be a limit to the effectiveness of attempting to arouse an audience emotionally. Disturbing TV images, for example, may distract a viewer from the intended message or, even if attended to, so upset the viewer that the entire episode is avoided.

In line with the dual-process models of information processing (see Chapters 2 and 5), Keller and Block (1995) argued that at a low level of fear a message probably does not spell out sufficiently the harmful consequences of an act. In contrast, a high-level scare tactic can rebound by interfering with the processing of a recommended change in behaviour.

Protection motivation theory (see Chapter 5) has offered further insights into the apparently contradictory role of fear appeals in eliminating dangerous health practices (see Wood, 2000, for a review). A threat should work if it includes an effective presentation of how to cope with the danger. Witte, Berkowitz, Cameron and McKeon (1998), for example, combined a fear appeal with the promotion of self-protective behaviours in a campaign to reduce the spread of genital warts.

These more modern approaches to the study of the differential effects of scary messages do not directly address the inverted U-curve hypothesis. Whether a message will achieve its result is determined by the trade-off between the perception of danger (*threat appraisal*) and whether people believe they can carry out the corrective behaviour (*coping appraisal*—see Figure 5.5 in Chapter 5).

Facts versus feelings

We note in Chapter 5 that a distinction is commonly drawn between belief and affect as components of an attitude. In the advertising industry, a related distinction is sometimes made between *factual* and *evaluative* advertising. The former deals with claims of fact and is thought to be objective, whereas the latter reflects opinion and is subjective. A factually oriented advertisement is high on information and is likely to emphasise one or more attributes among the following: price, quality, performance, components or contents, availability, special offer, taste, packaging, guarantees or warranties, safety, nutrition, independent research, company-sponsored research or new ideas. However, the simple recall of facts from an advertisement does not guarantee a change in the brand purchased. Furthermore, if there is factual content in a message, it is important for people to be able to assimilate and understand the general conclusion of the message (Albion & Faris, 1979; Beattie & Mitchell, 1985).

Even if a distinction is made between beliefs and feelings, evaluating an object (say, judging whether it is good or bad) is not identical to experiencing affect, or an emotion (see Chapter 5). From this point of view, we can repeat the argument that attitudes are fundamentally evaluations, which is where Thurstone (1928) started out. Applying this to an advertising context means that an evaluation refers to couching a message in such a way that it makes the consumer feel generally 'good' about the product, rather than attempting to convey a set of facts or objective claims.

A common method in evaluative advertising is to capitalise on the *transfer of affect*, which itself is based on associative learning. The tenor of evaluative advertising is caught in the following quotation (Sears, Peplau, & Taylor, 1991, p. 172):

Corporations pour millions of dollars into advertising aimed at convincing us that the lithest young women and the most athletic young men on the beach drink Coke (or Pepsi), the men who have the most fun in bars after work drink Bud (or Miller), and the fastest and smoothest cars, with the most beautiful drivers, are Pontiacs (or BMWs).

The distinction between facts and feelings does not imply that a given advertisement contains only factual or only evaluative material. On the contrary, modern marketing strategy favours using both approaches in an advertisement. A consumer can be led to *feel* that one product is superior to another by subtle associations with music or colour, or through the use of attractive models. The same consumer can be led to *believe* that the product is a better buy because it is better value for money.

Social psychological research debates whether the kind of appeal used should fit the basis on which an attitude is held. According to Edwards (1990), if the underlying attitude is emotional then the appeal should be as well, but if the attitude is centred on beliefs then a factual appeal should work better.

Millar and Millar (1990) argue for a mismatching— for example, using a factual appeal when the attitude is emotional. However, the attitude objects used by Edwards were not well known to the participants, whereas Millar and Millar tapped clearly held attitudes so that participants could counter with effective arguments.

This is an area awaiting further study (Petty & Wegener, 1998).

The medium and the message

Chaiken and Eagly (1983) have compared the relative effects on an audience of presenting messages in video, audio and written forms. This has obvious implications for advertising: which has more impact on the consumer—television, radio or printed media? It depends. If the message is simple, as much advertising is, the probable answer is: video > audio > written.

A mediating variable in this context is the relative ease or difficulty of comprehension for the audience. If the points of a message require considerable processing by the target person, a written medium is likely to be best. Readers have the chance to go back at will, mull over what is being said and then read on. If the material is quite complex, then newspapers and magazines come into their own. There is, however, an interesting *interaction* with the difficulty of the message. Look at the difference in effectiveness between various media in Figure 6.4. When the message was easy to comprehend,

Chaiken and Eagly found that a videotaped presentation brought about the greatest degree of opinion change. When the message was difficult, however, opinion change was greatest when the material was written.

Framing a message

The way is which a message is framed or slanted can have subtle effects on its meaning and, therefore, on whether it is accepted. For example, if the issue of 'affirmative action' is presented as 'equal opportunity' rather than 'reverse discrimination' people will view it more favourably (Bosveld, Koomen, & Vogelaar, 1997). In their review of how to promote health-related behaviours, Rothman and Salovey (1997) found that message framing has an important role. If the behaviour relates to detecting an illness, such as breast self-examination, the message should be framed in terms of preventing loss; but if the behaviour leads to a positive outcome, such as taking regular exercise, the message should be framed in terms of gain.

THE AUDIENCE
Self-esteem

In their 1950s studies, Hovland and his colleagues had noted that a distracted audience is more easily persuaded than one paying full attention, provided the message is simple, and that those who are low in self-esteem are more susceptible than those who have high self-esteem (refer back to Box 6.1). McGuire (1968) suggested that the relationship between persuasibility and self-esteem is actually curvilinear—that is, it follows an inverted U-curve of the kind shown in Figure 6.3 (substituting 'self-esteem' for 'fear'). This curve suggests that people who are either low or high on a measure of self-esteem are less persuasible than those in the middle. He reasoned that those with low self-esteem would either be less attentive or else more anxious when processing a message, whereas those high in self-esteem would be less susceptible to influence, presumably because they are generally more self-assured. (McGuire proposed a similar curvilinear relationship between intelligence and persuasability.)

With respect to the self-esteem connection, a review by Rhodes and Wood (1992) tested McGuire's proposition and concluded that the evidence overall supports his view.

Women and men

Another consistent, but more controversial, finding is that women are more easily persuaded than men (Cooper, 1979; Eagly, 1978). Crutchfield (1955) was the first to report this effect when he found that women were more conforming and susceptible to social

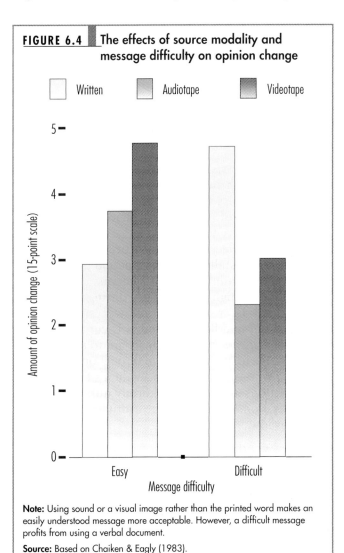

FIGURE 6.4 The effects of source modality and message difficulty on opinion change

Written   Audiotape   Videotape

Amount of opinion change (15-point scale)

Easy   Difficult
Message difficulty

Note: Using sound or a visual image rather than the printed word makes an easily understood message more acceptable. However, a difficult message profits from using a verbal document.

Source: Based on Chaiken & Eagly (1983).

influence than men. Some researchers have proposed that this difference exists because women are socialised to be cooperative and non-assertive and are therefore less resistant than men to attempts to influence them (Eagly, Wood, & Fishbaugh, 1981).

Sistrunk and McDavid (1971) suggested another explanation: women were more easily influenced than men, but only when the subject discussed was one with which men were more familiar. When the topic was female-oriented, men were more influenced than women (see also Chapters 7 and 10).

This finding led to the proposition that the consistent difference found in persuasibility had been due to a methodological bias. The persuasive messages used in attitude research had typically dealt with male-oriented topics and the researchers were usually male. If the topics had not been sex-biased, the male–female differences would not have been found. Because more recent studies are more sophisticated in both design and execution (e.g. Eagly & Carli, 1981), the conclusion they support is now widely accepted.

Carli (1990) investigated male–female differences in both the audience and the source. Participants heard a recorded message read by either a man or a woman, speaking either tentatively or assertively. When the reader was female and tentative rather than assertive, male listeners were more easily persuaded than female listeners. In contrast, male readers were equally influential under each condition. This suggests that there are variables of gender and gender-related persuasive effectiveness.

Covell, Dion and Dion (1994) investigated the effectiveness of tobacco and alcohol advertising as a function of gender and generation. The participants were female and male adolescents and their mothers and fathers. The participants indicated their rating of the image and of the quality of the advertised products, showing a preference for image-oriented over quality-oriented advertising. A gender difference was restricted to the adolescents, among whom female adolescents showed an even higher preference for image-oriented advertising. Covell, Dion and Dion suggested that, when advertisements target adolescents and feature alcohol and tobacco (seen so often in our cinemas), young women might be particularly attentive to image-oriented messages and judge drinking and smoking to be more desirable.

Individual differences

Consistent differences between individuals have been studied in relation to persuasibility. For example, Cacioppo and Petty (1982; see also Haugtvedt & Petty, 1992) reported that *need for cognition* (NC) played a significant role. A high scorer on their NC scale would agree with an item such as 'I really enjoy a task that involves coming up with new solutions to problems', but disagree with 'Thinking is not my idea of fun'. The high NC person should therefore be more likely to pay closer attention than a low NC person in reading a detailed verbal argument, such as a newspaper editorial.

There is a more general question here. When and why will people attend more clearly to some kinds of messages than others? We take this up when we look at dual-process models of persuasion in a later section. Other individual-difference variables that have been studied include *need for closure* (Kruglanski, Webster, & Klem, 1993), *need to evaluate* (Jarvis & Petty, 1995) and *preference for consistency* (Cialdini, Trost, & Newsom, 1995). Individual differences have also been found in *attitude importance* (Zuwerink & Devine, 1996). In these studies, high scorers on these dimensions were less likely to be persuaded than low scorers.

However, the relationship between personality variables and persuasion is rarely direct. Other variables, such as the social context, often moderate the relationship—which is consistent with the social psychological mantra that 'behaviour is a function of an interaction between the person and the situation'.

Age

Visser and Krosnick (1998) and Tyler and Schuller (1991) have suggested a relationship between age and susceptibility to attitude change, featuring five hypotheses:

1. *Increasing persistence*—susceptibility to attitude change is high in early adulthood and gradually decreases across the life span; attitudes reflect the accumulation of relevant experiences across the life span (a negative linear line).
2. *Impressionable years*—core attitudes, values and beliefs are crystallised during a period of great plasticity in early adulthood (an S-curve).
3. *Life stages*—high susceptibility during early adulthood and later life, but a lower susceptibility throughout middle adulthood (a U-curve).
4. *Lifelong openness*—individuals are to some extent susceptible to attitude change throughout their lives.
5. *Persistence*—most of an individual's fundamental orientations are established firmly during pre-adult socialisation; susceptibility to attitude change thereafter is low.

These hypotheses are derived as much from developmental psychology as social psychology, and which has the greatest explanatory power remains an open question. Tyler and Schuller's field study of attitudes towards the government supports the *lifelong openness* hypothesis: that is, age is generally irrelevant to attitude change. On the other hand, Visser and Krosnick's laboratory experiments support the *life stages* hypothesis.

The impressionable years: Respected adults, such as this teacher, are enormously influential in the development of young children's attitudes.

Other variables

Two other audience variables related to the persuasion process have attracted recent interest.

Prior beliefs affect persuasibility. There is evidence for a **disconfirmation bias** in argument evaluation: arguments incompatible with prior beliefs are scrutinised longer, subjected to more extensive refutational analyses and judged weaker than arguments compatible with prior beliefs. Furthermore, the magnitude and form of a disconfirmation bias is higher if prior beliefs are accompanied by emotional conviction (Edwards & Smith, 1996).

Even if arguments contain purely facts, prior beliefs affect whether factual information is considered at all. In a political discussion of the controversy over the causes for the stranding of a Soviet submarine near a Swedish naval base in 1981, the contending sides were most unwilling to accept facts introduced by each other into the debate, querying whether they were relevant and reliable (Lindstrom, 1997).

The disconfirmation bias is evident daily in media political discussions. For example, the disaster of the *Kursk*, a Russian submarine that sank in the Berent Sea in 2000, and the refusal of Western help in the rescue mission by Russian officials, sparked a debate similar to that in 1981.

Cognitive biases are important in both attitude formation and change (see also Chapter 3 for an overview). For example, Duck, Hogg and Terry (1999) demonstrated the third-person effect in media persuasion. According to this bias, people believe they are less influenced than others by persuasion attempts. Students' perceptions of the impact of AIDS advertisements on self, students (ingroup), non-students (outgroup) and people in general were examined.

Results showed that perceived self–other differences varied with how strongly students identified with being students. Those who did not identify strongly as students (low identifiers) exhibited the third-person effect, while those who did identify strongly as students (high identifiers) were more willing to acknowledge impact on themselves and the student ingroup.

Let us now consider how the persuasion process works.

COGNITIVE RESPONDING: TWO DUAL-PROCESS MODELS OF PERSUASION

Recent attitude research has focused on how we respond to the content of a message. Although different approaches have been taken by Petty and Cacioppo (Petty & Cacioppo, 1986b; Petty, Priester, & Wegener, 1994; Petty & Wegener, 1998) and by Chaiken (Bohner, Moskowitz, & Chaiken, 1995; Chaiken, 1980, 1987; Chaiken, Liberman, & Eagly, 1989; Eagly & Chaiken, 1993), there are elements in common. Each approach postulates two processes and draws on developments in research on memory from cognitive psychology (see Chapter 2). Both theories deal with persuasion cues. Sometimes, it may not be the quality or type of the persuasion cues that matters but rather the quantity of message processing that underlies attitude change (Mackie, Worth, & Asuncion, 1990).

Elaboration likelihood model

Adolph Hitler was convinced that ordinary people have only a feeble intellect for digesting arguments (see the opening quotation in this chapter). Closer to the truth is the fact that we often operate 'on automatic pilot'. According to Petty and Cacioppo's **elaboration likelihood model** (ELM), when people receive a persuasive message they think about the arguments it makes. However, they do not necessarily think deeply or carefully about the arguments, because to do so requires considerable cognitive effort. People are, after all, cognitive misers (see Chapter 2) who are motivated to expend cognitive effort only on issues that are important to them. Persuasion follows two routes, depending on whether people expend a great deal or very little cognitive effort on the message.

If the arguments of the message are closely followed, a *central route* is used. We learn the arguments in a message, extract a point that meets our needs, and even indulge mentally in counterarguments if we disagree with some of them. If the central route to persuasion is going to be used, the points in the message need to be convincingly put, as we will be required to expend considerable cognitive effort—that is, to work hard—on them. Suppose, for example, your doctor told you that you needed a major surgical procedure. The chances are that you would take a considerable amount of

Peripheral cues in advertising: Feeling hot and thirsty? Fancy buying a glass of cold water?

convincing, that you would listen carefully to what the doctor says, read what you could about the matter and even seek a second medical opinion.

On the other hand, when arguments are not well attended to, a *peripheral route* is followed. By using peripheral cues we act in a less diligent fashion, preferring a consumer product on a superficial basis, such as an advertisement in which the product is used by an attractive model. The alternative routes available according to the elaboration likelihood model are shown in Figure 6.5.

Heuristic–systematic model

In dealing with the same phenomena, Chaiken's **heuristic–systematic model** (HSM) uses slightly different concepts, distinguishing between *systematic* processing and *heuristic* processing. Systematic processing occurs when people scan and consider available arguments. In the case of heuristic processing we do not indulge in careful reasoning but instead use cognitive heuristics, or 'mental short-cuts', such as thinking that longer arguments are stronger. Persuasive messages are not always processed

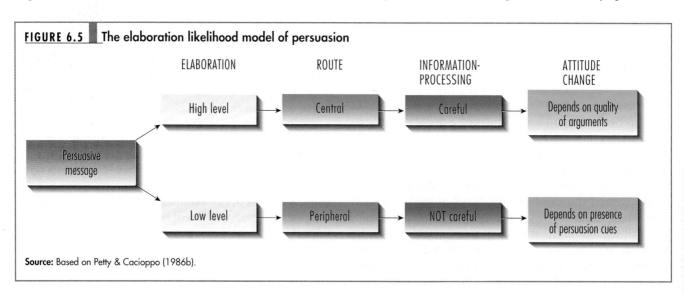

FIGURE 6.5 The elaboration likelihood model of persuasion

ELABORATION | ROUTE | INFORMATION-PROCESSING | ATTITUDE CHANGE

Persuasive message

High level → Central → Careful → Depends on quality of arguments

Low level → Peripheral → NOT careful → Depends on presence of persuasion cues

Source: Based on Petty & Cacioppo (1986b).

systematically. Chaiken has suggested that people will sometimes employ cognitive heuristics to simplify the task of handling information. You will recall that heuristics are a variety of simple decision rules or mental shortcuts that we use when we act like cognitive misers (see Chapter 2). So, when we are judging the reliability of a message, we may resort to such truisms as 'Statistics don't lie' or 'You can't trust a politician' as an easy way of making up our minds.

As previously discussed, this feature of judgment is actively exploited by advertising companies when they seek to influence consumers by portraying their products as supported by scientific research or expert opinion. For instance, washing detergents are often advertised in laboratory settings, showing much technical equipment and authoritative-looking people in white coats. At what point would we switch from heuristic to systematic processing? According to Petty (Petty & Wegener, 1998) people have a *sufficiency threshold*; heuristics will be used as long as they satisfy our need to be confident in the attitude we adopt. When we lack sufficient confidence we resort to the more effortful systematic mode of processing.

The emphasis on the strong role of cognition in relation to how we handle a persuasive message has been extended to cover the mediating role of transient states in the recipient, such as mood (e.g. Mackie & Worth, 1989; Petty, Schuman, Richman, & Strathman, 1993; Wegener, Petty, & Smith, 1995). Mackie and Worth (1989), for example, have shown that merely being in a good mood may change the way we attend to information.

Gorn (1982) reported that people were more likely to choose a product featured in an advertisement when the background music appealed to them. According to principles widely accepted in the fields of marketing and advertising (Belch & Belch, 2004), two factors underlie the use of background music:

- Music that appeals induces a good mood.
- Through classical conditioning, a product repeatedly associated with a good mood will come to be evaluated positively.

In addition, feeling 'good' makes it difficult to process a message systematically. Under time-limiting conditions, such as when watching a TV advertisement, a person already feeling good can be more susceptible to peripheral heuristic processing. Bohner, Chaiken and Hunyadi (1994) induced either a happy or a sad mood in 149 college students and then read them an argument that was strong, weak or ambiguous. All arguments were attributed to a highly credible source. They found that when the message was unambiguous, sad participants were more easily influenced by heuristic processing.

In a court of law, Schmidt and Brewer (2000) found that mood affected the way jurors process information

and come to a conclusion (see Chapter 5). Brewer and Hupfeld (2000) also found, in a mock-juror situation, that when the evidence presented does not lead to a reasonable level of judgmental confidence, heuristic processing takes over from systematic processing.

The degree of emotion associated with the content of a message can influence the 'choice' between processing methods. Hale, Lemieux and Mongeau (1995) investigated the type of processing used in response to a message varying in the degree of fear involved. Information tended to be processed centrally for low-fear messages and peripherally for high-fear messages.

Wegener, Petty and Smith (1995) demonstrated that, contrary to the common view that happy people scrutinise messages at a lower level, sometimes a happy mood can lead to more message processing. People who are happy may be more attentive, according to the *hedonic contingency* view (Wegener & Petty, 1994, cited in Wegener, Petty, & Smith, 1995).

Again, when individuals are impression-motivated—that is, aim to have a pleasant interaction—rather than accuracy-motivated, they express an attitude that is more consistent with their partner's in evaluative terms (Chen, Shechter, & Chaiken, 1996). This suggests that heuristic processing is associated with impression motivation (a desire to express socially acceptable attitudes) and systematic processing with being accurate.

As a reminder that social processes can be complex, consider a study by Chaiken and Maheswaran (1994), who argued that systematic processing can be eroded when certain variables interact (see Box 6.2).

In summary, when people are motivated to attend to a message and to deal with it *thoughtfully*, they use a central route to process it according to the ELM (Petty & Cacioppo) or process it systematically according to the HSM (Chaiken). When attention is reduced so that people become cognitively *lazy*, they use a peripheral route (Petty & Cacioppo) or resort to heuristics—simple decision rules (Chaiken).

Compliance: Interpersonal influence

The literature dealing with social influence sometimes uses the term **compliance** interchangeably with conformity. This can happen when 'conformity' is broadly defined to include a change in behaviour, as well as beliefs, as a consequence of group pressure. In this chapter, compliance refers to a *behavioural* response to a *request by another individual*, while conformity refers to the influence of a group on an individual.

We are daily confronted with demands and requests. Often they are put to us in a straightforward and clear manner, such as when a friend asks you to dinner, and

---

BOX 6.2 Systematic processing can be undermined

This study dealt with complex interactions between source and message variables, as well as task importance, in relation to whether people use heuristic or systematic processing. In New York, 367 students were asked to rate a new telephone-answering machine, the XT-100, in an experiment with three independent variables:

1. *Task importance* Some students believed that their opinion would weigh heavily, since sample size was small, in whether the machine would be distributed throughout New York; other students thought that their opinion would merely contribute to a much larger sample of New Yorkers and would not alter the outcome very much.

2. *Source credibility* The product description was supposedly written by either a high-credibility source (Consumer Reports) or a low-credibility source (the sales staff of KMart).

3. *Message type* A pretest established eight product features, four of which were important (e.g. could take different cassette types, screening of incoming calls) and four unimportant (e.g. colour range, special bolts for a wall). The important-to-unimportant ratio of these features was varied to create messages that were strong (4:2), ambiguous (3:3) or weak (2:4).

The findings for the students showed that:

- For the unimportant task (their opinion did not count for much), the machine was rated in terms of the credibility of the source—heuristic processing was used—regardless of whether the message was strong, ambiguous or weak.

- For the important task (their opinion really counted), the machine was rated in terms of message content—systematic processing was used—provided the message was clearly strong or clearly weak. Source credibility did not affect these ratings.

- However, source credibility did play a role when the task was important but the message was ambiguous. Both systematic and heuristic processing were used.

Source: Chaiken & Maheswaran (1994).

---

nothing more is requested. At other times, requests have a 'hidden agenda': for example, an acquaintance invites you to dinner to get you into the right mood to ask you to finance a new business venture. The result is often the same—we comply.

What are the factors and situations that make us more compliant, and why is it that we are more influenced on some occasions than others? According to Penner (1986), people influence us when they use effective tactics or have powerful attributes.

TACTICS FOR ENHANCING COMPLIANCE

A cornerstone of many economies has been to persuade people to comply with buying certain products. It is not surprising, therefore, that over the years many different tactics have been devised for enhancing compliance. Salespeople, especially, have designed and refined many indirect procedures for inducing compliance, as their livelihood depends on it. We have all come across these tactics.

One common tactic is **ingratiation**, in which a person attempts to influence others by first agreeing with them and getting them to like him/her. Next, various requests are made. You would be using ingratiation if you agreed with target people to appear similar, or to make them feel good; made yourself look attractive; gave compli-

ments; dropped names of those held in high esteem; or physically touched target people. Smith, Pruitt and Carnevale (1982) found that shoppers, when approached to sample a new food product, were more likely to sample and buy the item when they were touched in a socially acceptable way (though they did not think the food tasted any better!).

Use of the **reciprocity principle** is another tactic, based on the social norm that 'we should treat others the way they treat us'. If we do others a favour, they feel obliged to reciprocate. Regan (1971) showed that greater compliance was obtained from people who had previously received a favour than from those who had received none. Similarly, *guilt arousal* produces more compliance. When an experimenter induces feelings of guilt in a participant, the latter is ready to comply with a later request—for example, participation in future experiments, making a phone call to save native trees or agreeing to donate blood (Carlsmith & Gross, 1969; Darlington & Macker, 1966; Freedman, Wallington, & Bless, 1967). On the other hand, participants who were not made to feel guilty hardly ever complied.

Have you had your car's windscreen washed while you were waiting at traffic lights? If the cleaner washes it before you can refuse, there is a subtle pressure on you to pay for the service even though you didn't request it!

Multiple requests

A very effective tactic is the use of **multiple requests**. Instead of a single request, a two-step procedure is used, with the first request functioning as a set-up, or softener, for the second, real request. Three classic variations are the foot-in-the-door, the door-in-the-face and low-balling tactics (see Figure 6.6).

The **foot-in-the-door tactic** is based on the notion that if you get someone to agree to a small request, the person will later be more willing to comply with a large request. Some telephone salespeople use this approach. At first they might ask you to answer just a few questions 'for a small survey that we are doing' and then entice you to join 'the thousands of other Australians and New Zealanders' who subscribe to their product.

In a study by Freedman and Fraser (1966), participants were first contacted to answer a few simple questions about the kind of soap they used in the house. Later, they were more willing to comply with the larger request of allowing six people to come later and make a thorough inventory of all the household items present. Only 22% complied when they received the larger request 'cold', but 53% complied when they had been softened up by the initial questions about their soap.

DeJong (1979) suggested that the foot-in-the-door tactic can be understood in terms of self-perception theory (discussed later in this chapter). By complying with the small request, people become committed to their behaviour and develop a picture of themselves as 'giving'; the subsequent large request compels them to appear consistent.

The foot-in-the-door tactic may not always work. If the initial request appears too small or the second too large, the link between the multiple requests appears to break down (Foss & Dempsey, 1979; Zuckerman, Lazzaro, & Waldgeir, 1979). Nevertheless, a review by Saks (1978) suggested that, if the technique is carefully tuned, people can be induced to act as donors for organ and tissue transplants.

In a refinement of the tactic, students agreed to a series of graded requests rather than jumping from a small to a large request. In one line of research, people were presented with two requests (of increasing difficulty) prior to the third 'proper' or intended request (Goldman, Creason, & McCall, 1981; Dolinski, 2000). This has proven more effective than the classic foot-in-the-door technique. Think of this design as the 'two-feet-in-the-door technique'! Graded requests occur often among young dating adults. At first, a prospective partner might not agree to go with you on a 'date', but might well agree to go with you to study in the library. Your next tactic is to request another meeting and, eventually, a date.

In a Polish field experiment of the foot-in-the-door tactic, Dolinski (2000) arranged for a young man to ask people in the city of Wroclaw for directions to Zubrzyckiego Street. There is no such street. Most said they did not know, though a few gave precise directions! Further down the street, the same people were then asked by a young woman to look after a huge bag for five minutes while she went up to the fifth floor in an apartment building to see a friend. A control group was asked to look after the bag, but not for the street directions. Compliance with the second, more demanding, request was higher in the experimental group (see Figure 6.7; also Chapter 14 for a treatment of altruism).

As there is reasonable evidence across a variety of studies that the foot-in-the-door technique actually works, what psychological process could account for the phenomenon? Dolinski explained his results in terms of Bem's (1967) self-perception theory (see Chapter 4): in trying to help a stranger, although unsuccessfully, the participants inferred that they were altruistic and were therefore, more susceptible to later influence—even if that request was more demanding. Similarly, Cialdini

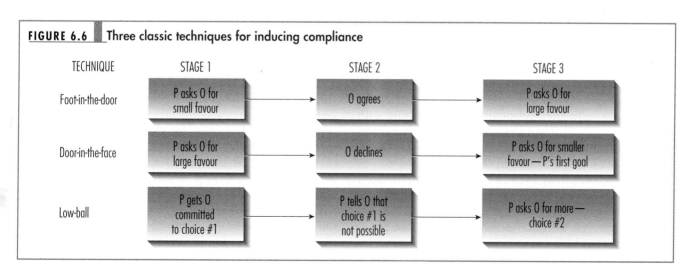

FIGURE 6.6 | Three classic techniques for inducing compliance

TECHNIQUE	STAGE 1	STAGE 2	STAGE 3
Foot-in-the-door	P asks O for small favour	O agrees	P asks O for large favour
Door-in-the-face	P asks O for large favour	O declines	P asks O for smaller favour — P's first goal
Low-ball	P gets O committed to choice #1	P tells O that choice #1 is not possible	P asks O for more — choice #2

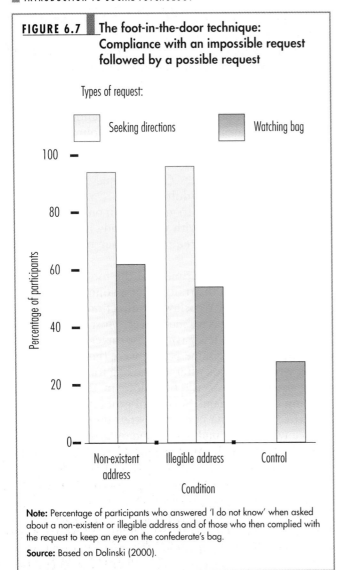

FIGURE 6.7 | The foot-in-the-door technique: Compliance with an impossible request followed by a possible request

Note: Percentage of participants who answered 'I do not know' when asked about a non-existent or illegible address and of those who then complied with the request to keep an eye on the confederate's bag.

Source: Based on Dolinski (2000).

Low ball: After consulting with his boss, a salesman tells a keen buyer that the quoted price for a new car no longer includes certain attractive 'extras'.

and Trost (1998) explain the effect in terms of the principle of *self-consistency*—we try to manage our self-concept is such a way that if we are charitable on one occasion then we should also be so on the second occasion.

Gorassini and Olson (1995), however, feel that it is a 'big ask' of this attitude change tactic to require an actual change in how people see themselves—the self-concept. Instead, they propose an explanation with fewer assumptions. The tactic alters the way we interpret situations that activate attitudes that enhance compliance. The self is left out of the loop.

What happens if an attempt to get a foot in the door fails? Common sense suggests that this should reduce the likelihood of future compliance. Surprisingly, the opposite strategy, the **door-in-the-face tactic**, can prove successful (Cialdini, Vincent, Lewis, Catalan, Wheeler, & Darby, 1975; Patch, 1986). Here, a person is asked

a large favour first and a small request second. Politicians especially are masters of this art. To illustrate, say that the government warns that student fees will go up 300%. Are you angry? Later, however, they announce officially that the rise will 'only' be 75%, the actual figure planned. You probably feel relieved and think 'That's not so bad' and, consequently, are more accepting.

Cialdini and his colleagues tested this tactic by approaching students with a huge request: 'Would you serve as a voluntary counsellor at a youth offenders centre two hours a week for the next two years?' Virtually no one agreed. However, when the researchers then made a considerably smaller request—'Would you chaperone a group of these offenders on a two-hour trip to the zoo?'—50% agreed. When the second request was presented alone, less than 17% complied. For the tactic to be effective, the researchers noted that the final request should come from the same person who asked the initial favour. According to them, participants perceive the scaled-down request as a concession by the influencer and, consequently, they feel pressure to reciprocate. If some other person were to make the second request, reciprocation would not be necessary.

According to Cialdini, the door-in-the-face technique may well capitalise on a contrast effect: just as lukewarm water feels cool when you have just taken your hand out of hot water, a second request seems more reasonable and acceptable when it is contrasted with a larger request. This procedure is prevalent in sales settings. If you inform a yacht broker that you will spend $20 000 on a small yacht and she then shows you a few run-down and overpriced examples, so that the higher-priced yachts (the ones she really wants to show you) look like bargains, she has used the door-in-the-face tactic.

The other multiple-request technique used in similar situations is the **low-ball tactic** (check the first focus question). Here, the influencer changes the rules halfway and manages to get away with it. Its effectiveness depends on inducing the customer to agree to a request, before revealing certain hidden costs. It is based on the principle that once people are committed to an action they are more likely to accept a slight increase in the cost of that action. This tendency for people to stick with decisions is also captured in the notion of *sunk costs* (e.g. Fox & Hoffman, 2002) where, once a course of action is decided on people will continue to invest in it even if the costs increase dramatically.

Suppose you shop around for a car and are confronted with the following chain of events. The car salesperson makes you a very attractive offer— a high trade-in price for your old car—and suggests a reduction on the marked purchase price for the car you have set your mind on. You decide to buy it and are ready to sign the papers. The salesperson then goes off to check the agreement with the boss, comes back, looks very disappointed and informs you that the boss will not sanction it, as they would lose money on the deal. You can still have the car, but at the marked price. What should you do? Surprisingly, many customers still go ahead with the deal. It seems that once you are committed you are hooked and reluctant to back out.

A commonplace example of low-balling is when someone asks 'Could you do me a favour?' and you agree before actually knowing what will be expected of you.

The effectiveness of low-balling was demonstrated by Cialdini, Cacioppo, Bassett and Miller (1978). They asked half the participants to be in an experiment that began at 7 am. The other half were asked first to commit themselves to participating in an experiment and then were informed that it would start at 7 am. The latter group, in the low-balling situation, complied more often

(56%) than the control group (31%) and also tended to keep the appointment.

These studies show us the circumstances in which compliance is likely to occur. In some situations our decision to comply may be a rational choice, in which we weigh the pros and cons of our action. Often, however, we act before we think. It has been argued that many of our compliant responses are 'mindless'—that is, we agree to many requests without even giving them a thought (Langer, Blank, & Chanowitz, 1978).

Langer and her colleagues conducted experiments in which people were asked to comply with requests with little or no justification. In one experiment, a person about to use a photocopy machine was interrupted by an experimenter who requested first use of the copier: (a) for no reason; (b) for a non-informative reason ('I have to make copies'); or (c) for a justified reason ('I'm in a rush'). Their findings indicated that as long as the request was a small one people were likely to agree to it, even if a spurious reason had been provided. They found that less compliance occurred when no reason at all was given.

Notwithstanding the fact that **mindlessness** may be a deciding factor in compliant behaviour, studies of power strategies indicate that this compliance often depends on the sources of power used.

ACTION RESEARCH

At about the time that Hovland and his associates were studying attitude change in the United States army, the expatriate German psychologist Kurt Lewin was undertaking another piece of practical wartime research on the home front for a civilian government agency. With the aim of conserving supplies in a time of food shortages and rationing, he tried to convince American housewives to feed their families unusual but highly nutritious foods, such as beef hearts and kidneys, rather than steak or roast beef.

Lewin considered that attitude change could best be achieved if the recipients were somehow actively engaged in the change process rather than just being passive recipients. He referred to this involvement of the participants in the actual research process, and its outcome, as **action research**. Lewin demonstrated that an active discussion between 'housewives' about how best to present beef hearts and other similar foods to their families was much more effective than merely giving them a persuasive lecture presentation. His data showed that 32% of the women in the first condition proceeded to serve the new food, compared with only 3% in the second condition (Lewin, 1943).

The emphasis on action by participants is not incompatible with the more passive approach to attitude change that characterised the work of Hovland and associates. For instance, Janis and King (1954)

investigated the effects of role-playing by their participants. They found that those who gave a speech arguing against something that they believed in (i.e. the participants acted out a role) experienced more attitude change than when they listened passively to a speech arguing against their position.

This early study of counterattitudinal behaviour foreshadowed research on cognitive dissonance (discussed in the next section). One of Lewin's students was Festinger, who believed that humans are active processors and organisers of the information they receive from the world around them and of the cognitions (attitudes, beliefs, ideas, opinions) they have about the world. He accepted the consistency principle, and argued that people will even change their ideas to make them consistent with what they are feeling or with how they are acting (Festinger, 1980). This would be the basis of the theory of cognitive dissonance.

In recent years, more and more social psychologists have used an action research approach to tackle community problems. An example is a study to combat skin cancer carried out in Melbourne by David Hill and his colleagues at the Centre for Behavioural Research in Cancer. Australia and New Zealand have the highest reported rates of melanoma in the world. One *SunSmart* health promotion program consisted of a three-year study dedicated to changing the sun-related attitudes and behaviours of Melbourne's residents (Hill, White, Marks, & Borland, 1993).

In the period 1988–90 the responses of nearly 4500 people were followed across a series of telephone interviews dealing with their views about being out in the sun. The campaign itself was called 'SLIP! SLOP! SLAP!' (slip on a shirt, slop on some sunscreen, slap on a hat) and was conducted over successive summers throughout Victoria, using various media.

An updated website for the SUNSMART PROGRAM 2003–2006 <http://www.sunsmart.com.au/s/about/about.htm> details changes in summer sun behaviour in 1988–2001. It points to a steady increase in the number of people who wear a hat, use a sunscreen, spend less time outside in the peak UV period and report less sunburn, although they are no more inclined to wear a long-sleeved top. Independent health statistics have also shown that rates of skin cancer have reached a plateau among people older than 40 years and begun to decline among younger people. By 2002 most primary schools in Victoria had adopted the *SunSmart* policy; as well, it has been implemented in other Australian states and in some parts of the United States, and has informed related programs for the World Health Organization.

The same team has tracked attitude and behaviour change in Victoria in relation to smoking (see Figure 6.8 and Box 6.3).

FIGURE 6.8 A set of six stickers offering positive anti-smoking slogans for use around children and babies

Source: Reproduced with permission from Quit Victoria.

Attitude–behaviour discrepancy and cognitive dissonance

Cognitive dissonance is a prime example of the cognitive approach in social psychology—emphasising beliefs as a central component of an attitude. As we see below, however, it also tackled the problem of attitude–behaviour discrepancy. Cognitive dissonance theory was developed by Festinger (1957) and became the most studied topic in social psychology during the 1960s. It states that cognitive dissonance is an unpleasant state of psychological tension generated when a person has two or more cognitions (bits of information) that are inconsistent or do not fit together. Cognitions are thoughts, attitudes, beliefs or states of awareness of behaviour. For example, if a husband believes that monogamy is an important feature of marriage, and yet is having an extramarital affair, he will probably experience a measure of guilt and discomfort (dissonance).

| BOX 6.3 | Quit smoking: Anti-smoking campaigns |

ANTI-SMOKING CAMPAIGNS SUCH AS *QUIT* HAVE REPORTED SOME SUCCESS IN CHANGING A HABIT THAT IS VERY RESISTANT TO CHANGE

Smoking has become an unfashionable activity in many countries over the last decade, and yet its incidence is still high. Even legislation against smoking in a shared work space and banning it on public transport has had limited success when measured by a decline in the percentage of people still addicted to smoking. According to the *Quit Evaluation Studies No. 6, 1990–1991*, the highest smoking rate in Victoria was found in the 20–29 years age group and it was more common in the working class ('lower blue collar') than in other groups.

Smokers tend to be well informed about illnesses related to their habit such as lung cancer, emphysema and heart disease. Despite this knowledge, current smokers tend to underestimate the risk of dying from smoking when compared with former smokers and those who have never smoked. This bias in risk perception has also been reported for those who use dangerous sexual practices (see Box 2.6 in Chapter 2, which deals with how the risk of contracting the HIV virus among practising male homosexuals can be underestimated).

There have been several concerted campaigns against smoking by a multidisciplinary team of health professionals, who have coordinated their activities within the Victorian Smoking and Health Program. They may have made a dent in the addiction figures. David Hill and his colleagues at the Centre for Behavioural Research in Cancer report that, from 1983 to 1991, there were 250 000 fewer smokers in the state: prevalence has declined from 34% to 26%, with comparable effects for men and women (Hill, White, Marks & Borland, 1993). The *Tobacco Act 1987* came into effect during this time, so it is probable that the decline in smoking is a product of the legislation combined with the *Quit* campaigns.

The Victorian *Quit* campaigns used different media and a variety of techniques to discourage smoking. One campaign adapted a television commercial and poster, while another used a direct-mail approach together with radio advertisements. Various celebrities helped by performing at places of work and by recording verbal messages. A classic, two-sided argument technique was tried, providing counterarguments for several commonly held self-exempting beliefs—that is, notions we apply to ourselves to exonerate the habit.

There have been different target groups. One campaign aimed to reach women, who outnumber men in the under-18 smokers' group, stressing the benefits of not smoking with respect to health, beauty and fitness. Another used baby and kid stickers (see Figure 6.8). One campaign highlighted the benefits of a smoke-free workplace and was conducted in major clothing chain stores throughout Victoria, supplemented by radio and television advertisements.

Nowadays there is a socially supportive context to quit, and the growing recognition that passive smoking is dangerous may help some in the future to quit permanently.

An interesting aspect of this work is how smoking cessation can be connected to the smoker's *intention to quit*: the act of giving up the habit can be traced through a series of stages. Biener and Abrams (1991) used the metaphor of a 'contemplation ladder' to suggest the stages that a person goes through in moving from thought to action when giving up smoking.

1. I'm taking action to quit—for example, cutting down (top of ladder).
2. I'm starting to think about how to change my smoking patterns.
3. I think I should quit, but I'm not quite ready.
4. I think I should consider quitting some day.
5. I have no thought of quitting (bottom of ladder).

This approach recognises that quitting is not an overnight decision, but a sequence of steps that a smoker can take. We can relate this analysis to the theoretical work of Ajzen and Fishbein (1980), which dealt with the relationship between attitude and intention, and to Ajzen's (1989) theory of planned behaviour (see Chapter 5).

Festinger proposed that we seek harmony in our attitudes, beliefs and behaviours and try to reduce tension from inconsistency among these elements. The unfaithful husband might try to reduce dissonance by changing one or more of the inconsistent cognitions (e.g. 'What's wrong with a little fun if no one finds out?'), by looking for additional evidence to bolster one side or the other ('My wife doesn't understand me') or by derogating the source of one of the cognitions ('Fidelity is an outcome of religious indoctrination'). The greater the dissonance, the stronger the attempts to reduce it. When people are in a state of dissonance, they become physiologically aroused. Changes in the electrical conductivity of the skin, typically associated with arousal, occur during dissonance and can be detected via a polygraph.

One great virtue of cognitive dissonance theory is

that it is stated in a broad and general way, which makes it applicable to many different situations in social psychology, particularly those involving attitude or behaviour change. For instance, it has been applied to understanding:

- people's feelings of regret and changes of attitude after making a decision;
- their patterns of exposing themselves to and searching for new information;
- reasons why people seek social support for their beliefs;
- attitude change in situations when non-support from a group acted as a dissonant cognition, when the self is tied to a salient common group membership;
- attitude change in situations where people have said or done something contrary to their customary beliefs or practice, as well as numerous other topics; and
- attitude change to reduce hypocritical behaviour (Stone, Wiegand, Cooper, & Aronson, 1997).

In Chapter 5 we noted that cognitive dissonance theory is often grouped with balance theory as one of a family of models that stress the human propensity for maintaining consistency in thought and action. However, a feature of dissonance theory that makes it unique is its ability to generate non-obvious predictions (Insko, 1967). This arises from the way the theory treats how we make choices and decisions in conflict situations—this becomes clearer in the sections that follow.

Three research paradigms can be distinguished in the many studies over the years since Festinger's original work (Worchel, Cooper, & Goethals, 1988): effort justification, induced compliance and free choice. Let's see how these differ.

EFFORT JUSTIFICATION

The moment we choose between two alternatives, we bring about a state of dissonance. Suppose you need some fast food tonight. You make the momentous decision to go to the hamburger bar rather than to the fried chicken outlet. The two alternatives will be mulled over, even after making your choice. The thought of that

Effort justification: She looks incredibly serene. All that dedication to yoga has paid off and, she believes, will ease the birth of her baby.

hamburger is getting better already. In terms of dissonance theory, the chosen alternative will be evaluated more favourably, or perhaps the other one will become less attractive, or both—at least for tonight. The way the **effort-justification** paradigm works is shown in Figure 6.9.

The notion of effort justification was explored in an early study by Aronson and Mills (1959). Female students volunteered to take part in a group discussion about sex, but were told that before they could join a group they must first pass a screening test for their capacity to speak openly. Those who agreed were assigned to one of two conditions. In the severe condition, they were given a list of obscene words and explicit sexual descriptions to read aloud; in the mild condition, they were to read a list that included words such as 'petting' and 'prostitution'.

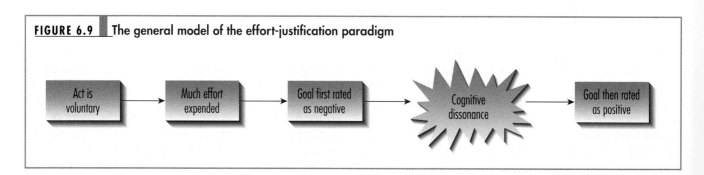

FIGURE 6.9 ▌ The general model of the effort-justification paradigm

Act is voluntary → Much effort expended → Goal first rated as negative → Cognitive dissonance → Goal then rated as positive

After being initiated, they listened over headphones to a discussion held by a group, with a view to joining in during the following week. What they heard was quite tame—far short of the embarrassing material they had been led to expect. The discussion was, in fact, a tape recording in which the participants had been primed to mumble, be incoherent and generally as boring as possible.

As well as the severe and mild initiation conditions, there was a control condition in which the participants did not undergo the screening experience.

The hypothesis was that the severe condition should have caused some suffering to the participants, and yet they had volunteered to participate in it. The act of volunteering to be embarrassed should cause dissonance. The predicted outcome would be increased liking for the chosen option (to participate in the discussion group), because the choice had entailed suffering. To make this sequence consonant would require the participant to rate the group discussion as more interesting than it really was.

Aronson and Mills found that the participants who had experienced the severe initiation rated both the group discussion and the other participants as much more interesting than did those in the mild or control conditions. The results are shown in Figure 6.10.

Later studies have demonstrated that the effort-justification effect can be particularly useful in inducing important behavioural changes relating to phobias and alcohol abuse. An interesting example is a study by Cooper and Axsom (1982), who assisted volunteers in a weight-reduction program. The participants were women who felt they needed assistance to lose body weight and were willing to try out a 'new experimental procedure'. Those wishing to participate were required to come to a laboratory where they were weighed and the procedure to be followed was explained to them.

In a high-effort condition, some women were told they needed to participate in a variety of time-consuming and effortful tasks, including the reading aloud of tongue-twisters for a session lasting 40 minutes. The investigators reasoned that the tasks used were based on psychological effort—that is, no physical exercise was involved. In a low-effort condition the tasks were shorter and easier; and in a control condition the volunteers did not participate in any tasks at all, but were simply weighed and asked to report again at a certain date.

The participants in the two experimental groups came to the laboratory for five sessions over a period of three weeks, at which point all the women were weighed again. The results are shown in Figure 6.11.

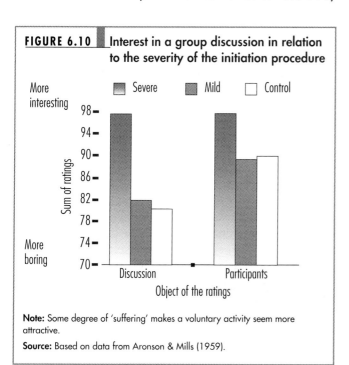

FIGURE 6.10 Interest in a group discussion in relation to the severity of the initiation procedure

Note: Some degree of 'suffering' makes a voluntary activity seem more attractive.

Source: Based on data from Aronson & Mills (1959).

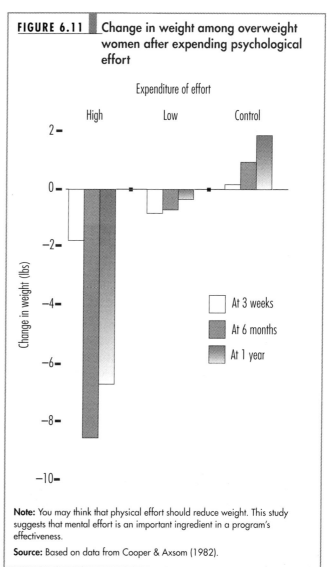

FIGURE 6.11 Change in weight among overweight women after expending psychological effort

Note: You may think that physical effort should reduce weight. This study suggests that mental effort is an important ingredient in a program's effectiveness.

Source: Based on data from Cooper & Axsom (1982).

Cooper and Axsom were encouraged to find that the weight loss effect in the high-effort group was not just an artifact of the interest shown in the women during the time of the five-week study. Without prior knowledge, the participants were contacted again after six months and after one year and agreed to be weighed again. The weight loss was much more marked after time had elapsed. After six months, a remarkable 94% of the high-effort group had lost some weight, while only 39% of the low-effort group had managed to do so.

INDUCED COMPLIANCE

Sometimes people are induced to act in a way that is inconsistent with their beliefs. An important aspect of the **induced-compliance** paradigm is that the inducement should not be perceived in terms of being forced against one's will.

Festinger and Carlsmith (1959) carried out an often-quoted experiment in which students who had volunteered to participate in a psychology experiment were asked to perform an extremely boring task for an hour, believing that they were contributing to research on 'measures of performance'.

Imagine that you are the volunteer and that in front of you is a board on which there are several rows of square pegs, each one sitting in a square hole. You are asked to turn each peg a quarter of a turn to the left and then a quarter of a turn back to the right. When you have finished turning all the pegs, you are instructed to start all over again, repeating the sequence over and over for 20 minutes. (This was not designed to be fun!)

When the 20 minutes are up, the experimenter tells you that you have finished the first part and you can now start on the second part, this time taking spools of thread off another pegboard and placing them all back on again, and again and again. Finally, the mind-numbing jobs are over.

At this point the experimenter lets you in on a secret: you were a control participant, but you can now be of 'real' help. It seems that a confederate of the experimenter has failed to show up. Could you fill in? All you have to do is tell the next person that the tasks are really very interesting. The experimenter explains that he is interested in the effects of preconceptions on people's work on a task. Later, the experimenter offers a monetary incentive if you would be willing to be on call to help again at some time in the future. Luckily, you are never called.

In the Festinger and Carlsmith study, participants in one condition were paid the princely sum of $1 for agreeing to cooperate in this way, while others in a second condition were paid $20 for agreeing to help. The experimental design also included a control group of participants who were not asked to tell anyone how interesting the truly boring experience had been, and

were paid no incentive. On a later occasion, all were asked to rate how interesting or otherwise this task had been.

According to the induced-compliance paradigm, dissonance follows from the fact that you have agreed to say things about what you have experienced when you know that the opposite is true. You have been induced to behave in a *counterattitudinal* way.

The variation in levels of incentive adds an interesting twist. Participants who had been paid $20 could explain their lie to themselves with the thought 'I did it for the $20. It must have been a lousy task indeed'. In other words, dissonance would probably not exist in this condition. (We should note that $20 was a sum of money not to be sneezed at by a student in the late 1950s.) On the other hand, those who told the lie and had been paid only $1 were confronted with a dilemma: 'I have done a really boring task, then told someone else that it is interesting, and finally even agreed to come back and do this again for a measly $1!'. Herein lies the dissonance.

One way of reducing the continuing arousal is to convince yourself that the experiment was really quite interesting after all. The results of this now-classic study are shown in Figure 6.12.

The interest ratings of the two reward groups confirmed the main predictions. The $1 group rated the task as fairly interesting, whereas the $20 group found it slightly boring (while control participants found it even more so). The $1 participants were also more willing to take part in similar experiments in the future. The main thrust of this experiment, which is to use a smaller reward to bring about a larger attitude change, has been replicated several times. To modify an old saying: 'If you are going to lead a donkey on, use a carrot, but make it a small one if you want the donkey to enjoy the trip'.

Talking of carrots, what about the 'fried grasshoppers' focus question? An intriguing experiment carried out in a military setting by Zimbardo and his colleagues (Zimbardo, Weisenberg, Firestone, & Levy, 1965) tackled this question. The participants were asked to comply with the aversive request of eating grasshoppers by an authority figure, whose interpersonal style was either positive (warm) or negative (cold).

According to the induced-compliance variation of cognitive dissonance, **post-decisional conflict** (and consequent attitude change) should be greater when the communicator is negative—how else could one justify behaving voluntarily in a counterattitudinal way?

Read what happened in this study in Box 6.4 and check the results in Figure 6.13.

Inducing people to act inconsistently with their attitudes is not an easy task and often requires a subtle approach. Counterattitudinal actions with foreseeable negative consequences, such as being quoted in a

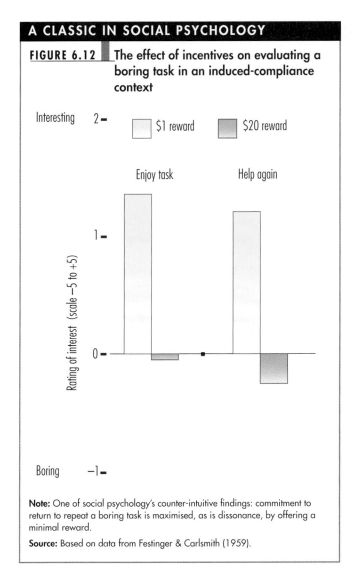

FIGURE 6.12 The effect of incentives on evaluating a boring task in an induced-compliance context

Note: One of social psychology's counter-intuitive findings: commitment to return to repeat a boring task is maximised, as is dissonance, by offering a minimal reward.

Source: Based on data from Festinger & Carlsmith (1959).

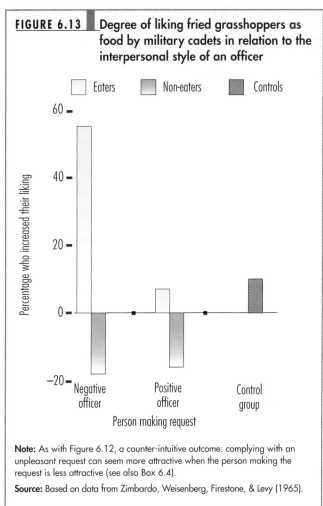

FIGURE 6.13 Degree of liking fried grasshoppers as food by military cadets in relation to the interpersonal style of an officer

Note: As with Figure 6.12, a counter-intuitive outcome: complying with an unpleasant request can seem more attractive when the person making the request is less attractive (see also Box 6.4).

Source: Based on data from Zimbardo, Weisenberg, Firestone, & Levy (1965).

Induced compliance: A celebrity in a reality television show about to eat a delicious little ant! If you think grasshoppers might be more to your taste, read Box 6.4.

newspaper saying that smoking is not harmful, require an intricate inducement, whereas actions with less serious or less negative consequences, like voting anonymously that smoking is harmless, may be less difficult to bring about. However, once people have been induced to act counterattitudinally, the theory predicts that dissonance will be strong and they will seek to justify their action (Riess, Kalle, & Tedeschi, 1981).

FREE CHOICE

Suppose that your choices between alternative courses of action are fairly evenly balanced, and that you are committed to making some kind of decision. This applies to numerous situations in our everyday lives: whether to buy this product or that, go to this tourist spot or another for a holiday, take this job offer or some other one. Based on Festinger's (1964) blueprint of the process of conflict in decision-making, the pre-decision period is marked by uncertainty and dissonance and the post-decision period by relative calm and confidence.

Free-choice dissonance reduction is likely to be a feature of wagers made on the outcome of sporting events, horse racing, gambling and so on. Once a person has made a choice between decision alternatives,

BOX 6.4   To know grasshoppers is to love them

ATTITUDE CHANGE FOLLOWING INDUCED COMPLIANCE

Think back to the focus question. This scenario, involving young military cadets, was actually researched in a famous study by Zimbardo and his colleagues. They arranged for an officer in command to suggest to the cadets that they might eat a few fried grasshoppers, and mild social pressure was put on them to comply. By administering a questionnaire about food habits earlier, they had ascertained that all the cadets thought there were limits to what they should be expected to eat, and that a meal of fried grasshoppers was one such limit. However, the officer gave them a talk indicating that modern soldiers in combat conditions should be mobile and, among other things, be ready literally to eat off the land. After his talk, the cadets were each given a plate with five fried grasshoppers and invited to try them out.

A critical feature of the experiment was the way in which the request was made. For half the cadets the officer was cheerful, informal and permissive. For the other half, he was cool, official and stiff. There was also a control group who gave two sets of food ratings but were never induced, or had the chance, to eat grasshoppers. The social pressure on the experimental participants had to be subtle enough for them to feel they had freely chosen whether or not to eat the grasshoppers. Indeed, an order to eat would not arouse dissonance, because a cadet could then justify his compliance by saying 'He made me do it'. Furthermore, the cadets who listened to the positive officer might justify complying by thinking 'I did it as a favour for this nice guy'. However, those who might eat the grasshoppers for the negative officer could not justify their behaviour in this way. The resulting experience should be dissonance, and the easy way of reducing this would be to change their evaluation of grasshoppers as a source of food.

As it turned out, about 50% of the cadets actually ate some grasshoppers. Those who complied ate, on average, two of the five hoppers sitting on their plate. The results in Figure 6.13 show the percentage of participants who changed their ratings of liking or disliking grasshoppers as food. It is interesting to note that in both the negative and positive officer conditions eaters were more favourable and non-eaters less favourable. This suggests that a degree of self-justification was required to account for an act that was voluntary but aversive. However, the most interesting result concerned the negative officer condition. This is the case in which dissonance should be maximal and, in line with the theory, it was here that the biggest change towards liking the little beasties was recorded.

Source: Based on Zimbardo, Ebbeson, & Maslash (1977); Zimbardo, Weisenberg, Firestone, & Levy (1965).

dissonance theory predicts that the person making a bet will become more confident about a successful outcome. Younger, Walker and Arrowood (1977) interviewed people at a Canadian national exposition who were either (a) about to bet, or (b) had just placed their bets, on games such as bingo and wheel of fortune, and asked them to rate their confidence in winning. They found that people who had already made their bet were more confident of winning (see Figure 6.14).

REDUCING DISSONANCE INDIRECTLY: THE ROLE OF SELF

In previous sections we looked at a variety of paradigms in which a person can reduce dissonance by directly (not necessarily consciously) confronting the conflict and attempting to solve it. Here we discuss two other aspects of dissonance reduction that seem to hinge on the role of self-conception.

Self-affirmation

According to Aronson (e.g. 1999), self-conception is central to dissonance. People strive for a view of them-selves as moral and competent human beings. Counter-attitudinal behaviour is inconsistent with this view and is thus distressing and motivates change, particularly among people who think relatively highly of themselves (i.e. they have higher self-esteem).

This idea that self-consistency is crucial for dissonance is taken up in a slightly different guise by **self-affirmation theory** (Steele, 1988; Steel, Spencer, & Lynch, 1993). The key idea is that if our self-concept is evaluatively challenged in one domain we can rectify the problem by publicly making positive statements about ourselves in another domain. For example, if my competence as a scholar is challenged I might emphasise (affirm) that I am a wonderful cook and a great athlete. From a dissonance point of view, negative behaviours are particularly threatening to our sense of self. People with high self-esteem can respond via self-affirmation—they experience no dissonance. Those with low self-esteem are less able to self-affirm and do experience dissonance.

Note that Aronson's (1999) self-consistency idea, above, predicts greater dissonance under high self-

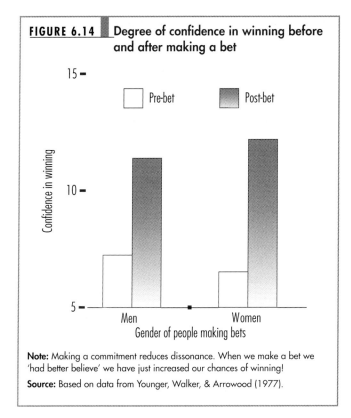

FIGURE 6.14 Degree of confidence in winning before and after making a bet

Note: Making a commitment reduces dissonance. When we make a bet we 'had better believe' we have just increased our chances of winning!

Source: Based on data from Younger, Walker, & Arrowood (1977).

esteem, while self-affirmation theory predicts greater dissonance under low self-esteem (Tesser, 2000).

Vicarious dissonance

New research provides some evidence for the intriguing idea that people can experience dissonance vicariously (Cooper & Hogg, 2002; Norton, Monin, Cooper, & Hogg, 2003). Where a strong bond exists between two people (e.g. when they identify strongly with the same group), dissonance experienced by one person can be experienced by the other. An implication is that advertisements promoting the public good may be able to induce dissonance in viewers by having them watch someone 'like them' engaging in counterattitudinal behaviour. The viewer does not actually have to behave counterattitudinally.

If the viewer also engages in counterattitudinal behaviour there may be a rebound effect, because the common-category member being observed provides social support for the viewer's dissonance. Research by Blake McKimmie, at Queensland University of Technology, and his colleagues found that ingroup social support for counterattitudinal behaviour reduces dissonance (McKimmie, Terry, Hogg, Manstead, Spears, & Doosje, in press).

ALTERNATIVE VIEWS TO DISSONANCE

Cognitive dissonance theory has had a chequered history in social psychology (see Visser & Cooper, 2003).

Festinger's original ideas have been refined and sharpened. Dissonance was not so easy to create as Festinger originally believed and, in some cases, other theories (such as self-perception theory) might provide a better explanation of attitude change than cognitive dissonance. Despite this, cognitive dissonance theory remains one of the most widely accepted explanations of attitude change and many other social behaviours. It has generated over 1000 research studies and will probably continue to be an integral part of social psychological theory for many years (Cooper & Croyle, 1984).

Some of the results of the dissonance experiments can also be explained by Bem's **self-perception theory** (Bem, 1972; see Chapter 4). Some researchers have suggested that attitude change does not occur according to the basic mechanisms proposed by dissonance theory. There have been several experimental attempts to compare dissonance and self-perception theory. Both theories have been shown to be helpful in understanding behaviour (Fazio, Zanna, & Cooper, 1977).

To understand the uses of each theory, imagine that attitudes fall on a continuum, spread over a range of acceptable choices. The idea that there are latitudes of acceptance and rejection around attitudes forms the basis of social judgment theory (Sherif & Sherif, 1967). If you are in favour of keeping the drinking age at 20, you might also agree to 19 or 21. There is a latitude of acceptance around your position. Alternatively, there is also a latitude of rejection: you might definitely be against a legal drinking age of either 17 or 23. Mostly we act within our own latitudes of acceptance. Sometimes, we may go outside them—for instance, when we pay $100 for dinner at a restaurant rather than the planned $50. If you feel you chose freely, you will experience dissonance about your decision: 'I wanted to pay only $50, was willing to go to $70 but actually paid $100'.

The view that integrates self-perception and dissonance theories suggests that, when your actions fall within your range of acceptance, self-perception theory best accounts for your response: 'I guess I was willing to pay more than I thought'. However, when you find yourself acting outside your previous range of acceptance, dissonance theory gives a better account of your response. We reduce our dissonance only by changing our attitude: 'I paid $100, but that's okay because I really thought it was a great meal' (Fazio, Zanna, & Cooper, 1977). Thus, attitudes may be changed either through a self-attributional process such as self-perception or through attempts to reduce the feeling of cognitive dissonance.

COGNITIVE DISSONANCE: ANOTHER LOOK

Cooper and Fazio (1984), in their *new look model*, have countered some of the objections to cognitive dissonance theory. A particular controversy is how to retain and defend the concept of attitudes when a person's observed behaviour and beliefs are in contradiction. According to Cooper and Fazio, when behaviour is counterattitudinal we try to figure out what the consequences might be. If these are thought to be negative and fairly serious, we must then check to see whether our action was voluntary. If it was, we then accept responsibility, experience arousal from the state of dissonance that follows and bring the relevant attitude into line, so reducing dissonance. This revision, shown in Figure 6.15, also includes attributional processes, in terms of whether we acted according to our free will and of whether external influences were more or less important.

The new look model is now supported by considerable evidence (Cooper, 1999), but so is the traditional cognitive dissonance theory that focuses on inconsistency rather then behavioural consequences (e.g. Harmon-Jones, 2000).

When attitude change fails: resistance to persuasion

When we feel strongly about an issue we can be quite stubborn in resisting attempts to change our position (Zuwerink & Devine, 1996). However, much of the coverage of material presented in this chapter highlights factors that are conducive to our altering our attitudes, very often beyond a level of direct awareness. Yet far more attempts at persuasion fail than ever succeed. Researchers have identified three major reasons: reactance, forewarning and inoculation.

FIGURE 6.15 A revised cognitive dissonance model of attitude-discrepant behaviour

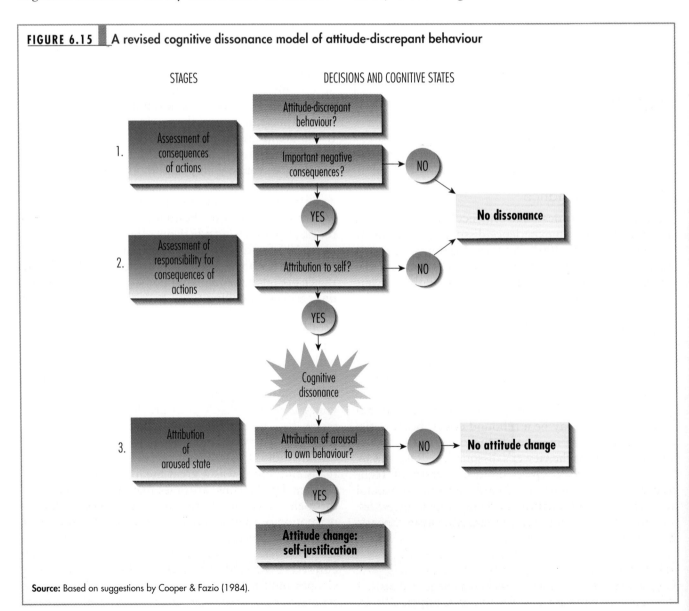

Source: Based on suggestions by Cooper & Fazio (1984).

REACTANCE

We note in Box 6.1 that we can be more easily persuaded if we think the message is not deliberately intended to be manipulative. To do otherwise may set off a process referred to as **reactance**. Think back to an occasion when someone obviously tried to change your attitudes. You might recall having an unpleasant reaction and even hardening your existing attitude—perhaps becoming even more opposed to the other person's position.

Brehm (1966) coined the term 'reactance' to describe this process, a psychological state that we experience when someone tries to limit our personal freedom. Research findings suggest that when we feel this way, we often tend to shift in the opposite direction, an effect known as *negative attitude change*. The treatment a doctor recommends to a patient is sometimes responded to in this way (Rhodewalt & Strube, 1985). What happened the last time you were told to ease up, maybe go to bed and miss a social function you had really been looking forward to?

Brehm felt that the underlying cause of reactance is the sense of having our personal freedom infringed.

FOREWARNING

Forewarning is prior knowledge of persuasive intent—that is, telling someone you are going to influence them. Research evidence suggests that, when we know in advance, persuasive effects are reduced (Cialdini & Petty, 1979; Johnson, 1994). This seems to be especially true with respect to attitudes and issues that we consider important (Petty & Cacioppo, 1979). It seems that what people do when they are forewarned that an attempt will be made to change their minds about an issue is to rehearse counterarguments that can be used as a defence. From this point of view, forewarning can be thought of as a special case of inoculation.

THE INOCULATION EFFECT

As the term suggests, **inoculation** is a form of protection. Just as in biology we can inject a weakened or inert form of disease-producing germs into the patient to build up resistance to a more powerful form, so in social psychology we might seek a way to provide a defence against persuasive ideas (McGuire, 1964). The technique is initiated by exposing a person to a weakened counterattitudinal argument.

McGuire and his associates (e.g. McGuire & Papageorgis, 1961; Anderson & McGuire, 1965) became interested in the technique following reports of the use of 'brainwashing' methods on American prisoners by Chinese forces during the Korean War of the early 1950s. Some of the American soldiers made public statements denouncing the American government and saying they wanted to remain in China when the war ended. McGuire reasoned that these soldiers were mostly inexperienced young men who had not been exposed before to attacks on the American way of life and were not forearmed with a defence against the subtleties of Marxist logic.

The biological analogy implies that a weak attack is mounted on the body's system, which in turn mobilises its defences, effects a recovery and is reinforced by antibodies against a subsequent stronger attack. McGuire continued the metaphor by observing that there is another major way of heading off illness, namely by strengthening our bodies against disease through diet, exercise and so on. In the case of persuasive communications, this led him to distinguish between two major kinds of defence:

1. The *supportive defence*—a person's resistance could be strengthened by providing additional arguments that support the original beliefs.
2. The *inoculation defence*—perhaps more effectively, the person might learn what the counterattitudinal arguments are and then hear them demolished.

Note that the inoculation defence picks up on the advantage of a two-sided presentation, discussed earlier in relation to the characteristics of a persuasive message. In general terms, this defence starts with a weak attack on a person's position, as a strong one might be fatal! The person can then be told that the weak argument is not too strong and should be easy to rebut, or else an argument is to be provided that deals directly with the weak attack. It is thought that increased resistance to persuasion comes about because (a) we become motivated to defend our beliefs, and (b) we acquire some skill in doing this.

In a study by McGuire and Papageorgis (1961), both forms of defence were put to the test. Students were asked to indicate their extent of agreement on a 15-point scale for a series of truisms relating to health beliefs, such as:

- It's a good idea to brush your teeth after every meal if at all possible.
- The effects of penicillin have been, almost without exception, of great benefit to mankind.
- Everyone should get a yearly chest X-ray to detect any signs of TB at an early stage.
- Mental illness is not contagious.

Before the experiment began, many of the students thoroughly endorsed these propositions by checking 15 on the response scale. The main variables of interest were the effects of introducing defences and attacks on these health beliefs in the form of essays offering arguments for or against the truisms. Students who were in the defence groups were allocated to one of two conditions, the first being a *supportive* defence group (the students received support for their position) and the second an *inoculation* defence group (their position was subjected to a weak attack which was then refuted). There were also two control groups, one in which the students were neither attacked nor defended, and another that read essays that strongly attacked the truisms but none defending them.

Not surprisingly, control participants who had been neither attacked nor defended continued to show the highest level of acceptance of the truisms. In dealing with their central hypotheses, McGuire and Papageorgis found that providing a supportive defence helped just a little when compared with the controls who had been attacked without any defence. Participants in the inoculation condition, however, were substantially strengthened in their defence against a strong attack, when compared with the same control group. The results are shown in Figure 6.16.

McGuire (1964) went on to argue that the supportive defence is not to be ignored, but that it is most effec-

tive when attacks on our position are well understood, so that established and rehearsed supportive arguments can be called up. For example, try persuading committed visitors to your door that they are in error when they are intent on telling you about the wonders of their religion. The chances are that they have heard your counterarguments before.

McGuire favoured the inoculation defence when the audience is to be exposed to a new argument. By having to deal with a mild, earlier attack on their position, they will be better equipped to innovate when a stronger one is mounted.

The inoculation phenomenon has been further applied to advertising practices with the introduction of 'issue/advocacy advertising campaigns'. Issue/advocacy refers to the instance of a company protecting consumer loyalty from 'attitude slippage' by issuing media releases on controversial issues (Burgoon, Pfau, & Birk, 1995). For example, a chemical company may issue a statement about environmental pollution in order to inoculate their consumers against allegations of environment misconduct from competing companies, or from other 'enemies' such as a local green party. This practice is now widespread: an alcohol company may fund alcohol research and alcohol-moderation campaigns, and a fashion company may support the protection of wildlife.

Role-play can be used as an extension of the inoculation approach to prepare an individual to withstand peer group pressure. For example, a young person trying to quit smoking can be trained to resist mockery by adolescent peers by acting out a verbal defence—such as 'Why should I be a nerd and smoke just to impress you?' (Chassin, Presson, & Sherman, 1990).

TRIVIALISATION

In addition to the supportive and inoculation defences proposed by McGuire, there is the *trivialisation defence*. This is not only a third way to resist a persuasive communication but also a method of reducing dissonance, a point neglected since Festinger (1957) first noted this possibility. To trivialise someone's argument is to minimise the perceived importance of the relevant cognitions. Simon, Greenberg and Brehm (1995) showed that, when pre-existing attitudes are made salient, participants choose to trivialise an argument that is inconsistent with their attitude rather than change the attitude itself.

ROLE OF ATTITUDE STRENGTH

Finally, we would expect intuitively that resistance to attitude change must be related to attitude strength, of which there are several indicators—for example, ego involvement, certainty, personal importance, knowledge and extremity of an attitude. These indicators may depend on different pathways to resistance. Using factor

FIGURE 6.16 Degree of acceptance of health truisms in modes of reading and writing as a function of supportive and inoculation defences

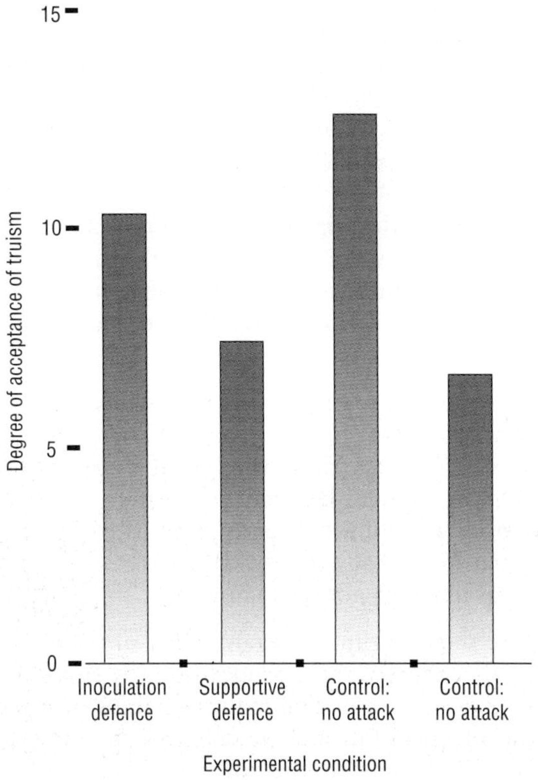

Note: One of the best forms of defence against counterarguments is to be exposed to small doses of these arguments.
Source: Based on data from McGuire & Papageorgis (1961).

analysis, Pomerantz, Chaiken and Tordesillas (1995) reported two dimensions of attitude strength, each with different resistance processes and outcomes, when people's beliefs are subjected to an attack:

1. *Commitment to a position* was associated with selective judgment, increased selective elaboration and attitude polarisation.

2. *Embeddedness*, or the linkage of the attitude to self-concept, value system and knowledge structure, was related to selective memory, decreased selective elaboration and increased information-seeking.

Attitude strength is an important concept to consider within both attitude formation and attitude change, and is an ongoing and developing research topic.

Summary

- The field of attitude change is vast and complex. Hovland headed the Yale approach to communication and persuasion, which studied variables dealing with the communicator, the source of the message, the message itself, and the context in which persuasion occurs.
- Two important areas of our lives that employ relevant principles from social psychological research are advertising and political propaganda.
- Two recent models, each dealing with how a persuasive message is learned, draw on developments in research on cognition. Petty and Cacioppo's elaboration likelihood model proposes that, when people attend to a message carefully, they use a central route to process it; otherwise they use a peripheral route. Chaiken's heuristic–systematic model suggests that people use systematic processing when they attend to a message carefully; otherwise they use heuristic processing.
- A variety of techniques that deal with ways of inducing another person to comply with our requests has been intensively studied: these include ingratiation, reciprocity and guilt arousal. There are also multiple-request techniques (foot-in-the-door, door-in-the-face and low-balling), in which a first request functions as a set-up for the second, real request.
- Festinger's cognitive dissonance theory is a major approach to the topic of attitude change. It addresses not only conflict between a person's beliefs but discrepancy between behaviour and underlying attitudes, and behaviour and self-conception. It includes three variations on the way in which dissonance is brought about: effort justification, induced compliance and free choice.
- Reactance is an increase in resistance to persuasion when the communicator's efforts to persuade are obvious. Techniques for building up resistance include forewarning and the inoculation defence. In recent years, manufacturing companies have used inoculating media releases to shore up consumer loyalty.

LINKS

YOU HAVE READ ABOUT:	WHICH LINKS TO:
Cognitive theories of attitude change	role of cognition in social processes (2, 3, 5)
Message acceptance and repetition	familiarity and interpersonal attraction (13)
Compliance	obedience (7)
Cognitive dissonance and attitude change	cognitive dissonance and initiation rites (8)

Key terms

action research *(p. 145)*
attitude change *(p. 130)*
audience *(p. 134)*
cognitive dissonance *(p. 130)*
compliance *(p. 141)*
disconfirmation bias *(p. 139)*
door-in-the-face tactic *(p. 144)*
effort justification *(p. 148)*
elaboration likelihood model
   (ELM) *(p. 139)*

foot-in-the-door tactic *(p. 143)*
forewarning *(p. 155)*
heuristic–systematic model
   (HSM) *(p. 140)*
induced compliance *(p. 150)*
ingratiation *(p. 142)*
inoculation *(p. 155)*
low-ball tactic *(p. 145)*
message *(p. 134)*
mindlessness *(p. 145)*

multiple requests *(p. 143)*
persuasive communication *(p. 130)*
post-decisional conflict *(p. 150)*
reactance *(p. 155)*
reciprocity principle *(p. 142)*
self-affirmation theory *(p. 152)*
self-perception theory *(p. 153)*
source *(p. 134)*
third-person effect *(p. 132)*

FURTHER READING

Belch, G. E., & Belch, M. A. (2004). *Advertising and promotion: An integrated marketing communications perspective* (6th ed.). New York: McGraw-Hill/Irwin. This latest edition of a well-known textbook uses a communications theory approach (source, message, receiver) to show how social psychological principles can be applied in changing consumer attitudes and behaviour. It is rich with examples and illustrations of advertisements.

Bohner, G., Moskowitz, G. B., & Chaiken, S. (1995). The interplay of heuristic and systematic processing of social information. *European Review of Social Psychology, 6,* 33–68. An in-depth overview of the extended heuristic–systematic model of social information processing, which links attitude change to the broader field of social influence.

Bohner, G., & Wänke, M. (2002). *Attitudes and attitude change.* Hove, UK: Psychology Press. A useful monograph with a treatment of persuasion, including dual-process models of information processing.

Eagly, A. H., & Chaiken, S. (1993). *The psychology of attitudes.* San Diego, CA: Harcourt Brace Jovanovich. A comprehensive and detailed review of attitude theory and research— probably already a classic, which rides the crest of an upsurge in attitude research.

Petty, R. E., & Wegener, D. T. (1998). Attitude change: Multiple roles for persuasion variables. In D. T. Gilbert, S. T. Fiske, & G. Lindzey (Eds.), *The handbook of social psychology* (4th ed., Vol. 1, pp. 323–390). New York: McGraw-Hill. An up-to-date coverage of historical foundations of attitude change. There is a useful comparison of the ELM and HSM attitude change models; also deals with cognitive dissonance, source, message, receiver and context variables.

Stroebe, W., & Stroebe, M. S. (1995). *Social psychology and health.* Buckingham, UK: Open University Press. A recent discussion of the application of principles of attitude change in the area of health behaviour.

Visser, P. S., & Cooper, J. (2003). Attitude change. In M. A. Hogg & J. Cooper (Eds.), *The Sage handbook of social psychology* (pp. 211–231). London: Sage. An up-to-date, comprehensive and accessible overview of research and theory on persuasion and attitude change.

Zimbardo, P. G., & Leippe, M. R. (1991). *The psychology of attitude change and social influence.* New York: McGraw-Hill. An in-depth and informative look at attitudes and social influences in society, with particular attention given to the areas of persuasion, influence and change. Well illustrated with relevant examples.

Social influence

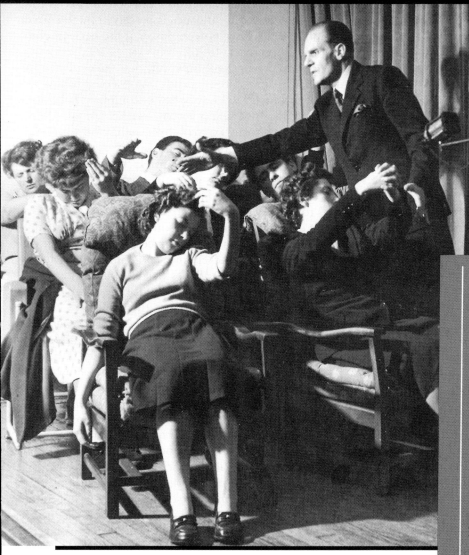

THIS CHAPTER DISCUSSES:

- types of social influence
- power and influence
- obedience to authority
- ethical issues in social psychological experiments
- classic studies of conformity
- modern theories of conformity
- minority influence and social change.

FOCUS QUESTIONS

1. During his tour of duty, Private Milkins committed a brutal act on a civilian. Almost straightaway, he felt quite bad about what he had done, since he had not been ordered specifically to do it. Later, he cheered up when his buddies said that in the same circumstances they would have done the same thing: their platoon commander expected it of them. What has Private Milkins experienced?
2. While playing Trivial Pursuit, Martha gives way to 'the boys' when they decide which plane first broke the sound barrier. They say she is a typical conformist female. What do you say?
3. Peter and Dudley work for a big corporation. They agree that certain conditions of their employment are highly exploitative. Peter wants to take the corporation on, but Dudley feels that 'there is no way we can succeed—there are only two of us up against the system'. What tips would you give them to improve their chance of success?

Types of social influence

Social psychology can be defined as 'an attempt to understand and explain how the thoughts, feelings, and behaviours of individuals are influenced by the actual, imagined, or implied presence of others' (Allport, 1954a, p. 5). This widely accepted and commonly quoted definition of social psychology (see Chapter 1) identifies a potential problem for the study of **social influence**—how does the study of social influence differ from the study of social psychology as a whole? There is no straightforward answer; instead, social influence research can be circumscribed by the sorts of issues addressed by social psychologists who consider themselves to be investigating social influence.

Social life is characterised by argument, conflict and controversy in which individuals or groups try to change the thoughts, feelings and behaviours of others, by persuasion, argument, example, command, propaganda or force. People can be quite aware of influence attempts, and can form impressions of how affected they and other people are by different types of influence (e.g. Duck, 1998; see Chapter 6).

Social life is also characterised by **norms**—that is, by attitudinal and behavioural uniformities among people, or what Turner has called 'normative social similarities and differences between people' (1991, p. 2). One of the most interesting sets of issues in social influence, perhaps even in social psychology, is how people construct norms, how they conform to or are regulated by those norms, and how those norms change. As norms are very much group phenomena, we discuss their structure, their origins and some of their effects in Chapter 8, reserving for this chapter discussion of the process of conformity to norms.

COMPLIANCE, OBEDIENCE, CONFORMITY

We are all familiar with the difference between yielding to direct or indirect social pressure from a group or an individual and being genuinely persuaded. For example, you may simply agree publicly with others' attitudes, comply with their requests or go along with their behaviour, yet privately not feel persuaded at all. On other occasions, you may privately change your innermost beliefs in accordance with the views or behaviours of others. This has not gone unnoticed by social psychologists, who generally find it useful to distinguish between coercive **compliance** on the one hand and persuasive influence on the other.

Some forms of social influence produce public compliance—a surface change in behaviour and expressed attitudes, often as a consequence of persuasion or coercion. As compliance does not reflect internal change, it usually persists only while behaviour is under surveillance. For example, children may obey parental directives to keep their room tidy, but only if they know that their parents are watching. An important prerequisite for coercive compulsion and compliance is that the source of social influence is perceived by the target of influence to have power; power is the basis of compliance (Moscovici, 1976).

It should be noted, however, that, as evidence for internal mental states depends on observed behaviour, it can be difficult to know whether compliant behaviour does or does not reflect internalisation (Allen, 1965). People's strategic control over behaviour for self-presentation and communicative purposes can accentuate this difficulty. Because research into compliance with direct requests has generally been conducted within an attitude-change and persuasion framework, we cover this topic in detail in Chapter 6.

In contrast to compliance, other forms of social influence produce private acceptance and internalisation. There is subjective acceptance and conversion (Moscovici, 1976), which produces true internal change that persists in the absence of surveillance. Conformity is not based on power, but rather on the subjective validity of social norms (Festinger, 1950)—that is, a feeling of confidence and certainty that the beliefs and actions described by the norm are correct, appropriate, valid and socially desirable. Under these circumstances, the norm becomes an internalised standard for behaviour, and thus surveillance is unnecessary.

Kelley (1952) has made a useful distinction between reference group and membership group. **Reference groups** are groups that are psychologically significant for our attitudes and behaviour, either in the positive sense that we seek to behave in accordance with their norms, or in the negative sense that we seek to behave in opposition to their norms. **Membership groups** are those groups to which we belong (which we are *in*) by some objective criterion, external designation or social consensus. A positive reference group is a source of conformity (which will be socially validated if that group happens also to be our membership group), while a negative reference group that is also our membership group has enormous coercive power to produce compliance.

For example, if I am a manual worker but I despise all the attributes of being a worker and I would rather be a member of management because I value management norms so much more, then 'worker' is my membership group, which is also a negative reference group, and 'management' is a positive reference group but not my membership group. I will comply with worker norms but conform to management norms.

The general distinction between coercive compliance and persuasive influence is a theme that surfaces repeatedly in different guises in social influence research. The distinction maps onto a general view in social psychology that there are two quite separate processes responsible for social influence phenomena—this dual-process approach is currently perhaps most obvious in Petty and Cacioppo's (1986) elaboration likelihood model, and Chaiken's (Bohner, Moskowitz, & Chaiken, 1995) heuristic–systematic model of attitude change (see Chapter 6; Eagly & Chaiken, 1993).

POWER AND INFLUENCE

As mentioned above, compliance tends to be associated with power relations whereas conformity is not. Compliance is influenced not only by the persuasive tactics people use to make requests, but also by how much power they are perceived to have. **Power** can be interpreted as the capacity or ability to exert influence; and influence is power in action. For example, French and Raven (1959) identified five bases of social power and later Raven (1965, 1993) expanded this to six: reward power, coercive power, informational power, expert power, legitimate power and referent power (see Figure 7.1). Because it is almost a truism in psychology

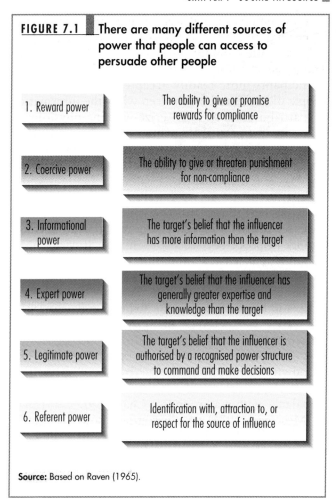

FIGURE 7.1 There are many different sources of power that people can access to persuade other people

1. Reward power	The ability to give or promise rewards for compliance
2. Coercive power	The ability to give or threaten punishment for non-compliance
3. Informational power	The target's belief that the influencer has more information than the target
4. Expert power	The target's belief that the influencer has generally greater expertise and knowledge than the target
5. Legitimate power	The target's belief that the influencer is authorised by a recognised power structure to command and make decisions
6. Referent power	Identification with, attraction to, or respect for the source of influence

Source: Based on Raven (1965).

Legitimate power: This executive may or may not have expertise, charisma, or even the respect of those responsible to him—but he is the boss.

that the power to administer reinforcements or punishments should influence behaviour, there have been virtually no attempts to demonstrate reward and coercive power (Collins & Raven, 1969).

One general problem is that reinforcement formulations, particularly of complex social behaviour, tend to strike enormous difficulty specifying in advance what is a reward and what is a punishment, and yet find it very easy to do so after the event. Thus, reinforcement formulations tend to be unfalsifiable, and it may be more useful to focus on the cognitive and social processes that cause specific individuals in certain contexts to treat some things as reinforcement and others as punishment.

While information may have the power to influence, it is clearly not true that all information has such power. If I were to tell you that I had information that pigs really do fly, it is very unlikely that you would be persuaded. For you to be persuaded, other influence processes would also have to be operating: for instance, the information might have to be perceived as consistent with normative expectations, or coercive or reward power might have to operate.

Information can, however, be influential when it originates in an expert source. Bochner, at the University of New South Wales (Bochner & Insko, 1966), provided a nice illustration of expert power. He found that participants more readily accepted information that people did not need much sleep when the information was attributed to a Nobel Prize-winning physiologist than to a less prestigious source. The information lost the power to influence only when it became intrinsically implausible—stating that almost no sleep was needed (see Figure 6.2 in Chapter 6).

Legitimate power is based in authority and is probably best illustrated by a consideration of obedience (see below). Referent power may operate through a range of processes (see also Collins & Raven, 1969), including consensual validation, social approval and group identification (all of which are discussed below in the section on conformity).

In addition to power as the ability to influence, there are other perspectives on social power (Keltner, Gruenfeld & Anderson, 2003; Ng, 1980, 1996). For example, Fiske (1993b; Fiske & Dépret, 1996; Goodwin, Gubin, Fiske, & Yzerbyt, 2000) presents a social cognitive and attributional analysis of power imbalance within a group (see Chapter 9).

Moscovici (1976) actually contrasts power with influence, treating them as two different processes. Power is the control of behaviour through domination that produces compliance and submission: if people have power, in this sense, they do not need influence; and if they can influence effectively, they need not resort to power.

There is an entire literature on intergroup power relations (e.g. Hornsey, Spears, Cremers, & Hogg, 2003; Jost & Major, 2001; see Chapter 11).

Power can also be considered as a role within a group that is defined by effective influence over followers— that is, as a leadership position. However, as we see in Chapter 9, the relationship between power and leadership is not clear-cut. Some leaders certainly do influence by the exercise of power through coercion, but others influence by persuasion and by instilling their vision in the rest of the group. Groups tend to permit leaders to be idiosyncratic and innovative (Hollander, 1985) and see their leaders as being charismatic (Bass, 1998) and having legitimate authority. Some leaders, however, are not perceived as having legitimate authority.

Generally, leadership researchers distinguish leadership from power (e.g. Chemers, 2001; Lord, Brown, & Harvey, 2001). Leadership is a process of influence that enlists and mobilises others in the attainment of collective goals—it imbues people with the group's attitudes and goals and inspires them to work towards achieving them. Leadership is not a process that requires people to exercise power over others in order to gain compliance or, more extremely, in order to coerce or force people. Leadership may actually be more closely associated with conformity processes than power processes (Hogg, 2001d; Hogg & Reid, 2001; Hogg & van Knippenberg, 2003; Reid & Ng, 1999).

Obedience to authority

In 1951 Asch published the results of a now-classic experiment on conformity, in which student participants conformed to erroneous judgments of line lengths made by a numerical majority (see later in this chapter for details). Some critics have been unimpressed by this study: the task, judging line length, was trivial, and there were no significant consequences for self and others of conforming or resisting.

Milgram (1974, 1992) was one of these critics; he tried to replicate Asch's study, but with a task that had important consequences attached to the decision to conform or remain independent. He decided to have experimental confederates apparently administer electric shocks to another person to see whether the true participant would conform. Before being able to start the study, Milgram needed to run a control group to obtain a base rate for people's willingness to shock someone *without* social pressure from confederates. For Milgram, this almost immediately became a crucial question in its own right. In fact, he never actually went ahead with his original conformity study and the control group became the basis of one of social psychology's most dramatic research programs.

Milgram was also influenced by a wider social issue. Adolf Eichmann was the Nazi official most directly responsible for the logistics of Hitler's Holocaust, in which six million Jews were systematically slaughtered. A book entitled *Eichmann in Jerusalem* (Arendt, 1963) was published reporting his trial. The subtitle of this book, *A Report on the Banality of Evil*, captures one of the most disturbing findings that emerged from Eichmann's trial and, indeed, from the trials of other war criminals. These 'monsters' did not appear to be monsters at all. They were often mild-mannered, softly spoken, courteous people, who repeatedly and politely explained that they did what they did, not because they hated Jews but because they were ordered to do it—they were simply following orders.

MILGRAM'S OBEDIENCE STUDIES
These two strands came together in a series of experiments conducted during the 1960s by Milgram (1963, 1974). Participants, recruited from the community by advertisement, reported to a laboratory at Yale University to participate in a study of the effect of punishment on human learning. They arrived in pairs, and

drew lots to determine their roles for the study (one was the 'learner', the other the 'teacher').

The learner's role was to learn a list of paired associates, and the teacher's role was to administer an electric shock to the learner every time the learner gave a wrong associate to the cue word. The teacher saw the learner being strapped to a chair and having electrode paste and electrodes attached to his arm, overheard the experimenter explain that the paste was to prevent blistering and burning, and overheard the learner telling the experimenter that he had a slight heart condition. The experimenter also explained that, although the shocks might be painful, they would cause no permanent tissue damage.

The teacher was now taken into a separate room containing a shock generator (see Figure 7.2). He was told to administer progressively larger shocks to the learner every time he made a mistake—15 V for the first mistake, 30 V for the next mistake, 45 V for the next, and so on. An important feature of the shock generator was the descriptive labels attached to the scale of increasing voltage. The teacher was given a sample shock of 45 V, and then the experiment began.

The learner got some pairs correct but also made some errors and very soon the teacher had reached 75 V, at which point the learner grunted in pain. At 120 V the learner shouted out to the experimenter that the shocks were becoming painful. At 150 V the learner, or now more accurately the 'victim', demanded to be released from the experiment and at 180 V he cried out that he could stand it no longer. The victim continued to cry out in pain at each shock, rising to an 'agonised scream' at 250 V. At 300 V the victim ceased responding to the cue words; the teacher was told to treat this as a 'wrong answer'.

Throughout the experiment the teacher was agitated and tense and often asked to break off. To such requests the experimenter responded with an ordered sequence of replies proceeding from a mild 'please continue', through 'the experiment requires that you continue' and 'it is absolutely essential that you continue' to the ultimate 'you have no other choice, you *must* go on'.

A panel of 110 experts on human behaviour, including 39 psychiatrists, were asked to predict how far a normal, psychologically balanced human being would go in this experiment. These experts believed that only about 10% would exceed 180 V and no one would obey to the end (these predictions are shown schematically in Figure 7.3). Compare this with the actual behaviour of the participants (Figure 7.3 also).

A CLASSIC IN SOCIAL PSYCHOLOGY

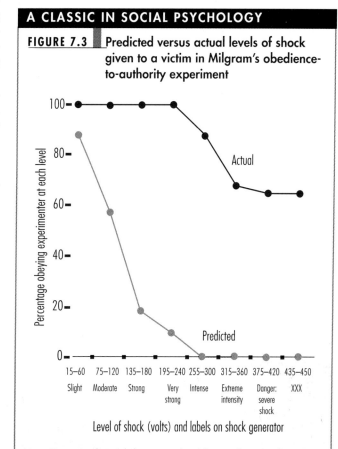

FIGURE 7.3 Predicted versus actual levels of shock given to a victim in Milgram's obedience-to-authority experiment

Level of shock (volts) and labels on shock generator

Note: 'Experts' on human behaviour predicted that very few normal, psychologically balanced people would obey orders to administer more than a 'strong' electric shock to the 'incompetent' learner in Milgram's experiment. In actual fact, 65% of people were obedient right to the very end, going beyond 'danger: severe shock' into a zone labelled 'XXX'.

Source: Based on data from Milgram (1974).

FIGURE 7.2 Milgram's shock generator

| 1 | 2 | 3 | 4 | 5 | 6 | 7 | 8 | 9 | 10 | 11 | 12 | 13 | 14 | 15 | 16 | 17 | 18 | 19 | 20 | 21 | 22 | 23 | 24 | 25 | 26 | 27 | 28 | 29 | 30 |

···15 ···················· 75 ···················· 135 ···················· 195 ···················· 255 ···················· 315 ···················· 375 ···················· 435   450

| VOLTS | 30 | 45 | 60 | VOLTS | 90 | 105 | 120 | VOLTS | 150 | 165 | 180 | VOLTS | 210 | 225 | 240 | VOLTS | 270 | 285 | 300 | VOLTS | 330 | 345 | 360 | VOLTS | 390 | 405 | 420 | VOLTS | VOLTS |

SLIGHT ···················· MODERATE ············· STRONG ···················· VERY ················· INTENSE ··············· EXTREME ·············· DANGER: ··················· X X X
SHOCK   SHOCK   SHOCK   STRONG   SHOCK   INTENSITY   EXTREME
                                                                               SHOCK   SHOCK   SHOCK

Note: Participants in Milgram's obedience studies were confronted with a 15–450 volt shock generator that had different descriptive labels, including the frighteningly evocative 'XXX', attached to the more impersonal voltage values.

Source: Milgram (1974). © 1974 by Stanley Milgram. Reprinted by permission of HarperCollins Publishers, Inc.

In a slight variant of the procedure described above, in which the victim could not be seen or heard but pounded on the wall at 300 V and 315 V and then went silent, almost everyone continued to 255 V, and 65% continued to the very end—administering massive electric shocks to someone who was not responding and who had previously reported having a heart complaint!

The participants in this experiment were quite normal people—forty 20–50-year-old men from a range of occupations. Unknown to them, however, the entire experiment involved an elaborate deception in which they were always the teacher, and the learner/victim was actually an experimental stooge (an avuncular-looking middle-aged man) who had been carefully briefed on how to react. No electric shocks were actually administered apart from the 45 V sample shock to the teacher.

FACTORS INFLUENCING OBEDIENCE

Milgram (1974) conducted a total of 18 experiments in which he varied different parameters to investigate factors influencing obedience. In all but one experiment the participants were 20–50-year-old male non-university students from a range of occupations and socioeconomic levels. In one study in which women were the participants, exactly the same level of obedience was obtained as with male participants. Milgram's experiment has been replicated in Italy, Germany, Australia, Britain, Jordan, Spain, Austria and Holland (Smith & Bond, 1998). Complete obedience ranged from over 90% in Spain and Holland (Meeus & Raaijmakers, 1986), through over 80% in Italy, Germany and Austria (Mantell, 1971) to a low of 40% among Australian men and only 16% among Australian women (Kilham & Mann, 1974).

One reason why people continue to administer electric shocks may be that the experiment starts very innocuously with quite trivial electric shocks. Once they have committed themselves to a course of action (i.e. to give shocks), it can be difficult subsequently to change their mind. The process may be similar to that involved in the foot-in-the-door technique of persuasion (Freedman & Fraser, 1966; see Chapter 6).

An important factor in obedience is *immediacy*—social proximity of the victim to the participant. Milgram (1974) varied the level of immediacy across a number of experiments. We saw above that 65% of people 'shocked to the limit' of 450 V when the victim was unseen and unheard except for pounding on the wall. In an even less immediate condition in which the victim was neither seen nor heard at all, 100% of people went to the end. The baseline condition (the one described in detail above) yielded 62.5% obedience. As immediacy increased from this baseline, obedience decreased: when the victim was visible in the same room, 40% obeyed to the limit; and, when the teacher actually had to hold the victim's hand down onto the electrode to receive the shock, obedience dropped to a still frighteningly high 30%.

Immediacy may make it easier to view a victim as a living and breathing person like ourselves and thus to empathise with their thoughts and feelings. Hence, pregnant women express greater commitment to their pregnancy after having seen an ultrasound that clearly reveals body parts (Lydon & Dunkel-Schetter, 1994); and it may be easier to press a button to wipe out a village from 12 000 metres, or deep under the ocean in a submarine, than it is to shoot an individual enemy from close range.

Another important factor is proximity/immediacy of the authority figure. Obedience was reduced to 20.5% when the experimenter was absent from the room and relayed directions by telephone. When the experimenter gave no orders at all and the participant was entirely free to choose when to stop, 2.5% still persisted to the end. Perhaps the most dramatic influence on obedience is group pressure. The presence of two disobedient peers (i.e. others who appeared to revolt and refused to continue after giving shocks in the 150–210 V range) reduced complete obedience to 10%, while two obedient peers raised complete obedience to 92.5%.

Group pressure probably has its effects because the actions of others help to confirm that it is either legitimate or illegitimate to continue administering the shocks. Another important factor is the legitimacy of

Obedience to authority: This guard's uniform symbolises complete unquestioning obedience to the British Monarch as a legitimate authority.

the authority figure, which allows people to abdicate personal responsibility for their actions.

For example, Bushman (1984, 1988) had confederates dressed in a uniform, neat attire or a shabby outfit stand next to someone fumbling for change for a parking meter. The confederate stopped passers-by and 'ordered' them to give the person change for the meter. Over 70% obeyed the uniformed confederate (giving 'because they had been told to' as the reason) and about 50% obeyed the non-uniformed confederate (generally giving altruism as a reason). These studies suggest that the mere emblems of authority can create unquestioning obedience.

Milgram's original experiments were conducted by lab-coated scientists at prestigious Yale University, and the purpose of the research was quite clearly the pursuit of scientific knowledge. What would happen if these trappings of legitimate authority were removed? Milgram ran one experiment in a run-down inner-city office building. The research was ostensibly sponsored by a private commercial research firm. Obedience dropped, but to a still remarkably high 48%.

Milgram's research addresses one of humanity's great failings—the tendency for people to obey orders without first thinking about (a) what they are being asked to do and (b) the consequences of their obedience for other living beings. Obedience can, of course, be beneficial—for example, many organisations would grind to a halt or would be catastrophically dysfunctional if their members continually painstakingly negotiated orders (think about an emergency surgery team, a flight crew, a commando unit). Now consider the first focus question. (See also the concept of the agentic model, Chapter 12.)

However, the pitfalls of blind obedience, contingent on immediacy, group pressure, group norms, legitimacy and so forth, are also many. For example, research in the United States has shown that medication errors in hospitals are significantly attributable to the fact that nurses overwhelmingly defer to doctors' orders, even when all sorts of alarm bells are ringing (Lesar, Briceland, & Stein, 1997).

In another study focusing on organisational obedience, 77% of participants who were role-playing board members of a pharmaceutical company advocated continued marketing of a hazardous drug, merely because they felt that the chair of the board favoured this decision (Brief, Dukerich, & Doran, 1991).

SOME ETHICAL CONSIDERATIONS

One enduring legacy of Milgram's experiments is the heated debate it stirred up over research ethics (Baumrind, 1964; Rosnow, 1981). Recall that Milgram's participants really believed they were administering severe electric shocks that were causing extreme pain to another human being. Milgram was careful to interview and, with the assistance of a psychiatrist, to follow up the more than 1000 participants in his experiments. There was no evidence of psychopathology and 83.7% of those who had taken part indicated that they were glad, or very glad, to have been in the experiment (Milgram, 1992, p. 186). Only 1.3% were sorry or very sorry to have participated.

The ethical issues really revolve around three questions concerning the ethics of subjecting experimental participants to short-term stress:

1. Is the research important? If not, then such stress is unjustifiable. However, it can be difficult to assess the 'importance' of research objectively.
2. Is the participant free to terminate the experiment at any time? How free were Milgram's participants? In one sense they were free to do whatever they wanted, but it was never made explicit to them that they could terminate whenever they wished—in fact, the very purpose of the study was to persuade them to remain!
3. Does the participant freely consent to being in the experiment in the first place? In Milgram's experiments the participants did not give fully informed consent: they volunteered to take part, but the true nature of the experiment was not explained to them.

This raises the issue of deception in social psychology research. Kelman (1967) distinguishes two reasons for deceiving people: the first is to induce them to take part in an otherwise unpleasant experiment. This is, ethically, a highly dubious practice. The second reason is that, in order to study the automatic operation of psychological processes, participants need to be naive regarding the hypotheses and this often involves some deception concerning the true purpose of the study and the procedures used. The fallout from this debate has been a code of ethics to guide psychologists in conducting research. The principal components of the code are:

- Participation must be based on fully informed consent.
- Participants must be explicitly informed that they can withdraw, without penalty, at any stage of the study.
- Participants must be fully and honestly debriefed at the end of the study.

Although it is probably no longer possible to get away with the impressively brazen deceptions that produced much of social psychology's classic research of the 1950s, 1960s and early 1970s, the use of minor and harmless procedural deceptions enshrined in clever cover stories is considered essential to preserve the scientific rigour of much experimental social psychology. The issue of research ethics in social psychology is discussed in full in Chapter 1.

Conformity

THE FORMATION AND INFLUENCE OF NORMS

Although much social influence is reflected in compliance with direct requests and obedience towards authority, social influence can also operate in a less direct manner, through **conformity** to social or group norms. For example, Allport (1924) observed that people in groups gave less extreme and more conservative judgments of odours and weights than when they were alone. It seemed as if, in the absence of direct pressure, the group could cause members to converge and thus become more similar to one another.

Sherif (1936) made a major step forward by explicitly linking this convergence effect to the development of *group norms*. Proceeding from the premise that people need to be certain and confident that what they are doing, thinking or feeling is correct and appropriate, Sherif argued that people use the behaviour of others to establish the range of possible behaviours: this we can call the **frame of reference**, or relevant *social comparative context*. Average, central or middle positions in such frames of reference are perceived to be more correct than fringe positions, and thus people tend to adopt them. Sherif believed that this explained the origins of social norms and concomitant convergence that accentuates consensus within groups.

To test this idea, he conducted his classic studies in **autokinesis** (see Box 7.1 and Figure 7.4 for details), in which two- or three-person groups making estimates of physical movement quickly converged over a series of trials on the mean of the group's estimates, and remained influenced by this norm even when subsequently making estimates alone.

The origins, structure, function and effects of norms are discussed fully in Chapter 8. It is, however, worth emphasising that normative pressure is one of the most effective ways of changing people's behaviour. For example, we noted in Chapter 6 that Lewin (1947) tried to encourage American housewives to change the eating habits of their families—specifically to eat more offal (kidneys, hearts, etc.). Three groups of 13–17 'housewives' attended an interesting factual lecture that, among other things, stressed how valuable such a change in eating habits would be to the war effort (in 1943). Another three groups were given information but were also encouraged to talk among themselves and arrive at some kind of consensus (i.e. to establish a norm) about buying the food.

A follow-up survey revealed that the norm was far more effective than the abstract information in causing some change in behaviour: only 3% of the information group had changed their behaviour compared with

A CLASSIC IN SOCIAL PSYCHOLOGY

BOX 7.1 Sherif's autokinetic study: The creation of arbitrary norms

Muzafer Sherif (1936) believed that social norms emerge in order to guide behaviour under conditions of uncertainty. To investigate this idea, he took advantage of a perceptual illusion—the autokinetic effect. Autokinesis is an optical illusion where a fixed pinpoint of light in a completely dark room appears to move: the movement is actually caused by eye movement in the absence of a physical frame of reference (i.e. objects). People asked to estimate how much the light moves find the task very difficult and generally feel uncertain about their estimates. Sherif presented the point of light a large number of times (i.e. trials) and had participants, who were unaware that the movement was an illusion, estimate the amount the light moved on each trial. He discovered that they used their own estimates as a frame of reference: over a series of 100 trials they gradually focused in on a narrow range of estimates, with different people adopting their own personal range, or norm (see session 1 in Figure 7.4a, when participants responded alone).

Sherif continued the experiment in further sessions of 100 trials on subsequent days, during which participants in groups of two or three took turns in a random sequence to call out their estimates. Now the participants used each other's estimates as a frame of reference and quickly converged on a group mean, so that they all gave very similar estimates (see sessions 2–4 in Figure 7.4a).

This norm seems to be internalised. When participants start and then continue as a group (sessions 1–3 in Figure 7.4b), the group norm is what they use when they finally make autokinetic estimates on their own (session 4 in Figure 7.4b).

Note: The results shown in Figure 7.4 are based on one set of three participants who made 100 judgments on each of eight sessions, spread over eight different days.

32% of the norm group. Subsequent research confirmed that it was the norm, not the attendant discussion, that was the crucial factor (Bennett, 1955).

YIELDING TO MAJORITY GROUP PRESSURE

Like Sherif, Asch (1952) believed that conformity reflects a relatively rational process, in which people construct a norm from other people's behaviour in order to determine correct and appropriate behaviour for themselves. Clearly, if you are already confident and certain about what is appropriate and correct, then others' behaviour will be largely irrelevant and thus socially not influential. In Sherif's study, the object of judgment was

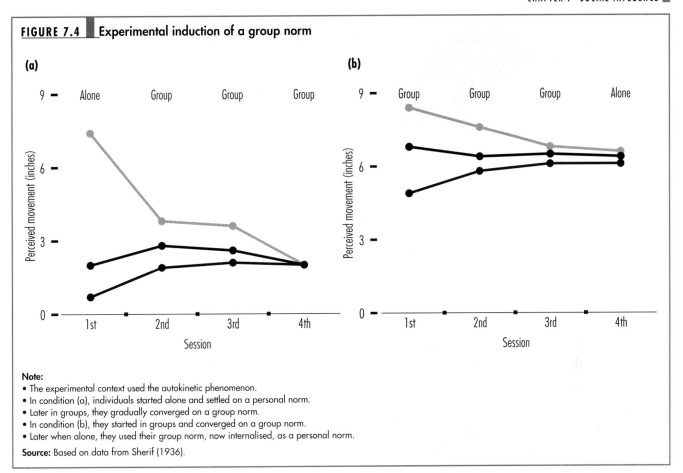

FIGURE 7.4 Experimental induction of a group norm

Note:
• The experimental context used the autokinetic phenomenon.
• In condition (a), individuals started alone and settled on a personal norm.
• Later in groups, they gradually converged on a group norm.
• In condition (b), they started in groups and converged on a group norm.
• Later when alone, they used their group norm, now internalised, as a personal norm.

Source: Based on data from Sherif (1936).

ambiguous: participants were uncertain, and so a norm arose rapidly and was highly effective in guiding behaviour. Asch argued that if the object of judgment was entirely unambiguous (i.e. no disagreement would be expected among judges) then disagreement, or alternative perceptions, would have no effect on behaviour: individuals would remain entirely independent of group influence.

To test this idea, Asch (1951, 1952, 1956) created a classic experimental paradigm. Male students, participating in what they thought was a visual discrimination task, seated themselves around a table in groups of seven to nine. They took turns in a fixed but apparently random order to call out publicly which of three comparison lines was the same length as a standard line (see Figure 7.5). There were 18 trials. In reality, only one person was a true naive participant and he answered second-to-last. The others were experimental confederates instructed to give erroneous responses on 12 focal trials: on six trials they picked a line that was too long, and on six a line that was too short. There was a control condition in which participants performed the task privately with no group influence; as less than 1% of control participants' responses were errors, it can be assumed that the task was unambiguous.

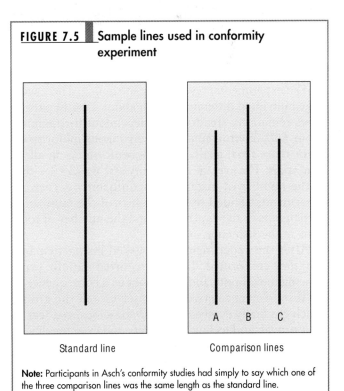

FIGURE 7.5 Sample lines used in conformity experiment

Standard line   Comparison lines

Note: Participants in Asch's conformity studies had simply to say which one of the three comparison lines was the same length as the standard line.
Source: Based on Asch (1951).

Conformity and group acceptance: How well would this woman fit in at a meeting of the board of directors of her multinational corporation?

The experimental results were intriguing. There were large individual differences, with about 25% of participants remaining steadfastly independent throughout, about 50% conforming to the erroneous majority on six or more focal trials, and 5% conforming on all 12 focal trials. The average conformity rate was 33%—that is, the number of instances of conformity across the experiment, divided by the product of the number of participants in the experiment and the number of focal trials in the sequence.

After the experiment, Asch asked his participants why they conformed. They all reported initially experiencing uncertainty and self-doubt as a consequence of the disagreement between themselves and the group, which gradually evolved into self-consciousness, fear of disapproval, and feelings of anxiety and even loneliness.

Different reasons were given for yielding. The majority knew they saw things differently from the group, but felt their perceptions may have been inaccurate and that the group was actually correct. Others did not believe the group was correct but simply went along with the group in order not to stand out. A small minority reported that they actually saw the lines as the group did. Independents were either entirely confident in the accuracy of their own judgments, or were emotionally affected but guided by a belief in individualism or in doing the task as directed (i.e. being accurate and therefore correct).

These subjective accounts suggest that one reason why people conform, even when the stimulus is completely unambiguous, may be to avoid censure, ridicule and social disapproval. This is a real fear. In another version of his experiment, Asch (1951) had 16 naive participants facing one confederate who gave incorrect answers. The participants found the confederate's behaviour ludicrous, and openly ridiculed him and laughed at him. Even the experimenter found the situation so bizarre that he could not contain his mirth and ended up laughing at the poor confederate!

Perhaps, then, if participants were not worried about social disapproval, there would be no subjective pressure to conform? To test this idea, Asch conducted another variation of the experiment, in which the incorrect majority called out their judgments publicly but the single naive participant wrote his down privately. Conformity dropped to 12.5%.

This modification was taken further by Deutsch and Gerard (1955), who believed that they could entirely eradicate pressure to conform if the task was unambiguous and the participant was anonymous, responded privately and was not under any sort of surveillance by the group. Why should you conform to an erroneous majority when there was an obvious, unambiguous and objectively correct answer, and the group had no way of knowing what you were doing?

To test this idea, Deutsch and Gerard confronted a naive participant face to face with three confederates who made unanimously incorrect judgments of lines on focal trials—exactly as in Asch's original experiment. In another condition, the naive participant was anonymous, isolated in a cubicle and allowed to respond privately—no group pressure existed. There was a third condition in which participants responded face to face but with an explicit group goal to be as accurate as possible—group pressure was maximised. Deutsch and Gerard also manipulated subjective uncertainty by having half the participants respond while the stimuli were present (the procedure used by Asch) and half respond after the stimuli had been removed (there would be scope for subjective uncertainty here).

As predicted, the results showed that both more certainty and decreasing group pressure (i.e. the motivation and ability of the group to censure lack of conformity) reduced conformity (Figure 7.6). Perhaps the most interesting finding was that people still conformed at a rate of about 23% even when uncertainty

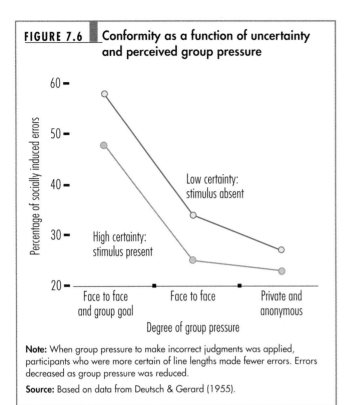

FIGURE 7.6 | Conformity as a function of uncertainty and perceived group pressure

Note: When group pressure to make incorrect judgments was applied, participants who were more certain of line lengths made fewer errors. Errors decreased as group pressure was reduced.

Source: Based on data from Deutsch & Gerard (1955).

investigation of factors influencing conformity. Crutchfield (1955) devised an apparatus in which participants in cubicles believed they were communicating with one another by pressing buttons on a console that illuminated responses, when in reality the cubicles were not interconnected and the experimenter was the source of all communication. In this way, many participants could be run simultaneously and yet all would believe they were being exposed to a unanimous group. The time-consuming, costly and risky practice of using confederates was no longer necessary, and data could now be collected much more quickly under more controlled and varied experimental conditions (Allen, 1965, 1975). Nowadays we can use a computerised variant of Crutchfield's methodology.

WHO CONFORMS? INDIVIDUAL AND GROUP CHARACTERISTICS

The existence of large individual differences in conformity has led some social psychologists to search for personality attributes that predispose some people to conform more than others. Those who conform tend to have low self-esteem, a high need for social support or social approval, a need for self-control, low IQ, high anxiety, feelings of self-blame and insecurity in the group, feelings of inferiority, feelings of relatively low status in the group and a generally authoritarian personality (Costanzo, 1970; Crutchfield, 1955; Elms & Milgram, 1966; Raven & French, 1958; Stang, 1972). However, the existence of negative findings, and

was low (stimulus present) and responses were private and anonymous.

The discovery that participants still conformed when isolated in cubicles has greatly facilitated the systematic

Group size and conformity: Could an individual in this throng resist joining in?

evidence that people who conform in one situation do not conform in another, suggests that situational factors may be more important than personality in conformity (Barocas & Gorlow, 1967; Barron, 1953; McGuire, 1968; Vaughan, 1964).

A similar conclusion can be drawn from research into sex differences in conformity. Women are typically found to conform slightly more than men in conformity studies. However, this can generally be explained in terms of the conformity tasks employed—ones with which women have less familiarity and expertise, experience greater subjective uncertainty and thus are influenced more than men (Eagly, 1978, 1983; Eagly & Carli, 1981; Eagly & Chrvala, 1986; Eagly & Wood, 1991).

For example, Sistrunk and McDavid (1971) exposed male and female participants to group pressure in identifying various stimuli. For some participants the stimuli were traditionally masculine items (e.g. identifying a special type of wrench), for some, traditionally feminine items (e.g. identifying types of needlework) and for others the stimuli were neutral (e.g. identifying popular rock stars). As expected, women conformed more on masculine items, men more on feminine items and both groups equally on neutral (non sex-stereotypical) items (Figure 7.7; see also second focus question).

Cultural norms

Do cultural norms affect conformity? Smith and Bond (1998) tabulated published conformity studies using Asch's paradigm or a variant thereof. There was significant intercultural variation. Level of conformity (i.e. percentage of incorrect responses) has been found to range from a low of 14% among Belgian students (Doms, 1983) to a high of 58% among Indian teachers in Fiji (Chandra, 1973), with an overall average of 31.2%. Conformity was lower among participants from individualist cultures in North America and northwestern Europe (25.3%) than from collectivist or interdependent cultures in Africa, Asia, Oceania and South America (37.1%).

A meta-analysis of 133 replications of the Asch paradigm in 17 different countries (R. Bond & Smith, 1996) confirmed that people who score high on Hofstede's (1980) collectivism scale conform more than people who score low (see also Figure 16.1, which shows summary data for non-Western versus various Western samples). The higher level of conformity in collectivist or interdependent cultures is because conformity is viewed favourably, as a form of social glue (Markus & Kitayama, 1991). What is perhaps more surprising is that, although conformity is lower in individualist Western societies, it is still remarkably high: even when conformity has negative overtones people find it difficult to resist conforming to group norms.

SITUATIONAL FACTORS IN CONFORMITY

The two situational factors in conformity that have been most exhaustively researched are group size and group unanimity (Allen, 1965, 1975). Asch (1952) found that, as the unanimous majority increased from 1 person to 2, to 3, to 4, to 8, to 10–15, the conformity rate increased and then decreased slightly: 3%, 13%, 33%, 35%, 32%, 31%. Although some research reports a linear relationship between size and conformity (e.g. Mann, 1977), the most robust finding is that conformity reaches its full strength with a three- to five-person majority and additional members have little effect (e.g. Stang, 1976).

Campbell and Fairey (1989) suggest that group size may have a different effect depending on the type of judgment being made and the motivation of the individual. With matters of taste, where there is no objectively correct answer (e.g. musical preference) and where you are concerned about 'fitting in', group size will have a relatively linear effect: the larger the majority, the more you will be swayed. When there is a correct response and you are concerned about being correct, the views of one or two others will usually be sufficient: the views of additional others will be largely redundant.

Finally, Wilder (1977) observed that size may not refer to the actual number of physically separate people in the group, but to the number of seemingly *independent* sources of influence in the group. For instance,

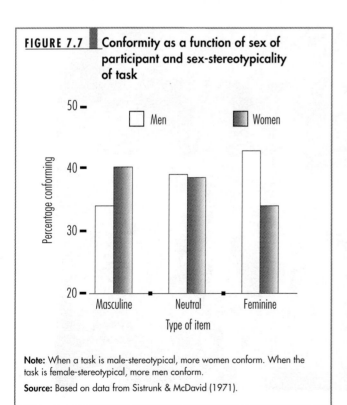

FIGURE 7.7 Conformity as a function of sex of participant and sex-stereotypicality of task

Percentage conforming

50 —
40 —
30 —
20 —

☐ Men   ▨ Women

Masculine   Neutral   Feminine

Type of item

Note: When a task is male-stereotypical, more women conform. When the task is female-stereotypical, more men conform.

Source: Based on data from Sistrunk & McDavid (1971).

CHAPTER 7 SOCIAL INFLUENCE

a majority of three individuals who are perceived to be independent will be more influential than a majority of, say, five who are perceived to be in collusion and thus represent a single information source. In fact, people may find it difficult to represent more than four or five discriminable or independent pieces of information and thus tend to assimilate additional group members into one or other of these initial sources of information—hence the relative lack of effect of group size above three to five members.

Asch's original experiment employed a unanimous erroneous majority to obtain a conformity rate of 33%. Subsequent experiments have shown that conformity is greatly reduced if the majority is not unanimous (Allen, 1975). Asch found that a correct supporter (i.e. a member of the majority who always gave the correct answer—and thus agreed with and supported the true participant) reduced conformity from 33% to 5.5%. The effectiveness of a supporter in reducing conformity is marginally greater if the supporter responds before rather than after the majority (Morris & Miller, 1975).

Support itself may not be the crucial factor in reducing conformity. Any sort of lack of unanimity among the majority seems to be effective. For example, Asch found that a dissenter who was even more incorrect than the majority was equally effective, and Shaw, Rothschild and Strickland (1957) found that a dithering and undecided deviate was also effective. Allen and Levine (1971) conducted an experiment in which participants who were asked to make visual judgments were provided with a supporter who had normal vision or a supporter who wore such thick glasses as to raise serious doubts about his ability to see anything at all, let alone judge lines accurately. In the absence of any support, participants conformed 97% of the time. The 'competent' supporter reduced conformity to 36% but most surprising was the fact that the 'incompetent' supporter reduced conformity as well, to 64% (see Figure 7.8).

Supporters, dissenters and deviates may be effective in reducing conformity because they shatter the unanimity of the majority and thus raise or legitimise the possibility of alternative ways of responding or behaving. For example, Nemeth and Chiles (1988) confronted participants with either four confederates who all correctly identified blue slides as blue, or four where one consistently called the blue slide 'green'. Participants were then exposed to another group who unanimously called red slides 'orange'. The participants who had previously been exposed to the consistent dissenter were more likely to correctly call the red slides 'red'.

NORMATIVE AND INFORMATIONAL INFLUENCE

Social psychologists generally believe that there are two processes of social influence responsible for conformity—called informational influence and normative

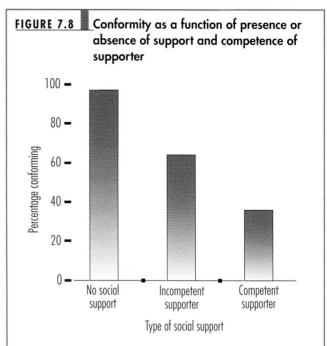

FIGURE 7.8 Conformity as a function of presence or absence of support and competence of supporter

Note: Social support on a line judgment task reduced conformity, even when the supporter was patently unable to make accurate judgments because he was visually impaired!

Source: Based on data from Allen & Levine (1971).

influence (Deutsch & Gerard, 1955; Kelley, 1952). **Informational influence** is an influence to accept information from another as *evidence* about reality. People have a need to feel confident that their perceptions, beliefs and feelings are correct. Informational influence comes into play when people are uncertain, either because stimuli are intrinsically ambiguous or because there is social disagreement. Under these circumstances, people initially make objective tests against reality, but if this is not possible then they make social comparisons (Festinger, 1950, 1954).

Effective informational influence causes true cognitive change.

Informational influence was probably partially responsible for the effects found by Sherif (1936) in his autokinetic studies. Reality was ambiguous and participants used other people's estimates as information to disambiguate reality and resolve subjective uncertainty. When participants were told that the apparent movement was in fact an illusion, they did not conform (e.g. Alexander, Zucker, & Brody, 1970): presumably, as reality itself was uncertain, their own subjective uncertainty was interpreted as a correct and valid representation of reality, and thus informational influence did not operate. Asch's stimuli were designed to be unambiguous in order to exclude informational influence. Asch (1952) found, however, that conformity increased as the comparison lines were made more similar to one another and the judgment task thus became more difficult.

Normative influence is an influence to conform to the positive expectations of others. People have a need for social approval and acceptance that causes them to 'go along with' the group for instrumental reasons—to cultivate approval and acceptance, avoid censure or disapproval, or achieve specific goals. Normative influence comes into play when the group is perceived to have the power and ability to mediate rewards and punishment contingent on our behaviour. An important precondition is that we are under surveillance by the group. Effective normative influence creates surface compliance rather than true cognitive change.

Normative influence was, no doubt, the principal cause of conformity in the Asch paradigm—the stimuli were unambiguous (informational influence would not be operating), but participants' behaviour was under direct surveillance by the group. We saw above how privacy, anonymity and lack of surveillance reduced conformity in the Asch paradigm, presumably because normative influence was weakened.

Deutsch and Gerard (1955) tried to remove normative influence entirely but, as we saw above, even under conditions in which neither informational nor normative influence would be expected to operate, they found residual conformity at a remarkably high rate of about 23%. From this we can conclude one of the following:

- The conditions of the experiment were such that informational and/or normative influence were not completely eradicated.
- They were inoperative but there is some third, as yet unspecified, social influence process.
- Social influence in groups needs to be explained in a different way.

REFERENT INFORMATIONAL INFLUENCE

The distinction between informational and normative influence is only one among many different terminologies that have been used in social psychology to distinguish between two types of social influence. It represents what has been called by Turner, at the Australian National University, and his colleagues a **dual-process dependency model** of social influence (Abrams & Hogg, 1990a; Hogg & Turner, 1987a; Turner, 1991). People are influenced by others because they are dependent on them either for information that clarifies reality and thus establishes subjective validity, or for reasons of social approval and acceptance.

This dual-process perspective has been challenged on the grounds that as an explanation of conformity it underemphasises the role of group belongingness. After all, an important feature of conformity is that we are influenced because we feel we belong, psychologically,

Marching to a different drum: An independent free-spirit? No. This young man is conforming to a sub-group norm.

to the group, and therefore the norms of the group are relevant standards for our behaviour. The dual-process model has drifted away from group norms and group belongingness and focused on *interpersonal* dependency, which could just as well occur between individuals as among group members.

This challenge has come from the **social identity approach** (Hogg, 2003b; Hogg & Abrams, 1988; Tajfel & Turner, 1979; see Chapter 11), which proposes a separate social influence process responsible for conformity to group norms—called **referent informational influence** (Hogg & Turner, 1987a; Turner, 1981b). Referent informational influence operates via the process of **self-categorisation**, which self-categorisation theorists believe is responsible for group belongingness and group behaviour (Turner, 1985; Turner, Hogg, Oakes, Reicher, & Wetherell, 1987; again see Chapter 11).

The categorisation of self and others present as members of the same social group occasions the search for a relevant group norm to describe and prescribe the group's, and hence our own, behaviour. The norm is constructed by the categorisation process according to the **metacontrast principle** (see Chapter 4)—that is, in such a way as to simultaneously minimise perceived differences among members of the group and accentuate differences between the group and people who are not in the group (e.g. outgroup members). The norm is internalised as a cognitive representation of the appropriate standard for behaviour as a group member. The self-categorisation process accentuates similarities between our own behaviour and that prescribed by the group norm—thus causing our own behaviour to conform to the norm.

To the extent that all members of the group construct a very similar group norm, self-categorisation produces intragroup convergence on that norm and increases intragroup uniformity—the typical conformity effect.

Referent informational influence differs from normative and informational influence in a number of important ways. For example, people conform because they are group members, not to validate physical reality or to avoid social disapproval. People do not conform to other people, but to a norm: other people (usually ingroup members, but they could be outgroup members) are a source of information about the appropriate ingroup norm. Because the norm is an internalised representation, people can conform to it in the absence of surveillance by group members or, for that matter, anybody else.

Referent informational influence has direct support from a series of four conformity experiments by Hogg and Turner (1987a). For example, under conditions of private responding (i.e. no normative influence) participants conformed to a non-unanimous majority containing a correct supporter (i.e. no informational influence) only if it was the participant's explicit or implicit ingroup (see also Abrams, Wetherell, Cochrane, Hogg, & Turner, 1990). Other support for referent informational influence comes from research into group polarisation (Chapter 9), crowd behaviour (Chapter 11) and social identity and stereotyping (Chapter 11).

leadership or (in the case of subgroups) legitimate power (leadership is discussed in Chapter 9).

However, there is an entire class of events where a minority that has little or no legitimate power can be innovative and sway the majority to its own viewpoint. For example, Asch (1952), as we have already seen, found that a single deviate (confederate) from a correct majority (true participants) was ridiculed and laughed at.

In another variant, however, Asch found a quite different response. When a correct majority of 11 true participants was confronted by a deviant/incorrect minority of nine confederates, the majority remained independent (i.e. continued responding correctly) but took the minority's responses far more seriously—no one laughed. Clearly, the minority had some influence over the majority, albeit not enough in this experiment to produce manifest conformity.

History illustrates the power of minorities. It could be argued that, if the only form of social influence was majority influence, then complete social homogeneity would have been reached tens of thousands of years ago—individuals and groups always being swayed to adopt the views and practices of the growing numerical majority. Minorities, particularly those that are active and organised, introduce innovations that ultimately produce social change: without **minority influence**, social change would be very difficult to explain. For example, the massive anti-war rallies during the 1960s in the United States had an effect on majority attitudes that hastened withdrawal from Vietnam. Similarly, the suffragettes of the 1920s gradually changed public opinion so that women were granted the vote, and the enormous CND (Campaign for Nuclear Disarmament) rallies in Western Europe in the early 1980s gradually shifted public opinion away from the 'benefits' of nuclear proliferation.

An excellent example of an active minority is Greenpeace: the group is numerically small (in terms of

Minority influence and social change

Our discussion of social influence, particularly conformity, has thus far been concerned with how individuals yield to direct or indirect social influence from a numerical majority—the usual Asch-type arrangement. Dissenters, deviates or independents have mainly been of interest indirectly, as a means of investigating either the effects of different types of majorities or conformist personality attributes. We are, however, all familiar with a very different, and very common, type of influence that can occur within a group: an individual or a numerical minority can change the views of the majority. Often such influence is based (in the case of individuals) on

Minority influence: Without active and organised minorities social change may not be possible.

'activist' members) but has had important and burgeoning influence on public opinion, through membership of the organisation and wider publicity of its views.

The sorts of questions that are important here are whether minorities and majorities gain influence via different social practices and, more fundamentally, whether the underlying psychology is different (see Wood, Lundgren, Ouellette, Busceme, & Blackstone, 1994, for a **meta-analysis** and overview of minority influence research).

THE CRITIQUE OF CONFORMITY RESEARCH

Social influence research has generally adopted a conformity perspective in which individuals depend on majorities for normative and informational reasons. Moscovici and colleagues launched an attack on this perspective (Moscovici, 1976; Moscovici & Faucheux, 1972; see Turner, 1991). Moscovici believes there is a **conformity bias** that considers all social influence as serving an adaptive requirement of human life—to adapt to the status quo and thus produce uniformity and perpetuate stability. Clearly, this is a valid and important need for individuals, groups and society. However, normative *change* is sometimes required to adapt to altered circumstances. Such change is difficult to understand from a conformity perspective, because it requires an understanding of the dynamics of active minorities.

Moscovici and Faucheux (1972) suggested that, in fact, it is minority influence that Asch observed in his classic studies. The Asch paradigm appears to pit a lone individual (true participant) against an erroneous majority (confederates) on an unambiguous physical perception task. Clearly, a case of majority influence in the absence of subjective uncertainty? Perhaps not.

The certainty with which we hold views lies in the amount of agreement we encounter for those views: ambiguity and uncertainty are not properties of objects 'out there', but of other people's disagreement with us. This point is just as valid for matters of taste (if everyone disagrees with your taste in music, it is very likely to change) as for matters of physical perception (if everyone disagrees with your perception of length, it is likely to change) (Moscovici, 1976, 1985a; Tajfel, 1969; Turner, 1985).

In this sense, Asch's lines were not 'unambiguous'—there was disagreement about their length. Furthermore, Asch's lone participant can be considered to be a member of a rather large majority (those people outside the experiment who would call the lines 'correctly'—i.e. the rest of humanity) confronted by a very small minority (the confederates who called the lines 'incorrectly') (see Tajfel, 1972a). Asch's participants were influenced by a minority: those who remained 'independent' can be considered to be the conformists!

'Independence' in this sense is nicely described by Henry Thoreau in his famous quote from *Walden* (1854): 'If a man does not keep pace with his companions, perhaps it is because he hears a different drummer'.

In contrast to traditional conformity research, Moscovici (1976, 1985a) believed that there is disagreement and conflict within groups and that there are three *social influence modalities* that define how people respond to such social conflict:

1. *conformity*—majority influence in which the majority persuades the minority, or deviates, to adopt the majority viewpoint;
2. *normalisation*—mutual compromise leading to convergence;
3. *innovation*—where a minority creates and accentuates conflict in order to persuade the majority to adopt the minority viewpoint.

INFLUENCE OF BEHAVIOURAL STYLE

Moscovici originally developed a **genetic model** of minority influence. He called it a 'genetic' model because it focused on the way in which the dynamics of social conflict can produce social change. People do not like social conflict. They try to avoid it or, if that is not possible, will often readily capitulate to resolve the situation. An active minority capitalises on this by going out of its way to create, draw attention to and accentuate conflict. Moscovici and colleagues believe that this can be a very effective way of winning over the majority, but it hinges on just *how* the minority goes about its task—on the *behavioural style* it adopts.

The single most important behavioural style is consistency. A *consistent minority*, one in which all members repeatedly promulgate the same message, has the following effects:

- It disrupts the majority norm and thus produces uncertainty and doubt.
- It draws attention to itself as an entity.
- It conveys the existence of an alternative coherent point of view.
- It demonstrates certainty in, and unshakable commitment to, its point of view.
- It shows that the only solution to the conflict that has arisen is espousal of the minority viewpoint (see third focus question).

The role of consistency is illustrated by Moscovici and his colleagues in a series of ingenious experiments—often referred to as the 'blue–green' studies (Maass & Clark, 1984). In a modified version of the Asch paradigm, Moscovici, Lage and Naffrechoux (1969) had four participants confront two confederates for a colour-perception task involving blue slides that varied only in intensity. The confederates were either consistent, always calling the slides 'green', or inconsistent, calling the slides 'green' two-thirds of the time and 'blue' one-

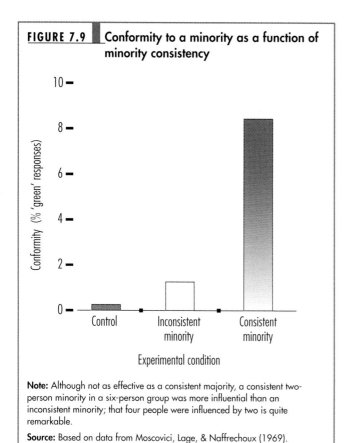

FIGURE 7.9 Conformity to a minority as a function of minority consistency

Conformity (% 'green' responses)

Experimental condition: Control, Inconsistent minority, Consistent minority

Note: Although not as effective as a consistent majority, a consistent two-person minority in a six-person group was more influential than an inconsistent minority; that four people were influenced by two is quite remarkable.

Source: Based on data from Moscovici, Lage, & Naffrechoux (1969).

The most important finding, however, was that the *only* participants in the entire experiment who actually changed their blue–green thresholds were those in the consistent minority condition.

There are two other properties of consistency that seem to be important: (a) it is perceived consistency, not merely objective repetition, that is important (Nemeth, Swedlund, & Kanki, 1974); and (b) the presence of consistency between members of the minority (i.e. consensus) is a crucial factor (Nemeth, Wachtler, & Endicott, 1977). Aside from consistency, there are at least three other *behavioural style factors* that may affect minority influence:

1. *Investment*—minorities are more effective if they are seen to have made significant personal or material sacrifices for their cause.
2. *Autonomy*—minorities are more effective if seen to be acting out of principle rather than from ulterior motives.
3. *Rigidity/flexibility*—a minority that is too rigid risks being rejected as dogmatic, while one that is too flexible risks being rejected as inconsistent.

There is a fine line to tread: a minority must be absolutely consistent with regard to its position, but should adopt a relatively open-minded and reasonable negotiating style (Moscovici & Mugny, 1983; Mugny, 1982).

GROUP MEMBERSHIP AND SOCIAL IDENTITY

Groups in society that promulgate minority viewpoints are generally widely stigmatised by the majority as social outgroups or are psychologised as deviant individuals. Their views are, at best, rejected as irrelevant, but are often ridiculed and trivialised in an attempt to discredit the minority (e.g. the treatment of gays, environmentalists, intellectuals) (see Chapter 10 for a discussion of discrimination against outgroups). All this makes it even more difficult for minorities to have effective influence: there is an enormous amount of resistance on the part of the majority.

From this it follows that minorities might be more effective if, in addition to promulgating a consistent view that differs from the majority position, they are also viewed by the majority as an ingroup. Indeed, research confirms that minorities do exert more influence if they are perceived by the majority as an ingroup (Maass, Clark, & Haberkorn, 1982; Martin, 1988; Mugny & Papastamou, 1982). How can minorities successfully have it both ways—be thought of as an ingroup *and* hold an unwavering outgroup position? The trick seems to be that effective minorities need to be able, psychologically, to establish their legitimate ingroup credentials before they draw undue critical attention to their distinct minority viewpoint (Crano & Alvaro, 1998; David & Turner, 1996; Turner, 1991).

third of the time. There was also a control condition with no confederates, just six real participants. Figure 7.9 shows that the consistent minority had significantly more influence than the inconsistent minority. Although the conformity rate is much lower than with a consistent majority, it is nevertheless remarkable that four people (a numerical majority) were influenced by two people (a minority).

There are two other notable results from an extension of this experiment, in which participants' actual colour thresholds were tested privately after the social influence stage: (a) both experimental groups showed a lower threshold for 'green' than the control group—that is, erred towards seeing ambiguous green–blue slides as 'green'; and (b) this effect was greater among experimental participants who were resistant to the minority—that is, did not publicly call the blue slides 'green'.

Moscovici and Lage (1976) employed the same colour-perception task to compare consistent and inconsistent minorities with consistent and inconsistent majorities. There was also a control condition. As before, the only minority to produce conformity was the consistent minority (10% conformity). Although this does not compare well with the rate of conformity to the consistent majority (40%), it is comparable with the rate of conformity to the inconsistent majority (12%).

The logic behind this is that disagreement among people who define themselves as members of the same group is both unexpected and unnerving—it raises subjective uncertainty about themselves and their attributes and motivates uncertainty reduction (Hogg, 2000a). Where common ingroup membership is important and 'inescapable', there will be a degree of redefinition of group attributes in line with the minority—the minority has been effective. Where common ingroup membership is unimportant and easily denied, there will be no redefinition of ingroup attributes in line with the minority—the minority will be ineffective.

CONVERSION

In 1980 Moscovici supplemented his earlier genetic model of social influence with a *dual-process model*. He argued that majorities and minorities exert influence through different processes (Moscovici, 1980). Majority influence brings about direct public compliance for reasons of normative or informational dependence. Majority views are accepted passively without much thought. In contrast, minority influence brings about indirect, often latent, private change in opinion due to the cognitive conflict and restructuring that deviant ideas produce. Minorities produce a **conversion effect** as a consequence of active consideration of the minority point of view.

This distinction is similar to that discussed earlier between normative and informational influence, and is related to Petty and Cacioppo's (1986a, b) distinction between peripheral and central processing, and Chaiken's (Bohner, Moskowitz, & Chaiken, 1995) distinction between heuristic and systematic processing (see Chapter 6; Eagly & Chaiken, 1993).

Conversion through minority influence would be expected to take longer to manifest itself than compliance through majority influence. Indeed, as we have already seen, Moscovici, Lage and Naffrechoux (1969) and Moscovici and Lage (1976) found evidence for private change in colour thresholds (i.e. conversion) among participants exposed to a consistent minority although they did not behave (or had not yet behaved) publicly in accordance with this change.

There is other evidence for the existence of two distinct processes. Nemeth (Nemeth, 1986; Nemeth & Wachtler, 1983) conducted a number of Asch-type and blue–green experiments in which participants exposed to majority or minority influence converged, with little thought, on majority responses; but minorities stimulated divergent, novel, creative thinking and more active information-processing, which increased the probability of correct answers.

Using a different paradigm, Mucchi-Faina, Maass and Volpato (1991) found that students at the University of Perugia generated more original and creative ideas for promoting the international image of the city of Perugia when they had been exposed to a conventional majority and a creative minority than vice versa, or where the majority and the minority were both original or both conventional.

Maass and Clark (1983, 1986) report three experiments investigating people's public and private reactions to majority and minority influence regarding the issue of gay rights. In one of these experiments (Maass & Clark, 1983), they found that publicly expressed attitudes conformed to the expressed views of the majority (i.e. if the majority was pro-gay, then so were the participants), while privately expressed attitudes shifted towards the position espoused by the minority (see Figure 7.10).

Perhaps the most intriguing series of experiments was by Moscovici and Personnaz (1980, 1986), who employed the blue–green paradigm as before. Individual participants, judging the colour of obviously blue slides that varied only in intensity, were exposed to a single confederate who always called the slides 'green'. They were led to believe that most people (82%) would respond as the confederate did, or that only very few people (18%) would. In this way, the confederate was a source of majority or minority influence. Participants publicly called out the colour of the slide and then (and this is the ingenious twist introduced by Moscovici and Personnaz) the

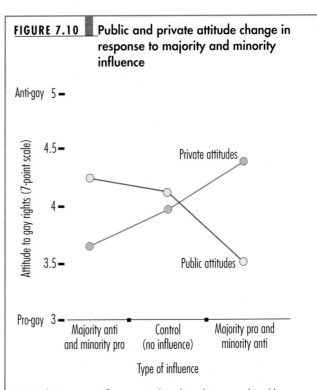

FIGURE 7.10 Public and private attitude change in response to majority and minority influence

Note: Relative to a no-influence control condition, heterosexuals' public attitudes towards gay rights closely reflected the pro- or anti-gay attitudes of the majority. However, private attitudes reflected the pro- or anti-gay attitudes of the minority.

Source: Based on data from Maass & Clarke (1983).

slide was removed and participants wrote down privately the colour of the after-image. Unknown to most people, including the participants, the after-image is always the complementary colour. So, for blue slides the after-image is yellow, and for green slides it would be purple.

There were three phases to the experiment: an influence phase where participants were exposed to the confederate, preceded and followed by phases where the confederate was absent and so there was no influence. The results were remarkable (see Figure 7.11). Majority influence hardly affected the chromatic after-image: it remained yellow, indicating that participants had seen a blue slide. Minority influence, however, shifted the after-image towards purple, indicating that participants had actually 'seen' a green slide! The effect persisted even when the minority confederate was absent.

This remarkable finding clearly supports the idea that minority influence produces indirect, latent internal change while majority influence produces direct, immediate behavioural compliance. Moscovici and Personnaz have been able to replicate it, but others have been less successful. For example, in a direct replication Doms and van Avermaet (1980) found after-image changes

Conversion: If you and your friends repeatedly and consistently told your friend Pierre that this was the Leaning Tower of Pisa, would he eventually believe you?

after both minority and majority influence, and Sorrentino, King and Leo (1980) found no after-image shift after minority influence, except among participants who were suspicious of the experiment.

To try to sort out the contradictory findings, Robin Martin at the University of Queensland conducted a series of five replications of Moscovici and Personnaz's (1980) paradigm (Martin, 1998). His pattern of findings revealed that participants tended to show a degree of after-image shift only if they paid close attention to the blue slides—and this occurred among participants who were either suspicious of the experiment or exposed to many rather than a few slides.

The key point here is that circumstances that made people attend more closely to the blue slides caused them to actually see more green in the slides and thus to report an after-image that had shifted towards that for green. This suggests that Moscovici and colleagues' intriguing after-image findings may not reflect distinct minority/majority influence processes but may be a methodological artifact. Of course, this does not mean that conversion theory is wrong but it does question the status of the blue–green studies as evidence for conversion theory.

ATTRIBUTION AND MINORITY INFLUENCE

There are many aspects of minority influence that suggest the operation of an underlying **attribution** process (Kelley, 1967; Hewstone, 1989; see Chapter 3). Effective minorities are consistent and consensual,

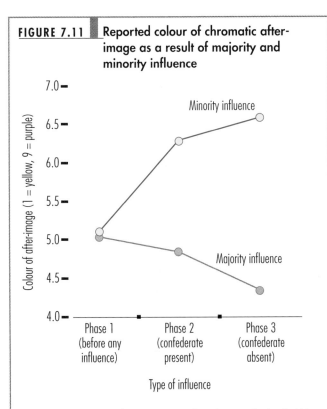

FIGURE 7.11 | Reported colour of chromatic after-image as a result of majority and minority influence

Colour of after-image (1 = yellow, 9 = purple)

Minority influence

Majority influence

Phase 1 (before any influence) — Phase 2 (confederate present) — Phase 3 (confederate absent)

Type of influence

Note: Participants exposed to a majority member who wrongly identified blue slides as green did not change their perception: their after-images did not alter. However, participants exposed to a minority member who called the blue slides green did change their perception: their after-images changed and continued to change even after influence had ceased.

Source: Based on data from Moscovici & Personnaz (1980).

distinct from the majority, unmotivated by self-interest or external pressures and flexible in style. This combination of factors encourages a perception that the minority has freely chosen its position. It is therefore difficult to explain away its position in terms of idiosyncrasies of individuals (though this is, as we saw above, a strategy that is attempted) or in terms of external inducements or threats. Perhaps, then, there is actually some intrinsic merit to its position.

This encourages people to take the minority seriously (though again social forces work against this) and at least consider its position; such cognitive work is an important precondition for subsequent attitude change.

SOCIAL IMPACT AND MINORITY INFLUENCE

Majorities and minorities can be defined in terms of power, but they also refer to numbers of people. Although 'minorities' are often both less powerful and less numerous (e.g. Aborigines in Australia), they can be less powerful but more numerous (e.g. Tibetans versus Chinese in Tibet). Perhaps not surprisingly, an attempt has been made to explain minority influence purely in terms of the social influence consequences of relative group size.

Latané and Wolf (1981) draw on **social impact** theory (e.g. Latané, 1981) to argue that as a source of influence increases in size (number) it has more influence. However, as the source of influence gets larger, the impact of each source is reduced: so, for instance, a single source has enormous impact, the addition of a second source increases impact but not by as much as the first, a third even less, and so on.

A good analogy is switching on a single light in a dark room—the impact is enormous. A second light improves things but only a little. If you have ten lights on, the impact of an eleventh will be negligible.

Evidence does support this idea: the larger the source of influence the more impact it has, with incremental changes due to additional sources decreasing with increasing size (e.g. Mullen, 1983; Tanford & Penrod, 1984). But how does this account for the fact that minorities can actually have influence?

There is a sense in which the effect of a large majority on an individual majority member has reached a plateau: additional members or 'bits' of majority influence have relatively little impact. Although a minority viewpoint has relatively little impact, it has not yet attained a plateau: additional members or 'bits' of minority influence have a relatively large impact. In this way, exposure to minority positions can, paradoxically, have relatively greater impact than exposure to majority viewpoints.

TWO PROCESSES OR ONE?

Although the social impact perspective can account for some quantitative differences between majority and minority influence at the level of overt public behaviour, even Latané and Wolf (1981) admit that it cannot explain the qualitative differences that seem to exist, particularly at the private level of covert cognitive changes. These qualitative differences, and particularly the process differences proposed by Moscovici's (1980) dual-process model are, however, themselves the focus of some debate. For instance, there is some concern (e.g. Abrams & Hogg, 1990a; Turner, 1991) that postulating separate processes to explain minority and majority influence has revived the opposition of informational and normative influence—an opposition which, as we saw earlier, has problems in explaining other social influence phenomena. Instead, whether minorities or majorities are influential or not may simply be a matter of social identity dynamics that determine whether people are able to define themselves as members of the minority (majority) group or not (e.g. Crano & Alvaro, 1998; David & Turner, 1996).

In addition, theoretical analyses by Kruglanski and Mackie (1990) and a meta-analysis by Wood and colleagues (Wood, Lundgren, Ouellette, Busceme, & Blackstone, 1994) together suggest that people who are confronted with a minority position, particularly under face-to-face conditions with real social minorities and majorities, tend not only to resist an overt appearance of alignment with the minority but also privately and cognitively avoid alignment with the minority. This conflicts with Moscovici's dual-process model.

Summary

- Social influence can produce surface compliance with requests, obedience to commands and internalised conformity to group norms.
- People tend to be more readily influenced by reference groups, because they are psychologically significant for our attitudes and behaviours, than by membership groups, as they are simply groups to which we belong by some external criterion.
- Given the right circumstances we all have the potential to obey commands blindly, even if the consequences of such obedience include harm to others.

- Obedience is affected by the proximity and legitimacy of authority, by the proximity of the victim and by the degree of social support for obedience or disobedience.
- Group norms are enormously potent sources of conformity: we all tend to yield to the majority.
- Conformity can be reduced if the task is unambiguous and people are not under surveillance—though even under these circumstances there is often residual conformity. Lack of unanimity among the majority is particularly effective in reducing conformity.
- People may conform in order to feel sure about the objective validity of their perceptions and opinions, to obtain social approval and avoid social disapproval or to express or validate their social identity as members of a specific group.
- Active minorities can sometimes influence majorities: this may be the very essence of social change.
- To be effective, minorities should be consistent but not rigid, should be seen to be making personal sacrifices and acting out of principle and should be perceived as being part of the ingroup.
- Minorities may be effective because, unlike majority influence which is based on 'mindless' compliance, they cause latent cognitive change as a consequence of thought produced by the cognitive challenge posed by the novel minority position.

LINKS

YOU HAVE READ ABOUT:	WHICH LINKS TO:
Compliance with requests	multiple-request compliance techniques (6)
Social power	centrality in communication networks (8)
Obedience to authority as a situational event	criticism of authoritarianism as a personality construct (10)
Minority influence and social change	power of minority groups (11)

Key terms

attribution *(p. 177)*
autokinesis *(p. 166)*
compliance *(p. 160)*
conformity *(p. 166)*
conformity bias *(p. 174)*
conversion effect *(p. 176)*
dual-process dependency model *(p. 172)*
frame of reference *(p. 166)*

genetic model *(p. 174)*
informational influence *(p. 171)*
membership group *(p. 160)*
meta-analysis *(p. 174)*
metacontrast principle *(p. 172)*
minority influence *(p. 173)*
normative influence *(p. 172)*
norms *(p. 160)*
power *(p. 161)*

reference group *(p. 160)*
referent informational influence *(p. 172)*
self-categorisation (theory) *(p. 172)*
social identity approach *(p. 172)*
social impact *(p. 178)*
social influence *(p. 160)*

FURTHER READING

Baron, R. S., & Kerr, N. (2003). *Group process, group decision, group action* (2nd ed.). Buckingham, UK: Open University Press. Up-to-date general overview of some major topics in the study of group processes; includes discussion of social influence phenomena.

Brown, R. J. (2000). *Group processes* (2nd ed.). Oxford, UK: Blackwell. A very readable introduction to group processes that also places an emphasis on social influence processes within groups—especially conformity, norms and minority influence.

Cialdini, R. B., & Trost, M. R. (1998). Social influence: Social norms, conformity, and compliance. In D. Gilbert, S. T. Fiske, & G. Lindzey (Eds.), *The handbook of social psychology* (4th ed., Vol. 2, pp. 151–192). New York: McGraw-Hill. Thorough overview of the field of social influence, in the most recent edition of this classic handbook; a primary source for theory and research.

Martin, R., & Hewstone, M. (2001). Conformity and independence. In M. A. Hogg & R. S. Tindale (Eds.), *Blackwell handbook of social psychology: Group processes* (pp. 209–234). Oxford, UK: Blackwell. Up-to-date overview of what we know about minority influence processes and how they relate to conformity and majority influence.

Martin, R., & Hewstone, M. (2003). Social influence processes of control and change: Conformity, obedience to authority, and innovation. In M. A. Hogg & J. Cooper (Eds.), *The Sage handbook of social psychology* (pp. 347–366). London: Sage. An up-to-date and comprehensive review of social influence research, including conformity, obedience and minority influence.

Mugny, G., & Pérez, J. A. (1991). *The social psychology of minority influence*. Cambridge, UK: Cambridge University Press. An overview of research into minority influence by two leading scholars on this notably European topic of research; also coverage of Mugny and Moscovici's own theories of minority influence.

Turner, J. C. (1991). *Social influence*. Buckingham, UK: Open University Press. Scholarly overview of the field of social influence that takes a critical stance from the viewpoint of European perspectives and places particular emphasis on social identity, minority influence and the role of group membership and group norms.

CHAPTER EIGHT

People in groups

THIS CHAPTER DISCUSSES:

- the nature of groups
- group effects on individual performance
- social facilitation
- group versus individual performance: social loafing
- group cohesiveness
- group socialisation
- group norms
- group structure: roles, status and communication networks
- why people join groups.

FOCUS QUESTIONS

1. James can play a difficult piano piece really well when he is alone, but finds it difficult to do as well when others are close by. He just knows they are waiting for him to make a mistake—and he usually does! How would you account for this?

2. You are debating a point about group processes with a classmate. She argues convincingly that a group that 'hangs together' must consist of members who liked each other in the first place. 'That's not so,' you point out. 'Haven't you heard how social attraction works?'

3. Terry wants to show the rest of the family that they are quite rule-bound in their everyday practices around the house, without even knowing it. How could she demonstrate this?

What is a group?

The social **group** occupies much of our day-to-day life. We work in groups, we socialise in groups, we play in groups, and we represent our views and attitudes through groups. Groups also largely determine the people we are and the sorts of lives we live. Selection panels, juries, committees and government bodies influence what we do, where we live, and how we live. The groups to which we belong determine what language we speak, what accent we have, what attitudes we hold, what cultural practices we adopt, what education we receive, what level of prosperity we enjoy and, ultimately, who we are. Even the groups to which we do not belong, either by choice or by exclusion, have a profound impact on our lives.

In this overwhelming matrix of group influences, the domain of the autonomous, independent, unique self may indeed be limited.

Groups differ in all sorts of respects (Deaux, Reid, Mizrahi, & Ethier, 1995). Some have a large number of members (e.g. a nation, a sex) and others are small (a committee, a family); some are relatively short-lived (a group of friends, a jury) and some endure for thousands of years (an ethnic group, a religion); some are concentrated (a road crew, a selection committee), others dispersed (academics, computer-mediated communication groups); some are highly structured and organised (an army, a flight crew), others more informally organised (a supporters' club, a community action group); some have highly specific purposes (an assembly line, an environmental protest group), others are more general (a tribal group, a teenage 'gang'); some are relatively autocratic (an army, a police force), others relatively democratic (a university department, a commune); and so on.

Any social group can thus be described in terms of an array of features that highlight its similarities to, and differences from, other groups. These can be very general features, such as membership size (e.g. a religion versus a committee), but they can also be very specific features, such as group practices and beliefs (e.g. Catholics versus Muslims, liberals versus conservatives, Maasai versus Kikuyu).

This enormous variety of groups could be reduced by limiting the number of significant dimensions to produce a restricted taxonomy of groups. Social psychologists have tended to focus more on group size, group 'atmosphere', task structure and leadership structure than other dimensions.

GROUPS AS CATEGORIES

One general distinction is made between similarity-based, or categorical, groups and interaction-based or dynamic groups (Arrow, McGrath, & Berdahl, 2000; Wilder & Simon, 1998). This distinction comes in different forms. For example, Prentice, Miller and Lightdale (1994) distinguish between *common-bond* groups (groups based upon attachment among members) and *common-identity* groups (groups based on direct attachment to the group). We can go further back to an important distinction in the social sciences originally made in 1857 by Tönnies (1955) between *Gemeinschaft* (i.e. community) and *Gesellschaft* (i.e. association)—that is, social organisation based on close interpersonal bonds and social organisation based on more formalised and impersonal associations.

Nevertheless, human groups are quite clearly categories—some people are in the group and some people are not. As such, human groups should differ in ways that all categories differ. One of the key ways in which categories differ is in terms of entitativity (Campbell, 1958). **Entitativity** is the property of a group that makes it appear to be a distinct, coherent and bounded entity. High entitativity groups have clear boundaries and are internally well structured and relatively homogeneous. Groups certainly differ in terms of entitativity (Hamilton & Sherman, 1996; Lickel, Hamilton, Wieczorkowska, Lewis, & Sherman, 2000).

GROUPS AND AGGREGATES

Not all collections of individuals can be considered groups in a psychological sense. For example, people with green eyes, strangers in a dentist's waiting room, people on a Gold Coast beach, locals fishing off a pier—are these groups? Perhaps not. More likely these are merely social aggregates, collections of unrelated individuals—not groups at all. The important social psychological question is what distinguishes groups from aggregates; it is by no means an easy question to answer. Social psychologists differ in their views on this issue. These differences are, to some extent, influenced by whether the researcher favours an individualistic or a collectivistic perspective on groups (Hogg & Abrams, 1988; Turner & Oakes, 1989).

Individualists believe that people in groups behave in much the same way as they do in pairs or by themselves, and that group processes are really nothing more than interpersonal processes among a number of people (e.g. Allport, 1924; Latané, 1981).

Collectivists believe that the behaviour of people in groups is influenced by unique social processes and cognitive representations that can only occur in and emerge from groups (e.g. Abrams & Hogg, 1988; McDougall, 1920; Sherif, 1936; Tajfel & Turner, 1979).

DEFINITIONS

Although there are almost as many definitions of the social group as there are social psychologists who research social groups, Johnson and Johnson (1987) have identified seven major emphases. The group is:

1. a collection of individuals who are interacting with one another;
2. a social unit consisting of two or more people who perceive themselves as belonging to a group;
3. a collection of individuals who are interdependent;
4. a collection of individuals who join together to achieve a goal;
5. a collection of individuals who are trying to satisfy a need through their joint association;
6. a collection of individuals whose interactions are structured by a set of roles and norms; and
7. a collection of individuals who influence each other.

Their definition incorporates all these emphases (Johnson & Johnson, 1987, p. 8):

A group is two or more individuals in face-to-face interaction, each aware of his or her membership in the group, each aware of the others who belong to the group, and each aware of their positive interdependence as they strive to achieve mutual goals.

You will notice that this definition, and many of the emphases in the previous paragraph cannot encompass large groups and/or do not distinguish between interpersonal and group relationships. This is a relatively accurate portrayal of the social psychology of group processes, which is generally restricted, explicitly or implicitly, to small, face-to-face, short-lived, interactive, task-oriented groups (but see Brown, 2000; Hogg & Tindale, 2001). In addition, 'group processes' generally

do not mean *group* processes but interpersonal processes among more than two people.

The effect of the group on individual performance

MERE PRESENCE AND AUDIENCE EFFECTS: SOCIAL FACILITATION

Perhaps the most basic and elementary *social* psychological question concerns the effect of the presence of other people on our behaviour: 'What changes in an individual's normal solitary performance occur when other people are present?' (Allport, 1954a, p. 46). You are playing a musical instrument, fixing the car, reciting a poem or working out in the gym, and someone comes to watch; what happens to your performance? Does it improve or deteriorate?

This question intrigued Norman Triplett (1898), credited by some as having conducted the first social psychology experiment, although there has been controversy about this (see Box 1.1 in Chapter 1). From observing that people cycled faster when paced than when alone, and faster in competition than when paced, Triplett hypothesised that competition between people energised and improved performance on motor tasks. To test this idea, he had young children reeling a continuous loop of line on a 'competition machine' and confirmed his hypothesis: more children reeled the line more quickly when racing against each other in pairs than when performing alone.

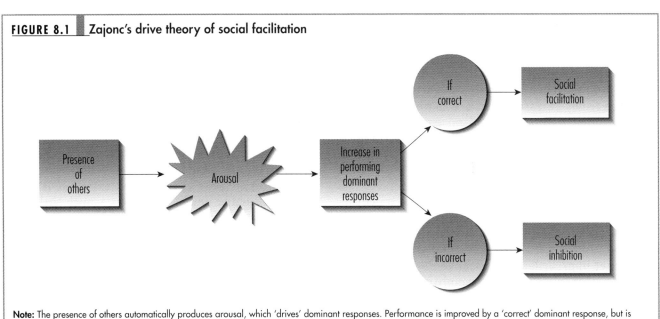

FIGURE 8.1 Zajonc's drive theory of social facilitation

Note: The presence of others automatically produces arousal, which 'drives' dominant responses. Performance is improved by a 'correct' dominant response, but is impaired by an 'incorrect' dominant response.
Source: Based on Zajonc (1965).

Drive theory: Would this young girl, playing her violin alone, play better or worse if there were an audience?

Allport (1920) termed this phenomenon **social facilitation**, but felt that Triplett's narrowing of the effect to competition could be widened to allow for a more general principle: that an improvement in performance could be due to the **mere presence** of conspecifics (i.e. members of the same species) as coactors (doing the same thing but not interacting) or as a passive audience (passively watching).

Until the late 1930s an enormous amount of social facilitation research was conducted, much of it with an exotic array of animals. For example, we now know that cockroaches run faster, chickens, fish and rats eat more, and pairs of rats copulate more when being 'watched' by conspecifics or when conspecifics are also running, eating or copulating! However, research has also revealed that social presence can produce quite the opposite effect—social inhibition, or a decrement in task performance.

Contradictory findings such as these, in conjunction with imprecision in defining the degree of social presence (early research used a coaction paradigm, whereas later research focused on passive **audience effects**), led to the near-demise of social facilitation research by about 1940.

Drive theory

In 1965 Zajonc published a classic theoretical statement called **drive theory** (see Figure 8.1, page 183), which revived social facilitation research and has kept it alive to the present day (see Geen, 1989; Guerin, 1986, 1993). Zajonc set himself the task of explaining what determines whether social presence (mainly in the form of a passive audience) facilitates or inhibits performance.

Drive theory argues that because people are relatively unpredictable (you can rarely know with any certainty exactly what they are going to do), there is a clear advantage to the species for their presence to cause us to be in a state of alertness and readiness. Increased arousal or motivation is thus an instinctive reaction to social presence. Such arousal functions as a 'drive' that energises (i.e. causes us to enact) those behaviours which are our dominant responses (i.e. best learned, most habitual) in that situation. If the dominant response is correct (we feel the task is easy), then social presence produces an improved performance; if it is incorrect (we feel the task is difficult), then social presence produces an impaired performance.

Let's illustrate this with an example. Toni is a novice violinist with a small repertoire of pieces to play. When playing alone, there is one piece that she finds extremely easy because it is very well learned—she almost never makes mistakes. If she were to play this piece in front of an audience (say, her friends), drive theory would predict that, because her dominant response is to make no mistakes, her performance would be greatly improved. In contrast, there is another piece which, when playing alone, she finds extremely difficult because it is not very well learned—she almost never gets it right. It would be a rash decision indeed to play this in front of an audience—drive theory would predict that, because the dominant response contains all sorts of errors, her performance would be truly awful, much worse than when she plays alone.

Evaluation apprehension

Although early research tends on the whole to support drive theory (Geen & Gange, 1977; Guerin & Innes, 1982), some social psychologists have questioned whether mere presence instinctively produces drive. Cottrell (1972) has proposed an **evaluation apprehension model**, in which he argues that we quickly learn that the social rewards and punishments we receive (e.g. approval and disapproval) are based on others' evaluations of us. Social presence thus produces an acquired arousal (drive) based on evaluation apprehension.

In support of this interpretation, Cottrell, Wack, Sekerak and Rittle (1968) found no social facilitation effect on three well-learned tasks when the two-person audience was inattentive (i.e. blindfolded) and merely present (i.e. only incidentally present while ostensibly waiting to take part in a different experiment). This audience would be unlikely to produce much evaluation apprehension. However, a non-blindfolded audience that attended carefully to the participant's performance and had expressed an interest in watching would be expected to produce a great deal of evaluation apprehension. Indeed, this audience did produce a social facilitation effect.

Other research is less supportive. For example, Markus (1978) had male participants undress, dress in unfamiliar clothing (laboratory coat, special shoes) and then dress in their own clothing again. To minimise apprehension about evaluation by the experimenter, the task was presented as an incidental filler activity. The task was performed under one of three conditions: (a) alone; (b) in the mere presence of an incidental audience (low evaluation apprehension)—a confederate who faced away and was engrossed in some other task; or (c) in the presence of an attentive audience (high evaluation apprehension)—a confederate who carefully and closely watched the participant dressing and undressing.

The results (Figure 8.2) confirmed evaluation apprehension theory on the relatively easy task of dressing in familiar clothing; only an attentive audience lessened the time taken to perform this task. However, on the more difficult task of dressing in unfamiliar clothing, mere presence was sufficient to slow performance down and an attentive audience had no additional effect; this supports drive theory rather than evaluation apprehension.

Schmitt, Gilovich, Goore and Joseph (1986) conducted a similarly conceived experiment. Participants were given what they thought was an incidental task that involved typing their name into a computer (a simple task), and then entering a code name by typing their name backwards interspersed with ascending digits (a difficult task). These tasks were performed (a) *alone* after the experimenter had left the room; (b) in the *mere presence* of only a confederate who was blindfolded, wore a headset and was allegedly participating in a separate experiment on sensory deprivation; or (c) under the *close observation of the experimenter*, who remained in the room carefully scrutinising the participant's performance.

The results of the study (Figure 8.3) show that mere presence produced a faster performance of the easy task and a slower performance of the difficult task, and that evaluation apprehension had little additional impact. Mere presence appears to be a sufficient cause of, and evaluation apprehension not necessary for, social facilitation effects (see first focus question).

Guerin, at Waikato University in Hamilton, and Innes, at the University of Adelaide, have suggested that social facilitation effects may occur only when people

FIGURE 8.2 Time taken to dress up in familiar and unfamiliar clothes as a function of social presence

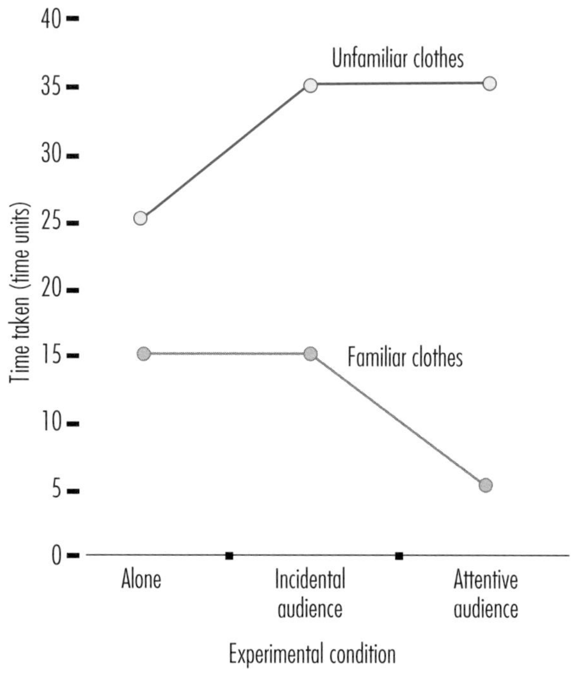

Note: Participants dressed in their own clothing (easy task) or in unfamiliar clothing (difficult task), alone, with an incidental audience present or with an attentive audience present. Evaluation apprehension occurred on the easy task: only the attentive audience reduced the time taken to dress up. There was a drive effect on the difficult task: both incidental and attentive audiences increased the time taken to dress.

Source: Based on data from Markus (1978).

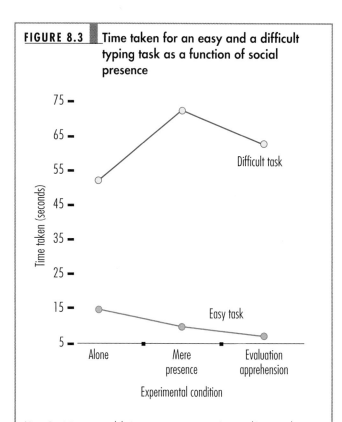

FIGURE 8.3 Time taken for an easy and a difficult typing task as a function of social presence

Note: Participants typed their name on a computer (easy task) or typed it backwards interspersed with digits (difficult task), alone, with an incidental audience present or with an attentive audience present. There was a drive effect on both the easy task and the difficult task: the incidental audience improved performance on the easy task and impaired it on the difficult task, and the attentive audience had no additional effect.

Source: Based on data from Schmitt, Gilovich, Goore, & Joseph (1986).

Distraction-conflict theory: Even an audience who cannot see what you are doing can be distracting, and can impair your performance.

are unable to monitor the audience and are therefore uncertain about the audience's evaluative reactions to their performance (Guerin & Innes, 1982). In support of this idea, Guerin (1989) found a social facilitation effect on a simple letter-copying task only among participants who were being watched by a confederate whom they could *not* see. When the confederate could be clearly seen, there was no social facilitation effect.

Distraction–conflict theory

The link between social presence and drive has been explained in another way by Baron and others (Baron, 1986; Sanders, 1983; Sanders, Baron, & Moore, 1978): **distraction–conflict theory** (see Figure 8.4). They argue

that people are a source of distraction that produces attentional conflict between attending to the task and attending to the audience or coactors. While distraction alone impairs task performance, attentional conflict also produces drive that facilitates dominant responses. Together these processes impair the performance of difficult tasks and, because drive usually overcomes distraction, improve the performance of easy tasks.

In support of distraction–conflict theory, Sanders, Baron and Moore (1978) had participants perform an easy and a difficult digit-copying task, alone, or coacting with someone performing either the same or a different task. They reasoned that someone performing a different task would not be a relevant source of social comparison and so distraction should be minimal, whereas someone performing the same task would be a relevant source of comparison and therefore highly distracting.

As predicted, they found that participants in the distraction condition made more mistakes on the difficult task, and copied more digits correctly on the simple task, than in the other conditions (again, see first focus question).

Distraction–conflict theory has other strengths. Experiments show that any form of distraction (noise, movement, flashing lights), not only social presence, can produce social facilitation effects. In addition, unlike the evaluation apprehension model, it can accommodate results from studies of social facilitation in animals. It is difficult to accept that cockroaches eat more while other roaches are watching because they are anxious

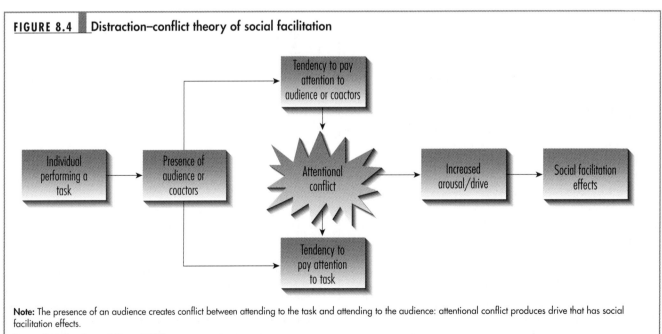

FIGURE 8.4 Distraction–conflict theory of social facilitation

Note: The presence of an audience creates conflict between attending to the task and attending to the audience: attentional conflict produces drive that has social facilitation effects.

Source: Based on Baron & Byrne (1987).

about evaluation; however, even the lowly roach can presumably be distracted.

Distraction–conflict theory also had the edge on evaluation apprehension in an experiment by Groff, Baron and Moore (1983). Whenever a tone sounded, participants had to rate the facial expressions of a person appearing on a TV monitor and, at the same time, as an ostensibly incidental activity, squeeze as firmly as possible a bottle held in the hand (latency and strength of squeeze were measures of arousal/drive). Participants undertook the experiment (a) alone; (b) closely scrutinised by a confederate sitting off to one side—this would be highly distracting, as the participant would need to look away from the screen to look at the observer; or (c) closely scrutinised by a confederate who was actually the person on the screen—no attentional conflict. As predicted from distraction–conflict theory, participants squeezed the bottle more strongly in the second condition.

Non-drive explanations of social facilitation

So far, we have discussed explanations of social facilitation that retain the notion of drive, and differ only about whether drive is an innate response to mere presence, a learned response based on evaluation apprehension or a product of attentional conflict. Although to date these are the best established and most researched explanations of social facilitation, there are other approaches that do not retain the notion of drive. After all, it is difficult to confirm or refute the existence of drive as a mediating mechanism. There are no unambiguous and direct ways to measure it: although physiological measures of arousal (e.g. palmar sweating) presumably may access drive, the absence of physiological arousal is no guarantee that drive is not operating, as drive is defined in psychological not physiological terms.

One non-drive explanation of social facilitation is based on *self-awareness theory* (Carver & Scheier, 1981; Duval & Wicklund, 1972; Wicklund, 1975). When people focus their attention on themselves as an object, they make comparisons between actual self (their actual task performance) and ideal self (how they would like to perform). The discrepancy between actual and ideal self increases motivation and effort to bring actual into line with ideal, so on easy tasks there is improved performance. On difficult tasks the discrepancy is too great, so people give up trying and thus there is a deterioration in performance.

Self-awareness can be produced by a range of circumstances, such as looking at oneself in a mirror, but also by the presence of coactors or an audience.

Still focusing on the role of self in social facilitation, Bond (1982) believes that people are concerned with presenting to others the best possible impression of themselves. As this is achievable on easy tasks, social

presence produces an improved performance. On more difficult tasks, people make, or anticipate making, errors: this creates embarrassment, and embarrassment impairs task performance.

Another way to explain social facilitation, without invoking self or drive, is in terms of the purely attentional consequences of social presence. This analysis is based on the general idea that people narrow the focus of their attention when they experience attentional overload (Easterbrook, 1959).

Baron (1986) believes people have a finite attention capacity that can be overloaded by the presence of an audience. Attention overload causes people to narrow their attention, give priority to attentional demands and focus on a small number of central cues. Difficult tasks are those that require attention to a large number of cues, and so attentional narrowing is likely to divert attention from cues that we really ought to attend to: thus social presence impairs performance.

Simple tasks require attention to only a small number of cues, and so attentional narrowing actually eliminates distraction caused by attending to extraneous cues and focuses attention onto central cues: thus social presence improves performance.

This general idea has been nicely supported in an experiment by Monteil and Huguet (1999). The task was a Stroop task, in which participants simply have to name the colour of ink that different words are written in. Some words are neutral or consistent with the colour of ink (e.g. 'red' written in red ink)—this is an easy task and people respond more quickly; others clash (e.g. 'red' written in blue)—this is a difficult task and people respond more slowly.

Monteil and Huguet had participants perform a Stroop task alone or in the presence of another person. They found that latencies on the difficult task were significantly lower in the social presence condition. Social presence had narrowed attention onto the colour of the ink, so that semantic interference from the word itself was reduced.

Manstead and Semin (1980) have proposed a similar attention-based model, but with the emphasis on automatic versus controlled task performance. They argue that difficult tasks require a great deal of attention because they are highly controlled. An audience distracts vital attention from task performance, which thus suffers. Easy tasks require little attention because they are fairly automatic. An audience causes more attention to be paid to the task, which thus becomes more controlled and better performed.

Social psychologists have suggested and investigated a large number of different explanations of what initially may have appeared to be a basic and straightforward social phenomenon. Some explanations fare better than others, some have not yet been properly tested, and after about 100 years of research a number of questions remain unanswered.

Nevertheless, the study of audience effects remains an important topic for social psychology, as much of our behaviour occurs in the physical presence of others as an audience. A survey administered by Borden (1980) revealed that people feared speaking in front of an audience more than heights, darkness, loneliness and even death!

However, we should perhaps keep in perspective the actual degree of impact that mere presence has on behaviour. From a review of 241 social facilitation experiments involving 24 000 participants, Bond and Titus (1983) concluded that mere presence accounted for only a tiny 0.3–3.0% of variation in behaviour. Bond and Titus used **meta-analysis** to arrive at these figures: this is a statistical technique that enables the analysis of data from different individual studies as if they came from one large study.

To explain some of the remaining variation, we now move from non-interactive contexts to more interactive contexts and true group processes.

CLASSIFICATION OF GROUP TASKS

Social facilitation research distinguishes between easy and difficult tasks, but restricts itself to tasks that do not of necessity involve interaction, interindividual coordination, division of labour, etc. While many tasks fall into this category (e.g. dressing, washing the car, surfing), many others do not (e.g. building a house, playing cricket, running a business). It is not unreasonable to assume that social presence will have entirely different effects on task performance, not only as a function of the degree of social presence (passive audience, coactor, interdependent interaction on a group task) but as a function of the specific task being performed.

What is needed is a taxonomy of types of task based on a limited number of psychologically meaningful parameters.

The pragmatic question of whether groups perform better than individuals has produced such a taxonomy (Steiner, 1972, 1976). Steiner's **task taxonomy** has three dimensions, which are best captured by asking three questions:

1. Is the task divisible or unitary? A *divisible* task is one that benefits from a division of labour, where different people perform different subtasks. A unitary task cannot sensibly be broken into subtasks. Building a house is a divisible task, and pulling a rope a unitary task.
2. Is it a maximising or an optimising task? A *maximising* task is an open-ended task that stresses quantity: the objective is to do as much as possible. An *optimising* task is one that has a predetermined standard to be met: the objective is to meet the standard, neither to exceed nor fall short of it. Pulling on a rope would be a maximising task, but maintaining a specified fixed force on the rope would be an optimising task.
3. How are individual inputs related to the group's product?
   An *additive* task is one where the group's product is the sum of all the individual inputs (e.g. a group of people planting trees).
   A *compensatory* task is one where the group's product is the average of the individuals' inputs (e.g. a group of people estimating the number of kauri trees in New Zealand).
   A *disjunctive* task is one where the group selects as its adopted product one individual's input (e.g. a group of people proposing different things to do over the weekend will adopt one person's suggestion).
   A *conjunctive* task is one where the group's product is determined by the rate or level of performance of the slowest or least able member (e.g. a group working on an assembly line).
   A *discretionary* task is one where the relationship between individual inputs and group product is not directly dictated by task features or social conventions; instead, the group is free to decide on its preferred course of action (e.g. a group that *decides* to shovel snow together).

These parameters allow us to classify tasks. For example, a tug-of-war is unitary, maximising and additive; assembling a car is divisible, optimising and conjunctive; and many group decision-making tasks are divisible, optimising and disjunctive (or compensatory).

As to whether groups are better than individuals, Steiner believes that in general the actual group product is always inferior to the group's potential (based on the potential of its human resources). This shortfall is due mainly to a **process loss** (e.g. losses due to the coordination of individual members' activities, disproportionate influence on the part of specific powerful group members, and various social distractors). However, against this background, Steiner's taxonomy makes predictions about what sort of tasks favour group performance.

For additive tasks, the group's performance is better than the best individual's performance. For compensatory tasks, the group's performance is better than most individuals—because the average is most likely to be correct. For disjunctive tasks, the group's performance is equal to or worse than the best individual—the group cannot do better than the best idea proposed. And for conjunctive tasks, the group's performance is equal to the worst individual's performance—unless the task is divisible, in which case a division of labour can redirect the weakest member to an easier task and so improve the group's performance.

Although Steiner emphasised the role of **coordination loss** in preventing a group from performing optimally in terms of the potential of its members, he also raised the possibility of an entirely different and more fundamentally psychological type of loss—motivation loss.

SOCIAL LOAFING AND SOCIAL IMPACT

Ringelmann (1913), a French professor of agricultural engineering, conducted a number of experiments to investigate the efficiency of various numbers of people, animals and machines performing agricultural tasks (Kravitz & Martin, 1986). In one study he had young men, alone or in groups of two, three or eight, pull horizontally on a rope attached to a dynamometer (an instrument that measures the amount of force exerted). He found that the force exerted per person decreased as a function of group size: the larger the group, the less hard each person pulled (see Figure 8.5). This is termed the **Ringelmann effect**.

Our previous discussion suggests two possible explanations for this:

Social loafing: An office environment often provides fertile ground for people to work less hard than if they were working alone.

1. *Coordination loss*—due to jostling, distraction, and the tendency for people to pull slightly against one another, participants were prevented from attaining their potential.
2. *Motivation loss*—participants were less motivated; they simply did not try so hard.

To investigate these explanations, Ingham, Levinger, Graves and Peckham (1974) replicated Ringelmann's study but with two experimental conditions: one in which real groups of varying size pulled on a rope, and the other involving pseudo-groups with only one true participant and a number of confederates. The confederates were instructed only to pretend to pull on the rope while making realistic grunts to indicate exertion. The true participant was in the first position and so did not know that the confederates were not actually pulling.

The results (Figure 8.6) indicate a decrement in individual performance in pseudo-groups. Because there was no coordination, there can be no loss due to poor coordination; the decrement can be attributed only to a loss of motivation. In real groups, there was an additional decrement in individual performance that can be attributed to coordination loss.

This motivation loss has been termed **social loafing** by Williams and his colleagues (Latané, Williams, & Harkins, 1979), who replicated the effect with shouting, cheering and clapping tasks. For instance, they had participants cheer and clap as loudly as possible alone or in groups of two, four or six. The amount of noise produced per person was reduced by 29% in two-person groups, 49% in four-person groups and 60% in six-person groups. For the shouting task, participants shouted alone or in two- or six-person real groups or pseudo-groups (they wore blindfolds and headsets transmitting continuous 'white noise').

A CLASSIC IN SOCIAL PSYCHOLOGY

FIGURE 8.5 The Ringelmann effect: Force per person as a function of group size

[Graph: x-axis labelled "Group size (persons)" from 1 to 8; y-axis labelled "Force per person (kg)" from 0 to 70. "Expected performance" line stays flat at about 63 kg. "Actual performance" line declines from about 63 kg at group size 1 to about 31 kg at group size 8.]

Note: As the number of people pulling horizontally on a rope increased, each person's exertion was reduced: people pulling in eight-person groups each exerted half the effort of a person pulling alone.

Source: Based on data from Ringelmann (1913).

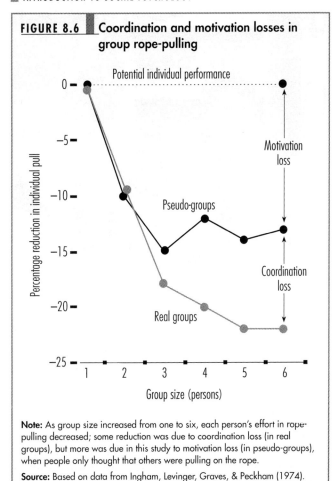

FIGURE 8.6 Coordination and motivation losses in group rope-pulling

Note: As group size increased from one to six, each person's effort in rope-pulling decreased; some reduction was due to coordination loss (in real groups), but more was due in this study to motivation loss (in pseudo-groups), when people only thought that others were pulling on the rope.

Source: Based on data from Ingham, Levinger, Graves, & Peckham (1974).

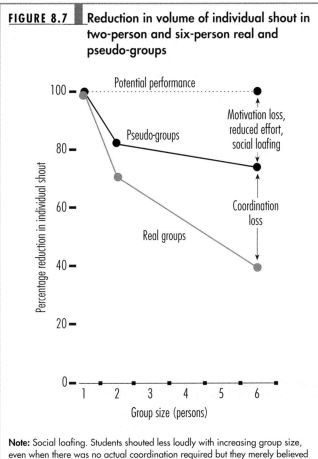

FIGURE 8.7 Reduction in volume of individual shout in two-person and six-person real and pseudo-groups

Note: Social loafing. Students shouted less loudly with increasing group size, even when there was no actual coordination required but they merely believed that they were in a group.

Source: Based on data from Latané, Williams, & Harkins (1979).

As in Ingham and colleagues' experiment, there was a clear reduction in effort for participants in pseudo-groups, with additional coordination loss for real groups (see Figure 8.7).

Social loafing, then, is a tendency for individuals to work less hard (i.e. loaf) on a task when they believe others are also working on the task. More formally, it refers to 'a reduction in individual effort when working on a collective task (in which one's outputs are pooled with those of other group members) compared to when working either alone or coactively' (Williams, Karau, & Bourgeois, 1993, p. 131).

A notable feature of loafing is that, as group size increases, the addition of new members to the group has a decreasingly significant impact on effort: the reduction of effort conforms to a negatively accelerating power function (see Figure 8.8). So, for example, the reduction in individual effort as the consequence of a third person joining a two-person group is relatively large, while the impact of an additional member on a 20-person group is minimal. The range within which group size seems to have a significant impact is about one to eight members.

Social loafing is related to the **free-rider effect** (Frohlich & Oppenheimer, 1970; Kerr, 1983) in research into social dilemmas and public goods (Chapter 11). A free rider is someone who takes advantage of a shared public resource, without contributing to its maintenance. For example, a tax evader who uses the road system, visits national parks and benefits from public medical provisions is a free rider.

The main difference between loafing and free riding is perhaps that, although loafers reduce effort on coactive tasks, they nevertheless do contribute to the group product (there is a *loss* of motivation); in contrast, free riders exploit the group product while contributing nothing to it (there is a *different* motivation) (see Williams, Karau, & Bourgeois, 1993).

Social loafing is a pervasive and robust phenomenon. A meta-analytic review by Karau and Williams (1993) of the 78 social loafing studies conducted up to the early 1990s found loafing in 80% of the individual–group comparisons that they made—this is an extraordinarily significant overall effect (see reviews by Harkins & Szymanski, 1987; Williams, Harkins, & Karau, 2003;

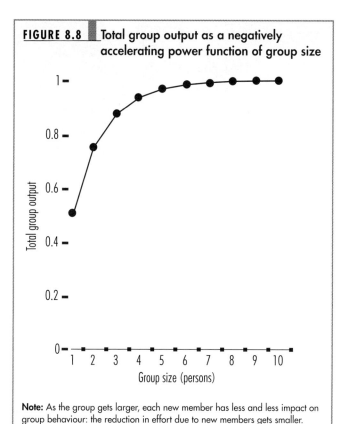

FIGURE 8.8 Total group output as a negatively accelerating power function of group size

Note: As the group gets larger, each new member has less and less impact on group behaviour: the reduction in effort due to new members gets smaller.

Williams, Karau, & Bourgeois, 1993). The general loafing paradigm is one in which individual or coactive performance is compared either with groups performing some sort of additive task (e.g. brainstorming) or with the performance of pseudo-groups, in which people are led to *believe* they are performing collectively with varying numbers of others but, in fact, circumstances are arranged so that they are performing individually.

Loafing has been obtained in the laboratory as well as in the field, on physical tasks (e.g. shouting, clapping, rope-pulling, pumping air and swimming), on cognitive tasks (e.g. generating ideas), on evaluative tasks (e.g. quality ratings of poems, editorials and clinical therapists) and on perceptual tasks (e.g. maze performance, vigilance performance) with a variety of participant populations from different cultures (e.g. the United States, France, Poland, Japan, Taiwan, Thailand, India).

Freeman, Walker, Bordon and Latané (1975) even found a loafing effect on restaurant tipping in the United States: roughly 20% of people gave tips when seated alone, but only about 13% when seated in groups of five or six.

Why do people loaf? Geen (1991) has suggested three explanations:

1. *Output equity*—people may loaf on collective tasks because they believe that people loaf in groups, thus

expect their partners to loaf, and therefore loaf themselves in order to maintain equity (Jackson & Harkins, 1985).

2. *Evaluation apprehension*—the presence of group members provides a sense of being anonymous and unidentifiable for people who are not motivated on a task (e.g. an uninteresting, boring or tiring task) (Kerr & Bruun, 1981). When performing individually or coactively, rather than collectively, people are identifiable and thus apprehensive about performance evaluation by others, and therefore overcome their unmotivated state (Harkins, 1987; Harkins & Szymanski, 1987).

3. *Matching to standard*—people loaf because they have no clear performance standard to match. The presence of a clear personal, social or group performance standard should reduce loafing (Goethals & Darley, 1987; Harkins & Szymanski, 1987; Szymanski & Harkins, 1987).

Group size may have the effect it does due to **social impact** (e.g. Latané, 1981; see also Chapter 14). The experimenter's instructions to clap, shout, brainstorm or whatever (i.e. the social obligation to work as hard as possible) are a source of social impact on the participants. To the extent that there is one participant and one experimenter, the experimenter's instructions have maximal impact. If there are two participants, the impact on each participant is halved, if three it is one-third, and so on. There is a diffusion of individual responsibility that grows with group size (see Chapter 14).

Loafing is not an inevitable consequence of group performance. Research has identified certain factors, apart from group size, that influence the tendency to loaf (see Geen, 1991; Williams, Karau, & Bourgeois, 1993). For example, personal identifiability by the experimenter (Williams, Harkins, & Latané, 1981), personal involvement in the task (Brickner, Harkins, & Ostrom, 1986), partner effort (Jackson & Harkins, 1985), intergroup comparison (Harkins & Szymanski, 1989) and a highly meaningful task in association with expectation of poor performance by co-workers (Williams & Karau, 1991) have all been shown to reduce loafing.

In some circumstances, people may even work harder collectively than coactively to compensate for anticipated loafing by others on important tasks or in important groups (Williams & Karau, 1991; Williams, Karau, & Bourgeois, 1993; Zaccaro, 1984).

This **social compensation** effect may be responsible for the results of an intriguing study by Zaccaro (1984). Zaccaro had male and female participants construct 'moon tents' out of sheets of paper in two- or four-person coactive groups. The usual loafing effect emerged (see Figure 8.9).

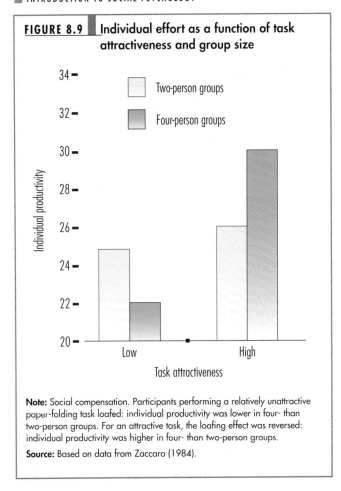

FIGURE 8.9 Individual effort as a function of task attractiveness and group size

Note: Social compensation. Participants performing a relatively unattractive paper-folding task loafed: individual productivity was lower in four- than two-person groups. For an attractive task, the loafing effect was reversed: individual productivity was higher in four- than two-person groups.

Source: Based on data from Zaccaro (1984).

Group cohesiveness: Is this team cohesive, or is it perhaps not a team at all?

However, other participants who believed they were competing against an outgroup, and for whom the attractiveness and social relevance of the task was accentuated, behaved quite differently. The loafing effect was actually reversed: individuals performed at a higher rate in the larger group. This was an unusual finding. In contrast to the rather pessimistic view of some social psychologists that groups inevitably inhibit individuals from attaining their true potential (e.g. Steiner, 1972), this study indicates that group life may, under certain circumstances, cause people to exceed their individual potential—there may be process gains in groups (e.g. Shaw, 1976).

There are other cases when people may work harder in groups than alone (e.g. Guzzo & Dickson, 1996). One is when people place greater value on groups than individuals—that is, they have a collectivist rather than an individualist social orientation (Hofstede, 1980). This difference in orientation is a significant difference between Western and Eastern cultures (R. Bond & Smith, 1996; Smith & Bond, 1998) and so it comes as no surprise to discover that people can work harder in groups than alone in, for example, China (Earley, 1989, 1994) and Japan (Matsui, Kakuyama, & Onglatco, 1987).

Another instance where people may be motivated to work harder in groups is when groups and their members believe and expect that the group will be effective in achieving important goals (Guzzo, Jost, Campbell, & Shea, 1993; Sheppard, 1993).

Recent years have witnessed a revival in interest in the possibility of process gains in groups and in the ability of groups to elevate task motivation (Brown, 2000; Kerr & Park, 2001). From their meta-analysis of 78 loafing studies, Karau and Williams (1993) identified task importance and the significance of the group to the individual as the two key factors that promote increased effort in groups. These factors may be related, in that people may be particularly motivated to work hard on tasks that are important precisely because they define membership of a group that is vital to their self-concept or social identity (see Fielding & Hogg, 2000).

For example, Worchel, Rothgerber, Day, Hart and Butemeyer (1998) had participants make paper chains alone and then as a group. In the group phase of the experiment participants simply worked in their groups, or they were also in competition against an outgroup;

they either had individual name tags and different-coloured coats, or everyone in the group had identical group name tags and wore identical-coloured coats. Worchel and his associates found clear evidence that people worked significantly harder in groups than alone when the group was highly salient—group name tags, identical-coloured coats and intergroup competition. The productivity increase was +5 paper chains. In the least salient condition there was loafing (productivity dropped by 4 paper chains), and in the intermediate salience conditions there was no significant departure from base rate (productivity changes of +1 or −1).

Karau and Hart (1998) found a similar process gain in groups that were highly cohesive because they contained people who liked one another.

Group cohesiveness

One of the most basic properties of a group is its **cohesiveness** (solidarity, esprit de corps, team spirit, morale)—the way it 'hangs together' as a tightly knit, self-contained entity characterised by uniformity of conduct and mutual support among members. Cohesiveness is a variable property: it differs between groups, between contexts and across time. Groups with extremely low levels of cohesiveness appear hardly to be groups at all, and so the term may also capture the very essence of being a group—the psychological process that transforms an aggregate of individuals into a group. Cohesiveness is thus a descriptive term, used to describe a property of the group as a whole—in this sense it is quite closely related to the property of entitativity possessed by categories, which we discussed at the beginning of this chapter. But, importantly, it is also a psychological term used to describe the individual psychological process underlying the cohesiveness of groups.

Herein lies a problem: it makes sense to say that a group is cohesive, but not that an individual is cohesive.

After almost a decade of informal usage, cohesiveness was formally defined by Festinger, Schachter and Back (1950). They believed that a field of forces, deriving from the attractiveness of the group and its members and the degree to which the group satisfies individual goals, acts on the individual. The resultant valence of these forces produces cohesiveness, which is responsible for group membership continuity and adherence to group standards (see Figure 8.10).

Because concepts such as 'field of forces' are difficult to operationalise, and also because the theory was not precise about exactly how to define cohesiveness operationally (i.e. in terms of specific measures or experimental manipulations), social psychologists almost immediately simplified their conception of cohesiveness.

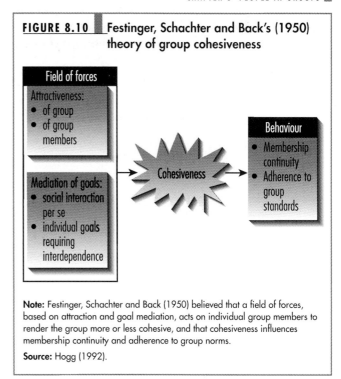

FIGURE 8.10 Festinger, Schachter and Back's (1950) theory of group cohesiveness

Note: Festinger, Schachter and Back (1950) believed that a field of forces, based on attraction and goal mediation, acts on individual group members to render the group more or less cohesive, and that cohesiveness influences membership continuity and adherence to group norms.

Source: Hogg (1992).

For instance, in their own research into the cohesiveness of postwar student housing projects at the Massachusetts Institute of Technology, Festinger, Schachter and Back simply asked students, 'What three people . . . do you see most of socially?' (1950, p. 37; see Chapter 13 for details of this study).

Major reviews (e.g. Cartwright, 1968; Hogg, 1992; Lott & Lott, 1965) indicate that the bulk of research conceptualises cohesiveness in terms of attraction to group or interpersonal attraction, derives the cohesiveness of the group as a whole from summing (or some other arithmetical procedure) and operationalises cohesiveness accordingly. Not surprisingly, this research reveals that factors which increase interpersonal attraction (e.g. similarity, cooperation, interpersonal acceptance, shared threat; see Chapter 13) generally elevate cohesiveness and elevated cohesiveness produces, for example, conformity to group standards, accentuated similarity, improved intragroup communication and enhanced liking.

It has been suggested (Hogg, 1987, 1992; Turner, 1982, 1984) that this perspective on group cohesiveness represents a much wider *social cohesion* or *interpersonal interdependence* model of the social group (see Figure 8.11), where researchers tend to differ only in which components of the model they emphasise.

Because social psychologists have not really resolved the problem of knowing unambiguously how to operationalise cohesiveness (Evans & Jarvis, 1980; Mudrack, 1989), more recent research has tended to be in applied areas (Levine & Moreland, 1990). In sports psychology,

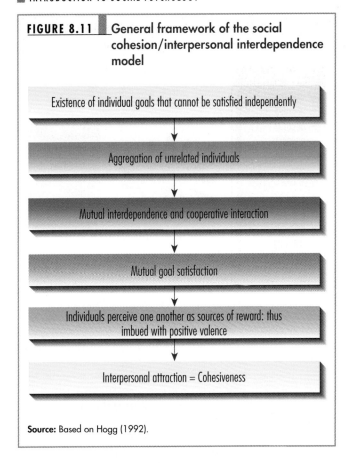

FIGURE 8.11 General framework of the social cohesion/interpersonal interdependence model

Existence of individual goals that cannot be satisfied independently

Aggregation of unrelated individuals

Mutual interdependence and cooperative interaction

Mutual goal satisfaction

Individuals perceive one another as sources of reward: thus imbued with positive valence

Interpersonal attraction = Cohesiveness

Source: Based on Hogg (1992).

in particular, some quite rigorous scales have been devised—for example, Widmeyer, Brawley and Carron's (1985) 18-item *group environment questionnaire* to measure the cohesiveness of sports teams.

A fundamental question raised by social identity researchers (Hogg, 1987, 1992; Turner, 1984, 1985; see Chapter 11) asks to what extent an analysis of group cohesiveness in terms of aggregation (or some other arithmetic integration) of interpersonal attraction really captures a group process at all. To all intents and purposes, the group has disappeared entirely from the analysis and we are simply left with interpersonal attraction, about which we already know a great deal (Berscheid & Reis, 1998; see Chapter 13).

Hogg, at the University of Queensland (Hogg, 1992, 1993), suggests that a distinction should be made between **personal attraction** (true interpersonal attraction based on close relationships and idiosyncratic preferences) and **social attraction** (interindividual liking based on perceptions of self and others in terms not of individuality but of group norms or prototypicality). Personal attraction is nothing to do with groups, while social attraction is the 'liking' component of group membership (see second focus question). Social attraction is merely one of a constellation of effects (ethnocentrism, conformity, intergroup differentiation, stereotyping,

ingroup solidarity) produced by the process of self-categorisation specified in self-categorisation theory (Turner, Hogg, Oakes, Reicher, & Wetherell, 1987; see Chapter 11).

This analysis has at least two major advantages over the traditional model:

1. It does not reduce group solidarity and cohesiveness to interpersonal attraction.
2. It is as applicable to small interactive groups (the only valid focus of traditional models) as to large-scale social categories, such as an ethnic group or a nation (people can feel attracted to one another on the basis of ethnic or national norms).

This perspective appears quite promising. For example, Hogg and Turner (1985) aggregated people with others whom they ostensibly would like or dislike (the fact that the others were people they would like or dislike was irrelevant to the existence of the group) or explicitly categorised them as a group on the basis of the criterion that they would like one another, or dislike one another. They found that interpersonal attraction was not automatically associated with greater solidarity (see Figure 8.12). Rather, where interpersonal liking was neither the implicit nor explicit basis for the group (i.e. in the random categorisation condition), group solidarity was unaffected by interpersonal attraction.

In another study, Hogg and Hardie (1991) gave a questionnaire to an Australian Rules football team in Melbourne. Perceptions of team prototypicality and of norms were significantly related to measures of group-based social attraction, but not related to measures of interpersonal attraction. This differential effect was strongest among members who themselves identified most strongly with the team. Another field study, this time of women's netball teams in an amateur league in Brisbane, revealed similar effects (Hogg & Hains, 1996).

Group socialisation

An obvious feature of many of the groups we are familiar with is that new members join, old members leave, members are socialised by the group, and the group in turn is imprinted with the contribution of individuals. Groups are dynamic structures that change continually over time; however, this dynamic aspect of groups is often neglected in social psychology: social psychologists have tended towards a rather static analysis that excludes time. Many social psychologists feel that this considerably weakens the explanatory power of social psychological theories of group processes and intergroup behaviour (Condor, 1996; Levine & Moreland, 1994; Tuckman, 1965; Worchel, 1996).

FIGURE 8.12 | Ingroup solidarity as a function of interpersonal attraction and social categorisation

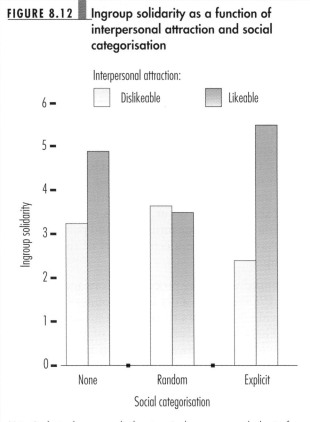

Note: Students who were explicitly categorised as a group on the basis of interpersonal liking or who were merely aggregated showed greater solidarity with likeable groups, while participants who were randomly categorised showed equal solidarity, irrespective of how likeable the group was.

Source: Hogg & Turner (1985).

Role transition: Graduation is a ritualised public ceremony that marks an important role transition in a student's life.

Time is taken more seriously by organisational psychology, where longitudinal analyses are relatively common and quite sophisticated (Wilpert, 1995). For instance, Cordery and his colleagues at Murdoch University in Perth (Cordery, Mueller, & Smith, 1991) studied job satisfaction, absenteeism and employee turnover for a 20-month period in two Australian mineral processing plants to discover that, although autonomous work groups improved work attitudes, they also increased absenteeism and employee turnover.

Another impressive longitudinal study was conducted by Hart and his colleagues at Melbourne University (Hart, Wearing, & Headey, 1994): they investigated the impact of work experiences on the psychological well-being of members of the Australian police force over a long period of time.

Within social psychology Tuckman (1965) described a now famous five-stage developmental sequence that small groups go through:

1. *forming*—an orientation and familiarisation stage;
2. *storming*—a conflict stage where members know each other well enough to start working through disagreements about goals and practices;
3. *norming*—having survived the storming stage, consensus, cohesion and a sense of common identity and purpose emerge;
4. *performing*—a period in which the group works smoothly as a unit that has shared norms and goals, and good morale and atmosphere; and
5. *adjourning*—the group dissolves because it has accomplished its goals, or because members lose interest and motivation and move on.

More recently, Moreland and Levine (1982, 1984; Levine & Moreland, 1994; Moreland, Levine, & Cini, 1993) have presented a model of **group socialisation** to describe and explain the passage of individuals through groups over time. They focus on the dynamic interrelationship of group and individual members across the life span of the group. A novel feature of this analysis is that it focuses not only on how individuals change in order to fit into the group, but also on how new members can, intentionally or unintentionally, be a potent source of innovation and change within the group (Levine, Moreland, & Choi, 2001).

There are three basic processes involved in group socialisation:

1. *Evaluation* refers to an ongoing comparison by individuals of the past, present and future rewards of the group with the rewards of potential alternative relationships (Thibaut & Kelley, 1959; see discussion of social exchange theory in Chapter 13). Simultaneously, the group evaluates individuals in terms of their contribution to the life of the group. Behind this idea lies an assumption that people have goals and needs that create expectations. To the extent that expectations are, or are likely to be, met, social approval is expressed. Actual or anticipated failure to fulfil expectations invites social disapproval and actions to modify behaviour or to reject individuals or the group.

2. Evaluation affects *commitment* of the individual to the group, and vice versa, in a relatively straightforward manner. However, at any given time, commitment disequilibrium may exist such that the individual is more committed to the group than the group is to the individual, or vice versa. This is an imbalanced and unstable relationship because the less committed party has less need of, and therefore more power over, the more committed party. There is pressure towards commitment equilibrium.

Commitment produces agreement on group goals and values, positive ties between individual and group, willingness to exert effort on the part of the group or the individual, and a desire for continued membership.

3. *Role transition* refers to discontinuities in the role relationship between individual and group. Although commitment varies smoothly in strength over time, the group and its members tend to see relatively sudden discontinuities in how they relate to one another, and therefore in what role the member has in the group.

There are three general types of role: (a) non-member, including prospective members who have not joined the group and ex-members who have left the group; (b) quasi-member, including new members who have not yet attained full member status and marginal members who have lost that status; and (c) full member. Full members are those who are most closely identified with the group and who have all the privileges and responsibilities associated with group membership.

Role transitions can be smooth and easy where individual and group are equally committed and share the same decision criteria. However, commitment disequilibrium and unshared decision criteria can introduce conflict over whether a role transition should or did occur. For this reason, transition criteria often become formalised and public, and rites of passage become a central part of the life of the group.

Equipped with these processes, Moreland and Levine (1982, 1984) provide a detailed account of the passage of individual members through the group (see Figure 8.13). There are five distinct phases of group socialisation, involving reciprocal evaluation and influence by group and individual, each heralded and/or concluded by a clear role transition (see Box 8.1).

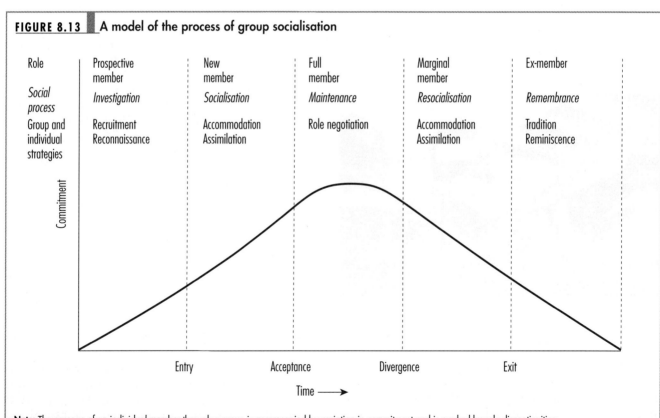

FIGURE 8.13 A model of the process of group socialisation

Role	Prospective member	New member	Full member	Marginal member	Ex-member
Social process	*Investigation*	*Socialisation*	*Maintenance*	*Resocialisation*	*Remembrance*
Group and individual strategies	Recruitment Reconnaissance	Accommodation Assimilation	Role negotiation	Accommodation Assimilation	Tradition Reminiscence

Commitment

Entry   Acceptance   Divergence   Exit

Time ⟶

Note: The passage of an individual member through a group is accompanied by variation in commitment and is marked by role discontinuities.
Source: Moreland & Levine (1982).

BOX 8.1   **Phases of group socialisation**

In their model of group socialisation Moreland and Levine (1982, 1984; Moreland, Levine & Cini, 1993) identify five distinct phases of group socialisation (see Figure 8.13).

1. *Investigation* The group recruits prospective members who in turn reconnoitre the group. This can be a formal process involving interviews and questionnaires (e.g. joining an organisation or learned society) or more informal (e.g. associating yourself with a student political society). Successful investigation leads to a role transition marking *entry* to the group.

2. *Socialisation* The group assimilates new members by educating them in the ways of the group. In turn, new members attempt to get the group to accommodate their views. Socialisation can be unstructured and informal, but also quite formal (e.g. induction programs for new members of organisations). Successful socialisation is marked by *acceptance*.

3. *Maintenance* Role negotiation among full members takes place. Role dissatisfaction can lead to a role transition called *divergence*, which can be unexpected and unplanned, but can also be an expected and quite ordinary feature of the group: for example, university students are expected to diverge as part of the process of graduating and leaving university.

4. *Resocialisation* In the case of expected divergence, there is little attempt at resocialisation. However, unexpected divergence marginalises the member into a deviant role and activates attempts at resocialisation. If successful, full membership is reinstated. If unsuccessful, the individual leaves the group—*exit*. This can be marked by elaborate retirement ceremonies, for example, or the ritualistic stripping of insignia in a court martial.

5. *Remembrance* After the individual has left the group both parties engage in reminiscence. This can take the form of fond recall of the 'Remember when . . .' type or the more extreme exercises in rewriting history engaged in by totalitarian regimes.

Source: Moreland & Levine (1982).

The occurrence of role transitions is considered an important aspect of group life. Indeed, Moreland and colleagues have conducted research on specific transitions, particularly those associated with becoming a member (Brinthaupt, Moreland, & Levine, 1991; Moreland, 1985; Moreland & Levine, 1989; Pavelchak, Moreland, & Levine, 1986). Generally, role transitions are ritualised public events—rites of passage—that is, **initiation rites**. They can be pleasant events marked by celebration and the giving of gifts (e.g. graduation, a wedding) but more often than not they involve a degree of pain, suffering, degradation or humiliation (e.g. circumcision, a wake).

These rites may serve a number of functions:

- *symbolic*—to allow a consensual and public recognition of identity discontinuity;
- *apprenticeship*—helping individuals to become accustomed to new roles and normative standards;
- *loyalty elicitation*—pleasant initiations involving gifts and special dispensations, which may elicit gratitude that should enhance commitment to the group.

In the light of this last function, the prevalence and apparent effectiveness of disagreeable initiation rites is puzzling. Surely people could avoid joining groups with severe initiations? If unfortunate enough not to be able to do this, then at the very least they should subsequently

hate the group and feel no sense of commitment. One way to explain this paradox is in terms of **cognitive dissonance** theory (Festinger, 1957), which is described in Chapter 6. An aversive initiation creates subsequent dissonance between the two cognitions 'I knowingly underwent a painful experience to join this group' and 'Some aspects of this group are not that good' (group life is usually a mixture of positive and negative aspects).

As the initiation cannot be denied (after all, it is usually a public event), dissonance can be reduced by revising your opinion of the group (downplaying negative aspects and focusing on more positive aspects). The consequence is a more favourable evaluation of the group and thus greater commitment.

This analysis clearly predicts that the more unpleasant the initiation is, the more positive the subsequent evaluation of the group will be. The Aronson and Mills (1959) experiment described in Chapter 6 is an investigation of this idea.

You will recall that Aronson and Mills recruited female students to participate in a group discussion of the psychology of sex. Before joining the group, they listened to and rated a short extract of the discussion—an extremely tedious and stilted discussion of the secondary sexual characteristics of lower animals. It was quite rightly rated as such by control participants, and also by a second group of participants who had gone through a mild initiation where they read out loud five words with vague sexual connotations. However, a third group, who underwent an extreme initiation where they read out loud explicit and obscene passages, rated the discussion as very interesting.

Gerard and Mathewson (1966) were concerned that the effect may have arisen because the severe-initiation participants were either sexually aroused by the obscene passage and/or relieved at discovering that the discussion was not as extreme as the passage. To discount these alternative explanations, they replicated Aronson and Mills' study. Participants, who audited and rated a boring discussion they were about to join, were given mild or severe electric shocks either explicitly as an initiation or under some other pretext completely unrelated to the ensuing discussion.

As predicted from cognitive dissonance theory, the painful experience enhanced evaluation of the group only when it was perceived to be an initiation (see Figure 8.14).

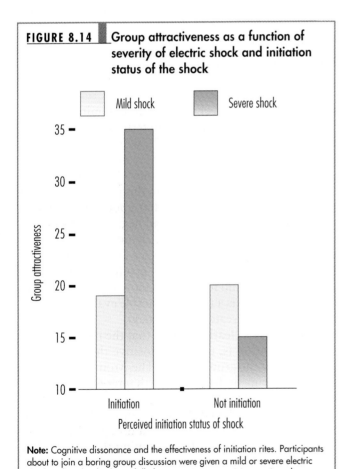

FIGURE 8.14 Group attractiveness as a function of severity of electric shock and initiation status of the shock

Note: Cognitive dissonance and the effectiveness of initiation rites. Participants about to join a boring group discussion were given a mild or severe electric shock. When the shock was billed as an initiation, participants given the severe shock rated the group as more attractive than participants given the mild shock.

Source: Based on data from Gerard & Mathewson (1966).

Norms

Norms are shared beliefs about the appropriate conduct for a group member: they are both descriptive ('is' statements) and prescriptive ('ought' statements). As such, norms describe the uniformities of behaviour that characterise groups, while normative discontinuities provide the contours of different social groups. For example, the behaviour of students and lecturers in a university is governed by very different norms: knowing whether someone is a student or a lecturer establishes clear expectations of appropriate normative behaviours.

Norms and **stereotypes** are closely related—the terms 'normative behaviour' and 'stereotypical behaviour' mean virtually the same thing. However, research traditions have generally separated the two areas, norms referring to behaviours that are shared in a group, and stereotypes (see Chapters 2, 10 and 11) to shared generalisations about other groups. Recently, self-categorisation theory (Turner, 1985; Turner, Hogg, Oakes, Reicher, & Wetherell, 1987; see Chapter 11) has tried to bridge this rather artificial distinction.

Let's return to norms. Norms can take the form of explicit rules that are enforced by legislation and sanctions (e.g. societal norms to do with private property, pollution and aggression) or they can be the implicit, unobserved, taken-for-granted background to everyday life (Garfinkel, 1967). Garfinkel believed that these norms are hidden because they are so integral to everyday life, and that they account for much behaviour that is often labelled native, instinctive or innate.

Garfinkel devised a particular methodology, called **ethnomethodology**, to detect these background norms. One method involved the violation of norms in order to attract people's attention to them. For example, Garfinkel had students act at home for 15 minutes as if they were boarders—that is, be polite, speak formally and speak only when spoken to. Their families reacted with astonishment, bewilderment, shock, embarrassment and anger, backed up with charges of selfishness, nastiness, rudeness and lack of consideration! An implicit norm for familial interaction was revealed, and its violation provoked a strong reaction (see third focus question).

Group norms can have a powerful effect on people. For example, Newcomb (1965) conducted a classic study of norms in the 1930s at a small American college called Bennington. The college had progressive and liberal norms but drew its students from conservative upper-middle-class families. The 1936 presidential election allowed Newcomb to conduct a confidential ballot. First-year students strongly favoured the conservative candidate, while third- and fourth-year

Ethnomethodology: Non-normative behaviour (playing with a yo-yo) draws attention to the implicit norm of being serious when meeting an important client.

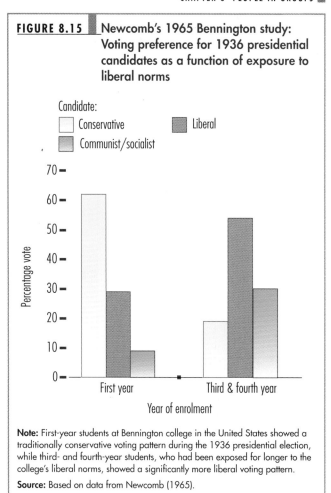

FIGURE 8.15 Newcomb's 1965 Bennington study: Voting preference for 1936 presidential candidates as a function of exposure to liberal norms

Note: First-year students at Bennington college in the United States showed a traditionally conservative voting pattern during the 1936 presidential election, while third- and fourth-year students, who had been exposed for longer to the college's liberal norms, showed a significantly more liberal voting pattern.

Source: Based on data from Newcomb (1965).

students had shifted their voting preference towards the liberal and communist/socialist candidates (Figure 8.15).

Presumably, prolonged exposure to liberal norms had produced change in political preference.

Siegel and Siegel (1957) conducted a slightly better controlled study, in which they took advantage of the random assignment of new students at a private American college to different types of student accommodation—called sororities or dormitories. At this particular college, sororities had a conservative ethos and the dormitories had more progressive liberal norms. Siegel and Siegel measured the students' degree of conservatism at the beginning and end of the year. Figure 8.16 clearly shows how exposure to liberal norms reduced conservatism.

Norms serve a function for the individual. They specify a limited range of behaviours that are acceptable in a certain context and thus reduce uncertainty and facilitate confident choice of the 'correct' course of action. Norms provide a **frame of reference** within which to locate our own behaviour. You will recall that this idea was explored by Sherif (1936) in his classic experiments dealing with norm formation (see Box 7.1 in Chapter 7 for details).

Sherif showed that, when people made perceptual judgments alone, they relied on their own estimates as a reference frame; however, when they were in a group, they used the group's range of judgments to converge quickly on the group mean.

Sherif believed that people were using other members' estimates as a social frame of reference to guide them: he felt he had experimentally produced a primitive group norm. The norm was an emergent property of interaction among group members but, once created, it acquired a life of its own. Members were later tested alone and still conformed to the norm.

This same point was strikingly demonstrated in a couple of related autokinetic studies (Jacobs & Campbell, 1961; MacNeil & Sherif, 1976). In a group comprising three confederates who gave extreme estimates and one true participant, a relatively extreme norm emerged. The group went through a number of 'generations' in which a confederate would leave and another true participant would join, until the membership of the group contained none of the original members. The original extreme norm still powerfully

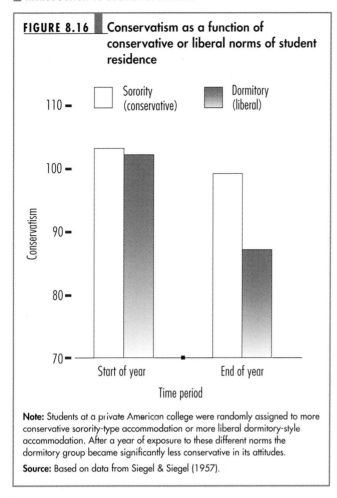

FIGURE 8.16 | Conservatism as a function of conservative or liberal norms of student residence

Note: Students at a private American college were randomly assigned to more conservative sorority-type accommodation or more liberal dormitory-style accommodation. After a year of exposure to these different norms the dormitory group became significantly less conservative in its attitudes.

Source: Based on data from Siegel & Siegel (1957).

influenced the participants' estimates. This is a very elegant demonstration that a norm is a true group phenomenon: it can emerge only from a group, and yet it can influence the behaviour of the individual in the physical absence of the group (Turner, 1991). It is as if the group is carried in the head of the individual in the form of a norm.

Norms also serve functions for the group, insofar as they coordinate the actions of members towards fulfilment of group goals. In an early study of factory production norms, Coch and French (1948) describe a group that set itself a standard of 50 units per hour as the minimum level to secure job tenure. New members quickly adopted this norm. Those who did not were strongly sanctioned by ostracism and, in some cases, had their work sabotaged. Generally speaking, there is good evidence from the study of goal-setting in organisational work teams that, where group norms embody clear group goals for performance and production, group members work harder and are more satisfied (Guzzo & Dickson, 1996; Weldon & Weingart, 1993).

Norms are inherently resistant to change—after all, their function is to provide stability and predictability. However, norms initially arise to deal with specific circumstances. They endure as long as those circumstances prevail, but ultimately change with changing circumstances.

Norms vary in their 'latitude of acceptable behaviour': some are narrow and restrictive (e.g. military dress codes) and others wider and less restrictive (e.g. dress codes for university lecturers). In general, norms that relate to group loyalty and to central aspects of group life have a narrow latitude of acceptable behaviour, while norms relating to more peripheral features of the group are less restrictive. Finally, certain group members are allowed a greater latitude of acceptable behaviour than others: higher-status members (e.g. leaders) can get away with more than lower-status members and followers (this phenomenon is discussed in Chapter 9 when we talk about leadership).

There is evidence for the patterning and structure of different types of norms from Sherif and Sherif's (1964) pioneering study of adolescent gangs in American cities. Participant observers infiltrated these gangs and studied them over several months. The gangs had given themselves names, adopted various insignia and had strict codes about how gang members should dress. Dress codes were important, as it was largely through dress that the gangs differentiated themselves from one another. The gangs also had strict norms concerning sexual mores and how to deal with outsiders (e.g. parents, police); however, leaders were allowed some latitude in their adherence to these and other norms.

Norms are the yardstick of group conduct, and it is through norms that groups influence the behaviour of their members. The exact processes responsible are the subject of much of Chapter 7, which deals with social influence.

Group structure

Cohesiveness, socialisation and norms refer mainly to uniformities in groups. However, we have just seen how there can also be a degree of patterning and differentiation of norms within groups. Here we develop this theme. In few groups indeed does it happen that all members are equal, perform identical activities and communicate freely with one another. **Group structure** is clearly reflected in roles, status relations and communication channels. Groups are also structured in terms of subgroups and in terms of the central or marginal group membership credentials of specific members.

ROLES

Roles are much like norms insofar as they describe and prescribe behaviour. However, while norms apply to the group as a whole, roles apply to a subgroup of people within the group. Furthermore, while norms may distinguish between groups, they are generally not intentionally derived to benefit the framework of groups in a society. In contrast, roles are specifically designed to differentiate among people within the group for the greater good of the group as whole.

Roles are not people but behavioural prescriptions that are assigned to people. They can be informal and implicit (e.g. in groups of friends) or formal and explicit (e.g. in aircraft flight crews). One quite general role differentiation within small groups is between task specialists (the 'ideas' people who get things done) and socioemotional specialists (the people everyone likes because they address relationships within the group) (e.g. Slater, 1955).

Roles may emerge in a group for a number of reasons:

- They represent a division of labour in the group; only in the simplest groups is there no division of labour.
- They furnish clear-cut social expectations within the group and provide information about how members relate to one another.
- They furnish members with self-definition and a place within the group.

Clearly, roles emerge to facilitate group functioning. However, there is evidence that inflexible role differentiation can sometimes be detrimental to the group. Gersick and Hackman (1990) found that rigid role differentiation relating to preflight checks among the flight crew of a passenger airliner caused the crew to fail to engage a de-icing device, with the tragic consequence that the plane crashed shortly after take-off.

Roles can sometimes also be associated with larger category memberships (e.g. professional groups) outside the specific task-oriented groups—in which case the task-oriented group can become a context for role conflict that is actually a manifestation of wider intergroup conflict (see below). A good example of this might be intergroup conflict between doctors and nurses.

Although we tend to adopt a dramaturgical perspective when we speak of people 'acting' or 'assuming' roles, we are probably only partly correct. We may assume roles much like actors taking different parts, but many people see us only in particular roles and so infer that that is how we really are; professional actors are easily typecast in exactly the same way. This tendency to attribute roles internally to dispositions of the role-player may be an example of the **fundamental attribution error** (Ross, 1977; see Chapter 3).

One practical implication of this is that you should avoid low-status roles in groups, or you will subsequently find it difficult to escape their legacy. Perhaps the most powerful and well-known social psychological illustration of the power of roles to modify behav-

iour is Zimbardo's (1971; Banuazizi & Movahedi, 1975) simulated prison experiment (see Box 8.2).

Ultimately, roles can actually influence who we are—our identity and concept of self. This idea has been extensively elaborated by sociologists to explain how social interaction and wider societal expectations about behaviour can create enduring and real identities for people—*role identity theory* (e.g. McCall & Simmons, 1978; Stryker & Statham, 1986; see Hogg, Terry, & White, 1995).

STATUS

All roles are not equal: some are consensually more valued and respected and thus confer greater **status** on the role occupant. The highest-status role in most groups is the role of leader (see Chapter 9). In general,

---

A CLASSIC IN SOCIAL PSYCHOLOGY

BOX 8.2 Guards versus prisoners: Role behaviour in a simulated prison

Philip Zimbardo (1971) was interested to investigate the way in which people can adopt and internalise roles to guide behaviour. He was also interested to establish that it is largely the prescription of the role rather than the personality of the role occupant that governs in-role behaviour.

In a famous role-playing exercise, 24 psychologically stable male Stanford University student volunteers were randomly assigned the roles of prisoners or guards. The prisoners were arrested at their homes and initially processed by the police, then handed over to the guards in a simulated prison constructed in the basement of the Psychology Department at Stanford University.

Zimbardo had planned to observe the role-playing exercise over a period of two weeks. However, he had to stop the study after six days. Although the students were psychologically stable and those assigned to the guard or prisoner roles had no prior dispositional differences, things got completely out of hand. The guards continually harassed, humiliated and intimidated the prisoners, and used psychological techniques to undermine solidarity and sow the seeds of distrust among them. Some guards increasingly behaved in a brutal and sadistic manner.

The prisoners initially revolted but gradually became passive and docile as they showed symptoms of individual and group disintegration and an acute loss of contact with reality. Some prisoners had to be released from the study because they showed symptoms of severe emotional disturbance (disorganised thinking, uncontrollable crying and screaming) and, in one case, a psychosomatic rash all over his body.

higher-status roles or their occupants tend to have two properties:

- consensual prestige, and
- a tendency to initiate ideas and activities that are adopted by the group.

For example, from his participant observation study of gangs in an American Italian immigrant community, Whyte (1943) reported that even the relatively inarticulate 'Doc', who described his assumption of leadership of the 13-member Norton gang in terms of who he 'walloped', found that the consensual prestige that such wallopings earned him was insufficient alone to ensure his high-status position. He admitted that his status also derived from the fact that he was the one who always thought of things for the group to do.

Status hierarchies in groups are not fixed: they can vary over time, and from situation to situation. Take an orchestra: the lead violinist may have the highest-status role at a concert, while the union representative has the highest-status role in negotiations with management. One explanation of why status hierarchies emerge so readily in groups is in terms of social comparison theory (Festinger, 1954; Suls & Miller, 1977)—status hierarchies are the expression and reflection of intragroup social comparisons. Groups furnish a pool of relevant others with whom we can make social comparisons so as to assess the validity of our opinions and abilities.

Certain roles in the group have more power and influence and, because they are therefore more attractive and desirable, have many more 'applicants' than can be accommodated. Fierce social comparisons on behavioural dimensions relevant to these roles inevitably mean that the majority of group members, who are unsuccessful in securing the role, cannot avoid the conclusion that they are less able than those who are successful. Thus arises a shared view that those occupying the attractive role are superior to the rest—consensual prestige and high status.

Status hierarchies often become institutionalised so that individual members do not engage in ongoing systematic social comparisons. Rather, they simply assume that particular roles or role occupants are of higher status than their own role or themselves. Research into the formation of status hierarchies in newly created groups tends to support this view. Strodtbeck, James and Hawkins (1957) assembled mock juries to consider and render a verdict on transcripts of actual trials. They found that the high-status role of jury foreman almost always went to people who had higher occupational status outside the context of the jury (e.g. teachers or psychologists rather than janitors or mechanics).

One explanation of this phenomenon is in terms of **expectation states theory** (Berger, Fisek, Norman, & Zelditch, 1977; Berger, Wagner, & Zelditch, 1985;

de Gilder & Wilke, 1994; Ridgeway, 2001). Status derives from two distinct sources:

1. **specific status characteristics**—characteristics that relate directly to ability on the group task (e.g. athletic ability in a sports team);
2. **diffuse status characteristics**—characteristics that do not relate directly to ability on the group task, but are nonetheless ones that are generally positively or negatively valued in society (e.g. sex, age, occupation, ethnicity).

Diffuse status characteristics are associated with favourable expectations that are generalised to all sorts of situations, even those that may not be relevant to the group task at all. Group members simply assume that someone who rates highly on diffuse status (e.g. a medical doctor) will be relatively more able than others to promote the group's goals (e.g. analysing trial transcripts in order to render a verdict) and therefore has higher specific status.

Specific and diffuse status are independent and additive sources of status in a newly formed group, according to a study by Knottnerus and Greenstein (1981). Female participants worked with a female confederate on two supposedly related tasks. Specific status was manipulated by informing participants that they had performed better or worse than the confederate on the first task—a perceptual task. Diffuse status was manipulated by leading participants to believe that they were either younger or older than the confederate. The second task, a word construction task, allowed measures of yielding to the confederate's suggestions to be used as an index of effective status. The results (Figure 8.17) showed that participants yielded more if they believed they were of lower specific or lower diffuse status than the confederate.

Other factors shown to contribute to high status in a group include seniority, assertiveness, past task success and high group orientation.

COMMUNICATION NETWORKS

People occupying different roles in a group need to coordinate their actions through communication, though not all roles need to communicate with one another. Thus, the structuring of a group with respect to roles entails an internal **communication network** that regulates who can communicate with whom. Although such networks can be informal, we are probably more familiar with the rigidly formalised ones in large organisations and bureaucracies (e.g. a university or government office). What are the effects on group functioning of different types of communication network, and what factors affect the sort of network that evolves?

Bavelas (1968) suggested that an important factor was the number of communication links to be crossed for one person to communicate with another. For

FIGURE 8.17 | Yielding as a function of specific and diffuse status of participants relative to a confederate

Diffuse status of participant relative to confederate:

☐ Low ■ High

Percentage of trials on which subject yielded to confederate

Specific status of participant relative to confederate

Note: Female participants yielded more often to a female confederate's suggestions in a word-construction task if the confederate had higher specific status (had performed well on a similar task) and had higher diffuse status (was older).

Source: Based on data from Knottnerus & Greenstein (1981).

example, if I can communicate with the dean of my faculty directly, there is one link; but if I have to go through the head of department, there are two. In Franz Kafka's (1925) classic novel *The Trial*, the central character 'K' was confronted by a bewildering and ever-increasing number of communication links in order to communicate with senior people in the organisation. Figure 8.18 shows some of the communication networks that have been researched experimentally; those on the left are more highly centralised than those on the right.

For relatively simple tasks, greater centralisation improves group performance (e.g. Leavitt, 1951): the hub person is quite able to receive, integrate and pass on information efficiently while allowing peripheral members to concentrate on their allotted roles. For more complex tasks, a less centralised structure is superior (e.g. Shaw, 1964) because the quantity and complexity of information communicated would overwhelm a hub person, who would be unable to integrate, assimilate and pass it on efficiently. Peripheral members would thus experience delays and miscommunication. For complex tasks, there are potentially serious coordination losses (Steiner, 1972) associated with overly centralised communication networks. However, centralisation for complex tasks may pay off in the long run once appropriate procedures have been well established and well learned.

Another important consideration is the degree of autonomy felt by group members. Because they depend on the hub for regulation and flow of information, peripheral members have less power in the group and can feel restricted and dependent. According to Mulder (1960), having more power leads to a greater sense of

Communication networks: A multifaceted activity like building a house requires a division of labour, and a centralised communication network focused on the team leader.

FIGURE 8.18 | Communication networks that have been studied experimentally

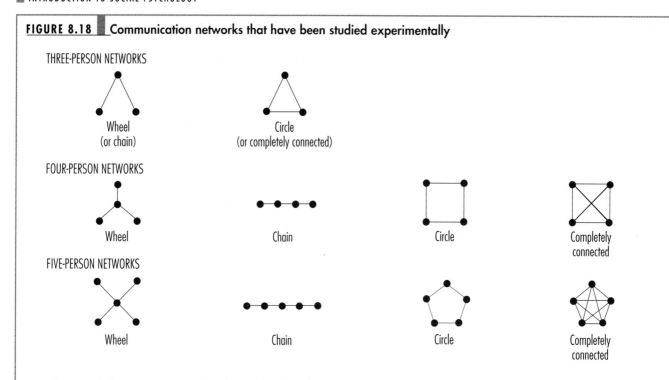

Note: The most studied communication networks are those involving three, four or five members (dots represent positions or roles or people, and lines represent communication channels). The networks on the left are highly centralised, and become increasingly less centralised as you move to the right of the figure.

autonomy and satisfaction, so peripheral members can become dissatisfied while hub members, who are often perceived to be group leaders, feel a sense of satisfaction. Centralised communication networks can thus reduce group satisfaction, harmony and solidarity and instead produce internal conflict.

Research on organisations confirms that job satisfaction and organisational commitment are influenced by the amount of control that employees feel they have, and that control is related to communication networks, in particular to employees' perceived participation in decision-making (e.g. Evans & Fischer, 1992).

In almost all groups, particularly organisational groups, the formal communication network is complemented by an informal communication 'grapevine'. You might be surprised to learn that, contrary to popular opinion and according to a study by Simmonds (1985), 80% of grapevine information is work-related and 70–90% of that information is accurate.

Finally, the rules for studying communication networks in organisations now need to be rewritten, with the explosion of computer-mediated communication (CMC) in recent years (Hollingshead, 2001). Organisations now have virtual groups and teams that rarely need to meet. They use electronic communication channels instead. One positive effect of CMC is that it can de-emphasise status differences and thus promote more equal participation among members.

SUBGROUPS AND CROSS-CUTTING CATEGORIES

Almost all groups are structurally differentiated into subgroups. These subgroups can be nested within the larger group—e.g. departments in a university, divisions in a company. However, many subgroups represent larger categories that have members outside the larger group—e.g. social psychologists in a psychology department are also members of the larger group of social psychologists. In this case the subgroups are not nested but are crosscutting categories (e.g. Crisp, Ensari, Hewstone, & Miller, 2003).

Group processes are significantly affected by subgroup structure. The main problem is that subgroups can engage in intergroup competition that can sometimes be harmful to the group as a whole. For example, divisions in a company can take healthy competition one step too far and slip into outright conflict. Research shows that, when one company takes over another company and therefore contains within it two subgroups, the original company and the new company, conflict between these two subgroups can be extreme (e.g. Terry, Carey, & Callan, 2001). When groups contain subgroups that differ ideologically or in their core values and attitudes, a **schism** can occur in which one group feels that the larger group no longer represents its values. The smaller group may then decide to split off and try to convert the larger group. This can create extreme conflict that can tear the larger group apart—this often happens in political, religious and scientific contexts (e.g. Sani & Reicher, 1998, 2000).

The problem of subgroup conflict is often most evident, and indeed harmful, when larger groups contain sociodemographic subgroups that have destructive intergroup relations in society as a whole—e.g. Protestants and Catholics who work together in a Northern Irish business (Hewstone, Cairns, Voci, Paolini, McLernon, Crisp, Niens, & Craig, in press). See Chapter 11 for a full treatment of intergroup relations, including intergroup relations among crosscutting and nested subgroups.

DEVIANTS AND MARGINAL MEMBERS

Many, if not most, groups are also structured in terms of two kinds of members:

1. those who best embody the group's attributes—core members who are highly prototypical of the group;
2. those who do not—marginal or non-prototypical members.

Highly prototypical members often have significant influence over the group and may occupy leadership roles—we discuss them in Chapter 9. Marginal members are an entirely different story.

Research by Marques and his colleagues shows that marginal members are often disliked by the group and treated as 'black sheep' (Marques & Páez, 1994) or deviants. People whose attributes place them on the boundary between ingroup and outgroup are actually disliked more if they are ingroup members than outgroup members—they are treated as deviants or even traitors. One reason for this is that they threaten the integrity of group norms by undermining normative consensus within the group (e.g. Marques, Abrams, & Serodio, 2001). Paradoxically, for this very reason, marginal members serve an important function for groups—groups, particularly their leaders, can engage in a rhetoric of vilification and exclusion of marginal members precisely to throw into stark relief what the group is and what the group is not.

Marginal members may play another important role in groups—they can be the agents of social change within the group. Under the right conditions, marginal members may be uniquely placed to act as critics of group norms, precisely because they are normatively marginal. Research by Matthew Hornsey and his associates, at the University of Queensland, shows that groups are more accepting of criticism from ingroup than outgroup members (Hornsey & Imani, 2004; Hornsey, Oppes, & Svensson, 2002). Of course, ingroup critics have an uphill struggle to be heard if they are labelled and treated as deviants. The task may be made easier if a number of dissenters unite as a subgroup— we then, effectively, have a schism or an active minority within the group.

The analysis of how marginal members, deviants and dissenters can influence the larger group is the analysis of minority influence, which we discuss at length in Chapter 7.

Why do people join groups?

This is not an easy question to answer. It depends on how we defines a group, and *why* people join groups is not the same thing as *how* people join groups. We also need to recognise that the groups to which we belong vary in the degree of free choice we had in joining. There is little choice in what sex, ethnic, national or social class groups we 'join': membership is largely externally designated. There is a degree of choice, though possibly less than we might think, in what occupational or political group we join; and there is a great deal of freedom in what clubs, societies and recreational groups we join. Even the most strongly externally designated social-category memberships, such as sex and ethnicity, can permit a degree of choice in what the implications of membership in that group may be (e.g. the group's norms and practices) and this may reflect the same sorts of motives and goals for choosing freely to join less externally designated groups (Hogg & Abrams, 1993).

However, we can identify a range of circumstances, motives, goals and purposes that tend to cause, in more or less immediate ways, people to join or form groups (e.g. aggregate, coordinate their actions, declare themselves members of a group). For example, physical proximity can promote group formation. We tend to get to like, or at least learn to put up with (Tyler & Sears, 1977), people we are in close proximity with. This appears to promote group formation: we form groups with those around us. Festinger, Schachter and Back's (1950) classic study of a student housing program, which we discussed earlier (see also Chapter 13), concerned just this—the role of proximity in group formation, group cohesiveness and subsequent adherence to group standards. The recognition of similar interests, attitudes and beliefs can also cause people to become or join a group.

If people share goals that require behavioural interdependence for their achievement, this is another strong and reliable reason for joining groups. This idea lies at the heart of Sherif's (1966) realistic conflict theory of intergroup behaviour (discussed in Chapter 11). For example, if we are concerned about degradation of the environment, we are likely ultimately to join an environmental conservation group, because division of labour and interdependent action among like-minded people will achieve a great deal more than the actions of a lone protester. People join groups to get things done that they cannot do on their own.

We can join groups for mutual positive support and the mere pleasure of affiliation—for example, to avoid loneliness (Peplau & Perlman, 1982). We can join groups for self-protection and personal safety; for example, adolescents join gangs (Ahlstrom & Havighurst, 1971) and bushwalkers often walk in groups for this reason. We can join groups for emotional support in times of stress; for example, a **social support network** for AIDS sufferers and their relatives and friends fulfils this function.

Oscar Lewis's (1969) account of a Catholic wake in Mexico in his novel *A Death in the Sanchez Family* describes the way in which people come together in stressful circumstances. Schachter (1959) has explored the same idea in controlled experimental circumstances. However, a word of qualification is needed. Extreme stress and deprivation (e.g. in concentration camps or after natural disasters) sometimes produce social disintegration and individual isolation rather than group formation (Middlebrook, 1980). This is probably because the link between stress and affiliation is not mechanical: if affiliation is not the effective solution to the stress, then it may not occur. Thomas Keneally's (1982) account, in his powerful biographical novel *Schindler's Ark*, of atrocities committed by the Nazis against Jews in the Polish city of Kracow supports this. Despite extreme stress, remarkably little affiliation occurred, because it was difficult to sustain and would probably have exacerbated the situation.

MOTIVATIONS FOR AFFILIATION AND GROUP FORMATION

The question of why people join groups can be reframed in terms of what basic motivations cause people to affiliate (see also Chapter 13). According to Baumeister and Leary (1995), human beings simply have a basic and overwhelming need to belong, and this causes them to affiliate and to join and be members of groups. The sense of belonging and being successfully connected to other human beings, interpersonally or in groups, produces a powerful and highly rewarding sense of self-esteem and self-worth (Leary, Tambor, Terdal, & Downs, 1995).

According to **terror management theory** (Greenberg, Pyszczynski, & Solomon, 1986; Greenberg, Solomon, & Pyszczynski, 1997; Solomon, Greenberg, & Pyszczynski, 1991; see Chapter 4), the most fundamental threat that people face is the inevitability of death and thus people live in perpetual terror of death. Fear of death is the most powerful motivating factor in human existence. People affiliate and join groups in order to reduce

fear of death. Affiliation and group formation are highly effective terror management strategies because they raise self-esteem and make people feel good about themselves—they feel immortal, and positive and excited about life.

One final and important motive for joining a group is to obtain a social identity (Hogg, 2003b; Hogg & Abrams, 1988; Tajfel & Turner, 1979). Groups provide us with a consensually recognised definition and evaluation of who we are, how we should behave and how we will be treated by others. There is thus a highly sought-after and satisfying reduction in subjective uncertainty. Hogg and his associates at the University of Queensland (see Hogg, 2000a) conducted a series of experiments to show that people who are randomly categorised as members of a group under highly abstract laboratory conditions (minimal group paradigm; see Chapter 11) actually identify with the group only if they are in a state of uncertainty and the group is able to reduce uncertainty.

In addition to uncertainty considerations, because we and others evaluate us in terms of the relative attractiveness, desirability and prestige of the groups to which we belong, we are motivated to join groups that are consensually positively evaluated—for example, high-status groups. We are motivated to join groups that will furnish a positive social identity (Hogg & Abrams, 1990; Tajfel & Turner, 1979; see Chapter 11).

WHY *NOT* JOIN GROUPS?

Perhaps the question 'Why do people join groups?' should be stood on its head: 'Why do people *not* join groups?' Not being a member of a group is a lonely existence, depriving us of social interaction, social and physical protection, the ability to achieve complex goals, a stable sense of who we are and confidence in how we should behave (see Chapter 13). Williams has devised an intriguing and powerful paradigm to study the consequences of being excluded from a group—**social ostracism** (Williams, 2002; Williams, Shore, & Grahe, 1998; Williams & Sommer, 1997). Three-person groups of students waiting for an experiment begin to throw a ball to one another across the room. After a while, two of the students (actually confederates) exclude the third student (true participant) by not throwing him the ball. It is very uncomfortable even to watch the video of this study (imagine how the participant felt!). True participants appear self-conscious and embarrassed, and many try to occupy themselves with other activities like playing with keys, staring out of the window or meticulously scrutinising their wallets.

Summary

- Although there are many definitions of the group, social psychologists generally agree that at the very least a group is a collection of people who define themselves as a group and whose attitudes and behaviours are governed by the norms of the group. Group membership often also entails shared goals, interdependence, mutual influence, and face-to-face interaction.
- People tend to perform easy, well-learned tasks better, and difficult, poorly learned tasks worse in the presence of other people than on their own.
- We may be affected in this way for a number of reasons. Social presence may instinctively drive habitual behaviours, we may learn to worry about performance evaluation by others, we may be distracted by others, or others may make us self-conscious or concerned about self-presentation.
- Tasks differ not only in difficulty but also in their structure and objectives. Whether a task benefits from division of labour, and how individual task performances are interrelated, have important implications for the relationship between individual and group performance.
- People tend to put less effort into task performance in groups than when alone, unless the task is involving and interesting, their individual contribution is clearly identifiable or the group is important to their self-definition, in which case they can sometimes exert more effort in a group than alone.
- Members of cohesive groups tend to feel more favourably inclined towards one another as group members, and are more likely to identify with the group and conform to its norms.
- Group membership is a dynamic process in which our sense of commitment varies, we occupy different roles at different times, we endure sharp transitions between roles and we are socialised by the group in many different ways.
- Groups develop norms in order to regulate the behaviour of members, to define the group and to distinguish the group from other groups.
- Groups are internally structured into different roles that regulate interaction and best serve the collective interest of the group. Roles prescribe behaviour. They also vary in their desirability and thus influence status within the group. Groups are also internally structured in terms of subgroups and central and marginal group members.
- People may join or form groups to get things done that cannot be done alone, to gain a sense of identity, to obtain social support or simply for the pleasure of social interaction.

LINKS

YOU HAVE READ ABOUT:	WHICH LINKS TO:
Group effects on the individual	conformity to group pressure (7)
Group cohesiveness	effective leadership (9)
Group socialisation and initiation	conformity (7); stereotyping outgroups (11)
Norms and group membership	norms and social influence (7)
Communication networks	group decision-making (9)

Key terms

audience effects *(p. 184)*
cognitive dissonance *(p. 197)*
cohesiveness *(p. 193)*
communication network *(p. 202)*
coordination loss *(p. 189)*
diffuse status characteristics
    (p. 202)
distraction–conflict theory *(p. 186)*
drive theory *(p. 184)*
entitativity *(p. 182)*
ethnomethodology *(p. 198)*
evaluation apprehension model
    (p. 184)
expectation states theory *(p. 202)*

frame of reference *(p. 199)*
free-rider effect *(p. 190)*
fundamental attribution error
    (p. 201)
group *(p. 182)*
group socialisation *(p. 195)*
group structure *(p. 200)*
initiation rites *(p. 197)*
mere presence *(p. 184)*
meta-analysis *(p. 188)*
norms *(p. 198)*
personal attraction *(p. 194)*
process loss *(p. 188)*
Ringelmann effect *(p. 189)*

roles *(p. 200)*
schism *(p. 204)*
social attraction *(p. 194)*
social compensation *(p. 191)*
social facilitation *(p. 184)*
social impact *(p. 191)*
social loafing *(p. 189)*
social ostracism *(p. 206)*
specific status characteristics
    (p. 202)
status *(p. 201)*
stereotype *(p. 198)*
task taxonomy *(p. 188)*
terror management theory *(p. 206)*

FURTHER READING

Baron, R. S., & Kerr, N. (2003). *Group process, group decision, group action* (2nd ed.). Buckingham, UK: Open University Press. Up-to-date general overview of some major topics in the study of group processes—takes a mainstream American perspective.

Brown, R. J. (2000). *Group processes* (2nd ed.). Oxford, UK: Blackwell. A very readable introduction to group processes, which takes a more European perspective and also covers intergroup work.

Guerin, B. (1993). *Social facilitation*. Cambridge, UK: Cambridge University Press. A scholarly overview of research and theory in the area of social facilitation.

Hogg, M. A., & Abrams, D. (1988). *Social identifications: A social psychology of intergroup relations and group processes*. London: Routledge. Detailed coverage of theory and research in group processes and intergroup relations from the perspective of social identity theory.

Hogg, M. A., & Tindale, R. S. (Eds.). (2001). *Blackwell handbook of social psychology: Group processes*. Oxford, UK: Blackwell. A comprehensive, detailed and up-to-date collection of 26 chapters from leading experts covering the entire field of group processes.

Levine, J., & Moreland, R. L. (1998). Small groups. In D. Gilbert, S. T. Fiske, & G. Lindzey (Eds.), *The handbook of social psychology* (4th ed., Vol. 2, pp. 415–469). New York: McGraw-Hill. Up-to-date and comprehensive overview of the field of small groups, in the most recent edition of this classic handbook. A primary source for theory and research.

Williams, K. D., Harkins, S. G., & Karau, S. J. (2003). Social performance. In M. A. Hogg & J. Cooper (Eds.), *The Sage handbook of social psychology* (pp. 327–346). London: Sage. A comprehensive and up-to-date overview of theory and research on how people's performance is affected by being in a group.

Leadership and **decision-making**

THIS CHAPTER DISCUSSES:

- definitions of leadership
- theories of leadership: personality traits, situational characteristics, leadership style, interaction of leadership style and situation, transactional and transformational leadership
- group decision-making
- brainstorming
- transactive memory
- groupthink
- group polarisation
- decision-making in juries.

Leaders and group decisions

We saw in Chapter 8 that groups vary in their size, composition, longevity and purpose. They also vary in cohesiveness, have different norms and are internally structured into roles in different ways. However, almost all groups, even those that are apparently most egalitarian, have some form of unequal distribution of power and influence, whereby some people lead and others follow. Although leadership can take a variety of forms (e.g. democratic, autocratic, informal, formal, intrusive, modest), it is a fundamental aspect of almost all social groups.

We know (see end of Chapter 8) that people can assemble as a group for many different reasons and to perform many different tasks. One of the most common reasons is to make decisions through some form of group discussion. In fact, many of the most important decisions that affect our lives are made by groups, often groups of which we are not members. Indeed, we could argue that most decisions that people make are actually group decisions: not only do we often make decisions as a group, but even those decisions that we seem to make on our own are made in reference to what groups of people may think or do.

This chapter continues the discussion of group processes begun in Chapter 8. It focuses on two of the most significant social psychological group phenomena—leadership and group decision-making.

Leadership

In the many groups to which we belong—teams, committees, organisations, friendship groups, gangs—we encounter leaders: people who have 'good' ideas that everyone else then agrees on, people everyone seems to follow, people who seem to have the power to make things happen. Leaders enable groups to function as productive and coordinated wholes: for example, Jacobs and Singell (1993) studied the performance records of American baseball teams over a 20-year period and found that successful teams had managers who exercised superior tactical skills or who were skilled in improving the performance of individual team members.

On a larger canvas, history and political news often comprise stories of the deeds of leaders and tales of leadership struggles—for an enthralling and beautifully written insight into the life of one of the 20th century's greatest leaders, read Nelson Mandela's (1994) autobiography, *Long Walk to Freedom*. Margaret Thatcher's

A great leader: Nelson Mandela, the first black president of South Africa.

(1993) autobiography, *The Downing Street Years*, also makes fascinating reading.

To understand how leaders lead, what factors influence who is likely to be a leader in a particular context, and what the social consequences of **leadership** may be, social psychology in earlier years embraced a range of theoretical emphases and perspectives. By the early 1980s research in social psychology gave scant attention to leadership, though there was still a full chapter on the topic in the 1985 third edition of the *Handbook of social psychology* (Hollander, 1985). In the 1998 fourth edition this chapter had disappeared. Instead, there has been a frenzy of research on leadership in organisational psychology (e.g. Bass, 1990a; Yukl, 2002). Leadership is a topic that transcends disciplinary boundaries and has obvious applied potential. Very recently, there has been a revival of interest in leadership among social psychologists—there are two chapters on leadership in Hogg and Tindale's (2001) *Blackwell Handbook of Social Psychology: Group Processes* (Chemers, 2001; Lord, Brown, & Harvey, 2001).

PERSONALITY TRAITS

Great or notorious leaders like Lenin, Mao Zedong, Hitler, Churchill, Gandhi, Thatcher and Mandela seem to have special and distinctive capabilities that mark them off from the rest of us. Not surprisingly, we tend to seek an explanation in the unique properties of these people—in terms of personality characteristics that predispose certain people to lead. This **great person theory** has an illustrious history that goes back to Plato and Classical Greece.

More recently, in the 19th century, Francis Galton believed that good leaders were born, not made. He investigated the hereditary background of 'great men' in order to discover inherited capabilities of great leaders (Stogdill, 1974).

Although social psychologists no longer believe that leadership potential is inborn, there is a tradition of research that pursues the possibility that it may be acquired early in life and, therefore, that a constellation of personality attributes may exist that imbues people with charisma and thus a predisposition to lead (Carlyle, 1841; House, 1977). The search for such characteristics has identified a handful of weak correlates of leadership. For example, leaders tend to be above average with respect to size, health, physical attractiveness, intelligence, self-confidence, sociability, talkativeness and need for dominance. Of these, intelligence (Mann, 1959) and talkativeness (Mullen, Salas, & Driskell, 1989) are two of the most reliable correlates. Intelligence is important probably because leaders are expected to be able to think and respond quickly and have more ready access to information than others, and talkativeness because it attracts attention and renders the individual perceptually salient (Mullen, Salas, & Driskell, 1989).

In general, however, the search for reliable personality correlates of leadership has been unsuccessful (Stogdill, 1974; Yukl, 2002). Correlations among traits, and between traits and effective leadership, are very low (Stogdill reports an average correlation of 0.30) and there is little evidence for the great person theory of leadership.

Nevertheless, folk wisdom prefers to interpret history in terms of the actions of great people: the French occupation of Moscow in 1812 was Napoleon's doing; the 1917 Russian Revolution was 'caused' by Lenin; the 1980s in Britain were 'the Thatcher years'; and it was Whitlam who single-handedly brought Australia out of the conservatism of the 1950s. Folk wisdom also tends to attribute great leaps forward in science —what Kuhn (1962) calls *paradigm shifts*—to the independent actions of such great people as Einstein, Freud, Darwin and Copernicus.

This preference for great person theories may be explained in terms of fundamental characteristics of the way people construct an understanding of their world.

- In the face of widespread, large-scale and complex phenomena (e.g. the economy, war, revolution, famine, the meaning of life, plague), non-experts readily resort to explanations in terms of the actions of groups (e.g. scapegoats; see Chapters 3, 10 and 11) or individuals (leaders).
- Having located an individual as the cause, we tend to attribute the behaviours internally to invariant dispositions of the leader (i.e. we commit the fundamental attribution error; see Chapter 3).

SITUATIONAL PERSPECTIVES

In contrast to explanations of leadership exclusively in terms of personality traits are explanations that emphasise the functional requirements of situations. The most extreme form of this perspective is to deny any influence at all to the leader. For example, much of Tolstoy's epic novel *War and Peace* is a vehicle for his critique of the great person account of history: 'To elicit the laws of history we must leave aside kings, ministers and generals, and select for study the homogeneous, infinitesimal elements which influence the masses' (Tolstoy, 1869, p. 977). Likewise, Marx's theory of history places explanatory emphasis on the actions of collectivities, not individuals.

Empirical tests of this extreme situationist perspective tend, however, to suggest that leaders do have a role. For example, Simonton (1980) analysed the outcome of 300 military battles for which there were reliable archival data on the generals and their armies. Although situational factors, such as size of the army and diversification of command structure, were correlated with casualties inflicted on the enemy, some personal attributes of the leader, to do with experience and previous battle record, were also associated with victory. In other words, although situational factors influenced outcome, so did attributes of the leader.

A second form of the situational perspective is one in which the leader is attributed an important role in group achievement, but leadership is not seen as an invariant property of individual personality. Different situations call for different leadership properties, and therefore the most effective leader in a given context is the group member who is best equipped to assist the group in achieving its objectives (Bales, 1950).

From time to time, then, we are likely to find ourselves in situations in which we are leaders. An often-cited illustration of this is the case of Winston Churchill. Although considered by many to be argumentative, opinionated and eminently unsuited to government, these were presumably precisely the characteristics needed in a great wartime leader. However, as soon as World War II was over he was voted out of government, as these were not thought to be the qualities most needed in a peacetime leader.

Social psychologists have found the same thing under more controlled conditions. For example, in their classic studies of intergroup relations at boys' summer camps in the United States (see Chapter 11 for details), Sherif, Harvey, White, Hood and Sherif (1961; Sherif, 1966) divided the boys into groups, and found that in one group there was a leadership change under conditions of intergroup competition: the former leader was displaced by someone with greater physical prowess, who was better equipped to lead the group successfully in the changed circumstances.

In an experimental study, Carter and Nixon (1949) demonstrated the same point by having pairs of high-school students perform three different tasks—an intellectual task, a clerical task and a mechanical assembly task. Those who took the lead in the first two tasks rarely led in the mechanical assembly task.

Overall, leadership seems to be a function of task or situational demands and is not purely a property of individual personality—though personal qualities may play a role. Balancing the Churchill example above, leaders can sometimes change to accommodate changed circumstances. When Nelson Mandela was released in 1990 from 26 years of imprisonment, most of it in isolation on Robben Island off Cape Town, the political terrain had altered dramatically. Yet he was able to read the changes and go on to lead the African National Congress to political victory in South Africa. Effective leadership is a matter of the right combination of personal characteristics and situational requirements.

The discussion so far leaves some questions unanswered, however: just exactly what do leaders do in order to lead? How do the 'person' and the 'situation' interact to produce effective leadership? Through what processes do leaders emerge in groups?

THE BEHAVIOUR OF LEADERS

While personality may not be particularly important to leadership success, perhaps behaviour is. This idea forms the basis of one of the earliest and most influential studies of leadership, published by Lippitt and White in 1943. Lippitt and White used after-school activities clubs for young boys as an opportunity to investigate the effects of different styles of leadership on group atmosphere, morale and effectiveness. The leaders of the clubs were confederates of the researchers and they were trained in each of three distinct leadership styles:

1. **Autocratic leaders** organised the club's activities, gave orders, were aloof and focused exclusively on the task at hand.
2. **Democratic leaders** called for suggestions, discussed plans and behaved like ordinary club members.
3. **Laissez-faire leaders** left the group to its own devices and generally intervened minimally.

Each club was assigned to a particular leadership style. One confederate was the leader for seven weeks and then the confederates were swapped around; this happened twice, so that each confederate adopted each leadership style, but each group was exposed to only one leadership style (though enacted by three different confederates). This important control allowed Lippitt and White to distinguish leadership behaviour per se from the specific leader who was behaving in that way, and therefore to rule out personality explanations.

Lippitt and White's findings are described in Figure 9.1. Democratic leaders were liked significantly more than autocratic or laissez-faire leaders. They created a friendly, group-centred, task-oriented atmosphere that was associated with relatively high group productivity, unaffected by the physical absence or presence of the leader.

In contrast, autocratic leaders created an aggressive, dependent and self-oriented group atmosphere, which was associated with high productivity only when the

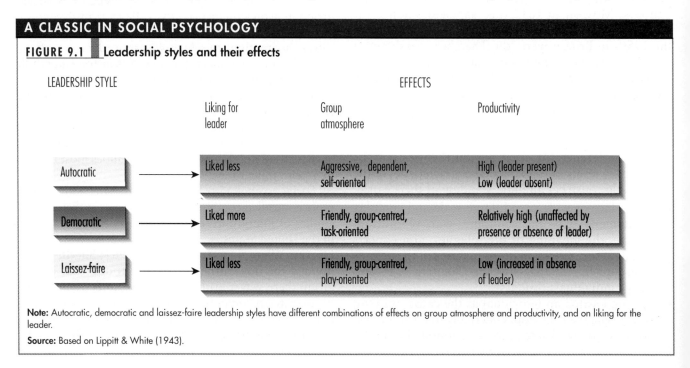

A CLASSIC IN SOCIAL PSYCHOLOGY

FIGURE 9.1 Leadership styles and their effects

LEADERSHIP STYLE	EFFECTS		
	Liking for leader	Group atmosphere	Productivity
Autocratic	Liked less	Aggressive, dependent, self-oriented	High (leader present) / Low (leader absent)
Democratic	Liked more	Friendly, group-centred, task-oriented	Relatively high (unaffected by presence or absence of leader)
Laissez-faire	Liked less	Friendly, group-centred, play-oriented	Low (increased in absence of leader)

Note: Autocratic, democratic and laissez-faire leadership styles have different combinations of effects on group atmosphere and productivity, and on liking for the leader.

Source: Based on Lippitt & White (1943).

Autocratic leaders: They give orders, are aloof, are focused on the task and are generally not liked very much.

leader was present (see first focus question). Laissez-faire leaders created a friendly, group-centred but play-oriented atmosphere, which was associated with low productivity that increased only if the leader was absent.

Lippitt and White used these findings to promote their view that democratic leadership was more effective than other leadership behaviours.

Lippitt and White's distinction between autocratic and democratic leadership styles re-emerges in a slightly different guise in later work. From his long series of studies of interaction styles in groups, Bales (1950) concluded that the two roles of task specialist and socioemotional specialist (Slater, 1955) were leadership roles in groups, but that no individual could occupy both roles simultaneously. Rather, the roles tend to devolve onto separate individuals and the person occupying the task-specialist role was more likely to be the dominant leader. Bales argued that task specialists tend to be centrally involved, often by offering opinions and giving directions, in the task-oriented aspects of group life. In contrast, socioemotional specialists tend to respond and pay attention to the feelings of other group members. Casual observation of groups and organisations supports this dual-leadership idea.

For example, the 1991 leadership struggle in the Australian Labor Party between Bob Hawke and Paul Keating tended to highlight their very different leadership styles—Bob Hawke being the friendly and approachable leader concerned with people's feelings, and Paul Keating the hard-headed, task-oriented economic rationalist.

Another major research program, the Ohio State leadership studies (e.g. Fleishman, 1973; Stogdill, 1974), draws a similar distinction. Questionnaires concerning the behaviour and effectiveness of leaders administered to subordinates mainly in military and industrial groups revealed a distinction between *initiating structure* and *consideration*. Leaders rating high on initiating structure define the group's objectives and organise members' work towards the attainment of these goals: they are task-oriented. Leaders rating high on consideration are concerned with the welfare of subordinates and seek to promote harmonious relationships in the group: they are relationship-oriented. While this distinction is similar to Bales' (1950) distinction between task-oriented and socioemotional leaders, there is one crucial difference. Bales considered his two dimensions to be inversely related—high scores on one entail low scores on the other. However, the Ohio State researchers considered, and obtained evidence for, the independence of their dimensions—that is, a particular leader could be high on both initiating structure and consideration.

In fact, research reveals that the most effective leaders are precisely those who score above average on both initiating structure and consideration (Stogdill, 1974). For example, Sorrentino and Field (1986) conducted detailed observations of 12 problem-solving groups over a five-week period. Those group members who had been observed to score high on both the task and socioemotional dimensions of Bales' (1950) system were subsequently elected by groups to be their leaders.

Taken together, research on leadership behaviour indicates a distinction between task and socioemotional leadership orientations. These distinct leadership functions may be fairly universal. Misumi and Peterson (1985) identify two similar functions, task performance and group maintenance, from their extensive program of leadership research in Japan. But he also notes that the way in which these functions are expressed differs from culture to culture: for example, eating lunch with workmates is associated with high group maintenance in some cultures but not others.

The same conclusion was drawn by Smith and colleagues (Smith, Misumi, Tayeb, Peterson, & Bond, 1989) from research in the United States, Britain, Hong Kong and Japan. They found that performance and maintenance behaviours were universally valued in leaders, but that what counted as each type of behaviour varied from culture to culture. For example, leaders need to assess workers' task performance: in Britain and America the considerate way to do this was by speaking directly with workers, while in Asia this was viewed as inconsiderate and the considerate way was to speak with the individual's co-workers.

This focus on leadership behaviour needs, however, to be complemented by an analysis of the role of situational factors in determining leadership effectiveness. In particular, we need to investigate the relationship between, and possible interaction of, leadership style and situational requirements.

CONTINGENCY THEORY

The need for an interactionist perspective became apparent from observations that effective leadership was not simply a matter of the right mixture of task and socioemotional orientation. The 'right mixture' seemed to depend on the nature of the group—whether it was an aircrew in combat, an organisational decision-making group, a ballet company, a nation in economic crisis. This led Fiedler (1965) to propose an interactionist model of leadership effectiveness in which the leadership effectiveness of particular leadership styles was *contingent* on situational factors—**contingency theory**.

Fiedler accepted Bales' distinction between task-oriented and **socioemotional-oriented leaders** and, like Bales, believed the dimensions to be inversely related, with people habitually adopting one or other leadership style. **Task-oriented leaders** are authoritarian, value group success and derive self-esteem from task accomplishment rather than being liked by the group; relationship-oriented leaders are relaxed, friendly, non-directive and sociable and gain self-esteem from happy and harmonious group relations.

To measure leadership style, Fiedler devised an instrument called the **least-preferred co-worker (LPC) scale**. Respondents think of all the people they have ever worked with, and then describe on 18 bipolar eight-point scales (e.g. pleasant/unpleasant, boring/interesting, friendly/unfriendly) the one person with whom they found it most difficult to work. The scores are summed so that higher LPC scores indicate a more favourable attitude towards this least-preferred co-worker. Thus, high-LPC leaders are relationship-oriented because their attitude towards a group member remains positive despite the fact that the member was extremely difficult to work with (relationships are more important than task performance); low-LPC leaders are task-oriented because their attitude towards a group member is unfavourable because the member was extremely hard to work with (task performance is more important than relationships).

The effectiveness of either style of leadership is contingent on the amount of control a leadership situation allows the leader to have over the group. **Situational control** is influenced by three factors, which decrease in relative importance: (1) the most important is *leader–member relations*—the affective relationship between leader and followers; (2) the next most important is *task structure*—the extent to which the group task is well or poorly structured; and (3) the least important is *position power*—the extent to which the leader has legitimate power and authority over followers. Good leader–member relations, a well-structured task and legitimate power together maximise situational control and make it easier for the leader to lead. Situational control can be classified quite precisely from I 'very high' to VIII 'very low', by dichotomising conditions under each of the three factors as good or bad (high or low) (see Figure 9.2).

Fiedler believed that low-LPC, mainly task-oriented leaders would excel under conditions of extremely low or extremely high situational control. Where control is extremely low, leader–member relations are poor, the task is unstructured and the leader has little power. Attempts to win over the group by being nice and supportive are unlikely to succeed and will, in any case, waste valuable time and hence reduce effectiveness. An autocratic style is the best bet. Where situational control is extremely high, leader–member relations are good, the task is clearly structured and the leader has power. There is little need to waste time worrying about group morale. The leader has the means and power to be wholly task-directive. For intermediate levels of situational control, high-LPC, mainly relationship-oriented leaders would be most effective, because improvement in morale might compensate for a poorly defined task or a lack of authority.

Fiedler's model predicts that, where situational control is extreme (high or low), group performance will be negatively correlated with LPC scores—that is, the lower the leader's LPC score, thus the more task-oriented the leadership style, the better the group performs. Where situational control is intermediate, group performance will be positively correlated with LPC scores—that is, the higher the leader's LPC score, thus the more relationship-oriented he is, the better the group performs. This prediction is illustrated in Figure 9.3, which also shows a composite of obtained LPC–performance correlations reported by Fiedler (1965) from published studies. The results match the prediction remarkably well.

In general, the contingency model has accumulated substantial empirical support. Strube and Garcia (1981) conducted a meta-analysis of 178 empirical tests of the theory, and Schriesheim, Tepper and Tetrault (1994) conducted a further meta-analysis of a subset of these studies. Despite some continuing controversy (Peters, Hartke, & Pohlmann, 1985), the contingency model is considered a useful approach to the analysis of leadership.

There are, however, three points worth considering. The first concerns Fiedler's view that leadership style is a characteristic of the individual that is invariant across

FIGURE 9.2 Fiedler's eight-category situational control scale as a function of leader–member relations, task structure and position power

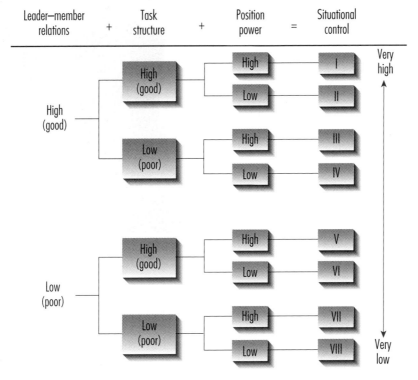

Note: An eight-category scale of situational control (I, very high, to VIII, very low) can be constructed by classifying situations as having good/bad leader–member relations, good/bad task structure, and high/low position power. The *a priori* assumption, that leader–member relations is more important than task structure which is more important than position power, means that a situation is first classified by leader–member relations, then within that by task structure, and then within that by position power.

Source: Based on Fiedler (1965).

time and situation. This view is inconsistent with, for example: (a) current conceptualisations of personality and research showing substantial temporal and situational variation in personality (e.g. Argyle & Little, 1972; Mischel, 1968); (b) evidence for relatively low test–retest reliability (correlations range from 0.01 to 0.93 with a median of 0.67) for LPC scores (Rice, 1978); and (c) the ease with which Lippitt and White (1943) trained their confederates to adopt different leadership styles in the study described earlier.

The second question concerns Fiedler's assumptions about the *a priori* relative importance of leader–member relations, task structure and position power in the assessment of overall situational control. It would not be surprising if the relative order of importance were itself a function of situational factors. Indeed, Singh, Bohra and Dalal (1979) obtained a better fit between prediction and results under conditions where the situational favourability of the eight octants was based on subjective ratings by participants rather than Fiedler's *a priori* classification.

A third problem is that contingency theory distinguishes between the leadership effectiveness of high- and low-LPC leaders, and generally classifies 'highs' as those with an LPC score greater than 64 and 'lows' as those with an LPC score less than 57. So, how do people in the 57–64 range behave? This is a valid question, as about 20% of people actually fall in this range. Kennedy (1982) conducted a study to answer this question. He found that high and low scorers behaved as predicted by contingency theory, but that middle scorers performed best of all and their effectiveness was uninfluenced by situational favourability.

This certainly limits contingency theory—it seems not to be able to explain the leadership effectiveness of approximately 20% of people or instances.

Finally, although contingency theory explores the interaction between properties of the person and properties of the situation in the assessment of leadership effectiveness, it neglects examination of the group processes that are responsible for the rise and fall of leaders and the situational complexion of leadership.

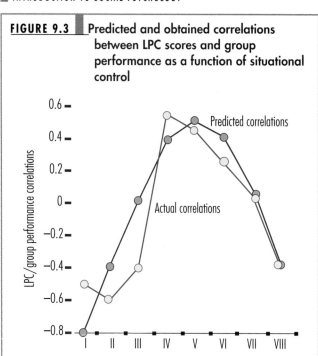

FIGURE 9.3 Predicted and obtained correlations between LPC scores and group performance as a function of situational control

Note: Where situational control is very high or very low, contingency theory predicts a negative correlation between LPC scores and quality of group performance: higher LPC, relationship-oriented leaders are associated with poor group performance, and lower LPC, task-oriented leaders with good performance. Where control is intermediate a positive correlation between LPC and group performance is predicted: relationship-oriented leaders are more effective. The obtained correlations from a series of studies support these predictions.

Source: Based on data from Fiedler (1965).

Least preferred co-worker: A first step in measuring your leadership style is to nominate the person with whom you find it most difficult to work.

LEADERSHIP AS A GROUP PROCESS

Explanations of leadership that focus on personality traits, situational demands, leadership behaviour or person–situation interaction neglect an essential aspect of leadership. Without followers there can be no leader. It is the members of the group who confer the role of leader on an individual, and it is they who finally topple the leader. There is a dynamic transaction between leaders and their followers (Bass, 1990b; Hollander, 1985). More generally, leadership can be defined as 'a process of social influence through which an individual enlists and mobilizes the aid of others in the attainment of a collective goal' (Chemers, 2001, p. 376).

Transaction, equity and power

One basis of this process may be an interpersonal equity transaction (Walster, Walster, & Berscheid, 1978; see Chapter 13). The distribution of skills and capabilities within a group almost inevitably means that some people are seen by most to be contributing more than others to the achievement of group goals. These individuals can be considered to be rewarding other group members more than they themselves are being rewarded. A state of inequity exists.

To redress the balance, group members reward the individual with social approval, praise, prestige, status and power—in other words, with the trappings of leadership. As the group's goals change, this transactional process ought to confer leadership on a different individual (someone who is better equipped in terms of capabilities to fulfil group goals). However, the course of equity is unlikely to be smooth. The incumbent leader has been given power and so has resources to resist being displaced: there is the familiar struggle for leadership among various contenders.

Incumbent leaders can be imbued with enduring charisma and mystique, perhaps through an attributional process based on power imbalance within the group. Fiske (1993b; Fiske & Dépret, 1996; Goodwin, Gubin, Fiske, & Yzerbyt, 2000) suggests that, once leaders are perceived to have power, people with relatively less power in the group (followers) are motivated to redress their perceived lack of control. One way in which they do this is by focusing attention on those who do have power (leaders) to find out what sort of people they are, in terms of their underlying dispositions and personality. There is an amplified dispositional attribution of power as charisma.

Leader–member exchange (LMX)

Looking more closely at social transactions between leaders and followers, **leader–member exchange (LMX)** theory describes how the quality of exchange relationships (i.e. relationships in which resources such as respect, trust, liking are exchanged) between leaders and followers can vary. Originally, LMX theory was called the *vertical dyad linkage* (VDL) model (Danserau, Graen, & Haga, 1975). According to the VDL model, leaders develop dyadic exchange relationships with different specific subordinates. In these dyadic relationships, the subordinate can either be treated as a close and valued 'ingroup' member or in a more remote manner as an 'outgroup' member who is separate from the leader.

LMX theory abandoned the ingroup/outgroup dichotomy and argued instead that there is a continuum of quality of exchange relationships (Graen & Uhl-Bien, 1995; Liden, Sparrowe & Wayne, 1997; Schriesheim, Castro, & Cogliser, 1999). This continuum ranges from relationships that are based on mutual trust, respect and obligation (high-quality LMX relationships) to those that are based simply on the terms of the formal employment contract between leader and subordinate (low-quality LMX relationships).

In high-quality LMX relationships subordinates are favoured by the leader and receive many valued resources, which can include both material benefits (e.g. money, privileges) and psychological benefits (e.g. trust, confidences). Leader-member exchanges go beyond the formal employment contract, with managers showing influence and support and giving the subordinate greater autonomy and responsibility. High-quality relationships motivate subordinates to internalise the group's and the leader's goals. In contrast, low-quality LMX relationships are those where subordinates are disfavoured by the leader and thus receive fewer valued resources. Leader-member exchanges simply adhere to the terms of the employment contract, with little attempt by the leader to develop or motivate the subordinate. Subordinates comply with the leader's goals without necessarily internalising them as their own.

Clearly, effective leadership requires leaders to develop high-quality LMX relationships with their subordinates, because these relationships enhance subordinates' wellbeing and work performance and bind the subordinate to the group more tightly through loyalty, gratitude and a sense of inclusion. Research finds that LMX relationships are positively related to supervisor ratings of job performance, objective job performance, job satisfaction, wellbeing, organisational commitment, organisational citizenship behaviour and member career outcomes. High-quality LMX relationships are also associated with lower employee turnover and with fewer retaliatory behaviours on the part of subordinates. There is also longitudinal research suggesting that, if leaders develop a *partnership* rather than just an exchange relationship with specific followers, there can be significant performance gains.

Overall, high-quality LMX relationships are associated with better performing and more satisfied workers who are more committed to the organisation and less likely to leave.

Trust, justice and the group value model

LMX theory emphasises the importance of trust in effective leadership. This idea also lies at the core of Tyler and Lind's (1992; Tyler, 1997) **group value model**, which contends that, although people in groups can tolerate some distributive injustice (e.g. some members of an organisation get paid more than others), they will not tolerate any procedural injustice (i.e. unfair procedures). All members need to be treated fairly and with respect as valued members by the leadership. Failure to ensure procedural justice will render leadership illegitimate and invalid, and the group will fragment as subordinates form warring factions or psychologically leave the group.

We are all familiar with how groups and their members use accusations of untrustworthiness to topple political or organisational leaders. The importance of being able to trust our leaders is probably an amplified manifestation of the wider need to be able to trust our fellow group members (Hogg, in press). Michael Platow at the Australian National University and his associates have published a number of studies supporting this general analysis (e.g. Platow, Hoar, Reid, Harley, & Morrison, 1997; Platow, Reid, & Andrew, 1998; Platow & van Knippenberg, 2001).

Leader categorisation

The analysis of leadership as a product of interaction among group members reminds us that leaders are *group*

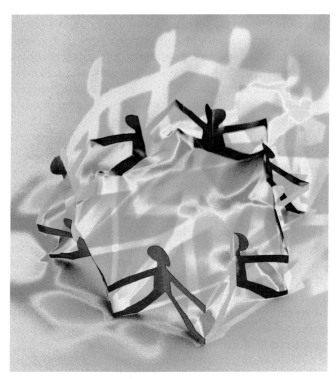

Group prototypicality: Where a group is cohesive, a leader who is a typical group member is often more effective than a leader who stands out as different to the group.

members. **Leader categorisation theory** (Lord, 1985; Lord, Foti, & De Vader, 1984) argues that we have schemas about how leaders should behave in specific group circumstances and that, once we categorise someone as a leader, the associated schema generates further information about that person (see Chapter 2 for a full discussion of schemas). Leader schemas exist at different levels of specificity—some being closely tied to specific tasks and activities, while others are much more generally applicable to most leadership situations. By virtue of their behaviours, leaders are more or less prototypical or schematic members of leader categories (hence *leader categorisation theory*).

Leader categories are not, however, real social groups. They are abstract cognitive clusterings of instances that share attributes, but do not have any psychological existence as a real social group. Indeed, the notion of a social group of leaders makes little sense: who would lead and who would follow? Recently, Lord and his colleagues have extended their model to include group prototypes as another leader schema (Lord & Brown, 2004; Lord, Brown, & Freiberg, 1999), drawing on the social identity theory of leadership.

Social identity and group prototypicality

An alternative model of leadership, based on the social identity perspective (e.g. Hogg, 2003b; see Chapter 11) has been proposed by Hogg at the University of Queensland (Hogg, 2001d; Hogg & van Knippenberg, 2003; van Knippenberg & Hogg, in press). Leader schemas do generally govern leader effectiveness but, when a social group becomes a salient and important basis for self-conception and identity, group prototypicality becomes important, perhaps more important than leader schemas. In salient groups, effective leadership depends to a much greater extent on how well someone embodies the ideal norms of the group.

This idea has support from a laboratory experiment conducted by Hains, Hogg and Duck (1997). Participants were explicitly categorised or merely aggregated as a group (the manipulation of group salience). Before participating in an interactive task they rated the leadership effectiveness of a randomly appointed leader who was described as being a prototypical or non-prototypical group member and as possessing or not possessing stereotypical leader characteristics. As predicted, stereotypical leaders were generally considered more effective than non-stereotypical leaders; however, when group membership was salient, group prototypicality became an important influence on perceived leadership effectiveness (see Figure 9.4).

These findings have been replicated in a longitudinal field study of Australian outward-bound groups (Fielding & Hogg, 1997) and in further experimental (Hogg, Hains, & Mason, 1998) and correlational

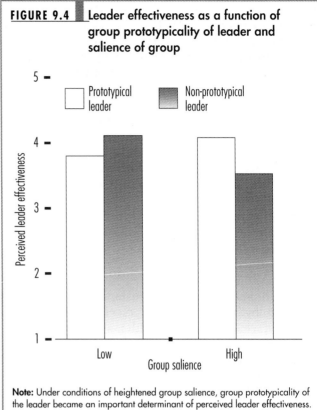

FIGURE 9.4 Leader effectiveness as a function of group prototypicality of leader and salience of group

Note: Under conditions of heightened group salience, group prototypicality of the leader became an important determinant of perceived leader effectiveness. Where group salience was low, prototypicality did not significantly affect perceptions of leader effectiveness.

Source: Based on data from Hains, Hogg, & Duck (1997).

studies (Platow & van Knippenberg, 2001). Other studies show that, in salient groups, ingroup leaders (more prototypical) are more effective than outgroup leaders (less prototypical) (Duck & Fielding, 1999; van Vugt & de Cremer, 1999).

The social identity analysis of leadership has a number of ramifications that stem from the fact that effective leaders often tend to be highly group prototypical.

- Being prototypical increases the probability that people, whether they are leaders or followers, identify strongly with the group and, therefore, behaves in a highly group-serving manner. Prototypical leaders are more likely to be trusted as 'one of us' than less prototypical leaders and, as we have seen above, trust is an important facilitator of effective leadership.
- Ironically, prototypical leaders do not actually have to behave highly prototypically. Their membership credentials are assured and they are trusted. This allows them to be innovative in moving the group in new directions—a key aspect of effective leadership. Less prototypical leaders do not have this luxury. They must be conformist in order to confirm their membership credentials and build trust (e.g. Platow & van Knippenberg, 2001; see also below).

- Because prototypicality is so important in a group, highly prototypical members attract attention and stand out—they are distinctive (see Chapter 2). The tendency to attribute others' behaviour internally to enduring personality (the fundamental attribution error—Ross, 1977; see Chapter 3) is stronger when the other person is distinctive. So, in groups where prototypical members are influential this greater influence is attributed to a disposition. In this way charisma, which facilitates leadership, is not a personality attribute so much as a contextual product of social identity processes.

- Prototypical leaders are viewed as charismatic, they are trusted and they are given leeway to act non-normatively. This allows them to act as 'entrepreneurs' of prototypicality and identity. They are effective in redefining group norms and, thus, the ingroup prototype in ways that reinforce their prototypicality (Reicher & Hopkins, 1996, 2004). Prototype management strategies can include direct rhetoric, identifying and marginalising ingroup deviants (see Chapter 8) and invoking different outgroups with which to compare. All these strategies directly influence perceptions of prototypicality.

Idiosyncrasy and transformation

The analysis of leaders as prototypical group members highlights a paradox, referred to above. On the one hand, leaders epitomise and represent the group—they embody the ideal standards and norms of the group. On the other hand, they are the agents of change within the group—they steer the group in new directions because they can alter prevailing group norms. They are simultaneously conformist and deviant. How can a leader be both a loyal member who adheres faithfully to group norms and an active deviant who influences the group to adopt new norms?

We have just seen how the social identity approach deals with this paradox. Originally, however, Hollander (1958; Hollander & Julian, 1970) provided an explanation in terms of the notion of **idiosyncrasy credit**. He argued that leaders initially need to build up 'credit' with the rest of the group. A good credit rating can be established by:

- initially conforming closely to established group norms;
- ensuring that the group feels it has democratically elected you as the leader;
- making sure that you are seen to have the competence to fulfil the group's objectives;
- being seen to identify with the group, its ideals and its aspirations.

A good credit rating gives a leader subsequent legitimacy to exert influence over the group and to deviate from existing norms—in other words, to be idiosyncratic (see second focus question).

Research supports this analysis. Merei (1949) introduced older children who had shown leadership potential into small groups of younger children in a Hungarian nursery. He reported that the most successful leaders were those who initially complied with existing group practices and who only gradually and later introduced minor variations. In another study, Hollander and Julian (1970) found that leaders of decision-making groups, who were led to believe they had been democratically elected, enjoyed more support from the group, felt more competent at the task and were more likely to suggest solutions that diverged from those of the group as a whole.

Finally, Kirkhart (1963) examined leadership choices in predominantly Black college fraternity houses in the United States. Members who identified with the social group Black were most likely to be selected, particularly in hypothetical situations involving Black–White relations.

A recent elaboration of transactional leadership has developed the notion of *transformational leadership* (Bass, 1990b, 1998; Bass & Avolio, 1993), which has become popular in organisational psychology (Yukl, 2002). Transformational leaders' transactions with followers are characterised by charisma, inspirational motivation, intellectual stimulation and individualised consideration, all of which motivate followers to work for group goals that transcend immediate self-interest. Transformational leaders are those who respond positively to change and who actively induce change. Great leaders often seem to behave in this way (Sooklal, 1991; also see the Mandela and Thatcher autobiographies mentioned earlier).

In addition, there is scientific evidence in support of the concept. Yammarino, Spangler and Bass (1993) conducted a longitudinal study of 186 randomly selected graduates from the United States Naval Academy; initial measures of transformational leadership predicted subsequent performance appraisal. In general, the correlation between transformational leadership and leadership effectiveness is high (typically 0.70–0.80) and certainly higher than the relationship between transactional leadership and leadership effectiveness (Bass, 1990b; Bryman, 1992).

There are, however, at least two questions to raise regarding transformational leadership.

1. By placing such emphasis on the leader's behavioural style (i.e. charisma), are we in danger of playing down transaction in favour of personality? Although Bass and Avolio (1993) assure us that this is not the case, the possibility exists. The notion of charismatic leadership does seem to return us, to some extent, to the 'great person' theory of leadership (Haslam & Platow, 2001).

2. Mowday and Sutton (1993) ask how much transformational leadership a group can bear or afford. Contextual factors presumably dictate an optimal level of transformational leadership: too much may be dysfunctional, because it imbues the leader with excessive power and fragments the group through continual change. The limits of transformational leadership are not specified.

Intergroup context

Something important is missing from almost all the perspectives on leadership we have discussed. Fiedler's contingency theory is an advance on purely personality, situational or behavioural perspectives insofar as it recognises the interaction between personal and situational characteristics; however, it suffers from being a static view of leadership. Transactional and transformational approaches overcome this problem by focusing on the forces in a group that render leadership a dynamic process. However, all these approaches neglect the *intergroup* dimension of leadership. The main exception is Hogg's (2001d; Hogg & van Knippenberg, 2003)

Trappings of leadership: In many cultures, leadership status is associated with an ornate dress style.

social identity analysis of leadership—leadership in salient groups rests on prototypicality, and prototypes gain their properties largely from intergroup comparisons. Indeed, much leadership rhetoric is all about defining the ingroup in contrast to specific outgroups or deviant ingroup factions (e.g. Reicher & Hopkins, 1996, 2004).

Leaders not only lead their groups—in different ways they lead their groups *against* other groups. The political and military leaders who are often invoked in discussions of leadership are, of course, leaders in a truly intergroup context—they lead their political parties, their nations or their armies *against* other political parties, nations or armies. It would be surprising if the nature of intergroup relations did not influence leadership by, for example, changing group goals or altering intragroup relations. Earlier we described how a leadership change in one of Sherif's groups of boys at a summer camp was produced by intergroup competition. More recently, Rabbie and Bekkers (1978) conducted a union–management bargaining simulation where relatively insecure leaders (i.e. leaders likely to be deposed by their group) actively sought competitive bargaining situations, particularly when their group was in a relatively strong bargaining position, in order to secure their leadership.

Perhaps this captures the familiar tactic where political leaders pursue an aggressive foreign policy (where they believe they can win) in order to combat unpopularity experienced at home (e.g. Thatcher's Falkland invasion of 1982, Bush senior's Gulf War of 1991, and perhaps Bush junior's current 'war on terror' and his 2003 war against Saddam Hussein's regime in Iraq).

Group decision-making

Groups perform many tasks, of which decision-making is probably one of the most important. The course of our lives is largely determined by decisions made by groups (e.g. selection committees, juries, parliament, committees of examiners, groups of friends). In addition, many of us spend a significant portion of our working lives engaged in group decision-making. Social psychologists have long been interested in the sorts of social processes involved in group decision-making, and in whether groups make better or different decisions than do individuals. Another dimension of group decision-making comes into play when members of the decision-making group are formally acting as representatives of different groups. This is more properly called intergroup decision-making and is dealt with in Chapter 11.

A variety of models has been developed to relate the distribution of initial opinions in a decision-making group to the final group decision (Stasser, Kerr, & Davis, 1989; Stasser & Dietz-Uhler, 2001). Some of these are complex computer-simulation models (Hastie, Penrod, & Pennington, 1983; Penrod & Hastie, 1980; Stasser & Davis, 1981), while others, although expressed in a formalised mathematical style, are more immediately related to real groups.

Davis's **social decisions schemes** model identifies a small number of explicit or implicit decision-making rules that groups can adopt (Davis, 1973; Stasser, Kerr, & Davis, 1989). Knowledge of the initial distribution of individual opinions in the group and what rule the group is operating under allows prediction, with a high degree of certainty, of the final group decision. These rules include:

- *unanimity*—discussion serves to pressurise deviants to conform;
- *majority wins*—discussion simply confirms the majority position, which is then adopted as the group position;
- *truth wins*—discussion reveals the position that is demonstrably correct;
- *two-thirds majority*—unless there is a two-thirds majority, the group is unable to reach a decision;
- *first shift*—the group ultimately adopts a decision consistent with the direction of the first shift in opinion shown by any member of the group.

For intellective tasks (those where there is a demonstrably correct solution—e.g. a mathematical puzzle) groups tend to adopt the truth-wins rule and, for judgmental tasks (no demonstrably correct solution—e.g. aesthetic preference), the majority-wins rule (Laughlin, 1980; Laughlin & Ellis, 1986). Rules differ in:

- their *strictness*—that is, the degree of agreement required by the rule (unanimity is extremely strict and majority less strict);

Social decision schemes: In a high level international political forum, like this one, would a decision be reached by a 'truth wins' rule?

- the *distribution of power* among members—that is, authoritarian rules concentrate power in one member, while egalitarian rules spread power among all members (Hastie, Peznrod, & Pennington, 1983).

In general, the stricter the rule the less the power concentration—unanimity is very strict but very low in power concentration, while two-thirds majority is less strict but has greater power concentration. The type of rule adopted can have an effect, largely as a function of its strictness, not only on the group's decision itself but also on members' preferences, their satisfaction with the group decision, the perception and nature of group discussion, and members' feelings for one another (Miller, 1989). For example, stricter decision rules can make final agreement in the group slower, more exhaustive and difficult to attain, but can enhance liking for fellow members and satisfaction with the quality of the decision.

Kerr's **social transition scheme** model focuses attention on the actual pattern of member positions moved through by a group operating under a particular decision rule, en route to its final decision (Kerr, 1981; Stasser, Kerr, & Davis, 1989). In order to do this, member opinions have to be monitored during the process of discussion (Kerr & MacCoun, 1985), either by periodically asking the discussants or by having them note any and every change in their opinion. These procedures can be intrusive, and so one issue is how much they affect the natural ongoing process of discussion.

BRAINSTORMING

An important part of the group decision-making process can be the generation of novel ideas. Indeed, some groups come together almost exclusively for this purpose—the goal being to be as creative as possible in generating ideas. The technique of **brainstorming**, initially popularised by Osborn (1957), is now commonly used for this purpose. Group members are instructed to generate as many ideas as possible as quickly as possible. They are told not to be inhibited or concerned about quality (simply say whatever comes to mind), not to be critical and to build on others' ideas when possible. Brainstorming is a group performance technique designed to facilitate creative thinking and thus make the group more creative. Popular opinion is so convinced that brainstorming works that it is widely used in business organisations and advertising agencies.

However, although research reveals that groups that have been given brainstorming instructions do generate more ideas than groups that have not been so instructed, there is no evidence that individuals in brainstorming groups are more creative than on their own (Diehl & Stroebe, 1987; Mullen, Johnson, & Salas, 1991; Stroebe & Diehl, 1994). On the contrary, *nominal* groups (i.e. brainstorming groups in which individuals create ideas

Brainstorming: We've been uninhibited and produced as many ideas as possible in a fairly short time. One of them is sure to be a brilliant idea! What do you think?

on their own and do not interact) are twice as creative as true interactive groups.

The inferior performance of brainstorming groups can be attributed to at least four factors (Paulus, Dzindolet, Poletes, & Camacho, 1993):

1. *Evaluation apprehension*—despite explicit instructions to encourage the uninhibited generation of as many ideas as possible, members may still be concerned about making a good impression. This introduces self-censorship and a consequent reduction in productivity.
2. *Social loafing and free riding*—there is motivation loss because of the collective nature of the task (see Chapter 8).
3. *Production matching*—because brainstorming is novel, members use average group performance to construct a performance norm to guide their own idea generation. This produces regression to the mean.
4. *Production blocking*—individual creativity and productivity are reduced due to interference effects from others who are generating ideas at the same time.

Stroebe and Diehl (1994) review evidence for these processes and conclude that production blocking is probably the main obstacle to unlocking the creative potential of brainstorming groups. They discuss a number of remedies, of which two have promise:

1. Electronic brainstorming reduces the extent to which the production of new ideas is blocked by such things as listening to others or waiting for a turn to speak (Hollingshead & McGrath, 1995): groups that brainstorm electronically via computer can produce more ideas than non-electronic groups (Gallupe, Cooper, Grise, & Bastianutti, 1994) and more ideas than nominal electronic groups (Dennis & Valacich, 1993).

2. Heterogeneous groups in which members have diverse types of knowledge about the brainstorming topic may create a particularly stimulating environment that alleviates the effects of production blocking; Stroebe and Diehl (1994) suggest that if production blocking is also reduced by other means, heterogeneous brainstorming groups might outperform heterogeneous nominal groups.

Given convincing evidence that face-to-face brainstorming does not actually improve individual creativity, why do people so firmly believe that it does and continue to use it as a technique for generating new ideas in groups? Diehl and Stroebe suggest that this paradox stems from the existence of an **illusion of group effectivity** (Diehl & Stroebe, 1991; Stroebe, Diehl, & Abakoumkin, 1992; see also Paulus, Dzindolet, Poletes, & Camacho, 1993). We all take part in group discussions from time to time and thus we all have some degree of personal experience with ideas generation in groups. The illusion of group effectivity is an experience-based belief that we actually produce more and better ideas in groups than alone.

This illusion may be generated by at least three processes. First, although groups produce fewer non-redundant original ideas than the sum of individuals working alone, they do produce more ideas than any single member would produce alone. In groups, therefore, people are exposed to more ideas than when alone. People find it difficult to remember which ideas they produced and which were produced by other people, and so tend to exaggerate their own contribution. They feel that they were individually more productive and were facilitated by the group, when in fact they were less productive.

Stroebe, Diehl and Abakoumkin (1992) had participants brainstorm in four-person nominal or real groups and asked them to estimate the percentage of ideas they had suggested, the percentage others had suggested but they had also thought of, and the percentage that others had suggested but they had not thought of. The results (see Figure 9.5) show that participants in real groups overestimate the percentage of ideas they thought they had but did not suggest, relative to participants in nominal groups.

Second, brainstorming is generally great fun. People enjoy brainstorming in groups more than alone and so feel more satisfied with their performance. Third, people in groups know that they only call out some of the ideas they have because others have already been mentioned. Of course, all group members are in the same position, but the participant is not privy to others' undisclosed ideas and so attributes the relatively low overt productivity of others to their own relatively high latent productivity. The group is seen to have enhanced or confirmed their own high level of performance.

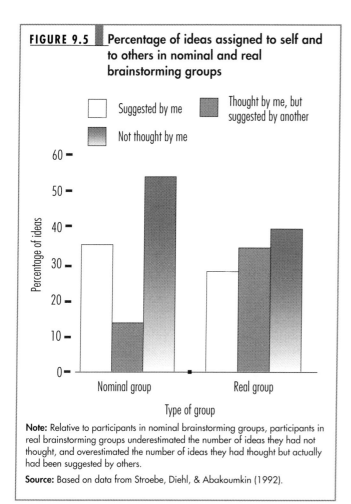

FIGURE 9.5 Percentage of ideas assigned to self and to others in nominal and real brainstorming groups

☐ Suggested by me

▨ Thought by me, but suggested by another

▨ Not thought by me

Note: Relative to participants in nominal brainstorming groups, participants in real brainstorming groups underestimated the number of ideas they had not thought, and overestimated the number of ideas they had thought but actually had been suggested by others.

Source: Based on data from Stroebe, Diehl, & Abakoumkin (1992).

GROUP MEMORY

Another important component of group decision-making is the ability to recall information. For instance, juries need to recall a testimony in order to be able to arrive at a verdict, and personnel selection panels need to recall information that differentiates among candidates in order to make an appointment. Group remembering can even be the principal reason for certain groups to come together: for example, groups of old friends often meet mainly to reminisce. On a slightly larger scale, organisations need to acquire, distribute, interpret and store enormous amounts of information. The analysis of exactly how this complex task of *organisational learning* is accomplished is still in its infancy (Wilpert, 1995).

Group remembering

Do groups remember more material than individuals? In summarising research on group remembering, Clark and Stephenson (1989, 1995) conclude that groups remember more material than individuals and more material than the best individual in the group. According to Lorge and Solomon (1955), groups recall more

than individuals because members communicate unshared information and because the group recognises true information when it hears it. There is, however, some evidence that the superiority of groups over individuals varies depending on the memory task. On simplistic and artificial tasks (e.g. nonsense words), group superiority is more marked than on complex and realistic tasks (e.g. a story).

One explanation of this is in terms of 'process loss' (Steiner, 1976; see Chapter 8). Faced with the task of recalling complex information, groups fail to adopt appropriate recall and decision strategies and, therefore, do not fully utilise all the human resources available in the group.

But group remembering is more than a simple collective regurgitation of facts. It is often a constructive process, characterised by negotiation of an agreed joint account of some part of experience. Some individuals' memories will contribute to the developing consensus while others' will not. In this way the group shapes a version of the truth that gains its subjective veracity from the degree of consensus. The group effectively constructs a version of the truth that guides individual members about what to store as a true memory and what to discard as an incorrect memory. The process of reaching consensus is subject to the entire range of social influence processes discussed in Chapter 7 as well as the group decision-making biases discussed in this chapter.

Most research into group remembering focuses on how much is remembered by individuals and by groups. Recently, however, other approaches have emerged: Clark and Stephenson and their associates have looked at the content and structure of what is remembered (see Box 9.1 and Figure 9.6) and Middleton and Edwards (1990) have adopted a discourse analysis approach (discussed in Chapter 15).

Transactive memory

A different perspective on group remembering has been proposed by Wegner (1987, 1995; Wegner, Erber, & Raymond, 1991; see also Moreland, Argote, & Krishnan, 1996). Individuals in couples and groups have a **transactive memory** that is greater than their individual memories. This idea refers to the way in which couples and groups can share memory load so that each individual is responsible for remembering only part of what the group needs to know, but all members know who is responsible for each memory domain. Transactive memory is a shared system for encoding, storing and retrieving information. It allows a group to remember significantly more information than if no transactive memory system was present (Hollingshead, 1998).

For example, the psychology departments at our universities need to remember an enormous amount of

BOX 9.1 Can two heads remember better than one?

DIFFERENCES BETWEEN INDIVIDUAL AND COLLECTIVE REMEMBERING

Noel Clark and Geoffrey Stephenson and their associates have conducted a series of experiments on group remembering (e.g. Clark, Stephenson & Rutter, 1986; Stephenson, Abrams, Wagner & Wade, 1986; Stephenson, Clark & Wade, 1986). Clark and Stephenson (1989, 1995) give an integrated overview of this research. Generally, students or police officers individually or collectively (four-person groups) recalled information from a five-minute police interrogation of a female who had allegedly been raped. The interrogation was real, or it was staged and presented as an audio recording or a visual transcript. The participants had to recall freely the interrogation and answer specific factual questions (cued recall). The way in which they recalled the information was analysed for content to investigate:

1. the amount of correct information recalled;
2. the number of reconstructive errors made—that is, inclusion of material that was consistent with but did not appear in the original stimulus;
3. the number of confusional errors made—that is, inclusion of material that was inconsistent with the original stimulus;
4. the number of metastatements made—that is, inclusion of information that attributed motives to characters or went beyond the original stimulus in other ways.

Figure 9.6 shows that groups recalled significantly more correct information and made fewer metastatements than individuals, but did not differ in the number of reconstructions or confusional errors.

Source: Clark & Stephenson (1989).

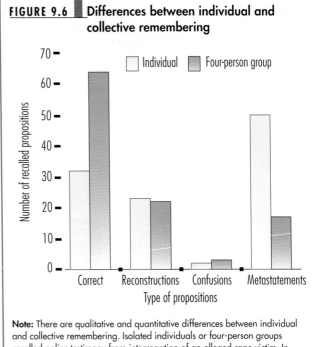

FIGURE 9.6 Differences between individual and collective remembering

Note: There are qualitative and quantitative differences between individual and collective remembering. Isolated individuals or four-person groups recalled police testimony from interrogation of an alleged rape victim. In comparison to individuals, groups recalled more information that was correct and made fewer metastatements (statements making motivational inferences and going beyond the information in other related ways).

Source: Based on data from Clark & Stephenson (1989).

practical information to do with research, postgraduate supervision, undergraduate teaching, equipment and administrative matters. This is far too much information for a single individual to remember. Instead, certain individuals are formally responsible for individual domains (e.g. research), but all of us have a transactive memory insofar as we know who is responsible for each domain.

Transactive memory is also very common in close relationships such as marriage: for example, both partners know that one of them remembers financial matters and the other remembers travel directions.

Transactive memory is a group-level representation because, although it is represented in the mind of the individual, it can emerge only through psychological involvement in a group and has no value or utility outside group membership. There can be no such thing as individual transactive memory. In this respect the concept of transactive memory is related to McDougall's (1920) notion of a **group mind** (Chapters 1 and 11)—a state of mind and mode of cognition found in groups that is qualitatively different from that found in individuals.

Wegner, Erber and Raymond (1991) describe the development of transactive memory. When groups or couples first form, the basis of transactive memory is usually social categorisation. People stereotypically assign memory domains to individuals on the basis of their category memberships. For example, members of heterosexual couples might initially develop a transactive memory in which there is sex-role stereotypical allocation of memory (the woman remembers things to do with cooking and believes that information to do with the car can be obtained from the man, and vice versa). Category-based transactive memory is the default mode.

In most cases, however, groups go on to develop more sophisticated memory-assignment systems:

- They can negotiate responsibility for different memory domains—for instance, couples can decide through discussion who will be responsible for bills, who for groceries, who for cars and so forth.
- They can assign memory domains on the basis of relative expertise—for instance, a conference-organising committee might assign responsibility for

the social program to someone who has successfully discharged that duty before.

- They can assign memory domains on the basis of access to information—for instance, the conference-organising committee might assign responsibility for publicity to someone who has a good graphics package, a list of potential registrants and is friendly with some advertising people in the city.

There is a potential pitfall to transactive memory—the uneven distribution of memory in a couple or a group. This means that when an individual leaves there is a temporary loss of, or reduction in, group memory (see Box 9.2). This can be very disruptive: for example, if the person in my department who is responsible for remembering undergraduate teaching matters should suddenly leave, a major crisis would arise. Groups often recover quickly, as there may be other people (often already with some expertise and access to information) who can immediately shoulder the responsibility.

In couples, however, partners are usually irreplaceable. Once one person leaves the couple, perhaps through death or separation, a whole section of group memory vanishes. It is possible that the depression usually associated with bereavement is, at least in part, due to the loss of memory. Happy memories are lost, our sense of who we are is undermined by lack of information, and we have to take responsibility for remembering a variety of things we did not have to remember before.

Group culture

The analysis of group memory in terms of group remembering and transactive memory can be viewed as part of a broader analysis of socially shared cognition and group culture (Tindale, Meisenhelder, Dykema-Engblade, & Hogg, 2001). We tend to think of culture as something that exists at the societal level—the customs (routines, rituals, symbols, jargon and so on) that describe large-scale social categories such as ethnic or national groups (see Chapter 16). However, there is no reason to restrict culture to such groups. Moreland, Argote and Krishnan (1996) argue that culture is an instance of group memory and thus can exist within smaller groups such as organisations, sports teams, work groups and even families.

The analysis of group culture is most developed in the study of work groups (Levine & Moreland, 1991): such groups develop detailed knowledge about norms, allies and enemies, cliques, working conditions, motivation to work, performance and performance appraisal, who fits in, and who is good at what.

GROUPTHINK

Groups sometimes employ deficient decision-making procedures that produce poor decisions. The consequences of such decisions can be disastrous. Janis (1972) used an archival method, relying on retrospective

---

BOX 9.2 | **The group that learns together stays together**

TRANSACTIVE MEMORY: COMBATING ITS LOSS AND FACILITATING ITS DEVELOPMENT

Transactive memory means that when an individual leaves a group there is a temporary loss of, or reduction in, group memory, which can be very disruptive for group functioning. Argote, Insko, Yovetich and Romero (1995) performed an experiment in which laboratory groups met over a number of consecutive weeks to produce complex origami objects. Member turnover did indeed disrupt group learning and performance, and its impact grew worse over time, presumably because more established groups had more established transactive memories. Attempts to reduce the problem by providing newcomers with individual origami training were unsuccessful.

The productivity implications for work groups and organisations are very serious, given that staff turnover is a fact of organisational life and that new members are almost always trained individually. Moreland, Argote and Krishnan (1996) argue that transactive memory systems develop more rapidly and operate more efficiently if group members learn together rather than individually. Thus new members of organisations or work groups should be trained together rather than apart. Moreland and associates report a series of laboratory experiments in which group training is indeed superior to individual training for the development and operation of transactive memory.

Groupthink: With one voice those present decide what action should be followed.

accounts and content analysis, to compare a number of American foreign policy decisions that had unfavourable outcomes (e.g. the 1961 Bay of Pigs fiasco, the 1941 defence of Pearl Harbor) with others that had favourable outcomes (e.g. the 1962 Cuban missile crisis). Janis coined the term **groupthink** to describe the group decision-making process that produced the poor decisions. Groupthink was defined as a mode of thinking in which the desire to reach unanimous agreement overrides the motivation to adopt proper rational decision-making procedures (Janis, 1982; Janis & Mann, 1977).

The antecedents, symptoms and consequences of groupthink are displayed in Figure 9.7. The principal cause of groupthink is excessive group cohesiveness (see Chapter 8 for a discussion of cohesiveness), but there are other antecedents that relate to basic structural faults in the group and to the immediate decision-making

context. Together these factors generate a range of symptoms that are associated with defective decision-making procedures: for example, there is inadequate and biased discussion and consideration of objectives and alternative solutions and a failure to seek the advice of experts outside the group (see the third focus question).

Descriptive studies of groupthink (e.g. Hensley & Griffin, 1986; Tetlock, 1979; Tetlock, Peterson, McGuire, Chang, & Feld, 1992) largely support the general model, whereas experimental studies tend to find mixed or little support for the role of cohesiveness. Experiments establish background conditions for groupthink in four-person laboratory or quasi-naturalistic groups and then manipulate cohesiveness (usually as friends versus strangers) and either a leadership variable (directiveness or need-for-power) or procedural directions for effective decision-making.

Some have found no relationship between cohesiveness and groupthink (Flowers, 1977; Fodor & Smith, 1982), some have found a positive relationship only under certain conditions (Callaway & Esser, 1984; Courtright, 1978; Turner, Pratkanis, Probasco, & Leve, 1992) and some have found a negative relationship (Leana, 1985).

These problems have led people to suggest other ways to approach the explanation of groupthink (Aldag & Fuller, 1993; Hogg, 1992). For example, group cohesiveness may need to be more precisely defined before its relationship to groupthink can be specified (Longley & Pruitt, 1980; McCauley, 1989); at present it ranges from close friendship to group-based liking. Hogg and Hains (1998) conducted a laboratory study of four-person discussion groups involving 472 participants to find that symptoms of groupthink were associated with cohesiveness, but only where cohesion represented group-based liking, not friendship or interpersonal attraction.

It has also been suggested that groupthink is merely a specific instance of 'risky shift', in which a group that already tends towards making a risky decision polarises through discussion to an even more risky decision (Myers & Lamm, 1975; see below). Others have suggested that groupthink may not really be a group process at all, but just an aggregation of individual coping responses to excessive stress (Callaway, Marriott, & Esser, 1985). Group members are under decision-making stress and thus adopt defensive coping strategies, which involve suboptimal decision-making procedures that are symptomatic of groupthink. These behaviours are mutually reinforced by members of the group and thus produce defective group decisions.

GROUP POLARISATION

Folk wisdom has it that groups, committees and organisations are inherently more conservative in their

FIGURE 9.7 Antecedents, symptoms and consequences of groupthink

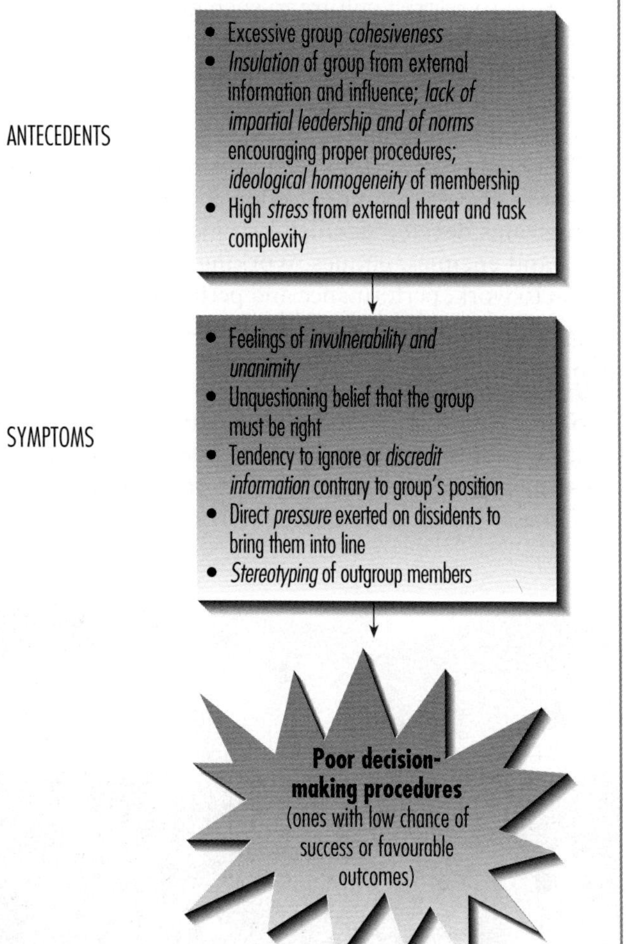

ANTECEDENTS
- Excessive group *cohesiveness*
- *Insulation* of group from external information and influence; *lack of impartial leadership* and of norms encouraging proper procedures; *ideological homogeneity* of membership
- High *stress* from external threat and task complexity

SYMPTOMS
- Feelings of *invulnerability and unanimity*
- Unquestioning belief that the group must be right
- Tendency to ignore or *discredit information* contrary to group's position
- Direct *pressure* exerted on dissidents to bring them into line
- *Stereotyping* of outgroup members

Poor decision-making procedures (ones with low chance of success or favourable outcomes)

Source: Janis & Mann (1977).

decisions than individuals. Individuals are likely to take risks, while group decision-making is very much a tedious averaging process that errs towards caution. This is consistent with much of what social psychologists know about conformity and social influence processes in groups (see Chapter 7). Sherif's (1936) autokinetic studies, discussed in Chapters 7 and 8, illustrate this averaging process very well.

Imagine, then, the excitement with which social psychologists greeted the results of Stoner's (1961) unpublished Masters thesis. Stoner had participants play the role of counsellor/adviser to imaginary people faced by choice dilemmas (Kogan & Wallach, 1964), in which there was a desirable but risky course of action contrasted with a less desirable but more cautious course of action (see Box 9.3). Participants made their own private recommendations and then met in small groups to discuss each dilemma and reach a unanimous group recommendation. Stoner found that groups tended to recommend the risky alternative more than did individuals. Stoner's (1961) finding was quickly replicated by Wallach, Kogan and Bem (1962). This phenomenon has been called **risky shift**, but later research documented group recommendations that were more cautious than those of individuals, and caused the risky shift to be treated as part of a much wider phenomenon of **group polarisation** (Moscovici & Zavalloni, 1969).

Group polarisation (Isenberg, 1986; Myers & Lamm, 1976; Wetherell, 1987) is defined as a tendency for groups to make decisions that are more extreme than the mean of individual members' initial positions, in the direction already favoured by that mean. So, for example, group discussion among a collection of people who already slightly favour capital punishment is likely to produce a group decision that strongly favours capital punishment.

Although 40 years of research have produced many different theories to explain polarisation, they can perhaps be simplified to three major perspectives: persuasive arguments, social comparison/cultural values, and self-categorisation theories.

Persuasive arguments theory

Persuasive arguments theory focuses on the persuasive impact of novel arguments in changing people's opinions (Burnstein & Vinokur, 1977; Vinokur & Burnstein, 1974). People tend to rest their opinions on a body of supportive arguments that they express publicly in group discussion. So people in a group that leans in a particular direction will hear not only familiar arguments they have heard before, but also some novel ones not heard before but supportive of their own position (Gigone & Hastie, 1993; Larson, Foster-Fishman, & Keys, 1994). As a consequence, their opinions will become more entrenched and extreme and, thus, the view of the group as a whole will become polarised.

For example, someone who already favours capital punishment is likely, through discussion with like-minded others, to hear new arguments in favour of capital punishment and come to favour its introduction more strongly. The process of thinking about an issue strengthens our opinions (Tesser, Martin, & Mendolia, 1995), as does the public repetition of our own and others' arguments (Brauer, Judd, & Gliner, 1995).

Social comparison/cultural values theory

According to this view, referred to as either **social comparison theory** or **cultural values theory** (Jellison & Arkin, 1977; Sanders & Baron, 1977), people are motivated to avoid social censure and to seek social approval. Group discussion reveals which views are socially desirable or culturally valued, and so group members shift

---

A CLASSIC IN SOCIAL PSYCHOLOGY

BOX 9.3   Giving advice on risk-taking

AN EXAMPLE OF A CHOICE DILEMMA

Suppose that the participant's task was to advise someone else on a course of action that could vary between two extremes—risky and cautious. The following is an example of such a choice dilemma (Kogan & Wallach, 1964):

Mr L, a married 30-year-old research physicist, has been given a five-year appointment by a major university laboratory. As he contemplates the next five years, he realises that he might work on a difficult long-term problem which, if a solution can be found, would resolve basic scientific issues in the field and bring him scientific honours. If no solution were found, however, Mr L would have little to show for his five years in the laboratory and this would make it hard for him to get a good job afterwards.

On the other hand, he could, as most of his professional associates are doing, work on a series of short-term problems where solutions would be easier to find but where the problems are of lesser scientific importance.

Imagine that you (the subject) are advising Mr L. Listed below are several probabilities or odds that a solution would be found to the difficult, long-term problem that Mr L has in mind. Please put a cross beside the LOWEST probability that you would consider acceptable to make it worthwhile for Mr L to work on the more difficult, long-term problem.

The participant then responds on a ten-point scale, indicating the odds that Mr L would solve the long-term problem.

Source: Based on Kogan & Wallach (1964).

---

in the direction of the group in order to gain approval and avoid disapproval. For example, favouring capital punishment and finding yourself surrounded by others who also favour capital punishment might be a strong basis for the (not necessarily accurate or valid) assumption that this is the socially valued attitude to hold. Social desirability considerations would cause people in the group to become more extreme in their support for capital punishment.

There are two variants of the social comparison perspective. One proposes that there is a bandwagon effect. On learning which is the socially desirable attitudinal pole, people in an interactive discussion will overtly compete with one another to appear to be stronger advocates of that pole. Codol (1975), in a series of 20 experiments, called this the 'primus inter pares' (PIP—first among equals) effect.

The other variant is pluralistic ignorance (Miller & McFarland, 1987; Prentice & Miller, 1993). Because people often behave publicly in ways that do not reflect their internal beliefs (see Chapters 5 and 6), people are often quite ignorant of what others really think—this is called pluralistic ignorance. One thing that group discussion can do is dispel pluralistic ignorance. Where people have relatively extreme attitudes but believe that most other people are moderate, group discussion can reveal the extremity of others' true attitudes. This liberates people to be true to their underlying beliefs. Polarisation is not so much a shift in attitude as an expression of true attitudes.

Self-categorisation theory

The persuasive arguments and social comparison approaches are supported by some studies but not by others (Mackie, 1986; Turner, 1991; Wetherell, 1987). For example, polarisation has been obtained under circumstances (e.g. perceptual tasks) where arguments and persuasion are unlikely to play a role (Baron & Roper, 1976), and under circumstances where lack of surveillance by the group should minimise the role of social desirability (Goethals & Zanna, 1979; Teger & Pruitt, 1967).

In general, it is not possible to argue that one perspective has a clear empirical advantage over the other. Isenberg (1986) has suggested that both are correct (they explain polarisation under different circumstances) and that we should seek to specify the range of applicability of each.

There is a third perspective, advanced by Turner at the Australian National University and his colleagues (Turner, 1985; Turner, Hogg, Oakes, Reicher, & Wetherell, 1987; see also Chapter 11). Unlike persuasive arguments and social comparison/cultural values theories, **self-categorisation theory** treats polarisation as a regular conformity phenomenon (Turner & Oakes,

1989). People in discussion groups actively construct a representation of the group norm from the positions held by group members in relation to those positions assumed to be held by people not in the group, or known to be held by people explicitly in an outgroup.

Because such norms not only minimise variability within the group (i.e. among ingroup members) but also distinguish the ingroup from outgroups, they are not necessarily the mean ingroup position: they can be polarised away from an explicit or implicit outgroup (see Figure 9.8). Self-categorisation, the process responsible for identification with a group, produces conformity to the ingroup norm—and thus, if the norm is polarised, group polarisation. If the norm is not polarised, self-categorisation produces convergence on the mean group position.

Research supports this perspective in (a) confirming how a norm can be polarised (Hogg, Turner, & Davidson, 1990); (b) showing that people are more persuaded by ingroup members than outgroup members or individuals; and (c) showing that group polarisation occurs only if an initial group tendency is perceived to represent a norm, rather than an aggregate of individual opinions (Mackie, 1986; Mackie & Cooper, 1984; Turner, Wetherell, & Hogg, 1989).

FIGURE 9.8 Group polarisation as self-categorisation induced conformity to a polarised group

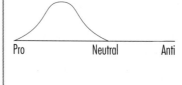

Stage 1:
Actual distribution of ingroup positions on an attitudinal dimension. Scale positions not under the bell curve are positions held by people not in the group.

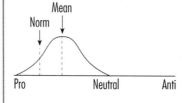

Stage 2:
Perceptual polarisation of the ingroup norm away from positions not held by ingroup members.

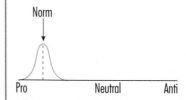

Stage 3:
Ingroup members conform to the polarised ingroup norm, causing the distribution of ingroup positions to be both homogenised and polarised.

Note: Group polarisation can occur because people categorise themselves in terms of, and conform to, an ingroup defined by a norm that is polarised away from positions not held by ingroup members.

Jury decision-making

People are fascinated by juries. They are the focus of a disproportionate number of novels and movies—John Grisham's novel *The Runaway Jury* and the 2003 movie adaptation dramatically highlight many of the important social psychological points made below about jury decision-making. Returning to reality, the 1995 murder trial of O.J. Simpson virtually brought the United States to a standstill because people couldn't miss the exciting televised instalments. Juries represent one of the most significant decision-making groups, not only because they are brandished as a symbol of all that is democratic, fair and just in a society, but because of the consequences of their decisions for defendants, victims and the community.

A case in point is the 1992 Los Angeles riots, which were sparked by an unexpected 'not guilty' verdict delivered by an all-White jury in the case of the police beating of a Black suspect (see Box 11.1 in Chapter 11). Juries are groups, and thus are potentially prey to the deficiencies of group decision-making discussed in this chapter (e.g. decision schemes, leadership, groupthink and group polarisation) (Hastie, 1993; Hastie, Penrod, & Pennington, 1983; Tindale, Nadler, Krebel, & Davis, 2001).

In addition to these problems, research has identified a number of issues specifically related to the task confronted by juries. Characteristics of the defendant and the victim can affect the jury. Physically attractive defendants are more likely to be acquitted (Michelini & Snodgrass, 1980) or to receive a lighter sentence (Stewart, 1980), although biases can be reduced by furnishing sufficient factual evidence (Baumeister & Darley, 1982), by presenting the jury with written rather than spoken, face-to-face testimony (Kaplan, 1977; Kaplan & Miller, 1978) or by explicitly directing the jury to consider the evidence alone (Weiten, 1980).

Race can also affect the jury. In the United States, for example, Blacks are more likely to receive prison sentences (Stewart, 1980), and people who murder a White are more likely than those who murder a Black to receive the death penalty (11.1% versus 4.5%; Henderson & Taylor, 1985).

Another issue is the influence of laws and penalties on the jury. Harsh laws with stiff penalties (e.g. the death penalty) tend to discourage juries from convicting (Kerr, 1978)—quite the reverse of the intention of legislators who introduce such laws. Consider some of the pressures on an Australian jury discussing evidence relating to an Aboriginal defendant, given that there is a high incidence of suicide among Aborigines serving custodial sentences.

More recent research in the United States has tended to show that whether jurors do or do not support the death penalty has a reliable but small impact on the verdict—1 to 3 verdicts out of 100 would be affected (Allen, Mabry, & McKelton, 1998).

Juries have to deal with enormous amounts of information presented in court. Research suggests that there is a recency effect in which information delivered later in the trial is more heavily weighted in decision-making (Horowitz & Bordens, 1990), and that inadmissible evidence (evidence that is given by witnesses or interjected by counsel, but is subsequently ruled inadmissible for procedural reasons by the judge) still has an effect on jury deliberation (Thompson & Fuqua, 1998). Juries also deal with complex evidence, enormous amounts of evidence, and complex laws and legal jargon—all three of which make the jury deliberation process extremely complex and prey to suboptimal decision-making (Heuer & Penrod, 1994).

The jury foreperson is important in guiding the jury to its verdict, as he/she occupies the role of leader. Research suggests that the foreperson is most likely to be someone of higher socioeconomic status, someone who has had previous experience as a juror, or simply the person who occupies the seat at the head of the table at the first sitting of the jury (Strodtbeck & Lipinski, 1985). This is perhaps of some concern, as diffuse status characteristics (Berger, Fisek, Norman, & Zelditch, 1977; Ridgeway, 2001), discussed in Chapter 8, are then influencing the jury process.

Research indicates that jurors who are older, less well educated or of lower socioeconomic status are more likely to vote to convict, but that men and women do not differ, except that women are more likely to convict defendants in rape trials (Nemeth, 1981). Jurors who score high on authoritarianism favour conviction when the victim is an authority figure (e.g. police officer), while jurors who are more egalitarian have the opposite bias of favouring conviction when the defendant is, say, a police officer (Mitchell, 1979).

In general, if two-thirds or more of the jurors initially favour one alternative, then that is likely to be the jury's final verdict (Stasser, Kerr, & Bray, 1982). Without such a majority, a hung jury is the likely outcome. The two-thirds majority rule is modified by a tendency for jurors to favour acquittal, particularly where evidence is not highly incriminating; under these circumstances a minority favouring acquittal may prevail (Tindale, Davis, Vollrath, Nagao, & Hinsz, 1990).

Jury size itself may matter (Saks & Marti, 1997). Juries of, say, 12 rather than six members are more likely to empanel representatives of minority groups. If a particular minority is 10% of the jury pool, random selection means that a minority member will be included in each 12-person jury but in only 50% of six-person juries. Furthermore, if minority or dissident viewpoints matter, they have more impact in larger juries than in smaller ones. If one-sixth of a jury favours acquittal, then in a six-person jury the 'deviate' has no social support, whereas in a 12-person jury he/she does.

Research on conformity and independence, and on minority influence (see Chapter 7) suggests that the dissident viewpoint is more likely to prevail in the 12-person jury than in the six-person one.

Summary

- Although certain personality traits are often associated with leadership, there are too many exceptions to support an explanation of leadership purely in terms of personality.
- Although almost all of us are suited to be leaders in the right circumstances, some individuals may have the edge over others.
- Leadership is best explained as an interaction of leadership style (task-oriented versus relationship-oriented) and task demands; depending on the nature of the task, one leadership style is more effective than the other.
- Leaders exist only insofar as there are followers. It is the followers who provide leaders with the trappings of power usually associated with leadership.
- Leadership is a group process that is affected by leader–member relations and the extent to which members and the leader identify strongly with the group and are prototypical of the group or not.
- Group decisions can sometimes be predicted accurately from the pre-discussion distribution of opinions in the group, and from the decision-making rule that prevails in the group at that time.
- People believe that group brainstorming enhances individual creativity, despite evidence that groups do no better than non-interactive individuals and that individuals do not perform better in groups than alone. This illusion of group effectivity may be due to distorted perceptions during group brainstorming and to the enjoyment people derive from group brainstorming.
- Groups, particularly established groups that have a transactive memory structure, are often more effective than individuals at remembering information.
- Highly cohesive groups with directive leaders are prone to groupthink—poor decision-making based on an overzealous desire to reach consensus.
- Groups that already tend towards an extreme position on a decision-making dimension often make even more extreme decisions than the average of the members' initial positions would suggest.
- Juries are not free from the usual range of group decision-making biases and errors.

LINKS

YOU HAVE READ ABOUT:	WHICH LINKS TO:
Leadership as a function of the person	enduring personal characteristics (1)
Leadership as a function of the situation	leadership change in intergroup competition (11)
Leadership as a group process	group cohesiveness, role and status (8)
Brainstorming and relying on others' opinions	social loafing (8)
Group remembering and truth shaping	social influence (7)
Transactive memory	group mind (1, 11)

Key terms

autocratic leadership *(p. 212)*
brainstorming *(p. 221)*
contingency theory *(p. 214)*
cultural values theory *(p. 227)*
democratic leadership *(p. 212)*
great person theory *(p. 210)*
group mind *(p. 224)*
group polarisation *(p. 227)*
group value model *(p. 217)*
groupthink *(p. 226)*
idiosyncrasy credit *(p. 219)*

illusion of group effectivity *(p. 222)*
laissez-faire leadership *(p. 212)*
leader categorisation theory *(p. 218)*
leader-member exchange (LMX) *(p. 216)*
leadership *(p. 210)*
least-preferred co-worker (LPC) scale *(p. 214)*
persuasive arguments theory *(p. 227)*

production blocking *(p. 222)*
risky shift *(p. 227)*
self-categorisation theory *(p. 228)*
situational control *(p. 214)*
social comparison theory *(p. 227)*
social decisions schemes *(p. 221)*
social transition scheme *(p. 221)*
socioemotional-oriented leaders *(p. 214)*
task-oriented leaders *(p. 214)*
transactive memory *(p. 223)*

FURTHER READING

Baron, R. S., & Kerr, N. (2003). *Group process, group decision, group action* (2nd ed.). Buckingham, UK: Open University Press. Up-to-date general overview of some major topics in the study of group processes—takes a mainstream American perspective, and has excellent coverage of group decision-making.

Bass, B. M. (1990a). *Bass & Stogdill's handbook of leadership.* New York: Free Press. A comprehensive overview of leadership research, which also includes the enormous quantity of leadership research done by organisational psychologists and in organisational settings.

Brown, R. J. (2000). *Group processes* (2nd ed.). Oxford, UK: Blackwell. A very readable introduction to group processes, which takes a more European perspective and also covers intergroup work. Good section on leadership.

Goethals, G. R., & Sorenson, G. (Eds.). (2004). *Encyclopedia of leadership.* Thousand Oaks, CA: Sage. Very large and comprehensive assembly of short essays on all aspects of leadership across the social and behavioural sciences, by virtually everyone who is anyone in leadership research. A wonderful resource to dip into.

Hogg, M. A., & Abrams, D. (1988). *Social identifications: A social psychology of intergroup relations and group processes.* London: Routledge. Detailed coverage of theory and research in group processes and intergroup relations from the perspective of social identity theory.

Hogg, M. A., & Tindale, R. S. (Eds.). (2001). *Blackwell handbook of social psychology: Group processes.* Oxford, UK: Blackwell. A comprehensive, detailed and up-to-date collection of 26 chapters from leading experts covering the entire field of group processes.

Hollander, E. P. (1985). Leadership and power. In G. Lindzey & E. Aronson (Eds.), *Handbook of social psychology* (3rd ed., Vol. 2, pp. 485–537). New York: Random House. Still one of the most comprehensive reviews of leadership research in social psychology; the fourth edition (1998) of the handbook does not have a leadership chapter.

Levine, J., & Moreland, R. L. (1998). Small groups. In D. Gilbert, S. T. Fiske, & G. Lindzey (Eds.), *The handbook of social psychology* (4th ed., Vol. 2, pp. 415–469). New York: McGraw-Hill. A comprehensive overview of the field of small groups, in the most recent edition of the classic handbook. A primary source for theory and research.

Tindale, R. S., Kameda, T., & Hinsz, V. B. (2003). Group decision making. In M. A. Hogg & J. Cooper (Eds.), *The Sage handbook of social psychology* (pp. 381–403). London: Sage. Comprehensive and up-to-date coverage of research on group decision-making, with a particular emphasis on the shared nature of group decisions.

van Knippenberg, D., & Hogg, M. A. (Eds.). (2004). *Leadership and power: Identity processes in groups and organizations.* London: Sage. An up-to-date collection of chapters, which captures the new directions that leadership research has taken since mainstream social psychology's new interest in leadership in the past five to ten years.

Yukl, G. (2002). *Leadership in organizations* (5th ed.). Upper Saddle River, NJ: Prentice Hall. Straightforward, comprehensive and very readable coverage of leadership from the perspective of organisations, where most leadership research tends to be done.

CHAPTER TEN

Prejudice and discrimination

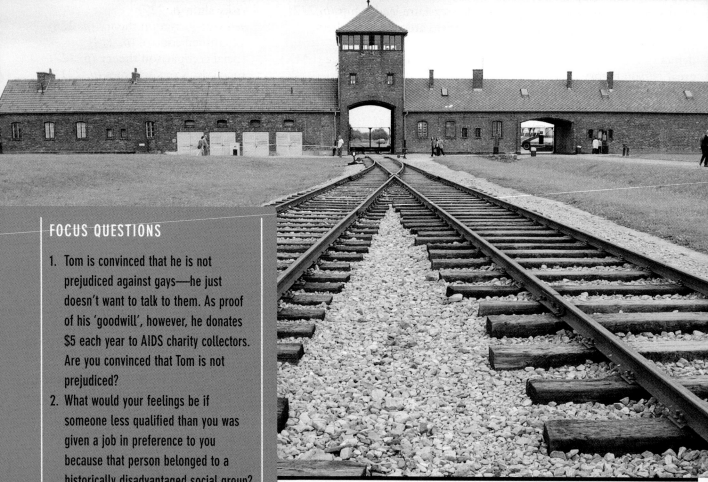

FOCUS QUESTIONS

1. Tom is convinced that he is not prejudiced against gays—he just doesn't want to talk to them. As proof of his 'goodwill', however, he donates $5 each year to AIDS charity collectors. Are you convinced that Tom is not prejudiced?

2. What would your feelings be if someone less qualified than you was given a job in preference to you because that person belonged to a historically disadvantaged social group?

3. A neighbourhood group proposes to separate the children of immigrants into a special school, where first they can learn to speak English and later continue the rest of their education there. The group says that this is for the good of these children. Would you have any concerns about this?

4. If you were frustrated in your ambitions or came from a harsh and repressive family background, do you think you might develop a tendency to vent your frustrations and anger, from time to time, on minority social groups rather than other targets?

THIS CHAPTER DISCUSSES:

- the nature and dimensions of prejudice
- prejudice and discrimination
- targets of prejudice: sex, race, age, sexual preference, physical and mental health
- forms of discrimination: reluctance to help, tokenism, reverse discrimination
- stigma and other effects of prejudice on victims
- explanations, at the personality and individual levels, of prejudice and discrimination.

Nature and dimensions of prejudice

Prejudice and discrimination are unquestionably two of the greatest problems faced by humanity. When one group of people hates another group of people so profoundly that they can torture and murder children and babies, we have a serious problem on our hands. Because prejudice and discrimination stand squarely in the path of enlightenment, an understanding of the causes and consequences of prejudice is one of humanity's great challenges. We can put people on the moon, we can genetically modify living organisms, we can replace dysfunctional organs, we can whizz around the world at an altitude of 10 000 metres and we can communicate with almost anyone anywhere via the Internet. But we seem unable to stop the Palestinians and the Israelis fighting over Jerusalem, the Catholics and Protestants tearing Northern Ireland apart and various groups in Africa hacking each other to death with machetes.

One of the awful aspects of prejudice is that it involves the **dehumanisation** of an outgroup. If people can be viewed as less than human, then atrocities against them become essentially no different from squashing an insect. Dehumanisation is commonplace. Take the following quotation, cited by Vaughan (1988, p. 1), which describes how a 16th-century Confucian scholar viewed Jesuit priests:

These 'Ocean Men' are tall beasts with deep sunken eyes and beak-like noses . . . Although undoubtably men, they seem to possess none of the mental faculties of men. The most bestial of peasants is far more human . . . It is quite possible that they are susceptible to training, and could with patience be taught the modes of conduct proper to a human being.

Prejudice is responsible for or associated with much of the pain and human suffering in the world—ranging from restricted opportunities and narrowed horizons to physical violence and **genocide**. It has always been with us and it is a depressing thought that it may remain with us as a fundamental part of the human condition.

Most people in liberal democratic societies consider prejudice a particularly unpalatable aspect of human behaviour, with terms such as 'racist' and 'bigot' being reserved as insults. And yet almost all of us experience prejudice in one form or another, ranging from relatively minor assumptions that people make about us to crude and offensive bigotry or violence. People make, and behave in accordance with, assumptions about our abilities and aspirations on the basis of, for example, our age, ethnicity, race or sex and we often find ourselves automatically making the same sorts of assumptions about others.

Herein lies a paradox: prejudice is socially undesirable and yet it pervades social life. Even in societies where prejudice is institutionalised, sophisticated justifications are used to deny that it is actually prejudice that is being practised. The system of apartheid in South Africa was a classic case of institutionalised prejudice and yet it was publicly packaged as recognition of and respect for cultural differences (see Nelson Mandela's fascinating autobiography, 1994).

Prejudice is a topic of research in its own right, but it is also a topic that draws on a range of other aspects of social psychology. In this chapter we discuss the nature of prejudice, what forms it takes and what its consequences are, and we also discuss some theories of prejudice. In Chapter 11 we continue our treatment but focus more widely on intergroup relations—prejudice and discrimination are intergroup phenomena—and thus Chapters 10 and 11 go together. However, prejudice rests on negative stereotypes of groups (see Chapter 2), it often translates into aggression towards an outgroup (see Chapter 12) and it pivots on the sort of people we think we are (see Chapter 4) and the sorts of people we think others are (see Chapters 2 and 3). The relationship between prejudice and discrimination can also be viewed as the attitude–behaviour relationship in the context of attitudes towards a group (see Chapters 5 and 6).

In many respects it is social psychology that is uniquely placed to rise to the challenge of understanding prejudice. Prejudice is a social psychological phenomenon. In fact, prejudice is doubly social—it involves people's feelings about and actions towards other people, and it is guided and given a context by the groups we belong to and the historical circumstances of specific intergroup relations in which these groups find themselves.

Prejudiced attitudes and discriminatory behaviour

As the term 'prejudice' literally means prejudgment (from the Latin *prae* and *judicium*), it is usual to consider prejudice as an attitude (see Chapter 5) where the attitude object is a social group (e.g. Americans, Tasmanians, Aborigines, musicians). A traditional view (e.g. Allport, 1954b) of prejudice is that it has three components:

1. *cognitive*—beliefs about the attitude object;
2. *affective*—strong feelings (usually negative) about the attitude object and the qualities it is believed to possess;
3. *conative*—intentions to behave in certain ways towards the attitude object (the conative component is an *intention* to act in certain ways, not the action itself).

However, not all attitude theorists are comfortable with the *tripartite model* of attitude (see Chapter 5) and there are other definitions of prejudice that do include discriminatory behaviour. For example, Brown (1995, p. 8) defines prejudice as:

the holding of derogatory social attitudes or cognitive beliefs, the expression of negative affect, or the display of hostile or discriminatory behaviour towards members of a group on account of their membership of that group.

Box 10.1 provides a fanciful account of how prejudice may arise and become the basis for discrimination. Although a fictional example, it does capture many of the principal features of prejudice that need to be explained.

The first issue, which is essentially the attitude–behaviour relationship (see Chapter 5), is the relationship between prejudiced beliefs and the practice of discrimination. You will recall from Chapter 5 that LaPiere (1934), a social scientist, spent two years travelling around the United States with a young Chinese American couple. They visited 250 hotels, caravan parks, tourist homes and restaurants and were refused service in only one (i.e. 0.4%); it would appear that there was little anti-Chinese prejudice. After returning home,

LaPiere contacted 128 of these establishments with the question, 'Will you accept members of the Chinese race as guests in your establishment?' The responses included 92% 'No', 7% 'Uncertain, depends on circumstances' and 1% 'Yes'. It appears that there was, after all, massive prejudice!

A controlled experiment was conducted later by Gaertner and Dovidio (1977). White female undergraduates waiting to participate in an experiment overheard a supposed 'emergency' in an adjoining room in which several chairs seemed to fall on a female confederate who was either White or Black. The participants were led to believe that they were alone with the confederate or that there were two other potential helpers. Ordinarily, we would expect the usual bystander effect (see Chapter 14 for details), in which participants would be less willing to go to the aid of the 'victim' when other potential helpers were available. Figure 10.1 shows that there was only a weak bystander effect when the victim was White, but that the effect was greatly amplified when the victim was Black. The White participants discriminated overtly against the Black victim only when other potential helpers were present.

There is an important lesson here: under certain circumstances, prejudice may go undetected. If the 'two

---

BOX 10.1   Prejudice and discrimination on campus

THE EMERGENCE OF A FICTIONAL 'STIGMATISED GROUP'

A study by Joseph Forgas (1983) at the University of New South Wales showed that students can have clear beliefs about different campus groups. One such target group was 'engineering students', who have often been described in terms of their drinking habits (beer, and lots of it), their cultural preferences (sports and little else) and their style of dress (practical and conservative). This is a prejudgment, in so far as it is assumed that all engineering students are like this. If these beliefs (the cognitive component) are not associated with any strong feelings (affect) or any particular intention to act (conation) then no real problem exists and we would probably not call this a prejudice—simply a harmless generalisation (see Chapter 5 for a discussion of the tripartite model of attitude).

However, if these beliefs were associated with strong negative feelings about engineering students and their characteristics then a pattern of conations would almost inevitably arise. If you hated and despised engineering students and their characteristics, you would probably intend to avoid them, perhaps humiliate them whenever possible and even dream of a brave new world without them.

This is now quite clearly prejudice, but it may still not be much of a social problem. Strong pressures would exist to inhibit expression of such views or the realisation of conation in action, so people with such prejudices would probably be unaware that others shared their views. However, if people became aware that their prejudices were widely shared, they might engage in discussion and form organisations to represent their views. Under these circumstances, more extreme conations might arise, such as suggestions to isolate engineering students in one part of the campus and deny them access to certain resources on campus (e.g. the bar, the refectory). Individuals or small groups might now feel strong enough to discriminate against individual engineering students, although wider social pressures would probably prevent widespread discrimination.

However, if the students gained legitimate overall power in the university, they would be free to put their plans into action. They could indulge in dehumanising engineering students: deny them their human rights, degrade and humiliate them, herd them into ghettos behind barbed wire and systematically exterminate them. Prejudice would have become enshrined in, and legitimated by, the norms and practices of the community.

FIGURE 10.1 | Bystander apathy as a function of race of victim

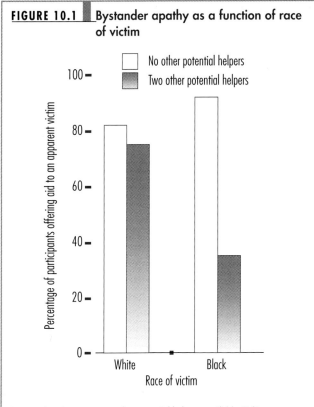

Note: When there were no other potential helpers available, White women were about equally likely to go to the aid of a Black or a White confederate who had suffered an emergency. However, when other helpers were available they were not inclined to assist the Black confederate: weak bystander apathy in the presence of a White victim was amplified many times over when the victim was Black.

Source: Based on data from Gaertner & Dovidio (1977).

potential helpers' condition had not been included, this experiment would have revealed that White women were somewhat more willing to aid a Black victim than a White victim. It was only with the inclusion of the 'two potential helpers' condition that underlying prejudice was revealed. The absence of overt discrimination should always be treated with caution, as prejudice can be expressed in indirect and subtle ways (see below).

Targets of prejudice and discrimination

Prejudice knows no cultural or historical boundaries—it is certainly not the exclusive province of people who are middle-aged, white, heterosexual or male. Human beings are remarkably versatile in being able to make almost any social group a target of prejudice. However, certain groups are the enduring victims of prejudice because they are formed by social categorisations that are vivid, omnipresent and socially functional, and the target groups themselves occupy low power positions in society. These groups are those based on sex, race, ethnicity, age, sexual preference, and physical and mental health. Research shows that, of these, sex, race and age are the most prevalent bases for stereotyping (Mackie, Hamilton, Susskind, & Rosselli, 1996).

Not surprisingly, most research on prejudice has focused on these three dimensions, in particular sex and race/ethnicity. For example, in his 1995 book on the social psychology of prejudice, Brown has a great deal to say about sexism and racism but merely touches on ageism and on handicap and disability, and says nothing about homophobia and discrimination based on sexual preference.

SEXISM

Almost all research on **sexism** focuses on prejudice and discrimination against women (Deaux & LaFrance, 1998). This is because women have historically suffered most as the victims of sexism—primarily because of their low power position relative to men in business, government and employment. It should, however, be noted that sex roles may have persisted because, although they provide men with structural power, they have provided women with dyadic or interpersonal power (e.g. Jost & Banaji, 1994).

Sex stereotypes

Research on sex stereotypes has revealed that both men and women believe that men are competent and independent and women are warm and expressive (Broverman, Vogel, Broverman, Clarkson, & Rosenkrantz, 1972; Spence, Helmreich, & Stapp, 1974). As Fiske (1998, p. 377) puts it: 'The typical woman is seen as nice but incompetent, the typical man as competent but maybe not so nice'. These beliefs have substantial cross-cultural generality: they prevail in Europe, North and South America, Australia and parts of the Middle East (Deaux, 1985; Williams & Best, 1982). These are really consensual social **stereotypes**.

Knowledge of such stereotypes is not inevitably associated with a stereotype-consistent personal belief about the target group. In fact, it seems that such a correspondence between knowledge and belief occurs only among highly prejudiced individuals (Devine, 1989). There is some evidence that, all things being equal, men and women do not describe themselves in such strongly sex-stereotypical terms (e.g. Martin, 1987) and that women deny feeling that they have been personally discriminated against: sex discrimination is something experienced by *other* women (Crosby, Cordova, & Jaskar, 1993; Crosby, Pufall, Snyder, O'Connell, & Whalen, 1989; see below).

Although there are generic stereotypes of men and women, people tend to represent the sexes in terms of

Sex stereotypes: How do you think this man will react to a smartly dressed woman walking by?

subtypes (Deaux & LaFrance, 1998; Fiske, 1998). Western research identifies four dominant female subtypes (housewife, sexy woman, career woman, and feminist/athlete/lesbian) that emphasise interpersonal versus competence dimensions. The typical woman is closest to the housewife or sexy woman subtype. Male subtypes are less clear-cut, but the two main ones are businessman and macho man. Here the emphasis is very much on the competence dimension. The typical man falls between the two poles. Generally speaking, research shows that both men and women see women as a more homogeneous group than men (Lorenzi-Cioldi, Eagly, & Stewart, 1995).

Presumably, competence, independence, warmth and expressiveness are all highly desirable and valued human attributes. But if this were true, there would be no differential evaluative connotation of the stereotype. Research, however, suggested that female-stereotypical traits are significantly less valued than male-stereotypical traits. Broverman and colleagues (Broverman, Broverman, Clarkson, Rosencrantz, & Vogel, 1970) asked 79 practising mental health clinicians (clinical psychologists, psychiatrists, social workers) to describe a healthy, mature, socially competent individual who was either (a) 'a male', (b) 'a female' or (c) 'a person'. Both male and female clinicians described a healthy adult man and

a healthy adult person in almost exactly the same terms (reflecting competency). The healthy adult woman was seen to be significantly more submissive, excitable and appearance-oriented—characteristics not attached to either the healthy adult or the healthy man. It is ominous that women are not considered to be normal, healthy adult people!

Behaviour and roles

Might sex stereotypes accurately reflect sex differences in personality and behaviour? Perhaps men and women really do have different personalities. Bakan (1966), for example, has argued that men are more *agentic* (i.e. action-oriented) than women, and women are more *communal* than men (see also Williams, 1984). This is a complicated issue. Traditionally, men and women have each occupied a different **sex role** in society (men pursue full-time out-of-home jobs, while women are 'home-makers') and, as we saw in Chapter 8, roles constrain behaviour in line with role requirements. Sex differences, if they do exist, may simply reflect roles, not sex, and role assignment may be determined and perpetuated by the social group that has more power (in most cases, men). An alternative argument might be that there are intrinsic personality differences between men and women that suit the sexes to different roles—that is, there is a biological imperative behind role assignments. This is a debate that can be, and is, highly politicised.

Social psychological research indicates that there is a small number of systematic differences between the sexes, but that they are not very diagnostic: in other words, knowing someone's position on one of these dimensions is not a reliable predictor of that person's sex (Parsons, Adler, & Meece, 1984). For example, research on male and female military cadets (Rice, Instone, & Adams, 1984) and male and female managers (Steinberg & Shapiro, 1982) indicated that perceived stereotypical differences were an exaggeration of minor differences. In general, sex stereotypes are more myth than a reflection of reality (Eagly & Carli, 1981; Swim, 1994).

One reason why sex stereotypes persist is that role assignment according to **gender** persists. In general, women make up the overwhelming majority of restaurant servers, telephone operators, secretaries, nurses, babysitters, dental hygienists, librarians and elementary/kindergarten teachers, while most lawyers, dentists, truck drivers, accountants, top executives and engineers are male (Greenglass, 1982). Certain occupations become labelled as 'women's work' and are accordingly valued less.

To investigate this idea, Eagly and Steffen (1984) asked male and female students to rate, on sex-stereotypical dimensions, an imaginary man or woman who was described as being either a 'homemaker' or employed full-time outside the home. In a third condition, no employment information was given. Figure 10.2 shows that, irrespective of sex, homemakers were perceived to be significantly more feminine (in their traits) than full-time employees. This indicates that certain roles may be sex-typed and suggests the possibility that, as women increasingly take on masculine roles, there will be substantial change in sex stereotypes. However, the converse may also occur: as a traditionally male role becomes increasingly occupied by women, that role may become less valued.

Any analysis of intergroup relations between the sexes should not lose sight of the fact that, in general, men still have more sociopolitical power than women to define the relative status of different roles in society. Not surprisingly, women can find it difficult to gain access to higher-status masculine roles/occupations. Older research found that in some universities women applicants for doctoral positions could be discouraged by condescending reactions from male peers and academic staff members (e.g. 'You're so cute, I can't see you as a professor of anything'; Harris, 1970) and that there was a bias against hiring women for academic positions (e.g. Fidell, 1970; Lewin & Duchan, 1971). Things have changed in the past 35 years, so it would be alarming to find this form of blatant discrimination in modern universities (see below).

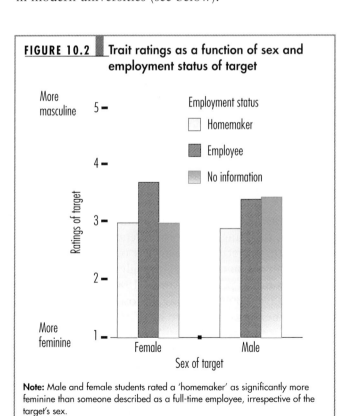

FIGURE 10.2 | Trait ratings as a function of sex and employment status of target

Note: Male and female students rated a 'homemaker' as significantly more feminine than someone described as a full-time employee, irrespective of the target's sex.

Source: Based on data from Eagly & Steffen (1984).

However, changes have been slower and less extensive outside the more progressive environment of universities and women still find it difficult to attain the very top leadership positions in large organisations—a phenomenon called the *glass ceiling effect* (e.g. Eagly, 2004; Eagly, Karau, & Makhijani, 1995). Women are well represented in middle management but on the way up, and just within sight of the very top, they hit an invisible ceiling—a glass ceiling. One explanation is that male prejudice, or backlash against women with power, constructs the glass ceiling (e.g. Rudman & Glick, 1999, 2001). Again, either sex can hit a glass ceiling if gender stereotypes are inconsistent with the organisation's norms. For example, Young and James (2001) found that male flight attendants hit a glass ceiling because, to put it simply, stereotypes about men prevent people from expecting men to make 'good' flight attendants—male stereotypes block promotion.

Maintenance of sex stereotypes and roles

One of the most powerful forces in the transmission and maintenance of traditional sex stereotypes is the media. We are all familiar with the unsubtle forms this may take: semi-clad women draped over boats, cars, motorcycles and other consumer products; the purely decorative role of women in TV game shows; the way in which women are often extraneous to the plot of a drama and are presented only as sexual/romantic embellishment. Although the cumulative power of these images should not be underestimated, there are more subtle forms that may be equally or even more powerful, as they are more difficult to detect and thus combat.

For example, Archer, Iritani, Kimes and Barrios (1983) have coined the term **face-ism** to describe the way in which depictions of men give greater prominence to the head, while depictions of women give greater prominence to the body. Archer and colleagues analysed 1750 visual images of men and women (newspaper and magazine pictures, as well as drawings made by students) and discovered that in almost all instances this was the case. Next time you watch, for example, a TV interview or documentary, note how the camera tends to focus on the face of men but on the face and upper body of women. Face-ism conveys the view that, relative to men, women are more important for their physical appearance than their intellectual capacity: facial prominence in photos has been shown to signify ambition and intelligence (Schwartz & Kurz, 1989).

Ng has noted another subtle form of sexism in the use of the generic masculine (Ng, 1990; see also Wetherell, 1986)—people's use of the masculine pronouns (he, him, his, etc.) and terms such as 'mankind' when they are talking about people in general. This practice conveys the impression that women are an aberration from the basic masculine mould of humanity. The sex-typing of occupations and roles is also maintained by terms such as 'housewife', 'chairman' and so on. Because it is largely through language that we represent our world (see Chapter 15), it is important, in order to change sex stereotypes, that the implicit meanings of words and phrases be considered and those expressions that are clearly sexist (or prejudiced in other ways) be changed.

For example, language codes such as the publication manual for the American Psychological Association (adhered to by psychologists around the world) have enshrined within them clear guidelines for non-sexist language use.

There is now substantial evidence that success or failure is explained in different ways depending on the sex of the actor (see Chapter 3). In general, successful performance by a man is attributed to ability, while an identical performance by a woman is attributed to luck or the ease of the task (see Figure 10.3). For example, Deaux and Emswiller (1974) had students watch fellow students perform well on perceptual tasks that were male-stereotypical (e.g. identifying a tyre jack) or female-stereotypical (e.g. identifying types of needlework). On the masculine tasks, male success was attributed to ability more than was female success (see Figure 10.4). On feminine tasks there was no differential **attribution**.

There are some circumstances when this bias may be overturned. For example, sex-stereotypical attributions disappear when the attention of the person who is evaluating performance is firmly directed onto the performance and away from the actor (Izraeli, Izraeli, & Eden, 1985). There is also evidence that women who succeed in traditionally masculine activities (e.g. becoming a top manager) are seen as more deserving than a similarly successful man (Taynor & Deaux, 1973).

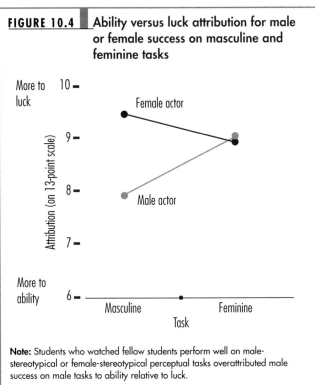

FIGURE 10.4 | Ability versus luck attribution for male or female success on masculine and feminine tasks

Note: Students who watched fellow students perform well on male-stereotypical or female-stereotypical perceptual tasks overattributed male success on male tasks to ability relative to luck.

Source: Based on data from Deaux & Emswiller (1974).

In general, however, sex-stereotypical attributions (on the part of both men and women) tend to create different evaluations of our own worth as a man or a woman. That is, for the same level of achievement women may consider themselves less deserving than men. Indeed, Major and Konar (1984) found this among male and female management students. The women's estimates of their realistic starting salaries were approximately 14% lower than the men's estimates of their starting salaries, and 31% lower with regard to estimated peak salaries.

Changes in sexism

While these forms of discrimination are difficult, and thus slow, to change, there is evidence that in Western democratic societies some forms of blatant sex discrimination are on the wane—though sexual harassment in various forms persists (Gutek, 1985). In 1893, New Zealand gave women the vote, followed closely by Australia. Other countries have been much slower in this regard—Britain in 1928 and Switzerland, finally, only in 1971. In one canton (Appenzell Inner-Rhoden) in Switzerland, women were excluded from the cantonal vote until as recently as 1990. Societies are also increasingly passing antidiscrimination legislation and even (particularly in the United States) legislation for affirmative action. Affirmative action (see below) involves systematically appointing properly qualified minorities

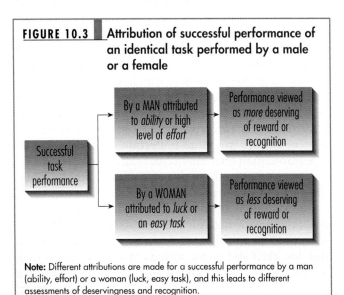

FIGURE 10.3 | Attribution of successful performance of an identical task performed by a male or a female

Note: Different attributions are made for a successful performance by a man (ability, effort) or a woman (luck, easy task), and this leads to different assessments of deservingness and recognition.

to positions in which they are historically underrepresented (e.g. senior management in organisations, senior government positions), with the aim of making such positions appear more attainable for minorities.

Social psychological research has perhaps detected some effects of these changes. For example, in the early 1970s, Bartol and Butterfield (1976) found that female leaders in organisations were valued less relative to male leaders. By the early 1980s this effect had vanished (Izraeli & Izraeli, 1985), though Eagly (2004) cites a Gallup Poll conducted in 1995 that found that, across 22 nations, both sexes still preferred to have a male boss.

In the mid-1960s, Goldberg (1968; also see Pheterson, Keisler, & Goldberg, 1971) had women students evaluate identical pieces of written work attributed to a man (John T. McKay) or a woman (Joan T. McKay) and found that those pieces ostensibly authored by a woman were downgraded relative to those ostensibly authored by a man.

A replication of this study in the late 1980s found no such effect and, indeed, a survey of 104 studies involving 20 000 people showed that the most common finding was no gender bias (Swim, Borgida, Maruyama, & Myers, 1989). Finally, no sex discrimination was found in a study of performance evaluations of more than 600 male and female store managers (Peters, O'Connor, Weekley, Pooyan, Frank, & Erenkrantz, 1984) nor in a study of the compensation worth of predominantly male or predominantly female occupations determined by experts in employment compensation (Schwab & Grams, 1985).

Because sexism is now illegal and unacceptable, particularly in certain segments of Western society, it can sometimes be difficult to detect traditional sexism (see below for an extensive discussion of this issue). Researchers have tried to measure sex stereotypes in more subtle and complex ways to reflect more modern forms of sexism (Glick & Fiske, 1996; Swim, Aikin, Hall, & Hunter, 1995). For example, Glick and Fiske (1996, 1997) have constructed an *ambivalent sexism inventory* that differentiates between hostile and benevolent attitudes to women on dimensions relating to attractiveness, dependence and identity. Sexists have benevolent attitudes (heterosexual attraction, protection, gender role complementarity) towards traditional women (e.g. pink-collar job holders, 'sexy chicks', housewives) and hostile attitudes (heterosexual hostility, domination, competition) towards non-traditional women (e.g. career women, feminists, athletes, lesbians). Interestingly, Glick and Fiske (1997) have extended their inventory to measure women's hostile and benevolent attitudes towards men.

From a recent review of scientific research into prejudice against women, Eagly and Mladinic (1994) optimistically comment that there is no longer any tendency to devalue women's work, that a positive stereotype of women relative to men is emerging, and that most people like women more than men. Although no doubt true, this conclusion must be tempered by the fact that most research is conducted in Western democratic societies; elsewhere the plight of women is not so rosy.

One particularly sobering statistic comes from Klasen (1994). Sex-selective abortions and infanticide have led to 76 000 000 (that's right, seventy-six *million*) 'missing women'. Of course, many regimes in many countries still legislate against women's rights: the denial of education to women in Afghanistan under the Taliban, women being sentenced to death by stoning for infidelity in Nigeria, and varying restrictions placed on women's choices about their bodies and reproduction. The list goes on and on.

RACISM

Discrimination on the basis of race or ethnicity is historically responsible for some of the most appalling acts of mass inhumanity. While sexism is responsible for the continuing practice of selective infanticide, in which female babies (and fetuses) are killed, this is largely restricted to a handful of developing countries (Freed & Freed, 1989). Genocide is universal: in recent times it has, for example, been carried out in Germany, Iraq, Yugoslavia and Rwanda.

Most social psychological research on **racism** has focused on anti-Black attitudes and behaviour in the United States. Historically, White people's stereotypes of Blacks in the United States are negative and reflect a general perception of rural, enslaved, manual labourers (LeVine & Campbell, 1972; Mackie, Hamilton, Susskind, & Rosselli, 1996; Plous & Williams, 1995). In this respect the stereotype is similar to that of Latino Americans, but quite different from that of Asians and Jews.

Research on anti-Black attitudes in the United States documents a dramatic reduction in unfavourable attitudes since the 1930s (e.g. Devine & Elliot, 1995; Dovidio, Brigham, Johnson, & Gaertner, 1996; Smedley & Bayton, 1978) (see Figure 10.5). This is a global trend in Western nations. The debate about attitudes towards Aborigines in Australia and Maoris in New Zealand has progressed—accelerated in recent years by a move towards reconciliation in Australia, and by a revisiting in New Zealand of the 1840 Treaty of Waitangi which protects Maori rights.

New racism

From this, should we conclude that racial prejudice is dying out in countries like Australia, New Zealand and the United States? Possibly not. Figure 10.5 shows a decline over 60 years in the characterisation of African Americans as superstitious, lazy and ignorant. What the figure does not show are data from a study by Devine and Elliot (1995) in which 45% of respondents felt

Sex discrimination on the wane: A budding chemist succeeds in what was once a male preserve.

African Americans were lazy. In addition, Devine and Elliot found that more than 25% of their respondents characterised African Americans as athletic, rhythmical, low in intelligence, criminal, hostile and loud. The stereotype has changed, not gone away. Nearer to home, a study by Oliver and Vaughan (1991) at Auckland University found that both positive and negative stereotypes, some of which are strong, may be privately expressed by Maori, Pacific Islander and Pakeha teenagers towards each outgroup. Furthermore, when a group of covert racists gets together, wider social mores of respect and tolerance hold little sway and the public expression of racist attitudes is common.

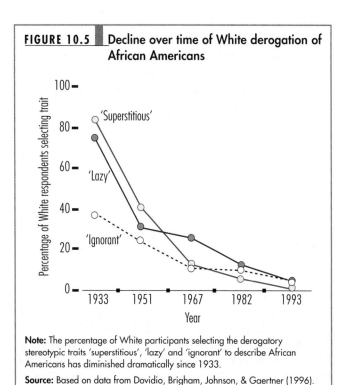

FIGURE 10.5 ▌ **Decline over time of White derogation of African Americans**

Note: The percentage of White participants selecting the derogatory stereotypic traits 'superstitious', 'lazy' and 'ignorant' to describe African Americans has diminished dramatically since 1933.

Source: Based on data from Dovidio, Brigham, Johnson, & Gaertner (1996).

Because explicit and blatant racism (derogatory stereotypes, ethnophaulisms (i.e. name-calling), abuse, persecution, assault and discrimination) is illegal and thus socially censured, it is now more difficult to find. Most people in most contexts do not behave in this way. However, racism may not merely have gone 'underground', it may actually have changed its form. This idea lies at the heart of a number of theories of new or modern racism. People may still be racist at heart, but in a different way—they may represent and express racism differently, perhaps more subtly (Crosby, Bromley, & Saxe, 1980).

This new form of racism has been called *aversive racism* (Gaertner & Dovidio, 1986), *modern racism* (McConahay, 1986), *symbolic racism* (Kinder & Sears, 1981; Sears, 1988), *regressive racism* (Rogers & Prentice-Dunn, 1981) and *ambivalent racism* (Hass, Katz, Rizzo, Bailey, & Eisenstadt, 1991). Although there are differences between these theories, they all share the view that people experience a conflict between negative emotional reactions towards racial outgroups and modern egalitarian values that exert pressure to behave in a non-prejudiced manner (see overviews by Brewer & Miller, 1996; Brown, 1995; Hilton & von Hippel, 1996). For example, according to Gaertner and Dovidio's (1986) notion of aversive racism, deep-seated racial antipathy expresses itself as overt racism when the situation is one in which egalitarian values are weak. According to Sears's (1988) notion of symbolic racism, negative feelings about Blacks (based on early learned racial fears and stereotypes) blend with moral values embodied in the Protestant ethic to justify some anti-Black attitudes and therefore legitimise their expression.

Generally, modern or subtle forms of racism reflect how people resolve an underlying antipathy based on race with their belief in equality between groups. This is achieved by avoidance and denial of racism—separate lives, avoidance of the topic of race, denial of being prejudiced, denial of racial disadvantage—and thus opposition to affirmative action or other measures to address racial disadvantage.

These ideas, although focused on race relations in the United States, have been applied to gender (Glick & Fiske, 1996; Swim, Aikin, Hall, & Hunter, 1995; see above) and to racial attitudes in Europe (Pettigrew & Meertens, 1995).

Detecting racism

The challenge to social psychology, then, is to be able to detect new racism. There are several scales associated with the various analyses of modern and subtle forms of racism. Generally, unobtrusive measures are needed to detect racism—otherwise people may simply respond in a socially desirable way (Crosby, Bromley, & Saxe, 1980; Devine, 1989; Greenwald & Banaji, 1995); see

Chapter 5 for a more general discussion of unobtrusive measures of attitudes (physiological indexes, behavioural measures, the bogus pipeline and the implicit association test (IAT)). One way to measure prejudice is in terms of social distance—how close, psychologically or physically, people are willing to get to one another. For example, racist attitudes persist in contexts of close social distance (e.g. marriage) although they may have disappeared in less close social relations (e.g. attending the same school) (Schofield, 1986). In India, people who subscribe to the caste system will typically accept a lower-caste person into their home but will not consider marrying one (Sharma, 1981).

Another way to uncover underlying prejudice is to isolate a response not usually thought of as discriminatory. For example, Rogers and Prentice-Dunn (1981) had a White or Black confederate insult White participants (in Alabama), who then had an opportunity to administer a shock to the confederate. Angered Whites gave larger shocks to the Black confederate. In another condition where no insults were forthcoming, participants gave smaller shocks to the Black confederate than the White confederate.

Prejudice can also surface inadvertently in people's relatively automatic cognition (see Chapter 2). For example, Duncan (1976) had White students in California observe on TV what they thought was a live conversation between a Black man and a White man. The conversation degenerated into an argument in which one lightly shoved the other. When the White did the shoving, the behaviour was interpreted as playful: only 13% of participants interpreted it as violent. When the Black did the shoving, 73% interpreted the action as violent.

Other evidence for well-concealed prejudice comes from an experiment by Gaertner and McLaughlin (1983). Participants were given pairings of the social categories White or Black with various positive or negative descriptive words; they had to decide whether the pairings were meaningful or not and then communicate their decision by pressing a button labelled 'yes' or 'no'. The latency of response is an index of how well the pairing represents an existing attitude in the mind of the participant—faster responses indicate an existing attitude. The results (see Figure 10.6) show no tendency among participants to pair negative words more strongly with Black or White. However, participants were much quicker at deciding whether positive words were meaningfully paired with White than with Black.

The general principle underlying this procedure for detecting prejudice is *automaticity* (Bargh, 1989). Stereotypes can be automatically generated by categorisation, and categorisation can automatically arise from **priming** a category (e.g. an accent, a face, a costume). If the primes or the categories are outside consciousness, then people can have little control over the stereotype.

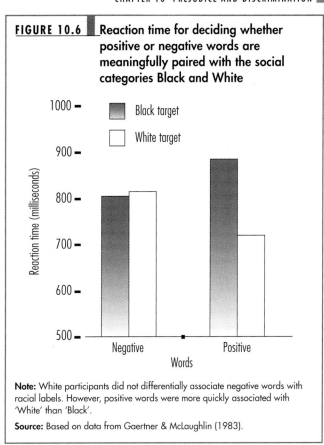

FIGURE 10.6 Reaction time for deciding whether positive or negative words are meaningfully paired with the social categories Black and White

Note: White participants did not differentially associate negative words with racial labels. However, positive words were more quickly associated with 'White' than 'Black'.

Source: Based on data from Gaertner & McLaughlin (1983).

Devine (1989) discovered that African American primes (e.g. lazy, slavery, Blacks, Negroes, niggers, athletic), which were presented too fast for anyone to be aware of them, caused people to interpret a subsequent neutral act by someone called 'Donald' in stereotypically negative ways. This showed that people had deep-seated negative stereotypes of African Americans. People of high or low prejudice did not differ in their susceptibility to preconscious priming, a provocative result that was conceptually replicated by Fazio, Jackson, Dunton and Williams (1995).

However, other research shows that the automatic effect is more marked for people who score high on prejudice on various modern racism scales (Lepore & Brown, 1997; Wittenbrink, Judd, & Park, 1997).

The notion of automaticity is related to the idea that categories and their stereotypical attributes are implicitly linked in memory. Thus, concealed prejudice can be detected by unobtrusive methods that reveal underlying stereotypical associations. This idea is the basis of the now very popular **implicit association test** described in detail in Chapter 5 (Greenwald, McGhee, & Schwartz, 1998—also see Ashburn-Nardo, Voils, & Monteith, 2001; Cunningham, Preacher & Banaji, 2001; Greenwald, Banaji, Rudman, Farnham, Nosek, & Mellott, 2002).

Finally, recent research shows how racism can very

subtly and quite unintentionally be imbedded in the words we use, the way we express ourselves and the way we communicate with and about racial outgroups (e.g. Potter & Wetherell, 1987; van Dijk, 1993; van Dijk & Wodak, 1988; see Chapter 15). An example of the meticulous attention to detail to be found in some of this work is Teun van Dijk's (1987) lengthy analysis of spontaneous everyday talk among Whites in the Netherlands and in Southern California about other races (e.g. Blacks, East Indians, North Africans, Hispanics, Asians). A total of 180 free-format interviews conducted between 1980 and 1985 were qualitatively analysed to show how racism is imbedded in and reproduced by everyday discourse. (See Wetherell, Taylor, & Yates, 2001, for an account of the methodology of discourse analysis.)

A slightly more cognitive index of language-based prejudice is the linguistic intergroup bias effect (Franco & Maass, 1996; Maass, 1999; Maass, Salvi, Arcuri, & Semin, 1989; see Chapter 5). Maass and her colleagues discovered that people tend to use very concrete language that simply describes events when talking about positive outgroup (and negative ingroup) characteristics, but use much more general and abstract terms that relate to enduring traits when talking about negative outgroup (and positive ingroup) characteristics. In this way we can detect negative outgroup attitudes: people become abstract and general when talking about their prejudices.

Finally, although we often have some control over what we say, we have less control over non-verbal communication channels; these can be a rich indicator of underlying emotions and prejudices (Burgoon, Buller, & Woodall, 1989; DePaulo & Friedman, 1998; see Chapter 15).

Racial and ethnic prejudices are extremely pervasive if, as is almost always the case, we have been brought up in societies in which such prejudices have prevailed. Most of us are aware of the relevant stereotypes and the task at hand is consciously to resist automatic stereotypic reactions—it would seem that less prejudiced people are more adept at this (Devine, 1989). Pettigrew noted (1987, p. 20):

Many Southerners have confessed to me . . . that even though in their minds they no longer feel prejudice toward Blacks, they still feel squeamish when they shake hands with a Black. These feelings are left over from what they learned in their families as children.

In summary, although overt racism and ethnic prejudice is both illegal and morally condemned, and most people think and act accordingly, a long history of such prejudices cannot easily be shrugged off. The germs of racism still exist and racism can be detected in various subtle forms. Racial and cultural resentment and partiality lurk beneath the surface—relatively dormant but

ready to be activated by a social environment (political regime) that might legitimise the expression of prejudice. The violence in Bosnia that began in 1992 and the more recent horrors in Rwanda have been chilling reminders of this. Closer to home, media coverage during 1996 and 1997 of Pauline Hanson's (then Federal Member for Oxley in southern Queensland) attitudes towards Aborigines and Asians created a supportive environment for the public expression of old-fashioned racist attitudes.

A final important point to bear in mind is that, although research suggests that overt discrimination may be on the wane in many Western democracies, this does not mean that the social consequences of decades or even centuries of racism will change as quickly. For example, although Australians' attitudes towards Australian Aborigines have improved dramatically in the past 25 years, the physical, material and spiritual plight of Aborigines has not.

AGEISM

In many cultures, particularly those in which the extended family thrives, older members of the community are often revered—they are considered to be wise and knowledgeable teachers and leaders. In other societies, largely those in which the nuclear family has displaced the extended family, this is often not the case (Oliver, 1986). Countries such as Australia, New Zealand, Canada, the United States and Britain fall into this latter category. In these societies the qualities of youth are highly valued and elderly people (a group that is rapidly increasing in relative number) attract generally unfavourable stereotypes. However, there is a range of subtypes that include the John Wayne conservative (patriotic, religious, nostalgic), the small-town neighbour (frugal, quiet, conservative), the perfect grandparent (wise, kind, happy), the golden-ager (adventurous, sociable, successful), the despondent (depressed, neglected), the severely impaired (incompetent, feeble) and the shrew/curmudgeon (bitter, complaining, prejudiced) (Brewer, Dull, & Lui, 1981).

Elderly people are generally treated as relatively worthless and powerless members of the community. They are denied many basic human rights and their special needs go untended. Social psychologists have only recently begun systematically to investigate **ageism** and much of the research has been done in the area of intergenerational communication (e.g. Fox & Giles, 1993; Harwood, Giles, & Ryan 1995; Hummert, 1990; Kite & Johnson, 1988; Williams, 1996; see Chapter 15).

Young adults may consider people over 65 to be grouchy, unhealthy, unattractive, unhappy, miserly, less efficient, less socially skilled, overly self-disclosing, overly controlling, feeble, egocentric, incompetent, abrasive, frail and vulnerable (see Noels, Giles, & Le Poire, 2003).

Furthermore, the young generally have little to do with the elderly and so intergenerational encounters tend to activate intergroup rather than interpersonal perceptions; these reinforce negative stereotypes that lead to avoidance and minimisation of intergenerational contact. The cycle continues and the elderly remain socially isolated and societally marginalised.

DISCRIMINATION AGAINST HOMOSEXUALS

The Romans were relatively tolerant of all forms of sexual preference, and in general there still is a great deal of cross-cultural variability in attitudes towards sexual preference (Gosselin & Wilson, 1980). It was with the advent of Christianity that social norms regarding sexual behaviour became more restrictive. Homosexuality was considered deviant and immoral, and the persecution of homosexuals became legitimate and quite acceptable.

Prejudice against homosexuals is widespread: for example, a survey in the United States showed that the majority of people believed that homosexuality was 'sick'

and should be outlawed (Levitt & Klassen, 1974) and, more recently, that only 39% of people 'would see a homosexual doctor' (Henry, 1994). Discrimination against homosexuals is often even legal: in the mid-1980s the National Party in Queensland actually passed legislation to prohibit the serving of liquor to 'perverts and deviants' (which included homosexuals) in bars. In Tasmania, many homosexual practices remained legally proscribed until very recently. It was only in 1973 that the American Psychiatric Association formally removed homosexuality from its list of mental disorders.

In general, since the late 1960s there has been a progressive liberalisation of attitudes towards homosexuals. However, the current HIV epidemic has, since the mid-1980s, whipped up a frenzy of hysteria against homosexuals (Altman, 1986; Herek & Glunt, 1988; see Box 10.2). Against this background, continued liberalisation often reveals deeply entrenched homophobia in certain sectors of the community. For example, the departure of the National Party from power in Queensland in 1989 was accompanied by swift new

---

BOX 10.2 | **AIDS and anti-gay prejudice**

FEAR SURROUNDING AIDS HAS BEEN USED TO JUSTIFY DISCRIMINATION AGAINST HOMOSEXUALS

AIDS is a serious and, as far as is known, fatal illness that develops in people infected with HIV. The virus is transmitted through exchange of certain bodily fluids—for example, through blood transfusions, by needle-sharing among intravenous drug users and by some sexual practices among gay men. Although AIDS is by no means a gay disease, the majority of people infected in Western countries have tended to be gay (63% of AIDS cases in the United States up to 1988 were gay: Herek & Glunt, 1988), so people assume a link between AIDS and homosexuality.

Fear and ignorance of AIDS, in conjunction with knowledge of its association with gays, has activated latent prejudices against gays. In many ways, AIDS has provided moral justification (grounded in fear for self and society) for overt discrimination against gay people: homophobics have felt free to come out of the closet. The promotion of gay rights can be seen by such people as tantamount to the promotion of AIDS itself.

Herek and Glunt's (1988, p. 888) discussion of public reaction in the United States to AIDS provided telling evidence for the way AIDS has been linked to homosexuality and used to justify anti-gay attitudes. The epidemic was virtually ignored by the US media in the early 1980s because it was merely a 'story of dead and dying homosexuals', and it was sometimes referred to as the 'gay plague'. Patrick Buchanan, a Republican columnist, wrote (1987, p. 23):

There is one, only one, cause of the AIDS crisis—the wilful refusal of homosexuals to cease indulging in the immoral, unnatural, unsanitary, unhealthy, and suicidal practice of anal intercourse, which is the primary means by which the AIDS virus is being spread.

He felt (Buchanan, 1987, p. 23) that the:

Democratic Party should be dragged into the court of public opinion as an un-indicted co-conspirator in America's AIDS epidemic [for] seeking to amend state and federal civil rights laws to make sodomy a protected civil right, to put homosexual behaviour, the sexual practice by which AIDS is spread, on the same moral plane with being female or being black.

The Catholic Church used the apparent link between AIDS and homosexuality to argue against civil rights protection for gay people. Others were more extreme: a mayoral candidate for the city of Houston was heard to joke publicly that his solution to the city's AIDS problem would be to 'shoot the queers' (quoted in Herek & Glunt, 1988, p. 888).

legislation by the Labor Party to repeal a mass of unenlightened laws, including those concerning homosexuality, and to pass new progressive legislation. This new legislation provoked fierce public reaction from a number of religious groups (there is good evidence for a correlation between prejudice and traditional or fundamentalist Christian attitudes; Batson, Schoenrade, & Ventis, 1993).

Similarly, in New Zealand in 1993, Parliament hotly debated the issue of whether the law should be amended to prevent discrimination against homosexuals entering the police force. In the same year, the then President Clinton met strong opposition to his proposal that homosexuals should be able to enlist in the United States armed forces. The HIV epidemic is, however, focusing the attention of social psychologists on homosexuality more strongly than in the past (e.g. Abrams, Carter, & Hogg, 1989; Cox & Gallois, 1996).

DISCRIMINATION ON THE BASIS OF PHYSICAL OR MENTAL HANDICAP

Prejudice and discrimination against the physically handicapped has a long history, in which such people have been considered repugnant and subhuman (Jodelet, 1991). For example, most circuses had a side-show alley in which various 'freaks' would be displayed (powerfully portrayed in Kevin Brownlow's movie *Freaks*) and many dramas hinge on the curiosity value of the physically handicapped (e.g. David Lynch's movie *Elephant Man*, Fellini's *Satyricon* and Victor Hugo's *Notre-Dame de Paris*).

Overt discrimination against people on the basis of physical handicap is now illegal and socially unacceptable, and societies such as Australia and New Zealand go out of their way to be sensitive to the special requirements of people with physical disabilities—for example, the provision of ramps for people in wheelchairs, and sound signals at pedestrian crossings. The staging of the para-Olympics (e.g. in Atlanta in 1996 and Sydney in 2000) is another step in the normalisation of physical handicap. Most people generally no longer derogate the physically handicapped, but we are often uneasy in their presence and uncertain how to interact with them (Heinemann, 1990). This can unintentionally produce patronising attitudes, speech and behaviour that serve to emphasise and perpetuate handicap (Fox & Giles, 1996a, 1996b; see Chapter 15).

The improvement of attitudes over the past 25 years towards physical handicap has not generalised to mental/psychological handicap. In the Middle Ages, women with schizophrenia were labelled witches and burned at the stake; Hitler's 'final solution' did not apply only to Jews but also to the insane; and in Stalin's Russia dissidents were labelled insane in order to justify their incarceration. Although Bedlam Hospital in London has long been closed, similar conditions prevail in asylums around the world: instances have recently been exposed in, for example, Greece and Romania. These are extreme cases, but ignorance and fear fuel strong prejudices and both institutionalised and face-to-face discrimination prevail.

The state of affairs in Australia was described in the Burdekin report (released in October 1993) from the Human Rights Commission—a damning indictment of Australia's violation of the human rights of the mentally ill. Society tries to overlook the existence of mental illness and to abdicate responsibility for the mentally ill. This is reflected in remarkably low funding for research into most mental illnesses—although most hospital beds are occupied by schizophrenics—and in poor resourcing for the care and therapy of psychiatric patients. Recently there has been a policy in Britain, the United States, Australia and New Zealand to 'deinstitutionalise' chronic psychiatric patients and simply to release them onto the streets—that is, release them from hospital without providing adequate alternative community resources for their support.

Another facet of prejudice against the mentally ill is the use of the 'mad' label to dehumanise and justify discrimination against minority-status groups as a whole. 'Different' becomes 'mad' (Szasz, 1970). This is the serious side of what we regularly do in jest—'You must be mad!' is a frequent exclamation on hearing someone outline a novel (read 'different') scheme. Research indicates that the stereotypical behaviours of women do not conform to what people consider to be the behaviours of a typical well-adjusted adult human being (Broverman, Broverman, Clarkson, Rosencrantz, & Vogel, 1970)—in this sense, women are 'maladjusted' (Chesler, 1972; Eichler, 1980). A similar process, in which cultural difference is made pathological by the dominant White middle-class group, occurs with respect to Blacks and other racial/ethnic minorities (Nahem, 1980; Waxman, 1977).

There is a further twist to the story. Prejudice often creates brutal conditions of existence (poverty, poor health, low self-esteem, violence, etc.) which may produce certain types of psychiatric disorder within minority groups. In this way, fear and ignorance about psychiatric illness dovetail with and may amplify ethnic or racial prejudices.

Forms of discrimination

The preceding discussion deals with some general targets of prejudice and, in so doing, inevitably speaks about different forms that discrimination can take. One important point to emerge is that a great deal of prejudice is expressed in subtle and often hidden ways—crude overt discrimination is now less frequent. We have already described modern forms of prejudice. Here we say a bit more about three types of behaviour that do not look so obviously like discrimination but nevertheless may conceal underlying prejudices: reluctance to help, tokenism and reverse discrimination.

RELUCTANCE TO HELP

Reluctance to help other groups to improve their position in society, by passively or actively declining to assist their efforts, is one way to make sure they remain disadvantaged. This strategy can be adopted by individuals (landlords may be reluctant to rent accommodation to ethnic minorities), organisations (organisations are reluctant to assist female employees by providing sensible maternity leave, flexible working hours or opportunities for job-sharing) or society as a whole (government resistance to legislate in favour of proper maternity leave provisions).

Reluctance to help can also, of course, be a hallmark of aversive racism (see above)—the combination of racial anxiety and antipathy, coupled with a belief that the magnitude of disadvantage is overstated, encourages people not to offer help. Studies show that reluctance to help is manifested only in certain conditions, specifically when such reluctance can be attributed to some factor other than prejudice. Gaertner and Dovidio's (1977) experiment, described earlier in this chapter, is an illustration of reluctance to help. White participants were more reluctant to help a Black confederate than a White confederate faced with an emergency, but only when they believed that other potential helpers were present.

TOKENISM

As the term implies, **tokenism** refers to a relatively small or trivial positive act towards members of a minority group. The action is then invoked as a defence against accusations of prejudice, and as a justification for declining to engage in larger and more meaningful positive acts or for subsequently engaging in discrimination ('Don't bother me, haven't I already done enough?'). For example, studies by Dutton and Lake (1973) and Rosenfield and colleagues (Rosenfield, Greenberg, Folger, & Borys, 1982) found that White participants who had performed a small favour for a Black stranger were subsequently less willing to engage in more effortful forms of helping than were those who had not performed the small favour. This effect was accentuated when the token action (the small favour) activated negative stereotypes about Blacks—for example, when the favour involved giving money to a Black panhandler (beggar) (see the first focus question).

Tokenism can be employed by organisations and society as a whole. In the United States there has been criticism of the token employment of minorities (Blacks, women, Hispanics) by organisations that then fail to take more fundamental and important steps towards equal opportunities. Such organisations may employ minorities as tokens to help deflect accusations of prejudice. Tokenism at this level can have damaging consequences for the self-esteem of those who are employed as token minorities (Chacko, 1982; see below).

REVERSE DISCRIMINATION

A more extreme form of tokenism is **reverse discrimination**. People with residual prejudiced attitudes sometimes go out of their way to favour members of a group against which they are prejudiced more than members of other groups. For example, Chidester (1986) had White students engage in a 'get-acquainted' conversation through audio equipment with another student who was ostensibly either Black or White. The White students systematically evaluated Black strangers more favourably than White strangers. Similar findings emerged from the Dutton and Lake (1973) study cited above.

Because reverse discrimination favours a minority group member, it can have beneficial effects in the short term. In the long run, however, it may have some harmful consequences for its recipients (Fajardo, 1985; see below), and there is as yet no evidence that reverse discrimination reduces or abolishes the deep-seated prejudices of the discriminator. Reverse discrimination is a very effective way to conceal prejudices, but it can also reflect ambivalence, the desire to appear egalitarian or genuine feelings of admiration and respect (Carver, Glass, & Katz, 1977; Gaertner & Dovidio, 1986).

For the researcher the challenge is to know when behaviour that goes out of its way to favour a minority is reverse discrimination or a genuine attempt to rectify disadvantage (e.g. affirmative action—see the second focus question).

Stigma and other effects of prejudice

The effects of prejudice on the victims of prejudice are diverse, ranging from relatively minor inconvenience to enormous suffering. In general, prejudice is harmful because it stigmatises groups and the people who belong to those groups (Crocker, Major, & Steele, 1998; Goffman, 1963; Swim & Stangor, 1998). Allport (1954) identified more than 15 possible consequences of being a victim of prejudice. Let us examine some of these effects.

SOCIAL STIGMA

Crocker and her associates define **stigma** as follows: 'Stigmatised individuals possess (or are believed to

Tokenism: She is happy now, but she may be less happy if she learned that she was hired merely to fill a gender quota.

possess) some attribute, or characteristic, that conveys a social identity that is devalued in a particular social context' (Crocker, Major, & Steele, 1998, p. 505). The targets of prejudice and discrimination are members of stigmatised groups, and thus they are stigmatised individuals. The subjective experience of stigma hinges on two factors: visibility/concealability and controllability.

Visible stigmas, such as race, gender and obesity, mean that people cannot avoid being the target of stereotypes and discrimination—being a member of a visibly stigmatised group makes the experience of prejudice inescapable (Steele & Aronson, 1995). Visibly stigmatised people cannot use concealment of the stigma to cope with the stereotypes, prejudice and harassment that the stigma may trigger. Concealable stigmas, such as homosexuality, some illnesses and some ideologies and religious affiliations, allow people to avoid the experience of prejudice. However, the cost of concealment can be high (Goffman, 1963). People have to be untrue to themselves and extra vigilant to make sure that their stigma does not inadvertently surface.

Controllable stigmas are those that people believe are chosen rather than assigned: for example, obesity, smoking and homosexuality are thought to be controllable—people are responsible for having chosen to be these things. Uncontrollable stigmas are those that people have little choice in possessing, such as race, sex and some illnesses. Controllable stigmas invite much harsher reactions and more extreme discrimination than uncontrollable stigmas. For example, Crandall (1994) has shown that fat people attract such negative reactions in contemporary Western cultures not only because

obesity is highly stigmatised but also because people believe it is controllable.

Those who believe they have a controllable stigma tend to try hard to escape the stigma. As with concealability, this can have a high cost. Many stigmas that people believe are controllable are actually not controllable or are extremely difficult to control (in many cases, obesity falls into this category). Attempts to control the stigma are largely futile, and people can experience profound feelings of failure and inadequacy in addition to the negativity of the stigma itself. Some people do, however, focus their energy on re-evaluating the stigma and on fighting prejudice and discrimination against their group (Crocker & Major, 1994).

Stigma persists for a number of fairly obvious reasons (see Crocker, Major, & Steele, 1998). Individuals and groups gain a relatively positive sense of self and social identity if they compare themselves or their group with other individuals or groups that are stigmatised—there is a self-evaluative advantage in having stigmatised outgroups as downward comparison targets (Hogg, 2000c). Stigma can legitimise inequalities of status and resource distribution that favour a dominant group: such groups are certainly going to ensure that the stigma remains in place, because it serves a system justification function—it justifies the status quo (Jost & Banaji, 1994; Jost & Kramer, 2002).

Finally, people may need to stigmatise groups that have different world views from their own; if they did not degrade and discredit outgroups in this way the frail sense of certainty in, and controllability over, life that they gained from their own world view would be shattered (Solomon, Greenberg, & Pyszczynski, 1991).

SELF-WORTH, SELF-ESTEEM AND PSYCHOLOGICAL WELLBEING

Stigmatised groups are, by definition, devalued in and by society. They are groups that have relatively low status and little power in society, and find it difficult to avoid society's consensual negative image of them. For example, African Americans past the age of 14 are aware that others have negative images of them (Rosenberg, 1979), as are Mexican Americans (Casas, Ponterotto, & Sweeney, 1987), homosexuals (D'Emilio, 1983) and many women (Crosby, 1982). Members of stigmatised groups tend to internalise these evaluations, forming an unfavourable self-image that can be manifested in relevant contexts as low **self-esteem**. For example, research reveals that women generally share men's negative stereotypes of them; women often evaluate themselves in terms of such stereotypes and, under circumstances where sex is the salient basis of self-perception, actually report a reduction in self-esteem (e.g. Hogg, 1985; Hogg & Turner, 1987b; Smith, 1985).

Groups and their members are, however, extremely ingenious in finding ways to combat low status and consensual low regard, and so depressed self-esteem is by no means an inevitable consequence of prejudice (e.g. Crocker, Blaine, & Luhtanen, 1993; Dion & Earn, 1975; Dion, Earn, & Yee, 1978; Tajfel & Turner, 1979; see Chapter 11). Although some stigmatised individuals are vulnerable to low self-esteem, diminished life satisfaction and in some cases depression, most members of stigmatised groups are able to weather the assaults and maintain a positive self-image (Crocker & Major, 1989; Crocker, Major, & Steele, 1998).

On a day-to-day basis, self-esteem can be assailed by prejudice. The experience can range from crude racial epithets and blatant physical attack to slights such as being ignored by a salesperson in a store or being served last in a bar. Cose (1993) describes the case of an African American partner in a law firm being denied access to his office because a young White lawyer who did not know him assumed that, because he was Black, he was engaged in criminal activity.

There is, however, evidence that more subtle forms of prejudice can also damage self-esteem. For example, Chacko (1982) asked women managers to rate the extent to which a number of factors (their ability, experience, education or sex) had influenced their being hired for the job. They also indicated their commitment to the organisation and their satisfaction with various aspects of the job. Those who felt that they had been hired only as token women reported less organisational commitment and job satisfaction than those who felt they had been hired on the basis of their ability (Figure 10.7). This is one way in which tokenism can have negative consequences.

Reverse discrimination can also affect self-esteem. Fajardo (1985) had White teachers grade essays that were designed to be poor, average or excellent in quality, and were attributed to either a Black or a White student. The teachers evaluated identical essays more favourably when they were attributed to Black students than to White students (Figure 10.8). Moreover, the reverse discrimination effect was more marked for average-quality essays. In the short run, this practice may furnish minority students with self-confidence. In the long run, however, some students will develop unrealistic opinions of their abilities and future prospects, resulting in severe damage to self-esteem when such hopes collide with reality.

Reverse discrimination may also prevent students from seeking the help they sometimes need early in their academic careers, with the consequence perhaps of contributing to educational disadvantage. Relatedly, the policy of affirmative action can have the unintended effect of provoking negative reaction from members of traditionally advantaged groups. They may experience a sense

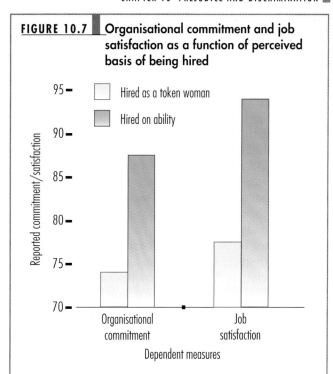

FIGURE 10.7 Organisational commitment and job satisfaction as a function of perceived basis of being hired

Note: A pitfall of tokenism. Women managers who felt they had been hired as a token woman reported less organisational commitment and less job satisfaction than women who felt they had been hired because of their ability.
Source: Based on data from Chacko (1982).

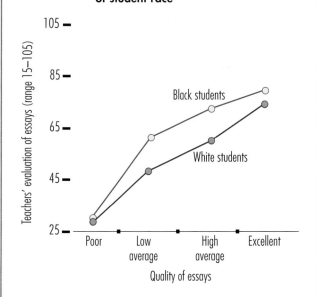

FIGURE 10.8 White teachers' evaluations of student essays of varying quality as a function of student race

Note: White teachers evaluated Black students' essays more favourably than White students' essays, particularly where the essays were of average, rather than poor or excellent, quality. An unintended consequence of reverse discrimination such as this is that Black students would be less likely to seek or be given guidance to improve their actually very average performance.
Source: Based on data from Fajardo (1985).

of injustice and relative deprivation (see Chapter 11) that provokes behaviours designed to re-establish equity (see Chapter 12) or reassert the superior status of their group. This can eventually affect minorities' self-esteem.

STEREOTYPE THREAT

Because stigmatised groups know exactly the negative stereotypes that others have of them, they experience what Steele and Aronson (1995; Steele, Spencer, & Aronson, 2002) have called **stereotype threat**. Stigmatised individuals are aware that others may judge and treat them stereotypically and, thus, on tasks that really matter to them, they worry that through their behaviour they may even confirm the stereotypes. These concerns not only increase anxiety but can also impair task performance. For example, an academically ambitious Aboriginal Australian, aware of stereotypes of intellectual inferiority, may be extremely anxious when answering a question in class—she would be worried that the slightest mistake would be interpreted stereotypically. This anxiety may actually affect behaviour adversely.

According to Steele, Spencer and Aronson (2002), stereotype threat is greatest when there are cues that the context is dominated by a cultural world view that differs from that of our own group.

To test the stereotype threat hypothesis, Steele and Aronson (1995) had Black and White students anticipate taking a 'very difficult' test that was defined as being 'diagnostic of intellectual ability' or 'just a laboratory exercise'. They then completed a number of measures designed to assess awareness of racial stereotypes—for example, completing ambiguous sentence fragments such as '____ CE' or '____ ERIOR'. As predicted, Black students who were anticipating a difficult test that was diagnostic of intellectual ability were more likely than other participants to complete the fragments with race-related words (e.g. race, inferior). Steele and Aronson also found that Black students actually performed worse on these tests than White students of equivalent scholastic aptitude.

Stereotype threat has now been found in many different contexts (see summary by Wright & Taylor, 2003)—for example, women and mathematics, low socioeconomic status and intelligence, the elderly and memory, women and negotiation skills, and Black and White men and athletic performance. One way of coping with stereotype threat is *domain disidentification*—that is, reducing the degree to which our identity is tied to the performance that may attract negative feedback (e.g. Major & Schmader, 1998).

FAILURE AND DISADVANTAGE

The victims of prejudice belong to groups that are denied access to those resources that society makes available for people to thrive and succeed, such as good education, health, housing and employment. Discrimination thus creates clearly visible evidence of real disadvantage and of manifest failure to achieve the high standards set by society. This sense of failure can be internalised by victims of prejudice so that they become chronically apathetic and unmotivated: they simply give up trying because of the obvious impossibility of succeeding.

There is some evidence that in certain circumstances women tend to anticipate failure more than men and lose motivation (e.g. Smith, 1985). As we saw earlier, when they do succeed they may attribute their success externally to factors such as luck or the ease of the task.

In Chapter 11 we discuss deprivation and disadvantage more fully. One observation that needs to be made is that, although stigmatised groups are clearly disadvantaged, members of those groups often deny any personal experience of discrimination. For example, Crosby (1982) found that employed women who were discriminated against with respect to pay rarely indicated that they had personally experienced any sex discrimination. The denial of personal discrimination was remarkably high (e.g. Crosby, 1984; Crosby, Cordova, & Jaskar, 1993; Crosby, Pufall, Snyder, O'Connell, & Whalen, 1989) and has been found among members of other stigmatised groups (Guimond & Dubé-Simard, 1983; Major, 1994; Taylor, Wright, & Porter, 1994).

ATTRIBUTIONAL AMBIGUITY

Attribution processes can affect stigmatised people in a rather unusual way, via attributional ambiguity. Stigmatised individuals are very sensitive to the causes of others' treatment of them (Crocker & Major, 1989): Did she fail to serve me at the bar because I am Black or simply because someone else shouted louder? Did she serve me ahead of all others because I am Black and she is trying to conceal her racism? Was I promoted quickly to comply with an affirmative action policy or because of my intrinsic ability? Attributional ambiguity can quite obviously lead to suspicion and mistrust in relationships.

Attributional ambiguity also does no favours to stigmatised individuals' self-esteem. Stigmatised people often fail to take personal credit for positive outcomes—they can attribute them to affirmative action, tokenism or reverse discrimination. Stigmatised individuals may also underattribute negative reactions from others to prejudice. For example, Ruggiero and Taylor (1995) had women receive negative evaluations from a male evaluator. The likelihood that the evaluator was prejudiced was varied experimentally. The women attributed the negative evaluation to prejudice only when the evaluator was almost 100% likely to be prejudiced. They attributed all of the more ambiguous evaluations to the inadequacy of their own work.

SELF-FULFILLING PROPHECIES

Prejudiced attitudes, covertly or overtly, produce discriminatory behaviour that cumulatively, across time and individuals, creates disadvantage. In this way, a stereotypical belief can create a material reality that confirms the belief: it is a **self-fulfilling prophecy** (see reviews by Jussim & Fleming, 1996; Jussim, Eccles, & Madon, 1996). For example, Eden (1990) primed platoon leaders in the Israeli Defence Force with high-performance expectations for their platoon. After an 11-week training program, platoons with high-expectation leaders outperformed platoons with 'no-expectation' leaders.

The most famous study of self-fulfilling prophecy is Rosenthal and Jacobson's (1968) classic experiment on teacher expectations in the classroom. Rosenthal and Jacobson administered an IQ test to elementary school children and told their teachers that the results of the test would be a reliable predictor of which children would 'bloom' (show rapid intellectual development in the near future). The teachers were given the names of the 20 'bloomers'; in fact, the 20 names were randomly chosen by the researchers and there were no IQ differences between bloomers and non-bloomers. Very quickly, the teachers rated the non-bloomers as being less curious, less interested and less happy than the bloomers—that is, the teachers developed stereotypical expectations about the two groups. Grades for work were consistent with these expectations.

Rosenthal and Jacobson measured the children's IQ at the end of the first year, and at the start and end of the second year. They found that in both years the bloomers showed a significantly greater IQ gain than the non-bloomers (see Figure 10.9). Sceptics simply did not believe this, so Rosenthal and Rubin (1978) conducted a **meta-analysis** of 345 follow-up studies to prove that the phenomenon really exists.

Another classic study of self-fulfilling prophecy was conducted by Word, Zanna and Cooper (1974). In a first experiment, White participants, acting as job interviewers, interviewed Black and White applicants. They were found to treat the Black and White applicants very differently—more speech errors (e.g. poor grammar, imprecision, disrupted fluency), shorter interviews and less non-verbal engagement with the Blacks than the Whites. In a second experiment, another set of White participants was trained to use either the Black or the White interview style obtained in the first experiment to interview a White job applicant. Interviewers who used the Black interview style subsequently considered that the White applicant had performed less well and was more nervous than did those interviewers who used the White interview style.

The process whereby beliefs create reality has been researched systematically over a number of years

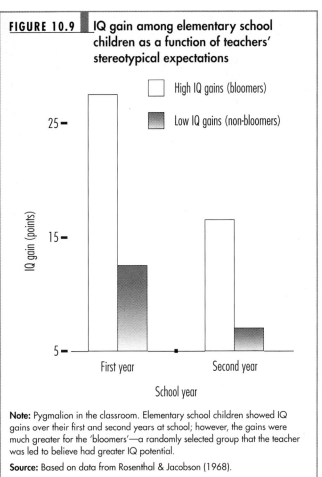

FIGURE 10.9 IQ gain among elementary school children as a function of teachers' stereotypical expectations

Note: Pygmalion in the classroom. Elementary school children showed IQ gains over their first and second years at school; however, the gains were much greater for the 'bloomers'—a randomly selected group that the teacher was led to believe had greater IQ potential.

Source: Based on data from Rosenthal & Jacobson (1968).

(Snyder, 1981, 1984). Snyder and his colleagues used a paradigm involving the creation of an expectation in the observer that someone he was going to meet had an extravert personality. (Note that the manipulation in this paradigm is limited to the observer.) The consequences for both the observer's and the actor's beliefs and behaviours were carefully tracked through the entire interaction process to an endpoint where the actor's behaviour and self-perception conformed to the initial expectation (see Figure 10.10).

According to Jussim and Fleming's (1996) review, there is good evidence for the creation of behavioural confirmation of stereotypical expectations based on gender, limited evidence in the case of race and ethnicity and no evidence for socioeconomic status.

Social psychological research on self-fulfilling prophecy has focused almost exclusively on dyadic (one-on-one) influence. Under these circumstances, expectations do create reality but the overall effect is small: only about 4% of a person's behaviour is affected by another's expectations. Jussim and associates reviewed the relevant literature (Jussim & Fleming, 1996; Jussim, Eccles, & Madon, 1996) and concluded that, although 4% may appear small, it is quite significant if you

Self-fulfilling prophecy: These children differ in personality, race and gender—all factors that can create in their teacher scholastic expectations that may become a reality.

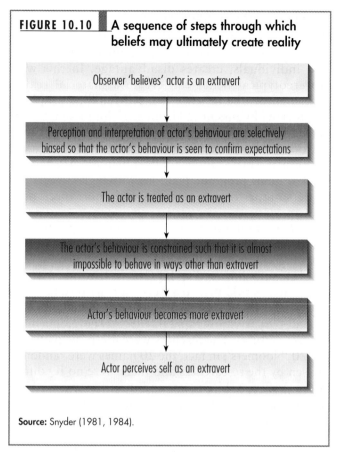

FIGURE 10.10 | A sequence of steps through which beliefs may ultimately create reality

Observer 'believes' actor is an extravert

Perception and interpretation of actor's behaviour are selectively biased so that the actor's behaviour is seen to confirm expectations

The actor is treated as an extravert

The actor's behaviour is constrained such that it is almost impossible to behave in ways other than extravert

Actor's behaviour becomes more extravert

Actor perceives self as an extravert

Source: Snyder (1981, 1984).

consider self-fulfilling prophecy effects in the real world of intergroup relations. In natural dyadic interactions people may be more inclined to perceive others in terms of personality rather than social stereotypes. In intergroup contexts, however, stereotypes and group perceptions come into play, the stereotypes match reality to some degree (stereotypes are not entirely arbitrary) and the actor encounters stereotypical expectations over and over again from many different outgroup members in a variety of social contexts. The 4% will probably be greatly magnified.

Stereotype threat (Steele, Spencer, & Aronson, 2002; see above) may also contribute to a self-fulfilling prophecy. Indeed, research on race-related academic underachievement in the United States invokes stereotype threat as a contributing factor. Black students are continually anxious about stereotypical interpretation of their academic failures. Cumulatively, this produces enormous anxiety and can encourage Black students to reduce their efforts, to have lower academic ambitions and, ultimately, to drop out of school altogether. A similar stereotype threat analysis has been used in the United States for women's underachievement and underrepresentation in mathematics and science.

VIOLENCE AND GENOCIDE

Much of the emphasis of this chapter has been on indirect or subtle forms of prejudice and their effects. This reflects relatively accurately the current state of affairs in most Western democracies in which antidiscrimination legislation is in place. For example, there is a lively campaign to purge language of racist and sexist terminology. It is important, however, not to lose sight of the extremes of prejudiced behaviour. Prejudiced attitudes tend to have common themes: the targets of prejudice are considered, for example, to be dirty, stupid, insensitive, repulsive, aggressive and psychologically unstable (Brigham, 1971; Katz & Braly, 1933). This is a constellation that evaluates others as relatively worthless human beings who do not need or deserve to be treated with consideration, courtesy and respect. Together with fear and hatred, this is a potent mix. It dehumanises other people and, given certain social circumstances, can permit individual violence, mass aggression or even systematic extermination.

In the absence of institutional or legislative support, dehumanisation usually sponsors individual acts of violence. For example, in Australia there are isolated attacks on South-East Asian immigrants; in the United States the Ku Klux Klan was notorious for its lynchings of Blacks (see the powerful movie *Mississippi Burning*); in Germany there are Nazi-style attacks on Turkish immigrants; and in India female infanticide is still practised—albeit covertly (Freed & Freed, 1989).

When prejudice is morally accepted and legally endorsed in a society, systematic acts of mass discrimination can be perpetrated. This can take the form of systems of apartheid, in which target groups are isolated from the rest of the community. South Africa is the most obvious recent example of this sort of system, but a similar system of segregation was practised in educational contexts in the United States until the mid-1950s, and the existence of reservations for native peoples in many countries (e.g. Australia, the United States) also attests to segregation.

Apartheid and segregation often come equipped with a formidable array of social justifications in terms of benefits for the segregated group (see the third focus question).

The most extreme form of legitimised prejudice is genocide (Staub, 1989), where the target group is systematically exterminated. The dehumanisation process makes it relatively easy for people to perpetrate the most appalling acts of degradation and violence on others (see Thomas Keneally's biographical novel *Schindler's Ark* (1982), or the movie *The Killing Fields*). The most chilling and best-documented recent instance of genocide is, of course, the Holocaust of the early 1940s, in which six million Jews (nearly twice the population of New Zealand) were systematically exterminated by the Nazis in death camps in Central Europe. At the massive Auschwitz complex in Poland, two million Jews were gassed to death between January 1942 and the summer of 1944 (a rate of 2220 men, women and children each day).

There are more recent examples of genocide: Pol Pot's 'killing fields' in Kampuchea in the 1970s; Saddam Hussein's extermination of Kurds in northern Iraq and Shi'ites in southern Iraq; the Bosnian Serbs' campaign of 'ethnic cleansing' in Bosnia; and the mutual genocide of the Hutu and Tutsi in Rwanda.

Genocide can also be practised more indirectly, by creating conditions of massive material disadvantage in which a group effectively exterminates itself through disease, and through suicide and murder based on alcoholism, drug abuse and acute despair. The plight of the Australian Aborigines and Brazilian Indians falls squarely in this camp.

Another form of genocide (although 'ethnic death' is a more appropriate term to distinguish it from the brutality of the Holocaust) is cultural assimilation, in which entire cultural groups disappear as discrete entities through widespread intermarriage and systematic suppression of their culture and language (e.g. Taft, 1973; see Chapter 15). This is particularly prevalent if societies do not practise multiculturalism (e.g. England's treatment of the Welsh and the Scottish, and Indonesia's stance towards the people of East Timor and other islands and enclaves across the vast archipelago).

Another form of ethnic death occurs when a group is excluded from the official history of a nation. Pilger (1989) notes that this is the case with the Australian Aborigines.

Explanations of prejudice and discrimination

Why are people prejudiced? Not surprisingly, theories of prejudice have tended to focus on the more extreme forms of prejudice, in particular the aggression and violence discussed above. At the beginning of the 20th century it was popular to consider prejudice to be an innate and instinctive reaction to certain categories of person (e.g. certain races), much as animals would react in instinctive ways to one another (Klineberg, 1940). This sort of approach is no longer popular, as it does not stand up well to scientific scrutiny. However, there may be an innate *component* to prejudice. There is some evidence that higher animals, including humans, have an inherent fear of the unfamiliar and unusual (Hebb & Thompson, 1968), which might set the mould for negative attitudes towards groups that are considered different in certain ways.

There is also evidence for a **mere exposure effect** (Zajonc, 1968), in which people's attitudes towards various stimuli (e.g. other people) improve as a direct function of repeated exposure to or familiarity with the stimulus, provided that initial reactions to the stimuli are not negative (Perlman & Oskamp, 1971).

Another perspective rests on the belief that prejudices are learned. Indeed, Tajfel (1981b) argues that hatred and suspicion of certain groups is learned early in life, before the child knows anything about the target group, and that this provides an emotional framework that colours all subsequent information about, and experience with, the group (see Brown, 1995; Durkin, 1995; Milner, 1996). For example, Barrett and Short (1992) found that 5–10-year-old English children had little factual knowledge about other European countries, yet expressed clear preferences; the French and Spanish were liked most, followed by Italians, and Germans were liked least. Generally speaking, ethnic biases are very marked among 4–5-year-olds because, at that age, the social-cognitive system relies on obvious perceptual features that are unambiguous bases for categorisation and social comparison (Aboud, 1988). These emotional preferences provide a potent framework for the acquisition of parental attitudes and behaviour (Goodman, 1964; Katz, 1976; see Chapter 5).

The transmission of parental prejudices can occur through parental modelling (e.g. the child witnesses parental expressions of racial hatred), instrumental/operant conditioning (e.g. parental approval for racist behaviour and disapproval for non-racist behaviour) or classical conditioning (e.g. a White child receives a severe parental beating for playing with an Australian Aboriginal child).

Below we discuss some major theories of prejudice.

These approaches focus largely on prejudice as the mass expression of aggression against certain groups. In Chapter 11 we continue with the theme of prejudice, but in a different guise—one that considers prejudice to be a form of intergroup behaviour based on social psychological processes associated with the categorisation of people into social categories.

FRUSTRATION–AGGRESSION

The rise of anti-Semitism in Europe, particularly Germany, during the 1930s placed the explanation of prejudice high on social psychology's agenda. In 1939 Dollard and colleagues published their **frustration–aggression hypothesis**, in which they argued that 'the occurrence of aggressive behaviour always presupposes the existence of frustration, and contrariwise, the existence of frustration always leads to some form of aggression' (Dollard, Doob, Miller, Mowrer, & Sears, 1939: 1). The theory was grounded in the psychodynamic assumption that there is a fixed amount of psychic energy available for the human mind to perform psychological activities, and that the completion of a psychological activity is *cathartic:* that is, it dissipates aroused energy and returns the system to psychological equilibrium.

Dollard and associates argued that personal goals entail arousal of psychic energy for their achievement, and that goal achievement is cathartic. If, however, goal achievement is impeded (i.e. frustrated), psychic energy remains activated and the system is in a state of psychological disequilibrium that can be corrected only by aggression. In other words, frustration produces an 'instigation to aggress' and the only way to achieve catharsis is through aggression.

The target of aggression is usually the perceived agent of frustration, but in many cases the agent of frustration is amorphous (e.g. a bureaucracy), indeterminate (the economy), too powerful (someone very big and strong wielding a weapon), unavailable (a specific individual bureaucrat) or someone you love (a parent). These, and many other circumstances, prevent or inhibit aggression against the perceived source of frustration and cause the entire amount of frustration-induced aggression to be *displaced* onto an alternative target (a person or an inanimate object) that can be legitimately aggressed against without fear. In other words, a **scapegoat** is found.

Although this theory has been applied extensively, and relatively successfully, to the study of interpersonal aggression (see Chapter 12), Dollard and associates' principal aim was to explain intergroup aggression—specifically, the violence and aggression associated with prejudice. If a large number of people (a group) is frustrated in its goals by another group which is too powerful or remote to be aggressed against, the aggression is displaced onto a weaker group that acts as a scapegoat. Figure 10.11 shows how the frustration–aggression hypothesis could be used to explain the rise of anti-Semitism in Germany in the 1920s and 1930s.

An archival study by Hovland and Sears (1940) provides some support for this sort of analysis. They correlated an economic index of frustrated ambitions (the price of cotton) with an index of racial aggression (number of lynchings of Blacks) in the southern United States over a 50-year period. The two indexes were negatively correlated: as the price of cotton fell (frustration), the number of lynchings rose (displaced aggression).

Much research on intergroup aggression has focused on the notion of **displacement** which lies at the heart of Dollard and associates' account of scapegoating and thus prejudice and intergroup aggression. In one study

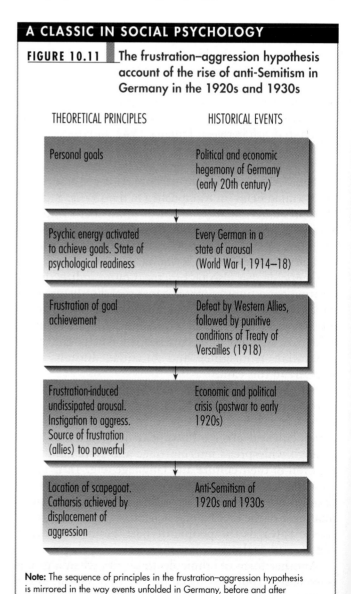

A CLASSIC IN SOCIAL PSYCHOLOGY

FIGURE 10.11 | The frustration–aggression hypothesis account of the rise of anti-Semitism in Germany in the 1920s and 1930s

THEORETICAL PRINCIPLES	HISTORICAL EVENTS
Personal goals	Political and economic hegemony of Germany (early 20th century)
Psychic energy activated to achieve goals. State of psychological readiness	Every German in a state of arousal (World War I, 1914–18)
Frustration of goal achievement	Defeat by Western Allies, followed by punitive conditions of Treaty of Versailles (1918)
Frustration-induced undissipated arousal. Instigation to aggress. Source of frustration (allies) too powerful	Economic and political crisis (postwar to early 1920s)
Location of scapegoat. Catharsis achieved by displacement of aggression	Anti-Semitism of 1920s and 1930s

Note: The sequence of principles in the frustration–aggression hypothesis is mirrored in the way events unfolded in Germany, before and after World War I, and led to blatant anti-Semitism.

(Miller & Bugelski, 1948), young men at a summer camp eagerly anticipated a night out on the town but had their goals frustrated by the camp authorities, who announced that they would have to stay behind to perform some uninteresting and difficult tests. Relative to a control group that was not frustrated in this way, the young men's stereotypical attitudes towards two minority groups were found to deteriorate as a consequence of the frustration.

Other research is inconclusive. For example, the frustration of doing badly on a test or experimental task has been shown to increase racial prejudice (Cowen, Landes, & Schaet, 1958), reduce prejudice (Burnstein & McRae, 1962) and leave prejudice unaffected (Stagner & Congdon, 1955); and there is no systematic evidence for an inverse correlation between international and intranational aggression (i.e. aggression displaced onto another nation is not available to be vented intranationally) (Tanter, 1966, 1969).

In some of this research it is difficult to know whether aggression is displaced (i.e. the entire quantity of aggression is vented on a specific scapegoat) or generalised (i.e. anger towards the agent of frustration spills over onto irrelevant other stimuli). For example, in the Miller and Bugelski (1948) study, the participants also felt angry towards the camp authorities. If both displacement and generalisation are operating, it becomes difficult to predict the target of aggression.

To address this problem, Miller (1948) suggested that displacement and generalisation might work against one another. Thus, scapegoats are likely to be not too similar to the real source of frustration (displacement is based on inhibition of aggression against the real source of frustration, and such inhibition will be stronger for targets that are more similar to the real source) but not too dissimilar either (generalisation implies that the magnitude of aggression will decrease as the potential target is less and less similar to the real source). Although it is often possible with the advantage of hindsight to use this principle to account for the scapegoat, it is difficult to predict it with any certainty (e.g. Horowitz, 1973).

The frustration–aggression hypothesis confronts another, major obstacle from research showing that frustration is neither necessary nor sufficient for aggression. Aggression can occur in the absence of frustration, and frustration does not necessarily result in aggression (Bandura, 1973; Berkowitz, 1962). The consequence is that the frustration–aggression hypothesis can explain only a limited subset of intergroup aggression. Other constructs are needed to explain other forms of intergroup aggression, or prejudice and intergroup aggression as a whole.

In an attempt to rescue the hypothesis, Berkowitz (1962) proposed three major changes:

1. The probability of frustration-induced aggression actually being vented is increased by the presence of situational cues to aggression, including past or present associations of a specific group (scapegoat) with conflict or dislike.
2. It is not objective frustration that instigates aggression but the subjective (cognitive) feeling of being frustrated.
3. Frustration is only one of a large number of aversive events (e.g. pain, extreme temperatures and other noxious stimuli) that can instigate aggression.

This revamped frustration–aggression theory has attracted empirical support for the role of environmental cues and cognitive mediators in controlling the amount and direction of aggression (Berkowitz, 1974; Konečni, 1979). However, its main application has been in the explanation of **collective behaviour** (riots) and **relative deprivation** (these are discussed in Chapter 11).

Despite these modifications, the frustration–aggression hypothesis has other limitations as an explanation of mass intergroup aggression and prejudice. The phenomenon to be explained is one in which the attitudes and behaviour of a large number of people are regulated and directed so that there is a great deal of uniformity as well as a clear logic to it. Critics have argued that the frustration–aggression hypothesis does not adequately explain this core feature of prejudice because it is a reductionist approach that arrives at group behaviour by aggregating individual psychological/emotional states in a communication vacuum (Billig, 1976; Brown, 2000; Hogg & Abrams, 1988).

For instance, the group members in this model do not speak to one another and are not exposed to mass communication or history. They are passive victims of individual frustration and anger rather than active participants in a social process involving construction, internalisation and the enacting of group norms (see Chapter 7). Aggression is only widespread and directed at the same target because a large number of people individually express aggression simultaneously, and coincidentally select the same target.

THE AUTHORITARIAN PERSONALITY

The liberation of Europe from the Nazis in 1945 revealed details of the Holocaust that were so appalling it seemed that only people with dysfunctional personalities could perpetrate such atrocities. It was in this context that Adorno, Frenkel-Brunswik, Levinson and Sanford (1950) developed their authoritarian personality explanation of prejudice. Unlike Dollard and associates, who believed that anyone could be prejudiced as it depended on the displacement of frustration-induced aggression, Adorno and associates believed that only people with prejudiced personalities could be prejudiced.

Authoritarianism and child-rearing: An authoritarian personality in the making?

They argued that certain people are bigots who are prejudiced against all minorities. They have an **authoritarian personality** that is defined by a constellation of characteristics. These include respect for and deference to authority and authority figures, obsession with rank and status, a tendency to displace anger and resentment onto weaker others, intolerance of ambiguity and uncertainty, a need for a rigidly defined world and problems with achieving intimacy.

This constellation originates in early childhood. Adopting a psychodynamic perspective, Adorno and associates argue that children whose parents employ excessively harsh and disciplinarian practices to secure emotional dependence and obedience develop an ambiguity in which they both love and hate their parents. This ambiguity is stressful and seeks resolution. Owing to guilt and fear the hatred cannot be expressed, so it is *repressed* and finds expression through displacement onto weaker others, while the parents and the power and authority they represent are idealised. This resolution of ambivalence provides an enduring framework for future life and is generalised to all authority figures (see the fourth focus question—though read the rest of this section and then think again).

For their original research, Adorno and associates distributed to 2000 members of organisations in California a questionnaire monitoring (a) anti-Semitism, (b) general ethnocentrism, (c) political and economic conservatism, and (d) potential for fascism. Some respondents responded to projective tests and were also interviewed about their childhood. The results were encouraging, although Brown (1965) raised several methodological criticisms. Among the most damning were:

- The scales were scored in such a way that people's tendency to agree with items (acquiescence response set) would inflate the correlation between the scales.

- Because the interviewers knew both the hypotheses and the authoritarianism scores of the interviewees, there was a danger of confirmatory bias (Rosenthal, 1966).

Nevertheless, the authoritarian personality has, over half a century, attracted an enormous amount of interest (e.g. Bray & Noble, 1978; Christie & Jahoda, 1954; Titus & Hollander, 1957; for an overview see Duckitt, 2000).

There are, however, a number of limitations to a personality explanation of prejudice (Billig, 1976; Brown, 1995, 2000; Hogg & Abrams, 1988; Reynolds, Turner, Haslam, & Ryan, in press). Powerful situational and sociocultural factors are underemphasised.

For instance, Pettigrew (1958) tested the authoritarian personality theory in a cross-cultural comparison between South Africa and the southern and the northern United States. He found that although Whites from South Africa and the southern United States were significantly more racist than those from the northern United States, they did not differ in terms of how authoritarian their personalities were. Pettigrew concluded from this and other findings that, while personality may predispose some people to be prejudiced in some contexts, a culture of prejudice that embodies societal norms legitimising prejudice is both necessary and sufficient.

This conclusion is supported by other findings. For example, Minard (1952) found that the majority (60%) of White miners in a West Virginian coal-mining community readily shifted from racist to non-racist attitudes and behaviours as a function of situational norms encouraging or inhibiting prejudice, and Stephan and Rosenfield (1978) found that interracial contact was a more important determinant than parental background of change in racial attitudes among children.

Adorno and associates believed that prejudice is laid down in childhood as an enduring personality style. This perspective is particularly troublesome in the light of evidence for sudden and dramatic changes in people's attitudes and behaviours regarding social groups. For example, the extreme anti-Semitism in Germany between the wars arose in a short period of only ten years—far too short a time for a whole generation of German families to adopt new child-rearing practices giving rise to authoritarian and prejudiced children.

Even more dramatic are sudden changes in attitudes and behaviours contingent on single events, such as the Japanese bombing of Pearl Harbor in 1941, the Argentinian occupation of the Falkland Islands in 1982, the French sinking of the *Rainbow Warrior* in Auckland Harbour in 1985 and the Indonesian massacre of East Timorese in Dili in 1991. Personalities did not have time to change, yet attitudes and behaviours did.

Power and authority: Respect for authority figures, deference to authority, and obsession with rank and status.

DOGMATISM AND CLOSED-MINDEDNESS

Another personality theory of prejudice has been proposed by Rokeach (1948, 1960). It is closely related to the authoritarian personality theory but, in the light of evidence that authoritarianism is not restricted to people who are politically and economically right-wing (e.g. Tetlock, 1984), focuses on cognitive style. Rokeach argues for the existence of a more generalised syndrome of intolerance called **dogmatism** or **closed-mindedness**. It is characterised by the isolation of contradictory belief systems from one another, resistance to belief change in the light of new information, and appeals to authority to justify the correctness of existing beliefs. Scales devised by Rokeach (1960) to measure these personality styles have good reliability, correlate well with measures of authoritarianism and have been used extensively.

However, the concept of dogmatism as an explanation of prejudice has the same limitations as the authoritarian personality theory. It is a concept that reduces a group phenomenon to an aggregation of individual personality predispositions and largely overlooks the wider sociocultural context of prejudice and the role of group norms (Billig, 1976; Billig & Cochrane, 1979).

RIGHT-WING AUTHORITARIANISM

Recently, the idea of authoritarianism has been revived but without the psychodynamic and personality aspect. Altemeyer (e.g. 1988, 1994, 1998; see also Duckitt, 1989) has approached authoritarianism as a collection of attitudes, with three components:

1. *conventionalism*—adherence to societal conventions that are endorsed by established authorities;
2. *authoritarian aggression*—support for aggression towards social deviants;
3. *authoritarian submission*—submission to society's established authorities.

Altemeyer (1981) devised the right-wing authoritarianism (RWA) scale to measure this constellation of attitudinal factors. From this perspective, authoritarianism is an ideology that varies from person to person; it suggests that positions of power within a social hierarchy come from correct and moral behaviour (i.e. following social conventions). Questioning authority and tradition are transgressions that ought to invite the wrath of legitimate authorities. Authoritarianism thus legitimises and maintains the status quo.

SOCIAL DOMINANCE THEORY

The role of ideology in prejudice is also important in work by Sidanius and Pratto and associates. They describe a relatively sophisticated but nonetheless 'individual differences' analysis of exploitative power-based intergroup relations—called **social dominance theory** (e.g. Pratto, 1999; Pratto, Sidanius, Stallworth, & Malle, 1994; Sidanius & Pratto, 1999).

Social dominance theory explains the extent to which people accept or reject societal ideologies or myths that legitimise hierarchy and discrimination, or legitimise equality and fairness. People who desire their own group to be dominant and superior to outgroups have a high social dominance orientation that encourages them to reject egalitarian ideologies and accept myths that legitimise hierarchy and discrimination. These kinds of people are more inclined to be prejudiced than people with a low social dominance orientation.

Social dominance theory was originally about the desire for ingroup domination over outgroups. More recently, it has offered a view of a more general desire for unequal relations between groups, irrespective of whether one's own group is at the top or bottom of the status hierarchy (e.g. Sidanius, Levin, Federico, & Pratto, 2001). This development makes social dominance theory look more like **system justification theory** (e.g. Jost & Hunyadi, 2002; see Chapter 11 for details). System justification theory argues that certain social conditions cause people to resist social change and instead justify and protect the existing social system, even if this maintains their own group's position of disadvantage.

BELIEF CONGRUENCE

At the same time as his personality theory of prejudice (above), Rokeach (1960) proposed a separate **belief congruence theory**. Belief systems are important anchoring points for individuals and, thus, interindividual similarity or congruence of belief systems confirms the validity of our own beliefs. Congruence is therefore rewarding and produces attraction and positive attitudes (Byrne, 1971; Festinger, 1954). The converse is that incongruence produces negative attitudes. For Rokeach, 'belief is more important than ethnic or racial membership as a determinant of social discrimination' (Rokeach, 1960, p. 135)—prejudice is not an attitude based on group memberships but an individual's reaction to perceived lack of congruence of belief systems.

Research using a paradigm in which participants report their attitudes towards others (presented photographically or as verbal descriptions), who are either of the same or a different race and have either similar or different beliefs to the participant, shows that belief does seem to be a more important determinant of attitude than race (e.g. Byrne & Wong, 1962; Hendrick, Bixenstine, & Hawkins, 1971; Rokeach & Mezei, 1966). However, when it comes to more intimate behaviours such as friendship, race is more important than belief (e.g. Insko, Nacoste, & Moe, 1983; Triandis & Davis, 1965).

There are at least two problems with belief congruence as an explanation of prejudice. The first is that Rokeach (1960) hedges his theory with an important qualification. Under circumstances where prejudice is institutionalised or socially sanctioned, belief congruence plays no part—prejudice is a matter of ethnic group membership (see Figure 10.12). This is a restrictive exemption clause that excludes what we would consider to be the most obvious and distressing manifestations of prejudice: for example, ethnic prejudice in Rwanda and religious prejudice in Northern Ireland would be excluded.

A second problem arises with the relatively small amount of prejudice that Rokeach has left himself to

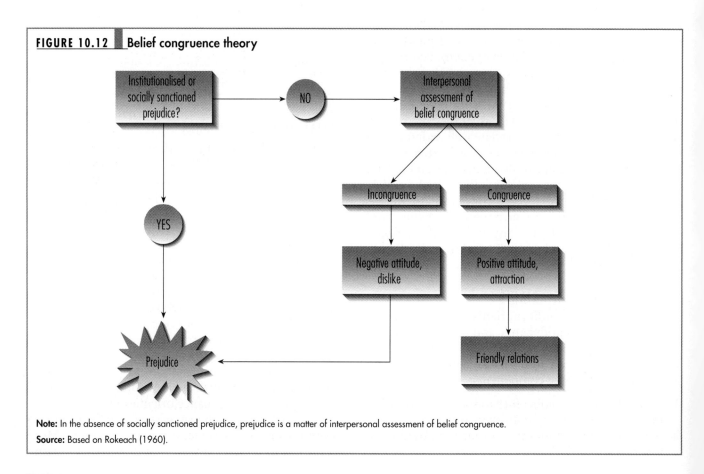

FIGURE 10.12 | Belief congruence theory

Note: In the absence of socially sanctioned prejudice, prejudice is a matter of interpersonal assessment of belief congruence.
Source: Based on Rokeach (1960).

Belief congruence: Similar clothes, similar behaviour, and similar beliefs—a potent recipe for liking and social harmony.

explain. His explanation of how belief congruence may influence prejudice in these circumstances may actually be an explanation of how belief similarity produces interpersonal attraction (Brown, 2000; Brown & Turner, 1981). The research paradigm used to test belief congruence theory has people rate their attitude towards a number of stimulus individuals presented in a repeated measures design (in which a series of treatments is applied to each individual). Some stimuli are of the same race and others of a different race (the race variable) and they all have different beliefs from one another (the belief variable). The absence of clear belief homogeneity within each group and belief discontinuity between groups may muddy intergroup boundaries and focus attention on differences among stimulus individuals rather than on their racial or ethnic group memberships. The research paradigm may inadvertently have diminished the contextual salience of race or ethnicity such that participants react to the stimulus individuals as individuals, not as members of racial or ethnic groups.

This interpretation has some support from experiments where group membership is clearly differentiated from belief similarity. For example, Billig and Tajfel (1973) had children allocate rewards to anonymous other children, who were defined either as having similar attitudes to them (on the basis of a bogus picture-preference task) or for whom no information on similarity was provided, and who were either explicitly categorised as being members of the same group (simply labelled X group) or for whom no categorisation information was provided. This research adopted the **minimal**

group paradigm, which is described in detail in Chapter 11. The focal outcome measure was **discrimination** in favour of some target individuals over others.

Figure 10.13 shows that, although belief similarity increased favouritism (as would be predicted from belief congruence theory), the effect of categorisation on favouritism was much stronger, and it was only in the two categorisation conditions that the amount of discrimination was statistically significant (i.e. discrimination scores were significantly greater than zero). Belief congruence theory would not predict these last two effects; similar findings emerged from an experiment by Allen and Wilder (1975).

Perhaps most conclusively, Diehl (1988) found that, although attitudinally similar individuals were liked more than dissimilar individuals (though there was little difference in discrimination), attitudinally similar outgroups were liked less (and discriminated against more) than dissimilar outgroups.

OTHER EXPLANATIONS

There are two other major perspectives on the explanation of prejudice. The first concerns how people construct and use stereotypes. This is dealt with mainly in Chapter 2 as part of our discussion of social cognition and social thinking, but it surfaces also in Chapter 11. The second perspective approaches prejudice and

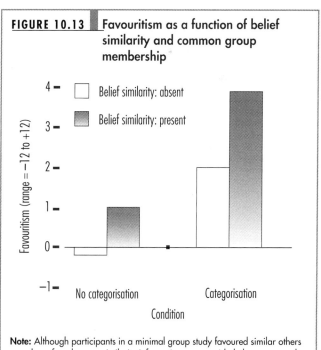

FIGURE 10.13 Favouritism as a function of belief similarity and common group membership

Favouritism (range = −12 to +12)

☐ Belief similarity: absent
▨ Belief similarity: present

Condition: No categorisation / Categorisation

Note: Although participants in a minimal group study favoured similar others over those for whom no similarity information was provided, there was much stronger favouritism for others who were simply explicitly categorised as being ingroup members: in fact, statistically significant favouritism was expressed only towards ingroup members.

Source: Based on data from Billig & Tajfel (1973).

discrimination as an aspect of intergroup behaviour as a whole. This is dealt with in Chapter 11.

Because the material in the next chapter can be treated as an extension of this chapter, we reserve our discussion of prejudice reduction for the end of Chapter 11. The main practical reason for studying the social psychology of prejudice is to gain sufficient understanding of the phenomenon to try to reduce its incidence and alleviate conflict. Arguments about ways in which prejudice may be reduced rest on the particular perspectives on, and theories of, prejudice to which we subscribe. The intergroup perspectives and theories dealt with in Chapter 11 suggest strategies that are different from those that derive from the person-centred explanations in this chapter.

Summary

- Prejudice can be considered to be an attitude about a social group, which may or may not be expressed in behaviour as overt discrimination.
- The most pervasive prejudices are based on sex, race, ethnicity, age, sexual orientation, and physical and mental handicap. In most Western nations, legislation and social attitudes have significantly reduced these prejudices in recent years (with the exception perhaps of the last two), but there is still a long way to go.
- Legislation and social disapproval have inhibited the more extreme expressions of prejudice. Prejudice is more difficult to detect when it is expressed covertly or in restricted contexts and may go almost unnoticed, imbedded in everyday assumptions, language and discourse.
- The victims of prejudice can suffer material and psychological disadvantage, low self-esteem, stigma, depressed aspirations, and physical and verbal abuse.
- Prejudice may be a relatively ordinary reaction to frustrated goals, in which people vent their aggression on weaker groups that serve as scapegoats for the original source of frustration. By no means can all prejudices be explained in this way.
- Prejudice may be abnormal behaviour expressed by people who have developed generally prejudiced personalities, perhaps as a consequence of being raised in harsh and restrictive families. This may explain why some individuals are prejudiced, but the presence of a social environment that encourages prejudice seems to be a much stronger and more diagnostic determinant.
- These sorts of explanations of prejudice do not deal well with the widespread collective nature of the phenomenon. They overlook the fact that people communicate with one another and are influenced by propaganda and mass communication.

LINKS

YOU HAVE READ ABOUT:	WHICH LINKS TO:
Prejudice linked to discrimination	attitudes linked to behaviour (5)
Sex, race and other stereotypes	categories and stereotyping (2)
Violence and genocide	collective behaviour (11); aggression (12)
Frustration–aggression hypothesis	frustration as a cause of aggression (12)
Difficulty in explaining prejudice in terms of personality, such as authoritarianism	obedience to authority as a situational event (7)

ageism *(p. 242)*
attribution *(p. 238)*
authoritarian personality *(p. 254)*
belief congruence theory
 (p. 256)
closed-mindedness *(p. 255)*
collective behaviour *(p. 253)*
dehumanisation *(p. 233)*
discrimination *(p. 257)*
displacement *(p. 252)*
dogmatism *(p. 255)*
face-ism *(p. 237)*

frustration–aggression hypothesis
 (p. 252)
gender *(p. 236)*
genocide *(p. 233)*
implicit association test *(p. 241)*
mere exposure effect *(p. 251)*
meta-analysis *(p. 249)*
minimal group paradigm *(p. 257)*
prejudice *(p. 233)*
priming *(p. 241)*
racism *(p. 239)*
relative deprivation *(p. 253)*

reverse discrimination *(p. 245)*
scapegoat *(p. 252)*
self-esteem *(p. 246)*
self-fulfilling prophecy *(p. 249)*
sex role *(p. 236)*
sexism *(p. 235)*
social dominance theory *(p. 255)*
stereotype *(p. 235)*
stereotype threat *(p. 248)*
stigma *(p. 245)*
system justification theory *(p. 256)*
tokenism *(p. 245)*

FURTHER READING

Augoustinos, M., & Reynolds, K. J. (Eds.). (2001). *Understanding the psychology of prejudice and racism*. London: Sage. An edited collection of chapters on different aspects of prejudice. The book includes chapters from leading Australian social psychologists who study prejudice.

Brewer, M. B. (2003). *Intergroup relations* (2nd ed.). Philadelphia, PA: Open University Press. A readable overview of research on intergroup relations, including coverage of issues more directly relating to prejudice.

Brewer, M. B., & Brown, R. J. (1998). Intergroup relations. In D. T. Gilbert, S. T. Fiske, & G. Lindzey (Eds.), *The handbook of social psychology* (4th ed., Vol. 2, pp. 554–594). New York: McGraw-Hill. A thorough overview of the field of intergroup relations, including discussion of prejudice and discrimination. This most recent edition of the classic handbook is a primary source for theory and research.

Brown, R. J. (1995). *Prejudice: Its social psychology*. Oxford, UK: Blackwell. Styled as the sequel to Allport's classic 1954 book, *The nature of prejudice*, this is an accessible, detailed and comprehensive coverage of what social psychology has learned about prejudice.

Brown, R. J. (2000). *Group processes* (2nd ed.). Oxford, UK: Blackwell. A readable introduction to group processes and intergroup relations that takes a more European perspective and also covers prejudice.

Brown, R. J., & Gaertner, S. (Eds.). (2001). *Blackwell handbook of social psychology: Intergroup processes*. Oxford, UK: Blackwell. An up-to-date collection of 25 chapters from leading social psychologists, covering the entire field of intergroup processes including aspects of prejudice and discrimination.

Crocker, J., Major, B., & Steele, C. (1998). Social stigma. In D. T. Gilbert, S. T. Fiske, & G. Lindzey (Eds.), *The handbook of social psychology* (4th ed., Vol. 2, pp. 504–553). New York: McGraw-Hill. A thorough overview of research into the experience of being the target of prejudice and a member of a stigmatised group.

Duckitt, J. (1992). *The social psychology of prejudice*. New York: Praeger. A comprehensive review of the literature on the nature and causes of prejudice and ethnocentrism.

Fiske, S. T. (1998). Stereotyping, prejudice, and discrimination. In D. T. Gilbert, S. T. Fiske, & G. Lindzey (Eds.), *The handbook of social psychology* (4th ed., Vol. 2, pp. 357–414). New York: McGraw-Hill. A thorough overview in this most recent edition of the classic handbook—a primary source of theory and research. Fiske takes a slightly more social cognitive approach to the study of prejudice and discrimination.

Hogg, M. A. (2003). Intergroup relations. In J. Delamater (Ed.), *Handbook of social psychology* (pp. 479–501). New York: Kluwer Academic/Plenum. Very accessible overview and review of social psychology research on intergroup relations, prejudice and discrimination.

Hogg, M. A., & Abrams, D. (1988). *Social identifications: A social psychology of intergroup relations and group processes*. London: Routledge. Detailed coverage of theory and research in group processes and intergroup relations from the perspective of social identity theory, with a strong emphasis on prejudice and discrimination.

Hogg, M. A., & Abrams, D. (2003). Intergroup behavior and social identity. In M. A. Hogg & J. Cooper (Eds.), *The Sage handbook of social psychology* (pp. 407–431). London: Sage. A comprehensive overview of research on intergroup relations that includes substantial coverage of prejudice and discrimination.

Jones, J. M. (1996). *The psychology of racism and prejudice*. New York: McGraw-Hill. An authoritative discussion of the causes and consequences of stereotyping and prejudice.

Oakes, P. J., Haslam, S. A., & Turner, J. C. (1994). *Stereotyping and social reality*. Oxford, UK: Blackwell. Detailed and technical discussion, mainly from a social identity perspective, of stereotyping as it relates to social cognition and intergroup relations.

Stangor, C. (Ed.). (2000). *Stereotypes and prejudice: Essential readings*. Philadelphia, PA: Psychology Press. Annotated collection of key publications on stereotyping and prejudice. There is an introductory overview chapter and a commentary chapter introducing each reading.

Wright, S. C., & Taylor, D. M. (2003). The social psychology of cultural diversity: Social stereotyping, prejudice, and discrimination. In M. A. Hogg & J. Cooper (Eds.), *The Sage handbook of social psychology* (pp. 432–457). London: Sage. A comprehensive overview of current research on prejudice and discrimination; deals with stereotyping and also tackles issues of social diversity.

CHAPTER ELEVEN

Intergroup behaviour

1. Richard, an old-fashioned conservative, agrees with the newspaper editorial: 'Nurses should stop complaining about their pay. After all, the hospital orderlies, with even less pay, keep their mouths shut and just get on with their job'. What can you say?

2. 'There is no other way. The rainforest has to go. We need the timber now.' The news bulletin gets you thinking about the way people abuse scarce resources. Is there a way forward?

3. Their teacher has allocated Jeanette and Marion to different work-and-play groups for the rest of the school day—on the basis of their hair colour! What is this teacher up to?

4. Oliver maintains that when a lot of people get together they become something else. This is because a crowd is a kind of super beast; it is emotional, fickle and dangerous. Can you enlighten him a little?

THIS CHAPTER DISCUSSES:

- the context of intergroup behaviour
- its relevance to an explanation of prejudice and discrimination
- relative deprivation, social unrest and aggression
- realistic conflict theory
- evidence from the study of games
- social identity theory: minimal group paradigm, social categorisation, self-categorisation theory
- cognitive and perceptual biases applied to intergroup behaviour
- collective behaviour and the crowd
- strategies for improving intergroup relations.

What is intergroup behaviour?

International and intranational conflicts, political confrontations, revolutions, interethnic relations, negotiations between unions and management and competitive team sports are all examples of **intergroup behaviour**. An initial definition of intergroup behaviour might therefore be: any behaviour that involves interaction between one or more representatives of two or more separate social groups. This sort of definition fairly accurately characterises much of the intergroup behaviour that social psychologists study; however, focusing on face-to-face 'interaction' might be a little restrictive.

A broader and perhaps more accurate definition would be that any perception, cognition or behaviour that is influenced by people's recognition that they and others are members of distinct social groups is intergroup behaviour. This broader definition has an interesting implication: it acknowledges that the real or perceived relations between social groups (e.g. between ethnic groups, between nations) can have far-reaching and pervasive effects on the behaviour of members of those groups—effects that go well beyond situations of face-to-face intergroup encounters. This type of definition stems from a particular perspective in social psychology—an intergroup perspective that argues that a great deal of social behaviour is fundamentally influenced by the social categories to which we belong, and the power and status relations between those social categories. A broad perspective such as this on the appropriate type of theory to develop is called a **metatheory** (see Chapter 1).

In many ways this chapter on intergroup behaviour brings together under one umbrella the preceding discussions of social influence (Chapter 7), group processes (Chapters 8 and 9) and prejudice and discrimination (Chapter 10). Social influence and group processes are generally treated as occurring within groups. But wherever there is a group to which people belong (i.e. an ingroup), there are other groups to which those people do not belong (outgroups). Thus, there is almost always an intergroup, or ingroup–outgroup, context for whatever happens within groups. It is unlikely that processes within groups will be unaffected by relations between groups. Prejudice and discrimination are, as we see in Chapter 10, clear instances of intergroup behaviour (e.g. between different races, between different age groups, between the sexes). One of the recurring themes of Chapter 10 is that personality or interpersonal explanations of prejudice and discrimination (e.g. authoritarian personality, dogmatism, frustration–aggression) may have limitations precisely because they do not adequately consider the intergroup aspect of the phenomena.

In dealing with intergroup behaviour, this chapter confronts important questions about the difference between individuals (and interpersonal behaviour) and groups (and intergroup behaviour) and the way in which harmonious intergroup relations can become conflictual, and vice versa.

Relative deprivation and social unrest

Our discussion in Chapter 10 of the frustration–aggression hypothesis (Dollard, Doob, Miller, Mowrer, & Sears, 1939) as an explanation of intergroup prejudice, discrimination and aggression concluded with Berkowitz's (1962) modification of the original theory. Berkowitz argued that subjective (not objective) frustration is one of an array of aversive events (e.g. heat, cold) that produce an instigation to aggress, and that the actual expression of aggression is strengthened by aggressive associations (e.g. situational cues, past associations).

Berkowitz (1972a) used this analysis to explain collective intergroup aggression—riots. The best-known application is to riots that occurred during long periods of hot weather in the United States—for example, the Watts riots in Los Angeles in August 1965 and the Detroit riots in August 1967 (see Figure 11.1). Heat can be an 'aversive event' that facilitates individual and collective aggression (e.g. Anderson & Anderson, 1984; Baron & Ransberger, 1978; Carlsmith & Anderson, 1979; see also Chapter 12).

Berkowitz (1972a) argues that, under conditions of perceived relative deprivation (e.g. Blacks in the United States in the late 1960s), people feel frustrated. The heat of a long hot summer amplifies the frustration (especially in poor, overcrowded neighbourhoods with little air conditioning or cooling vegetation) and increases the prevalence of individual acts of aggression, which are in turn exacerbated by the presence of aggressive stimuli (e.g. armed police). Individual aggression becomes widespread and is transformed into true collective violence by a process of social facilitation (Zajonc, 1965; see Chapter 8) whereby the presence of other people facilitates dominant behaviour patterns (in this case, aggression).

RELATIVE DEPRIVATION
A crucial precondition for intergroup aggression is **relative deprivation** (Walker & Smith, 2002). Deprivation is not an absolute condition but is always relative to other conditions: one person's new-found prosperity might be someone else's terrible deprivation. George Orwell captures this point very well in *The Road to Wigan Pier*—his essay on the plight of the British working class in the 1930s:

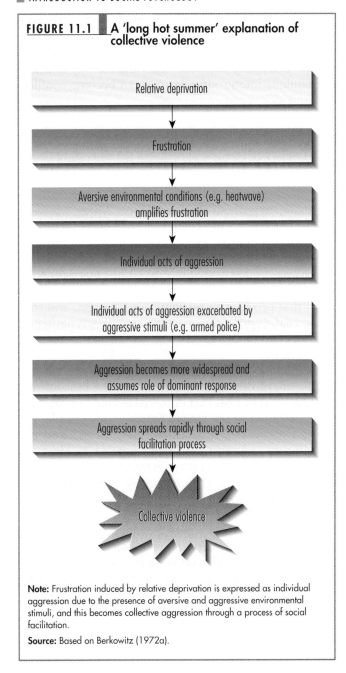

FIGURE 11.1 A 'long hot summer' explanation of collective violence

Relative deprivation

↓

Frustration

↓

Aversive environmental conditions (e.g. heatwave) amplifies frustration

↓

Individual acts of aggression

↓

Individual acts of aggression exacerbated by aggressive stimuli (e.g. armed police)

↓

Aggression becomes more widespread and assumes role of dominant response

↓

Aggression spreads rapidly through social facilitation process

↓

Collective violence

Note: Frustration induced by relative deprivation is expressed as individual aggression due to the presence of aversive and aggressive environmental stimuli, and this becomes collective aggression through a process of social facilitation.

Source: Based on Berkowitz (1972a).

Talking once with a miner I asked him when the housing shortage first became acute in his district; he answered, 'When we were told about it', meaning that ' 'til recently people's standards were so low that they took almost any degree of overcrowding for granted' (Orwell, 1962, p. 57).

The concept of relative deprivation was introduced by Stouffer, Suchman, DeVinney, Star and Williams (1949) in their classic wartime study of the American soldier. Its role in intergroup conflict and aggression was developed more formally by Davis (1959). Relative deprivation refers to a perceived discrepancy between

attainments or actualities ('what is') and expectations or entitlements ('what ought to be'). In its simplest form, relative deprivation arises from comparisons between our experiences and our expectations (Gurr, 1970) (see first focus question).

In his famous **J-curve** hypothesis, Davies (1969) has suggested that people construct their future expectations from past and current attainments and that, under certain circumstances, attainments may suddenly fall short of rising expectations. When this happens, relative deprivation is particularly acute, with the consequence of collective unrest—revolutions of rising expectations (see Box 11.1). The J-curve gets its name from the solid line in Figure 11.2.

BOX 11.1 | **Rising expectations and collective protest**

THE 1992 LOS ANGELES RIOTS PROVIDED A RIVETING, REAL-LIFE EXAMPLE OF RELATIVE DEPRIVATION PERCEIVED BY A LARGE GROUP OF PEOPLE

The Los Angeles riots that erupted on 29 April 1992 resulted in more than fifty dead and 2300 injured. The proximal cause was the acquittal by an all-White suburban jury of four Los Angeles police officers accused of beating a Black motorist, Rodney King. The assault with which the police officers were charged had been captured on video and played on national TV. Against a background of rising unemployment and deepening disadvantage, this acquittal was seen by Blacks as a particularly poignant symbol of the low value placed by White America on American Blacks.

The flashpoint for the riot was the intersection of Florence and Normandie Avenues in South Central Los Angeles. Initially, there was an outbreak of stealing liquor from a nearby liquor store, breaking of car windows and pelting of police. The police moved in en masse but then withdrew to try to de-escalate the tension. This left the intersection largely in the hands of the rioters, who attacked Whites and Hispanics. Reginald Denny, a White truck driver who happened to be driving through, was dragged from his cab and brutally beaten; the incident was watched live on TV by millions and has largely come to symbolise the riots.

South Central Los Angeles is relatively typical of Black ghettos in the United States. However, the junction of Florence and Normandie is not in the worst part of the ghetto by any means. It is a relatively well-off Black neighbourhood in which the poverty rate dropped during the 1980s from 33% to only 21%. That the initial outbreak of rioting would occur here, rather than in a more impoverished neighbourhood, is consistent with relative deprivation theories of social unrest.

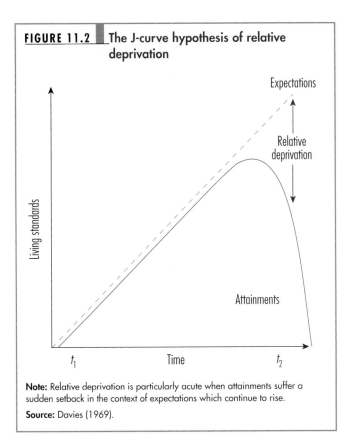

FIGURE 11.2 The J-curve hypothesis of relative deprivation

Note: Relative deprivation is particularly acute when attainments suffer a sudden setback in the context of expectations which continue to rise.

Source: Davies (1969).

Some historical events do seem to fit this model. For example, the Depression of the early 1930s caused a sudden fall in farm prices that was associated with increased anti-Semitism in Poland (Keneally, 1982, p. 95). In Australia, the Victorian goldrush of the early 1850s was followed by a rapid decline in average annual takings per person (from $780 in 1852 to $216 in 1857), which was directly associated with a marked increase in mob violence, harassment and the lynching of Chinese workers in the goldfields (Yarwood & Knowling, 1982, p. 168). Davies (1969) himself cites the French and Russian revolutions, the American Civil War, the rise of Nazism in Germany and the growth of Black Power in the United States in the 1960s. In all these cases, a long period (20–30 years) of increasing prosperity was followed by a steep and sudden recession.

Systematic tests of predictions from Davies' (1969) theory are less encouraging. For example, from a longitudinal survey of American political and social attitudes, Taylor (1982) found little evidence that people's expectations were constructed from their immediate past experience, or that satisfaction was based on the degree of match between actualities and these expectations.

Runciman (1966) made an important distinction between two forms of relative deprivation:

1. **egoistic relative deprivation**, which derives from the individual's sense of deprivation relative to other similar individuals;

2. **fraternalistic relative deprivation**, which derives from comparisons with dissimilar others or members of other groups.

Studies that include measures of both types of relative deprivation provide some evidence that they are independent (e.g. Crosby, 1982). Research indicates that it is fraternalistic, particularly intergroup, relative deprivation, not egoistic relative deprivation, that is associated with social unrest. Vanneman and Pettigrew (1972) conducted surveys in large cities in the United States to discover that Whites who expressed the most negative attitudes towards Blacks were those who felt most strongly that Whites as a group were poorly off relative to Blacks as a group. The deprivation is clearly fraternalistic and, as Whites were actually better off than Blacks, illustrates the subjective nature of relative deprivation.

Abeles (1976) found that Black militancy in the United States was more closely associated with measures of fraternalistic than egoistic relative deprivation, and Guimond and Dubé-Simard (1983) found that militant Francophones in Montreal felt more acute dissatisfaction and frustration when making intergroup salary comparisons between Francophones and Anglophones rather than egoistic comparisons. In India, where there had been a rapid decline in the status of Muslims relative to Hindus, Tripathi and Srivasta (1981) found that those Muslims who felt most fraternalistically deprived (e.g. in terms of job opportunities, political freedom) expressed the greatest hostility towards Hindus.

Finally, in a study of unemployed workers, Walker, at Murdoch University in Western Australia, found that it was principally those who reported most fraternalistic deprivation who were prepared to contemplate militant protest, such as demonstrations, law-breaking and destruction of private property (Walker & Mann, 1987). Those who felt egoistically deprived reported symptoms of individual stress (e.g. headaches, indigestion, sleeplessness). This study is particularly revealing in showing how egoistic and fraternalistic deprivation produce different outcomes, and how it is the latter that is associated with social unrest as intergroup or collective protest (see below) or aggression.

Although fraternalistic relative deprivation may be associated with competitive intergroup behaviours or with forms of social protest, there are at least four other factors that need to be considered. First, for fraternalistic relative deprivation to have sufficient subjective impact for people to take action, they may need to identify relatively strongly with their ingroup. This stands to reason: if you do not identify very strongly with your group, the fact that it is relatively deprived is merely academic. In support of this, Kelly and Breinlinger (1996) found, from a longitudinal study of women activists, that relative deprivation reliably predicted involvement in women's group activities only among women who showed a strong sense of identification with women as a group. Abrams (1990) found that Scottish teenagers indicated greater support for the Scottish Nationalist Party if they felt a sense of fraternalistic relative deprivation towards the English and identified strongly with being Scottish.

Second, groups that feel relatively deprived are unlikely to engage in collective action unless such action is considered to be a practical and feasible way of bringing about social change (see below). Martin, Brickman and Murray (1984) conducted a role-playing study that illustrates this rather nicely. They had women workers imagine they were managers who were slightly to greatly underpaid relative to men of comparable rank in the company. They were also given information that portrayed the women managers as well placed or poorly placed to mobilise resources to change their situation. Martin and his associates found that relative deprivation was closely tied to the magnitude of pay inequality, but that protest was tied much more closely to the perceived probability that protest would be successful.

Third, relative deprivation rests on perceptions of injustice. Generally, the injustice we have had in mind is distributive injustice—feeling that you have less than you are entitled to relative to expectations, other groups and so forth. There is, however, another form of injustice—procedural injustice, in which you feel that you have been the victim of unfair procedures. Tyler and his colleagues have explored this distinction between distributive and procedural justice (Tyler & Lind, 1992; Tyler & Smith, 1998). They suggest that the perception of procedural injustice may be a particularly potent motivation for intergroup protest. Procedural justice seems to be particularly important within groups: if people are subject to unfair procedures within a group, they tend to disidentify and lose commitment to group goals (see discussion of leadership in Chapter 9). In intergroup contexts, however, it may be very difficult to untangle unjust procedures from unjust distributions: for example, status differences (distributive injustice) between groups may rest on unfair procedures (procedural injustice) (Brockner & Weisenfeld, 1996).

Finally, as fraternalistic relative deprivation depends on the particular ingroup–outgroup comparison that is made, it is important to be able to predict whom we compare ourselves with (Martin & Murray, 1983; Walker & Pettigrew, 1984). From social comparison theory (Festinger, 1954; see Suls & Wheeler, 2000) we would expect comparisons to be made with similar others and some of the work cited above certainly supports this (e.g. Abeles, 1976; Runciman, 1966). For instance, Crosby's (1982) 'paradox of the contented female worker' may arise because women workers

compare their salaries and working conditions with those of other women, which narrows the potential for recognising much larger gender-based inequalities in pay and conditions (Major, 1994). However, many intergroup comparisons, particularly those that lead to the most pronounced conflict, are made between markedly different groups (e.g. Black and White South Africans).

One way to approach this issue is to consider the extent to which groups are involved in real conflict over scarce resources (see below).

SOCIAL PROTEST AND COLLECTIVE ACTION

Social unrest associated with relative deprivation often represents sustained social protest to achieve social change; however, the study of protest is complex, as it requires a sophisticated articulation of constructs from social psychology, sociology and political science (Klandermans, 1997; Reicher, 1996, 2001; Stürmer & Simon, in press). The study of protest is the study of how individual discontents or grievances are transformed into collective action: how and why do sympathisers become mobilised as activists or participants?

Klandermans (1997) argues that this involves the relationship between individual attitudes and behaviour (see Chapter 5): sympathisers hold, by definition, sympathetic attitudes towards an issue, yet these attitudes do not automatically translate into behaviour. Participation also resembles a social dilemma (see below). Protest is generally *for* a social good (e.g. equality) or *against* a social ill (e.g. pollution) and, as success benefits everyone irrespective of participation but failure harms participants more, it is tempting to 'free-ride' (see Chapter 8)—to remain a sympathiser rather than become a participant. Finally, Klandermans notes that protest can only be understood as intergroup behaviour that occurs in what he calls 'multiorganisational fields': that is, protest movements involve the clash of ideas and ideologies between groups, and politicised and strategic articulation with other more or less sympathetic organisations.

Klandermans (1997; for an overview see Stürmer & Simon, in press) described four steps in social movement participation:

1. *Becoming part of the mobilisation potential* First, you must be a sympathiser. The most important determinants of mobilisation potential are fraternalistic relative deprivation (feeling relatively deprived as a group), an us/them orientation that targets an outgroup that is responsible for your plight, and a belief that social change through collective action is possible.
2. *Becoming a target of mobilisation attempts* Being a sympathiser is not enough—you must also be informed about what you can do and what is being

done (e.g. sit-ins, demonstrations, lobbying). Media access and informal communication networks are critical here.

3. *Developing motivation to participate* Being a sympathiser and knowing what is going on is not sufficient—you must also be motivated to participate. Motivation arises from the value that you place on the outcome of protest and the extent to which you believe that the protest will actually deliver the goods (an expectancy-value analysis; Ajzen & Fishbein, 1980). Motivation is strongest if the collective benefit of the outcome of protest is highly valued (collective motive), if important others value your participation (normative motive) and if valued personal outcomes are anticipated (reward motive). The normative and reward motives are important to inhibit sympathisers from free-riding on others' participation. This analysis of motivation is strikingly similar to Ajzen and Fishbein's (1980) theory of reasoned action account of the attitude–behaviour relationship (see Chapter 5).

4. *Overcoming barriers to participation* Finally, even substantial motivation may not translate into action if there are insurmountable obstacles, such as no transport to the demonstration, or ill health. However, these obstacles are more likely to be overcome if motivation is very high.

Simon (2003; Stürmer & Simon, in press) argues that the cost–benefit aspect of Klanderman's model places too much emphasis on individual decision-making. Simon proposes a social identity analysis. Drawing on the social identity approach (e.g. Hogg, 2003b—see below for details), Simon argues further that when people identify very strongly with a group they have a powerfully shared perception of collective injustice, needs and goals. They also share behavioural intentions, trust and like one another, and are collectively influenced by group norms and legitimate group leaders. Furthermore, group motivation eclipses personal motivation. Provided that members believe that protest is an effective way forward, these processes increase the probability of participation in collective protest.

Realistic conflict

A key feature of intergroup behaviour is ethnocentrism (Brewer & Campbell, 1976; LeVine & Campbell, 1972), described by Sumner (1906, p. 13) as:

. . . a view of things in which one's own group is the centre of everything, and all others are scaled and rated with reference to it . . . Each group nourishes its own pride and vanity, boasts itself superior, exalts its own

divinities, and looks with contempt on outsiders. Each group thinks its own folkways the only right one . . . Ethnocentrism leads a people to exaggerate and intensify everything in their own folkways which is peculiar and which differentiates them from others.

In contrast to other perspectives on prejudice, discrimination and intergroup behaviour that explain the origin of ethnocentrism in terms of individual or interpersonal processes (e.g. frustration–aggression, relative deprivation, authoritarianism, dogmatism), Sherif believed that 'we cannot extrapolate from the properties of individuals to the characteristics of group situations' (Sherif, 1962, p. 8) and that the origins of ethnocentrism lie in the nature of intergroup relations. For Sherif (1962, p. 5):

Intergroup relations refer to relations between two or more groups and their respective members. Whenever individuals belonging to one group interact, collectively or individually, with another group or its *members in terms of their group identifications* we have an instance of intergroup behaviour.

Sherif believed that, where groups compete for scarce resources, intergroup relations become marked by conflict and ethnocentrism arises. To investigate this idea, Sherif and his colleagues conducted three famous field experiments in 1949, 1953 and 1954 at summer camps for young boys in the United States (Sherif, 1966), using the following general procedure:

- *Phase 1*—The children arrived at the camp which, unknown to them, was run by the experimenters. They engaged in various camp-wide activities through which they formed friendships.
- *Phase 2*—The camp was divided into two separate groups that split up friendships. The groups were entirely isolated from each other: they had separate living quarters, engaged in separate activities and developed their own norms and status differentials. Although little reference was made to the outgroup, there was some embryonic ethnocentrism.
- *Phase 3*—The two groups were brought together to engage in organised intergroup competitions embracing sports contests and other activities. This produced fierce competition and intergroup hostility that rapidly generalised to situations outside the organised competitions. Ethnocentric attitudes and behaviour were amplified and coupled with intergroup aggression and ingroup solidarity. Almost all intergroup encounters degenerated into intergroup hostility: for example, when the two groups ate together, the meal became an opportunity for the groups to throw food at each other. Intergroup relations deteriorated so dramatically that two of the experiments were hastily concluded at this stage.

In one experiment, however, it was possible to proceed to a fourth stage:

- *Phase 4*—The two groups were provided with **superordinate goals**, goals they both desired but were unable to achieve on their own. The groups had to work together in cooperation.

As an example of a superordinate goal (also dealt with later in this chapter), the groups were told that the truck bringing a movie they both wanted to watch had become bogged down and would need to be pulled out, but that everyone would be needed to help as the truck was very heavy. Sherif had a wonderful sense of symbolism: the rope used cooperatively by the boys to pull the truck was the same rope that had previously been used in an aggressive tug-of-war between the warring groups. Sherif and colleagues found a gradual improvement in intergroup relations as a consequence of a number of cooperative intergroup interactions in order to achieve superordinate goals.

There are some notable points about these experiments:

- There was a degree of latent ethnocentrism even in the absence of intergroup competition (more of this below).
- Prejudice, discrimination and ethnocentrism arose as a consequence of real intergroup conflict.
- The boys did not have authoritarian or dogmatic personalities.
- The less frustrated group (the winning group) was usually the one that expressed the greatest intergroup aggression.
- Ingroups formed despite the fact that friends were actually outgroup members (see Chapter 8).
- Simple contact between members of opposing groups did not improve intergroup relations (see below).

REALISTIC CONFLICT THEORY

To explain these phenomena, Sherif (1966) proposed a **realistic conflict theory** of intergroup behaviour, in which the nature of the goal relations among individuals and groups determines the nature of intergroup and interindividual relations. He argued that individuals who share goals requiring interdependence for their achievement tend to cooperate and form a group (Figure 11.3), while individuals who have mutually exclusive goals (i.e. a scarce resource that only one can obtain, such as winning a chess game) engage in interindividual competition that prevents group formation or contributes to the collapse of an existing group.

At the intergroup level, mutually exclusive goals produce realistic intergroup conflict and ethnocentrism, while shared goals requiring intergroup interdependence for their achievement (i.e. superordinate goals) reduce conflict and encourage intergroup harmony.

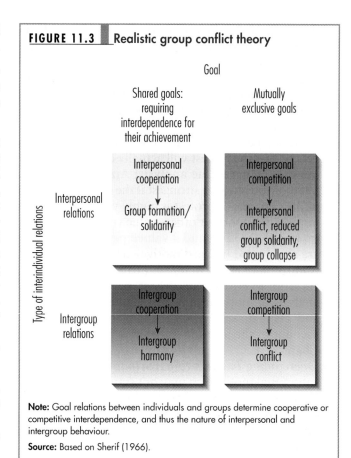

FIGURE 11.3 | **Realistic group conflict theory**

Note: Goal relations between individuals and groups determine cooperative or competitive interdependence, and thus the nature of interpersonal and intergroup behaviour.

Source: Based on Sherif (1966).

Sherif's model is generally supported by other naturalistic experiments (Fisher, 1990). For example, Blake and Mouton (1961) employed similar procedures in a series of 30 studies, each run for two weeks, involving more than 1000 business people on management training programs in the United States. Zimbardo's simulated prison experiment (Haney, Banks, & Zimbardo, 1973; see Chapter 8) also illustrates the way in which mutually exclusive intergroup goals produce conflict and hostile intergroup relations. Sherif's studies have been replicated successfully in Lebanon (Diab, 1970) and the former Soviet Union (Andreeva, 1984) but, in Britain, Tyerman and Spencer (1983) were not so successful. Tyerman and Spencer used an established scout group as participants and found that the different 'patrols' did not express anywhere near as much hostility as expected. Furthermore, it was easy to increase interpatrol cooperation even in the absence of a superordinate goal. Tyerman and Spencer attribute this to the fact that a well-established superordinate group already existed.

Realistic conflict theory makes good sense and is generally useful for understanding intergroup conflict, particularly in applied settings (Fisher, 1990). For example, Brewer and Campbell (1976; see also Chapter 13) conducted an ethnographic survey of 30 tribal groups in Africa and found, among other things, greater derogation of tribal outgroups that lived close by and were thus likely to be direct competitors for scarce resources such as water and land.

Realistic conflict theory does suffer from one problem. Because so many variables are operating together in the various studies, how can we know that it is the nature of goal relations that ultimately determines intergroup behaviour rather than, for example, the cooperative or competitive nature of interaction, or perhaps merely the existence of two separate groups (e.g. Dion, 1979; Turner, 1981b)? These causal agents are confounded—an observation that we pursue later in this chapter.

COOPERATION, COMPETITION AND SOCIAL DILEMMAS

Realistic conflict theory focuses attention on the relationship between people's goals, the competitive or cooperative nature of their behaviour, and the conflicting or harmonious nature of their relations. We can study these relationships in abstract settings by designing 'games' with different goal relations for two or more people to play. Von Neumann and Morgenstern (1944) introduced a model for analysing situations where people are in conflict over some non-trivial outcome (e.g. money, power). Variously called *decision theory*, *game theory* or *utility theory*, this initiated an enormous amount of research in the 1960s and 70s. (This topic is also dealt with in the context of interpersonal relations, in Chapter 13.) The highly abstract nature of the research raised questions about its relevance (generalisability) to real-world conflict and led to its decline in the 1980s (Apfelbaum & Lubek, 1976; Nemeth, 1970). Much of this research is concerned with interpersonal conflict; however, much of it also has important implications for intergroup conflict—for example, the prisoner's dilemma, the trucking game and the commons dilemma (e.g. Liebrand, Messick, & Wilke, 1992).

The prisoner's dilemma

Introduced by Luce and Raiffa (1957; Rapoport, 1976), the **prisoner's dilemma** is the most widely researched game. It is based on an anecdote. Two obviously guilty suspects are questioned separately by detectives who have only enough evidence to convict them of a lesser offence. The suspects are separately offered a chance to confess, knowing that if one confesses but the other does not, the confessor will be granted immunity and the confession will be used to convict the other of the more serious offence. If both confess, each will receive a moderate sentence. If neither confesses, each will receive a very light sentence. The dilemma faced by the prisoners can be summarised by a *payoff matrix* (Figure 11.4).

Although mutual non-confession produces the best joint outcome, mutual suspicion and lack of trust almost always encourages both to confess. This finding has been

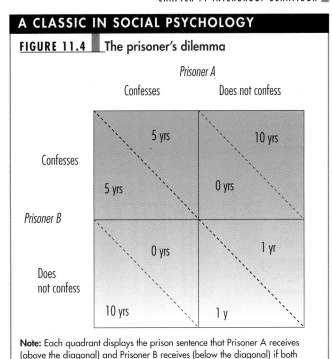

A CLASSIC IN SOCIAL PSYCHOLOGY

FIGURE 11.4 The prisoner's dilemma

Note: Each quadrant displays the prison sentence that Prisoner A receives (above the diagonal) and Prisoner B receives (below the diagonal) if both confess, one confesses or neither confesses.

replicated in literally hundreds of prisoner's dilemma experiments, using a variety of experimental conditions and payoff matrices (Dawes, 1991). The prisoner's dilemma is described as a 'two-person, mixed-motive, non-zero-sum game', meaning that two people are involved, they each experience a conflict between being motivated to cooperate and motivated to compete, and the outcome can be that both parties gain or both lose (in contrast, a zero-sum game is one in which one party's gain is always the other's loss).

The trucking game

In the trucking game there are two trucking companies, Acme and Bolt, who transport goods from one place to another (Deutsch & Krauss, 1960). Each company has its own private route, but there is a much faster shared route that has a major drawback—a one-lane section (see Figure 11.5). Clearly, the mutually beneficial solution is for the two companies to agree to take it in turns to use the one-lane section. Instead, research reveals again and again that participants prefer to fight for use of the one-lane section. Typically, both enter and meet head-on in the middle, and then waste time arguing until one backs up. Again, mutual mistrust has produced a suboptimal joint outcome.

These games highlight the detrimental consequences of lack of trust that have clear real-world analogues. For example, mutual distrust between Iran and Iraq fuelled their terrible conflict over which of them rightfully owned the Shatt al Arab waterway. When they laid

FIGURE 11.5 | The trucking game

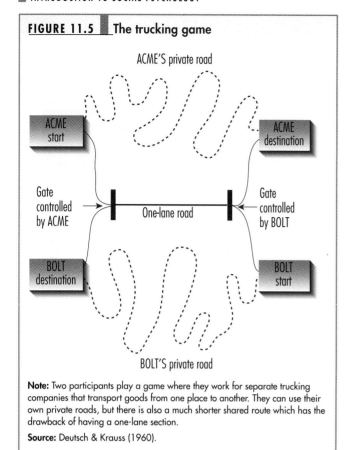

ACME'S private road

ACME start

ACME destination

Gate controlled by ACME

One-lane road

Gate controlled by BOLT

BOLT destination

BOLT start

BOLT'S private road

Note: Two participants play a game where they work for separate trucking companies that transport goods from one place to another. They can use their own private roads, but there is also a much shorter shared route which has the drawback of having a one-lane section.

Source: Deutsch & Krauss (1960).

down their arms in 1988 after horrific atrocities, more than a million civilian and military casualties and the devastation of their economies, the borders remained precisely where they were when the war began eight years earlier.

The commons dilemma

Many other social dilemmas involve a number of individuals or groups exploiting a limited resource (Foddy, Smithson, Schneider, & Hogg, 1999; Kerr & Park, 2001). These are essentially *n*-person prisoner's dilemmas—if everyone cooperates an optimal solution for all is reached, but if everyone competes then everyone loses. The **commons dilemma**, or 'tragedy of the commons' (Hardin, 1968), gets its name from the common pasture that English towns used to have. People were free to graze their cattle on this land and, if all used it in moderation it would replenish itself and continue to benefit them all. Imagine, however, 100 farmers surrounding a common that could support only 100 cows. If each grazed one cow, the common would be maximally utilised and minimally taxed. One farmer, however, reasons that if he grazed an additional cow output would be doubled, minus a very small cost due to overgrazing—a cost borne equally by all 100 farmers. So this farmer adds a second cow. If all 100 farmers

reasoned in this way they would rapidly destroy the pasture, thus producing the tragedy of the commons.

The commons dilemma is an example of a replenishable resource dilemma—the common is a renewable resource that will continually support many people provided they all show restraint in 'harvesting' the resource. Many of the world's most pressing environmental and conservation problems are replenishable resource dilemmas—for example, rainforests and the world's population of ocean fish are renewable resources if harvested appropriately (see second focus question).

Another type of social dilemma is called a *public goods dilemma*. Public goods are provided for everyone or nobody—for example, public health, national parks, clean air, a national road network, public radio and television. Because public goods are available to all, people are tempted to use them without contributing to their maintenance. There is a **free-rider effect** (Kerr, 1983; Kerr & Bruun, 1983; see also Chapter 8) in which people self-interestedly exploit a resource without caring for it. For example, if I own a cat, it contributes minimally to the disappearance of Australian native fauna, but if all 1.8 million people living in my city reason similarly and hence own cats, annihilation is assured. Likewise, if I fail to fix my car exhaust or fail to plant trees in my garden, it contributes minimally to noise, atmospheric and visual pollution; if everyone living in my neighbourhood did likewise, it would become uninhabitable.

Reflecting on the commons dilemma, Hardin (1968, p. 162) observed:

Ruin is the destination to which all men rush, each pursuing his own best interest in a society that believes in the freedom of the commons. Freedom in a commons brings ruin to all.

Experimental research on social dilemmas finds that, when self-interest is pitted against the collective good, the usual outcome is competition and resource destruction (Edney, 1979; Sato, 1987). However, laboratory and field studies also obtain high levels of voluntary social cooperation (Caporael, Dawes, Orbell, & van de Kragt, 1989). A series of studies by Brewer and her colleagues (Brewer & Kramer, 1986; Brewer & Schneider, 1990; Kramer & Brewer, 1984, 1986) identifies one condition under which this can occur. When individuals identify with the common good—in other words, they derive their social identity (see below) from the entire group that has access to the resource—self-interest becomes subordinate to the common good.

However, the same research indicates that when different *groups*, rather than individuals, have access to a public good the ensuing intergroup competition ensures ethnocentric actions that are far more destructive than mere self-interest. International competition over limited resources such as rainforests, whales and wetlands tragically accelerates their disappearance.

Resolving social dilemmas

People find it difficult to escape the trap of a social dilemma. Even appeals to altruistic norms are surprisingly ineffective (Kerr, 1992): if you know that others are free-riding, you do not want to be taken for a sucker (Kerr & Bruun, 1983). Because selfish behaviour is so prevalent in social dilemmas, structural solutions that cause the dilemma to disappear often have to be imposed (Kerr, 1992). Structural solutions include a range of measures such as limiting the number of people accessing the resource (e.g. via permits), limiting the amount of the resource that people can take (e.g. via quotas), handing over management of the resource to an individual (a leader) or a single group, facilitating free communication among those accessing the resource and shifting the payoff to favour cooperation over competition.

The problem with structural solutions is that they require an enlightened and powerful authority to implement measures, manage the bureaucracy and police violations. This can be hard to bring about. A case in point is the inability, in the face of global catastrophe, for the world's nations to put a structural solution in place to limit carbon emission and halt global warming. We've had the Rio summit, the Kyoto protocol and, in 2000, a meeting in The Hague and still selfishness prevails and the social dilemma persists.

A structural solution that has been well researched is the appointment of a leader to manage the resource (e.g. de Cremer & van Vugt, 2002; Rutte & Wilke, 1984; van Vugt & de Cremer, 1999). Leaders are very effective at resolving social dilemmas under certain circumstances. People with a generally prosocial orientation are relatively open to leadership when their group is faced with a social dilemma, particularly if they identify strongly with the group (de Cremer, 2000; de Cremer & van Vugt, 1999). Leader charisma is typically not critical, but it is important that the leader can be viewed as 'one of us', as a representative member of the group (de Cremer, 2002). People with a pro-self orientation are less open to leadership unless they identify strongly with the group, and the leader's behaviours and qualities are group-serving and representative of the group. Charismatic leaders are particularly good at helping pro-self members behave in prosocial and group-serving ways.

If structural solutions are so difficult, what other options do we have? One factor that seems particularly effective in resolving social dilemmas is group identification (Foddy, Smithson, Schneider, & Hogg, 1999; van Vugt & de Cremer, 1999). Where people identify very strongly with a group that accesses a shared resource, those people act in ways that benefit the group as a whole rather than themselves as separate from the group (e.g. Brewer & Kramer, 1986; Brewer & Schneider, 1990). It is as if a large number of individuals competing for access has been transformed into a single person who carefully tends the resource. Indeed, this is a good analogy. As we see shortly, identification with a group actually does psychologically transform people in this way. Identification seems to facilitate communication that develops conserving norms (e.g. Bouas & Komorita, 1996), it encourages adherence to those norms (e.g. Sattler & Kerr, 1991), it inspires perceptions of distributive and procedural justice (Tyler & Smith, 1998) and it makes people feel that their conserving actions really do have an effect (Kerr, 1992).

Social identity

MINIMAL GROUPS

We have seen that realistic conflict theory (Sherif, 1966) traces the origins and form of intergroup behaviour to goal interdependence, and that research tends to confound a number of possible causal agents. Research also suggests that ethnocentric attitudes and competitive intergroup relations are easy to trigger and difficult to suppress. For example, embryonic ethnocentrism was found in phase 2 of Sherif's summer-camp studies, when groups had just been formed but there was no realistic conflict between them (see also Blake & Mouton, 1961; Kahn & Ryen, 1972). Other researchers have found that competitive intergroup behaviour spontaneously emerges:

- even when intergroup goal relations are not interdependent (Rabbie & Horwitz, 1969);
- under conditions of explicitly non-competitive intergroup relations (Ferguson & Kelley, 1964; Rabbie & Wilkens, 1971);
- under conditions of explicitly cooperative intergroup relations (Rabbie & DeBrey, 1971).

What, then, are the minimal conditions for intergroup behaviour—that is, conditions that are both necessary and sufficient for a collection of individuals to be ethnocentric and to engage in intergroup competition? (See third focus question.)

Tajfel and his colleagues devised an intriguing paradigm to answer this question—the **minimal group paradigm** (Tajfel, Billig, Bundy, & Flament, 1971). British schoolboys, participating in what they believed was a study of decision-making, were assigned to one of two groups completely randomly, but allegedly on the basis of their expressed preference for paintings by the artists Kandinsky or Klee. The children knew only which group they themselves were in (Kandinsky group or Klee group), with the identity of outgroup and fellow ingroup members concealed by the use of code numbers. The children then individually distributed money between pairs of recipients identified only by code number and group membership.

This paper-and-pencil task was repeated for a number of different pairs of ingroup and outgroup members, excluding self, on a series of distribution matrices carefully designed to tease out the sorts of strategies that were being used. The results indicated that, although they showed a degree of fairness, the children strongly favoured their own group: they adopted the ingroup favouritism strategy (FAV) described in Box 11.2.

This is a rather startling finding, as the groups were indeed minimal. They were created on the basis of a flimsy criterion, had no past history or possible future, the children did not know the identity of other members of each group, and there was no self-interest involved in the money-distribution task as self was not a recipient.

Subsequent experiments were even more minimal. For example, Billig and Tajfel (1973) explicitly randomly categorised their participants as X- or Y-group members, thereby eliminating any possibility that they might infer that people in the same group were interpersonally similar because they ostensibly preferred the same artist. Turner (1978) abolished the link between points and money. The task was simply to distribute points. Other studies have included, in addition to the points-distribution task, measures of attitudinal, affective and conative aspects of ethnocentrism.

The robust finding, from hundreds of minimal group experiments conducted with a wide range of participants, is that the mere fact of being categorised as a group member seems to be necessary and sufficient to produce ethnocentrism and competitive intergroup behaviour (Bourhis, Sachdev, & Gagnon, 1994; Diehl, 1990; Tajfel, 1982).

More accurately, **social categorisation** is necessary but may not be sufficient for intergroup behaviour. For example, Hogg and his colleagues conducted a number of minimal group experiments to show that, if participants are made more certain and confident about how to use the complex and unusual minimal group matrices, categorisation does *not* produce group identification and intergroup discrimination (e.g. Grieve & Hogg, 1999; see Hogg, 2000a). It seems that one reason why people identify with groups, even minimal groups, is to reduce subjective uncertainty (see below). Thus categorisation will produce identification and discrimination only if people identify with the category, and they will identify with the category only if the categorisation reduces subjective uncertainty in the situation.

The minimal group paradigm has not gone unchallenged. There has been a lively debate over the measures,

---

A CLASSIC IN SOCIAL PSYCHOLOGY

BOX 11.2   Tajfel's minimal group paradigm

DISTRIBUTION STRATEGIES AND SAMPLE DISTRIBUTION MATRICES (PARTICIPANTS CIRCLED PAIRS OF NUMBERS TO INDICATE HOW THEY WISHED TO DISTRIBUTE THE POINTS)

A. *Two sample distribution matrices.* Within each matrix (1 and 2), participants circle the column of numbers that represents how they would like to distribute the points (representing real money) in the matrix between ingroup and outgroup members.

1. Ingroup member	7	8	9	10	11	12	13	14	15	16	17	18	19
Outgroup member	1	3	5	7	9	11	13	15	17	19	21	23	25
2. Ingroup member	18	17	16	15	14	13	12	11	10	9	8	7	6
Outgroup member	5	6	7	8	9	10	11	12	13	14	15	16	17

B. *Distribution strategies.* From an analysis of responses on a large number of matrices it is possible to determine the extent to which the participants' distribution of points is influenced by each of the following strategies.

- Fairness — F — Equal distribution of points between groups
- Maximum joint profit — MJP — Maximise total number of points obtained by both recipients together, irrespective of which group receives most
- Maximum ingroup profit — MIP — Maximise number of points for the ingroup
- Maximum difference — MD — Maximise the difference in favour of the ingroup in the number of points awarded
- Favouritism — FAV — Composite employment of MIP and MD

Note: Distribution strategies, and sample distribution matrices (participants circled pairs of numbers to indicate how they wished to distribute the points).

Source: Based on Hogg & Abrams (1988).

procedures and statistics used (Aschenbrenner & Schaefer, 1980; Bornstein, Crum, Wittenbraker, Harring, Insko, & Thibaut, 1983; Branthwaite, Doyle, & Lightbown, 1979; Turner, 1980, 1983) and over the extent to which favouritism reflects rational economic self-interest rather than social identity-based intergroup differentiation (Rabbie, Schot, & Visser, 1989; Turner & Bourhis, 1996).

Another objection is that the conditions of the experiments create a demand characteristic whereby participants conform to transparent expectations of the experimenters or simply to general norms of intergroup competitiveness (Gerard & Hoyt, 1974). This interpretation seems unlikely in the light of evidence that discrimination is not associated with awareness of being under surveillance (Grieve & Hogg, 1999) and that discrimination can be reduced when adherence to and awareness of discriminatory norms is increased (Billig, 1973; Tajfel & Billig, 1974). In fact, people not actually participating in such experiments tend to predict significantly less discrimination (i.e. no norm of discrimination) than is actually expressed by those who do take part (St Claire & Turner, 1982) and it can be almost impossible to encourage participants to follow an explicitly cooperative norm in a minimal intergroup situation (Hogg, Turner, Nascimento-Schulze, & Spriggs, 1986).

Although not a criticism of the minimal group paradigm, Mummendey and her associates have identified a positive–negative asymmetry in the minimal group effect (Mummendey, Simon, Dietze, Grünert, Haeger, Kessler, Lettben, & Schäferhoff, 1992; Otten, Mummendey, & Blanz, 1996; see also Peeters & Czapinski, 1990). In the usual paradigm participants give positively valued resources (points); the effect is much weaker or can disappear when they give negatively valued resources (e.g. punishment) or when, instead of giving resources, they subtract them.

SOCIAL IDENTITY APPROACH

The pivotal role of social categorisation in intergroup behaviour, as demonstrated by minimal group studies, led to the development by Tajfel and, now at the Australian National University, Turner of **social identity theory** (Tajfel & Turner, 1979). This theory has developed exponentially over the intervening years to become perhaps the pre-eminent contemporary social psychological analysis of group processes, intergroup relations and the collective self. Perhaps the most significant development was **self-categorisation theory** (Turner, Hogg, Oakes, Reicher, & Wetherell, 1987). Because this expansion has involved the development of many compatible subtheories and emphases, it is more appropriate to characterise it as the **social identity approach** or perspective—though it is convenient to refer to it as a theory (see Abrams & Hogg, 2001; Hogg, 2001a, 2003b; Hogg & Abrams, 1988, 2003; Turner, 1999; see also Chapter 4).

Social identity and group membership

Based on the assumption that society is hierarchically structured into different social groups that stand in power and status relations to one another (e.g. Blacks and Whites in the United States, Catholics and Protestants in Northern Ireland, Malays and Chinese in Malaysia), a core premise of the social identity approach is that social categories (large groups such as a nation or church, intermediate groups such as an organisation, or small groups such as a club) provide members with a **social identity**—a definition and evaluation of who they are and a description and evaluation of what this entails. Social identities not only describe members but prescribe appropriate behaviour and specific tactics for them. So, for example, being a member of the social category 'gypsy' means not only defining and evaluating themselves, and being defined and evaluated by others, as gypsies, but thinking and behaving in characteristically gypsy ways.

Social identity is that part of the self-concept that derives from group membership. It is associated with group and intergroup behaviours that have some notable general characteristics: **ethnocentrism**, **ingroup favouritism**, **intergroup differentiation**; conformity to ingroup norms; ingroup solidarity and cohesion; and perception of self, outgroupers and fellow ingroupers in terms of relevant group **stereotypes**.

Social identity is quite separate from personal identity, which is the part of the self-concept that derives from personality traits and the idiosyncratic personal relationships we have with other people (Turner, 1982). Personal identity is not associated with group and intergroup behaviours—it is related to interpersonal and individual behaviour. We have a repertoire of as many social and personal identities as we have groups with which we identify, or close relationships and idiosyncratic attributes in terms of which we define ourselves. Although we have many discrete social and personal identities, we subjectively experience the self as an integrated whole person with a continuous and unbroken biography—the subjective experience of self as fragmented discontinuous selves would be problematic and associated with psychopathology.

The social identity approach distinguishes social from personal identity as a deliberate attempt to avoid explaining group and intergroup processes in terms of personality attributes or interpersonal relations. Social identity theorists believe that many social psychological theories of group processes and intergroup relations are limited because they explain the phenomena simply by combining the effects of personality predispositions or interpersonal relations.

The **authoritarian personality** theory and the **frustration–aggression hypothesis** are examples of this type of explanation of prejudice and discrimination (Billig, 1976; see Chapter 10). To illustrate: if a social psychologist asks why people stick their arms out of car windows to indicate a turn, the question would remain unanswered by an explanation in terms of the biochemistry of muscle action. An explanation in terms of adherence to social norms would be more appropriate (though inappropriate to a biochemist asking the same question). It is the problem of **reductionism** (see Chapter 1 for details) that prompts social identity theorists to distinguish between social and personal identity (Doise, 1986; Israel & Tajfel, 1972; Moscovici, 1972; Taylor & Brown, 1979; Turner & Oakes, 1986).

Social categorisation, prototypes and depersonalisation

Self-categorisation theory (Turner, 1985; Turner, Hogg, Oakes, Reicher, & Wetherell, 1987) specifies the social cognitive underpinnings of social identity phenomena. Categorisation lies at the heart of social identity phenomena. People cognitively represent social categories/groups as prototypes. A **prototype** is a fuzzy set of attributes (perceptions, beliefs, attitudes, feelings, behaviours) that describes one group and distinguishes it from relevant other groups. Prototypes obey the **metacontrast principle**—they maximise the ratio of intergroup differences to intragroup differences and, in so doing, they accentuate group entitativity. **Entitativity** (Campbell, 1958; Hamilton & Sherman, 1996) is the property of a group that makes it seem like a coherent, distinct and unitary entity (see Chapter 8).

An implication of metacontrast and entitativity is that group prototypes are not simply the average of ingroup attributes, and the most prototypical person in a group is not simply the average group member. Because of the important intergroup distinctiveness function, group prototypes are typically displaced from the group average in a direction that is further away from the relevant comparison outgroup. Prototypes are thus *ideal types* rather than average types. It is quite conceivable that a group prototype may be so ideal that no single member actually embodies it.

Prototypes are cognitive representations of groups and, as such, are very closely related to stereotypes (see Chapter 2). However, from a social identity perspective, a prototype is a stereotype only if it is *shared* by group members (Tajfel, 1981a). Finally, prototypes are context dependent. What this means is that the content of a specific prototype changes as a function of the comparison outgroup and the relevant ingroup members present. This context dependence can be quite extreme in newly forming groups (a task group), but is probably less extreme in more established groups (e.g. ethnic groups) that are better anchored in well-known global intergroup stereotypes.

The process of categorising another person, including self, leads to **depersonalisation**. When we categorise others we see them through the lens of the relevant ingroup or outgroup prototype—we view them as members of a group, not as idiosyncratic individuals. We perceptually accentuate their similarity to (i.e. assimilate them to) the relevant prototype, thus perceiving them stereotypically and ethnocentrically. When we categorise ourselves exactly the same happens—we define, perceive and evaluate ourselves in terms of our ingroup prototype and behave in accordance with that prototype. Self-categorisation produces ingroup normative behaviour (conformity to group norms; see Chapter 7) and self-stereotyping (see Chapter 2) and is thus the process that causes us to behave like group members. Depersonalisation is not the same thing as dehumanisation—though it can produce dehumanisation (see Chapter 10) if the outgroup is deeply hated and is stereotyped in terms that deny its members any respect or human dignity.

Salience

What determines the point at which one social identity or another becomes the psychologically salient basis for social categorisation of self and others? Without an answer to this question, social identity researchers would have a serious scientific problem—they would be unable to predict or manipulate social identity-contingent behaviours. Penelope Oakes and her associates at the Australian National University have drawn on work by Campbell (1958) to answer this critical question (Oakes, 1987; Oakes, Haslam, & Turner, 1994; Oakes & Turner, 1990; see Chapter 2). Social categories that are (a) chronically accessible to us (e.g. in memory), and/or (b) accessible in the situation (e.g. there are obvious cues to category), come into operation as the basis of self-categorisation if they make good sense of the situation (a) by accounting for similarities and difference between people (i.e. they fit the way the situation is structured) and (b) by accounting for why people behave as they do (i.e. they fit the norms that people seem to adhere to). This can be put technically: salience is an interactive function of chronic accessibility and situational accessibility on the one hand, and the structural fit and normative fit on the other.

Self-enhancement and uncertainty reduction

Social identity phenomena are motivated by two underlying processes: self-enhancement and uncertainty reduction. One of the key premises of the social identity approach is that groups stand in status and prestige relations to one another—some groups are simply more prestigious and of higher status than others, and most people in a given social context know this. Intergroup relations are characterised by a struggle over prestige and status (Tajfel & Turner, 1979; see also Hogg & Abrams, 1988). From a social identity point of view groups compete to be different from one another in favourable ways because positive intergroup distinctiveness provides group members with a favourable (positive) social identity. Unlike interpersonal comparisons, which generally strive for similarity (e.g. Festinger, 1954; Suls & Wheeler, 2000), intergroup comparisons strive to maximise differences in ways that evaluatively favour the ingroup. This group-level process is believed to map onto a very basic human motivation for self-enhancement (Sedikides & Strube, 1997; see Chapter 4).

Drawing on this analysis, social identity researchers have suggested that self-esteem is a key motive in social identity contexts. Research (Abrams & Hogg, 1988; Crocker & Luhtanen, 1990; Crocker & Major, 1989; Hogg & Abrams, 1990; Long & Spears, 1997; Rubin & Hewstone, 1998) on self-esteem motivation has shown that:

• intergroup differentiation tends to elevate self-esteem;
• depressed self-esteem does not motivate intergroup differentiation;
• it is collective self-esteem, not personal self-esteem, that is related to group processes;
• people in groups are highly creative and competent at protecting themselves from the low self-esteem consequences of low-status group membership.

Social identity processes are also motivated by uncertainty reduction (Hogg, 2000a, 2001c). In life, people are fundamentally motivated to know who they are and how they relate to other people—they need to feel relatively certain about what to think, feel and do and about what others will think, feel and do. We need to know what to expect from other people in order to make life predictable and allow us to plan effective action. Group identification is a highly effective way of reducing uncertainty. Identification with a group, through relevant prototypes, immediately and automatically defines our relationships with ingroup and outgroup others and sets out how we and others will act. Experimental research, largely using the minimal group paradigm, has shown that people do not identify with groups unless they are motivated to do so because they are in a state of subjective uncertainty (e.g. Grieve & Hogg, 1999; see Hogg, 2000a).

Social identity and intergroup relations

The social identity approach was founded on an attempt to explain intergroup conflict and social change—this was Tajfel's original social identity theory (Tajfel, 1972b; Tajfel, 1974; Tajfel & Turner, 1979).

In pursuit of positive social identity, groups and individuals can adopt an array of different behavioural strategies, the choice of which is determined by people's beliefs about the nature of relations between their own and other groups (Ellemers, 1993; Hogg & Abrams, 1988; Tajfel & Turner, 1979; Taylor & McKirnan, 1984)—see Figure 11.6. These beliefs, which may or may not accord with the reality of intergroup relations (they are ideological constructs), hinge first on whether

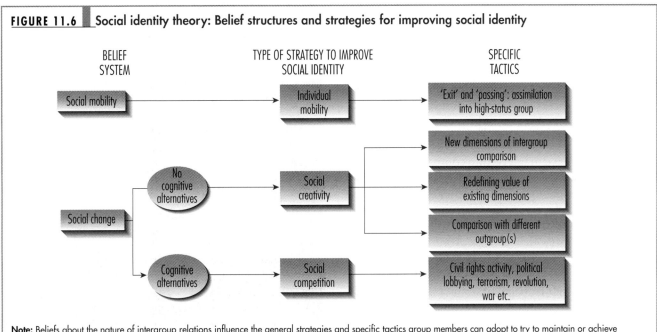

FIGURE 11.6 | Social identity theory: Belief structures and strategies for improving social identity

Note: Beliefs about the nature of intergroup relations influence the general strategies and specific tactics group members can adopt to try to maintain or achieve positive social identity.

Social action: When minorities demonstrate for equal rights they challenge the status quo and the majority's power base.

it is possible, as an individual, to 'pass' from a lower-status group and gain acceptance in a higher-status group. A **social mobility belief system** inhibits group action on the part of subordinate groups and instead encourages individuals to dissociate themselves from the group and try to gain acceptance for themselves and their immediate family in the dominant group. A belief in social mobility is enshrined in Western democratic political systems.

Where individuals believe that intergroup boundaries are impermeable to 'passing', a **social change belief system** exists (e.g. the Hindu caste system in India). In these circumstances, positive social identity can be achieved only by group action and the sort of action taken is influenced by whether the status quo (the existing status and power hierarchy) is perceived to be secure or insecure. If the status quo is considered stable, legitimate and thus secure, it is difficult to conceive of an alternative social structure (i.e. no **cognitive alternatives** exist), let alone a path to real social change. Groups tend to adopt **social creativity** strategies.

- They can engage in intergroup comparisons on novel or unorthodox dimensions that tend to favour the subordinate group. For example, Lemaine (1966, 1974) had children engage in an intergroup competition to build the best hut and found that groups which were provided with poor building materials, and thus had no possibility of winning, went on to emphasise how good a garden they had made.
- They can attempt to change the consensual value attached to ingroup characteristics (e.g. the slogan 'Black is beautiful').
- They can compare themselves with other low- or lower-status groups (e.g. 'poor-White racism').

Where social change is associated with recognition that the status quo is illegitimate, unstable and thus insecure, and where cognitive alternatives (i.e. conceivable and attainable alternative social orders) exist, then direct **social competition** occurs—that is, direct intergroup conflict (e.g. political action, collective protest, revolutions, war). Social movements typically emerge under these circumstances (e.g. Klandermans, 1997; Milgram & Toch, 1969; Reicher, 2001; Tyler & Smith, 1998; see earlier in this chapter).

In a manner closely related to social identity theory, Jost and his associates (Jost & Banaji, 1994; Jost & Hunyadi, 2002; Jost & Kramer, 2002; see Chapter 10), in their **system justification theory**, attribute social stasis to an ideology that justifies the status quo. This is an ideology that subordinate group members subscribe to even though it legitimises current status relations and encourages people to protect it and thus maintain their position of disadvantage. It is quite possible that the motivation to do this is uncertainty reduction—better to live in disadvantage but be certain of one's place than to challenge the status quo and face an uncertain future (Hogg, 2000a, 2001c).

Social identity theory, as the macrosocial dimension of the social identity approach, has been tested successfully in a range of laboratory and naturalistic contexts (Hogg & Abrams, 1988; Ellemers, 1993; see

Social change: After winning her event at the 2000 Olympics, Cathy Freeman reported that she carried the aspirations of her people on her shoulders.

Box 11.3 and Figure 11.7 for a New Zealand study) and has been elaborated and extended in many areas of social psychology (e.g. the study of language and ethnicity; see Chapter 15). The social identity approach attributes the general form of intergroup behaviour (e.g. ethnocentrism, stereotyping) to processes related to social categorisation and the specific manifestation (e.g. conflict, harmony) to people's beliefs about the nature of intergroup relations.

Haslam and associates at the Australian National University (Haslam, Turner, Oakes, McGarty, & Hayes, 1992) capture this nicely in a study of subtle changes in Australians' stereotypes of Americans that occurred as a consequence of changes in intergroup attitudes caused by the 1991 Gulf War. They discovered that Australians who were making comparisons between Australia, Britain and the United States had a relatively unfavourable stereotype of Americans and this deteriorated further during the course of the Gulf conflict, particularly on dimensions reflecting arrogance, argumentativeness and traditionalism. The authors argue that the reason why attitudes deteriorated on these particular dimensions rather than others was that these dimensions related directly to the perceived actions of Americans in relation to other nations during the war.

Other aspects

The social identity approach has a number of other important components, which are discussed elsewhere in this book. These include:

- referent informational influence theory (Abrams & Hogg, 1990a; Turner, 1991; Turner & Oakes, 1989),

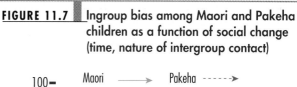

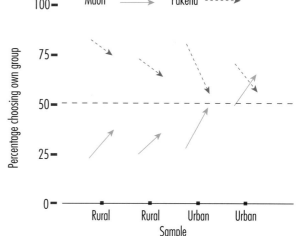

FIGURE 11.7 | Ingroup bias among Maori and Pakeha children as a function of social change (time, nature of intergroup contact)

Note: The direction of the arrows emphasises an age trend from younger to older children within each group. Between 1963 and 1971 there was a systematic decrease in Pakeha ingroup bias and Maori outgroup bias, which was more pronounced for older than younger children. By 1971, older Maori were exhibiting more ingroup bias than older Pakeha (see Box 11.3).

Source: Vaughan (1978b); in Tajfel (1978).

which deals with conformity (Chapter 7) and group polarisation (Chapter 9);
- the social attraction hypothesis (Hogg, 1993), which deals with cohesion and attraction phenomena in groups (Chapter 8);

The Maori are New Zealand's indigenous people and make up about 10% of the population. The remainder of the population is predominantly Pakeha (i.e. European). Graham Vaughan collected data on ingroup (ethnic) preferences of younger (6–8 years) and older (10–12 years) Maori and Pakeha children from urban and rural backgrounds (Vaughan, 1978a, 1978b). The data were collected at various times during the 1960s, which was a period of considerable social change in New Zealand, and are displayed in Figure 11.7. The arrows represent an age trend from younger to older children within each ethnic group at each time and at each location. Choices above 50% represent ingroup preference and those below 50% outgroup preference.

Against an overall reduction in ethnocentrism for older children (presumably a developmental trend), the data show that urban Pakeha preferred their own group but were less ethnocentric than rural Pakeha, and rural Maori showed more marked outgroup preference than urban Maori. The most interesting finding was that, between 1961 and 1971, urban Maori actually changed from making outgroup to making ingroup preferences—a change that reflected the rise in the late 1960s and early 1970s of an assertive Brown (Maori) Power movement modelled on the American Black Power movement of the 1960s.

Intergroup perceptions may be less ethnocentric in the city for a number of reasons, including perhaps interethnic contact. Maori who moved to the city were often cut off from the traditional Polynesian extended family (and from other aspects of Maori culture) and found they had to compete with Pakeha for work. There was a gradual realignment of ethnic power relations and greater possibility of less unequal-status interethnic contact. Perhaps this contributed to some extent to reduced prejudice on the part of Pakeha and elevated ethnic pride on the part of Maori.

- the theory of subjective group dynamics (Marques, Abrams, & Serodio, 2001), which deals with deviance processes in groups (Chapter 8);
- the social identity theory of leadership (Hogg, 2001d; Hogg & van Knippenberg, 2003; Chapter 9);
- the social identity analysis of attitude–behaviour relations (Terry & Hogg, 1996; Chapter 5);
- the social identity theory of deindividuation phenomena (Reicher, Spears & Postmes, 1995; see below).

Social cognition

Although self-categorisation theory is a social cognitive theory that emphasises the role of cognitive processes and cognitive representations in intergroup behaviour (Farr, 1996), it is a theory that explicitly articulates with a more broadly social analysis (Doise, 1986; see Chapter 1). This is because, as we have seen, it is part of the general social identity approach. Social cognition (see Chapter 2 for full coverage), however, provides a number of other more purely cognitive explanations that focus on certain cognitive and perceptual effects with implications for intergroup behaviour.

CATEGORISATION AND RELATIVE HOMOGENEITY

The most obvious effect is stereotyping. The categorisation of people (or objects) has been shown to cause an **accentuation effect** (Tajfel, 1959): the perceptual accentuation of similarities among people within a category and of differences between people from different categories, on those dimensions believed to be associated with the categorisation—that is, stereotypical dimensions (Doise, 1978; Eiser & Stroebe, 1972; Tajfel & Wilkes, 1963). There is some evidence that people perceptually homogenise outgroup members more than ingroup members: '*they* all look alike, but *we* are diverse' (Brigham & Malpass, 1985; Quattrone, 1986).

For example, Brigham and Barkowitz (1978) had Black and White college students indicate for 72 photographs of Black and White faces how certain they were that they had seen each photograph in a previously presented series of 24 photographs (12 of Blacks and 12 of Whites). Figure 11.8 shows that participants found it more difficult to recognise outgroup than ingroup faces. This effect is quite robust. It has emerged from other studies comparing 'Anglos' with Blacks (Bothwell, Brigham, & Malpass, 1989), Hispanics (Platz & Hosch, 1988) and Japanese (Chance, 1985), and from studies of student eating clubs (Jones, Wood, & Quattrone, 1981), college sororities (Park & Rothbart, 1982) and artificial laboratory groups (Wilder, 1984).

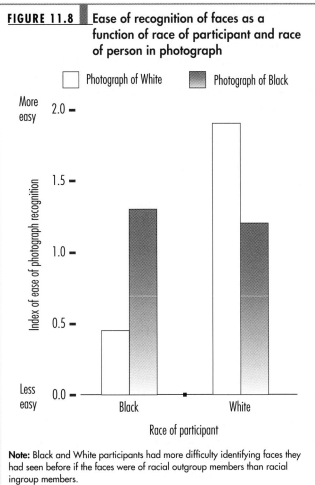

FIGURE 11.8 Ease of recognition of faces as a function of race of participant and race of person in photograph

□ Photograph of White   ▨ Photograph of Black

Index of ease of photograph recognition

More easy — 2.0

1.5

1.0

0.5

Less easy — 0.0

Black   White

Race of participant

Note: Black and White participants had more difficulty identifying faces they had seen before if the faces were of racial outgroup members than racial ingroup members.

Source: Based on data from Brigham & Barkowitz (1978).

The **relative homogeneity effect** is enhanced on group-defining dimensions (Lee & Ottati, 1993) and when groups are in competition (Judd & Park, 1988)—see Ostrom and Sedikides (1992).

The principal explanation for this effect is that, because we are generally more familiar with ingroup than outgroup members, we have more detailed knowledge about them and thus are better able to differentiate them (Linville, Fischer, & Salovey, 1989; Wilder, 1986). Although quite sensible, this may not be the complete story. For example, the outgroup homogeneity effect occurs when participants report no greater familiarity with the ingroup than the outgroup (Jones, Wood, & Quattrone, 1981) and when there is equally minimal information about both groups (Wilder, 1984). Stephan (1977) found that children in both segregated and integrated schools (i.e. with lower or higher intergroup familiarity) actually rated their own group as more homogeneous than two outgroups. If outgroup homogeneity is not inevitable, what factors influence the relative homogeneity effect?

One clue is that, while most research has used majority or equal-sized groups, Stephan's (1977) groups were minority groups (Chicanos and Blacks). Also, the relative outgroup homogeneity effect is enhanced when the outgroup is perceived to be relatively small—a minority (Bartsch & Judd, 1993; Mullen & Hu, 1989). To test the idea that relative homogeneity is influenced by the majority–minority status of the ingroup, Simon and Brown (1987) conducted a minimal group study. Relative group size was varied and participants were asked to rate the variability of both ingroup and outgroup, and to indicate how much they identified with the ingroup. Figure 11.9 shows that, while majorities rated the outgroup as less variable than the ingroup (the usual outgroup homogeneity effect), minorities did the opposite. In addition, this latter ingroup homogeneity effect was accompanied by greater group identification. This is consistent with self-categorisation and social identity theories: minorities categorise themselves more strongly as a group and are thus more strongly depersonalised (see above) in their perceptions, attitudes and behaviour.

MEMORY

Social categorisation is associated with category-based person memory effects (Fiske & Taylor, 1991). For example, Taylor, Fiske, Etcoff and Ruderman (1978) had participants listen to taped mixed-sex or mixed-race discussion groups and later attribute various statements to the correct speaker. They rarely attributed the statements to the wrong category, but within categories they were not good at identifying the correct speaker—that is, they made few between-category errors but many within-category errors. The category-based memory effect can be quite selective. For example, Howard and Rothbart (1980) had participants attribute statements about behaviours to ingroup and outgroup members: some of the behaviours reflected favourably and others unfavourably on the actor. The participants were equally accurate at recalling whether it was an ingroup or outgroup member who performed the favourable behaviours, but they were more accurate at recalling outgroup than ingroup actors who performed unfavourable behaviours (see Figure 11.10).

These two experiments illustrate the way in which information about individuals can be cognitively represented and organised as category attributes that

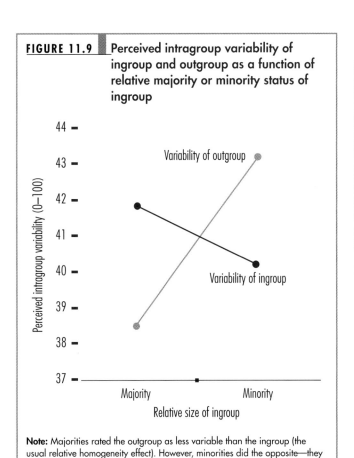

FIGURE 11.9 Perceived intragroup variability of ingroup and outgroup as a function of relative majority or minority status of ingroup

Note: Majorities rated the outgroup as less variable than the ingroup (the usual relative homogeneity effect). However, minorities did the opposite—they rated the outgroup as more variable than the ingroup.

Source: Based on data from Simon & Brown (1987).

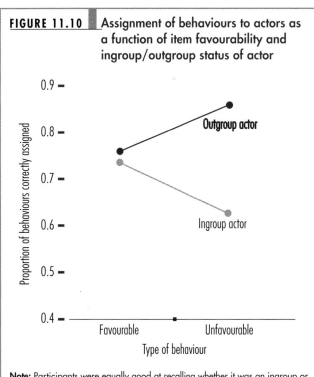

FIGURE 11.10 Assignment of behaviours to actors as a function of item favourability and ingroup/outgroup status of actor

Note: Participants were equally good at recalling whether it was an ingroup or outgroup member who performed favourable behaviours, but they were better at recalling outgroup than ingroup actors who performed unfavourable behaviours.

Source: Based on Howard & Rothbart (1980).

submerge individual differences between people within the same category. Furthermore, evaluative biases may influence what information is associated with a particular category.

DISTINCTIVE STIMULI AND ILLUSORY CORRELATION
A particularly important influence on what information is associated with which categories is the distinctiveness of the information. Anything that is out of the ordinary (objects, events and people who are statistically infrequent, rare, unusual, relatively vivid or conspicuous) tends to attract our attention and engage a disproportionate amount of cognitive activity (Taylor & Fiske, 1978). So, for example, we will attend more to a single man in a group of women, a single Black in a group of Whites, or a person we understand to be a genius, a homosexual or a movie star. Distinctive individuals can also disproportionately influence the generalised images we construct of groups. There is a tendency to generalise from distinctive individuals to the group as a whole, particularly when we have few prior expectations and/or are unfamiliar with the category (Quattrone & Jones, 1980). For instance, on the basis of meeting one extremely stupid (i.e. distinctive individual) Martian (i.e. unfamiliar group), we would be apt to stereotype the group as stupid.

Another effect of distinctiveness is that people tend to perceive an **illusory correlation**, based on *paired distinctiveness* or *associative meaning*, between distinctive events that occur at the same time (Chapman, 1967; illusory correlation is discussed fully in Chapter 2). Distinctiveness-based illusory correlation may help to explain stereotyping, in particular negative stereotypes of minority groups (Hamilton, 1979; Hamilton & Sherman, 1989; Mullen & Johnson, 1990): negative events are distinctive because they are subjectively less frequent than positive events; and minority groups are distinctive because people have relatively few contacts with them. Illusory correlation based on associative meaning may also be involved in negative stereotyping of minority groups: people have preconceptions that negative attributes go with minority groups (McArthur & Friedman, 1980).

Distinctiveness-based illusory correlation is a robust empirical effect that is stronger for negative behaviours and under conditions of high memory load (McConnell, Sherman, & Hamilton, 1994; Mullen & Johnson, 1990), and when people are aroused (Kim & Baron, 1988). Once an illusory correlation between a group and a negative attribute in one domain (e.g. intellectual) has been established, there is a tendency to generalise the negative impression to other domains (e.g. social) (Acorn, Hamilton, & Sherman, 1988).

A limitation of seeing illusory correlation as an explanation of stereotyping is that it does not consider the emotional and self-conceptual investment that people have in stereotyping, nor the material bases of power and status differentials between groups that stereotype one another. As we have seen in this chapter and in Chapter 10, the construction and use of stereotypes is framed by intergroup relations and governed by cognitive, affective and rhetorical motives (Leyens, Yzerbyt, & Schadron, 1994; McGarty, Haslam, Turner, & Oakes, 1993; Oakes, Haslam, & Turner, 1994).

OPTIMAL DISTINCTIVENESS
Distinctiveness enters into intergroup behaviour in a different way in Brewer's (1991, 1993) theory of **optimal distinctiveness**. Building on her dual-process model of information processing (Brewer, 1988, 1994; see Chapter 2), Brewer argues that people are driven by conflicting motives for inclusion/sameness (satisfied by group membership) and for distinctiveness/uniqueness (satisfied by individuality), and that they try to strike a balance between these two motives in order to achieve optimal distinctiveness. Small groups oversatisfy the need for distinctiveness and so people strive for greater inclusiveness, while large groups oversatisfy the need for inclusiveness and so people strive for distinctiveness. In small groups, then, people identify and assimilate strongly, whereas in large groups people disidentify and emphasise their individuality or their membership of smaller subgroups.

Intergroup emotions

People in groups that are important to them tend to have strong emotions about outgroups and fellow members of their own groups. Mackie and Smith and their associates have recently proposed **intergroup emotions theory** (IET) to address emotions in group contexts (Mackie, Devos, & Smith, 2000; Mackie & Smith, 2002a; see also Mackie & Smith, 2002b).

IET argues that individuals' emotions are based on appraisals of whether a situation is going to harm or benefit them personally. Drawing on the social identity approach, IET goes on to argue that, in group contexts, the self is a collective self and so appraisals operate at the level of whether a situation is going to harm or benefit 'us'. When people identify with a group, intergroup emotions come into play. Harm to the ingroup, which often emanates from the actions of outgroups is seen as self-harming and will generate negative emotions about the outgroup. Behaviour that promotes the ingroup, often coming from fellow ingroup members, will generate positive emotions about the ingroup and its members. Emotions have an action tendency and so outgroup emotions may translate into discrimination and ingroup emotions into solidarity and cohesion.

From IET it can also be predicted that emotions felt by fellow ingroup members will quickly be felt by self—due to the common identity bond that exists.

Collective behaviour and the crowd

Collective behaviour usually refers to large numbers of people who are in the same place at the same time, and who behave in a uniform manner that is volatile, highly emotional and in violation of social norms (Graumann & Moscovici, 1986; Milgram & Toch, 1969; Moscovici, 1985b). Some social psychologists interpret this to include the study of rumours (see Chapter 3), fads and fashions, social movements and cults, and contagions of expression, enthusiasm, anxiety, fear and hostility.

Contagions include some of the most bizarre behaviours imaginable (Klapp, 1972). In the 1630s tulip mania swept north-western Europe, with people trading small fortunes for a single, ultimately worthless bulb; in the 15th century there was an epidemic in Europe in which nuns bit each other; in the 18th century there was an epidemic of nuns meowing like cats; between the 10th and the 14th century in Europe there were frequent episodes of dancing mania, with people continually dancing from town to town until they dropped and even died; and in the mid- and late 1980s there were epidemics in China of men complaining hysterically about shrinkage of the penis and an overwhelming fear of impending death!

Usually, however, the study of collective behaviour is a more sober business. It is the study of crowd behaviour. The crowd is a vivid social phenomenon for both those who are involved and those who witness the events first-hand or through literature and the media. Consider the Tian'anmen Square protest in 1989, the Los Angeles riots of 1992, the Nazi rallies of the 1930s, the celebrations at the fall of the Berlin wall in 1990, the huge anti-war demonstrations of the late 1960s, the enormous rock festivals of the 1970s, and the crowd scenes in Richard Attenborough's movie *Gandhi* or in the novels of Emile Zola or Victor Hugo. More recently, we witnessed the crowd scenes in East Timor and then, around Sydney Harbour, the millennium celebrations followed by the 2000 Olympics. Crowd events are nothing if not varied.

Crowd behaviour, in its full manifestation, can be difficult to research in the laboratory, though attempts have been made. For example, French (1944) locked his participants in a room and then wafted smoke under the door while sounding the fire alarm. Ethics aside, the study was not successful as an attempt to create panic in the laboratory. One group kicked open the door and knocked over the smoke generator, and another group calmly discussed the possibility that its reactions were being observed by the experimenters!

EARLY THEORIES

One of the earliest theories of collective behaviour was proposed by LeBon (1896/1908). LeBon, who lived in France during a period of great social turmoil, observed and read accounts of the great revolutionary crowds of the French Revolution of 1848 and the Paris Commune of 1871—accounts such as those to be found in Zola's novels *Germinal* and *La Débacle* and Hugo's *Les Misérables*. He was appalled by the 'primitive, base and ghastly' behaviour of the crowd and the way in which people's civilised conscious personality seemed to vanish and be replaced by savage animal instincts. LeBon (1908, p. 12) believed that:

. . . by the mere fact that he forms part of an organised crowd, a man descends several rungs in the ladder of civilisation. Isolated, he may be a cultivated individual; in a crowd he is a barbarian—that is, a creature acting by instinct.

According to LeBon, crowds produce primitive and homogeneous behaviour because (see Figure 11.11):

- members are anonymous and thus lose personal responsibility for their actions;
- ideas and sentiments spread rapidly and unpredictably through a process of contagion;
- unconscious antisocial motives ('ancestral savagery') are released through suggestion (a process akin to hypnosis).

LeBon is still important nowadays (see Apfelbaum & McGuire, 1986; Hogg & Abrams, 1988; Reicher, 1987, 1996, 2001), due mainly to the influence of his perspective, in which crowd behaviour is considered to

Crowd behaviour: Primitive aggressive instincts, or normatively regulated goal-oriented action?

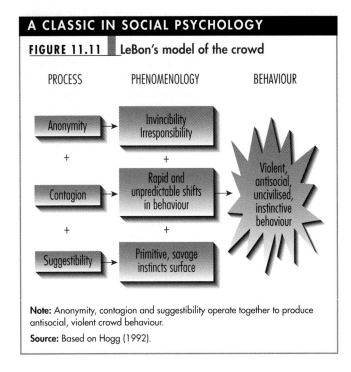

A CLASSIC IN SOCIAL PSYCHOLOGY

FIGURE 11.11 | LeBon's model of the crowd

PROCESS · PHENOMENOLOGY · BEHAVIOUR

Anonymity → Invincibility Irresponsibility

+

Contagion → Rapid and unpredictable shifts in behaviour

+

Suggestibility → Primitive, savage instincts surface

→ Violent, antisocial, uncivilised, instinctive behaviour

Note: Anonymity, contagion and suggestibility operate together to produce antisocial, violent crowd behaviour.

Source: Based on Hogg (1992).

be pathological/abnormal, on later theories of collective behaviour (e.g. Freud, 1921; McDougall, 1920; Zimbardo, 1970).

Freud, for example, argued that the crowd 'unlocks' the unconscious. Society's moral standards maintain civilised behaviour because they are installed in the human psyche as the super-ego. However, in crowds the super-ego is supplanted by the leader of the crowd, who now acts as the hypnotist controlling unconscious and uncivilised id impulses. Crowd leaders have this effect because of a deep and primitive instinct in all of us to regress, in crowds, to the 'primal horde'—the original brutal human group at the dawn of existence. Civilisation is able to evolve and thrive only to the extent that the leader of the primal horde, the 'primal father', is overthrown. This analysis has been used to explain how the 'Reverend' Jim Jones had such enormous power over his cult followers that more than 900 of them participated in collective suicide at Jonestown in Guyana in 1978 (Ulman & Abse, 1983).

Another important early theorist is McDougall, who characterised the crowd as (McDougall, 1920, p. 45):

. . . excessively emotional, impulsive, violent, fickle, inconsistent, irresolute and extreme in action, displaying only the coarser emotions and the less refined sentiments; extremely suggestible, careless in deliberation, hasty in judgment, incapable of any but the simpler and imperfect forms of reasoning, easily swayed and led, lacking in self-consciousness, devoid of self-respect and of a sense of responsibility, and apt to be carried away by the consciousness of its own force, so that it tends to

produce all the manifestations we have learnt to expect of any irresponsible and absolute power.

McDougall believed that the most widespread instinctive emotions are the simple primitive ones (e.g. fear, anger) and that these would therefore be the most common and widely shared emotions in any human aggregate. More complex emotions would be rare and less widely shared. Stimuli eliciting the primitive simple emotions would therefore cause a strong consensual reaction, while those eliciting more complex emotions would not. Primary emotions spread and strengthen rapidly in a crowd, as each member's expression of the emotion acts as a further stimulus to others—a snowball effect dubbed 'primitive sympathy'. This effect is not easily modulated, as individuals feel depersonalised and have a lowered sense of personal responsibility.

DEINDIVIDUATION AND SELF-AWARENESS

More recent explanations of collective behaviour discard some of the specifics of earlier approaches (e.g. the emphasis on instinctive emotions, the psychodynamic framework), but retain the overall perspective. People usually refrain from exercising their basically impulsive, aggressive and selfish nature because of their identifiability as unique individuals in societies that have strong norms against 'uncivilised' conduct. In crowds, these restraints are relaxed and we can revert to type, embarking on an orgy of aggressive, selfish, antisocial behaviour. The mediating mechanism is **deindividuation**.

The term 'deindividuation', coined by Festinger, Pepitone and Newcomb (1952), originates in Jung's definition of 'individuation' as 'a process of differentiation, having for its goal the development of the individual personality' (Jung, 1946, p. 561). It was Zimbardo (1970) who developed the concept most fully. He believed that being in a large group provides people with a cloak of anonymity that diffuses personal responsibility for the consequences of their actions. This leads to a loss of identity and a reduced concern for social evaluation: that is, to a state of deindividuation that causes behaviour to become impulsive, irrational, regressive and disinhibited because it is not under the usual social and personal controls.

Research on deindividuation has tended to focus on the effects of anonymity on behaviour in groups. Festinger, Pepitone and Newcomb (1952) found that participants dressed in grey laboratory coats and seated in a poorly lit room for a group discussion of their parents made more negative comments about their parents than did participants in a control condition (see also Cannavale, Scarr, & Pepitone, 1970). Similarly, participants dressed in laboratory coats used more obscene language when discussing erotic literature than did more easily identifiable individuals (Singer, Brush, & Lublin, 1965).

Zimbardo (1970) conducted a series of experiments in which participants were deindividuated by wearing cloaks and hoods (reminiscent of the Ku Klux Klan). In one such experiment, deindividuated female students gave electric shocks to a female confederate in a paired-associate learning task that were twice the duration of those given by conventionally dressed participants. In another classic study, in which a simulated prison was constructed in the basement of the psychology department of Stanford University, Zimbardo (Zimbardo, Haney, Banks, & Jaffe, 1982; see Chapter 8) found that students who were deindividuated by being dressed as guards were extremely brutal to other students who were deindividuated as prisoners.

There is also evidence that people are more willing to lynch someone (Mullen, 1986) or bait a disturbed person to jump from a building if it is dark and if they are in a larger group (Mann, 1981; see Chapter 12).

Finally, Diener and colleagues (Diener, Fraser, Beaman, & Kelem, 1976) conducted a clever study that took advantage of Halloween—when the streets are filled with children, disguised and thus anonymous, who are trick-or-treating. The researchers observed the behaviour of 1352 children, alone or in groups, who approached 27 focal homes in Seattle where they were warmly invited in and told to 'take *one* of the candies' on a table. Half the children were first asked their names and where they lived, to reduce deindividuation. Groups and deindividuated children were more than twice as likely to take extra candy. The transgression rate varied from 8% of individuated individuals to 80% of deindividuated groups.

Although, in general, anonymity seems to increase aggressive antisocial behaviour (Dipboye, 1977), there are problematic findings. Zimbardo (1970) employed his deindividuation paradigm with Belgian soldiers and found that they gave shorter-duration electric shocks when dressed in cloaks and hoods. Zimbardo suggests this might be because the soldiers were an intact group (i.e. already deindividuated) and the 'cloak and hood' procedure had the paradoxical effect of reducing deindividuation. However, other studies have found a reduction in aggression as a consequence of anonymity or group membership (Diener, 1976).

Johnson and Downing (1979) had female participants administer shocks to confederate 'learners' in a paired-associate learning task. The women were deindividuated by wearing either clothing resembling a Ku Klux Klan robe or a nurse's uniform. The experimenter highlighted the impact of the clothing by explicitly commenting on the resemblance. Although all participants wore the special clothing, half also wore a large badge displaying their name in order to individuate them (reduce deindividuation). Deindividuation failed to increase aggression, even among those dressed as Ku

Klux Klan members (see Figure 11.12). Those dressed as nurses were significantly less aggressive than those dressed as Ku Klux Klan members, and deindividuated nurses were the least aggressive of all.

These studies tell us two important things:

1. Aggression and antisocial behaviour are not automatic and inevitable consequences of anonymity.
2. Normative expectations surrounding situations of deindividuation may influence behaviour.

Regarding this second point, Jahoda (1982) has noted the similarity between Zimbardo's method of deindividuation (i.e. hood and robe) and the wearing of the *chadoor* (full-length veil) by women in some Islamic countries. Far from setting free antisocial impulses, the chadoor very precisely specifies a woman's social obligations.

More recently, Diener (1980) has assigned Duval and Wicklund's (1972) notion of objective self-awareness (awareness of oneself as an object of attention) a central role in the deindividuation process (Diener, 1980, p. 210):

A deindividuated person is prevented by situational factors present in a group from becoming self-aware. Deindividuated persons are blocked from awareness of

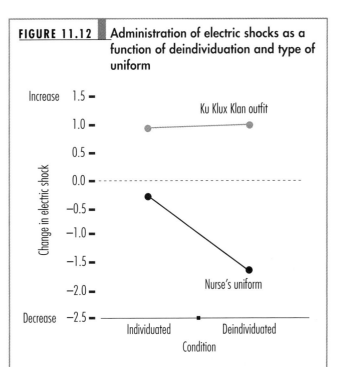

FIGURE 11.12 | Administration of electric shocks as a function of deindividuation and type of uniform

Note: In a paired-associate learning task, participants dressed as Ku Klux Klan members gave slightly increased shocks, and participants dressed as nurses gave reduced shocks, to a confederate learner; additionally, deindividuated participants (that is, they did not wear large personal name badges) were not more aggressive, and in fact those deindividuated as nurses were the least aggressive of all.

Source: Based on data from Johnson & Downing (1979).

Deindividuation: People in uniforms, and in a large group, have a cloak of anonymity.

themselves as separate individuals and from monitoring their own behaviour.

Factors present in crowds reduce self-awareness and create a psychological state of deindividuation that has specific consequences for behaviour (Figure 11.13). Although these consequences do not inevitably include aggression, they tend to facilitate the emergence of anti-social behaviour. In support of Diener's model, Prentice-Dunn and Rogers (1982) found that participants who were prevented from becoming self-aware, by being subjected to loud rock music in a darkened room while working on a collective task, subsequently administered more intense electric shocks to a 'learner' than did participants who had been working individually in a quiet, well-illuminated room under instructions to concentrate on their own thoughts and feelings.

Another perspective on deindividuation distinguishes between public and private self-awareness (Carver & Scheier, 1981; Scheier & Carver, 1981). Reduced attention to our private self (feelings, thoughts, attitudes and other private aspects of self) is equated with deindividuation, but does not necessarily produce antisocial behaviour unless the appropriate norms are in place (Figure 11.14). It is reduced attention to our public self (how we want others to view our conduct) that causes behaviour to be independent of social norms and thus to become antisocial.

All models of deindividuation, including the latter ones that focus on self-awareness, dwell on *loss*—loss of individuality, loss of identity, loss of awareness and 'loss' of desirable behaviour. Critics have suggested that all this talk about 'loss' may at best seriously restrict the range of collective behaviours we can talk about, and at worst provide an inadequate understanding altogether. Instead we should be focusing on *change*—change of identity, change of awareness and change of behaviour (e.g. Reicher, Spears, & Postmes, 1995) (see fourth focus question).

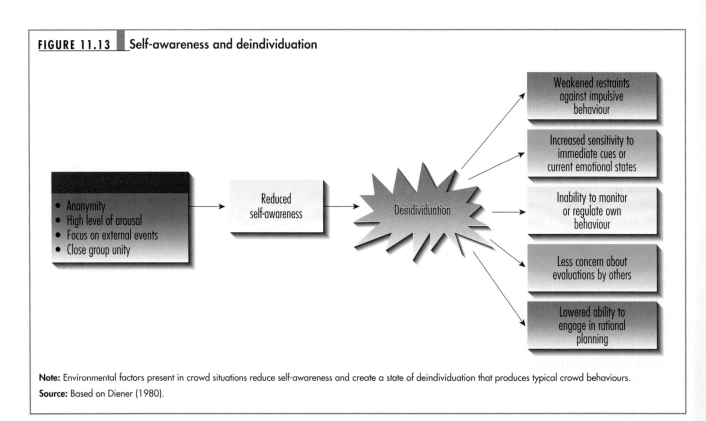

FIGURE 11.13 Self-awareness and deindividuation

- Anonymity
- High level of arousal
- Focus on external events
- Close group unity

→ Reduced self-awareness → Deindividuation →

- Weakened restraints against impulsive behaviour
- Increased sensitivity to immediate cues or current emotional states
- Inability to monitor or regulate own behaviour
- Less concern about evaluations by others
- Lowered ability to engage in rational planning

Note: Environmental factors present in crowd situations reduce self-awareness and create a state of deindividuation that produces typical crowd behaviours.
Source: Based on Diener (1980).

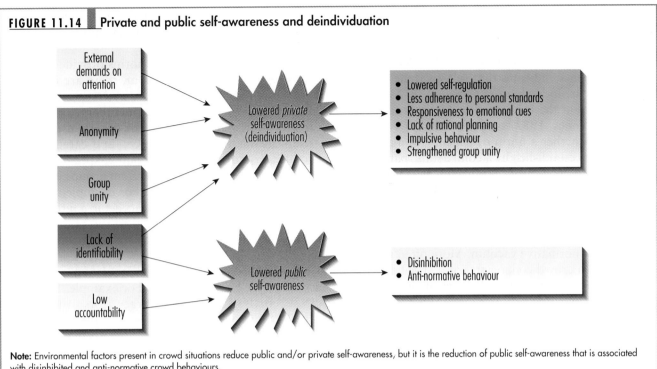

FIGURE 11.14 Private and public self-awareness and deindividuation

Note: Environmental factors present in crowd situations reduce public and/or private self-awareness, but it is the reduction of public self-awareness that is associated with disinhibited and anti-normative crowd behaviours.

Source: Based on Hogg & Abrams (1988).

EMERGENT NORM THEORY

Emergent norm theory takes a very different approach to the explanation of collective behaviour (Turner, 1974; Turner & Killian, 1957). Rather than treating collective behaviour as pathological or instinctual behaviour, it focuses on collective action as norm-governed behaviour, much like any other group behaviour. Turner (the sociologist R.H. Turner, not the social psychologist J.C. Turner) believes that what is distinct about the crowd is that it has no formal organisation or tradition of established norms to regulate behaviour, and so the problem of explaining crowd behaviour is to explain how a norm emerges from within the crowd (hence, 'emergent norm theory'; Figure 11.15). People in a crowd find themselves together under circumstances in which there are no clear norms to indicate how to behave. Their attention is attracted by distinctive behaviours (or the behaviour of distinctive individuals). These behaviours imply a norm and consequently there is pressure against non-conformity. Inaction on the part of the majority is interpreted as tacit confirmation of the norm, which consequently amplifies pressures against non-conformity.

By focusing on norms, emergent norm theory acknowledges that members of a crowd may communicate with one another in the elaboration of appropriate norms of action. However, the general nature of crowd behaviour is influenced by the role of distinctive behaviours,

which are presumably behaviours that are relatively rare in most people's daily lives—for instance, antisocial behaviours. Two other critical observations have been

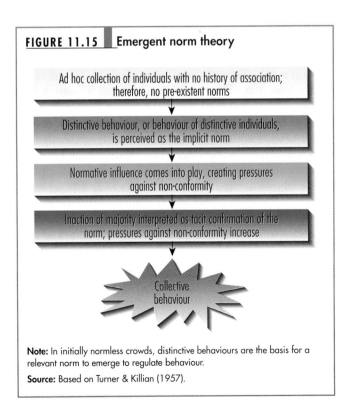

FIGURE 11.15 Emergent norm theory

Ad hoc collection of individuals with no history of association; therefore, no pre-existent norms

Distinctive behaviour, or behaviour of distinctive individuals, is perceived as the implicit norm

Normative influence comes into play, creating pressures against non-conformity

Inaction of majority interpreted as tacit confirmation of the norm; pressures against non-conformity increase

Collective behaviour

Note: In initially normless crowds, distinctive behaviours are the basis for a relevant norm to emerge to regulate behaviour.

Source: Based on Turner & Killian (1957).

made. Diener (1980) correctly observes that a norm-regulated crowd would have to be a self-aware crowd (there is no need for people to comply with norms unless they are identifiable and thus individuated and self-aware) and yet evidence indicates that self-awareness is very low in crowds. Indeed, an experiment by Mann and his associates at the University of Melbourne (Mann, Newton, & Innes, 1982) supports Diener's view: irrespective of whether a norm of leniency or aggressiveness had been established by a confederate, participants were more aggressive when anonymous than when identifiable. Anonymous participants were also more aggressive when the aggressive norm was in place.

The second critical observation comes from Reicher (1982, 1987), who reminds us that crowds rarely come together in a normative vacuum. More often than not, members of a crowd congregate for a specific purpose and thus bring with them a clear set of shared norms to regulate their behaviour as members of a specific group (e.g. a crowd of people welcoming the Queen, watching the Olympics, demonstrating outside parliament or protesting on campus). The lack of tradition of established norms that Turner refers to may be more myth than reality. There is a logic to the crowd, Reicher argues, that is not adequately captured by emergent norm theory.

SOCIAL IDENTITY APPROACH

An important aspect of crowd behaviour that is usually ignored is that it is actually an *intergroup* phenomenon (Reicher & Potter, 1985). Many crowd events involve, for instance, a direct collective confrontation between police and rioters or rival gangs or team supporters, and even where no direct confrontation occurs there is symbolic confrontation in that the crowd event symbolises a confrontation between, for instance, the crowd (or the wider group it represents) and the state.

A second point is that, far from losing identity, people in the crowd actually assume the identity provided by the crowd: there is a change from idiosyncratic personal identity to shared social identity as a crowd member. These points are made by Reicher (1982, 1987, 1996, 2001), who applies the social identity approach (this chapter) to collective behaviour. This analysis has been extended and called the SIDE model, or social identity model of deindividuation phenomena (Reicher, Spears, & Postmes, 1995).

Individuals come together, or find themselves together, as members of a specific social group for a specific purpose (e.g. conservationists protesting against environmental destruction). There is a high degree of shared social identity that promotes social categorisation of self and others in terms of that group membership. It is this wider social identity that provides the limits for crowd behaviour. For example, for certain groups violence may be legitimate (e.g. neo-Nazi groups in Germany), while for others it may not (e.g. supporters at a Test match).

While these general group norms provide the limits for acceptable crowd behaviour, there are often few norms to indicate how to behave in the specific context of the crowd event. Crowd members look to the identity-consistent behaviour of others, usually core group members, for guidance. Self-categorisation produces conformity to these context-specific norms of conduct. This explains why different groups in a crowd event often behave differently. For example, the police act in one way while the protesters act in a different way because, despite being exposed to the same environmental stimuli, their behaviours are being controlled by different group memberships.

This analysis seems to be consistent with what actually goes on in the crowd. For example, Fogelson's (1970) analysis of American race riots of the 1960s showed one noteworthy feature: that the violence was not arbitrary and without direction; and Milgram and Toch (1969) report accounts from participants in the Watts riot in which a sense of positive social identity is strongly emphasised. Reicher (1984; Reicher & Potter, 1985) uses his analysis to account for a specific riot, which occurred in the spring of 1980 in the St Paul's district of Bristol (this was a forerunner of subsequent widespread rioting in other cities in Britain during the early 1980s).

Three important points that emerged from this analysis were:

1. The violence, burning and looting were not unconstrained: the crowd was 'orderly' and the rioters were selective. Aggression was directed only at symbols of the state—the bank, the police, and entrepreneurial merchants in the community.
2. The crowd remained within the bounds of its own community—St Paul's.
3. During and as a consequence of the riot, rioters felt a strong sense of positive social identity as members of the St Paul's community.

All this makes sense when it is recognised that the riot was an anti-government protest on the part of the St Paul's community—an economically deprived area of Bristol with very high unemployment during a time of severe national unemployment.

Improving intergroup relations

Different theories of prejudice and intergroup behaviour spawn different emphases in the explanation of prejudice and conflict reduction. From the perspective of personality theories (e.g. authoritarian personality, dogmatism; Chapter 10), prejudice reduction entails changing the personality of the prejudiced person. More precisely, it would involve ensuring that particular parental strategies of child-rearing were avoided in order to prevent the creation of bigoted people. From the perspective of frustration–aggression theory (Chapter 10) or relative deprivation theory (this chapter), prejudice and intergroup conflict can be minimised by preventing frustration, lowering people's expectations, distracting people from realising that they are frustrated, providing people with harmless (non-social) activities through which to vent their frustration, or ensuring that aggressive associations are minimised among frustrated people.

Minimisation of aggressive cues and increase of non-aggressive cues seem to be important. For example, there is substantial research showing that, if weapons are made less available, aggression is reduced. When Jamaica implemented strict gun control and censorship of gun scenes on TV and in the movies in 1974, robbery and shooting rates dropped dramatically (Diener & Crandall, 1979). When Washington, DC, introduced handgun control laws there was a similar reduction in violent crime (Loftin, McDowall, Wiersema, & Cottey, 1991). The mere sight of a gun, either real or an image of one, can actually induce the **weapons effect** (see Chapter 12). On the other hand, the presence of non-aggressive cues such as infants and laughter can actually reduce aggression (Berkowitz, 1984; see also an account in Chapter 12 of how the depiction of violence in the media can increase the incidence of later antisocial acts).

For realistic conflict theory (this chapter), it is the existence of superordinate goals and cooperation for their achievement that gradually reduces intergroup hostility and conflict. The avoidance of mutually exclusive goals would also help. Finally, from a social identity perspective (this chapter), prejudice and overt conflict will wane to the extent that intergroup stereotypes become less derogatory and polarised and there exists mutually legitimised non-violent forms of intergroup competition.

PROPAGANDA AND EDUCATION

Propaganda messages, such as official exhortations that people should not be prejudiced, are usually formulated with reference to an absolute standard of morality (e.g. humanism). This may be effective for those people who subscribe to the standard of morality that is being invoked. It may also suppress more extreme forms of discrimination because it communicates social disapproval of discrimination.

As prejudice is at least partly based in ignorance (Stephan & Stephan, 1984), education—particularly the formal education of children—that promotes tolerance of diversity may reduce bigotry (Stephan & Stephan,

Traditional sex-roles: Stereotypes are difficult to change when billboards like this exist.

2001). This can involve teaching children about the moral implications of discrimination or teaching them facts about different groups. One problem with this strategy is that formal education has only marginal impact if children are systematically exposed to prejudice outside the classroom (e.g. bigoted parents, chauvinistic advertising and the material consequences of discrimination).

An educational strategy that may be more effective is to allow children to experience being a victim of prejudice. Jane Elliot, an Iowa school teacher, made a short movie called *The Eye of the Storm* of a classroom demonstration in which she divided her class of very young children into those with blue and those with brown eyes. For one day the 'brown eyes', and then for one day the 'blue eyes', were assigned inferior status: they were ridiculed, denied privileges, accused of being dull, lazy and sloppy and made to wear a special collar. It was hoped that the experience would be unpleasant enough to make the children think twice about being prejudiced against others (see third focus question).

One problem about prejudice is that it is *mindless*—a knee-jerk reaction to others as stereotypes. Perhaps if people, particularly when they were children, were taught to be mindful of others—to think about others not as stereotypes but as complex, whole individuals—then stereotypic reactions would be reduced. Langer, Bashner and Chanowitz (1985) explored this idea in the context of young children's attitudes towards the handicapped. They found a definite improvement in attitudes towards and treatment of handicapped children by children who had been trained to be *mindful* of others. Generally, the development of an ability to empathise with others significantly reduces people's capacity to harm those others physically, verbally, or indirectly via decisions and institutions (Miller & Eisenberg, 1988).

INTERGROUP CONTACT

A core feature of prejudice and conflict is the existence of unfavourable stereotypic outgroup attitudes. Such attitudes are enshrined in widespread social ideologies, and are maintained by lack of access to information that may disconfirm or improve negative attitudes. In most cases, such isolation is reinforced by real social and physical isolation of different groups from one another—the Protestant–Catholic situation in Northern Ireland is a case in point (Hewstone et al., in press). In other words, there is simply a chronic lack of intergroup contact and little opportunity to meet real members of the outgroup. The groups are kept apart by educational, occupational, cultural and material differences, as well as by anxiety about the personal negative consequences of contact (Stephan & Stephan, 1985). In fact, intergroup anxiety is one of the most significant hurdles to greater contact (Stephan & Stephan, 2000) and contact, under the right circumstances, does reduce intergroup anxiety (e.g. Hewstone et al., in press).

It is this state of affairs that spawns the popular view that, if there were greater intergroup contact, social harmony would prevail. This view is known as the **contact hypothesis** and was proposed on a scientific basis in 1954 by Allport, in the same year as the United States Supreme Court paved the way for the racial desegregation of the American education system. Contact is likely to be effective only under certain conditions (Allport, 1954b):

• It should be prolonged and involve cooperative activity, rather than casual and purposeless interaction. It was precisely this sort of contact that improved relations in Sherif's (1966) summer camp studies.

The contact hypothesis: Sushi for beginners. Under what conditions can contact between cultures improve intergroup relations?

• It should occur within the framework of official and institutional support for integration. Although legislation against discrimination, or for equal opportunities, will not in itself abolish prejudice, it provides a social climate that is conducive to the emergence of more tolerant social practices.

• It should involve people (or groups) of equal social status. Unequal status contact is more likely to confirm stereotypes and thus entrench prejudices.

Although this makes good sense (refer back to Box 11.3 and Figure 11.7 for a New Zealand example of contact in operation), almost half a century of research on the contact hypothesis yields a complex picture (e.g. Amir, 1976; Cook, 1985; Fox & Giles, 1993; Schofield, 1991)—at least partly due to the predominance of uncontrolled field studies, and partly because Allport's list of conditions has been extended to become overly specific. Nevertheless, there is generally good evidence for Allport's core contention that cooperation, shared goals, equal status, and the support of local authorities and norms are important preconditions to positive intergroup attitude change (Pettigrew & Tropp, 2000).

There are, however, some unresolved issues concerning precisely how contact may have effects (see recent overviews by Brewer and Miller, 1996; Brown, 1995, 1996; Hewstone, 1994, 1996; and Pettigrew, 1998). These issues include the role of similarity, and the generalisation of favourable interindividual attitudes to favourable intergroup attitudes.

Similarity

It has long been believed that prejudice is based in ignorance and the perception of irreconcilable intergroup differences (Pettigrew, 1971; Stephan & Stephan, 1984). Contact causes people to recognise that they are in fact a great deal more similar than they had thought, and hence to get to like one another (Byrne, 1971). There are some problems with this perspective:

• Because groups are often very different, contact is likely to bring to light more profound or more widespread differences, and hence to reduce liking further and produce a deterioration in intergroup attitudes (e.g. Bochner, 1982).

• As groups are actually so different, it may be misleading to promulgate the view that they are similar; this will establish false-positive expectations that are disconfirmed by contact.

• Research indicates that intergroup attitudes are not merely a matter of ignorance or unfamiliarity—rather, they reflect real conflict of interest between groups and are often maintained by the very existence of social categories. New knowledge made available by contact is unlikely to change attitudes.

Generalisation

Contact between representatives of different groups is supposed to improve attitudes towards the group as a whole—not just the specific outgroup members involved in the encounter. Weber and Crocker (1983) suggested three models of how this might happen:

1. *Bookkeeping*—the accumulation of favourable information about an outgroup gradually improves the stereotype. If outgroup information is stored in terms of exemplars, dramatic attitude changes can occur as new exemplars are added or retrieved (Smith & Zárate, 1992).
2. *Conversion*—dramatically counter-stereotypical information about an outgroup causes a sudden change in attitudes.
3. *Subtyping*—stereotype-inconsistent information produces a subtype, so that the outgroup stereotype becomes more complex but the superordinate category remains unchanged.

In general, research indicates that contact improves attitudes towards the participants but does not generalise to the group as a whole (Amir, 1976; Cook, 1978). One explanation is that most intergroup contact is actually *interpersonal* contact—contact between individuals as individuals, not group members. There is no good reason why an attitude towards one person should generalise to other people who are not categorically related to that person. For example, if you like John as a friend, and the fact that he happens to be Canadian is irrelevant, then your liking for John will not generalise to anyone else who just happens to be Canadian, or to the category 'Canadian' as a whole.

This raises an interesting paradox: perhaps intergroup contact is more likely to generalise if people's group affiliations are made *more*, not less, salient during contact—the *mutual-differentiation model* (Hewstone & Brown, 1986; Johnston & Hewstone, 1990). There is some support for this idea. Wilder (1984) had participants from rival colleges come into contact over a cooperative task in which the outgroup person, who was either highly typical or highly atypical of that college, behaved in a pleasant or unpleasant manner. Those taking part evaluated the other college as a whole after the contact. Figure 11.16 shows that, relative to a no-contact control, it was only where contact was both pleasant and with a typical outgroup member that there was generalised improvement of attitude (see also Rothbart & John, 1985; Weber & Crocker, 1983).

Miller and Brewer (1984; Miller, Brewer, & Edwards, 1985) have a different perspective—the *decategorisation model*. They argue that contact which draws attention to people's group affiliations will rapidly degenerate into conflict and thus a deterioration of

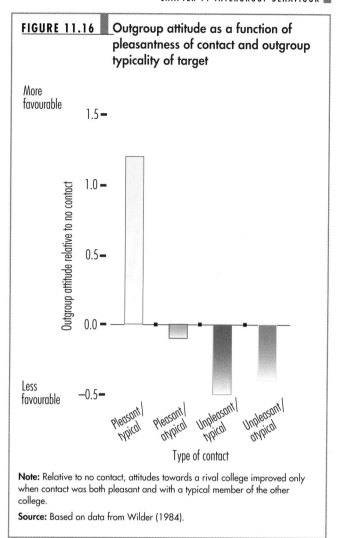

FIGURE 11.16 Outgroup attitude as a function of pleasantness of contact and outgroup typicality of target

Note: Relative to no contact, attitudes towards a rival college improved only when contact was both pleasant and with a typical member of the other college.

Source: Based on data from Wilder (1984).

generalised attitudes. Instead, they recommend interpersonal encounters that stress socioemotional aspects and avoid group or task-related aspects of the encounter—that is, 'decategorisation' or personalisation. This seems to work (Hamburger, 1994), but as yet the idea has been tested only in abstract experimental settings, where intergroup relations lack the powerful emotions and personal investments associated with 'real' intergroup relations. Where real intergroup conflict exists (e.g. between Catholics and Protestants in Northern Ireland), it may be almost impossible to distract people from their group affiliations.

A more promising variant of the interpersonal contact idea, called the **extended contact effect**, has been proposed by Wright, Aron, McLaughlin-Volpe and Ropp (1997). Wright and his colleagues suggest, and provide some evidence, that intergroup attitudes can improve if people witness or have knowledge of rewarding intergroup friendships between others—if my friend John has close outgroup friends then maybe the outgroup isn't quite as bad as I thought. This can happen because members of the same group are linked by a common identity; this allows them, in the words of Wright, Aron and Tropp (2002), *to include the other in the self*—that is, to develop a degree of intersubjectivity that allows them to experience others as themselves. Intersubjectivity may also be implicated in vicarious dissonance (Cooper & Hogg, 2002; see Chapter 6) and intergroup emotions (Mackie & Smith, 2002a; see above).

Related to the extended contact idea is the notion that perspective-taking plays a role in improving intergroup attitudes. If we are able to take the perspective of another person and experience the world as they do, we are less likely to harbour harmful negative attitudes about that person and perhaps more likely to behave prosocially towards them (see Chapter 14). There is now some evidence that perspective-taking can improve intergroup attitudes (Galinsky, 2002; Galinsky & Moskowitz, 2000; Vescio, Sechrist, & Paoluci, 2003).

Another process that does not involve drawing attention to the original intergroup context is 'recategorisation'. Gaertner's *common ingroup identity model* (Gaertner & Dovidio, 2000; Gaertner, Dovidio, Anastasio, Bachman, & Rust, 1993; Gaertner, Mann, Murrell, & Dovidio, 1989; Gaertner, Rust, Dovidio, Bachman, & Anastasio, 1996) suggests that, if members of opposing groups can be encouraged to recategorise themselves as members of the same group, intergroup attitudes will, by definition, not only improve but actually disappear (see below for some limitations of this process).

Contact policy in multicultural contexts

Initially, it might seem that the most non-discriminatory and unprejudiced way to approach interethnic relations is simply to be 'colour-blind'—that is, to ignore group differences completely (Berry, 1984; Schofield, 1986). This is a 'melting-pot' policy, where all groups are ostensibly treated as equal (see also the concept of *assimilation* discussed in Chapter 16). There are at least three problems with this approach:

1. It ignores the fact that discrimination has disadvantaged certain groups (e.g. regarding education or health) and that, unless positive steps are taken to rectify the problem, the disadvantage will simply persist.
2. It ignores the reality of ethnic/cultural differences (e.g. Muslim dress code for women).
3. The melting pot is not really a melting pot at all but rather a 'dissolving' pot, where ethnic minorities are dissolved and assimilated by the dominant social group: minority groups are stripped of their cultural heritage and cease to exist.

The alternative approach is pluralism or multiculturalism—an approach that draws attention and responds to the reality of cultural diversity and group differences in an attempt to improve negative attitudes and redress disadvantage, at the same time as the cultural integrity of different groups is preserved. This approach aims to achieve a multicultural society in which intergroup relations among the constituent groups is harmonious (see also Chapter 16). Empirical research suggests that intergroup arrangements that resemble multiculturalism are quite effective in reducing intergroup conflict (Hornsey & Hogg, 2000a; see below).

SUPERORDINATE GOALS

In his summer camp studies, Sherif (1966) managed to improve intergroup relations between the warring factions by allowing them to cooperate in order to achieve a number of superordinate goals (shared goals that were unachievable by either group alone). The effectiveness of providing a superordinate goal has been confirmed by other studies (Brown & Abrams, 1986; Ryen & Kahn, 1975; Turner, 1981b; Worchel, 1979). One particularly effective superordinate goal is resistance against a shared threat from a common enemy (Dion, 1979; Wilder & Shapiro, 1984). This is the basis of alliances that can temporarily improve relations between erstwhile opponents (e.g. the existence for almost 45 years of the former Soviet Union as a common foe to unite Western nations).

There is an important qualification. Superordinate goals do not reduce intergroup conflict if the groups fail to achieve the goal. For example, Worchel, Andreoli and Folger (1977) created competitive, cooperative or independent relations between two groups and then provided a superordinate goal that the groups either achieved or failed to achieve. The superordinate goal improved intergroup relations in all cases except where previously competitive groups failed to achieve the goal. In this condition, relations actually deteriorated. Unsuccessful intergroup cooperation to achieve a superordinate goal appears to worsen intergroup relations only when the failure can be attributed, rightly or wrongly, to the actions of the outgroup (Worchel & Novell, 1980). Where there is sufficient external justification, and the outgroup is not blamed, there is the more usual improvement in intergroup relations.

For example, the 1982 Falklands conflict between Britain and Argentina provided a superordinate goal to reduce factional conflict within Argentina. The cooperative exercise failed (Argentina lost the war) and, because the actions of the junta could easily be blamed, there was renewed factional conflict that almost immediately overthrew the junta (Latin American Bureau, 1982).

PLURALISM AND DIVERSITY

One of the main problems of intergroup relations is that, in most contexts, groups are actually subgroups wholly nested within larger groups or cross-cut with them (Crisp, Ensari, Hewstone, & Miller, 2003; see Chapter 8). For example, the psychology department at your university is a group nested with the larger university, whereas the group of social psychologists is a cross-cutting category because its membership stretches across many universities around the world. In these situations it is rare for all subgroups to have an equal representation in the defining features of the overarching identity—more often than not one group is much better represented, with the consequence that other groups feel subordinate (Mummendey & Wenzel, 1999). A similar problem exists when one organisation merges with or takes over another organisation: the post-merger entity contains within it both pre-merger entities and, usually, one pre-merger entity has lower status and poor representation in the post-merger entity (e.g. Terry, Carey, & Callan, 2001).

Even where relations among subgroups are reasonably good, another problem, associated with superordinate goals, emerges. Intense or prolonged cooperation to achieve a shared goal can gradually blur intergroup boundaries (Gaertner & Dovidio, 2000; see discussion above of the common ingroup identity model). Although this may seem an ideal solution to intergroup conflict, it can backfire. Even though the groups have superordinate goals, they may also wish to maintain their individual identities and so resist the perceived threat of becoming a single entity. New conflicts can thus arise to maintain intergroup distinctiveness. This effect has been observed in a chemical plant (Blake, Shepard, & Mouton, 1964), an engineering factory (Brown, 1978) and the laboratory (Brown & Wade, 1987; Deschamps & Brown, 1983). It will be interesting to see if the current pressures in Europe for international cooperation in the service of superordinate economic goals (the European Union) increase international conflict on other dimensions in order to maintain national distinctiveness.

Hornsey, at the University of Queensland, has conducted a program of research suggesting that a careful balancing of superordinate identity and positive subgroup distinctiveness may provide a promising blueprint for social harmony (Hornsey & Hogg, 2000a, 2000b, 2000c). This mimics the sociopolitical strategy of multiculturalism, or cultural pluralism, that is pursued by countries such as Australia and Canada. This arrangement works because by retaining distinct cultural identities, there is no threat that would provoke intergroup hostility. At the same time, the existence of a superordinate identity can cause subgroups to see themselves as distinct groups, with complementary roles, all working on the same team towards integrative goals.

More broadly, this idea suggests that the answer to intergroup conflict may be to build groups that are not only based on tolerance for diversity but actually celebrate diversity as a defining feature of their social identity (Niedenthal & Beike, 1997; Roccas & Brewer, 2002; Wright, Aron, & Tropp, 2002; see also Hogg & Hornsey, in press).

A final point about goal relations and social harmony picks up on our earlier discussion of zero-sum and non-zero-sum goals. Where two groups see their goal relations as zero-sum they are characterising their relationship as competitive—if they get a lot, we get a little. There is a limited pie to divide up and thus their actions are frustrating our goals. Where two groups see their goal relations as non-zero-sum they are characterising their relationship as cooperative—if they get a lot, we get a lot. The pie can get bigger if we work together and thus their actions are helping us achieve our goals.

Goal relations do not have to be accurate perceptions—they are subject to ideology and rhetoric. Take the immigration debates in Australia and New Zealand (and in most countries around the world). One side argues that immigration is bad because immigrants come along and take people's jobs and soak up public money—a zero-sum rhetoric that is associated with xenophobia, prejudice and intolerance towards immigrants. The other side argues that immigration is good because immigrants bring skills, energy and enthusiasm that create new jobs and additional wealth—a non-zero-sum rhetoric that is associated with internationalism and positive attitudes towards immigrants and immigration.

COMMUNICATION

Groups in conflict can try to improve intergroup relations by communicating directly about the conflict and attempting to resolve it. This can be done through bargaining, mediation or arbitration. These are very complex procedures that are prey to all sorts of psychological barriers to dispute resolution (e.g. self-esteem, emotion, misattribution; Ross & Ward, 1995; Thompson & Loewenstein, 2003; Thompson, Medvex, Seiden, & Kopelman, 2001). One real problem is that it can be difficult for negotiators to take the perspective of the other—a failure that is amplified by the intergroup nature of the negotiation, making compromise almost impossible (Carroll, Bazerman, & Maury, 1988; Galinsky & Mussweiler, 2001). In addition, many crucial negotiations are between cultures and thus a host of cross-cultural communication issues can arise to complicate things (e.g. Carnevale & Leung, 2001; Kimmel, 1994; see also M.H. Bond & Smith, 1996; Smith & Bond, 1998).

Bargaining

Intergroup negotiations usually take place between representatives of the opposing groups: for example, union and management may try to resolve disputes by direct negotiation between representatives. One of the most significant intergroup negotiations of the 20th century was the 1945 meeting in Yalta in the Crimea between Stalin, Churchill and Roosevelt, as representatives of the victorious Allies of World War II: the Soviet Union, Britain and the United States. The negotiation of international differences at that meeting has determined the nature of the world to the present day. Social psychological research indicates that when people are **bargaining** on behalf of a social group to which they belong, they tend to bargain much more fiercely and less compromisingly than if they were bargaining for themselves (Benton & Druckman, 1974; Breaugh & Klimoski, 1981). The effect is enhanced when negotiators are aware that they are being observed by their constituents, either directly or through the media (Carnevale, Pruitt, & Britton, 1979).

This 'bullish' strategy of relative intransigence is less likely to secure a satisfactory compromise than a more interpersonal orientation in which both parties make reciprocal concessions (Esser & Komorita, 1975; Komorita & Esser, 1975). Direct negotiation between group representatives is therefore quite likely to reach an impasse, in which neither group feels it can compromise without losing face. A case in point is George Bush senior and Saddam Hussein's media-orchestrated bargaining over the plight of Kuwait in 1990, which seemed mainly to involve Bush threatening to 'kick Saddam's ass', and Hussein threatening to make 'infidel' Americans 'swim in their own blood'—not a good start.

Mediation

To break the deadlock, a third party can be brought in for **mediation** between the groups (Pruitt, 1981). To be effective, mediators should have power, must be seen by both groups to be impartial (Lim & Carnevale, 1990), and the groups should already be fairly close in their positions (Rubin, 1980). Biased mediators are ineffective because they are not trusted, and weak mediators

are ineffective because they exert little pressure on intransigent groups to be reasonable.

Although mediators have no power to impose a settlement, they can help in several important ways:

- They are able to *reduce the emotional heat* associated with deadlock (Tetlock, 1988).
- They can help to *reduce misperceptions*, encourage understanding and establish trust.
- They can propose *novel compromises* that allow both groups to appear to win—that is, to change a zero-sum conflict (one in which one group's gains are precisely the other group's losses; the more one gains, the more the other loses) into a non-zero-sum conflict (where both groups can gain).
- They can help both parties to make a *graceful retreat*, without losing face, from untenable positions.
- They can inhibit unreasonable claims and behaviours by threatening public exposure of unreasonable groups.
- They can reduce intragroup conflict and thus help a group to clarify its consensual position.

History provides instances of effective mediation. For example, Henry Kissinger's shuttle diplomacy of the mid-1970s, which involved meeting separately with each side over a period of two years after the 1973 Arab–Israeli conflict, produced a number of significant agreements between Israel and its Arab neighbours (Pruitt, 1981). In the late 1970s, using a slightly different strategy, Jimmy Carter secluded Egypt's President Sadat and Israel's Prime Minister Begin at Camp David near Washington in the United States. After 13 days an agreement was reached that ended a state of war that had existed between Israel and Egypt since 1948.

Arbitration

Many intergroup conflicts are so intractable, the underlying interests so divergent, that mediation is ineffective. The last resort is **arbitration**, in which the mediator or some other third party is invited to impose a mutually binding settlement. Research shows that arbitration really is the last resort for conflict resolution (McGillicuddy, Welton, & Pruitt, 1987). The prospect of arbitration can backfire because both groups adopt outrageous final positions in the hope that arbitration will produce a more favourable compromise (Pruitt, 1986). One way to combat this is through *final-offer arbitration*, where the third party chooses one of the final offers. This tends to encourage more reasonable final positions.

Conciliation

Although direct communication may help to improve intergroup relations, tensions and suspicions often run so high that direct communication is all but impossible.

Mediation: An effective mediator needs to have power and to be seen as impartial.

Instead, conflicting groups threaten, coerce or retaliate against one another and, if this behaviour is reciprocated there is an escalation of the conflict. For example, during World War II, Germany believed it could move Britain to surrender by bombing its cities and the Allies believed they could break Germany's will by bombing its cities. Similarly, Japan believed it could dissuade the United States from interfering in its imperial expansion in Asia by bombing Pearl Harbor, and the United States believed it could bring North Vietnam to the negotiation table by sustained bombing of cities and villages.

There are uncountable examples of the terrible consequences of threat, coercion and retaliation. Can this cycle be broken? Might one group adopt an unconditionally cooperative strategy in the hope that the other group will reciprocate? Laboratory research suggests this does not work: unilateral unconditional cooperation simply invites retaliation and exploitation (Shure, Meeker, & Hansford, 1965).

Osgood (1962) suggested a more effective alternative that involves **conciliation** (i.e. not retaliation), but with enough strength to discourage exploitation. Called 'graduated and reciprocated initiatives in tension-reduction' (with the acronym GRIT), it invokes social psychological principles to do with the norm of reciprocity and the attribution of motives. GRIT involves at least two stages:

1. One party announces its conciliatory intent (allowing a clear attribution of non-devious motive), clearly specifies a small concession it is about to make (activates reciprocity norm) and invites its opponent to do likewise.
2. The initiator makes the concession exactly as announced and in a publicly verifiable manner. There is now strong pressure on the other group to reciprocate.

Laboratory research provides evidence for the effectiveness of this procedure. For example, a *tit-for-tat* strategy that begins with one cooperative act and proceeds by matching the other party's last response is both conciliatory and strong and can improve interparty relations (Axelrod & Dion, 1988; Komorita, Parks, & Hulbert, 1992). Direct laboratory tests of GRIT by Linskold and his colleagues (e.g. Linskold, 1978; Linskold & Han, 1988) confirm that announcement of cooperative intent boosts cooperation, repeated conciliatory acts breed trust and maintenance of power equality protects against exploitation. GRIT-type strategies have been used effectively from time to time in international relations (e.g. between the former Soviet Union and the United States during the Berlin crisis of the early 1960s, and between Israel and Egypt on a number of occasions).

Summary

- Intergroup behaviour can be defined as any behaviour that is influenced by group members' perceptions of an outgroup.
- Group members may engage in collective protest to the extent that they subjectively feel deprived as a group relative to their aspirations or to other groups.
- Competition for scarce resources tends to produce intergroup conflict. Cooperation to achieve a shared goal reduces conflict.
- Social categorisation may be the only necessary precondition for being a group and engaging in intergroup behaviour, provided that people identify with the category.
- Self-categorisation is the process responsible for psychologically identifying with a group and behaving as a group member (e.g. conformity, stereotyping,

ethnocentrism, ingroup solidarity). Social comparison and the need for self-esteem motivate groups to compete in different ways (depending on the nature of intergroup relations) for relatively positive social identity.
- Crowd behaviour may not represent a loss of identity and regression to primitive antisocial instincts. Instead, it may be group behaviour that is governed by local contextual norms that are framed by a wider social identity.
- Prejudice, discrimination and intergroup conflict are difficult to reduce. Together, education, propaganda and shared goals together may help, but simply bringing groups into contact with one another is unlikely to be effective. Other strategies include bargaining, mediation, arbitration and conciliation.

LINKS

YOU HAVE READ ABOUT:	WHICH LINKS TO:
Relative deprivation	modification of the frustration–aggression hypothesis (10)
Realistic conflict	an intergroup explanation of prejudice and discrimination (10)
Social identity	intergroup attributions (3); why people join groups (8)
Self-categorisation theory	prototypes (2) applied at an intergroup level
Collective behaviour and the crowd	violence on a grand scale (12)
Improving intergroup relations	reducing aggression and violence (12)

Key terms

accentuation effect *(p. 276)*
arbitration *(p. 290)*
authoritarian personality *(p. 272)*
bargaining *(p. 290)*
cognitive alternatives *(p. 274)*
collective behaviour *(p. 279)*
commons dilemma *(p. 268)*
conciliation *(p. 291)*
contact hypothesis *(p. 286)*
deindividuation *(p. 280)*
depersonalisation *(p. 272)*
egoistic relative deprivation *(p. 263)*
emergent norm theory *(p. 283)*
entitativity *(p. 272)*
ethnocentrism *(p. 271)*
extended contact effect *(p. 287)*
fraternalistic relative deprivation *(p. 263)*

free-rider effect *(p. 268)*
frustration–aggression hypothesis *(p. 272)*
illusory correlation *(p. 278)*
ingroup favouritism *(p. 271)*
intergroup behaviour *(p. 261)*
intergroup differentiation *(p. 271)*
intergroup emotions theory (IET) *(p. 278)*
J-curve *(p. 262)*
mediation *(p. 290)*
metacontrast principle *(p. 272)*
metatheory *(p. 261)*
minimal group paradigm *(p. 269)*
optimal distinctiveness *(p. 278)*
prisoner's dilemma *(p. 267)*
prototype *(p. 272)*
realistic conflict theory *(p. 266)*
reductionism *(p. 272)*

relative deprivations *(p. 261)*
relative homogeneity effect *(p. 276)*
self-categorisation theory *(p. 271)*
social categorisation *(p. 270)*
social change belief system *(p. 274)*
social competition *(p. 274)*
social creativity *(p. 274)*
social identity *(p. 271)*
social identity approach *(p. 271)*
social identity theory *(p. 271)*
social mobility belief system *(p. 274)*
stereotype *(p. 271)*
superordinate goals *(p. 266)*
system justification theory *(p. 274)*
weapons effect *(p. 285)*

FURTHER READING

Brewer, M. B., & Brown, R. J. (1998). Intergroup relations. In D. T. Gilbert, S. T. Fiske, & G. Lindzey (Eds.), *The handbook of social psychology* (4th ed., Vol. 2, pp. 554–594). New York: McGraw-Hill. Up-to-date and comprehensive overview of the field of intergroup relations. This most recent edition of the classic handbook is a primary source for theory and research.

Brewer, M. B. (2003). *Intergroup relations* (2nd ed.). Philadelphia, PA: Open University Press. A readable and wide-ranging overview of research on intergroup relations, including prejudice reduction.

Brown, R. J. (1995). *Prejudice: Its social psychology.* Oxford, UK: Blackwell. Prejudice is treated as intergroup behaviour in this accessible, detailed and comprehensive discussion of the social psychology of intergroup behaviour.

Brown, R. J. (2000). *Group processes* (2nd ed.). Oxford, UK: Blackwell. Readable introduction to group processes and intergroup relations, with a relatively European perspective.

Brown, R. J., & Gaertner, S. (Eds.). (2001). *Blackwell handbook of social psychology: Intergroup processes.* Oxford, UK: Blackwell. An up-to-date collection of 25 chapters from leading social psychologists, covering the entire field of intergroup processes.

Fiske, S. T. (1998). Stereotyping, prejudice, and discrimination. In D. T. Gilbert, S. T. Fiske, & G. Lindzey (Eds.), *The handbook of social psychology* (4th ed., Vol. 2, pp. 357–414).

New York: McGraw-Hill. Up-to-date overview that also covers social cognitive aspects of intergroup behaviour.

Hogg, M. A. (2003). Social identity. In M. R. Leary & J. P. Tangney (Eds.), *Handbook of self and identity* (pp. 462–479). New York: Guilford. Entirely up-to-date and easily readable coverage of the social identity perspective in social psychology.

Hogg, M. A. (2003). Intergroup relations. In J. Delamater (Ed.), *Handbook of social psychology* (pp. 479–501). New York: Kluwer Academic/Plenum. Very accessible overview and review of social psychology research on intergroup relations, prejudice, discrimination and social identity.

Hogg, M. A., & Abrams, D. (1988). *Social identifications: A social psychology of intergroup relations and group processes*. London: Routledge. Detailed coverage of theory and research on group processes and intergroup relations—probably still the most comprehensive overview of the social identity approach.

Hogg, M. A., & Abrams, D. (Eds.). (2001). *Intergroup relations: Essential readings*. Philadelphia, PA: Psychology Press. Annotated collection of key publications on intergroup relations. There is an introductory overview chapter and commentary chapters introducing each reading.

Hogg, M. A., & Abrams, D. (2003). Intergroup behavior and social identity. In M. A. Hogg & J. Cooper (Eds.), *Sage handbook of social psychology* (pp. 407–431). London: Sage. A comprehensive overview of research on intergroup relations and social identity; includes substantial coverage of prejudice and discrimination.

Hogg, M. A., & Tindale, R. S. (Eds.). (2001). *Blackwell handbook of social psychology: Group processes*. Oxford, UK: Blackwell. A comprehensive, detailed and completely up-to-date collection of 26 chapters from leading social psychologists covering the entire field of group processes. Many chapters also deal with intergroup relations.

Oakes, P. J., Haslam, S. A., & Turner, J. C. (1994). *Stereotyping and social reality*. Oxford, UK: Blackwell. Detailed and technical discussion, mainly from a social identity perspective, of stereotyping as it relates to social cognition and intergroup relations.

Robinson, W. P. (Ed.). (1996). *Social groups and identities: Developing the legacy of Henri Tajfel*. Oxford, UK: Butterworth–Heinemann. An interesting collection of chapters from almost everyone who was closely associated with Tajfel's far-reaching insights into intergroup relations; although social identity and self-categorisation theory are well represented, there is also intriguing diversity and breadth in these chapters.

Stangor, C. (Ed.). (2000). *Stereotypes and prejudice: Essential readings*. Philadelphia, PA: Psychology Press. Annotated collection of key publications on stereotyping and prejudice, but also covering some cognitive aspects of intergroup relations. There is an introductory overview chapter and commentary chapters introducing each reading.

Wright, S. C., & Taylor, D. M. (2003). The social psychology of cultural diversity: Social stereotyping, prejudice, and discrimination. In M. A. Hogg & J. Cooper (Eds.), *Sage handbook of social psychology* (pp. 432–457). London: Sage. A comprehensive overview of the current state of research on prejudice and discrimination; deals with stereotyping and prejudice reduction.

Aggression

FOCUS QUESTIONS

1. Some people argue that 'Humans are real losers. We are like the biblical Cain, born to harm others.' Do you agree with this point of view?
2. Other people argue that 'Humans are real losers. We learn how to hurt people because it is an inevitable part of living.' Do you prefer this point of view?
3. Anyway, some people say you shouldn't let feelings like that remain bottled up. You should let them hang out, at least part of the time—shouldn't you?
4. Is it true that porn movies make men violent towards women?
5. May wiped her blood onto the back of her hand. 'Sorry babe, you had it coming!', Mitch explained. How can violence occur within intimate relationships?

THIS CHAPTER DISCUSSES:

- aggression and violence in the community
- definitions and measurement of aggression
- biological and social theories of aggression
- personal and situational factors
- the effects of mass media
- domestic violence
- institutionalised aggression
- group-centred versus person-centred explanations
- reducing aggression at interpersonal and intergroup levels.

Aggression in our community

We are continually reminded of the violence that surrounds us. The mass media, the entertainment industry and even our personal experience provide examples from everyday life. Occasionally, we may talk about someone behaving like an animal, but the most bestial of acts are those committed by humans against humans. In aggression's most extreme forms, entire races or nations are threatened. In our own cities, at a more mundane level, banks are robbed regularly, citizens are mugged for their wallets every day, children are beaten and people are raped. Are things getting worse?

Nearly every year, we read of reports from our police departments that crime in general, and especially crime against individuals and property, is becoming more frequent. Consider how often a murder takes place in our communities. The figures in Table 12.1 show comparative murder rates (for every 100 000 people) in the Australian states and territories and in New Zealand in 1999. As a yardstick, in 1994 the comparative rate in the United States was nearly nine, but in Colombia it was a staggering 78 (United Nations Statistics, 1994; cited in Brehm, Kassin, & Fein, 1999). Maguire and Pastore (2001) report 1995 homicide rates that vary from a low of less than 1 per 100 000 in Singapore to a high of 35 in South Africa, with the United States at nine and Europe at two.

What is the evidence that violent crime is increasing in our communities? Consider the trend for rates of violent crimes recorded in New Zealand over the decade 1989–99 (see Figure 12.1). Although there is an increase in the rate at which violent crime occurs, there are peaks and troughs across individual years. The number of convictions for violent crimes in New Zealand nearly doubled from 1991 to 1998, but peaked in 1995 (New Zealand Police Statistics, 2000). Of the 461 677 offences recorded by the New Zealand Police in 1998 (excluding traffic offences), violent crimes constituted nearly 9%. The US Department of Justice (2001) reports homicide rates per 100 000 people in the United States from 1900 to 1997: the rate fluctuates, with troughs in 1900 (1:100 000) and 1957 (3:100 000), and peaks in 1930 (9:100 000) and in 1980 (10:100 000).

The effects of mass murders can make quite a difference in one year in a state or country with a relatively small population (say, less than 5 million people). For example, the number of murders in Australia in 1999 was 342—a 29% increase on the 285 murders in the previous year. However, the 1999 figure includes the mass murder of 12 people in Snowtown in South Australia and two incidents of murder-suicides in Western Australia, which claimed another nine lives.

If we broaden the picture to include other classes of violent crime, statistics from an international survey

TABLE 12.1	Murder rates in Australia and New Zealand 1999
LOCATION	RATE PER 100 000 PEOPLE
Australian Capital Territory	1.61
New South Wales	5.40
Northern Territory	7.26
Queensland	6.18
South Australia	6.50
Tasmania	2.13
Victoria	3.50
Western Australia	4.89
National Australian average	4.98
New Zealand average	2.59

Source: Australian Bureau of Statistics (2000); International Comparisons of Recorded Violent Crime Rates for 2000.

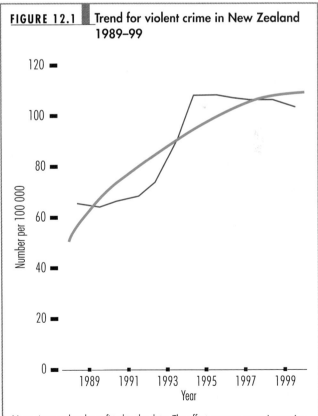

FIGURE 12.1 Trend for violent crime in New Zealand 1989–99

Note: A curve has been fitted to the data. The effect appears as an increasing trend.

Source: New Zealand Police Statistics (2000).

found that New Zealanders reported being victims of assault or threatened assault on more occasions than others in the study, followed in frequency by Australians, Americans and Canadians (Harland, 1995; see Figure 12.2).

In a New Zealand survey, it was estimated that domestic violence (assault, rape and incest within the home) accounts for as much as 80% of all violent offences, although most of it remains unreported (Roper Report, 1987). The phenomenon of underreporting makes it difficult to establish reliable prevalence rates of crimes such as aggression against the person or against property. Often, crimes are not reported for reasons such as fear of reprisal, lack of faith in the possibility of resolution, apathy or ignorance of available legal help. An Australian report compared two measures: (1) official data—the number of crimes *reported* to police, and (2) unofficial data—the number of *unreported* crimes, according to a Crime and Safety Survey of 42 200 adults from 21 000 households (see Figure 12.3). The reporting rates of different categories of crime varied. For example, most car thefts were reported (95%) and half of the robberies, but few of the assaults (28%) and sexual assaults (33%).

For many people, even if they are not immediate victims, there are more indirect and insidious effects of violence at the societal level. We are changing aspects of our lifestyle because of fear of attack: more people carry weapons of some kind, take special precautions to avoid vulnerability or take lessons in self-defence. The media report a constant, depressing barrage of violent behaviour at the interpersonal, societal and international

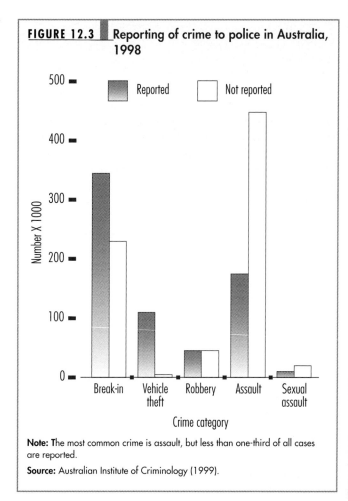

FIGURE 12.3 Reporting of crime to police in Australia, 1998

Note: The most common crime is assault, but less than one-third of all cases are reported.

Source: Australian Institute of Criminology (1999).

level. At the individual level, it is likely that most of us experience feelings of aggression towards others quite regularly, although our response may stop short of acting out those feelings through aggressive behaviour.

Violence and aggression are not limited to the adult world but are well established—and some would say originate—in childhood. In a survey of New Zealand school children, mostly 11- and 12-year-olds, Lind and Maxwell (1996) found that half had been punched, kicked, beaten or hit by other children, and two-thirds had been threatened with physical abuse or had experienced emotional abuse by their peers.

It would therefore seem reasonable to conclude that aggression is both omnipresent and an integral part of human nature. Some theorists (e.g. Ardrey, 1961) claim that aggression is a basic human instinct, an innate fixed action pattern that we share with other species (see also the bodily expression of emotions, Chapter 15). It is thus an inevitable and inescapable aspect of our lives. Other theorists are more optimistic about our ability to prevent and control violence and aggression, but nonetheless concede that aggression will continue to be an aspect of human behaviour. We explore these different emphases concerning the origins of aggression in a later section.

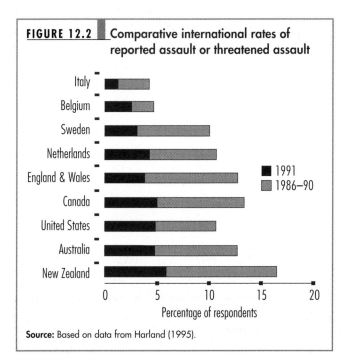

FIGURE 12.2 Comparative international rates of reported assault or threatened assault

Source: Based on data from Harland (1995).

The immediate challenges for psychologists are to identify the reasons why people aggress against others, and to find ways of reducing the harmful effects of aggression on the victims, the aggressor and society. But, first, how are we to define 'aggression'?

Defining aggression

Psychological definitions are to an extent determined by theoretical perspectives. We discuss the main theoretical perspectives of aggression later in this chapter, but the concept itself presents a special problem for social psychologists that arises within the context of empirical research methods. The study of aggressive behaviour, whether in experimental or in naturalistic settings, requires some agreement in description and explanation. Here we have a problem: although most of us will talk about aggression in everyday conversation with a reasonably clear idea of what we mean, there is still no consensus within or across the sciences about its components. One researcher may define aggression using physical parameters—pushing, shoving, striking—while another may add other features—threatening speech, verbal insults, facial expressions. To an extent, what is considered to be aggressive is determined by the social and cultural characteristics of the perceiver. There are cultures and subcultures that regard violence as ordinary

and even necessary, an analysis that Elkin (1961) has applied to Australian Aborigines (see also Chapter 16). On the other hand, there are those who consider that most Western societies are unacceptably violent.

There is no shortage of social psychological definitions of aggression. Here are a few:

- behaviour that results in personal injury or destruction of property (Bandura, 1973);
- behaviour intended to harm another of the same species (Scherer, Abeles, & Fischer, 1975);
- behaviour directed towards the goal of harming or injuring another living being who is motivated to avoid such treatment (Baron, 1977);
- the intentional infliction of some form of harm on others (Baron & Byrne, 2000);
- behaviour directed towards another individual carried out with the proximate (immediate) intent to cause harm (Anderson & Huesmann, 2003).

Conceptual differences between these definitions are apparent. In Baron's case, it is interesting to see how he has simplified his later definition.

Now check the kinds of behaviour listed in Box 12.1. Should they be included as components in a satisfactory definition? Although most textbooks offer a definition of aggression, no definition is generally agreed upon. In reviewing various attempts, Carlson, Marcus-Newhall and Miller (1989) argued that more common ground is achieved, across findings and contexts, by defining

---

BOX 12.1   Applying two definitions of aggression

WHAT IS AGGRESSION? CONSIDER THE TWO DEFINITIONS THAT FOLLOW AND THEN TRY TO APPLY EACH ONE TO THE DIFFERENT KINDS OF BEHAVIOUR THAT ARE LISTED

1. Behaviour that results in personal injury or destruction of property (Bandura, 1973).
2. The intentional infliction of some type of harm upon others (Baron & Byrne, 2000).

How do these two definitions, one stressing *outcomes* and the other stressing *intentions*, stand up when you classify the following kinds of behaviour? Can you decide which behaviours are necessary components of aggression? Also, which ones in combination are sufficient to define aggression?

- actual harm (although not unsuccessful hostility, even if it was intended);
- physical injury (although not psychological harm, such as verbal abuse);
- any kind of harm to a person (although not to an animal or to property);
- harm to a person in a rule-governed context (such as a boxing match);
- intention to do harm (although not careless or negligent harm, or accidental injury caused by self-serving behaviour);
- belief by the victim that harm has occurred (although not sado-masochistic injury);
- injury in the victim's alleged 'best interests' (such as smacking a child);
- harm to another (although not self-injury, such as self-mutilation or suicide).

This list is not exhaustive. You may think of other elements of behaviour that may or may not render it aggressive, according to your perspective. Discuss some of these issues with a friend. Is it difficult to agree on a definition?

aggression as 'the intent to harm'. After you have checked Box 12.1 you may well agree that this definition is a major compromise!

Measuring aggression

In practice, scientists tend to use definitions that correspond to their own social values. As a result, the behaviour studied may differ in crucial ways from one researcher to another, and across different cultures, and yet be given the same label of 'aggression'. For example, are bodily cues of anger directed towards someone else the same as actually fighting? Are protests by indigenous peoples about their traditional lands comparable to acts of international terrorism? Is spanking a child in the same category as the grisly deeds of a serial killer?

As the problem of definition is not fully resolved, we might ask how aggression has been operationalised. We note in Chapter 1 that the scientific social psychologist should offer a definition of a social process in such a way that it is rendered capable of measurement—that is, use an **operational definition**. The difficulty is that different researchers have used different measures for the same term. Look at the examples, drawn from different researchers, shown in Box 12.2. Each of these measures has been used as a substitute, or an **analogue**, for the real thing. The major reason for this is ethical (see Chapter 1), as it is very difficult to justify an actual physical assault against a person in an experimental setting.

But can we generalise any of the findings of research using an analogue measure to a larger population in real-life settings? For example, what is the **external validity** of the aggression machine developed by Buss (1961), which is similar to the apparatus used by Milgram (1963) in his studies of obedience (see Chapter 7)?

BOX 12.2 Experimental analogues of aggression

Aggression has been operationally defined and then measured in research in many different ways.

- Punching an inflated plastic doll (Bandura, Ross, & Ross, 1963).
- Pushing a button that is supposed to deliver an electric shock to someone else (Buss, 1961).
- Pencil-and-paper ratings by teachers and classmates of a child's level of aggressiveness (Eron, 1982).
- Written self-report by institutionalised teenage boys about their prior aggressive behaviour (Leyens, Camino, Parke, & Berkowitz, 1975).
- A verbal expression of willingness to use violence in an experimental laboratory setting (Geen, 1978).

Cherek, Schnapp, Moeller and Dougherty (1996) tested this device among prisoners and found that those with histories of violence administered higher levels of shock to a confederate. Anderson and Bushman (1997) have reported other validity checks: there is a parallel between the laboratory and real life for the effects on aggression of alcohol, high temperatures, direct provocation and violence in the media (topics dealt with later in this chapter).

This chapter explores only some of the extensive range of behaviours that are labelled 'aggressive' and it will become clear that it is inappropriate to attempt a single definition for such a variety of complex, and perhaps qualitatively different, phenomena.

Major theoretical positions

Trying to understand why humans aggress against their own kind, and the factors that make them behave with viciousness and brutality towards one another in ways and degrees unparalleled in other animals, has led to much speculation since ancient times (Geen & Donnerstein, 1983). Explanations of aggression fall into two broad classes, the biological and the social, although this distinction is not rigid. A debate about which of the two is the crucial component is an example of the **nature–nurture controversy**: is human action determined by our biological inheritance or by our social environment? (A further instance of this debate involves the origins of prosocial behaviour; see Chapter 14.)

Our interest in social psychology favours a focus on social factors and, therefore, a class of theories that incorporates a learning component. Interest in the biological dimension, however, cannot be ignored. After all, violence is a reaction of our bodily system. And some theories are so thoroughly biological that they might seem to constitute a threat to any form of theory that is social. We deal with each class in turn.

BIOLOGICAL EXPLANATIONS
The starting point for these explanations is that aggression is an innate action tendency. Although modification of the consequent behaviour is possible, the wellspring is not. Aggression is an instinct—that is, a pattern of responses that is genetically predetermined. If so, it should show certain characteristics of an instinct. According to Riopelle (1987), an **instinct** is:

- *goal-directed* and terminates in a specific consequence (e.g. an attack);
- *beneficial* to the individual and to the species;
- *adapted* to a normal environment (though not to an abnormal one);

- *shared* by most members of the species (though its manifestation can vary from individual to individual);
- *developed* in a clear way as the individual matures;
- *unlearned* on the basis of individual experience (though it can become manifest in relation to learned aspects within a context).

Three major views have shared most, if not all, of these biological attributes in their treatment of human aggression. All argue cogently that aggressive behaviour is an inherent part of human nature, that we are programmed at birth to act in that way. The oldest is the psychodynamic position, dating back to the earlier part of the 20th century. This was followed a little later by the ideas of the ethologists, based on their studies of animal behaviour. The third view, which is more recent and startling, comes mainly from the field of evolutionary social psychology.

Psychodynamic theory

Freud (1930) proposed that human aggression stems from an innate 'death instinct', *Thanatos*, which is in opposition to a 'life instinct', *Eros*. Thanatos is initially directed at self-destruction, but later in development becomes redirected outwards at others. Freud's background as a physician heavily influenced his theorising, and his notion of Thanatos was partly a response to the large-scale destruction of World War I. Like the sexual urge that stems from Eros, an aggressive urge from Thanatos builds up from bodily tensions and needs to be expressed. This is essentially a one-factor theory: aggression builds up naturally and must be released. Freud's ideas were revised by later theorists, known as **neo-Freudians**, who viewed aggression as a more rational but nonetheless innate process whereby people sought a healthy release for primitive survival instincts that are basic to all animal species (Hartmann, Kris, & Loewenstein, 1949).

Ethological theory

In the 1960s, three books made a strong case for the instinctual basis of human aggression, on the basis of a comparison with animal behaviour: Lorenz's *On Aggression* (1966), Ardrey's *The Territorial Imperative* (1966) and Morris's *The Naked Ape* (1967). The general perspective that underpins this explanation of aggression is referred to as **ethology**, a branch of biology devoted to the study of instincts, or fixed-action patterns, among all members of a species when living in their natural environment.

Like the neo-Freudians, ethologists stressed the positive, functional aspects of aggression but they also recognised that, while the potential or instinct for aggression may be innate, actual aggressive behaviour

Threat displays: 'Nice little puppy!' Aggression in animals is often limited by appeasement gestures. Do you think appeasement will work with 'Mad Max'?

is elicited by specific stimuli in the environment, known as **releasers**. Lorenz invoked evolutionary principles to propose that aggression has survival value. An animal is considerably more aggressive towards other members of its species, which serves to distribute the individuals and/or family units in such a way as to make the most efficient use of available resources, such as sexual selection and mating, food and territory. Most of the time, intraspecies aggression may not even result in actual violence, as one animal will display instinctual threat gestures that are recognised by the other animal, who can then depart the scene—'the rottweiler growls so the chihuahua runs'. Even if fighting does break out it is unlikely to result in death, as the losing animal can display instinctual appeasement gestures that divert the victor from actually killing—for example, some animals will lie on the ground belly up in an act of subordination. Over time, in animals such as monkeys that live in colonies, appeasement gestures can help to establish dominance hierarchies or 'pecking orders'.

This is a two-factor theory: (1) there is an innate urge to aggress, which (2) depends on appropriate stimulation by the environmental releasers.

Lorenz extended the argument to humans, who must also have an inherited **fighting instinct**. Unfortunately, its survival value is much less clear than is the case for other animals. This is largely because humans lack well-developed killing appendages, such as large teeth or claws, so that clearly recognisable appeasement gestures seem not to have evolved (or may have disappeared through evolution).

There are two implications from this approach: (1) once we start being violent, we do not seem to know when to stop; (2) in order to kill we generally need to resort to weapons. The advanced technology of our times has produced frightful devices that can slaughter people in large numbers. Furthermore, this can be accomplished at a great distance, so that even the visual and auditory feedback cues of the victim's anguish are not available to persuade the victor to desist. In short, humans have the ability to harm others easily, with very little effort.

Evolutionary social psychology

The field of **evolutionary social psychology** first appeared under the guise of **sociobiology** (Krebs & Miller, 1985; Wilson, 1978) but has recently been promulgated as a virtual revision of the discipline of social psychology. Evolutionary social psychology is an ambitious approach that not only assumes an innate basis for aggression but also claims a biological basis for all social behaviour (Buss, 1990, 1999; Simpson & Kenrick, 1997; see Chapter 1). We revisit the theory in treating interpersonal attraction and altruism (see Chapters 13 and 14).

Derived from Darwinian theory, the evolutionary argument is provocative: specific behaviours have evolved because they promote the survival of genes that allow the individual to live long enough to pass the same genes on to the next generation. Aggression is adaptive because it must be linked to living long enough to procreate. As such, it is helpful to the individual and to the species. Consider the situation where danger threatens the offspring of a species. Most animals, and usually the mother, will react with a high level of aggression, often higher than they would normally exhibit in other situations. A mother bird, for example, may take life-threatening risks to protect her young. In common with the ethological view, being aggressive also increases access to resources. For humans, the goals for which aggressive behaviour is adaptive include social and economic advantage, either to defend the resources that we already have or to acquire new ones.

Limitations of biological arguments

Biological explanations of aggression have considerable appeal, picking up as they do on the popular assumption that violence is part of human nature. The 17th-century philosopher Thomas Hobbes saw fit to remark that people's lives are 'short, nasty and brutish'. Biological explanations also allow for our common experience of the power of strong bodily reactions that accompany some emotions—in this case, anger. Broadly speaking, however, social scientists (Goldstein, 1987; Ryan, 1985) question the sufficiency of the explanation of aggression when it is based totally on the cornerstone of instinct, on the grounds that this concept:

- depends on energy that is unknown, unknowable and immeasurable;

- is supported by only limited and biased empirical observation of actual human behaviour;
- has little utility in the prevention or control of aggression;
- relies on circular logic, proposing causal connections for which there is no evidence.

In summary, the view among most social psychologists who research human aggression is that evolutionary social psychology's overall contribution to an understanding of the incidence and maintenance of aggression (as distinct from its expression) is limited (Geen, 1998) (see first focus question).

SOCIAL AND BIOSOCIAL EXPLANATIONS

Few social psychologists favour theories of aggression defined in terms of an instinct, preferring instead to emphasise learning processes and factors within the social context that appear to be linked to aggressive behaviour. Even though most social psychologists do not accept that aggression is necessarily innate and instinctual, there are some who regard it as a general drive that can be either innate or learned, and which is elicited by social events or circumstances. As these approaches incorporate a biological element, we refer to them as **biosocial theories**. The two outlined below both consider a drive (or state of arousal) to be a precondition for aggression, although they differ in the ways in which internal and external factors are thought to interact to promote aggressive reactions.

Frustration and aggression

In its original form, the **frustration–aggression hypothesis** linked aggression to an antecedent condition of frustration. It derived from the work of a group of psychologists at Yale University in the 1930s, and it has been used to explain prejudice (see Chapter 10 for details). The anthropologist John Dollard and his psychologist colleagues (Dollard, Doob, Miller, Mowrer, & Sears, 1939) proposed that aggression was always caused by some kind of frustrating event or situation; conversely, frustration invariably led to aggression. In recent times, this reasoning has been applied to the effects of job loss on violence (Catalano, Novaco, & McConnell, 1997), while 'ethnic cleansing' in the former Yugoslavia may have had its origins in social and economic deprivation (Staub, 1996). We might also speculate that terrorism is spawned by chronic and acute frustration over the ineffectiveness of other mechanisms to achieve socioeconomic and cultural goals—people are unlikely to become suicide bombers unless all other channels of social improvement have proved ineffective.

Frustration–aggression theory had considerable appeal, inasmuch as it was decidedly different from the Freudian approach. According to Goldstein (1980,

Road rage: Sitting in traffic is a daily frustration for many people that occasionally spills over into aggression.

pp. 262–263), 'it was a theory with no psychoanalytic mumbo jumbo. No need to bother about such phantoms as ids, egos, superegos, and ego defence mechanisms'. Later research was to show that the basic hypothesis was simplistic and far from a complete explanation for aggressive behaviour (see Berkowitz, 1993). One major flaw is the theory's loose definition of 'frustration' and the difficulty in predicting which kinds of frustrating circumstances may lead to aggression. As we shall see, there are many factors other than frustration that can cause violence between people.

Excitation transfer

A later approach to aggression that features a drive concept is Zillmann's (1979, 1988) **excitation-transfer model**. The expression of aggression (or any other emotion, for that matter) is a function of three factors:

1. a learned aggressive behaviour;
2. arousal or excitation from another source;
3. the person's interpretation of the arousal state, such that an aggressive response seems appropriate.

Zillmann suggests that this residual arousal transfers from one situation to another in such a way that it promotes or contributes to the likelihood of the person interpreting a situation in an aggressive way, especially if aggressive behaviour is well established within that person's usual behaviour patterns. According to Zillmann, any experience that markedly increases the level of overall excitation can lead to unintended consequences.

Look at the example shown in Figure 12.4. Imagine that a student (not you, of course) has been working out at the gym and is still in a state of physical arousal when driving to the local supermarket. Here, another customer's car sneaks forward into the parking space that the student is trying to reverse into. Although this would ordinarily be only mildly annoying, the residual excitation from the workout (now forgotten) triggers verbal abuse from the student.

It is not difficult to think of instances where heightened arousal can lead people to react more aggressively than they normally would: aggressive acts while driving a car in stressful conditions; a greater tendency to yell angrily at our spouse when we are already upset about something quite unrelated; the mother who smacks a child for accidentally getting lost; the fights that break

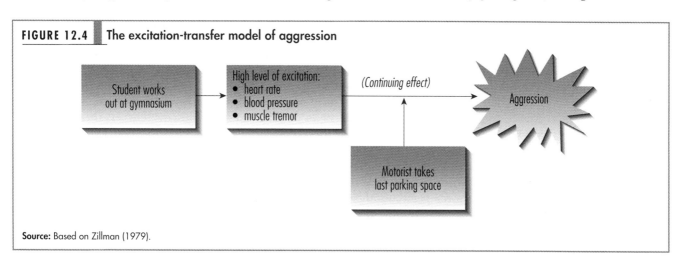

FIGURE 12.4 The excitation-transfer model of aggression

Student works out at gymnasium → High level of excitation:
• heart rate
• blood pressure
• muscle tremor

(Continuing effect) → Aggression

Motorist takes last parking space

Source: Based on Zillman (1979).

out so readily among children on exciting occasions. Kerr (1994) has noted the extreme level of excitement that often occurs at football matches, which can spill over into violence between rival groups of fans. All these instances make some sense in terms of Zillmann's theory. It can be applied to the experience of sexual arousal as well (see the section on erotica below) or to any kind of former stimulation whose effects linger over time.

Hate crimes

Biological and social models of aggression can provide us with plausible reasons why people aggress against others. Sometimes, violence is linked to prejudice, as noted in our discussion of the frustration–aggression hypothesis above (see also Chapter 10). **Hate crimes** are an instance, although some of the old targets of prejudice have been replaced: the lynchings of African Americans in the South during the 1930s have given way to different forms of persecution, and the persecution of other minorities (Green, Glaser, & Rich, 1998; see Box 12.3).

Aggression can be learned

The gradual control of aggressive impulses in an infant clearly depends on an extensive learning process (Miles & Carey, 1997). **Social learning theory** is a wide-ranging behavioural approach in psychology and features the processes responsible for:

- the *acquisition* of a behaviour or a behavioural sequence;
- the *instigation* of overt acts; and
- the *maintenance* of the behaviour.

Learning by vicarious experience: Children can learn to be aggressive by playing video games in which heroic characters are reinforced for aggression.

Its best known proponent is probably Bandura (Bandura, 1977; Bandura & Walters, 1963), who also applied it specifically to the understanding of aggression (Bandura, 1973). Of course, if antisocial behaviour can be learned, so can prosocial behaviour (see Chapter 14). Although Bandura acknowledges the role of biological factors in relation to aggression, the emphasis is on the role of experience, which can be direct or vicarious.

BOX 12.3 | **Hate crimes, gays and the case of Matthew Shepard**

A subpopulation whose members have been the victims of frequent and extreme hate crimes is the gay community. Aggression is frequently perpetrated against homosexuals by people who have no direct dealings with their victims other than being motivated by strong negative feelings about homosexuality. Many homosexual people report being the victims of such hate crimes: one study found that 94% of its homosexual participants had been victimised for reasons associated with their sexuality (National Gay and Lesbian Task Force, 1990). Franklin (2000) surveyed 489 racially and economically diverse students at a community college in North Carolina in the United States: 10% reported that they had physically assaulted or threatened to assault a person whom they knew or assumed to be homosexual; 24% reported that they had verbally abused people they thought were homosexual.

Matthew Shepard was a 21-year-old gay college student in Wyoming who was the victim of a hate crime against gay people. He was murdered in 1998 by two 22-year-old men. Matthew was taken from a bar to a remote prairie, where he was tied to a fence and whipped in the face with a gun until he lost consciousness. He was then left to die in the freezing weather. His killers admitted to laughing as they attacked him. Each assailant received two life sentences. Attempts by the prosecution to secure the death penalty were thwarted by Matthew's mother, who appealed for clemency for the men. The girlfriends of the two men were charged with being an accessory to the crime.

This hate crime, although not uncommon, sparked worldwide outrage in gay and lesbian communities, and Matthew has become of a symbol for the persecution that many minority group members experience.

(See the Matthew Shepard Foundation website at <http://www.matthewshepard.org>; but see also the Westborough Baptist anti-gay home page, some of whose members picketed his funeral, at <http://www.godhatesfags.com/home.html>).

Through socialisation, children learn to aggress because either they are directly rewarded or someone else appears to be rewarded for their actions.

The idea of **learning by direct experience** is based on Skinner's operant reinforcement principles: a behaviour is maintained by rewards and punishments actually experienced by the child. For example, if Jonathan takes Margaret's biscuit from her and no one intervenes, he is reinforced by now having the biscuit. The idea of **learning by vicarious experience** is a contribution made by social learning theorists, who argue that learning occurs through the processes of modelling and imitation of other people. The concept of imitation is not new in social theory. The French sociologist Tarde (1890), for example, devoted a whole book to the subject and boldly asserted that 'Society is imitation'. What is unique in social learning theory is the proposition that the behaviour to be imitated must be seen to be rewarding in some way. Some models—for example, parents, siblings and peers—are more appropriate for the child than others. The learning sequence of aggression can be extended beyond direct interactions between people to include media images, such as on television. It can also be applied to learning by adults in later life.

According to Bandura, whether a person is aggressive in a particular situation depends on:

- the person's previous experiences of aggressive behaviour, including both that of the individual and of others;
- the success of aggressive behaviour in the past;
- the current likelihood of the aggression being either rewarded or punished;
- the complex array of cognitive, social and environmental factors in the situation.

Bandura's studies used a variety of experimental settings to show that children will quite readily mimic the aggressive acts of others. In particular, an adult makes a potent model, no doubt because children perceive their elders as responsible and authoritative figures (see also Chapters 5 and 14). His early findings pointed to a clear **modelling** effect when the adult was seen acting aggressively in a live setting. Even more disturbing, this capacity to acquire aggression was also demonstrated when the adult model was seen acting violently on television (see Box 12.4 and Figure 12.5).

An interesting and recent theoretical development is a blending of social learning theory with the learning of a particular kind of cognitive schema—the **script** (see Chapter 2). Children learn rules of conduct from those

A CLASSIC IN SOCIAL PSYCHOLOGY
BOX 12.4   Sock it to the Bobo doll!

Can the mere observation of an act be sufficient to learn how to perform it? Albert Bandura and his colleagues addressed this question in a series of experiments at Stanford University. This work had a considerable impact on the acceptance of social factors within the narrower field of experimental research on learning, but it also had a long-term effect on wider thinking about the origins of aggression. According to the social learning theory of observational learning, observing a behaviour produces a cognitive representation in the observer, who then experiences vicarious reinforcement. This kind of reinforcement refers to a process whereby the outcome for the model, whether rewarding or punishing, becomes a remote reinforcement for the observer. If this is so, then aggression is likely to be one of many forms of behaviour that can be learned.

Bandura, Ross and Ross (1963) tested this idea in one study of 4- and 5-year-old children who watched a male or female adult play with a commercially popular inflated Bobo doll. There were four conditions:

1. *Live*—the adult model came into the room where the child was playing. After playing with some tinker toys, the adult began to act aggressively towards the Bobo doll. The acts included sitting on the doll, hitting its nose, banging it on the head with a mallet and kicking it around the room. The words used were 'Sock him in the nose', 'pow', 'kick him', 'hit him down' and the like. After this, the child was left to play with the Bobo doll.
2. *Videotape*—this was the same as the live sequence but had been filmed on videotape for the child to view.
3. *Cartoon*—the model acted in the same way but was dressed in a cat uniform, and the room was decorated as if it were in a cartoon.
4. *Control*—the child skipped all these conditions and went directly to play with the Bobo doll.

The results in Figure 12.5 show that the children who watched an adult behave aggressively in any condition behaved more aggressively later. The most effective condition for modelling aggressive behaviour was the live sequence. However, the finding that the cartoon and videotaped conditions also increased imitative aggression in children provided fuel for critics who argued that graphic presentations of violence in films and television could have serious consequences for children's later behaviour.

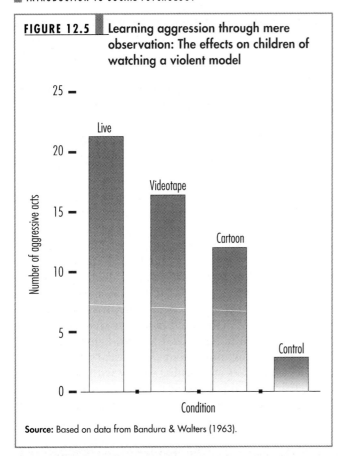

FIGURE 12.5 | Learning aggression through mere observation: The effects on children of watching a violent model

Number of aggressive acts

Live
Videotape
Cartoon
Control

Condition

Source: Based on data from Bandura & Walters (1963).

around them, so that aggression becomes internalised. A situation is recognised as frustrating or threatening—for example, a human target is identified—and a learned routine of aggressive behaviour is enacted (Perry, Perry, & Boldizar, 1990). Once established in childhood, an aggressive sequence is persistent (Huesmann, 1988; Anderson & Huesmann, 2003). Research on age trends for murder and manslaughter in the United States shows that this form of aggression quickly peaks among 15–25-year-olds and then declines systematically (US Department of Justice, 2001).

In summary, the social learning approach has had a major impact on research into aggression, stimulating many other studies. It has also touched a chord in our community about the causes of aggression, and has directly sparked research into the effects of violence in the visual media on both children and adults. If violence is learned, exposure to aggressive and successful models leads people to imitate them. Being aggressive can become an established pattern of behaving, even a way of life, which is likely to repeat itself by imitation across generations (Huesmann, Eron, Lefkowitz, & Walder, 1984). This does not necessarily mean that change is impossible. If aggression can be learned, presumably it can also be modified and remedied. This is the basis of behaviour modification programs, such as anger management,

used by clinical and community psychologists to help people find more peaceful ways of dealing with others.

Finally, what effects does spanking have on the social development of children? Considering the thrust of social learning theory, you might deduce that children will learn that the act of striking another is not punished, at least if the aggressor is more powerful! In a longitudinal study of children and their parents, Strauss, Sugarman and Giles-Sims (1997) recorded how often a child was spanked (0–3 or more times) each week. Across a two-year span, they found an almost linear relationship over time between the rate of spanking and the level of antisocial behaviour. What is more, children who were not spanked at all showed less antisocial behaviour after two years (see second focus question).

DOES THEORY HAVE ANY POINT?

As each chapter in this book attests, social psychology is replete with theory. In the case of aggression, theories are numerous and vigorously debated. There is no sign of change in the search for explanation—and little wonder, as aggression is part of a community's everyday experience and it is every person's wish to account for it (see Chapter 3). Despite this, Geen and Donnerstein (1983) argued that little theoretical progress has been made. Many investigations have been criticised for being aimless and contributing little to our understanding of the nature of aggression and violence (Lubek, 1979).

Some of this criticism relates to problems involving both definitions and ethics, described at the beginning of this chapter. Some critics have concluded that theory based on case studies and experimentation has doubtful validity. This criticism applies in some degree to all the theories we have considered, and all have some difficulty in accounting for the diverse dimensions of aggression. No available theory can provide a full explanation for the diversity of aggression, and, even when the precipitating factor for an aggressive act may be apparent, there will invariably be several other contributing factors that are not so obvious.

Consider how cultural values (see Chapter 16) and social pressures may contribute to a pub brawl involving unemployed immigrants, even though drunkenness may initially appear to be the cause. Other examples include the underlying effects of poverty, chronic frustration and social disadvantage that cumulatively often lead to acts of both public and domestic violence. Some of these factors are explored next.

Personal and situational factors

Although it is possible to distinguish conceptually between the person and the situation when dealing with any social behaviour, common sense suggests that an interaction of both determines how people behave. Ross and Nisbett (1991) have cogently argued in this way. Like an echo of Lewin's early field theory doctrine of a tension between the person and the environment (see Chapter 1), people bring their unique characteristics to any situation and their individual way of construing it. When we apply such thinking to the study of aggression, the separation of person variables from situation variables is a matter of convenience and even of oversimplification. It reflects the way in which most research has been performed, and belies the reality that the causes of aggression are complex and interactive.

Consider some contexts in which people may show aggression. It could be in response to being teased, a carry-over from a near traffic accident, a continuing way of responding to the burden of poverty, someone's method for dealing with a nagging partner, a parent's control over a fractious child. Some of these instances appear to be situational variables, but closer inspection shows that some go with the person or with a category of person (the poor, the partner, the parent). What is more, not all people in that category respond in that way, or even in the same way in identical situations. With that caveat in mind, we shall move on.

INDIVIDUAL DIFFERENCES
Personality

The tendency to aggress develops quite early in life and becomes a stable behavioural pattern. Huesmann and Guerra (1997) found that children who are aggressive at eight years of age are more likely to be aggressive in later years. It also seems likely that chronic aggression is linked to a tendency to attribute hostile intentions to others (Graham, Hudley, & Williams, 1992).

When a behavioural pattern is stable, and found in children, it is an attractive proposition to claim that people aggress because they have an 'aggressive personality'. Can you rate your friends according to how much or how little they typically tend towards aggressive behaviour? The ability to evaluate people in terms of their aggressiveness is an important part of some psychometric (psychological test-based) and clinical assessments (Sundberg, 1977)—for example, in determining the likelihood of reoffending among violent offenders (Mullen, 1984).

It is simplistic to think of people as somehow naturally aggressive but, for a variety of reasons, including age, gender, culture and personal experiences, some people tend to be more aggressive in their behaviour than others. There are several personal characteristics which are common to violent offenders, including low self-esteem and poor frustration tolerance. Narcissistic people seem to be particularly prone to aggression (Bushman & Baumeister, 1998). Social workers often

recognise children who have been exposed to higher than average levels of violence, particularly in the home, as being 'high-risk' and in need of primary intervention.

Type A personality and ADHD

Research in recent years has suggested the existence of a behaviour pattern called **type A personality** (Matthews, 1982). This syndrome is associated with susceptibility to coronary heart disease. People showing this pattern are overactive and excessively competitive in their encounters with others. A study by Carver and Glass (1978) found that type A people were also more aggressive towards others who were perceived to be competing with them on an important task. According to Dembroski and MacDougall (1978), type A people prefer to work alone rather than with others when they are under stress, as if to avoid exposure to incompetence in others and to feel in control of the situation. Although type A people may have found that behaving in this way was rewarding at certain points in their life, it can have some very destructive effects for themselves and for those who are close to them. For example, type A personalities were reported to be more prone to engage in child abuse (Strube, Turner, Cerro, Stevens, & Hinchey, 1984). In an organisational setting, Baron (1989) found that managers who were classified as type A experienced more conflict with peers and subordinates, though not with their supervisors. They apparently knew where to draw the line!

ADHD (attention deficit hyperactivity disorder) has received a great deal of press in recent years. It is a collection of behaviours that includes poor attention span, hyperactivity and poor impulse control. To the extent that ADHD is an individual difference, it has been strongly associated with aggression in childhood and it also predicts aggression in adolescents and young adults (Hinshaw, 1987). Pharmacological interventions reduce ADHD symptoms and concurrent aggression, although they have little effect on long-term aggression.

Hormones

Is it a popular fallacy that hormonal activity could relate to the rate at which aggression occurs? Recent research actually suggests a link. Gladue (1991) reported higher levels of overt aggression in men than in women, but also that this sex difference applied equally to both heterosexual and homosexual men, when compared with women. In other words, biology (male/female) rather than gender orientation was the main contributing variable. In a second study, Gladue and his colleagues measured testosterone levels through saliva tests in their male participants and also assessed whether they were type A or type B personalities (Berman, Gladue, & Taylor, 1993). The levels of shock administered to a contrived opponent in an experimental setting were higher when the man was higher in testosterone, a type A personality, or both. Overall, there is a small correlation of 0.14 between elevated testosterone (in both males and females) and aggression (Book, Starzyk, & Quinsey, 2002)—if it was causal, testosterone would explain 2% of variation in aggression.

However, a correlation between levels of testosterone and aggression does not, of course, establish causality. In fact, causality could operate in the opposite direction: for example, playing and winning at chess or tennis can cause a temporary elevation of testosterone level (Gladue, Boechler, & McCall, 1989; Mazur, Booth, & Dabbs, 1992). A more convincing link between the two was pinpointed in two studies in the Netherlands (van Goozen, Cohen-Kettenis, Gooren, Frijda, & van der Poll, 1995; Cohen-Kettenis & van Goozen, 1997). Transsexuals who were treated with sex hormones as part of their sex reassignment showed increased or decreased proneness to aggression according to whether the direction of change was female to male or male to female.

Gender and socialisation

A learned source of individual difference lies in the differential socialisation of the sexes. This occurs in subtle ways, such that men in our society are encouraged from early childhood to be more aggressive than women, who in turn are discouraged from such behaviour (Condry & Ross, 1985). A wealth of research has now confirmed this male–female difference in many societies and across socioeconomic groups. However, the size of the difference varies according to the mode and context of aggression; for example, men are more likely than women to be physically violent and to hold more aggressive attitudes. On the other hand, women are almost as likely as men to use verbal attack in similar contexts, although the degree to which they aggress may be less (Eagly & Steffen, 1986; Harris, 1992).

Frustration

The consequences of being frustrated figure prominently in our account of the frustration–aggression hypothesis (see above and Chapter 10). It is difficult to measure frustration empirically. Perhaps you can recall personal instances when you become angry and lash out verbally or physically when some circumstance gets in your way—thumping a photocopying machine, fuming at another motorist who slows you down, kicking a reluctant lawnmower, or chastising a family member for making you late for an engagement. Although there is little doubt that frustration may lead to aggression, the frustration–aggression formula is unpredictable. Two factors help to predict whether frustration will result in aggression: the intensity of the frustrating event and how apparently legitimate, reasonable or unavoidable it is (Kulik & Brown, 1979).

Catharsis

An instrumental reason for aggression that has popular appeal is **catharsis**, which refers to the use of a behaviour as an outlet or release for pent-up emotion—the **cathartic hypothesis**. Although associated with Freud, the idea can be traced back to Aristotle and ancient Greek tragedy: by acting out their emotions, people can purify their feelings (Scherer, Abeles, & Fischer, 1975). The idea makes sense, arguing that we have a need to 'let off steam' from frustration in order to get back to a stable level of functioning, and that acting aggressively helps to get rid of the stressful emotion. In Japan, some companies have acted on this hypothesis by providing a special room with a toy replica of the boss on which employees can relieve their tensions by 'bashing the boss' (Middlebrook, 1980)! However, research in this area shows that the relationship between frustration and catharsis is quite complex; catharsis appears to have reduced feelings of aggression in some studies, but actually increased it in others (Konečni & Ebbesen, 1976) (see third focus question).

Some recent research has rejected the efficacy of catharsis for reducing later aggression (see Box 12.5). Other factors contribute to feelings of aggression, such as our normal level of aggression, whether the catharsis is in fact sufficient release for the feelings, whether it induces guilt, and any consequences of the aggression (Geen & Quanty, 1977).

Direct provocation

It is clear that people might aggress when directly provoked, even when the provocation is quite mild. Laboratory research has shown that this is so for both verbal

Catharsis: This is an anger management centre where you can drop by to let it all hang out—in this case by beating someone up.

BOX 12.5	Letting it 'all hang out' may be worse than useless

Have you ever felt really angry and then 'let it all out' by screaming, punching a pillow or breaking a plate? Did you feel better afterwards? There is a common perception that such 'designer outbursts' of aggression are a good and effective way of reducing anxiety and aggression. Wann and his colleagues (Wann, Carlson, Holland, Jacob, Owens, & Wells, 1999) found that many participants in their experiments believed that catharsis, achieved in particular by viewing violent sports, can lower the likelihood of subsequent aggression. However, the cathartic hypothesis has little support; research suggests that the opposite is true: cathartic aggression actually increases aggression in general. If so, then the common belief that catharsis is an effective remedy for pent-up anger and aggression is a dangerous misconception.

A study by Bushman, Baumeister and Stack (1999) tested the cathartic hypothesis by asking students to read one of three fake newspaper articles: (1) a pro-catharsis article in which a prominent university researcher claimed that cathartic behaviour relieved the tendency to aggress; (2) an anti-catharsis article quoting a research finding of no link between catharsis and a reduction in later aggression; (3) a 'control' article completely unrelated to aggression or catharsis.

The students were then asked to write an essay that was critiqued by another student (in fact, by the experimenter) while they waited. The essays were returned with very negative written comments designed to induce anger, such as 'This is one of the worst essays I have ever read!' Angered students who had read the pro-catharsis article were more inclined to choose a punching bag exercise as an optional task than those who had read either the anti-catharsis or control article. Those who had not been angered by the critique of their essays were still more likely to choose to punch a bag if they had read the pro-catharsis article than those who had not. The results of this study highlight how the media or popular belief can influence people to choose cathartic stress relief, and how this choice is affected by the amount of anger people are feeling.

The initial study was extended to a situation where an essay writer could later interact with the essay critic. After reading one of the three articles, some students were asked to spend two minutes punching a bag. Next, they completed a competitive reaction time task in which they selected a degree of punishment (noise volume) to deliver to the competitor (supposedly in another room) when the competitor was slower. As a final twist, just before this encounter, a group of students was led to believe that this competitor was the person who had negatively critiqued their essays.

Those who expected to interact with their critic were more willing to engage in punching a bag before their 'meeting'. Also, those who had read the pro-catharsis article were more aggressive in the task (delivering louder noises) even after punching the bag—which, according to popular belief, should be a cathartic exercise and reduce aggression. This study suggests that catharsis does not relieve stress and is actually 'worse than useless'!

and physical provocation (Geen, 1968), and you may recall past incidents of responding aggressively to being teased or taunted. Moreover, provocation can readily escalate into quite vicious fighting, as occurs in brawls in bars or in sports and sometimes in street demonstrations. This suggests that a **reciprocity principle** is operating—that is, we tend to strike back rather than turn the other cheek. (See how reciprocity operates in relation to interpersonal attraction in Chapter 13 and to prosocial behaviour in Chapter 14.) Of course, there will always be other contributing factors, such as whether we have viable alternative responses (a school child might 'tell the teacher'), the likely consequences of aggression in the particular situation, and factors such as age and gender. For example, young children, especially boys, are more likely to reciprocate with aggressiveness than older people (Eagly & Steffen, 1986). In real life, aggression in the form of self-defence might save a life and this is recognised in law as justification for some cases of homicide.

Alcohol

It is often assumed that alcohol befuddles the brain. This is a particular form of the *disinhibition hypothesis* (see below): that is, alcohol detracts from cortical control and increases activities of more primitive brain areas. The link of alcohol to aggressive behaviour seems firmly established (see a meta-review by Bushman & Cooper, 1990) and controlled behavioural studies suggest a causal relationship. Additionally, people who drink more are more aggressive (Bailey & Taylor, 1991). Even people who do not often consume alcohol can become aggressive when they do (LaPlace, Chermack, & Taylor, 1994).

The effects of alcohol on aggression have been studied experimentally. In one study, male students were assigned to either an alcohol or a placebo condition (Taylor & Sears, 1988). They were placed in a competition involving reaction time with another participant. In each pair, the person who responded more slowly on a given trial would receive an electric shock from the opponent. The level of shock to be delivered could be set at various intensity levels and was selected by each person before the trial commenced. In reality, the opponent's shock settings, which were always low-intensity (i.e. fairly passive) and the win/loss frequency (50%) were determined by the experimenter. The results in Figure 12.6 show the proportions of high-intensity shocks given by participants who were in either an alcohol or a placebo condition.

In four sequential stages (none, mild, strong, none) social pressure, by way of encouragement to give a shock, was sometimes exerted on the participant by a confederate who was watching the proceedings. The results show an interaction between taking alcohol and being pressured to aggress: participants who had imbibed were more susceptible to influence and continued to give high-intensity shocks even after the pressure was later withdrawn. In an extension by Gustafson (1992), men who were intoxicated were more aggressive than those who were sober and delivered a higher shock intensity when they were provoked.

The analogy to real life is the context of social drinking, such as at a party or a bar, where others may goad the drinker to be aggressive. Actual statistics on the connection between alcohol and aggression are suggestive, not clear-cut. Although alcohol consumption is disproportionately associated with physical violence, the causal pathways are complex. According to

Bradbury (1984), the links between violent offending and drinking patterns occur because:

- stress and lifestyle factors may contribute to high levels of both alcohol consumption and aggressiveness; and
- violent people tend to drink a lot, and alcohol promotes violent behaviour.

Alcohol is also known for its disinhibiting powers. Behaviour and attitudes that are normally kept under control, due to their antisocial, illegal, immoral or embarrassing nature might be released following alcohol consumption. How many people sing karaoke only when intoxicated?

Disinhibition

Another phenomenon that often leads to aggression, even where such reactions are not typical of the aggressor, is **disinhibition**, which refers to any kind of reduction in the usual social forces that operate to restrain us from acting antisocially, illegally or immorally. There appear to be several ways in which people lose their normal inhibitions about aggressing against others. In Box 12.6, we consider the case in which the *aggressor* experiences a state of **deindividuation**. This process (discussed in more detail in Chapter 11) involves changes controlled by situational factors affecting the aggressor, such as the presence of others or lack of identifiability. Box 12.7 looks at how other factors that focus on how the aggressor perceives the victim, such as being less than human (**dehumanisation**), can increase the probability that a hostile act will follow.

Mann, at the University of Melbourne, applied the concept of deindividuation to a particular context relating to **collective aggression**, the 'baiting crowd'. The typical situation involves a person threatening to jump from a high building; a crowd gathers below and some begin to chant 'Jump, jump'. In one dramatic case in New York in 1938, thousands of people waited at ground level, some for 11 hours, until a man jumped to his death from a 17th-storey hotel ledge.

Mann (1981) analysed 21 cases of suicides reported in newspapers in the 1960s and 1970s. He found that, in 10 out of the 21 cases where there had been a crowd watching, baiting had occurred. He examined other features of these reports that distinguished between crowds that bait and those that do not. Baiting was more likely to occur at night and when the crowd was large (more than 300 people). Also, the crowd was typically a long way from the victim, usually at ground level. These features are likely to produce a state of deindividuation in the individual. Furthermore, the longer the crowd waited the more likely it was that baiting would start, perhaps egged on by irritability and frustration (see Figure 12.7).

FIGURE 12.6 The effects of alcohol and social pressure on men's willingness to deliver electric shocks to a passive opponent

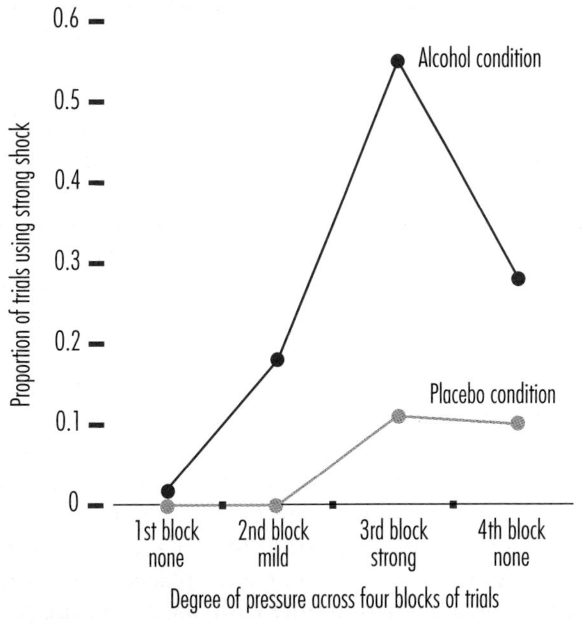

Source: Based on Taylor & Sears (1988).

BOX 12.6 Disinhibition, deindividuation and violence

DEINDIVIDUATION BRINGS A SENSE OF REDUCED LIKELIHOOD OF PUNISHMENT

A dramatic example of how a real, or perceived, reduction in the likelihood of punishment can enhance aggression and violence was seen in the My Lai incident in the war in Vietnam, where American soldiers slaughtered an entire village of innocent civilians. In the official inquiry, it was revealed that the same unit had previously killed and tortured civilians without any disciplinary action; that the area was a designated 'free-fire' zone, so that it was considered legitimate to shoot at anything that moved; and, indeed, that the whole ethos of the war was one of glorified violence (Hersh, 1970).

In addition, there was a sense of anonymity, or deindividuation, that came from being part of a large group and this further enhanced the soldiers' perception that they would not be punished as individuals. (See the effects of deindividuation in Chapter 11.) This sense of anonymity is thought to contribute to the translation of aggressive emotion into actual violence: it may occur through being part of a large group or gathering, as in the crowd that baits a suicide to jump (Mann, 1981) or a pack rape at a gang convention; or it may happen through something that protects anonymity in another way, such as the white hoods worn by Ku Klux Klan members (Middlebrook, 1980), the stocking worn over the face of an armed robber or the Hallowe'en masks that prompt children to steal candy and money (Diener, Fraser, Beaman, & Kelem, 1976).

A study by Malamuth (1981) found that almost one-third of male students questioned at an American university admitted there was a likelihood they would rape if they were certain of not getting caught!

BOX 12.7 Deindividuation induced by dehumanising the victim

A variation of deindividuation in the aggressor can occur when the victim, rather than the aggressor, is anonymous or dehumanised in some way, so that the aggressor cannot easily see the personal pain and injury suffered by the victim. This can weaken any control that may be applied through feelings of shame and guilt.

Terrible examples of this phenomenon have been documented, such as the violent treatment of psychiatric patients and prisoners who were either kept naked or dressed identically so that they were indistinguishable as individuals (Steir, 1978). And having faceless and deindividuated victims in violent films and television programs has been shown to have a disinhibiting effect on some viewers, encouraging them to play down the injury and thus be more likely to imitate the violent acts (Bandura, 1986).

Extreme and inhumane instances of disinhibition come from war: for example, the extermination of tens of thousands of people by a single atomic blast in Hiroshima and again in Nagasaki in 1945. Cohen (1987) presented a revealing analysis of the ways in which military personnel 'sanitise', and thereby justify, the use of nuclear weaponry by semantics that dehumanise the likely or actual victims, referring to them as 'targets', 'the aggressed' or even 'collateral damage'. American military personnel used the same semantic strategies during the Vietnam War to rationalise and justify the killing of Vietnamese civilians, who were known as 'gooks' (Sabini & Silver, 1982).

In 1993 Bosnian Serbs, in what was once part of Yugoslavia, referred to acts of genocide against the Muslim population as 'ethnic cleansing'. The media can also unwittingly lessen the impact of the horror of large-scale killing. A phrase often used on television during the Allied bombing campaigns in Iraq in 1991 was 'theatre of war', inviting the audience to sit back and be entertained.

In a study in Israel, Struch and Schwartz (1989) investigated aggression among non-orthodox Jews towards highly orthodox Jews, measured in terms of strong opposition to orthodox institutions. They found two factors underlying the aggression. The first was a perception of intergroup conflict of interests (see Chapter 11); the second was a tendency to regard orthodox Jews as 'inhuman'.

Other factors

There is a diverse range of other factors that have been implicated in aggression. For example, a need for personal space has been found to predispose prisoners to greater violence in crowded prison conditions in New Zealand (Walkley, 1984). Personal attitudes about the acceptability of aggressiveness will naturally be an important source of individual difference in levels of aggressive behaviour. Although there is a correlation between some psychological disturbances and interpersonal violence, it seems that mental abnormality in itself, contrary to common myth, does not predispose people to aggression (Mullen, 1984).

Another myth that can be laid to rest is the notion that having an extra Y chromosome—XYY rather than XY—can predispose men to be violent. An extensive survey by Witkin and associates (Witkin, Mednick, Schulsinger, Bakkestrom, Christiansen, Goodenough, Philip, Rubin, & Stocking, 1976) reported that XYY male prisoners showed rates of violence and criminality that were similar to those of XY prisoners. It also

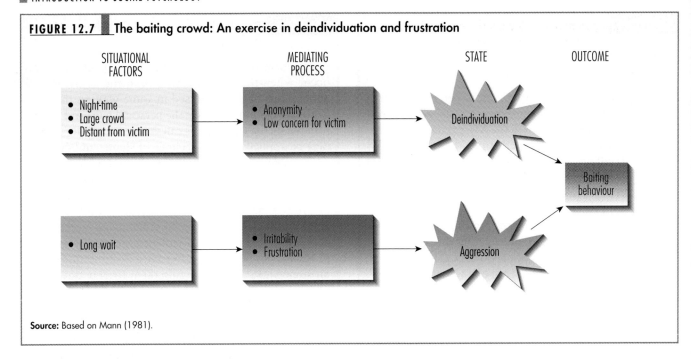

FIGURE 12.7   The baiting crowd: An exercise in deindividuation and frustration

Source: Based on Mann (1981).

seems doubtful that brain tumours or unusual hormonal levels in some people can be linked directly to levels of aggression (Montague, 1973; Valenstein, 1975), as there is no evidence of a simple control centre for violence in the brain (Simmel, Hahn, & Walters, 1983).

SITUATION VARIABLES

Physical environment

Various aspects of our physical environment may contribute to violence. Heat and crowding are two such factors.

That heat affects aggression is not surprising, given that our language commonly links *body temperature* to aggression. For example, if someone is irate we may say they are 'hot under the collar' or 'simmering with rage'. Conversely, we may tell people to 'cool down' if they are angry. Research has found that, as the ambient temperature rises, there is an increase in domestic violence (Cohn, 1993), violent suicide (Maes, De Meyer, Thompson, Peeters, & Cosyns, 1994) and collective violence (Carlsmith & Anderson, 1979).

Harries and Stadler (1983) examined the incidence of aggravated assault in Dallas over the 12 months of 1980, and found that assaults were more evident when it was hotter and more humid than normal, but not when it was excessively hot and humid. Another study, of the incidence of murders and rapes over a two-year period, found a positive relationship with fluctuations in the daily average temperature (Anderson & Anderson, 1984). Another study gauged motorists' responses to a car blocking the road at a green light by recording the amount of horn-honking. As the temper-

ature rose, so did the amount of honking (Kenrick & MacFarlane, 1986). There is evidence that the relationship between heat and aggression was recorded in Ancient Rome (Anderson, Bushman, & Groom, 1997) and that even in normally very hot climates, such as India's, people report more negative moods on the hottest days (Ruback & Pandey, 1992).

The relationship between heat and aggression actually follows an inverted U (Halpern, 1995): as the temperature rises, so does aggression, at least to a certain level. When it gets very hot, aggression levels out and then declines, suggesting that extreme heat saps our energy. We should note here that the critical variable is likely to be the *ambient temperature*. Cohn and Rotton (1997) tracked rates of physical assaults according to temperature throughout each day over a two-year period in Minneapolis (1987–88). Their data reflect an inverted U-curve (see Figure 12.8).

Cohn and Rotton also found that assaults were more frequent later in the evening than at other times. The reason was that most people in Minneapolis work in temperature-controlled environments during the day; therefore, the effects of ambient temperature did not show up until people left work. Finally, Cohn and Rotton reported a link between heat and *alcohol consumption*. It is likely that people drink more alcohol in the evening to quench their thirst, so that alcohol becomes a mediating variable leading to aggression.

A relationship between heat and aggression does not apply to all classes of violent crime. No correlation with temperature was found in a study of factors affecting rape (Rotton, 1993). This points to a subtlety in the way the terms 'aggression' and 'violence' are used. Anderson,

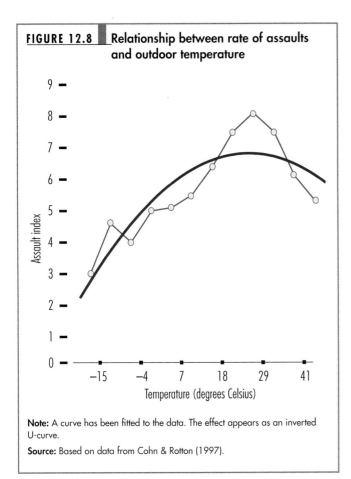

FIGURE 12.8 Relationship between rate of assaults and outdoor temperature

Assault index (y-axis): 0 to 9

Temperature (degrees Celsius) (x-axis): −15, −4, 7, 18, 29, 41

Note: A curve has been fitted to the data. The effect appears as an inverted U-curve.

Source: Based on data from Cohn & Rotton (1997).

Bushman and Groom (1997) note a difference between *affective aggression*, in which the primary end-goal of the behaviour is to harm another person, and *instrumental aggression*, in which harm to another (even death) is a means to an end, as in a robbery. The findings suggest that only affective aggression is correlated with a rise in temperature.

The effects of crowding and invasion of personal space on aggressiveness have already been mentioned. At peak hours in some large drinking taverns, there may be several hundred people in various stages of intoxication, so that even a small incident might lead to a brawl (Roper Report, 1987). In such a context there may be a series of contributory factors: heat, crowding, alcohol, provocation and disinhibition.

Disadvantaged groups

At a societal level social disadvantage can sometimes produce aggression, although disadvantaged groups often become passive victims or engage in conventional political activity or non-violent protest. In Chapter 11 we explore in detail the relationship between disadvantage and intergroup behaviour. A key factor in the relationship between disadvantage and aggression is the extent to which a disadvantaged group has a sense of **relative deprivation** and, in particular, a sense that the group is deprived relative to other groups (called fraternalistic relative deprivation—Runciman, 1966); or that, against a background of rising expectations, the group has suddenly experienced a dramatic setback (Davies, 1969).

Relative deprivation is a sense of discontent that can be associated with a feeling that the chance of improving one's condition is slight. In such a context, if improvement cannot be achieved legitimately, a deprived person or group may act aggressively. At an individual level this could include vandalism, assault or burglary; at an intergroup level it could extend to collective aggression, such as violent protest or rioting. The Los Angeles race riots of 1992 were ostensibly triggered by a jury verdict that acquitted White police officers of extended physical battery of a Black motorist. Although this was the proximal cause, there was also a marked undercurrent of relative deprivation among African Americans in the neighbourhood of Los Angeles where the rioting occurred (see Box 11.1 in Chapter 11).

There is a reasonable level of support for the validity of the concept of relative deprivation, from both experiments and historical analyses (Walker & Smith, 2002). Relative deprivation provides a plausible, partial explanation for recent events close to home, such as the coups in 2000 in Fiji and in the Solomons. In Fiji, less economically advantaged indigenous Fijians translated their frustrations into racial hatred and violence against the more commercially successful Indian community. Other examples include the dramatic rise in crime among and between young Maori and Pacific Island people in New Zealand in recent years.

Criminality and women

Gender stereotypes characterise men as significantly more aggressive than women. Recent research suggests that the increasing emancipation of women in Western societies over the past 30 years may be changing this by removing women's inhibitions against violence—emancipation may be criminogenic. It has been suggested that by removing some of the restraints on women from being assertive or aggressive, the women's movement may have contributed to a substantial increase in violent crime committed by women in recent decades (Hall, 1984). This notion requires more investigation. Although violent offending by women is more common now, the trend is more pronounced in lower socioeconomic groups, and it could be argued that such groups are the least likely to have been influenced by the women's movement. Nevertheless, the redefinition of male and female roles in most Western societies in recent decades can be linked to a rise in alcohol and drug abuse among women. The return of women to the workforce has coincided more recently with widespread unemployment, a further trigger for increased offences against persons (and property).

Although convictions for violent offending have increased more rapidly among women than men, male criminal violence is still enormously prevalent. In the United States in 1990 the ratio of male to female arrests for murder and manslaughter was 43 to 3 among 15–19-year-olds. This dropped to 5 to 1 among 55–59-year-olds (US Department of Justice, 2001). In New Zealand 96% of prison inmates are male. Just more than half of these are violent offenders, the most common crimes being aggravated robbery, rape, unlawful sexual connection, murder, and injuring or wounding.

It is the relative increase in female crime that is a telling statistic. The number of men sentenced to prison terms grew by 19% from 1995 to 1997, but there was a 37% increase in the number of women sentenced to prison for the same period (Census of Prison Inmates, 1997).

Cultural variation

Attitudes towards aggression and violence vary over time, between cultures, and also between groups within cultures and nations. Although Western nations such as Australia and New Zealand view democracy, human rights and non-violence as core cultural values, other cultures view things differently and, of course, within our own cultures there are individuals and groups who think differently (e.g. skinheads). The Western emphasis on non-violence is a sociocultural norm, not a universal morality.

Throughout history there have always been differences in **cultural norms** and **values** that have shaped some societies as more, and some as less, aggressive than others. Usually, it is not difficult to identify the reasons. Historical factors such as repeated invasions, geographic factors that made some societies more competitive or more vulnerable than others, and even bioevolutionary factors that simply permitted some groups to be more aggressive by virtue of their greater size, have all played a part in shaping the social philosophies of particular societies. Moreover, these philosophies are dynamic and can change rapidly with a change in context.

Examples of this in recent years are the development of aggressive Zionism following the Jewish Holocaust in World War II, altering a religious philosophy of pacifism that had endured for centuries; and in Australia the emergence of Black activism among Aborigines, whose generally low level of aggression towards outsiders probably contributed to their initial exploitation (Rowley, 1971).

The ethic of non-violence in our own society is actually quite recent. In earlier times the violence of soldiery, and physical pursuits for schoolboys such as boxing and football, were not only approved but even considered an essential element of masculinity (Phillips, 1987). Just think of corporal punishment—there are still people who believe it is right to hit small children who have been naughty.

While most societies in the world do show forms of interpersonal violence (Rohner, 1976), there are some that still actively practise a lifestyle of non-aggression. These include the Hutterite and Amish communities in the United States and the Pygmies of Central Africa. Although this appears to support Bandura's claims that aggression is learned rather than instinctual, it is noteworthy that all the societies that remain peaceful in the 21st century are both small and relatively isolated, suggesting that these may be necessary preconditions for peaceful existence (see Gorer, 1968, for a social anthropological review of peaceful societies).

The fact remains that different societies view aggressive behaviour in very different ways, according to historical, normative and social–contextual factors, and that sometimes this can lead to damaging misunderstandings in this age of increasingly multicultural societies. An example of relevance locally is that Samoan people have viewed violent drunken behaviour as a bout of sickness rather than aggression; and rape as an offence against the victim's entire family, not just the woman personally (Kinloch, 1985). These cultural differences have had important implications for police intervention with Samoan and possibly other Pacific Islands offenders in Australia or New Zealand.

A different kind of evidence in support of social learning theory comes from the study of the **subculture of violence** (Toch, 1969). Within societies there are often smaller groups or minority subcultures in which violence is legitimised as a lifestyle, initially perhaps because it is seen as a way of improving the group's status and power within the larger society. The beliefs, values and norms of the group reflect an approval of aggressiveness, and there will be both social rewards for violent behaviour and negative sanctions for not going along with the group's violent activities. In urban settings, these groups are often labelled, and self-styled, as gangs, and the importance of violence is reflected in their appearance as well as in their behaviour. Violence is a way of life for such groups, both towards the greater society and among themselves. Baumeister and Heatherton (1996) suggest that, rather than valuing violence, these groups define in different ways to mainstream society the *conditions* under which violence is disinhibited.

Nieburg (1969) provided a graphic example of the traditional initiation rite for the Sicilian Mafia. After a long lead-up period of observation, the new Mafia member would attend a candle-lit meeting of other members and be led to a table showing the image of a saint, an emblem of high religious significance. Blood taken from his right hand would be sprinkled on the saint and he would swear an oath of allegiance, binding him to the brotherhood. In a short time he would prove

Culture of violence: These young people are members of rival gangs whose norm for solving intergroup disputes is violence. The traffic can wait.

himself worthy by executing a suitable person selected by the Mafia. Ingoldsby (1991) points to the existence of **machismo** among Latin American families. In Italy, Tomada and Schneider (1997) report that aggression is still encouraged in adolescent boys from traditional villages, in the belief that it shows sexual prowess and shapes a dominant male in the household. They link this in turn to a higher rate of male bullying at school than in England, Spain, Norway or Japan (Genta, Menesini, Fonzi, Costabile, & Smith, 1996).

Such a subculture exists in many prison communities, where the factions often parallel gang membership. Violence in most prisons in Western society is actually *institutionalised* (a term discussed in a later section) in ways that are informal but clearly recognised by both inmates and prison staff. Paradoxically, this is believed to account for much of the control and discipline within prisons (Calkin, 1985). (See also the discussion of the culture of honour in the American South (Nisbett & Cohen, 1996)—Chapter 16 and Box 16.2.)

INTERACTIONISM

By now it should be evident that aggression is never a simple act resulting from one specific cause. There will be contributing factors at each of the **levels of explanation** (personal, social, situational and cultural) discussed above (see Chapter 1 for further discussion of the way in which levels of explanation are used across different theoretical approaches in psychology). While the most obvious cause may often appear to be some aspect of the immediate situation, a fuller explanation for the behaviour will always require a search for underlying social and cultural factors as well. Part of this picture is the role of the mass media.

Mass media

The impact of *mass media*, especially visual media, on aggressive behaviour has been a controversial focus of research and theory in the past two decades or more. There are many examples of people emulating violent acts such as assault, rape and murder in almost identical fashion to portrayals in a film or television program and, likewise, of the disinhibitory effects on the general population of watching an excessive amount of sanitised violence on the screen. Attempts by laboratory researchers to establish a causal link between viewing violence and acting aggressively have been flawed both methodologically and theoretically. For example, much of the work on the effects of **desensitisation** to media violence has involved exposure to rather mild forms of television violence for relatively short periods of time (Freedman, 1984; Geen & Donnerstein, 1983).

Bandura (1973, 1986) has demonstrated how film and television violence distorts the perceived outcomes of violence by sanitising both the aggressive acts and the injuries received by the victim. This suggests to the viewer that the aggression is not actually harmful. Moreover, the aggressor is often portrayed as the good guy in the situation and is rarely punished for his acts of violence. Social learning theory (Bandura, 1973) has taken a strong position on this point: children will readily mimic the behaviour of a model who is reinforced for aggressing, or at least escapes punishment. There has been considerable debate about whether violent video games can also have harmful effects on children (see Box 12.8).

BOX 12.8   **Do gory video games make children more aggressive?**

There has been frequent and often heated debate in recent years about the effects of violence in video games. Some believe these games increase levels of aggression in children, whereas others argue that such games actually reduce aggression. Proponents claim that contact between characters in the games is often graphically violent, and that children will copy this in their everyday interactions with others; *social learning theory* is sympathetic to this view. We noted in Box 12.4, for example, that even cartoon characters might be imitated by young children. Those disagreeing with this view believe that children may experience the benefits of *catharsis* from playing the games, by venting some energy and by relaxing. Again, we have already called into question the efficacy of catharsis in this connection (see Box 12.5).

Will children become desensitised to the consequences of acting aggressively in real-life situations by playing out violent scenes? Certainly, the content of the games themselves is of some concern. Dietz (1998) examined 33 popular video games and found that nearly 80% contained aggression as part of either the immediate object or the long-term strategy.

Griffiths (1997) reviewed research into the effects of video games on aggression in children and concluded that aggression levels increase in younger children but not in teenage children. However, he cautioned on methodological grounds that most of the research in this field is restricted to observations of children's free play activity following game-playing.

In a large-scale study, van Schie and Wiegman (1997) investigated game-playing among 346 children. Their findings were multi-faceted:

- There was no significant relationship between the amounts of time spent gaming and subsequent levels of aggression.
- Video gaming did not replace children's other leisure activities.
- The amount of time spent gaming was positively correlated with the child's measured level of intelligence.

On the other hand, they also found that children who spent more time playing video games were less likely to behave prosocially (see Chapter 13 for a full discussion of factors associated with prosocial behaviour in children).

Ultimately, ethical considerations prevent researchers from experimental manipulation, such as exposing children to aggressive video games to observe subsequent changes in aggressive behaviour. To date, the evidence is inconclusive about the effects of playing violent video games on children's behaviour.

Sheehan (1983) presents evidence of a correlation between children's television-viewing habits and their levels of aggressive behaviour. His samples were upper-middle-class boys and girls aged 5–10 years at primary schools in 1979–81 in Brisbane. Some of these samples were age cohorts tested more than once across different years. The behaviour variable consisted of ratings by peers of each child's acts that physically injured or irritated another person. Other data relating to the use of aggressive fantasies by the children, and parental variables, were also gathered. Correlations between viewing violent programs and peer-rated aggression were consistently significant only among older children (approximately 8–10 years), mostly close to $r = 0.25$, and were stronger among boys than among girls.

Although Sheehan also carried out multiple-regression analyses to try to determine causal relationships, he was unable to show a direct connection between early (younger age) viewing habits and later (older age) aggression. According to these longitudinal regressions, the best predictors were ratings of aggression for the same child (from younger to older), parental

characteristics (income, rejection of child, use of punishment, television-viewing habits) and the use of aggressive fantasies by the child. In other words, there were multiple links, involving several factors, between the viewing of television violence and aggressive behaviour in children. In contrast to the use of experimental techniques, it is difficult in a field study to confirm causal relationships between variables, a point that Sheehan noted (see also Chapter 1).

Several other non-experimental studies have demonstrated a generalised connection between mass media violence and both intrapersonal and interpersonal aggression (see Phillips, 1986, for a comprehensive review). Longitudinal research points to a correlation between overall amount of violent television watched and aggressive behaviour (Huesmann & Miller, 1994). The effect is not simply one of the imitation of violence modelled on the screen or read about in newspapers and magazines, nor just of desensitisation and disinhibition; there is evidence that seeing and reading about violence in general promotes greater aggression in some people.

Black and Bevan (1992) investigated reported levels of aggression among 129 film-goers who watched either a very violent or a non-violent film. The participants completed an aggression questionnaire either entering or leaving the cinema. The researchers found higher pre-viewing aggression scores among participants who chose the violent film, and noted that their scores were even higher after seeing the film. Gender differences were minimal (see Figure 12.9).

The bottom line from an extensive and rigorous **meta-analysis** by Anderson and Bushman (2002) is that, regardless of how we study the media violence/aggression link, the outcomes are the same—significant, substantial positive relations.

A COGNITIVE INTERPRETATION

Recent views on the idea that the media can trigger violence have featured the manner in which people process information and, in this case, automatically react to aggressive scenes or descriptions (Berkowitz, 1984; Eron, 1994; Huesmann, 1988). Berkowitz's (1984) **neo-associationist analysis** picked up on old themes in psychology, including the 19th-century notion of *ideo-motor response*—that merely thinking about an act can facilitate its performance (see Box 1.2 in Chapter 1). According to neo-associationism, real or fictional images of violence that are presented to an audience can translate later into antisocial acts. Conversely, exposure to images of people helping others can lead later to pro-social acts (see Figure 12.10).

Berkowitz drew on cognitive psychological literature in which memory is treated as a collection of networks, each of which consists of nodes. A node can include substantive elements of thoughts and feelings, connected through associative pathways. When a thought comes into focus, its activation radiates out from that particular node via the associative pathways to other nodes, which in turn can lead to a **priming** effect (see also Chapter 2). Consequently, if you have been watching a movie depicting a violent gang 'rumble', other semantically related thoughts can be primed, such as *punching*, *kicking*, *shooting a gun* and so forth. This process can be mostly automatic, without much conscious thinking involved.

Similarly, feelings associated with aggression, such as some components of the emotion of anger, may be activated. The outcome is an overall increase in the probability that an aggressive act will follow. Such action could be of a generalised nature or it may be similar to that portrayed in the media—in which case, it could be an example of a 'copy-cat crime' (Phillips, 1986).

Can the mere sight of a gun provoke a person to use it? Perhaps. The **weapons effect** is a phenomenon that can be accounted for by a neo-associationist approach. Berkowitz asked the question 'Does the finger pull the trigger or the trigger pull the finger?' (Berkowitz & LePage, 1967). If weapons suggest aggressive images not associated with most other stimuli, a person's range of attention could be severely curtailed—a possibility tested in a priming experiment by Anderson, Anderson and Deuser (1996). Their participants first viewed either

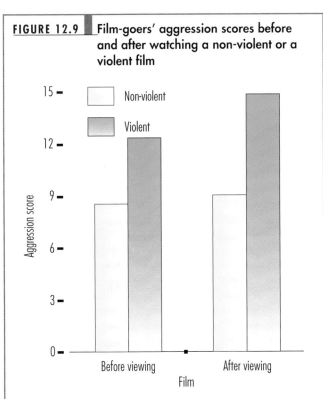

FIGURE 12.9 Film-goers' aggression scores before and after watching a non-violent or a violent film

Aggression score (y-axis): 0, 3, 6, 9, 12, 15

Before viewing / After viewing (x-axis)
Film

Non-violent
Violent

Note: People who attend screenings of violent films may be generally more disposed to aggression, according to their scores on an aggression questionnaire. Furthermore, their aggression scores rise after attending a violent film.

Source: Based on data from Black & Bevan (1992).

The weapons effect: Guns evoke images associated with few other stimuli. They shoot, they kill. A firearm is unlikely to have neutral connotations.

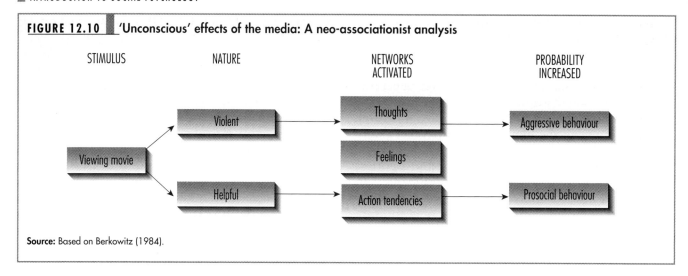

FIGURE 12.10 'Unconscious' effects of the media: A neo-associationist analysis

Source: Based on Berkowitz (1984).

pictures of guns or scenes of nature. They were then presented with words printed in different colours which had either aggressive or neutral connotations. Their task was to report the colours of the words. Their response speed was slowest in the condition where pictures of weapons preceded aggressive words. We should not infer from this that weapons always invite violent associations. A gun might, for example, be associated with sport rather than being a destructive weapon (Berkowitz, 1993)—hence the more specific term 'weapons effect'.

EROTICA AND AGGRESSION

If exposure to erotica, such as magazines and films, can lead to sexual arousal, might it also be related to later aggression? The evidence points to a U-function, depending on the kind of erotica viewed. Looking at pictures of attractive nudes, for example, seems to reduce aggression when compared with a control condition of neutral pictures, pointing to a distracting effect caused by mild erotica (Baron, 1979; Ramirez, Bryant, & Zillmann, 1983). On the other hand, the viewing of highly erotic materials showing explicit love-making can increase aggression (Baron & Bell, 1977; Zillmann, 1984, 1996). Sexual arousal from non-violent erotica could lead to aggression because of the excitation-transfer effect (refer back to Figure 12.4). This phenomenon, however, depends on the person experiencing a later frustrating event, which acts as a trigger to aggress. In short, there has been no convincing demonstration of a direct link between erotica and aggression.

In an experiment by Zillmann and Bryant (1984), participants were exposed to a massive amount of violent pornography, after which they were annoyed by a confederate. Following this, they became more callous about what they had seen: they viewed rape more tolerantly and became more lenient about prison sentences they would recommend (see Figure 12.11). However,

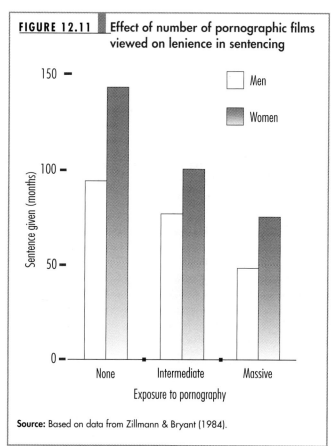

FIGURE 12.11 Effect of number of pornographic films viewed on lenience in sentencing

Source: Based on data from Zillmann & Bryant (1984).

the experimental design involves a later provoking event, so the outcome can be explained as an instance of excitation transfer.

When violence is mixed with sex in films there is, at least, evidence of male desensitisation to aggression against women—in the form of callous and demeaning attitudes (Donnerstein & Linz, 1994; Mullin & Linz, 1995). In a meta-analysis by Paik & Comstock (1994), sexually violent TV programs have been linked to later aggression, most clearly in male aggression against women (Donnerstein & Malamuth, 1997).

Linz, Donnerstein and Penrod (1988) reported that, when women were shown enjoying violent pornography, men were later more willing to aggress against women (though, interestingly, not against men). Perhaps just as telling are other consequences of such material: it can perpetuate the myth that women actually enjoy sexual violence. It has been demonstrated that portrayals of women apparently enjoying such acts reinforce rape myths and weaken social and cognitive restraints against violence towards women (Malamuth & Donnerstein, 1982). Zillmann and Bryant (1984) pointed out that the cumulative effect of exposure to violent pornography trivialises rape by portraying women as 'hyperpromiscuous and socially irresponsible'.

There has been a growth of resistance to such materials by women's movements in recent years. A *feminist perspective* emphasises two concerns about continual exposure of men to media depicting violence and/or sexually explicit material involving women:

1. that exposure to violence will cause men to become callous or desensitised to violence against female victims; and
2. that exposure to pornography will contribute to the development of negative attitudes towards women.

Some feminist writers (see Gubar & Hoff, 1989) maintain that pornography is a blight when it depicts women as subordinate to men and existing solely to satisfy men's sexual needs. In Geen's (1998) review, an attitude—perhaps a value—developed by long-term use of pornography is callousness. A woman is reduced to being a sexual reward for the conquering male (Mosher & Anderson, 1986).

In summary, Linz, Wilson and Donnerstein (1992) isolate two culprits relevant to an otherwise confusing mix of violence, sex and women in the media:

1. The portrayal of violence can beget violence.
2. Degrading messages about women institutionalise a demeaning and one-dimensional image of women.

Finally, issues concerning the links between media violence, media pornography and real-life violence have extended to the role of the Internet (see Durkin & Bryant, 1995). This latest electronic medium brings massive amounts of information directly into the privacy of our homes. Concern is mounting steadily about the type of material that can be accessed and the difficulty of monitoring it. There have been revelations of international paedophilia and child pornography networks, and the likelihood of a connection between these networks and child sexual abuse. However, even if there are correlations between these variables, care must be exercised in drawing a causal inference (see fourth focus question).

Domestic violence

Domestic violence is a topic of great concern in our community and has prompted considerable research in recent years. According to actual reports made to the police in New Zealand, 18 500 domestic disputes were attended each year in the period 1988–95 (New Zealand Now Crime Tables, 1996). However, it is difficult to assess whether domestic violence is actually increasing or whether supporting data reflect a higher level of vigilance and reporting, more media publicity or even unreliable statistics. We note earlier in this chapter that there are difficulties in assessing the prevalence of violence. People are often reluctant to report or admit to violence within their homes, so it is difficult to know how commonly it occurs (Haines, 1987; see also Box 12.9). A study in 1996 on women's safety reported that only 8% of women who disclosed abuse by a current partner had reported the violence to the police (New Zealand Police Statistics, 2000).

A survey of more than 2000 families in the United States revealed that some kind of physical assault with intent to injure had occurred, at some point, in 28% of the married couples sampled, and in 16% of the cases within the past year (Straus, Gelles, & Steinmetz, 1980). These were not trivial acts, but behaviours such as pushing, hitting with the fist, slapping, kicking, throwing something and beating up; 7% reported being threatened with a gun or knife. More than 70% of parents reported using slaps and spankings on children and 20% admitted to hitting children with an object. The phenomenon also extends with equal or greater frequency to intimate relationships outside families (Sigelman,

Domestic violence: Within relationships and families people can use whatever advantage they have (physical strength, verbal dexterity) as a means of control—which can sometimes spill over into aggression or violence.

BOX 12.9 | Domestic violence

THERE'S NO PLACE LIKE HOME

We like to think that we are safe in our own homes but cross-national comparisons between the United Kingdom and New Zealand suggest otherwise.

In 1995 more than 45 000 violent offences were reported to the New Zealand police—double the annual rate for the preceding five years (New Zealand Now Crime Tables, 1996). Although we cannot conclude that violence has increased so dramatically in one year, clearly the rate of reporting has. A remarkable feature of these data is that nearly half the offences occurred at home.

The consequences for the mental health of the victims are telling. Tham, Ford and Wilkinson (1995) investigated nearly 200 male and female patients in the United Kingdom who presented with acute symptoms to a psychiatric hospital over a five-month period. One-quarter reported being victims of domestic violence, and three out of four of these were women. In all, 25% felt that their mental condition was related to their abuse.

In the case of rape and sexual assault, a New Zealand study of 1000 victims found that 97% were female (Holdt, 1996). Nearly three-quarters of the attacks took place in the victim's home, and the victim knew the offender in 90% of cases. As two-thirds of the victims did not report the attack, the reported levels of domestic violence are almost certainly well below actual levels.

At the same time, some reports of domestic abuse are false. These may arise, for example, from paternity disputes or from the 'divorce-related malicious mother syndrome' (Turkat, 1995)—false allegations of violence and other malicious acts against fathers. Abuse in the home extends beyond partners, to include their children and even their parents as victims.

There is evidence of a link between the experience of being a victim of violence and lack of adequate pro-social behaviours towards others. When abused toddlers were compared with other preschool children who had affectionate and caring parents, they were found to be quite unsympathetic towards age-mates in distress (Zahn-Waxler, Radke-Yarrow, & King, 1979).

Why do people remain silent about the physically and psychologically traumatic attacks they suffer? Personal pride; fear of reprisals, either on oneself or another family member (Fergusson, Horwood, Kershaw, & Shannon, 1986); fear of blame or social ridicule; and the perceived and actual failure of the police and others to provide any real help—these have all been found to prevent people in Australia and New Zealand from telling others about the violence that occurs behind closed doors. Thus, the majority of instances go unreported and, therefore, unpunished and without constructive or protective intervention (see fifth focus question).

GENDER

We have seen that the view that only men aggress against women and children is not true. It is also challenged by studies of same-sex relationships: lesbians, bisexual people and gay men are also victims of acts of violence in the home (Klinger & Stein, 1996), suggesting that earlier theories of domestic violence are insufficient and heterosexist (Letellier, 1994). What seems more accurate is that, when men and women are aggressive, men tend to do more physical damage.

Nevertheless, the image of a man being battered by a woman may be difficult to envisage. Harris and Cook (1994) investigated students' responses to three scenarios: a husband battering his wife, a wife battering her husband, and a gay man battering his male partner, each in relation to verbal provocation. Battering of the wife was rated as more violent than the other two scenarios. Further, 'victim blaming' (see Chapter 3) was attributed most often to a gay victim, who was also judged most likely to leave the relationship. It seems that the one act takes on a different meaning according to the gender of the aggressor and the victim.

HURTING THE ONES WE 'LOVE'

Assault, rape and incest within intimate relationships may account for as much as 80% of all violent offending. Although there is evidence that women attack men (O'Leary, Barling, Arias, Rosenbaum, Malone, & Tyree, 1989), male violence is, as we have seen, usually more severe so that the term *battered woman* is often apt (Walker 1993). Why do people want to hurt those closest to them? There are no simple answers, but some of the most influential factors are these:

- *learned patterns of aggression*, imitated from parents and significant others, together with low competence

Berry, & Wiles, 1984) and the difference between the sexes appears to relate to the degree of violence of the acts, but not to the frequency with which they occur (Straus, Gelles, & Steinmetz, 1980). In fact, women are slightly more likely than men to use physical aggression against their partners in heterosexual relationships (Archer, 2000). However male violence tends to do more harm—women account for only 35% of serious injuries and 44% of deaths.

Consider these sobering statistics: in Queensland, it is estimated that 29% of homicides where the killer knows the victim are committed by a spouse (Strang, 1991, cited in *We Can Stop Domestic Violence*, 1994); in New Zealand, between 1993 and 1998, 43% of murders and 37% of manslaughter cases were domestically related (New Zealand Police Statistics, 2000).

in other non-aggressive ways of responding; the generational cycle of child abuse is a well-established phenomenon (Straus, Gelles, & Steinmetz, 1980) and the chronic repetition of violence within some families has been identified now as an **abuse syndrome**;

- the *proximity* of family members, which makes them more likely to be sources of annoyance or frustration, and targets when these feelings are generated externally;
- *stresses*, especially financial difficulties, unemployment and illnesses (including postnatal depression; see Searle, 1987); this accounts partly for domestic violence being much more common in poorer families;
- the division of *power* within traditional nuclear families, favouring the man, which makes it easier for less democratic styles of interaction to predominate (Claes & Rosenthal, 1990); and
- a high level of *alcohol* consumption, which is a common correlate of male abuse of a spouse (Stith & Farley, 1993).

The interaction of these factors, heightened by the normal stresses of day-to-day living that we all encounter, means that those we live closest to are, ironically, the most likely targets of our aggression. A further irony is that domestic violence seems to be most common in, if not endemic to, industrialised societies, and relatively uncommon in non-industrialised ones (Steinmetz & Straus, 1973). This suggests that factors associated with the industrialisation process, such as urbanisation, population increase and density, and competition for resources, may play an important part in the cycle of domestic abuse.

Institutionalised aggression: Many sports involve aggression, but aggression that is carefully governed by rules and regulations.

Institutionalised aggression

ROLE OF SOCIETY
Not all societies define aggression as a totally bad thing. In our society, the emphasis on non-violence is an outcome of historical and sociocultural factors. It is an ethic that derives from a combination of politics, religion, philosophy, events in recent history, including the atrocities of World War II and the Vietnam War, and the threat of nuclear annihilation. Our emphasis on non-violence is a sociocultural value judgment about aggression, and we should remember that each society views the different kinds of aggression in different ways.

We noted at the outset that biological theories usually argue that aggression is functional—that is, it has useful properties. Can we find examples of human aggression, apart from personal self-defence, that seem reasonable?

Issues of definition reappear: there are ways in which aggression has been used, at both interpersonal and societal levels, in an attempt to bring about positive outcomes for individuals or particular groups, which have in common the characteristic of preserving the **social order** (see Kelvin, 1970).

Human societies depend for their continuity on social norms; those that are well established may become embedded as values that are widely shared in a community, such as caring for our fellows. Ultimately, law provides protection for a social system. Occasionally, the mechanisms of social order even sanction the use of violence. Table 12.2 sets out some legitimate functions of **institutionalised aggression**, but suggests that they can have either socially desirable or undesirable effects, depending on the degree of violence used and the motives underlying the acts. In recent years we saw the emergence of vigilante groups on the New York subway system. Group members occasionally use force and violence to assert citizens' rights to safe passage. Although unsanctioned, vigilante groups are gaining favour with ordinary citizens, who judge that the police are simply unable to provide adequate protection.

Moral issues underlie the judgments we might make, as they do when we debate issues such as suicide, abortion and euthanasia—all of which can be made to fit a definition of aggression.

WAR: AGGRESSION ON A GRAND SCALE
Large-scale aggression and war, which can be linked to the topics of prejudice and discrimination (discussed in Chapters 10 and 11), are, tragically, part of the human

TABLE 12.2 Social control functions of aggression

BONA FIDE OR INTENDED FUNCTION	'DESIRABLE' EFFECTS (?)	'UNDESIRABLE' EFFECTS (?)
• National defence • Policing; law and order • Behaviour control • Protection of civilians • Self-defence	• Australian and New Zealand forces in Vietnam • Use of 'bouncers' in night clubs • Scolding young children • Australian and New Zealand soldiers in Iraq • Martial arts (e.g. karate)	• My Lai massacre in Vietnam • Death penalty for drug trafficking • Smacking young children • British occupation of Northern Ireland • Police or civilian ownership of guns

condition. Two million years of human evolution, industrialisation, the communications revolution, philosophy, art and poetry have had no effect whatsoever—collective violence continues unabated. Recent years have witnessed horrific violence in Somalia, Bosnia, Croatia, Kosovo, Rwanda, Chechnya and East Timor.

One way of glimpsing the continuing tragedy is to consider the incidence and severity of wars. In World War I (1914–18) four million people died directly from the conflict. The figure was 15 million in World War II (1939–45), even disregarding acts of genocide such as six million Jews exterminated during the Holocaust, deaths in concentration camps and civilians killed in bombing raids in Europe. Table 12.3 includes interstate wars between 1946 and 1979 in which more than 1000 deaths have been documented. Even these estimates (Dupuy & Dupuy, 1977; Hartman & Mitchell, 1984; Singer & Small, 1972) are conservative; and the list does not include fatal casualties in civil wars and wars of independence during the period covered.

ROLE OF THE STATE

The worst acts of inhumanity are committed against humanity itself. Warfare is not possible without a supporting psychological structure involving the beliefs and emotions of a people. If such a structure is lacking, national leaders can create one by means of propaganda (as noted in Chapter 6). In times of war, both the soldiers who are fighting and the people at home need to maintain good morale. We note in Chapter 11 that genocide can be thought of as a kind of legitimised prejudice, carried through into behaviour. Some political regimes have fostered beliefs in genetic differences between groups of people to justify oppression and slaughter. Ideologies of racial, moral and social inferiority were the cornerstones of the Nazi programs directed against gypsies, political non-conformists, homosexuals, the mentally handicapped, the ill, Blacks and, of course, Jews. Open antagonism expressed by Hitler led German citizens to especially avoid Jews, who were sometimes neighbours and friends. This climate paved the way for the enactment of the Nuremberg laws

TABLE 12.3 Interstate wars 1946–79 with deaths exceeding 1000

WAR	PERIOD	DEATHS
Palestine	1948–49	16 000
Korea	1950–53	2 000 000
Hungary	1956	39 000
Sinai	1956	4 000
Sino-India	1962	5 000
First Kashmir	1947–49	1 000
UK–India	1946–48	800 000
Yugoslavia	1946–48	45 000
Egypt	1948–59	8 000
Indo-China	1946–54	105 000
Madagascar	1947–49	1 000
Laos	1953–73	10 000
Algeria	1954–62	115 000
Tibet	1956–59	14 000
Suez	1957	3 500
Lebanon	1958–81	45 000
Vietnam	1961–75	1 000 000
Second Kashmir	1965	14 000
Six-day (Israeli)	1967	21 000
Honduras–El Salvador	1969	2 000
Bangladesh	1971	17 000
Cambodia	1975–79	2 500 000
Angola	1961–75	38 000
Angola	1979	6 000
China–Vietnam	1979	70 000

Source: Vaughan (1988).

of discrimination. It was a small step to the burning of synagogues, huge numbers of arrests and street attacks on Jews. The horrific last link in the chain was the killing of millions of people.

The role of the state, then, can be to suggest to its citizens that aggression is reasonable in certain circumstances. Our earlier treatment of authoritarianism (Chapter 10) linked obedience to a set of personality characteristics, although this research has been found wanting as a major explanation of prejudice and aggressive behaviour. However, a powerful autocracy constrains its citizens to obey without question.

People as agents

In this context, Milgram's (1974) experiment on blind destructive obedience (covered in full in Chapter 7) is worthy of further mention. Milgram showed how ordinary people could do terrible things (give apparently lethal electric shocks to a stranger who simply made mistakes on a learning task in a laboratory) when conditions encouraged blind obedience to authority. Just think about it—Milgram's participants were prepared to electrocute someone who had not learned properly which words went together, simply because someone in a white coat told them to do so! Milgram gave the lie to the idea that terrible things are done by terrible psychopathic people; on the contrary, his results suggested that many of us would have responded in the same way.

Although his work was criticised for its supposed artificiality, as well as for his deception of participants to induce an 'immoral act', Milgram defended himself on the grounds of his contribution to the understanding of ordinary people's willingness to aggress when obeying a legitimate authority. A few years after the original experiment (Milgram, 1963) came the news of the massacre by American forces of men, women and children in Vietnam in 1969, at a village called My Lai (see Box 12.6). The Vietnam War scarred the American psyche more than any other, and this incident has acquired a uniqueness by exploding the myth that atrocities are committed only by the 'enemy'.

Milgram generalised from the context of war to the everyday life of citizens in any country: people are taught from childhood to obey both the laws of the state and the orders of those who represent its authority. In so doing, citizens enter an **agentic mode** of thinking and distance themselves from personal responsibility for their actions.

Levels of explanation

We note earlier in this chapter that different levels of explanation are adopted to account for aggression and for a wide variety of social behaviours (see Chapter 1). In the context of war, psychological explanations have varied from being heavily person-centred to being group-centred. Studies of authoritarianism have argued that prejudice, discrimination, violence and war atrocities reside in extreme or deviant personalities. Milgram moved away from this by suggesting that ordinary people can feel they are agents of the state, and will carry out orders that can harm others when the voice of authority seems legitimate. Sherif (Sherif & Sherif, 1953) moved well away from an individual level of explana-

tion by relating large-scale conflict to the nature of *intergroup relations*, suggesting that discriminatory acts against an outgroup will flourish only when the objective interests of a group are threatened. Tajfel refined this group-centred approach by suggesting that the very existence of ingroups is the essential cause of prejudice, discrimination and conflict. Outgroups provide a reference and must be kept at bay. These issues are examined in detail in Chapter 11.

Tajfel (1974) contrasted an account of aggression based on the person with one based on the group (see Box 12.10). The first account in Box 12.10 is an individualist perspective offered by Berkowitz (1962). The second account, by Tajfel, has taken Berkowitz's own words and made crucial substitutions of terms that implicate society as 'the cause'.

Reducing aggression

With the development of behavioural technologies based on social learning theory, and attention given to the social costs of increasing violence, greater effort has been put into the prevention and control of aggression. The effectiveness of interventions to reduce both interpersonal and intergroup aggression is contentious and may involve political decisions about the costs incurred. To make an impact on the underlying causes of violence, significant changes are required at the societal level to improve the conditions of groups that are plagued by stresses that exacerbate the cyclic repetition of violence. A major underlying factor is poverty (Belsky, 1993). In families, parents can raise more peaceful children by not rewarding acts of violence, by rewarding behaviour that is not compatible with violence and by avoiding the use of punishing behaviour themselves.

At the interpersonal level there is probably more optimism; techniques of behaviour modification, social skills training, non-aggressive modelling, anger management and assertiveness training have been shown to be effective in teaching people self-control.

Mass violence such as genocide and war is quite a different matter (see Chapter 11). There is room for the introduction of **peace studies** into the education system and there is evidence that children are frightened by the prospect of war, especially nuclear war (Fernando & Vaughan, 1992; Prior, 1989). Peace education is more than an anti-war campaign: it has broadened to cover all aspects of peaceful relationships and coexistence. By teaching young children how to build and maintain self-esteem without being aggressive (the culture of self-esteem may nourish aggression—see Chapter 4), it is hoped that there will be a long-term impact which will expand into all areas of people's lives (Oliver, 1990).

| BOX 12.10 | Two levels of explanation of aggression and war |

An explanation of prejudice and discrimination was once offered in terms of person characteristics, namely the authoritarian personality (Adorno, Frenkel-Brunswik, Levinson, & Sanford, 1950). The use of a similar individual level of explanation is clear in the views of Berkowitz (1962, p. 167) in his account of the causes of aggression:

> Granting all this, the present writer is still inclined to emphasise the importance of individualistic considerations in the field of group relations. Dealings between groups ultimately become problems of the psychology of the individual. Individuals decide to go to war; battles are fought by individuals; and peace is established by individuals. It is the individual who adopts the beliefs prevailing in his society, even though the extent to which these opinions are shared by many people is a factor governing his readiness to adopt them, and he transmits these views to other individuals. Ultimately, it is the single person who attacks the feared and disliked ethnic minority group, even though many people around him share his feelings and are very important in determining his willingness to aggress against this minority.

The social psychologist Tajfel, working at Bristol in the early 1970s, regarded this view as typical of the restricted level of explanation offered by American social psychology. In an unpublished paper written in 1974, he deliberately rewrote Berkowitz's words as follows, using word in italics to emphasise where an individual focus is replaced by a societal one:

> Granting all this, the present writer is still inclined to emphasise the importance of considering the field of group relations in terms of *social structure*. Dealings between groups cannot be accounted for by the psychology of the individual. *Governments* decide to go to war; battles are fought by *armies*; and peace is established by *governments*. The *social conditions* in which groups live largely determine their beliefs and the extent to which they are shared. Ultimately, a single person's attack on an ethnic minority group that he dislikes or fears would remain a trivial occurrence had it not been for the fact that he acts in *unison with others* who share his feelings and are very important in determining his willingness to aggress against this minority.

Source: Tajfel (1974); cited in Vaughan (1988).

We cannot wave a magic wand and banish violence. At an interpersonal level, it is linked to a variety of factors—a person's social learning history, alcohol abuse, the way people handle frustration and so on. At a societal level, aggression is maintained to a large degree by inequitable relationships between groups (see Chapters 10 and 11). There is room at both levels for social psychologists and others to work towards harmony in a world of increasing stress and dwindling resources.

Summary

- Aggression has been defined in many ways. These definitions reflect differences in underlying theories about its nature and causes. One simple definition is 'the intentional infliction of some type of harm on others'.
- There are two major classes of theory about the origins of aggression, one stressing its biological origins and the other stressing social influences.
- Biological explanations can be traced to Darwinian theory and include the views of Freud, ethological theory and, more recently, evolutionary social psychology. These approaches emphasise genetically determined behaviour patterns shared by a species.
- Social explanations usually stress the role of societal influences and/or learning processes. Some incorporate a biological component as well, such as the frustration–aggression hypothesis and excitation-transfer theory. Social learning theory is a developmental approach that stresses reinforcement principles and the influence that models have on the young child.
- Some research into causes has concentrated on factors thought to be part of the person, such as personality correlates and gender. Other work has looked at transitory states: the experience of frustration, the role of catharsis, the effects of

provocation and alcohol, the role of brain injury or mental illness and the experience of disinhibition.

- Other studies have focused on situational factors. These include stressors in the physical environment, such as heat and crowding. A major societal variable is the perceived disadvantage that some groups have in relation to those holding power. This analysis is basic to relative deprivation theory.

- A social approach to aggression allows for the possibility of change in patterns over time and cultural context. Aggression is increasing in women. Rates of physical aggression vary across cultures, reflecting long-standing differences in norms and values.

- The role of the mass media, particularly television, is controversial. It is fashionable to argue that the continued portrayal of violence at the very least desensitises young people to the consequences of violence. A stronger argument is that it provides a model for future behaviour. The debate continues.

- Reports of domestic violence against spouse and children now have a high profile in our community. Whether these trends are actually more common is unclear.

- War is a continuing and massive blight on humanity. Arguments about its causes and its prevention that are defined purely in political terms miss many crucial points: the role of intergroup relations themselves, the fact that people actually hurt other people, and the perpetuation across generations of outgroup stereotypes and prejudice.

LINKS

YOU HAVE READ ABOUT:	WHICH LINKS TO:
Measurement of aggression	operational definitions (1)
Biological theories	evolutionary social psychology (1); attraction (13); altruism (14)
Learning to aggress	modelling and attitude learning (5); modelling and prosocial behaviour (14)
Personal and situational factors affecting aggression	personality, the situation and leadership (9); personal and situational factors affecting prosocial behaviour (14)
Mass media effects on violence	mass media and attitude change (6)
Role of cognition	priming (2)
Institutionalised aggression	legitimising prejudice (10)
Reducing aggression	role of inequity in intergroup relations (11)

Key terms

abuse syndrome (p. 319)
agentic mode (p. 321)
analogue (p. 298)
biosocial theories (p. 300)
catharsis (p. 306)
cathartic hypothesis (p. 306)
collective aggression (p. 308)
cultural norms (p. 312)
dehumanisation (p. 308)
deindividuation (p. 308)
desensitisation (p. 313)
disinhibition (p. 308)

ethology (p. 299)
evolutionary social psychology (p. 300)
excitation-transfer model (p. 301)
external validity (p. 298)
fighting instinct (p. 299)
frustration–aggression hypothesis (p. 300)
hate crimes (p. 302)
instinct (p. 298)
institutionalised aggression (p. 319)

learning by direct experience (p. 303)
learning by vicarious experience (p. 303)
level of explanation (p. 313)
machismo (p. 313)
meta-analysis (p. 315)
modelling (p. 303)
nature–nurture controversy (p. 298)
neo-associationist analysis (p. 315)

neo-Freudians *(p. 299)*
operational definition *(p. 298)*
peace studies *(p. 321)*
priming *(p. 315)*
reciprocity principle *(p. 307)*

relative deprivation *(p. 311)*
releasers *(p. 299)*
script *(p. 303)*
social learning theory *(p. 302)*
social order *(p. 319)*

sociobiology *(p. 300)*
subculture of violence *(p. 312)*
type A personality *(p. 305)*
values *(p. 312)*
weapons effect *(p. 315)*

FURTHER READING

Anderson, C. A., & Huesmann, L. R. (2003). Human aggression: A social-cognitive view. In M. A. Hogg & J. Cooper (Eds.), *The Sage handbook of social psychology* (pp. 296–323). London: Sage. Up-to-date and comprehensive overview of research on human aggression by two of the world's leading aggression researchers.

Baron, R. A., & Richardson, D. R. (1994). *Human aggression* (2nd ed.). New York: Plenum. A recognised source of psychological research findings spanning the whole field.

Berkowitz, L. (1993). *Aggression: Its causes, consequences and control*. Philadelphia, PA: Temple University Press. Another work by an authority in the field with a good coverage of the topic.

Bradby, H. (Ed.). (1996). *Defining violence*. Aldershot, UK: Avebury. A compilation of recent research into the definition, causes and effects of violence.

Buford, B. (1993). *Among the thugs*. New York: Vintage. An inside look at the operation of English soccer thugs in British and other European settings. The work is compelling—one reviewer describes it as '*A Clockwork Orange* comes to life'.

Campbell, A. (1993). *Men, women and aggression*. New York: Harper Collins. The concepts of violence and aggression are explored with particular focus on roles and the implications regarding gender and culture.

Geen, R. (1998). Aggression and antisocial behaviour. In D. T. Gilbert, S. T. Fiske, & G. Lindzey (Eds.), *The handbook of social psychology* (4th ed., Vol. 2, pp. 317–356). New York: McGraw-Hill. An authoritative overview of the field of aggression, including biological aspects, psychological theories, individual differences, effects of the media, spouse bashing and sexual violence.

Glick, R. A., & Roose, S. P. (Eds.). (1993). *Rage, power, and aggression*. New Haven, CT: Yale University Press. A review of research accompanied by clinical and theoretical perspectives and a treatment of the origins and development of aggression.

Goldstein, A. P. (1994). *The ecology of aggression*. New York: Plenum. As the title suggests, the focus is on how aggression can be influenced by ecological factors, which can be both physical and social.

Krahé, B. (1996). Aggression and violence in society. In G. R. Semin & K. Fiedler (Eds.), *Applied social psychology* (pp. 343–373). London: Sage. A compact introduction to problems of definition and explanation. Personal and situational variables are explored, together with domestic violence, rape and bullying.

Loeber, R., & Hay, D. (1997). Key issues in the development of aggression and violence from childhood to early adulthood. *Annual Review of Psychology, 48*, 371–410. A review of the prediction of childhood factors that may lead to aggression in adolescence and on into adulthood.

Rose, H., & Rose, S. (2000). *Alas, poor Darwin: Arguments against evolutionary psychology*. London: Vintage. A group of scholars from a variety of biological, philosophical and social science backgrounds raise major concerns about the adequacy of genetic accounts of social behaviour, including aggression.

Affiliation, attraction and love

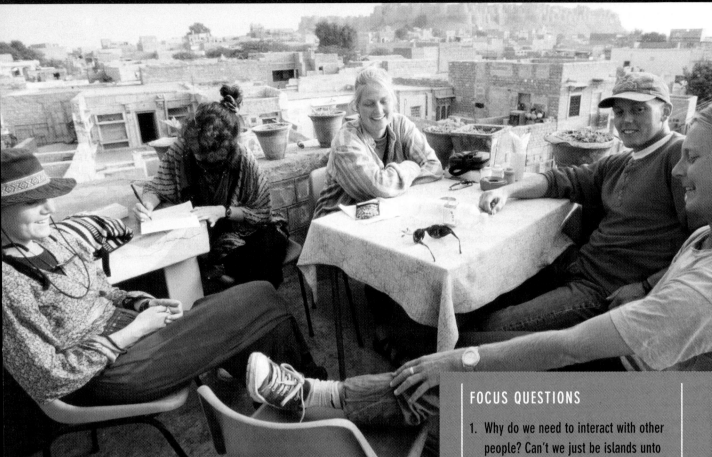

THIS CHAPTER DISCUSSES:

- the need to affiliate: effects of long-term and short-term social isolation
- evidence indicating a need for affiliation with others in times of stress and anxiety: the stress-shared model
- factors affecting attraction: physical attractiveness, reciprocity, proximity, similarity, need complementarity
- theories of attraction: balance, reinforcement and social exchange theories
- loving versus liking relationships
- maintaining and ending relationships: the effects of loneliness.

FOCUS QUESTIONS

1. Why do we need to interact with other people? Can't we just be islands unto ourselves?
2. Have you ever taken your mother and father for granted? Join the club. We are told from childhood that we owe parents a great deal, but would you believe that their role as caretaker is crucial to your intellectual and social development, setting you on the path to proper functioning as a human being?
3. You have just been introduced to an attractive stranger. How fairly can you judge this person's other attributes, such as his/her intelligence?
4. 'Wham! She walked out on me—just like that!' What do *you* think? Can the ending of a relationship come right out of the blue?

Why affiliate?

The **need to affiliate,** to be with others, is powerful and pervasive and underlies the way in which we form positive and lasting interpersonal relationships (Baumeister & Leary, 1995; see also Chapter 8). Although most of us from time to time want to be alone, to enjoy our own company, the effects of enduring social isolation can be extremely dire (Perlman & Peplau, 1998; see below).

In the early part of the 20th century, affiliative behaviour was understood in terms of instinct. McDougall (1908), for example, put it down to a gregarious propensity—that is, an inborn tendency to gather together. In this respect, he thought, we have something in common with other animals that live in herds or colonies. Simplistic instinct theories fell out of favour with the arrival of the behaviourist revolution spearheaded by Watson (1913), who argued that simply calling a behaviour like herding 'a herding instinct' is no explanation at all. An attempt to find some biological basis for social behaviour persists, most evidently in the field of **evolutionary social psychology** (see also Chapters 12, 14 and 15).

In the following sections we look first at two social psychological models put forward to account for variation in **affiliative behaviour,** ranging from wanting to be with others to wanting to be alone. Then we examine the effects of isolation on social functioning, the way that childhood attachments can influence adult relationships, and the effects of anxiety on wanting to be with others. From there we turn our attention to the attraction process, focusing on why we choose some people rather than others as the ones we would prefer to interact with. The question of attraction leads naturally to the area of long-term relationships and the exciting topic of love.

TOGETHER OR ALONE?

According to Altman's (1975, 1993) **privacy regulation theory** (PRT), affiliative behaviour is an outcome of a person's desire to be 'more or less accessible and open to others' (Altman, 1975, p. 3). For example, if Jane could satisfy her wish to be more private, she would feel that her **personal space** was larger and, if necessary, she would become more territorial in its protection. Privacy can fluctuate considerably over time and operates according to two principles (see Figure 13.1):

1. A *dialectic* principle—Jane's desire for privacy can vary between two poles, even within a few hours, from openness to closedness towards others.
2. An *optimisation* principle—Jane tries to match her desired and actual levels of contact with others. If the actual level of contact is too low, Jane will feel

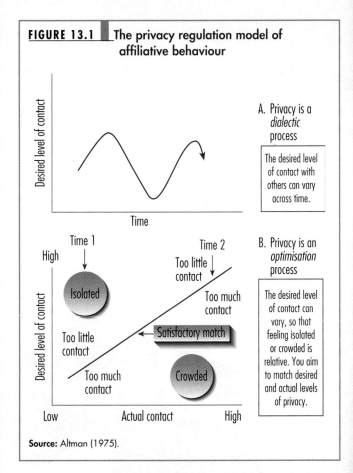

FIGURE 13.1 The privacy regulation model of affiliative behaviour

A. Privacy is a *dialectic* process

The desired level of contact with others can vary across time.

B. Privacy is an *optimisation* process

The desired level of contact can vary, so that feeling isolated or crowded is relative. You aim to match desired and actual levels of privacy.

Source: Altman (1975).

socially isolated; if it is too high, she will feel crowded.

Thus the need to affiliate is not a blind pursuit of constant interaction with others. In this way, PRT is able to account not only for changes in affiliative behaviour but also for the way that people regulate the physical distance between themselves and others.

O'Connor and Rosenblood (1996) have proposed an alternative model, called the **social affiliation model** (SAM). It retains the optimisation principle of PRT but replaces the dialectic property with the principle of *homeostasis.* Just as humans regulate their calorie intake, so they control their level of contact with others, keeping it both stable and close to their desired level.

In an innovative study, O'Connor and Rosenblood had students carry portable beepers on their bodies for four days. Most of the students lived with friends, family or a partner. The beepers went off at intermittent intervals, but on average every hour, signalling students to write down whether they were: (a) completely alone, (b) in the company of others but without interacting, or (c) in the company of others and interacting. This was a measure of their actual level of contact. They were also asked whether they wanted to be alone or not, which was a measure of their desired level of contact. Most of the students reported interacting with others at the rate that they intended across the four-day period; they had been successful in regulating their own personal needs for affiliation. There was a sex difference: women were with others more often than men were. However, both women and men were usually in the state they had desired, either alone or with others (see first focus question).

LONG-TERM ISOLATION

One way of learning what it means to affiliate is to ask what happens when people are prevented from being with others. We shall see that even relatively short-term separation from other people can be a nasty experience. Even more compelling, long-term separation can have serious and, in the case of the young, permanently damaging outcomes.

Stories from the field

There have been many instances of people being isolated and returning to the company of others to tell their stories—for example, prisoners in solitary confinement and shipwreck survivors. However, in these situations the experience of isolation has been accompanied by deprivation in another form (e.g. lack of food) or it has been enforced as punishment. For this reason, the experiences of Admiral Byrd are perhaps the most interesting example we have, as his isolation was voluntary and planned, thus ensuring he had adequate supplies to cater to his physical needs.

Byrd volunteered to spend six months alone at an Antarctic weather station observing and recording conditions. Although he had radio contact with the main base of the expedition, he had no other contact with people. He reported looking forward to the experience, as he wanted to 'be by myself for a while and to taste peace and quiet and solitude long enough to find out how good they really are' (Byrd, 1938, p. 4). However, after 24 days he began to write of the loneliness he felt and how this caused him to feel 'lost and bewildered' (1938, p. 95). He began embroidering his experience by imagining that he was among familiar people.

After 63 days he became preoccupied with religious questions and dwelt on the 'meaning of life'. His thoughts turned to ways of believing that he was not alone: 'The human race, then, is not alone in the universe. Though I am cut off from human beings, I am not alone' (1938, p. 185). After three months, he became severely depressed and apathetic. He was beset with hallucinations and bizarre ideas.

The mental health effects of 'wintering over' among both navy and civilian personnel in the harsh climate of the Antarctic have been well-documented (Taylor, 1987; Palinkas, Cravalho, & Browner, 1995), and are now taken into account in the selection of personnel (Rothblum, 1990).

Although this evidence is based on reports from people who have left the trappings of 'normal civilisation' behind, it is supported by other accounts of those for whom long periods of isolation is part of their annual experience of seasonal cycles. For example, the Inuit of Northern Canada go fishing in groups to prevent hallucinations and thereby avert disasters, such as drowning. Young men of the American Plains Indians deliberately isolated themselves for several days to await a visitation from benevolent spirits, for them a positive experience. However, Westerners who experience hallucinations generally seem to have found them and the other correlates of isolation an extremely stressful experience. Some never recover. Lilly (1956) reviewed autobiographies of people who had endured isolation and concluded that they displayed many, if not all, of the symptoms of mental illness.

Short-term sensory deprivation

One way of testing the question of whether we really are 'social animals' is to ask what happens to an individual who experiences a period of isolation from others. Bexton, Heron and Scott (1954) carried out a dramatic experiment at McGill University in Canada on the effects of almost complete sensory isolation. This work grew out of interest in how enforced isolation was thought to contribute to the phenomenon of **brainwashing**, an experience that received media publicity following reports of the solitary confinement, sleep deprivation and intensive interrogation of Western prisoners during the Korean War of the 1950s (see Chapter 6).

The participants in the McGill experiment were 22 paid volunteer students who were surprised to find that their task was to lie on a bed, wearing opaque goggles, cardboard cuffs and heavy gloves, and do nothing! They lay in a sound-deadened cubicle where there was a masking hum and a foam pillow fitted around their ears. After nearly three days of this dramatic reduction in sensory input, participants reported fuzzy vision, difficulties in focusing, the appearance of the visual environment as two-dimensional and deterioration on a number of cognitive tasks.

In a follow-up study by Bexton (cited in Kubzansky, 1961), participants were also persuaded to change their views on psychic phenomena after listening to a long and monotonous recorded propaganda message.

The effects reported in this research followed short-term sensory and social isolation and the outcomes, even if immediate, were transitory. Nevertheless, **sensory deprivation** studies of human volunteers provide an interesting example of the enormous power of the social context over the individual. We come to understand something of the importance of having others near us by experimentally impoverishing the social environment—that is, by taking these other people away. We return to this theme later in dealing with the topic of loneliness.

Studies of long-term deprivation in animals

Some of the most penetrating insights into factors that are crucial to normal social development were provided by Harlow, in studies of relationships between newborn rhesus monkeys and their mothers (Harlow, 1958; Harlow & Harlow, 1965; Harlow & Zimmermann, 1959). He studied **maternal deprivation** at the University of Wisconsin at the same time that Bowlby was working with deprived children in London (see below), each being aware of the other's ideas. Bowlby (1988) discussed Harlow's work in a way that showed that, although one set of studies was carried out on human infants and the other on monkeys, he was not concerned about comparability. The principles uncovered have much in common.

In one of Harlow's experiments, baby monkeys were separated from their mothers at birth and raised in isolation for up to 12 months. Each baby's home was a wire cage containing an artificial mother. In one condition, the mother surrogate was no more than a wire frame. In a second condition, this frame was covered with towelling cloth and topped with a primitive face. As an additional variable, each 'mother' was either equipped or not with a lactating nipple (see Figure 13.2).

Lactation had little effect on the number of hours per day that a baby spent in contact with the surrogate mother; more crucial was the soft cloth covering provided, something to which the baby could cling. The baby monkey preferred a soft, dry (non-lactating)

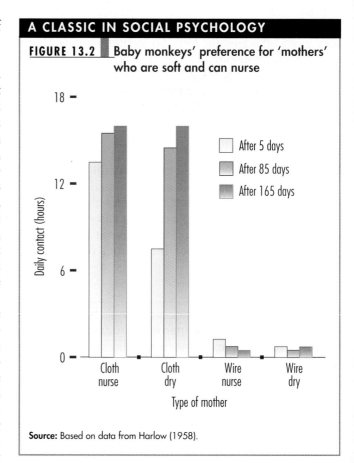

A CLASSIC IN SOCIAL PSYCHOLOGY

FIGURE 13.2 Baby monkeys' preference for 'mothers' who are soft and can nurse

Daily contact (hours)

18 —

12 —

6 —

0 —

After 5 days
After 85 days
After 165 days

Cloth nurse · Cloth dry · Wire nurse · Wire dry

Type of mother

Source: Based on data from Harlow (1958).

Attachment: Infants thrive on food, but they also need nurturing—cuddling, warmth, and softness.

surrogate to a wire, nursing (lactating) surrogate. At these extreme limits of 'motherhood', contact comfort was a major factor in forming an affectionate bond between baby and mother. Follow-up research showed that the baby monkey would spend more time on a rocking mother than on a stationary mother; and, in the early days of life, on a warm mother than on a cold mother.

A monkey mother, however, provides more than contact, food, rocking and warmth: she is the first link in the chain of the baby's experience of socialisation. Harlow's investigation was extended to baby monkeys who were totally isolated from contact with any living being for up to 12 months. Such long periods of solitary confinement had terrible consequences. The infant monkeys would sometimes huddle in a corner, rock back and forth repetitively and bite themselves. When later exposed to normal peers, they did not enter into the rough-and-tumble play of the others and failed to defend themselves from attack. As adults, they were sexually incompetent. As parents, a state achieved by artificial insemination, there was an absence of adequate parenting behaviour. There were also examples of violent 'child abuse', such as a mother biting her baby to death. In all, there was a marked failure by monkeys who had been reared in total isolation to make a satisfactory or acceptable adjustment to the needs of living a normal social life.

Harlow's study is an example of an artificially contrived laboratory situation for monkeys, which would not occur in their natural habitat. In the wild, motherless young animals are either adopted or killed very quickly. However, its relevance to humans is clear enough when we look at the following studies by child psychiatrist Bowlby (1988) and others.

Studies of long-term deprivation in infants

According to Bowlby (1988), the release of two movies had a profound effect on research workers studying children in the 1950s—one by René Spitz, *Grief: A Peril in Infancy* (1947) and the other by James Robertson, *A Two-Year-Old Goes to Hospital* (1952). Survival, it transpired, depends on physical needs but also on a quite independent need for care and intimate interaction.

Spitz (1945) reported on babies who had been left in an overcrowded institution for a two-year period by mothers unable to look after them. These babies were essentially deprived of a caregiver during this period of time. They were fed but rarely handled, and were confined to their cots for most of their sleeping and waking hours. Not only were they later found to be less advanced, mentally and socially, when compared with other institutionalised children who had been given adequate care, but the mortality rate was extremely high. Spitz coined the term **hospitalism** to describe the psychological condition in which he found these children.

'Hospitalism' probably comes to life most vividly for many of us when recalling the heart-wrenching TV footage of little children in Romanian orphanages in the early 1990s.

Systematic research of infant behaviour would seem to support this view. Bowlby (1969) and his colleagues

Maternal deprivation? These children in day care have working parents, but they are certainly not socially deprived—they benefit from contact with peers and compassionate adult caregivers.

at the Tavistock Institute in England studied the **attachment behaviour** of infants to their mothers, noting that young children maintain physical proximity with their mothers or restore it if disrupted. Behaviours observed were signal behaviours such as crying and smiling and also behaviours that physically maintained proximity, such as clinging or following, all of which Bowlby attributed to an innate affiliative drive. Innate predispositions are anathema to learning theorists, who would prefer to argue that infants come to associate their mothers with need-reduction and pleasure, and seek them out on this basis.

Whatever its origin, the tendency to affiliate is both strong and observable. For Bowlby and many other social psychologists, attachment behaviour is not limited to the mother–infant experience, but can be observed throughout the life cycle.

ATTACHMENT STYLES

Berscheid (1994) noted that relatively stable adult relationships 'come from somewhere' and that research into the genesis of adult attachment in relationships is increasingly dependent on developmental theory. It is in this way that Bowlby's work on attachment behaviour in young children has stimulated recent studies on **attachment styles** in adults.

According to Feeney and Noller (1990) at the University of Queensland, different attachment styles (*anxious*, *secure*, *avoidant*), thought to develop in childhood, influence the way romantic relationships are formed in later life. For example, Feeney (1994) assessed levels of attachment, communication patterns and relationship satisfaction within married couples and found that securely attached individuals (comfortable with closeness and having low anxiety about relationships) were more often paired with similarly secure spouses.

In another study, those who were secure in a love relationship scored higher on companionate love scales than others who were avoidantly or anxiously attached (Doherty, Hatfield, Thompson, & Choo, 1994). Rholes, Simpson and Blakely (1995) examined the relationship between a mother's feelings of closeness to her children and her own attachment style in adult relationships. Avoidant mothers felt less close to their children than did securely attached mothers and were less supportive of their children during a teaching task in the research laboratory.

Rholes and colleagues also investigated the levels of certainty that college men and women felt regarding their ability to relate to children. Avoidant participants were less certain about their capacity to relate to children, even about whether they wanted to have children. Such research suggests that attachment should be viewed as a process that is active throughout life rather than as a feature of infancy, and that attachment styles adopted early in life may prevail in relationship dynamics in adulthood.

Brennan and Shaver (1995) looked at three attachment styles in adulthood (secure, avoidant, anxious/ambivalent) and their effects on the quality of people's romantic relationships. Securely attached adults felt it was relatively easy to get close to others and to enjoy affectionate and long-lasting relationships. Avoidant adults reported discomfort in getting close to others and said that their relationships were hampered by a lack of disclosure and by jealousy. Anxious/ambivalent adults tended to fall in love easily; however, subsequent relationships were full of emotional highs and lows and more likely to be rated as unhappy (see second focus question).

Most research into attachment styles has not been genuinely developmental. The studies referred to above typically measure the attachment style of adult participants and have no independent estimate of children's attachment style. Even cross-sectional studies, in which different age groups are studied simultaneously, are not, strictly speaking, developmental. Aware of these concerns, Klohnen and Bera (1998) conducted a longitudinal analysis of data that had been collected over 31 years. The participants were women who had been avoidant or secure in their attachment styles at 27 years of age, and were later followed up at 43 and 52 years of age. When compared with securely attached women, avoidantly attached women were found to be less interpersonally close, less socially confident, more emotionally distant, more self-reliant and more distrustful. These differences in the youngest women continued through later life (see Figure 13.3).

REDUCING ANXIETY: A SHORT-TERM MOTIVE

The need for affiliation can be both transitory and situation-specific. Sometimes we seek to affiliate with others, even strangers, for brief moments in order to cope with immediate circumstances.

To investigate this, Schachter (1959) conducted a now classic study of the role that the company of others can play in reducing anxiety. Female psychology students were led to believe that they were to receive electric shocks. One group was told that the shocks would be painful (high-anxiety condition); another group was told that the shocks would not be at all painful (low-anxiety condition). Participants were then told that there would be a delay while the equipment was set up. They were given the option of waiting either alone or with another participant. Once this choice was made, the experiment was terminated (see Case 1 in Figure 13.4). Results supported Schachter's **shared-stress** hypothesis that a greater preference for company would occur among high-anxiety participants: 20 of the

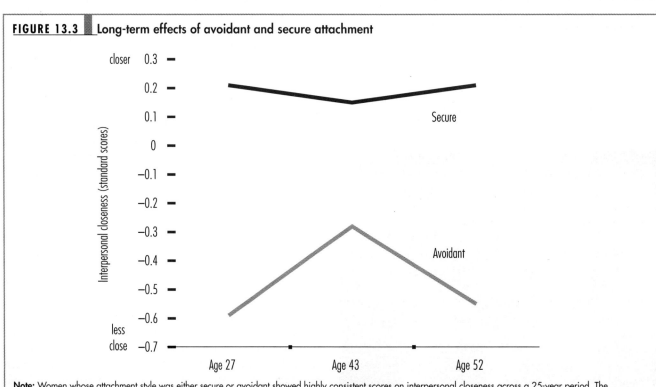

FIGURE 13.3 Long-term effects of avoidant and secure attachment

Note: Women whose attachment style was either secure or avoidant showed highly consistent scores on interpersonal closeness across a 25-year period. The dependent variable is a set of standard scores (ranging from −1 to +1) that indicate the size of the effect.

Source: Klohnen & Bera (1998).

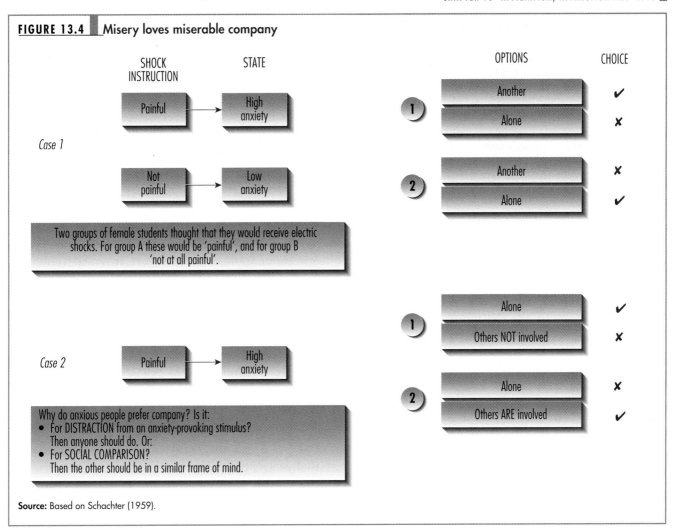

FIGURE 13.4 Misery loves miserable company

SHOCK INSTRUCTION | STATE

Case 1

Painful → High anxiety

Not painful → Low anxiety

Two groups of female students thought that they would receive electric shocks. For group A these would be 'painful', and for group B 'not at all painful'.

OPTIONS | CHOICE

1. Another ✔ / Alone ✗
2. Another ✗ / Alone ✔

Case 2

Painful → High anxiety

Why do anxious people prefer company? Is it:
- For DISTRACTION from an anxiety-provoking stimulus? Then anyone should do. Or:
- For SOCIAL COMPARISON? Then the other should be in a similar frame of mind.

1. Alone ✔ / Others NOT involved ✗
2. Alone ✗ / Others ARE involved ✔

Source: Based on Schachter (1959).

32 high-anxiety participants elected to wait with others, while only 10 of the 30 low-anxiety participants chose this option.

Schachter also asked why it is that anxious people prefer company (see Case 2 in Figure 13.4). It could be hypothesised either that the presence of another person provided a distraction from the anxiety-provoking stimulus or that participants wanted company for **social comparison** (e.g. Suls & Wheeler, 2000)—that is, to provide a yardstick against which to validate their own reactions. If distraction was wanted, then any person would suffice for company. However, if company was desired for social-comparison purposes, the other person would need to be in a similar situation for the comparison to be valid.

Participants in this experiment (Case 2) were told that they were to receive painful electric shocks, so they were all in a high-anxiety condition. They were given the choice of waiting alone or waiting with others. The characteristics of the others formed the independent variable. Some participants were given the choice of waiting alone or waiting with others involved in the same experiment. For other participants the choice was between waiting alone or waiting with students who were not involved in the experiment but merely there to see their teachers.

The results for Case 2 in Figure 13.4 show that participants preferred to wait with similar others rather than alone and that, when the others were dissimilar, they actually preferred to wait alone. This suggests that similarity-based social comparison may be the motive for affiliation in times of fear. It seems that, if we have something to worry about, we prefer to wait with another worrier! Putting this into a practical context, it suggests that patients awaiting surgery would rather be with others like themselves or, by extension, with someone who has just successfully survived the operation in question. (See Box 13.1 and Figure 13.5 for an example of how this idea has been used in a health setting.)

In summary, the need to affiliate can be affected by temporary states such as fear. It is not just any person

BOX 13.1 | Heart to heart: Effects of room-sharing before surgery

WHAT HAPPENS WHEN CORONARY BYPASS PATIENTS SHARE A ROOM?

Kulik, Mahler and Moore (1996) studied the effects of preoperative room-mate assignments on patterns of affiliation, preoperative anxiety and postoperative recovery among heart patients. Patients engaged significantly more in discussion of issues relating to their surgery if their room-mate was cardiac rather than non-cardiac and postoperative rather than preoperative (as measured by actual recording of interactions). Those patients assigned to a room-mate who was postoperative rather than preoperative were less anxious (as measured by the number of anxiety-reducing drugs and sedatives requested by patients the night before surgery). Patients were also more likely to be discharged sooner if assigned to a room-mate who was cardiac rather than non-cardiac (as measured by postoperative length of stay in days). Patients without room-mates generally had the slowest recoveries (see the results in Figure 13.5).

FIGURE 13.5 | Social comparison and affiliation under threat: Effects on recovery from major surgery

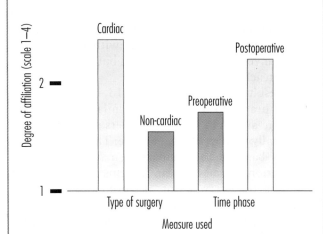

Note: Patients gave estimates (ranging from 1 *not at all* to 4 *very much so*) of how much they discussed with a room-mate what it would feel like after surgery and how they might ease recovery. Affiliation increased when the room-mate was also a cardiac patient and when the time phase was postoperative.

Source: Based on Kulik, Mahler, & Moore (1996).

that we want to be with, but someone specific. Schachter's original assertion can be amended to read: 'Misery loves the company of those in the same miserable situation' (Gump & Kulik, 1997). The reduction of anxiety is only one condition that invokes the process of social comparison. In a broader context, we make these comparisons whenever we look to the views of a special group—our friends. How people come to be part of this special group is discussed below.

Why are some people attractive?

Attraction refers to what makes one person feel positively about another. When we are attracted to (allured by, charmed by) someone, we want to know that person—to spend some time with them. Attraction is necessary for friendships to begin and yet we meet many people who do not become our friends. There are many bases for our friendship choices.

PHYSICAL ATTRACTIVENESS: EVOLUTION OR CULTURE?

Social psychologists have recently engaged in vigorous debate about the role of evolutionary and cultural factors in detemining how we perceive beauty (see Box 13.2).

In a **meta-analysis** of 919 studies of attraction by Langlois and colleagues (Langlois, Kalakanis, Rubenstein, Larson, Hallam, & Smoot, 2000), the validity of three common maxims about beauty was tested: 'Beauty is in the eye of the beholder', 'Never judge a book by its cover' and 'Beauty is only skin-deep'. These all suggest that physical beauty is not important in life. In contrast, both evolutionary theory and socialisation/social expectancy theory suggest that physical appeal influences how people develop and interact. Evolutionary theory emphasises the role played by mate selection, good genes and the differential care given to attractive young by their parents. Socialisation theory emphasises the effects, on judgments of beauty, of social and cultural norms (see Chapters 7 and 16) and of experience; social expectancy theory argues that social stereotypes (see Chapter 2) create their own reality.

The meta-analysis showed that people agree about who is and is not attractive, both within and across cultures, and that individuals were treated differently according to whether they were perceived as being attractive or not. Attractive people were judged more positively than unattractive people, even by those who knew them, and attractive people exhibited more positive behaviours and traits than unattractive people.

There are some intriguing findings about the logic of how we perceive attractiveness and, in the case of the opposite sex, how this relates to reproductive fitness.

IS YOUR NOTION OF BEAUTY A MATTER OF PERSONAL OR CULTURAL PREFERENCE, OR IS IT HARD-WIRED?

Is beauty really a matter of personal preference? A contrary view is that what is regarded as beautiful is a matter of fashion, a function of a particular society and its history. Recently, however, a debate has re-emerged that pits the opposing forces of the cultural versus the universal against each other as forms of explanation.

An intriguing study by Cunningham (1986) argued that American men found women with 'cute' faces more attractive. Cuteness was a function of being relatively childlike (the eyes are large and set well apart, and the nose and chin are small). No doubt the sociobiologist could interpret this as indicating youth and, therefore, fertility in the woman!

Is physical beauty a composite, or average, of symmetrical physical qualities or do unusual or striking features make a face more appealing? Gillian Rhodes and her colleagues at the University of Western Australia had participants judge caricatures of faces, each of which was systematically varied from average to distinctive (Rhodes & Tremewan, 1996). She found that averageness, rather than distinctiveness, was correlated with facial attractiveness (see also Rhodes, Sumich, & Byatt, 1999). Reviewing evidence that infants also show a preference for faces that are more average, Rhodes suggested an evolutionary basis for preferring average faces that directs infants to prefer the most human-face-like objects in their environment.

The averageness effect has been confirmed in other studies by Langlois, Roggman and Musselman (1994) and Penton-Voak, Perrett and Peirce (1999).

For example, according to Gangestad and Simpson (2000), women apparently prefer the smell of T-shirts that have been worn by symmetrical men! These women had no idea who had actually worn the T-shirts. It is also interesting that this preference occurs only among women about to ovulate. The underlying evolutionary argument is that symmetry signifies genetic good health.

Other research focuses on women's waist-to-hip ratio (WHR) (Singh, 1993). Typically, men prefer the classic hourglass figure (a ratio of .70), probably because it signifies youthfulness, good health and fertility. However, there are cultural and environmental effects: in foraging societies, being thin may mean illness and so men prefer their women to be heavier (i.e. larger WHRs). In Western societies, where heaviness may indicate ill health, men prefer slimmer women (i.e smaller WHRs) (Marlowe & Wetsman, 2001).

If a relationship is to continue, however, factors other than physical attractiveness become important, as we see later in this chapter.

CORRELATES OF BEING ATTRACTIVE

The primary cue that we use in evaluating other people is how they look (Langlois et al. 2000); the more attractive you are, the more positively people will judge you. Even babies gaze longer at more attractive female faces (Slater, Von der Schulenburg, Brown, Badenoch, Butterworth, Parsons, & Samuels, 1998). Later in life, people with attractive faces are more likely to score a date (Rowatt, Cunningham, & Druen, 1999).

The studies in Box 13.2 indicate that facial attractiveness is related to *averageness*. Recent research has also associated attractiveness with:

- some feminisation of facial features (computer-simulated), including male faces (Rhodes, Hickford, & Jeffrey, 2000);
- being youthful (Buss & Kenrick, 1998; Perlini, Bertolissi, & Lind, 1999);
- having a slimmer (computer-simulated) figure (Gardner & Tockerman, 1994);
- being judged as more honest (Yarmouk, 2000);
- earning more money (Hamermesh & Biddle, 1994).

Earlier research is consistent with the tenor of these findings. Attractive people were:

- judged as less maladjusted and disturbed (Cash, Kehr, Polyson, & Freeman, 1977; Dion, 1972);
- judged as more likely to be hired after a job interview (Dipboye, Arvey, & Terpstra, 1977);
- rated as happier, more successful, having a better personality and more likely to get married (Dion, Berscheid, & Walster, 1972);
- given an easier time by jurors, if they were female defendants (Sigall & Ostrove, 1975);
- evaluated more highly on their written work, if they were female students (Landy & Sigall, 1974).

Landy and Sigall (1974) studied the last effect experimentally. Male students graded one or other of two essays of different quality, attached to which was a photograph of the supposed writer, a female student. The same essays were rated by control participants, but without any photograph. In one condition, the 'good' essay was paired with an attractive photograph and then with a relatively unattractive photograph; in the other condition, the 'poor' essay was paired with each of the photographs. Sad to relate, better grades were given to the attractive female student (see Figure 13.6; but also see Chapter 10 for more details on sex discrimination and the findings of more recent studies).

With attractiveness being such an asset, those who spend big on cosmetics and fashion could be making a

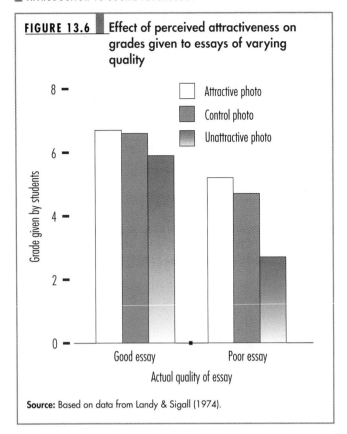

FIGURE 13.6 Effect of perceived attractiveness on grades given to essays of varying quality

Legend:
□ Attractive photo
▨ Control photo
▨ Unattractive photo

y-axis: Grade given by students (0 to 8)
x-axis: Actual quality of essay — Good essay, Poor essay

Source: Based on data from Landy & Sigall (1974).

Proximity: High-density living is often associated with crowding. However, as the washing lines strung across this Neapolitan street suggest, it can also promote cooperative social interaction.

real investment in their future! Short of this, just a smile can also work wonders. Joseph Forgas and his colleagues at the University of New South Wales (Forgas, O'Connor, & Morris, 1983) found that students who smile are punished less after a misdemeanour than those who do not (see third focus question).

PROXIMITY

Self-evident as it might seem, the physical **proximity** of one person to another is a potent facilitator of attraction (Sprecher, 1998). Chance occurrences, such as who is allocated the adjoining room in college, or who catches the same bus home, play an important role in determining friendships. In a famous study of a housing complex, Festinger, Schachter and Back (1950) found that more people chose as friends others who were living on the same floor, rather than on other floors or in more distant buildings. Even subtle architectural features, such as the location of a staircase, can affect the process of making acquaintances and, therefore, the choice of our friends.

Look at the apartment block in Figure 13.7. Of the lower-floor residents, those in apartments 1 and 5 interacted most often with people living on the upper floor. Note that the residents in apartments 1 and 5 are close to the staircases used by upper-floor residents and are therefore more likely to encounter them. Friendships occurred more often between 1 and 6 than 2 and 7; and

likewise between 5 and 10 than 4 and 9. Although the physical distance between residents within each pair is the same, the interaction rate varied: becoming acquainted depended on the traffic flow.

Proximity permits several other factors to come into play in determining a choice of friends and acquaintances: familiarity, availability and expectation of continued interaction. Let us consider these factors.

FIGURE 13.7 Friendship choice, physical proximity and housing design

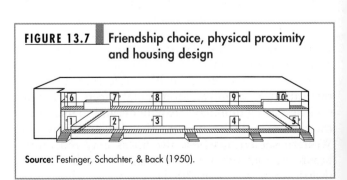

Source: Festinger, Schachter, & Back (1950).

Familiarity

Proximity generally leads to repeated exposure and greater familiarity and, therefore, more liking—a friend is rather like your favourite pair of shoes, something that you feel comfortable about. Familiarity enhances liking as part of a more general effect in which repetitive presentation of stimuli increases liking for them (Zajonc, 1968; Moreland & Zajonc, 1982; see also the effect of repetitive advertising in Chapter 6). This **familiarity** effect extends to the faces of strangers, which are liked more when they are seen more often (Jorgensen & Cervone, 1978).

In contrast, when something familiar seems different, people feel uncomfortable. For example, people do not usually like mirror reversals of photos of their own or others' faces (Mita, Dermer, & Knight, 1977). The effect of repeated exposure may be stronger when the repetition occurs without our awareness, such as when stimuli are presented to us subliminally (Bornstein & D'Agostino, 1992). The familiarity effect extends to classroom settings: Moreland and Beach (1992) found that students rated the tutors whom they saw most often as more likeable. If you want to be liked, be around!

Availability

People who live close by are accessible, so that interaction with them requires little effort and the rewards of interacting are at a low cost. (This notion of cost is considered in more detail below in terms of social exchange theory.) Think of what happens when a friend shifts to a distant place. Do you keep up the promised contact?

Expectation of continued interaction

In line with Heider's (1958) balance theory (see Chapter 5), we can predict that it would be an uncomfortable experience not to get on with our neighbours. More specifically, this includes the process of being aware that neighbours are people with whom further interaction is anticipated. An experiment by Berscheid, Graziano, Monson and Dermer (1976), for example, showed that university students who thought they might actually date someone seen only on videotape liked that person more than someone else with whom they were led to believe they might not have a continued interaction.

RECIPROCITY

Liking and disliking often follow the **reciprocity principle**: that is, we tend to like those who like us and dislike those who dislike us. (See also how reciprocity can operate in the area of aggression in Chapter 12.) In a classic study, Dittes and Kelley (1956) led students in small discussion groups to believe, by way of anonymous written evaluations (actually written by the experimenters), that other group members either liked or disliked them. Results showed that students who believed they were liked were more attracted to the group than those who believed they were disliked. More recently, Sprecher (1998) found reciprocal liking to be one of the major determinants of interpersonal attraction.

Individual differences

Reciprocity may not operate uniformly between people. An influential mediating variable is the attachment style (see above) of individuals. Sperling and Borgaro (1995) found a strong link between attraction and the effect of receiving interpersonal feedback, in relation to a person's level of security. If people are insecurely attached, positive interpersonal feedback leads to greater attraction. Furthermore, negative feedback from other people appears to affect women's attraction ratings of another (in an interpersonal relationship) to a greater extent than men's (Sperling & Borgaro, 1995).

Another variable affecting the impact of reciprocity on attraction is level of self-esteem. Dittes (1959) found that, for those with high self-esteem, liking did not seem to be affected by acceptance or rejection. In contrast, those with low self-esteem liked the group a lot when they were accepted, but disliked the group a lot when rejected. Dittes carried out an experiment in which the participants were classified as high or low on self-esteem. They were placed in a satisfying condition, where the group's behaviour towards them was positive, or in a frustrating condition, where it was negative. For participants who were low in self-esteem, attraction to the group depended on how the group behaved; for those high in self-esteem, the difference in attraction was not significant. These results are shown in Figure 13.8 (for more on self-esteem, see Chapter 4).

It could be argued that people who have high self-esteem do not need the bolster of assurances from others, whereas those who are low in self-esteem do. An alternative explanation suggests a reverse causality. In a study by Minahan (1971), teenage schoolgirls with higher self-esteem gave more favourable ratings to their bodies, in terms of perceived physical attractiveness, than did those lower in self-esteem. The girls with higher self-esteem had more dates with boys and expected to marry earlier. The line of inference is that girls who were judged as more attractive by boys in turn judged themselves to be more attractive, leading to a more favourable self-image.

Situational variables

The effects of reciprocity can interact with the nature of the situation. If reciprocity is based on the power of praise as a social reward, the outcome can vary with how much value is placed on the praise. For example, praise from a flatterer with ulterior motives will not be highly valued and will therefore not elicit liking. We also attach lower value to praise from a friend than a

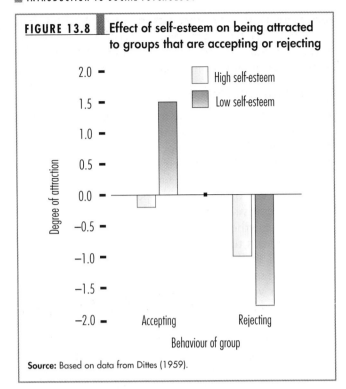

FIGURE 13.8 Effect of self-esteem on being attracted to groups that are accepting or rejecting

Source: Based on data from Dittes (1959).

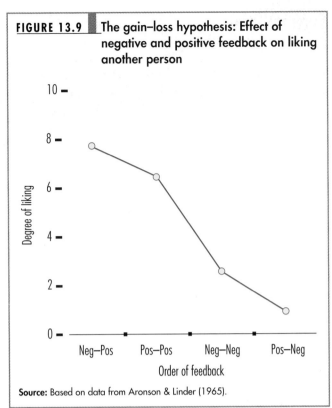

FIGURE 13.9 The gain–loss hypothesis: Effect of negative and positive feedback on liking another person

Source: Based on data from Aronson & Linder (1965).

stranger, as we expect praise from our friends. The pattern in which the praise is received is also influential. An interesting example is the **gain–loss hypothesis**: we tend to like most those who initially dislike us but then warm to us; and we dislike most those people who initially like us but turn cold (Aronson & Linder, 1965). This phenomenon is slightly puzzling, as it runs counter to a reinforcement model—the person who is constantly praised receives more rewards but likes the praiser less.

Aronson has suggested two explanations. The first involves anxiety reduction: when experiencing rejection, anxiety rises; when rejection changes to acceptance, the anxiety is reduced so that we experience the pleasure of being liked. Alternatively, it is possible that we regard those who like us from the beginning as undiscriminating, and this reduces the value of their praise. Those who dislike us to begin with but then re-evaluate as they get to know us better are discerning people, so their praise is worth more.

Aronson and Linder (1965) carried out an experiment designed to test the effect of the order in which we receive feedback from another person. Participants heard feedback about themselves, across seven meetings, from a confederate. The quality of the feedback was either all negative or all positive for the first three meetings. Then, depending on the condition, the quality was either reversed or remained the same. Of the four conditions, liking for the confederate was greatest when the order was negative-positive and least when it was positive-negative. The results in Figure 13.9 indicate that

we are most likely to be attracted to someone when that person's early dislike for us changes to liking.

An interesting line of recent research studies relationships on the Internet (see Box 13.3). When communicating by computer, many of the normal cues we use to form an impression of another person are not available (see also Chapters 2 and 15).

SIMILARITY

Similarity of attitudes or values is one of the most important determinants of attraction and hence one of the most often studied (Sprecher, 1998). For example, Newcomb (1961) gave students rent-free accommodation in return for filling out questionnaires about their attitudes and values. The first questionnaires were filled out before the students arrived at the university. Over the course of a semester, attraction among the students and attitude changes were measured. Results showed that in the first few weeks attraction was related to proximity. However, as the semester progressed, attraction related most closely to similarity of pre-acquaintance attitudes.

Byrne (1971) confirmed, in a series of laboratory experiments, the important role of attitude similarity in relationships. The results were so reliable and consistent that Byrne formulated a 'law of attraction'—attraction towards a person bears a linear relationship to the proportion of attitudes associated with the person (Clore

BOX 13.3 Meeting on the Net

Access to a computer and the Internet allows people to meet, form friendships, fall in love and arrange marriage or cohabitation. Relationships that begin in cyberspace do not necessarily stay there. In a study of online friendship formation, Katz and Aspden (1998) found that three out of five participants who had Internet friends eventually met that friend in person. In cyberspace, traditional variables controlling interest in another person, such as proximity or physical appeal, are severely reduced. Cyber-relationships can progress rapidly from knowing little about the other person to being very intimate; equally, they can be ended very quickly, literally with the 'click of a button'.

From the outset, Internet-mediated relationships differ markedly from offline relationships. A first meeting via the Internet does not give access to the usual range of physical and spoken linguistic cues that help to form an impression, although this may change as the use of digital cameras to exchange images and live video over the Internet increases.

Jacobson (1999) investigated impression formation in cyberspace and compared online expectation with offline experiences: that is, when people who had met online actually met in person. He found significant discrepancies—people often formed erroneous impressions about characteristics such as talkativeness ('they seemed so quiet in person') and expansiveness ('they seemed so terse online but were very expressive offline'). People online often constructed images based on stereotypes, such as the vocation of the unseen person. One participant reported:

> I had no idea what to expect with Katya. From her descriptions I got the impression she would be overweight, kinda hackerish, but when we met, I found her very attractive. Normal sized, nice hair, not at all the stereotypical programmer. (Jacobson, 1999, p. 13)

& Byrne, 1974). According to Clore (1976), the law is actually intended to be more generally applicable than just to attitudes in common between two people. Anything that other people do that agrees with your perception of things is reinforcing. The more other people agree, the more reinforcing they are and the more you like them. For example, if you suddenly discover that someone you are dating likes the same obscure rock band as you, your liking for that person will suddenly increase.

Conversely, differences in attitudes and interests can lead to dislike and avoidance (Singh & Ho, 2000; Tan & Singh, 1995). Cognitive consistency theories (see Chapter 6) may provide an explanation for this. The recognition that you like something but that someone else does not is a cognitively unbalanced state that makes us feel uncomfortable. One way to resolve this is by deciding that you do not like that person—cognitive consistency has then been re-established. Thus, people usually choose or preserve the company of similar others—it makes us feel comfortable.

Cross-cultural research offers evidence on a wider scale that similarity increases liking. In an extensive study of 30 different tribal groups in East Africa, Brewer (1968) found that perceived similarity was one of several factors that determined liking. Her 1500 interviews highlighted three variables affecting intertribal attraction. In order of importance, they were:

1. perceived similarity;
2. physical distance between tribes;
3. perceived educational and economic advancement.

When another tribe was thought to have quite different attitudes, social contact was avoided; if they were perceived as quite similar, intimate contact was possible. The physical distance factor meant that neighbours were generally liked more than more distant tribes. The more advanced a tribe was seen to be also increased liking, but this appeared to play a role only when a tribe was judged to be dissimilar in attitudes. The most disliked tribe would be one that was dissimilar and least advanced.

Matching

Dating partners often try to match each other. People who are evenly matched in their physical appearance, social background and personality (Stevens, Owens, & Schaefer, 1990; Sprecher, 1998), sociability (Joiner, 1994; Sprecher, 1998) and interests and leisure activities (Sprecher, 1998) are more likely to be attracted to one another. A longitudinal study of married couples over 21 years (Gruber-Baldini, Schaie, & Willis, 1995) confirmed that, at the time of initial testing, spouses were similar in a number of aspects such as age and education. Over time, these spouses became even more similar on measures of mental abilities and attitudes.

It appears that birds of a feather not only flock together, they also stay together (Byrne, 1997)—and, to take the feather analogy further, their plumage becomes more and more similar! See Table 13.1 for evidence of similarity and other factors in relationships.

Other characteristics

Although similarity is an important predictor of attraction there are other characteristics that people consistently find attractive. In a study of three kinds of relationship (romantic, and same-gender and opposite-gender friendships), Sprecher (1998) confirmed that similarity of interests, leisure activities, attitudes, values and social skills were determinants of attraction. However, these factors were less important than other personal characteristics—for example, having a 'desirable personality', warmth and kindness, and reciprocal liking. Proximity and familiarity were also important; intelligence, earning potential and competence were relatively unimportant (see Table 13.1).

NEED COMPLEMENTARITY

In contrast to the theory of similarity, Winch (1958) formulated a theory of **need complementarity**. Winch hypothesised that we seek others who can best satisfy our needs—for example, the pairing of apparent opposites when a dominant person is attracted to a submissive partner. Although Winch found some support for his theory, later studies have been less encouraging (e.g. Levinger, Senn, & Jorgensen, 1970). One reason for this apparent contradiction is that need complementarity may be more important at a particular stage in the development of a relationship. One study found that social-status factors were the most important predictors early in a dating relationship. Later, similarity of values became more important, which, in turn, was followed by need complementarity (Kerckhoff & Davis, 1962). However, this pattern has not been replicated by other studies.

A second reason, proposed by Levinger (1964), is that studies of need complementarity usually measure personality characteristics globally, such as whether a person has a general need for dominance, rather than specific measures of needs relevant to close relationships. Supportive evidence comes from Lipetz, Cohen, Dworin and Rogers (1970), who found that complementarity of needs in marriage correlated with marital satisfaction,

even though complementarity of general psychological needs did not.

SELF-DISCLOSURE

Self-disclosure in conversation is an important determinant of long-term intimacy in a relationship. According to Altman and Taylor's model (1973) of *social penetration*, people share more intimate topics with a close friend than with a casual acquaintance or a stranger. Based on the reciprocity principle (see earlier), people tend to reveal more to people they like and trust. The converse is also true. People tend to prefer people who reveal more about their feelings and thoughts (Collins & Miller, 1994). Disclosing personal information and being sensitive and responsive to our partner's disclosures are central processes, both in developing relationships (Laurenceau, Barrett, & Pietromonaco, 1998) and in maintaining them (Cross, Bacon, & Morris, 2000). Collins & Miller give three reasons:

1. We disclose to those we like.
2. We like those who disclose to us.
3. We like those to whom we have disclosed.

In a study by Vittengl and Holt (2000), students who did not know one another engaged in brief conversations, before and after which they rated their positive and negative affect as well as their level of self-disclosure. Greater self-disclosure led to an increase in positive affect.

Despite this, self-disclosure is not universal; the amount and depth of information shared with another vary according to culture and gender. For example, a meta-analysis of 205 studies of self-disclosure showed that women reveal more about themselves than men (Dindia & Allen, 1992).

TABLE 13.1 Determinants of initial attraction for three types of relationships

	TYPE OF RELATIONSHIP OR FRIENDSHIP			
	ALL MEASURES	ROMANTIC	SAME GENDER	OPPOSITE GENDER
Other's desirable personality	3.41	3.50[1]	3.33[1]	3.37[2]
Other's warmth and kindness	3.31	3.43[2]	3.08[5]	3.40[1]
Reciprocal liking	3.09	3.17[3]	2.99[7]	3.11[4]
Something specific about the other	3.05	3.14[4]	2.91[8]	3.11[3]
Similarity of interests and leisure activities	3.02	2.79[8]	3.29[2]	3.02[6]
Similarity of attitudes and values	2.99	2.96[5]	3.10[4]	2.88[8]
Similarity on social skills	2.97	2.87[7]	3.01[6]	3.07[5]
Proximity	2.91	2.76[10]	3.11[3]	2.88[9]
Similarity in background characteristics	2.81	2.74[11]	2.89[9]	2.82[10]
Familiarity of the other	2.76	2.77[9]	2.73[10]	2.79[7]

Note: Mean ratings on a 4-point scale of importance are shown in each column. Numbers in parentheses represent the rank order of the mean in the column.
Source: Sprecher (1998).

With respect to culture, Lewin (1936) long ago observed differences between Americans and Germans. Americans disclosed more than Germans in initial encounters but did not become as intimate as Germans as their relationships progressed. People from individualist cultures self-disclose more information than people from collectivist cultures (see Chapter 16). When information is shared, individualists give more personal information whereas collectivists share information about group membership (Gudykunst, Matsumoto, Ting-Toomey, Nishida, Kim, & Heyman, 1996). (For a review of cultural differences in disclosure, see Goodwin, 1999.)

Another reason why self-disclosure is important in relationships may be that trust sustains relationships. In life, people try to reduce risk, but they also need and seek out relationships. The problem is that relationships are a risky business in which people make themselves vulnerable to others. We need to build interpersonal trust to manage relationship-based risk (Cvetkovich &

Löfstedt, 1999; Earle & Cvetkovich, 1995). Self-disclosure plays an important role in reducing risk and building trust—the more that your friend or partner self-discloses the safer you feel in the relationship and the more you trust them. Trust and good relationships go hand in hand (e.g. Boon & Holmes, 1999; Holmes, 2002; Rempel, Ross, & Holmes, 2001).

THE DATING GAME

Have you ever been advised to be somewhat distant or aloof to attract the partner you desire in the dating game? Many know this tactic as 'playing hard to get'. Presumably, the hypothesis guiding this behaviour is this: by ensuring that a potential partner's early advances seem less than successful, you increase your 'value' as a mate and appear more desirable. However, research suggests that this is not as simple as it first appears (see Box 13.4).

Studies of interethnic or cross-cultural dating also reveal a complex interplay of factors that influence

---

BOX 13.4   Strategic subtleties in the dating game

IS PLAYING 'HARD TO GET' A GOOD IDEA?

One common piece of advice, especially to females, is that playing 'hard to get' will help you to attract the partner that you desire in the dating game. However, research suggests that this strategy is not as simple as it seems.

Walster, Walster, Piliavin and Schmidt (1973) reported negative results on several studies looking at the 'hard-to-get' hypothesis. The first experiment involved college men who were recruited ostensibly to help to improve a computer dating service. They filled in a questionnaire and returned two weeks later to pick up the phone number of their prospective date. They were asked to call her from the office so that their first impressions could easily be recorded. To those in the *easy-to-get* condition, the confederate responded with delight at the phone call and being asked out. In the *hard-to-get* condition, the confederate reluctantly accepted a date, conveying the impression that she had many other dates. The subjects' evaluations of the confederate were uniformly high across conditions and therefore did not support the hypothesis.

The second study was a field experiment, in which a prostitute conveyed the impression either that she was welcoming of all clients or that she had to be selective about whom she could see. The clients' evaluations were rated in three ways: the prostitute's own estimation of how much they liked her, how much the client paid her, and how soon afterwards the client called for a second appointment. Again, the hypothesis was not supported, as clients in both conditions responded in the same way, although it should be noted that two of the ratings in this experiment are confounded by financial factors and the third is a subjective measure, which could easily be influenced by other factors.

Faced with this lack of support, the experimenters revisited the factors involved, such as how relaxing each type of woman would be on a date. They produced a reworked hypothesis, which proposed that the maximally rewarding date would be one that was easy for the subject to get but hard for anyone else to get.

This hypothesis was tested using the computer dating system again. Subjects filled in questionnaires then returned several weeks later. On their return, they were told that the computer had identified five possible dates for them. The subjects were able to read biographies of these five so they could indicate their preference. Together with the biography was a supposed evaluation, made by the woman, of the dates the computer had matched for her. These evaluations were manipulated so that one woman appeared easy to get, as she rated all her dates highly. Another woman appeared hard to get, as she did not rate any of her dates particularly highly. A third woman appeared selectively hard to get by having rated only the subject highly. The other two women constituted a control condition, having not made any evaluations. The results showed strong support for the revised hypothesis. The women in all conditions were liked equally except for the selectively hard-to-get woman, who was uniformly the most popular.

attraction. Liu, Campbell and Condie (1995) studied heterosexual dating preferences and ingroup bias among four ethnic groups in the United States (Asian, African, Latino and Euro/White Americans) and found that participants from all groups preferred to choose partners from their own ethnic group. However, Asians and Latinos rated Whites as more physically attractive than typical members of their own group, and Latinos and Blacks rated Whites and Asians as higher in status. Social network approval was the most powerful predictor for partner preferences, followed by similarity and physical attractiveness.

Yancey and Yancey (1998) studied personal advertisements from magazines and found that ethnic affiliation was insignificant relative to physical attractiveness or financial security. Availability was found to be the best predictor of why people entered into interethnic relationships.

Thus, in multiethnic societies, such as Australia and New Zealand, there is an intergroup dimension to dating and relationship development that needs to be considered along with other factors such as proximity and similarity.

Theories of attraction and relationships

Rarely in psychology does a theory account for a phenomenon in its totality. More often, several theories contribute perspectives that focus on different aspects of the same process. Theories of attraction are no exception. At the broadest level, theories of attraction can be divided into those (cognitive approaches) that view human nature as a striving to maintain cognitive consistency or balance and those (behaviourist or reinforcement approaches) that view human nature as the pursuit of pleasure and the avoidance of pain. Here we discuss cognitive balance theory, two relatively traditional reinforcement approaches, and two less traditional reinforcement approaches that are based on an economic model of people's behaviour.

BALANCE THEORY

Balance theory focuses on people's mental processes rather than objective reality (see also Chapter 5). The key idea is that people like others who are similar to them because agreement is an affirming experience involving positive affect. If people who like one another discover a disagreement (e.g. an attitude about something), this produces aversive psychological tension based on cognitive imbalance. Both parties will try hard to modify their attitudes in order to restore balance based on attitudinal agreement. If relative strangers discover a disagreement, there is no interpersonal liking

to produce a sense of imbalance, and so all that will happen to maintain balance is that they will tend not to come to like one another.

This theory does not hold for every interaction we have. There are times when we like to be regarded as dissimilar, as this can make us feel unique and special. It has also been found that if the threat of rejection by the dissimilar other is removed, by knowing in advance that they are willing to discuss other points of view, the dissimilarity is no longer a barrier to interaction and attraction (Broome, 1983; Sunafrank & Miller, 1981).

REINFORCEMENT THEORIES

According to a simple reinforcement model of attraction, we may like people who happen to be present when we receive a reward even if they have nothing to do with the rewarding event (Lott & Lott, 1972, 1974). Griffit and Guay (1969) had a non-involved bystander present while someone else administered either a reward or a punishment to various participants. Although the bystander was merely present when the reinforcement was delivered, he was liked more when a participant was rewarded than when punished. Lott, Aponte, Lott and McGinley (1969) applied the principle that immediate reinforcement is sometimes stronger than delayed reinforcement. They found that children liked a person more who was associated with immediate reward for task completion than one associated with reward after a 10-second delay.

Another variation derived from learning theory is Byrne and Clore's (1970) **reinforcement–affect model**. The logic is drawn from classical (Pavlovian) conditioning. Just as a dog learns to associate the sound of a bell with the positive reinforcement of food, so humans can associate another person with other positive features of the immediate environment. The way the model works is shown in Figure 13.10.

The reinforcement–affect model includes the following features:

1. People identify stimuli as *rewarding* or *punishing* and then seek out the former while avoiding the latter.
2. *Positive feelings* are associated with rewarding stimuli and *negative feelings* with punishing stimuli.
3. A stimulus is evaluated in terms of the feelings it arouses. An *evaluation* is good if the feelings are positive and bad if the feelings are negative.
4. Any background *neutral* stimuli that happen to be associated with reward will elicit positive feelings, while those associated with punishment will elicit negative feelings.

Consequently, people can be liked or disliked depending on whether they are associated with positive or negative feelings. Griffit and Veitch (1971) presented neutral statements by a stranger to participants who

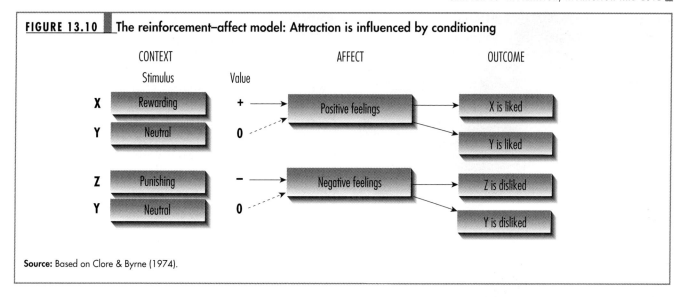

FIGURE 13.10   The reinforcement–affect model: Attraction is influenced by conditioning

Source: Based on Clore & Byrne (1974).

were in either physically uncomfortable conditions (hot and crowded) or physically comfortable conditions. Participants liked the stranger less in the more uncomfortable conditions: the stranger's statements (the neutral stimulus) had become associated with negative feelings about physical comfort in the uncomfortable condition.

Finally, Lewicki (1985) had an experimenter be unfriendly towards some students participating in an experiment. Later, the students were asked to hand in their data to either of two other assistants, one of whom physically resembled the experimenter. The students chose to hand their data in to the other person!

SOCIAL EXCHANGE THEORY

Although social exchange theory can be considered a member of the general family of behaviourist theories, as an approach to the topic of interpersonal relationships it goes beyond reinforcement theory by taking an interactive approach. It also deals more directly with close relationships (but see Chapter 8, where a social exchange perspective is described to help explain group socialisation). A recent extension of this general approach maps out very broadly how the structure of different types of social situations impacts on people's social interactions and social outcomes (Kelley, Holmes, Kerr, Reis, Rusbult, & van Lange, 2003).

Social exchange theory focuses on the fact that there are at least two people in a relationship and, as its name suggests, is concerned with how these people proceed to exchange rewards. A major proponent was Homans (1961), a sociologist who made it clear that he was adapting the blueprint from Skinner's operant psychology. As a model of behaviour, it proposes several economic concepts, wedded to behaviourism, to account for our interpersonal relationships. Whether we like someone else is determined by the **cost–reward ratio**: 'What will it cost me to get a positive reward from that person?' Social exchange theory, however, takes an additional step in arguing that the outcomes for the two participants are *jointly* determined by their actions.

Even though the consequences of this may not be dramatic, the process is ongoing in much of our everyday behaviour. We seek to obtain, preserve or exchange things of value with other human beings. We bargain over what we are prepared to give to another in exchange for what they will give us. Some of these exchanges are brief and perhaps without deep meaning, while others are ongoing and long-term and may be extremely important to us. In all cases, we experience outcomes or payoffs that depend on the behaviour of others. Over time, people will try to develop a pattern of interaction that is rational and mutually beneficial. We can think of social exchange as a give-and-take relationship between people and relationships as business transactions. So far, you might be thinking that this is a fairly dry approach to the study of important relationships. If so, you are right. Its proponents would argue, however, that this does not detract from its validity.

Box 13.5 gives an example of how social exchange theory might be applied to the development of a relationship.

At a broad level, Foa and Foa (1975) set out six kinds of interpersonal relationships, each involving an exchange of resources:

1. *goods*—any products or objects;
2. *information*—advice, opinion or instructions;
3. *love*—affectionate regard, warmth and comfort;
4. *money*—any coin or token that has some value;
5. *services*—activities of the body or belonging to the individual;
6. *status*—an evaluative judgment that conveys high or low prestige.

Any of these resources can be exchanged in a

Social exchange: Marriage is not entered into lightly. In a long-term relationship, partners carefully weigh up their respective costs and benefits.

Stages in the development of a social exchange relationship

BUILDING A RELATIONSHIP: STEPS ALONG THE WAY

When we are attracted to others, we hope that they feel the same way about us. Thibaut and Kelley (1959) suggested four stages in the development of a relationship:

1. *Sampling.* When people consider a new relationship, they check its potential costs and rewards and compare it with other relationships available.
2. *Bargaining.* As an interaction takes place, there is a giving and receiving of rewards that test whether a deeper relationship is worthwhile.
3. *Commitment.* Sampling and bargaining are reduced and the focus is now on one other person. Most relationships are between people equal in status (Homans, 1961) or in popularity (Jennings, 1943), both of which assist predictability in a relationship. Attraction will increase further if the costs of interacting are lowered. You are less likely to misunderstand your partner's intentions as you get to know them better. In addition, the ability to predict allows each partner to know how to elicit rewards from the other.
4. *Institutionalisation.* Finally, norms are developed that recognise the legitimacy of a particular relationship and the specific pattern of rewards and costs for each partner.

Source: Based on Thibaut & Kelley (1959).

relationship between people. In most relationships, according to this point of view, we try to use a **minimax strategy**: that is, we aim to minimise costs and maximise rewards, although we may not be conscious of doing so and would probably object to the idea that we do.

The social psychologists Thibaut and Kelley (1959) provided impetus to social exchange theory in a major work, *The Social Psychology of Groups*, which underpinned much subsequent research. They argued that we must understand the *structure* of a relationship in order to deal with the behaviour that takes place, as it is the structure that defines the rewards and punishments available. A relationship between people is a series of trading interactions or business transactions. We have already noted that a guiding aim, according to the minimax strategy, is that a relationship is unsatisfactory when the costs exceed the rewards. In practice, people exchange resources with one another in the hope that they will earn a **profit**—that is, the rewards will exceed the costs. This is a novel way of defining a 'good relationship'.

Rewards for interacting with someone else can include satisfaction, gratification and pleasure. Costs include effort, embarrassment, time wasted and money spent. This is a deliberate and explicitly economic approach to human behaviour and relationships. In common with other theories that stress the importance of behavioural principles, exchange theory argues that socially significant behaviour is repeated only if it has been suitably reinforced.

A final important concept in social exchange theory is each person's **comparison level** (CL). This is a standard against which all our relationships are judged. People's comparison levels are the product of their past experiences with other parties in the exchange, their past experiences in other similar exchanges and their general views of what can be expected from the exchange.

If the final result in a particular exchange is positive (i.e. the profit exceeds the person's comparison level), the relationship will be perceived as satisfying and the other person will seem attractive. However, if the final result is negative (i.e. the profit falls below the CL), then dissatisfaction will follow. Fortunately, it is possible for both people in a relationship to be making a profit and therefore gaining satisfaction. The CL concept is helpful in accounting for why some relationships might be acceptable at some times but not at others. See Box 13.6 for a further discussion of comparison level.

A strong feature of exchange theory is that it accommodates the individual *differences* that are apparent in interpersonal relationships in two ways: (1) differences between people in perceiving what are rewards and what are costs (some would think of the free advice of a

partner as being a reward, others wouldn't); and (2) differences within the person based on variations in comparison levels, both over time and across different contexts (I like companionship, but I prefer to shop for clothes alone).

Equity in relationships

Western society may actually be founded on a system of social exchange within which we strive for equity, or balance, in our relationships with others (Walster, Walster, & Berscheid, 1978). Accordingly, people generally believe that outcomes for participants in a social exchange should be fair and just. This view is reinforced by societal laws and norms, which provide both internal and external pressure to comply with the 'rules'. Justice and fairness perceptions play important roles in group processes (e.g. leadership—Chapter 9) and in intergroup relations (see Chapters 10 and 11) (Tyler & Smith, 1998). Note that equity and equality are not the same thing—*equality* requires, for example, that everyone gets paid the same, whereas *equity* requires that those who work hardest or do the most important jobs get paid more.

Equity theory is a more specific model within social exchange theory, which asks how people decide when an exchange is fair and what they do if they decide it is not. It was popularised in social psychology by Adams (1965) and deals with two main social situations:

1. a mutual exchange of resources (e.g. a marriage relationship);
2. an exchange in which limited resources must be distributed (e.g. a judge awarding compensation for injury).

In both situations, an equity model predicts that people expect resources to be given out *fairly*—that is, in proportion to their contribution. (The idea of equity can also be extended to an understanding of *altruism*; see the work of Piliavin and colleagues in Chapter 14.) If we help others—that is, act altruistically—then it is fair to expect them to help us. According to Adams (1965), equity exists between two people, A and B, when:

A's outcomes ÷ A's inputs = B's outcomes ÷ B's inputs

Accordingly, an individual first estimates the ratio of what has been put into a relationship to what has been received from it. This ratio is then compared with the ratio applying to the other person (see Figure 13.11). If these ratios are equal, people feel they are being treated fairly or equitably. If the ratios are not equal, in either direction, people feel treated unfairly or inequitably. For example, if John thinks he does not get much out of his relationship with Gavin, feeling that the costs exceed the rewards, he can check his judgment against the relationship he has with Fred.

BOX 13.6 Using a comparison level in a relationship

WHAT DO YOU GET FROM A RELATIONSHIP? AN EXERCISE IN SOCIAL EXCHANGE THEORY

An individual's comparison level (CL) is an idiosyncratic judgment point, as each person has had unique experiences. Your CL is the average value of all outcomes of relationships with others in your past, and also of outcomes for others that you may have heard about. It can vary across different kinds of relationship, so your CL for your doctor will be different from that for a lover.

Your entry point into a new relationship is seen against a backdrop of the other people you have known (or known about) in that context, together with the profits and losses you have encountered in relating to them. This running average constitutes a baseline for your relationships in that particular sphere. A new encounter could only be judged as satisfactory if it exceeds this baseline.

Take as an example a date that you have had with another person. The outcome is defined as the rewards (having a nice time, developing a potential relationship) minus the costs (how much money it cost you, how difficult or risky it was to arrange, whether you feel you blew your chance to make a good impression). The actual outcome will be determined by how it compares with other dates you have had in similar circumstances in the past or at present, and perhaps by how successful other people's dates have seemed to you.

To complicate matters a little, your CL can change over time. Although age may not make you any wiser, as you get older you are likely to expect more of some future commitment to another person than when you were younger. There is an additional concept—the comparison level for alternatives. Suppose that you are in an already satisfying relationship but then meet someone new, an enticing stranger. As the saying goes, 'The grass is always greener on the other side of the fence'. In social exchange language, there is the prospect here of an increase in rewards over costs.

Does all this sound too calculating to you? Be honest, now! Whatever the outcome, the situation has become unstable. Decisions, decisions . . .

Equity in a relationship, therefore, is defined as a situation where all participants' outcomes (rewards minus costs) are proportional to their inputs or contributions to the relationship. This is usually referred to as the rule of **distributive justice**, another concept originally propounded by Homans. Distributive justice, however, appears to depend on a person's gain–loss frame as well as on the other party's gain–loss frame (De Dreu, Lualhati, & McCusker, 1994). A *gain frame* implies the likelihood of an outcome being evaluated as a gain, and a *loss frame* refers to the perception of the outcome being evaluated as a loss. The frame effect in turn is related to the cooperative or non-cooperative nature of the relationship between individuals.

Consistent with equity theory, the study conducted by de Dreu, Lualhati and McCusker (1994) found that gain-framed individuals found equity more pleasing than advantageous inequity in a cooperative decision-making context, whereas in a non-cooperative context gain-framed individuals were as pleased with equity as with advantageous inequity.

Equity theory is applicable to many areas of social life, such as exploitative relationships, helping relationships and intimate relationships (Walster, Walster, & Berscheid, 1978). The more inequitably people are treated, the more distress they will feel. People who believe they are getting less than their fair share will experience distress, though people who are aware that they are receiving more can also experience distress (Adams, 1965). Most distress, however, is felt when people feel they are victims, rather than beneficiaries, of inequitable relationships (Lane & Messé, 1971).

Whenever we experience inequity, we are motivated in one of two ways to do something about it. We can:

1. alter our inputs to, or outcomes from, the exchange; or

2. restructure our perceptions of inputs and outcomes so that the ratios no longer appear inequitable.

Generally, only one method is used to restore equity in a given situation. If neither method works, and if the ratio is below an individual's comparison levels, the relationship is likely to end (Adams, 1965). How relationships end is dealt with at the end of this chapter.

As noted, the process of deciding what is a fair allocation of resources is often complex and difficult. A key issue is how an allocation can be worked out to everyone's satisfaction. In practice, a society operates according to a set of standards, or *norms*, which guide social behaviour. We can then be guided by common rules of practice, such as the following:

- an equity norm, such as the rule of distributive justice;
- a *social welfare norm*, or a rule that the amount of resources allocated to people should be proportional to their needs;
- an *equality norm*, or a rule that everyone should get an equal amount.

According to Adams (1965), people always prefer the equity norm when allocating resources, though this has been questioned (Deutsch, 1975; Mikula, 1980). It now seems probable that different norms are preferred in different situations. When allocations are made on the basis of inputs, people may evaluate a friend's inputs differently from a stranger's. Strangers tend to allocate resources on the basis of *ability*, whereas friends allocate on the basis of both *ability* and *effort* (Lamm & Kayser, 1978).

Individual differences, such as gender, also play a role. Women tend to allocate resources on the basis of an equality norm, whereas men tend to use an equity norm (Kahn, O'Leary, Krulewitz, & Lamm, 1980; Major & Adams, 1983; Major & Deaux, 1982). The reasons for this difference is not clear, although Kahn and colleagues attributed it to a traditional female role of maintaining group harmony and peace, which might best be achieved through treating people equally. In contrast, Tyler has suggested that in groups people actually consider procedural justice rather than distributive justice or equality to be more important (Tyler & Lind, 1992; see Chapters 9 and 11).

Differential value of costs and benefits

Behaviours that are interpreted by one's partner as constructive are particularly beneficial (Yovetich & Rusbult, 1994). Showing forgiveness for transgressions is a benefit with high value (McCullough, Worthington, & Rachal, 1997), as is apologising for giving offence (Azar, 1997).

FIGURE 13.11 Equity theory applied to two equitable and two inequitable relationships

	PETER		**OLIVIA**			**PETER**		**OLIVIA**
Outputs / Inputs	★★★ / ★★★	=	★ / ★		Equity perceived	★★ / ★★	=	★ / ★
Outputs / Inputs	★★★ / ★★	≠	★★ / ★★★		Equity not perceived	★ / ★★	≠	★★ / ★

Inputs or outputs are:
★   Few
★★   Average
★★★   Many

Source: Adapted from Baron & Byrne (1987).

RELATIONSHIPS AND WELLBEING

According to Argyle (1992), the most important thing about relationships is that they are good for us. One benefit is health, both physical and mental. *Physical health* has repeatedly been linked to positive relationships (for a meta-analysis, see Schwarzer & Leppin, 1989). Intimate relationships contribute to our physical health, including lower rates of heart attack, stroke, lung cancer and tuberculosis (Argyle, 1992). Married couples also display better health behaviour and better diet (Feist & Brannon, 1988). Similarly, *mental health* appears to be affected by intimate relationships. Depression is markedly lower among married women (Brown & Harris, 1978) and stress is reduced by social support (Williams, Ware, & Donald, 1981). Campbell, Sedikides and Bosson (1994) found that people who were romantically involved reported a higher sense of **wellbeing** than did romantically uninvolved individuals.

Marriage affects people's happiness and, like love, wellbeing (Diener, Suh, Lucas, & Smith, 1999). Being happy in marriage may differ for men and women (Wood, Rhodes, & Whelan, 1989). Diener et al. (1999) studied 'never married' and 'married' women and men longitudinally, 1972–89 (Figure 13.12). They found that marriage benefited men more than women in terms of positive emotions. However, married men and women did not differ in overall life satisfaction. An Australian study supported these findings but emphasised that the quality of a relationship is a critical mediator of both physical and mental health and subjective wellbeing (McCabe, Cummins, & Romeo, 1996).

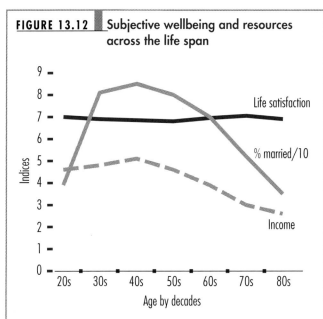

FIGURE 13.12 Subjective wellbeing and resources across the life span

Note: Overall satisfaction with one's life remains steady throughout the life span, according to this cross-national study carried out in 40 countries. This points to people's resilience in adapting to different circumstances, such as their marital status or income.

Source: Diener, Suh, Lucas, & Smith (1999). Copyright © 1999 by the American Psychological Association. Reprinted with permission.

Love relationships

LIKING AND LOVING: ARE THEY DIFFERENT?

We have discussed the general process of interpersonal attraction in terms of a powerful need to affiliate with others, and extended our discussion to deal with the way in which we choose our acquaintances and friends. Can we extend these principles to the important topic of the very special people we love? Once a neglected topic in psychology, **love** is now a popular focus for systematic research (Dion & Dion, 1996). What, indeed, is love, and is it a qualitatively different experience from liking? Intuition tells us: yes! Let's explore this further.

We are only gradually beginning to gain a scientific understanding of love. In common parlance we use terms such as passion, romance, companionship, infatuation and sexual attraction, but what are the differences between these states? Couple this with the way love is regarded as magical and mysterious—the stuff of poetry and song rather than science—and the difficulty of taking love into the laboratory becomes compounded. Not surprisingly, most research on love has used survey and interview methods.

Rubin (1973) maintained that 'liking' refers to a different state from 'loving' and developed scales to measure each separately. Regan and Berscheid (1999) distinguish between 'love' and 'being in love', the former not containing the sexual desire and excitement which is an essential part of the latter. Similarly, Lamm and Wiesmann (1997) used the term 'liking' to mean the desire to interact with a person, 'loving' to have the distinctive characteristic of trusting a person and 'being in love' to mean being aroused by a person.

Kinds of love

In a **cluster analysis** of love prototypes such as romantic love, parental love and infatuation, Fehr (1994) confirmed previous findings by Hatfield and Walster (1981), who distinguished between:

- passionate love (or romantic love); and
- companionate love.

Passionate love is an intensely emotional state and a confusion of feelings: tenderness, sexuality, elation and pain, anxiety and relief, altruism and jealousy. **Companionate love**, in contrast, is a less intense emotion, combining feelings of friendly affection and deep attachment. It is characterised by friendship, understanding and a concern for the welfare of the other (Hatfield, 1987).

Love: Romantic love involves intense and occasionally confused emotions. Companionate love develops slowly from the continuous sharing of intimacy.

Shaver, Morgan and Wu (1996) argue that love is an emotion—like sadness, anger, fear and happiness (see Chapter 15 for a discussion of these 'primary' emotions).

A distinction between passionate and companionate love makes good sense. There are many people with whom we may find it pleasant and comforting to share time, without the suggestion that we are 'in love' with them. Argyle and Henderson (1985) have extended the distinction to couples who have been married for some time, noting that people report that their passion evolves into a relationship marked more by attachment and affection, and reduced sexual excitement.

TABLE 13.2	How many loves?	
	LOVE STYLE	CHARACTERISTICS
EROS	Passionate love	Love is an all-consuming emotional experience. Love at first sight is typical, and physical love is essential.
STORGE	Friendship or companionate love	Love is a comfortable intimacy that slowly grows out of companionship, mutual sharing and self-disclosure. A best-friend lover is thoughtful, warm and companionate.
LUDUS	Game-playing love	This person plays at love as others play tennis or chess: to enjoy the 'love game' and to win it. No relationship lasts for long, usually ending when the partner becomes boring or too serious.
MANIA	Possessive love	The possessive lover is emotionally intense, jealous, obsessed with the beloved. The possessive lover is highly dependent on the beloved and therefore fears rejection.
PRAGMA	Logical love	This is 'love shopping for a suitable mate' and all it asks is that the relationship works well, that the two partners be compatible and that they satisfy each other's basic needs. The pragmatic lover seeks contentment rather than excitement.
AGAPE	Selfless (altruistic) love	This style of love is unconditionally caring, giving and forgiving. Love means a duty to give to the loved one with no strings attached.

Source: Based on Hendrick & Hendrick (1995).

In addition to the distinction between passionate and companionate love, other styles of love have been proposed. For example, drawing on philosophy and literature, Lee (1988) offered a fine-grained taxonomy of six love styles. These were used by Hendrick and Hendrick (1995) to develop a scale to measure gender differences in the 'colours of love'. They found that men scored higher than women on *ludus*, *mania* and *pragma* (see Table 13.2). We deal with a dimensional analysis of love below in considering Sternberg's (1988) work.

Love and marriage

Does love go with marriage 'like a horse and carriage', as a popular song once claimed? In Western culture there appears to have been a change in attitude over time, even across a single generation. Simpson, Campbell and Berscheid (1986) compared responses across three time samples, from the 1960s to the 1980s. Would you be surprised to learn that 'young people' in a later generation expected a causal connection more than young people 20 years earlier? The respondents answered the same question: 'If a man (woman) had all the qualities you desired, would you marry this person if you were not in love with him (her)?' The number of those, especially women, who answered 'No' increased over time (see Figure 13.13). Presumably, marrying for conferred status or security was less required or favoured among young people in the 1980s than in the 1960s.

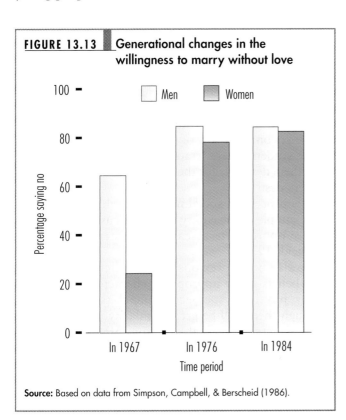

FIGURE 13.13 Generational changes in the willingness to marry without love

Source: Based on data from Simpson, Campbell, & Berscheid (1986).

Hill and Peplau (1998) offered a further perspective on the link between love and marriage. Even though there is a far greater percentage of long-term relationships outside marriage in Western cultures, recent American survey data suggest that love is still an accurate predictor of whether a couple would get married or not—even though it is not enough to guarantee a happy and stable relationship.

Most research on marriage is Western and may seem culturally myopic. In one sense it is—because marriage, as a social contract, takes varying forms in different cultures and groups. However, almost all love relationships in all cultures and groups have some public contractual aspect to identify the relationship and one's membership of it.

ROMANTIC LOVE

Though many songwriters have attempted to answer the elusive question 'What is love?', social psychologists tend to stick more to descriptions of behavioural and cognitive tendencies that are indicative of the state of being 'in love'. Such things may include thinking of the lover constantly, wanting to spend as much time as possible with her/him and, often, being unrealistic in judgments about the lover (Murstein, 1980). This usually results in the lover becoming the focus of the person's life, to the exclusion of other friends (Milardo, Johnson, & Huston, 1983). It is perceived as a very intense emotion, one over which the individual has little control. Is it a good thing?

In a longitudinal study of students, Aron, Paris and Aron (1995) found that those who had fallen in love reported positive experiences: they felt that their self had 'expanded' and reported an increase in self-efficacy and self-esteem.

However, we speak of 'falling' in love as though it is some sort of accident, something that happens to us rather than some process in which we actively participate. It is interesting that we perceive love in this manner. One of the most widely accepted claims about love among social psychologists is that a prerequisite for falling in love is to have been raised in a culture that believes in the concept and teaches it to young people, both in fiction and real-life depictions. If it really was an accident that happened to us, we would expect people from all cultures to fall in love, but this is not the case. (See the later discussion on arranged marriages.)

As with many other situations in life, our beliefs determine what happens to us. According to Noller at the University of Queensland, love 'can be strongly affected by the beliefs about love that are present in the culture . . . these beliefs can be either functional or dysfunctional. Particularly dysfunctional beliefs include those emphasising that love is blind, external, and beyond the control of the lovers' (Noller, 1996, p. 97).

Not only do you need to have a concept of love before it happens to you, but the more you think about love, the more likely you are to fall in love (Tesser & Paulhus, 1976); and if you believe that 'love at first sight' is possible, the chances are that it will happen to you (Averill & Boothroyd, 1977).

Is love just a label?

Now, we don't want to spoil your fun, but some social psychologists have argued that romantic love is merely a label we apply to the product of interacting variables. In their **three-factor theory of love**, Hatfield and Walster (1981) distinguished three variables that underlie the experience of love:

1. a cultural determinant that acknowledges love as a state;
2. an appropriate love object present—in most cultures the norm is a member of the opposite sex, and of similar age;
3. emotional arousal, self-labelled 'love', that is felt when interacting with, or even thinking about, an appropriate love object.

Label or not, most who have been smitten report feeling powerful effects. Although the idea of labelling arousal may not seem intuitively appealing, it has a basis in research. Our physiological reactions do not seem to be well differentiated across the emotions: that is, similar reactions seem to occur regardless of whether we describe ourselves as angry, fearful, joyful or sexually aroused (Fehr & Stern, 1970).

Taking this into account, Schachter and Singer (1962) proposed that, when events elicit internal physiological arousal, we look for external cues in the world around us to discover the reason for the arousal. We then label the arousal as an emotion consistent with what we see as possible cues. For example, if we feel arousal following insult, we are likely to label the arousal as anger. However, if we experience arousal while interacting with an attractive member of the appropriate sex, we are likely to label the arousal sexual attraction, liking or love. Mixed evidence, some of which provides support for the proposal (e.g. Schachter & Singer, 1962) and some of which does not (e.g. Marshall & Zimbardo, 1979), means that we cannot say with confidence that we exclusively label arousal according to external cues. It is probable that the relationship is rather more complex and that external cues are one factor in our perception of arousal (see Chapter 3 on attribution and the cognitive labelling of arousal).

The effects of arousal in love can also be looked at from the perspective of the reinforcement–affect model discussed earlier in this chapter. According to this model, any positive arousal experienced while with a possible love object is associated with, or attributed to, that person. In this way, the belief of being in love can grow.

Regardless of whether we accept the mislabelling hypothesis and/or the reinforcement–affect model, according to the three-factor theory love depends on past learning of the concept, the presence of someone to love, and arousal. It would be difficult to dispute the involvement of these factors in love. However, though they may be necessary for the state of love to occur, they do not seem to be sufficient. If they were, love could easily be taken into the laboratory. The ingredients required would be that Peter's culture includes a concept of love and Olivia provides arousal by being attractive, or by chasing Peter around the room, or by paying him a compliment and, hey presto, 'Love'!

It is at this point that we run into problems with Schachter's mislabelling hypothesis. Although love can be accompanied by sexual arousal, the latter itself is not a reliable indicator of love. Anecdotal evidence provides the best support for this—when a person is called to account for an extramarital affair by a spouse, the classic response is often 'But, dear, it didn't mean anything!'

What process is it that sometimes leads us both to be aroused and to fall in love? Or, how is it that we feel sexual attraction ('lust'), without any glimmerings of love, towards someone else? Although conclusive answers are not available, several contributing factors can be identified. A major variable highlighted by research has been the degree of appropriateness of another person as a partner. Field research (Silverman, 1971) has shown that the couples who seem happiest with their dating partners are those who are fairly well matched with regard to physical attractiveness. Elder (1969) tracked down female students who had been rated for attractiveness in the 1930s. He found that the more attractive the female student had been, the 'better' she had achieved in marriage with regard to social status. This supported the belief that couples match themselves on some sort of social desirability scale—the female students were 'trading' the attractiveness that made them desirable for the social status that made their partners desirable.

This process of **social matching**, which we can see is an example of the equity theory discussed earlier, has been supported in research (Walster, Walster, & Berscheid, 1978).

We also bring previously held beliefs to the situation—beliefs about appropriate characteristics such as gender, physique, socioeconomic class and religion. Although there will be great similarity of these beliefs in any society, individual variations are extensive. For example, most people would regard a sibling as an inappropriate love object; however, a brother and sister in Britain were reported as being prepared to go to prison to defend their love (Russell, 1987). Again, many people will not fall in love with others who are already involved in a relationship, on the basis that these others are judged unavailable from the outset.

Love in the workplace

In Western nations, the participation rate of women in the workforce has increased steadily over several decades (with consequent changes in gender role, as noted later; see Box 13.8). The increase in the proportion of female to male workers provides greater opportunity (through the principle of proximity) for romantic relationships. However, research on love in the workplace remains in its infancy (Powell & Foley, 1999). A practical issue is the effect of a workplace love affair on co-workers and, indeed, on management (see Box 13.7).

Love and illusions

People bring various ideals or images into a love relationship that can affect the way it develops. A person

---

BOX 13.7   Gossip in the workplace

Have you ever gossiped about a workmate's romantic involvement with another workmate? Until recently, romantic relationships in organisational settings have attracted little research attention (Powell & Foley, 1999).

A workplace relationship is currently defined as any heterosexual relationship between two members of the same organisation that entails mutual sexual attraction and is jointly desired (Pierce, Byrne, & Aguinis, 1996). Workplace romances follow the patterns of attraction outlined in this chapter, with some extra variables such as consequences in the workplace and managerial actions. Consequences for an employee include productivity, morale, motivation, job satisfaction, job involvement—and gossip, which is usually negative.

In their review, Pierce and his colleagues concluded that romantically involved employees exhibit a decrease in productivity, motivation and job involvement in the early stages of their romance but an increase in all three of these during the later stages. Productivity is more affected when the employees differ in status.

Decision-making can be difficult when employees are romantically involved. For example, a manager may feel obliged to avoid perceived favouritism and inequity with respect to promotions. Some organisations are concerned enough about perceived injustice to be reluctant to promote employees who are in a romantic relationship (Spelman & Crary, 1984; cited in Pierce, Byrne, & Aguinis, 1996).

One outcome can be to relocate employees. Low-status employees involved in a workplace romance are more likely than high-status employees to be relocated, or even sacked, especially if they are female.

---

can fall out of love quickly if the partner is not what (or who) they were first thought to be. The initial love was not for the partner, but for some *ideal image* that the person had formed of this partner, such as 'the knight in shining armour'. Possible sources of these images are previous lovers, characters from fiction, or childhood love objects such as parents. A physical characteristic similar to one held by the image can start a chain reaction whereby other characteristics from the image are transferred onto the partner.

This use of images seems to be the factor that best differentiates love from liking (though not love from sexual arousal). Love seems to be inextricably tied up with fantasy and positive illusion, both of which can create better relationships (Martz, Verette, Arriaga, Slovic, Cox, & Rusbult, 1998; Murray & Holmes, 1997), and with a biased image of the other person (Klohnen & Mendelsohn, 1998).

One illusion is the belief in romantic destiny—the idea that two people are 'meant for each other'. Such a relationship is based on a positive start and is likely to be maintained longer and perceived as happier (Knee, 1998).

Another illusion is that people project their own ideal self onto another person. The clinical psychologist Reik (1944) found support for his idea that, when we are dissatisfied with ourselves we are vulnerable to love, because this is the time that we fantasise about having our needs met. We then proceed to drape these fantasies around another person (Berscheid & Walster, 1978).

Evidence to support Reik's hypothesis comes from work on deprivation. Leiman and Epstein (1961) showed that when people are sexually aroused they usually have sexual fantasies. Stephan, Berscheid and Walster (1971) proposed that, when we are sexually aroused, fantasising occurs and we mix up these fantasies with the reality of another person.

Their study asked college men to give their impressions of a blind date who had been picked for them. While they were waiting, they were given something to read. For one condition, the reading material was designed to dampen sexual feelings, being a boring account of the sex life of the herring gull! Those in the other condition were given a story of sexual seduction designed to stimulate their sexual feelings. The same date, a pretty blonde who was active, intelligent and easy to get on with, was described to all the participants. The men in the aroused condition thought the date more beautiful and more likely to be receptive to sexual advances. Also, the more sexually inexperienced participants found the date more attractive—supposedly, a reflection of their greater need—than those who reported having had sex often and recently.

These results demonstrate that arousal does alter the perception of a member of the opposite sex. However, the results are limited, as the study had only male participants and looked at sexual arousal and assumptions about sexual response rather than love.

No greater love

Sternberg (1988) has proposed a model of love in which commitment and intimacy are factors as crucial as passion to some experiences of love. *Passion* is roughly equivalent to sexual attraction; *intimacy* refers to feelings of warmth, closeness and sharing; *commitment* is our resolve to maintain the relationship, even in moments of crisis. In an Australian study, Forgas and Dobosz (1980) found that women tended to show higher levels of commitment than men.

An interesting notion in Sternberg's proposal is that romance is exceeded by one other experience, **consummate love**, which includes all three factors. By systematically creating combinations of the presence or absence of each factor we can distinguish eight cases, ranging in degree of bonding from no love at all to consummate love. Out of this some interesting relationships emerge. Fatuous love is characterised by passion and commitment but no intimacy (e.g. the 'whirlwind Hollywood romance'). Do you recognise some of the relationships in Figure 13.14?

EMOTION IN CLOSE RELATIONSHIPS

We tend to think of close relationships as characterised by strong feelings—typically, love. However, such relationships are a crucible for a host of strong emotions: the interdependence and general closeness of such relationships guarantee an elevated level of emotion (Fitness & Fletcher, 1993; Fitness, Fletcher, & Overall, 2003). According to Berscheid and Ammazzalorso's (2001) **emotion-in-relationships model** (ERM), relationships pivot on strong, well-established and wide-ranging interpersonal expectations about how partners should/will behave. It is when behaviour interrupts expectations that strong emotions are felt, and the probability of interruptions is much greater in close relationships.

Emotional expressiveness is generally valued in close relationships (Huston & Houts, 1998), particularly by people who have a secure attachment style (Feeney, 1999). There is, however, a caveat. According to research by Julie Fitness at Macquarie University, the elevated tendency to feel *all* emotions in close relationships makes it important to be able to manage the expression of emotions, particularly negative ones (Fitness, 2001). If I engage in an orgy of uninhibited expression of all I feel for my partner then, unfortunately, the relationship is not long for this world. Emotional expression for my partner needs to be carefully, dare one say strategically, managed (see above on self-disclosure).

ARRANGED MARRIAGES

Despite the romantic Western ideal of meeting Mr or Ms Right—falling in love, getting married and living happily ever after—some cultures have a quite calculating approach to the union of marriage, preferring the careful

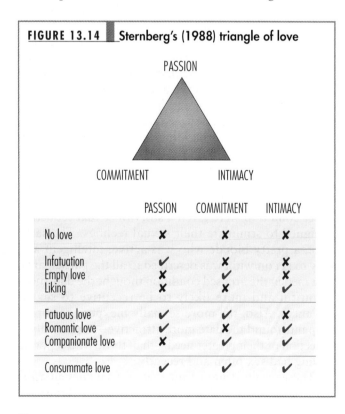

FIGURE 13.14 ▌ Sternberg's (1988) triangle of love

	PASSION	COMMITMENT	INTIMACY
No love	✗	✗	✗
Infatuation	✓	✗	✗
Empty love	✗	✓	✗
Liking	✗	✗	✓
Fatuous love	✓	✓	✗
Romantic love	✓	✗	✓
Companionate love	✗	✓	✓
Consummate love	✓	✓	✓

Arranged marriages: Marriage serves such an important function for the community that in many traditional cultures young people are not left to choose their own marriage partner.

arrangement of 'suitable' partners for their children. Although this traditional Eastern practice is viewed by many Westerners as mysterious and perhaps undesirable, it can be very successful, particularly if we view the success of a marriage in terms of its duration and its social function (having children, caring for aged parents, reinforcing the extended family and building a stronger community). Arranged marriages also recognise a wider social function: they integrate a community through building bonds and alliances among extended families or tribal groups. This function has always been critical— it is only weak in post-industrial societies that are organised around nuclear families (i.e. in Western societies).

Three studies of arranged marriages were carried out in India. Gupta and Singh (1982) compared arranged marriages and 'love' marriages and found that, at the beginning, the arranged couples rated their love for each other at a lower level than did the 'love' couples. Over time, this trend reversed. We might conclude that (a) love can be learned, especially if we feel we 'must make it work'; and (b) it is possible that others can successfully match couples according to attributes that are not obvious at first to either party.

Umadevi, Venkataramaiah and Srinivasulu (1992) found that female students preferred the idea of an arranged marriage, though with their consent, but also endorsed the idea of a 'love marriage', with their parents' consent. Saroja and Surendra (1991) compared students' preferences for arranged and love marriages and found that students who preferred love marriages were also more liberal in terms of their mate's sociocultural background, whereas students who endorsed arranged marriages preferred a partner from within their own kin group.

Some research has challenged the dichotomy of arranged and love marriages as oversimplified. De Munck (1996) investigated love and marriage in a Sri Lankan Muslim community, finding that arranged marriages were the cultural preference. However, romantic love also contributed to the decision, even when parents officially selected the partner. De Munck concluded that the concept of romantic love should be included in any analyses of marriage practices in different cultures.

In general, such research highlights the importance and respect that some cultures afford their elders as legitimate match-makers. Many Westerners believe that they would never consider an arranged marriage. However, dating and international marriage-match agencies are rapidly growing in popularity in Western culture, reflecting perhaps a decline in opportunities for those who have to seek a partner.

MAINTAINING RELATIONSHIPS

The relevant literature deals mostly with marriage, as it has been assumed that this is the most obvious rela-

tionship to be preserved. However, in view of what we have discussed above, marriage is only one of a number of love relationships. Marriage involves other factors that make it unlike most others: it is a contractual arrangement; it can be a financial partnership with accumulating assets; it usually involves parenting; and the nature of the initial attraction transforms over a lengthy period of time. And, of course, marriage remains, due to legislation, largely a heterosexual phenomenon and thus excludes love and sexual relationships between members of the same sex.

External influences, such as pressure from in-laws, are other factors beyond love that can perpetuate a marriage relationship—but when weakened can be linked to an escalating divorce rate (Attridge & Berscheid, 1994). Karney and Bradbury (1995) looked at nearly 200 variables in marital satisfaction and stability longitudinally and found that highly valued variables such as education, employment and supportive behaviour predicted a positive outcome, whereas negatively valued variables such as neuroticism, unhappy childhood and negative behaviour predicted negative marital outcomes. However, no single factor appeared to be a reliable predictor of satisfaction.

A study by Cotton, Cunningham and Antill (1993) at Macquarie University investigated the relationship between spousal marital satisfaction and couples' social and support networks. A wife would report more marital satisfaction when members of her network were related to one another, when her husband's network included some relatives, and when she was a friend of some members of her husband's network. A husband would report more marital satisfaction when he was a friend of some members of his wife's network, and when some members of his network were related to those in his wife's network. Marriage is more than a union of two individuals: it includes interaction of the partners with, and overlap between, two larger networks of people. Satisfaction is higher when individuals who might have been 'worlds apart' become 'worlds together'.

Nevertheless, it is an interesting question whether a love relationship is *ever* maintained. Some works of literature lead us to believe that 'love endures', whereas TV soap operas often focus on relationship break-ups. The reason for the latter's appeal is intriguing in a society where marriage 'till death do us part' is still the ideal. In previous generations, love was the prerequisite for marriage in Western societies. In a study by Burgess and Wallin (1953), 1000 young people who were engaged to be married were asked, 'Do you think that a person should ever marry someone they do not love?' The results showed that 82% of men and 80% of women said 'No'; only 12% of men and 15% of women said 'Yes'.

Despite the precondition put on love, there is general agreement that a relationship that survives time is one in which the partners adapt and change with respect to what they expect of each other. What counts in maintaining a relationship is companionate love (see above). Such love involves deep friendship and caring, and arises from the sharing of lives and the myriad experiences that only time can provide. From such a starting point, we can get a glimmering of how both the Western 'love' marriage and the Eastern arranged marriage could result in a similar perception of powerful bonding between partners.

In companionate love, the ambivalence of feeling that 'I can't live with him and I can't live without him' recedes. However, even companionate love cannot guarantee a lasting relationship. *Security* is a critical variable that can exert influence in several different ways. When one partner feels insecure, the emotion of *jealousy* can follow, a state expressed by extreme possessiveness and suspicion that accelerates the deterioration of the relationship.

Jealousy as a consequence of insecurity has been linked to the perception of being inadequate in a relationship or falling short of one's own expectations (Attridge, Berscheid, & Sprecher, 1998). On the other hand, feeling secure in a relationship can bring its own problems. Companionate love might imply that the 'magic' of romantic love has disappeared. In this case, security can lead to boredom and a consequent search for new stimulation, often away from the partner. Despite this risk, security can enhance a relationship if the search for new stimulation is undertaken together.

Commitment

A crucial variable in maintaining a relationship is **commitment**—the desire or intention to continue. Highly committed partners have a greater chance of staying together (Adams & Jones, 1997). The very idea of subjectively committing ourselves to a relationship can be more important than the conditions that led to commitment (Berscheid & Reis, 1998). Subjective commitment may be related to our self-construal, the way we think about ourselves (see Chapter 4). In a study by Cross, Bacon and Morris (2000), people who construed themselves as relations-interdependent (i.e. generally more connected with other people) were more committed to important relationships than individuals who did not.

Commitment has also been linked to the level of marital satisfaction, pro-relationship behaviour and trust. Two longitudinal studies by Wieselquist, Rusbult, Foster and Agnew (1999) revealed that commitment-inspired acts, such as accommodation and willingness to sacrifice, are good indicators of someone's pro-relationship motives. This is a *cyclical* model: such acts in turn elicit the partner's trust and reciprocal commitment and subsequent dependence on the relationship.

Johnson (1991) proposed that relationship mainte-

nance depends on people's feelings that: (a) they want to continue the relationship; (b) they ought to continue it; (c) they must continue it. All three forms of commitment can have different behavioural consequences. Similarly, Adams and Jones (1997) pinpointed three factors that contribute to an ongoing relationship:

1. *personal dedication*—positive attraction to a particular partner and relationship;
2. *moral commitment*—a sense of obligation, religious duty or social responsibility, as controlled by a person's values and moral principles;
3. *constraint commitment*—factors that make it costly to leave a relationship, such as lack of attractive alternatives and various social, financial or legal investments in the relationship.

Role complementarity

Role complementarity is a major factor in maintaining any relationship. Any change in a relationship requires a renegotiation of roles. For example, if the female partner has been ill for a long time and then recovers, her partner may feel down even though he believes he should be happy about it. He may feel that his role of caregiver is now redundant, so that it becomes difficult for him to see where he fits in.

Even without a radical change in roles in a relationship, people do change over time; if this change occurs in different directions or at different rates, a breakdown of the relationship often results. A societal change in the latter half of the 20th century was the changing role of women. The redefinition of women as a group that is economically equal to men has caused both sexes to reconsider their status (see Box 13.8). For many couples the outcome is the experience of role strain for each partner and the possibility of a broken relationship.

ENDING A RELATIONSHIP

The deterioration of a relationship involves the perception by one or both partners that it is not as desirable as it once was. Levinger (1980) points to four factors that herald the end of a relationship:

1. A new life seems to be the only solution.
2. Alternative partners are available.
3. There is an expectation that the relationship will fail.
4. There is a lack of commitment to a continuing relationship.

Most research in this area deals with heterosexual relationships, but a study by Schullo and Alperson (1984) has shown these factors to be valid for homosexual relationships as well.

Rusbult and Zembrodt (1983) believe that, once deterioration is identified, it can be responded to in any of four ways. A partner can take a passive stance and show:

The changing role of women

ROLE CHANGE CAN STRAIN A RELATIONSHIP

The manner in which role relationships are defined is especially important in the way men and women respond to each other. Traditional gender role stereotypes have been going through a process of change in our society for about a generation, with the larger degree of reconstruction taking place for women. For example, in an Australian study of 18–34-year-olds Carmichael (1983) found that young women (57%) were even less likely than young men (78%) to endorse the item 'People should consider needs of spouse and children as more important than their own'.

Women taking assertiveness training courses have become less prepared to play a submissive role. This will inevitably put a strain on their relationship if their male partner expects to continue in a dominant role. His traditional role of breadwinner has been eroded to differing degrees for different couples. Welfare payments from the state system lessen the extent to which women need to be directly dependent on men for the financial means of caring for children.

Participation by women in the workforce enables a degree of financial independence that in many cases raises self-esteem and changes perceptions of equity. Economic factors, allied to the changed status and work expectations of women compared with a generation ago, mean that in many families in Western nations the woman is working while the man is unemployed. This reversal of the breadwinner role can be difficult to reconcile with the traditional roles of husband and wife.

1. *loyalty*, by waiting for an improvement to occur; or
2. *neglect*, by allowing the deterioration to continue.

Alternatively, a partner can take an active stance and show:

3. *voice behaviour*, by working at improving the relationship; or
4. *exit behaviour*, by choosing to end the relationship.

It is not easy to determine whether the passive or the active approach leads to more pain at the final break-up, as many other factors are involved, such as previous levels of attraction, amount of time and effort invested and the availability of new partners. It can also depend on the person's general level of social contact, such as support from family and friends. It is often loneliness that adds to the pain and makes life seem unbearable; if this is minimised, recovery from the end of a relationship can be faster.

Duck (1988, 1992) has offered a detailed **relationship dissolution model** of four phases that partners pass through when a break-up occurs. Each phase culminates in a threshold which, when reached, leads to the behaviours shown in Figure 13.15.

1. The *intrapsychic phase* starts as a period of brooding with little outward show, perhaps in the hope of putting things right. This can give way to needling the partner and seeking out a third party to be able to express one's concern.
2. The *dyadic phase* takes the person to the point of deciding that something needs to be done, short of leaving the partner, an act that is usually easier said than done. There are arguments and differences

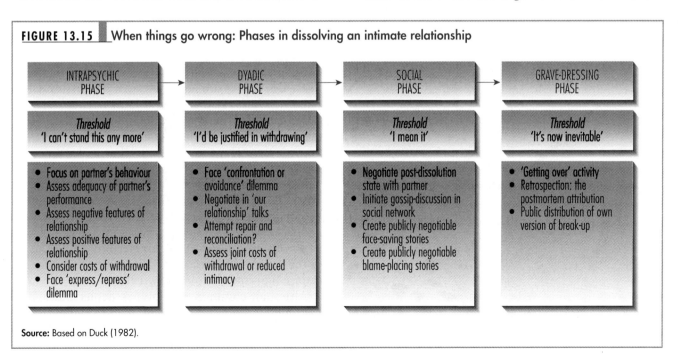

FIGURE 13.15 When things go wrong: Phases in dissolving an intimate relationship

INTRAPSYCHIC PHASE	DYADIC PHASE	SOCIAL PHASE	GRAVE-DRESSING PHASE
Threshold 'I can't stand this any more'	*Threshold* 'I'd be justified in withdrawing'	*Threshold* 'I mean it'	*Threshold* 'It's now inevitable'
• Focus on partner's behaviour • Assess adequacy of partner's performance • Assess negative features of relationship • Assess positive features of relationship • Consider costs of withdrawal • Face 'express/repress' dilemma	• Face 'confrontation or avoidance' dilemma • Negotiate in 'our relationship' talks • Attempt repair and reconciliation? • Assess joint costs of withdrawal or reduced intimacy	• Negotiate post-dissolution state with partner • Initiate gossip-discussion in social network • Create publicly negotiable face-saving stories • Create publicly negotiable blame-placing stories	• 'Getting over' activity • Retrospection: the postmortem attribution • Public distribution of own version of break-up

Source: Based on Duck (1982).

between the pair in attributing responsibility for what is going wrong. With luck, they may talk their problems through.

3. The *social phase* involves a new element: in saying that the relationship is near an end, the partners may negotiate with friends, both as a means of social support for an uncertain future and for reassurance of being right. The social network will probably take sides, pronounce on guilt and blame and, like a court, sanction the dissolution.

4. The final *grave-dressing phase* can involve more than leaving a partner. It may include the division of property and of access to children, and a further working towards an assurance for one's reputation. In the individual's community, it is probably important to emerge with a self-image of relationship reliability for the future. The partners know that the relationship is dead, and metaphorically its burial is marked by erecting a tablet. This 'grave-dressing' activity seeks a socially acceptable version of the life and death of the relationship (see fourth focus question).

In the case of the institution of marriage, divorce is now so common that postmarital relationships can be anticipated. Noller and Callan (1990), at the University of Queensland, reported that the rate of divorce in Australia is actually overestimated by people who were asked to imagine a normal family with two children. Divorce can no longer be considered deviant or pathological; it is an institution in its own right (Ahrons & Rodgers, 1987).

LONELINESS

One way of defining loneliness is as dissatisfaction with our relationships. This can come about when the desired rate of interaction with others is not satisfied by the actual rate that we experience (see Altman's privacy regulation model in this chapter). Loneliness is a 'normal' experience: according to Perlman and Peplau (1998),

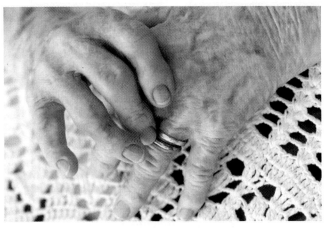

Loneliness: Her rings are a reminder of her loss. Loneliness and depression, among the elderly, can be reduced by having a social support network.

25% of Americans report that they have felt lonely or remote from others in the past two weeks. Perlman and Peplau distinguish between *loneliness*, which is a feeling within a person, and *aloneness*, which is a person's observable state of being physically apart from others.

Along similar lines, Williams and Solano (1983) have argued that the *quality* of relationships, defined as a lack of closeness, contributes to feeling lonely. In a study of first-year university students, they found that there was no difference between lonely and non-lonely people in terms of the number of best friends they listed, or in the number of people who reciprocated the best friend's choice. Instead, lonely students perceived a lack of intimacy with their friends.

Maxwell and Coebergh (1986) isolated four predictors of loneliness: how close people are to the closest person in their life; how many close friends they have; how satisfied they are with their relationships; and whether they have daily contacts with others. Buunk and Prins (1998) found that Dutch students linked reciprocity to loneliness when assessing their relationship with their best friend. Those who felt they were not receiving an equitable share of benefits from their friend were the most lonely.

In their review, Berscheid and Reis (1998) identified three variables associated with loneliness:

1. *dispositional factors*—such as shyness, depression, introversion, self-consciousness, low self-esteem, lack of self-disclosure and reduced responsiveness to partners and others;
2. *social circumstances*—reduced time spent with women, by either men or women, along with lower intimacy and disclosure;
3. *social cognitive tendencies*—harshness in judging others, and self-defeating attributions.

There is a special case of loneliness following the loss of a partner that can have severely disruptive effects, even when the person has access to a reasonably active social network (also see the role of networks in the earlier section on maintaining relationships). The media often report cases of elderly couples where the partners die within a short time of each other and, while it is possible that these events occur by chance, there is compelling evidence suggesting a causal link (Stroebe, Stroebe, Gergen, & Gergen, 1982). The death of a loved one can lead to prolonged grief, bodily neglect and even immune deficiencies (Jemmott & Locke, 1984)—all hallmarks of the broken-heart effect (see Box 13.9). Caring for the bereaved is a secondary, but major, target for the hospice movement (Youngson, 1989).

Although common stereotypes depict old age as the time of loneliness, Perlman (1988) has found that loneliness is in fact highest among teenagers and young people. This may be due to the number of social transitions young people undergo when leaving home to live independently, often on their own, when they get a job or go to university. As people grow older, these situations become more stable and social skills improve, making it easier to build up social networks and commit to close relationships.

BOX 13.9 **Health risks among the bereaved**

DYING OF A BROKEN HEART

'I care for you,' she said, 'but what if we lose one another?'
'Well,' he said, 'that is the price we must pay.' Raphael, 1985, p. 402

The death of a spouse may be followed in a short period of time by the death of the remaining partner. Stroebe and his colleagues (Stroebe, Stroebe, Gergen, & Gergen, 1982) suggested a connection.

They averaged across age categories to show that the death rate among bereaved spouses was three times higher than for other people of similar age, and in the 20–29-year-old group it was a staggering ten times higher. Death of a loved one can lead to a prolonged period of grief in which the first six months after the loss is a particularly critical period. Although some deaths among bereaved spouses could be attributed to a tendency to neglect their body, there is some evidence of a related deterioration in the immune system following an extended period of grieving (Jemmott & Locke, 1984). Carers in the hospice movement, who support the terminally ill, are well aware of the broken-heart effect and continue to support the family of the bereaved for a time after the patient's death. This post-death care of others deliberately targets the first of several of a bereaved person's anniversaries, such as birthdays, Christmas, the wedding and the actual death.

In a study carried out in Sydney (Raphael, 1985), 56 widows who were judged to be both lacking a supportive network and at risk of poor resolution of their spouse's death were allocated randomly to either an intervention or a non-intervention group. The intervention group received on average four two-hour counselling sessions, usually in their homes. These were distributed over a 13-month period in order to include all first anniversaries. A comparison of the two groups, carried out by an independent rater, showed that the intervention group was coping significantly better with their loss. The non-intervention group showed substantial health impairment.

Summary

- Studies of isolation show that long-term separation from others can have disturbing intellectual and social outcomes. Young children who are deprived for a long period of physical and social contact with others, especially adults, may suffer irreversible psychological damage.
- Various researchers have emphasised a need to affiliate that is clearly not satisfied by prolonged periods of isolation.
- According to Schachter's shared-stress model, being in the company of others who are experiencing a similar psychological state to ourselves helps to reduce anxiety.
- Variables that play a significant role in determining why people are attracted to each other include: how attractive they are, whether they live or work close by, whether they reciprocate positive reinforcers, and how similar they are in terms of attitudes and values. In a long-term relationship, it can also be important that the needs of the parties are complementary.

- Theories of attraction include balance theory (which is also a consistency theory of attitude), reinforcement theories (stressing mutual reinforcement) and social exchange theories (which use a cost–benefit analysis).
- Love is distinguished by some theorists (such as Hatfield & Walster, and Sternberg) from mere liking. Different kinds of love have also been distinguished, particularly romantic and companionate love.
- The break-up of long-term relationships can be traced through a series of stages. Duck's relationship dissolution model notes four phases: intrapsychic, dyadic, social and grave-dressing.
- Loneliness is a serious problem for people who have ended a relationship or who have suffered bereavement. Its effects on both physical and psychological health can be profound. There is a need for a social support network to help people through this experience.

LINKS

YOU HAVE READ ABOUT:	WHICH LINKS TO:
The tendency to affiliate	why people join groups (8)
Learning to be sociable	modelling and attitudes (5); learning to aggress (12); learning to help others (14)
Liking those who like us	reciprocity principle of aggression (12)
Balance theory and liking	cognitive consistency (5)
Social exchange theory of relationships	connection to another social science (economics, 1)
Emotional component of love	primary emotions (15)
Internet relationships	computer-mediated communications (15)

Key terms

affiliative behaviour *(p. 326)*
attachment behaviour *(p. 329)*
attachment styles *(p. 329)*
brainwashing *(p. 327)*
cluster analysis *(p. 345)*
commitment *(p. 352)*
companionate love *(p. 345)*
comparison level *(p. 342)*
consummate love *(p. 350)*
cost–reward ratio *(p. 341)*
distributive justice *(p. 344)*
emotion-in-relationships model
   (p. 350)
equity theory *(p. 343)*
evolutionary social psychology
   (p. 326)

familiarity *(p. 335)*
gain–loss hypothesis *(p. 336)*
hospitalism *(p. 329)*
love *(p. 345)*
maternal deprivation *(p. 328)*
meta-analysis *(p. 332)*
minimax strategy *(p. 342)*
need complementarity *(p. 338)*
need to affiliate *(p. 326)*
passionate (or romantic) love
   (p. 345)
personal space *(p. 326)*
privacy regulation theory *(p. 326)*
profit *(p. 342)*
proximity *(p. 334)*
reciprocity principle *(p. 335)*

reinforcement–affect model
   (p. 340)
relationship dissolution model
   (p. 353)
role complementarity *(p. 352)*
self-disclosure *(p. 338)*
sensory deprivation *(p. 327)*
shared stress *(p. 330)*
similarity of attitudes or values
   (p. 336)
social affiliation model *(p. 326)*
social comparison *(p. 331)*
social matching *(p. 348)*
three-factor theory of love *(p. 348)*
wellbeing *(p. 345)*

FURTHER READING

Berscheid, E. (1994). Interpersonal relationships. *Annual Review of Psychology, 45*, 79–129. This review, by an acknowledged leader in the area of interpersonal attraction, covers the major topics in the field.

Berscheid, E., & Reis, H. T. (1998). Attraction and close relationships. In D. T. Gilbert, S. T. Fiske, & G. Lindzey (Eds.), *The handbook of social psychology* (4th ed., Vol. 2, pp. 193–281). New York: McGraw-Hill. Authoritative overview of the field of attraction and related topics in the most recent edition of the classic handbook—a primary source for theory and research.

Blank, P. D. (Ed.). (1993). *Interpersonal expectations: Theory, research and applications.* Cambridge, UK: Cambridge University Press. An interesting and informative collection of the work of experts on interpersonal expectations, with particular attention and focus on the research, study and mediation of non-verbal behaviour.

Duck, S. (1992). *Human relationships* (2nd ed.). London: Sage. A perspective by a major theorist on people's interactions, acquaintances, friendships and relationships.

Fehr, B. (1996). *Friendship processes.* Thousand Oaks, CA: Sage. An in-depth analysis of friendship in modern society based on recent research.

Fitness, J., Fletcher, G., & Overall, N. (2003). Interpersonal attraction and intimate relationships. In M. A. Hogg & J. Cooper (Eds.), *The Sage handbook of social psychology* (pp. 258–278). London: Sage. Up-to-date overview of research on close relationships, including emotion in relationships and the evolutionary dimensions of relationships.

Goodwin, R. (1999). *Personal relationships across cultures.* London: Routledge. Draws together research from across the world to explore how fundamental differences in cultural values influence the ways we form and maintain various kinds of relationships.

Rose, H., & Rose, S. (Eds.). (2000). *Alas, poor Darwin: Arguments against evolutionary psychology*. London: Vintage. A group of scholars from a variety of biological, philosophical and social science backgrounds raise major concerns about the adequacy of genetic accounts of social behaviour, including partner selection.

Wilson, J. (1995). *Love between equals: A philosophical study of love and sexual relationships*. London: Macmillan. An exploration of the concept of love and its origins, with applications to relationships. Topics also include friendship, power and altruism.

Prosocial behaviour

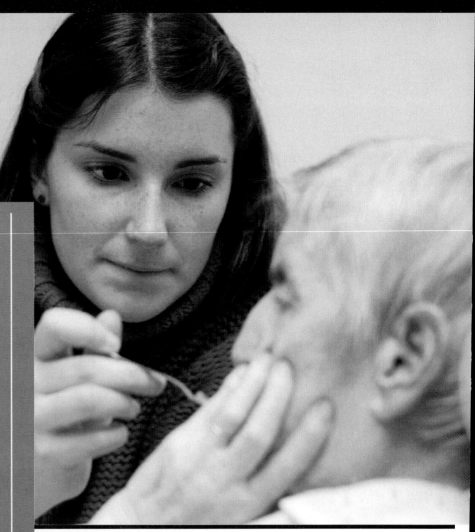

FOCUS QUESTIONS

1. Arthur spots this headline in his local newspaper: 'Horse saves rider!' Interesting, he notes, but that's not altruism . . . or is it?

2. Lily is 13 years old and tall for her age. One afternoon, she confronts a suspicious-looking stranger loitering near a young girl playing in the local park. The stranger takes to his heels when Lily challenges him. It's the talk of the neighbourhood and there's mention of a medal for bravery. On hearing this, your social psychology classmate points out: 'It's just as well that Lily's usual playmates were not around or that little girl might not have received any help.' What could your classmate mean?

3. You turn the corner of a city street to see a man sprawled across the footpath in front of you. What do you do? Probably, it depends. Before you read further in this chapter, make a brief checklist of the things you might want to know more about before deciding on your action. We will ask you to look back at this list later to see how you fared against the experts!

THIS CHAPTER DISCUSSES:

- prosocial behaviour, helping and altruism
- traditional theories of helping: evolutionary social psychology, social learning, empathy and arousal
- recent situational models of helping: cognitive and bystander–calculus
- personal characteristics and prosocial behaviour
- applications: exam cheating, shoplifting, interventions to increase prosocial behaviour
- receiving help: cultural and interracial contexts, social support networks.

Background

In Chapter 10 we saw how people can hate others simply because they are not members of their group. Chapter 11 looked at how groups discriminate and compete destructively against each other and Chapter 12 at the aggressiveness of human beings. We would be forgiven for gloomily concluding that people are basically full of hatred and aggression. It was the philosopher Thomas Hobbes who famously proclaimed in *Leviathan*, his 1651 treatise on the human condition, that life is 'solitary, poor, nasty, brutish and short'.

Chapter 13 gives us some hope for optimism, with its discussion of liking, love and close relationships. In this chapter we continue the uplifting theme by asking why, when and how people decide to help others even if they themselves have to pay the ultimate sacrifice. We try to explain phenomena like soldiers throwing themselves on live grenades to save their comrades, firemen losing their lives while rescuing people from the collapsing World Trade Center towers in New York on September 11, 2001, and people like Oscar Schindler and Miep Gies taking huge personal risks to save Jews in Nazi Europe.

PROSOCIAL BEHAVIOUR, HELPING BEHAVIOUR AND ALTRUISM

Researchers typically refer to acts that benefit another person as prosocial behaviour, helping behaviour or altruistic behaviour. Although people often use these three terms interchangeably, they are actually quite distinct and there are considerable differences in the way they are used in the scientific literature.

Prosocial behaviour as a broad category refers to acts that are positively valued by society—simply contrast it with antisocial behaviour. In our culture, helping others is socially valued. Thus helpful responses are a form of prosocial behaviour. Wispé (1972) defined prosocial behaviour as behaviour that has positive social consequences and contributes to the physical or psychological wellbeing of another person. It can further be defined as voluntary and having the intention of being of benefit to others (Eisenberg, Fabes, Karbon, Murphy, Wosinski, Polazzi et al., 1996).

Behaviours that fall into this category include altruism, aiding, attraction, bystander intervention (helping a stranger in need), charity, cooperation, friendship, helping, rescue, sacrifice, sharing, sympathy and trust. It is important to remember, however, that the determining factor is the perspective of the society being considered. Aggression, for example, is typically considered to be antisocial behaviour but, if it were valued by society (e.g. when fighting an enemy), it could also be considered prosocial behaviour.

Helping behaviour is a term most commonly used to denote a subcategory of prosocial behaviour. It can further be defined as an intentional act that benefits another living being or group. The *intention to benefit* is the key aspect of this definition. If you accidentally drop $10 and someone finds it, you have not performed a helping behaviour. However, if you decided to give $10 to someone who needed it with the intention of aiding them, this would clearly be helping. On the other hand, making a large public donation to a charity for no other reason than to appear generous is not helping behaviour. Some corporate donations to a good cause may even be driven by product image—for example, with the expectation of a long-term increase in profit. Helping may even be antisocial—as with overhelping, which involves giving help to make others look incompetent or inferior (Gilbert & Silvera, 1996).

Altruism is a subcategory of helping behaviour, and refers to an act that is motivated by the desire to benefit another rather than oneself (Batson & Coke, 1981; Macaulay & Berkowitz, 1970). It is difficult to show unequivocally that an act is altruistic, as we would need to eliminate other long-term ulterior motives, such as ingratiation (Rushton & Sorrentino, 1981). Staub (1977) noted that there may also be 'private' rewards associated with acting prosocially, such as feeling good or being virtuous. Even as a subset of prosocial behaviour, altruistic behaviour can sometimes be antisocial. For example, over a three-year period the famous psychologist Henry Murray conducted a series of cruel experiments with students at Harvard. There were painful and negative consequences in both the short and the long term. One of his participants later took the name 'Unabomber' and became a serial killer. Ironically, Murray thought that his experiments would help humanity and contribute to world happiness (Chase, 2000).

THE KITTY GENOVESE MURDER

Social psychological research into helping behaviour began in the late 1950s. As a result of over a thousand articles dealing with altruism and helpfulness (Dovidio, 1984), social psychologists have learned a great deal in the past three or four decades about why we sometimes turn our backs on people requiring assistance, and why we also often go out of our way to help those in need. However, one single event is credited with providing a major impetus to this research—the murder of a young woman called Kitty Genovese in New York in 1964. The report of her murder appalled New York residents (see Box 14.1).

Prosocial behaviour is difficult to explain using traditional theories of human behaviour. Most psychologists, and philosophers before them, have conceptualised human behaviour as *egoistic*. Everything

A SAD NIGHT IN NEW YORK CITY

Late at night in 1964, Kitty Genovese was on her way home from work when a maniac attacked her with a knife. The attack took place in Kew Gardens in the borough of Queens, a respectable neighbourhood. Her screams and struggles drove off the attacker at first but, seeing no one come to the woman's aid, the man attacked again. Once more she escaped, shouting and crying for help. Yet her screams were to no avail and she was soon cornered again. She was stabbed eight more times and then sexually molested. In the half-hour or so that it took for the man to kill Kitty, not one of her neighbours helped her.

About half an hour after the attack began, the local police received a call from an anonymous witness. He reported the attack but would not give his name because he did not want to 'get involved'. The next day, when the police interviewed the area's residents, 38 people openly admitted to hearing the screaming. They had all had time to do something but failed to act. It is perhaps understandable that some of these people had not rushed out into the street for fear that they would also be attacked, but why did they not at least call the police?

This particularly tragic and horrific event received national media attention in America, all asking why none of the neighbours had helped. Not surprisingly, this resulted in heightened interest from social psychologists, including Latané and Darley (1976, p. 309):

> This story became the journalistic sensation of the decade. 'Apathy,' cried the newspapers. 'Indifference,' said the columnists and commentators. 'Moral callousness', 'dehumanisation', 'loss of concern for our fellow man' added preachers, professors and other sermonisers. Movies, television specials, plays and books explored this incident and many like it. Americans became concerned about their lack of concern.

we do is ultimately done to benefit ourselves—self-interest reigns supreme. Prosocial behaviour is unusual because it seems to be independent of reinforcement. It highlights an optimistic and positive view of human beings. How can effort and sacrifice for another person be reinforcing in the usual sense?

A recurring theme in psychology is the **nature–nurture controversy**, the debate over the roles of biological versus learned determinants of behaviour. We see it in relation to aggression in Chapter 12 and it crops up again here in connection with prosocial behaviour.

Why do people help?

The question of why people help others has been addressed from two major perspectives: a biological approach and a social learning approach. This distinction is significant and represents important differences among psychologists generally, as well as social psychologists. A third approach, combining aspects of both biological and social learning approaches, has been developed more recently.

THE BIOLOGICAL APPROACH

The biological position is that, just as humans have innate tendencies to eat and drink, so they have innate tendencies to help others. This may seem strange at first, but such a need to help others is seen as one reason why human beings have been so successful in an evolutionary sense. Recently, there has been a great deal of interest in the possibility that altruism is a trait that has evolutionary survival value (Campbell, 1975; Krebs & Miller, 1985; Wilson, 1978).

This explanation of helping arises primarily from **evolutionary social psychology**. Sociobiologists approach human social behaviour from quite a different perspective from most social psychologists. They view social behaviour in general as an outcome of our human genetic heritage (see Chapters 1, 12, 13). The basic contention is that we may be biologically predisposed to respond with aid to the suffering of others (Barash, 1977). Sociobiology contends that the essence of life is gene survival and that our genes drive us in ways that maximise their chance of survival, so that when we die they live on. Sociobiologists believe there is such a thing as strong altruism, which occurs in the absence of any obvious benefit for the helper. The benefit is actually genetic, because the behaviour is not affected by obvious rewards or punishments. Stories like the one that follows are seen as showing strong altruism caused by certain genetic characteristics.

A small child, Margaret, and her friend, Red, were seated in the back seat of Margaret's parents' car. Suddenly the car burst into flames. Red jumped from the car, but realised Margaret was still inside. He jumped back into the burning vehicle, grabbed Margaret by the jacket and pulled her to safety (Batson, 1983). Should we view these actions as being caused by an altruistic impulse inherited from our ancestors? The answer is still being debated, but the fact that Red was an Irish setter—yes, a dog!—tends to add weight to the argument that there is a genetic aspect to altruism and prosocial behaviour.

Sociobiologists point out that such acts of altruism are commonly observed in a variety of animal species. They consider these behaviours to be not learned but inborn and the same argument applies to humans. For humans, modifications of Darwin's theory of evolution are used to explain why altruism is a positive evolutionary trait. Sociobiologists such as Wilson (1975, 1978) have argued that genes responsible for self-sacrificial behaviour might be selected for over generations because, in the long run, self-sacrifice increases the probability that the species will survive, even though the specific individual perishes (see first focus question).

The idea that we have a biological predisposition to help others is a fascinating one and has generated a great deal of controversy pitting psychologists against sociobiologists (Vine, 1983). In general, social psychologists have not accepted biological explanations of human social behaviour. In more recent years, an evolutionary perspective on altruism has been acknowledged to some extent, but continues to be heavily criticised—sometimes from outside social psychology (see Rose & Rose, 2000). The major criticisms by social psychologists are that no good studies with humans have supported the biological explanation of helping, and that sociobiologists have ignored the social learning theorists' extensive research on the causes of helping in humans. The Kitty Genovese case, for instance, is difficult to explain from a biological perspective.

Buck and Ginsburg (1991) have softened the strong version of an 'altruistic gene' with a proposed 'communicative gene', according to which both animals and humans are disposed to communicate. Communication includes emotional signals (see Chapter 15), the formation of social bonds (see Chapter 13) and the possibility of prosocial behaviour. Such an argument has merit, but is a long way from the main sociobiological point that helping is due to innate drives. Perhaps of more practical value is to explore the social structures that actually promote prosocial behaviour (Darley, 1991).

Burnstein, Crandall and Kitayama (1994) investigated neo-Darwinian decision rules in a set of studies sympathetic to the role of sociobiological factors in altruism. In one study, the researchers asked participants to state how likely they would be to help others in several hypothetical situations (see Figure 14.1). People favoured the sick over the healthy in everyday situations, but favoured the healthy over the sick in life-or-death situations. They gave more weight to kinship in life-or-death situations than in everyday situations. Help is more likely to be given to the poor in everyday situations, and to the wealthy in life-or-death situations. Finally, people were more likely to assist the very young or the very old in everyday situations, but under famine conditions people are more likely to help 10-year-olds or 18-year-olds than infants or older people.

LEARNING TO BE HELPFUL

A stronger explanation of helping is that the display of prosocial behaviour is intricately bound up in the

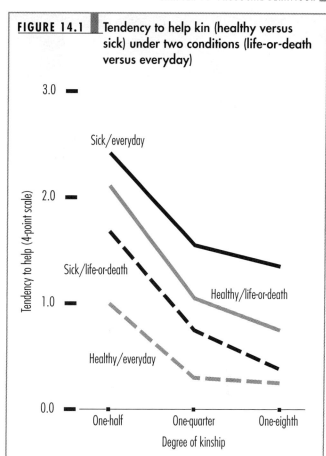

FIGURE 14.1 Tendency to help kin (healthy versus sick) under two conditions (life-or-death versus everyday)

Note: There is an interaction between health, kinship and willingness to help. Participants chose between people who varied in kinship in two conditions: healthy versus sick individuals, and giving help in a situation which was life-or-death versus merely 'everyday'. The participants were more willing to help closer kin than more distant kin. They also preferred to help people who were sick rather than healthy in a mundane situation, but who were healthy rather than sick in a perilous situation.

Source: Burnstein, Crandall, & Kitayama (1994).

socialisation process: it is learned, not inborn. Various theorists have argued that classical conditioning, instrumental conditioning and observational learning all play a role in the development of human prosocial behaviour. The focus of recent research seems to be shifting: interest is being directed more towards the way in which prosocial behaviour is acquired in childhood (Eisenberg & Fabes, 1991; Grusec, 1991). The phenomena of altruism and helping behaviour are being investigated more from within developmental and educational paradigms, and less from traditional social psychological perspectives.

However, traditional research carried out with adults in earlier decades—some of which was experimental—dealt with a variety of conditions that appear to control the display of helping. These are covered later in this chapter. First, we deal with studies of childhood, the period in which so much important learning takes place. It has even been argued that children's responses to

Learning to be prosocial: Young children soon learn the value of cooperative play and helping one another.

distress that they cause or observe in others include sharing, helping and providing comfort, and that these emerge between the ages of 1 and 2 years (Zahn-Waxler, Radke-Yarrow, Wagner, & Chapman, 1992). There are several ways in which these actions can be learned.

Giving instructions

Telling children to be helpful to others does increase their helpfulness (Grusec, Kuczynski, Rushton, & Simutis, 1978). Telling a child what is appropriate behaviour establishes an expectation about the desired behaviour and may later guide the child's behaviour. Simply preaching about being good to others is of doubtful value (Rushton, 1980), unless a fairly strong form is used (Rice & Grusec, 1975). Further, telling children to be generous if the 'preacher' behaves inconsistently is probably useless: 'Do as I say, not as I do' does not work. When an adult acted selfishly but urged children to be generous, the children were actually less generous.

Using reinforcement

When behaviour is rewarded it is more likely to be repeated. When young children are in natural settings and are rewarded by others for offering to help, they are more likely to offer help again later. Similarly, if they are not rewarded they are less likely to offer help again (Grusec, 1991). When children in an experiment are praised or reinforced with bubblegum for their sharing, they will learn to share what they have with other children (Fischer, 1963).

Rushton and Teachman (1978) studied children who saw a second person behaving generously by donating tokens to a third person. Most children tended to imitate by also donating tokens in a later play situation. Next, the second person either rewarded or punished the child

for behaving generously. Both tactics had strong effects on how children behaved, both immediately and after a two-week interval (see Figure 14.2). This study employed not only reinforcement principles but also the effects of watching a model, which leads into the next section.

Exposure to models

People also learn to be helpful by observing another person engaging in a helping act, and by generalising their helping behaviour to other tasks. Consider the young child who, after helping a parent carry some shopping, wants to help in putting it away and other related tasks. Laboratory research has shown that setting an example has a strong effect on helping behaviour. Learning to be helpful through observation is a particular case of **modelling**, a process which we have noted can help to account for the learning of attitudes (Chapter 5) and aggressive behaviour (Chapter 12). Children who win tokens in games, and who then see an adult model donating tokens to help a needy child, are more likely to be generous themselves (Grusec & Skubiski, 1970).

In studies of the effects of viewing prosocial behaviour on television in America, the general finding has been that children's attitudes towards prosocial behaviour are improved (Coates, Pusser, & Goodman, 1976; Rushton, 1979). There was less direct effect on actual prosocial behaviours and less effect over longer time periods. Further, children who exhibit prosocial

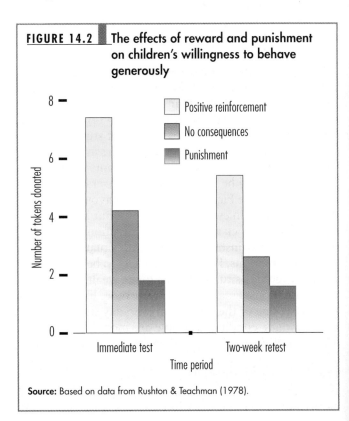

FIGURE 14.2 | **The effects of reward and punishment on children's willingness to behave generously**

Source: Based on data from Rushton & Teachman (1978).

behaviours also tend to be able to delay gratification (Long & Lerner, 1974) and are more popular with their peers (Dekovic & Janssens, 1992). Coping and social competence and prosocial skills are closely linked during a child's development (Eisenberg, Fabes, Karbon, Murphy, Wosinski, Polazzi et al., 1996).

Adults can also be influenced by models who help others. Check the example in Box 14.2.

When a person observes a model and behaves in kind, is this just a matter of mechanical imitation? The work of Bandura (1973) suggests otherwise (see also Chapter 12). According to his **social learning theory**, it is the knowledge of what happens to the model that largely determines whether or not the observer will help. As with direct learning experience, positive outcomes should increase a model's effectiveness in influencing the observer to help, while negative outcomes should decrease the model's effectiveness. Hornstein (1970) conducted an experiment where people saw a model returning a lost wallet. They either appeared pleased to be able to help, displeased at the bother of having to help, or showed no strong reaction. Later, the participant came across another 'lost' wallet. Those who had seen the pleasant consequences helped the most; others who saw the unpleasant consequences helped the least.

Observing the outcomes for another person is called **learning by vicarious experience** (see also Chapter 12); it can increase the rates at which both selfishness and selflessness take place (Midlarsky & Bryan, 1972).

BOX 14.2 The case of the helpful motorist

A model who shows us how to perform a helpful act reminds us that helping is appropriate, increases our confidence in being able to help and gives us information about the consequences of helping others (Rushton, 1980).

In a study of the modelling effect, Bryan and Test (1967) investigated whether a model would influence the number of people who might stop to help a woman change a car tyre. There were two conditions:

1. In the *experimental* condition, motorists first passed a woman whose car had a flat tyre; another car had pulled to the side of the road and the male driver was apparently helping her to change the tyre. This condition provided a helping model for participants who shortly came upon another car with a flat tyre. This time, the woman was alone and needed assistance.
2. In the *control* condition, only the second car and driver were present; there was no model. The results were clear. The motorists who were exposed to a prosocial model were over 50% more likely to help than those in the no-model condition.

Finally, a recent study by Rosenkoetter (1999) emphasised the need for a degree of moral reasoning in children. Children who watched television situation comedies that often included a moral lesson engaged more often in prosocial behaviour than children who did not—provided they understood the principle underlying the lesson.

Attribution processes

The attributions that people make about their own helping or non-helping behaviour and about people who are in need of help can play a role. Even if a person is helpful on a first occasion, in order for helpfulness to continue the idea of helpfulness must be internalised. Attribution theory (see Chapter 3, also self-perception theory in Chapter 4) suggests that this occurs through developing self-attributions of helpfulness. A child who decides 'I am a helpful person' makes an attribution that will guide future behaviour in situations where helping is an option.

Self-attributions of helpfulness are even more powerful than reinforcement for helping behaviour in young children: those who were told they were 'helpful people' donated more marbles to a needy child than those who were reinforced with verbal praise, and this effect persisted over time (Grusec & Redler, 1980). Indeed, children may experience self-criticism and bad feelings when they fail to live up to the standards implied by their attributions (Perry, Perry, Bussey, English, & Arnold, 1980).

Attributions about the person in need are also important and likely to influence whether help is offered. Under some conditions, people do not help and may even blame an innocent victim. According to the **just-world hypothesis** (Lerner & Miller, 1978), people have a need to believe—perhaps for their own security—that the world is a just place where people get what they deserve (see also Chapter 3).

If, for instance, someone has an accident, it may have been deserved (Bulman & Wortman, 1977). Consequently, if some victims deserved their fate (which means that blame is attributed to them), the bystander is less likely to help. Some of the witnesses in the Kitty Genovese case may well have believed that it was her fault for being out so late. This is a familiar response to many crimes. A rape victim, for example, might have 'deserved' what happened because her clothing was tight or revealing. Accepting that the world must necessarily be a just place begins in childhood and is a learned attribution.

Fortunately, evidence of people's undeserved suffering can undermine this belief in a just world and one way to re-establish justice is to compensate or, in this case, help the victim. Miller (1977), however, argued that a necessary precondition of actually helping is the belief that such help will be effective. He distinguished two kinds of need that may convince a would-be helper: (1) need extent, and (2) need persistence. Each of these should operate at a fairly low level if the giving of help is likely to be judged effective.

An example of this line of thinking is a study carried out at Murdoch University in Western Australia by Warren and Walker (1991) which showed that, if the needs of a person in distress can be evaluated, they can be used by others to determine whether giving help is justified. In a field study of more than 2500 adults in Perth, letters were mailed out soliciting donations for a refugee family from Sudan. Covering letters with slightly different wording were used. A higher rate of giving was recorded when the letter highlighted that: (a) the donation was restricted to this particular family rather than being extended to other people in Sudan; and (b) the family's need was only short-term. In short, the case was just and action would be effective.

Normative influences

Often we help others simply because 'something tells us' we should. We ought to help that little old lady cross the street, we ought to return a wallet we found, we ought to help a child in distress. An important influence on the development and maintenance of prosocial behaviour is the existence of a cultural norm. **Norms** provide background social influence on human behaviour (see Chapter 7) and are, of course, quintessentially learned rather than innate. A norm is a standard of action that specifies what behaviour is expected, or 'normal', and what behaviour is abnormal. Norms are social expectations, prescribing proper social behaviour.

Almost every culture has a norm that concern for others is good and that selfishness is bad. The unwritten rule in most societies is that, when the cost is not very great and another person is in need, we should do all we can to help that person. The universality of some type of norm of social responsibility indicates that this standard has functional value and that it operates to facilitate social life. One way of accounting for helping others, therefore, is to say that it is *normative*. There are social rewards for behaving in accord with the norm and sanctions for violating the norm. Sanctions may range from mild disapproval to incarceration or worse, depending on the threat posed to the existing social order.

Two specific norms have been proposed as a basis for altruism:

1. The *reciprocity norm*—we should help those who help us. Gouldner (1960) argued that this norm, which is also referred to as the **reciprocity principle**, is as universal as the incest taboo. Nevertheless, the extent of our obligation to reciprocate varies according to circumstance. We feel deeply indebted when someone freely makes a big sacrifice for us, but much less so if the sacrifice is smaller and expected (Tesser, Gatewood, & Driver, 1968; Wilke & Lanzetta, 1970). Additionally, in terms of the concept of social exchange (see Chapter 13), people might give help only in return for help given in the past or anticipated in the future.

2. The **social responsibility norm**—help should be freely given to those in need, without regard to future exchanges (Berkowitz, 1972b; Schwartz, 1975). Members of a community are often willing to help needy people, even when they remain anonymous and have no expectation of any social reward (Berkowitz, 1972b). Charitable donations given to callers at the front door are an example. In practice, people usually apply this norm selectively, to those in need through no fault of their own. Consistent with the just-world hypothesis, the social responsibility norm dictates that we should give to people in line with what they deserve. If they are victims of a natural disaster, by all means help but, if they are drunk and injure themselves falling over, they should suffer what they deserve. The application of the norm depends on the attribution of causes of the need for help. Ironically, it can run counter to a norm that we should not interfere in other people's lives.

Teger (1970) has suggested that a norm of helping is often endorsed verbally but is really an ideal rather than an actual behaviour; even then, it is not a very compelling force. As an ideal norm, the prosocial ethic is an expression of people paying lip service to being responsible citizens. The question, then, is when and why do people actually adhere to such social norms? Schwartz (1977) has identified certain conditions that determine whether or not a person is sensitive to internalised norms or feelings of moral obligation. This, however, brings us to the area of situational influences on prosocial behaviour, which is covered later in this chapter.

WHY DO WE ACT PROSOCIALLY?

Batson (1994; Batson, van Lange, Ahmad, & Lishner, 2003) frames this question in terms of motivation—what motivates helping? Treating motivation as a goal-directed force, Batson distinguishes between instrumental goals, ultimate goals and unintended consequences. An *instrumental goal* is sought as a means to reach some other goal. An *ultimate goal* is sought as an end in itself. An *unintended consequence* is a result of acting to reach a goal but is not itself sought as a goal.

These distinctions make it clear that the debate over why people help is a debate over whether benefiting others is an instrumental goal on the way to a self-interested ultimate goal or an ultimate goal in its own right with the self-benefits being unintended consequences.

Batson postulates four ultimate goals (motives) for benefiting other people:

- *Egoism* (self-benefit)—prosocial acts contribute to the welfare of the actor. We may help others in order to secure material, social and self-rewards; and to escape material, social and self-punishments.

- *Altruism* (benefiting another individual)—prosocial acts contribute to the welfare of other people. Acting altruistically does not imply the need for someone to reciprocate. This kind of prosocial motivation is held in high esteem in many cultures.

- *Collectivism* (benefiting a group)—prosocial acts contribute to the welfare of a social group—for example, one's family, ethnic group or country (see Chapter 16). Of course, actions that benefit one's ingroup may come at a cost to an outgroup (see Chapter 11).

- *Principalism* (upholding a moral rule)—prosocial acts follow from a moral principle, such as 'the greatest good for the greatest number'. The philosopher Kant's categorical imperative, 'Act only on that maxim whereby thou canst at the same time will that it should become a universal law', is another example. Even though the correlation between moral reasoning and prosocial behaviour is not powerful, studies tend to support the view that these two processes are at least correlated (Eisenberg, 1991; Underwood & Moore, 1982).

EMPATHY AND AROUSAL

As with other social behaviours, both genetic and environmental factors seem to be involved in helping others and there have been attempts to offer a compromise between sociobiological and social learning approaches in explaining altruism. For example, Vine (1983) and Hoffman (1981) argued that a motive to help has evolved through natural selection, but that it is also sensitive to environmental influences. Biological mechanisms may predispose a person to act, but how that person ultimately responds is affected by past experiences and immediate circumstances.

It is likely that a state of arousal is necessary before we act prosocially and that **empathy** then motivates us to help others (Gaertner & Dovidio, 1977; Hoffman, 1981; Hornblow, 1980). Empathy is an emotional response to someone else's distress, a reaction to witnessing a disturbing event. There is considerable evidence that both adults and children respond empathically to the distress of another person, suggesting that it is unpleasant to watch someone else suffer. Even infants of one or two days of age can respond to the distress of another infant (Sagi & Hoffman, 1976; Simner, 1971). However, when we actually help, are we merely trying to reduce the unpleasant feelings that others' distress or pain arouses in us? The extra ingredient suggested is empathy, or the ability to identify with another's experiences, particularly their feelings (Krebs, 1975).

A major model of prosocial behaviour by Piliavin, Piliavin and Rodin (1975) proposed that people will intervene in an emergency because they find it unpleasantly arousing and they seek relief (see reviews by Batson & Oleson, 1991; Dovidio, Piliavin, Gaertner, Schroeder, & Clark, 1991). As a result, 'altruism' is a misnomer because it is really motivated by self-interest, or egoism, as we have already noted. A person helps out of a desire to deal with an unpleasant emotion. Helping is an act that rapidly and completely reduces the unpleasant feelings. Piliavin's approach is dealt with in detail later.

One factor mediating empathy is *similarity*: we are more likely to feel empathy towards someone we perceive as being similar to ourselves. Krebs (1975) has demonstrated that people show a physiological response when they see someone like themselves being shocked; the greater the similarity the greater the arousal, and also the greater the later altruism to the victim.

If it is true that prosocial behaviour is based only on self-interest, is there such a thing as an altruist? Batson and colleagues (Batson, Duncan, Ackerman, Buckley, & Birch, 1981) argued that an act is truly altruistic only if people seek to help even when they will no longer be troubled by observing the suffering of another person (e.g. turning back to help after passing a stranded motorist). This approach could offer a different perspective to the Genovese case, with the bystanders feeling disturbed but not sufficiently so to act: perhaps they could not identify with the victim.

Oswald (1996) has argued that empathy requires us to demonstrate *perspective-taking*—being able to see the position of another person from that person's point of view. For example, Maner, Luce, Neuberg, Cialdini, Brown and Sagarin (2002) used a perspective-taking manipulation to increase empathy and found this was indeed associated with increased helping—however, they were sceptical that helping was the same as altruism.

Oswald (1996) also distinguished between cognitive perspective-taking (understanding what the other person is thinking) and affective perspective-taking (experiencing what the other person is feeling). In a study of empathy and helping, Oswald cued participants to take either a cognitive or an affective perspective and found that those engaged in cognitive perspective-taking showed higher empathic concern and were willing to give more help. However, being cued to take either perspective was more effective than not being cued at all (in a control group). Both kinds of perspective-taking led to more empathy than that shown by the control group. In a later study, however, Oswald (2002) found the opposite—affective perspective-taking increased helping more than cognitive perspective-taking.

Batson, Early and Salvarani (1997) made a further

Empathy and perspective taking: These shoes weren't meant for walking! 'Super-model' Naomi Campbell takes a tumble at a Paris fashion show. How much do you 'feel her pain'?

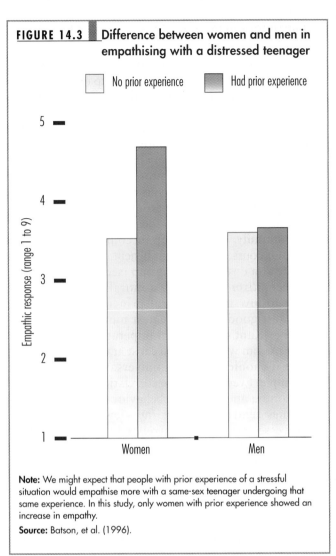

FIGURE 14.3 Difference between women and men in empathising with a distressed teenager

Note: We might expect that people with prior experience of a stressful situation would empathise more with a same-sex teenager undergoing that same experience. In this study, only women with prior experience showed an increase in empathy.

Source: Batson, et al. (1996).

distinction concerning perspective-taking: between understanding and experiencing how another person feels and how you would feel in the same situation. Different kinds of empathy lead to different kinds of motivations to help. Their study showed that actively imagining how another feels produces empathy (which leads to altruistic motivation), while actively imagining how *you* would feel produces both empathy and self-oriented distress (which leads to a mixture of altruistic and egoistic motivations).

Perhaps people who have experienced something stressful will empathise more with a person who is in a similar situation. For example, those who were once homeless or have been extremely ill may empathise more with a person in the same condition. Are women more empathic than men?

To test this, Batson and colleagues (Batson, Sympson, Hindman, Decruz, Todd, Weeks et al., 1996) had participants read a same-sex adolescent's description of a stressful life event (e.g. being the object of ridicule and teasing because of acne, or being betrayed and rejected). They found that women reported more empathy with the same-sex teenager when they had had similar experiences during their adolescence. However, men with a similar experience showed no more empathy than those without a similar experience (see Figure 14.3). Batson and colleagues accounted for this sex difference by suggesting that women are socialised to value interdependence and are more likely to be other-oriented, while men are socialised to value independence and are more likely to be self-oriented.

Situational models of helping

We noted above that social psychologists were curious and concerned about the lack of involvement of witnesses or bystanders during the Kitty Genovese murder. As a result, there was a frenzy of research to identify when people will help in an emergency. More recently, the question has been broadened to ask: when will people help in non-emergencies by performing such deeds as giving money, donating blood or contributing their time and effort? The focus here is on the situational factors that affect **bystander intervention** in real-life situations in the real world, rather than on the origins of helping behaviour or how it is learned. Furthermore, there has been an attempt to develop models of the helping process, largely from a cognitive viewpoint. The initial emphasis was on helping in emergencies, but this has now widened to prosocial behaviour in general.

Perhaps the most influential and thoroughly studied factor that affects prosocial behaviour and responding is whether the potential helper is alone or in the company of others. What is now known is that a lone bystander is more likely to help than any of several bystanders, a phenomenon known as the **bystander effect** (see second focus question).

A number of general models attempt to explain situational influences on bystander intervention. We consider two, the first by Latané and Darley (1970) and the second by Piliavin and colleagues (Piliavin, Dovidio, Gaertner, & Clark, 1981).

LATANÉ AND DARLEY'S COGNITIVE MODEL

Stemming directly from the wide public discussion and concern about the Genovese case, Latané and Darley began a program of research (Darley & Latané, 1968), now considered a classic in its field. Surely, these researchers asked, empathy for another's suffering or, at the very least, a sense of civic responsibility should lead to an intervention in a situation of danger; furthermore, where several bystanders are present, there should be a correspondingly greater probability that someone will help?

Before looking at this theory, consider first the elements of an **emergency situation**, which:

- may involve danger, for person or property;
- is an unusual event, rarely encountered by the ordinary person;
- can differ widely in nature, from a bank on fire to a pedestrian being mugged;
- is not foreseen, so that prior planning of how to cope is improbable;
- requires instant action, so that leisurely consideration of options is not feasible.

We note here a similarity between the nature of an emergency and that of the autokinetic phenomenon used by Sherif (e.g. Sherif, 1935) in his study of the way in which social norms develop (see Chapters 7 and 8). Both involve uncertainty, ambiguity and a lack of structure in terms of a proper basis for judgment or action. Consequently, there should be a greater probability in each case that the individual will look to others for guidance on how to think and act. So a core prediction about an emergency is that people will react quite differently according to whether others are present or absent.

Latané and Darley noted that it would be easy simply to label the failure to help a victim in an emergency as apathy—an uncaring response to the problems of others. They reasoned, however, that the apparent lack of concern of the witnesses in the Genovese case could conceal other processes. An early finding was that failure to help occurred more often when the size of the group of witnesses increased. Latané and Darley's cognitive model of bystander intervention proposes that whether a person helps depends on the outcomes of a series of decisions. At any point along this path a decision could be made that would terminate helping behaviour.

The steps in this model are described in Box 14.3 and the decision process is illustrated in Figure 14.4. A series of experiments is outlined below to illustrate how this model works.

'Where there's smoke there's fire'

In an illustrative experiment (Latané & Darley, 1970), male students were invited to an interview to discuss some of the problems involved in life at a large university. While they were filling out a preliminary questionnaire, smoke began to pour into the room from a wall vent. This continued for six minutes until the room was full of smoke. Participants were alone, or with two other participants they did not know, or with two confederates who ignored the smoke. The issue was what the participant did and how long he took. The authors hypothesised that people in such situations look to others around them to decide what to do. The results supported this. Participants who were alone were more likely to report the smoke than those who were with strangers. While 75% of the participants who were alone took positive action, only 38% of the two-stranger groups intervened. Participants in the presence of two passive confederates, who had been instructed to ignore the smoke, were even less likely to report the situation, taking action only 10% of the time!

The curious case of the solitary bystander: Your best chance of getting help is if there is only one bystander.

A CLASSIC IN SOCIAL PSYCHOLOGY

BOX 14.3 Steps in Latané and Darley's cognitive model

DECIDING WHETHER TO HELP

1. Does the bystander even notice an event where helping may be required, such as an accident?

2. How is the event interpreted? We are most likely to define a situation as an emergency, and most likely to help, when we believe that the victim's condition is serious and is about to deteriorate rapidly. Shotland and Huston (1979) showed in a field experiment that people were more likely to help in emergencies (e.g. someone needs an insulin shot for diabetes) than in non-emergencies (e.g. needing some allergy medicine).

   Verbal distress cues (e.g. screaming) are particularly effective and increase the likelihood of bystander intervention (Clark & Word, 1972, 1974; Gaertner & Dovidio, 1977): the act of screaming can lead to receiving help 75% or more of the time. These studies suggest that bystander apathy is markedly reduced once people interpret a situation as an emergency.

3. Does the bystander accept personal responsibility for helping? Sometimes, a person witnessing an emergency knows that there are other onlookers but cannot see their reactions. This was clearly the case in the Genovese incident. Sometimes, the decision to assume responsibility is determined by how competent the bystander feels in the particular situation. For both steps 2 and 3, the influence of other people is clearly a determining factor.

4. What does the bystander decide to do?

5. Is help given? If we doubt whether the situation is an emergency, or we do not know what to do if it is, the behaviour of others around us can influence how we respond.

   These steps are illustrated in Figure 14.4.

Source: Based on Darley & Latané (1968).

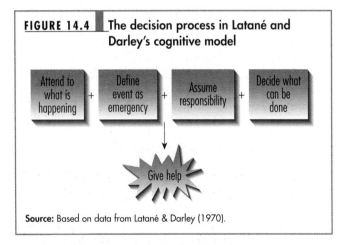

FIGURE 14.4 The decision process in Latané and Darley's cognitive model

Source: Based on data from Latané & Darley (1970).

Latané and Darley's interpretation was that the presence of others can inhibit people from responding to an emergency: the more people, the slower the response. Even worse, many of the people who did not respond were persuaded by the passive behaviour of others that the situation was not an emergency. Some later reported that they believed there was no danger from the smoke. In a real emergency this could easily have proved fatal.

'A lady in distress'

Latané and Rodin (1969) replicated these results, extending the argument to situations where others might be in danger. Male participants were alone or in pairs filling out a questionnaire and heard a woman in another room struggle to open a filing cabinet. They then heard a loud crash followed by a cry of pain and moans and groans.

Participants who were alone helped 70% of the time but, when in pairs, only 40% of the time. Participants who were with a passive confederate, a manipulation that suggested the situation was not critical, helped only 7% of the time. One further refinement was added and it was found that pairs of friends helped more often— 70% of the time.

'He's having a fit'

Must bystanders be physically present to reduce the probability of a person giving help? Darley and Latané (1968) devised an experiment where students could communicate with each other only via microphones while in separate cubicles. They were led to believe that the group consisted of two people (self and a victim), four people or six people. The 'victim' told the others over the intercom system that he was an epileptic. Later, he was heard to choke and gasp, apparently having a seizure, and then became quiet. The important question was whether the number of presumed bystanders that might help influenced how long the participant took to help.

The results showed that the more bystanders people thought there were, the less likely they were to help. Before the end of the seizure, 85% of the participants who were alone helped, but only 62% of the participants who believed that two other people were present helped, and 31% of those who thought there were four others present. Within six minutes after the event began, the respective figures were 100%, 81% and 62%.

Processes contributing to bystander apathy

Let's take stock. To respond to an emergency, people must stop whatever they are doing and engage in some unusual, unexpected behaviour. Lone bystanders will usually do just that, often without hesitation. However, when several bystanders are present there is a clear tendency to hold back and perhaps not to respond at all. Multiply this effect across each individual and a whole group of onlookers may fail to intervene. What is it about a group that can produce this effect?

As the data from their own and others' experiments were gathered, Latané and Darley (1976) puzzled over which of several possible social processes could underlie the reluctance of groups to help a victim. Three major explanations were available. In distinguishing between them, we can use the analogy of the nature of the communication channel open to the onlookers. Three questions can be asked:

1. Is the individual aware that others are present?
2. Can the individual actually see or hear the others, and be aware of how they are reacting?
3. Can these others monitor the behaviour of the individual?

Each of the following processes is distinctive in terms of how these questions are answered:

- *Diffusion of responsibility.* Think back to the phenomenon of social loafing (discussed in Chapter 8), in which a person who is part of a group often tends to offload responsibility for action to others. In the case of an emergency, the presence of other onlookers provides the opportunity to transfer the responsibility for acting, or not acting, onto them. The communication channel does not imply that the individual can be seen by the others, or can see them. It is necessary only that they be available, somewhere, for action. People who are alone are most likely to help a victim because they believe they carry the entire responsibility for action. If they do not act, nobody else will. Ironically, the presence of just one other witness allows **diffusion of responsibility** to operate among all present.
- *Audience inhibition.* Other onlookers can make a person self-conscious about an intended action; people do not want to appear foolish by overreacting. In the context of prosocial behaviour, this process is sometimes referred to as a **fear of social blunders**. Have you felt a dread of being laughed at

for misunderstanding little crises involving others? What if it is not as it seems? What if someone is playing a joke? Am I on *Candid Camera*? The communication channel implies that the others can see or hear the individual, but it is not necessary that they be seen.
- *Social influence.* Other onlookers provide a model for action. If they are passive and unworried, the situation may seem less serious. The communication channel implies that the individual can see the others, but not vice versa.

The three-in-one experiment

We can now consider the most complicated of Latané and Darley's experiments, designed specifically to detect the operation of each of the three processes just outlined. By the use of TV monitors and cameras, participants were induced to believe that they were in one of four conditions with respect to other onlookers. They could: (1) see and be seen; (2) see, but not be seen; (3) not see, but be seen; or (4) neither see nor be seen. This complexity was necessary to allow for the consequences of sequentially adding social influence and audience inhibition effects to that of diffusion of responsibility.

We should note that diffusion of responsibility must always be involved if a bystander is, or is thought to be, present at the moment of the emergency. However, the additive effect of another process can be assessed and then compared with the effect of diffusion acting on its own. You will get a good idea of how this was done by studying Box 14.4.

The results measured in seconds the amount of time that elapsed before the participant moved to help the prostrate experimenter. Figure 14.5 shows the cumulative number of participants who intervened as time went by. The analysis also distinguishes between the 'alone' condition and three sets of bystander conditions. The investigators collapsed the data for two of these (diffusion of responsibility plus either audience inhibition or social influence), as they did not differ significantly and both involved one-way communication.

The results in Figure 14.5 show that the probability of help being offered decreases as the amount of communicated information increases. Simple diffusion of responsibility (no communication) reduces helping behaviour and this declines further when either social influence or audience inhibition is added (one-way communication). When all three processes are allowed to operate (two-way communication), the least help is given.

Limits to these effects

Bystanders who are strangers to each other inhibit helping even more because communication between

---

BOX 14.4   The conditions in the three-in-one experiment

A SHOCKING EXPERIENCE

The participants were students who had agreed to take part in a study of 'repression'. Their supposed task was to rate whether the way in which a target person responded to verbal stimuli indicated whether they had received an electric shock or not. When certain words were presented, the target person would receive a shock from the experimenter. The participant would watch this on closed-circuit television in another room and judge when shocks had been delivered by studying the target person's overall behaviour. The experiment was carried out at night in a deserted building at Princeton University. Participants were to work in pairs (except in the 'alone' condition), although in fact the second rater in each case was a confederate of the experimenter.

Each pair of participants was initially taken to a control room, where there was an antiquated shock generator. Commenting on it, the experimenter said that the parts were from army surplus and were not reliable. In front of the generator was a chair, with a TV camera pointing at it. The experimenter then noted that the target person was late and that time could be saved by filling in a background questionnaire. The participants were ushered to their individual cubicles, each of which contained two TV monitors and a camera. Monitor #1 was operating and showed the control room they had just left, with the shock generator in clear view. The experimenter apologised for the presence of monitor #2 and the camera, saying they belonged to another, absent staff member and could not be touched. Both items were operating. This extra, supposedly superfluous, equipment provided the basis for several experimental conditions. Monitor #2 could show the neighbour in the next cubicle and the camera could show the participant to the neighbour. There were five conditions:

1. *Alone*. This is a baseline condition in which no other person is present with the real participant. The camera in the real participant's room is pointing at the ceiling and monitor #2 shows a shot of the ceiling of the second cubicle but no sign of anybody else.
2. *Diffusion of responsibility*. As in the remaining conditions, there are two people, but no communication. Monitor #2 shows only the ceiling of the other cubicle (where its camera is pointing). The camera in the real participant's room is pointing at the ceiling. It is different from the 'alone' condition, however, as the participant knows that a bystander is present.
3. *Diffusion plus social influence*. The participant sees the other's response, but not vice versa. One camera is trained on someone, in this case the bystander. The confederate can be seen working on a questionnaire on monitor #2.
4. *Diffusion plus audience inhibition*. The other sees the participant's response, but not vice versa. One camera is trained on someone, in this case the participant. Although the bystander cannot be seen, presumably the participant can.
5. *Diffusion plus social influence plus audience inhibition*. The two people see each other. Both cameras are trained on them and they can be seen on the respective monitors.

The emergency was created when the experimenter left the participant in the cubicle and returned to the control room to adjust the shock generator, visible in monitor #1. On the screen, the experimenter could be seen to pick up some wires.

They must not have been the right wires, because the experimenter screamed, jumped in the air, threw himself against the wall, and fell to the floor out of camera range with his feet sticking up. About 15 seconds later he began to moan softly, and he continued until help was received or for about six minutes. (Latané & Darley, 1976, p. 327)

What will the real participant do in each condition? See the accompanying results in Figure 14.5.

---

them is slower. When bystanders are known to each other, there is much less inhibition of prosocial behaviour than in a group of strangers (Latané & Rodin, 1969; Rutkowski, Gruder, & Romer, 1983). Gottlieb and Carver (1980) showed, however, that even among strangers inhibition is reduced if they know there will be an opportunity to interact later and possibly explain their actions. Overall, the bystander effect is strongest when the bystanders are anonymous strangers who do not expect to meet again, which could have been the situation in the Genovese case. Christy and Voigt (1994) found that bystander apathy is reduced if the victim is an acquaintance, friend or relative, or a child being abused in a public place.

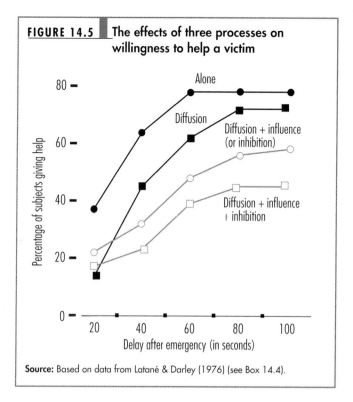

FIGURE 14.5 The effects of three processes on willingness to help a victim

Source: Based on data from Latané & Darley (1976) (see Box 14.4).

PILIAVIN'S BYSTANDER–CALCULUS MODEL

Whereas Latané and Darley's approach is cognitive, the **bystander–calculus model** is a mixture of cognitive and physiological processes. According to Piliavin and colleagues (Piliavin, Dovidio, Gaertner, & Clark, 1981), when bystanders perceive someone in trouble they work their way through three stages before they respond. This process involves a set of calculations, hence the notion of calculus. At first, bystanders become physiologically aroused by the sight of another's distress. Next, this arousal is labelled as an emotion. Finally, the consequences of helping or not are evaluated. Let's look at these three steps.

Physiological arousal

When we see another person in distress, our first reaction is physiological, an empathic response. However, Piliavin and colleagues showed that there is often a decline in physiological responses when someone first sees an emergency: for example, heart rate drops. This is an *orienting reaction*, designed to allow us to figure out what is going on. It is quickly followed by a dramatic rise in physiological reactions, a *defence reaction*, which prepares an observer to act. This pattern of arousal is typical when people encounter a strong stimulus; in the case of an emergency involving another person it is an empathic response, as it is caused by something that happens to someone else.

The greater the arousal in emergencies, the greater the chance a bystander will help (Piliavin et al.).

Gaertner and Dovidio (1977) found a strong correlation between the speed of participants' responses and their heart rate, when they helped a woman who had been hurt by falling chairs.

The strength of a bystander's empathic physiological reaction is also influenced by non-social factors. For example, as the severity and clarity of the victim's plight increases, so does the strength of a bystander's physiological arousal (Geer & Jarmecky, 1973).

Labelling the arousal

Being aroused is one thing, but feeling a specific emotion (fear, anger, love) is another. Generally, arousal does not automatically produce specific emotions; people's cognitions or thoughts about the arousal play a critical role in determining the nature of the emotions they feel (Schachter & Singer, 1962). When another person is distressed, the situational cues trigger two distinct sets of responses: personal distress and empathic concern (Batson & Coke, 1981; Davis, 1980; Piliavin et al., 1981). Personal distress is an experience of anxiety when someone else is upset. Empathic concern is a response to another person in which the bystander feels compassion.

According to Piliavin, a bystander often labels physiological arousal as *personal distress*. If you believe that someone is hurt, you feel aroused—that is, tense and anxious. You label this personal distress: 'I feel upset because of this'. This is more likely to occur if you do not have a close personal relationship with the victim, or if the situation involves a highly arousing emergency. Piliavin proposed that helping others reduces a bystander's personal distress (see also Gaertner & Dovidio, 1977).

This unflattering idea, that helping is motivated by the self-serving needs of the bystander and not because it serves the needs of the victim, has been disputed by others. Batson and his associates (Batson & Coke, 1981; Batson, Duncan, Ackerman, Buckley, & Birch, 1981; Toi & Batson, 1982) have suggested that, when bystanders believe they are similar to a victim and identify with that person, they experience **empathic concern**. The difference here is that helping is motivated by concern for the other, not by a desire to reduce our own distress. Helping that is motivated by empathic concern could, therefore, accurately be called altruistic.

Evaluating the consequences

Piliavin went on to argue that bystanders evaluate the consequences of acting before helping a victim. They weigh the costs of either direct helping or indirect helping. They then choose the action that will reduce their personal distress at the lowest cost (note the strong social exchange flavour here; see Chapter 13). The two main costs of helping are time and effort: the greater

Empathic concern: Helping someone in need is a matter of compassion, not simply an act that reduces one's own sense of distress.

(1980) of more than 50 studies dealing with the effect of group size on helping concluded that the higher the number of bystanders, the less likely anyone will intervene to help. A Piliavin interpretation is that the presence of others reduces the cost of not helping, a subtly different perspective on the concept of diffusion of responsibility.

The personal costs of not helping are many and varied, such as public censure or self-blame. Certain characteristics of the person in distress also affect the costs of not helping: for instance, the greater the victim's need for help, the greater the costs of not helping (Piliavin, Dovidio, Gaertner, & Clark, 1981). If you believe a victim might die if you do not help, the personal costs are likely to be high. If a tramp in the street asked you for money to buy alcohol, the personal costs of refusing might not be high; but if the request was for money for food or medicine, the costs might be quite high.

Other things being equal, the more similar the victim is to the bystander, the more likely the bystander is to help (Gross, Wallston, & Piliavin, 1975; Krebs, 1975; Pandey & Griffitt, 1974). Similarity causes greater physiological arousal in bystanders and thus greater empathy costs of not helping. Similar victims may also be friends, for whom the costs of not helping would probably be high. Recall the sociobiological position that preservation of our genes is the basis of protecting our kin. The Piliavin model would simply note the high level of similarity between bystander and victim, thereby increasing the cost of not helping to an excruciating level. Think of the agony if you did not try to enter a blazing house to rescue your own child.

Piliavin and colleagues (1981) used the reward–cost matrix shown in Figure 14.6 and Box 14.5 to describe how these costs affect bystanders' responses in an emergency.

these costs, the less likely a bystander will help (Batson, Cochran, Biederman, Blosser, Ryan, & Vogt, 1978; Darley & Batson, 1973). So, in the Genovese case, the fear of being attacked may have reduced the likelihood of the bystanders helping (McGovern, 1976; Midlarsky & Midlarsky, 1973).

Now, not helping can also involve costs. Piliavin distinguished between **empathy costs of not helping** and **personal costs of not helping**. A critical intervening variable is the relationship between the bystander and the victim. We have already seen that empathic concern was one motive for helping a distressed person; conversely, not helping when you feel empathic concern results in empathy costs. These consist of continued unpleasant feelings (tension, anxiety) in response to the other's plight. Thus, the clarity of the emergency, its severity, and the closeness of the bystander to the victim will increase the costs of not helping. Anything that increases the impact of the victim's state on the bystander will increase the empathy costs if help is not given.

You will remember that Latané and Darley (1970) noted that helping was reduced when more people witnessed an emergency. A review by Latané and Nida

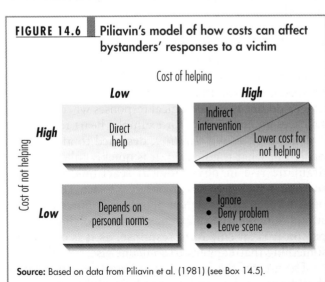

FIGURE 14.6 | **Piliavin's model of how costs can affect bystanders' responses to a victim**

Source: Based on data from Piliavin et al. (1981) (see Box 14.5).

BOX 14.5 Differences in costs in Piliavin's model

THE COSTS OF HELPING

- *Lower right cell*—the costs of helping are high and the costs of not helping are low. For example, suppose 50 people witness a knife fight between two drunks outside a pub at closing time. Fear of being injured would be an obvious high possible cost of intervening. The costs of not helping are low because (1) you can diffuse responsibility for not helping across all the others present; and (2) the victims are not deserving of help as they brought it on themselves. In such instances, bystanders are likely to leave the scene or to ignore a victim's plight.

- *Lower left cell*—both types of cost are low. Personal norms are likely to guide whether help is offered. Such a situation might be helping a market researcher on the street with a brief survey.

- *Upper left cell*—the cost of helping is low and the cost of not helping is high. For example, most people would intervene directly by giving aid to a child accident victim lying on the side of the road after a car crash.

- *Upper right cell*—both kinds of cost are high. Here, bystanders may engage in indirect intervention (e.g. calling the police, ambulance or fire engine). This action could help the victim but involves a low cost. If such indirect intervention is not possible (e.g. no telephone is at hand), bystanders may resolve their dilemma by lowering the costs of not helping—by, for example, deciding that the situation does not really require their help (reinterpretation) or that the victim deserves what is happening (derogation).

Let's take an experimental example (Piliavin, Piliavin, & Rodin, 1975). Each participant saw a person fall over and apparently require help. In a high-cost condition this person had an extensive birthmark and in a low-cost condition did not. You might think this a little strange, but it seems that many people find physical disfigurement aversive. There was also a second bystander. For half the participants the other bystander was dressed like a medical intern, and dressed ordinarily for the other half.

In the low-cost (no birthmark) condition, people helped equally, regardless of how the other bystander was dressed. In the high-cost (birthmark) condition, it depended on dress: with the ordinary person 72% helped, but with an intern present only 48% helped. The Piliavin interpretation is that, in the high-cost condition, the first bystander could more easily refer responsibility for helping to the intern, thereby lowering the costs of not helping.

With regard to the Genovese case, the bystander–calculus model suggests that, although the onlookers would have been aroused and felt personal distress and empathic concern, the empathy costs and personal costs were not sufficient. Personal costs, in particular, may have deterred people from intervening. What if they got killed? In terms of the matrix in Figure 14.6, the costs of helping directly would be high; the costs of not helping could be either high or low, depending on how people interpreted the situation: for example, was it (at least initially) just a marital dispute?

In this case, the outcome is contained in the two right-hand cells of the matrix. People either ignored the problem or denied it existed, or lowered the costs of not helping (perhaps help was not really needed; maybe someone else has done something by now). If someone had called the police, it would have been an instance of indirect intervention.

You can now see some of the complications involved in asking why people did not help in the Genovese murder. Most of the research on situational influences on helping among adults has focused on the bystander effect. Check the various points made by comparing Latané and Darley's step-by-step decision approach in Figure 14.4 with Piliavin's reward–cost matrix approach in Figure 14.6.

Lest we conclude this section with the feeling that Piliavin's model is unacceptably mechanistic, consider a view expressed by Piliavin and Charng (1990, p. 27):

There appears to be a 'paradigm' shift away from [an] earlier position that behaviour that appears to be altruistic must, under close scrutiny, be revealed as reflecting egoistic motives. Rather, theory and data now being advanced are more compatible with the view that true altruism—acting with the goal of benefiting another—does exist and is part of human nature.

Experiencing empathy can make people uncomfortable—feeling empathic may have motivational consequences. How often do you actively avoid thinking about people in need? Do you sometimes change the television channel when disturbing images of starving children appear? Shaw, Batson and Todd (1994) argued that, in addition to other mechanisms (outlined above), people often fail to act prosocially because they are actively engaged in avoiding empathy.

The person in the equation

With so many situational factors affecting prosocial behaviour, we might wonder if aspects of the person have much effect. We can re-establish some balance by noting the psychological maxim that 'behaviour is a product of the individual and the environment'.

Are there personal characteristics that are relatively independent of the situation? Research has concentrated on two areas: transitory psychological states and personality characteristics. The former includes passing moods and feelings, which all of us may experience; the latter implies relatively permanent attributes.

TRANSITORY PSYCHOLOGICAL STATES

We have all experienced days when things seem to go perfectly and other days when things go totally wrong, and we know that this can affect how we interact with other people. Prosocial research has shown that people who feel good are much more likely to help someone in need than are people who feel bad.

Good moods

A typical experimental approach is to get participants to believe that they have succeeded or failed at a task they are asked to perform. It then transpires that those who believe they have been successful are more helpful than those who believe they have failed or those who have received no feedback. Isen (1970) found that teachers who were more successful on a task were more likely to contribute later to a school fundraising drive. Those who had done well, in fact, donated seven times as much as the others! So, such momentary feelings as success on a relatively innocuous task can dramatically affect prosocial behaviour.

Isen suggested that doing well creates a 'warm glow of success', which makes people more likely to help. (You can compare this effect with the *reinforcement–affect model* of interpersonal liking in Chapter 13.) When people feel good, they are less preoccupied with themselves and are more sensitive to the needs and problems of others. Being in a good mood means people are more likely to focus on positive things (Isen, Clark, & Schwartz, 1976), to have a more optimistic outlook on life and to see the world in pleasant ways (Isen & Stalker, 1982).

People who hear good news on the radio show greater attraction towards strangers and greater willingness to help, compared with people who hear bad news (Holloway, Tucker, & Hornstein, 1977); people are in better moods and are more helpful on sunny, temperate days than on overcast, cold days (Cunningham, 1979). Even experiences such as reading aloud statements expressing elation, or recalling pleasant events from childhood, can increase the rate of helping. The evidence consistently demonstrates that good moods produce helpful behaviour under a variety of circumstances.

Bad moods

In contrast to people who are in good moods, people who feel bad, sad or depressed are internally focused.

They concentrate on themselves, their problems and worries (Berkowitz, 1970), are less concerned with the welfare of others and help others less (Weyant, 1978). Berkowitz (1972b) showed that self-concern lowered the rate and amount of helping among students awaiting the outcome of an important exam. In a similar experiment, Darley and Batson (1973) led seminary students who were due to give a speech to think they were quite late, just in time, or early. They then had the opportunity to help a man who had apparently collapsed in an alley. The percentages that helped were: quite late, 10%; just in time, 45%; and early, 63%.

However, not all bad moods produce the effect of lowered helping. Isen, Horn and Rosenhan (1973) have shown that some kinds of self-concern may cause people to be more helpful. Guilt is one such feeling (see Box 14.6).

Overall, the research on mood and similar psychological states is complex (see Chapter 2), and indicates that experiencing success and feeling good generally lead to prosocial helping behaviour, but that bad moods may or may not lead to helping, depending on whether they are moderated by self-concern. Nevertheless, a common feature derived from providing help is that the helper ends up 'feeling good' (Williamson & Clark, 1989) and experiences, at least for a while, a more positive self-evaluation.

ATTRIBUTES OF THE PERSON

Special interpersonal relationships can increase the feeling of personal responsibility a bystander in an emergency will experience. It is increased, for example, if there is a special bond with or commitment to the victim (Geer & Jarmecky, 1973; Moriarty, 1975; Tilker, 1970) or if the victim is especially dependent on the bystander (Berkowitz, 1978).

Are there other intrapersonal factors that can make people more helpful, even temporarily? Are there factors that make some people consistently more helpful than others? Famous figures such as Florence Nightingale, Mahatma Gandhi, Albert Schweitzer and Mother Teresa come to mind. This area of research has been described as the attempt to identify or profile the 'Good Samaritan'. In reaction to earlier work, Huston and Korte (1976) argued that there had been an overemphasis on situational factors in helping and that personal factors had been neglected. Let's ask whether their confidence in individual-level predictors has been justified.

Demographic variables

Several studies (see Huston & Korte, 1976) have attempted to identify why some individuals are likely to be helpers, with inconclusive results. Latané and Darley (1970) found that fairly obvious demographic variables, such as father's occupation and number of siblings, were

The case of the guilty helper

'OH DEAR! YOU'VE SMASHED MY CAMERA.'

People who have accidentally broken something or injured someone show increases in helping behaviour. When participants believed they had ruined an experiment, cheated on a test, broken expensive equipment or inflicted pain on another, they were much more likely to help the person against whom they had transgressed (Cialdini, Darby, & Vincent, 1973; Katz, Glass, Lucido, & Farber, 1979).

Regan, Williams and Sparling (1972) led a group of female participants to believe they had broken an expensive camera. Later, when they had the chance to help another woman who had dropped some groceries, 50% of the 'guilty' participants intervened to help, whereas only 15% of a control group did so.

One explanation offered to account for the guilty helper is the image-reparation hypothesis: people want to make amends. If you have hurt someone, you can restore self-esteem by making it up. However, the complication is that the guilty party will actually help anyone in need, not just the person towards whom they feel guilty. It is difficult to see how their self-esteem can be threatened in this way.

According to Cialdini's negative relief state model (Cialdini et al., 1973; Cialdini & Kenrick, 1976; Cialdini, Baumann, & Kenrick, 1981), hurting another person, or even seeing this happen, causes a bystander to experience a negative affect state. This motivates them to do something to relieve this feeling. We come to learn that helping can alleviate negative moods. Consequently, people are motivated to *feel* good rather than *look* good. If so, this process is better described as hedonism than altruism, as it is motivated by self-interest.

This view gains support from the finding that people who have inflicted, or who have witnessed, harm or pain, and then receive an unexpected monetary reward or social approval immediately afterwards, are less helpful than participants who are left in a bad mood (Cialdini et al., 1973; McMillen, 1971).

not correlated with helping behaviour. However, there was the intriguing suggestion that size of home town might be connected. People from small-town backgrounds were more likely to help than those from larger cities, a finding replicated by Gelfand, Hartmann, Walder and Page (1973).

Amato (1983) at James Cook University in Townsville studied size of population in a direct fashion. He investigated people's willingness to help in 55 Australian cities and towns, focusing on acts such as picking up fallen envelopes, giving a donation to charity, stating

one's favourite colour in response to a student survey, correcting inaccurate directions that were overheard, and helping a stranger who had hurt a leg and collapsed onto the footpath. With the exception of picking up the fallen envelope, the results showed that, as population size rose (i.e. in the larger towns and cities), acts of helping decreased.

The results for four of the helping measures are shown in Figure 14.7. Best-fitting regression lines for each set of data points are shown. You can see that there is a consistent trend downwards for helping a stranger as population levels rise.

Personality variables

Latané and Darley (1970) reported that none of several personality test measures predicted helping behaviour. Such measures included authoritarianism, alienation, trustworthiness, Machiavellianism (the tendency to manipulate others) and need for approval.

On the other hand, positive relationships between helping behaviour have been noted with: the belief that our fate lies within our control; mature moral judgment; need for social approval or self-esteem; and the tendency to take responsibility for others' welfare (Eisenberg-Berg, 1979; Schwartz & Clausen, 1970; Staub, 1974). None of this evidence, however, is strong enough to distinguish clearly the Good Samaritans from the rest of humanity and there is some doubt whether the attempt

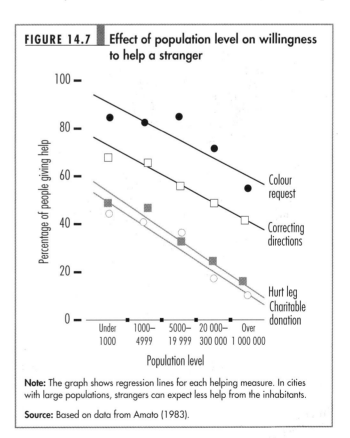

FIGURE 14.7 Effect of population level on willingness to help a stranger

Percentage of people giving help (y-axis): 0, 20, 40, 60, 80, 100

Population level (x-axis): Under 1000, 1000–4999, 5000–19 999, 20 000–300 000, Over 1 000 000

Colour request
Correcting directions
Hurt leg
Charitable donation

Note: The graph shows regression lines for each helping measure. In cities with large populations, strangers can expect less help from the inhabitants.

Source: Based on data from Amato (1983).

is meaningful (Bar-Tal, 1976; Schwartz, 1977) or even useful. Even the strongest reported correlates of helping are weak predictors.

Gergen, Gergen and Meter (1972) summarised this situation by concluding that the characteristics of the situation, and of the request for help, can interact in complex ways with personality characteristics. An individual's personality and background are bound to interact with a situation and influence how the individual interprets and responds to it.

Competence: 'Have skills, will help'

While it is clear that many situational cues and characteristics influence whether prosocial behaviour occurs, at another level the reactions of all bystanders are those of individuals. Each person must interpret, process and react to the situation. As noted above, the bystander effect is diminished if the bystanders are friends or know each other well. The interpretation of the situation is critical: anything that makes the situation less ambiguous decreases the bystander effect (Clark & Word, 1972).

An important individual factor that affects the likelihood of helping is the feeling of competence to deal with the emergency (Korte, 1971)—an awareness that 'I know what I'm doing'. As costs are determinants of helping, people who feel competent to deal with the potential costs of helping are more likely to intervene than people who feel unable to handle the situation. (As discussed here, competence is examined in a context of spontaneous helping. For a review of non-spontaneous helping, such as volunteering for neighbourhood duties, see Clary & Snyder, 1991.)

Feelings of competence for a specific task have been clearly shown to increase helping.

- People who were told they had a high tolerance for electric shock were more willing to help others move electrically charged objects (Midlarsky & Midlarsky, 1976).
- People who were told they were good at handling rats were more likely to help recapture a possibly dangerous laboratory rat (Schwartz & David, 1976).
- There is some evidence that the competence effect may even generalise beyond being specifically linked to the nature of the prosocial act. Kazdin and Bryan (1971) found that participants who were led to believe they had done well on either a creativity task or a health examination were later more willing to donate blood.

Certain 'packages' of skills should be perceived as being relevant to many emergencies. In a study of reactions to a stranger who was bleeding, people with first-aid training intervened more often than those who were untrained (Shotland & Heinold, 1985).

Pantin and Carver (1982) similarly 'created' competence by showing female students a series of films on first aid and emergencies. Three weeks later they provided an opportunity to help a confederate who was apparently choking. The bystander effect was reduced by having previously seen the films. This simple educational experience reduced the inhibiting consequence of the presence of others. It could be argued that these results might depend on a transitory state of feeling skilled. Pantin and Carver, however, reported that the increase in helping persisted over time.

The role that skills can play should be easily tested by comparing the degree of help offered by professionals with that offered by novices. An experiment by Cramer, McMaster, Bartell and Dragna (1988) provided such evidence. Their participants were female students, of whom half were actually registered nurses (high competence) and half general-course students (low competence). In the main condition, each participant waited with a non-helping confederate. The nurses were more

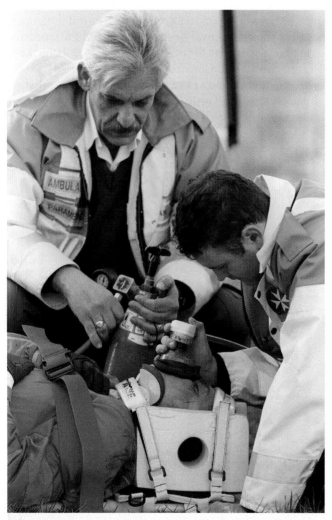

Competence in an emergency: 'Trust us—we know what we're doing.' People with the appropriate knowledge, skills and equipment are much more likely to help someone in difficulty.

likely than the general students to help a workman, seen earlier, who had apparently fallen off a ladder in an adjoining corridor (a rigged accident, with prerecorded moans). In responding to a post-experimental questionnaire, the nurses specified that they felt they had the skills to help.

To sum up how competence relates to helping: a situational role that highlights the fact that a person possesses clearly relevant skills implies that they should be used. The self-perception is: 'I know what to do, so I have the responsibility to act'. Competence may be situation-specific, but there is the tantalising possibility that it may not only last over time but also generalise to non-related situations.

Leaders and followers

A variation on the theme of competence is the instance of acting as a leader. We might think that a leader is, by definition, more generally competent than followers and more likely to initiate all kinds of actions, including helping in an emergency. The skills component of leadership could probably be used to account for some helping outcomes. Even so, a study by Baumeister and his colleagues (Baumeister, Chesner, Senders, & Tice, 1988) specified an additional feature of the leadership role (see also Chapter 9) that goes beyond the 'Have skills, will help' explanation: being a leader acts as a cue to gener-

alised responsibility. In an emergency situation, Baumeister hypothesised, the leader does not experience the same degree of diffusion of responsibility as ordinary group members. Read how they tested for this in Box 14.7.

Male–female interactions

Are men meant to be gallant? It seems that men are more likely to help women than vice versa (Latané & Dabbs, 1975).

Typically, the research paradigm has involved helping a motorist in distress (flat tyre, stalled car); another is offering a ride to a hitchhiker. When the person in need of such help is female, passing cars are much more likely to stop than for a man or for a male–female pair (Pomazal & Clore, 1973; Snyder, Grether, & Keller, 1974; West, Whitney, & Schnedler, 1975). Those who stop are typically young men driving alone.

It is interesting that the male tendency to be more helpful to women stands up in a **meta-analysis** of research findings, despite a baseline difference of women showing more empathy generally than men (Eagly & Crowley, 1986).

A question is whether men might be motivated by sexual attraction to help women in trouble. Benson, Karabenick and Lerner (1976) and West and Brown (1975) found that those who are physically attractive are more likely to get help, suggesting that sexual cues

---

BOX 14.7 Acting like a leader counteracts diffusion of responsibility

'WHO'S IN CHARGE AROUND HERE?'

A major requirement of effective leadership is to guide decision-making for a group (see Chapter 9) and, in an emergency, to provide control and direction for action. In an experiment by Baumeister, Chesner, Senders, & Tice, (1988), 32 male and female students (seven others were dropped because they suspected a deception) were led to believe they had been allocated to four-person groups, in which one member was thought to be randomly assigned to act as leader. The students were told that their task was to decide which survivors of a nuclear war should be allowed to join the group in its bomb shelter. The assistants could make recommendations, but their designated leader would make the final decision.

Participants were actually tested individually, half as leaders and half as followers, and group discussion was simulated using tape recordings over an intercommunication system. At a critical point, each participant was exposed to a simulated emergency, when the recorded voice of a male group member faltered and said, 'Somebody come help me, I'm choking!' He then had a bout of coughing and went silent.

The experimenter met those who came out of the test room to help, telling them there was no problem. All were later debriefed.

Those designated as leaders were much more likely to help than assistants: as high as 80% (12 of 15) leaders helped, but only 35% (6 of 17) followers did so.

Now, the leaders in this study were randomly allocated to their role, so the outcome cannot be explained in terms of their merely having a set of personal skills. In Baumeister's view, acting as a leader brings with it a generalised responsibility, which:

- goes beyond the immediate requirement of the group task to involve other external events;
- provides a buffer against the usual process of diffusion of responsibility to which ordinary members are prone, and which can mediate the seeming indifference to helping a victim.

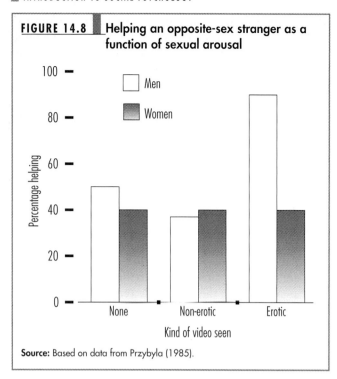

FIGURE 14.8 Helping an opposite-sex stranger as a function of sexual arousal

Percentage helping

Kind of video seen: None, Non-erotic, Erotic

Men / Women

Source: Based on data from Przybyla (1985).

may be important. Przybyla (1985) clarified the motivation involved by manipulating people's sexual arousal. Male and female students watched an erotic (sexually explicit) videotape, a non-erotic videotape or none at all. When leaving the laboratory, the participants passed either a male or a female confederate who accidentally knocked over a stack of papers.

The results are shown in Figure 14.8. Almost all the male participants who had seen an erotic tape were motivated to help a female stranger. They also spent more time helping a woman (a relaxed six minutes) than they spent helping a fellow man (about 30 seconds)!

Przybyla noted that both men and women reported degrees of arousal in response to viewing the sexually explicit tape. In the case of men, the more aroused the man felt, the longer he spent helping a woman, an effect not extended to another man. In contrast, the more aroused women spent less time helping anyone. Thus, it seems that male altruism towards women is confounded with a desire to be romantic. On the other hand, women are less likely to initiate such interactions with strangers (especially men), due perhaps to socialisation experiences (see third focus question).

Applied contexts

HELPING TO PREVENT CRIME

An interesting line of research has focused on the causes and prevention of petty and non-violent crime, such as

property theft and shoplifting, and of misdemeanours, such as classroom cheating. Preventing crime can involve a class of prosocial behaviours. The development of neighbourhood-watch schemes and accompanying media campaigns are examples of the promotion of prosocial behaviour. People are most likely to engage in non-violent crime if the benefits are high and the costs are low. Fraud (Lockard, Kirkevold, & Kalk, 1980) and tax evasion (Hassett, 1981) are often perceived this way by offenders.

A riskier crime is property theft, which is statistically more common among younger men. As individuals mature, their assessment of the costs and benefits change. Older people are more likely to deceive a customer or lie about a product or service than actually steal something. Research on property theft, however, illustrates two important phenomena related to prosocial behaviour: responsibility and commitment.

People are most likely to be helpful to others if they have a feeling of *responsibility* for providing assistance. We saw earlier, for example, that people feel responsible if they are the only witness to a crime or accident, or if they have been trained in dealing with emergencies. Feeling responsible for providing aid increases the likelihood of prosocial behaviour.

Prior commitment is a specific form of responsibility that can be experimentally manipulated to induce a prosocial act. Consider the study by Moriarty (1975) in Box 14.8.

Cheating, stealing, lying and other unethical acts have also been of interest to social psychologists. Massive American surveys (Gallup, 1978; Hassett, 1981) revealed that about two-thirds of the population had cheated in school at least once. In a study of over 24 000 people, Hassett found that surprisingly high numbers of people had broken various rules of ethical conduct. About 25% had cheated on an expense account, 40% had driven while drunk and 65% had stolen office supplies from their employers. Understanding the types of situations that can induce such behaviours, or the types of people most likely to commit such acts, could give clues to how to reduce their occurrence and even to replace them with prosocial alternatives.

Shoplifting

Stealing goods from shops is a crime that has been of interest to psychologists investigating prosocial behaviour (Gelfand, Hartmann, Walder, & Page, 1973). Bickman and Rosenbaum (1977) showed that most people would report a thief to the management if reminded by an experimental confederate. In contrast, it is clear that posters or other mass media messages have not been effective in reducing shoplifting. It is possible that impersonal reminders like these influence attitudes about shoplifting and about reporting thieves, but do

BOX 14.8 Preventing theft as a consequence of prior commitment

BEING RESPONSIBLE: THE COMMITTED MINDER

In a series of real-life encounters, Moriarty chose individuals who were sitting alone on a crowded beach and then sat next to them with a radio and blanket. Shortly afterwards, he talked to the participants and either:

- simply asked for a match;

or, to create commitment,

- asked them to watch his things while he went for a short walk.

All participants agreed to the second request, thereby committing themselves to be *responsible bystanders*. Then a confederate came along, picked up the radio and walked away. Of participants who were only asked for a match, just 20% did anything about this, compared with 95% for those specifically asked to be responsible. These participants even ran after and grabbed the confederate until the experimenter returned.

The powerful effects of such prior commitments have been demonstrated in other ways: for example, watching a stranger's suitcase in a laundrette (Moriarty, 1975), watching another student's books in a library (Shaffer, Rogel, & Hendrick, 1975) and watching a stranger's books in a classroom (Austin, 1979). The results were similar, with a high likelihood of prosocial interventions following explicit prior commitment.

BOX 14.9 Cheating in the good old days

AN EARLY STUDY OF DISPOSITIONAL FEATURES ASSOCIATED WITH EXAM CHEATING

As far back as 1933 MacKinnon investigated the role of personality in cheating. In this experiment, participants were required to solve a series of problems, knowing that the answers were in books next to them. They were allowed to look at only a few examples from this book and then had to work out the rest themselves, not knowing that they were being observed. The question was who would cheat and look up more answers than was permitted.

Participants were divided into cheaters and non-cheaters. Cheaters tended to express anger towards the task more than non-cheaters; non-cheaters blamed themselves for not solving the problems more than cheaters did; non-cheaters tended to verbalise the problems and develop other strategies to help to solve them; cheaters were more destructive or aggressive (kicking the table leg or pounding their fists on the table); non-cheaters behaved more nervously and fidgeted more.

Several weeks later, the students were asked if they had cheated. Those who had not readily said so; those who had cheated either denied it or admitted it but said they felt no guilt about it. Further research showed that such guilt feelings were a critical variable in determining whether a person cheated or not: 84% of the non-cheaters said they would feel guilty if they cheated. Those who did not cheat reported the highest degree of guilt, whereas feeling guilty was relatively rare among those who had cheated.

This early example of research assumed that cheating was dispositional—a personality characteristic of a 'cheater'. Since this research, many other psychologists have considered that cheating is influenced more by situational variables and that research should concentrate on these factors, especially if methods to deter it are to be developed. However, guilt has been identified in a number of ways as leading to prosocial behaviour.

Source: MacKinnon (1933).

---

not change the behaviour itself (Bickman & Green, 1977).

A specific program was developed to reduce shoplifting by informing people about its nature and costs, in both financial and human terms. The most effective method for increasing prosocial interventions in shoplifting was found to be a lecture stressing how and why to report this crime and the reasons that bystanders are sometimes inhibited from taking action (Klentz & Beaman, 1981).

Exam cheating

Are there personality correlates? Cheating in examinations has been well researched by social psychologists. An early study of the character and disposition of cheaters was carried out by MacKinnon (1933; see Box 14.9).

More recent studies have also pursued links between cheating and personality. The following links have been reported. Students who cheat tend to be low in the ability to delay gratification (Yates & Mischel, 1979), high in sociopathic tendencies (Lueger, 1980), high in need for approval (Milham, 1974), low in interpersonal trust (Rotter, 1980), high in chronic self-destructive tendencies (Kelley, Byrne, Przybyla, Eberly, Eberly, Greenlinger et al., 1985), low in adherence to the work ethic and in the desire to perform tasks industriously (Eisenberger & Shank, 1985) and high in the belief that transgressions are not automatically punished (Karniol, 1982). Persistent cheaters have been found to be emotionally and morally immature individuals who are not committed to hard work, who are unable to give up

Cheating: Given the opportunity would you take a peek at your neighbour's exam script?

immediate pleasures in order to obtain future goals, and who believe that they are likely to get away with breaking the rules.

Despite these findings, correlations are typically modest, so that situational factors are thought to be more important.

An area of some interest has been the influence of *arousal* or, more specifically, the feelings of excitement or the thrills that occur when people take a chance and cheat, at least when there is little chance of being caught (Scitovsky, 1980).

Lueger (1980) took a different line by suggesting that any type of arousal is distracting and makes us less able to regulate our behaviour. In his study, participants saw either an arousing film or a relaxing one and then had the chance to cheat while undergoing an intelligence test. In the relaxed condition 43% cheated, but 70% in the aroused condition cheated. It is possible that the build-up of arousal accounts for the finding that warning students about to sit an exam of the penalties for being caught cheating can paradoxically increase cheating (Heisler, 1974).

The object of much of this research has been to find a way to *discourage cheating*. A traditional reaction has been to increase the severity of punishments available. The efficacy of a punitive approach, however, can be diminished by the arousal that accompanies its publicity, and by the fact that only about one in five self-reported cheaters are ever caught (Gallup, 1978). Consider again the early research results shown in Box 14.9. These suggest an alternative: would something that increases feelings of guilt lead to a decrease in cheating? Most people agree that cheating is wrong and those who do cheat disapprove as strongly as those who do not (Hughes, 1981). Some high schools have introduced programs to raise the ethical awareness of their students

and, hence, to promote prosocial behaviour in a variety of ways (see Britell, 1981; Dienstbier, Kahle, Willis, & Tunnell, 1980; Hechinger, 1980).

Dienstbier and colleagues (1980) reported some success with a program that compared externally oriented guilt with internally oriented guilt. Cheating was lower in the internally oriented guilt condition, which suggests that the problem is not a lack of morality and ethical standards—rather how to make ethical standards salient. This also reflects an emphasis on situational rather than dispositional causes of cheating and is a fairly optimistic view of human beings.

In summary, it is clear that a large number of people readily confess to a wide variety of unethical or illegal behaviours at one time or another. Non-violent crimes such as fraud, tax evasion and insurance fraud are prevalent in our society (as well as violent crime, of course), and social psychologists have become interested in the causes of such behaviour in an attempt to promote prosocial behaviour campaigns such as neighbourhood-watch schemes. Shoplifting is another area of interest.

Research has concentrated on cheating in school students in an attempt to understand the situational and dispositional causes of such behaviours. Such research provides an interesting and potentially useful application of social psychology to real-life problems, especially in terms of devising advertising campaigns and interventions to increase prosocial behaviour in our communities.

Receiving help

We have based this chapter around the psychology of the 'helper': when will we help, why do we hesitate, how can we improve the rate of helping in our community? There is another perspective that we should consider. Does the recipient always want help? Just as we have noted that there can be psychological costs in helping (Piliavin, Dovidio, Gaertner, & Clark, 1981), is it possible to expand this argument to the person who is seen to need help?

Nadler (1986, 1991) believes that it can. He notes that Western society encourages people to be self-reliant and to achieve as individuals. To ask for help, then, confronts people with a dilemma: the benefits of being aided are tempered by the costs of appearing dependent on others. In a study in Israel, Nadler (1986) introduced a cultural dimension to this issue by comparing the help-seeking tendencies of kibbutz dwellers with city dwellers. People in kibbutzim are socialised to cherish collectivism and sought help on a difficult task only when they thought the performance of their group as a whole was to be compared with other groups. Israeli city people, however, are typically Western and individualistic and sought help only when they thought their individual performance was to be compared with other individuals. (For details of this research see Figure 16.3 and Box 16.3 in Chapter 16.)

AN INTERETHNIC CONTEXT

In Chapter 13 we noted that a reinforcement approach to the study of interpersonal attraction investigated how liking for our workmates can be affected by whether help is received when the individual has trouble doing a job properly (Cook & Pelfrey, 1985). A variable in this study compared own-ethnicity with mixed-ethnicity work groups. The participants were 84 White male airforce trainees, selected for their negative orientation towards African Americans; they came from geographic regions in the United States where racial prejudice was relatively high. Each group consisted of an experimental participant and two confederates and their task was to run a simulated freight business. The group interacted over five days. Each member had specific duties as shipping officer, equipment officer or communications officer and needed to collaborate with the others to run the business successfully. The task was structured so that the unfortunate participant (as victim) experienced task overload in trying to deal with his duties as shipping officer.

The confederate who was the communications officer 'noticed' the participant's difficulties and reacted as a 'helper' in one of three ways: (1) voluntarily offering help; (2) giving help, but only after being instructed to do so by the experimenter; (3) making no effort to help. In an additional condition, the helper was either White or African American. At the end of five days, the participants reported privately how much they liked their workmates.

There was a strong, and not surprising, effect for participants to like most those confederates who volunteered help. Even helpers who were instructed to act were liked more than those who did not help at all. The most interesting outcome, however, was that this applied equally to African American helpers and White helpers. This was particularly interesting in view of the high level of racial prejudice in the White participants in this study.

A HEALTH SUPPORT NETWORK

The frequent use of the term 'victim' in this chapter reaches out to another field, the function of a **social support network**. We look at just one example from the extensive literature, a study by Dakof and Taylor (1990) dealing with cancer patients. A victimising event such as cancer has profound effects on how significant others (family, friends, workmates, medical staff) might interact with a patient: an initial reaction of aversion can give way to a facade projecting good cheer. Not surprisingly, the victim can feel stigmatised and unwanted.

Dakof and Taylor argued that the reactions of members of a support network are moderated by the nature of the relationship that people have with the victim and, in a wider sense, by the cultural constraints imposed on social interactions. In most nuclear families, those close to a cancer victim are more likely to be overprotective than withdrawing. Their study concentrated on how a victim views the nature of help and how this interacts with its source.

Their participants were 55 cancer patients, mostly Whites, in Los Angeles. In terms of the source of help,

A social support network: Surrounding yourself with others who care can help you cope with life's trials and tribulations.

patients generally valued helpful acts by intimate providers (family, friends) that related to the victim's self-esteem and emotional support, such as concern, empathy and affection. In contrast, helpful acts by medical staff and other cancer patients were viewed as informational and tangible support, such as prognosis and technical or medical care. When either group stepped out of the appropriate role, the act became misguided and unhelpful. In the case of nursing staff, helpful acts tended to be closer to those appreciated among people intimate to the victim.

Summary

- Prosocial behaviour is a broad category that refers to all acts positively valued by society, and includes helping and altruistic behaviours. Helping behaviour refers to intentional acts designed to benefit another person. Altruistic behaviour refers to behaviours motivated by the desire to benefit another with no expectation of personal gain or reward. It is difficult to identify purely altruistic behaviour clearly, because motives or rewards may be entirely internal.
- The Kitty Genovese murder stimulated and heavily influenced the entire field of prosocial behaviour in human beings, and research into bystander intervention specifically.
- Two major developmental approaches have attempted to explain the origin and nature of prosocial behaviour in humans: a biological approach, known as evolutionary social psychology, and a social learning theory approach. Most social psychologists reject too heavy an emphasis on the biological approach. A third, integrative approach attempts to combine aspects of both approaches, focusing on arousal and empathy.
- Attempts to understand situational effects on bystander intervention have focused on explaining the bystander effect—that is, that there is less help given, or it takes longer, when a crowd of bystanders is present than when a single bystander witnesses an emergency. Two major models have been developed, one by Latané and Darley and the other by Piliavin and colleagues.
- Individual characteristics influencing prosocial behaviour have tended to be overlooked, with greater emphasis placed on situational determinants. However, such factors as mood, background, personality characteristics and competence can have an influence in certain circumstances. For example, people who feel guilty about transgressing show an increased desire to help others in need.
- Other strands of research on prosocial behaviour have been developed that are less influenced by the Genovese case and are good examples of applied social psychology. These include research into male–female differences in helping behaviour (especially with the 'stranded motorist' paradigm), research into preventing or reporting theft or shoplifting, and research into examination cheating.

LINKS

YOU HAVE READ ABOUT:	WHICH LINKS TO:
Evolutionary social psychology and altruism	biological theories of aggression (12)
Empathy and arousal	emotions as a form of communication (15)
Learning to help	modelling and attitude learning (5); modelling and aggression (12)
Cognitive model of bystander intervention	role of cognition in social behaviour (2)
Personal and situational factors affecting prosocial behaviour	personality, the situation and leadership (9); personal and situational factors affecting aggression (12)
Collectivism and the tendency to seek help	nature of values as broad constructs guiding behaviour (5); collectivism across cultures (16)

Key terms

altruism *(p. 359)*
bystander–calculus model *(p. 371)*
bystander effect *(p. 367)*
bystander intervention *(p. 367)*
diffusion of responsibility *(p. 369)*
emergency situation *(p. 367)*
empathic concern *(p. 371)*
empathy *(p. 365)*
empathy costs of not helping
  (p. 372)

evolutionary social psychology
  (p. 360)
fear of social blunders *(p. 369)*
helping behaviour *(p. 359)*
just-world hypothesis *(p. 363)*
learning by vicarious experience
  (p. 363)
meta-analysis *(p. 377)*
modelling *(p. 362)*
nature–nurture controversy *(p. 360)*

norms *(p. 364)*
personal costs of not helping
  (p. 372)
prior commitment *(p. 378)*
prosocial behaviour *(p. 359)*
reciprocity principle *(p. 364)*
social learning theory *(p. 363)*
social responsibility norm *(p. 364)*
social support network *(p. 381)*

FURTHER READING

Batson, C. D. (1998). Altruism and prosocial behaviour. In D. T. Gilbert, S. T. Fiske, & G. Lindzey (Eds.), *The handbook of social psychology* (4th ed., Vol. 2, pp. 282–316.) New York: McGraw-Hill. Authoritative overview of the field of prosocial behaviour, in the most recent edition of the classic handbook—a primary source for theory and research.

Batson, C. D., van Lange, P. A. M., Ahmad, N., & Lishner, D. A. (2003). Altruism and helping behaviour. In M. A. Hogg & J. Cooper (Eds.), *The Sage handbook of social psychology* (pp. 279–295). London: Sage. Comprehensive, up-to-date and easily accessible overview of research on altruism and prosocial behaviour.

Clark, M. S. (Ed.). (1991). *Prosocial behavior.* Newbury Park, CA: Sage. A comprehensive coverage by the major theorists who have helped to build the social psychology of helping behaviour.

Eisenberg, N., & Mussen, P.H. (1989). *The roots of prosocial behaviour in children.* Cambridge, UK: Cambridge University Press. A concise introduction to the methods and main concepts used in this field, with an emphasis on the socialisation process and the connections of prosocial behaviour with the development of moral reasoning.

Rose, H., & Rose, S. (Eds.). (2000). *Alas, poor Darwin: Arguments against evolutionary psychology.* London: Vintage. A group of scholars from a variety of biological, philosophical and social science backgrounds raise major concerns about the adequacy of genetic accounts of social behaviour, including altruism.

Spacapan, S., & Oskamp, S. (Eds.). (1992). *Helping and being helped.* Newbury Park, CA: Sage. The contributors deal with a wide range of real-life altruisms, including spouse support of stroke patients, family support for people with Alzheimer's disease, and kidney donors.

1. Kamalini lived most of her early life in Sri Lanka. When she shops for rice in Brisbane, she checks for colour, smell and whether it is free from grit, and she can put names to at least seven varieties. Are her senses more acute than yours? Is her vocabulary richer than yours?

2. En Li worked as a shop assistant in Shanghai after leaving school at 14 years of age, and arrived in Edinburgh at 18 with just a smattering of English. What support factors might help her master English?

3. James has been in trouble at school, but his mother is still not sure what the problem is. 'When I see him,' she thinks, 'I will ask him to look me in the eye and tell the truth.' Does she have a good chance of spotting any lies?

THIS CHAPTER DISCUSSES:

- the social basis of communication
- the meaning of language, its species-specificity, and the ways in which language determines or affects thought
- paralinguistic cues and speech style
- intergroup perspectives on language: ethnolinguistic identity theory, speech accommodation
- social factors affecting second-language learning
- age and sex differences in speech style
- the nature and function of non-verbal communication
- impression management and deception
- conversation and discourse
- computer-mediated communication.

Communication

Communication is the essence of social interaction. Indeed, it is almost impossible to conceive of a social interaction that is free of communication. People constantly communicate information, intentionally or unintentionally, about their perceptions, thoughts, feelings, intentions and identity. They do this through direct contact, various electronic or written media, and with words, expressions, gestures or signs. Communication is social in a variety of ways:

- It involves interrelationships among people.
- It requires that people acquire a shared understanding of what particular sounds, words, signs and gestures mean.
- It is the means by which people influence others and are, in turn, influenced by them.

Communication requires a sender, a message, a receiver and a channel of communication. However, any two-way communicative event is enormously complex: the sender becomes the receiver, and vice versa, and there may be multiple, sometimes contradictory, messages communicated simultaneously via an array of different verbal and non-verbal channels.

Communication has also been considered by some social psychologists to be the missing dimension from social cognition. Social cognition (i.e. socially influenced/determined thought; Chapter 2) has generally focused on individual information processing and storage and has underemphasised the important role of communication in structuring cognition (Forgas, 1981; Markus & Zajonc, 1985; Zajonc, 1989).

The study of communication is potentially an enormous undertaking that can draw on a wide range of disciplines, such as psychology, social psychology, sociology, linguistics, sociolinguistics, philosophy and literary criticism. Social psychologists have tended broadly to distinguish between the study of language and the study of non-verbal communication. Recently, some social psychologists have focused on discourse. The structure of this chapter reflects the existence of these three overlapping areas of research. Scholars find that a full understanding of communication needs to incorporate verbal and non-verbal communication (Cappella & Palmer, 1993; Gallois, Giles, Jones, Cargile, & Ota, 1995). We also touch briefly on computer-mediated communication (Hollingshead, 2001).

Language

Spoken languages are based on rule-governed structuring of meaningless sounds (**phonemes**) into basic units of meaning (**morphemes**), which are further structured by morphological rules into words and by syntactic rules into sentences. The meanings of words, sentences and entire utterances are determined by semantic rules. Together, all these rules represent grammar. It is because shared knowledge of morphological, syntactic and semantic rules permits the generation and comprehension of almost limitless meaningful utterances that **language** is such a powerful communication medium.

Meaning can be communicated by language at a number of levels. These range from a simple **utterance** (a sound made by one person to another), to a **locution** (words placed in sequence: e.g. 'It is hot in this room'), to an **illocution** (the locution and the context in which it is made: 'It is hot in this room' may be a statement, or a criticism of the institution for not providing cooled rooms, or a request to turn on the air conditioner, or a plea to move to another room) (Austin, 1962).

Mastery of language also requires knowledge of the cultural rules for what it is appropriate to say, when, where, how and to whom. This has spawned the field of sociolinguistics (Fishman, 1972; see also Forgas, 1985b) and, more recently, an emphasis in social psychology on the study of discourse as the basic unit of analysis (Edwards & Potter, 1992; Potter & Wetherell, 1987; see also below).

Finally, Searle (1979) identifies five sorts of meanings that people can intentionally use language to communicate:

1. to say how something is;
2. to get someone to do something;
3. to express feelings and attitudes;
4. to make a commitment;
5. to accomplish something directly.

Language is a distinctly human form of communication (see Box 15.2 on page 400). Although young apes have been taught to combine basic signs in order to communicate meaningfully (Gardner & Gardner, 1971; Patterson, 1978), even the most precocious ape cannot match the complexity of hierarchical language structure used by a normal 3-year-old child (Limber, 1977). The species-specificity of language has caused some theorists to believe that there must be an innate component to language. Specifically, Chomsky (1957) argued that the most basic universal rules of grammar are innate (called a 'language acquisition device') and are activated by interaction to 'crack the code' of language. Others argue that the basic rules of language do not have to be innate—they can easily be learned through prelinguistic interaction between a child and its parents (Lock, 1978, 1980). And the meanings of utterances are so dependent on social context that they are unlikely to be innate (Bloom, 1970; Rommetveit, 1974; see Durkin, 1995).

LANGUAGE, THOUGHT AND COGNITION

Language is social in all sorts of ways: as a system of symbols, it lies at the heart of social life (G.H. Mead, 1934). It may be even more important than this. Perhaps thought itself is determined by language. We tend to perceive and think about the world in terms of linguistic categories, and thinking often involves a silent internal conversation with ourselves. Vygotsky (1962) believes that inner speech is the medium of thought and that it is mutually interdependent with external speech (the medium of social communication). This interdependence suggests that cultural differences in language and speech are reflected in cultural differences in thought. A more extreme version of this idea was proposed by Sapir and Whorf in their theory of **linguistic relativity** (Whorf, 1956).

The strong version of this theory is that language entirely determines thought, and so people who speak different languages see the world in entirely different ways and, effectively, live in entirely different cognitive universes. The Inuit (Eskimos) have a much more textured vocabulary for snow than other people; does this mean they actually see more differences than we do?

In English we differentiate between living and non-living flying things, while the Hopi of North America do not; does this mean that they actually see no difference between a bee and an aeroplane? Japanese personal pronouns differentiate between interpersonal relationships more subtly than do English personal pronouns; does this mean that English-speakers cannot tell the difference between different relationships? (See the first focus question.)

The strong form of the Sapir–Whorf hypothesis is now considered too extreme and a weak form seems to accord better with the facts (Hoffman, Lau, & Johnson, 1986). Language does not determine thought, but rather permits us to communicate more easily about those aspects of the physical or social environment that are important for the community (e.g. Krauss & Chiu, 1998). If it is important to be able to communicate about snow, it is likely that a rich vocabulary concerning snow will develop. If you want or need to discuss wine in any detail and with any ease, it is useful to be able to master the arcane vocabulary of the wine aficionado.

Although language may not determine thought, it can certainly constrain thought so that it is more or less easy to think about some things than others. If there is no simple word for something, it is more difficult to think about it. Nowadays there is, for this reason, a great deal of borrowing of words from one language to another—for example, English has borrowed *Zeitgeist* from German, *raison d'être* from French, *aficionado* from Spanish and *verandah* from Hindi. This idea is powerfully illustrated in George Orwell's novel *1984*, in which is described a fictional totalitarian regime, based on Stalin's Russia. The regime develops its own highly restricted language, called Newspeak, specifically designed to inhibit people from even thinking non-orthodox or heretical thoughts because the words don't exist (see Chapter 3).

PARALANGUAGE AND SPEECH STYLE

Language communicates not only by *what* is said but by *how* it is said. **Paralanguage** refers to all the non-linguistic accompaniments of speech—volume, stress, pitch, speed, tone of voice, pauses, throat-clearing, grunts and sighs (Knapp, 1978; Trager, 1958). Timing, pitch and loudness (the *prosodic* features of language; Argyle, 1975) are particularly important, as they can dramatically change the meaning of utterances: a rising intonation at the end of a statement transforms it into a question or communicates uncertainty, doubt or need for approval (Lakoff, 1973). Prosodic features are important cues to underlying emotions: low pitch can communicate sadness or boredom, while high pitch can communicate anger, fear or surprise (Frick, 1985). Fast speech often communicates power and control (Ng & Bradac, 1993).

Scherer (1974) systematically varied, by means of a synthesiser, a range of paralinguistic features of short neutral utterances and then had people identify the emotion that was being communicated. Table 15.1 shows how different paralinguistic features communicate information about the speaker's feelings.

In addition to these paralinguistic cues, something can be said in different accents, different language varieties and different languages. These are important **speech style** differences that have been the subject of an enormous amount of research in social psychology (Giles & Coupland, 1991). In general, the social psychology of language tends to be more concerned with how something is said than with what is said—with speech style rather than speech content—though this is changing with the advent of discourse analysis (see later in this chapter).

SOCIAL MARKERS IN SPEECH

There are few significant or reliable interpersonal differences in speech style (Giles & Street, 1985). People generally have a repertoire of speech styles and they automatically or deliberately tailor the way they speak to the context of the communicative event. For instance, we tend to speak slowly and use short words and simple

TABLE 15.1 Emotions displayed through paralinguistic cues

ACOUSTIC VARIABLE	QUALITY	PERCEIVED AS
Amplitude variation	Moderate	Pleasantness, activity, happiness
	Extreme	Fear
Pitch variation	Moderate	Anger, boredom, disgust, fear
	Extreme	Pleasantness, activity, happiness, surprise
Pitch contour	Down	Pleasantness, boredom, sadness
	Up	Potency, anger, fear, surprise
Pitch level	Low	Pleasantness, boredom, sadness
	High	Activity, potency, anger, fear, surprise
Tempo	Slow	Boredom, disgust, sadness
	Fast	Pleasantness, activity, potency, anger, fear, happiness, surprise
Duration (shape)	Round	Potency, boredom, disgust, fear, sadness
	Sharp	Pleasantness, activity, happiness, surprise
Filtration (lack of overtones)	Low	Pleasantness, happiness, boredom, sadness
	Moderate	Potency, activity
	Extreme	Anger, disgust, fear, surprise
	Atonal	Disgust
Tonality	Tonal-minor	Anger
	Tonal-major	Pleasantness, happiness
Rhythm	Not rhythmic	Boredom
	Rhythmic	Activity, fear, surprise

Source: Scherer (1974).

grammatical constructions when we speak to foreigners and children (Clyne, 1981; Elliot, 1981), and longer and more complex constructions, or more formalised language varieties or standard accents, when we are in a formal context such as an interview.

Brown and Fraser (1979) have charted the different components of a communicative situation that may influence speech style and distinguish between two broad features: (1) the scene (e.g. its purpose, time of day, whether there are bystanders); (2) the participants (e.g. their personality, ethnicity, whether they like each other). Since this is an objective classification of situations, it is important to bear in mind that different people may not define the same objective situation in the same way. What seems a formal context to one person may seem quite informal to another. It is the subjective perception of the situation that influences speech style.

Furnham (1986) goes one step further in pointing out that not only do we tailor speech style to perceived situational demands, but we also seek out situations that are appropriate to a preferred speech style. (If you want to have an informal chat, you are more likely to choose a pleasant café than a seminar room as the venue.)

Contextual variation in speech style means that speech style itself can tell us something about the context: in other words, speech contains clues to who is speaking to whom, in what context and about what. Speech contains **social markers** (Scherer & Giles, 1979) and some of the most-researched markers are of group memberships such as social class, ethnicity, sex and age.

Social markers are often clearly identifiable and act as very reliable clues to group membership. For instance, Australians can quite easily identify New Zealanders and Americans from speech style alone. Speech style alone can thus be sufficient to elicit a listener's attitudes towards the group that the speaker represents. You will recall the lengths to which Eliza Doolittle went in the movie *My Fair Lady* to acquire a standard English accent in order to conceal her cockney origins.

This idea is the basis of one of the most widely used research paradigms in the social psychology of language—the **matched-guise technique**. Lambert, Hodgson,

Gardner and Fillenbaum (1960) devised this technique to investigate language attitudes (people's attitudes towards a person as a function of speech alone). The method involves people rating short extracts of speech that are identical in all paralinguistic, prosodic and content respects, differing only in speech style (accent, dialect, language). All the speech extracts are spoken by the same person—someone who is fluently bilingual. The speaker is rated on a number of evaluative dimensions, which often fall into two distinct clusters:

1. *status* variables (e.g. intelligent, competent, powerful); and
2. *solidarity* variables (e.g. close, friendly, warm).

The matched-guise technique has been used extensively in a large range of cultural contexts to investigate the social evaluation of speakers of standard and non-standard language varieties. The standard language variety is the one that is associated with high economic status, power and media usage; in the Anglophone world, including Australia and New Zealand, it is what is called **received pronunciation** (RP) English. Non-standard varieties include regional accents (e.g. Yorkshire in the UK), non-standard urban accents (e.g. Birmingham in the UK) and minority ethnic languages (e.g. Greek in Australia). Research reveals that standard varieties are more favourably evaluated on status and competence dimensions (e.g. intelligence, confidence, ambition) than non-standard varieties (e.g. Giles & Powesland, 1975).

There is also a tendency for non-standard speakers to be more favourably evaluated on solidarity dimensions. Gallois and her associates at the University of Queensland (Gallois, Callan, & Johnstone, 1984) found that both White Australians and Australian Aborigines upgraded Aboriginal-accented English on solidarity dimensions. In another study, Hogg, Joyce and Abrams (1984) found that Swiss Germans upgraded speakers of non-standard Swiss German relative to speakers of High German, on solidarity dimensions.

LANGUAGE AND ETHNICITY

Matched-guise and other studies suggest that how we speak (our accent or even language) can affect how others evaluate us. This is unlikely to be because certain speech styles are intrinsically more pleasing than others, but rather because speech styles are associated with particular social groups that are consensually evaluated more or less positively in society. Use of a speech style that is associated with a lower-status group may cause people to regard you in terms of their evaluation of that group—with all sorts of potential implications for how you may perceive yourself, your group and other groups, and how you may act in society. This idea suggests that processes associated with intergroup relations and group membership can affect language behaviour.

Communication: Communication involves spoken and written language and a rich mix of expressions, gestures and emblems—all contextualised by ethnicity and nationality.

Giles and Bourhis and colleagues have employed and extended principles from **social identity theory** (see Chapter 11) to develop an intergroup perspective on the social psychology of language (Giles, Bourhis, & Taylor, 1977; Giles & Johnson, 1981, 1987). Because the analysis focuses mainly on ethnic groups that differ in speech style, the theory is called **ethnolinguistic identity theory**. Ethnic groups can differ from one another in appearance, dress, cultural practices, religious beliefs, and language or speech style.

Language or speech style is often one of the most distinct and clear markers of *ethnic identity* (see Chapter 4)—social identity as a member of an **ethnolinguistic group** (an ethnic group defined by language or speech style). For instance, the Welsh and the English in the UK are most distinctive in terms of accent and language. Speech style, then, is an important and often central stereotypical or normative property of group membership: one of the most powerful ways to display your Welshness is to speak Welsh.

Language or speech style cues ethnic identity. Therefore, whether people accentuate or de-emphasise their ethnic language will be influenced by the extent to which they see their ethnic identity as being a source of self-respect and pride. This perception will in turn be influenced by the real nature of the power and status relations between ethnic groups in society. Almost all societies are multicultural, containing a single dominant high-status group whose language is the *lingua franca* of the nation and a number of other ethnic groups whose languages are subordinate. Australia is a perfect example and, indeed, a great deal of the research on ethnicity and language has been conducted in Australia. In Australia, English is the lingua franca but there are also, for example, large Italian-, Greek- and Vietnamese-Australian communities.

Language research has been conducted in all these communities (e.g. Gallois & Callan, 1986; Giles, Rosenthal, & Young, 1985; Hogg, D'Agata, & Abrams, 1989; McNamara, 1987; Smolicz, 1983). For example, Gallois, Barker, Jones and Callan (1992) studied ethnic Chinese students at the University of Queensland to discover how their speech style affected perceptions and interpretations of their scholastic ability and their academic needs (for details of this research see Box 16.5 in Chapter 16).

Giles, Bourhis and Taylor (1977) introduced the term **ethnolinguistic vitality** to describe those objective features of an interethnic context that influence language behaviour (see Figure 15.1). Ethnic groups that are high on status and on demographic and institutional support variables have high ethnolinguistic vitality. This encourages continued use of the language, thus ensuring its survival and the survival of the ethnolinguistic group itself as a distinct entity in society. Low vitality is associated with declining use of the ethnic language, its gradual disappearance, and often the disappearance of the ethnolinguistic group as a distinct entity: that is, there is language death or language suicide.

Objective ethnolinguistic vitality configurations can be calculated for different groups (Giles, 1978; Saint-Blancat, 1985), but it is **subjective vitality**—that is, people's subjective perception of the vitality of their group—that more directly influences language usage (Bourhis, Giles, & Rosenthal, 1981; Harwood, Giles, & Bourhis, 1994; Sachdev & Bourhis, 1993). In general, there is a correspondence between objective and subjective vitality, but the two need not be identical.

Ethnic minorities may consider their language to have more or less vitality than an objective index indicates. Under some circumstances, a dominant group may actively encourage a minority to underestimate the vitality of its language, in order to inhibit ethnolinguistic revival movements that may threaten the status quo.

Interethnic relations, and subjective perceptions of these relations, may thus influence language behaviour. In Canada, the past 35 years has witnessed a strong French language revival in the province of Quebec, which can be understood in terms of changes in subjective vitality (Bourhis, 1984; Sachdev & Bourhis, 1990). Other language revivals include Hebrew, which was considered a dead language half a century ago, in Israel; Flemish in Belgium; Welsh in the UK; and Hindi in India (Fishman, 1989).

Language death also occurs. For example, Italian and Scottish Canadians generally consider themselves Anglo-Canadian (Edwards & Chisholm, 1987) and third-generation Japanese in Brazil have entirely lost their Japanese culture (Kanazawa & Loveday, 1988). Closer to home, there are very different vitality configurations for first- and second-generation Greek, Italian and Vietnamese Australians, and this has implications for the

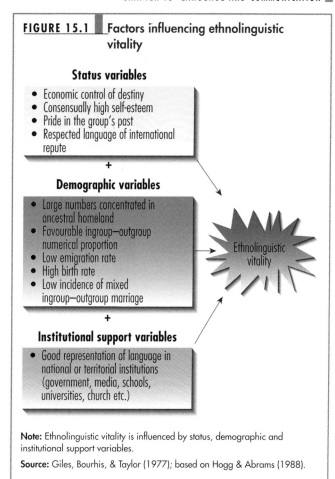

FIGURE 15.1 Factors influencing ethnolinguistic vitality

Status variables
- Economic control of destiny
- Consensually high self-esteem
- Pride in the group's past
- Respected language of international repute

+

Demographic variables
- Large numbers concentrated in ancestral homeland
- Favourable ingroup–outgroup numerical proportion
- Low emigration rate
- High birth rate
- Low incidence of mixed ingroup–outgroup marriage

+

Institutional support variables
- Good representation of language in national or territorial institutions (government, media, schools, universities, church etc.)

Ethnolinguistic vitality

Note: Ethnolinguistic vitality is influenced by status, demographic and institutional support variables.

Source: Giles, Bourhis, & Taylor (1977); based on Hogg & Abrams (1988).

extent to which these cultural groups will maintain or lose their ethnolinguistic identity (Clyne, 1985; Currie & Hogg, 1994; Hogg, D'Agata, & Abrams, 1989).

A 21-item subjective vitality questionnaire administered to 40 middle-aged Sicilian/Italian Australians in Melbourne (Hogg, D'Agata, & Abrams, 1989) revealed a generally low subjective vitality profile (see Figure 15.2 for mean ratings on each of four vitality dimensions). However, among these participants, those who gave higher subjective vitality ratings tended to upgrade an Italian-speaker and downgrade an English-speaker more strongly than those who gave lower vitality ratings.

Allard and Landry (1994) have recently extended the subjective vitality notion to place greater emphasis on interpersonal communicative environments. They argue that what really counts in whether an ethnic language thrives is not subjective beliefs about the vitality of the language, but rather the interpersonal network of linguistic contacts that people have. This makes good sense: a language will not thrive unless it is used. However, perceived vitality may still be important—it influences linguistic opportunities, linguistic and identity motivations and linguistic evaluations. A study of Italian Australians living in Brisbane (Hogg & Rigoli, 1996)

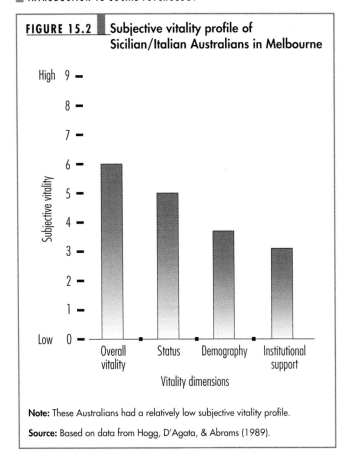

FIGURE 15.2 Subjective vitality profile of Sicilian/Italian Australians in Melbourne

Note: These Australians had a relatively low subjective vitality profile.

Source: Based on data from Hogg, D'Agata, & Abrams (1989).

particular, the listener. This idea is the basis of **speech accommodation theory** (Giles, 1984; Giles, Taylor, & Bourhis, 1973), which explains the ways in which people accommodate their speech style to those who are present, in terms of specific motivations. The motives that may be involved include a desire to help the listener understand what you are saying or a desire to promote a specific impression of yourself in order to obtain social approval.

Based on the assumption that most talk involves people of unequal status, speech accommodation theory describes the type of accommodation that might occur as a function of the sort of social orientation that the speakers have towards one another (Table 15.2). Where a simple interpersonal orientation exists (e.g. between two friends), bilateral **speech convergence** occurs. Higher-status speakers shift their accent or speech style 'down-wards' towards that of lower-status speakers, who in turn shift 'upwards'. In this context, convergence satis-fies a need for approval or liking. Convergence increases interpersonal speech style similarity and thus enhances interpersonal approval and liking (Bourhis, Giles, & Lambert, 1975), particularly if the convergence behav-iour is clearly intentional (Simard, Taylor, & Giles, 1976).

Now consider the case where an intergroup orien-tation exists. If the lower-status group has low subjec-tive vitality coupled with a belief in social mobility (i.e. that one can pass, linguistically, into the higher-status group), there is unilateral upward convergence on the part of the lower-status speaker and unilateral **speech divergence** on the part of the higher-status speaker. In intergroup contexts, divergence achieves psycholinguistic distinctiveness: it differentiates the speaker's ingroup on linguistic grounds from the outgroup. Where an inter-group orientation exists and the lower-status group has high subjective vitality coupled with a belief in social change (i.e. that one cannot pass into the higher-status group; see Chapter 11), bilateral divergence occurs. Both speakers pursue *psycholinguistic distinctiveness*.

Speech accommodation theory has been well supported empirically (Giles & Coupland, 1991). For

found that Italian-language competence was not related to interpersonal linguistic contacts but to subjective vitality (see second focus question).

SPEECH ACCOMMODATION

Social categories, such as ethnic groups, may develop and maintain or lose their distinctive languages or speech styles as a consequence of intergroup relations. However, categories do not speak. People speak, and they speak to one another, usually in face-to-face interaction. As described above, when people speak they tend to adapt their speech style to the context—the situation and, in

TABLE 15.2 Speech accommodation as a function of status, social orientation and subjective vitality

	SOCIAL ORIENTATION AND VITALITY OF LOWER STATUS GROUP		
	INTERPERSONAL	INTERGROUP	
Speaker status		Low vitality (Social mobility)	High vitality (Social change)
Higher	Downward convergence	Upward divergence	Upward divergence
Lower	Upward convergence	Upward convergence	Downward divergence

example, Bourhis and Giles (1977) found that Welsh adults accentuated their Welsh accent in the presence of RP English-speakers (i.e. the standard non-regional variety of English). Bourhis, Giles, Leyens and Tajfel (1979) obtained a similar finding in Belgium, with Flemish-speakers in the presence of French-speakers. In both cases there was a language revival under way at the time and thus an intergroup orientation with high vitality was salient. In a low-vitality social mobility context, Hogg (1985) found that female students in Britain shifted their speech style 'upwards' towards that of their male partners.

Accommodation in intergroup contexts reflects an intergroup or social identity mechanism in which speech style is dynamically governed by the speakers' motivations to adopt ingroup or outgroup speech patterns. These motivations are formed by perceptions of:

- the relative status and prestige of the speech varieties and their associated groups; and
- the vitality of their own group.

What may actually govern changes in speech style is conformity to stereotypical perceptions of the appropriate speech norm (see Chapter 7). Thakerar, Giles and Cheshire (1982) have recognised this in distinguishing between objective and subjective accommodation. People converge on or diverge from what they perceive to be the relevant speech style. Objective accommodation may reflect this, but in some circumstances it may not: for instance, subjective convergence may look like objective divergence if the speech style **stereotype** is different from the actual speech behaviour of the other speaker.

Recently, speech accommodation theory has been extended in recognition of the role of non-verbal behaviours in communication (non-verbal behaviour is discussed below). Now more accurately called **communication accommodation theory** (Giles, Mulac, Bradac, & Johnson, 1987; Giles & Noels, 2002; see also Gallois, Giles, Jones, Cargile, & Ota, 1995), it acknowledges that convergence (increase in similarity) and divergence (decrease in similarity) can occur non-verbally as well as verbally. For instance, in mixed-sex dyads women's gaze was found to converge towards their partner's eyes (Mulac, Studley, Wiemann, & Bradac, 1987). While verbal and non-verbal channels are often accommodatively synchronised, this is not necessarily the case. Bilous and Krauss (1988) found that women in mixed-sex dyads converged towards men on some dimensions (e.g. total words uttered and interruptions) but diverged on others (e.g. laughter).

BILINGUALISM AND SECOND-LANGUAGE ACQUISITION

We note above that most countries are bilingual or multilingual—in some instances people need to be trilingual (see Box 15.1). Such countries contain a variety of ethnolinguistic groups, with a single dominant group whose language is the *lingua franca*. Very few countries are monolingual (e.g. Portugal). Bilingualism or second-language acquisition for most people is not simply a recreational activity—it is a vital necessity for survival. For example, Vietnamese immigrants have to learn English in order to be educated and to be able to participate in employment, culture and day-to-day life in Australia.

In a study in Melbourne of bilingual school children, Lotherington (2003) focused on Vietnamese, now Australia's fifth largest language group, and Khmer-speaking Cambodians. Even a host society (such as the state of Victoria) that explicitly supports multiculturalism can present immigrants with mixed messages, including the nature of their ethnic identity. Immigrant children in Australia are often instructed by a variety of LOTE and ESL teachers. (LOTE refers to languages other than English and ESL to English as a second language.)

LOTE teachers saw their students as *Australians*, while English and ESL teachers saw the same students as *Asians*. (Lotherington, 2003, p. 209; italics ours)

Acquisition of a second language is not so much a matter of acquiring basic classroom proficiency but rather the wholesale acquisition of a language embedded in its cultural context (Gardner, 1979). Second-language acquisition requires native-like mastery (being able to speak like a native speaker), and this hinges more on the motivations of the second-language learner than on linguistic aptitude or pedagogical factors.

BOX 15.1 | **Being trilingual in Montreal**

Since the 1970s Montreal has become a bilingual city, whereas in earlier decades its natives were far more likely to be bilingual Francophones than bilingual Anglophones (Lamarre & Paredes, 2003). This past asymmetry reflected the relative status of the two language groups—English was the dominant group. Social change, specifically in the use of French, was enacted in law as part of Quebec's language policy—its 1977 *Charte de la langue francaise* gave French official status in schools alongside English—and in the following decades the perceived status of French improved.

This change in relative French–English status has had major consequences for the children of new immigrants: they are now mostly *trilingual*. At one time they would have preferred to learn English as their second language, on the basis that Anglophones were perceived to be the dominant group, but now they choose to speak three languages—a degree of their ancestral language at home and the two local languages in public.

Bilingualism: A street sign in the Indian city of Pondicherry.

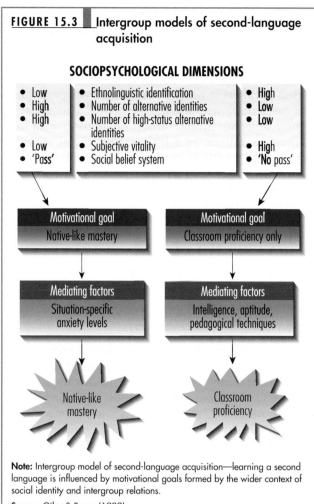

FIGURE 15.3 | Intergroup models of second-language acquisition

SOCIOPSYCHOLOGICAL DIMENSIONS

• Low • High • High • Low • 'Pass'	• Ethnolinguistic identification • Number of alternative identities • Number of high-status alternative identities • Subjective vitality • Social belief system	• High • Low • Low • High • 'No pass'

Motivational goal Native-like mastery	Motivational goal Classroom proficiency only
Mediating factors Situation-specific anxiety levels	Mediating factors Intelligence, aptitude, pedagogical techniques
Native-like mastery	Classroom proficiency

Note: Intergroup model of second-language acquisition—learning a second language is influenced by motivational goals formed by the wider context of social identity and intergroup relations.

Source: Giles & Byrne (1982).

Failure to acquire native-like mastery can undermine self-confidence and cause physical and social isolation, leading to material hardship and psychological suffering. For example, Noels, Pon and Clément (1996) found low self-esteem and marked symptoms of stress among Chinese Canadians with poor English skills.

Building on earlier models by Gardner (1979) and Clément (1980), Giles and Byrne (1982) proposed an intergroup model. There are five *sociopsychological dimensions* that influence a subordinate group member's motivational goals in learning the language of a dominant group (see Figure 15.3):

1. ethnolinguistic identification;
2. number of alternative identities available;
3. number of high-status alternative identities available;
4. subjective vitality;
5. social belief system about whether it is possible to pass linguistically into the dominant group.

Low identification with the ethnic ingroup, low subjective vitality and a belief that we can 'pass' linguistically, coupled with a large number of other potential identities of which many are high status, are conditions that motivate the individual to acquire native-like mastery in the second language. Proficiency in the second language is seen to be economically and culturally useful; it is considered *additive* to our identity. Realisation of this goal will be facilitated or inhibited by the extent to which we are made to feel confident or anxious about using the second language in specific contexts. The converse set of sociopsychological conditions (see Figure 15.3) motivates people to acquire only classroom proficiency. Through fear of assimilation, the second language is considered *subtractive* in that it may attract ingroup hostility and accusations of ethnic betrayal. Intelligence and aptitude will also affect proficiency.

This model found broad support in a study by Hall and Gudykunst (1986) in Arizona. The English-language ability of over 200 international students from a wide range of cultural and linguistic backgrounds could be explained in terms of Giles and Byrne's (1982) intergroup model. The model is, however, still being developed and modified in recognition of the enormous complexity of accurately modelling second-language learning in multicultural contexts (Garrett, Giles, & Coupland, 1989; Giles & Coupland, 1991).

For instance, Lambert, Mermigis and Taylor (1986) have proposed a *multiculturalism hypothesis*. Secure ethnolinguistic minorities do not inevitably consider native-like mastery to be subtractive—on the contrary, they can sometimes consider it to be additive. Examples of this process include English-language mastery among Japanese (San Antonio, 1987) and Hong Kong Chinese (Bond & King, 1985), and Italian-language mastery among Valdotans (a French-speaking community in northern Italy; Saint-Blancat, 1985). These groups acquire native-like mastery in the dominant language and yet maintain their own cultural and ethnolinguistic heritage.

This analysis of second-language acquisition grounds language firmly in its cultural context and, thus, relates language acquisition to broader acculturation processes. For example, Berry, Trimble and Olmedo (1986; see also Chapter 16) distinguish between *integration* (people maintain their ethnic culture and relate to the dominant culture), *assimilation* (people give up their ethnic culture and wholeheartedly embrace the dominant culture), *separation* (people maintain their ethnic culture and isolate themselves from the dominant culture) and *marginalisation* (people give up their ethnic culture and fail to relate properly to the dominant culture). The consequences for second-language learning are quite dramatic.

Majority group members do not generally have the motivation to acquire native-like mastery of another language. According to Edwards (1994), it is precisely the international prestige and utility of English that makes native English-speakers such poor foreign-language students: they are simply not motivated to become proficient. Sachdev and Wright (1996) pursued this point. They found that White English children were more motivated to learn European languages than Asian languages: the former were considered more useful and of higher status, even though the children in their sample had immeasurably more day-to-day contact with Asian than European languages and people.

GENDER, AGE AND LANGUAGE

Much of the social psychology of language focuses on ethnicity and language. The analyses are, however, intended to deal generally with intergroup aspects of language behaviour and so are intended, all things being equal, to apply to any intergroup context.

Gender

Gender differences in speech style have been investigated principally in Western countries (Aries, 1996; Smith, 1985), where there are strong stereotypes about sex differences in speech (Haas, 1979; see Chapter 10). For example, women are said to be more talkative, polite, emotional, positive, supportive and tentative, less assertive, and more likely to talk about home and family. Real speech differences are much smaller than stereotypes lead us to believe (Aries, 1997) and such differences are highly context-dependent. Even paralinguistic differences that are grounded in physiology (women's voices have a higher pitch, softer volume, greater variability and more relaxed and pleasant tone) are influenced by context and show great within-sex variability (Montpare & Vega, 1988).

Because speech style has become stereotypically sex-typed (Weatherall, 1998), it is not surprising to discover that both men and women can adopt more or less masculine or feminine speech styles depending on whether they have a more or less traditional sex-role orientation (Smith, 1985). Non-traditional men tend to eschew more masculine speech styles and non-traditional women eschew more feminine speech styles.

Speech style can also vary as a function of the immediate communicative context, in accordance with the principles of speech accommodation theory. Women tend to adopt a more masculine speech style when speaking to male strangers or acquaintances (Hall & Braunwald, 1981; Hogg, 1985), but a more feminine style when speaking to intimate male friends (Montpare & Vega, 1988).

There is some evidence that women adopt a 'power-less' form of speech when addressing men or in the company of men (O'Barr & Atkins, 1980; Wiemann & Giles, 1988). Powerless speech involves greater use of *intensifiers* (e.g. 'very', 'really', 'so'), *hedges* (e.g. 'kind of', 'sort of', 'you know'), *tag questions* (e.g. '. . . didn't they?'), rising intonation that transforms a declarative statement into a question and *polite forms of address* (Lakoff, 1975).

Power can also be associated with the ability to interrupt and take control of the floor (Reid & Ng, 1999; Ng, Bell, & Brooke, 1993; Ng & Bradac, 1993). In mixed-sex conversations, women have been shown to interrupt less often than men: Zimmerman and West (1975) reported that 98% of interruptions were by men. However, other research suggests that women can interrupt more often than men (Dindia, 1987).

Powerless speech is not confined to women; it simply reflects status differences in interactions and so has been shown to characterise low-status speakers in general (Lind & O'Barr, 1979).

To the extent that boys and girls are socialised in relatively sex-segregated groups, the two sexes acquire different kinds of interaction and communication styles that carry over into adulthood. Girls emphasise cooperation and equality and attend sensitively to relationships and situations. Boys emphasise competition and hierarchical relations and assert their individual identity. Much like interactions between cultural groups with different language communication norms, men and women interact with different assumptions and goals in a conversation. Since some of the same forms can carry different meanings and serve different functions for men and women, intersex miscommunication is almost inevitable (e.g. Mulac, Bradac, & Gibbons, 2001).

One criticism that has been raised about research on gender differences in language and communication is that it is hard to generalise because contextual factors are underplayed and because the research is culturally constrained largely to White, middle-class, Western men and women (e.g. Crawford, 1995; Eckert & McConnell-Ginet, 1999).

Age

Through life we all move into and out of a sequence of age groups—infant, child, teenager, youth, young adult,

adult, middle-aged, old. Society has stereotypical beliefs and expectations about the attitudes and behaviours associated with these categories. In Western society, for instance, old people are generally considered to be frail, incompetent, of low status and largely worthless (Baker, 1985; Noels, Giles, & Le Poire, 2003; see Chapter 10). This attitude is reflected in an intergenerational speech accommodation strategy, where younger people (in the United States) adopt a sort of 'baby talk' to communicate with both institutionalised and non-institutionalised elderly people (Caporael, Lukaszewski, & Cuthbertson, 1983; Ryan, Giles, Bartolucci, & Henwood, 1986). The elderly find this rather insulting, though some see it as nurturant.

At the same time, young people feel that the elderly fail to accommodate their speech, and find this irritating (Fox & Giles, 1993; Williams, 1996). Intergenerational encounters between the young and the elderly are thus likely to reinforce stereotypes rather than disconfirm them (see discussion of intergroup contact in Chapter 11). These intergenerational effects are widespread, and some recent research by Giles and his associates has found, quite surprisingly, that they are more pronounced in East Asian settings (Giles, Noels, Ota, Ng, Gallois, Ryan et al., 2001).

Because age categories are so pervasive, we all know what is expected of us once we reach a particular age. Furthermore, 'age group' is one of the most salient and often used social categorisations (Mackie, Hamilton, Susskind, & Rosselli, 1996): almost every official form you complete asks your age and sex. Together, these are likely to make it difficult for elderly people not to 'act their age'. The social costs of not acting our age can be extreme—as was entertaininingly illustrated in the movie *Cocoon*.

Perhaps, then, elderly people talk a great deal about their age, make painful disclosures about their health, and exhibit other symptoms of elderly speech not so much because of their age but because they are constrained to conform to social expectations (Coupland, Coupland, Giles, & Henwood, 1988; Giles & Coupland, 1991). Intergenerational communication can certainly be problematic and can even have effects on psychological and physical wellbeing (Williams & Nussbaum, 2001).

Non-verbal communication

Speech rarely occurs in isolation from non-verbal cues. Even on the telephone, people tend automatically to use all sorts of gestures that cannot possibly be 'seen' by the person at the other end of the line. Telephone and computer-mediated communication (CMC) conversations can often be difficult precisely because many non-verbal cues are not accessible. However, non-verbal channels do not necessarily work in concert with speech to facilitate understanding. Sometimes the non-verbal message starkly contradicts the verbal message (e.g. threats, sarcasm and other negative messages accompanied by a smile; Bugental, Love, & Gianetto, 1971; Noller, 1984).

The importance of non-verbal behaviour for communication is now well recognised in social psychology (Argyle, 1988; Burgoon, Buller, & Woodall, 1989; DePaulo & Friedman, 1998; Rimé, 1983). Doing research in this area is, however, a major challenge. People can produce about 20 000 different facial expressions (Birdwhistell, 1970) and about 1000 different paralanguages (Hewes, 1957). In all, there are about 700 000 different physical gestures, facial expressions and movements (Pei, 1965). Even the briefest interaction can involve the fleeting and simultaneous use of a large number of these communicative devices, making it enormously difficult even to code behaviour, let alone analyse the causes and consequences of particular **non-verbal communications**.

Non-verbal behaviours can serve a variety of purposes (Patterson, 1983):

- They can provide information about feelings and intentions (e.g. non-verbal cues are often reliable indicators of whether someone likes you).
- They can be used to regulate interactions (e.g. non-verbal cues can signal the approaching end of an utterance, or that someone else wishes to speak).
- They can be used to express intimacy (e.g. touching and mutual eye contact).
- They can be used to establish dominance or control (e.g. non-verbal threats).
- They can be used to facilitate goal attainment (e.g. pointing).

These functions will be evident in our discussion of specific non-verbal behaviours—gaze, facial expressions, body language, touch and interpersonal distance. One final general point about non-verbal behaviours: people acquire, without any formal training, consummate mastery of a rich repertoire of non-verbal behaviours very early in life. Perhaps partly because we acquire non-verbal behaviours unawares, we tend not to be conscious that we are using non-verbal cues or that we are being influenced by others' use of such cues: non-verbal communication goes largely unnoticed, yet has enormous impact.

This is not to say that non-verbal behaviours are completely uncontrolled. On the contrary, social norms can influence their expression. For example, even if delighted at the demise of a foe, we are unlikely to smile at his or her funeral. There are also individual and group differences, with some people being better than others at noticing and using non-verbal cues. Rosenthal, Hall, DiMatteo, Rogers and Archer (1979) have devised a Profile of Nonverbal Sensitivity (PONS) test that has been used to help chart these individual and group differences. All things being equal, non-verbal sensitivity improves with age, is more advanced among successful people and is compromised among people with a range of psychopathologies.

One of the most robust findings is that women are more non-verbally sensitive than men. Research shows that women are generally more adept than men at detecting and sending non-verbal communications. However, they differ less in conscious awareness of precisely what information has been communicated by which non-verbal channel, and they are worse than men at recognising covert messages such as discrepant or deceptive communications (Brown, 1986; Eagly, 1987; E. T. Hall, 1979; J. A. Hall, 1984). These differences are usually attributed to sex-specific child-rearing strategies that encourage girls more than boys to be emotionally expressive and attentive.

Finally, there is also scope for all of us to improve our non-verbal skills. As they can be useful for improving interpersonal communication, detecting deception, presenting a good impression and hiding our feelings, practical books and courses on communications skills are popular.

GAZE AND EYE CONTACT

The eyes are often considered to be the windows of the soul and so it is not surprising to learn that people spend a great deal of time gazing at each other's eyes. In dyads, people spend 61% of the time gazing and a **gaze** lasts about three seconds (Argyle & Ingham, 1972). Eye contact, an older term for this non-verbal channel, refers more precisely to mutual gaze. People in dyads spend on average 31% of the time engaging in mutual gaze, and a mutual gaze lasts less than a second.

In many respects, gaze is perhaps the most information-rich and important of the non-verbal communication channels (Kleinke, 1986). We are driven to seek out the information communicated by others' eyes, even though under certain circumstances (e.g. passing a stranger in the street) eye contact itself is uncomfortable and even embarrassing.

Absence of eye behaviour can be equally unnerving. Consider how disorienting it can be to interact with someone whose eyes you cannot see (e.g. someone wearing dark glasses) or someone who continually avoids eye contact. Conversely, obscuring your own eye behaviour from others can increase your sense of security and privacy: for example, female tourists visiting notably chauvinistic societies are often encouraged to wear dark glasses and to avoid eye contact with male

strangers. In many societies, women secure privacy in public places by wearing a veil.

The amount and pattern of gazing is a rich source of information about people's feelings, their relative status, their credibility and honesty, and their competence and attentiveness (Kleinke, 1986). People tend to look more at people they like than those they dislike. Likewise, intimacy is communicated by greater gaze, particularly mutual gaze. This appears to be such common knowledge that even false information about how much someone has looked at you can influence your liking for that person. In one study, mixed-sex couples who had engaged in a 10-minute conversation were given false feedback on gaze (Kleinke, Bustos, Meeker, & Staneski, 1973). Individuals who were told they had been gazed at less than average were less attracted to their partners. Above-average gaze increased men's liking for their female partners, but did not affect women's liking for their male partners.

Gaze can communicate status. From studies using experimentally manipulated or real-life status differences between interactants, it has been found that lower-status individuals gaze at their partners more than do higher-status individuals (e.g. Exline, 1971; Dovidio & Ellyson, 1985). To the extent that the traditional power difference between men and women casts women in a relatively low-status position, this may explain why women engage in more eye contact than men (Duncan, 1969; Henley, 1977; Henley & Harmon, 1985).

Dovidio, Ellyson, Keating, Heltman and Brown (1988) investigated this idea by having mixed-sex pairs discuss three topics of conversation—one where the man had more expertise, one where the woman had more expertise, and one where the partners had equal expertise. The percentage of speaking time, and separately of listening time, spent gazing was recorded. Figure 15.4 shows that both men and women in a position of relatively high expertise displayed their power non-verbally (gazing almost as much or more while speaking as listening), whereas men and women in a position of relatively lower expertise exhibited the usual lower-status pattern (gazing more while listening than speaking).

The interesting finding is that, under conditions of equal expertise, women displayed a lower-status non-verbal pattern and men a higher-status pattern.

Gaze regulates interaction. Mutual gaze, making eye contact, is an important means of initiating conversation (Argyle, 1971; Cary, 1978) and we tend to avoid eye contact if we do not want to be drawn into conversation. Gaze plays an important role in regulating the course of a conversation once started. White adults spend on average 75% of the time gazing when listening and 41% of the time gazing when speaking (Argyle & Ingham, 1972); thus, a listener can decrease gaze in order to signal an intention to gain the floor, while a

FIGURE 15.4 | Gaze as a function of sex and relative expertise

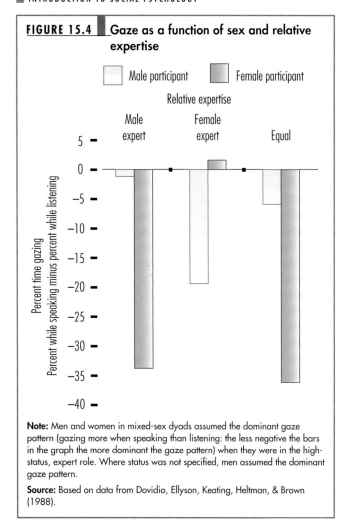

Note: Men and women in mixed-sex dyads assumed the dominant gaze pattern (gazing more when speaking than listening: the less negative the bars in the graph the more dominant the gaze pattern) when they were in the high-status, expert role. Where status was not specified, men assumed the dominant gaze pattern.

Source: Based on data from Dovidio, Ellyson, Keating, Heltman, & Brown (1988).

(Kleinke, 1986). A stern stare can also express disapproval, dominance or threat. It can stop someone talking or even cause flight. For instance, Ellsworth, Carlsmith and Henson (1972) found that drivers waiting at an intersection departed much more rapidly when stared at than not stared at by a person standing on the corner. Higher-status people, who, as described above, generally gaze less than lower-status people at a partner, can adopt a specific pattern of gaze behaviour in order to exert control. This **visual dominance behaviour** is a tendency to gaze fixedly at a lower-status speaker. Leaders who adopt this visual dominance pattern tend to be given higher leadership ratings than leaders who do not (Exline, Ellyson, & Long, 1975; see also Chapter 8).

Finally, gaze can facilitate the accomplishment of various tasks. A gaze can be used secretly to communicate information (e.g. surprise at an outrageous statement) to a partner in the presence of a third party. A gaze can be used to signal a routine activity in an established working relationship (e.g. sailing a boat) or a noisy environment (e.g. a production line). A gaze can also serve to communicate something that is too complex, difficult or long-winded to explain in words in that context (e.g. a dental patient).

FACIAL EXPRESSION

The scientific study of facial expression has largely focused on the way in which facial expressions communicate emotions. Darwin (1872) believed that there is a small number of universal emotions and that, associated with these emotions, are universal facial expressions. Subsequent research generally identified six basic emotions (happiness, surprise, sadness, fear, disgust, anger), from which more complex or blended emotions are derived (Ekman, 1982; Scherer, 1986; see also Ortony & Turner, 1990). Basic emotions are associated with quite distinctive patterns of facial muscle activity: for instance, surprise is associated with raised eyebrows, dropped jaw, horizontal wrinkles across the forehead, raised upper eyelid and lowered lower eyelid (Ekman & Friesen, 1975).

Figure 15.5 shows posed versions of the six basic emotions. See if you can identify the emotions intended by our models.

To facilitate research on facial expression of emotion, researchers at the University of Adelaide developed a computer program that can simultaneously vary different facial components (e.g. roundness of eyes, thickness of lips, curve of eyebrows, distance between mouth and eyes) to reproduce on a computer screen recognisable emotional expressions (Katsikitis, Pilowsky, & Innes, 1990).

The facial expressions associated with basic emotions appear to be relatively universal. Ekman and colleagues showed people a series of posed photographs of faces

speaker can increase gaze to indicate an intention to stop speaking.

LaFrance and Mayo (1976) have shown that this pattern is reversed among African Americans, who gaze more when speaking than listening. This produces some complicated communication problems in interracial interactions. For example, a White speaker may interpret a Black listener's *low* rate of gaze as lack of interest, rudeness or an attempt to butt in and take the floor, while a Black speaker may interpret a White listener's *high* rate of gaze in the same way. From the perspective of the listener, a White may interpret a Black speaker's high rate of gaze as arrogance and/or an invitation to take the floor, while a Black may interpret a White speaker's low rate of gaze in the same way.

It gets pretty confusing, but it is easy to see how smooth and harmonious interaction may be hindered by non-verbal miscommunication such as this. It is obviously important for people to be aware of cultural differences in non-verbal communication (see Chapter 16).

Gaze exercises control. People gaze more when they are trying to be persuasive or ingratiate themselves

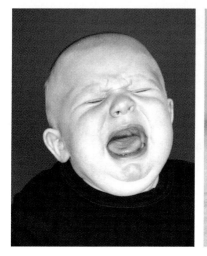

Unlearned facial displays: Crying and smiling—innate expressions of emotion. Later in life we learn when to display different feelings.

FIGURE 15.5 | Facial expression of six fundamental emotions

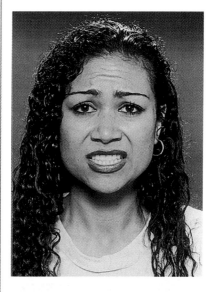

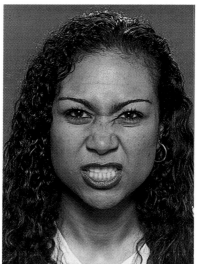
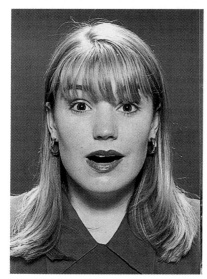

Six basic emotions: Anger, happiness, surprise, fear, sadness and disgust. But which is which?

expressing the six basic emotions and had them report the emotions being expressed (Ekman, 1971; Ekman & Friesen, 1971; Ekman, Friesen, O'Sullivan, Chan, Diacoyanni-Tarlatzis, Heider et al., 1987). People from a variety of Western cultures (Argentina, Brazil, Chile, Greece, Germany, Italy, Scotland, the United States), Asian cultures (Japan, Hong Kong, Sumatra, Turkey) and tribal cultures (Borneo, New Guinea) were remarkably accurate at identifying the six emotions from facial expression by people from both the same and different cultures.

Ekman's dependence on the use of posed expressions in representing the emotions, and his arguments for the universality of primary emotions have attracted some criticism (see overviews in Russell, Bachorowski, and Fernandez-Dols (2003), and in Russell and Fernandez-Dols, 1997).

Krauss, Curran and Ferleger (1983) adopted a more naturalistic technique in which, rather than using static and largely decontextualised photographs, people identified emotions as they occurred on videotapes of Japanese and American soap operas. Again, there was remarkable cross-cultural agreement. The apparent universality of facial expressions of emotion may reflect universals of ontogeny (i.e. cross-cultural commonalities in early socialisation) or may reflect phylogeny (i.e. an innate link between emotions and facial muscle activity).

The contribution of phylogeny has some support from research with people born deaf, blind and without hands. Although these people have limited access to the normal cues we would use to learn which facial expressions go with which emotions, they express basic emotions in much the same manner as people who are not handicapped in this way (Eibl-Eibesfeldt, 1972).

Despite the apparent universality of facial expressions associated with particular basic emotions, there are marked cultural and situational rules, called **display rules**, governing the expression of emotions (see Figure 15.6). These rules exist because of the important communicative function of facial expressions (Gallois, 1993). For instance, the expression of emotion is encouraged for women and in Mediterranean cultures, but discouraged for men and in Northern European and Asian cultures (Argyle, 1975). In Japan, people are taught to control facial expressions of negative emotion and to use laughter or smiling to conceal anger or grief.

In our own culture it is considered impolite to display happiness at beating an opponent in squash by laughing, and yet laughter is quite acceptable to display happiness at a party. Similarly, tears are an acceptable display of sadness at a funeral but not on hearing disappointing news in a business setting.

The **nature-nurture controversy** is nicely illustrated by Russell's (1994) investigation of the varying success that people from different parts of the world have in labelling

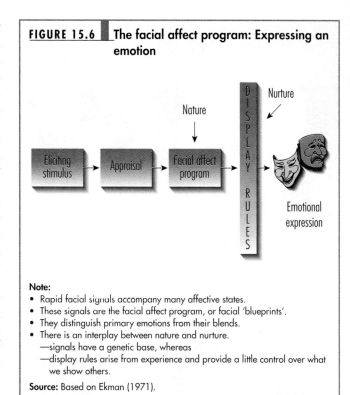

FIGURE 15.6 | The facial affect program: Expressing an emotion

Note:
- Rapid facial signals accompany many affective states.
- These signals are the facial affect program, or facial 'blueprints'.
- They distinguish primary emotions from their blends.
- There is an interplay between nature and nurture.
  —signals have a genetic base, whereas
  —display rules arise from experience and provide a little control over what we show others.

Source: Based on Ekman (1971).

the six primary or fundamental emotions (shown in Figure 15.5). His results are displayed in Figure 15.7.

Expressive and communicative functions of facial expression can be distinguished. In a series of naturalistic studies of smiling, Kraut and Johnston (1979) observed the frequency of smiling in a range of settings, including bowling alleys, hockey arenas and public footpaths. People were more likely to smile when talking to others than alone, and whether they were really happy or not seemed to have little influence on whether they smiled or not: smiling seemed to be more important as a communication of happiness than an expression of happiness.

Figure 15.8 shows the percentage of bowlers in a bowling competition who smiled when facing their team-mates (social interaction) or facing the pins (no social interaction), as a function of whether they had scored well or poorly.

Focusing on cross-cultural differences in emotional expression, Ekman (1973) monitored facial expressions of American students in America and Japanese students in Japan watching a very stressful film in private and talking about it to the experimenter afterwards. In private, both groups displayed negative emotions, but in public only the Americans gave facial expressions indicating negative emotions. In public, the Japanese students' facial expressions were indicative of positive emotions. This finding clearly reflects the existence of different cultural display rules.

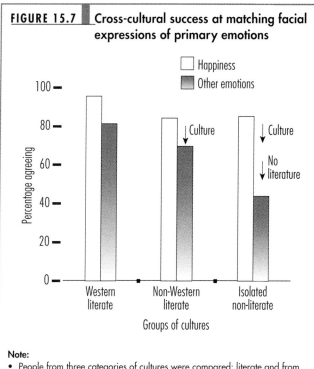

FIGURE 15.7 Cross-cultural success at matching facial expressions of primary emotions

Percentage agreeing

☐ Happiness
■ Other emotions

↓ Culture
↓ Culture
↓ No literature

Western literate   Non-Western literate   Isolated non-literate

Groups of cultures

Note:
• People from three categories of cultures were compared: literate and from the West (20 studies) or elsewhere (11 studies), and non-literate from elsewhere (three studies).
• Recognition of happiness is high in all cultures.
• Agreement about other emotions falls away, depending on: (a) what is thought to be a culturally appropriate expression, and (b) exposure to a literature that provides models of how to express an emotion.

Source: Based on data from Russell (1994).

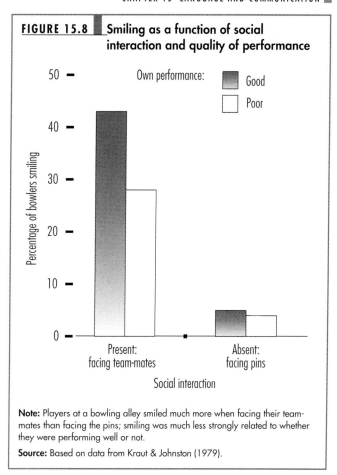

FIGURE 15.8 Smiling as a function of social interaction and quality of performance

Percentage of bowlers smiling

Own performance:
■ Good
☐ Poor

Present: facing team-mates   Absent: facing pins

Social interaction

Note: Players at a bowling alley smiled much more when facing their team-mates than facing the pins; smiling was much less strongly related to whether they were performing well or not.

Source: Based on data from Kraut & Johnston (1979).

POSTURES AND GESTURES

Not only the eyes and the face but also the head, hands, legs, feet and torso communicate information. Birdwhistell (1970) embarked on an ambitious attempt to construct an entire linguistics of body communication, called **kinesics**. From extensive observations, mainly in the United States, he identified 60 or 70 basic units of body movement (e.g. flared nostrils) and described rules of combination that produce meaningful units of body communication (e.g. the combination of a shoulder shrug, raised eyebrows and upturned palms). While some scholars feel that this may be somewhat ambitious, there is general agreement with Ekman and Friesen's (1972) distinction between illustrators and emblems.

Body movements and **postures** that accompany spoken language are **illustrators**: for example, the use of your hands can help to explain directions to someone. The communicative importance of illustrators becomes apparent when conversing on the phone, when they cannot be used. **Emblems**, on the other hand, are **gestures** that replace or stand in for spoken language, such as the wave of the hand in greeting, or less friendly hand signals. There has been a recent argument from

evolutionary social psychology that *manual gestures* are the precursor of human language (see Box 15.2).

Some emblems are widely understood across cultures, but many are culture-specific. The same thing can be indicated by different gestures in different cultures, and the same gesture can mean different things in different cultures. For instance, we refer to 'self' by pointing at

Phone language: Not another automated menu! Body movements and facial expressions are superfluous when we talk on the telephone.

BOX 15.2   The gestural origins of language

THE HANDS HAVE IT

Can chimps talk? Not as we know it. Animal vocalisation in general is stimulus-bound—a relatively small number of utterances connected to specific cues, such as a food source or a predator. Our own cries that sometimes accompany the primary emotions (see later in this chapter) may be the vestiges of the utterances of our primate ancestors.

According to Corballis (1999) the evolution of language may have proceeded like this:

1. 6–7 million years ago—hominids diverged from the other great apes;
2. 5 million years ago—*Australopithecus* may have used hand signals;
3. 2 million years ago—gestures were used syntactically but vocalisation became prominent;
4. 100 000 years ago—speech now dominated gesture in *Homo sapiens*.

However, chimpanzees and other primates could undoubtedly vocalise well before the arrival of *Homo sapiens*. Two questions follow: (1) could simple and primitive utterances have developed into language; and (2) could speech have happened relatively suddenly—arriving with *Homo sapiens*? Corballis's answer to the first is 'probably no' and to the second 'probably yes'. Gestural communication is the most likely predecessor to spoken language.

A limited use of gesture and reciprocal gesture for communication may extend back more than 25 million years to the common ancestors of humans, apes and monkeys. However, when hominids (our human line) stood up and walked, their hands were no longer instruments of locomotion and could serve extensively as tools for gestural communication.

In today's world, examples of gestural language include:

- sign languages used by the deaf;
- communicating with someone who speaks a different language;
- hand signals used superfluously, as when talking on the phone;
- religious communities bound by a vow of silence;
- sophisticated manual communication among Australian Aborigines and American Plains Indians.

Source: Based on Corballis (1999).

Gestures: Rude gestures can cross cultural boundaries. Does the double gesture make it twice as bad?

our chest, while in Japan they put a finger to the nose (DeVos & Hippler, 1969). A sideways nod of the head means 'no' in Australia but 'yes' in India, and in Turkey 'no' is indicated by moving the head backwards and rolling the eyes upwards (Rubin, 1976). In Australia we invite people to approach by beckoning with an upturned finger, while Indians use all four downturned fingers. If you were to draw your finger across your throat it would mean, in Australia, that you'd 'had it'. The same gesture would be interpreted in Swaziland as 'I love you'. Cross-cultural differences in the meaning of gestures can have serious consequences. Argyle (1975) recounted the tale of a missionary girl who tried to shake hands with an African chieftain, who interpreted this as an attempt to throw him to the ground.

Body language can serve other functions apart from illustrating or replacing spoken language. The relative status of interactants can be very evident from body cues (Mehrabian, 1972). Higher-status individuals adopt a relaxed, open posture, with arms and legs asymmetrically positioned and a backward lean to the body. Lower-status individuals adopt a more rigid, closed and upright posture, with arms close to the body and feet together. Status differences between men and women in society may explain why, all things being equal, men tend to adopt a higher-status body posture and women a lower-status posture (Henley, 1977).

Finally, posture communicates information about attraction. People who like one another tend to lean forward, maintain a relaxed posture and face one another (Mehrabian, 1972).

TOUCH

Touch is perhaps the earliest form of communication we learn. Long before we learn language, and even before we are adept at using body illustrators or gestures, we give and receive information by touch. There are many different types of touch (e.g. brief, enduring, firm, gentle) to different parts of the body (e.g. hand, shoulder, chest). The meaning of a touch varies as a function of the type of touch, the context within which the touch occurs, who touches whom, and what the relationship is between the interactants (e.g. man and wife, doctor and patient, strangers). From an analysis of 1500 bodily contacts between people, Jones and Yarbrough (1985) identified five discrete categories of touch:

1. *positive affect*—to communicate appreciation, affection, reassurance, nurturance or sexual interest;
2. *playful*—to communicate humour and playfulness;
3. *control*—to draw attention or induce compliance;
4. *ritualistic*—to satisfy ritualised requirements (e.g. greetings and departures);
5. *task-related*—to accomplish tasks (e.g. a nurse taking a pulse, or violin teacher positioning a student's hand).

To these can be added *negative affect* (gently pushing an annoying hand away) and *aggressive touches* (slaps, kicks, shoves, punches) (Burgoon, Buller, & Woodall, 1989). Even the most incidental and fleeting touches can have significant effects. Male and female customers in a restaurant gave larger tips if they had been touched incidentally on the hand by their female waiting person (Crusco & Wetzel, 1984). In another study (Fisher, Rytting, & Heslin, 1976), university library clerks briefly touched the hand of students checking out books. Women who had been touched indicated greater liking for the clerk, and even for the library, than those who had not been touched. Male students were unaffected.

Whitcher and Fisher (1979) reported a similar sex difference in a health setting. They arranged for patients to be touched or not touched by a female nurse during a preoperative teaching interaction. Although the touches were brief and 'professional', they had significant effects on postoperative physiological and questionnaire measures. Female patients who had been touched reported less fear and anxiety, and had lower blood pressure readings, than those who had not been touched. Unfortunately, male patients who had been

touched were more anxious and had higher blood pressure!

In general, men touch women more often than women touch men, and people are more likely to touch members of the opposite than the same sex (Henley, 1973). Women derive greater pleasure from being touched than do men (Major, 1981), but the circumstances of the touch are important. Heslin (1978) asked men and women how much they would enjoy being 'squeezed and patted' in various parts of the body by strangers or close friends of the same or the opposite sex. Figure 15.9 shows that both sexes agreed that being touched by someone of the same sex was relatively

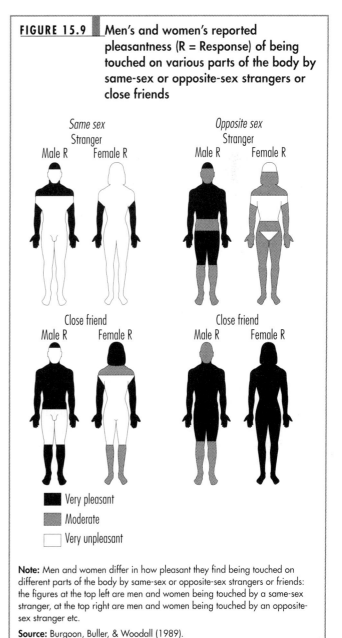

FIGURE 15.9 Men's and women's reported pleasantness (R = Response) of being touched on various parts of the body by same-sex or opposite-sex strangers or close friends

Note: Men and women differ in how pleasant they find being touched on different parts of the body by same-sex or opposite-sex strangers or friends: the figures at the top left are men and women being touched by a same-sex stranger, at the top right are men and women being touched by an opposite-sex stranger etc.

Source: Burgoon, Buller, & Woodall (1989).

unpleasant and that being touched by an opposite-sex close friend was relatively pleasant, but disagreed about the pleasantness of being touched by an opposite-sex stranger. Women did not enjoy being touched by strange men, but men enjoyed being touched by strange women!

Heslin (1978) also found that men were much more likely than women to read sexual connotations into touch, with all sorts of obvious implications for mis-communication and misinterpretation (Heslin & Alper, 1983).

Apparent sex differences in touch may reflect more general status differences in touch: people who initiate touch are perceived to be of higher status than those who receive a touch (Major & Heslin, 1982). Major (1981) has argued that the usual sex differences in touch (women react more positively than men) occur only when status differences between interactants are ambiguous or negligible; under these circumstances, wider societal assumptions about sex-linked status differences come into play. When the toucher is clearly higher in status than the recipient, both men and women react positively to being touched.

In addition to sex and status differences in touch, there is substantial cross-cultural variation in the amount of actual use made of touch. People from Latin American, Mediterranean and Arab countries touch a great deal, while people from Australia, North America, Northern Europe and Asia do not (Argyle, 1975). From a study of the touching behaviour of couples in cafés in different countries, Jourard (1966) observed, in a one-hour period, no touching in London, two touches in Florida, 110 touches in Paris, and 180 in Puerto Rico. Clearly, a Londoner in Puerto Rico or a Puerto Rican in London would feel very uncomfortable!

INTERPERSONAL DISTANCE

The forms of communication discussed so far involve parts of the body as a means of transmitting messages. Now we consider the distance between bodies as a communication channel. The study of interpersonal distance is often called **proxemics**. The closer two people are to one another, the greater the number of non-verbal cues that can be detected and so non-verbal communication can become richer. One implication is, therefore, that interpersonal distance can be used to regulate privacy and intimacy: the greater the distance, the more private you can be. On the basis of extensive observational studies, mainly in the United States, Hall (1966) has identified the existence of four discrete *interpersonal distance zones*—an intimate zone, a personal zone, a social zone and a public zone—each a little more removed from the individual's body (see Table 15.3).

Interpersonal distance can be used to communicate intimacy and associated information about liking (Hayduk, 1983) and status. For instance, Rosenfeld

Interpersonal distance: Her personal space is being invaded—or is it?

(1965) had female students talk with a female confederate with the goal of either appearing friendly or of avoiding the appearance of friendliness. The friendly participants placed their chairs on average 1.5 metres from the confederate, while those who did not want to appear friendly placed their chairs 2.25 metres away. Dean, Willis and Hewitt (1975) found that navy personnel maintained greater interpersonal distance when interacting with someone of a different rank than someone of the same rank, and the effect was stronger as the difference in rank grew.

Interpersonal distance is such a potent cue to intimacy that it can be disconcerting to find ourselves at an inappropriate distance from someone. Argyle and Dean (1965) proposed an intimacy-equilibrium theory, which predicts that when intimacy signals are increased in one modality they are decreased in other modalities (e.g. eye contact). For instance, on approaching a stranger in the street people are quite content to gaze; as soon as the approaching stranger crosses into their social zone (about 3.5 metres), people avert their gaze or feel compelled to engage in some form of ritualised recognition (a smile or mumbled greeting). Intimacy-

A CLASSIC IN SOCIAL PSYCHOLOGY

TABLE 15.3 Four zones of space in social interaction: How close is comfortable?

ZONE	DISTANCE	DESCRIPTION
Intimate distance	Up to 0.5 m	At this distance, which may involve physical contact, much is exposed about a person. Cues can come from sight, sound, smell, body temperature and depth and pace of breath.
Personal distance	0.5–1.25 m	This is the transitional area between intimate contact and formal behaviour. It is the normal distance for everyday interactions with friends and acquaintances. Touching is still possible at this distance. Although a lot of cues are still available, the effects of body temperature, smell and breathing are greatly reduced.
Social distance	1.25–4 m	This is the typical distance for casual interactions with people who are not well known, and for business interactions. Many cues are lost at this distance, but verbal contact is still easily maintained. Furniture arrangement usually falls within this distance. For example, the typical office desk is about 75 cm deep. Allowing for chair space on either side, people interacting across the desk are usually 1.2m apart. (Differences attributable to rank are also observable with personal space: managers usually have much wider desks.)
Public distance	4–8 m	At this distance communication cues become quite gross. This distance is common for lecturers, public speakers and celebrities. In a lecture hall, lecterns are usually placed about 3.5m back from the first row of seats. Courtrooms also use this spacing to remove the judge from easy communication. In these situations, interaction is often unwanted and the distance conveys this message.

Source: Hall (1966).

equilibrium theory is nicely illustrated by how people behave in elevators. Interpersonal distance is inappropriately close, and so people reduce intimacy cues in other modalities by assiduously avoiding eye contact (Zuckerman, Miserandino, & Bernieri, 1983).

Elevator behaviour is only one example of the way in which physical space can enforce inappropriate levels of intimacy. Inappropriate seating arrangements can have a similar effect (Sommer, 1969). Seating people in a large-diameter circle facing each other would be an inappropriate way to promote a friendly, relaxed atmosphere: interpersonal distance is inappropriately great and there is a confrontational orientation between people across the circle. We can also find examples of appropriate seating. In some transport lounges, for instance, where people are forced to be overly close to strangers, seats are oriented away from one another to inhibit eye contact, and TV screens may be used to distract attention.

Inappropriate interpersonal distance can be stressful. Middlemist, Knowles and Mutter (1976) conducted a memorable study in which a male confederate loitered outside a men's urinal until someone entered. The confederate followed the man into the urinal and stood in another cubicle that varied in distance from him. The closer they were, the longer the man took to begin urinating and the faster the act was completed!

Interpersonal distance violations can also occur as a consequence of interaction between people with different interpersonal distance zones. There are notable differences in interpersonal distance zones as a function of culture, age and sex. For instance, Aiello and Jones (1971) found that Black and working-class children in the United States tend to stand closer to people than do White or non-working-class children. Other research reveals that Southern Europeans prefer closer interactions to Northern Europeans, children tolerate closer distances than adults and women interact more closely, especially with other women, than do men.

IMPRESSION MANAGEMENT AND DECEPTION

Non-verbal communication can be subliminal and automatic, and we are often unaware that we and others are using it. However, we do have some control and awareness, and we can use non-verbal cues strategically to create an impression of ourselves or to influence other people's beliefs, attitudes and behaviour (DePaulo, 1992). Sometimes, we can detect others' strategic use of non-verbal cues. This raises the possibility that people may try to hide their true feelings or communicate false feelings or information by the controlled use of appropriate non-verbal cues. In general, such attempts at deception are not completely successful as there is information leakage via non-verbal channels. As Freud (1905) so eloquently remarked:

He that has eyes to see and ears to hear may convince himself that no mortal can keep a secret. If his lips are silent, he chatters with his fingertips; betrayal oozes out of him at every pore.

Research indicates that people are relatively good at controlling the verbal content of a message to conceal deception. Liars try to avoid saying things that might give them away and so they tend to make fewer factual statements, are prone to making vague, sweeping statements and leave gaps in the conversation (Knapp, Hart, & Dennis, 1974). There is also a tendency for attempts at deception to be accompanied by a slightly raised vocal pitch (Ekman, Friesen, & Scherer, 1976). Facial expressions are generally not very 'leaky': people tend to make a special and concerted effort to control facial cues to deception. However, with so much attention diverted to facial cues, other channels of non-verbal communication are left unguarded. For example, deceivers tend to touch their face more often (Ekman & Friesen, 1974) or fiddle with their hands, their glasses or other external objects (Knapp, Hart, & Dennis, 1974) (see third focus question).

Some people are better than others at concealing deception. For instance, people who habitually monitor their own behaviour carefully tend to be better liars (Siegman & Reynolds, 1983; see Chapter 4 for further information about self-monitoring). People who are highly motivated to deceive because, for instance, they believe it to be necessary for career advancement tend to be adept at controlling verbal channels (DePaulo, Lanier, & Davis, 1983) but, ironically, poor at controlling other channels. This is often their downfall.

However, people are generally poor at detecting deception (DePaulo, 1994). Even those whose jobs are essentially the detection of deception (e.g. in the customs, police, legal and intelligence professions) are often not significantly better than the general population (Kraut & Poe, 1980). People who do detect deception tend to feel only generally suspicious and are not sure exactly what false information is being communicated (DePaulo & Rosenthal, 1979; DePaulo & DePaulo, 1989). Interestingly, although women are superior to men at reading other people's non-verbal cues (Hall, 1978), they are no better than men at detecting deception (Rosenthal & DePaulo, 1979).

Does this discussion of deception lead to the conclusion that we are more likely to get away with a lie than to be detected? Zuckerman, DePaulo and Rosenthal (1981) have reviewed research on deception and conclude that, overall, receivers have the edge: they are slightly better at detecting deception than senders are at concealing it.

Impression management and deception have another consequence that we have already discussed (see Chapters 4, 5 and 10). Social psychology often tries to gain insight into people's underlying attitudes and feelings by administering questionnaires or conducting surveys or interviews. In the context of our discussion of impression management and deception, we can see that this enterprise is fraught with difficulties. Social psychologists are continually seeking non-reactive unobtrusive measures. For example, there is the **bogus pipeline technique** (Jones & Sigall, 1971), where research participants are led to believe that the researchers have unambiguous physiological measures against which to check the validity of their attitudinal responses (see Chapter 5 for details).

Another example: Maass and her associates take advantage of the linguistic intergroup bias effect (Franco & Maass, 1996; Maass, 1999; Maass & Arcuri, 1996; Maass, Salvi, Arcuri, & Semin, 1989) to detect underlying prejudices through speech style. Prejudiced people talk about the negative attributes of outgroups in broad and general terms that nevertheless make the attributes appear to be enduring and immutable, whereas they talk about the positive attributes of outgroups in very concrete, specific terms that are transitorily tied to the specific context.

Conversation and discourse

Although language and non-verbal communication are considered separately in this chapter, they usually occur together in communication (Cappella & Palmer, 1993). Non-verbal and paralinguistic behaviours can influence the meaning of what is said and also serve important functions in regulating the flow of conversation.

CONVERSATION

Conversations have distinct phases (e.g. opening and closing) and an array of complex cultural rules that govern every phase of the interaction (Clark, 1985). For instance, there are ritualistic openings (e.g. 'Hello') and closings (e.g. 'Well, I must go'). We can signal the end of a face-to-face conversation non-verbally by moving apart and looking away (looking at your watch is a common but unsubtle way of doing this) and end a telephone conversation by lengthening pauses before responding. During a conversation it is important to have rules about turn-taking, otherwise there would be conversational chaos. Argyle (1975) describes a number of signals that people use to indicate they are ending their turn and giving the listener an opportunity to take the floor:

- coming to the end of a sentence;
- raising or lowering the intonation of the last word;

- drawing out the last syllable;
- leaving a sentence unfinished to invite a continuation (e.g. 'I was going to go to the beach, but, uh . . .');
- body motions such as ceasing hand gestures, opening the eyes wide or lifting the head with the last note of a question, sitting back or looking directly at the listener.

Attempts to butt in before the speaker is ready to yield the floor invite *attempt-suppressing* signals. The voice maintains the same pitch, the head remains straight, the eyes remain unchanged, the hands maintain the same gesture, the speaker may speak louder or faster and may keep a hand in mid-gesture at the end of sentences. At the same time, listeners may regularly signal that they are still listening and not seeking to interrupt. We do this by using **back-channel communication**: the listener nods or says 'mm-hmm' or 'okay' or 'right'. Ng reviewed and extended the relationship between conversational turn-taking and power to show that interruptions can convey different information. Depending on context, an interruption may be considered rude, may signify greater influence and power, and can also signify involvement, interest and support (Dindia, 1987; Ng, 1996; Ng, Bell, & Brooke, 1993; Ng & Bradac, 1993; Reid & Ng, 1999).

See Box 15.3 for an example between people of unequal power.

The course of conversation differs depending on how well the interactants know one another. Close friends are more interpersonally responsive, and tend to raise more topics and disclose more about themselves (Hornstein, 1985). Under these circumstances, women are more likely than men to talk about and self-disclose relational and personal topics (Davidson & Duberman, 1982; Jourard, 1971), but both sexes adhere to a reciprocity norm governing the intimacy of self-disclosure (Cozby, 1973). The reciprocity norm is relaxed in longer-term relationships (Morton, 1978).

In marriage, one of the most intimate of relationships, communication is a central process—and, as we have seen above, there is genuine potential for miscommunication between men and women (e.g. Mulac, Bradac, & Gibbons, 2001). Effective communication is one of the strongest correlates of marital satisfaction (Snyder, 1979), and marital therapists identify communication problems as one of the major features of marital distress (Craddock, 1980).

Noller (1984), at the University of Queensland, has analysed communication between married partners in detail by asking people to imagine situations in which they have to communicate something to their partners and to verbalise the communication (i.e. encode what they intend to communicate). The partner then has to decode the communication to discover what was

---

BOX 15.3 | **Speaking with your doctor**

POWER AND STATUS IMBALANCE IN DOCTOR–PATIENT COMMUNICATION

Effective communication is of paramount importance in the doctor–patient consultation. In order to make a correct diagnosis and provide proper treatment, the communicative context should be one in which the doctor can obtain as much relevant information as possible. To do this, the doctor should develop rapport with the patient, appear empathic, encourage the patient to speak frankly and openly and, generally, do a substantial amount of listening. Is this your experience of visiting a doctor?

Research in the United States reveals a marked conversational imbalance, with the doctor controlling the conversation (Fisher & Todd, 1983; West, 1984). The doctor does most of the talking, initiates 99% of utterances, leaves only 9% of questions to be asked by the patient, asks further questions before the patient has finished answering the last one, interrupts the patient, determines agenda and topic shifts and controls the termination of the consultation.

This communication pattern reflects a power and status imbalance between doctor and patient that resides in social status differences, unshared expertise and knowledge, and uncertainty and to some extent anxiety on the part of the patient. This is all accentuated by the context of the consultation—the doctor's surgery. Far from encouraging communicative openness, this conversational imbalance may inhibit it and, in many instances, communication may be counterproductive as far as diagnosis and treatment are concerned.

---

intended; several choices are given and only one can be selected.

Using this paradigm, Noller was able to discover that couples who scored high on a scale of marital adjustment were much more accurate at encoding their own communications, and decoding their partner's, than were couples who scored low. In general, women were better than men at encoding messages, particularly positive ones. Maritally dissatisfied couples tended to spend more time arguing, nagging, criticising and being coercive, and were poor and unresponsive listeners.

On balance, it seems that poor marital communication may be a symptom of a distressed relationship rather than something brought to the relationship by partners (Noller, 1984; Noller & Fitzpatrick, 1990). People who have problems encoding and decoding messages within the marriage may have no such problems in their non-marital relationships with others.

DISCOURSE

The social psychology of language and communication tends to analyse speech styles and non-verbal communication rather than the actual text of the communication. It tends also to break the communicative act down into components, and then reconstructs more complex communications from the interaction of different channels (e.g. verbal, visual). This approach may have some limitations. For example, a great deal of language research has rested on the use of the matched-guise technique (Lambert, Hodgson, Gardner, & Fillenbaum, 1960; see above). This technique isolates the text of a speech from the speech style (i.e. non-text) in order to see how the speaker is evaluated on the basis of the group that is marked by the speech style. However, the text of a speech is rarely truly neutral—that is, rarely carries no information on group membership (e.g. older and younger people talk about different things). Furthermore, the meaning of the text can itself be changed by speech style. Thus text and non-text features of utterances are inextricable, together conveying meaning that influences attitude (Giles, Coupland, Henwood, Harriman, & Coupland, 1990).

This suggests that we might need to look to the entire **discourse** (what is said, in what way, by whom and for what purpose) in order to understand the contextualised attitudes that emerge (e.g. Billig, 1987; Edwards & Potter, 1992; Giles & Coupland, 1991; Potter & Wetherell, 1987).

This idea has been taken up by a number of researchers in the study of racism and sexism, which are embedded in and created by discourse (Condor, 1988; Potter & Wetherell, 1987; van Dijk, 1987, 1993; see Chapter 10). It has also been employed in the study of intergenerational talk (Giles & Coupland, 1991), homophobia and prejudice against people with HIV (Pittam & Gallois, 1996), political rhetoric (Billig, 1987, 1991, 1996) and collective action and protest (Reicher, 1996, 2001). The entire discourse is considered the unit of analysis, and it is through discourse that people construct categories of meaning. For instance, 'the economy' does not really exist for most of us. It is something that we bring into existence through talk (see discussion of **social representations** in Chapters 3 and 5).

A good example of discourse analysis is Rapley's (1998) analysis of Pauline Hanson's maiden speech to the Australian Federal Parliament in September 1996. Hanson suddenly rose to prominence in Australia in 1996 when she was unexpectedly elected federal member for the seat of Oxley in greater Brisbane. She immediately formed, and was leader of, the eponymous 'Pauline Hanson's One Nation Party'. One Nation's platform was nationalism, monoculturalism, opposition to affirmative action, anti-immigration, anti-intellectualism, anti-arts, economic isolationism and promotion of the right to own and bear arms. The party's organisational structure was highly authoritarian.

One Nation polled 23% of the state vote at the early 1998 Queensland state election and 8% of the national vote at the October 1998 federal election. Rapley, at Murdoch University in Perth, conducted a very careful analysis of Hanson's speeches to identify One Nation's true agenda. Rapley believed, and was able to show, that a relatively thin veneer of modern prejudice (see Chapter 10) concealed an underlying current of old-fashioned prejudice.

The analysis of discourse is clearly a useful tool for revealing hidden agendas and laying bare concealed prejudices (Wetherell, Taylor, & Yates, 2001). However, the discourse analysis approach in social psychology often goes one step further by arguing that many social psychological concepts such as attitude, motivation, cognition and identity may likewise be constituted through discourse and, therefore, any discussion of them as real causal processes or structures is misguided. If accepted in its extreme form, this idea necessarily rejects much of social psychology and invites a new social psychology that focuses on talk, not people, groups or cognition, as the basic social psychological unit. This interesting and provocative idea forms the core of the *discourse analysis* approach to social psychology (e.g. Edwards, 1997; Potter, 1996; Potter & Wetherell, 1987; Potter, Wetherell, Gill, & Edwards, 1990). It has its origins in post-structuralism (Foucault, 1972), ethnomethodology (Garfinkel, 1967), ethogenics (Harré, 1979) and dramaturgical perspectives (Goffman, 1959). Critics believe, however, that it can be extreme in its rejection of cognitive processes and structures (Abrams & Hogg, 1990c; Zajonc, 1989) and that it may be more profitable to retain cognition and theorise how it articulates with language (Giles & Coupland, 1991).

Computer-mediated communication

No chapter on communication in the 21st century would be complete without recognition that increasingly, people in the developed world communicate electronically with one another via phone, email and the Internet. The biggest development, of course, is the explosion of *computer-mediated communication* (CMC) over the past 10 years. Not surprisingly, research in this area is in its infancy—it is as yet relatively fragmented, unprogrammatic and atheoretical (Hollingshead, 2001; McGrath & Hollingshead, 1994). There are, however, four general findings:

1. CMC restricts paralanguage and non-verbal communication channels. This has little effect on

Gender-specific email: 'Believe me. Only a guy would write that!'

communication between strangers, but negatively affects interaction between people who have a closer relationship (Hollingshead, 1998). Non-verbal and paralanguage cues can be introduced into CMC by emphasis (e.g. 'YES!!!') or by means of what are called *emoticons* (e.g. the 'smiley' :-)).

2. CMC can suppress the amount of information that is exchanged, which in turn can lead to poorer communicative outcomes. Generally, procedural aspects of group discussion that improve information exchange and group decisions in face-to-face settings may not have the same effect in computer-mediated settings (Hollingshead, 1996; Straus & McGrath, 1994).

3. CMC has a 'participation equalisation effect' that evens out many of the status effects that occur in face-to-face communicative contexts. People may feel less inhibited because they are less personally identifiable (see **deindividuation** in Chapter 11). The effect depends on how effectively identity and status markers are concealed by the electronic medium (Spears & Lea, 1994). For example, emails usually have a signature that clearly indicates the identity and status of the communicator. According to the social identity analysis of deindividuation phenomena

(Reicher, Spears, & Postmes, 1995), personal anonymity in the presence of a highly salient social identity will make people conform strongly to identity-congruent norms, and be easily influenced by group leaders and normative group members. CMC research has confirmed this (Postmes, Spears, & Lea, 1998; Postmes, Spears, Sakhel, & de Groot, 2001).

4. Although, on balance, CMC hinders interaction and group performance initially, over time people adapt quite successfully to this mode of communication (Arrow, Berdahl, Bouas, Craig, Cummings, Lebie et al., 1996; Walther, 1996). Indeed, in many ways people gradually respond to CMC as if it were not computer-mediated. Williams and his associates found that, when people are ignored in email interactions or chat rooms, they can interpret it as ostracism (called cyberostracism) and react much as they would in face-to-face settings (Williams, Cheung, & Choi, 2000; see Chapter 13 for more on ostracism).

We have already noted that men and women differ in how they communicate non-verbally when interacting with each other. Let us close with an example from local CMC research. Thomson and Murachver (2001) at Otago University investigated gender-preferential communication in students' email messages. Surprisingly, there are male–female differences in electronic communication, even when the sex of the target person is unknown to the sender. The differences are small but, when used in combination, allow quite accurate classification of a male or female sender.

Here are some of the differences. Female senders used more intensive adverbs (e.g. 'It was *really* good'), hedges (e.g. 'It was *sort of* interesting'), emotive references (e.g. 'I was *upset*') and provided more personal information (e.g. where they worked). On the other hand, male senders were more insulting (e.g. 'You were *stupid* to take that course') and offered more opinions (e.g. 'The protest was worthwhile'). Perhaps with your own knowledge of sex-stereotypical behaviour you will not be surprised at these findings after all!

Summary

- Language is a shared, rule-governed and meaningfully structured system of elementary sounds. Speech is the articulation of language.
- Language does not determine thought, but makes it easier to think about things that have communicative importance in our social and physical environment.

- The way we speak carries information about our feelings and motives, our membership of social groups (e.g. sex, ethnicity, region, age), to whom we are talking and in what context.
- Ethnic groups may actively promote their own language, or gradually abandon it, depending on the

degree of vitality they consider their ethnolinguistic group to possess in a multi-ethnic context.

- People tailor their speech style to the communicative context, either automatically or consciously. Minority ethnic groups tend to converge on higher-status speech styles unless they consider the status hierarchy illegitimate and the vitality of their own group is high.
- For ethnolinguistic minority groups, vitality considerations provide the motivational framework for the acquisition of native-like mastery, as opposed to classroom proficiency, of the dominant group's language as a second language.
- Non-verbal channels of communication (e.g. gaze, facial expression, posture, gesture, touch, interpersonal distance) carry important information about

our feelings and emotions, as well as about relative status.

- We have less awareness of and control over non-verbal communication than spoken language. For this reason, non-verbal cues can often give away a lie.
- Non-verbal cues play an important role in regulating turn-taking and other features of conversation.
- As with language and speech style, there are large cross-cultural differences in non-verbal communication.
- A great deal of information about communication can be learned from an analysis of what is said, in what way, by whom and in what context—by focusing on complete communicative events (i.e. discourse).

LINKS

YOU HAVE READ ABOUT:	WHICH LINKS TO:
Language and ethnicity	social identity theory of intergroup relations (11)
Language vitality and speech accommodation	social mobility and social change belief structures (11)
Sex, age and language	sexism and ageism as categories of prejudice (10)
Emotion as a form of communication	distress in others as a cue to empathy (14)
Interpersonal distance	interpersonal attraction (13)
Collectivism and the tendency to seek help	individualism versus collectivism across cultures (16)
Discourse as a method of analysing conversation	discourse analysis as a replacement for attitude measurement (5)

Key terms

back-channel communication (p. 405)
bogus pipeline technique (p. 404)
communication (p. 385)
communication accommodation theory (p. 391)
deindividuation (p. 407)
discourse (p. 406)
display rules (p. 398)
emblems (p. 399)
ethnolinguistic group (p. 388)
ethnolinguistic identity theory (p. 388)
ethnolinguistic vitality (p. 389)
evolutionary social psychology (p. 399)

gaze (p. 395)
gestures (p. 399)
illocution (p. 385)
illustrators (p. 399)
impression management (p. 404)
kinesics (p. 399)
language (p. 385)
linguistic relativity (p. 386)
locution (p. 385)
matched-guise technique (p. 387)
morpheme (p. 385)
nature–nurture controversy (p. 398)
non-verbal communication (p. 394)
paralanguage (p. 386)
phonemes (p. 385)
postures (p. 399)

proxemics (p. 402)
received pronunciation (RP) (p. 388)
social identity theory (p. 388)
social markers (p. 387)
social representations (p. 406)
speech (p. 394)
speech accommodation theory (p. 390)
speech convergence (p. 390)
speech divergence (p. 390)
speech style (p. 386)
stereotype (p. 391)
subjective vitality (p. 389)
utterance (p. 385)
visual dominance behaviour (p. 396)

FURTHER READING

Bayley, B., & Schechter, S. R. (Eds.). (2003). *Language sociali-sation in bilingual and multilingual societies*. Clevedon, UK: Multilingual Matters. Sociolinguists, educationists and other social scientists take an international perspective on language socialisation and bilingualism from early childhood to adult-hood. Contexts include home, schools, communities and workplaces.

DePaulo, B. M., & Friedman, H. S. (1998). Nonverbal commu-nication. In D. T. Gilbert, S. T. Fiske, & G. Lindzey (Eds.), *The handbook of social psychology* (4th ed., Vol. 2, pp. 3–40). New York: McGraw-Hill. Detailed and scholarly overview of the field of non-verbal communication in the most recent edition of the classic handbook—a primary source for theory and research.

Giles, H., & Coupland, N. (1991). *Language: Contexts and con-sequences*. Milton Keynes, UK: Open University Press. Readable introduction and overview of the social psychology of language, with an emphasis on intergroup dimensions and a balanced coverage of discourse perspectives.

Giles, H., & Robinson, W. P. (Eds.). (1993). *Handbook of language and social psychology*. Oxford, UK: Pergamon. Comprehensive collection of critical and review chapters, covering interpersonal communication from a language and social psychology perspective.

Grasser, A. C., Millis, K. K., & Swan, R. A. (1997). Discourse comprehension. *Annual Review of Psychology, 48*, 163–189. A dispassionate overview of the technical contributions of dis-course analysis to psychology in general.

Knapp, M. L., & Miller, G. R. (Eds.). (1994). *The handbook of interpersonal communication* (2nd ed.). Thousand Oaks, CA: Sage. Invaluable source book for in-depth knowledge of vir-tually all areas of interpersonal communication.

Krauss, R. M., & Chiu, C. Y. (1998). Language and social behavior. In D. T. Gilbert, S. T. Fiske, & G. Lindzey (Eds.), *The handbook of social psychology* (4th ed., Vol. 2, pp. 41–88). New York: McGraw-Hill. Detailed and scholarly overview of the field of language, in the most recent edition of the classic handbook—a primary source for theory and research.

Noels, K. A., Giles, H., & Le Poire, B. (2003). Language and com-munication processes. In M. A. Hogg & J. Cooper (Eds.), *The Sage handbook of social psychology* (pp. 232–257). London: Sage. A very accessible review, from a social psychological perspective, of research on language and communication, including both verbal and non-verbal communication.

Russell, J. A., & Fernandez-Dols, J. M. (Eds.). (1997). *The psychology of facial expression: Studies in emotion and social interaction*. Cambridge, UK: Cambridge University Press. A critical overview of major theoretical perspectives on facial expression, including ethological, neurobehavioural and devel-opmental views.

Culture

FOCUS QUESTIONS

1. John is Australian and has been brought up to defend what he thinks is true. After living in South Korea for a few months, he has noticed that the locals are more concerned about maintaining harmony in their social relationships than in deciding who's right and who's wrong. Why, he wonders, can't they just speak their minds?

2. Bernice and Inga have studied social psychology at the University of the South Pacific. They are concerned that what they have studied is based on Western theory, with limited relevance to the traditional group-centred values of people in their community. Do they have a point?

3. Keiko and her new husband are Japanese. After a traditional wedding in Hokkaido they emigrate to San Francisco. Then a dilemma arises: should they maintain the customs of their homeland or should they become entirely American? Do they have any other choices?

THIS CHAPTER DISCUSSES:

- culture, society and social behaviour
- links with cultural anthropology
- cultural variations in social processes
- the two psyches: East and West
- intercultural communication
- social action in the global village.

The cultural context

Culture is a pervasive but slippery construct. There is a great deal of popular talk about culture, cultural differences, cultural sensitivity, cultural change, culture shock, subcultures and culture contact; but what precisely is culture and how much and through what processes does it affect people, and how in turn is it affected by people? In his Presidential Address to the American Association for the Advancement of Science in 1932, the sociologist Franz Boas (cited in Kluckhohn, 1954, p. 921) made a plea for his own discipline to pay much greater attention to cultural variation in behaviour:

It seems a vain effort to search for sociological laws disregarding what should be called social psychology, namely, the reaction of the individual to culture. They can be no more than empty formulas that can be imbued with life only by taking account of individual behaviour in cultural settings.

Boas believed that culture is central to social science and that the study of culture's influence on people is the definition of the discipline of social psychology. This is not an isolated view. Wundt (1897, 1916), the founder of psychology as an experimental science, believed that social psychology was all about collective phenomena such as culture—a position shared by Durkheim (1898), one of the founders of sociology (see Farr, 1996; Hogg & Williams, 2000; also Chapter 1).

Throughout this book we have repeatedly drawn attention to the impact of culture on behaviour—for example, in Chapter 3 we discuss how culture intrudes upon intergroup attributions (see Figure 3.7). In this chapter we draw together and integrate these observations, but go further to ask some fundamental questions about the universality of social psychological laws, and about the relevance of social psychological principles to cultures in which such principles were not developed.

Cross-cultural psychologists, and some social psychologists, have provided evidence for considerable cultural variation in a range of quite basic human behaviours and social psychological processes. Most of this research identifies a general difference between Eastern and Western cultures—indeed, the contemporary debate in social psychology about 'culture' is largely restricted to this contrast or, more accurately, the contrast between (Eastern) collectivism and (Western) individualism.

The big question then is 'How deep do these differences go?' Are they simply differences in normative practices, or do they go much deeper to affect basic cognitive and perceptual processes? In this chapter we also explore the role of language barriers to effective communica-

tion, the nature of acculturation, and what role social and cross-cultural psychologists can play in helping to improve intercultural relations.

The issues discussed in this final chapter of our book build upon and reflect back on many of the themes and ideas explored in earlier chapters: we hope that this chapter provides a cultural context and a cultural challenge to what has gone before.

Locating culture in social psychology

Has social psychology neglected culture?

If you are an Australian or a New Zealander, which of these countries have you visited: Indonesia, Fiji, Japan, the United States, England, Italy? You could add some more to this list. One of the first things that strikes you in a foreign land is the different language, along with the appearance and dress of the local people. Other differences may be more subtle and slower to emerge—they are to do with underlying values and attitudes. Culture infuses behaviour and is the lifeblood of ethnic and national groups. In unravelling the properties and processes of *groups*, social psychologists have usually eschewed culture, focusing instead on normative differences between groups and subgroups (see Chapter 9). The social psychological historian Robert Farr (1996) has argued that psychological theory and research in social psychology has been dominated by one cultural perspective—that of a middle-class, largely Anglo-Saxon, America. In itself this is not surprising, as so many psychologists have been middle-class White Americans. A leading cross-cultural psychologist, Harry Triandis, once noted (1980, p. ix) that:

One of the key facts about psychology is that most of the psychologists who have ever lived and who are now living can be found in the United States . . . The rest of the world has only about 20% of the psychologists that are now or have ever been alive.

There is a natural tendency for people to fail to recognise that their life is only one of many possible lives—that what may appear natural may merely be normative (Garfinkel, 1967). The problem for social psychology is that this cultural perspective is dominant—social psychology is **culture-bound** and also, to a significant extent, **culture-blind**. For example, almost all major social psychology texts are American (one reason we wrote this book was to balance this; see the Preface and Chapter 1). They are well produced and highly scholarly, but they are written by Americans for Americans—and yet these are authoritative texts in many countries around the world.

Another reason why social psychologists have under-emphasised culture may be the experimental method (Vaughan & Guerin, 1997). As explained in Chapter 1, social psychologists generally, and with good cause, consider laboratory experiments to be the most rigorous way to establish causal theories, a love affair with laboratory experimentation that dates back to the early 20th century. Laboratory experiments tend, by definition, to focus on the manipulation of focal variables in isolation from other variables, such as participants' biographical and cultural backgrounds. However, people *do*, of course, bring their autobiographical and cultural baggage into the laboratory—as Tajfel (1972a) so eloquently put it, you simply cannot do experiments in a cultural vacuum. This is not a trivial problem. Because experiments regard culture as the unproblematic backdrop to research, this method may prevent researchers from realising that culture itself may be a variable that influences the processes being studied.

DEFINITIONS

Boas (1930, p. 30) defined culture as 'the social habits of a community' and Smith & Bond (1998, p. 69) as 'systems of shared meanings'. These elements, shared activity and shared meaning, should both be included in a definition of culture, according to Greenfield and her colleagues (Greenfield, Keller, Fuligni, & Maynard, 2003). In dealing with variations in definition, Brislin (1987, p. 275) noted:

Kroeber and Kluckhohn [1952] concluded that many definitions contained 'patterns . . . of behaviour transmitted by symbols, constituting the distinctive achievements of human groups . . . [and] ideas and their attached values'. Herskovits proposed the equally influential generalization that culture is 'the man-made part of the human environment'. Triandis made a distinction between physical [e.g. houses and tools] and subjective culture [e.g. peoples' values, roles, and attitudes].

Despite these difficulties, in this chapter we focus on culture and its impact on us as social beings. We view culture as the set of cognitions and practices that identifies a specific social group and distinguishes it from others. In essence, 'culture' is the expression of group norms at the national and ethnic level (see Chapter 8 on norms, Chapter 4 on self and identity, and Chapter 11 on intergroup behaviour).

Culture, history and social psychology

In discussing Anglo-European influences on the development of social psychology in 19th-century Germany we noted the contribution of the *folk psychologists*.

Their *Völkerpsychologie* was sufficiently well established for Steinthal and Lazarus to devote a journal to it in 1860 (see Chapter 1). By the beginning of the 20th century, anthropologists were devoting time to the concept of culture and the process of cultural transmission. The task became easier with the decline of instinct-based explanations, such as that espoused by McDougall (1908; see Murphy & Murphy, 1931).

Are the social scientists who study culture today ethnocentric? The answer is probably 'no', in the stronger sense of that term (see Chapter 3). However, they are vulnerable to assumptions based on their own cultural world view in terms of what data they collect in another cultural setting and how they go about the enterprise.

CONTRIBUTION OF CULTURAL ANTHROPOLOGY

A scientific interest in culture and in social groups generally is imbedded in the social history of Western Europe. We note in Chapter 4 that, during and after the 16th century, there was a confluence of factors contributing to new ways of construing both the individual and the wider social group: (a) *secularisation*—dealing with the here and now rather than the afterlife; (b) *industrialisation*—people being mobile in order to seek work and therefore needing to have a portable personal identity rather than one imbedded in a static structure such as the extended family; and (c) *enlightenment*—a philosophy that endowed individuals with rationality and acknowledged that they had the intellect to manage their social lives (see also Allport, 1954a; Fromm, 1941; Weber, 1930).

By the late 19th and early 20th century, the development of cross-cultural research is virtually the history of the origins of modern cultural anthropology. Some major works that guided thinking were, in the United Kingdom, Frazer's (1890) *The Golden Bough* and Malinowski's (1927) *Sex and Repression in Savage Society* and, in the United States, Boas's (1911) *The Mind of Primitive Man*. In terms of what was to follow, the most influential of these early figures was Franz Boas at Columbia University, who single-mindedly advanced the proposition that personality is formed by culture. This was not easy going in a context where behaviour was thought to be biologically determined, as in Freudian theory (see Chapter 12).

Cultural studies were treated by psychology as 'unassimilatable objects' (Mead, 1974). Margaret Mead (1928/1961) and Ruth Benedict (1934) each studied with Boas and wrote graphically, on the basis of **ethnographic research**, of cultures—where the norms that encouraged some actions but sanctioned others—differed enormously. Mead, who was also trained in psychology, made a determined effort to divert anthropology from a universal biological model towards a treatment of how differences between cultures affected psychological development (Price-Williams, 1976). By the 1950s, cross-cultural research had made a major impact on theories of child development and socialisation (Child, 1954).

There have been isolated but influential instances of early psychological studies that drew on cultural anthropology. At Cambridge University, Bartlett conducted a series of experiments (e.g. Bartlett, 1923, 1932) on social and cultural factors affecting memory. In one, he borrowed a folk tale, *The War of the Ghosts*, from Boas. His participants read the tale and later reconstructed it as precisely as possible from memory. In a variation using serial reproduction, each participant in a group passed a recalled version on to the next participant, in an analogue of spreading a rumour. In both cases the original story was systematically reconstructed to bring it more into line with what they would remember easily. The consequence was a 'cultural' transformation of the tale.

This early research is remarkably consistent with Moscovici's (e.g. 1988) more recent notion of **social representations** which is discussed fully in Chapter 3. You will recall that social representations are shared frameworks for rendering the world meaningful, and that they are developed and maintained by social interaction.

In his influential text, *Social Psychology*, Klineberg (1940) introduced findings from ethnology (the 'science of races') and comparative sociology, an unusual innovation well ahead of its time. For much of the 20th century social psychologists distanced themselves from cross-cultural material. There were two reasons: they were unwilling to be seen as 'tender-minded', particularly as anthropologists were often wedded to psychoanalytic theory and methods (Segall, 1965); they were also increasingly committed to using experimental methods (Vaughan & Guerin, 1997; see Chapter 1).

RISE OF CROSS-CULTURAL PSYCHOLOGY

The birth of cross-cultural psychology was marked by the publication of the *International Journal of Psychology* in Paris in 1966 and the *Journal of Cross-Cultural Psychology* in the United States in 1970. Two eminent social psychologists, Lois and Gardner Murphy (1970), contributed their thoughts in the latter journal on what cross-cultural psychology might achieve. Just as the independence of social psychology has been marked by the arrival of handbooks, so has that of cross-cultural psychology, with works published in 1980 and 1997 (Triandis et al., 1980; Berry, Poortinga, & Pandey, 1997). Cross-cultural psychologists wanted answers to three questions:

1. Are Western psychological theories valid in other cultures?
2. Are there psychological constructs that are culture-specific?
3. How can we evolve a psychology with universal relevance?

Cultural anthropologists have long been interested in the second and third of these questions (Kluckhohn, 1954). With the arrival of the new subdiscipline came new terminology and a new distinction: the **etic–emic distinction**, drawn by analogy from the linguistic distinction between phon*etics* and phon*emics*. As Smith and Bond (1998, p. 57) noted:

. . . Berry [1969] argues that 'etic' analyses of behaviour are those that focus on universals, principally those that . . . are either simple or variform. For example, we all eat, we almost all have intimate relations with certain others, and we all have ways of attacking enemies. An 'emic' analysis of these behaviours, on the other hand, would focus on the different, varied ways in which each of these activities was carried out in any specific cultural setting. Successful emic analyses could be expected to establish generalisations that were only valid locally.

Power distance, for example, is an etic construct because it can be observed in most cultures, while *amae*, or passive love, is an emic construct that is probably limited to Japanese culture. (Power distance and *amae* are discussed further below.) Emic constructs may 'grow' into etic ones if they are appropriately investigated and established across cultures.

The formal recognition of the subdiscipline is complete. In addition to the journals and books, there are now university courses devoted to cross-cultural psychology in various countries. In recent years, however, further terms have been added to describe slightly different activities undertaken by some groups of researchers. **Cross-cultural psychologists** generally use traditional social psychological (questionnaires, interviews) and statistical methods to compare and contrast ethnic and national groups. **Cultural psychologists** tend to study cultural transmission and change, and prefer qualitative methodology (including discourse analysis). **Intercultural psychologists** usually concentrate on how people communicate across cultures and emphasise the dynamic qualities of interactions.

Cultural variations in behaviour

In considering some of the major scientific effects underlying theory in social psychology, Smith and Bond (1998) concluded that the solitary finding that clearly replicated across cultures is obedience to authority (see Chapter 7). This would hardly be surprising, given that authority is a cornerstone of any major social system. Below, we touch on some more substantial differences and several interesting variations by culture. These are by no means exhaustive. A target for the future is for psychologists who are social, cross-cultural, cultural and intercultural to be alive to processes that are relatively universal and those that are relatively culturally specific.

VARIATION IN ATTRIBUTIONAL STYLE

In Chapter 3 we discuss how people make causal attributions for their own and other's behaviours (e.g. Hewstone, 1989). A key point that emerged from attribution research was that people are not naïve scientists or, more properly, are *very naïve* scientists in the way they make attributions. The sorts of attributions they make are influenced by motivations, by social orientations and by cultural perspectives. More specifically, it is culture that allows us to make an attribution that is appropriate to the context—failure to pay attention to culture would have 'interesting' consequences for the unfortunate attributor.

Of more direct interest to mainstream social psychologists are variations in *attributional style*. One example concerns the differences in the degree to which Malay and Chinese people in Singapore show ethnocentric bias (Hewstone & Ward, 1985). This kind of difference is known as the **ultimate attribution error** (see Chapter 3, Figure 3.6). Another example involves the **fundamental attribution error**. Miller (1984) found that Hindu Indians were much less likely than North Americans to make dispositional rather than situational attributions (see Chapter 3, Figure 3.7).

VARIATION IN CONFORMITY

Smith and Bond (1998, p. 15) referred to Asch's (1951) study as the 'most widely replicated social psychology experiment of all time'. In a **meta-analysis** of studies carried out in the United States and 16 other countries they found considerable cultural variation in conformity to group pressure. It was generally stronger outside Western Europe and North America (see Figure 16.1). The authors cautioned that such a difference should not be interpreted as indicating weakness of character among non-Western cultures. The experimental context, where conformity is equivalent to making incorrect responses (see Chapter 7), could be interpreted as indicating escape from embarrassment (saving face) as much as capitulation to pressure (conformity).

Conformity in subsistence cultures

The way people function interpersonally and in groups can be profoundly affected by where they work and live. For example, people from both Western and Eastern cultures experience considerable physical and psychological stress when they live for extended periods of time in polar regions (Taylor, 1987). Furthermore, our geographical location can interact with kinship and family

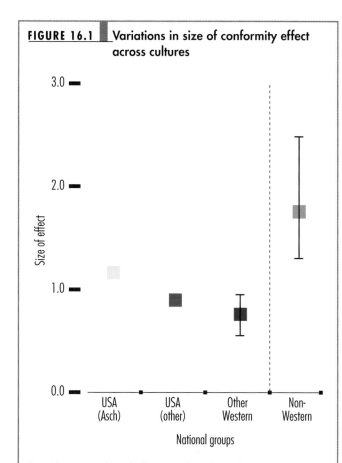

FIGURE 16.1 Variations in size of conformity effect across cultures

Note: This meta-analysis of 'effect sizes' shows that conformity rates were lower among American and other Western samples than among samples from other parts of the world. The rates among Americans have also dropped since the time in which Asch conducted his studies.

Source: Based on data from Smith & Bond (1998).

structure, child development, and group norms regarding economic practices (e.g. Price-Williams, 1976; Smith & Bond, 1998).

An early study of two subsistence cultures compared response differences in an Asch-type conformity setting.

Conformity as a necessity: This young Laplander lives in a harsh environment where survival depends on strict adherence to communal norms.

One was a food-accumulating culture, the Temne from Sierra Leone, and the other a hunter-gatherer society, the Canadian Eskimos (or Inuit) (Berry, 1967; see Box 16.1).

CULTURE AND SOCIALISATION

By the 1930s, anthropologists at Columbia University (Boas, Benedict and Mead) had established that child development was inextricably bound up with cultural norms. According to Mead, Samoan norms dictate that young people 'should keep quiet, wake up early, obey, and work hard and cheerfully' (Mead, 1928/1961, p. 130), whereas among the Manus in New Guinea there was a culturally induced disposition towards being 'the aggressive, violent, overbearing type' (Mead, 1930/1962, p. 233).

Recent research, along with older observations, has taken this argument forward to cover the phenomenon of higher rates of violence in the south and south-western regions of the United States; the trends are confined to situations involving individuals, their family or their possessions (see Box 16.2 and Table 16.1). The studies use the concept of **culture of honour** (Nisbett & Cohen, 1996) to give meaning to a regional pattern of behaviour. In this instance, it is linked to a tradition of aggression in dealing with threat and is related clearly to **machismo** in Latin American families (see Chapter 12). It can also be linked to acts of beneficence, however a person can be honour-bound to help as well as hurt. The Arabic term *izzat* has the same sense.

BOX 16.1 | **No room for dissenters among the Temne**

Berry (1967) provides an intriguing insight into the way in which culture may influence conformity. Using a variant of Asch's conformity paradigm, Berry hypothesised that a people's hunting and food-gathering practices should affect the extent to which individuals conform to their group's norms. On this basis, he compared the Temne people of Sierra Leone with the Eskimos of Canada and found a much higher conformity rate among the Temne.

The Temne subsist on a single crop, which they harvest in one concerted effort once a year. As this requires enormous cooperation and coordination of effort, consensus and agreement are strongly represented in Temne culture. Berry quotes one participant as saying 'When Temne people choose a thing, we must all agree with the decision—this is what we call cooperation' (Berry, 1967, p. 417). In contrast, the Eskimo economy involves continual hunting and gathering on a relatively individual basis. An Inuit looks after himself and his immediate family; thus, consensus is less strongly emphasised in Eskimo culture.

BOX 16.2 | **Southern honour**

Historically, Southern United States has had higher homicide rates than the rest of the country. Cohen and Nisbett (Cohen, 1996; Cohen & Nisbett, 1994, 1997; Nisbett, 1993) link greater violence in the South to the herding economy that developed in its early settlements. In other parts of the world, herders have typically resorted to force more readily when they needed to protect their property, especially in contexts where their animals can roam widely.

When self-protection can be so important, a culture of honour may develop. An individual must let an adversary know that intrusion will not be tolerated. In old Louisiana, a wife and her lover were surrendered by law to the husband, who might punish as he saw fit, including killing them. Even today, laws in the South relating to violent actions are more tolerant of violence than those in the North—for example, relating to gun ownership, spouse abuse, corporal punishment and capital punishment. According to Fischer (1989), Southern violence is not indiscriminate. For example, rates for robbery in the South are no higher than those in the North. The culture of honour would apply to self-protection, protection of the family, or when affronted.

The persistence of higher levels of violence so long after the pioneering days may follow from the use of more violent child-rearing patterns in the South (see the discussion of learned patterns of aggression and the *abuse syndrome* in Chapter 12). Boys are told to stand up for themselves and to use force in so doing, while spanking is regarded as the normal solution for misbehaviour.

See Table 16.1 for comparative responses, from the South and elsewhere, of appropriate ways of using violence for self-protection (Blumenthal, Kahn, Andrews, & Head, 1972).

Source: Based on Taylor, Peplau, & Sears (2000).

Two psyches: East meets West

Fiske, Kitayama, Markus and Nisbett (1998) refer to two culturally patterned social systems, or psyches: the European American (called, loosely, Western) and East Asian (called, loosely, Eastern). These groupings best reflect the spectrum of available research findings when dealing with cultural differences at the broadest level, although the use of these categories runs the risk of being simplistic. A further description of the two regions is that people in Western cultures have an *independent* self-concept and people in Eastern cultures have an *interdependent* self-concept (Markus & Kityama, 1991). (See

TABLE 16.1 Using violence in self-defence

Differences in the United States between Southern and non-Southern views

QUESTION AND REGION	PERCENTAGE AGREEING	PERCENTAGE AGREEING STRONGLY
A man has a right to kill:		
(a) *in self-defence*		
South	92	70
Non-South	88	57
(b) *to defend his family*		
South	97	80
Non-South	92	67
(c) *to defend his house*		
South	69	56
Non-South	52	18

Source: Based on Blumenthal, Kahn, Andrew, & Head (1972).

also the discussion in Chapter 4 of the debate about whether the self is an individual or a collective phenomenon.)

Using a cognitive metaphor, Triandis (Triandis, 1989, 1994; Triandis & Suh, 2002) has suggested that cultures provide conventions for people to sample information in their environment. When sampling for clues, those from Western cultures use elements of the personal self, such as 'I am kind', whereas those from Eastern cultures use elements of the collective self, such as '*my co-workers think* I am kind' (italics ours).

We need to keep the looseness of the dichotomies, East–West and independent–interdependent, in mind. For example, Mexican and some Latin American cultures are usually strongly based on interdependence between individuals (Diaz-Guerrero, 1987). We note that the terms 'collectivism' and 'individualism' have not been used in a consistent way (Oyserman, Coon, & Kemmelmeier, 2002) and that other terms are used interchangeably to define these orientations (e.g. independence versus interdependence; private self versus collective self).

The meanings attached to the Western and Eastern cultural models, when applied to the individual, are shown in Table 16.2. In Figure 16.2, these ideas are further elaborated to show how the self can be represented in quite different ways—the independent self and the interdependent self. These two conceptions have important implications for how the individual relates to significant others. After looking at these illustrations, think back to John's concern about 'speaking out' in South Korea (the first focus question).

We now consider two major systems, one defined in terms of values and the other in terms of relationships, that are used in modern theory to compare a wide variety of cultures. While they resonate with the broad East–West distinction outlined above, they also permit a more fine-grained comparison between individual societies.

Systems for comparing cultures

CHARACTERISING CULTURES BY VALUES

The study of **values** has a long history with a two-fold **level of explanation**—one at an individual level in psychology (see Chapter 5) and the other at a societal level in sociology. Within both disciplines a value is a broad construct. In the case of making cultural (societal) comparisons, it has provided an approach heavily used in research (Fiske et al., 1998). In this section we consider the research of Hofstede and Schwartz.

Hofstede's (1980) work was a *tour de force*. He distributed a questionnaire to 117 000 IBM respondents

TABLE 16.2 Western and Eastern cultural models of the person

THE *INDEPENDENT* PERSON:	THE *INTERDEPENDENT* PERSON:
• is bounded, stable, autonomous	• is connected, fluid, flexible
• has personal attributes that guide action	• participates in social relationships that guide action
• is achievement-oriented	• oriented to the collective
• formulates personal goals	• meets obligations and conforms to norms
• defines life by successful goal achievement	• defines life by contributing to the collective
• is responsible for own behaviour	• is responsible with others for joint behaviour
• is competitive	• is cooperative
• strives to feel good about the self	• subsumes self in the collective

Source: Based on Fiske, Kitayama, Markus, & Nisbett (1998).

FIGURE 16.2 Representations of the self: Independent versus interdependent

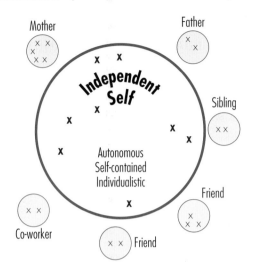

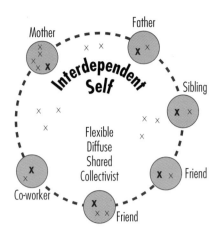

Note:
- A person's culture (see Table 16.2) may be mapped into self–other relationships.
- For the *independent* self:
  —the boundaries are impermeable
  —strong and unique traits are internalised
  —the traits of significant others, including key figures, are muted and external.
- For the *interdependent* self:
  —the boundaries are permeable
  —strong traits are shared with key figures
  —unique and internalised traits are muted.

Source: Based on Markus & Kitayama (1991).

in 40 countries and used factor analysis to isolate four dimensions (although in 1991 he added the dimension of time perspective) on which these countries could be compared:

1. *Power distance*: the degree to which unequal power in institutions and practices is accepted or, alternatively, egalitarianism is endorsed (e.g. can employees freely express disagreement with their manager?).
2. *Uncertainty avoidance*: planning for stability in dealing with life's uncertainties (e.g. believing that company rules should never be broken).
3. *Masculinity–femininity*: valuing attributes that are either masculine (e.g. achieving, gaining material success) or feminine (e.g. promoting interpersonal harmony, caring).
4. *Individualism–collectivism*: whether your identity is determined by personal choices or by the collective (e.g. having the freedom to adapt your approach to the job).

These four dimensions are the basis of the data shown in Table 16.3. The top and bottom quartiles among the 40 countries have been ranked by an index on each dimension. Take the following examples:

1. Denmark is low on power distance (0.18), uncertainty avoidance (0.23) and masculinity (0.16), but high on individualism (0.74)—Danes do not easily accept hierarchical relationships, they tolerate uncertain outcomes, are caring and egalitarian, but individualistic.
2. Japan is high on uncertainty avoidance (0.92) and masculinity (0.95)—Japanese plan to reduce life's uncertainties and want to achieve material success.
3. Singapore is high on power distance (0.74) but low on individualism (0.20)—Singaporeans tend to accept hierarchical relationships and are collectivist.

An interesting aspect of this analysis is that Eastern and Western countries do not always follow an East–West dichotomy.

Of these dimensions, by far the most popular for the work that was to follow was individualism–collectivism (Fiske, Kitayama, Markus, & Nisbett, 1998; Smith & Bond, 1998). It was the one deemed to capture the essence of the East–West dichotomy discussed above.

Schwartz and his colleagues (Schwartz, 1992; Schwartz & Bardi, 1997) offered an alternative approach, based on a tradition dating back to the work of Rokeach (1973; see Chapter 5). They started with 56 values thought to exist in different cultures. They then had more than 40 000 teachers and students from 56 nations rate these values for their relevance to themselves. Using a multidimensional scaling analysis, he found two dimensions with stable meanings:

1. *openness to change versus conservatism*—e.g. ranging from autonomy to security and tradition;

A CLASSIC IN SOCIAL PSYCHOLOGY

TABLE 16.3 | Cross-cultural differences in work-related values

	POWER DISTANCE		UNCERTAINTY AVOIDANCE		INDIVIDUALISM		MASCULINITY	
LOWEST QUARTILE	Austria	0.11	Singapore	0.08	Venezuela	0.12	Sweden	0.05
	Israel	0.13	**Denmark**	0.23	Colombia	0.13	Norway	0.08
	Denmark	0.18	Hong Kong	0.29	Pakistan	0.14	Netherlands	0.14
	New Zealand	0.22	Sweden	0.29	Peru	0.16	**Denmark**	0.16
	Ireland	0.28	Great Britain	0.35	Taiwan	0.17	Yugoslavia	0.21
	Norway	0.31	Ireland	0.35	**Singapore**	0.20	Finland	0.26
	Sweden	0.31	India	0.40	Thailand	0.20	Chile	0.28
	Finland	0.33	Philippines	0.44	Chile	0.23	Portugal	0.31
	Switzerland	0.34	USA	0.46	Hong Kong	0.25	Thailand	0.34
	Great Britain	0.35	Canada	0.48	Portugal	0.27	Spain	0.42
	Turkey	0.66	Turkey	0.85	France	0.71	Colombia	0.64
	Colombia	0.67	Argentina	0.86	Sweden	0.71	Philippines	0.64
	France	0.68	Chile	0.86	**Denmark**	0.74	Germany (FR)	0.66
	Hong Kong	0.68	France	0.86	Belgium	0.75	Great Britain	0.66
	Brazil	0.69	Spain	0.86	Italy	0.76	Ireland	0.68
	Singapore	0.74	Peru	0.87	New Zealand	0.79	Mexico	0.69
	Yugoslavia	0.76	Yugoslavia	0.88	Canada	0.80	Italy	0.70
	India	0.77	**Japan**	0.92	Netherlands	0.80	Switzerland	0.70
	Mexico	0.81	Belgium	0.94	Great Britain	0.89	Venezuela	0.73
HIGHEST	Venezuela	0.81	Portugal	1.04	Australia	0.90	Austria	0.79
QUARTILE	Philippines	0.94	Greece	1.12	USA	0.91	**Japan**	0.95

Source: Based on Hofstede (1980).

2. *self-enhancement versus self-transcendence*—e.g. ranging from mastery and power to egalitarianism and harmony with nature.

There are similarities between Schwartz's first dimension and Hofstede's individualism–collectivism, and between Schwartz's second dimension and Hofstede's power distance. An advantage of Schwartz's approach is that he carried out separate analyses, one at the level of individuals and another at the level of cultures.

Fiske and colleagues (1998) concluded that the body of cross-cultural work on values, together with other research (e.g. Smith, Dugan, & Trompenaars, 1996), indicated three groupings of nations in terms of value orientations:

1. Western European nations are individualistic and egalitarian;
2. Eastern European nations are individualistic and hierarchical;
3. East Asian nations are collectivist and hierarchical.

Research on the nature of values expressed through culture continues to flourish and some connections between the various approaches have been noted. For example, Smith and Bond (1998) point to a similarity between the concept of power distance in Hofstede's theory (see above) and authority ranking (where power and status define relationships) in Fiske's relationship models theory (see below). Bond (1996) has suggested that there is a fundamental Chinese value not captured by Western research—Confucian work dynamism.

What can we learn from this section to address the concerns of the Fijian students Bernice and Inga (see the second focus question)?

INDIVIDUALISM AND COLLECTIVISM

We have already noted that traditional and agrarian societies were collectivist. The very term 'tribe' has the sense of a collective. As far as we know, **collectivism** characterised preliterate communities as well. A shift to **individualism** has been gradual (see our earlier treatment of the rise of cultural anthropology). We consider below two examples of research based on individualism and collectivism selected from fields that have featured in earlier chapters.

Cooperation, competition and social identity

A social situation may be structured in ways that favour cooperative or competitive interactions, involving individuals or groups. In gaming research, this was encapsulated in the **prisoner's dilemma** (see Chapter 11).

Hinkle and Brown (1990) pursued this idea and suggested an important qualification to **social identity theory** (see Chapter 11). They argue that groups can vary in terms of their social orientation, from *collectivist* to *individualist*. However, groups can also vary in their orientation towards defining themselves through comparisons or not—they can vary from a *comparative* ideology to a *non-comparative* ideology. For example, some groups, such as sports teams, are intrinsically comparative—they often require a comparison group to estimate their worth. Other groups are non-comparative, such as a family whose members are close, and would think it unnecessary to compare their group's qualities with, say, those of their neighbours (see Figure 16.3).

The implication of this analysis is that not all intergroup contexts generate discrimination; groups vary in the extent to which they engage in intergroup discrimination. Those located in the upper-left quadrant of Figure 16.3 show most (or any) discrimination.

Brown and his colleagues (Brown, Hinkle, Ely, Fox-Cardamone, Maras, & Taylor, 1992) confirmed this idea in a study in which they measured individualistic and collectivist values among British participants who were members of groups that were either relatively comparative or non-comparative. They found that outgroup discrimination was highest when an individual's orientation was collectivist and the ingroup was comparative. (We should note here that conformity rates are also higher in non-Western collectivist cultures—refer back to Figure 16.1—which might be expected if collectivism implies higher ingroup identification.)

The relationship between cultural orientation and social identity has been taken further in three studies designed to show that the more strongly people identify with a (cultural) group the more strongly they will endorse and conform to the norms of individualism or collectivism that define the relevant (cultural) group.

In the first study (Jetten, Postmes, & McAuliffe, 2002), North Americans (individualist culture) were more individualistic when they identified highly with their culture than when they did not; Indonesians (collectivist culture) were less individualistic when they identified more strongly with their culture.

In the second and third studies (McAuliffe, Jetten, Hornsey, & Hogg, 2003), participants were categorised as members of an ad hoc group described as having

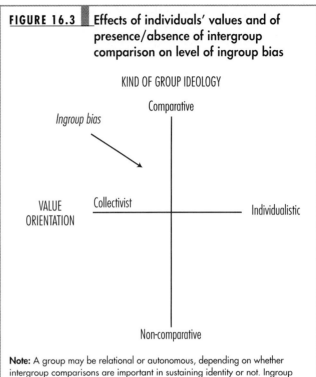

FIGURE 16.3 Effects of individuals' values and of presence/absence of intergroup comparison on level of ingroup bias

Note: A group may be relational or autonomous, depending on whether intergroup comparisons are important in sustaining identity or not. Ingroup bias occurs when a person has a collectivist value orientation and is a member of a group with a comparative ideology. This combination occurs in the upper-left quadrant.

Source: Based on Hinkle & Brown (1990, p. 48).

either an individualist or a collectivist group culture. They then evaluated a group member based on a series of statements, manipulated to reflect individualism or collectivism, ostensibly made by the group member. It was found that collectivist behaviour was evaluated more positively than individualist behaviour when the group norm prescribed collectivism, but that this preference was attenuated when group norms prescribed individualism. Furthermore, consistent with the idea that evaluations were driven by conformity to *salient norms*, attenuation occurred only for high identifiers, not for low identifiers.

In two further studies (McAuliffe, Jetten, Hornsey, & Hogg, in press) dissenting group members were better tolerated and less likely to be rejected when the group had an individualistic norm and participants identified strongly with the group.

Prosocial behaviour

We note in Chapter 14 that **prosocial behaviour** is more likely to occur in rural areas than in cities. It is tempting to ask on this basis whether people whose orientation is collectivist rather than individualistic are more likely to help others and to receive help from them. According to Nadler (1986, 1991), self-reliance and individual achievement is fostered by Western cultures.

In a study in Israel (Nadler, 1986), he compared the help-seeking tendencies of Israeli high school students living in kibbutzim with those dwelling in cities. In Israel, socialisation in a *kibbutz* stresses collectivist values, a lifestyle in which a communal and egalitarian outlook is important and being cooperative with peers is crucial. Kibbutz-dwellers rely on being comrades, depend heavily on group resources and treat group goals as paramount. In contrast, the Israeli *city* context is typically Western, with an emphasis on individualist values, including personal independence and individual achievement.

Help-seeking has a strong sociocultural component. Nadler found that the two groups treated a request for aid in dramatically different ways. If it was clear that the situation affected the outcome for the group as a whole, kibbutz-dwellers were much more likely than city-dwellers to seek help, and vice versa if the benefit was defined in individual terms. There were no differences between men and women in these trends. The results are shown in Figure 16.4. See how Nadler tested this idea in Box 16.3.

CHARACTERISING CULTURES BY RELATIONSHIPS

The protagonist for a thoroughgoing cultural psychology might argue that our psyche works in tandem with our social relationships. A. P. Fiske (Fiske, 1992; Fiske & Haslam, 1996; Haslam, 1995) developed a **relational theory** based on the concept of the **schema** (Fiske,

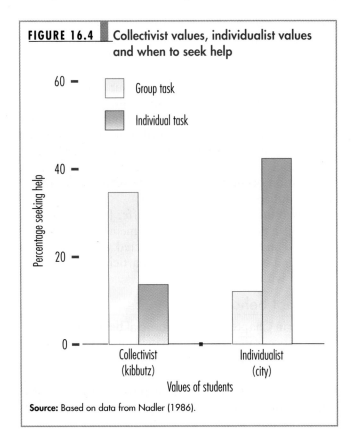

FIGURE 16.4 Collectivist values, individualist values and when to seek help

Source: Based on data from Nadler (1986).

'FOR MY COMRADE'S SAKE, WILL YOU HELP ME?'

Nadler's (1986) study was conducted among 110 male and female high school students in Israel. Half grew up and lived with their families on various kibbutzim and attended a high school catering to the needs of kibbutz-dwellers. The city-dwellers grew up and lived with their families in two middle-sized towns in northern Israel, attended their local high school and were mostly of middle-class background. The study was conducted in the students' classrooms.

The task consisted of solving 20 anagrams and its importance was made salient by suggesting that performance could predict success in other domains in life. They were told that people in the past had failed to solve several of the problems. They were also told that, if they could not solve certain anagrams, they could seek help from the investigator. The dependent variable was the percentage of occasions that a student sought help; for example, if help was requested on five anagrams out of ten unsolved ones, the help-seeking score was 50%.

In a 2 × 2 design, half the kibbutz group and half the city group were tested after receiving a group-oriented instruction and the remaining half after an individual-oriented instruction. In the group condition, the students believed that their scores would be compared with the average scores of other classes. In the individual condition, they would be compared with other individuals.

In terms of a cost–benefit analysis, Nadler hypothesised that help-seeking by these two groups would vary according to the nature of the instruction. Kibbutz-dwellers would seek help more often if the instruction was group-oriented, while city-dwellers would look for help if it was individual-oriented.

See the results in Figure 16.4.

Source: Based on Nadler (1986).

Kitayama, Markus, & Nisbett, 1998, p. 950; see Chapter 2 for full discussion of schemas):

People in every culture use just four elementary models to generate, understand, coordinate, evaluate, and contest most social interaction. Each of these four models is a motivated, affectively colored, cognitive schema . . . [by] which people jointly construct meaningful social relations.

1. *Communal sharing (CS)*—the group transcends the individual. People in a CS relationship experience solidarity and a corporate identity. Examples include lovers, teams, family.
2. *Authority ranking (AR)*—the AR relationship is defined by precedence and a linear hierarchy.

Collective decision making: In making group decisions people can be concerned not to damage their relationships with fellow group members—this is particularly true of Eastern cultures.

In practice, people may use any of Fiske's four relationship models in accordance with the multiple roles that people play at different moments in time.

Sally is John's mother. In the course of a normal day, they adopt different ways of relating to each other without being very conscious of the changes that take place. At home in the morning, Sally prepares breakfast with John. She makes the drinks, while he checks the food and places utensils on the table—neither one minding who puts in more effort (CS). Later that morning Sally goes to work, where she is a company manager. John, a sales representative in the same company, is told by his mother that his sales figures are improving (AR). After dinner that night they play a game of chess, which the better player will win (EM). Before going to bed, John asks Sally for a loan to buy a car. She thinks carefully and they discuss his proposition. Finally she agrees, provided that he paints the house and makes a good job of it (MP).

Together, they feel that their overall relationship is complex and that life is rich.

Examples include how a subordinate individual relates to an army officer and, in Chinese society, the custom of filial piety (see Liu, Ng, Weatherall, & Loong, 2000 for a study of filial piety among Chinese in New Zealand).

3. *Equality matching (EM)*—based on attending to balance in a social exchange. Examples of an EM relationship include reciprocating in a tit-for-tat manner, taking biblical vengeance, being egalitarian and car-pooling.

4. *Market pricing (MP)*—based on a sense of proportional outcomes. Examples of MP are prices, rents, salary and taxes. In an MP interpersonal relationship, the partners calculate their relative costs and benefits (see the discussion of the cost–reward ratio in Chapter 14).

Before linking relational theory to cultural variation, first consider how they can operate within the same culture. An example of how the four relationship models work is given in Box 16.4.

Since the models operate as schemas, they are available for use in ways that make sense within a culture, and are not necessarily used identically across cultures. They provide a 'grammar' for defining work, distributing resources and giving meaning to time and land. Fiske and colleagues (1998) provide this illustration with respect to land: it can be an investment (MP), a kingdom (AR), a mark of equal status if all citizens can own it or not own it (EM), a motherland, or even a common, defining a collective identity (CS). Relational theory is an innovative and promising approach to understanding fundamental ways that cultures can be similar or different.

Fiske and his colleagues (e.g. Fiske & Haslam, 1996) also make a strong claim. The four relationship models are not commensurate: there is no higher-order schema that mediates between them. Although the models are

Authority ranking: Respect for elders, such as this man in rural China, is a cornerstone of collective societies.

'in the culture', they are also 'in the head'—when a person is in, say, CS mode it is not easy to switch into AR mode. It can affect the ease or the difficulty of retrieving people from memory (see person memory in Chapter 2). If you are thinking in AR terms about your present boss, for example, you are more likely to recall your last boss and other bosses before that.

Finally, there is a link between the four relational models and cultural variations in independence–interdependence. MP is more common in individualistic cultures and CS in collectivist cultures. Further, AR occurs relatively more frequently in East Asian cultures, as it once did in feudal Europe. Likewise, the incidence of EM is higher in interdependent cultures, in some Asian countries and in Melanesia. This points to some convergence between the two major systems we have discussed. There are common features in characterising cultures, whether we use *values* or *relational models*.

Culture, norms and identity

An underlying theme of our discussion of culture is that culture does not just influence social psychological processes but is a product of social psychological processes. In this short section we elaborate this point by reflecting back on the way in which some of the basic social psychological processes discussed in earlier chapters may generate and influence culture.

Our culture provides us with an identity and a set of attributes that defines that identity. Culture influences what we think, how we feel, how we dress, what and how we eat, how we speak, what values and moral principles we hold, how we interact with one another and how we understand the world around us. Culture pervades almost all aspects of our existence. Perhaps because of this, culture is often the taken-for-granted background to everyday life (e.g. Garfinkel, 1967) and we may only really become aware of features of our culture when we encounter other cultures or when our own culture is threatened. Culture, like other entrenched normative systems, may only be revealed to us by intercultural exposure or intercultural conflict.

A key feature of cultural attributes is that they are tightly integrated in a logical way that makes our lives and the world we live in meaningful. In this sense, culture has some of the attributes of social attributions (see Hewstone, 1989), social representations (see Lorenzi-Cioldi & Clémence, 2001) and ideologies (Thompson, 1990)—see Chapter 3. At the cognitive level, our own culture might be represented schematically as a well-organised and compact prototype (see Chapter 2).

Because culture makes the world meaningful, we might expect cultural revivals to occur under conditions of societal uncertainty (e.g. Hogg, 2000a): for example, prolonged economic crises. Because culture defines identity, we would also expect cultural revivals when the prestige or distinctiveness of our culture is threatened by other cultural groups. In these respects, culture would be expected to obey the principles of intergroup behaviour described by the social identity approach (see Chapter 11). Indeed, research on language revivals, where language is central to culture, shows precisely this (e.g. Giles & Johnson, 1987; see Chapter 15).

Another key feature of cultural attributes is that they are shared among members of the culture and they differentiate between cultures—they are normative and thus obey the general principles of norms (Chapter 8). For example, cultural leaders may be allowed greater latitude for cultural divergence than other members of the culture (e.g. Sherif & Sherif, 1964; see Chapter 8). Cultural forms may emerge and be sustained or modified through human interaction—as described by Moscovici's (e.g. 1988) theory of social representations (Chapter 3)—and through talk, as described by discourse analytic perspectives on social psychology (e.g. Potter, 1996; see Chapter 15).

The dynamics of large-scale cultures may be very similar to the dynamics of small-scale cultures in organisations and small groups. In such cases, the processes of group socialisation (e.g. Levine & Moreland, 1994; see Chapter 8) and group memory (e.g. Moreland, Argote, & Krishnan, 1996; see Chapter 9) may operate at the societal level.

The main message of this necessarily brief section is that, while culture can be studied as an independent topic in its own right, there is a real sense in which it is actually an integral part of social psychology.

Contact between cultures

Cultural groups do not live in isolation: they come into contact with one another, increasingly so with each passing decade. You do not need to be a tourist to taste another culture. New York City is probably the best example of a cultural mélange, though the same can be seen in other large gateway cities like London, Paris and Sydney. It is similar, on a smaller scale, in the major cities of Australia and New Zealand, even those with fewer people than the very large metropolises.

Intercultural contact should be an enriching experience, a force for good and for beneficial change. But it can also be a pressure cooker, in which perceived threats and ancient animosities boil over into conflict (see Prentice & Miller, 1999).

Casual intercultural contact is unlikely to bring about a change in people's attitudes or behaviour. Recall the complexities of the **contact hypothesis**—creating conditions where contact will improve intergroup relations is very difficult (see Chapter 11 for full details). A brief interpersonal encounter with someone from a different culture will be interpreted according to an individual's existing stereotypes (see Chapter 2).

LANGUAGE AND LANGUAGE STYLE

We note elsewhere that multilingual and, therefore, multicultural societies usually have a dominant high-status group (Chapter 15). Consequently, a *language barrier* can be a major obstacle to a comfortable intercultural encounter. Quite clearly, if you are in France and cannot speak French very well, you have a major hurdle in communicating with one of the locals. Phrase books and sign language can take you only so far. Even accent and speech style present a problem, according to Gallois and her colleagues at the University of Queensland. Native English-speakers were less attentive to Italians for whom English was a second language, an effect probably compounded by negative stereotypes about immigrants from Southern Europe (Gallois & Callan, 1986). In another study, when the speech style of a second-language speaker was thought to be submissive it may have reinforced a negative stereotype about an ethnic group—in this case about Chinese students (Gallois, Barker, Jones, & Callan, 1992; see Box 16.5).

The magnitude of cultural difference can mediate intercultural contact. The extent to which a culture is perceived to be dissimilar to our own can affect intercultural interaction. An early social distance study by Vaughan (1962) showed that the more dissimilar a culture is perceived to be, the more people wish to distance themselves from members of that cultural group. Thus, the likelihood of some intercultural contacts is reduced.

The setting of a cross-cultural contact is also important. Smith and Bond (1998) distinguished between interpersonal contacts that are within the same society (e.g. between African and White Americans) and those that are international. By comparison with international contacts same-society contacts are in a joint territory, are longer-term, have a higher frequency of contact and are more variable in intimacy and in relative status and power. Kochman (1987) has shown that African Americans use an intonation and expressive intensity in their speech that marks them out from the White majority. This can be an intentional sociolinguistic marker, drawing an intergroup line and acting to protect their ethnic identity (see Chapters 11 and 15).

In the remainder of this section we deal with intercultural communication that is cross-national.

A quite substantial East–West difference is that Asians are more likely to use 'code'—messages with implicit meanings for each communicator (Burgoon,

---

BOX 16.5 | **Communication mismatch**

ETHNIC DIFFERENCES IN COMMUNICATION STYLE MAY HAVE IMPLICATIONS FOR A STUDENT'S PERCEIVED ACADEMIC ABILITY

Chinese students have recently become the largest single ethnic group of overseas students enrolled in Australian tertiary institutions. Due to cultural differences in communication styles, these students often find it difficult to adjust to local communication norms, which encourage students to speak out in class and in interaction with academic staff.

Gallois and her associates (Gallois, Barker, Jones, & Callan, 1992) studied this phenomenon. They prepared 24 carefully scripted videotapes of communications between a student and a lecturer, in which the student adopted a submissive, assertive or aggressive communication style to ask for help with an assignment or to complain about a grade. The student was either a male or a female Anglo-Australian or an ethnic Chinese (the lecturer was always Anglo-Australian and the same sex as the student).

The investigators had Australian students, ethnic Chinese students (i.e. from Hong Kong, Singapore or Malaysia) and lecturers view the videotaped vignettes and rate the students on a number of behavioural dimensions and on the effectiveness of their communication style. All participants agreed that the aggressive style was inappropriate, ineffective and atypical of students of any ethnic background. Consistent with stereotypes, submissiveness was considered more typical of Chinese than Australian students, and assertiveness more typical of Australian than Chinese students. Chinese students felt that the submissive style was more effective than the assertive style. However, lecturers and Australian students interpreted the submissive style as being less effective and indicating less need for assistance.

Clearly, this assumption that a submissive style indicates lack of need and interest could nourish a view that Chinese students are less talented than their Australian counterparts.

Buller, & Woodall, 1989). This is recognised in Chinese society, for example, as *hanxu* (Gao, Ting-Toomey, & Gudykunst, 1996). Consequently, an East–West interaction can sometimes be unfortunate (Gallois & Callan, 1997). In a conversation between an Australian and a Japanese, for example, the Australian might seem blunt and the Asian ambiguous.

We have noted certain cultural differences in *nonverbal behaviour* (see Chapter 15). The use of **display rules** is evidence of the importance of culture in communicating emotional states through facial expression.

Language barrier? Not in this case. Multinationals and cheap air travel are two factors that may contribute to the dilution of cultural difference.

Similarly, **kinesics** provides clues to a person's cultural origin, as do variations in touching and interpersonal distance. There is less eye contact during the course of an interview in Japan than in the West. Unlike Western listeners, who are socialised to look at a speaker's eyes, Japanese listeners focus on the speaker's neck (Bond & Komai, 1976), a practice that might be unnerving to some!

As another example, suppose someone gestured to you with a finger and thumb forming a circle: you would probably think they meant 'it's okay' or 'great'. However, there are cultures where this is the symbol for 'money', 'worthless' or even 'screw you!' (Burgoon, Buller, & Woodall, 1989; Morris, Collett, Marsh, & O'Shaughnessy, 1979).

Sometimes, an action that is normal in one culture violates a moral standard in another. Western women, for example, should avoid wearing revealing clothing in some Islamic countries. Unfortunately, breaches of a cultural norm are often committed in ignorance; for example, sitting or standing on a table in an area where food is served offends Maori custom in New Zealand. Intergroup and, therefore, intercultural contact can be severely curtailed if it leads to anxiety and uncertainty (Hogg, 2000a; Stephan & Stephan, 1985; see Chapter 11).

LANGUAGE AND UNDERSTANDING

English-speakers may underestimate the difficulty of preserving meaning when translating into another language. Glenn (1976) demonstrated various examples of differences in word meanings when changing from English to French or Russian. The use of the personal pronoun 'I', for example, usually has a subjective connotation in English but extends to objective connotations in French or Russian. In English, 'as long as I understand that . . .' could be rendered in French as '*s'il s'agit de . . .*', an idiom meaning 'if what is being dealt with is . . .'. In English there is a single word for 'here', whereas in Spanish there is a distinction between right here (*aquí*) and hereabouts (*acá*).

In addition to seeking words or idioms to communicate meaning accurately across cultures, a language can pose a larger problem when words, or word usage, are entwined with culture-specific concepts. Consider two instances in Japanese:

1. Yoshihisa Kashima at the University of Melbourne and Emiko Kashima at the Swinburne University of Technology have shown that, for certain statements, the first personal pronoun 'I' is dropped in Japanese but not in English (Kashima & Kashima, 1998). What is intriguing is that this may reflect the conceptual difference between the independent self and the interdependent self dealt with above (see Table 16.2 and Figure 16.2). This implies that the individualistic English-speaker uses 'I' to represent the self as separate from all others, whereas the collectivist Japanese-speaker drops 'I' to incorporate significant others into the self.

2. Doi (1976, p. 188) provided a classic case of the term *amae*—an emotional state with communicative implications that is fundamental in traditional Japanese culture. In the following quotation, the context is that of adult and child, but it can also be applied to students and professors, and to work teams and their supervisors:

   Amaeru [amae is its noun form] can be translated as 'to depend and presume upon another's love' . . . [It] has a distinct feeling of sweetness, and is generally used to express a child's attitude toward an adult, especially his parents. I can think of no English word equivalent to amaeru except for 'spoil', which, however, is a transitive verb and definitely has a bad connotation . . . I think most Japanese adults have a dear memory of the taste of sweet dependency as a child and, consciously or unconsciously, carry a lifelong nostalgia for it.

   By custom, Japanese people have a powerful need to experience *amae*, and knowledge of this state provides an emotional basis for interpersonal communication. According to Doi, a person who experiences *amae* during conversation will provide non-verbal cues (e.g. silences, pensive looks and even unnatural smiles) to 'soften the atmosphere' for the other person.

These two examples illustrate how some subtle language cues are unlikely to be interpreted appropriately in an intercultural setting by someone unfamiliar with the language and the culture.

At a political level, language sometimes gives an appearance of a game in which outcomes are negotiated to minimise public humiliation (see Box 16.6).

ACCULTURATION AND CULTURE CHANGE

When people migrate they find it almost impossible to avoid close contact with members of the host culture and with other immigrant cultural groups. Long ago, Gordon Allport (1954b) suggested that most members of ethnic minorities are of two minds—cultural pluralism or assimilation?

Extended contact inevitably produces changes in behaviour and thinking among new migrants. The process of internalising the rules of behaviour characteristic of another culture is **acculturation**, and when it applies to a whole group we have culture change. We should note in passing that culture change is not restricted to immigrants, since it can apply to indigenous peoples. Culture change can lead to *acculturative stress* (Ward & Kennedy, 1992). For example, look again at how ethnic minorities can suffer depressed self-esteem when their culture is eroded by an ethnic majority (see Box 4.3 in Chapter 4).

An acculturating individual can have *dual identities*—for example, a feeling that one is both a Mexican-American and an Anglo-American (Buriel, 1987), a Greek and an Australian (Rosenthal, 1987) or a Croatian and a New Zealander (Jankovic, 2001). A similar concept, *bicultural identity*, is used in research on ethnic socialisation in children (see Phinney & Rotheram, 1987). Immigrants face a dilemma: will they maintain their social identity as defined by their home

Acculturation: New immigrants face a dilemma—assimilate entirely to the new culture or retain aspects of their original culture?

culture identity or will it be defined by the host culture? How can this be resolved?

We note in our treatment of second-language learning (see Chapter 15) that Berry and his colleagues offered several solutions. In weighing up home culture (HC) and dominant culture (DC), immigrants can choose between: *integration* (maintaining HC but also relating to DC), *assimilation* (giving up HC and embracing DC), *separation* (maintaining HC and being isolated from DC) and *marginalisation* (giving up HC and failing to relate properly to DC) (e.g. Berry, Trimble, & Olmedo, 1986). Reflect on the third focus question. These are the paths that Keiko and her husband must consider.

Leaving aside the issue of language learning, the most popular path for immigrants is integration and is the one associated with least acculturative stress (Berry, Kim, Minde, & Mok, 1987). A key factor in stress reduction is the availability of a **social support network** (just as it is for the loss of loved ones; see Chapter 13). Choosing to integrate, however, is a process that takes considerable time and, in many instances, competes with a host culture's emphasis on assimilation.

In a pre- and post-migration study of Hong Kong Chinese adolescents who came to New Zealand, Ho (1995) found that the separation path was the overwhelming choice for young people prior to emigrating. After four years, however, the percentages choosing each of the four paths were: integration (38%), assimilation (18%), separation (36%) and marginalisation (8%). We would expect different outcomes for older people (less integration) and for immigrating minorities from another Western culture (more integration).

The choice to integrate fits well with current theories of intergroup arrangements that maximise social

---

BOX 16.6 | When is being 'sorry' an apology?

An international event in April 2001 highlighted how language differences can reflect conceptual differences.

An American surveillance aircraft was damaged in an accident with a Chinese plane off the coast of China and was forced to land in Chinese territory. The Chinese pilot was lost at sea. The Chinese government insisted that the American government make a formal apology before they would return the American crew. Such an apology (*dao qian*) is an admission of responsibility and an expression of remorse.

At first, the American expression was one of 'regret' (*yihan*), which carries no acknowledgement of guilt. The American president next expressed 'sincere regret' (*shen biao qian yi*) for the missing pilot and said he was 'very sorry (*zhen cheng yihan*) for the unauthorised landing. Both expressions are ambiguous with respect to implying blame.

The American crew was finally released and both governments may have felt that face was saved.

harmony and stability (e.g. Hornsey & Hogg, 2000a; see Chapter 11). Groups tend to get on better together when their cherished identities and practices are respected and allowed to flourish within a superordinate culture that also allows groups to feel that their relations to one another are not competitive, but more in the nature of different teams 'pulling together'.

Cultural challenges to social psychology

The publication of Bond's (1988) *The Cross-cultural Challenge to Social Psychology* was a call to arms. When would social psychologists pay heed to the limitations of untested universal assumptions in developing their theories? The challenges are multiple, occuring across cultures as nations and within a culture when addressing majority–minority group relations. We deal elsewhere with the latter topic in the context of intergroup theory (see Chapter 11). In a later section we revisit it in the setting of the consequences of policy-making for ethnic minorities.

THE CROSS-CULTURAL CHALLENGE

Although the cross-cultural challenge is typically targeted at social psychology, it actually cuts both ways. Cross-cultural, cultural and intercultural psychologists can draw on many principles from social psychology and use them beyond the culture in which they were developed, a point noted by Smith and Bond (1998) and Moghaddam (1998). Take the instance of planning to improve *intercultural relations*. Social psychologists can argue cogently that intercultural relations are a special case of intergroup relations. As such, an understanding of what drives intercultural conflict, discrimination and stereotyping is covered by the social psychology of intergroup behaviour (Chapter 11), of prejudice and discrimination (Chapter 10) and of stereotyping (Chapters 2 and 10).

What are the challenges, in the reverse direction, to social psychologists?

Indigenous social psychologies

Smith and Bond (1998) pose the question: should we promulgate an **indigenous psychology**? Or, put differently, should each culture have its own social psychology that reflects its own world view in its topics and constructs?

The most successful example of an indigenous *social* psychology is the development of a relatively distinct European social psychology (see Chapter 1). As a consequence of fascism and World War II, social psychology in Europe in the 1940s, 50s and early 60s was largely an outpost of American social psychology. In this context, Moscovici (1972) worried that American social

psychology was culturally alien for Europeans because it did not address European priorities and interests and adopted an interpretive framework or **metatheory** that clashed with European metatheory. He advocated a European social psychology grounded specifically in the cultural context of Europe.

Although Europe (particularly north-west Europe) and the United States have different traditions, histories and world views, as cultures they are remarkably similar—both are industrialised, individualistic Western democratic cultures. They can largely be grouped together (also of course with Australia and New Zealand) and contrasted with non-industrialised and collectivist cultures around the world. Thus, even if we make a distinction between European and American social psychology, we may not go far enough.

Malpass (1988), an American, reminds us that scientific psychology is a Euro-American enterprise (see also the historical origins of social psychology in Chapter 1). As such, people from Western cultures are the objects of study. Thus, we should not be surprised at a call for indigenous psychologies from the Asian region—for Filipinos by Enriquez (1993), for Chinese by Yang (Yang & Bond, 1990) and for Indians by Sinha (1997).

The point of an indigenous social psychology is that theories are developed and applied within the same culture. This issue is particularly relevant for developing nations that have serious social problems to solve: the well-meaning application of theories that are developed, say, in Europe or the United States may simply not work. For example, Moghaddam (1998) describes how the application of the Western idea that modernisation can be achieved by motivating people to act like entrepreneurs has backfired—it brought about a collapse of traditional communities (e.g. among Pygmies in central Africa) and ecologies (e.g. in parts of Brazil). Indeed, one of the fundamental problems of globalisation is precisely the assumption that people in developing nations have the same social psychological resources as people in the West (Stiglitz, 2002).

Another problem is the tendency for social psychological theory, and social action, to focus on static social relations rather than on dynamic processes that may change those relations (Moghaddam, 1990). There have, of course, been some notable exceptions, such as the social identity approach (e.g. Tajfel & Turner, 1979; Hogg & Abrams, 1988; see Chapter 11) and minority influence theory (e.g. Moscovici, 1976; see Chapter 7). These theoretical orientations, from Europe, were part of a deliberate strategy to address a European scientific and social agenda and to differentiate European from American social psychology (see Chapter 1; also Israel & Tajfel, 1972).

Whether an independent indigenous psychology is required to solve problems in each and every culture is a moot point. Neglected in the current debate is an older question of linking theory to practice, culture notwithstanding. The question arises as to whether an **action research** approach (see Chapter 6), which is oriented towards practical outcomes, is more useful. In a similar vein, Moghaddam (1990, 1998) has advocated a **generative psychology**; he cites examples of the success of such an approach in the 1990s in Latin America and Turkey.

The search for universals

We have already noted that tabulating human attributes and classes of behaviour with universal application was a characteristic of early cultural anthropology. This is still the case today with respect to most social psychologists, who are generally committed to the very search that concerned Boas, a quest for universal laws of social behaviour. A call for multiple indigenous psychologies that apply to a host of specific cultural groups raises issues that touch on the relationship between science and ideology, and issues of epistemology and the constitution of valid knowledge. For every new indigenous psychology there may be a different set of laws and principles. Do we run the risk of scientific Balkanisation?

Smith and Bond (1998) suggest that we find a way to classify national cultures in order to test the limits of culture-specific knowledge. While this is possible, we feel it is a more realistic target to encourage social psychologists to broaden their discipline to articulate:

- fundamental social–cognitive and social–perceptual processes, such as social categorisation (see Chapter 2); with
- emergent social properties, such as group norms and social representations (see Chapters 5, 7 and 9); and
- to gain insight into the general form of human behaviour and its context-specific cultural and historical manifestation. The universal and the 'cultural' are the two interdependent moments of the dialectic of a mature social psychology.

The question is not the absence of universals in behaviour or in what social psychology has so far unearthed about social behaviour. Virtually all the major topics in this book are relevant across cultures. Pause to think about the following: all people use schemas, are guided by values, have leaders and fear group ostracism. They seek causes for behaviour, have families, help others and fight wars. On the other hand, major variations are brought about by cultural difference. Social psychology is more interested in this enterprise now and examples of cultural diversity abound in a number of modern textbooks.

The challenge of cross-cultural research for social psychologists is not that it can be difficult to do cross-cultural research. Although cross-cultural research is

difficult so, for example, is social cognition research (Devine, Hamilton, & Ostrom, 1994; see Chapter 2) and research on small interactive task-oriented groups (e.g. Moreland, Hogg, & Hains, 1994; see Chapters 2 and 8).

The real challenge is to try to overcome our own cultural perspective—to try to see things from different cultural perspectives as well as being aware of the cultural limitations of our own thinking. Social psychologists, like all people, are blinkered by their own cultural parameters, adopting perspectives and addressing questions that are culturally relevant. They incline us towards culture-specific psychologies rather than a universal science. A collateral problem of this is, of course, that the psychology of the dominant scientific culture can oust all other psychologies and hinder the development of true universalism.

A social psychology that is relevant to all peoples would have a laudable sociopolitical role to play on the global stage, perhaps guiding humanitarians dedicated to solving widespread and pressing problems in the developing world. As well, social psychology could help to explain how basic social psychological processes interact with socioculturally specific processes. Activities like these may help us to understand intergroup conflict, family violence, social dilemmas, social change and destructive blind obedience. They may also tell us why noble attitudes rarely translate into noble acts.

THE MULTIPLE-CULTURES CHALLENGE

There is another wider challenge to the many societies of the world: can multiple cultures coexist? In a society of diverse cultures, should all cultural forms be permitted to flourish (even if they engage in such practices as infanticide and genital mutilation) or should cultures change with changing global values? For example, consider George W. Bush's 'war against terror' and the 2003 toppling of Saddam Hussein's B'ath party in Iraq. Are these struggles against universal evils or the forceful imposition of one cultural world view over another? This is, of course, a highly politicised question and beyond the scope of a scientific text. It confronts issues of cultural relativism and what has been called the postmodern paradox: the tendency for people to embrace fundamentalist belief systems in order to find a distinct and prescriptive identity that resolves the sense of anomie and moral vacuum in modern industrialised society.

Managing cultural diversity

Less problematic is the 'simple' question of how to manage cultural diversity in pluralistic societies. This is the cultural application of resolving intergroup conflict that we discussed in Chapter 11 and also mentioned in passing earlier in this chapter. At the intergroup level, you will recall, there is increasing support for the idea

Cultural diversity: These workmates have different ethnic origins and clearly enjoy each others'company.

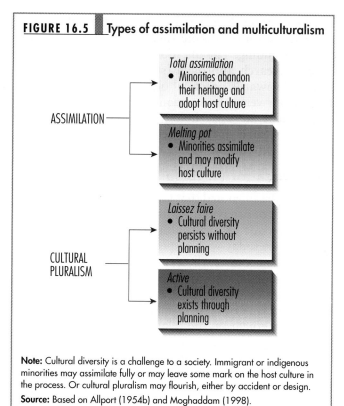

FIGURE 16.5 | Types of assimilation and multiculturalism

ASSIMILATION

Total assimilation
• Minorities abandon their heritage and adopt host culture

Melting pot
• Minorities assimilate and may modify host culture

CULTURAL PLURALISM

Laissez faire
• Cultural diversity persists without planning

Active
• Cultural diversity exists through planning

Note: Cultural diversity is a challenge to a society. Immigrant or indigenous minorities may assimilate fully or may leave some mark on the host culture in the process. Or cultural pluralism may flourish, either by accident or design.
Source: Based on Allport (1954b) and Moghaddam (1998).

that groups live more harmoniously together if their cherished identities and practices are respected. Groups will flourish within a superordinate culture that also allows them to feel that their relations to one another are cooperative rather than competitive (e.g. Hornsey & Hogg, 2000a).

At the cultural level the debate is largely about the relative merits of assimilationism and multiculturalism (see Prentice & Miller, 1999). For example, Moghaddam (1998) has contrasted assimilationist policies with those that manage cultural diversity by promoting multiculturalism (see Figure 16.5). Assimilation can be of two kinds—total and 'melting-pot'. The former implies the obliteration of a culture, whereas the latter is less extreme and allows a new form of the dominant culture to emerge.

Multiculturalism is a more positive and embracing view of dominant and minority cultures. In its laissez-faire form, cultural diversity can continue without help from the host culture. Ethnic enclaves, such as the many Chinatowns that can be found in various cities of the world, Little India in Singapore and expatriate European communities in some Asian cities, are examples of laissez-faire multiculturalism. In its active form, a

nation's policy sustains cultural diversity. For example, in Canada there is government support for a variety of minority activities; in New Zealand there is recognition of the Treaty of Waitangi and ongoing land settlements, and Australia has started down a similar path for Aboriginal people.

At the psychological level, active multiculturalism sustains cultural units that can be either individualistic or collectivist. Belanger and Pinard (1991) have suggested that there is a worldwide trend to sustain collectivist cultures. In the past decade, however, world history has not revealed a kind picture of support for minorities from powerful and dominant cultures.

Summary

• The roots of social psychology are Western and the discipline has underemphasised the impact of culture. If social psychological processes are really universal, they should stand up to cross-cultural scrutiny.
• People, including psychologists, often use their own cultural standards to interpret the behaviour of culturally different people.
• Anthropologists, rather than psychologists, fostered almost all research dealing with culture and behaviour in the early 20th century.

• Cultures vary considerably in social behaviour, including attributional style, conformity and socialisation practices.
• The way people in the East view themselves and the way they relate to each other can be very different from the view of people in the West. Eastern or collectivist cultures nurture interdependence, whereas Western or individualistic cultures nurture independence.
• Modern systems that characterise cultures include crucial differences in values and a different distrib-

ution of individualism and collectivism.
- Intercultural communication can sometimes lead to misunderstandings in meaning and intentions.
- Acculturating groups such as migrants face different acculturative choices, varying from retaining their ethnic identity to merging with the dominant culture. Acculturative stress is a common problem.

- Some social psychological principles may be applied across cultures and some may not. There is a tension between fostering principles that may apply only to an indigenous people and the pursuit of principles that are universal.
- In most of the world's societies there is the challenge to maintain cultural diversity.

LINKS

YOU HAVE READ ABOUT:	WHICH LINKS TO:
A culturally restricted social psychology	American influence in social psychology (1)
Values and cultures	values and attitudes (5)
Individualism and collectivism	personal and social identities (4, 11)
Improving intercultural relations	reducing prejudice (10); improving intergroup relations (11)
Universal behaviours (emic constructs)	principles of evolutionary social psychology (1, 12, 13, 14, 15)

Key terms

acculturation *(p. 425)*
action research *(p. 427)*
collectivism *(p. 418)*
contact hypothesis *(p. 423)*
cross-cultural psychologists *(p. 413)*
cultural psychologists *(p. 413)*
culture-blind *(p. 411)*
culture-bound *(p. 411)*
culture of honour *(p. 415)*
display rules *(p. 423)*
ethnographic research *(p. 412)*

etic–emic distinction *(p. 413)*
fundamental attribution error *(p. 414)*
generative psychology *(p. 427)*
indigenous psychology *(p. 426)*
individualism *(p. 418)*
intercultural psychologists *(p. 413)*
kinesics *(p. 424)*
level of explanation *(p. 416)*
machismo *(p. 415)*
meta-analysis *(p. 414)*

metatheory *(p. 426)*
prisoner's dilemma *(p. 419)*
prosocial behaviour *(p. 419)*
relational theory *(p. 420)*
schema *(p. 420)*
social identity theory *(p. 419)*
social representations *(p. 413)*
social support network *(p. 425)*
ultimate attribution error *(p. 414)*
values *(p. 416)*
Völkerpsychologie (p. 412)

FURTHER READING

Adamopoulos, J., & Kashima, Y. (1999). *Social psychology and cultural context*. London: Sage. A discussion of the cultural context of social psychology and how social psychological phenomena are influenced by culture.
Berry, J. W., Segall, M. H., & Kagitçibasi, C. (Eds.). (1997). *Handbook of cross-cultural psychology* (2nd ed.). Boston: Allyn & Bacon. A three-volume presentation and up-to-date review of the major areas of cross-cultural psychology.
Brislin, R. (1993). *Understanding culture's influence on behavior*. Fort Worth, TX: Harcourt Brace. An undergraduate text that treats both cross-cultural psychology and intercultural psychology.
Fiske, A. P., Kitayama, S., Markus, H. R., & Nisbett, R. E. (1998). The cultural matrix of social psychology. In D.T. Gilbert, S.T.
Fiske, & G. Lindzey (Eds.), *The handbook of social psychology* (4th ed., Vol. 2, pp. 915–981). New York: McGraw-Hill. A major review of theories and processes underlying the connection between social psychology and culture.
Moghaddam, F. M. (1998). *Social psychology: Exploring universals across cultures*. New York: Freeman. This is a text that explicitly builds cultural constructs and analysis into the treatment of traditional social psychological topics.
Smith, P. B., & Bond, M. H. (1998). *Social psychology across cultures* (2nd ed.). London: Prentice Hall. This work covers most of the topics dealt with in Chapter 16 and includes some additional material relevant to organisational psychology.
Triandis, H. (1994). *Culture and social behavior*. New York: McGraw-Hill. A good source for material showing cross-cultural differences in behaviour.

Glossary

abuse syndrome Factors of proximity, stress and power that are associated with the cycle of abuse in some families. *(p. 319)*

accentuation effect Overestimation of similarities among people within a category and dissimilarities between people from different categories. *(p. 276)*

accentuation principle Categorisation accentuates perceived similarities within and differences between groups on dimensions believed to be correlated with the categorisation. The effect is amplified where the categorisation and/or dimension has subjective importance, relevance or value. *(p. 35)*

accessibility Ease of recall of categories or *schemas* that we already have in mind. *(p. 37)*

acculturation The process whereby individuals learn about the rules of behaviour characteristic of another culture. *(p. 425)*

acquiescent response set Tendency to agree with items in an attitude questionnaire. This leads to an ambiguity in interpretation if a high score on an attitude questionnaire can be obtained only by agreeing with all or most items. *(p. 119)*

action research The simultaneous activities of undertaking social science research, involving participants in the process, and addressing a social problem. *(p. 145)*

actor–observer effect Tendency to attribute our own behaviours externally and others' behaviours internally. *(p. 60)*

affect–infusion model Cognition is infused with affect such that social judgments reflect current mood. *(p. 47)*

affiliative behaviour Acts that indicate that a person (or an animal) chooses to be with others. *(p. 326)*

ageism Prejudice and discrimination against people because of their age. *(p. 242)*

agentic mode State of mind thought by Milgram to characterise unquestioning obedience, in which people transfer personal responsibility to the person giving orders. *(p. 321)*

altruism A special form of *helping behaviour*, sometimes costly, that shows concern for fellow human beings and is performed without expectation of personal gain. *(p. 359)*

analogue Device or measure intended to faithfully mimic the 'real thing'. *(p. 298)*

anchoring and adjustment A cognitive shortcut in which inferences are tied to initial standards or *schemas*. *(p. 45)*

arbitration Process of intergroup conflict resolution in which a neutral third party is invited to impose a mutually binding settlement. *(p. 290)*

archival research Non-experimental method involving the assembly of data, or reports of data, collected by others. *(p. 8)*

associative meaning *Illusory correlation* in which items are seen as belonging together because they 'ought' to, on the basis of prior expectations. *(p. 44)*

associative network Model of memory in which nodes or ideas are connected by associative links along which cognitive activation can spread. *(p. 33)*

attachment behaviour The tendency of an infant to maintain close physical proximity with the mother or primary caregiver. *(p. 329)*

attachment styles Descriptions of the nature of people's close relationships, thought to be established in childhood. *(p. 329)*

attitude (a) A relatively enduring organisation of beliefs, feelings and behavioural tendencies towards socially significant objects, groups, events or symbols. (b) A general feeling or evaluation—positive or negative—about some person, object or issue. *(p. 97)*

attitude change Any significant modification of an individual's attitude. In the persuasion process this involves the communicator, the communication, the medium used, and the characteristics of the audience. Attitude change can also occur by inducing someone to perform an act that runs counter to an existing attitude. *(p. 130)*

attitude formation The process of forming our attitudes, mainly from our own experiences, the influences of others and our emotional reactions. *(p. 112)*

attribution The process of assigning a cause to our own behaviour, and that of others. *(p. 27)*

attributional style An individual (personality) predisposition to make a certain type of causal attribution for behaviour. *(p. 57)*

audience Intended target of a persuasive communication. *(p. 134)*

audience effects Impact on individual task performance of the presence of others. *(p. 184)*

authoritarian personality Personality syndrome originating in childhood that predisposes individuals to be prejudiced. *(p. 254)*

autocratic leadership Leadership style based on giving orders to followers. *(p. 212)*

autokinesis Optical illusion in which a pinpoint of light shining in complete darkness appears to move about. *(p. 166)*

automatic activation According to Fazio, attitudes that have a strong evaluative link to situational cues are more likely to automatically come to mind from memory. *(p. 108)*

availability heuristic A cognitive shortcut in which the frequency or likelihood of an event is based on how quickly instances or associations come to mind. *(p. 45)*

averaging A method of forming positive or negative impressions by averaging the valence of all the constituent attributes. *(p. 30)*

back-channel communication Verbal and non-verbal ways in which listeners let speakers know they are still listening. *(p. 405)*

balance theory According to Heider, people prefer attitudes that are consistent with each other, over those that are inconsistent. A person (P) tries to maintain consistency in attitudes to, and relationships with, other people (O) and elements of the environment (X). *(p. 99)*

bargaining Process of intergroup conflict resolution where representatives reach agreement through direct negotiation. *(p. 290)*

base-rate information Pallid, factual, statistical information about an entire class of events. *(p. 44)*

behaviour What people actually do that can be objectively measured. *(p. 2)*

behavioural decision theory Set of normative models (ideal processes) for making accurate social inferences. *(p. 43)*

behaviourism An emphasis on explaining observable behaviour in terms of reinforcement schedules. *(p. 17)*

belief congruence theory The theory that similar beliefs promote liking and social harmony among people while dissimilar beliefs produce dislike and prejudice. *(p. 256)*

belief in a just world Belief that the world is a just and predictable place where good things happen to 'good people' and bad things to 'bad people'. *(p. 62)*

biosocial theories In the context of aggression, theories that emphasise an innate component, though not the existence of a full-blown instinct. *(p. 300)*

BIRGing Basking In Reflected Glory—that is, name-dropping to link yourself with desirable people or groups and thus improve other people's impression of you. *(p. 80)*

bogus pipeline technique A measurement technique that leads people to believe that a 'lie detector' can monitor their emotional responses, thus measuring their true attitudes. *(p. 124)*

bookkeeping Gradual *schema* change through the accumulation of bits of schema-inconsistent information. *(p. 38)*

brainstorming Uninhibited generation of as many ideas as possible in a group, in order to enhance group creativity. *(p. 221)*

brainwashing The experience of extensive social isolation, broken sleep and intensive interrogation. This can produce a high level of susceptibility to political propaganda. *(p. 327)*

bystander–calculus model In attending to an emergency, the bystander calculates the perceived costs and benefits of providing help compared with those associated with not helping. *(p. 371)*

bystander effect People are less likely to help in an emergency when they are with others than when alone. The greater the number, the less likely it is that anyone will help. *(p. 367)*

bystander intervention This occurs when an individual breaks out of the role of a bystander and helps another person in an emergency.

case study In-depth analysis of a single case (or individual). *(p. 8)*

catharsis A dramatic release of pent-up feelings: the idea that aggressive motivation is 'drained' by acting against a frustrating object (or substitute), or by a vicarious experience. *(p. 306)*

cathartic hypothesis The notion that acting aggressively, or even just viewing aggressive material, reduces feelings of anger and aggression. *(p. 306)*

causal schemata Experience-based beliefs about how certain types of causes interact to produce an effect. *(p. 65)*

central traits Traits that have a disproportionate influence on the configuration of final impressions, in Asch's configural model of impression formation. *(p. 27)*

closed-mindedness A cognitive style that is rigid and intolerant, predisposing people to be prejudiced. *(p. 255)*

cluster analysis A statistical classification of data into groups or clusters based on similarity or likeness. *(p. 345)*

cognition The knowledge, beliefs, thoughts and ideas that people have about themselves and their environment. May also refer to mental processes through which knowledge is acquired, including perception, memory and thinking. *(p. 99)*

cognitive algebra Approach to the study of impression formation that focuses on how people combine attributes that have valence into an overall positive or negative impression. *(p. 30)*

cognitive alternatives Belief that the status quo is unstable and illegitimate, and that social competition with the dominant group is the appropriate strategy to improve *social identity*. *(p. 274)*

cognitive consistency A model of *social cognition* in which people try to reduce inconsistency among their cognitions, because they find inconsistency unpleasant. *(p. 27)*

cognitive consistency theories A group of attitude theories stressing that people try to maintain internal consistency, order and agreement among their various cognitions. *(p. 99)*

cognitive dissonance State of psychological tension, produced by simultaneously having two opposing *cognitions*. People are motivated to reduce the tension, often by changing or rejecting one of the cognitions. Festinger proposed that we seek harmony in our attitudes, beliefs and behaviours, and try to reduce tension from inconsistency among these elements. *(p. 130)*

cognitive miser A model of *social cognition* that characterises people as using the least complex and least demanding *cognitions* that are able to produce generally adaptive behaviours. *(p. 27)*

cognitive theories These attempt to explain behaviour in terms of the way people actively interpret and represent their experiences and then plan action. *(p. 13)*

cohesiveness The property of a group that affectively binds people, as group members, to one another and to the group as a whole, giving the group a sense of solidarity and oneness. *(p. 193)*

collective aggression Unified aggression by a group of individuals, who may not even know one another, against another individual or group. *(p. 308)*

collective behaviour The behaviour of people en masse—such as in a crowd, protest or riot. *(p. 253)*

collectivism Societal structure and world view in which people prioritise group loyalty, commitment and conformity, and belonging and fitting in to groups, over standing out as an isolated individual. *(p. 418)*

commitment The desire or intention to continue an interpersonal relationship. *(p. 352)*

commons dilemma Social dilemma in which cooperation by all benefits all, but competition by all harms all. *(p. 268)*

communication Transfer of meaningful information from one person to another. *(p. 385)*

communication accommodation theory Modification of verbal and non-verbal communication styles to the context (e.g. listener, situation) of a face-to-face interaction—an extension of speech accommodation theory to incorporate non-verbal communication. *(p. 391)*

communication network Set of rules governing the possibility or ease of communication between different roles in a group. *(p. 202)*

companionate love The caring and affection for another person that usually arises from sharing time together. *(p. 345)*

comparison level A standard that develops over time, allowing us to judge whether a new relationship is profitable or not. *(p. 342)*

compliance Superficial, public and transitory change in behaviour and expressed attitudes in response to requests, coercion or group pressure. *(p. 141)*

conciliation Process whereby groups make cooperative gestures to one another in the hope of avoiding an escalation of conflict. *(p. 291)*

configural model Asch's *Gestalt*-based model of impression formation, in which central traits play a disproportionate role in configuring the final impression. *(p. 27)*

conformity Deep-seated, private and enduring change in behaviour and attitudes due to group pressure. *(p. 166)*

conformity bias Tendency for social psychology to treat group influence as a one-way process in which individuals or minorities always conform to majorities. *(p. 174)*

confounding Where two or more independent variables covary in such a way that it is impossible to know which has caused the effect. *(p. 6)*

consensus information Information about the extent to which other people react in the same way to a stimulus X. *(p. 54)*

consistency information Information about the extent to which a behaviour Y always co-occurs with a stimulus X. *(p. 54)*

conspiracy theories Explanations of widespread, complex and worrying events in terms of the premeditated actions of small groups of highly organised conspirators. *(p. 67)*

construal An automatic judgment that underlies an attitude. *(p. 101)*

consummate love Sternberg argues that this is the ultimate form of love, involving passion, intimacy and commitment. *(p. 350)*

contact hypothesis The view that bringing members of opposing social groups together will improve intergroup relations and reduce prejudice and discrimination. *(p. 286)*

contingency theory Fiedler's interactionist theory that the effectiveness of particular leadership styles depends on situational and task factors. *(p. 214)*

conversion Sudden *schema* change as a consequence of gradual accumulation of schema-inconsistent information. *(p. 38)*

conversion effect When minority influence brings about a sudden and dramatic internal and private change in the attitudes of a majority *(p. 176).*

coordination loss Deterioration in group performance compared with individual performance, due to problems in coordinating behaviour. *(p. 189)*

correlation Where changes in one variable reliably map onto changes in another variable, but it cannot be determined which of the two variables *caused* the change. *(p. 8)*

correspondent inference Causal attribution of behaviour to underlying dispositions. *(p. 53)*

cost–reward ratio Tenet of social exchange theory, according to which liking for another is determined by calculating what it will cost to be reinforced by that person. *(p. 341)*

covariation model Kelley's theory of causal attribution—people assign the cause of behaviour to the factor that covaries most closely with the behaviour. *(p. 54)*

cross-cultural psychologists Psychologists who test theories about differences between selected ethnic groups or nations. *(p. 413)*

cultural norms *Norms* whose origin is part of the tradition of a culture. *(p. 312)*

cultural psychologists Psychologists who focus on universal processes whereby cultures are transmitted or transformed. *(p. 413)*

cultural values theory The view that people in groups use members' opinions about the position valued in the wider culture, and then adjust their views in that direction for social approval reasons. *(p. 227)*

culture-blind Theory and data untested outside the host culture. *(p. 411)*

culture-bound Theory and data conditioned by a specific cultural background. *(p. 411)*

culture of honour A culture that endorses male violence as a way of addressing threats to social reputation or economic position. *(p. 415)*

data Publicly verifiable observations. *(p. 2)*

dehumanisation Stripping people of their dignity and humanity. *(p. 233)*

deindividuation Process whereby people lose their sense of socialised individual identity and engage in unsocialised, often antisocial, behaviours. *(p. 76)*

demand characteristics Features of an experiment that seem to 'demand' a certain response. *(p. 7)*

democratic leadership Leadership style based on consultation and obtaining agreement and consent from followers. *(p. 212)*

dependent variables Variables that change as a consequence of changes in the independent variable. *(p. 5)*

depersonalisation The perception and treatment of self and others not as unique individual persons but as *prototypical* embodiments of a social group. *(p. 272)*

desensitisation A serious reduction in a person's responsiveness to material that usually evokes a strong emotional reaction, such as violence or sexuality. *(p. 313)*

diffuse status characteristics Information about a person's abilities that are only obliquely relevant to the group's task, and derive mainly from large-scale category memberships outside the group. *(p. 202)*

diffusion of responsibility Tendency of an individual to assume that others will take responsibility (as a result, no one does). This is a hypothesised cause of the *bystander effect*. *(p. 369)*

disconfirmation bias The tendency to notice, refute and regard as weak, arguments that contradict our prior beliefs. *(p. 139)*

discounting If there is no consistent relationship between a specific cause and a specific behaviour, that cause is discounted in favour of some other cause. *(p. 54)*

discourse Entire communicative event or episode located in a situational and sociohistorical context. *(p. 406)*

discrimination The behavioural expression of prejudice. *(p. 257)*

disinhibition A breakdown in the learned controls (social mores) against behaving impulsively or, in this context, aggressively. For some people, alcohol has a disinhibiting effect. *(p. 308)*

displacement Psychodynamic concept referring to the transfer of negative feelings onto an individual or group other than that which originally caused the negative feelings. *(p. 252)*

display rules Cultural and situational rules that dictate how appropriate it is to express emotions in a given context. *(p. 398)*

distinctiveness information Information about whether a person's reaction occurs only with one stimulus, or is a common reaction to many stimuli. *(p. 54)*

distraction–conflict theory The physical presence of members of the same species causes drive because people are distracting and produce conflict between attending to the task and to the audience. *(p. 186)*

distributive justice A concern with whether the outcome of a decision in distributing resources has been fair. *(p. 344)*

dogmatism Cognitive style that is rigid and intolerant and predisposes people to be prejudiced. *(p. 255)*

door-in-the-face tactic Multiple-request technique to gain compliance, in which the focal request is preceded by a larger request that is bound to be refused. *(p. 144)*

double blind Procedure to reduce experimenter effects, in which the experimenter is unaware of the experimental conditions. *(p. 7)*

drive theory Zajonc's theory that the physical presence of members of the same species instinctively causes arousal that motivates performance of habitual behaviour patterns. *(p. 184)*

dual-process dependency model General model of social influence in which two separate processes operate—dependency on others for social approval and for information about reality. *(p. 172)*

effort justification A special case of *cognitive dissonance*: inconsistency is experienced when a person makes a considerable effort to achieve a modest goal. *(p. 148)*

egoistic relative deprivation A feeling of personally having less than we feel we are entitled to, relative to our aspirations or to other individuals. *(p. 263)*

elaboration likelihood model Petty and Cacioppo's model of attitude change: when people attend to a message carefully, they use a central route to process it; otherwise they use a peripheral route. This model competes with the *heuristic–systematic model*. *(p. 139)*

emblems Gestures that replace or stand in for spoken language *(p. 399)*

emergency situation Often involves an unusual event, can vary in nature, is unplanned, and requires a quick response. *(p. 367)*

emergent norm theory Collective behaviour is regulated by *norms* based on distinctive behaviour that arises in the initially normless crowd. *(p. 283)*

emotion-in-relationships model Close relationships provide a context that elicits strong emotions due to the increased probability of behaviour interrupting interpersonal expectations. *(p. 350)*

empathic concern An element in Batson's theory of helping behaviour. In contrast to personal distress (which may lead us to flee from the situation), it includes feelings of warmth, being softhearted, and having compassion for a person in need. *(p. 371)*

empathy Ability to feel another person's experiences; identifying with and experiencing another person's emotions, thoughts and attitudes. *(p. 365)*

empathy costs of not helping Piliavin's view that failing to help can cause distress to a bystander who empathises with a victim's plight. *(p. 372)*

entitativity The property of a group that makes it seem like a coherent, distinct and unitary entity. *(p. 182)*

equity theory A special case of social exchange theory that defines a relationship as equitable when the ratio of inputs to outcomes are seen to be the same by both partners. *(p. 343)*

ethnocentrism Evaluative preference for all aspects of our own group relative to other groups. *(p. 63)*

ethnographic research Descriptive study of a specific society, based on fieldwork, and requiring immersion of the researcher in the everyday life of its people. *(p. 412)*

ethnolinguistic group Social group defined principally in terms of its language. *(p. 388)*

ethnolinguistic identity theory Application and extension of *social identity theory* to deal with the language behaviour of ethnolinguistic groups. *(p. 388)*

ethnolinguistic vitality Concept describing objective features of an interethnic context that influence language, and ultimately the cultural survival or disappearance of an ethnolinguistic group. *(p. 389)*

ethnomethodology Method devised by Garfinkel, involving the violation of hidden norms to reveal their presence. *(p. 198)*

ethology Approach that argues that animal behaviour should be studied in the species' natural physical and social environment. Behaviour is genetically determined and is controlled by natural selection. *(p. 299)*

etic–emic distinction Contrast between psychological constructs that are relatively culture-universal and those that are relatively culture-specific. *(p. 413)*

evaluation apprehension model The argument that the physical presence of members of the same species causes drive because people have learned to be apprehensive about being evaluated. *(p. 184)*

evolutionary social psychology A biological theory claiming that complex social behaviour is adaptive and helps (a) the individual, (b) kin and (c) the species as a whole to survive. *(p. 13)*

excitation-transfer model The expression of aggression is a function of learned behaviour, some excitation from another source, and the person's interpretation of the arousal state. *(p. 301)*

exemplars Specific instances of a member of a category. *(p. 33)*

expectancy-value model Direct experience with an attitude object informs a person how much that object should be liked or disliked in the future. *(p. 122)*

expectation states theory Theory of the emergence of *roles* as a consequence of people's status-based expectations about others' performance. *(p. 202)*

experimental method Intentional manipulation of *independent variables* in order to investigate effects on one or more *dependent variables*. *(p. 17)*

experimental realism Psychological impact of the manipulations in an experiment. *(p. 7)*

experimenter effect Effect that is produced or influenced by clues to the hypothesis under examination, inadvertently given by the experimenter. *(p. 7)*

extended contact effect Knowing about an ingroup member who shares a close relationship with an outgroup member can improve one's own attitudes towards the outgroup. *(p. 287)*

external (or situational) attribution Assigning the cause of our own or others' behaviour to external or environmental factors. *(p. 53)*

external validity Similarity between circumstances surrounding an experiment and circumstances encountered in everyday life. *(p. 7)*

face-ism Media depiction that gives greater prominence to the head and less prominence to the body for men, but vice versa for women. *(p. 237)*

false consensus effect Seeing our own behaviour as being more typical than it really is. *(p. 61)*

familiarity As we become more familiar with a stimulus (even another person), we feel more comfortable with it and we like it more. *(p. 335)*

family resemblance Defining property of category membership. *(p. 32)*

fear of social blunders The dread of acting inappropriately or of making a foolish mistake witnessed by others. The desire to avoid ridicule inhibits effective responses to an emergency by members of a group. *(p. 369)*

fighting instinct Innate impulse to aggress which ethologists claim is shared by humans with other animals. *(p. 299)*

foot-in-the-door tactic Multiple-request technique to gain compliance, in which the focal request is preceded by a smaller request that is bound to be accepted. *(p. 143)*

forewarning Advance knowledge that one is to be the target of a persuasion attempt. Forewarning often produces resistance to persuasion. *(p. 155)*

frame of reference Complete range of subjectively conceivable positions that relevant people can occupy in that context on some attitudinal or behavioural dimension. *(p. 166)*

fraternalistic relative deprivation Sense that our group has less than it is entitled to, relative to its aspirations or to other groups. *(p. 263)*

free-rider effect Gaining the benefits of group membership by avoiding costly obligations of membership and by allowing other members to incur those costs. *(p. 190)*

frustration–aggression hypothesis Theory that all frustration leads to aggression, and all aggression comes from frustration. Used to explain prejudice and intergroup aggression. *(p. 252)*

fundamental attribution error Bias in attributing another's behaviour more to internal than to situational causes. *(p. 59)*

fuzzy sets Categories are considered to be fuzzy sets of features organised around a *prototype*. *(p. 32)*

gain–loss hypothesis Paradox of liking people more if they initially dislike us and then later like us; and of liking them less if the sequence is reversed. *(p. 336)*

gaze Looking at someone's eyes. *(p. 395)*

gender Sex-stereotypical attributes of a person. *(p. 236)*

generative psychology Psychology intended to generate positive social change through direct intervention. *(p. 427)*

genetic model Moscovici's early focus on how social conflict between minority and majority can change the attitudes and behaviours of the majority. *(p. 174)*

genocide The ultimate expression of prejudice by exterminating an entire social group. *(p. 233)*

gestalt psychology Perspective in which the whole influences constituent parts rather than vice versa. *(p. 26)*

gestures Meaningful body movements and postures. *(p. 399)*

great person theory Perspective on leadership that attributes effective leadership to innate or acquired individual characteristics. *(p. 210)*

group Two or more people who share a common definition and evaluation of themselves and behave in accordance with such a definition. *(p. 182)*

group mind McDougall's idea that people adopt a qualitatively different mode of thinking when in a group. *(p. 224)*

group polarisation Tendency for group discussion to produce more extreme group decisions than the mean of members' prediscussion opinions, in the direction favoured by the mean. *(p. 227)*

group socialisation Dynamic relationship between the group and its members that describes the passage of members through a group in terms of commitment and of changing roles. *(p. 195)*

group structure Division of a group into different *roles* that often differ with respect to status and prestige. *(p. 200)*

group value model View that procedural justice within groups makes members feel valued, and thus leads to enhanced *commitment* to and identification with the group. *(p. 217)*

groupthink A mode of thinking in highly cohesive groups in which the desire to reach unanimous agreement overrides the motivation to adopt proper rational decision-making procedures. *(p. 226)*

Guttman scale A scale that contains either favourable or unfavourable statements arranged hierarchically. Agreement with a strong statement implies agreement with weaker ones; disagreement with a weak one implies disagreement with stronger ones. *(p. 120)*

hate crimes A class of violence against members of a stereotyped minority group. *(p. 302)*

hedonic relevance Refers to behaviour that has important direct consequences for self. *(p. 53)*

helping behaviour Acts that intentionally benefit someone else. *(p. 359)*

heuristics Cognitive short-cuts that provide adequately accurate inferences for most of us most of the time. *(p. 45)*

heuristic–systematic model Chaiken's model of attitude change: when people attend to a message carefully, they use systematic processing; otherwise they process information by using *heuristics*, or 'mental short-cuts'. This model competes with the elaboration likelihood model. *(p. 140)*

hospitalism A state of apathy and depression noted among institutionalised infants deprived of close contact with a caregiver. *(p. 329)*

hypothesis Empirically testable prediction about what goes with what, or what causes what. *(p. 4)*

ideology A systematically interrelated set of beliefs whose primary function is explanation. It circumscribes thinking, making it difficult for the holder to escape from its mould. *(p. 115)*

idiosyncrasy credit Hollander's transactional theory, that followers reward leaders for achieving group goals by allowing them to be relatively idiosyncratic. *(p. 219)*

illocution Words placed in sequence and the context in which this is done. *(p. 385)*

illusion of control Belief that we have more control over our world than we really do. *(p. 62)*

illusion of group effectivity Experience-based belief that we produce more and better ideas in groups than alone. *(p. 222)*

illusory correlation Cognitive exaggeration of the degree of co-occurrence of two stimuli or events, or the perception of a co-occurrence where none exists. *(p. 44)*

illustrators Body movements and postures that accompany spoken language. *(p. 399)*

implicit association test Reaction-time test to measure attitudes, particularly unpopular attitudes that people might conceal. *(p. 126)*

implicit personality theories Idiosyncratic and personal ways of characterising other people and explaining their behaviour. *(p. 29)*

impression management People's use of various strategies to get other people to view them in a positive light. *(p. 90)*

independent variables Features of a situation that change of their own accord, or can be manipulated by an experimenter to have effects on a *dependent variable*. *(p. 5)*

indigenous psychology A psychology created by and for a specific cultural group, based on the claim that culture can be understood only from within its own perspective. *(p. 426)*

individualism Societal structure and world view in which people prioritise standing out as an individual over fitting in as a group member. *(p. 418)*

induced compliance A special case of *cognitive dissonance*: inconsistency is experienced when a person is persuaded to behave in a way that is contrary to an attitude. *(p. 150)*

information integration theory The idea that a person's attitude can be estimated by averaging across the positive and negative ratings of the object. *(p. 101)*

information processing The evaluation of information; in relation to attitudes, the means by which people acquire knowledge, and form and change attitudes. *(p. 101)*

informational influence An influence to accept information from another as evidence about reality. *(p. 171)*

ingratiation Strategic attempt to get someone to like you in order to obtain compliance with a request. *(p. 142)*

ingroup favouritism Behaviour that favours one's own group over other groups. *(p. 271)*

initiation rites Often painful or embarrassing public procedure to mark group members' movements from one *role* to another. *(p. 197)*

inoculation A way of making people resistant to persuasion. By providing them with a diluted counterargument, they can build up effective refutations to a later, stronger argument. *(p. 155)*

instinct Innate drive or impulse, genetically transmitted. *(p. 298)*

institutionalised aggression Aggression which is given formal or informal recognition and social legitimacy by being incorporated into rules and norms. *(p. 319)*

intercultural psychologists Psychologists who deal with social processes that allow members of different cultural groups to interact. *(p. 413)*

intergroup attributions Process of assigning the cause of one's own or others' behaviour to group membership. *(p. 63)*

intergroup behaviour Behaviour among individuals that is regulated by those individuals' awareness of and identification with different social groups. *(p. 261)*

intergroup differentiation Behaviour that emphasises differences between our own group and other groups. *(p. 271)*

intergroup emotions theory (IET) Theory that, in group contexts, appraisals of personal harm or benefit in a situation operate at the level of social identity and thus produce mainly positive ingroup and negative outgroup emotions. *(p. 278)*

internal (or dispositional) attribution Process of assigning the cause of our own or others' behaviour to internal or dispositional factors. *(p. 53)*

internal validity Psychological impact of the manipulations in an experiment. *(p. 7)*

J-curve A graphical figure that captures the way in which relative deprivation arises when attainments suddenly fall short of rising expectations. *(p. 262)*

just-world hypothesis According to Lerner, people need to believe that the world is a just place where they get what they deserve. As evidence of undeserved suffering undermines this belief, people may conclude that victims deserve their fate. *(p. 363)*

kinesics Linguistics of body communication. *(p. 399)*

laboratory A place, usually a room, in which data are collected, usually by experimental methods. *(p. 6)*

laissez-faire leadership Leadership style based on disinterest in followers. *(p. 212)*

language A system of sounds that convey meaning because of shared grammatical and semantic rules. *(p. 385)*

leader categorisation theory We have a variety of *schemas* about how different types of leaders behave in different leadership situations. When a leader is categorised as a particular type of leader, the schema fills in details about how that leader will behave. *(p. 217)*

leader–member exchange (LMX) Theory of leadership in which effective leadership rests on the ability of the leader to develop good-quality personalised exchange relationships with individual members. *(p. 216)*

leadership Getting group members to achieve the group's goals. *(p. 210)*

learning by direct experience Acquiring a behaviour because we were rewarded for it. *(p. 303)*

learning by vicarious experience Acquiring a behaviour after observing that another person was rewarded for it. *(p. 303)*

least-preferred co-worker (LPC) scale Fiedler's scale for measuring leadership style in terms of favourability of attitude towards one's least-preferred co-worker. *(p. 214)*

level of explanation The types of concepts, mechanisms and language used to explain a phenomenon. *(p. 14)*

Likert scale Scale that evaluates how strongly people agree/disagree with favourable/unfavourable statements about an attitude object. Initially, many items are tested. After item analysis, only those items that correlate with each other are retained. *(p. 119)*

linguistic relativity View that language determines thought and, therefore, people who speak different languages see the world in very different ways. *(p. 386)*

locution Words placed in sequence. *(p. 385)*

looking-glass self The self derived from seeing ourselves as others see us. *(p. 75)*

love A combination of emotions, cognitions and behaviours that can be involved in intimate relationships. *(p. 345)*

low-ball tactic Technique for inducing compliance in which a person who agrees to a request still feels committed after finding that there are hidden costs. *(p. 145)*

machismo A code in which challenges, abuse and even differences of opinion must be met with fists or other weapons. *(p. 313)*

matched-guise technique Research methodology to measure people's attitudes towards a speaker based solely on speech style. *(p. 387)*

maternal deprivation An extended period of separation of an infant from its principal caregiver. The consequences can be irreversible damage to both intellectual and social functioning. *(p. 328)*

mediation Process of intergroup conflict resolution where a neutral third party intervenes in the negotiation process to facilitate a settlement. *(p. 290)*

membership group Kelley's term for a group to which we belong by some objective external criterion. *(p. 160)*

mere exposure effect Repeated exposure to an object results in greater attraction to that object. *(p. 112)*

mere presence Refers to an entirely passive and unresponsive audience that is only physically present. *(p. 184)*

message Communication from a source directed to an audience. *(p. 134)*

meta-analysis Statistical procedure that combines data from different studies to measure the overall reliability and strength of specific effects. *(p. 103)*

metacontrast principle The prototype of a group is that position within the group that has the largest ratio of 'differences to ingroup positions' to 'differences to outgroup postions'. *(p. 83)*

metatheory Set of interrelated concepts and principles concerning which theories or types of theory are appropriate. *(p. 12)*

mindlessness The act of agreeing to a request without giving it a thought. A small request is likely to be agreed to, even if a spurious reason is provided. *(p. 145)*

minimal group paradigm Experimental methodology to investigate the effect of *social categorisation* alone on behaviour. *(p. 257)*

minimax strategy In relating to others, we try to minimise the costs and maximise the rewards that accrue. *(p. 342)*

minority influence Social influence processes whereby numerical or power minorities change the attitudes of the majority. *(p. 173)*

modelling Tendency for a person to reproduce the actions, attitudes and emotional responses exhibited by a real-life or symbolic model. Also called observational learning. *(p. 113)*

moderator variable A variable that qualifies an otherwise simple hypothesis with a view to improving its predictive power (e.g. A causes B, but only when C (the moderator) is present). *(p. 110)*

morpheme Basic unit of meaning: elementary word or part of a word that has meaning. *(p. 385)*

motivated tactician A model of *social cognition* that characterises people as having multiple cognitive strategies available, from which they choose on the basis of personal goals, motives and needs. *(p. 27)*

multiple-act criterion Term for a general behavioural index based on an average or combination of several specific behaviours. *(p. 103)*

multiple requests Tactics for gaining compliance using a two-step procedure: the first request functions as a set-up for the second, real request. *(p. 143)*

mundane realism Similarity between circumstances surrounding an experiment and circumstances encountered in everyday life. *(p. 7)*

naive scientist (or psychologist) Model of *social cognition* that characterises people as using rational, scientific-like, cause–effect analyses to understand their world. *(p. 27)*

nature–nurture controversy Classic debate about whether genetic or environmental factors determine human behaviour. Scientists generally accept that it is an interaction of both. *(p. 298)*

need complementarity Winch's theory that we seek out apparent opposites, as they can best satisfy our needs. *(p. 338)*

need to affiliate The urge to form connections and make contact with other people. *(p. 326)*

neo-associationist analysis A view of aggression according to which mass media may provide images of violence to an audience that later translate into antisocial acts. *(p. 315)*

neo-behaviourist One who attempts to explain observable behaviour in terms of contextual factors and unobservable intervening constructs such as beliefs, feelings and motives. *(p. 13)*

neo-Freudians Psychoanalytic theorists who modified the original theories of Freud. *(p. 299)*

non-common effects Effects of behaviour that are relatively exclusive to that behaviour rather than other behaviours. *(p. 53)*

non-verbal communication Transfer of meaningful information from one person to another by means other than written or spoken language (e.g. gaze, facial expression, posture, touch). *(p. 394)*

normative influence An influence to conform with the positive expectation of others, to gain social approval or to avoid social disapproval. *(p. 172)*

normative models Ideal processes for making accurate social inferences. *(p. 43)*

norms Attitudinal and behavioural uniformities that define group membership and differentiate between groups. *(p. 110)*

one-component attitude model An attitude consists of affect towards or evaluation of the object. *(p. 97)*

operational definition Defines a theoretical term in a manner that renders it susceptible to manipulation or measurement. *(p. 15)*

optimal distinctiveness People strive to achieve a balance between conflicting motives for inclusiveness and separateness, expressed in groups as a balance between intragroup differentiation and intragroup homogenisation. *(p. 278)*

outcome bias Belief that the outcomes of a behaviour were intended by the person who chose the behaviour. *(p. 62)*

overjustification effect In the absence of obvious external determinants of our behaviour, we assume that we freely choose the behaviour because we enjoy it. *(p. 78)*

paired distinctiveness *Illusory correlation* in which items are seen as belonging together because they share some unusual feature. *(p. 44)*

paralanguage The non-linguistic accompaniments of speech (e.g. stress, pitch, speed, tone, pauses). *(p. 386)*

passionate (or romantic) love State of intense absorption in another person involving physiological arousal. *(p. 345)*

peace studies Multidisciplinary movement dedicated to the study and promotion of peace. *(p. 321)*

peripheral traits Traits that have an insignificant influence on the configuration of final impressions, in Asch's configural model of impression formation. *(p. 27)*

personal attraction Liking for someone based on idiosyncratic preferences and interpersonal relationships. *(p. 194)*

personal constructs Idiosyncratic and personal ways of characterising other people. *(p. 28)*

personal costs of not helping Piliavin's view that not helping a victim in distress can be costly to a bystander (e.g. experiencing blame). *(p. 372)*

personal identity The self defined in terms of unique personal attributes or unique interpersonal relationships. *(p. 80)*

personal space Physical space around people's bodies which they treat as a part of themselves. *(p. 326)*

personalism Behaviour that appears to be directly intended to benefit or harm oneself rather than others. *(p. 53)*

persuasive arguments theory View that people in groups are persuaded by novel information that supports their initial position, and thus become more extreme in their endorsement of their initial position. *(p. 227)*

persuasive communication Message intended to change an attitude and related behaviours of an audience. *(p. 130)*

phonemes Elementary and meaningless sounds that are combined in various ways to produce meaningful sound units. *(p. 385)*

positivism Non-critical acceptance of science as the only way to arrive at true knowledge: science as religion. *(p. 15)*

post-decisional conflict The dissonance associated with behaving in a counterattitudinal way. Dissonance can be reduced by bringing the attitude into line with the behaviour. *(p. 150)*

postures Meaningful positionings of parts of the body (e.g. hands, head, arms). *(p. 399)*

power Capacity to influence others while resisting their attempts to influence. *(p. 161)*

prejudice Unfavourable attitude towards a social group and its members. *(p. 233)*

primacy An order of presentation effect in which earlier presented information has a disproportionate influence on social cognition. *(p. 28)*

priming The procedure of recalling accessible categories or schemas that we already have in mind. *(p. 39)*

prior commitment An individual's agreement in advance to be responsible if trouble occurs: for example, committing oneself to protect the property of another person against theft. *(p. 372)*

prisoner's dilemma Two-person game in which both parties are torn between competition and cooperation and, depending on mutual choices, both can win or both can lose. *(p. 267)*

privacy regulation theory Altman's model, in which people control how much contact they have with others in order to satisfy their need to affiliate (which can vary widely). *(p. 326)*

process loss Deterioration in group performance in comparison to individual performance due to the whole range of possible interferences among members. *(p. 188)*

production blocking Reduction in individual creativity and productivity in *brainstorming* groups due to interruptions and turn-taking. *(p. 222)*

profit This flows from a relationship when the rewards that accrue from continued interaction exceed the costs. *(p. 342)*

prosocial behaviour Acts that are positively valued by society. *(p. 359)*

protection motivation theory Adopting a healthy behaviour requires cognitive balancing between the perceived threat of illness and one's capacity to cope with the health regimen. *(p. 107)*

prototype Cognitive representation of the typical/ideal defining features of a category. *(p. 32)*

proxemics Study of interpersonal distance. *(p. 402)*

proximity The factor of living close by is known to play an important role in the early stages of forming a friendship. *(p. 334)*

racism Prejudice and discrimination against people based on their ethnicity or race. *(p. 239)*

radical behaviourist One who explains observable behaviour in terms of reinforcement schedules, without recourse to any intervening unobservable (e.g. cognitive) constructs. *(p. 13)*

reactance Brehm's theory that people try to protect their freedom to act. When they perceive that this freedom has been curtailed, they will act to regain it. *(p. 155)*

realistic conflict theory Sherif's theory of intergroup conflict that explains intergroup behaviour in terms of the nature of goal relations between groups. *(p. 266)*

received pronunciation (RP) Standard, high-status, spoken variety of English. *(p. 388)*

recency An order of presentation effect in which later presented information has a disproportionate influence on social cognition. *(p. 28)*

reciprocity principle The law of 'doing unto others as they do to you'. It can refer to an attempt to gain compliance by first doing someone a favour, or to mutual aggression or mutual attraction. *(p. 142)*

reductionism Explanation of a phenomenon in terms of the language and concepts of a lower level of analysis, usually with a loss of explanatory power. *(p. 14)*

reference group Kelley's term for a group that is psychologically significant for our behaviour and attitudes. *(p. 160)*

referent informational influence Pressure to conform with a group norm that defines oneself as a group member. *(p. 172)*

regression Tendency for initial observations of instances from a category to be more extreme than subsequent observations. *(p. 43)*

reinforcement–affect model Model of attraction which postulates that we like people who are around when we experience a positive feeling (which itself is reinforcing). *(p. 340)*

relational theory An analysis based on structures of meaningful social relationships that recur across cultures. *(p. 420)*

relationship dissolution model Duck's proposal of the sequence through which most long-term relationships proceed if they finally break down. *(p. 353)*

relative deprivation A sense of having less than we feel entitled to *(p. 253)*

relative homogeneity effect Tendency to see outgroup members as all the same, and ingroup members as more differentiated. *(p. 276)*

releasers Specific stimuli in the environment thought by *ethologists* to trigger aggressive responses. *(p. 299)*

representativeness heuristic A cognitive shortcut in which instances are assigned to categories or types on the basis of overall similarity or resemblance to the category. *(p. 45)*

reverse discrimination The practice of publicly being prejudiced in favour of a minority group in order to deflect accusations of prejudice and discrimination against that group. *(p. 245)*

Ringelmann effect Individual effort on a task diminshes as group size increases. *(p. 189)*

risky shift Tendency for group discussion to produce group decisions that are more risky than the mean of members' prediscussion opinions, but only if the prediscussion mean already favoured risk. *(p. 227)*

role complementarity A successful relationship requires role negotiation, some 'give and take'. *(p. 352)*

roles Patterns of behaviour that distinguish between different activities within the group, and that interrelate to one another for the greater good of the group. *(p. 32)*

salience Property of a stimulus that makes it stand out in relation to other stimuli and attract attention. *(p. 38)*

scapegoat Individual or group that becomes the target for anger and frustration caused by a different individual or group or some other set of circumstances. *(p. 252)*

schema Cognitive structure that represents knowledge about a concept or type of stimulus, including its attributes and the relations among those attributes. *(p. 31)*

schism Division of a group into subgroups that differ in their attitudes, values or ideology. *(p. 204)*

science Method for studying nature that involves the collecting of data to test *hypotheses*. *(p. 2)*

script A *schema* about an event. *(p. 31)*

self-affirmation theory Steele's theory of how people who have been derogated on one dimension of self will publicly affirm one or more other positive aspects of self. *(p. 84)*

self-assessment The motivation to seek out new information about ourselves in order to find out what sort of person we really are. *(p. 83)*

self-categorisation theory Turner and associates' theory of how the process of categorising oneself as a group member produces *social identity* and group and intergroup behaviours. *(p. 35)*

self-disclosure The sharing of intimate information and feelings with another person. *(p. 338)*

self-discrepancy theory Higgins' theory about the consequences of making actual–ideal and actual–'ought' self comparisons that reveal self-discrepancies. *(p. 77)*

self-efficacy Expectations that we have about our capacity to succeed in particular tasks. *(p. 107)*

self-enhancement The motivation to develop and promote a favourable image of self. *(p. 84)*

self-esteem Feelings about and evaluations of oneself. *(p. 85)*

self-evaluation maintenance model People who are constrained to make esteem-damaging upward comparisons can underplay or deny similarity to the target, or they can withdraw from their relationship with the target. *(p. 79)*

self-fulfilling prophecy Expectations and assumptions about a person that influence our interaction with that person and eventually change their behaviour in line with our expectations. *(p. 249)*

self-handicapping Publicly making advance external attributions for our anticipated failure or poor performance in a forthcoming event. *(p. 62)*

self-monitoring Carefully controlling how we present ourselves. There are situational differences and individual differences in self-monitoring. *(p. 90)*

self-perception theory Bem's idea that we gain knowledge of ourselves only by making self-attributions: for example, we infer our own attitudes from our own behaviour. *(p. 56)*

self-presentation A deliberate effort to act in ways that create a particular impression, usually favourable, of ourselves. *(p. 91)*

self-rating scale An attitude measure that asks for agreement or disagreement with an attitude position. *(p. 117)*

self-serving biases Attributional distortions that protect or enhance self-esteem or the self-concept. *(p. 62)*

self-verification Seeking out information that verifies and confirms what we already know about ourselves. *(p. 83)*

semantic differential An attitude measure that asks for a rating on a scale composed of bipolar (opposite) adjectives. (Also a technique for measuring the connotative meaning of words or concepts.) *(p. 120)*

sensory deprivation The experience of an impoverished environment that contains very few stimuli for the senses. *(p. 327)*

sex role Behaviour deemed sex-stereotypically appropriate. *(p. 236)*

sexism Prejudice and discrimination against people based on their gender. *(p. 235)*

shared stress Condition noted by Schachter in which anxiety is reduced by sharing the experience with others. *(p. 330)*

similarity of attitudes or values One of the most important positive determinants of attraction. *(p. 336)*

situational control Fiedler's classification of task characteristics in terms of how much control effective task performance requires. *(p. 214)*

social affiliation model People's need to affiliate follows a homeostatic principle and is not marked by wide fluctuations. Variation between people, however, can be marked. *(p. 326)*

social attraction Liking for someone based on common group membership and determined by the person's *prototypicality* of the group. *(p. 194)*

social categorisation Classification of people as members of different social groups. *(p. 270)*

social change belief system Belief that intergroup boundaries are impermeable. Therefore, a lower-status individual can improve social identity only by challenging the legitimacy of the higher-status group's position. *(p. 274)*

social cognition Cognitive processes and structures that influence and are influenced by social behaviour. *(p. 26)*

social comparison (theory) Comparing our behaviours and opinions with those of others in order to establish the correct or socially approved way of thinking and behaving. *(p. 79)*

social compensation Increased effort on a collective task to compensate for other group members' actual, perceived or anticipated lack of effort or ability. *(p. 191)*

social competition Group-based behavioural strategies that improve *social identity* by directly confronting the dominant group's position in society. *(p. 274)*

social creativity Group-based behavioural strategies that improve *social identity* but do not directly attack the dominant group's position. *(p. 274)*

social decisions schemes Explicit or implicit decision-making rules that relate individual opinions to a final group decision. *(p. 221)*

social dominance theory Theory that attributes prejudice to an individual's acceptance of an ideology that legitimises ingroup-serving hierarchy and domination, and rejects egalitarian ideologies. *(p. 255)*

social facilitation An improvement in the performance of well-learned/easy tasks and a deterioration in the performance of poorly learned/difficult tasks in the mere presence of members of the same species. *(p. 184)*

social identity That part of the self-concept that derives from our membership of social groups. *(p. 80)*

social identity approach Theory of the relationship between collective self-conception and group and intergroup processes. It subsumes *social identity theory*, *self-categorisation theory* and other social identity theories of, for example, motivation and social influence. *(p. 172)*

social identity theory Theory of group membership and intergroup relations based on self-categorisation, social comparison and the construction of a shared self-definition in terms of ingroup-defining properties. *(p. 35)*

social impact The effect that other people have on our attitudes and behaviour, usually as a consequence of factors such as group size, and temporal and physical immediacy. *(p. 178)*

social influence Process whereby attitudes and behaviour are influenced by the real or implied presence of other people. *(p. 160)*

social learning theory The view championed by Bandura that human social behaviour is not innate but learned from appropriate models. *(p. 302)*

social loafing A reduction in individual effort when working on a collective task (one in which our outputs are pooled with those of other group members) compared with working either alone or coactively (our outputs are not pooled). *(p. 189)*

social markers Features of *speech style* that convey information about mood, context, status and group membership. *(p. 387)*

social matching The way people are attracted to partners of approximately the same level of social desirability. *(p. 348)*

social mobility belief system Belief that intergroup boundaries are permeable. Thus, it is possible for someone to pass from a lower-status into a higher-status group to improve *social identity*. *(p. 274)*

social order The balance and control of a social system, regulated by *norms*, values, rules and law. *(p. 319)*

social ostracism Exclusion from a group by common consent. *(p. 206)*

social psychology Scientific investigation of how the thoughts, feelings and behaviour of individuals are influenced by the actual, imagined or implied presence of others. *(p. 2)*

social representations Collectively elaborated explanations of unfamiliar and complex phenomena that transform them into a familiar and simple form. *(p. 66)*

social responsibility norm The idea that we should help people who are dependent and in need. It is contradicted by another norm that discourages interfering in other people's lives. *(p. 364)*

social support network People who know and care about us and who can provide back-up during a time of stress. *(p. 381)*

social transition scheme Method for charting incremental changes in member opinions as a group moves towards a final decision. *(p. 221)*

sociobiology A biological view that aggression, altruism and some other social behaviours serve to protect the survival of one's genes. *(p. 300)*

sociocognitive model Attitude theory highlighting an evaluative component. Knowledge of an object is represented in memory along with a summary of how to appraise it. *(p. 99)*

socioemotional-oriented leaders Leaders who are concerned with group members' feelings and relationships rather than the group task. *(p. 214)*

source The point of origin of a persuasive communication. *(p. 134)*

specific status characteristics Information about those abilities of a person that are directly relevant to the group's task. *(p. 202)*

speech Vocal production of language. *(p. 394)*

speech accommodation theory Modification of *speech style* to the context (e.g. listener, situation) of a face-to-face conversation. *(p. 390)*

speech convergence Accent or *speech style* shift towards that of the other person. *(p. 390)*

speech divergence Accent or speech style shift away from that of the other person. *(p. 390)*

speech style The way in which something is said (e.g. accent, language), rather than the content of what is said. *(p. 386)*

statistical significance An effect is statistically significant if statistics reveal that it, or a larger effect, is unlikely to occur by chance more often than one in twenty times. *(p. 9)*

statistics Formalised numerical procedures performed on data to investigate the magnitude and/or significance of effects. *(p. 9)*

status Consensual evaluation of the prestige of a *role* or role occupant in a group, or of the prestige of a group and its members as a whole. *(p. 201)*

stereotype Widely shared and simplified evaluative image of a social group and its members. *(p. 29)*

stereotype threat Feeling that we will be judged and treated in terms of negative stereotypes of our group, and that we will inadvertently confirm these stereotypes through our behaviour. *(p. 248)*

stigma Group attributes that mediate a negative social evaluation of people belonging to the group. *(p. 245)*

subculture of violence A subgroup of society in which a higher level of violence is accepted as the norm. *(p. 312)*

subject effects Effects that are not spontaneous, due to demand characteristics and/or participants wishing to please the experimenter. *(p. 7)*

subjective vitality Individual group members' representation of the objective *ethnolinguistic vitality* of their group. *(p. 389)*

subtyping *Schema* change as a consequence of schema-inconsistent information, causing the formation of subcategories. *(p. 38)*

summation A method of forming positive or negative impressions by summing the valence of all the constituent person attributes. *(p. 30)*

superordinate goals Goals that both groups desire but which can be achieved only by both groups cooperating. *(p. 266)*

symbolic interactionism Theory of how the self emerges from human interaction that involves people trading symbols (through language and gesture) that are usually consensual, and represent abstract properties rather than concrete objects. *(p. 74)*

system justification theory Theory that attributes social stasis to people's adherence to an ideology that justifies and protects the status quo. *(p. 256)*

t-test Statistical procedure to test the statistical significance of an effect in which the mean for one condition is greater than the mean for another. *(p. 9)*

'tall poppy' syndrome Tendency to denigrate a person or group whose behaviour or physical or intellectual attributes are judged to be superior to the average. *(p. 115)*

task-oriented leaders Leaders who are concerned with the group task rather than relationships among members. *(p. 214)*

task taxonomy Group tasks can be classified according to whether a division of labour is possible; whether there is a predetermined standard to be met; and how an individual's inputs can contribute. *(p. 188)*

terror management theory The notion that the most fundamental human motivation is to reduce the terror of the inevitability of death. *Self-esteem* may be centrally implicated in effective terror management. *(p. 89)*

theory Set of interrelated concepts and principles that explain a phenomenon. *(p. 2)*

theory of planned behaviour Modification by Ajzen of the *theory of reasoned action*. It suggests that predicting a behaviour from an attitude measure is improved if people believe they have control over that behaviour. *(p. 105)*

theory of reasoned action Fishbein and Ajzen's model of the links between attitude and behaviour. A major feature is the proposition that the best way to predict a behaviour is to ask whether the person intends to do it. *(p. 104)*

third-person effect Most people think that they are less influenced than others by advertisements. *(p. 132)*

three-component attitude model An attitude consists of cognitive, affective and behavioural components. This three-fold division has an ancient heritage, stressing thought, feeling and action as basic to human experience. *(p. 98)*

three-factor theory of love Hatfield and Walster distinguished three components of what we label 'love': a cultural concept of love, an appropriate person to love, and emotional arousal. *(p. 348)*

Thurstone scale An 11-point scale with 22 items, two for each point. Each item has a value ranging from very unfavourable to very favourable. Respondents check the items with which they agree. Their attitude is the average scale value of these items. *(p. 118)*

tokenism Practice of publicly making small concessions to a minority group in order to deflect accusations of *prejudice* and *discrimination*. *(p. 245)*

transactive memory Group members have a shared memory for who within the group remembers what and is the expert on what. *(p. 223)*

two-component attitude model An attitude consists of a mental readiness to act. It also guides evaluative (judgmental) responses. *(p. 98)*

type A personality The 'coronary-prone' personality—a behavioural correlate of heart disease characterised by striving to achieve, time urgency, competitiveness and hostility. *(p. 305)*

ultimate attribution error Tendency to internally attribute bad outgroup and good ingroup behaviour, and to externally attribute good outgroup and bad ingroup behaviour. *(p. 63)*

unidimensionality A Guttman scale is cumulative: that is, agreement with the highest-scoring item implies agreement with all lower-scoring items. *(p. 120)*

unobtrusive measures Observational approaches that neither intrude on the processes being studied nor cause people to behave unnaturally. *(p. 123)*

utterance Sounds made by one person to another. *(p. 385)*

values A higher-order concept thought to provide a structure for organising attitudes. *(p. 114)*

visual dominance behaviour Tendency to gaze fixedly at a lower-status speaker. *(p. 396)*

vividness An intrinsic property of a stimulus on its own that makes it stand out and attract attention. *(p. 39)*

Völkerpsychologie Early precursor of social psychology, as the study of the collective mind, in Germany in the mid- to late 19th century. *(p. 16)*

weapons effect The mere presence of a weapon increases the probability that it will be used aggressively. *(p. 285)*

weighted averaging Method of forming positive or negative impressions by first weighting and then averaging the valence of all the constituent person attributes. *(p. 30)*

wellbeing A broad category of subjective phenomena, including emotional responses and global judgments of life satisfaction. *(p. 345)*

Photo credits

Action Plus	p. 169
Age	p. 388
Alamy	pp. 41, 260, 325, 384, 392
Andrew Barr	p. 19
Andrew Lukey	pp. 119, 285, 317, 367, 380
Angela Colbert	p. 7
Associated Press	pp. 63, 109, 255,
BBC	p. 189
Camera Press	p. 54
Corbis	pp. 125, 181, 232, 414
David Hoffman Library	p. 96
DK	pp. 25, 72, 81, 130, 177
Eye Ubiquitous	p. 334
Gabriele Schäfer	p. 220
Getty News	p. 279
Godfrey Bohnke	p. 397 (bottom)
Goldfields Children's Centre	p. 329
Michelle Duddey	p. 33
Mirrorpix	pp. 133, 209, 376
Narelle Beer	p. 328
Nathan Gaunt	p. 302
New Zealand Herald	pp. 61, 102, 210, 221, 274, 286, 313, 424, 425
Photobank Image Library	pp. 4, 9, 29, 44, 58, 68, 92, 161, 199, 236, 290, 319, 346 (right), 350, 354, 410, 421 (bottom)
Photos 12	p. 36
popperfoto	p. 159
PYMCA	pp. 12, 91
Rex	pp. 56, 129, 151, 225, 294, 306, 358, 366, 372
Science Photo Library	p. 6
Stock Image Group	pp. 1, 20, 38, 51, 76, 89, 104, 140, 164, 186, 192, 213, 240, 282, 299, 315, 342, 402, 421 (top), 428
Sunday News	p. 17

References

Abeles, R. P. (1976). Relative deprivation, rising expectations, and black militancy. *Journal of Social Issues, 32,* 119–137.

Abelson, R. P. (1968). Computers, polls and public opinion—some puzzles and paradoxes. *Transaction, 5,* 20–27.

Abelson, R. P. (1972). Are attitudes necessary? In B. T. King (Ed.), *Attitudes, conflict and social change* (pp. 19–32). New York: Academic Press.

Abelson, R. P. (1981). The psychological status of the script concept. *American Psychologist, 36,* 715–729.

Abelson, R. P., Aronson, E., McGuire, W. J., Newcomb, T. M., Rosenberg, M. J., & Tannenbaum, P. H. (Eds.). (1968). *Theories of cognitive consistency: A sourcebook.* Chicago: Rand McNally.

Aboud, F. E. (1987). The development of ethnic self-identification and attitudes. In J. S. Phinney & M. J. Rotheram (Eds.), *Children's ethnic socialisation: Pluralism and development* (pp. 32–55). Beverly Hills, CA: Sage.

Aboud, F. (1988). *Children and prejudice.* Oxford: Blackwell.

Abrams, D. (1990). Political identity: Relative deprivation, social identity and the case of Scottish Nationalism. *ESRC 16–19 Initiative Occasional Papers.* London: Economic & Social Research Council.

Abrams, D., Carter J., & Hogg, M. A. (1989). Perceptions of male homosexuality: An application of social identity theory. *Social Behaviour, 4,* 253–264.

Abrams, D., & Hogg, M. A. (1988). Comments on the motivational status of self-esteem in social identity and intergroup discrimination. *European Journal of Social Psychology, 18,* 317–334.

Abrams, D., & Hogg, M. A. (1990a). Social identification, self-categorisation, and social influence. *European Review of Social Psychology, 1,* 195–228.

Abrams, D., & Hogg, M. A. (Eds.). (1990b). *Social identity theory: Constructive and critical advances.* London: Harvester Wheatsheaf.

Abrams, D., & Hogg, M. A. (1990c). The social context of discourse: Let's not throw out the baby with the bath water. *Philosophical Psychology, 3,* 219–225.

Abrams, D., & Hogg, M. A. (Eds.). (1999). *Social identity and social cognition.* Oxford, UK: Blackwell.

Abrams, D., & Hogg, M. A. (2001). Collective identity: Group membership and self-conception. In M. A. Hogg & R. S. Tindale (Eds.), *Blackwell handbook of social psychology: Group processes* (pp. 425–460). Oxford, UK: Blackwell.

Abrams, D., Wetherell, M. S., Cochrane, S., Hogg, M. A., & Turner, J. C. (1990). Knowing what to think by knowing who you are: Self-categorization and the nature of norm formation, conformity, and group polarization. *British Journal of Social Psychology, 29,* 97–119.

Abramson, L. Y., Metalsky, G. I., & Alloy, L. B. (1989). Hopelessness depression: A theory-based subtype of depression. *Psychology Review, 96,* 358–372.

Abramson, L. Y., Seligman, M. E. P., & Teasdale, J. D. (1978). Learned helplessness in humans: Critique and reformulation. *Journal of Abnormal and Social Psychology, 87,* 49–74.

Acorn, D. A., Hamilton, D. L., & Sherman, S. J. (1988). Generalisation of biased perceptions of groups based on illusory correlations. *Social Cognition, 6,* 345–372.

Adair, J., Dushenko, T. W., & Lindsay, R. C. L. (1985). Ethical regulations and their impact on research practice. *American Psychologist, 40,* 59–72.

Adamopoulos, J., & Kashima, Y. (1999). *Social psychology and cultural context.* London: Sage.

Adams, J. (1965). Inequity in social exchange. In L. Berkowitz (Ed.), *Advances in experimental social psychology* (Vol. 2, pp. 267–299). New York: Academic Press.

Adams, J. M., & Jones, W. H. (1997). The conceptualisation of marital commitment: An integrative analysis. *Journal of Social and Personal Relationships, 11,* 1177–1196.

Adorno, T. W., Frenkel-Brunswik, E., Levinson, D. J., & Sanford, R. M. (1950). *The authoritarian personality.* New York: Harper.

Ahlstrom, W., & Havighurst, R. (1971). *400 losers: Delinquent boys in high school.* San Francisco, CA: Jossey-Bass.

Ahrons, C., & Rodgers, R. (1987). *Divorced families.* New York: Norton.

Aiello, J. R., & Jones, S. E. (1971). Field study of the proxemic behaviour of young children in three subcultural groups. *Journal of Personality and Social Psychology, 19,* 351–356.

Ajzen, I. (1989). Attitude structure and behaviour. In A. R. Pratkanis, S. J. Breckler, & A. G. Greenwald (Eds.), *Attitude structure and function* (pp. 241–274). Hillsdale, NJ: Erlbaum.

Ajzen, I., & Fishbein, M. (1980). *Understanding attitudes and predicting social behavior.* Englewood Cliffs, NJ: Prentice Hall.

Ajzen, I., & Madden, T. J. (1986). Prediction of goal-directed behaviour: Attitudes, intentions and perceived behavioural control. *Journal of Experimental Social Psychology, 22,* 453–474.

Albion, M. S., & Faris, P. W. (1979). *Appraising research on advertising's economic impacts* (Report no. 79–115). Cambridge, MA: Marketing Science Institute.

Aldag, R. J., & Fuller, S. R. (1993). Beyond fiasco: A reappraisal of the groupthink phenomenon and a new model of group decision processes. *Psychological Bulletin, 113,* 533–552.

Alexander, C. N., Zucker, L. G., & Brody, C. L. (1970). Experimental expectations and autokinetic experiences: Consistency theories and judgemental convergence. *Sociometry, 33,* 108–122.

Allard, R., & Landry, R. (1994). Subjective ethnolinguistic vitality: A comparison of two measures. *International Journal of the Sociology of Language, 108,* 117–144.

Allen, M., Mabry, E., & McKelton, D. (1998). Impact of juror attitudes about the death penalty on juror evaluations of guilt and punishment. *Law and Human Behavior, 23,* 715–732.

Allen, V. L. (1965). Situational factors in conformity. In L. Berkowitz (Ed.), *Advances in experimental social psychology* (Vol. 2, pp. 133–175). New York: Academic Press.

Allen, V. L. (1975). Social support for non-conformity. In L. Berkowitz (Ed.), *Advances in experimental social psychology* (Vol. 8, pp. 1–43). New York: Academic Press.

Allen, V. L., & Levine, J. M. (1971). Social support and conformity: The role of independent assessment of reality. *Journal of Experimental Social Psychology, 7,* 48–58.

Allen, V. L., & Wilder, D. A. (1975). Categorisation, belief similarity, and group similarity. *Journal of Personality and Social Psychology, 32,* 971–977.

Allison, S. T., Mackie, D. M., & Messick, D. M. (1996). Outcome biases in social perception: Implications for dispositional inference, attitude change, stereotyping, and social behavior. *Advances in Experimental Social Psychology, 28,* 53–93.

Alloy, L. B., & Tabachnik, N. (1984). Assessment of covariation by humans and animals: The joint influence of prior expectations and current situational information. *Psychological Review, 91,* 112–149.

Allport, F. H. (1920). The influence of the group upon association and thought. *Journal of Experimental Psychology, 3,* 159–182.

Allport, F. H. (1924). *Social psychology*. Boston, MA: Houghton-Mifflin.

Allport, G. W. (1935). Attitudes. In C. M. Murchison (Ed.), *Handbook of social psychology* (pp. 789–844). Worcester, MA: Clark University Press.

Allport, G. W. (1954a). The historical background of modern social psychology. In G. Lindzey (Ed.), *Handbook of social psychology* (Vol. 1, pp. 3–56). Reading, MA: Addison-Wesley.

Allport, G. W. (1954b). *The nature of prejudice*. Reading, MA: Addison-Wesley.

Allport, G. W., & Postman, L. J. (1945). Psychology of rumour. *Transactions of the New York Academy of Sciences*, 8, 61–81.

Allport, G. W., & Vernon, P. E. (1931). *A study of values*. Boston: Houghton-Mifflin.

Allyn, J., & Festinger, L. (1961). The effectiveness of unanticipated persuasive communications. *Journal of Abnormal and Social Psychology*, 62, 35–40.

Altemeyer, B. (1981). *Right-wing authoritarianism*. Winnipeg, Canada: University of Manitoba Press.

Altemeyer, B. (1988). *Enemies of freedom: Understanding right-wing authoritarianism*. San Francisco, CA: Jossey-Bass.

Altemeyer, B. (1994). Reducing prejudice in right-wing authoritarians. In M. P. Zanna & J. M. Olsen (Eds.), *The psychology of prejudice: The Ontario symposium* (pp. 131–148). Hillsdale, NJ: Erlbaum.

Altemeyer, B. (1998). The other "authoritarian personality'. In M. Zanna (Ed.), *Advances in experimental social psychology* (Vol. 30, pp. 47–92). Orlando, FL: Academic Press.

Altman, D. (1986). *AIDS and the new Puritanism*. London & Sydney: Pluto Press.

Altman, I. (1975). *The environment and social behavior*. Monterey, CA: Brooks/Cole.

Altman, I. (1993). Dialectics, physical environments and personal relationships. *Communication Monographs*, 60, 26–34.

Altman, I., & Taylor, D. A. (1973). *Social penetration: The development of interpersonal relationships*. New York: Holt, Rinehart & Winston.

Amato, P. R. (1983). Helping behavior in urban and rural environments: Field studies based on a taxonomic organisation of helping episodes. *Journal of Personality and Social Psychology*, 45, 571–586.

American Psychological Association. (2002). Ethical principles of psychologists and code of conduct. *American Psychologist, 57(12)*.

Amir, Y. (1976). The role of intergroup contact in change of prejudice and ethnic relations. In P. A. Katz (Ed.), *Towards the elimination of racism* (pp. 245–308). Elmsford, NY: Pergamon Press.

Anderson, C. A., & Anderson, D. C. (1984). Ambient temperature and violent crime: Tests of the linear and curvilinear hypothesis. *Journal of Personality and Social Psychology*, 46, 91–97.

Anderson, C. A., Anderson, K. B., & Deuser, W. E. (1996). Examining an affective framework: Weapon and temperature effects on aggressive thoughts, affect, and attitudes. *Personality and Social Psychology Bulletin*, 22, 366–376.

Anderson, C. A., & Bushman, B. J. (1997). External validity of trivial experiments: The case of laboratory aggression. *Review of General Psychology*, 1, 19–41.

Anderson, C. A., & Bushman, B. J. (2002). The effects of media violence on society. *Science, 295*, 2377–2378.

Anderson, C. A., Bushman, B. J., & Groom, R. W. (1997). Hot years and serious and deadly assault: Empirical tests of the heat hypothesis. *Journal of Personality and Social Psychology, 73*, 1213–1223.

Anderson, C. A., & Godfrey, S. S. (1987). Thoughts about actions: The effects of specificity and availability of imagined behavioral scripts on expectations about oneself and others. *Social Cognition*, 5, 238–258.

Anderson, C. A., & Huesmann, L. R. (2003). Human aggression: A social-cognitive view. In M. A. Hogg & J. Cooper (Eds.), *The Sage handbook of social psychology* (pp. 296–323). London: Sage.

Anderson, C. A., & Slusher, M. P. (1986). Relocating motivational effects: A synthesis of cognitive and motivational effects on attributions for success and failure. *Social Cognition*, 4, 250–292.

Anderson, J. R. (1990). *Cognitive psychology and its implications* (3rd ed.). New York: Freeman.

Anderson, J., & McGuire, W. J. (1965). Prior reassurance of group consensus as a factor in producing resistance to persuasion. *Sociometry*, 28, 44–56.

Anderson, N. H. (1965). Adding versus averaging as a stimulus combination rule in impression formation. *Journal of Experimental Psychology*, 70, 394–400.

Anderson, N. H. (1971). Integration theory and attitude change. *Psychological Review*, 78, 171–206.

Anderson, N. H. (1978). Cognitive algebra: Integration theory applied to social attribution. In L. Berkowitz (Ed.), *Cognitive theories in social psychology* (pp. 1–126). New York: Academic Press.

Anderson, N. H. (1980). Integration theory applied to cognitive responses and attitudes. In R. E. Petty, T. M. Ostrom, & T. C. Brock (Eds.), *Cognitive responses in persuasion*. New York: Erlbaum.

Anderson, N. H. (1981). *Foundations of information integration theory*. New York: Academic Press.

Andreeva, G. (1984). Cognitive processes in developing groups. In L. H. Strickland (Ed.), *Directions in Soviet social psychology* (pp. 67–82). New York: Springer.

Apfelbaum, E., & Lubek, I. (1976). Resolution vs. revolution? The theory of conflicts in question. In L. Strickland, F. Aboud, & K. J. Gergen (Eds.), *Social psychology in transition* (pp. 71–94). New York: Plenum.

Apfelbaum, E., & McGuire, G. R. (1986). Models of suggestive influence and the disqualification of the social crowd. In C. F. Graumann & S. Moscovici (Eds.), *Changing conceptions of crowd mind and behavior* (pp. 27–50). New York: Springer-Verlag.

Archer, D., Iritani, B., Kimes, D. D., & Barrios, M. (1983). Face-ism: Five studies of sex differences in facial prominence. *Journal of Personality and Social Psychology*, 45, 725–735.

Archer, J. (2000). Sex differences in aggression between heterosexual partners: A meta-analytic review. *Psychological Bulletin*, 126, 697–702.

Ardrey, R. (1961). *African genesis*. New York: Delta Books.

Ardrey, R. (1966). *The territorial imperative*. New York: Atheneum.

Arendt, H. (1963). *Eichmann in Jerusalem: A report on the banality of evil*. New York: Viking.

Argote, L., Insko, C. A., Yovetich, N., & Romero, A. A. (1995). Group learning curves: The effects of turnover and task complexity on group performance. *Journal of Applied Social Psychology*, 25, 512–529.

Argyle, M. (1971). *The psychology of interpersonal behaviour*. Harmondsworth: Penguin.

Argyle, M. (1975). *Bodily communication*. London: Methuen.

Argyle, M. (1988). *Bodily communication* (2nd ed.). London: Methuen.

Argyle, M. (1992). Benefits produced by supportive social relationships. In H. Veiel & U. Baumann (Eds.), *The meaning and measurement of social support*. New York: Hemisphere.

Argyle, M., & Dean, J. (1965). Eye-contact, distance and affiliation. *Sociometry, 28,* 289–304.

Argyle, M., & Henderson, M. (1985). *The anatomy of relationships*. London: Heinemann & Harmondsworth: Penguin.

Argyle, M., & Ingham, R. (1972). Gaze, mutual gaze, and proximity. *Semiotica, 6,* 32–49.

Argyle, M., & Little, B. R. (1972). Do personality traits apply to social behavior? In N. S. Endler & D. Magnusson (Eds.), *Interactional psychology and personality* (pp. 30–57). New York: Wiley.

Aries, E. (1996). *Men and women in interaction: Considering the differences*. New York: Oxford University Press.

Aries, E. (1997). Women and men talking: Are they worlds apart? In W. R. Walsh (Ed.), *Women, men and gender: Ongoing debates* (pp. 79–100). New Haven, CT: Yale University Press.

Arkes, H. R., Boehm, L. E., & Xu, G. (1991). Determinants of judged validity. *Journal of Experimental Social Psychology, 27,* 576–605.

Aron, A., Paris, M., & Aron, E. N. (1995). Falling in love: Prospective studies of self-concept change. *Journal of Personality and Social Psychology, 69,* 1102–1112.

Aronson, E. (1984). *The social animal* (4th ed.). New York: W. H. Freeman.

Aronson, E. (1999). Dissonance, hypocrisy, and the self-concept. In E. Harmon-Jones & J. Mills (Eds.), *Cognitive dissonance: Progress on a pivotal theory in social psychology* (pp. 103–126). Washington, DC: American Psychological Association.

Aronson, E., Ellsworth, P. C., Carlsmith, J. M., & Gonzales, M. H. (1990). *Methods of research in social psychology* (2nd ed.). New York: McGraw-Hill.

Aronson, E., & Linder, D. (1965). Gain and loss of esteem as determinants of interpersonal attractiveness. *Journal of Experimental Social Psychology, 1,* 156–171.

Aronson, E., & Mills, J. (1959). The effects of severity of initiation on liking for a group. *Journal of Abnormal and Social Psychology, 59,* 177–181.

Arrow, H., Berdahl, J. L., Bouas, K. S., Craig, K. M., Cummings, A., Lebie, L., McGrath, J. E., O'Connor, K. M., Rhoades, J. A., & Schlosser, A. (1996). Time, technology, and groups: An integration. *Computer Supported Cooperative Work, 4,* 253–261.

Arrow, H., McGrath, J. E., & Berdahl, J. L. (2000). *Small groups as complex systems: Formation, coordination, development, and adaptation*. Thousand Oaks, CA: Sage.

Asch, S. E. (1946). Forming impressions of personality. *Journal of Abnormal and Social Psychology, 41,* 258–290.

Asch, S. E. (1951). Effects of group pressure upon the modification and distortion of judgements. In H. Guetzkow (Ed.), *Groups, leadership and men* (pp. 177–190). Pittsburg, PA: Carnegie Press.

Asch, S. E. (1952). *Social psychology*. Englewood Cliffs, NJ: Prentice Hall.

Asch, S. E. (1956). Studies of independence and conformity: A minority of one against a unanimous majority. *Psychological Monographs: General and Applied, 70,* 1–70 (whole no. 416).

Aschenbrenner, K. M., & Schaefer, R. E. (1980). Minimal group situations: Comments on a mathematical model and on the research paradigm. *European Journal of Social Psychology, 10,* 389–398.

Ashburn-Nardo, L., Voils, C. I., & Monteith, M. J. (2001). Implicit associations as the seeds of intergroup bias: How easily do they take root? *Journal of Personality and Social Psychology, 81,* 789–799.

Ashmore, R. D. (1981). Sex stereotypes and implicit personality theory. In D. L. Hamilton (Ed.), *Cognitive processes in stereotyping and intergroup behavior* (pp. 37–81). Hillsdale, NJ: Erlbaum.

Ashmore, R .D., & Jussim, L. (1997). Towards a second century of the scientific analysis of self and identity. In R. Ashmore & L. Jussim (Eds.), *Self and identity: Fundamental issues* (pp. 3–19). New York: Oxford University Press.

Assael, H. (1981). *Consumer behavior and marketing action*. Boston: Kent.

Atkin, C. K. (1977). Effects of campaign advertising and newscasts on children. *Journalism Quarterly, 54,* 503–58.

Atkin, C. K. (1980). *Effects of the mass media*. New York: McGraw-Hill.

Attridge, M., & Berscheid, E. (1994). Entitlement in romantic relationships in the United States: A social exchange perspective. In M. J. Lerner & G. Mikula (Eds.), *Entitlement and the affectional bond: Justice in close relationships* (pp. 117–148). New York: Plenum.

Attridge, M., Berscheid, E., & Sprecher, S. (1998). Dependency and insecurity in romantic relationships: Development and validation of two companion scales. *Personal Relationships, 5,* 31–58.

Augoustinos, M. (1991). Consensual representations of social structure in different age groups. *British Journal of Social Psychology, 30,* 193–205.

Augoustinos, M., & Innes, J. M. (1990). Towards an integration of social representations and social schema theory. *British Journal of Social Psychology, 29,* 213–231.

Augoustinos, M., & Walker, I. (1995). *Social cognition: An integrated introduction*. London: Sage.

Austin, J. L. (1962). *How to do things with words*. Oxford: Clarendon Press.

Austin, W. (1979). Sex differences in bystander intervention in a theft. *Journal of Personality and Social Psychology, 37,* 2110–2120.

Australian Bureau of Statistics. (2000). Retrieved January 21, 2001, from http://www.abs.gov.au

Australian Institute of Criminology. (1999). *Australian crime: Facts and figures*. Retrieved January 21, 2001, from http://www.aic.gov.au/stats/facts99/sec1.html#css

Averill, J. R., & Boothroyd, P. (1977). On falling in love in conformance with the romantic ideal. *Motivation and Emotion, 1,* 235–247.

Azar, B. (1997). Forgiveness helps keep relationships steadfast. *APA Monitor*, November 14.

Axelrod, R., & Dion, D. (1988). The further evolution of cooperation. *Science, 242,* 1385–1390.

Bailey, D. S., & Taylor, S. P. (1991). Effects of alcohol and aggressive disposition on human physical aggression. *Journal of Research in Personality, 25,* 334–342.

Bains, G. (1983). Explanations and the need for control. In M. Hewstone (Ed.), *Attribution theory: Social and functional extensions* (pp. 126–143). Oxford: Blackwell.

Bakan, D. (1966). *The duality of human existence*. Chicago, IL: Rand McNally.

Baker, P. M. (1985). The status of age: Preliminary result. *Journal of Gerontology, 40,* 506–508.

Baldwin, J. M. (1897). *Social and ethical interpretations in mental development*. New York: Macmillan.

Bales, R. F. (1950). *Interaction process analysis: A method for the study of small groups*. Reading, MA: Addison-Wesley.

Ballard, K. D. (1973). A scale for measuring adolescents' attitudes toward school. *The New Zealand Psychologist, 2*, 83–88.

Banaji, M. R., & Prentice, D. J. (1994). The self in social contexts. *Annual Review of Psychology, 45*, 297–332.

Bandura, A. (1973). *Aggression: A social learning analysis*. Englewood Cliffs, NJ: Prentice Hall.

Bandura, A. (1977). *Social learning theory*. Englewood Cliffs, NJ: Prentice Hall.

Bandura, A. (1986). *Social foundations of thought and action: A social cognitive theory*. Englewood Cliffs, NJ: Prentice Hall.

Bandura, A. (1992). Exercise of personal agency through the self-efficacy mechanism. In R. Schwarzer (Ed.), *Self-efficacy: Thought control of action* (pp. 3–38). Washington, DC: Hemisphere.

Bandura, A., Ross, D., & Ross, S. A. (1963). Imitation of film-mediated aggressive models. *Journal of Abnormal and Social Psychology, 66*, 3–11.

Bandura, A., & Walters, R. H. (1963). *Social learning and personality development*. New York: Holt, Rinehart & Winston.

Banks, W. C. (1976). White preference in Blacks: A paradigm in search of a phenomenon. *Psychological Bulletin, 83*, 1179–1186.

Banuazizi, A., & Movahedi, S. (1975). Interpersonal dynamics in a simulated prison: A methodological analysis. *American Psychologist, 30*, 152–160.

Barash, D. P. (1977). *Sociobiology of behavior*. New York: Elsevier.

Bargh, J. A. (1984). Automatic and conscious processing of social information. In R. S. Wyer Jr. & T.K. Srull (Eds.), *Handbook of social cognition* (Vol. 3, pp. 1–44). Hillsdale, NJ: Erlbaum.

Bargh, J. A. (1989). Conditional automaticity: Varieties of automatic influence in social perception and cognition. In J. S. Uleman & J. A. Bargh (Eds.), *Unintended thought* (pp. 3–51). New York: Guilford.

Bargh, J. A., Chaiken, S., Govender, R., & Pratto, F. (1992). The generality of the automatic attitude activation effect. *Journal of Personality and Social Psychology, 62*, 893–912.

Bargh, J. A., Lombardi, W. J., & Higgins, E. T. (1988). Automaticity of chronically accessible constructs in person X situation effects on person perception: It's just a matter of time. *Journal of Personality and Social Psychology, 55*, 599–605.

Bargh, J. A., & Pratto, F. (1986). Individual construct accessibility and perceptual selection. *Journal of Experimental Social Psychology, 22*, 293–311.

Bargh, J. A., & Tota, M. E. (1988). Context-dependent automatic processing in depression: Accessibility of negative constructs with regard to self but not others. *Journal of Personality and Social Psychology, 54*, 925–939.

Bar-Hillel, M. (1980). The base-rate fallacy in probability judgements. *Acta Psychologica, 44*, 211–233.

Barjonet, P. E. (1980). L'influence sociale et des représentations des causes de l'accident de la route. *Le Travail Humain, 43*, 243–253.

Barney, W. D. (1973). TV viewing habits of 3-, 4- and 5-year old children. *The New Zealand Psychologist, 2*, 15–27.

Barocas, R., & Gorlow, L. (1967). Self-report personality measurement and conformity behaviour. *Journal of Social Psychology, 71*, 227–234.

Baron, R. A. (1977). *Human aggression*. New York: Plenum.

Baron, R. A. (1979). Aggression, empathy, and race: Effects of victim's pain cues, victim's race, and level of instigation on physical aggression. *Journal of Applied Social Psychology, 9*, 103–114.

Baron, R. A. (1989). Personality and organisational conflict: The type A behavior pattern and self-monitoring. *Organisational Behavior and Human Decision Processes, 44*, 281–297.

Baron, R. A., & Bell, P. (1977). Sexual arousal and aggression by males: Effects of types of erotic stimuli and prior provocation. *Journal of Personality and Social Psychology, 35*, 79–87.

Baron, R. A., & Byrne, D. (1987). *Social psychology: Understanding human interaction* (5th ed.). Boston: Allyn & Bacon.

Baron, R. A., & Byrne, D. (1994). *Social psychology: Understanding human interaction* (7th ed.). Boston: Allyn & Bacon.

Baron, R. A., & Ransberger, V. M. (1978). Ambient temperature and the occurrence of collective violence: The 'long hot summer' revisited. *Journal of Personality and Social Psychology, 36*, 351–360.

Baron, R. S. (1986). Distraction-conflict theory: Progress and problems. In L. Berkowitz (Ed.), *Advances in experimental social psychology* (Vol. 20, pp. 1–40). New York: Academic Press.

Baron, R. S., & Byrne, D. (2000). *Social psychology* (9th ed.). Boston: Allyn & Bacon.

Baron, R. S., & Kerr, N. (2003). *Group process, group decision, group action* (2nd ed.). Buckingham, UK: Open University Press.

Baron, R. S., & Roper, G. (1976). Reaffirmation of social comparison views of choice shifts: Averaging and extremity effects in an autokinetic situation. *Journal of Personality and Social Psychology, 33*, 521–530.

Barrett, M., & Short, J. (1992). Images of European people in a group of 5–10 year old English school children. *British Journal of Developmental Psychology, 10*, 339–363.

Barron, F. (1953). Some personality correlates of independence of judgment. *Journal of Personality, 21*, 287–297.

Bar-Tal, D. (1976). *Prosocial behavior: Theory and research*. Washington, DC: Hemisphere Press.

Bartlett, F. C. (1923). *Psychology and primitive culture*. Cambridge: Cambridge University Press.

Bartlett, F. C. (1932). *Remembering: A study in experiential and social psychology*. Cambridge: Cambridge University Press.

Bartol, K. M., & Butterfield, D. A. (1976). Sex effects in evaluating leaders. *Journal of Applied Psychology, 61*, 446–454.

Bartsch, R. A., & Judd, C. M. (1993). Majority–minority status and perceived ingroup variability revisited. *European Journal of Social Psychology, 23*, 471–483.

Basow, S. A. (1992). *Gender stereotypes and roles* (3rd ed.). Belmont, CA: Brooks/Cole.

Bass, B. M. (1990a). *Bass & Stogdill's handbook of leadership*. New York: Free Press.

Bass, B. M. (1990b). From transactional to transformational leadership: Learning to share the vision. *Organizational Dynamics, 18*, 19–31.

Bass, B. M. (1998). *Transformational leadership: Industrial, military, and educational impact*. Mahwah, NJ: Erlbaum.

Bass, B. M., & Avolio, B. J. (1993). Transformational leadership: A response to critiques. In M. M. Chemers & R. A. Ayman (Eds.), *Leadership theory and research: Perspectives and directions* (pp. 49–80). London: Academic Press.

Batson, C. D. (1983). Sociobiology and the role of religion in promoting prosocial behavior: An alternative view. *Journal of Personality and Social Psychology, 45*, 1380–1385.

Batson, C. D. (1994). Why act for the public good? Four answers. *Personality and Social Psychology Bulletin, 20*, 603–610.

Batson, C. D., Cochran, P. J., Biederman, M. F., Blosser, J. L., Ryan, M. J., & Vogt, B. (1978). Failure to help when in a hurry: Callousness or conflict? *Journal of Personality and Social Psychology Bulletin, 4*, 97–101.

Batson, C. D., & Coke, J. S. (1981). Empathy: A source of altruistic motivation for helping? In J. P. Rushton & R. M. Sorrentino (Eds.), *Altruism and helping behavior: Social, personality, and developmental perspectives* (pp. 167–183). Hillsdale, NJ: Erlbaum.

Batson, C. D., Duncan, B., Ackerman, P., Buckley, T., & Birch, K. (1981). Is empathic emotion a source of altruistic motivation? *Journal of Personality and Social Psychology, 40*, 290–302.

Batson, C. D., Early, S., & Salvarani, G. (1997). Perspective taking: Imagining how another feels versus imagining how you would feel. *Personality and Social Psychology Bulletin, 23*, 751–758.

Batson, C. D., & Oleson, K. C. (1991). Current status of the empathy–altruism hypothesis. In M. S. Clark (Ed.), *Prosocial behaviour* (pp. 62–85). Newbury Park, CA: Sage.

Batson, C. D., Schoenrade, P., & Ventis, W. L. (1993). *Religion and the individual: A social-psychological perspective*. New York: Oxford University Press.

Batson, C. D., Sympson, S. C., Hindman, J. L., Decruz, P., Todd, R. M., Weeks, J. L., Jennings, G., & Burris, C. T. (1996). 'I've been there, too': Effect on empathy of prior experience with a need. *Personality and Social Psychology Bulletin, 22*, 474–482.

Batson, C. D., van Lange, P. A. M., Ahmad, N., & Lishner, D. A. (2003). Altruism and helping behavior. In M. A. Hogg & J. Cooper (Eds.), *The Sage handbook of social psychology* (pp. 279–295). London: Sage.

Battisch, V. A., Assor, A., Messe, L. A., & Aronoff, J. (1985). Personality and person perception. In P. Shaver (Ed.), *Review of personality and social psychology* (Vol. 6, pp. 185–208). Beverly Hills, CA: Sage.

Baumeister, R. F. (1987). How the self became a problem: A psychological review of historical research. *Journal of Personality and Social Psychology, 52*, 163–176.

Baumeister, R. F. (1989). The optimal margin of illusion. *Journal of Social and Clinical Psychology, 8*, 176–189.

Baumeister, R. F. (1991). *Escaping the self: Alcoholism, spirituality, masochism, and other flights from the burden of selfhood*. New York: Basic Books.

Baumeister, R. F. (1998). The self. In D. T. Gilbert, S. T. Fiske, & G. Lindzey (Eds.), *Handbook of social psychology* (4th ed., Vol. 1, pp. 680–740). New York: McGraw-Hill.

Baumeister, R. F., Chesner, S. P., Senders, P. S., & Tice, D. M. (1988). Who's in charge here? Group leaders do lend help in emergencies. *Personality and Social Psychology Bulletin, 14*, 17–22.

Baumeister, R. F., & Covington, M. V. (1985). Self-esteem, persuasion, and retrospective distortion of initial attitudes. *Electronic Social Psychology, 1*, 1–22.

Baumeister, R. F., & Darley, J. M. (1982). Reducing the biasing effect of perpetrator attractiveness in jury simulation. *Personality and Social Psychology Bulletin, 8*, 286–292.

Baumeister, R. F., & Heatherton, T. F. (1996). Self-regulation failure: An overview. *Psychological Inquiry, 7*, 1–15.

Baumeister, R. F., & Leary, M. R. (1995). The need to belong: Desire for interpersonal attachments as a fundamental human motivation. *Psychological Bulletin, 117*, 497–529.

Baumeister, R. F., Smart, L., & Boden, J. M. (1996). Relation of threatened egotism to violence and aggression: The dark side of high self-esteem. *Psychological Review, 103*, 5–33.

Baumeister, R. F., Tice, D. M., & Hutton, D. G. (1989). Self-presentational motivations and personality differences in self-esteem. *Journal of Personality, 57*, 547–579.

Baumrind, D. (1964). Some thoughts on ethics of research: After reading Milgram's 'Behavioral study of obedience'. *American Psychologist, 19*, 421–443.

Bavelas, A. (1968). Communications patterns in task-oriented groups. In D. Cartwright & A. Zander (Eds.), *Group dynamics: Research and theory* (3rd ed., pp. 503–511). London: Tavistock.

Baxter, T. L., & Goldberg, L. R. (1988). Perceived behavioral consistency underlying trait attributions to oneself and another: An extension of the actor–observer effect. *Personality and Social Psychology Bulletin, 13*, 437–447.

Bayley, B., & Schechter, S. R. (Eds.). (2003). *Language socialization in bilingual and multilingual societies*. Clevedon, UK: Multilingual Matters.

Beattie, A. E., & Mitchell, A. A. (1985). The relationship between advertising recall and persuasion: An experimental investigation. In L. F. Alwitt & A. A. Mitchell (Eds.), *Psychological processes and advertising effects: Theory, research and applications*. Hillsdale, NJ: Erlbaum.

Beauvois, J. L., & Dubois, N. (1988). The norm of internality in the explanation of psychological events. *European Journal of Social Psychology, 18*, 299–316.

Beck, L., & Ajzen, I. (1991). Predicting dishonest actions using the theory of planned behavior. *Journal of Research in Personality, 25*, 285–301.

Belanger, S., & Pinard, M. (1991). Ethnic movements and the competition model: Some missing links. *American Sociological Review, 56*, 446–457.

Belch, G. E., & Belch, M. A. (2004). *Advertising and promotion: An integrated marketing communications perspective* (6th ed.). New York: McGraw-Hill/Irwin.

Bell, L. G., Wicklund, R. A., Manko, G., & Larkin, C. (1976). When unexpected behaviour is attributed to the environment. *Journal of Research in Personality, 10*, 316–327.

Belsky, J. (1993). Etiology of child maltreatment: A developmental-ecological analysis. *Psychological Bulletin, 114*, 413–434.

Bem, D. J. (1967). Self perception: An alternative interpretation of cognitive dissonance. *Psychological Review, 74*, 183–200.

Bem, D. J. (1972). Self-perception theory. In L. Berkowitz (Ed.), *Advances in experimental social psychology* (Vol. 6, pp. 1–62). New York: Academic Press.

Bem, D. J., & Allen, A. A. (1974). On predicting some of the people some of the time: The search for cross-situational consistencies in behavior. *Psychological Review, 81*, 506–520.

Bem, D. J., & McConnell, H. K. (1970). Testing the self-perception explanation of dissonance phenomena: On the salience of premanipulation attitudes. *Journal of Personality and Social Psychology, 14*, 23–31.

Bem, S. L. (1981). Gender schema theory: A cognitive account of sex typing. *Psychological Review, 88*, 354–364.

Benedict, R. (1934). *Patterns of culture*. Boston: Houghton Mifflin.

Bennett, E. B. (1955). Discussion, decision, commitment and consensus in group decision. *Human Relations, 8*, 25–73.

Benson, P. L., Karabenick, S. A., & Lerner, R. M. (1976). Pretty pleases: The effects of physical attractiveness, race, and sex on receiving help. *Journal of Experimental Social Psychology, 12*, 409–415.

Benton, A. A., & Druckman, D. (1974). Constituent's bargaining orientation and intergroup negotiations. *Journal of Applied Social Psychology, 4*, 141–150.

Berger, J., Fisek, M. H., Norman, R. Z., & Zelditch, M. Jr. (1977). *Status characteristics and social interaction*. New York: Elsevier.

Berger, J., Wagner, D., & Zelditch, M. Jr. (1985). Expectation states theory: Review and assessment. In J. Berger & M. Zelditch Jr. (Eds.), *Status, rewards and influence* (pp. 1–72). San Francisco, CA: Jossey-Bass.

Berglas, S. (1987). The self-handicapping model of alcohol abuse. In H. T. Blane & K. E. Leonard (Eds.), *Psychological theories of drinking and alcoholism* (pp. 305–345). New York: Guilford Press.

Berglas, S., & Jones, E. E. (1978). Drug choice as a self-handicapping strategy in response to noncontingent success. *Journal of Personality and Social Psychology, 36,* 405–417.

Berkowitz, L. (1962). *Aggression: A social psychological analysis.* New York: McGraw-Hill.

Berkowitz, L. (1970). The self, selfishness and altruism. In J. Macaulay & L. Berkowitz (Eds.), *Altruism and helping behavior.* New York: Academic Press.

Berkowitz, L. (1972a). Frustrations, comparisons, and other sources of emotion arousal as contributors to social unrest. *Journal of Social Issues, 28,* 77–91.

Berkowitz, L. (1972b). Social norms, feelings, and other factors affecting helping and altruism. In L. Berkowitz (Ed.), *Advances in experimental social psychology* (Vol. 6, pp. 63–108). New York: Academic Press.

Berkowitz, L. (1974). Some determinants of impulsive aggression: Role of mediated associations with reinforcements for aggression. *Psychological Review, 81,* 165–176.

Berkowitz, L. (1978). Decreased helpfulness with increased group size through lessening the effects of the needy individual's dependency. *Journal of Personality, 46,* 299–310.

Berkowitz, L. (1984). Some effects of thoughts on anti- and pro-social influences of media events: A cognitive–neoassociation analysis. *Psychological Bulletin, 95,* 410–427.

Berkowitz, L. (1993). *Aggression: Its causes, consequences and control.* Philadelphia, PA: Temple University Press.

Berkowitz, L., & LePage, A. (1967). Weapons as aggression-eliciting stimuli. *Journal of Personality and Social Psychology, 7,* 202–207.

Berman, M., Gladue, B., & Taylor, S. (1993). The effects of hormones, type A behaviour pattern, and provocation on aggression in men. *Motivation and Emotion, 17,* 125–138.

Berry, J. W. (1967). Independence and conformity in subsistence level societies. *Journal of Personality and Social Psychology, 7,* 415–418.

Berry, J. W. (1984). Multicultural policy in Canada: A social psychological analysis. *Canadian Journal of Behavioural Science, 16,* 353–370.

Berry, J. W., Kim, U., Minde, T., & Mok, D. (1987). Comparative studies of acculturative stress. *International Migration Review, 21,* 491–511.

Berry, J. W., Poortinga, Y. H., & Pandey, J. (Eds.). (1997). *Handbook of cross-cultural psychology, Vol 1: Theory and method* (2nd ed.). Boston, MA: Allyn & Bacon.

Berry, J. W., Trimble, J. E., & Olmedo, E. L. (1986). Assessment of acculturation. In W. J. Lonner & J. W. Berry (Eds.), *Field methods in cross-cultural research* (pp. 290–327). Beverly Hills, CA: Sage.

Berscheid, E. (1994). Interpersonal relationships. *Annual Review of Psychology, 45,* 79–129.

Berscheid, E., & Ammazzalorso, H. (2001). Emotional experience in close relationships. In G. J. O. Fletcher & M. Clark (Eds.), *Blackwell handbook of social psychology: Interpersonal processes* (pp. 253–278). Oxford: Blackwell Publishers.

Berscheid, E., Graziano, W., Monson, T., & Dermer, M. (1976). Outcome dependency: Attention, attribution, and attraction. *Journal of Personality and Social Psychology, 34,* 978–979.

Berscheid, E., & Reis, H. T. (1998). Attraction and close relationships. In D. T. Gilbert, S. T. Fiske, & G. Lindzey (Eds.), *The handbook of social psychology* (4th ed., Vol. 2, pp. 193–281). New York: McGraw-Hill.

Berscheid, E., & Walster, E. H. (1978). *Interpersonal attraction* (2nd ed.). Reading, MA: Addison-Wesley.

Bexton, W. H., Heron, W., & Scott, T. H. (1954). Effects of decreased variation in the sensory environment. *Canadian Journal of Psychology, 8,* 70–76.

Bickman, L., & Green, S. K. (1977). Situational cues and crime reporting: Do signs make a difference? *Journal of Applied Social Psychology, 7,* 1–8.

Bickman, L., & Rosenbaum, D. P. (1977). Crime reporting as a function of bystander encouragement, surveillance, and credibility. *Journal of Personality and Social Psychology, 35,* 577–586.

Biener, L., & Abrams, D. (1991). The contemplation ladder: Validation of a measure of readiness to consider smoking cessation. *Health Psychology, 10,* 360–365.

Billig, M. (1973). Normative communication in a minimal inter-group situation. *European Journal of Social Psychology, 3,* 339–343.

Billig, M. (1976). *Social psychology and intergroup relations.* London: Academic Press.

Billig, M. (1978). *Fascists: A social psychological view of the national front.* London: Harcourt Brace Jovanovich.

Billig, M. (1987). *Arguing and thinking: A rhetorical approach to social psychology.* Cambridge: Cambridge University Press.

Billig, M. (1991). *Ideology and opinions: Studies in rhetorical psychology.* London: Sage.

Billig, M. (1996). *Arguing and thinking: A rhetorical approach to social psychology.* Cambridge, UK: Cambridge University Press.

Billig, M., & Cochrane, R. (1979). Values of political extremists and potential extremists: A discriminant analysis. *European Journal of Social Psychology, 9,* 205–222.

Billig, M., & Tajfel, H. (1973). Social categorisation and similarity in intergroup behaviour. *European Journal of Social Psychology, 3,* 27–52.

Bilous, F. R., & Krauss, R. M. (1988). Dominance and accommodation in the conversational behaviours of same- and mixed-gender dyads. *Language and Communication, 8,* 183–194.

Birdwhistell, R. (1970). *Kinesics and context: Essays on body movement communication.* Philadelphia, PA: University of Pennsylvania Press.

Black, S. L., & Bevan, S. (1992). At the movies with Buss and Durkee: A natural experiment on film violence. *Aggressive Behavior, 18,* 37–45.

Blake, R. R., & Mouton, J. S. (1961). Reactions to intergroup competition under win/lose conditions. *Management Science, 7,* 420–435.

Blake, R. R., Shepard, H. A., & Mouton, J. S. (1964). *Managing intergroup conflict in industry.* Texas: Gulf Publishing.

Blascovich, J., & Mendes, W. B. (2000). Challenge and threat appraisals: The role of affective cues. In J. P. Forgas (Ed.), *Feeling and thinking: The role of affect in social cognition* (pp. 59–82). New York: Cambridge University Press.

Bloom, L. (1970). *Language development: Form and function in emerging grammars.* Cambridge, MA: MIT Press.

Blumenthal, M. D., Kahn, R. L., Andrews, F. M., & Head, K. B. (1972). *Justifying violence: Attitudes of American men.* Ann Arbor, MI: Institute for Social Research.

Blumer, H. (1969). *Symbolic interactionism: Perspective and method.* Englewood Cliffs, NJ: Prentice Hall.

Boas, F. (1911). *The mind of primitive man.* New York: Macmillan.

Boas, F. (1930). Anthropology. *Encyclopedia of the Social Sciences, 2,* 73–110.

Bochner, S. (1982). The social psychology of cross-cultural relations. In S. Bochner (Ed.), *Cultures in contact: Studies in cross-cultural interaction.* Oxford: Pergamon.

Bochner, S., & Insko, C. A. (1966). Communicator discrepancy, source credibility, and opinion change. *Journal of Personality and Social Psychology, 4,* 614–621.

Bodenhausen, G. V., & Lichtenstein, M. (1987). Social stereotypes and information-processing strategies: The impact of task complexity. *Journal of Personality and Social Psychology, 52,* 871–880.

Bogardus, E. S. (1925). Measuring social distances. *Journal of Applied Sociology, 9,* 299–308.

Bohner, G., Bless, H., Schwarz, N., & Strack, F. (1988). What triggers causal attributions? The impact of valence and subjective probability. *European Journal of Social Psychology, 18,* 335–345.

Bohner, G., Chaiken, S., & Hunyadi, P. (1994). The role of mood and message ambiguity in the interplay of heuristic and systematic processing, special issue: Affect in social judgments and cognition. *European Journal of Social Psychology, 24,* 207–221.

Bohner, G., Moskowitz, G. B., & Chaiken, S. (1995). The interplay of heuristic and systematic processing of social information. *European Review of Social Psychology, 6,* 33–68.

Boldero, J., Sanitioso, R., & Brain, B. (1999). Gay Asian Australians' safer-sex behaviour and behavioral skills: The predictive utility of the theory of planned behaviour and cultural factors. *Journal of Applied Social Psychology, 29,* 2143–2163.

Bond, C. F. Jr. (1982). Social facilitation: A self-presentational view. *Journal of Personality and Social Psychology, 42,* 1042–1050.

Bond, C. F. Jr. & Titus, L. J. (1983). Social facilitation: A meta-analysis of 241 studies. *Psychological Bulletin, 94,* 265–292.

Bond, M. H. (Ed.). (1988). *The cross-cultural challenge to social psychology.* Newbury Park, CA: Sage.

Bond, M. H. (1996). Chinese values. In M. H. Bond (Ed.), *The handbook of Chinese psychology* (pp. 208–227). Hong Kong: Oxford University Press.

Bond, M. H., & King, A. Y. C. (1985). Coping with the threat of westernisation in Hong Kong. *International Journal of Intercultural Relations, 9,* 351–364.

Bond, M. H. & Komai, H. (1976). Targets of gazing and eye contact during interviews: Effects on Japanese nonverbal behaviour. *Journal of Personality and Social Psychology, 34,* 1276–1284.

Bond, M. H., & Smith, P. B. (1996). Cross-cultural social and organizational psychology. *Annual Review of Psychology, 47,* 205–235.

Bond, R. & Smith, P. B. (1996). Culture and conformity: A meta-analysis of the Asch line judgment task. *Psychological Bulletin, 119,* 111–137.

Book, A. S., Starzyk, K. B., & Quinsey, V. L. (2002). The relationship between testosterone and aggression: A meta-analysis. *Aggression and Violent Behavior, 6,* 579–599.

Boon, S. D., & Holmes, J. G. (1999). Interpersonal risk and the evaluation of transgressions in close relationships. *Personal Relationships, 6,* 151–168.

Borden, R. J. (1980). Audience influence. In P. B. Paulus (Ed.), *Psychology of group influence* (pp. 99–131). Hillsdale, NJ: Erlbaum.

Bornstein, G., Crum, L., Wittenbraker, J., Harring, K., Insko, C. A., & Thibaut, J. (1983). On the measurement of social orientations in the minimal group paradigm. *European Journal of Social Psychology, 13,* 321–350.

Bornstein, R. F. (1989). Exposure and affect: Overview and meta-analysis of research, 1968–1987. *Psychological Bulletin, 106,* 265–289.

Bornstein, R. F., & D'Agostino, P. R. (1992). Stimulus recognition and the mere exposure effect. *Journal of Personality and Social Psychology, 63,* 545–552.

Bosveld, W., Koomen, W., & Vogelaar, R. (1997). Construing a social issue: Effects on attitudes and the false consensus effect. *British Journal of Social Psychology, 36,* 263–272.

Bothwell, R. K., Brigham, J. C., & Malpass, R. S. (1989). Cross-racial identification. *Personality and Social Psychology Bulletin, 15,* 19–25.

Bouas, K. S., & Komorita, S. S. (1996). Group discussion and cooperation in social dilemmas. *Personality and Social Psychology Bulletin, 22,* 1144–1150.

Bourhis, R. Y. (1984). *Conflict and language planning in Quebec.* Clevedon: Multilingual Matters.

Bourhis, R. Y., & Giles, H. (1977). The language of intergroup distinctiveness. In H. Giles (Ed.), *Language, ethnicity and intergroup relations* (pp. 119–135). London: Academic Press.

Bourhis, R. Y., Giles, H., & Lambert, W. E. (1975). Social consequences of accommodating one's style of speech: A cross-national investigation. *International Journal of the Sociology of Language, 6,* 55–72.

Bourhis, R. Y., Giles, H., Leyens, J. P., & Tajfel, H. (1979). Psycholinguistic distinctiveness: Language divergence in Belgium. In H. Giles & R. St Clair (Eds.), *Language and social psychology* (pp. 158–185). Oxford: Blackwell.

Bourhis, R. Y., Giles, H., & Rosenthal, D. (1981). Notes on the construction of a 'subjective vitality questionnaire' for ethnolinguistic groups. *Journal of Multilingual and Multicultural Development, 2,* 144–155.

Bourhis, R. Y., Sachdev, I., & Gagnon, A. (1994). Intergroup research with the Tajfel matrices: Methodological notes. In M. Zanna & J. Olson (Eds.), *The psychology of prejudice: The Ontario symposium* (Vol. 7, pp. 209–232). Hillsdale, NJ: Erlbaum.

Bowlby, J. (1969). *Attachment and loss: (Vol. 1) Attachment.* London: Hogarth.

Bowlby, J. (1988). *A secure base: Parent–child attachment and healthy human development.* New York: Basic Books.

Bowman, C. H., & Fishbein, M. (1978). Understanding public reaction to energy proposals: An application of the Fishbein model. *Journal of Applied Social Psychology, 8,* 319–340.

Bradbury, J. (1984). Violent offending and drinking patterns. *Institute of Criminology Monograph.* Victoria University of Wellington, Wellington.

Branthwaite, A., Doyle, S., & Lightbown, N. (1979). The balance between fairness and discrimination. *European Journal of Social Psychology, 9,* 149–163.

Brauer, M., Judd, C. M., & Gliner, M. D. (1995). The effects of reoperated expressions on attitude polarisation during group discussion. *Journal of Personality and Social Psychology, 68,* 1014–1029.

Bray, R. M., & Noble, A. M. (1978). Authoritarianism and decisions of mock juries: Evidence of jury bias and group polarisation. *Journal of Personality and Social Psychology, 36,* 1424–1430.

Breakwell, G. M., & Canter, D. V. (1993). *Empirical approaches to social representations.* Oxford, UK: Clarendon Press.

Breaugh, J. A., & Klimoski, R. J. (1981). Social forces in negotiation simulations. *Personality and Social Psychology Bulletin, 7,* 290–295.

Breckler, S. J. (1984). Empirical validation of affect, behavior, and cognition as distinct components of attitude. *Journal of Personality and Social Psychology, 47,* 1191–1205.

Breckler, S. J., Pratkanis, A. R., & McCann, C. D. (1991). The representation of self in multidimensional cognitive space. *British Journal of Social Psychology, 30,* 97–112.

Breckler, S. J., & Wiggins, E. C. (1989a). On defining attitude and attitude theory: Once more with feeling. In A. R. Pratkanis, S. J. Breckler, & A. G. Greenwald (Eds.), *Attitude structure and function* (pp. 407–427). Hillsdale, NJ: Erlbaum.

Breckler, S. J., & Wiggins, E. C. (1989b). Affect versus evaluation in the structure of attitudes. *Journal of Experimental Social Psychology, 25,* 253–271.

Brehm, J. W. (1966). *A theory of psychological reactance.* New York: Academic Press.

Brehm, S. S., Kassin, S. M., & Fein, S. (1999). *Social psychology* (4th ed.). Boston, MA: Houghton Mifflin.

Brennan, K. A., & Shaver, P. R. (1995). Dimensions of adult attachment, affect regulation, and romantic relationship functioning. *Personality and Social Psychology Bulletin, 21,* 267–283.

Brewer, M. B. (1968). Determinants of social distance among East African tribal groups. *Journal of Personality and Social Psychology, 10,* 279–289.

Brewer, M. B. (1988). A dual process model of impression formation. In T. K. Srull & R. S. Wyer (Eds.), *Advances in social cognition: A dual process model of impression formation* (Vol. 1, pp. 1–36). Hillsdale, NJ: Erlbaum.

Brewer, M. B. (1991). The social self: On being the same and different at the same time. *Personality and Social Psychology Bulletin, 17,* 475–482.

Brewer, M. B. (1993). The role of distinctiveness in social identity and group behaviour. In M. A. Hogg & D. Abrams (Eds.), *Group motivation: Social psychological perspectives* (pp. 1–16). London: Harvester Wheatsheaf.

Brewer, M. B. (1994). Associated systems theory: If you buy two representational systems, why not many more? In R. Wyer & T. Srull (Eds.), *Advances in social cognition* (Vol. 7, pp. 141–147). Hillsdale, NJ: Erlbaum.

Brewer, M. B. (2001). The many faces of social identity: Implications for political psychology. *Political Psychology, 22,* 115–125.

Brewer, M. B. (2003). *Intergroup relations* (2nd edn.). Philadelphia, PA: Open University Press.

Brewer, M. B., & Campbell, D. T. (1976). *Ethnocentrism and intergroup attitudes: East African evidence.* New York: Sage.

Brewer, M. B., Dull, V., & Lui, L. (1981). Perceptions of the elderly: Stereotypes as prototypes. *Journal of Personality and Social Psychology, 41,* 656–670.

Brewer, M. B., & Gardner, W. (1996). Who is this 'We'? Levels of collective identity and self representation. *Journal of Personality and Social Psychology, 71,* 83–93.

Brewer, M. B., & Kramer, R. M. (1986). Choice behavior in social dilemmas: Effects of social identity, group size, and decision framing. *Journal of Personality and Social Psychology, 50,* 543–549.

Brewer, M. B., & Lui, L. L. (1989). The primacy of age and sex in the structure of person categories. *Social Cognition, 7,* 262–274.

Brewer, M. B., & Miller, N. (1984). Beyond the contact hypothesis: Theoretical perspectives on desegregation. In N. Miller & M. B. Brewer (Eds.), *Groups in contact: The psychology of desegregation* (pp. 281–302). New York: Academic Press.

Brewer, M. B., & Miller, N. (1996). *Intergroup relations.* Buckingham, UK: Open University Press.

Brewer, M. B., & Schneider, S. (1990). Social identity and social dilemmas: A double-edged sword. In D. Abrams & M. A. Hogg (Eds.), *Social identity theory: Constructive and critical advances* (pp. 169–184). London: Harvester Wheatsheaf.

Brewer, N., & Hupfeld, R. M. (2000). Effects of testimonial inconsistencies and witness group identity on mock-juror processing. Paper presented at the Society of Australasian Social Psychologists Conference, Fremantle.

Brickner, M. A., Harkins, S. G., & Ostrom, T. M. (1986). Effects of personal involvement: Thought provoking implications of social loafing. *Journal of Personality and Social Psychology, 51,* 763–770.

Brief, A. P., Dukerich, J. M., & Doran, L. I. (1991). Resolving ethical dilemmas in management: Experimental investigation of values, accountability, and choice. *Journal of Applied Social Psychology, 21,* 380–396.

Brigham, J. C. (1971). Ethnic stereotypes. *Psychological Bulletin, 76,* 15–38.

Brigham, J. C. (1991). *Social psychology.* New York: Harper Collins.

Brigham, J. C., & Barkowitz, P. B. (1978). Do 'they all look alike'? The effect of race, sex, experience and attitudes on the ability to recognise face. *Journal of Applied Social Psychology, 8,* 306–318.

Brigham, J. C., & Malpass, R. S. (1985). The role of experience and contact in the recognition of faces of own and other-race persons. *Journal of Social Issues, 41,* 139–156.

Brinthaupt, T. M., Moreland, R. L., & Levine, J. M. (1991). Sources of optimism among prospective group members. *Personality and Social Psychology Bulletin, 17,* 36–43.

Brislin, R. W. (1987). Cross-cultural psychology. In R. J. Corsini (Ed.), *Concise encyclopedia of psychology* (pp. 274–287). New York: Wiley.

Britell, J. K. (1981). Ethics courses are making slow inroads. *New York Times, Education Section,* 26 April, vp. 44.

Broadbent, D. E. (1985). *Perception and communication.* London: Pergamon.

Brockner, J., & Weisenfeld, B. M. (1996). The interactive impact of procedural and outcome fairness on reactions to a decision: The effects of what you do depend on how you do it. *Psychological Bulletin, 120,* 189–208.

Broome, B. J. (1983). The attraction paradigm revisited: Response to dissimilar others. *Human Communication Research, 10,* 137–151.

Broverman, I. K., Broverman, D. M., Clarkson, F., Rosencrantz, P. S., & Vogel, S. (1970). Sex-role stereotypes and clinical judgments in mental health. *Journal of Consulting and Clinical Psychology, 34,* 1–7.

Broverman, I. K., Vogel, S. R., Broverman, D. M., Clarkson, F. E., & Rosenkrantz, P. S. (1972). Sex-role stereotypes: A current appraisal. *Journal of Social Issues, 28,* 59–78.

Brown, G. W., & Harris, T. (1978). *Social origins of depression.* London: Tavistock.

Brown, P., & Fraser, C. (1979). Speech as a marker of situation. In K. R. Scherer & H. Giles (Eds.), *Social markers in speech* (pp. 33–108). Cambridge: Cambridge University Press.

Brown, R. (1965). *Social psychology.* New York: Free Press.

Brown, R. (1986). *Social psychology* (2nd ed.). New York: Free Press.

Brown, R., & Fish, D. (1983). The psychological causality implicit in language. *Cognition, 14,* 237–273.

Brown, R., Hinkle, S., Ely, P. C., Fox-Cardamone, L., Maras, P., & Taylor, L. A. (1992). Recognising group diversity: Individualist–collectivist and autonomous–relational social orientations and their implications for intergroup processes. *British Journal of Social Psychology, 31,* 327–342.

Brown, R. J. (1978). Divided we fall: An analysis of relations between sections of a factory workforce. In H. Tajfel (Ed.), *Differentiation between social groups: Studies in the social psychology of intergroup relations* (pp. 395–429). London: Academic Press.

Brown, R. J. (1995). *Prejudice: Its social psychology.* Oxford, UK: Blackwell.

Brown, R. J. (1996). Tajfel's contribution to the reduction of intergroup conflict. In W. P. Robinson (Ed.), *Social groups and identities: Developing the legacy of Henri Tajfel* (pp. 169–189). Oxford, UK: Butterworth-Heinemann.

Brown, R. J. (2000). *Group processes* (2nd ed.). Oxford, UK: Blackwell.

Brown, R. J., & Abrams, D. (1986). The effects of intergroup similarity and goal interdependence on intergroup attitudes and task performance. *Journal of Experimental Social Psychology, 22,* 78–92.

Brown, R. J., & Gaertner, S. (Eds.). (2001). *Blackwell handbook of social psychology: Intergroup processes.* Oxford, UK: Blackwell.

Brown, R. J., & Turner, J. C. (1981). Interpersonal and intergroup behaviour. In J. C. Turner & H. Giles (Eds.), *Intergroup behaviour* (pp. 33–65). Oxford: Blackwell.

Brown, R. J., & Wade, G. S. (1987). Superordinate goals and intergroup behavior: The effects of role ambiguity and status on intergroup attitudes and task performance. *European Journal of Social Psychology, 17,* 131–142.

Bruner, J. S. (1957). On perceptual readiness. *Psychological Review, 64,* 123–152.

Bruner, J. S. (1958). Social psychology and perception. In E. E. Maccoby, T. M. Newcomb, & E. L. Hartley (Eds.), *Readings in social psychology* (3rd ed., pp. 85–94). New York: Henry Holt & Company.

Bruner, J. S., & Goodman, C. C. (1947). Value and need as organising factors in perception. *Journal of Abnormal and Social Psychology, 42,* 33–44.

Brunswik, E. (1956). *Perception and the representative design of psychological experiments* (2nd ed.). Berkeley, CA: University of California Press.

Bryan, J. H., & Test, M. A. (1967). Models and helping: Naturalistic studies in aiding behavior. *Journal of Personality and Social Psychology, 6,* 400–407.

Bryman, A. (1992). *Charisma and leadership in organizations.* London: Sage.

Buchanan, G. M., & Seligman, M. E. P. (1995). *Explanatory style.* Hillsdale, NJ: Erlbaum.

Buchanan, P. J. (1987). AIDS and moral bankruptcy. *New York Post,* December 2, p. 23.

Buck, R., & Ginsburg, B. (1991). Spontaneous communication and altruism: The communicative gene hypothesis. In M. S. Clark (Ed.), *Prosocial behaviour* (pp. 149–175). Newbury Park, CA: Sage.

Buckner, H. T. (1965). A theory of rumour transmission. *Public Opinion Quarterly, 29,* 54–70.

Budd, R. J., North, D., & Spencer, C. (1984). Understanding seatbelt use: A test of Bentler and Speckart's extension of the 'theory of reasoned action'. *European Journal of Social Psychology, 14,* 69–78.

Bugental, D. E., Love L. R., & Gianetto, R. M. (1971). Perfidious feminine faces. *Journal of Personality and Social Psychology, 17,* 314–318.

Bulman, R. J., & Wortman, C. B. (1977). Attributions of blame and coping in the 'real world': Severe accident victims react to their lot. *Journal of Personality and Social Psychology, 35,* 351–363.

Bunge, C. (1903). *Principes de psychologie individuelle et sociale.* Paris: Alcan.

Burger, J. M. (1981). Motivational biases in the attribution of responsibility for an accident: A meta-analysis of the defensive attribution hypothesis. *Psychological Bulletin, 90,* 496–513.

Burger, J. M. (1986). Increasing compliance by improving the deal: The that's-not-all technique. *Journal of Personality and Social Psychology, 51,* 277–283.

Burgess, E. W., & Wallin, P. (1953). *Engagement and marriage.* PA: Lipppencott.

Burgoon, J. K., Buller, D. B., & Woodall, W. G. (1989). *Nonverbal communication: The unspoken dialogue.* New York: Harper & Row.

Burgoon, M., Pfau, M., & Birk T. S. (1995). An inoculation theory explanation for the effects of corporate issue/advocacy advertising campaigns. *Communication Research 22,* 485–505.

Buriel, R. (1987). Ethnic labelling and identity among Mexican Americans. In J. S. Phinney & M. J. Rotheram (Eds.). *Children's ethnic socialisation: Pluralism and development.* (pp. 134–152). Newbury Park, CA: Sage.

Burnham, W. H. (1910). The group as a stimulus to mental activity. *Science, 31,* 761–767.

Burnstein, E., Crandall, C., & Kitayama, S. (1994). Some neo-Darwinian decision rules for altruism: Weighing cues for inclusive fitness as a function of the biological importance of the decision. *Journal of Personality and Social Psychology, 67,* 773–789.

Burnstein, E., & McRae, A. (1962). Some effects of shared threat and prejudice in racially mixed groups. *Journal of Abnormal and Social Psychology, 64,* 257–263.

Burnstein, E., & Vinokur, A. (1977). Persuasive argumentation and social comparison as determinants of attitude polarisation. *Journal of Experimental Social Psychology, 13,* 315–332.

Bushman, B. J. (1984). Perceived symbols of authority and their influence on compliance. *Journal of Applied Social Psychology, 14,* 501–508.

Bushman, B. J. (1988). The effects of apparel on compliance: A field experiment with a female authority figure. *Personality and Social Psychology Bulletin, 14,* 459–467.

Bushman, B. J., & Baumeister, R. F. (1998). Threatened egotism, narcissism, self-esteem, and direct and displaced aggression: Does self-love or self-hate lead to violence? *Journal of Personality and Social Psychology, 75,* 219–229.

Bushman, B. J., Baumeister, R. F., & Stack, A. D. (1999). Catharsis, aggression, and persuasive influence: Self-fulfilling or self-defeating prophecies? *Journal of Personality and Social Psychology, 76,* 367–376.

Bushman, B. J., & Cooper, H. M. (1990). Effects of alcohol on human aggression: An integrative research review. *Psychological Bulletin, 107,* 341–354.

Buss, A. H. (1961). *The psychology of aggression.* New York: Wiley.

Buss, D. M. (1990). Evolutionary social psychology: Prospects and pitfalls. *Motivation and Emotion, 14,* 265–286.

Buss, D. M. (1999). *Evolutionary psychology: The new science of the mind*. Boston: Allyn & Bacon.

Buss, D. M., & Kenrick, D. T. (1998). Evolutionary social psychology. In D. T. Gilbert, S. T. Fiske, & G. Lindzey (Eds.), *The handbook of social psychology* (4th ed., Vol. 2, pp. 982–1026). New York: McGraw-Hill.

Buunk, B. P., & Prins, K. S. (1998). Loneliness, exchange orientation, and reciprocity in friendships. *Personal Relationships, 5,* 1–14.

Byrd, R. E. (1938). *Alone*. New York: Putnam.

Byrne, D. (1971). *The attraction paradigm*. New York: Academic Press.

Byrne, D. (1997). An overview (and underview) of research and theory within the attraction paradigm. *Journal of Social and Personal Relationships, 14,* 1167–1170.

Byrne, D., & Clore, G. L. (1970). A reinforcement model of evaluative responses. *Personality: An International Journal, 1,* 103–128.

Byrne, D., & Wong, T. J. (1962). Racial prejudice, interpersonal attraction, and assumed dissimilarity of attitudes. *Journal of Abnormal and Social Psychology, 65,* 246–252.

Cacioppo, J. T., & Petty, R. E. (1979). Attitudes and cognitive response: An electrophysiological approach. *Journal of Personality and Social Psychology, 37,* 2181–2199.

Cacioppo, J. T., & Petty, R. E. (1981). Electromyograms as measures of extent and affectivity of information processing. *American Psychologist, 36,* 441–456.

Cacioppo, J. T., & Petty, R. E. (1982). The need for cognition. *Journal of Personality and Social Psychology, 42,* 116–131.

Cacioppo, J. T., & Tassinary, L. G. (1990). Inferring psychological significance from physiological signals. *American Psychologist, 45,* 16–28.

Calder, B. J., & Ross, M. (1973). *Attitudes and behavior*. Morristown, NJ: General Learning Press.

Calkin, B. (1985). 'Joe Lunch Box': Punishment and resistance in prisons. *Race Gender Class, 1,* 5–16.

Callaway, M. R., & Esser, J. K. (1984). Groupthink: Effects of cohesiveness and problem-solving procedures on group decision making. *Social Behavior and Personality, 12,* 157–164.

Callaway, M. R., Marriot, R. G., & Esser, J. K. (1985). Effects of dominance on group decision making: Towards a stress-reduction explanation of groupthink. *Journal of Personality and Social Psychology, 49,* 949–952.

Campbell, D. T. (1957). Factors relevant to the validity of experiments in social settings. *Psychological Bulletin, 54,* 297–312.

Campbell, D. T. (1958). Common fate, similarity, and other indices of the status of aggregates of persons as social entities. *Behavioral Science, 3,* 14–25.

Campbell, D. T. (1975). On the conflict between biological and social evolution and between psychology and moral tradition. *American Psychologist, 30,* 1103–1126.

Campbell, D. T., & Fairey, P. J. (1989). Informational and normative routes to conformity: The effect of faction size as a function of norm extremity and attention to the stimulus. *Journal of Personality and Social Psychology, 57,* 457–468.

Campbell, J. D. (1986). Similarity and uniqueness: The effects of attribute type, relevance, and individual differences in self-esteem and depression. *Journal of Personality and Social Psychology, 50,* 281–294.

Campbell, J. D. (1990). Self-esteem and clarity of the self-concept. *Journal of Personality and Social Psychology, 59,* 538–549.

Campbell, J. D., & Fairey, P. J. (1985). Effects of self-esteem, hypothetical explanations, and verbalisations of expectancies on future performance. *Journal of Personality and Social Psychology, 48,* 1097–1111.

Campbell, W. K., Sedikides, C., & Bosson, J. (1994). Romantic involvement, self-discrepancy, and psychological well-being: A preliminary investigation. *Personal Relationships, 1,* 399–404.

Cannavale, F. J., Scarr, H. A., & Pepitone, A. (1970). Deindividuation in the small group: Further evidence. *Journal of Personality and Social Psychology, 16,* 141–147.

Cantor, N., & Kihlstrom, J. F. (1987). *Personality and social intelligence*. Englewood Cliffs, NJ: Prentice Hall.

Cantor, N., & Mischel, W. (1977). Traits as prototypes: Effects on recognition memory. *Journal of Personality and Social Psychology, 35,* 38–48.

Cantor, N., & Mischel, W. (1979). Prototypes in person perception. In L. Berkowitz (Ed.), *Advances in experimental social psychology* (Vol. 12, pp. 3–52). New York: Academic Press.

Caplow, T. (1947). Rumours in war. *Social Forces, 25,* 298–302.

Caporael, L., Dawes, R., Orbell, J., & van de Kragt, A. (1989). Selfishness examined: Cooperation in the absence of egoistic incentives. *Behavioral and Brain Sciences, 12,* 683–699.

Caporael, L. R., Lukaszewski, M. P., & Cuthbertson, G. H. (1983). Secondary baby talk: Judgments by institutionalised elderly and their caregivers. *Journal of Personality and Social Psychology, 44,* 746–754.

Cappella, J. N., & Palmer, M. (1993). The structure and organisation of verbal and non-verbal behavior: Data for models of production. In H. Giles & W. P. Robinson (Eds.), *Handbook of language and social psychology* (pp. 141–161). Oxford, UK: Pergamon.

Carli, L. L. (1990). Gender, language, and influence. *Journal of Personality and Social Psychology, 59,* 941–951.

Carlsmith, J. M., & Anderson, C. A. (1979). Ambient temperature and the occurrence of collective violence: A new analysis. *Journal of Personality and Social Psychology, 37,* 337–344.

Carlsmith, J. M., & Gross, A. E. (1969). Some effects of guilt on compliance. *Journal of Personality and Social Psychology, 11,* 232–239.

Carlson, M., Marcus-Newhall, A., & Miller, N. (1989). Evidence for a general construct of aggression. *Personality and Social Psychology Bulletin, 15,* 377–389.

Carlyle, T. (1841). *On heroes, hero-worship, and the heroic*. London: Fraser.

Carmichael, G. (1983). The transition to marriage: Trends in age at first marriage in Australia. Cited in V. J. Callan, C. Gallois, P. Noller, & Y. Kashima (1991), *Social psychology* (2nd ed.). Sydney: Harcourt Brace Jovanovich.

Carnevale, P. J., & Leung, K. (2001). Cultural dimensions of negotiation. In M. A. Hogg & R. S. Tindale (Eds.), *Blackwell handbook of social psychology: Group processes* (pp. 482–496). Oxford, UK: Blackwell.

Carnevale, P. J. D., Pruitt, D. G., & Britton, S. D. (1979). Looking tough: The negotiator under constituent surveillance. *Personality and Social Psychology Bulletin, 5,* 118–121.

Carrithers, M., Collins, S., & Lukes, S. (Eds.). (1986). *The category of the person*. Cambridge: Cambridge University Press.

Carroll, J. S., Bazerman, M. H., & Maury, R. (1988). Negotiator cognitions: A descriptive approach to negotiators' understanding of their opponents. *Organizational Behavior and Human Decision Processes, 41,* 352–370.

Carter, L. F., & Nixon, M. (1949). An investigation of the relationship between four criteria of leadership ability for three different tasks. *The Journal of Psychology, 27*, 245–261.

Cartwright, D. (1968). The nature of group cohesiveness. In D. Cartwright & A. Zander (Eds.), *Group dynamics: Research and theory* (3rd ed., pp. 91–109). London: Tavistock.

Cartwright, D., & Harary, F. (1956). Structural balance: A generalisation of Heider's theory. *Psychological Review, 63*, 277–293.

Carver, C. S., & Glass, D. C. (1978). Coronary-prone behavior pattern and interpersonal aggression. *Journal of Personality and Social Psychology, 36*, 361–366.

Carver, C. S., Glass, D. C., & Katz, I. (1977). Favorable evaluations of Blacks and the disabled: Positive prejudice, unconscious denial, or social desirability. *Journal of Applied Social Psychology, 8*, 97–106.

Carver, C. S., & Scheier, M. F. (1981). *Attention and self-regulation: A control theory approach to human behavior.* New York: Springer-Verlag.

Cary, M. S. (1978). The role of gaze in the initiation of conversation. *Social Psychology, 41*, 269–271.

Casas, J. M., Ponterotto, J. G., & Sweeney, M. (1987). Stereotyping the stereotyper: A Mexican American perspective. *Journal of Cross-Cultural Psychology, 18*, 45–57.

Cash, T. F., Kehr, J. A., Polyson, J., & Freeman, V. (1977). Role of physical attractiveness in peer attribution of psychological disturbance. *Journal of Consulting and Clinical Psychology, 45*, 987–993.

Catalano, R., Novaco, R., & McConnell, W. (1997). A model of the net effect of job loss on violence. *Journal of Personality and Social Psychology, 72*, 1440–1447.

Census of Prison Inmates (1997). Retrieved January 21, 2001, from http://www.justice.govt.nz

Chacko, T. I. (1982). Women and equal employment opportunity: Some unintended effects. *Journal of Applied Psychology, 67*, 119–123.

Chaffee, S. H., Jackson-Beeck, M., Durall, J., & Wilson, D. (1977). Mass communication in political communication. In S. A. Renshon (Ed.), *Handbook of political socialization: Theory and research* (pp. 223–258) New York: Free Press.

Chaiken, S. (1979). Communicator physical attractiveness and persuasion. *Journal of Personality and Social Psychology, 37*, 1387–1397.

Chaiken, S. (1980). Heuristic versus systematic information processing and the use of source versus message cues in persuasion. *Journal of Personality and Social Psychology, 39*, 752–766.

Chaiken, S. (1983). Physical appearance variables and social influence. In C. P. Herman, E. T. Higgins, & M. P. Zanna (Eds.), *Physical appearance, stigma, and social behavior: Third Ontario symposium* (pp. 143–178). Hillsdale, NJ: Erlbaum.

Chaiken, S. (1987). The heuristic model of persuasion. In M. P. Zanna, J. M. Olsen, & C. P. Herman (Eds.), *Social influence: The Ontario symposium* (Vol. 5, pp. 3–39). Hillsdale, NJ: Erlbaum.

Chaiken, S., & Eagly, A. H. (1983). Communication modality as a determinant of persuasion: The role of communicator salience. *Journal of Personality and Social Psychology, 45*, 241–256.

Chaiken, S., Liberman, A., & Eagly, A. H. (1989). Heuristic and systematic processing within and beyond the persuasion context. In J. S. Uleman & J. A. Bargh (Eds.), *Unintended thought* (pp. 215–252). New York: Guilford.

Chaiken, S., & Maheswaran, D. (1994). Heuristic processing can bias systematic processing: Effects of source credibility, argument ambiguity, and task importance on attitude judgement. *Journal of Personality and Social Psychology, 66*, 460–473.

Chance, J. E. (1985). *Faces, folklore, and research hypotheses.* Presidential address to the Midwestern Psychological Association convention, Chicago.

Chandra, S. (1973). The effects of group pressure in perception: A cross-cultural conformity study. *International Journal of Psychology, 8*, 37–39.

Chaplin, W. F., John, O. P., & Goldberg, L. R. (1988). Conceptions of states and traits: Dimensional attributes with ideals as prototypes. *Journal of Personality and Social Psychology, 54*, 541–557.

Chapman, L. J. (1967). Illusory correlation in observational report. *Journal of Verbal Learning and Verbal Behavior, 6*, 151–155.

Chase, A. (2000). Harvard and the making of the Unabomber. *The Atlantic Monthly, 285* (6), June, 41.

Chassin, L., Presson, C. C., & Sherman, S. J. (1990). Social psychological contributions to the understanding and prevention of adolescent cigarette smoking. *Personality and Social Psychology Bulletin, 16*, 135-151.

Chemers, M. M. (2001). Leadership effectiveness: An integrative review. In M. A. Hogg & R. S. Tindale (Eds.), *Blackwell handbook of social psychology: Group processes* (pp. 376–399). Oxford, UK: Blackwell.

Chen, H., Yates, B.T., & McGinnies, E. (1988). Effects of involvement on observers' estimates of consensus, distinctiveness, and consistency. *Personality and Social Psychology Bulletin, 14*, 468–478.

Chen, S., Shechter, D., & Chaiken, S. (1996). Getting at the truth or getting along: Accuracy versus impression motivated heuristic and systematic processing. *Journal of Personality and Social Psychology, 71*, 2.

Cherek, D. R., Schnapp, W., Moeller, F., & Dougherty, D. M. (1996). Laboratory measures of aggressive responding in male parolees with violent and nonviolent histories. *Aggressive Behaviour, 22*, 27–36.

Chesler, P. (1972). *Women and madness.* Garden City, NY: Doubleday.

Chidester, T. R. (1986). Problems in the study of interracial interaction: Pseudo-interracial dyad paradigm. *Journal of Personality and Social Psychology, 50*, 74–79.

Child, I. L. (1954). Socialization. In G. Lindzey (Ed.), *A handbook of social psychology* (Vol. 2, pp. 655–692). Cambridge, MA: Addison-Wesley.

Chomsky, N. (1957). *Syntactic structures.* The Hague: Mouton.

Chomsky, N. (1959). Verbal behavior [Review of Skinner's book]. *Language, 35*, 26–58.

Christensen, L. (1988). Deception in psychological research: When is its use justified? *Personality and Social Psychology Bulletin, 14*, 664–675.

Christie, R., & Jahoda, M. (Eds.). (1954). *Studies in the scope and method of 'the authoritarian personality'.* New York: Free Press.

Christy, C. A., & Voigt, H. (1994). Bystander responses to public episodes of child abuse. *Journal of Applied Social Psychology, 24*, 824–847.

Cialdini, R. B., Baumann, D. J., & Kenrick, D. T. (1981). Insights from sadness: A three-step model of the development of altruism as hedonism. *Developmental Review, 1*, 207–223.

Cialdini, R. B., Borden, R. J., Thorne, A., Walker, M. R., Freeman, S., & Sloan, L. R. (1976). Basking in reflected glory: Three (football) field studies. *Journal of Personality and Social Psychology, 34*, 366–375.

Cialdini, R. B., Cacioppo, J. T., Bassett, R., & Miller, J. A. (1978). Low-balling procedure for producing compliance: Commitment then cost. *Journal of Personality and Social Psychology, 36,* 463–476.

Cialdini, R. B., Darby, B. L., & Vincent, J. E. (1973). Transgression and altruism: A case for hedonism. *Journal of Personality and Social Psychology, 9,* 502–516.

Cialdini, R. B., & Kenrick, D. T. (1976). Altruism as hedonism: A social development perspective on the relationship of negative mood state and helping. *Journal of Personality and Social Psychology, 34,* 907–914.

Cialdini, R. B., & Petty, R. E. (1979). Anticipatory opinion effects. In R. Petty, T. Ostrom, & T. Brock (Eds.), *Cognitive responses in persuasion.* Hillsdale, NJ: Erlbaum.

Cialdini, R. B., & Trost, M. R. (1998). Social influence: Social norms, conformity, and compliance. In D. T. Gilbert, S. T. Fiske, & G. Lindzey (Eds.), *The handbook of social psychology* (4th ed., Vol. 2, pp. 151–192). New York: McGraw-Hill.

Cialdini, R. B., Trost, M. R., & Newsom, J. T. (1995). Preference for consistency: The development of a valid measure and the discovery of surprising behavioral implications. *Journal of Personality and Social Psychology, 69,* 318–328.

Cialdini, R. B., Vincent, J. E., Lewis, S. K., Catalan, J., Wheeler, D., & Darby, B. L. (1975). Reciprocal concessions procedure for inducing compliance: The door-in-the-face technique. *Journal of Personality and Social Psychology, 31,* 206–215.

Claes, J. A., & Rosenthal, D. M. (1990). Men who batter women: A study in power. *Journal of Family Violence, 5,* 215–224.

Clark, H. H. (1985). Language use and language users. In G. Lindzey & E. Aronson (Eds.), *Handbook of social psychology* (3rd ed., Vol. 2, pp. 179–232). New York: Random House.

Clark, K. B., & Clark, M. P. (1939a). The development of consciousness of self and the emergence of racial identification in Negro preschool children. *Journal of Social Psychology, 10,* 591–599.

Clark, K. B., & Clark, M. P. (1939b). Segregation as a factor in the racial identification of Negro preschool children. *Journal of Experimental Education, 8,* 161–163.

Clark, K. B., & Clark, M. P. (1940). Skin color as a factor in racial identification and preference in Negro children. *Journal of Negro Education, 19,* 341–358.

Clark, N. K., & Stephenson, G. M. (1989). Group remembering. In P. B. Paulus (Ed.), *Psychology of group influence* (2nd ed., pp. 357–391). Hillsdale, NJ: Erlbaum.

Clark, N. K., & Stephenson, G. M. (1995). Social remembering: Individual and collaborative memory for social information. *European Review of Social Psychology, 6,* 127–160.

Clark, N. K., Stephenson, G. M., & Rutter, D. R. (1986). Memory for a complex social discourse: The analysis and prediction of individual and group remembering. *Journal of Memory and Language, 25,* 295–313.

Clark, R. D., III & Word, I. E. (1972). Why don't bystanders help? Because of ambiguity? *Journal of Personality and Social Psychology, 24,* 392–400.

Clark, R. D., III & Word, I. E. (1974). Where is the apathetic bystander? Situational characteristics of the emergency. *Journal of Personality and Social Psychology, 29,* 279–287.

Clark, T. N. (1969). *Gabriel Tarde: On communication and social influence.* Chicago, IL: University of Chicago Press.

Clary, E. G., & Snyder, M. (1991) A functional analysis of altruism and prosocial behaviour: The case of volunteerism. In M. S. Clarke (Ed.), *Prosocial behaviour* (pp. 119–147). Newbury Park. CA: Sage.

Clément, R. (1980). Ethnicity, contact and communication competence in a second language. In H. Giles, W. P. Robinson & P. M. Smith (Eds.), *Language: Social psychological perspectives* (pp. 147–154). Oxford: Pergamon.

Clore, G. L. (1976). Interpersonal attraction: An overview. In J. W. Thibaut, J. T. Spence & R. C. Carson (Eds.), *Contemporary topics in social psychology* (pp. 135–175). Morristown, NJ: General Learning Press.

Clore, G. L., & Byrne, D. (1974). A reinforcement–affect model of attraction. In T. L. Huston (Ed.), *Foundations of interpersonal attraction* (pp. 143–165). New York: Academic Press.

Clyne, M. G. (1981). 'Second generation' foreigner talk in Australia. *International Journal of the Sociology of Language, 28,* 69–80.

Clyne, M. G. (1985). *Multilingual Australia* (2nd ed.). Melbourne: River Seine.

Coates, B., Pusser, H. E., & Goodman, I. (1976). The influence of 'Sesame Street' and 'Mister Rogers' Neighbourhood' on children's prosocial behavior in preschool. *Child Development, 47,* 138–144.

Coch, L., & French, J. R. P. Jr. (1948). Overcoming resistance to change. *Human Relations, 1,* 512–532.

Codol, J.-P. (1975). On the so-called 'superior conformity of the self' behaviour: Twenty experimental investigations. *European Journal of Social Psychology, 5,* 457–501.

Cohen, C. (1987). Nuclear language. *Bulletin of the Atomic Scientist,* June, 17–24.

Cohen, D. (1996). Law, social policy, and violence: The impact of regional cultures. *Journal of Personality and Social Psychology, 70,* 961–978.

Cohen, D., & Nisbett, R. E. (1994). Self-protection and the culture of honor: Explaining southern violence. *Personality and Social Psychology Bulletin, 20,* 551–567.

Cohen, D., & Nisbett, R. E. (1997). Field experiments examining the culture of honor: The role of institutions in perpetuating norms about violence. *Personality and Social Psychology Bulletin, 23,* 1188–1199.

Cohen-Kettenis P. T., & van Goozen, S. H. M. (1997). Sex reassignment of adolescent transsexuals: A follow-up study. *Journal of the American Academy of Child and Adolescent Psychiatry, 36,* 263–271.

Cohn, E. G. (1993). The prediction of police calls for service: The influence of weather and temporal variables on rape and domestic violence. *Journal of Environmental Psychology, 13,* 71–83.

Cohn, E. G., & Rotton, J. (1997). Assault as a function of time and temperature: A moderator-variable time-series analysis. *Journal of Personality and Social Psychology, 72,* 1322–1334.

Cohn, N. (1966). *Warrant for genocide: The myth of the Jewish world conspiracy and the Protocol of the Elders of Zion.* New York: Harper & Row.

Cohn, N. (1975). *Europe's inner demons: An enquiry inspired by the great witch hunt.* London: Chatto.

Collins, B. E. (1974). Four separate components of the Rotter I–E scale: Belief in a difficult world, a just world, a predictable world, and a politically responsive world. *Journal of Personality and Social Psychology, 29,* 381–391.

Collins, B., & Raven, B. H. (1969). Group structure: Attraction, coalitions, communication, and power. In G. Lindzey & E. Aronson (Eds.), *Handbook of social psychology* (Vol. 4, pp. 102–204). Reading, MA: Addison-Wesley.

Collins, N. L., & Miller, L. C. (1994). Self-disclosure and liking: A meta-analytic review. *Psychological Bulletin, 116,* 457–475.

Colvin, C. R., & Block, J. (1994). Do positive illusions foster mental health? An examination of the Taylor and Brown formulation. *Psychological Bulletin, 116,* 3–20.

Colvin, C. R., Block, J., & Funder, D. C. (1995). Overly positive evaluations and personality: Negative implications for mental health. *Journal of Personality and Social Psychology, 68,* 1152–1162.

Commonwealth of Australia (1996). *Psychological science in Australia.* Canberra: Australian Government Publishing Service.

Condor, S. (1988). Race stereotypes and racist discourse. *Text, 8,* 69–90.

Condor, S. (1996). Social identity and time. In W. P. Robinson (Ed.), *Social groups and identities: Developing the legacy of Henri Tajfel* (pp. 285–315). Oxford, UK: Butterworth-Heinemann.

Condry, J. (1977). Enemies of exploration: Self-initiated versus other-initiated learning. *Journal of Personality and Social Psychology, 35,* 459–477.

Condry, J. C., & Ross, D. F. (1985). Sex and aggression: The influence of gender label. *Child Development, 56,* 225–233.

Conley, T. D., Collins, B. E., & Garcia, D. (2000). Perceptions of women condom proposers among Chinese Americans, Japanese Americans, and European Americans. *Journal of Applied Social Psychology, 30,* 389–406.

Connell, R.W. (1972). Political socialisation in the American family: The evidence reexamined. *Public Opinion Quarterly, 36,* 323–333.

Conner, M., Warren, R., Close, S., & Sparks, P. (1999). Alcohol consumption and the theory of planned behaviour: An examination of the cognitive mediation of past behaviour. *Journal of Applied Social Psychology, 28,* 1676–1704.

Cook, S. W. (1978). Interpersonal and attitudinal outcomes in cooperating interracial groups. *Journal of Research and Development in Education, 12,* 97–113.

Cook, S. W. (1985). Experimenting on social issues: The case of school desegregation. *American Psychologist, 40,* 452–460.

Cook, S. W., & Pelfrey, M. (1985). Reactions to being helped in cooperating interracial groups: A context effect. *Journal of Personality and Social Psychology, 49,* 1231–1245.

Cooper, H. M. (1979). Statistically combining independent studies: Meta-analysis of sex differences in conformity. *Journal of Personality and Social Psychology, 37,* 131–146.

Cooper, J. (1999). Unwanted consequences and the self: In search of the motivation for dissonance reduction. In E. Harmon-Jones & J. Mills (Eds.), *Cognitive dissonance: Progress on a pivotal theory in social psychology* (pp. 149–174). Washington, DC: American Psychological Association.

Cooper, J., & Axsom, D. (1982). Effort justification in psychotherapy. In G. Weary & H. Mirels (Eds.), *Integrations of clinical and social psychology.* London: Oxford University Press.

Cooper, J., & Croyle, R. T. (1984). Attitudes and attitude change. *Annual Review of Psychology, 35,* 395–426.

Cooper, J., & Fazio, R. H. (1984). A new look at dissonance theory. In L. Berkowitz (Ed.), *Advances in experimental social psychology* (Vol. 17, pp. 229–265). New York: Academic Press.

Cooper, J., & Hogg, M. A. (2002). Dissonance arousal and the collective self: Vicarious experience of dissonance based on shared group membership. In J. P. Forgas & K. D. Williams (Eds.), *The social self: Cognitive, interpersonal, and intergroup perspectives* (pp. 327–341). New York: Psychology Press.

Corballis, M. C. (1999). The gestural origins of language. *American Scientist, 87,* 138–145.

Cordery, J. L., Mueller, W. S., & Smith, L. M. (1991). Attitudinal and behavioral effects of autonomous group working: A longitudinal field study. *Academy of Management Journal, 34,* 464–476.

Correia, H. (2000). *Mental illness and the psychologist: Social representations and education.* Paper presented at the Society of Australasian Social Psychologists Conference, Fremantle.

Cose, E. (1993). *Rage of a privileged class.* New York: Harper Collins.

Costanzo, P. R. (1970). Conformity development as a function of self-blame. *Journal of Personality and Social Psychology, 14,* 366–374.

Cotton, S., Cunningham, J. D., & Antill, J. (1993). Network structure, network support and the marital satisfaction of husbands and wives. *Australian Journal of Psychology, 45,* 176–181.

Cottrell, N. B. (1972). Social facilitation. In C. McClintock (Ed.), *Experimental Social Psychology* (pp. 185–236). New York: Holt, Rinehart & Winston.

Cottrell, N. B., Wack, D. L., Sekerak, G. J., & Rittle, R. H. (1968). Social facilitation of dominant responses by the presence of others. *Journal of Personality and Social Psychology, 9,* 245–250.

Coupland, N., Coupland, J., Giles, H., & Henwood, K. (1988). Accommodating the elderly: Invoking and extending a theory. *Language in Society, 17,* 1–41.

Courtright, J. A. (1978). A laboratory investigation of groupthink. *Communication Monographs, 45,* 229–246.

Covell, K., Dion, K. L., & Dion, K. K. (1994). Gender differences in evaluations of tobacco and alcohol advertisements. *Canadian Journal of Behavioural Science, 26,* 404–420.

Cowen, W. L., Landes, J., & Schaet, D. E. (1958). The effects of mild frustration on the expression of prejudiced attitudes. *Journal of Abnormal and Social Psychology, 58,* 33–38.

Cox, S., & Gallois, C. (1996). Gay and lesbian identity development: A social identity perspective. *Journal of Homosexuality, 30,* 1–30.

Cozby, P. C. (1973). Self-disclosure: A literature review. *Psychological Bulletin, 79,* 73–91.

Craddock, A. (1980). The impact of social change on Australian families. *Australian Journal of Sex, Marriage and the Family, 1,* 4–14.

Cramer, R. E., McMaster, M. R., Bartell, P. A., & Dragna, M. (1988). Subject competence and minimization of the bystander effect. *Journal of Applied Social Psychology, 18,* 1133–1148.

Crandall, C. S. (1994). Prejudice against fat people: Ideology and self-interest. *Journal of Personality and Social Psychology, 66,* 882–894.

Crano, W. D., & Alvaro, E. M. (1998). The context/comparison model of social influence: Mechanisms, structure, and linkages that underlie indirect attitude change. In W. Stroebe & M. Hewstone (Eds.), *European Review of Social Psychology* (Vol. 8, pp. 175–202). Chichester, UK: Wiley.

Crawford, M. (Ed.) (1995). *Talking difference: On gender and language.* London: Sage.

Crisp, R. J., Ensari, N., Hewstone, M., & Miller, N. (2003). A dual-route model of crossed categorization effects. In W. Stroebe & M. Hewstone (Eds.), *European Review of Social Psychology* (Vol. 13, pp. 35–74). New York: Psychology Press.

Crocker, J. (1981). Judgement of covariation by social perceivers. *Psychological Bulletin, 90,* 272–292.

Crocker, J., Alloy, L. B., & Kayne, N. T. (1988). Attributional style, depression, and perceptions of consensus for events. *Journal of Personality and Social Psychology, 54,* 840–846.

Crocker, J., Blaine, B., & Luhtanen, R. (1993). Prejudice, intergroup behaviour and self-esteem: Enhancement and protection motives.

In M. A. Hogg & D. Abrams (Eds.), *Group motivation: Social psychological perspectives* (pp. 52–67). London: Harvester Wheatsheaf.

Crocker, J., Fiske, S. T., & Taylor, S. E. (1984). Schematic bases of belief change. In J. R. Eiser (Ed.), *Attitudinal judgment* (pp. 197–226). New York: Springer-Verlag.

Crocker, J., & Luhtanen, R. (1990). Collective self-esteem and ingroup bias. *Journal of Personality and Social Psychology, 58,* 60–67.

Crocker, J., & Major, B. (1989). Social stigma and self-esteem: The self-protective properties of stigma. *Psychological Review, 96,* 608–630.

Crocker, J., & Major, B. (1994). Reactions to stigma: The moderating role of justifications. In M. P. Zanna & J. M. Olson (Eds.), *The psychology of prejudice: The Ontario symposium* (Vol. 7, pp. 289–314). Hillsdale, NJ: Erlbaum.

Crocker, J., Major, B., & Steele, C. (1998). Social stigma. In D. T. Gilbert, S. T. Fiske, & G. Lindzey (Eds.), *The handbook of social psychology* (4th ed, Vol. 2, pp. 504–553). New York: McGraw-Hill.

Crockett, W. H. (1965). Cognitive complexity and impression formation. In B. A. Maher (Ed.), *Progress in experimental personality research* (Vol. 2, pp. 47–90). New York: Academic Press.

Crosby, F. (1982). *Relative deprivation and working women.* New York: Oxford University Press.

Crosby, F. (1984). The denial of personal discrimination. *American Behavioral Scientist, 27,* 371–386.

Crosby, F., Bromley, S., & Saxe, L. (1980). Recent unobtrusive studies of black and white discrimination and prejudice: A literature review. *Psychological Bulletin, 87,* 546–563.

Crosby, F., Cordova, D., & Jaskar, K. (1993). On the failure to see oneself as disadvantaged: Cognitive and emotional components. In M. A. Hogg & D. Abrams (Eds.), *Group motivation: Social psychological perspectives* (pp. 87–104). London: Harvester Wheatsheaf.

Crosby, F., Pufall, A., Snyder, R. C., O'Connell, M., & Whalen, P. (1989). The denial of personal disadvantage among you, me, and all the other ostriches. In M. Crawford & M. Gentry (Eds.), *Gender and thought* (pp. 79–99). New York: Springer-Verlag.

Cross, P. (1977). Not can but will college teaching be improved? *New Directions for Higher Education, 17,* 1–15.

Cross, S. E., Bacon, P. L., & Morris, M. L. (2000). The relational-interdependent self-construal and relationships. *Journal of Personality and Social Psychology, 78,* 791–808.

Cross, W. E. (1987). A two-factor theory of black identity: Implications for the study of identity development in minority children. In J. S. Phinney & M. J. Rotheram (Eds.), *Children's ethnic socialisation: Pluralism and development* (pp. 117–133). Beverly Hills, CA: Sage.

Crusco, A. H., & Wetzel, C. G. (1984). The Midas touch: The effects of interpersonal touch on restaurant tipping. *Personality and Social Psychology Bulletin, 10,* 512–517.

Crutchfield, R. A. (1955). Conformity and character. *American Psychologist, 10,* 191–198.

Cunningham, M. R. (1979). Weather, mood, and helping behavior: Quasi-experiments with the sunshine samaritan. *Journal of Personality and Social Psychology, 37,* 1947–1956.

Cunningham, M. R. (1986). Measuring the physical in physical attraction: Quasi-experiments on the sociobiology of female beauty. *Journal of Personality and Social Psychology, 50,* 925–935.

Cunningham, W. A., Preacher, K. J., & Banaji, M. R. (2001). Implicit attitude measures: Consistency, stability, and convergent validity. *Psychological Science, 12,* 163–170.

Currie, M., & Hogg, M. A. (1994). Subjective ethnolinguistic vitality and social adaptation among Vietnamese refugees in Australia. *International Journal of the Sociology of Language, 108,* 97–115.

Cutrona, C. E., Russell, D., & Jones, R. D. (1985). Cross-situational consistency in causal attributions: Does attributional style exist? *Journal of Personality and Social Psychology, 47,* 1043–1058.

Cvetkovich, G., & Löfstedt, R. E. (Eds.). (1999). *Social trust and the management of risk.* London: Earthscan.

Dakof, G. A., & Taylor, S. E. (1990). Victims' perceptions of social support: What is helpful from whom? *Journal of Personality and Social Psychology, 58,* 80–89.

Danserau, F., Jr., Graen, G., & Haga, W. J. (1975). A vertical dyad linkage approach to leadership within formal organizations: A longitudinal investigation of the role making process. *Organizational Behavior and Human Performance, 13,* 46–78.

Darley, J. M. (1991). Altruism and prosocial behaviour: Reflections and prospects. In M. S. Clark (Ed.), *Prosocial behaviour* (pp. 312–327). Newbury Park, CA: Sage.

Darley, J. M., & Batson, C. D. (1973). From Jerusalem to Jericho: A study of situational and dispositional variables in helping behavior. *Journal of Personality and Social Psychology, 27,* 100–108.

Darley, J. M., & Latané, B. (1968). Bystander intervention in emergencies: Diffusion of responsibility. *Journal of Personality and Social Psychology, 8,* 377–383.

Darlington, R. B., & Macker, D. F. (1966). Displacement of guilt-produced altruistic behavior. *Journal of Personality and Social Psychology, 4,* 442–443.

Darwin, C. (1872). *The expression of emotions in man and animals.* Chicago, IL: University of Chicago Press.

David, B., & Turner, J. C. (1996). Studies in self-categorization and minority conversion. Is being a member of the outgroup an advantage? *British Journal of Social Psychology, 35,* 179–199.

Davidowicz, L. C. (1975). *The war against the Jews, 1933–1945.* New York: Holt, Rinehart & Winston.

Davidson, A. R., & Jacard, J. (1979). Variables that moderate the attitude–behavior relation: Results of a longitudinal survey. *Journal of Personality and Social Psychology, 37,* 1364–1376.

Davidson, L. R., & Duberman, L. (1982). Friendship: Communication and interactional patterns in same-sex dyads. *Sex Roles, 8,* 809–822.

Davies, J. C. (1969). The J-curve of rising and declining satisfaction as a cause of some great revolutions and a contained rebellion. In H. D. Graham & T. R. Gurr (Eds.), *The history of violence in America: Historical and comparative perspectives* (pp. 690–730). New York: Praeger.

Davis, J. A. (1959). A formal interpretation of the theory of relative deprivation. *Sociometry, 22,* 280–296.

Davis, J. H. (1973). Group decision and social interaction: A theory of social decision schemes. *Psychological Review, 80,* 97–125.

Davis, M. H. (1980). Measuring individual differences in empathy. *JSAS Catalog of Selected Documents in Psychology, 10,* 85.

Dawes, R. M. (1991). Social dilemmas, economic self-interest, and evolutionary self-interest. In D. R. Brown & J. E. Keith-Smith (Eds.), *Frontiers of mathematical psychology: Essays in honour of Clyde Coombs* (pp. 53–79). New York: Springer-Verlag.

Dawes, R. M., Faust, D., & Meehl, P. E. (1989). Clinical versus actuarial judgment. *Science, 243,* 1668–1674.

Dean, L. M., Willis, F. N., & Hewitt, J. (1975). Initial interaction distance among individuals equal and unequal in military rank. *Journal of Personality and Social Psychology, 32*, 294–299.

Deaux, K. (1976). *The behavior of women and men.* Monterey, CA: Brooks/Cole.

Deaux, K. (1984). From individual differences to social categories. *American Psychologist, 39*, 105–116.

Deaux, K. (1985). Sex and gender. *Annual Review of Psychology, 36*, 49–81.

Deaux, K., & Emswiller, T. (1974). Explanations of successful performance on sex-linked tasks: What is skill for the male is luck for the female. *Journal of Personality and Social Psychology, 29*, 80–85.

Deaux, K., & LaFrance, M. (1998). Gender. In D. T. Gilbert, S. T. Fiske, & G. Lindzey (Eds.), *The handbook of social psychology* (4th ed., Vol. 1, pp. 788–827). New York: McGraw-Hill.

Deaux, K., & Wrightsman, L. S. (1988). *Social psychology* (5th ed.). Belmont, CA: Brooks/Cole.

Deaux, K., Reid, A., Mizrahi, K., & Ethier, K. A. (1995). Parameters of social identity. *Journal of Personality and Social Psychology, 68*, 280–291.

Deci, E. L., & Ryan, R. M. (1985). *Intrinsic motivation and self-determination in human behavior.* New York: Plenum.

de Cremer, D. (2000). Leadership selection in social dilemmas— Not all prefer it: The moderating effect of social value orientation. *Group Dynamics, 4*, 330–337.

de Cremer, D. (2002). Charismatic leadership and cooperation in social dilemmas: A matter of transforming motives? *Journal of Applied Social Psychology, 32*, 997–1016.

de Cremer, D., & van Vugt, M. (1999). Social identification effects in social dilemmas: A transformation of motives. *European Journal of Social Psychology, 29*, 871–893.

de Cremer, D., & van Vugt, M. (2002). Intergroup and intragroup aspects of leadership in social dilemmas: A relational model of cooperation. *Journal of Experimental Social Psychology, 38*, 126–136.

de Dreu, C. K. W., Lualhati, J. C., & McCusker, C. (1994). Effects of gain–loss frames on satisfaction with self–other outcome-differences. *European Journal of Social Psychology, 24*, 497–510.

de Gilder, D., & Wilke, H. A. M. (1994). Expectation states theory and motivational determinants of social influence. *European Review of Social Psychology, 5*, 243–269.

de Jong, P. F., Koomen, W., & Mellenbergh, G. J. (1988). Structure of causes for success and failure: A multidimensional scaling analysis of preference judgments. *Journal of Personality and Social Psychology, 55*, 1024–1037.

DeJong, W. (1979). An examination of self-perception mediation of the foot in the door effect. *Journal of Personality and Social Psychology, 37*, 2171–2180.

Dekovic, M., & Janssens, J. M. (1992). Parents' child-rearing style and child's sociometric status. *Developmental Psychology, 28 (2)*, 925–932.

Delamater, J. (Ed.). (2003). *Handbook of social psychology.* New York: Kluwer Academic/Plenum.

Dembroski, T. M., & MacDougall, J. M. (1978). Stress effects on affiliation preferences among subjects possessing the type A coronary-prone behavior pattern. *Journal of Personality and Social Psychology, 36*, 23–33.

D'Emilio, J. (1983). *Sexual politics, sexual communities: The making of a homosexual minority in the United States.* Chicago: University of Chicago Press.

De Munck, V. C. (1996). Love and marriage in a Sri Lankan Muslim community: Toward an evaluation of Dravidian marriage practices. *American Ethnologist, 23*, 698–716.

Dennis, A. R., & Valacich, J. S. (1993). Computer brainstorms: More heads are better than one. *Journal of Applied Psychology, 78*, 531–537.

DePaulo, B. (1992). Nonverbal behavior and self-presentation. *Psychological Bulletin, 111*, 203–243.

DePaulo, B. (1994). Spotting lies: Can humans learn to do better? *Current Directions in Psychological Science, 3*, 83–86.

DePaulo, B., & Friedman, H. S. (1998). Nonverbal communication. In D. T. Gilbert, S. T. Fiske, & G. Lindzey (Eds.), *The handbook of social psychology* (4th ed., Vol. 2, pp. 3–40). New York: McGraw-Hill.

DePaulo, B. M., Lanier, K., & Davis, T. (1983). Detecting the deceit of the motivated liar. *Journal of Personality and Social Psychology, 45*, 1096–1103.

DePaulo, B. M., & Rosenthal, R. (1979). Telling lies. *Journal of Personality and Social Psychology, 37*, 1713–1722.

DePaulo, P. J., & DePaulo, B. M. (1989). Can deception by salespersons and customers be detected through nonverbal behavioral cues? *Journal of Applied Social Psychology, 19*, 1552–1577.

Deschamps, J.-C. (1983). Social attribution. In J. Jaspars, F. D. Fincham, & M. Hewstone (Eds.), *Attribution theory and research: Conceptual, developmental and social dimensions* (pp. 223–240). London: Academic Press.

Deschamps, J.-C., & Brown, R. J. (1983). Superordinate goals and intergroup conflict. *British Journal of Social Psychology, 22*, 189–195.

Deutsch, M. (1975). Equity, equality and need: What determines which value will be used as a basis of distributive justice? *Journal of Social Issues, 31*, 137–149.

Deutsch, M., & Gerard, H. B. (1955). A study of normative and informational social influences upon individual judgment. *Journal of Abnormal and Social Psychology, 51*, 629–636.

Deutsch, M., & Krauss, R. M. (1960). The effect of threat upon interpersonal bargaining. *Journal of Abnormal and Social Psychology, 61*, 181–189.

Devine, P. G. (1989). Stereotypes and prejudice: Their automatic and controlled components. *Journal of Personality and Social Psychology, 56*, 5–18.

Devine, P. G., & Elliot, A. (1995). Are racial stereotypes really fading? The Princeton trilogy revisited. *Personality and Social Psychology Bulletin, 22*, 22–37.

Devine, P. G., Hamilton, D. L., & Ostrom, T. M. (Eds.). (1994). *Social cognition: Impact on social psychology.* San Diego, CA: Academic Press.

Devine, P. G., & Malpass, R. S. (1985). Orienting strategies in differential face recognition. *Personality and Social Psychology Bulletin, 11*, 33–40.

DeVos, G. A., & Hippler, A. E. (1969). Cultural psychology: Comparative studies of human behavior. In G. Lindzey & E. Aronson (Eds.), *Handbook of social psychology* (2nd ed., Vol. 4, pp. 322–417). Reading, MA: Addison-Wesley.

Diab, L. N. (1970). A study of intragroup and intergroup relations among experimentally produced small groups. *Genetic Psychology Monographs, 82*, 49–82.

Diaz-Guerrero, R. (1987). Historical sociocultural premises and ethnic socialization. In M. J. Rotheram (Ed.), *Children's ethnic socialization: Pluralism and development* (pp. 239–250). Newbury Park, CA: Sage.

Dickens, C. (1854). *Hard times.* Harmondsworth: Penguin.

Diehl, M. (1988). Social identity and minimal groups: The effects of interpersonal and intergroup attitudinal similarity on intergroup discrimination. *British Journal of Social Psychology, 27*, 289–300.

Diehl, M. (1990). The minimal group paradigm: Theoretical explanations and empirical findings. *European Review of Social Psychology, 1*, 263–292.

Diehl, M., & Stroebe, W. (1987). Productivity loss in brainstorming groups: Toward the solution of a riddle. *Journal of Personality and Social Psychology, 53*, 497–509.

Diehl, M., & Stroebe, W. (1991). Productivity loss in idea-generating groups: Tracking down the blocking effect. *Journal of Personality and Social Psychology, 61*, 392–403.

Diener, E. (1976). Effects of prior destructive behavior, anonymity, and group presence on deindividuation and aggression. *Journal of Personality and Social Psychology, 33*, 497–507.

Diener, E. (1980). Deindividuation: The absence of self-awareness and self-regulation in group members. In P. B. Paulus (Ed.), *Psychology of group influence* (pp. 209–242). Hillsdale, NJ: Erlbaum.

Diener, E., & Crandall, R. (1979). An evaluation of the Jamaican anticrime program. *Journal of Applied Social Psychology, 9*, 135–146.

Diener, E., Fraser, S. C., Beaman, A. L., & Kelem, R. T. (1976). Effects of deindividuation variables on stealing by Halloween trick-or-treaters. *Journal of Personality and Social Psychology, 33*, 178–183.

Diener, E., Suh, E. M., Lucas, R. E., & Smith, H. L. (1999). Subjective well-being: Three decades of progress. *Psychological Bulletin, 125*, 276–302.

Dienstbier, R. A., Kahle, L. R., Willis, K. A., & Tunnell, G. B. (1980). The impact of moral theories on cheating: Studies of emotion attribution and schema activation. *Motivation and Emotion, 4*, 193–216.

Dietz, T. L. (1998). An examination of violence and gender role portrayals in video games: Implications for gender socialization and aggressive behavior. *Sex Roles, 38*, 425–442.

Dindia, K. (1987). The effects of sex of subject and sex of partner in interruptions. *Human Communication Research, 13*, 345–371.

Dindia, K., & Allen, M. (1992). Sex differences in self-disclosure: A meta-analysis. *Psychological Bulletin, 112*, 106–124.

Dion, K. K. (1972). Physical attractiveness and evaluation of children's transgressions. *Journal of Personality and Social Psychology, 24*, 207–213.

Dion, K. K, Berscheid, E., & Walster, E. (1972). What is beautiful is good. *Journal of Personality and Social Psychology, 24*, 285–290.

Dion, K. K., & Dion, K. L. (1996). Toward understanding love. *Personal Relationships, 3*, 1–3.

Dion, K. L. (1979). Intergroup conflict and intragroup cohesiveness. In W. G. Austin & S. Worchel (Eds.), *The social psychology of intergroup relations* (pp. 211–224). Monterey, CA: Brooks/Cole.

Dion, K. L., & Earn, B. M. (1975). The phenomenology of being a target of prejudice. *Journal of Personality and Social Psychology, 32*, 944–950.

Dion, K. L., Earn, B. M., & Yee, P. H. N. (1978). The experience of being a victim of prejudice: An experimental approach. *International Journal of Psychology, 13*, 197–214.

Dipboye, R. L. (1977). Alternative approaches to deindividuation. *Psychological Bulletin, 84*, 1057–1075.

Dipboye, R. L., Arvey, R. D., & Terpstra, D. E. (1977). Sex and physical attractiveness of raters and applicants as determinants of résumé evaluations. *Journal of Applied Psychology, 62*, 288–294.

Dittes, J. E. (1959). Attractiveness of group as function of self-esteem and acceptance by group. *Journal of Abnormal and Social Psychology, 59*, 77–82.

Dittes, J. E., & Kelley, H. H. (1956). Effects of different conditions of acceptance upon conformity to group norms. *Journal of Abnormal and Social Psychology, 53*, 100–107.

Doherty, R. W., Hatfield, E., Thompson, K., & Choo, P. (1994). Cultural and ethical influences on love and attachment. *Personal Relationships, 1*, 391–398.

Doi, L. T. (1976). The Japanese patterns of communication and the concept of *amae*. In L. A. Samovar & R. E. Porter (Eds.). *Intercultural communication: A reader* (2nd ed., pp. 188–193).

Doise, W. (1978). *Groups and individuals: Explanations in social psychology.* Cambridge: Cambridge University Press.

Doise, W. (1986). *Levels of explanation in social psychology.* Cambridge: Cambridge University Press.

Doise, W., Clemence, A., & Lorenzi-Cioldi, F. (1993). *The quantitative analysis of social representations.* London: Harvester Wheatsheaf.

Dolinski, D. (2000). On inferring one's beliefs from one's attempt and consequences for subsequent compliance. *Journal of Personality and Social Psychology, 78*, 260–272.

Doll, J., & Ajzen, I. (1992). Accessibility and stability of predictors in the theory of planned behaviour. *Journal of Personality and Social Psychology, 63*, 754–765.

Dollard, J., Doob, L. W., Miller, N. E., Mowrer, O. H., & Sears, R. R. (1939). *Frustration and aggression.* New Haven, CT: Yale University Press.

Doms, M. (1983). The minority influence effect: An alternative approach. In W. Doise & S. Moscovici (Eds.), *Current issues in European social psychology* (Vol. 1, pp. 1–32). Cambridge: Cambridge University Press.

Doms, M., & van Avermaet, E. (1980). Majority influence, minority influence, and conversion behavior: A replication. *Journal of Experimental Social Psychology, 16*, 283–292.

Donnerstein, E., & Linz, D. (1994). Sexual violence in the mass media. In M. Costanzo & S. Oskamp (Eds.), *Violence and the law* (pp. 9–36). Thousand Oaks, CA: Sage.

Donnerstein, E., & Malamuth, N. (1997). Pornography: Its consequences on the observer. In L. B. Schlesinger & E. Revitch (Eds.), *Sexual dynamics of anti-social behaviour* (2nd ed., pp. 30–49). Springfield, IL: Charles C. Thomas.

Dovidio, J. F. (1984). Helping behaviour and altruism: An empirical and conceptual overview. In L. Berkowitz (Ed.), *Advances in experimental social psychology* (Vol. 17, pp. 361–427). New York: Academic Press.

Dovidio, J. F., Brigham, J. C., Johnson, B. T., & Gaertner, S. L. (1996). Stereotyping, prejudice, and discrimination: Another look. In C. N. Macrae, C. Stangor & M. Hewstone (Eds.), *Stereotypes and stereotyping* (pp. 276–319). New York: Guilford.

Dovidio, J. F., & Ellyson, S. L. (1985). Patterns of visual dominance behavior in humans. In S. Ellyson & J. Dovidio (Eds.), *Power, dominance, and nonverbal behavior* (pp. 129–149). New York: Springer-Verlag.

Dovidio, J. F., Ellyson, S. L., Keating, C. J., Heltman, K., & Brown, C. E. (1988). The relationship of social power to visual displays of dominance between men and women. *Journal of Personality and Social Psychology, 54*, 233–242.

Dovidio, J. F., Kawakami, K., & Beach, K. R. (2001). Implicit and explicit attitudes: Examination of the relationship between measures of intergroup bias. In R. Brown & S. Gaertner (Eds.), *Blackwell handbook of social psychology: Intergroup processes* (Vol. 4, pp. 175–197). Oxford: Blackwell.

Dovidio, J. F., Piliavin, J. A., Gaertner, S. L., Schroeder, D. A., & Clark, R. D., III (1991). The arousal: Cost–reward model and the process of intervention: A review of the evidence. In M. S. Clark (Ed.), *Prosocial behaviour* (pp. 86–118). Newbury Park, CA: Sage.

Duck, J. M. (1998). People's perceptions of being influenced by mass communication. In D. J. Terry & M. A. Hogg (Eds.), *Attitudes, behavior, and social context: The role of norms and group membership*. Mahwah, NJ: Erlbaum.

Duck, J. M., & Fielding, K. S. (1999). Leaders and sub-groups: One of us or one of them? *Group Processes and Intergroup Relations*, 2, 203–230.

Duck, J. M., Hogg, M. A., & Terry, D. J. (1995). Me, us and them: Political identification and the third person effect in the 1993 Australian federal election. *European Journal of Social Psychology*, 25, 195–215.

Duck, J. M., Hogg, M. A., & Terry, D. J. (1998). Perceived self–other differences in persuasibility: The effects of interpersonal and group-based similarity. *European Journal of Social Psychology*, 28, 1–21.

Duck, J. M., Hogg, M. A., & Terry, D. J. (1999). Social identity and perceptions of media persuasion: Are we always less influenced than others? *Journal of Applied Social Psychology*, 29, 1879–1899.

Duck, J. M., Terry, D. J., & Hogg, M. A. (1995). The perceived influence of AIDS advertising: Third-person effects in the context of positive media content. *Basic and Applied Social Psychology*, 17, 305–325.

Duck, J. M., Terry, D. J., & Hogg, M. A. (1998). Perceptions of a media campaign: The role of social identity and the changing intergroup context. *Personality and Social Psychology Bulletin*, 24, 3–16.

Duck, S. W. (1977). *The study of acquaintance*. Farnborough, UK: Saxon House.

Duck, S. W. (Ed.). (1982). *Personal relationships, 4: Dissolving personal relationships*. London: Academic Press.

Duck, S. W. (1988). *Relating to others*. Milton Keynes: Open University Press.

Duck, S. W. (1992). *Human relationships* (2nd ed.). London: Sage.

Duckitt, J. (1989). Authoritarianism and group identification: A new view of an old construct. *Political Psychology*, 10, 63–84.

Duckitt, J. (2000). Culture, personality and prejudice. In S. A. Renshon & J. Duckitt (Eds.), *Political psychology* (pp. 89–107). London: Macmillan.

Duncan, S. (1969). Nonverbal communication. *Psychological Bulletin*, 72, 118–137.

Duncan, S. L. (1976). Differential social perception and attribution of intergroup violence: Testing the lower limits of stereotyping of blacks. *Journal of Personality and Social Psychology*, 34, 590–598.

Dunning, D., Meyerowitz, J. A., & Holzberg, A. (1989). Ambiguity and self-evaluation: The role of idiosyncratic trait definitions in self-serving assessments of ability. *Journal of Personality and Social Psychology*, 57, 1082–1090.

Dupuy, R. E., & Dupuy, T. N. (1977). *The encyclopedia of military history*. London: Janes.

Durkheim, E. (1898). Représentations individuelles et représentations collectives. *Revue de Metaphysique et de Morale*, 6, 273–302.

Durkheim, E. (1912/1995). *The elementary forms of the religious life*. New York: Free Press.

Durkin, K. (1995). *Developmental social psychology: From infancy to old age*. Oxford, UK: Blackwell.

Durkin, K. F., & Bryant, C. D. (1995). 'Log on to sex': Some notes on the carnal computer and erotic cyberspace as an emerging research frontier. *Deviant Behavior*, 16, 179–200.

Dutton, D. G., & Lake, R. (1973). Threat of own prejudice and reverse discrimination in interracial situations. *Journal of Personality and Social Psychology*, 28, 94–100.

Duval, S., & Wicklund, R. A. (1972). *A theory of objective self-awareness*. New York: Academic Press.

Eagly, A. H. (1978). Sex differences in influenceability. *Psychological Bulletin*, 85, 86–116.

Eagly, A. H. (1983). Gender and social influence: A social psychological analysis. *American Psychologist*, 38, 971–981.

Eagly, A. H. (1987). *Sex differences in social behavior: A social-role analysis*. Hillsdale, NJ: Erlbaum.

Eagly, A. H. (1995). The science and politics of comparing women and men. *American Psychologist*, 50, 145–158.

Eagly, A. H. (2004). Few women at the top: How role incongruity produces prejudice and the glass ceiling. In D. van Knippenberg & M. A. Hogg (Eds.), *Leadership and power: Identity processes in groups and organizations* (pp. 79–93). London: Sage.

Eagly, A. H., & Carli, L. (1981). Sex of researcher and sex-typed communications as determinants of sex differences in influenceability: A meta-analysis of social influence studies. *Psychological Bulletin*, 90, 1–20.

Eagly, A. H., & Chaiken, S. (1984). Cognitive theories of persuasion. In L. Berkowitz (Ed.), *Advances in experimental social psychology* (Vol. 17, pp. 268–359). New York: Academic Press.

Eagly, A. H., & Chaiken, S. (1993). *The psychology of attitudes*. San Diego, CA: Harcourt Brace Jovanovich.

Eagly, A. H., & Chaiken, S. (1998). Attitude structure and function. In D. T. Gilbert, S. T. Fiske, & G. Lindzey (Eds.), *The handbook of social psychology* (Vol. 1, pp. 269–322). Boston, MA: McGraw-Hill.

Eagly, A. H., & Chrvala, C. (1986). Sex differences in conformity: Status and gender role interpretations. *Psychology of Women Quarterly*, 10, 203–220.

Eagly, A. H., & Crowley, M. (1986). Gender and helping behavior: A meta-analytic review of the social psychological literature. *Psychological Review*, 100, 283–308.

Eagly, A. H., Karau, S. J., & Makhijani, M. G. (1995). Gender and the effectiveness of leaders: A meta-analysis. *Psychological Bulletin*, 117, 125–145.

Eagly, A. H., & Mladinic, A. (1994). Are people prejudiced against women? Some answers from research on attitudes, gender stereotypes, and judgments of competence. *European Review of Social Psychology*, 5, 1–35.

Eagly, A. H., & Steffen, V. J. (1984). Gender stereotypes stem from the distribution of women and men into social roles. *Journal of Personality and Social Psychology*, 46, 735–754.

Eagly, A. H., & Steffen, V. J. (1986). Gender and aggressive behavior: A meta-analytic review of the social psychological literature. *Psychological Bulletin*, 100, 309–330.

Eagly, A. H., & Wood, W. (1991). Explaining sex differences in social behaviour: A meta-analytic perspective. *Personality and Social Psychology Bulletin*, 17, 306–315.

Eagly, A. H., Wood, W., & Fishbaugh, L. (1981). Sex differences in conformity: Surveillance by the group as a determinant of male nonconformity. *Journal of Personality and Social Psychology, 40,* 384–394.

Earle, T. C., & Cvetkovich, G. T. (1995). *Social trust: Toward a cosmopolitan society.* Westport, CT: Praeger.

Earley, P. C. (1989). Social loafing and collectivism: A comparison of the United States and the People's Republic of China. *Administrative Science Quarterly, 34,* 565–581.

Earley, P. C. (1994). Self or group: Cultural effects of training on self-efficacy and performance. *Administrative Science Quarterly, 39,* 89–117.

Easterbrook, J. A. (1959). The effect of emotion on cue utilization and organization of behavior. *Psychological Review, 66,* 183–201.

Ebbinghaus, H. (1885). *Memory: A contribution to experimental psychology.* H. A. Ruger & C. E. Bussenius (trans), New York: Dover, 1964.

Eckert, P., & McConnell-Ginet, S. (1999). New generalizations and explanations in language and gender research. *Language in Society, 28,* 185–201.

Eden, D. (1990). Pygmalion without interpersonal contrast effects: Whole groups gain from raising manager expectations. *Journal of Applied Psychology, 75,* 394–398.

Edney, J. J. (1979). The nuts game: A concise commons dilemma analog. *Environmental Psychology and Nonverbal Behavior, 3,* 252–254.

Edwards, A. L. (1957). *Techniques of attitude scale construction.* New York: Appleton-Century-Crofts.

Edwards, D. (1997). *Discourse and cognition.* London: Sage.

Edwards, D., & Potter, J. (Eds.). (1992). *Discursive psychology.* London: Sage.

Edwards, J. (1994). *Multilingualism.* London: Routledge.

Edwards, J., & Chisholm, J. (1987). Language, multiculturalism and identity: A Canadian study. *Journal of Multilingual and Multicultural Development, 8,* 391–407.

Edwards, K. (1990). The interplay of affect and cognition in attitude formation and change. *Journal of Personality and Social Psychology, 59,* 202–216.

Edwards, K., & Smith, E. E. (1996). A disconfirmation bias in the evaluation of arguments. *Journal of Personality and Social Psychology, 71,* 5–24.

Ehrlich, H. J. (1973). *The social psychology of prejudice.* New York: Wiley.

Eibl-Eibesfeldt, I. (1972). Similarities and differences between cultures in expressive movements. In R. Hinde (Ed.), *Non-verbal communication* (pp. 297–314). Cambridge: Cambridge University Press.

Eichler, M. (1980). *The double standard: A feminist critique of feminist social science.* London: Croom Helm.

Einhorn, H. J., & Hogarth, R. M. (1981). Behavioral decision theory: Processes of judgment and choice. *Annual Review of Psychology, 32,* 53–88.

Eisen, S. V. (1979). Actor-observer differences in information inference and causal attribution. *Journal of Personality and Social Psychology, 37,* 261–272.

Eisenberg, N. (1991). Meta-analytic contributions to the literature on prosocial behaviour. *Personality and Social Psychology Bulletin, 17,* 273–282.

Eisenberg, N., & Fabes, R. A. (1991). Prosocial behaviour and empathy: A multimethod development perspective. In M. S. Clark (Ed.), *Prosocial behaviour* (pp. 34–61). Newbury Park, CA: Sage.

Eisenberg, N., Fabes, R. A., Karbon, M., Murphy, B. C., Wosinski, M., Polazzi, L., Carlo, G., & Juhnke, C. (1996). The relationship of children's dispositional prosocial behaviour to emotionality, regulation, and social functioning. *Child Development, 67,* 974–992.

Eisenberg-Berg, N. (1979). Relationship of prosocial moral reasoning to altruism, political liberalism and intelligence. *Developmental Psychology, 15,* 87–89.

Eisenberger, R., & Shank, D. M. (1985). Personal work ethic and effort training affect cheating. *Journal of Personality and Social Psychology, 49,* 520–528.

Eiser, J. R. (1986). *Social psychology: Attitudes, cognition and social behaviour.* Cambridge: Cambridge University Press.

Eiser, J. R., & Stroebe, W. (1972). *Categorization and social judgement.* London: Academic Press.

Ekman, P. (1971). Universals and cultural differences in facial expressions of emotion. In J. K. Cole (Ed.), *Nebraska symposium on motivation* (Vol. 19, pp. 207–284). Lincoln, NE: University of Nebraska Press.

Ekman, P. (1973). Cross-cultural studies of facial expression. In P. Ekman (Ed.), *Darwin and facial expression* (pp. 169–222). New York: Academic Press.

Ekman, P. (1982). *Emotion in the human face.* New York: Cambridge University Press.

Ekman, P., & Friesen, W. V. (1971). Constants across cultures in the face and emotion. *Journal of Personality and Social Psychology, 17,* 124–129.

Ekman, P., & Friesen, W. V. (1972). Hand movements. *Journal of Communication, 22,* 353–374.

Ekman, P., & Friesen, W. V. (1974). Detecting deception from the body or face. *Journal of Personality and Social Psychology, 29,* 188–198.

Ekman, P., & Friesen, W. V. (1975). *Unmasking the face.* Englewood Cliffs, NJ: Prentice Hall.

Ekman, P., Friesen, W. V., & Scherer, K. R. (1976). Body movement and voice pitch in deceptive interaction. *Semiotica, 16,* 23–27.

Ekman, P., Friesen, W. V., O'Sullivan, M., Chan, A., Diacoyanni-Tarlatzis, I., Heider, K., Krause, R., Lecompte, W. A., Pitcairn, T., Riccibitti, P. E., Scherer, K., Tomita, M., & Tzavaras, A. (1987). Universals and cultural differences in the judgements of facial expressions of emotion. *Journal of Personality and Social Psychology, 53,* 712–717.

Elder, G. H. Jr. (1969). Appearance and education in marriage mobility. *American Sociological Review, 34,* 519–533.

Elkin, A. P. (1961). *The Aboriginal Australians.* London: Longmans.

Ellemers, N. (1993). The influence of socio-structural variables on identity management strategies. *European Review of Social Psychology, 4,* 27–57.

Elliot, A. J. (1981). *Child language.* Cambridge: Cambridge University Press.

Ellis, R. J., Olson, J. M., & Zanna, M. P. (1983). Stereotypic personality inferences following objective versus subjective judgments of beauty. *Canadian Journal of Behavioral Science, 15,* 35–42.

Ellsworth, P. C., Carlsmith, J. M., & Henson, A. (1972). The stare as a stimulus to flight in human subjects: A series of field experiments. *Journal of Personality and Social Psychology, 21,* 302–311.

Elms, A. C. (1975). The crisis of confidence in social psychology. *American Psychologist, 30,* 967–976.

Elms, A. C. (1982). Keeping deception honest: Justifying conditions for social scientific research strategies. In T. L. Beauchamp &

R. Faden (Eds.), *Ethical issues in social science research*. Baltimore, MD: Johns Hopkins University Press.

Elms, A. C., & Milgram, S. (1966). Personality characteristics associated with obedience and defiance toward authoritative command. *Journal of Experimental Research in Personality, 1,* 282–289.

Emler, N., & Reicher, S. D. (1995). *Adolescence and delinquency: The collective management of reputation*. Oxford, UK: Blackwell.

Enriquez, V. G. (1993). Developing a Filipino psychology. In U. Kim & J. W. Berry (Eds.), *Indigenous psychologies: Research and experience in cultural context* (pp. 152–169). Newbury Park, CA: Sage.

Erber, R. (1991). Affective and semantic priming: Effects of mood on category accessibility and inference. *Journal of Experimental Social Psychology, 27,* 480–498.

Erber, R., & Fiske, S. T. (1984). Outcome dependency and attention to inconsistent information. *Journal of Personality and Social Psychology, 47,* 709–726.

Eron, L. D. (1982). Parent–child interaction, television violence, and aggression of children. *American Psychologist, 37,* 197–211.

Eron, L. D. (1994). Theories of aggression: From drives to cognitions. In L. R. Huesmann (Ed.), *Aggressive behavior: Current perspectives* (pp. 3–11). New York: Plenum.

Esser, J. K., & Komorita, S. S. (1975). Reciprocity and concession making in bargaining. *Journal of Personality and Social Psychology, 31,* 864–872.

Evans, B. K., & Fischer, D. G. (1992). A hierarchical model of participatory decision-making, job autonomy, and perceived control. *Human Relations, 45,* 1169–1189.

Evans, N. J., & Jarvis, P. A. (1980). Group cohesion: A review and re-evaluation. *Small Group Behavior, 11,* 359–370.

Evans-Pritchard, E. E. (1937). *Witchcraft, oracles and magic among the Azande*. Oxford: Oxford University Press.

Exline, R. V. (1971). Visual interaction: The glances of power and preference. In J. K. Cole (Ed.), *Nebraska symposium on motivation* (Vol. 19, pp. 163–206). Lincoln, NE: University of Nebraska Press.

Exline, R. V., Ellyson, S. L., & Long, B. (1975). Visual behavior as an aspect of power role relationships. In P. Pliner, L. Krames, & T. Alloway (Eds.), *Nonverbal communication of aggression* (Vol. 2, pp. 21–52). New York: Plenum.

Fajardo, D. M. (1985). Author race, essay quality, and reverse discrimination. *Journal of Applied Social Psychology, 15,* 255–268.

Farr, R. M. (1996). *The roots of modern social psychology: 1872–1954*. Oxford, UK: Blackwell.

Farr, R. M., & Moscovici, S. (Eds.). (1984). *Social representations*. Cambridge: Cambridge University Press.

Fazio, R. H. (1986). How do attitudes guide behavior? In R. M. Sorrentino & E. T. Higgins (Eds.), *The handbook of motivation and cognition*. New York: Guilford Press.

Fazio, R. H. (1989). On the power and functionality of attitudes: The role of attitude accessibility. In A. R. Pratkanis, S. Breckler, & A. G. Greenwald (Eds.), *Attitude structure and function* (pp. 153–179). Hillsdale, NJ: Erlbaum.

Fazio, R. H. (1995). Attitudes as object-evaluation associations: Determinants, consequences, and correlates of attitude accessibility. In R. E. Petty & J. A. Krosnick (Eds.), *Attitude strength: Antecedents and consequences* (pp. 247–282). Mahwah, NJ: Erlbaum.

Fazio, R. H., Blascovich, J., & Driscoll, D. M. (1992). On the functional value of attitudes: The influence of accessible attitudes upon the ease and quality of decision making. *Personality and Social Psychology Bulletin, 18,* 388–401.

Fazio, R. H., Effrein, E. A., & Falender, V. J. (1981). Self-perceptions following social interactions. *Journal of Personality and Social Psychology, 41,* 232–242.

Fazio, R. H., Jackson, J. R., Dunton, B. C., & Williams, C. J. (1995). Variability in automatic activation as an unobtrusive measure of racial attitudes: A bona fide pipeline. *Journal of Personality and Social Psychology, 69,* 1013–1027.

Fazio, R. H., Ledbetter, J. E., & Towles-Schwen, T. (2000). On the costs of accessible attitudes: Detecting that the attitude object has changed. *Journal of Personality and Social Psychology, 78,* 197–210.

Fazio, R. H., & Olson, M. A. (2003). Attitudes: Foundations, functions, and consequences. In M. A. Hogg & J. Cooper (Eds.), *The Sage handbook of social psychology* (pp. 139–160). London: Sage.

Fazio, R. H., & Powell, M. C. (1997). On the value of knowing one's likes and dislikes: Attitude accessibility, stress and health in college. *Psychological Science, 8,* 430–436.

Fazio, R. H., Sanbonmatsu, D. M., Powell, M. C., & Kardes, F. R. (1986). On the automatic activation of attitudes. *Journal of Personality and Social Psychology, 50,* 229–238.

Fazio, R. H., & Zanna, M. P. (1978). Attitudinal qualities relating to the strength of the attitude–behaviour relation. *Journal of Experimental Social Psychology, 14,* 398–408.

Fazio, R. H., & Zanna, M. P. (1981). Direct experience and attitude–behavior consistency. In L. Berkowitz (Ed.), *Advances in experimental social psychology* (Vol. 14, pp. 161–202). New York: Academic Press.

Fazio, R. H., Zanna, M. P., & Cooper, J. (1977). Dissonance and self-perception: An integrative view of each theory's proper domain of application. *Journal of Experimental Social Psychology, 13,* 464–479.

Feagin, J. (1972). Poverty: We still believe that God helps them who help themselves. *Psychology Today, 6,* 101–129.

Feather, N. T. (1974). Explanations of poverty in Australian and American samples: The person, society and fate. *Australian Journal of Psychology, 26,* 199–216.

Feather, N. T. (1985). Attitudes, values, and attributions: Explanations of unemployment. *Journal of Personality and Social Psychology, 48,* 876–889.

Feather, N. T. (1989). Attitudes towards the high achiever: The fall of the tall poppy. *Australian Journal of Psychology, 41,* 239–267.

Feather, N. T. (1991). Human values, global self-esteem, and belief in a just world. *Journal of Personality, 59,* 83–106.

Feather, N. T. (1993a). Attitudes towards the high achiever: Value correlates and family resemblances. Unpublished research manuscript.

Feather, N. T. (1993b). Authoritarianism and attitudes towards high achievers. *Journal of Personality and Social Psychology, 65,* 152–164.

Feather, N. T. (1994). Attitudes toward high achievers and reactions to their fall: Theory and research toward tall poppies. In L. Berkowitz (Ed.), *Advances in experimental social psychology* (Vol. 26, pp. 1–73). New York: Academic Press.

Feather, N. T. (1995). Psychology at Flinders University: Some reflections on the first 28 years. *Bulletin of the American Psychological Society, 17,* 21–25.

Feather, N. T., & Barber, J. G. (1983). Depressive reactions and unemployment. *Journal of Abnormal Psychology, 92,* 185–195.

Feather, N. T., & Davenport, P. R. (1981). Unemployment and depressive affect: A motivational and attributional analysis. *Journal of Personality and Social Psychology, 41,* 422–436.

Feather, N. T., & Simon, J. G. (1975). Reactions to male and female success and failure in sex-linked occupations: Impressions of personality, causal attributions, and perceived likelihood of different consequences. *Journal of Personality and Social Psychology, 31,* 20–31.

Feather, N. T., & Tiggerman, M. (1984). A balanced measure of attributional style. *Australian Journal of Psychology, 36,* 267–283.

Feeney, J. A. (1994) Attachment style, communication patterns, and satisfaction across the life cycle of marriage. *Personal Relationships, 1,* 333–348.

Feeney, J. A. (1999). Adult attachment, emotional control, and marital satisfaction. *Personal Relationships, 6,* 169–185.

Feeney, J. A., & Noller, P. (1990). Attachment style as a predictor of adult romantic relationships. *Journal of Personality and Social Psychology, 58,* 281–291.

Fehr, B. (1994). Prototype based assessment of laypeople's views of love. *Personal Relationships, 1,* 309–331.

Fchr, R. S., & Stern, J. A. (1970). Peripheral physiological variables and emotion: The James–Lange theory revisited. *Psychological Bulletin, 74,* 411–424.

Feist, J., & Brannon, L. (1988). *Health psychology.* Belmont, CA: Wadsworth.

Fenigstein, A. (1984). Self-consciousness and the overperception of self as a target. *Journal of Personality and Social Psychology, 47,* 860–870.

Ferguson, C. K., & Kelley, H. H. (1964). Significant factors in overevaluation of own group's product. *Journal of Abnormal and Social Psychology, 69,* 223–228.

Fergusson, D. M., Horwood, L. J., Kershaw, K. L., & Shannon, F. T. (1986). Factors associated with reports of wife assault in New Zealand. *Journal of Marriage and the Family, 48,* 407–412.

Fernando, K., & Vaughan, G. M. (1992). Young New Zealanders' knowledge and concern about nuclear war. *Interdisciplinary Peace Research, 4,* 31–57.

Festinger, L. (1950). Informal social communication. *Psychological Review, 57,* 271–282.

Festinger, L. (1954). A theory of social comparison processes. *Human Relations, 7,* 117–140.

Festinger, L. (1957). *A theory of cognitive dissonance.* Stanford, CA: Stanford University Press.

Festinger, L. (1964). *Conflict, decision and dissonance.* Stanford, CA: Stanford University Press.

Festinger, L. (1980). *Retrospections on social psychology.* New York: Oxford University Press.

Festinger, L., & Carlsmith, J. M. (1959). Cognitive consequences of forced compliance. *Journal of Abnormal and Social Psychology, 58,* 203–210.

Festinger, L., Pepitone, A., & Newcomb, T. M. (1952). Some consequences of deindividuation in a group. *Journal of Personality and Social Psychology, 47,* 382–389.

Festinger, L., Schachter, S., & Back, K. (1950). *Social pressures in informal groups: A study of human factors in housing.* New York: Harper.

Fidell, L. S. (1970). Empirical verification of sex discrimination in hiring practices in psychology. *American Psychologist, 25,* 1094–1098.

Fiedler, F. E. (1965). A contingency model of leadership effectiveness. In L. Berkowitz (Ed.), *Advances in experimental social psychology* (Vol. 1, pp. 149–190). New York: Academic Press.

Fiedler, K. (1982). Casual schemata: Review and criticism of research on a popular construct. *Journal of Personality and Social Psychology, 42,* 1001–13.

Fielding, K. S., & Hogg, M. A. (1997). Social identity, self-categorisation and leadership: A field study of small interactive groups. *Group Dynamics, Theory, Research, and Practice, 1,* 39–51.

Fielding, K. S., & Hogg, M. A. (2000). Working hard to achieve self-defining group goals: A social identity analysis. *Zeitschrift für Sozialpsychologie, 31,* 191–203.

Fincham, F. D. (1985). Attributions in close relationships. In J. H. Harvey & G. Weary (Eds.), *Attribution: Basic issues and applications.* Orlando, FL: Academic Press.

Fincham, F. D., & Bradbury, T. N. (1987). Cognitive processes and conflict in close relationships: An attribution–efficacy model. *Journal of Personality and Social Psychology, 53,* 1106–1118.

Fincham, F. D., & Bradbury, T. N. (1991). Cognition in marriage: A program of research on attributions. In W. H. Jones & D. Perlman (Eds.), *Advances in personal relationships* (Vol. 2, pp. 159–204). London: Jessica Kingsley.

Fincham, F. D., & Bradbury, T. N. (1993). Marital satisfaction, depression, and attributions: A longitudinal analysis. *Journal of Personality and Social Psychology, 64,* 442–452.

Fincham, F. D., & O'Leary, K. D. (1983). Causal inferences for spouse behavior in maritally distressed and nondistressed couples. *Journal of Social and Clinical Psychology, 1,* 42–57.

Fischer, D. (1989). *Albion's seed: Four British folkways in America.* New York: Oxford University Press.

Fischer, W. F. (1963). Sharing in preschool children as a function of amount and type of reinforcement. *Genetic Psychology Monographs, 68,* 215–245.

Fishbein, M. (1967a). A behavior theory approach to the relation between beliefs about an object and the attitude toward the object. In M. Fishbein (Ed.), *Readings in attitude theory and measurement* (pp. 389–400). New York: Wiley.

Fishbein, M. (1967b). A consideration of beliefs and their role in attitude measurement. In M. Fishbein (Ed.), *Readings in attitude theory and measurement* (pp. 257–266). New York: Wiley.

Fishbein, M. (1971). Attitudes and the prediction of behaviour. In K. Thomas (Ed.), *Attitudes and behaviour* (pp. 52–83). London: Penguin.

Fishbein, M., & Ajzen, I. (1974). Attitudes toward objects as predictors of single and multiple behavior criteria. *Psychological Review, 81,* 59–74.

Fishbein, M., & Ajzen, I. (1975). *Belief, attitude, intention and behavior: An introduction to theory and research.* Reading, MA: Addison-Wesley.

Fishbein, M., Ajzen, I., & Hinkle, R. (1980). Predicting and understanding voting in American elections: Effects of external variables. In I. Ajzen & M. Fishbein (Eds.), *Understanding attitudes and predicting human behavior* (pp. 173–195). Englewood Cliffs, NJ: Prentice Hall.

Fishbein, M., Bowman, C. H., Thomas, K., Jacard, J. J., & Ajzen, I. (1980). Predicting and understanding voting in British elections and American referenda: Illustrations of the theory's generality. In I. Ajzen & M. Fishbein (Eds.), *Understanding attitudes and predicting human behavior* (pp. 196–216). Englewood Cliffs, NJ: Prentice Hall.

Fishbein, M., & Coombs, F. S. (1974). Basis for decision: An attitudinal analysis of voting behavior. *Journal of Applied Social Psychology, 4,* 95–124.

Fishbein, M., & Feldman, S. (1963). Social psychological studies in voting behavior: I. Theoretical and methodological considerations. *American Psychologist, 18,* 388.

Fisher, J. D., Rytting, M., & Heslin, R. (1976). Hands touching hands: Affective and evaluative effects of an interpersonal touch. *Sociometry, 39,* 416–421.

Fisher, R. J. (1990). *The social psychology of intergroup and international conflict resolution.* New York: Springer-Verlag.

Fisher, S., & Todd, A. D. (1983). *The social organization of doctor–patient communication.* Washington, DC: Centre for Applied Linguistics.

Fishman, J. A. (1972). *Language and nationalism.* Rowley, MA: Newbury House.

Fishman, J. A. (1989). *Language and ethnicity in minority sociolinguistic perspective.* Clevedon: Multilingual Matters.

Fiske, A. P. (1992). The four elementary forms of sociality: Framework for a unified theory of social relations. *Psychological Review, 99,* 689–723.

Fiske, A. P., & Haslam, N. (1996). Social cognition is thinking about relationships. *Current Directions in Psychological Science, 5,* 143–148.

Fiske, A. P., Kitayama, S., Markus, H. R., & Nisbett, R. E. (1998). The cultural matrix of social psychology. In D. T. Gilbert, S. T. Fiske, & G. Lindzey (Eds.), *The handbook of social psychology* (4th ed., Vol. 2, pp. 915–981). New York: McGraw-Hill.

Fiske, S. T. (1980). Attention and weight on person perception. *Journal of Personality and Social Psychology, 38,* 889–906.

Fiske, S. T. (1993a). Social cognition and social perception. *Annual Review of Psychology, 44,* 155–194.

Fiske, S. T. (1993b). Controlling other people: The impact of power on stereotyping. *American Psychologist, 48,* 621–628.

Fiske, S. T. (1998). Stereotyping, prejudice, and discrimination. In D. T. Gilbert, S. T. Fiske, & G. Lindzey (Eds.), *The handbook of social psychology* (4th ed., Vol. 2, pp. 357–414). New York: McGraw-Hill.

Fiske, S. T., & Dépret, E. (1996). Control, interdependence and power: Understanding social cognition in its social context. *European Review of Social Psychology, 7,* 31–61.

Fiske, S. T., Lau, R. R., & Smith, R. A. (1990). On the varieties and utilities of political expertise. *Social Cognition, 8,* 31–48.

Fiske, S. T., & Neuberg, S. L. (1990). A continuum of impression formation, from category-based to individuating processes: Influences of information and motivation on attention and interpretation. In L. Berkowitz (Ed.), *Advances in experimental social psychology* (Vol. 23, pp. 1–74). New York: Academic Press.

Fiske, S. T., & Taylor, S. E. (1991). *Social cognition* (2nd ed.). New York: McGraw-Hill.

Fitness, J. (2001). Emotional intelligence in intimate relationships. In J. Ciarrochi, J. Forgas, & J. Mayer (Eds.), *Emotional intelligence in everyday life: A scientific enquiry* (pp. 98–112). Philadelphia: Taylor & Francis.

Fitness, J., & Fletcher, G. J. O. (1993). Love, hate, anger, and jealousy in close relationships: A cognitive appraisal and prototype analysis. *Journal of Personality and Social Psychology, 65,* 942–958.

Fitness, J., Fletcher, G., & Overall, N. (2003). Interpersonal attraction and intimate relationships. In M. A. Hogg & J. Cooper (Eds.), *The Sage handbook of social psychology* (pp. 258–278). London: Sage.

Fleishman, E. A. (1973). Twenty years of consideration and structure. In E. A. Fleishman & J. F. Hunt (Eds.), *Current developments in the study of leadership.* Carbondale, IL: South Illinois University Press.

Fletcher, G. J. O., & Clark, M. S. (Eds.). (2001). *Blackwell handbook of social psychology: Interpersonal processes.* Oxford, UK: Blackwell.

Fletcher, G. J. O., Danilovics, P., Fernandez, G., Peterson, D., & Reeder, G. D. (1986). Attributional complexity: An individual differences measure. *Journal of Personality and Social Psychology, 51,* 875–884.

Fletcher, G. J. O., Fincham, F. D., Cramer, L., & Heron, N. (1987). The role of attributions in the development of dating relationships. *Journal of Personality and Social Psychology, 53,* 481–489.

Fletcher, G. J. O., & Thomas, G. (2000). Behavior and on-line cognition in marital interaction. *Personal Relationships, 7,* 111–130.

Fletcher, G. J. O., & Ward, C. (1988). Attribution theory and processes: A cross-cultural perspective. In M. H. Bond (Ed.), *The cross-cultural challenge to social psychology* (pp. 230–244). Newbury Park, CA: Sage.

Flowers, M. L. (1977). A laboratory test of some implications of Janis's groupthink hypothesis. *Journal of Personality and Social Psychology, 35,* 888–896.

Floyd, D. L., Prentice-Dunn, S., & Rogers, R. W. (2000). A meta-analysis of research on protection motivation theory. *Journal of Applied Social Psychology, 30,* 407–429.

Foa, E. B., & Foa, U. G. (1975). *Resource theory of social exchange.* Morristown, NJ: General Learning Press.

Foddy, M., Smithson, M., Schneider, S., & Hogg, M. A. (Eds.). (1999). *Resolving social dilemmas: Dynamic, structural, and intergroup aspects.* Philadelphia, PA: Psychology Press.

Fodor, E. M., & Smith, T. (1982). The power motive as an influence on group decision making. *Journal of Personality and Social Psychology, 42,* 178–185.

Fogelson, R. M. (1970). Violence and grievances: Reflections on the 1960s riots. *Journal of Social Issues, 26,* 141–163.

Fong, G. T., Krantz, D. H., & Nisbett, R. E. (1986). The effects of statistical training on thinking about everyday problems. *Cognitive Psychology, 18,* 253–292.

Forgas, J. P. (Ed.) (1981). *Social cognition: Perspectives on everyday understanding.* London: Academic Press.

Forgas, J. P. (1983). The effects of prototypicality and cultural salience on perceptions of people. *Journal of Research in Personality, 17,* 153–173.

Forgas, J. P. (1985a). Person prototypes and cultural salience: The role of cognitive and cultural factors in impression formation. *British Journal of Social Psychology, 24,* 3–17.

Forgas, J. P. (1985b). *Interpersonal behaviour.* Sydney: Pergamon.

Forgas, J. P. (1994). The role of emotion in social judgments: An introductory review and an affect infusion model (AIM). *European Journal of Social Psychology, 24,* 1–24.

Forgas, J. P. (1995). Mood and judgment: The affect infusion model. *Psychological Bulletin, 117,* 39–66.

Forgas, J. P. (2002). Feeling and doing: Affective influences on interpersonal behavior. *Psychological Inquiry, 13,* 1–28.

Forgas, J. P., & Dobosz, B. (1980). Dimensions of romantic involvement: Towards a taxonomy of heterosexual relationships. *Social Psychology Quarterly, 43,* 290–300.

Forgas, J. P., & Fiedler, K. (1996). Us and them: Mood effects on intergroup discrimination. *Journal of Personality and Social Psychology, 70,* 36–52.

Forgas, J. P., Morris, S., & Furnham, A. (1982). Lay explanations of wealth: Attributions for economic success. *Journal of Applied Social Psychology, 12,* 381–397.

Forgas, J. P., O'Connor, K., & Morris, S. (1983). Smile and punishment: The effects of facial expression on responsibility attributions by groups and individuals. *Personality and Social Psychology Bulletin, 9,* 587–596.

Forgas, J. P., & Smith, C. A. (2003). Affect and emotion. In M. A. Hogg & J. Cooper (Eds.), *The Sage handbook of social psychology* (pp. 161–189). London: Sage.

Forsterling, F. (1988). *Attribution theory in clinical psychology.* Chichester, UK: Wiley.

Forsterling, F. & Rudolph, U. (1988). Situations, attributions and the evaluation of reactions. *Journal of Personality and Social Psychology, 54,* 225–232.

Foss, R. D., & Dempsey, C. B. (1979). Blood donation and the foot-in-the-door technique. *Journal of Personality and Social Psychology, 37,* 580–590.

Foucault, M. (1972). *The archaeology of knowledge.* London: Tavistock.

Fox, S., & Hoffman, M. (2002). Escalation behavior as a specific case of goal-directed activity: A persistence paradigm. *Basic and Applied Social Psychology, 24,* 273–285.

Fox, S. A., & Giles, H. (1993). Accommodating intergenerational contact: A critique and theoretical model. *Journal of Aging Studies, 7,* 423–451.

Fox, S. A., & Giles, H. (1996a). 'Let the wheelchair through!': An intergroup approach to interability communication. In W. P. Robinson (Ed.), *Social groups and identities: Developing the legacy of Henri Tajfel* (pp. 215–248). Oxford, UK: Butterworth-Heinemann.

Fox, S. A., & Giles, H. (1996b). Interability communication: Evaluating patronizing encounters. *Journal of Language and Social Psychology, 15,* 265–290.

Fox-Cardamone, L., Hinkle, S., & Hogue, M. (2000). The correlates of antinuclear activism: Attitudes, subjective norms, and efficacy. *Journal of Applied Social Psychology, 30,* 484–498.

Franco, F. M., & Maass, A. (1996). Implicit versus explicit strategies of outgroup discrimination: The role of intentional control in biased language use and reward allocation. *Journal of Language and Social Psychology, 15,* 335–359.

Frank, M. G., & Gilovich, T. (1989). Effect of memory perspective on retrospective causal attributions. *Journal of Personality and Social Psychology, 57,* 399–403.

Franklin, K. (2000) Antigay behaviours among young adults: Prevalence, patterns, and motivators in a noncriminal population. *Journal of Interpersonal Violence, 15,* 339–362.

Frazer, J. G. (1890). *The golden bough.* London: Macmillan.

Fredericks, A. J., & Dossett, D. L. (1983). Attitude–behavior relations: A comparison of the Fishbein–Ajzen and the Bentler–Speckart models. *Journal of Personality and Social Psychology, 45,* 501–512.

Freed, R. S., & Freed, S. A. (1989). Beliefs and practices resulting in female deaths and fewer females than males in India. *Population and Environment, 10,* 144–161.

Freedman, J. L. (1984). Effect of television violence on aggressiveness. *Psychological Bulletin, 96,* 227–246.

Freedman, J. L., & Fraser, S. C. (1966). Compliance without pressure: The foot-in-the-door technique. *Journal of Personality and Social Psychology, 4,* 195–202.

Freedman, J. L., Wallington, S. A., & Bless, E. (1967). Compliance without pressure: The effect of guilt. *Journal of Personality and Social Psychology, 7,* 117–124.

Freeman, S., Walker, M. R., Bordon, R., & Latané, B. (1975). Diffusion of responsibility and restaurant tipping: Cheaper by the bunch. *Personality and Social Psychology Bulletin, 1,* 584–587.

Freides, D. (1974). Human information processing and sensory modality: Cross-modal functions, information complexity, memory, and deficit. *Psychological Bulletin, 81,* 284–310.

French, J. R. P. (1944). Organised and unorganised groups under fear and frustration. *University of Iowa Studies of Child Welfare, 20,* 231–308.

French, J. R. P., & Raven, B. H. (1959). The bases of social power. In D. Cartwright (Ed.), *Studies in social power* (pp. 118–149). Ann Arbor, MI: Institute for Social Research.

Freud, S. (1905). *Three contributions to the theory of sex.* New York: Dutton.

Freud, S. (1921). Group psychology and the analysis of the ego. In J. Strachey (Ed.), *Standard edition of the complete psychological works* (Vol. 18, pp. 1953–1964). London: Hogarth Press.

Freud, S. (1930). *Civilization and its discontents.* London: Hogarth Press.

Frick, R. W. (1985). Communication emotions: The role of prosodic features. *Psychological Bulletin, 97,* 412–429.

Frieze, I., & Weiner, B. (1971). Cue utilisation and attributional judgments for success and failure. *Journal of Personality, 39,* 591–605.

Frohlich, N., & Oppenheimer, J. (1970). I get by with a little help from my friends. *World Politics, 23,* 104–120.

Fromm, E. (1941). *Escape from freedom.* New York: Farrar & Rinehart.

Funder, D. C. (1982). On the accuracy of dispositional vs. situational attributions. *Social Cognition, 1,* 205–222.

Funder, D. C. (1987). Errors and mistakes: Evaluating the accuracy of social judgment. *Psychological Bulletin, 101,* 75–90.

Furnham, A. (1982). Explanations for unemployment in Britain. *European Journal of Social Psychology, 12,* 335–352.

Furnham, A. (1983). Attributions for affluence. *Personality and Individual Differences, 4,* 31–40.

Furnham, A. (1986). Some explanations for immigration to, and emigration from, Britain. *New Community, 13,* 65–78.

Furnham, A., & Bond, M. H. (1986). Hong Kong Chinese explanations for wealth. *Journal of Economic Psychology, 7,* 447–460.

Gaertner, S. L., & Dovidio, J. F. (1977). The subtlety of white racism, arousal, and helping behavior. *Journal of Personality and Social Psychology, 35,* 691–707.

Gaertner, S. L., & Dovidio, J. F. (1986). The aversive form of racism. In J. F. Dovidio & S. L. Gaertner (Eds.), *Prejudice, discrimination, and racism* (pp. 61–89). New York: Academic Press.

Gaertner S. L., & Dovidio, J. F. (2000). *Reducing intergroup bias: The common ingroup identity model.* New York: Psychology Press.

Gaertner, S. L., Dovidio, J., Anastasio, P., Bachman, B., & Rust, M. (1993). The common ingroup identity model: Recategorization and the reduction of intergroup bias. *European Review of Social Psychology, 4,* 1–26.

Gaertner, S. L., Mann, J., Murrell, A., & Dovidio, J. F. (1989). Reducing intergroup bias: The benefits of recategorization. *Journal of Personality and Social Psychology, 57,* 239–249.

Gaertner, S. L., & McLaughlin, J. P. (1983). Racial stereotypes: Associations and ascriptions of positive and negative characteristics. *Social Psychology Quarterly, 46,* 23–40.

Gaertner, S. L., Rust, M. C., Dovidio, J. F., Bachman, B. A., & Anastasio, P. A. (1996). The contact hypothesis: The role of a common ingroup identity on reducing intergroup bias among majority and minority group members. In J. L. Nye & A. M. Bower (Eds.), *What's social about social cognition: Research on socially shared cognition in small groups* (pp. 230–260). Thousand Oaks, CA: Sage.

Galinsky, A. D. (2002). Creating and reducing intergroup conflict: The role of perspective-taking in affecting out-group evaluations. In H. Sondak (Ed.), *Toward phenomenology of groups and group membership. Research on managing groups and teams* (Vol. 4, pp. 85–113). New York: Elsevier.

Galinsky, A. D., & Moskowitz, G. B. (2000). Perspective-taking: Decreasing stereotype expression, stereotype accessibility, and in-group favoritism. *Journal of Personality and Social Psychology, 78*, 708–724.

Galinsky, A. D., & Mussweiler, T. (2001). First offers as anchors: The role of perspective-taking and negotiator focus. *Journal of Personality and Social Psychology, 81*, 657–669.

Galizio, M., & Hendrick, C. (1972). Effect of musical accompaniment on attitude: The guitar as a prop for persuasion. *Journal of Applied Social Psychology, 2*, 350–359.

Gallois, C. (1993). The language and communication of emotion: Interpersonal, intergroup, or universal. *American Behavioral Scientist, 36*, 309–338.

Gallois, C., Barker, M., Jones, E., & Callan, V. J. (1992). Intercultural communication: Evaluations of lecturers and Australian and Chinese students. In S. Iwawaki, Y. Kashima, & K. Leung (Eds.), *Innovations in cross-cultural psychology* (pp. 86–102). Amsterdam: Swets & Zeitlinger.

Gallois, C., & Callan, V. J. (1986). Decoding emotional messages: Influence of ethnicity, sex, message type, and channel. *Journal of Personality and Social Psychology, 51*, 755–762.

Gallois, C., & Callan, V. J. (1997). *Communication and culture: A guide for practice.* Chichester: John Wiley & Sons.

Gallois, C., Callan, V. J., & Johnstone, M. (1984). Personality judgements of Australian Aborigine and white speakers: Ethnicity, sex and context. *Journal of Language and Social Psychology, 3*, 39–57.

Gallois, C., Giles, H., Jones, C., Cargile, A., & Ota, G. (1995). Accommodating intercultural encounters: Elaborations and extensions. In R. Wiseman (Ed.), *Theories of intercultural communication* (pp. 115–147). Thousand Oaks, CA: Sage.

Gallup, G. (1978). Gallup youth survey. *Indianapolis Star*, 18 October.

Gallupe, R. B., Cooper, W. H., Grise, M.-L., & Bastianutti, L. M. (1994). Blocking electronic brainstorms. *Journal of Applied Psychology, 79*, 77–86.

Gangestad, S. W., & Simpson, J. A. (2000). The evolution of human mating: Trade-offs and strategic pluralism. *Behavioral and Brain Sciences, 23*, 573–644.

Gao, G. (1996). Self and other: A Chinese perspective on interpersonal relationships. In W. B. Gudykunst, S. Ting-Toomey, & T. Nishida (Eds.), *Communication in personal relationships across cultures* (pp. 81–101). Thousand Oaks, CA: Sage.

Gao, G., Ting-Toomey, S., & Gudykunst, W. B. (1996). Chinese communication processes. In M. H. Bond (Ed.), *Handbook of Chinese psychology* (pp. 280–293). Hong Kong: Oxford University Press.

Gardner, R. A., & Gardner, B. T. (1971). Teaching sign language to a chimpanzee. *Science, 165*, 664–672.

Gardner, R. C. (1979). Social psychological aspects of second language acquisition. In H. Giles & R. St Clair (Eds.), *Language and social psychology* (pp. 193–220). Oxford: Blackwell.

Gardner, R. M., & Tockerman, Y. R. (1994). A computer-TV methodology for investigating the influence of somatotype on perceived

personality traits. *Journal of Social Behavior and Personality, 9*, 555–563.

Garfinkel, H. (1967). *Studies in ethnomethodology.* Englewood Cliffs, NJ: Prentice Hall.

Garrett, P., Giles, H., & Coupland, N. (1989). The contexts of language learning: Extending the intergroup model of second language acquisition. In S. Ting-Toomey & F. Korzenny (Eds.), *Language, communication, and culture* (pp. 201–221). Newbury Park, CA: Sage.

Gaskell, G., & Smith, P. (1985). An investigation of youths' attributions for unemployment and their political attitudes. *Journal of Economic Psychology, 6*, 65–80.

Geen, R. G. (1968). Effects of frustration, attack, and prior training in aggressiveness upon aggressive behavior. *Journal of Personality and Social Psychology, 9*, 316–321.

Geen, R. G. (1978). Some effects of observing violence on the behaviour of the observer. In B. A. Maher (Ed.), *Progress in experimental personality research* (Vol. 8, pp. 49–93). New York: Academic Press.

Geen, R. G. (1989). Alternative conceptions of social facilitation. In P.B. Paulus (Ed.), *Psychology of group influence* (2nd ed., pp. 15–51). Hillsdale, NJ: Erlbaum.

Geen, R. G. (1991). Social motivation. *Annual Review of Psychology, 42*, 377–399.

Geen, R. G. (1998). Aggression and antisocial behaviour. In D. T. Gilbert, S. T. Fiske, & G. Lindzey (Eds.), *The handbook of social psychology* (4th ed., Vol. 2, pp. 317–356). New York: McGraw-Hill.

Geen, R. G., & Donnerstein, E. (Eds.). (1983). *Aggression: Theoretical and empirical reviews.* New York: Academic Press.

Geen, R. G., & Gange, J. J. (1977). Drive theory of social facilitation: Twelve years of theory and research. *Psychological Bulletin, 84*, 1267–1288.

Geen, R. G., & Quanty, M. (1977). The catharsis of aggression: An evaluation of a hypothesis. In L. Berkowitz (Ed.), *Advances in experimental social psychology* (Vol. 10, pp. 2–37). New York: Academic Press.

Geer, J. H., & Jarmecky, L. (1973). The effect of being responsible for reducing another's pain on subject's response and arousal. *Journal of Personality and Social Psychology, 26*, 232–237.

Geertz, C. (1975). On the nature of anthropological understanding. *American Scientist, 63*, 47–53.

Gelfand, D. M., Hartmann, D. P., Walder, P., & Page, B. (1973). Who reports shoplifters? A field-experimental study. *Journal of Personality and Social Psychology, 25*, 276–285.

Genta, M. L., Menesini, E., Fonzi, A., Costabile, A., & Smith, P. K. (1996). Bullies and victims in schools in Central and South Italy. *European Journal of Psychology of Education, 11*, 97–110.

Gerard, H. B., & Hoyt, M. F. (1974). Distinctiveness of social categorisation and attitude toward ingroup members. *Journal of Personality and Social Psychology, 29*, 836–842.

Gerard, H. B., & Mathewson, G. C. (1966). The effects of severity of initiation on liking for a group: A replication. *Journal of Experimental Social Psychology, 2*, 278–287.

Gergen, K. J. (1971). *The concept of self.* New York: Holt, Rinehart & Winston.

Gergen, K. J. (1973). Social psychology as history. *Journal of Personality and Social Psychology, 26*, 309–320.

Gergen, K. J., Gergen, M. M., & Meter, K. (1972). Individual orientations to prosocial behavior. *Journal of Social Issues, 28*, 105–130.

Gersick, C. J., & Hackman, J. R. (1990). Habitual routines in task performing groups. *Organizational Behavior and Human Decision Processes, 47,* 65–97.

Gigone, D., & Hastie, R. (1993). The common knowledge effect: Information sharing and group judgment. *Journal of Personality and Social Psychology, 65,* 959–974.

Gilbert, D. T. (1995). Attribution and interpersonal perception. In A. Tesser (Ed.), *Advanced social psychology* (pp. 99–147). New York: McGraw-Hill.

Gilbert, D. T. (1998). Ordinary personology. In D. T. Gilbert, S. T. Fiske, & G. Lindzey (Eds.), *The handbook of social psychology* (4th ed., Vol. 2, pp. 89–150). New York: McGraw-Hill.

Gilbert, D. T., Fiske, S. T., & Lindzey, G. (Eds.). (1998). *The handbook of social psychology* (4th ed.). New York: McGraw-Hill.

Gilbert, D. T., & Malone, P. S. (1995). The correspondence bias. *Psychological Bulletin, 117,* 21–38.

Gilbert, D. T., & Silvera, D. H. (1996). Overhelping. *Journal of Personality and Social Psychology, 70,* 678–690.

Giles, H. (1978). Linguistic differentiation in ethnic groups. In H. Tajfel (Ed.), *Differentiation between social groups: studies in the social psychology of intergroup relations* (pp. 361–393). London: Academic Press.

Giles, H. (Ed.). (1984). The dynamics of speech accommodation theory. *International Journal of the Sociology of Language, 46,* whole issue.

Giles, H., Bourhis, R. Y., & Taylor, D. M. (1977). Towards a theory of language in ethnic group relations. In H. Giles (Ed.), *Language, ethnicity, and intergroup relations* (pp. 307–348). London: Academic Press.

Giles, H., & Byrne, J. L. (1982). The intergroup model of second language acquisition. *Journal of Multilingual and Multicultural Development, 3,* 17–40.

Giles, H., & Coupland, N. (1991). *Language: Contexts and consequences.* Milton Keynes, UK: Open University Press.

Giles, H., Coupland, N., Henwood, K., Harriman, J., & Coupland, J. (1990). The social meaning of RP: An intergenerational perspective. In S. Ramsaran (Ed.), *Studies in the pronunciation of English: A commemorative volume in honour of A.C. Gimson* (pp. 191–211). London: Routledge.

Giles, H., & Johnson, P. (1981). The role of language in ethnic group relations. In J. C. Turner & H. Giles (Eds.), *Intergroup behaviour* (pp. 199–243). Oxford: Blackwell.

Giles, H., & Johnson, P. (1987). Ethnolinguistic identity theory: A social psychological approach to language maintenance. *International Journal of the Sociology of Language, 68,* 66–99.

Giles, H., Mulac, A., Bradac, J. J., & Johnson, P. (1987). Speech accommodation theory: The next decade and beyond. In *Communication yearbook* (Vol. 10, pp. 13–48). Newbury Park, CA: Sage.

Giles, H., & Noels, K. A. (2002). Communication accommodation in intercultural encounters. In T. K. Nakayama & L. A. Flores (Eds.), *Readings in cultural contexts* (pp. 117–126). Boston: McGraw-Hill.

Giles, H., Noels, K., Ota, H., Ng, S. H., Gallois, C., Ryan, E. B., et al. (2001). Age vitality in eleven nations. *Journal of Multilingual and Multicultural Development, 21,* 308–323.

Giles, H., & Powesland, P. F. (1975). *Speech style and social evaluation.* London: Academic Press.

Giles, H., Rosenthal, D., & Young, L. (1985). Perceived ethnolinguistic vitality: The Anglo- and Greek-Australian setting. *Journal of Multilingual and Multicultural Development, 6,* 253–269.

Giles, H., & Street, R. (1985). Communicator characteristics and behaviour. In M. L. Knapp & G. R. Miller (Eds.), *Handbook of interpersonal communication* (pp. 205–261). Beverly Hills, CA: Sage.

Giles, H., Taylor, D. M., & Bourhis, R. Y. (1973). Towards a theory of interpersonal accommodation through language: Some Canadian data. *Language in Society, 2,* 177–192.

Gladue, B. (1991). Aggressive behavioral characteristics, hormones, and sexual orientation in men and women. *Aggressive Behavior, 17,* 313–326.

Gladue, B. A., Boechler, M., & McCall, K. D. (1989). Hormonal response to competition in human males. *Aggressive Behavior, 15,* 409–422.

Glaser, J., & Banaji, M. R. (1999). When fair is foul and foul is fair: Reverse priming in automatic evaluation. *Journal of Personality and Social Psychology, 77,* 669–687.

Glenn, E. S. (1976). Meaning and behaviour: Communication and culture. In L. A. Samovar & R. E. Porter (Eds.), *Intercultural communication: A reader* (2nd ed., pp. 170–193). Belmont, CA: Wadsworth.

Glick, P., & Fiske, S. T. (1996). The Ambivalent Sexism Inventory: Differentiating hostile and benevolent sexism. *Journal of Personality and Social Psychology, 70,* 491–512.

Glick, P., & Fiske, S. T. (1997). Hostile and benevolent sexism: Measuring ambivalent sexist attitudes toward women. *Psychology of Women Quarterly, 21,* 119–135.

Godin, G., Valois, P., Lepage, L., & Desharnais, R. (1992). Predictors of smoking behaviour: An application of Ajzen's theory of planned behaviour. *British Journal of Addiction, 87,* 1335–1343.

Goethals, G. R., & Darley, J. M. (1987). Social comparison theory: Self-evaluation and group life. In B. Mullen & G. Goethals (Eds.), *Theories of group behavior* (pp. 21–48). New York: Springer-Verlag.

Goethals, G. R., & Nelson, R. E. (1973). Similarity in the influence process: The belief–value distinction. *Journal of Personality and Social Psychology, 25,* 117–122.

Goethals, G. R., & Sorenson, G. (Eds.). (2004). *Encyclopedia of leadership.* Thousand Oaks, CA: Sage.

Goethals, G. R., & Zanna, M. P. (1979). The role of social comparison in choice shifts. *Journal of Personality and Social Psychology, 37,* 1469–1476.

Goffman, E. (1959). *The presentation of self in everyday life.* New York: Doubleday Anchor.

Goffman, E. (1963). *Stigma: Notes on the management of spoiled identity.* Englewood-Cliffs, NJ: Prentice Hall.

Goldberg, M. E., & Gorn, G. J. (1974). Children's reactions to television advertising: An experimental approach. *Journal of Consumer Research, 1,* 69–75.

Goldberg, P. (1968). Are some women prejudiced against women? *Trans-Action, 5,* 28–30.

Goldman, M., Creason, C. R., & McCall, C. G. (1981). Compliance employing a two-feet-in-the-door procedure. *Journal of Social Psychology, 114,* 259–265.

Goldstein, A. P. (1987). Aggression. In R. J. Corsini (Ed.), *Concise encyclopedia of psychology* (pp. 35–39). New York: Wiley.

Goldstein, J. H. (1980). *Social psychology.* New York: Academic Press.

Gollwitzer, P. M., & Bargh, J. A. (Eds.). (1996). *The psychology of action: Linking cognition and motivation to behavior.* New York: Guilford.

Gollwitzer, P. M., & Kinney, R. F. (1989). Effects of deliberative and implemental mind-sets on illusion of control. *Journal of Personality and Social Psychology, 56*, 531–542.

Goodman, M. E. (1946). Evidence concerning the genesis of interracial attitudes. *American Anthropologist, 38*, 624–630.

Goodman, M. E. (1952). *Race awareness in young children.* Cambridge: Addison-Wesley.

Goodman, M. E. (1964). *Race awareness in young children* (2nd ed.). New York: Cromwell-Collier.

Goodwin, R. (1999). *Personal relationships across cultures.* London: Routledge.

Goodwin, S. A., Gubin, A., Fiske, S. T., & Yzerbyt, V. Y. (2000). Power can bias impression processes: Stereotyping subordinates by default and by design. *Group Processes and Intergroup Relations, 3*, 227–256.

Gorassini, D. R., & Olson, J. M. (1995). Does self-perception change explain the foot-in-the-door effect? *Journal of Personality and Social Psychology, 69*, 91–105.

Gordon, R. A. (1996). Impact of ingratiation on judgments and evaluations: A meta-analytic investigation. *Journal of Personality and Social Psychology, 71*, 54–70.

Gorer, G. (1968). Man has no 'killer' instinct. In M. F. A. Montagu (Ed.), *Man and aggression* (pp. 27–36). New York: Oxford University Press.

Gorn, G. J. (1982). The effects of music in advertising on choice: A classical conditioning approach. *Journal of Marketing, 46*, 94–101.

Gorsuch, R. L., & Ortbergh, J. (1983). Moral obligation and attitudes: Their relation to behavioral intentions. *Journal of Personality and Social Psychology, 44*, 1025–1028.

Gosselin, C., & Wilson, G. (1980). *Sexual variations.* New York: Simon & Schuster.

Gottlieb, J., & Carver, C. S. (1980). Anticipation of future interaction and the bystander effect. *Journal of Experimental Social Psychology, 16*, 253–260.

Gouldner, A. W. (1960). The norm of reciprocity: A preliminary statement. *American Sociological Review, 25*, 161–178.

Graen, G. B., & Uhl-Bien, M. (1995). Relationship-based approach to leadership: Development of leader–member exchange (LMX) theory of leadership over 25 years: Applying a multi-level multi-domain approach. *Leadership Quarterly, 6*, 219–247.

Graham, S., Hudley C., & Williams, E. (1992). An attributional approach to aggression in African-American children. *Developmental Psychology, 28*, 731–740.

Granberg, D. (1987). Candidate preference, membership group, and estimates of voting behavior. *Social Cognition, 5*, 323–335.

Graumann, C. F., & Moscovici, S. (Eds.). (1986). *Changing conceptions of crowd mind and behavior.* New York: Springer-Verlag.

Graumann, C. F., & Moscovici, S. (Eds.). (1987). *Changing conceptions of conspiracy.* New York: Springer-Verlag.

Green, D. P., Glaser, J., & Rich, A. (1998). From lynching to gay bashing: The elusive connection between economic conditions and hate crime. *Journal of Personality and Social Psychology, 75*, 82–92.

Greenberg, J., Pyszczynski, T., & Solomon, S. (1986). The causes and consequences of self-esteem: A terror management theory. In R. Baumeister (Ed.), *Public self and private self* (pp. 189–212). New York: Springer-Verlag.

Greenberg, J., & Rosenfield, D. (1979). Whites' ethnocentrism and their attributions for the behavior of blacks: A motivational bias. *Journal of Personality, 47*, 643–657.

Greenberg, J., Solomon, S., & Pyszczynski, T. (1997). Terror management theory of self-esteem and cultural worldviews: Empirical assessments and conceptual refinements. In M. Zanna (Ed.), *Advances in experimental social psychology* (Vol. 29, pp. 61–139). Orlando, FL: Academic Press.

Greenberg, J., Solomon, S., Pyszczynski, T., Rosenblatt, A., Burling, J., Lyon, D., Simon, L., & Pinel, E. (1992). Why do people need self-esteem? Converging evidence that self-esteem serves an anxiety-buffering function. *Journal of Personality and Social Psychology, 63*, 913–922.

Greenberg, J., Williams, K. D., & O'Brien, M. K. (1986). Considering the harshest verdict first: Biasing effects on mock juror verdict. *Personality and Social Psychology Bulletin, 12*, 41–50.

Greenfield, P. M., Keller, H., Fuligni, A., & Maynard, A. (2003). Cultural pathways through universal development. *Annual Review of Psychology, 54*, 461–490.

Greenglass, E. R. (1982). *A world of difference: Gender roles in perspective.* Toronto: Wiley.

Greenwald, A. G. (1980). The totalitarian ego: Fabrication and revision of personal history. *American Psychologist, 35*, 603–618.

Greenwald, A. G., & Banaji, M. R. (1995). Implicit social cognition: Attitudes, self-esteem, and stereotypes. *Psychological Review, 102*, 4–27.

Greenwald, A. G., Banaji, M. R., Rudman, L. A., Farnham, S. D., Nosek, B. A., & Mellott, D. S. (2002). A unified theory of implicit attitudes, stereotypes, self-esteem, and self-concept. *Psychological Review, 109*, 3–25.

Greenwald, A. G., McGhee, D. E., & Schwartz, J. L. K. (1998). Measuring individual differences in implicit cognition: The Implicit Association Test. *Journal of Personality and Social Psychology, 74*, 1464–1480.

Greenwald, A. G., & Pratkanis, A. R. (1984). The self. In R. S. Wyer, Jr. & T. K. Srull (Eds.), *Handbook of social cognition* (Vol. 3, pp. 129–178). Hillsdale, NJ: Erlbaum.

Greenwald, A. G., & Pratkanis, A. R. (1988). On the use of 'theory' and the usefulness of theory. *Psychological Review, 95*, 575–579.

Gregson, R. A. M., & Stacey, B. G. (1980). Components of some New Zealand attitudes to alcohol and drinking in 1978–79: A preliminary report. *New Zealand Psychologist, 9*, 29–33.

Gregson, R. A. M., & Stacey, B. G. (1981). Attitudes and self-reported alcohol consumption in New Zealand. *New Zealand Psychologist, 10*, 15–23.

Grieve, P., & Hogg, M. A. (1999). Subjective uncertainty and intergroup discrimination in the minimal group situation. *Personality and Social Psychology Bulletin, 25*, 926–940.

Griffit, W. B., & Guay, P. (1969). 'Object' evaluation and conditioned affect. *Journal of Experimental Research in Psychology, 4*, 1–8.

Griffit, W. B., & Veitch, R. (1971). Hot and crowded: Influence of population density and temperature on interpersonal affective behavior. *Journal of Personality and Social Psychology, 17*, 92–98.

Griffiths, M. (1997). Video games and aggression. *The Psychologist,* September, 397–401.

Groff, B. D., Baron, R. S., & Moore, D. L. (1983). Distraction, attentional conflict, and drivelike behavior. *Journal of Experimental Social Psychology, 19*, 359–380.

Gross, A. E., & Fleming, J. (1982). Twenty years of deception in social psychology. *Personality and Social Psychology Bulletin, 8*, 402–408.

Gross, A. E., Wallston, B. S., & Piliavin, I. M. (1975). Beneficiary attractiveness and cost as determinants of responses to routine requests for help. *Sociometry, 38*, 131–140.

Gruber-Baldini, A. L., Schaie, K. W., & Willis, S. L. (1995). Similarity in married couples: A longitudinal study of mental abilities and rigidity–flexibility. *Journal of Personality and Social Psychology, 69*, 191–203.

Grusec, J. E. (1991). The socialisation of altruism. In M. S. Clark (Ed.), *Prosocial behaviour* (pp. 9–33). Newbury Park, CA: Sage.

Grusec, J. E., & Redler, E. (1980). Attribution, reinforcement and altruism: A developmental analysis. *Developmental Psychology, 16*, 525–534.

Grusec, J. E., & Skubiski, S. L. (1970). Model nurturance, demand characteristics of the modeling experiment, and altruism. *Journal of Personality and Social Psychology, 14*, 352–359.

Grusec, J. E., Kuczynski, L., Rushton, J. P., & Simutis, Z. M. (1978). Modelling, direct instruction, and attributions: Effects on altruism. *Developmental Psychology, 14*, 51–57.

Gubar, S., & Hoff, J. (Eds.). (1989). *For adult users only: The dilemma of violent pornography.* Bloomington, IN: Indiana University Press.

Gudykunst, W. B., Matsumoto, Y., Ting-Toomey, S., Nishida, T., Kim, K., & Heyman, S. (1996). The influence of cultural individualism–collectivism, self-construals, and individual values on communication styles across cultures. *Human Communication Research, 22*, 510–543.

Guerin, B. (1986). Mere presence effects in humans: A review. *Journal of Experimental Social Psychology, 22*, 38–77.

Guerin, B. (1989). Reducing evaluation effects in mere presence. *Journal of Social Psychology, 129*, 183–190.

Guerin, B. (1993). *Social facilitation.* Cambridge: Cambridge University Press.

Guerin, B., & Innes, J. M. (1982). Social facilitation and social monitoring: A new look at Zajonc's mere presence hypothesis. *British Journal of Social Psychology, 21*, 7–18.

Guimond, S., & Dubé-Simard, L. (1983). Relative deprivation theory and the Québec Nationalist Movement: The cognitive-emotion distinction and the personal-group deprivation issue. *Journal of Personality and Social Psychology, 44*, 526–535.

Gump, B. B., & Kulik, J. A. (1997). Stress, affiliation, and emotional contagion. *Journal of Personality and Social Psychology, 72*, 305–319.

Gupta, U., & Singh, P. (1982). An exploratory study of love and liking and types of marriages. *Indian Journal of Applied Psychology, 19*, 92–97.

Gurr, T. R. (1970). *Why men rebel.* Princeton, NJ: Princeton University Press.

Gustafson, R. (1992). Alcohol and aggression: A replication study controlling for potential confounding variables. *Aggressive Behavior, 18*, 21–28.

Gutek, B. A. (1985). *Sex and the workplace.* San Francisco, CA: Jossey-Bass.

Guttman, L. A. (1944). A basis for scaling qualitative data. *American Sociological Review, 9*, 139–150.

Guzzo, R. A., & Dickson, M. W. (1996). Teams in organizations: Recent research on performance and effectiveness. *Annual Review of Psychology, 47*, 307–338.

Guzzo, R. A., Jost, P. R., Campbell, R. J., & Shea, G. P. (1993). Potency in groups: Articulating a construct. *British Journal of Social Psychology, 32*, 87–106.

Haas, A. (1979). Male and female spoken language differences: Stereotypes and evidence. *Psychological Bulletin, 86*, 616–626.

Haddock, G., Rothman, A. J., Reber, R., & Schwarz, N. (1999). Forming judgements of attitude certainty, intensity, and impor-

tance: The role of subjective experiences. *Personality and Social Psychology Bulletin, 25*, 231–232.

Haines, H. (1980). *The origins of modern social psychology.* Unpublished doctoral dissertation, University of Auckland, Auckland.

Haines, H. (1987). *Mental health for women.* Auckland: Reed Methuen.

Haines, H., & Vaughan, G. M. (1979). Was 1898 a great date in the history of social psychology? *Journal for the History of the Behavioural Sciences, 15*, 323–332.

Hains, S. C., Hogg, M. A., & Duck, J. M. (1997). Self-categorization and leadership: Effects of group prototypicality and leader stereotypicality. *Personality and Social Psychology Bulletin, 23*, 1087–1100.

Haire, M., & Grune, W. E. (1950). Perceptual defenses: Processes protecting an organised perception of another personality. *Human Relations, 3*, 403–412.

Hale, J. L., Lemieux, R., & Mongeau, P. A. (1995). Cognitive processing of fear-arousing message content. *Communication Research, 22*, 459–474.

Hall, B. J., & Gudykunst, W. B. (1986). The intergroup theory of second language ability. *Journal of Language and Social Psychology, 5*, 291–302.

Hall, E. T. (1966). *The hidden dimension.* New York: Doubleday.

Hall, E. T. (1979). Gender, gender roles, and nonverbal communication. In R. Rosenthal (Ed.), *Skill in nonverbal communication* (pp. 32–67). Cambridge, MA: Oelgeschlager, Gunn & Hain.

Hall, E. T., & Braunwald, K. G. (1981). Gender cues in conversations. *Journal of Personality and Social Psychology, 40*, 99–110.

Hall, G. (1984). Women and violent crime: New Zealand 1950–1979. *Papers of the Women's Studies Association Conference*, no. 6. Christchurch.

Hall, J. A. (1978). Gender effects in decoding nonverbal cues. *Psychological Bulletin, 85*, 845–857.

Hall, J. A. (1984). *Nonverbal sex differences: Communication accuracy and expressive style.* Baltimore: Johns Hopkins University Press.

Halpern, D. (1995). *Mental health and the built environment: More than bricks and mortar?* London, UK: Taylor & Francis.

Hamburger, Y. (1994). The contact hypothesis reconsidered: Effects of the atypical outgroup member on the outgroup stereotype. *Basic and Allied Social Psychology, 15*, 339–358.

Hamermesh, D. S., & Biddle, J. E. (1994). Beauty and the labour market. *American Economic Review, 84*, 1174–1195.

Hamilton, D. L. (1979). A cognitive attributional analysis of stereotyping. In L. Berkowitz (Ed.), *Advances in experimental social psychology* (Vol. 12, pp. 53–84). New York: Academic Press.

Hamilton, D. L., & Gifford, R. K. (1976). Illusory correlation in interpersonal personal perception: A cognitive basis of stereotypic judgments. *Journal of Experimental Social Psychology, 12*, 392–407.

Hamilton, D. L., & Sherman, J. W. (1989). Illusory correlations: Implications for stereotype theory and research. In D. Bar-Tal, C. F. Graumann, A. W. Kruglanski & W. Stroebe (Eds.), *Stereotyping and prejudice: Changing conceptions* (pp. 59–82). New York: Springer-Verlag.

Hamilton, D. L., & Sherman, J. W. (1994). Stereotypes. In R. S. Wyer, Jr. & T. K. Srull (Eds.), *Handbook of social cognition* (Vol. 2, pp. 1–68). Hillsdale, NJ: Erlbaum.

Hamilton, D. L., & Sherman, S. J. (1996). Perceiving persons and groups. *Psychological Review, 103*, 336–355.

Hamilton, D. L., Stroessner, S. J., & Driscoll, D. M. (1994). Social cognition and the study of stereotyping. In P. G. Devine, D. L.

Hamilton, & T. M. Ostrom (Eds.), *Social cognition: Impact on social psychology* (pp. 291–321). San Diego, CA: Academic Press.

Hamilton, D. L., & Zanna, M. P. (1974). Context effects in impression formation: Changes in connotative meaning. *Journal of Personality and Social Psychology, 29,* 649–654.

Hampson, S. E., John, O. P., & Goldberg, L. R. (1986). Category breadth and hierarchical structure in personality: Studies in asymmetries in judgments of trait implications. *Journal of Personality and Social Psychology, 51,* 37–54.

Haney, C., Banks, C., & Zimbardo, P. (1973). Interpersonal dynamics in a simulated prison. *International Journal of Criminology and Penology, 1,* 69–97.

Hansen, S. (2000). *Social representation of the Internet and of Internet addiction.* Paper presented at the Society of Australasian Social Psychologists Conference, Fremantle.

Hardin, G. (1968). The tragedy of the commons. *Science, 162,* 1243–1248.

Harkins, S. G. (1987). Social loafing and social facilitation. *Journal of Experimental Social Psychology, 23,* 1–18.

Harkins, S. G., & Szymanski, K. (1987). Social loafing and social facilitation: New wine in old bottles. In C. Hendrick (Ed.), *Review of personality and social psychology: Group processes and intergroup relations* (Vol. 9, pp. 167–188). Newbury Park, CA: Sage.

Harkins, S. G., & Szymanski, K. (1989). Social loafing and group evaluation. *Journal of Personality and Social Psychology, 56,* 934–941.

Harland, A. (1995). *Victimisation in New Zealand.* Ministry of Justice New Zealand: Strategic Assessment Group.

Harlow, H. F. (1958). The nature of love. *American Psychologist, 13,* 673–685.

Harlow, H. F., & Harlow, M. K. (1965). The affectional systems. In A. M. Schrier, H. F. Harlow, & F. Stollnitz (Eds.), *Behavior of non-human primates* (Vol. 2). New York: Academic Press.

Harlow, H. F., & Zimmermann, R. R. (1959). Affectional responses in the infant monkey. *Science, 130,* 421.

Harmon-Jones, E. (2000). Cognitive dissonance and experienced negative affect: Evidence that dissonance increases experienced negative affect even in the absence of aversive consequences. *Personality and Social Psychology Bulletin, 27,* 889–898.

Harré, R. (1979). *Social being: A theory for social psychology.* Oxford: Blackwell.

Harries, K. D., & Stadler, S. J. (1983). Determinism revisited: Assault and heat stress in Dallas, 1980. *Environment and Behavior, 15,* 235–256.

Harris, E. E. (1970). *Hypothesis and perception.* London: Allen & Unwin.

Harris, N. B. (1992). Sex, race, and experiences of aggression. *Aggressive Behavior, 18,* 201–217.

Harris, R. J., & Cook C. A. (1994). Attributions about spouse abuse: It matters who the batterers and victims are. *Sex Roles, 30,* 553–564.

Hart, P. M., Wearing A. J., & Headey, B. (1994). Perceived quality of life, personality and work experience: Construct validation of the Police Daily Hassles and Uplifts Scales. *Criminal Justice and Behaviour, 27(3),* 283–311.

Hartman, T., & Mitchell, J. (1984). *A world atlas of military history 1945–1984.* London: Cooper/Secker & Warburg.

Hartmann, H., Kris, E., & Loewenstein, R. M. (1949). Notes on a theory of aggression. *Psychoanalytic Study of the Child, 3–4:* 9–36.

Harvey, J. H. (1987). Attributions in close relationships: Research and theoretical developments. *Journal of Social and Clinical Psychology, 5,* 420–434.

Harvey, J. H., & Weary, G. (1981). *Perspectives on attributional processes.* Dubuque, IA: W.C. Brown.

Harwood, J., Giles, H., & Bourhis, R. Y. (1994). The genesis of vitality theory: Historical patterns and discoursal dimensions. *International Journal of the Sociology of Language, 108,* 167–206.

Harwood, J., Giles, H., & Ryan, E. B. (1995). Aging, communication, and intergroup theory: Social identity and intergenerational communication. In J. Nussbaum & J. Coupland (Eds.), *Handbook of communication and aging research* (pp. 133–159). Mahwah, NJ: Erlbaum.

Haslam, N. (1995). Factor structure of social relationships: An examination of relational models and resource exchange theories. *Journal of Social and Personal Relationships, 12,* 217–227.

Haslam, S. A. (2000). *Psychology in organisations: The social identity approach.* London: Sage.

Haslam, S. A., & Platow, M. J. (2001). Your wish is our command: The role of shared social identity in translating a leader's vision into followers' action. In M. A. Hogg & D. J. Terry (Eds.), *Social identity processes in organizational contexts* (pp. 213–228). Philadelphia, PA: Psychology Press.

Haslam, S. A., Turner, J. C., Oakes, P. J., McGarty, C., & Hayes, B. K. (1992). Context-dependent variation in social stereotyping 1: The effects of intergroup relations as mediated by social change and frame of reference. *European Journal of Social Psychology, 22,* 3–20.

Hass, R. G., Katz, I., Rizzo, N., Bailey, J., & Eisenstadt, D. (1991). Cross-racial appraisal as related to attitude ambivalence and cognitive complexity. *Personality and Social Psychology Bulletin, 17,* 83–92.

Hassett, J. (1981). But that would be wrong . . . *Psychology Today,* November, 34–50.

Hastie, R. (1984). Causes and effects of causal attribution. *Journal of Personality and Social Psychology, 46,* 44–56.

Hastie, R. (1988). A computer simulation model of person memory. *Journal of Experimental Social Psychology, 24,* 423–447.

Hastie, R. (Ed.) (1993). *Inside the juror: The psychology of juror decision making.* Cambridge: Cambridge University Press.

Hastie, R., & Park, B. (1986). The relationship between memory and judgment depends on whether the judgment task is memory-based or on-line. *Psychological Review, 93,* 258–268.

Hastie, R., Penrod, S. D., & Pennington, N. (1983). *Inside the jury.* Cambridge, MA: Harvard University Press.

Hatfield, E. (1987). Love. In R. J. Corsini (Ed.), *Concise encyclopedia of psychology* (pp. 676–677). New York: Wiley.

Hatfield, E., & Walster, G.W. (1981). *A new look at love.* Reading, MA: Addison-Wesley.

Haugtvedt, C. P., & Petty, R. E. (1992). Personality and persuasion: Need for cognition moderates the persistence and resistance of attitude changes. *Journal of Personality and Social Psychology, 63,* 308–319.

Hawking, S. W. (1988). *A brief history of time: From the Big Bang to black holes.* London: Bantam.

Hayduk, L. A. (1983). Personal space: Where we now stand. *Psychological Bulletin, 94,* 293–335.

Heaven, P. C. L. (1990). Human values and suggestions for reducing unemployment. *British Journal of Social Psychology, 29,* 257–264.

Hebb, D. O., & Thompson, W. R. (1968). The social significance of animal studies. In G. Lindzey & E. Aronson (Eds.), *Handbook of social psychology* (2nd ed., Vol. 2, pp. 729–774). Reading, MA: Addison-Wesley.

Hechinger, F. M. (1980). Studies examine the issue of ethics. *New York Times*, 30 December, pp. C1, C3.

Heider, F. (1946). Attitudes and cognitive organisation. *Journal of Psychology*, 21, 107–112.

Heider, F. (1958). *The psychology of interpersonal relations*. New York: Wiley.

Heider, F., & Simmel, M. (1944). An experimental study of apparent behavior. *American Journal of Psychology*, 57, 243–259.

Heilman, M. E., & Stopeck, M. H. (1985). Attractiveness and corporate success: Different causal attributions for males and females. *Journal of Applied Psychology*, 70, 379–388.

Heinemann, W. (1990). Meeting the handicapped: A case of affective-cognitive inconsistency. *European Review of Social Psychology*, 1, 323–338.

Heisler, G. (1974). Ways to deter law violators: Effects of levels of threat and vicarious punishment on cheating. *Journal of Consulting and Clinical Psychology*, 42, 577–582.

Henderson, J., & Taylor, J. (1985). Study finds bias in death sentences: Killers of whites risk execution. *Times Union*, 17 November, p. A19.

Hendrick, C., Bixenstine, V. E., & Hawkins, G. (1971). Race vs. belief similarities as determinants of attraction: A search for a fair test. *Journal of Personality and Social Psychology*, 17, 250–258.

Hendrick, C., & Hendrick, S. S. (1995). Gender differences and similarities in sex and love. *Personal Relationships*, 2, 55–65.

Henley, N. M. (1973). The politics of touch. In P. Brown (Ed.), *Radical psychology* (pp. 421–433). New York: Harper & Row.

Henley, N. M. (1977). *Body politics: Power, sex, and nonverbal communication*. Englewood Cliffs, NJ: Prentice Hall.

Henley, N. M., & Harmon, S. (1985). The nonverbal semantics of power and gender: A perceptual study. In S. L. Ellyson & J. F. Dovidio (Eds.), *Power, dominance, and nonverbal behavior* (pp. 151–164). New York: Springer-Verlag.

Henriques, J., Holloway, W., Urwin, C., Venn, C., & Walkerdine, V. (1984). *Changing the subject: psychology, social regulation, and subjectivity*. London: Methuen.

Henry, W. A. III. (1994). Pride and prejudice. *Time*, 27 June, pp. 54–59.

Hensley, T. R., & Griffin, G. W. (1986). Victims of groupthink: The Kent State University Board of Trustees and the 1977 gymnasium controversy. *Journal of Conflict Resolution*, 30, 497–531.

Herek, G. M., & Glunt, E. K. (1988). An epidemic of stigma: Public reaction to AIDS. *American Psychologist*, 43, 886–891.

Herr, P. M., Sherman, S. J., & Fazio, R. H. (1983). On the consequences of priming: Assimilation and contrast effects. *Journal of Experimental Social Psychology*, 19, 323–340.

Hersh, S. (1970). *My Lai: A report on the massacre and its aftermath*. New York: Vintage Books.

Heslin, R. (1978). Responses to touching as an index of sex-role norms and attitudes. Paper presented at the annual meeting of the American Psychological Association, Toronto, August.

Heslin, R., & Alper, T. (1983). Touch: A bonding gesture. In J. M. Wiemann & R. P. Harrison (Eds.), *Nonverbal interaction* (pp. 47–75). Beverly Hills, CA: Sage.

Hess, E. H. (1965). The pupil responds to changes in attitude as well as to changes in illumination. *Scientific American*, 212, 46–54.

Heuer, L., & Penrod, S. (1994). Trial complexity: A field investigation of its meaning and its effect. *Law and Human Behavior*, 18, 29–51.

Hewes, G. W. (1957). The anthropology of posture. *Scientific American*, 196, 123–132.

Hewstone, M. (1989). *Causal attribution: From cognitive processes to collective beliefs*. Oxford, UK: Blackwell.

Hewstone, M. (1990). The 'ultimate attribution error': A review of the literature on intergroup causal attribution. *European Journal of Social Psychology*, 20, 311–335.

Hewstone, M. (1994). Revision and change of stereotypic beliefs: In search of the elusive subtyping model. *European Review of Social Psychology*, 5, 69–109.

Hewstone, M. (1996). Contact and categorization: Social psychological interventions to change intergroup relations. In C. N. Macrae, C. Stangor, & M. Hewstone (Eds.), *Stereotypes and stereotyping* (pp. 323–368). New York: Guilford.

Hewstone, M., & Antaki, C. (1988). Attribution theory and social explanations. In M. Hewstone, W. Stroebe, J.-P. Codol, & G. M. Stephenson (Eds.), *Introduction to social psychology: A European perspective* (pp. 111–141). Oxford, UK: Blackwell.

Hewstone, M., & Brown, R. J. (Eds.). (1986). *Contact and conflict in intergroup encounters*. Oxford, UK: Blackwell.

Hewstone, M., Cairns, E., Voci, A., Paolini, S., McLernon, F., Crisp, R., Niens, U., & Craig, J. (in press). Intergroup contact in a divided society: Challenging segregation in Northern Ireland. In D. Abrams, J. M. Marques, & M. A. Hogg (Eds.), *The social psychology of inclusion and exclusion*. New York: Psychology Press.

Hewstone, M., & Jaspars, J. M. F. (1982). Intergroup relations and attribution processes. In H. Tajfel (Ed.), *Social identity and intergroup relations* (pp. 99–133). Cambridge: Cambridge University Press.

Hewstone, M., & Jaspars, J. M. F. (1984). Social dimensions of attribution. In H. Tajfel (Ed.), *The social dimension* (pp. 379–404). Cambridge: Cambridge University Press.

Hewstone, M., Jaspars, J. M. F., & Lalljee, M. (1982). Social representations, social attribution and social identity: The intergroup images of 'public' and 'comprehensive' schoolboys. *European Journal of Social Psychology*, 12, 241–269.

Hewstone, M., & Stroebe, W. (Eds.). (2001). *Introduction to social psychology* (3rd ed.). Oxford, UK: Blackwell.

Hewstone, M., & Ward, C. (1985). Ethnocentrism and causal attribution in Southeast Asia. *Journal of Personality and Social Psychology*, 48, 614–623.

Higgins, E. T. (1981). The 'communication game': Implications for social cognition. In E. T. Higgins, C. P. Herman, & M. Zanna (Eds.), *Social cognition: The Ontario symposium* (Vol. 1, pp. 343–392). Hillsdale, NJ: Erlbaum.

Higgins, E. T. (1987). Self-discrepancy: A theory relating self and affect. *Psychological Review*, 94, 319–340.

Higgins, E. T. (1996). Knowledge activation: Accessibility, applicability, and salience. In E. T. Higgins & A. W. Kruglanski (Eds.), *Social psychology: Handbook of basic principles* (pp. 133–168). New York: Guilford.

Higgins, E. T. (1998). Promotion and prevention: Regulatory focus as a motivational principle. In M. P. Zanna (Ed.), *Advances in experimental social psychology* (Vol. 30, pp. 1–46). New York: Academic Press.

Higgins, E. T., & Bargh, J. A. (1987). Social cognition and social perception. *Annual Review of Psychology*, 38, 369–425.

Higgins, E. T., Bargh, J. A., & Lombardi, W. (1985). The nature of priming effects on categorization. *Journal of Experimental Psychology: Learning, Memory, and Cognition, 11,* 59–69.

Higgins, E. T., Bond, R. N., Klein, R., & Strauman, T. (1986). Self-discrepancies and emotional vulnerability: How magnitude, accessibility, and type of discrepancy influence affect. *Journal of Personality and Social Psychology, 51,* 5–15.

Higgins, E. T., van Hook, E., & Dorfman, D. (1988). Do self-attributes form a cognitive structure? *Social Cognition, 6,* 177–207.

Hill, C., & Peplau, L. (1998). Premarital predictors of relationship outcomes: A 15-year follow up of the Boston Couples Study. In T. N. Bradbury (Ed.), *The developmental course of marital dysfunction.* New York: Cambridge University Press.

Hill, D., White, V., Marks, R., & Borland, R. (1993). Changes in sun-related attitudes and behaviours and reduced sunburn prevalence in a population at high risk of melanoma. *European Journal of Cancer Prevention, 1,* 447–456.

Hilton, D. J. (1988). Logic and causal attribution. In D. J. Hilton (Ed.), *Contemporary science and natural explanation: Commonsense conceptions of causality.* Brighton: Harvester Press.

Hilton, D. J. (1990). Conversational processes and causal explanation. *Psychological Bulletin, 107,* 65–81.

Hilton, D. J., & Karpinski, A. (2000). *Attitudes and the implicit associations test.* Michigan: University of Michigan.

Hilton, J. L., & von Hippel, W. (1996). Stereotypes. *Annual Review of Psychology, 47,* 237–271.

Himmelfarb, S., & Eagly, A. H. (Eds.). (1974). *Readings in attitude change.* New York: Wiley.

Hinde, R. A. (1982). *Ethology: Its nature and relations with other sciences.* London: Fontana.

Hinkle, S., & Brown, R. (1990). Intergroup comparisons and social identity: Some links and lacunae. In D. Abrams & M. Hogg (Eds.), *Social identity theory: Constructive and critical advances* (pp. 48–70). Hemel Hempstead: Harvester Wheatsheaf.

Hinshaw, S. P. (1987). On the distinction between attentional deficits/hyperactivity and conduct problems/aggression in child psychopathology. *Psychological Bulletin, 101,* 443–463.

Hitler, A. (1933). *Mein Kampf.* Retrieved November 11, 2003, from http://www.stormfront.org/books/mein_kampf/mkv1ch06.html

Ho, E. S. (1995). *The challenge of culture change: The cross-cultural adaptation of Hong Kong Chinese adolescent immigrants in New Zealand.* PhD thesis, Waikato University.

Hodges, S. D., Klaaren, K. J., & Wheatley, T. (2000). Talking about safe sex: The role of expectations and experience. *Journal of Applied Social Psychology, 30,* 330–349.

Hoffman, C., Lau, I., & Johnson, D. R. (1986). The linguistic relativity of person cognition: An English–Chinese comparison. *Journal of Personality and Social Psychology, 51,* 1097–1105.

Hoffman, C., Mischel, W., & Mazze, K. (1981). The role of purpose in the organisation of information about behavior: Trait-based versus goal-based categories in person cognition. *Journal of Personality and Social Psychology, 40,* 211–225.

Hoffman, M. L. (1981). Is altruism part of human nature? *Journal of Personality and Social Psychology, 40,* 121–137.

Hofstede, G. (1980). *Culture's consequences: International differences in work-related values.* Beverly Hills, CA: Sage.

Hogg, M. A. (1985). Masculine and feminine speech in dyads and groups: A study of speech style and gender salience. *Journal of Language and Social Psychology, 4,* 99–112.

Hogg, M. A. (1987). Social identity and group cohesiveness. In J. C. Turner, M. A. Hogg, P. J. Oakes, S. D. Reicher, & M. S. Wetherell

(Eds.), *Rediscovering the social group: A self-categorization theory* (pp. 89–116). Oxford: Blackwell.

Hogg, M. A. (1992). *The social psychology of group cohesiveness: From attraction to social identity.* London: Harvester Wheatsheaf.

Hogg, M. A. (1993). Group cohesiveness: A critical review and some new directions. *European Review of Social Psychology, 4,* 85–111.

Hogg, M. A. (2000a). Subjective uncertainty reduction through self-categorization: A motivational theory of social identity processes. *European Review of Social Psychology, 11,* 223–255.

Hogg, M. A. (2000b). Social processes and human behavior: Social psychology. In K. Pawlik & M. R. Rosenzweig (Eds.), *International handbook of psychology* (pp. 305–327). London: Sage.

Hogg, M. A. (2000c). Social identity and social comparison. In J. Suls & L. Wheeler (Eds.), *Handbook of social comparison: Theory and research* (pp. 401–421). New York: Kluwer/ Plenum.

Hogg, M. A. (2001a). Social categorization, depersonalization, and group behavior. In M. A. Hogg & R. S. Tindale (Eds.), *Blackwell handbook of social psychology: Group processes* (pp. 56–85). Oxford, UK: Blackwell.

Hogg, M. A. (2001b). Social identity and the sovereignty of the group: A psychology of belonging. In C. Sedikides & M. B. Brewer (Eds.), *Individual self, relational self, and collective self: Partners, opponents, or strangers.* Philadelphia, PA: Psychology Press.

Hogg, M. A. (2001c). Self-categorization and subjective uncertainty resolution: Cognitive and motivational facets of social identity and group membership. In J. P. Forgas, K. D. Williams, & L. Wheeler (Eds.), *The social mind: Cognitive and motivational aspects of interpersonal behavior* (pp. 323–349). New York: Cambridge University Press.

Hogg, M. A. (2001d). A social identity theory of leadership. *Personality and Social Psychology Review, 5,* 184–200.

Hogg, M. A. (2003a). Intergroup relations. In J. Delamater (Ed.), *Handbook of social psychology* (pp. 479–501). New York: Kluwer Academic/Plenum.

Hogg, M. A. (2003b). Social identity. In M. R. Leary & J. P. Tangney (Eds.), *Handbook of self and identity* (pp. 462–479). New York: Guilford.

Hogg, M. A. (Ed.). (2003c). *Sage benchmarks in psychology: Social psychology.* London: Sage.

Hogg, M. A. (in press). Social identity and the group context of trust: Managing risk and building trust through belonging. In M. Siegrist & H. Gutscher (Eds.), *Trust, technology, and society: Studies in cooperative risk management.* London: Earthscan.

Hogg, M. A., & Abrams, D. (1988). *Social identifications: A social psychology of intergroup relations and group processes.* London: Routledge.

Hogg, M. A., & Abrams, D. (1990). Social motivation, self-esteem and social identity. In D. Abrams & M. A. Hogg (Eds.), *Social identity theory: Constructive and critical advances* (pp. 28–47). London: Harvester Wheatsheaf.

Hogg, M. A., & Abrams, D. (1993). Towards a single-process uncertainty-reduction model of social motivation in groups. In M. A. Hogg & D. Abrams (Eds.), *Group motivation: Social psychological perspectives* (pp. 173–190). London: Harvester Wheatsheaf.

Hogg, M. A., & Abrams, D. (1999). Social identity and social cognition: Historical background and current trends. In D. Abrams & M. A. Hogg (Eds.), *Social identity and social cognition* (pp. 1–25). Oxford, UK: Blackwell.

Hogg, M. A., & Abrams, D. (2003). Intergroup behavior and social identity. In M. A. Hogg & J. Cooper (Eds.), *The Sage handbook of social psychology* (pp. 407–431). London: Sage.

Hogg, M. A., & Cooper, J. (Eds.). (2003). *The Sage handbook of social psychology.* London: Sage.

Hogg, M. A., D'Agata, P., & Abrams, D. (1989). Ethnolinguistic betrayal and speaker evaluations among Italian Australians. *Genetic, Social and General Psychology Monographs, 115,* 153–181.

Hogg, M. A., & Hains, S. C. (1996). Intergroup relations and group solidarity: Effects of group identification and social beliefs on depersonalized attraction. *Journal of Personality and Social Psychology, 70,* 295–309.

Hogg, M. A., & Hains, S. C. (1998). Friendship and group identification: A new look at the role of cohesiveness in groupthink. *European Journal of Social Psychology, 28,* 323–341.

Hogg, M. A., Hains, S. C., & Mason, I. (1998). Identification and leadership in small groups: Salience, frame of reference, and leader stereotypicality effects on leader evaluations. *Journal of Personality and Social Psychology, 75,* 1248–1263.

Hogg, M. A., & Hardie, E. A. (1991). Social attraction, personal attraction, and self-categorisation: A field study. *Personality and Social Psychology Bulletin, 17,* 175–180.

Hogg, M. A., & Hornsey, M. J. (in press). Self-concept threat and multiple categorization within groups. In R. J. Crisp & M. Hewstone (Eds.), *Multiple social categorization: Processes, models, and applications.* New York: Psychology Press.

Hogg, M. A., Joyce, N., & Abrams, D. (1984). Diglossia in Switzerland? A social identity analysis of speaker evaluations. *Journal of Language and Social Psychology, 3,* 185–196.

Hogg, M. A., & McGarty, C. (1990). Self-categorization and social identity. In D. Abrams & M. A. Hogg (Eds.), *Social identity theory: Constructive and critical advances* (pp. 10–27). London: Harvester Wheatsheaf.

Hogg, M. A., & Reid, S. A. (2001). Social identity, leadership, and power. In A. Y. Lee-Chai & J. A. Bargh (Eds.), *The use and abuse of power: Multiple perspectives on the causes of corruption* (pp. 159–180). Philadelphia, PA: Psychology Press.

Hogg, M. A., & Rigoli, N. (1996). Effects of ethnolinguistic vitality, ethnic identification, and linguistic contacts on minority language use. *Journal of Language and Social Psychology, 15,* 76–89.

Hogg, M. A., Terry, D. J., & White, K. M. (1995). A tale of two theories: A critical comparison of identity theory with social identity theory. *Social Psychology Quarterly, 58,* 255–269.

Hogg, M. A., & Tindale, R. S. (Eds.). (2001). *Blackwell handbook of social psychology: Group processes.* Oxford, UK: Blackwell.

Hogg, M. A., & Turner, J. C. (1985). Interpersonal attraction, social identification and psychological group formation. *European Journal of Social Psychology, 15,* 51–66.

Hogg, M. A., & Turner, J. C. (1987a). Social identity and conformity: A theory of referent informational influence. In W. Doise & S. Moscovici (Eds.), *Current issues in European social psychology* (Vol. 2, pp. 139–182). Cambridge: Cambridge University Press.

Hogg, M. A., & Turner, J. C. (1987b). Intergroup behaviour, self-stereotyping and the salience of social categories. *British Journal of Social Psychology, 26,* 325–340.

Hogg, M. A., Turner, J. C., & Davidson, B. (1990). Polarized norms and social frames of reference: A test of the self-categorization theory of group polarization. *Basic and Applied Social Psychology, 11,* 77–100.

Hogg, M. A., Turner, J. C., Nascimento-Schulze, C., & Spriggs, D. (1986). Social categorization, intergroup behaviour and self-esteem: Two experiments. *Revista de Psicología Social, 1,* 23–37.

Hogg, M. A., & van Knippenberg, D. (2003). Social identity and leadership processes in groups. In M. P. Zanna (Ed.), *Advances in experimental social psychology* (Vol. 35, pp. 1–52). San Diego, CA: Academic Press.

Hogg, M. A., & Vaughan, G. M. (2002). *Social psychology: An introduction* (3rd ed.). London: Pearson Education.

Hogg, M. A., & Williams, K. D. (2000). From I to we: Social identity and the collective self. *Group Dynamics: Theory, Research, and Practice, 4,* 81–97.

Holdt, J. (1996). *1996 clients: Aggregate report 2. Initial contact & work record information.* Auckland: National Collective of Rape Crisis & Related Groups of Aotearoa Inc.

Hollander, E. P. (1958). Conformity, status, and idiosyncrasy credit. *Psychological Review, 65,* 117–127.

Hollander, E. P. (1967). *Principles and methods of social psychology.* New York: Oxford University Press.

Hollander, E. P. (1985). Leadership and power. In G. Lindzey & E. Aronson (Eds.), *Handbook of social psychology* (3rd ed., Vol. 2, pp. 485–537). New York: Random House.

Hollander, E. P., & Julian, J. W. (1970). Studies in leader legitimacy, influence, and innovation. In L. Berkowitz (Ed.), *Advances in experimental social psychology* (Vol. 5, pp. 34–69). New York: Academic Press.

Hollingshead, A. B. (1996). The rank order effect: Decision procedure, communication technology and group decisions. *Organizational Behavior and Human Decision Processes, 68(3),* 1–13.

Hollingshead, A. B. (1998). Retrieval processes in transactive memory systems. *Journal of Personality and Social Psychology, 74,* 659–671.

Hollingshead, A. B. (2001). Communication technologies, the internet, and group research. In M. A. Hogg & R. S. Tindale (Eds.), *Blackwell handbook of social psychology: Group processes* (pp. 557–573). Oxford, UK: Blackwell.

Hollingshead, A. B., & McGrath, J. E. (1995). Computer-assisted groups: A critical review of the empirical research. In R. A. Guzzo & E. Salas (Eds.), *Team effectiveness and decision making in organizations* (pp. 46–78). San Francisco: Jossey-Bass.

Holloway, S., Tucker, L., & Hornstein, H. A. (1977). The effects of social and nonsocial information on interpersonal behavior of males: The news makes news. *Journal of Personality and Social Psychology, 35,* 514–522.

Holmes, J. G. (2002). Interpersonal expectations as the building blocks of social cognition: An interdependence theory perspective. *Personal Relationships, 9,* 1–26.

Holtgraves, T., & Lasky, B. (1999). Linguistic power and persuasion. *Journal of Language and Social Psychology, 18,* 196–205.

Holtzworth-Munroe, A., & Jacobson, N. S. (1985). Causal attributions of married couples. When do they search for causes? What do they conclude when they do? *Journal of Personality and Social Psychology, 48,* 1398–1412.

Homans, G. C. (1961). *Social behavior: Its elementary forms.* New York: Harcourt, Brace & World.

Horai, J. (1977). Attributional conflict. *Journal of Social Issues, 33,* 88–100.

Hornblow, A. R. (1980). The study of empathy. *New Zealand Psychologist, 9,* 19–28.

Hornsey, M. J., & Hogg, M. A. (2000a). Assimilation and diversity: An integrative model of subgroup relations. *Personality and Social Psychology Review, 4*, 143–156.

Hornsey, M. J., & Hogg, M. A. (2000b). Subgroup relations: A comparison of mutual intergroup differentiation and common ingroup identity models of prejudice reduction. *Personality and Social Psychology Bulletin, 26*, 242–256.

Hornsey, M. J., & Hogg, M. A. (2000c). Intergroup similarity and subgroup relations: Some implications for assimilation. *Personality and Social Psychology Bulletin, 26*, 948–958.

Hornsey, M. J., & Imani, A. (2004). Criticising groups from the inside and the outside: An identity perspective on the intergroup sensitivity effect. *Personality and Social Psychology Bulletin, 30*, 365–383.

Hornsey, M. J., Oppes, T., & Svensson, A. (2002). 'It's OK if we say it, but you can't': Responses to intergroup and intragroup criticism. *European Journal of Social Psychology, 32*, 293–307.

Hornsey, M. J., Spears, R., Cremers, I., & Hogg, M. A. (2003). Relations between high and low power groups: The importance of legitimacy. *Personality and Social Psychology Bulletin, 29*, 216–227.

Hornstein, G. A. (1985). Intimacy in conversational style as a function of the degree of closeness between members of a dyad. *Journal of Personality and Social Psychology, 49*, 671–681.

Hornstein, H. A. (1970). The influence of social models on helping. In J. Macaulay & L. Berkowitz (Eds.), *Altruism and helping behavior* (pp. 29–42). New York: Academic Press.

Horowitz, D. L. (1973). Direct, displaced and cumulative ethnic aggression. *Comparative Politics, 6*, 1–16.

Horowitz, E. L. (1936). The development of attitudes towards the Negro. *Archives of Psychology, 194*.

Horowitz, E. L. (1939). Racial aspects of self-identification in nursery school children. *Journal of Psychology, 7*, 91–99.

Horowitz, I. A., & Bordens, K. S. (1990). An experimental investigation of procedural issues in complex tort trials. *Law and Human Behavior, 14*, 269–285.

House, R. (1977). A 1976 theory of charismatic leadership. In J. G. Hunt & L. Larson (Eds.), *Leadership: The cutting edge* (pp. 189–207). Carbondale, IL: Southern Illinois University Press.

Hovland, C. I., Janis, I. L., & Kelley, H. H. (1953). *Communication and persuasion*. New Haven, CT: Yale University Press.

Hovland, C. I., Lumsdaine, A. A., & Sheffield, F. D. (1949). *Experiments in mass communication*. Princeton, NJ: Princeton University Press.

Hovland, C. I., & Sears, R. R. (1940). Minor studies in aggression: VI. Correlation of lynchings with economic indices. *Journal of Psychology, 9*, 301–310.

Hovland, C. I., & Weiss, W. (1952). The influence of source credibility in communication effectiveness. *Public Opinion Quarterly, 15*, 635–650.

Howard, J. A. (1985). Further appraisal of correspondent inference theory. *Personality and Social Psychology Bulletin, 11*, 467–477.

Howard, J. W., & Rothbart, M. (1980). Social categorization and memory for ingroup and outgroup behavior. *Journal of Personality and Social Psychology, 38*, 301–310.

Hraba, J. (1972). A measure of ethnocentrism? *Social Forces, 50*, 522–527.

Hraba, J., & Grant, G. (1970). Black is beautiful: A reexamination of racial preference and identification. *Journal of Personality and Social Psychology, 16*, 398–402.

Huesmann, L. R. (1988). An information processing model for the development of aggression. *Aggressive Behavior, 14*, 13–24.

Huesmann, L. R., Eron, L. D., Lefkowitz, M. M., & Walder, L. O. (1984). Stability of aggression over time and generations. *Developmental Psychology, 20*, 1120–1134.

Huesmann, L. R., & Guerra, N. G. (1997). Children's normative beliefs about aggression and aggressive behavior. *Journal of Personality and Social Psychology, 72*, 408–419.

Huesmann, L. R., & Miller, L. S. (1994). Long-term effects of repeated exposure to media violence in childhood. In L. R. Huesmann (Ed.), *Aggressive behavior: Current perspectives* (pp. 153–186). New York: Plenum.

Hughes, M. T. (1981). To cheat or not to cheat? *Albany Times–Union*, 26 July, pp. B–1, B–3.

Hummert, M. L. (1990). Multiple stereotypes of elderly and young adults: A comparison of structure and evaluations. *Psychology and Aging, 5*, 182–193.

Huston, T. L., & Houts, R. M. (1998). The psychological infrastructure of courtship and marriage: The role of personality and compatibility in romantic relationships. In T. Bradbury (Ed.), *The developmental course of marital dysfunction* (pp. 114–151). New York: Cambridge University Press.

Huston, T. L., & Korte, C. (1976). The responsive bystander: Why he helps. In T. Lickona (Ed.), *Morality: A handbook of moral behavior and development* (pp. 269–283). New York: Holt, Rinehart & Winston.

Ingham, A. G., Levinger, G., Graves, J., & Peckham, V. (1974). The Ringelmann effect: Studies of group size and group performance. *Journal of Experimental Social Psychology, 10*, 371–384.

Ingoldsby, B. B. (1991). The Latin American family: Familism vs machismo. *Journal of Comparative Family Studies, 23*, 47–62.

Insko, C. A. (1965). Verbal reinforcement of attitude. *Journal of Personality and Social Psychology, 2*, 621–623.

Insko, C. A. (1967). *Theories of attitude change*. New York: Appleton-Century-Crofts.

Insko, C. A., Nacoste, R. W., & Moe, J. L. (1983). Belief congruence and racial discrimination: Review of the evidence and critical evaluation. *European Journal of Social Psychology, 13*, 153–174.

International Comparisons of Recorded Violent Crime Rates for 2000. Retrieved 16 February 2004 from http://www.justice.govt.nz/pubs/reports/2002/intl-comparisons-crime/index.html

Isen, A. M. (1970). Success, failure, attention, and reaction to others: The warm glow of success. *Journal of Personality and Social Psychology, 15*, 294–301.

Isen, A. M., Clark, M., & Schwartz, M. (1976). Duration of the effect of good mood on helping: 'footprints on the sands of time'. *Journal of Personality and Social Psychology, 34*, 385–393.

Isen, A. M., Horn, N., & Rosenhan, D. L. (1973). Effects of success and failure on children's generosity. *Journal of Personality and Social Psychology, 27*, 239–247.

Isen, A. M., & Stalker, T. E. (1982). The effect of feeling state on evaluation of positive, neutral, and negative stimuli when you 'accentuate the positive': Do you 'eliminate the negative'? *Social Psychology Quarterly, 45*, 58–63.

Isenberg, D. J. (1986). Group polarization: A critical review. *Journal of Personality and Social Psychology, 50*, 1141–1151.

Islam, M., & Hewstone, M. (1993). Intergroup attributions and affective consequences in majority and minority groups. *Journal of Personality and Social Psychology, 65*, 936–950.

Israel, J., & Tajfel, H. (Eds.). (1972). *The context of social psychology: A critical assessment*. London: Academic Press.

Izraeli, D. N., & Izraeli, D. (1985). Sex effects in evaluating leaders: A replication study. *Journal of Applied Psychology, 70*, 540–546.

Izraeli, D. N., Izraeli, D., & Eden, D. (1985). Giving credit where credit is due: A case of no sex bias in attribution. *Journal of Applied Social Psychology, 15,* 516–530.

Jackson, J., & Harkins, S. G. (1985). Equity in effort: An explanation of the social loafing effect. *Journal of Personality and Social Psychology, 49,* 1199–1206.

Jacobs, D., & Singell, L. (1993). Leadership and organisational performance: Isolating links between managers and collective success. *Social Science Research, 22,* 165–189.

Jacobs, R., & Campbell, D. T. (1961). The perpetuation of an arbitrary tradition through several generations of a laboratory microculture. *Journal of Abnormal and Social Psychology, 62,* 649–658.

Jacobson, D. (1999). Impression formation in cyberspace: Online expectations and offline experiences in text-based virtual communities [Electronic version]. *Journal of Computer-Mediated Communication 5* (1).

Jacoby, L. L., Kelly, C., Brown, J., & Jasechko, J. (1989). Becoming famous overnight: Limits on the ability to avoid unconscious influences of the past. *Journal of Personality and Social Psychology, 56,* 326–338.

Jahoda, G. (1979). A cross-cultural perspective on experimental social psychology. *Personality and Social Psychology Bulletin, 5,* 142–148.

Jahoda, G. (1982). *Psychology and anthropology: A psychological perspective.* London: Academic Press.

James, W. (1890). *The principles of psychology* (Vol. 1). New York: Holt.

Jamieson, D. W., & Zanna, M. P. (1989). Need for structure in attitude formation and expression. In A. R. Pratkanis, S. J. Breckler, & A. G. Greenwald (Eds.), *Attitude structure and function* (pp. 383–406). Hillsdale, NJ: Erlbaum.

Janis, I. L. (1954). Personality correlates of susceptibility to persuasion. *Journal of Personality, 22,* 504–518.

Janis, I. L. (1967). Effects of fear arousal on attitude change: Recent developments in theory and experimental research. In L. Berkowitz (Ed.), *Advances in experimental social psychology* (Vol. 3, pp. 167–224). New York: Academic Press.

Janis, I. L. (1972). *Victims of groupthink: A psychological study of foreign policy decisions and fiascoes.* Boston, MA: Houghton-Mifflin.

Janis, I. L. (1982). *Groupthink: Psychological studies of policy decisions and fiascoes* (2nd ed.). Boston, MA: Houghton-Mifflin.

Janis, I. L., & Feshbach, S. (1953). Effects of fear-arousing communications. *Journal of Abnormal and Social Psychology, 48,* 78–92.

Janis, I. L., & Hovland, C. I. (1959). An overview of persuasibility research. In C. I. Hovland and I. L. Janis (Eds.), *Personality and persuasibility* (pp. 1–26). New Haven: Yale University Press.

Janis, I. L., & King, B. T. (1954). The influence of role-playing on opinion change. *Journal of Abnormal and Social Psychology, 49,* 211–218.

Janis, I. L., & Mann, L. (1977). *Decision making.* New York: Free Press.

Janis, I. L., Kaye, D., & Kirschner, P. (1965). Facilitating effects of 'eating-while-reading' on responsiveness to persuasive communications. *Journal of Personality and Social Psychology, 1,* 181–186.

Jankovic, J. (2001). *Ethnic identity among the Croatian community in Auckland.* Masters thesis, University of Auckland.

Jarvis, W. B. G., & Petty, R. E. (1995). The need to evaluate. *Journal of Personality and Social Psychology, 70,* 172–192.

Jaspars, J. M. F. (1980). The coming of age of social psychology in Europe. *European Journal of Social Psychology, 10,* 421–428.

Jellison, J., & Arkin, R. (1977). Social comparison of abilities: A self-presentation approach to decision making in groups. In J. M. Suls & R. L. Miller (Eds.), *Social comparison processes: Theoretical and empirical perspectives* (pp. 235–257). Washington, DC: Hemisphere.

Jellison, J. M., & Green, J. (1981). A self-presentation approach to the fundamental attribution error: The norm of internality. *Journal of Personality and Social Psychology, 40,* 643–649.

Jemmott, J., & Locke, S. (1984). Psychosocial factors, immunologic mediation, and human susceptibility to infectious diseases: How much do we know? *Psychological Bulletin, 95,* 78–108.

Jennings, H. H. (1943). *Leadership and isolation.* New York: Longmans, Green.

Jennings, M. K., & Niemi, R. G. (1968). The transmission of political values from parent to child. *American Political Science Review, 62,* 546–575.

Jetten, J., Postmes, T., & McAuliffe, B. J. (2002). We're all individuals: Group norms of individualism and collectivism, levels of identification, and identity threat. *European Journal of Social Psychology, 32,* 189–207.

Jodelet, D. (1991). *Madness and social representations.* Hemel Hempstead, UK: Harvester Wheatsheaf.

Johnson, B. T. (1994). Effects of outcome-relevant involvement and prior information on persuasion. *Journal of Experimental Social Psychology, 30,* 556–579.

Johnson, B. T., & Eagly, A. H. (1989). Effects of involvement on persuasion: Meta-analysis. *Psychological Bulletin, 106,* 290–314.

Johnson, D. W., & Johnson, F. P. (1987). *Joining together: Group theory and group skills* (3rd ed.). Englewood Cliffs, NJ: Prentice Hall.

Johnson, M. P. (1991). Commitment to personal relationships. In W. H. Jones & D. Perlman (Eds.), *Advances in personal relationships* (Vol. 3, pp. 117–143). London: Jessica Kingley.

Johnson, R. D., & Downing, L. L. (1979). Deindividuation and valence of cues: Effects on prosocial and antisocial behavior. *Journal of Personality and Social Psychology, 37,* 1532–1538.

Johnston, L., & Hewstone, M. (1990). Intergroup contact: Social identity and social cognition. In D. Abrams & M. A. Hogg (Eds.), *Social identity theory: Constructive and critical advances* (pp. 185–210). London: Harvester Wheatsheaf.

Joiner, T. E. Jr. (1994). The interplay of similarity and self-verification in relationship formation. *Social Behavior and Personality, 22,* 195–200.

Jones, E. E. (1979). The rocky road from acts to dispositions. *American Psychologist, 34,* 107–117.

Jones, E. E. (1990). *Interpersonal perception.* New York: Freeman.

Jones, E. E. (1998). Major developments in five decades of social psychology. In D. T. Gilbert, S. T. Fiske, & G. Lindzey (Eds.), *The handbook of social psychology* (4th ed., Vol. 1, pp. 3–57). New York: McGraw-Hill.

Jones, E. E., & Davis, K. E. (1965). From acts to dispositions: The attribution process in person perception. In L. Berkowitz (Ed.), *Advances in experimental social psychology* (Vol. 2, pp. 219–266). New York: Academic Press.

Jones, E. E., Davis, K. E., & Gergen, K. (1961). Role playing variations and their informational value for person perception. *Journal of Abnormal and Social Psychology, 63,* 302–310.

Jones, E. E., & Goethals, G. R. (1972). Order effects in impression formation: Attribution context and the nature of the entity. In E. E. Jones, D. E. Kanouse, H. H. Kelley, R. E. Nisbett, S. Valins,

& B. Weiner (Eds.), *Attribution: Perceiving the causes of behavior* (pp. 27–46). Morristown, NJ: General Learning Press.

Jones, E. E., & Harris, V. A. (1967). The attribution of attitudes. *Journal of Experimental Social Psychology, 3*, 1–24.

Jones, E. E., & McGillis, D. (1976). Correspondent inferences and the attribution cube: A comparative reappraisal. In J. H. Harvey, W. J. Ickes, & R. F. Kidd (Eds.), *New directions in attribution research* (Vol. 1, pp. 389–420). Hillsdale, NJ: Erlbaum.

Jones, E. E., & Nisbett, R. E. (1972). The actor and the observer: Divergent perceptions of the causes of behavior. In E. E. Jones, D. E. Kanouse, H. H. Kelley, R. E. Nisbett, S. Valins, & B. Weiner (Eds.), *Attribution: Perceiving the causes of behavior* (pp. 79–94). Morristown, NJ: General Learning Press.

Jones, E. E., & Pittman, T.S. (1982). Toward a general theory of strategic self-presentation. In J. Suls (Ed.), *Psychological perspectives on the self* (Vol. 1, pp. 231–262). Hillsdale, NJ: Erlbaum.

Jones, E. E., & Sigall, H. (1971). The bogus pipeline: A new paradigm for measuring affect and attitude. *Psychological Bulletin, 76*, 349–364.

Jones, E. E., Wood, G. C., & Quattrone, G. A. (1981). Perceived variability of personal characteristics in ingroups and outgroups: The role of knowledge and evaluation. *Personality and Social Psychology Bulletin, 7*, 523–528.

Jones, S. E., & Yarbrough, A. E. (1985). A naturalistic study of the meanings of touch. *Communication Monographs, 52*, 19–56.

Jordan, N. (1953). Behavioral forces that are a function of attitudes and of behavioral organisation. *Human Relations, 6*, 273–287.

Jorgensen, B. W., & Cervone, J. C. (1978). Affect enhancement in the pseudo recognition task. *Personality and Social Psychology Bulletin, 4*, 285–288.

Jost, J. T., & Banaji, M. R. (1994). The role of stereotyping in system-justification and the production of false consciousness. *British Journal of Social Psychology, 33*, 1–27.

Jost, J. T., & Hunyadi, O. (2002). The psychology of system justification and the palliative function of ideology. *European Review of Social Psychology, 13*, 111–153.

Jost, J. T., & Kramer, R. M. (2003). The system justification motive in intergroup relations. In D. M. Mackie & E. R. Smith (Eds.), *From prejudice to intergroup emotions: Differentiated reactions to social groups* (pp. 227–246). New York: Psychology Press.

Jost, J. T., & Major, B. (Eds.). (2001). *The psychology of legitimacy: Emerging perspectives on ideology, justice, and intergroup relations.* New York: Cambridge University Press.

Jourard, S. M. (1966). An exploratory study of body-accessibility. *British Journal of Social and Clinical Psychology, 5*, 221–231.

Jourard, S. M. (1971). *The transparent self.* New York: Van Nostrand.

Judd, C. M., & Park, B. (1988). Out-group homogeneity: Judgments of variability at the individual and group levels. *Journal of Personality and Social Psychology, 54*, 778–788.

Jung, C. G. (1946). *Psychological types or the psychology of individuation.* New York: Harcourt Brace. (Originally published 1922.)

Jussim, L., & Fleming, C. (1996). Self-fulfilling prophecies and the maintenance of social stereotypes: The role of dyadic interactions and social forces. In C. N. Macrae, C. Stangor, & M. Hewstone (Eds.), *Stereotypes and stereotyping* (pp. 161–192). New York: Guilford.

Jussim, L., Eccles, J., & Madon, S. (1996). Social perception, social stereotypes, and teacher expectations: Accuracy and the quest for

the powerful self-fulfilling prophecy. *Advances in Experimental Social Psychology, 28*, 281–388.

Kafka, F. (1925). *The trial.* Harmondsworth: Penguin.

Kahn, A., O'Leary, V. E., Krulewitz, J. E., & Lamm, H. (1980). Equity and equality: Male and female means to a just end. *Basic and Applied Social Psychology, 1*, 173–197.

Kahn, A., & Ryen, A. H. (1972). Factors influencing the bias towards one's own group. *International Journal of Group Tensions, 2*, 33–50.

Kahneman, D., & Tversky, A. (1973). On the psychology of prediction. *Psychological Review, 80*, 237–251.

Kanazawa, H., & Loveday, L. (1988). The Japanese immigrant community in Brazil: Language contact and shift. *Journal of Multilingual and Multicultural Development, 9*, 423–435.

Kanouse, D. E., & Hanson, L. R. Jr. (1972). Negativity in evaluations. In E. E. Jones, D. E. Kanouse, H. H. Kelley, R. E. Nisbett, S. Valins, & B. Weiner (Eds.), *Attribution: Perceiving the causes of behavior* (pp. 47–62). Morristown, NJ: General Learning Press.

Kaplan, M. F. (1977). Discussion polarization effects in a modified jury decision paradigm: Informational influence. *Sociometry, 40*, 262–271.

Kaplan, M. F., & Miller, L. E. (1978). Reducing the effects of juror bias. *Journal of Personality and Social Psychology, 36*, 1443–1455.

Karau, S. J., & Hart, J. W. (1998). Group cohesiveness and social loafing: Effects of a social interaction manipulation on individual motivation within groups. *Group Dynamics, 2*, 185–191.

Karau, S. J., & Williams, K. D. (1993). Social loafing: A meta-analytic review and theoretical integration. *Journal of Personality and Social Psychology, 65*, 681–706.

Karney, B. R., & Bradbury, T. N. (1995). Assessing longitudinal change in marriage: An introduction to the analysis of growth curves. *Journal of Marriage and the Family, 57*, 1091–1108.

Karniol, R. (1982). Behavioral and cognitive correlates of various immanent justice responses in children: Deterrent versus punitive moral systems. *Journal of Personality and Social Psychology, 43*, 881–920.

Kashima, Y., & Kashima, E. (1998). Culture, connectionism, and the self. In J. Adamopoulos & Y. Kashima (Eds.) (1999). *Social psychology and cultural context* (pp. 77–92). London: Sage.

Kassin, S. M. (1979). Consensus information, prediction and causal attribution: A review of the literature and issues. *Journal of Personality and Social Psychology, 37*, 1966–1981.

Kassin, S. M., Ellsworth, P. C., & Smith, V. L. (1989). The 'general acceptance' of psychological research on eyewitness testimony. *American Psychologist, 44*, 1089–1098.

Kassin, S. M., & Pryor, J. B. (1985). The development of attribution processes. In J. Pryor & J. Day (Eds.), *The development of social cognition* (pp. 3–34). New York: Springer-Verlag.

Katsikitis, M., Pilowsky, I., & Innes, J. M. (1990). The quantification of smiling using a microcomputer-based approach. *Journal of Nonverbal Behavior, 14*, 3–17.

Katz, D. (1960). The functional approach to the study of attitudes. *Public Opinion Quarterly, 24*, 163–204.

Katz, D., & Braly, K. (1933). Racial stereotypes of one hundred college students. *Journal of Abnormal and Social Psychology, 28*, 280–290.

Katz, I., Glass, D. C., Lucido, D., & Farber, J. (1979). Harm-doing and victim's racial or orthopaedic stigma as determinants of helping behavior. *Journal of Personality, 47*, 340–364.

Katz, I., & Haas, R. G. (1988). Racial ambivalence and American value conflict: Correlational and priming studies of dual cognitive structures. *Journal of Personality and Social Psychology*, 55, 893–905.

Katz, J. E., & Aspden, P. (1998). Friendship formation in cyberspace: Analysis of a national survey of users. Retrieved January 21, 2001, from http://www.iaginteractive.com/emfa/friendship.htm

Katz, P. A. (1976). *Towards the elimination of racism*. New York: Pergamon.

Kazdin, A. E., & Bryan, J. H. (1971). Competence and volunteering. *Journal of Experimental Social Psychology*, 7, 87–97.

Keller, P. A., & Block, L. G. (1995). Increasing the persuasiveness of fear appeals: The effect of arousal and elaboration. *Journal of Consumer Research*, 22, 448–459.

Kelley, H. H. (1950). The warm–cold variable in first impressions of persons. *Journal of Personality*, 18, 431–439.

Kelley, H. H. (1952). Two functions of reference groups. In G. E. Swanson, T. M. Newcomb, & E. L. Hartley (Eds.), *Readings in social psychology* (2nd ed., pp. 410–414). New York: Holt, Rinehart & Winston.

Kelley, H. H. (1967). Attribution theory in social psychology. In D. Levine (Ed.), *Nebraska symposium on motivation* (pp. 192–238). Lincoln, NE: University of Nebraska Press.

Kelley, H. H. (1972a). Causal schemata and the attribution process. In E. E. Jones, D. E. Kanouse, H. H. Kelley, R. E. Nisbett, S. Valins, & B. Weiner (Eds.), *Attribution: Perceiving the causes of behavior* (pp. 151–174). Morristown, NJ: General Learning Press.

Kelley, H. H. (1972b). Attribution in social interaction. In E. E. Jones, D. E. Kanouse, H. H. Kelley, R. E. Nisbett, S. Valins, & B. Weiner (Eds.), *Attribution: Perceiving the causes of behavior* (pp. 1–26). Morristown, NJ: General Learning Press.

Kelley, H. H. (1973). The process of causal attribution. *American Psychologist*, 28, 107–128.

Kelley, H. H. (1979). *Personal relationships: Their structures and processes*. Hillsdale, NJ: Erlbaum.

Kelley, H. H., Holmes, J. G., Kerr, N. L., Reis, H. T., Rusbult, C. E., & van Lange, P. A. M. (2003). *An atlas of interpersonal situations*. New York: Cambridge University Press.

Kelley, H. H., & Michela, J. L. (1980). Attribution theory and research. *Annual Review of Psychology*, 31, 457–501.

Kelley, H. H., & Thibaut, J. (1978). *Interpersonal relations: A theory of interdependence*. New York: Wiley.

Kelley, K., Byrne, D., Przybyla, D. P. J., Eberly, C. C., Eberly, B. W., Greenlinger, V., Wan, C. K., & Grosky, J. (1985). Chronic self-destructiveness: Conceptualisation, measurement, and initial validation of the construct. *Motivation and Emotion*, 9, 35–151.

Kelly, C., & Breinlinger, S. (1996). *The social psychology of collective action*. London: Taylor & Francis.

Kelly, G. A. (1955). *The psychology of personal constructs*. New York: Norton.

Kelman, H. C. (1967). Human use of human subjects: The problem of deception in social psychology. *Psychological Bulletin*, 67, 1–11.

Keltner, D., Gruenfeld, D. H., & Anderson, C. (2003). Power, approach, and inhibition. *Psychological Review*, 110, 265–284.

Kelvin, P. (1970). *The bases of social behaviour: An approach in terms of order and value*. London: Holt, Rinehart & Winston.

Keneally, T. (1982). *Schindler's ark*. Washington, DC: Hemisphere.

Kennedy, J. (1982). Middle LPC leaders and the contingency model of leader effectiveness. *Organizational Behavior and Human Performance*, 30, 1–14.

Kenny, D. A., & DePaulo, B. M. (1993). Do people know how others view them? An empirical and theoretical account. *Psychological Bulletin*, 114, 145–161.

Kenrick, D. T., & MacFarlane, S. W. (1986). Ambient temperature and horn honking: A field study of the heat/aggression relationship. *Environment and Behavior*, 18, 179–191.

Kerckhoff, A. C., & Davis, K. E. (1962). Value consensus and need complementarity in mate selection. *American Sociological Review*, 27, 295–303.

Kernis, M. H., Granneman, B. D., & Barclay, L. C. (1989). Stability and level of self-esteem as predictors of anger arousal and hostility. *Journal of Personality and Social Psychology*, 56, 1013–1022.

Kerr, J. H. (1994). *Understanding soccer hooliganism*. Buckingham: Open University.

Kerr, N. L. (1978). Beautiful and blameless: Effects of victim attractiveness and responsibility on mock jurors' verdicts. *Journal of Personality and Social Psychology*, 4, 479–482.

Kerr, N. L. (1981). Social transition schemes: Charting the group's road to agreement. *Journal of Personality and Social Psychology*, 41, 684–702.

Kerr, N. L. (1983). Motivation losses in small groups: A social dilemma analysis. *Journal of Personality and Social Psychology*, 45, 819–828.

Kerr, N. L. (1992). Norms in social dilemmas. In D. Schroeder (Ed.), *Social dilemmas: Psychological perspectives*. New York: Praeger.

Kerr, N. L., & Bruun, S. (1981). Ringelmann revisited: Alternative explanations for the social loafing effect. *Personality and Social Psychology Bulletin*, 7, 224–231.

Kerr, N. L., & Bruun, S. (1983). The dispensability of member effort and group motivation losses: Free rider effects. *Journal of Personality and Social Psychology*, 44, 78–94.

Kerr, N. L., & MacCoun, R. J. (1985). The effects of jury size and polling method on the process and product of jury deliberation. *Journal of Personality and Social Psychology*, 48, 349–363.

Kerr, N. L., & Park, E. S. (2001). Group performance in collaborative and social dilemma tasks: Progress and prospects. In M. A. Hogg & R. S. Tindale (Eds.), *Blackwell handbook of social psychology: Group processes* (pp. 107–138). Oxford, UK: Blackwell.

Kiesler, C. A., & Kiesler, S. B. (1969). *Conformity*. Reading, MA: Addison-Wesley.

Kilham, W., & Mann, L. (1974). Level of destructive obedience as a function of transmitter and executant roles in the Milgram obedience paradigm. *Journal of Personality and Social Psychology*, 29, 696–702.

Kihlstrom, J. F. (2004). Implicit methods in social psychology. In C. Sansone, C. C. Morf, & A. T. Panter (Eds.), *The Sage handbook of methods in social psychology* (pp. 195–212). London: Sage.

Kim, H. S., & Baron, R. S. (1988). Exercise and the illusory correlation: Does arousal heighten stereotypic processing? *Journal of Experimental Social Psychology*, 24, 366–380.

Kimble, G. A. (1961). *Hilgard and Marquis' conditioning and learning* (2nd ed.). New York: Appleton-Century-Crofts.

Kimmel, P. R. (1994). Cultural perspectives on international negotiations. *Journal of Social Issues*, 50, 179–196.

Kinder, D. R., & Sears, D. O. (1981). Symbolic racism vs. threats to the good life. *Journal of Personality and Social Psychology*, 40, 414–431.

Kinloch, P. (1985). Alcohol, violence, and rape. In P. Kinloch (Ed.), *Talking health, doing sickness: Studies in Samoan health.* Wellington, NZ: Victoria University Press.

Kirkhart, R. O. (1963). Minority group identification and group leadership. *Journal of Social Psychology, 59,* 111–117.

Kitayama, S., Markus, H. R., Matsumoto, H., & Norasakkunkit, V. (1997). Individual and collective processes in the construction of the self: Self-enhancement in the United States and self-criticism in Japan. *Journal of Personality and Social Psychology, 72,* 1245–1267.

Kite, M. E., & Johnson, B. T. (1988). Attitudes toward older and younger adults: A meta-analysis. *Psychology and Aging, 3,* 233–244.

Klandermans, B. (1997). *The social psychology of protest.* Oxford, UK: Blackwell.

Klapp, O. E. (1972). *Currents of unrest.* New York: Holt, Rinehart & Winston.

Klasen, S. (1994). 'Missing women' re-considered. *World Development, 22,* 1061–1071.

Klein, S. B., Loftus, J., Trafton, J. G., & Fuhrman, R. W. (1992). Use of exemplars and abstractions in trait judgments: A model of trait knowledge about self and others. *Journal of Personality and Social Psychology, 63,* 739–753.

Kleinke, C. L. (1986). Gaze and eye contact: A research review. *Psychological Bulletin, 100,* 78–100.

Kleinke, C. L., Bustos, A. A., Meeker, F. B., & Staneski, R. A. (1973). Effects of self-attributed and other-attributed gaze on interpersonal evaluations between males and females. *Journal of Experimental Social Psychology, 9,* 154–163.

Klentz, B., & Beaman, A. L. (1981). The effects of type of information and method of dissemination on the reporting of a shoplifter. *Journal of Applied Psychology, 11,* 64–82.

Klineberg, O. (1940). *Social psychology.* New York: Holt.

Klinger, R. L., & Stein, T. S. (1996). Impact of violence, childhood sexual abuse, and domestic violence and abuse on lesbians, bisexuals, and gay men. In R. P. Cabaj & T. S. Stein (Eds.), *Textbook of homosexuality and mental health* (pp. 801–818). Washington, DC: American Psychiatric Press.

Klohnen, E. C., & Bera, S. (1998). Behavioral and experiential patterns of avoidantly and securely attached women across adulthood: A 31-year longitudinal perspective. *Journal of Personality and Social Psychology, 74,* 211–223.

Klohnen, E. C., & Mendelsohn, G. A. (1998). Partner selection for personality characteristics: A couple-centered approach. *Personality and Social Psychology Bulletin, 24,* 268–278.

Kluckhohn, C. (1954). Culture and behavior. In G. Lindzey (Ed.), *A handbook of social psychology* (Vol. 2, pp. 921–976). Cambridge, MA: Addison-Wesley.

Knapp, M. L. (1978). *Nonverbal communication in human interaction* (2nd ed.). New York: Holt, Rinehart & Winston.

Knapp, M. L., Hart, R. P., & Dennis, H. S. (1974). An exploration of deception as a communication construct. *Human Communication Research, 1,* 15–29.

Knee, C. R. (1998). Implicit theories of relationships: Assessment and prediction of romantic relationship initiation, coping, and longevity. *Journal of Personality and Social Psychology, 74,* 360–370.

Knottnerus, J. D., & Greenstein, T. N. (1981). Status and performance characteristics: A theory of status validation. *Social Psychology Quarterly, 44,* 338–349.

Kochman, T. (1987). The ethnic component in Black language and culture. In M. J. Rotheram (Ed.), *Children's ethnic socialization: Pluralism and development* (pp. 219–238). Newbury Park, CA: Sage.

Koffka, K. (1935). *Principles of gestalt psychology.* New York: Harcourt, Brace & World.

Kogan, N., & Wallach, M. A. (1964). *Risk taking: A study in cognition and personality.* New York: Holt.

Komorita, S. S., & Esser, J. K. (1975). Frequency of reciprocated concessions in bargaining. *Journal of Personality and Social Psychology, 32,* 699–705.

Komorita, S. S., Parks, C. D., & Hulbert, L. G. (1992). Reciprocity and the induction of cooperation in social dilemmas. *Journal of Personality and Social Psychology, 62,* 607–617.

Koneçni, V. J. (1979). The role of aversive events in the development of intergroup conflict. In W. G. Austin & S. Worchel (Eds.), *The social psychology of intergroup relations* (pp. 85–102). Monterey, CA: Brooks/Cole.

Koneçni, V. J., & Ebbesen, E. (1976). Disinhibition versus the cathartic effect: Artifact and substance. *Journal of Personality and Social Psychology, 34,* 352–365.

Korte, C. (1971). Effects of individual responsibility and group communication on help-giving in an emergency. *Human Relations, 24,* 149–159.

Kramer, R. M., & Brewer, M. B. (1984). Effects of identity on resource use in a simulated commons dilemma. *Journal of Personality and Social Psychology, 46,* 1044–1057.

Kramer, R. M., & Brewer, M. B. (1986). Social group identity and the emergence of cooperation in resource conservation dilemmas. In H. Wilke, D. Messick, & C. Rutte (Eds.), *Psychology of decisions and conflict* (Vol. 3). Frankfurt: Verlag Peter Lang.

Kraus, S. J. (1995). Attitudes and the prediction of behaviour. A meta-analysis of the empirical literature. *Psychological Bulletin, 21,* 58–75.

Krauss, R. M., & Chiu, C. Y. (1998). Language and social behavior. In D. T. Gilbert, S. T. Fiske, & G. Lindzey (Eds.), *The handbook of social psychology* (4th ed., Vol. 2, pp. 41–88). New York: McGraw-Hill.

Krauss, R. M., Curran, N. M., & Ferleger, N. (1983). Expressive conventions and the cross-cultural perception of emotion. *Basic and Applied Social Psychology, 4,* 295–305.

Kraut, R. E., & Higgins, E. T. (1984). Communication and social cognition. In R. S. Wyer, Jr. & T. K. Srull (Eds.), *Handbook of social cognition* (Vol. 3, pp. 87–127). Hillsdale, NJ: Erlbaum.

Kraut, R. E., & Johnston, R. E. (1979). Social and emotional messages of smiling: An ethological approach. *Journal of Personality and Social Psychology, 37,* 1539–1553.

Kraut, R. E., & Poe, D. (1980). Behavioral roots of person perceptions: The deception judgments of the customs inspectors and laymen. *Journal of Personality and Social Psychology, 39,* 784–798.

Kravitz, D. A., & Martin, B. (1986). Ringelmann rediscovered: The original article. *Journal of Personality and Social Psychology, 50,* 936–941.

Krebs, D. L. (1975). Empathy and altruism. *Journal of Personality and Social Psychology, 32,* 1134–1146.

Krebs, D. L., & Miller, D. T. (1985). Altruism and aggression. In G. Lindzey & E. Aronson (Eds.), *Handbook of social psychology* (3rd ed., Vol. 2, pp. 1–71). New York: Random House.

Krech, D., & Crutchfield, R. S. (1948). *Theory and problems of social psychology.* New York: McGraw-Hill.

Krech, D., Crutchfield, R., & Ballachey, R. (1962). *Individual in society.* New York: McGraw-Hill.

Kroeber, A.L., & Kluckhohn, L. (1952). *Culture: A critical review of concepts and definitions*. Cambridge, MA: Peabody Museum.

Krosnick, J. A. (1990). Expertise and political psychology. *Social Cognition*, 8, 1–8.

Krosnick, J. A., Boninger, D. S., Chuang, Y. C., Berent, M. K., & Carnot, C. G. (1993). Attitude strength: One construct or many related constructs? *Journal of Personality and Social Psychology*, 65, 1132–1151.

Kruger, J., & Dunning, D. (1999). Unskilled and unaware of it: How difficulties in recognizing one's own incompetence lead to inflated self-assessments. *Journal of Personality and Social Psychology*, 77, 1121–1134.

Kruglanski, A. W. (1975). The endogenous–exogenous partition in attribution theory. *Psychological Review*, 82, 387–406.

Kruglanski, A. W., & Mackie, D. M. (1990). Majority and minority influence: A judgmental process analysis. *European Review of Social Psychology*, 1, 229–261.

Kruglanski, A. W., Webster, D. M., & Klem, A. (1993). Motivated resistance and openness to persuasion in the presence or absence of prior information. *Journal of Personality and Social Psychology*, 65, 861–876.

Krull, D. S. (1993). Does the grist change the mill? The effect of the perceiver's inferential goal on the process of social inference. *Personality and Social Psychology Bulletin*, 19, 340–348.

Kubzansky, P. E. (1961). The effects of reduced environmental stimulation on human behavior: A review. In A. D. Biderman & H. Zimmer (Eds.), *The manipulation of human behavior* (pp. 51–95). New York: Wiley.

Kuhn, T. S. (1962). *The structure of scientific revolutions*. Chicago, IL: University of Chicago Press.

Kulik, J. A. (1983). Confirmatory attribution and the perpetuation of social beliefs. *Journal of Personality and Social Psychology*, 44, 1171–1181.

Kulik, J. A., & Brown, R. (1979). Frustration, attribution of blame, and aggression. *Journal of Experimental Social Psychology*, 15, 183–194.

Kulik, J. A., Mahler, H. I. M., & Moore, P. J. (1996). Social comparison and affiliation under threat: Effects on recovery from major surgery. *Journal of Personality and Social Psychology*, 71, 967–979.

Kun, A., & Weiner, B. (1973). Necessary versus sufficient causal schemata for success and failure. *Journal of Research on Psychology*, 7, 197–207.

Kunda, Z. (1990). The case for motivated reasoning. *Psychological Bulletin*, 108, 480–498.

Kunda, Z., & Sanitoso, R. (1989). Motivated changes in the self-concept. *Journal of Experimental Social Psychology*, 25, 272–285.

LaFrance, M., & Mayo, C. (1976). Racial differences in gaze behavior during conversations: Two systematic observational studies. *Journal of Personality and Social Psychology*, 33, 547–552.

Lakoff, R. (1973). Language and woman's place. *Language in Society*, 2, 45–80.

Lakoff, R. (1975). *Language and woman's place*. New York: Harper & Row.

Lalljee, M. (1981). Attribution theory and the analysis of explanations. In C. Antaki (Ed.), *The psychology of ordinary explanations of social behaviour* (pp. 119–138). London: Academic Press.

Lamarre, P., & Paredes, J. R. (2003). Growing up trilingual in Montreal: Perceptions of college students. In B. Bayley & S. R. Schechter (Eds.), (2003), *Language socialization in bilingual and multilingual societies* (pp. 62–80). Clevedon, UK: Multilingual Matters.

Lambert, W. E., Hodgson, R. C., Gardner, R. C., & Fillenbaum, S. (1960). Evaluation reactions to spoken language. *Journal of Abnormal and Social Psychology*, 60, 44–51.

Lambert, W. E., Mermigis, L., & Taylor, D. M. (1986). Greek Canadians' attitudes toward own group and other Canadian ethnic groups: A test of the multiculturalism hypothesis. *Canadian Journal of Behavioural Sciences*, 18, 35–51.

Lambert, W. W., Solomon, R. L., & Watson, P. D. (1949). Reinforcement and extinction as factors in size estimation. *Journal of Experimental Psychology*, 39, 637–641.

Lamm, H., & Kayser, E. (1978). The allocation of monetary gain and loss following dyadic performance: The weight given effort and ability under conditions of low and high intradyadic attraction. *European Journal of Social Psychology*, 8, 275–278.

Lamm, H., & Wiesmann, U. (1997). Subjective attributes of attraction: How people characterize their liking, their love, and their being in love. *Personal Relationships*, 4, 271–284.

Landman, J., & Manis, M. (1983). Social cognition: Some historical and theoretical perspectives. In L. Berkowitz (Ed.), *Advances in experimental social psychology* (Vol. 16, pp. 49–123). New York: Academic Press.

Landy, D., & Sigall, H. (1974). Beauty is talent: Task evaluation as a function of the performer's physical attractiveness. *Journal of Personality and Social Psychology*, 29, 299–304.

Lane, I. M., & Messé, L. A. (1971). Equity and the distribution of rewards. *Journal of Personality and Social Psychology*, 20, 1–17.

Langer, E. J. (1975). The illusion of control. *Journal of Personality and Social Psychology*, 32, 311–328.

Langer, E. J. (1978). Rethinking the role of thought in social interaction. In J. H. Harvey, W. I. Ickes, & R. F. Kidd (Eds.), *New directions in attribution research* (Vol. 2, pp. 35–58). Hillsdale, NJ: Erlbaum.

Langer, E. J., Bashner, R. S., & Chanowitz, B. (1985). Decreasing prejudice by increasing discrimination. *Journal of Personality and Social Psychology*, 49, 113–120.

Langer, E. J., Blank, A., & Chanowitz, B. (1978). The mindlessness of ostensibly thoughtful action. *Journal of Personality and Social Psychology*, 36, 635–642.

Langlois, J. H., Kalakanis, L., Rubenstein, A. J., Larson, A., Hallam, M., & Smoot, M. (2000). Maxims or myths of beauty? A meta-analytic and theoretical review. *Psychological Bulletin*, 126, 390–423.

Langlois, J. H., Roggman, L. A., & Musselman, L. (1994). What is average and what is not average about attractive faces? *Psychological Science*, 5, 214–220.

LaPiere, R. T. (1934). Attitudes vs actions. *Social Forces*, 13, 230–237.

LaPiere, R. T., & Farnsworth, P.R. (1936). *Social psychology*. New York: McGraw-Hill.

LaPlace, A. C., Chermack S. T., & Taylor, S. P. (1994). Effects of alcohol and drinking experience on human physical aggression. *Personality and Social Psychology Bulletin*, 20, 439–444.

Larson, J. R. Jr., Foster-Fishman, P. G., & Keys, C. B. (1994). Discussion of shared and unshared information in decision-making groups. *Journal of Personality and Social Psychology*, 67, 446–461.

Latané, B. (1981). The psychology of social impact. *American Psychologist*, 36, 343–356.

Latané, B., & Dabbs, J. M. Jr. (1975). Sex, group size and helping in three cities. *Sociometry*, 38, 180–194.

Latané, B., & Darley, J. M. (1970). *The unresponsive bystander: Why doesn't he help?* New York: Appleton-Century-Crofts.

Latané, B., & Darley, J. M. (1976). Help in a crisis: Bystander response to an emergency. In J. W. Thibaut & J. T. Spence (Eds.), *Contemporary topics in social psychology* (pp. 309–332). Morristown, NJ: General Learning Press.

Latané, B., & Nida, S. (1980). Social impact theory and group influence: A social engineering perspective. In P. B. Paulus (Ed.), *Psychology of group influence*. Hillsdale, NJ: Erlbaum.

Latané, B., & Rodin, J. (1969). A lady in distress: Inhibiting effects of friends and strangers on bystander intervention. *Journal of Experimental Social Psychology, 5,* 189–202.

Latané B., Williams, K. D., & Harkins, S. G. (1979). Many hands make light the work: The causes and consequences of social loafing. *Journal of Personality and Social Psychology, 37,* 822–832.

Latané, B., & Wolf, S. (1981). The social impact of majorities and minorities. *Psychological Review, 88,* 438–453.

Latin American Bureau. (1982). *Falklands/Malvinas: Whose crisis?* London: Latin American Bureau.

Laughlin, P. R. (1980). Social combination processes of cooperative problem solving groups on verbal intellective tasks. In M. Fishbein (Ed.), *Progress in social psychology* (Vol. 1, pp. 127–155). Hillsdale, NJ: Erlbaum.

Laughlin, P. R., & Ellis, A. L. (1986). Demonstrability and social combination processes on mathematical intellective tasks. *Journal of Experimental Social Psychology, 22,* 177–189.

Laurenceau, J. P., Barrett, L. F., & Pietromonaco, P. R. (1998). Intimacy as an interpersonal process: The importance of self-disclosure, partner disclosure, and perceived partner responsiveness in interpersonal exchanges. *Journal of Personality and Social Psychology, 74,* 1238–1251.

Lavine, H., Huff, J. W., Wagner, S. H., & Sweeney, D. (1998). The moderating influence of attitude strength on the susceptibility to context effects in attitude surveys. *Journal of Personality and Social Psychology, 75,* 359–373.

Leana, C. R. (1985). A partial test of Janis's groupthink model: Effects of group cohesiveness and leader behavior on defective decision making. *Journal of Management, 11,* 5–17.

Leary, M. R. (1995). *Self-presentation: Impression management and interpersonal behavior.* Madison, WI: Brown & Benchmark.

Leary, M. R., & Kowalski, R. (1995). *Social anxiety.* New York: Guilford.

Leary, M. R., Tambor, E. S., Terdal, S. K., & Downs, D. L. (1995). Self-esteem as an interpersonal monitor: The sociometer hypothesis. *Journal of Personality and Social Psychology, 68,* 518–530.

Leary, M. R., & Tangney, J. P. (2003). *Handbook of self and identity.* New York: Guilford.

Leavitt, H. J. (1951). Some effects of certain communication patterns on group performance. *Journal of Abnormal and Social Psychology, 46,* 38–50.

LeBon, G. (1908). *The crowd: A study of the popular mind.* London: Unwin. (Original work published 1896.)

Lee, J. A. (1988). Love styles. In R. J. Sternberg & M. L. Barnes (Eds.), *The psychology of love* (pp. 38–67). New Haven, CT: Yale University Press.

Lee, Y. T., & Ottati, V. (1993). Determinants of ingroup and outgroup perceptions of heterogeneity. *Journal of Cross-Cultural Psychology, 24,* 298–318.

Leiman, A. H., & Epstein, S. (1961). Thematic sexual responses as related to sexual drive and guilt. *Journal of Abnormal and Social Psychology, 63,* 169–175.

Lemaine, G. (1966). Inégalité, comparison et incomparabilité: Esquisse d'une théorie de l'originalité sociale. *Bulletin de Psychologie, 20,* 24–32.

Lemaine, G. (1974). Social differentiation and social originality. *European Journal of Social Psychology, 4,* 17–52.

Lepore, L., & Brown, R. (1997). Category and stereotype activation: Is prejudice inevitable? *Journal of Personality and Social Psychology, 72,* 275–287.

Lepper, M. R., Greene, D., & Nisbett, R. E. (1973). Undermining children's intrinsic interest with extrinsic reward: A test of the over-justification hypothesis. *Journal of Personality and Social Psychology, 28,* 129–137.

Lerner, M. J. (1977). The justice motive: Some hypotheses as to its origins and forms. *Journal of Personality, 45,* 1–52.

Lerner, M. J., & Miller, D. T. (1978). Just-world research and the attribution process: Looking back and ahead. *Psychological Bulletin, 85,* 1030–1051.

Lesar, T. S., Briceland, L., & Stein, D. S. (1997). Factors related to errors in medication prescribing. *Journal of the American Medical Association, 277,* 312–317.

Letellier, P. (1994). Gay and bisexual domestic violence victimisation: Challenges to feminist theories and responses to violence. *Violence and Victims, 9,* 95–106.

Leventhal, H., Singer, R., & Jones, S. (1965). Effects of fear and specificity of recommendations upon attitudes and behavior. *Journal of Personality and Social Psychology, 2,* 20–29.

Leventhal, H., Watts, J. C., & Pagano, R. (1967). Effects of fear and instructions on how to cope with danger. *Journal of Personality and Social Psychology, 6,* 313–321.

Levine, J. M., & Moreland, R. L. (1990). Progress in small group research. *Annual Review of Psychology, 41,* 585–634.

Levine, J. M., & Moreland, R. L. (1991). Culture and socialization in work groups. In L. B. Resnick, J. M. Levine, & S. D. Teasley (Eds.), *Perspectives on socially shared cognition* (pp. 257–279). Washington, DC: American Psychological Association.

Levine, J. M., & Moreland, R. L. (1994). Group socialization: Theory and research. *European Review of Social Psychology, 5,* 305–336.

Levine, J. M., Moreland, R. L., & Choi, H.-S. (2001). Group socialization and newcomer innovation. In M. A. Hogg & R. S. Tindale (Eds.), *Blackwell handbook of social psychology: Group processes* (pp. 86–106). Oxford, UK: Blackwell.

Levine, J. M., Resnick, L. B., & Higgins, E. T. (1993). Social foundations of cognition. *Annual Review of Psychology, 44,* 585–612.

LeVine, R. A., & Campbell, D. T. (1972). *Ethnocentrism: Theories of conflict, ethnic attitudes and group behavior.* New York: Wiley.

Levinger, G. (1964). Note on need complementarity in marriage. *Psychological Bulletin, 61,* 153–157.

Levinger, G. (1980). Toward the analysis of close relationships. *Journal of Experimental Social Psychology, 16,* 510–544.

Levinger, G., Senn, D. J., & Jorgensen, B. W. (1970). Progress toward permanence in courtship: A test of the Kerckhoff–Davis hypothesis. *Sociometry, 33,* 427–443.

Levitt, E., & Klassen, A. (1974). Public attitudes towards homosexuality: Part of the 1970 national survey by the Institute for Sex Research. *Journal of Homosexuality, 1,* 29–43.

Lévy-Bruhl, L. (1925). *How natives think.* New York: Alfred A. Knopf.

Lewicki, P. (1985). Nonconscious biasing effects of single instances on subsequent judgments. *Journal of Personality and Social Psychology, 48,* 563–574.

Lewin, A. Y., & Duchan, L. (1971). Women in academia. *Science, 173,* 892–895.

Lewin, K. (1936). Some socio-psychological differences between the United States and Germany. *Character and Personality*, 4, 265–293.

Lewin, K. (1943). Forces behind food habits and methods of change. *Bulletin of National Research Council*, 108, 35–65.

Lewin, K. (1947). Frontiers in group dynamics. *Human Relations*, 1, 5–42.

Lewin, K. (1951). *Field theory in social science*. New York: Harper.

Lewin, K., Lippitt, R., & White, R. K. (1939). Patterns of aggressive behavior in experimentally created 'social climates'. *Journal of Social Psychology*, 10, 271–299.

Lewis, A., Snell, M., & Furnham, A. (1987). Lay explanations for the causes of unemployment in Britain: Economic, individualistic, societal or fatalistic? *Political Psychology*, 8, 427–439.

Lewis, O. (1969). *A death in the Sanchez family*. New York: Secker & Warburg.

Leyens, J. P., Camino, L., Parke, R. D., & Berkowitz, L. (1975). Effects of movie violence on aggression in a field setting as a function of group dominance and cohesion. *Journal of Personality and Social Psychology*, 32, 346–360.

Leyens, J.-P., Yzerbyt, V., & Schadron, G. (1994). *Stereotypes and social cognition*. London: Sage.

Lickel, B., Hamilton, D. L., Wieczorkowska, G., Lewis, A. C., & Sherman, S. (2000). Varieties of groups and the perception of group entitativity. *Journal of Personality and Social Psychology*, 78, 223–246.

Liden, R. C., Sparrowe, R. T., & Wayne, S. J. (1997). Leader-Member Exchange theory: The past and potential for the future. *Research in Personnel and Human Resources Management*, 15, 47–119.

Lieberman, M. D. (2000). Intuition: A social cognitive neuroscience approach. *Psychological Bulletin*, 126, 109–137.

Liebrand, W., Messick, D., & Wilke, H. (Eds.). (1992). *Social dilemmas: Theoretical issues and research findings*. Oxford: Pergamon.

Likert, R. (1932). A technique for the measurement of attitudes. *Archives of Psychology*, 22, no. 140, 44–53.

Lilly, J. C. (1956). Mental effects of reduction of ordinary levels of physical stimuli on intact, healthy persons. *Psychiatric Research Reports*, 5, 1–9.

Lim, R. G., & Carnevale, P. J. D. (1990). Contingencies in the mediation of disputes. *Journal of Personality and Social Psychology*, 58, 259–272.

Limber, J. (1977). Language in child and chimp? *American Psychologist*, 32, 280–295.

Lind, E. A., & O'Barr, W. M. (1979). The social significance of speech in the courtroom. In H. Giles & R. N. St. Clair (Eds.), *Language and social psychology*. Oxford, UK: Blackwell.

Lind, J., & Maxwell, G. (1996). Children's experiences of violence in schools. *Children*, March. Wellington, NZ: Office of the Commissioner for Children.

Lindstrom, P. (1997). Persuasion via facts in political discussion. *European Journal of Social Psychology*, 27, 145–163.

Linskold, S. (1978). Trust development, the GRIT proposal, and the effects of conciliatory acts on conflict and cooperation. *Psychological Bulletin*, 85, 772–793.

Linskold, S., & Han, G. (1988). GRIT as a foundation for integrative bargaining. *Personality and Social Psychology Bulletin*, 14, 335–345.

Linville, P. W. (1982). Affective consequences of complexity regarding the self and others. In M. S. Clark & S. T. Fiske (Eds.), *Affect and cognition: The 17th annual Carnegie symposium on cognition* (pp. 79–109). Hillsdale, NJ: Erlbaum.

Linville, P. W. (1985). Self-complexity and affective extremity: Don't put all of your eggs in one cognitive basket. *Social Cognition*, 3, 94–120.

Linville, P. W. (1987). Self-complexity as a cognitive buffer against stress-related depression and illness. *Journal of Personality and Social Psychology*, 52, 663–676.

Linville, P. W., Fischer, G. W., & Salovey, P. (1989). Perceived distributions of the characteristics of ingroup and outgroup members: Empirical evidence and a computer simulation. *Journal of Personality and Social Psychology*, 57, 165–188.

Linz, D. G., Donnerstein, E., & Penrod, S. (1988). Effects of long-term exposure to violent and sexually degrading depictions of women. *Journal of Personality and Social Psychology*, 55, 758–768.

Linz, D., Wilson, B. J., & Donnerstein, E. (1992). Sexual violence in the mass media: Legal solutions, warnings, and mitigation through education. *Journal of Social Issues*, 48, 145–171.

Lipetz, M. E., Cohen, I. H., Dworin, J., & Rogers, L. (1970). Need complementarity, marital stability and marital satisfaction. In T. L. Huston (Ed.), *Personality and social behavior* (pp. 143–165). New York: Academic Press.

Lippa, R. A. (1990). *Introduction to social psychology*. Belmont, CA: Brooks Cole.

Lippitt, R., & White, R. (1943). The 'social climate' of children's groups. In R. G. Barker, J. Kounin, & H. Wright (Eds.), *Child behavior and development* (pp. 485–508). New York: McGraw-Hill.

Lippman, W. (1922). *Public opinion*. New York: Harcourt Brace.

Litton, I., & Potter, J. (1985). Social representations in the ordinary explanation of a 'riot'. *European Journal of Social Psychology*, 15, 371–388.

Liu, J. H. (2000). *Nation building in Malaysia & Singapore: Social representations of history, authority, and legitimising myths*. Paper presented at the Society of Australasian Social Psychologists Conference, Fremantle.

Liu, J. H., Campbell, S. M., & Condie, H. (1995). Ethnocentrism in dating preferences for an American sample: The ingroup bias in social context. *European Journal of Social Psychology*, 25, 95–115.

Liu, J. H., Ng, S. H., Weatherall, A., & Loong, C. (2000). Filial piety, acculturation and intergenerational communication among New Zealand Chinese. *Basic and Applied Social Psychology*, 22, 213–223.

Liu, T. J., & Steele, C. M. (1986). Attributional analysis and self-affirmation. *Journal of Personality and Social Psychology*, 51, 531–540.

Lock, A. (Ed.). (1978). *Action, gesture and symbol: The emergence of language*. London: Academic Press.

Lock, A. (1980). *The guided reinvention of language*. London: Academic Press.

Lockard, J. S., Kirkevold, B. C., & Kalk, D. F. (1980). Cost–benefit indexes of deception in nonviolent crime. *Bulletin of the Psychonomic Society*, 16, 303–306.

Loftin, C., McDowall, D., Wiersema, B., & Cottey, T. J. (1991). Effects of restrictive licensing of handguns on homicide and suicide in the District of Columbia. *New England Journal of Medicine*, 325, 1615–1620.

Loftus, E. F. (1979). *Eyewitness testimony*. Cambridge, MA: Harvard University Press.

Long, K., & Spears, R. (1997). The self-esteem hypothesis revisited: Differentiation and the disaffected. In R. Spears, P. J. Oakes, N. Ellemers, & S. A. Haslam (Eds.), *The social psychology of stereotyping and group life* (pp. 296–317). Oxford, UK: Blackwell.

Long, G. T., & Lerner, M. J. (1974). Deserving the 'personal contract' and altruistic behavior by children. *Journal of Personality and Social Psychology, 29,* 551–556.

Longley, J., & Pruitt, D. G. (1980). Groupthink: A critique of Janis's theory. In L. Wheeler (Ed.), *Review of personality and social psychology* (Vol. 1, pp. 74–93). Beverly Hills, CA: Sage.

Lord, R. G. (1985). An information processing approach to social perception, leadership and behavioral measurement in organizations. *Research in Organizational Behavior, 7,* 87–128.

Lord, R. G., & Brown, D. J. (2004). *Leadership processes and follower self-identity.* Mahwah, NJ: Erlbaum.

Lord, R. G., Brown, D. J., & Freiberg, S. J. (1999). Understanding the dynamics of leadership: The role of follower self-concepts in the leader/follower relationship. *Organizational Behavior and Human Decision Processes, 78,* 1–37.

Lord, R. G., Brown, D. J., & Harvey, J. L. (2001). System constraints on leadership perceptions, behavior and influence: An example of connectionist level processes. In M. A. Hogg & R. S. Tindale (Eds.), *Blackwell handbook of social psychology: Group processes* (pp. 283–310). Oxford, UK: Blackwell.

Lord, R. G., Foti, R. J., & De Vader, C. L. (1984). A test of leadership categorization theory: Internal structure, information processing, and leadership perceptions. *Organizational Behavior and Human Performance, 34,* 343–378.

Lorenz, K. (1966). *On aggression.* New York: Harcourt, Brace & World.

Lorenzi-Cioldi, F., & Clémence, A. (2001). Group processes and the construction of social representations. In M. A. Hogg & R. S. Tindale (Eds.), *Blackwell handbook of social psychology: Group processes* (pp. 311–333). Oxford, UK: Blackwell.

Lorenzi-Cioldi, F., & Doise, W. (1990). Levels of analysis and social identity. In D. Abrams & M. A. Hogg (Eds.), *Social identity theory: Constructive and critical advances* (pp. 71–88). London: Harvester Wheatsheaf.

Lorenzi-Cioldi, F., Eagly, A. H., & Stewart, T. L. (1995). Homogeneity of gender groups in memory. *Journal of Experimental Social Psychology, 31,* 193–217.

Lorge, I., & Solomon, H. (1955). Two models of group behavior in the solution of eureka-type problems. *Psychometrika, 20,* 139–148.

Lotherington, H. (2003). Multiliteracies in Springvale: Negotiating language, culture and identity in suburban Melbourne. In B. Bayley & S. R. Schechter (Eds.), (2003), *Language socialization in bilingual and multilingual societies* (pp. 200–217). Clevedon, UK: Multilingual Matters.

Lott, A. J., Aponte, J. F., Lott, B. E., & McGinley, W. H. (1969). The effect of delayed reward on the development of positive attitudes towards persons. *Journal of Experimental Social Psychology, 5,* 101–113.

Lott, A. J., & Lott, B. E. (1965). Group cohesiveness as interpersonal attraction. *Psychological Bulletin, 64,* 259–309.

Lott, A. J., & Lott, B. E. (1972). The power of liking: Consequences of interpersonal attitudes derived from a liberalized view of secondary reinforcement. In L. Berkowitz (Ed.), *Advances in experimental social psychology* (Vol. 6, pp. 109–148). New York: Academic Press.

Lott, A. J., & Lott, B. E. (1974). The role of reward in the formation of positive interpersonal attitudes. In T. L. Huston (Ed.), *Foundations of interpersonal attraction* (pp. 171–189). New York: Academic Press.

Lott, B. E. (1961). Group cohesiveness: A learning phenomenon. *Journal of Social Psychology, 55,* 275–286.

Lubek, I. (1979). A brief social psychological analysis of research on aggression in social psychology. In A. R. Buss (Ed.), *Psychology in social context* (pp. 259–306). New York: Irvington.

Luce, R. D., & Raiffa, H. (1957). *Games and decisions.* New York: Wiley.

Lueger, R. J. (1980). Person and situation factors influencing transgression in behavior-problem adolescents. *Journal of Abnormal Psychology, 89,* 453–458.

Lumsdaine, A. A., & Janis, I. L. (1953). Resistance to 'counterpropaganda' produced by one-sided and two-sided 'propaganda' presentations. *Public Opinion Quarterly, 17,* 311–318.

Lydon, J., & Dunkel-Schetter, C. (1994). Seeing is committing: A longitudinal study of bolstering commitment in amniocentesis patients. *Personality and Social Psychology Bulletin, 20,* 218–227.

Maass, A. (1999). Linguistic intergroup bias: Stereotype-perpetuation through language. In M. P. Zanna (Ed.), *Advances in experimental social psychology* (Vol. 31, pp. 79–121). San Diego, CA: Academic Press.

Maass, A., & Arcuri, L. (1996). Language and stereotyping. In C. N. Macrae, C. Stangor, & M. Hewstone (Eds.), *Stereotypes and stereotyping* (pp. 193–226). New York: Guilford.

Maass, A., & Clark, R. D. III (1983). Internalisation versus compliance: Differential processes underlying minority influence and conformity. *European Journal of Social Psychology, 13,* 197–215.

Maass, A., & Clark, R. D. III (1984). Hidden impact of minorities: Fifteen years of minority influence research. *Psychological Bulletin, 95,* 428–450.

Maass, A., & Clark, R. D. III (1986). Conversion theory and simultaneous majority/minority influence: Can reactance offer an alternative explanation? *European Journal of Social Psychology, 16,* 305–309.

Maass, A., Clark, R. D. III, & Haberkorn, G. (1982). The effects of differential ascribed category membership and norms on minority influence. *European Journal of Social Psychology, 12,* 89–104.

Maass, A., Salvi, D., Arcuri, L., & Semin, G. (1989). Language use in intergroup contexts: The linguistic intergroup bias. *Journal of Personality and Social Psychology, 57,* 981–993.

Macaulay, J. R., & Berkowitz, L. (Eds.). (1970). *Altruism and helping behavior: Social psychological studies of some antecedents and consequences.* New York: Academic Press.

MacKay, N. J., & Covell, K. (1997). The impact of women in advertisements on attitudes toward women. *Sex Roles, 36,* 573–579.

Mackie, D. M. (1986). Social identification effects in group polarization. *Journal of Personality and Social Psychology, 50,* 720–728.

Mackie, D. M., & Cooper, J. (1984). Attitude polarization: The effects of group membership. *Journal of Personality and Social Psychology, 46,* 575–585.

Mackie, D. M., Devos, T., & Smith, E. R. (2000). Intergroup emotions: Explaining offensive action tendencies in an intergroup context. *Journal of Personality and Social Psychology, 79,* 602–616.

Mackie, D. M., Hamilton, D. L., Susskind, J., & Rosselli, F. (1996). Social psychological foundations of stereotype formation. In C. N. Macrae, C. Stangor, & M. Hewstone (Eds.), *Stereotypes and stereotyping* (pp. 41–78). New York: Guilford.

Mackie, D. M., & Smith, E. R. (2002a). Intergroup emotions and the social self: Prejudice reconceptualized as differentiated reactions to outgroups. In J. P. Forgas & K. D. Williams (Eds.),

The social self: Cognitive, interpersonal, and intergroup perspectives (pp. 309–326). New York: Psychology Press.

Mackie, D. M., & Smith, E. R. (2002b). *From prejudice to intergroup emotions: Differentiated reactions to social groups.* New York: Psychology Press.

Mackie, D. M., & Worth, L. T. (1989). Processing deficits and the mediation of positive affect in persuasion. *Journal of Personality and Social Psychology, 57,* 27–40.

Mackie, D. M., & Worth, L. T. (1990). Processing of persuasive in-group messages. *Journal of Personality and Social Psychology, 58,* 812–822.

Mackie, D. M., Worth, L. T., & Asuncion, A. G. (1990). Processing of persuasive in-group messages. *Journal of Personality and Social Psychology, 58,* 812–822.

MacKinnon, D. W. (1933). *The violation of prohibitions in the solving of problems.* Doctoral dissertation, Harvard University, Cambridge.

MacNeil, M., & Sherif, M. (1976). Norm change over subject generations as a function of arbitrariness of prescribed norms. *Journal of Personality and Social Psychology, 34,* 762–773.

Macrae, C. N., Stangor, C., & Hewstone, M. (Eds.). (1996). *Stereotypes and stereotyping.* New York: Guilford.

Madden, T. J., Ellen, P. S., & Ajzen, I. (1992). A comparison of the theory of planned behavior and the theory of reasoned action. *Personality and Social Psychology Bulletin, 18,* 3–9.

Maes, M., De Meyer, F., Thompson, P., Peeters D., & Cosyns, P. (1994). Synchronised annual rhythms in violent suicide rate, ambient temperature and the light–dark span. *Acta Psychiatrica Scandinavica, 90,* 391–396.

Maguire, K., & Pastore, A. L. (Eds.). (2001). *Sourcebook of criminal justice statistics.* Retrieved January 1, 2002, from http://www.albany.edu/sourcebook

Maio, G. R., & Olson, J. M. (1994). Value–attitude–behaviour relations: The moderating role of attitude functions. *British Journal of Social Psychology, 33,* 301–312.

Major, B. (1981). Gender patterns in touching behavior. In C. Mayo & N. M. Henley (Eds.), *Gender and nonverbal behavior* (pp. 15–37). New York: Springer-Verlag.

Major, B. (1994). From social inequality to personal entitlement: The role of social comparisons, legitimacy appraisals and group memberships. In M. P. Zanna (Ed.), *Advances in experimental social psychology* (Vol. 26, pp. 293–355). San Diego, CA: Academic Press.

Major, B., & Adams, J. B. (1983). Role of gender, interpersonal orientation, and self-presentation in distributive justice behaviour. *Journal of Personality and Social Psychology, 45,* 598–608.

Major, B., & Deaux, K. (1982). Individual differences in justice behavior. In J. Greenberg & R. L. Cohen (Eds.), *Equity and justice in social behavior* (pp. 43–76). New York: Academic Press.

Major, B., & Heslin, R. (1982). Perceptions of same-sex and cross-sex reciprocal touch: It's better to give than to receive. *Journal of Nonverbal Behavior, 3,* 148–163.

Major, B., & Konar, E. (1984). An investigation of sex differences in pay expectations and their possible causes. *Academy of Management Journal, 27,* 777–792.

Major, B., & Schmader, T. (1998). Coping with stigma through psychological disengagement. In J. K. Swim & C. Stangor (Eds.), *Prejudice: The target's perspective* (pp. 219–242). San Diego, CA: Academic Press.

Malamuth, N. M. (1981). Rape proclivity among males. *Journal of Social Issues, 37,* 138–157.

Malamuth, N. M., & Donnerstein, E. (1982). The effects of aggressive-pornographic mass media stimuli. In L. Berkowitz (Ed.), *Advances in experimental social psychology* (Vol. 15, pp. 104–136). New York: Academic Press.

Malinowski, B. (1927). *Sex and repression in savage society.* New York: Harcourt Brace.

Malpass, R. S. (1988). Why not cross-cultural psychology? A characterization of some mainstream views. In M. H. Bond (Ed.), *The cross-cultural challenge to social psychology* (pp. 29–35). Newbury Park, CA: Sage.

Malpass, R. S., & Kravitz, J. (1969). Recognition for faces of own and other race. *Journal of Personality and Social Psychology, 13,* 330–334.

Mandela, N. (1994). *The long walk to freedom: The autobiography of Nelson Mandela.* London: Little Brown.

Maner, J. K., Luce, C. L., Neuberg, S. L., Cialdini, R. B., Brown, S., & Sagarin, B. J. (2002). The effects of perspective taking on motivations for helping: Still no evidence for altruism. *Personality and Social Psychology Bulletin, 28,* 1601–1610.

Manis, M. (1977). Cognitive social psychology. *Personality and Social Psychology Bulletin, 3,* 550–566.

Mann, L. (1981). The baiting crowd in episodes of threatened suicide. *Journal of Personality and Social Psychology, 41,* 703–709.

Mann, L., Newton, J. W., & Innes, J. M. (1982). A test between deindividuation and emergent norm theories of crowd aggression. *Journal of Personality and Social Psychology, 42,* 260–272.

Mann, R. D. (1959). A review of the relationship between personality and performance in small groups. *Psychological Bulletin, 56,* 241–270.

Manstead, A. S. R., & Parker, D. (1995). Evaluating and extending the theory of planned behaviour. *European Review of Social Psychology, 6,* 69–95.

Manstead, A. S. R., Proffitt, C., & Smart, J. L. (1983). Predicting and understanding mother's infant-feeding intentions and behavior: Testing the theory of reasoned action. *Journal of Personality and Social Psychology, 44,* 657–671.

Manstead, A. S. R., & Semin, G. R. (1980). Social facilitation effects: Mere enhancement of dominant responses? *British Journal of Social and Clinical Psychology, 19,* 119–136.

Mantell, D. M. (1971). The potential for violence in Germany. *Journal of Social Issues, 27,* 101–112.

Marks, G., & Miller, N. (1985). The effect of certainty on consensus judgments. *Personality and Social Psychology Bulletin, 2,* 165–177.

Marks, G., & Miller, N. (1987). Ten years of research on the false-consensus effect: An empirical and theoretical review. *Psychological Bulletin, 102,* 72–90.

Markus, H. (1977). Self-schemata and processing information about the self. *Journal of Personality and Social Psychology, 35,* 63–78.

Markus, H. (1978). The effect of mere presence on social facilitation: An unobtrusive test. *Journal of Experimental Social Psychology, 14,* 389–397.

Markus, H. R., & Kitayama, S. (1991). Culture and the self: Implications for cognition, emotion, and motivation. *Psychological Review, 98,* 224–253.

Markus, H., Kitayama, S., & Heiman, R. J. (1996). Culture and basic psychological principles. In E. T. Higgins & A. W. Kruglanski (Eds.), *Social psychology: Handbook of basic principles* (pp. 857–914). New York: Guilford.

Markus, H., & Nurius, P. (1986). Possible selves. *American Psychologist, 41,* 954–969.

Markus, H., & Sentis, K. P. (1982). The self in social information processing. In J. Suls (Ed.), *Psychological perspectives on the self* (Vol. 1, pp. 41–70). Hillsdale, NJ: Erlbaum.

Markus, H., Smith, J., & Moreland, R. L. (1985). Role of the self-concept in the social perception of others. *Journal of Personality and Social Psychology, 49,* 1494–1512.

Markus, H., & Zajonc, R. B. (1985). The cognitive perspective in social psychology. In G. Lindzey & E. Aronson (Eds.), *Handbook of social psychology* (3rd ed., Vol. 1, pp. 137–230). New York: Random House.

Marlowe, F., & Wetsman, A. (2001). Preferred waist-to-hip ratio and ecology. *Personality and Individual Differences, 30,* 481–489.

Marques, J. M, Abrams, D., & Serodio, R. (2001). Being better by being right: Subjective group dynamics and derogation of in-group deviants when generic norms are undermined. *Journal of Personality and Social Psychology, 81,* 436–447.

Marques, J. M., & Páez, D. (1994). The black sheep effect: Social categorization, rejection of ingroup deviates, and perception of group variability. *European Review of Social Psychology, 5,* 37–68.

Marrow, A. J. (1969). *The practical theorist: The life and work of Kurt Lewin.* New York: Basic Books.

Marshall, G. O., & Zimbardo, P. G. (1979). Affective consequences of inadequately explained physiological arousal. *Journal of Personality and Social Psychology, 37,* 970–988.

Martin, C. L. (1986). A ratio measure of sex stereotyping. *Journal of Personality and Social Psychology, 52,* 489–499.

Martin, J., Brickman, P., & Murray, A. (1984). Moral outrage and pragmatism: Explanations for collective action. *Journal of Experimental Social Psychology, 20,* 484–496.

Martin, J., & Murray, A. (1983). Distributive injustice and unfair exchange. In K. S. Cook & D. M. Messick (Eds.), *Theories of equity: Psychological and sociological perspectives.* New York: Praeger.

Martin, L. L., & Clark, L. F. (1990). Social cognition: Exploring the mental processes involved in human social interaction. In M. W. Eysenck (Ed.), *Cognitive psychology: An international review* (Vol. 1, pp. 266–310). Sussex: Wiley.

Martin, R. (1987). Influence minorité et relations entre groupe. In S. Moscovici & G. Mugny (Eds.), *Psychologie de la conversion.* Paris: Cossett de Val.

Martin, R. (1988). Ingroup and outgroup minorities: Differential impact upon public and private response. *European Journal of Social Psychology, 18,* 39–52.

Martin, R. (1998). Majority and minority influence using the after-image paradigm: A series of attempted replications. *Journal of Experimental Social Psychology, 34,* 1–26.

Martin, R., & Hewstone, M. (2003). Social influence processes of control and change: Conformity, obedience to authority, and innovation. In M. A. Hogg & J. Cooper (Eds.), *The Sage handbook of social psychology* (pp. 347–366). London: Sage.

Martz, J. M., Verette, J., Arriaga, X. B., Slovic, L. F., Cox, C. L., & Rusbult, C. E. (1998). Positive illusion in close relationships. *Personal Relationships, 5,* 159–181.

Maslach, C. (1979). Negative emotional biasing of unexplained arousal. *Journal of Personality and Social Psychology, 37,* 953–969.

Matsui, T., Kakuyama, T., & Onglatco, M. L. (1987). Effects of goals and feedback on performance in groups. *Journal of Applied Psychology, 72,* 407–415.

Matthews, K. A. (1982). Psychological perspectives on the type A behaviour pattern. *Psychological Bulletin, 91,* 293–323.

Maxwell, G. M., & Coebergh, B. (1986). Patterns of loneliness in a New Zealand population. *Community Mental Health in New Zealand, 2,* 48–61.

Mazur, A., Booth, A., & Dabbs, J. M. (1992). Testosterone and chess competition. *Social Psychology Quarterly, 55,* 70–77.

McArthur, L. A. (1972). The how and what of why: Some determinants of consequences of causal attributions. *Journal of Personality and Social Psychology, 22,* 171–193.

McArthur, L. Z. (1981). What grabs you? The role of attention in impression formation and causal attribution. In E. T. Higgins, C. P. Herman, & M. P. Zanna (Eds.), *Social cognition: The Ontario symposium* (Vol. 1, pp. 201–246). Hillsdale, NJ: Erlbaum.

McArthur, L. Z., & Baron, R. (1983). Toward an ecological theory of social perception. *Psychological Review, 90,* 215–238.

McArthur, L. Z., & Friedman, S. A. (1980). Illusory correlation in impression formation: Variations in the shared distinctiveness effect as a function of the distinctive person's age, race, and sex. *Journal of Personality and Social Psychology, 39,* 615–624.

McArthur, L. Z., & Post, D. L. (1977). Figural emphasis and person perception. *Journal of Experimental Social Psychology, 13,* 520–535.

McAuliffe, B. J., Jetten, J., Hornsey, M. J., & Hogg, M. A. (2003). Individualist and collectivist group norms: When it's OK to go your own way. *European Journal of Social Psychology, 33,* 57–70.

McAuliffe, B. J., Jetten, J., Hornsey, M. J., & Hogg, M. A. (in press). The impact of individualist and collectivist group norms on evaluations of dissenting group members. *Journal of Experimental Social Psychology.*

McCabe, M. P., Cummins, R. A., & Romeo, Y. (1996). Relationship status, relationship quality, and health. *Journal of Family Studies, 2,* 109–120.

McCall, G., & Simmons, R. (1978). *Identities and interactions* (2nd ed.). New York: Free Press.

McCauley, C. (1989). The nature of social influence in groupthink: Compliance and internalisation. *Journal of Personality and Social Psychology, 57,* 250–260.

McClure, J. (1998). Discounting causes of behavior: Are two reasons better than one? *Journal of Personality and Social Psychology, 74,* 1–14.

McConahay, J. G. (1986). Modern racism, ambivalence, and the modern racism scale. In J. F. Dovidio & S. L. Gaertner (Eds.), *Prejudice, discrimination, and racism* (pp. 91–125). New York: Academic Press.

McCullough, M. E., Worthington, E. L., & Rachal, K. C. (1997). Interpersonal forgiving in close relationships. *Journal of Personality and Social Psychology, 73,* 321–336.

McConnell, A. R., Sherman, S. J., & Hamilton, D. L. (1994). On-line and memory-based aspects of individual and group target judgments. *Journal of Personality and Social Psychology, 67,* 173–185.

McDougall, W. (1908). *An introduction to social psychology.* London: Methuen.

McDougall, W. (1920). *The group mind.* London: Cambridge University Press.

McGarty, C., & Penny, R. E. C. (1988). Categorization, accentuation and social judgement. *British Journal of Social Psychology, 27,* 147–157.

McGarty, C., Haslam, S.A., Turner, J. C., & Oakes, P.J. (1993). Illusory correlation as accentuation of actual intercategory difference: Evidence for the effect with minimal stimulus information. *European Journal of Social Psychology, 23*, 391–410.

McGarty, C., & Turner, J. C. (1992). The effects of categorization on social judgement. *British Journal of Social Psychology, 31*, 253–268.

McGillicuddy, N. B., Welton, G. L., & Pruitt, D. G. (1987). Third-party intervention: A field experiment comparing three different models. *Journal of Personality and Social Psychology, 53*, 104–112.

McGinnies, E. (1966). Studies in persuasion: III. Reactions of Japanese students to one-sided and two-sided communications. *Journal of Social Psychology, 70*, 87–93.

McGovern, L. P. (1976). Dispositional social anxiety and helping behavior under three conditions of threat. *Journal of Personality, 44*, 84–97.

McGrath, J. E., & Hollingshead, A. B. (1994). *Groups interacting with technology.* Newbury Park, CA: Sage.

McGuire, W. J. (1964). Inducing resistance to persuasion. In L. Berkowitz (Ed.), *Advances in experimental social psychology* (Vol. 1, pp. 191–229). New York: Academic Press.

McGuire, W. J. (1968). Personality and susceptibility to social influence. In E. F. Borgatta & W. W. Lambert (Eds.), *Handbook of personality: Theory and research* (pp. 1130–1187). Chicago, IL: Rand-McNally.

McGuire, W. J. (1969). The nature of attitudes and attitude change. In G. Lindzey & E. Aronson (Eds.), *Handbook of social psychology* (2nd ed., Vol. 3, pp. 136–314). Reading, MA: Addison-Wesley.

McGuire, W. J. (1986). The vicissitudes of attitudes and similar representational constructs in twentieth century psychology. *European Journal of Social Psychology, 16*, 89–130.

McGuire, W. J. (1989). The structure of individual attitudes and attitude systems. In A. R. Pratkanis, S. J. Breckler, & A. G. Greenwald (Eds.), *Attitude structure and function* (pp. 37–69). Hillsdale, NJ: Erlbaum.

McGuire, W. J., & Papageorgis, D. (1961). The relative efficacy of various types of prior belief-defence in producing immunity against persuasion. *Journal of Abnormal and Social Psychology, 62*, 327–337.

McKiethen, K. B., Reitman, J. S., Rueter, H. H., & Hirtle, S. C. (1981). Knowledge organisation and skill differences in computer programmers. *Cognitive Psychology, 13*, 307–325.

McKimmie, B. M., Terry, D. J., Hogg, M. A., Manstead, A. S. R., Spears, R., & Doosje, B. (in press). I'm a hypocrite, but so is everyone else: Group support and the reduction of cognitive dissonance. *Group Dynamics: Theory, Research and Practice.*

McMillen, D. L. (1971). Transgression, self-image, and compliant behavior. *Journal of Personality and Social Psychology, 20*, 176–179.

McNamara, T. F. (1987). Language and social identity: Israelis abroad. *Journal of Language and Social Psychology, 6*, 215–228.

Mead, G. H. (1934). *Mind, self and society.* Chicago, IL: University of Chicago Press.

Mead, M. (1928/1961). *Coming of age in Samoa.* New York: Morrow.

Mead, M. (1930/1962). *Growing up in New Guinea.* New York: Morrow.

Mead, M. (1974). [Untitled article]. In G. Lindzey (Ed.), *A history of psychology in autobiography* (Vol. 6, pp. 295–326). Englewood Cliffs, NJ: Prentice Hall.

Medvec, V. H., Madley, S. F., & Gilovich, T. (1995). When less is more: Counterfactual thinking and satisfaction among Olympic medalists. *Journal of Personality and Social Psychology, 69*, 603–610.

Meeus, W., & Raaijmakers, Q. (1986). Administrative obedience as a social phenomenon. In W. Doise & S. Moscovici (Eds.), *Current issues in European social psychology* (Vol. 2, pp. 183–230). Cambridge: Cambridge University Press.

Mehrabian, A. (1972). Nonverbal communication. In J. Cole (Ed.), *Nebraska symposium on motivation* (Vol. 19, pp. 107–162). Lincoln, NE: University of Nebraska Press.

Merei, F. (1949). Group leadership and institutionalization. *Human Relations, 2*, 23–39.

Mervis, C. B., & Rosch, E. (1981). Categorization of natural objects. *Annual Review of Psychology, 32*, 89–115.

Metalsky, G. I., & Abramson, L. Y. (1981). Attributional styles: Toward a framework for conceptualization and assessment. In P. C. Kendall & S. D. Hollon (Eds.), *Cognitive-behavioral intentions: Assessment methods.* New York: Academic Press.

Michelini, R. L., & Snodgrass, S. R. (1980). Defendant characteristics and juridic decisions. *Journal of Research in Personality, 14*, 340–350.

Middlebrook, P. N. (1980). *Social psychology and modern life* (2nd ed.). New York: Knopf.

Middlemist, R. D., Knowles, E. S., & Mutter, C. F. (1976). Personal space invasions in the lavatory: Suggestive evidence for arousal. *Journal of Personality and Social Psychology, 33*, 541–546.

Middleton, D., & Edwards, D. (Eds.). (1990). *Collective remembering.* London: Sage.

Midlarsky, E., & Bryan, J. H. (1972). Affect expressions and children's imitative altruism. *Journal of Experimental Research in Personality, 6*, 195–203.

Midlarsky, E., & Midlarsky, M. (1973). Some determinants of aiding under experimentally induced stress. *Journal of Personality, 41*, 305–327.

Midlarsky, M., & Midlarsky, E. (1976). Status inconsistency, aggressive attitude, and helping behavior. *Journal of Personality, 44*, 371–391.

Mikula, G. (1980). On the role of justice in allocation decisions. In G. Mikula (Ed.), *Justice and social interaction.* New York: Springer-Verlag.

Milardo, R. M., Johnson, M. P., & Huston, T. L. (1983). Developing close relationships: Changing patterns of interaction between pair members and social networks. *Journal of Personality and Social Psychology, 44*, 964–976.

Miles, D. R., & Carey, G. (1997). Genetic and environmental architecture of human aggression. *Journal of Personality and Social Psychology, 72*, 207–217.

Milgram, S. (1963). Behavioral study of obedience. *Journal of Abnormal and Social Psychology, 67*, 371–378.

Milgram, S. (1974). *Obedience to authority.* London: Tavistock.

Milgram, S. (1992). *The individual in a social world: Essays and experiments* (2nd ed.). New York: McGraw-Hill.

Milgram, S., & Toch, H. (1969). Collective behavior: Crowds and social movements. In G. Lindzey & E. Aronson (Eds.), *Handbook of social psychology* (2nd ed., Vol. 4, pp. 507–610). Reading, MA: Addison-Wesley.

Milham, J. (1974). Two components of need for approval score and their relationship to cheating following success and failure. *Journal of Research in Personality, 8*, 378–392.

Mill, J. S. (1869). *The analysis of the phenomenon of the human mind.* New York: Kelley.

Millar, M. G., & Millar, K. U. (1990). Attitude change as a function of attitude type and argument type. *Journal of Personality and Social Psychology, 59*, 217–228.

Millar, M. G., & Tesser, A. (1986). Effects of affective and cognitive focus on the attitude–behavior relation. *Journal of Personality and Social Psychology, 51*, 270–276.

Miller, C. E. (1989). The social psychological effects of group decision rules. In P. B. Paulus (Ed.), *Psychology of group influence* (2nd ed., pp. 327–355). Hillsdale, NJ: Erlbaum.

Miller, D. T. (1977). Altruism and the threat to a belief in a just world. *Journal of Experimental Social Psychology, 13*, 113–124.

Miller, D. T., & McFarland, C. (1987). Pluralistic ignorance: When similarity is interpreted as dissimilarity. *Journal of Personality and Social Psychology, 53*, 298–305.

Miller, D. T., & Porter, C. A. (1980). Effects of temporal perspective on the attribution process. *Journal of Personality and Social Psychology, 39*, 532–541.

Miller, D. T., & Porter, C. A. (1983). Self-blame in victims of violence. *Journal of Social Issues, 39*, 139–152.

Miller, D. T., & Ross, M. (1975). Self-serving biases in the attribution of causality: Fact or fiction? *Psychological Bulletin, 82*, 213–225.

Miller, J. G. (1984). Culture and the development of everyday social explanation. *Journal of Personality and Social Psychology, 46*, 961–978.

Miller, N. E. (1948). Theory and experiment relating psychoanalytic displacement to stimulus-response generalisation. *Journal of Abnormal and Social Psychology, 43*, 155–178.

Miller, N. E., & Bugelski, R. (1948). Minor studies in aggression: The influence of frustrations imposed by the ingroup on attitudes toward outgroups. *Journal of Psychology, 25*, 437–442.

Miller, N., & Brewer, M. B. (Eds.). (1984). *Groups in contact: The psychology of desegregation*. New York: Academic Press.

Miller, N., Maruyama, G., Beaber, R. J., & Valone, K. (1976). Speed of speech and persuasion. *Journal of Personality and Social Psychology, 34*, 615–625.

Miller, N., Brewer, M. B., & Edwards, K. (1985). Cooperative interaction in desegregated settings: A laboratory analogue. *Journal of Social Issues, 41*, 63–79.

Miller, P. A., & Eisenberg, N. (1988). The relation of empathy to aggressive and externalizing/antisocial behavior. *Psychological Bulletin, 103*, 324–344.

Milner, D. (1996). Children and racism: Beyond the value of the dolls. In W. P. Robinson (Ed.), *Social groups and identities: Developing the legacy of Henri Tajfel* (pp. 246–268). Oxford, UK: Butterworth-Heinemann.

Minahan, N. M. (1971). Relationships among self-perceived physical attractiveness, body shape, and personality of teen-age girls. *Dissertation Abstracts International, 32*, 1249–1250.

Minard, R. D. (1952). Race relations in the Pocahontas coal field. *Journal of Social Issues, 8*, 29–44.

Mischel, W. (1968). *Personality and assessment*. New York: Wiley.

Mischel, W., Ebbesen, E. B., & Zeiss, A. R. (1976). Determinants of selective memory about the self. *Journal of Consulting and Clinical Psychology, 44*, 92–103.

Misumi, J., & Peterson, M. F. (1985). The performance-maintenance (P-M) theory of leadership: Review of a Japanese research program. *Administrative Science Quarterly, 30*, 198–223.

Mita, T. H., Dermer, M., & Knight, J. (1977). Reversed facial images and the mere exposure hypothesis. *Journal of Personality and Social Psychology, 35*, 597–601.

Mitchell, H. E. (1979). *Informational and affective determinants of juror decision making*. Doctoral dissertation, Purdue University.

Moghaddam, F. M. (1990). Modulative and generative orientations in psychology: Implications for psychology in the three worlds. *Journal of Social Issues, 46(3)*, 21–41.

Moghaddam, F. M. (1998). *Social psychology: Exploring universals across cultures*. New York: Freeman.

Moghaddam, F. M., Taylor, D. M., & Wright, S. C. (1993). *Social psychology in cross-cultural perspective*. New York: Freeman.

Moliner, P., & Tafani, E. (1997). Attitudes and social representations: A theoretical and experimental approach. *European Journal of Social Psychology, 27*, 687–702.

Moloney, G., & Walker, I. (2000). Past and present: Social representations and organ donation. Paper presented at the Society of Australasian Social Psychologists Conference, Perth, Australia.

Monson, T. C., & Hesley, J. W. (1982). Causal attributions for behavior consistent or inconsistent with an actor's personality traits: Differences between those offered by actors and observers. *Journal of Experimental Social Psychology, 18*, 426–432.

Montague, A. (1973). *Man and aggression* (2nd ed.). London: Oxford University Press.

Monteil, J. M., & Huguet, P. (1999). *Social context and cognitive performance*. Philadelphia, PA: Psychology Press.

Monteith, M. J. (1993). Self-regulation of prejudiced responses: Implication for progress in prejudice-reduction efforts. *Journal of Personality and Social Psychology, 65*, 469–485.

Montepare, J. M., & Vega, C. (1988). Women's vocal reactions to intimate and casual male friends. *Personality and Social Psychology Bulletin, 14*, 103–112.

Moore, B. S., Sherrod, D. R., Liu, T. J., & Underwood, B. (1979). The dispositional shift in attribution over time. *Journal of Experimental Social Psychology, 15*, 553–569.

Moreland, R. L. (1985). Social categorization and the assimilation of 'new' group members. *Journal of Personality and Social Psychology, 48*, 1173–1190.

Moreland, R. L., & Beach, S. R. (1992). Exposure effects in the classroom: The development of affinity among students. *Journal of Experimental Social Psychology, 28*, 255–276.

Moreland, R. L., & Levine, J. M. (1982) Socialization in small groups: Temporal changes in individual–group relations. In L. Berkowitz (Ed.), *Advances in experimental social psychology* (Vol. 15, pp. 137–192). New York: Academic Press.

Moreland, R. L., & Levine, J. M. (1984). Role transitions in small groups. In V. Allen & E. van de Vliert (Eds.), *Role transitions: Explorations and explanations* (pp. 181–195). New York: Plenum.

Moreland, R. L., & Levine, J. M. (1989). Newcomers and oldtimers in small groups. In P. B. Paulus (Ed.), *Psychology of group influence* (2nd ed., pp. 143–186). Hillsdale, NJ: Erlbaum.

Moreland, R.L., & Zajonc, R. B. (1982). Exposure effects in person perception: Familiarity, similarity, and attraction. *Journal of Experimental Social Psychology, 18*, 395–415.

Moreland, R. L., Levine, J. M., & Cini, M. (1993). Group socialisation: The role of commitment. In M. A. Hogg & D. Abrams (Eds.), *Group motivation: Social psychological perspectives* (pp. 105–129). London: Harvester Wheatsheaf.

Moreland, R. L., Argote, L., & Krishnan, R. (1996). Socially shared cognition at work: Transactive memory and group performance. In J. L. Nye & A. M. Bower (Eds.), *What's social about social cognition: Research on socially shared cognition in small groups* (pp. 57–84). Thousand Oaks, CA: Sage.

Moreland, R. L., Hogg, M. A., & Hains, S. C. (1994). Back to the future: Social psychological research on groups. *Journal of Experimental Social Psychology, 30,* 527–555.

Moriarty, T. (1975). Crime, commitment and the responsive bystander: Two field experiments. *Journal of Personality and Social Psychology, 31,* 370–376.

Morris, D. (1967). *The naked ape.* New York: McGraw-Hill.

Morris, D., Collett, P., Marsh, P., & O'Shaughnessy, M. (1979). *Gestures: Their origins and distribution.* New York: Stein & Day.

Morris, M. W., & Peng, K. P. (1994). Culture and cause: American and Chinese attributions for social and physical events. *Journal of Personality and Social Psychology, 67,* 949–971.

Morris, W. N., & Miller, R. S. (1975). The effects of consensus-breaking and consensus pre-empting partners on reduction of conformity. *Journal of Experimental Social Psychology, 11,* 215–223.

Morton, T. L. (1978). Intimacy and reciprocity of exchange: A comparison of spouses and strangers. *Journal of Personality and Social Psychology, 36,* 72–81.

Moscovici, S. (1961). *La psychanalyse: Son image et son public.* Paris: Presses Universitaires de France.

Moscovici, S. (1972). Society and theory in social psychology. In J. Israel & H. Tajfel (Eds.), *The context of social psychology: A critical assessment* (pp. 17–68). New York: Academic Press.

Moscovici, S. (1976). *Social influence and social change.* London: Academic Press.

Moscovici, S. (1980). Toward a theory of conversion behavior. In L. Berkowitz (Ed.), *Advances in experimental social psychology* (Vol. 13, pp. 202–239). New York: Academic Press.

Moscovici, S. (1981). On social representation. In J. P. Forgas (Ed.), *Social cognition: Perspectives on everyday understanding* (pp. 181–209). London: Academic Press.

Moscovici, S. (1982). The coming era of representations. In J.-P. Codol & J. P. Leyens (Eds.), *Cognitive analysis of social behaviour* (pp. 115–150). The Hague: Martinus Nijhoff.

Moscovici, S. (1985a). Social influence and conformity. In G. Lindzey & E. Aronson (Eds.), *Handbook of social psychology* (3rd ed., Vol. 2, pp. 347–412). New York: Random House.

Moscovici, S. (1985b). *The age of the crowd.* Cambridge: Cambridge University Press.

Moscovici, S. (1988). Notes towards a description of social representations. *European Journal of Social Psychology, 18,* 211–250.

Moscovici, S., & Faucheux, C. (1972). Social influence, conforming bias, and the study of active minorities. In L. Berkowitz (Ed.), *Advances in experimental social psychology* (Vol. 6, pp. 149–202). New York: Academic Press.

Moscovici, S., & Lage, E. (1976). Studies in social influence: III. Majority vs. minority influence in a group. *European Journal of Social Psychology, 6,* 149–174.

Moscovici, S., Lage, E., & Naffrechoux, M. (1969). Influence of a consistent minority on the responses of a majority in a colour perception task. *Sociometry, 32,* 365–380.

Moscovici, S., & Mugny, G. (1983). Minority influence. In P. B. Paulus (Ed.), *Basic group processes* (pp. 41–64). New York: Springer-Verlag.

Moscovici, S., & Personnaz, B. (1980). Studies in social influence: V. Minority influence and conversion behavior in a perceptual task. *Journal of Experimental Social Psychology, 16,* 270–282.

Moscovici, S., & Personnaz, B. (1986). Studies on latent influence by the spectrometer method: I. The impact of psychologization in the case of conversion by a minority or a majority. *European Journal of Social Psychology, 16,* 345–360.

Moscovici, S., & Zavalloni, M. (1969). The group as a polarizer of attitudes. *Journal of Personality and Social Psychology, 12,* 125–135.

Mosher, D. L., & Anderson, R. D. (1986). Macho personality, sexual aggression, and reactions to guided imagery of realistic rape. *Journal of Research in Personality, 20,* 77–94.

Mowday, R. T., & Sutton, R. I. (1993). Organisational behavior: Linking individuals and groups to organisational contexts. *Annual Review of Psychology, 44,* 195–229.

Mucchi-Faina, A., Maass, A., & Volpato, C. (1991). Social influence: The role of originality. *European Journal of Social Psychology, 21,* 183–197.

Mudrack, P. E. (1989). Defining group cohesiveness: A legacy of confusion. *Small Group Behavior, 20,* 37–49.

Mugny, G. (1982). *The power of minorities.* London: Academic Press.

Mugny, G., & Papastamou, S. (1982). Minority influence and psychosocial identity. *European Journal of Social Psychology, 12,* 379–394.

Mulac, A., Bradac, J. J., & Gibbons, P. (2001). Empirical support for the gender-as-culture hypothesis: An intercultural analysis of male/female language differences. *Human Communication Research, 27,* 121–152.

Mulac, A., Studley, L. B., Wiemann, J. M., & Bradac, J. J. (1987). Male/female gaze in same-sex and mixed-sex dyads: Gender-linked differences and mutual influence. *Human Communication Research, 13,* 323–343.

Mulder, M. (1960). Communication structure, decision structure and group performance. *Sociometry, 23,* 1–14.

Mullen, B. (1983). Operationalizing the effect of the group on the individual: A self-attention perspective. *Journal of Experimental Social Psychology, 19,* 295–322.

Mullen, B. (1986). Atrocity as a function of lynch mob composition: A self-attention perspective. *Personality and Social Psychology Bulletin, 12,* 187–197.

Mullen, B., Atkins, J. L., Champion, D. S., Edwards, C., Hardy, D., Story, J. E., & Vanderklok, M. (1985). The false consensus effect: A meta-analysis of 115 hypothesis tests. *Journal of Experimental Social Psychology, 21,* 262–283.

Mullen, B., & Hu, L. (1989). Perceptions of ingroup and outgroup variability: A meta-analytic integration. *Basic and Applied Social Psychology, 10,* 233–252.

Mullen, B., & Johnson, C. (1990). Distinctiveness-based illusory correlations and stereotyping: A meta-analytic integration. *British Journal of Social Psychology, 29,* 11–28.

Mullen, B., Johnson, C., & Salas, E. (1991). Productivity loss in brainstorming groups. *Basic and Applied Social Psychology, 12,* 3–24.

Mullen, B., & Riordan, C. A. (1988). Self-serving attributions for performance in naturalistic settings: A meta-analytic review. *Journal of Applied Social Psychology, 18,* 3–22.

Mullen, B., Salas, E., & Driskell, J. E. (1989). Salience, motivation, and artifact as contributions to the relation between participation rate and leadership. *Journal of Experimental Social Psychology, 25,* 545–559.

Mullen, P. E. (1984). Mental disorder and dangerousness. *Australian and New Zealand Journal of Psychiatry, 18,* 8–17.

Mullin, C. R., & Linz, D. (1995). Desensitisation and resensitisation to violence against women: Effects of exposure to sexually violent films on judgments of domestic violence victims. *Journal of Personality and Social Psychology, 69,* 449–459.

Mummendey, A., Simon, B., Dietze, C., Grünert, M., Haeger, G., Kessler, S., Lettben, S., & Schäferhoff, S. (1992). Categorization is not enough: Intergroup discrimination in negative outcome allocation. *Journal of Experimental Social Psychology, 28,* 125–144.

Mummendey, A., & Wenzel, M. (1999). Social discrimination and tolerance in intergroup relations: Reactions to intergroup difference. *Personality and Social Psychology Review, 3,* 158–174.

Murchison, C. (Ed.). (1935). *Handbook of social psychology.* Worcester, MA: Clark University Press.

Murphy, G., & Murphy, L. B. (1931). *Experimental social psychology.* New York: Harper. (Rev. ed. published with T. M. Newcomb in 1937.)

Murphy, L., & Murphy, G. (1970). Perspectives in cross-cultural research. *Journal of Cross-Cultural Psychology, 1,* 1–4.

Murphy, S. T., Monahan, J. L., & Zajonc, R. B. (1995). Additivity of nonconscious affect: Combined effects of priming and exposure. *Journal of Personality and Social Psychology, 69,* 589–602.

Murphy, S. T., & Zajonc, R. B. (1993). Affect, cognition, and awareness: Affective priming with optimal and suboptimal stimulus exposures. *Journal of Personality and Social Psychology, 64,* 723–739.

Murray, S. L., & Holmes, J. G. (1997). A leap of faith? Positive illusions in romantic relationships. *Personality and Social Psychology Bulletin, 23,* 586–604.

Murstein, B. I. (1980). Love at first sight: A myth. *Medical Aspects of Human Sexuality, 14,* 34, 39–41.

Myers, D. G., & Lamm, H. (1975). The polarising effect of group discussion. *American Scientist, 63,* 297–303.

Myers, D. G., & Lamm, H. (1976). The group polarisation phenomenon. *Psychological Bulletin, 83,* 602–627.

Nadler, A. (1986). Help seeking as a cultural phenomenon: Differences between city and kibbutz dwellers. *Journal of Personality and Social Psychology, 51,* 976–982.

Nadler, A. (1991). Help-seeking behavior: Psychological costs and instrumental benefits. In M. S. Clark (Ed.), *Prosocial behavior* (pp. 290–311). Newbury Park, CA: Sage.

Nahem, J. (1980). *Psychology and psychiatry today: A Marxist view.* New York: International Publishers.

Neisser, U. (1967). *Cognitive psychology.* Englewood Cliffs, NJ: Prentice Hall.

Nemeth, C. (1970). Bargaining and reciprocity. *Psychological Bulletin, 74,* 297–308.

Nemeth, C. (1981). Jury trials: Psychology and law. In L. Berkowitz (Ed.), *Advances in experimental social psychology* (Vol. 14, pp. 309–367). New York: Academic Press.

Nemeth, C. (1986). Differential contributions of majority and minority influence. *Psychological Review, 93,* 23–32.

Nemeth, C., & Chiles, C. (1988). Modelling courage: The role of dissent in fostering independence. *European Journal of Social Psychology, 18,* 275–280.

Nemeth, C., Swedlund, M., & Kanki, B. (1974). Patterning of the minority's response and their influence on the majority. *European Journal of Social Psychology, 4,* 53–64.

Nemeth, C., & Wachtler, J. (1983). Creative problem solving as a result of majority vs. minority influence. *European Journal of Social Psychology, 13,* 45–55.

Nemeth, C., Wachtler, J., & Endicott, J. (1977). Increasing the size of the minority: Some gains and some losses. *European Journal of Social Psychology, 7,* 15–27.

Nesdale, D. (in press). Social identity processes and children's ethnic prejudice. In M. Bennett & F. Sani (Eds.), *The Development of the Social Self.* London: Psychology Press.

Neuberg, S. L., & Fiske, S. T. (1987). Motivational influences on impression formation: Outcome dependency, accuracy-driven attention, and individuating processes. *Journal of Personality and Social Psychology, 53,* 431–444.

New Zealand Police Statistics (2000). Retrieved January 21, 2001, from http://www.police.govt.nz/download/nzpolice-stats-apr2000.pdf

Newcomb, T. M. (1961). *The acquaintance process.* New York: Holt, Rinehart & Winston.

Newcomb, T. M. (1965). Attitude development as a function of reference groups: The Bennington study. In H. Proshansky & B. Seidenberg (Eds.), *Basic studies in social psychology* (pp. 215–225). New York: Holt, Rinehart & Winston.

Ng, S. H. (1980). *The social psychology of power.* London: Academic Press.

Ng, S. H. (1990). Androgenic coding of man and his in memory by language users. *Journal of Experimental Social Psychology, 26,* 455–464.

Ng, S. H. (1996). Power: An essay in honour of Henri Tajfel. In W. P. Robinson (Ed.), *Social groups and identities: Developing the legacy of Henri Tajfel* (pp. 191–214). Oxford, UK: Butterworth-Heinemann.

Ng, S. H., & Bradac, J. J. (1993). *Power in language.* Thousand Oaks, CA: Sage.

Ng, S. H., Bell, D., & Brooke, M. (1993). Gaining turns and achieving high influence in small conversational groups. *British Journal of Social Psychology, 32,* 265–275.

Nieburg, H. (1969). *Political violence: The behavioural process.* New York: St Martin's Press.

Niedenthal, P. M., & Beike, D. R. (1997). Interrelated and isolated self-concepts. *Personality and Social Psychology Review, 1,* 106–128.

Nisbett, R. E. (1993). Violence and US regional culture. *American Psychologist, 48,* 441–449.

Nisbett, R. E., & Cohen, D. (1996). *Culture of honor: The psychology of violence in the South.* Boulder, CO: Westview Press.

Nisbett, R. E., Krantz, D. H., Jepson, C., & Fong, G. T. (1982). Improving inductive inference. In D. Kahneman, P. Slovic, & A. Tversky (Eds.), *Judgment under uncertainty: Heuristics and biases* (pp. 445–462). New York: Cambridge University Press.

Nisbett, R. E., & Ross, L. (1980). *Human inference: Strategies and shortcomings of social judgment.* Englewood Cliffs, NJ: Prentice Hall.

Nisbett, R. E., & Wilson, T. D. (1977). Telling more than we can know: Verbal reports on mental behavior. *Psychological Review, 84,* 231–259.

Nisbett, R. E., Zukier, H., & Lemley, R. E. (1981). The dilution effect: Non-diagnostic information weakens the implications of diagnostic information. *Cognitive Psychology, 13,* 248–277.

Noels, K. A., Giles, H., & Le Poire, B. (2003). Language and communication processes. In M. A. Hogg & J. Cooper (Eds.), *The Sage handbook of social psychology* (pp. 232–257). London: Sage.

Noels, K. A., Pon, G., & Clément, R. (1996). Language and adjustment: The role of linguistic self-confidence in the acculturation process. *Journal of Language and Social Psychology, 15,* 246–264.

Nolen-Hoeksma, S., Girgus, J. S., & Seligman, M. E. P. (1992). Predictors and consequences of childhood depressive symptoms: Five year longitudinal study. *Journal of Abnormal Psychology, 101,* 405–422.

Noller, P. (1984). *Nonverbal communication and marital interaction.* Oxford: Pergamon.

Noller, P. (1996). What is this thing called love? Defining the love that supports marriage and family. *Personal Relationships, 3,* 97–115.

Noller, P., & Callan, V. J. (1990). *Adolescents in the family.* London: Routledge & Kegan Paul.

Noller, P., & Fitzpatrick, M. A. (1990). Marital communication in the eighties. *Journal of Marriage and the Family, 52,* 832–843.

Noller, P., & Ruzzene, M. (1991). Communication in marriage: The influence of affect and cognition. In G. J. O. Fletcher & F. D. Fincham (Eds.), *Cognition and close relationships* (pp. 203–233). Hillsdale, NJ: Erlbaum.

Norton, M. I., Monin, B., Cooper, J., & Hogg, M. A. (2003). Vicarious dissonance: Attitude change from the inconsistency of others. *Journal of Personality and Social Psychology, 85,* 47–62.

Nye, J. L., & Bower, A. M. (Eds.). (1996). *What's social about social cognition: Research on socially shared cognition in small groups.* Thousand Oaks, CA: Sage.

O'Barr, W. M., & Atkins, B. K. (1980). 'Women's language' or 'powerless language'? In S. McConnell-Ginet, R. Borker, & N. Furman (Eds.), *Women and language in literature and society* (pp. 93–110). New York: Praeger.

O'Connor, S., & Rosenblood, L. (1996). Affiliation motivation in everyday experience: A theoretical perspective. *Journal of Personality and Social Psychology, 70,* 513–522.

O'Leary, K. D., Barling, J., Arias, I., Rosenbaum, A., Malone, J., & Tyree, A. (1989). Prevalence and stability of physical aggression between spouses: A longitudinal analysis. *Journal of Consulting and Clinical Psychology, 57,* 263–268.

Oakes, P. J. (1987). The salience of social categories. In J. C. Turner, M. A. Hogg, P. J. Oakes, S. D. Reicher, & M. S. Wetherell, *Rediscovering the social group: A self categorization theory* (pp. 117–141). Oxford, UK: Blackwell.

Oakes, P. J., Haslam, S. A., & Reynolds, K. J. (1999). Social categorization and social context: Is stereotype change a matter of information or of meaning? In D. Abrams & M. A. Hogg (Eds.), *Social identity and social cognition* (pp. 55–79). Oxford, UK: Blackwell.

Oakes, P. J., Haslam, S. A., & Turner, J. C. (1994). *Stereotyping and social reality.* Oxford: Blackwell.

Oakes, P. J., & Turner, J. C. (1990). Is limited information processing capacity the cause of social stereotyping? *European Review of Social Psychology, 1,* 111–135.

Oliver, P. (1986). Rest home accommodation for the elderly: A civil rights perspective. *Community Mental Health in New Zealand, 3,* 74–91.

Oliver, P. (1990). Nuclear freedom and young people's sense of efficacy in relation to the prevention of nuclear war. *American Journal of Orthopsychiatry, 60,* 611–621.

Oliver, P., & Vaughan, G. M. (1991). How we see one another: Interethnic perceptions of New Zealand teenagers. *Journal of Intercultural Studies, 12,* 17–38.

Olson, J. M. (1988). Misattribution, preparatory information, and speech anxiety. *Journal of Personality and Social Psychology, 54,* 758–767.

Olson, J. M., & Zanna, M. P. (1993). Attitudes and attitude change. *Annual Review of Psychology, 44,* 117–154.

Oppenheim, A. N. (1992). *Questionnaire design, interviewing and attitude measurement* (2nd ed.). London: Pinter.

Orano, P. (1901). *Psicologia sociale.* Bari: Lacerta.

Orne, M. T. (1962). On the social psychology of the psychology experiment: With particular reference to demand characteristics and their implications. *American Psychologist, 17,* 776–783.

Ortony, A., & Turner, T. J. (1990). What's basic about basic emotions? *Psychological Review, 97,* 315–331.

Orvis, B. R., Kelley, H. H., & Butler, D. (1976). Attributional conflicts in young couples. In J. H. Harvey, W. J. Ickes, & R. F. Kidd (Eds.), *New directions in attribution research* (Vol. 1, pp. 353–386). Hillsdale, NJ: Erlbaum.

Orwell, G. (1962). *The road to Wigan pier.* Harmondsworth: Penguin.

Osborn, A. F. (1957). *Applied imagination* (Rev. ed.). New York: Scribners.

Osgood, C. E. (1962). *An alternative to war or surrender.* Urbana, IL: University of Illinois Press.

Osgood, C. E., Suci, G. J., & Tannenbaum, P. H. (1957). *The measurement of meaning.* Urbana, IL: University of Illinois Press.

Oskamp, S. (1977). *Attitudes and opinions.* Englewood Cliffs, NJ: Prentice Hall.

Oskamp, S. (1984). *Applied social psychology.* Englewood Cliffs, NJ: Prentice Hall.

Ostrom, T. M. (1968). The relationship between the affective, behavioural, and cognitive components of attitude. *Journal of Experimental Social Psychology, 5,* 12–30.

Ostrom, T. M. (1989a) Three catechisms for social memory. In P. R. Solomon, G. R. Goethals, C. M. Kelley, & B. R. Stephens (Eds.), *Memory: Interdisciplinary approaches* (pp. 201–220). New York: Springer.

Ostrom, T. M. (1989b). Interdependence of attitude theory and measurement. In A. R. Pratkanis, S. J. Breckler, & A. G. Greenwald (Eds.), *Attitude structure and function* (pp. 11–36). Hillsdale, NJ: Erlbaum.

Ostrom, T. M., & Sedikides, C. (1992). Outgroup homogeneity effects in natural and minimal groups. *Psychological Bulletin, 112,* 536–552.

Oswald, P. A. (1996). The effects of cognitive and affective perspective taking on empathic concern and altruistic helping. *Journal of Social Psychology, 136,* 613–623.

Oswald, P. A. (2002). The interactive effects of affective demeanor, cognitive processes, and perspective-taking focus on helping behavior. *Journal of Social Psychology, 142,* 120–132.

Otten, S., Mummendey, A., & Blanz, M. (1996). Intergroup discrimination in positive and negative outcome allocations: Impact of stimulus valence, relative group status, and relative group size. *Personality and Social Psychology Bulletin, 22,* 568–581.

Oyserman, D., Coon, H. M., & Kemmelmeier, M. (2002). Rethinking individualism and collectivism: Evaluation of theoretical assumptions and meta-analyses. *Psychological Bulletin, 128,* 3–72.

Pagel, M. D., & Davidson, A. R. (1984). A comparison of three social-psychological models of attitude and behavioral plan: Prediction of contraceptive behavior. *Journal of Personality and Social Psychology, 47,* 517–533.

Paglia, A., & Room, R. (1999). Expectancies about the effects of alcohol on the self and on others as determinants of alcohol policy. *Journal of Applied Social Psychology, 29,* 2632–2651.

Paik, H., & Comstock, G. (1994). The effects of television violence on antisocial behaviour: A meta-analysis. *Communication Research, 21,* 516–546.

Palinkas, L. A., Cravalho, M., & Browner, D. (1995). Seasonal variation of depressive symptoms in Antarctica. *Acta Psychiatrica Scandinavica, 91,* 423–429.

Pandey, J., & Griffitt, W. (1974). Attraction and helping. *Bulletin of Psychonomic Psychology, 3,* 123–124.

Pandey, J., Sinha, Y., Prakash, A., & Tripathi, R. C. (1982). Right–Left political ideologies and attribution of the causes of poverty. *European Journal of Social Psychology, 12,* 327–331.

Pantin, H. M., & Carver, C. S. (1982). Induced competence and the bystander effect. *Journal of Applied Social Psychology, 12,* 100–111.

Parducci, A. (1968). The relativism of absolute judgments. *Scientific American, 219,* 84–90.

Park, B. (1986). A method for studying the development of impressions of real people. *Journal of Personality and Social Psychology, 51,* 907–917.

Park, B., & Hastie, R. (1987). Perception of variability in category development: Instance versus abstraction-based stereotypes. *Journal of Personality and Social Psychology, 53,* 621–635.

Park, B., & Rothbart, M. (1982). Perception of outgroup homogeneity and levels of social categorization: Memory for the subordinate attributes of ingroup and outgroup members. *Journal of Personality and Social Psychology, 42,* 1051–1068.

Parker, D., Manstead, A. S. R., & Stradling, S. G. (1995). Extending the theory of planned behaviour: The role of personal norm. *British Journal of Social Psychology, 34,* 127–137.

Parkinson, B. (1985). Emotional effects of false autonomic feedback. *Psychological Bulletin, 98,* 471–494.

Parsons, J. E., Adler, T., & Meece, J. L. (1984). Sex differences in achievement: A test of alternate theories. *Journal of Personality and Social Psychology, 46,* 26–43.

Patch, M. E. (1986). The role of source legitimacy in sequential request strategies of compliance. *Personality and Social Psychology Bulletin, 12,* 199–205.

Patterson, F. (1978). Conversations with a gorilla. *National Geographic, 154,* 438–465.

Patterson, M. L. (1983). *Nonverbal behavior: A functional perspective.* New York: Springer.

Paulhus, D. L., & Levitt, K. (1987). Desirable responding triggered by affect: Automatic egotism. *Journal of Personality and Social Psychology, 52,* 245–259.

Paulus, P. B., Dzindolet, M. T., Poletes, G., & Camacho, L. M. (1993). Perception of performance in group brainstorming: The illusion of group productivity. *Personality and Social Psychology Bulletin, 19,* 78–89.

Pavelchak, M. A., Moreland, R. L., & Levine, J. M. (1986). Effects of prior group memberships on subsequent reconnaissance activities. *Journal of Personality and Social Psychology, 50,* 56–66.

Pechmann, C., & Esteban, G. (1994). Persuasion processes associated with direct comparative and noncomparative advertising and implications for advertising effectiveness. *Journal of Consumer Psychology, 2,* 403–432.

Pedersen, A., & Dudgeon, P. (2003). *Indigenous children at school: A look beyond the scenes.* Perth: Gunada Press, Curtin Indigenous Research Centre.

Pedersen, A., Walker I., & Glass, C. (1999). Experimenter effects on ingroup preference and self-concept of urban Aboriginal children. *Australian Journal of Psychology, 51,* 82–89.

Peeters, G., & Czapinski, J. (1990). Positive–negative asymmetry in evaluations: The distinction between affective and informational negativity effects. *European Review of Social Psychology, 1,* 33–60.

Pei, M. (1965). *The story of language* (2nd ed.). Philadelphia, PA: Lippincott.

Pennebaker, J. W. (1997). Writing about emotional experiences as a therapeutic process. *Psychological Science, 8,* 162–166.

Penner, L. A. (1986). *Social psychology: Concepts and applications.* St Paul, MN: West Publishing Company.

Penrod, S. (1983). *Social psychology.* Englewood Cliffs, NJ: Prentice Hall.

Penrod, S., & Hastie, R. (1980). A computer simulation of jury decision making. *Psychological Review, 87,* 133–159.

Penton-Voak, I. S., Perrett, D. I., & Peirce, J. W. (1999). Computer graphic studies of the role of facial similarity in judgements of attractiveness. *Current Psychology: Developmental, Learning, Personality, Social, 1(8),* 104–117.

Pepitone, A. (1981). Lessons from the history of social psychology. *American Psychologist, 36,* 972–985.

Peplau, L. A., & Perlman, D. (Eds.). (1982). *Loneliness: A sourcebook of current theory, research and therapy.* New York: Wiley.

Perlini, A. H., Bertolissi, S., & Lind, D. L. (1999). The effects of women's age and physical appearance on evaluations of attractiveness and social desirability. *Journal of Social Psychology, 1999, 139,* 343–354.

Perlman, D. (1988). Loneliness: A life-span, family perspective. In R. M. Milardo (Ed.), *Families and social networks: New perspectives on family* (pp. 190–220). Newbury Park, CA: Sage.

Perlman, D., & Oskamp, S. (1971). The effects of picture content and exposure frequency on evaluations of Negroes and Whites. *Journal of Experimental Social Psychology, 7,* 503–514.

Perlman, D., & Peplau, L. A. (1998). Loneliness. *Encyclopedia of mental health* (Vol. 2, pp. 571–581). New York: Academic Press.

Perry, D. G., Perry L. C., & Boldizar, J. P. (1990). Learning of aggression. In M. Lewis & S. Miller (Eds.), *Handbook of developmental psychopathology* (pp. 135–146). New York: Plenum.

Perry, D. G., Perry, L., Bussey, K., English, D., & Arnold, G. (1980). Processes of attribution and children's self-punishment following misbehaviour. *Child Development, 51,* 545–551.

Peters, L. H., Hartke, D. D., & Pohlmann, J. T. (1985). Fiedler's contingency theory of leadership: An application of the meta-analytic procedure of Schmidt and Hunter. *Psychological Bulletin, 97,* 274–285.

Peters, L. H., O'Connor, E. J., Weekley, J., Pooyan, A., Frank, B., & Erenkrantz, B. (1984). Sex bias and managerial evaluation: A replication and extension. *Journal of Applied Psychology, 69,* 349–352.

Peterson, C. (1980). Memory and the 'dispositional shift'. *Social Psychology Quarterly, 43,* 372–380.

Peterson, C., Semmel, A., von Baeyer, C., Abramson, L. Y., Metalsky, G. I., & Seligman, M. E. P. (1982). The Attributional Style Questionnaire. *Cognitive Therapy and Research, 6,* 287–300.

Pettigrew, T. F. (1958). Personality and sociocultural factors in intergroup attitudes: A cross-national comparison. *Journal of Conflict Resolution, 2,* 29–42.

Pettigrew, T. F. (1971). *Racially separate or together.* New York: McGraw-Hill.

Pettigrew, T. F. (1979). The ultimate attribution error: Extending Allport's cognitive analysis of prejudice. *Personality and Social Psychology Bulletin, 5,* 461–476.

Pettigrew, T. F. (1981). Extending the stereotype concept. In D. L. Hamilton (Ed.), *Cognitive processes in stereotyping and intergroup behavior* (pp. 303–332). Hillsdale, NJ: Erlbaum.

Pettigrew, T. F. (1987). *Modern racism: American black–white relations since the 1960s.* Cambridge, MA: Harvard University Press.

Pettigrew, T. F. (1998). Intergroup contact theory. *Annual Review of Psychology, 49,* 65–85.

Pettigrew, T. F., & Meertens, R.W. (1995). Subtle and blatant prejudice in western Europe. *European Journal of Social Psychology, 25*, 57–75.

Pettigrew, T. F. & Tropp, L. (2000). Does intergroup contact reduce prejudice? Recent meta-analytic findings. In S. Oskamp (Ed.), *Reducing prejudice and discrimination: Social psychological perspectives* (pp. 93–114). Mahwah, NJ: Erlbaum.

Petty, R. E., & Cacioppo, J. T. (1979). Issue-involvement can increase or decrease persuasion by enhancing message-relevant cognitive responses. *Journal of Personality and Social Psychology, 37,* 1915–1926.

Petty, R. E., & Cacioppo, J. T. (1981). *Attitudes and persuasion: Classic and contemporary approaches.* Dubuque, IA: Brown.

Petty, R. E., & Cacioppo, J. T. (1986a). *Communication and persuasion: Central and peripheral routes to attitude change.* New York: Springer.

Petty, R. E., & Cacioppo, J. T. (1986b). The elaboration likelihood model of persuasion. In L. Berkowitz (Ed.), *Advances in experimental social psychology* (Vol. 19, pp. 123–205). New York: Academic Press.

Petty, R. E., Priester, J. H. R., & Wegener, D. T. (1994). Cognitive processes in attitude change. In R. S. Wyer, Jr. & T. K. Srull (Eds.), *Handbook of social cognition* (Vol. 2, pp. 69–142). Hillsdale, NJ: Erlbaum.

Petty, R. E., Schuman, D. W., Richman, S. A., & Strathman, A. J. (1993). Positive mood and persuasion: Different roles for affect under high- and low-elaboration conditions. *Journal of Personality and Social Psychology, 64,* 5–20.

Petty, R. E., & Wegener, D. (1998). Attitude change: Multiple roles for persuasion variables. In D. T. Gilbert, S. T. Fiske, & G. Lindzey (Eds.), *The handbook of social psychology* (4th ed.). New York: McGraw-Hill.

Pevers, B. H., & Secord, P. F. (1973). Developmental changes in attribution of descriptive concepts to persons. *Journal of Personality and Social Psychology, 27,* 120–128.

Pheterson, G. I., Keisler, S. B., & Goldberg, P. A. (1971). Evaluation of the performance of women as a function of their success, achievements, and personal history. *Journal of Personality and Social Psychology, 19,* 114–118.

Phillips, D. P. (1986). Natural experiments on the effects of mass media violence on fatal aggression: Strengths and weaknesses of a new approach. In L. Berkowitz (Ed.), *Advances in experimental social psychology* (Vol. 19, pp. 207–250). New York: Academic Press.

Phillips, J. (1987). *A man's country? The image of the pakeha male, a history.* Auckland: Penguin.

Phinney, J. S., & Rotheram, M. J. (Eds.). (1987). *Children's ethnic socialisation: Pluralism and development.* Newbury Park, CA: Sage.

Pierce, C. A., Byrne, D., & Aguinis, H. (1996). Attraction in organizations: A model of workplace romance. *Journal of Organizational Behavior, 17,* 5–32.

Pilger, J. (1989). *A secret country.* London: Vantage.

Piliavin, I. M., Piliavin, J. A., & Rodin, J. (1975). Costs, diffusion and the stigmatised victim. *Journal of Personality and Social Psychology, 32,* 429–438.

Piliavin, J. A., & Charng, H.-W. (1990). Altruism: A review of recent theory and research. *Annual Review of Sociology, 16,* 27–65.

Piliavin, J. A., Dovidio, J. F., Gaertner, S. L., & Clark, R. D. III (1981). *Emergency intervention.* New York: Academic Press.

Pittam, J., & Gallois, C. (1996). The mediating role of narrative in intergroup processes: Talking about AIDS. *Journal of Language and Social Psychology, 15,* 312–334.

Platow, M. J., Hoar, S., Reid, S. A., Harley, K., & Morrison, D. (1997). Endorsement of distributively fair and unfair leaders in interpersonal and intergroup situations. *European Journal of Social Psychology, 27,* 465–494.

Platow, M. J., Reid, S. A., & Andrew, S. (1998). Leadership endorsement: The role of distributive and procedural behavior in interpersonal and intergroup contexts. *Group Processes and Intergroup Relations, 1,* 35–47.

Platow, M. J., & van Knippenberg, D. (2001). A social identity analysis of leadership endorsement: The effects of leader ingroup prototypicality and distributive intergroup fairness. *Personality and Social Psychology Bulletin, 27,* 1508–1519.

Platz, S. J., & Hosch, H. M. (1988). Cross-racial/ethnic eyewitness identification: A field study. *Journal of Applied Social Psychology, 18,* 972–984.

Plous, S., & Williams, T. (1995). Racial stereotypes from the days of American slavery: A continuing legacy. *Journal of Applied Social Psychology, 25,* 795–817.

Pomazal, R. J., & Clore, G. L. (1973). Helping on the highway: The effects of dependency and sex. *Journal of Applied Social Psychology, 3,* 150–164.

Pomerantz, E. M., Chaiken, S., & Tordesillas, R. S. (1995). Attitude strength and resistance processes. *Journal of Personality and Social Psychology, 69,* 408–419.

Popper, K. (1969). *Conjectures and refutations* (3rd ed.). London: Routledge & Kegan Paul.

Postmes, T., Spears, R., & Lea, M. (1998). Breaching or building social boundaries? SIDE-effects of computer-mediated communication. *Communication Research, 25,* 689–715.

Postmes, T., Spears, R., Sakhel, K., & de Groot, D. (2001). Social influence in computer-mediated communication: The effects of anonymity on group behavior. *Personality and Social Psychology Bulletin, 27,* 1243–1254.

Potter, J. (1996). *Representing reality.* London: Sage.

Potter, J., Stringer, P., & Wetherell, M. S. (1984). *Social texts and context: Literature and social psychology.* London: Routledge & Kegan Paul.

Potter, J., & Wetherell, M. S. (1987). *Discourse and social psychology: Beyond attitudes and behaviour.* London: Sage.

Potter, J., Wetherell, M. S., Gill, R., & Edwards, D. (1990). Discourse: Noun, verb or social practice? *Philosophical Psychology, 3,* 205–217.

Powell, G., & Foley, S. (1999). Romantic relationships in organizational settings: Something to talk about. In G. Powell (Ed.), *Handbook of gender and work.* Thousand Oaks, CA: Sage Publications.

Powell, M. C., & Fazio, R. M. (1984). Attitude accessibility as a function of repeated attitudinal expression. *Personality and Social Psychology Bulletin, 10,* 139–148.

Pratkanis, A. R., & Greenwald, A. G. (1989). A sociocognitive model of attitude structure and function. In L. Berkowitz (Ed.), *Advances in experimental social psychology* (Vol. 22, pp. 245–285). New York: Academic Press.

Pratto, F. (1999). The puzzle of continuing group inequality: Piecing together psychological, social and cultural forces in social dominance theory. In M. P. Zanna (Ed.), *Advances in experimental social psychology* (Vol. 31, pp. 191–263). New York: Academic Press.

Pratto, F., Sidanius, J., Stallworth, L. M., & Malle, B. F. (1994). Social dominance orientation: A personality variable predicting social and political attitudes. *Journal of Personality and Social Psychology*, 67, 741–763.

Prentice, D. A., & Miller, D. T. (1993). Pluralistic ignorance and alcohol use on campus: Some consequences of misperceiving the social norm. *Journal of Personality and Social Psychology*, 64, 243–256.

Prentice, D. A., & Miller, D. T. (Eds.). (1999). *Cultural divides: Understanding and overcoming group conflict*. New York: Russell Sage Foundation.

Prentice, D. A., Miller, D., & Lightdale, J. R. (1994). Asymmetries in attachment to groups and to their members: Distinguishing between common-identity and common-bond groups. *Personality and Social Psychology Bulletin*, 20, 484–493.

Prentice-Dunn, S., & Rogers, R. W. (1982). Effects of public and private self-awareness on deindividuation and aggression. *Journal of Personality and Social Psychology*, 43, 503–513.

Price-Williams, D. (1976). Cross-cultural studies. In L. A. Samovar & R. E. Porter (Eds.), *Intercultural communication: A reader* (2nd ed., pp. 32–48). Belmont, CA: Wadsworth.

Prior, M. (1989). Australian adolescents' views of the nuclear threat. *Interdisciplinary Peace Research*, 1, 61–85.

Pruitt, D. G. (1981). *Negotiation behavior*. New York: Academic Press.

Pruitt, D. G. (1986). Achieving integrative agreements in negotiation. In R. K. White (Ed.), *Psychology and the prevention of nuclear war* (pp. 463–478). New York: New York University Press.

Pryor, J. B., & Ostrom, T. M. (1981). The cognitive organisation of social information: A converging-operations approach. *Journal of Personality and Social Psychology*, 41, 628–641.

Przybyla, D. P. J. (1985). *The facilitating effects of exposure to erotica on male prosocial behavior*. Doctoral dissertation, State University of New York at Albany.

Purkhardt, S. C. (1995). *Transforming social representations*. London: Routledge.

Pyszczynski, T. A., & Greenberg, J. (1981). Role of disconfirmed expectancies in the instigation of attributional processing. *Journal of Personality and Social Psychology*, 40, 31–38.

Quattrone, G. A. (1986). On the perception of a group's variability. In S. Worchel & W. Austin (Eds.), *The psychology of intergroup relations* (Vol. 2, pp. 25–48). New York: Nelson-Hall.

Quattrone, G. A., & Jones, E. E. (1980). The perception of variability within ingroups and outgroups: Implications for the law of small numbers. *Journal of Personality and Social Psychology*, 38, 141–152.

Quigley-Fernandez, B., & Tedeschi, J. T. (1978). The bogus pipeline as lie detector: Two validity studies. *Journal of Personality and Social Psychology*, 36, 247–256.

Rabbie, J. M., & Bekkers, F. (1978). Threatened leadership and intergroup competition. *European Journal of Social Psychology*, 8, 9–20.

Rabbie, J. M., & DeBrey, J. H. C. (1971). The anticipation of intergroup cooperation and competition under private and public conditions. *International Journal of Group Tensions*, 1, 230–251.

Rabbie, J. M., & Horwitz, M. (1969). Arousal of ingroup–outgroup bias by a chance win or loss. *Journal of Personality and Social Psychology*, 13, 269–277.

Rabbie, J. M., & Wilkens, G. (1971). Ingroup competition and its effect on intragroup relations. *European Journal of Social Psychology*, 1, 215–234.

Rabbie, J. M., Schot, J. C., & Visser, L. (1989). Social identity theory: A conceptual and empirical critique from the perspective of a behavioural interaction model. *European Journal of Social Psychology*, 19, 171–202.

Ramirez, J., Bryant, J., & Zillman, D. (1983). Effects of erotica on retaliatory behavior as a function of level of prior provocation. *Journal of Personality and Social Psychology*, 43, 971–978.

Rankin, R. E., & Campbell, D. T. (1955). Galvanic skin response to Negro and White experimenters. *Journal of Abnormal and Social Psychology*, 51, 30–33.

Raphael, B. (1985). *The anatomy of bereavement: A handbook for the caring professions*. London: Hutchinson.

Rapley, M. (1998). 'Just an ordinary Australian': Self-categorization and the discursive construction of facticity in 'new racist' political rhetoric. *British Journal of Social Psychology*, 37, 325–344.

Rapoport, A. (1976). *Experimental games and their uses in psychology*. Morristown, NJ: General Learning Press.

Raven, B. H. (1965). Social influence and power. In I. D. Steiner & M. Fishbein (Eds.), *Current studies in social psychology* (pp. 371–382). New York: Holt, Rinehart & Winston.

Raven, B. H. (1993). The bases of power: Origins and recent developments. *Journal of Social Issues*, 49, 227–251.

Raven, B. H., & French, J. R. P. (1958). Legitimate power, coercive power and observability in social influence. *Sociometry*, 21, 83–97.

Ray, M. L. (1988). *Short-term evidence of advertising's long-term effect* (Report no. 88–107). Cambridge, MA: Marketing Science Institute.

Reeder, G. D., & Brewer, M. B. (1979). A schematic model of dispositional attribution in interpersonal perception. *Psychological Review*, 86, 61–79.

Regan, D. T., & Fazio, R. H. (1977). On the consistency of attitudes and behavior: Look to the method of attitude formation. *Journal of Experimental Social Psychology*, 13, 38–45.

Regan, D. T., Williams, M., & Sparling, S. (1972). Voluntary expiation of guilt: A field experiment. *Journal of Personality and Social Psychology*, 24, 42–45.

Regan, J. (1971). Guilt, perceived injustice, and altruistic behaviour. *Journal of Personality and Social Psychology*, 18, 124–132.

Regan, P. C., & Berscheid, E. (1999). *Lust: What we know about human sexual desire*. Thousand Oaks, CA: Sage.

Reicher, S. D. (1982). The determination of collective behaviour. In H. Tajfel (Ed.), *Social identity and intergroup relations* (pp. 41–83). Cambridge: Cambridge University Press.

Reicher, S. D. (1984). Social influence in the crowd: Attitudinal and behavioural effects of deindividuation in conditions of high and low group salience. *British Journal of Social Psychology*, 23, 341–350.

Reicher, S. D. (1987). Crowd behaviour as social action. In J. C. Turner, M. A. Hogg, P. J. Oakes, S. D. Reicher, & M. S. Wetherell (Eds.), *Rediscovering the social group: A self-categorization theory* (pp. 171–202). Oxford: Blackwell.

Reicher, S. D. (1996). Social identity and social change: Rethinking the context of social psychology. In W. P. Robinson (Ed.), *Social groups and identities: Developing the legacy of Henri Tajfel* (pp. 317–336). Oxford, UK: Butterworth-Heinemann.

Reicher, S. D. (2001). The psychology of crowd dynamics. In M. A. Hogg & R. S. Tindale (Eds.), *Blackwell handbook of social psychology: Group processes* (pp. 182–207). Oxford, UK: Blackwell.

Reicher, S. D., & Hopkins, N. (1996). Seeking influence through characterising self-categories: An analysis of anti-abortionist rhetoric. *British Journal of Social Psychology*, 35, 297–311.

Reicher, S., & Hopkins, N. (2004). On the science and art of leadership. In D. van Knippenberg & M. A. Hogg (Eds.), *Leadership and power: Identity processes in groups and organizations* (pp. 197–209). London: Sage.

Reicher, S. D., & Potter, J. (1985). Psychological theory as intergroup perspective: A comparative analysis of 'scientific' and 'lay' accounts of crowd events. *Human Relations*, 38, 167–189.

Reicher, S. D., Spears, R., & Postmes, T. (1995). A social identity model of deindividuation phenomena. *European Review of Social Psychology*, 6, 161–198.

Reid, S. A., & Ng, S. H. (1999). Language, power, and intergroup relations. *Journal of Social Issues*, 55, 119–139.

Reik, T. (1944). *A psychologist looks at love*. New York: Farrar & Rinehart.

Reisenzein, R. (1983). The Schachter theory of emotion: Two decades later. *Psychological Bulletin*, 94, 239–264.

Rempel, J. K., Ross, M., & Holmes, J. G. (2001). Trust and communicated attributions in close relationships. *Journal of Personality and Social Psychology*, 81, 57–64.

Reynolds, K. J., Turner, J. C., Haslam, S. A., & Ryan, M. K. (in press). The role of personality and group factors in explaining prejudice. *Journal of Experimental Social Psychology*.

Rhodes, G., Hickford, C., & Jeffrey, L. (2000). Sex-typicality and attractiveness: Are supermale and superfemale faces superattractive? *British Journal of Psychology*, 91, 125–140.

Rhodes, G., Sumich, A., & Byatt, G. (1999). Are average facial configurations attractive only because of their symmetry? *Psychological Science*, 10, 52–58.

Rhodes, G., & Tremewan, T. (1996). Averageness, exaggeration, and facial attractiveness. *Psychological Science*, 2, 105–110.

Rhodes, N., & Wood, W. (1992). Self-esteem and intelligence affect influenceability: The mediating role of message reception. *Psychological Bulletin*, 111, 156–171.

Rhodewalt, F., & Strube, M. J. (1985). A self-attribution reactance model for health outcomes. *Journal of Applied Social Psychology*, 15, 330–344.

Rhodewalt, F., Madrian, J. C., & Cheney, S. (1998). Narcissism, self-knowledge, organization, and emotional reactivity: The effects of daily experiences on self-esteem and affect. *Personality and Social Psychology Bulletin*, 24, 75–86.

Rholes, W. S., & Pryor, J. B. (1982). Cognitive accessibility and causal attributions. *Personality and Social Psychology Bulletin*, 8, 719–727.

Rholes, W. S., Simpson, J. A., & Blakely, B. S. (1995). Adult attachment styles and mothers' relationships with their young children. *Personal Relationships*, 2, 35–54.

Rice, M. E., & Grusec, J. E. (1975). Saying and doing: Effects on observer performance. *Journal of Personality and Social Psychology*, 32, 584–593.

Rice, R. W. (1978). Construct validity of the least preferred co-worker score. *Psychological Bulletin*, 85, 1199–1237.

Rice, R. W., Instone, D., & Adams, J. (1984). Leader sex, leader success, and leadership process: Two field studies. *Journal of Applied Psychology*, 69, 12–31.

Richards, M. J. (1991). *Perceptions of HIV infection and risk behaviours in men who have sex with men*. Unpublished master's thesis, University of Auckland, Auckland, New Zealand.

Ridgeway, C. L. (2001). Social status and group structure. In M. A. Hogg & R. S. Tindale (Eds.), *Blackwell handbook of social psychology: Group processes* (pp. 352–375). Oxford, UK: Blackwell.

Riess, M., Kalle, R. J., & Tedeschi, J. T. (1981). Bogus pipeline attitude assessment, impression management, and misattribution in induced compliance settings. *Journal of Social Psychology*, 115, 247–258.

Riess, M., Rosenfield, R., Melburg, V., & Tedeschi, J. T. (1981). Self-serving attributions: Biased private perceptions and distorted public descriptions. *Journal of Personality and Social Psychology*, 41, 224–231.

Rimé, B. (1983). Nonverbal communication or nonverbal behaviour. In W. Doise & S. Moscovici (Eds.), *Current issues in European social psychology* (Vol. 1, pp. 85–141). Cambridge: Cambridge University Press.

Ringelmann, M. (1913). Recherches sur les moteurs animés: Travail de l'homme. *Annales de l'Institut National Agronomique*, 2(12), 1–40.

Riopelle, A. J. (1987). Instinct. In R. J. Corsini (Ed.), *Concise encyclopedia of psychology* (pp. 599–600). New York: Wiley.

Robinson, R. J., Keltner, D., Ward, A., & Ross, L. (1995). Actual versus assumed differences in construal: Realism in intergroup perception and conflict. *Journal of Personality and Social Psychology*, 68, 404–417.

Roccas, S., & Brewer, M. B. (2002). Social identity complexity. *Personality and Social Psychology Review*, 6, 88–109.

Roethlisberger, F., & Dickson, W. (1939). *Management and the worker*. Cambridge, MA: Harvard University Press.

Rogers, R. W., & Prentice-Dunn, S. (1981). Deindividuation and anger-mediated interracial aggression: Unmasking regressive racism. *Journal of Personality and Social Psychology*, 41, 63–73.

Rohner, R. P. (1976). A worldwide study of sex differences in aggression: A universalist perspective. Paper presented at the meeting of the Eastern Psychological Association, New York.

Rohner, R. P. (1984). Toward a conception of culture for cross-cultural psychology. *Journal of Cross-Cultural Psychology*, 15, 111–138.

Rokeach, M. (1948). Generalized mental rigidity as a factor in ethnocentrism. *Journal of Abnormal and Social Psychology*, 43, 259–278.

Rokeach, M. (Ed.). (1960). *The open and closed mind*. New York: Basic Books.

Rokeach, M. (1973). *The nature of human values*. New York: Free Press.

Rokeach, M., & Mezei, L. (1966). Race and shared belief as factors in social choice. *Science*, 151, 167–172.

Rommetveit, R. (1974). *On message structure: A framework for the study of language and communication*. New York: Wiley.

Roper Report (1987). *Report of ministerial committee of inquiry into violence*. Wellington, NZ: Government Printer.

Rosch, E. (1978). Principles of categorization. In E. Rosch & B. B. Lloyd (Eds.), *Cognition and categorization* (pp. p. 27–48). Hillsdale, NJ: Erlbaum.

Rose, H., & Rose, S. (Eds.). (2000). *Alas, poor Darwin: Arguments against evolutionary psychology*. London: Vintage.

Rosenberg, M. (1979). *Conceiving the self*. New York: Basic Books.

Rosenberg, M. J. (1969). The conditions and consequences of evaluation apprehension. In R. Rosenthal & R. L. Rosnow (Eds.), *Artifact in behavioral research* (pp. 280–349). New York: Academic Press.

Rosenberg, M. J., & Hovland, C. I. (1960). Cognitive, affective, and behavioral components of attitude. In M. J. Rosenberg, C. I. Hovland, W. J. McGuire, R. P. Abelson, & J. W. Brehm (Eds.),

Attitude organization and change: An analysis of consistency among attitude components. New Haven, CT: Yale University Press.

Rosenberg, S. W., & Wolfsfeld, G. (1977). International conflict and the problem of attribution. *Journal of Conflict Resolution, 21,* 75–103.

Rosenberg, S., Nelson, C., & Vivekanathan, P.S. (1968). A multi-dimensional approach to the structure of personality impressions. *Journal of Personality and Social Psychology, 39,* 283–294.

Rosenberg, S., & Sedlak, A. (1972). Structural representations of implicit personality theory. In L. Berkowitz (Ed.), *Advances in experimental social psychology* (Vol. 6, pp. 235–297). New York: Academic Press.

Rosenfeld, H. M. (1965). Effect of approval-seeking induction on interpersonal proximity. *Psychological Reports, 17,* 120–122.

Rosenfeld, D., Greenberg, J., Folger, R., & Borys, R. (1982). Effect of an encounter with a black panhandler on subsequent helping for blacks: Tokenism or conforming to a negative stereotype? *Personality and Social Psychology Bulletin, 8,* 664–671.

Rosenfeld, D., & Stephan, W. G. (1977). When discounting fails: An unexpected finding. *Memory and Cognition, 5,* 97–102.

Rosenkoetter, L. I. (1999). The television situation comedy and children's prosocial behavior. *Journal of Applied Social Psychology, 29,* 979–993.

Rosenthal, D. (1987). Ethnic identity development in adolescents. In J. S. Phinney & M. J. Rotheram (Eds.). (1987). *Children's ethnic socialisation: Pluralism and development* (pp. 156–179). Newbury Park, CA: Sage.

Rosenthal, R. (1966). *Experimenter effects in behavioral research.* New York: Appleton-Century-Crofts.

Rosenthal, R., & DePaulo, B. M. (1979). Sex differences in eavesdropping on nonverbal cues. *Journal of Personality and Social Psychology, 37,* 273–285.

Rosenthal, R., Hall, J. A., DiMatteo, M. R., Rogers, P. L., & Archer, D. (1979). *Sensitivity to nonverbal communication: The PONS test.* Baltimore: Johns Hopkins University Press.

Rosenthal, R., & Jacobson, L. F. (1968). *Pygmalion in the classroom.* New York: Holt, Rinehart & Winston.

Rosenthal, R., & Rubin, D. B. (1978). Interpersonal expectancy effects: The first 345 studies. *Behavioral and Brain Sciences, 3,* 377–386.

Roskos-Ewoldsen, D. R., & Fazio, R. H. (1992). On the orienting value of attitudes: Attitude accessibility as a determinant of an object's attraction of visual attention. *Journal of Personality and Social Psychology, 63,* 198–211.

Rosnow, R. L. (1980). Psychology of rumour reconsidered. *Psychological Bulletin, 87,* 578–591.

Rosnow, R. L. (1981). *Paradigms in transition: The methodology of social enquiry.* Oxford: Oxford University Press.

Ross, E. A. (1908). *Social psychology.* New York: Macmillan.

Ross, L. (1977). The intuitive psychologist and his shortcomings. In L. Berkowitz (Ed.), *Advances in experimental social psychology* (Vol. 10, pp. 174–220). New York: Academic Press.

Ross, L., Greene, D., & House, P. (1977). The 'false consensus effect': An egocentric bias in social perception and attribution processes. *Journal of Experimental Social Psychology, 13,* 279–301.

Ross, L., Lepper, M. R., & Hubbard, M. (1975). Perseverance in self-perception and social perception: Biased attribution processes in the debriefing paradigm. *Journal of Personality and Social Psychology, 32,* 880–892.

Ross, L., & Nisbett, R. E. (1991). *The person and the situation: Perspectives of social psychology.* New York: McGraw-Hill.

Ross, L., & Ward, A. (1995). Psychological barriers to dispute resolution. *Advances in experimental social psychology, 27,* 255–304.

Ross, M., & Fletcher, G. J. O. (1985). Attribution and social perception. In G. Lindzey & E. Aronson (Eds.), *Handbook of social psychology* (3rd ed., Vol. 2, pp. 73–122). New York: Random House.

Rosser, B. R. S. (1991). *Male homosexual behavior and the effects of AIDS education.* New York: Praeger.

Rothbart, M. (1981). Memory processes and social beliefs. In D. L. Hamilton (Ed.), *Cognitive processes in stereotyping and intergroup behavior* (pp. 145–182). Hillsdale, NJ: Erlbaum.

Rothbart, M., & John, O. P. (1985). Social categorization and behavioral episodes: A cognitive analysis of intergroup contact. *Journal of Social Issues, 41,* 81–104.

Rothbart, M., & Park, B. (1986). On the confirmability and disconfirmability of trait concepts. *Journal of Personality and Social Psychology, 50,* 131–142.

Rothblum, E. D. (1990). Psychological factors in the Antarctic. *Journal of Psychology, 124,* 253–273.

Rothman, A. J., & Salovey, P. (1997). Shaping perceptions to motivate healthy behaviour: The role of message framing. *Psychological Bulletin, 121,* 3–19.

Rotter, J. B. (1966). Generalized expectancies for internal versus external control of reinforcement. *Psychological Monographs, 80,* whole no. 609.

Rotter, J. B. (1980). Trust and gullibility. *Psychology Today, 14 (5),* pp. 35–38, 40, 42, 102.

Rotton, J. (1993) Atmospheric and temporal correlates of sex crimes: Endogenous factors do not explain seasonal differences in rape. *Environment and Behavior, 25,* 625–642.

Rowatt, W. C., Cunningham, M. R., & Druen, P. B. (1999). Lying to get a date: The effect of facial physical attractiveness on the willingness to deceive prospective dating partners. *Journal of Social & Personal Relationships, 16,* 209–223.

Rowley, C. D. (1971). *Outcasts in white Australia.* Canberra: Australian National University Press.

Ruback, R. B., & Pandey, J. (1992). Very hot and really crowded: Quasi-experimental investigations of Indian 'tempos'. *Environment and Behavior, 24,* 527–554.

Rubin, A. M. (1978). Child and adolescent television use and political socialization. *Journalism Quarterly, 55,* 125–129.

Rubin, J. (1976). How to tell when someone is saying no. *Topics in Culture Learning, 4,* 61–65.

Rubin, J. (1980). Experimental research on third-party intervention in conflict: Toward some generalizations. *Psychological Bulletin, 87,* 379–391.

Rubin, M., & Hewstone, M. (1998). Social identity theory's self-esteem hypothesis: A review and some suggestions for clarification. *Personality and Social Psychology Review, 2,* 40–62.

Rubin, Z. (1973). *Liking and loving: An invitation to social psychology.* New York: Holt, Rinehart & Winston.

Ruckmick, C. A. (1912). The history and status of psychology in the United States. *American Journal of Psychology, 23,* 517–531.

Rudman, L. A., & Glick, P. (1999). Feminized management and backlash toward agentic women: The hidden costs to women of a kinder, gentler image of middle-managers. *Journal of Personality and Social Psychology, 77,* 1004–1010.

Rudman, L. A., & Glick, P. (2001). Prescriptive gender stereotypes and backlash against agentic women. *Journal of Social Issues, 57,* 743–762.

Ruggiero, K. M., & Taylor, D. M. (1995). Coping with discrimination: How disadvantaged group members perceive the discrimination that confronts them. *Journal of Personality and Social Psychology, 68,* 826–838.

Rumelhart, D. E., & Ortony, A. (1977). The representation of knowledge in memory. In C. R. Anderson, R. J. Spiro, & W. E. Montague (Eds.), *Schooling and the acquisition of knowledge* (pp. 99–136). Hillsdale, NJ: Erlbaum.

Runciman, W. G. (1966). *Relative deprivation and social justice.* London: Routledge & Kegan Paul.

Rusbult, C. E., & Zembrodt, I. M. (1983). Responses to dissatisfaction in romantic involvements: A multi-dimensional scaling analysis. *Journal of Experimental Social Psychology, 19,* 274–293.

Rushton, J. P. (1979). Effects of prosocial television and film material on the behavior of viewers. In L. Berkowitz (Ed.), *Advances in experimental social psychology* (Vol. 12, pp. 322–351). New York: Academic Press.

Rushton, J. P. (1980). *Altruism, socialisation, and society.* Englewood Cliffs, NJ: Prentice Hall.

Rushton, J. P., & Sorrentino, R. M. (1981). *Altruism and helping behavior: Social, personality, and developmental perspectives.* Hillsdale, NJ: Erlbaum.

Rushton, J. P., & Teachman, G. (1978). The effects of positive reinforcement, attributions, and punishment on model induced altruism in children. *Personality and Social Psychology Bulletin, 4,* 322–325.

Russell, C. (1987). The brother and sister who fell in love. *Women's Day,* November (Australia).

Russell, J. A. (1994). Is there universal recognition of emotion from facial expressions? A review of the cross-cultural studies. *Psychological Bulletin, 115,* 102–141.

Russell, J. A., Bachorowski, J.-A., & Fernandez-Dols, J.M. (2003). Facial and vocal expressions of emotion. *Annual Review of Psychology, 54,* 329–349.

Russell, J. A., & Fernandez-Dols, J. M. (Eds.). (1997). *The psychology of facial expression: Studies in emotion and social interaction.* Cambridge, UK: Cambridge University Press.

Rutkowski, G. K., Gruder, C. L., & Romer, D. (1983). Group cohesiveness, social norms, and bystander intervention. *Journal of Personality and Social Psychology, 44,* 545–552.

Rutte, C. G., & Wilke, H. A. M. (1984). Social dilemmas and leadership. *European Journal of Social Psychology, 14,* 105–121.

Ryan, E. B., Giles, H., Bartolucci, G., & Henwood, K. (1986). Psycholinguistic and social psychological components of communication by and with the elderly. *Language and Communication, 6,* 1–24.

Ryan, T. (1985). Human nature and the origins of war. *Hurupaa, 3,* 46–54.

Ryen, A. H., & Kahn, A. (1975). Effects of intergroup orientation on group attitudes and proxemic behavior. *Journal of Personality and Social Psychology, 31,* 302–310.

Sabini, J., & Silver, M. (1982). *The moralities of everyday life.* New York: Oxford University Press.

Sachdev, I., & Bourhis, R. Y. (1990). Language and social identification. In D. Abrams & M. A. Hogg (Eds.), *Social identity theory: Constructive and critical advances* (pp. 211–229). London: Harvester Wheatsheaf.

Sachdev, I., & Bourhis, R. Y. (1993). Ethnolinguistic vitality: Some motivational and cognitive considerations. In M. A. Hogg & D. Abrams (Eds.), *Group motivation: Social psychological perspectives* (pp. 33–51). Hemel Hempstead, UK: Harvester Wheatsheaf.

Sachdev, I., & Wright, A. (1996). Social influence and language learning: An experimental study. *Journal of Language and Social Psychology, 15,* 230–245.

Sagi, A., & Hoffman, M. (1976). Empathic distress in the newborn. *Developmental Psychology, 12,* 175–176.

Saint-Blancat, C. (1985). The effect of minority group vitality upon its sociopsychological behaviour and strategies. *Journal of Multilingual and Multicultural Development, 6,* 31–44.

Saks, M. J. (1978). Social psychological contributions to a legislative committee on organ and tissue transplants. *American Psychologist, 33,* 680–690.

Saks, M. J., & Marti, M. W. (1997). A meta-analysis of the effects of jury size. *Law and Human Behavior, 21,* 451–467.

Salovey, P., Rothman, A. J., & Rodin, J. (1998). Health behaviour. In D. T. Gilbert, S. T. Fiske, & G. Lindzey (Eds.), *The handbook of social psychology* (4th ed., Vol. 2, pp. 633–683). New York: McGraw-Hill.

Samovar, L. A., & Porter, R. E. (Eds.). (1976). *Intercultural communication: A reader* (2nd ed.). Belmont, CA: Wadsworth.

Sampson, E. E. (1977). Psychology and the American ideal. *Journal of Personality and Social Psychology, 35,* 767–782.

San Antonio, P. M. (1987). Social mobility and language use in an American company in Japan. *Journal of Language and Social Psychology, 6,* 191–200.

Sanders, G. S. (1983). An attentional process model of social facilitation. In A. Hare, H. Blumberg, V. Kent, & M. Davies (Eds.), *Small groups.* London: Wiley.

Sanders, G. S., & Baron, R. S. (1977). Is social comparison relevant for producing choice shifts? *Journal of Experimental Social Psychology, 13,* 303–314.

Sanders, G. S., Baron, R. S., & Moore, D. L. (1978). Distraction and social comparison as mediators of social facilitation. *Journal of Experimental Social Psychology, 14,* 291–303.

Sanders, G. S., & Mullen, B. (1983). Accuracy in perceptions of consensus: Differential tendencies of people with majority and minority positions. *European Journal of Social Psychology, 13,* 57–70.

Sani, F., & Reicher, S. D. (1998). When consensus fails: An analysis of the schism within the Italian Communist Party (1991). *European Journal of Social Psychology, 28,* 623–645.

Sani, F., & Reicher, S. D. (2000). Contested identities and schisms in groups: Opposing the ordination of women as priests in the Church of England. *British Journal of Social Psychology, 39,* 95–112.

Sargant, W. (1957). *Battle for the mind: A physiology of conversion and brainwashing.* Garden City, NY: Doubleday.

Saroja, K., & Surendra, H. S. (1991). A study of postgraduate students' endogamous preference in mate selection. *Indian Journal of Behaviour, 15,* 1–13.

Sato, K. (1987). Distribution of the cost of maintaining common resources. *Journal of Experimental Social Psychology, 23,* 19–31.

Sattler, D. N., & Kerr, N. L. (1991). Might versus morality explored: Motivational and cognitive bases for social motives. *Journal of Personality and Social Psychology, 60,* 756–765.

Saucier, G. (2000). Isms and the structure of social attitudes. *Journal of Personality and Social Psychology, 78,* 366–385.

Schachter, S. (1959). *The psychology of affiliation.* Stanford, CA: Stanford University Press.

Schachter, S. (1964). The interaction of cognitive and physiological determinants of emotional state. In L. Berkowitz (Ed.), *Advances in experimental social psychology* (Vol. 1, pp. 49–80). New York: Academic Press.

Schachter, S. (1971). *Emotion, obesity, and crime.* New York: Academic Press.

Schachter, S., & Burdeck, H. (1955). A field experiment on rumour transmission and distortion. *Journal of Abnormal and Social Psychology, 50,* 363–371.

Schachter, S., & Singer, J. E. (1962). Cognitive, social and physiological determinants of emotional state. *Psychological Review, 69,* 379–399.

Schank, R. C., & Abelson, R. P. (1977). *Scripts, plans, goals, and understanding: An inquiry into human knowledge structures.* Hillsdale, NJ: Erlbaum.

Scheier, M. F., & Carver, C. S. (1981). Private and public aspects of self. In L. Wheeler (Ed.), *Review of personality and social psychology* (Vol. 2, pp. 189–216). London: Sage.

Scherer, K. R. (1974). Acoustic concomitants of emotional dimensions: Judging affect from synthesised tone sequences. In S. Weitz (Ed.), *Nonverbal communication* (pp. 249–253). New York: Oxford University Press.

Scherer, K. R. (1978). Personality inference from voice quality: The loud voice of extroversion. *European Journal of Social Psychology, 8,* 467–488.

Scherer, K. R. (1986). Vocal affect expression: A review and model for future research. *Psychological Bulletin, 99,* 143–165.

Scherer, K. R., Abeles, R. P., & Fischer, C. S. (1975). *Human aggression and conflict.* Englewood Cliffs, NJ: Prentice Hall.

Scherer, K. R., & Giles, H. (Eds.). (1979). *Social markers in speech.* Cambridge: Cambridge University Press.

Schiller, J. C. F. (1882). *Essays, esthetical and philosophical, including the dissertation on the 'Connexions between the animal and the spiritual in man'.* London: Bell.

Schlenker, B. R. (1980). *Impression management: The self-concept, social identity, and interpersonal relations.* Monterey, CA: Brooks/Cole.

Schlenker, B. R., Dlugolecki, D. W., & Doherty, K. (1994). The impact of self-presentation on self-appraisal and behavior: The roles of commitment and biased scanning. *Personality and Social Psychology Bulletin, 20,* 20–33.

Schlenker, B. R., Weingold, M. F., & Hallam, J. R. (1990). Self-serving attributions in social context: Effects of self-esteem and social pressure. *Journal of Personality and Social Psychology, 58,* 855–863.

Schmidt, C. F. (1972). Multidimensional scaling of the printed media's explanations of the riot of the summer of 1967. *Journal of Personality and Social Psychology, 24,* 59–67.

Schmidt, T., & Brewer, N. (2000). *Effects of mood and emotion on juror processing and judgements.* Paper presented at the Society of Australasian Social Psychologists Conference, Fremantle.

Schmitt, B. H., Gilovich, T., Goore, N., & Joseph, L. (1986). Mere presence and socio-facilitation: One more time. *Journal of Experimental Social Psychology, 22,* 242–248.

Schneider, D. J. (1973). Implicit personality theory: A review. *Psychological Bulletin, 79,* 294–309.

Schneider, D. J., Hastorf, A. H., & Ellsworth, P. C. (1979). *Person perception.* Reading, MA: Addison-Wesley.

Schofield, J. W. (1986). Black–white contact in desegregated schools. In M. Hewstone & R. J. Brown (Eds.), *Contact and conflict in intergroup encounters* (pp. 79–92). Oxford: Blackwell.

Schofield, J. W. (1991). School desegregation and intergroup relations: A review of the literature. In G. Grant (Ed.), *Review of research in education* (Vol. 17, pp. 335–409). Washington, DC: American Education Research Association.

Schriesheim, C. A., Castro, S. L., & Cogliser, C. C. (1999). Leader-member exchange (LMX) research: A comprehensive review of theory, measurement, and data-analytic practices. *Leadership Quarterly, 10,* 63–113.

Schriesheim, C. A., Tepper, B. J., & Tetrault, L. A. (1994). Least preferred co-worker score, situational control, and leadership effectiveness: A meta-analysis of contingency model performance predictions. *Journal of Applied Psychology, 79,* 561–573.

Schul, Y. (1983). Integration and abstraction in impression formation. *Journal of Personality and Social Psychology, 44,* 45–54.

Schul, Y., & Burnstein, E. (1985). The informational basis of social judgments: Using past impression rather than the trait description in forming new impression. *Journal of Experimental Social Psychology, 21,* 421–439.

Schullo, S. A., & Alperson, B. L. (1984). Interpersonal phenomenology as a function of sexual orientation, sex, sentiment, and trait categories in long-term dyadic relationships. *Journal of Personality and Social Psychology, 47,* 983–1002.

Schwab, D. P., & Grams, R. (1985). Sex-related errors in job evaluation: A 'real-world' test. *Journal of Applied Psychology, 70,* 533–539.

Schwartz, N., & Kurz, E. (1989). What's in a picture? The impact of face-ism on trait attribution. *European Journal of Social Psychology, 19,* 311–316.

Schwartz, S. H. (1975). The justice need and the activation of humanitarian norms. *Journal of Social Issues, 31,* 111–136.

Schwartz, S. H. (1977). Normative influences on altruism. In L. Berkowitz (Ed.), *Advances in experimental social psychology* (Vol. 10, pp. 222–279). New York: Academic Press.

Schwartz, S. H. (1992). Universals in the content and structure of values: Theoretical advances and empirical tests in 20 cultures. In M. P. Zanna (Ed.), *Advances in experimental social psychology* (Vol. 25, pp. 1–65). San Diego: Academic Press.

Schwartz, S. H., & Bardi, A. (1997). Influences of adaptation to communist rule on value priorities in Eastern Europe. *Political Psychology, 18,* 385–410.

Schwartz, S. H., & Clausen, G. T. (1970). Responsibility, norms and helping in an emergency. *Journal of Personality and Social Psychology, 16,* 299–310.

Schwartz, S. H., & David, T. B. (1976). Responsibility and helping in an emergency: Effects of blame, ability and denial of responsibility. *Sociometry, 39,* 406–415.

Schwarz, N. (2000). Social judgement and attitudes: Warmer, more social, and less conscious. *European Journal of Social Psychology, 30,* 149–176.

Schwarzer, R., & Leppin, A. (1989). Social support and health: A meta-analysis. *Psychology and Health, 3,* 1–15.

Schwerin, H. S., & Newell, H. H. (1981). *Persuasion in marketing.* New York: Wiley.

Scitovsky, T. (1980). Why do we seek more and more excitement? *Stanford Observer,* October, p. 13.

Searle, A. (1987). The effects of postnatal depression on mother–infant interaction. *Australian Journal of Sex, Marriage & Family, 8,* 79–88.

Searle, J. (1979). *Expression and meaning: Studies in the theory of speech acts.* Cambridge: Cambridge University Press.

Sears, D. O. (1983). The person-positivity bias. *Journal of Personality and Social Psychology, 44,* 233–250.

Sears, D. O. (1986). College sophomores in the laboratory: Influences of a narrow data base on social psychology's view of human nature. *Journal of Personality and Social Psychology, 51,* 515–530.

Sears, D. O. (1988). Symbolic racism. In P. Katz & D. Taylor (Eds.), *Towards the elimination of racism: Profiles in controversy* (pp. 53–84). New York: Plenum.

Sears, D. O., Peplau, L. A., & Taylor, S. E. (1991). *Social psychology* (7th ed.). Englewood Cliffs, NJ: Prentice Hall.

Sedikides, C. (1993). Assessment, enhancement, and verification determinants of the self-evaluation process. *Journal of Personality and Social Psychology, 65,* 317–338.

Sedikides, C. (1995). Central and peripheral self-conceptions are differentially affected by mood: Tests of the differential sensitivity hypothesis. *Journal of Personality and Social Psychology, 69,* 759–777.

Sedikides, C., & Brewer, M. B. (Eds.). (2001). *Individual self, relational self, collective self.* Philadelphia, PA: Psychology Press.

Sedikides, C., & Gregg, A. P. (2003). Portraits of the self. In M. A. Hogg & J. Cooper (Eds.), *The Sage handbook of social psychology* (pp. 110–138). London: Sage.

Sedikides, C., & Ostrom, T. M. (1988). Are person categories used when organizing information about unfamiliar sets of persons? *Social Cognition, 6,* 252–267.

Sedikides, C., & Strube, M. J. (1997). Self-evaluation: To thine own self be good, to thine own self be sure, to thine own self be true, and to thine own self be better. In M. P. Zanna (Ed.), *Advances in experimental social psychology* (Vol. 29, pp. 209–296). New York: Academic Press.

Segall, M. H. (1965). Anthropology and psychology. In O. Klineberg & R. Christie (Eds.), *Perspectives in social psychology* (pp. 53–74). New York: Holt Rinehart Winston.

Seligman, M. E. P., Abramson, L. Y., Semmel, A., & von Baeyer, C. (1979). Depressive attributional style. *Journal of Abnormal Psychology, 88,* 242–247.

Semin, G. R. (1980). A gloss on attribution theory. *British Journal of Social and Clinical Psychology, 19,* 291–300.

Semin, G. R., & Fiedler, K. (1991). The linguistic category model, its bases, applications and range. *European Review of Social Psychology, 2,* 1–30.

Senchak, M., & Leonard, K. E. (1993). The role of spouses' depression and anger in the attribution–marital satisfaction relation. *Cognitive Therapy and Research, 17,* 397–409.

Shaffer, D. R., Rogel, M., & Hendrick, C. (1975). Intervention in the library: The effect of increased responsibility on bystanders' willingness to prevent a theft. *Journal of Applied Psychology, 5,* 303–319.

Shapiro, P. N., & Penrod, S. (1986). Meta-analysis of facial identification studies. *Psychological Bulletin, 100,* 139–156.

Sharma, N. (1981). Some aspect of attitude and behaviour of mothers. *Indian Psychological Review, 20,* 35–42.

Shaver, P. R., Morgan, H. J., & Wu, S. (1996). Is love a 'basic' emotion? *Personal Relationships, 3,* 81–96.

Shaw, L. L., Batson, C. D., & Todd, R. M. (1994). Empathy avoidance: Forestalling feeling for another in order to escape the motivational consequences. *Journal of Personality and Social Psychology, 67,* 879–887.

Shaw, M. E. (1964). Communication networks. In L. Berkowitz (Ed.), *Advances in experimental social psychology* (Vol. 1, pp. 111–147). New York: Academic Press.

Shaw, M. E. (1966). Social psychology and group processes. In J. B. Sidowski (Ed.), *Experimental methods and instrumentation in psychology* (pp. 607–643). New York: McGraw-Hill.

Shaw, M. E. (1976). *Group dynamics* (2nd ed.). New York: McGraw-Hill.

Shaw, M. E., & Costanzo, P. R. (1982). *Theories of social psychology* (2nd ed.). New York: McGraw-Hill.

Shaw, M. E., Rothschild, G., & Strickland, J. (1957). Decision process in communication networks. *Journal of Abnormal and Social Psychology, 54,* 323–330.

Sheehan, P. W. (1983). Age trends and the correlates of children's television viewing. *Australian Journal of Psychology, 35,* 417–431.

Sheeran, P., & Taylor, S. (1999). Predicting intentions to use condoms: A meta-analysis and comparison of the theories of reasoned action and planned behavior. *Journal of Applied Social Psychology, 29,* 1624–1675.

Sheppard, J. A. (1993). Productivity loss in performance groups: A motivational analysis. *Psychological Bulletin, 113,* 67–81.

Sherif, M. (1935). A study of some social factors in perception. *Archives of Psychology, 27,* 1–60.

Sherif, M. (1936). *The psychology of social norms.* New York: Harper.

Sherif, M. (Ed.). (1962). *Intergroup relations and leadership.* New York: Wiley.

Sherif, M. (1966). *In common predicament: Social psychology of intergroup conflict and cooperation.* Boston, MA: Houghton-Mifflin.

Sherif, M., Harvey, O. J., White, B. J., Hood, W., & Sherif, C. (1961). *Intergroup conflict and cooperation: The Robbers Cave experiment.* Norman, OK: University of Oklahoma Institute of Intergroup Relations.

Sherif, M., & Sherif, C. W. (1953). *Groups in harmony and tension: An integration of studies in intergroup behavior.* New York: Harper & Row.

Sherif, M., & Sherif, C. W. (1964). *Reference groups.* New York: Harper & Row.

Sherif, M., & Sherif, C. W. (1967). Attitude as an individual's own categories: The social judgement–involvement approach to attitude and attitude change. In C. W. Sherif & M. Sherif (Eds.), *Attitude, ego-involvement, and change* (pp. 105–139). New York: Wiley.

Sherman, S. J., Presson, C. C., & Chassin, L. (1984). Mechanisms underlying the false consensus effect: The special role of threats to the self. *Personality and Social Psychology Bulletin, 10,* 127–138.

Shibutani, T. (1966). *Improvised news: A sociological study of rumor.* Indianapolis, IA: Bobbs-Merrill.

Shotland, R. L., & Huston, T. L. (1979). Emergencies: What are they and do they influence bystanders to intervene? *Journal of Personality and Social Psychology, 37,* 1822–1834.

Shotland, R. L., & Heinold, W. D. (1985). Bystander response to arterial bleeding: Helping skills, the decision-making process, and differentiating the helping response. *Journal of Personality and Social Psychology, 49,* 347–356.

Shotter, J. (1984). *Social accountability and selfhood.* Oxford: Blackwell.

Showers, C. (1992). Compartmentalization of positive and negative self-knowledge: Keeping bad apples out of the bunch. *Journal of Personality and Social Psychology, 62,* 1036–1049.

Showers, C., & Cantor, N. (1985). Social cognition: A look at motivated strategies. *Annual Review of Psychology, 36,* 275–305.

Shrauger, J. S., & Schoeneman, T. J. (1979). Symbolic interactionist view of self-concept: Through the looking glass darkly. *Psychological Bulletin, 86,* 549–573.

Shure, G. H., Meeker, R., & Hansford, E. A. (1965). The effectiveness of pacifist strategies in bargaining games. *Journal of Conflict Resolution*, 9, 106–117.

Shweder, R. A., & Bourne, E. J. (1982). Does the concept of the person vary cross-culturally? In A. J. Marsella & G. M. White (Eds.), *Cultural conceptions of mental health and therapy* (pp. 97–137). Dordrecht, Holland: D. Reidel.

Sidanius, J., Levin, S., Federico, C. M., & Pratto, F. (2001). Legitimizing ideologies: The social dominance approach. In J. T. Jost & B. Major (Eds.), *The psychology of legitimacy: Emerging perspectives on ideology, justice, and intergroup relations* (pp. 307–331). New York: Cambridge University Press.

Sidanius, J., & Pratto, F. (1999). *Social dominance: An intergroup theory of social hierarchy and oppression.* New York: Cambridge University Press.

Siegel, A. E., & Siegel, S. (1957). Reference groups, membership groups, and attitude change. *Journal of Abnormal and Social Psychology*, 55, 360–364.

Siegman, A. W., & Reynolds, M. A. (1983). Self-monitoring and speech in feigned and unfeigned lying. *Journal of Personality and Social Psychology*, 45, 1325–1333.

Sigall, H., & Ostrove, N. (1975). Beautiful but dangerous: Effects of offender attractiveness and the nature of the crime on juristic judgment. *Journal of Personality and Social Psychology*, 31, 410–414.

Sigelman, C. K., Berry, C. J., & Wiles, K. A. (1984). Violence in college students' dating relationships. *Journal of Applied Social Psychology*, 5, 530–548.

Sillars, A. L. (1981). Attributions and interpersonal conflict resolution. In J. H. Harvey, W. J. Ickes, & R. F. Kidd (Eds.), *New directions in attribution research* (Vol. 3, pp. 281–305). Hillsdale, NJ: Erlbaum.

Silverman, I. (1971). Physical attractiveness and courtship. *Sexual Behavior*, September, 22–25.

Simard, L., Taylor, D. M., & Giles, H. (1976). Attribution processes and interpersonal accommodation in a bilingual setting. *Language and Speech*, 19, 374–387.

Simmel, E. C., Hahn, M. E., & Walters, J. K. (Eds.). (1983). *Aggressive behavior: Genetic and neural approaches.* Hillsdale, NJ: Erlbaum.

Simmonds, D. B. (1985). The nature of the organizational grapevine. *Supervisory Management*, 39–42.

Simner, M. (1971). Newborn's response to the cry of another infant. *Developmental Psychology*, 5, 136–150.

Simon, B., & Brown, R. J. (1987). Perceived intragroup homogeneity in minority–majority contexts. *Journal of Personality and Social Psychology*, 53, 703–711.

Simon, L., Greenberg, J., & Brehm, J. (1995). Trivialisation: The forgotten mode of dissonance reduction. *Journal of Personality and Social Psychology*, 68, 247–260.

Simon, S. (2003). *Identity in modern society: A social psychological perspective.* Oxford, UK: Blackwell.

Simonton, D. K. (1980). Land battles, generals and armies: Individual and situational determinants of victory and casualties. *Journal of Personality and Social Psychology*, 38, 110–119.

Simpson, J. A., Campbell, B., & Berscheid, E. (1986). The association between romantic love and marriage: Kephart (1967) twice revisited. *Personality and Social Psychology Bulletin*, 12, 363–372.

Simpson, J. A., & Kenrick, D. (1997). *Evolutionary social psychology.* Mahway, NJ: Erlbaum.

Singer, J. D., & Small, M. (1972). *The wages of war 1816–1965: A statistical handbook.* New York: Wiley.

Singer, J., Brush, C., & Lublin, S. (1965). Some aspects of deindividuation: Identification and conformity. *Journal of Experimental Social Psychology*, 1, 356–378.

Singh, D. (1993). Adaptive significance of female physical attractiveness: Role of waist-to-hip ratio. *Journal of Personality and Social Psychology*, 65, 293–307.

Singh, R., Bohra, K. A., & Dalal, A. K. (1979). Favourableness of leadership situations studies with information integration theory. *European Journal of Social Psychology*, 9, 253–264.

Singh, R., & Ho, S. Y. (2000). Attitudes and attraction: A new test of the attraction, repulsion and similarity–dissimilarity asymmetry hypotheses. *British Journal of Social Psychology*, 39, 197–211.

Sinha, D. (1997). Indigenising psychology. In J. W. Berry, Y. Poortinga, & J. Pandey (Eds.), *Handbook of cross-cultural psychology: Vol. 1. Theory and method* (2nd ed., pp. 129–169). Boston, MA: Allyn & Bacon.

Sistrunk, F., & McDavid, J. W. (1971). Sex variable in conforming behavior. *Journal of Personality and Social Psychology*, 2, 200–207.

Skinner, B. F. (1963). Operant behavior. *American Psychologist*, 18, 503–515.

Skowronski, J. J., & Carlston, D. E. (1989). Negativity and extremity biases in impression formation: A review of explanations. *Psychological Bulletin*, 105, 131–142.

Slater, A., Von der Schulenburg, C., Brown, E., Badenoch, M., Butterworth, G., Parsons, S., & Samuels, C. (1998). Newborn infants prefer attractive faces. *Infant Behavior & Development*, 21, 345–354.

Slater, P. E. (1955). Role differentiation in small groups. *American Sociological Review*, 20, 300–310.

Smedley, J. W., & Bayton, J. A. (1978). Evaluative race–class stereotypes by race and perceived class of subjects. *Journal of Personality and Social Psychology*, 3, 530–535.

Smith, B. N., & Stasson, M. F. (2000). A comparison of health behaviour constructs: Social psychological predictors of AIDS-preventive behavioural intentions. *Journal of Applied Social Psychology*, 30, 443–462.

Smith, C. A., & Lazarus, R. S. (1990). Emotion and adaptation. In L. A. Pervin (Ed.), *Handbook of personality: Theory and research* (pp. 609–637). New York: Guilford.

Smith, C. P. (1983). Ethical issues: Research on deception, informed consent, and debriefing. In L. Wheeler & P. Shaver (Eds.), *Review of Personality and Social Psychology* (Vol. 4, pp. 297–328). Beverly Hills, CA: Sage.

Smith, D. L., Pruitt, D. G., & Carnevale, P. J. D. (1982). Matching and mismatching: The effect of own limit, other's toughness, and time pressure on concession rate in negotiation. *Journal of Personality and Social Psychology*, 42, 876–883.

Smith, E. R., Fazio, R. H., & Cejka, M. A. (1996). Accessible attitudes influence categorization of multiple categorizable objects. *Journal of Personality and Social Psychology*, 71, 888–898.

Smith, E. R., & Zárate, M. A. (1992). Exemplar-based model of social judgment. *Psychological Review*, 99, 3–21.

Smith, M. B., Bruner, J. S., & White, R. W. (1956). *Opinions and personality.* New York: Wiley.

Smith, P. B., & Bond, M. H. (1998). *Social psychology across cultures* (2nd ed.). London: Prentice Hall Europe.

Smith, P. B., Dugan, S., & Trompenaars, F. (1996). National culture and the values of organisational employees. *Journal of Cross-Cultural Psychology*, 27, 231–264.

Smith, P. B., Misumi, J., Tayeb, M., Peterson, M., & Bond, M. (1989). On the generality of leadership style measures across cultures. *Journal of Occupational Psychology*, 62, 97–109.

Smith, P. M. (1985). *Language, the sexes and society*. Oxford: Blackwell.

Smolicz, J. J. (1983). Modification and maintenance: Language among school children of Italian background in South Australia. *Journal of Multilingual and Multicultural Development*, 4, 313–337.

Sniderman, P. M., Hagen, M. G., Tetlock, P. E., & Brady, H. E. (1986). Reasoning chains: Causal models of policy reasoning in mass publics. *British Journal of Political Science*, 16, 405–430.

Snyder, M. (1974). The self-monitoring of expressive behavior. *Journal of Personality and Social Psychology*, 30, 526–537.

Snyder, M. (1979). Self-monitoring processes. In L. Berkowitz (Ed.), *Advances in experimental social psychology* (Vol. 12, pp. 88–131). New York: Academic Press.

Snyder, M. (1981). On the self-perpetuating nature of social stereotypes. In D. L. Hamilton (Ed.), *Cognitive processes in stereotyping and intergroup behavior* (pp. 183–212). Hillsdale, NJ: Erlbaum.

Snyder, M. (1984). When belief creates reality. In L. Berkowitz (Ed.), *Advances in experimental social psychology* (Vol. 18, pp. 248–306). New York: Academic Press.

Snyder, M., & Gangestad, S. (1982). Choosing social situations: Two investigations of self-monitoring processes. *Journal of Personality and Social Psychology*, 43, 123–135.

Snyder, M., Grether, J., & Keller, K. (1974). Staring and compliance: A field experiment on hitchhiking. *Journal of Applied Social Psychology*, 4, 165–170.

Snyder, M. L., Stephan, W. G., & Rosenfield, D. (1978). Attributional egotism. In J. H. Harvey, W. Ickes, & R. F. Kidd (Eds.), *New directions in attribution research* (Vol. 2, pp. 91–120). Hillsdale, NJ: Erlbaum.

Solomon, S., Greenberg, J., & Pyszczynski, T. (1991). A terror management theory of social behavior: The psychological functions of self-esteem and cultural worldviews. In M. Zanna (Ed.), *Advances in experimental social psychology* (Vol. 24, pp. 93–159). San Diego, CA: Academic Press.

Sommer, R. (1969). *Personal space: The behavioral basis of design*. Englewood Cliffs, NJ: Prentice Hall.

Sooklal, L. (1991). The leader as a broker of dreams. *Human Relations*, 44, 833–857.

Sorrentino, R. M., & Field, N. (1986). Emergent leadership over time: The functional value of positive motivation. *Journal of Personality and Social Psychology*, 50, 1091–1099.

Sorrentino, R. M., King, G., & Leo, G. (1980). The influence of the minority on perception: A note on a possible alternative explanation. *Journal of Experimental Social Psychology*, 16, 293–301.

Sorrentino, R. M., & Roney, C. J. R. (1999). *The uncertain mind: Individual differences in facing the unknown*. Philadelphia, PA: Psychology Press.

Spears, R., & Lea, M. (1994). Panacea or panopticon? The hidden power in computer-mediated communication. *Communication Research*, 21, 427–459.

Spence, J. T., Helmreich, R. L., & Stapp, J. (1974). The personal attributes questionnaire: A measure of sex role stereotypes and masculinity–femininity. *JSAS Catalog of Selected Documents in Psychology*, 4, 127.

Sperling, M. B., & Borgaro, S. (1995). Attachment anxiety and reciprocity as moderators of interpersonal attraction. *Psychological Reports*, 76, 323–335.

Spitz, R. A. (1945). Hospitalism: An inquiry into the genesis of psychiatric conditions in early childhood. In A. Freud, H. Hartman, & E. Kris (Eds.), *The psychoanalytic study of the child* (Vol. 1, pp. 53–74). New York: International University Press.

Sprecher, S. (1998). Insiders' perspectives on reasons for attraction to a close other. *Social Psychology Quarterly*, 61, 287–300.

Srull, T. K. (1983). Organisational and retrieval processes in person memory: An examination of processing objectives, presentation format, and the possible role of self-generated retrieval cues. *Journal of Personality and Social Psychology*, 44, 1157–1170.

Srull, T. K., & Wyer, R. S., Jr. (1986). The role of chronic and temporary goals in social information processing. In R. M. Sorrentino & E. T. Higgins (Eds.), *Handbook of motivation and cognition: Foundations of social behavior* (pp. 503–549). New York: Guilford Press.

Srull, T. K., & Wyer, R. S. (1989). Person memory and judgement. *Psychological Review*, 96, 58–83.

Staats, C. K., & Staats, A. W. (1957). Meaning established by classical conditioning. *Journal of Experimental Social Psychology*, 54, 74–80.

Stagner, R., & Congdon, C. S. (1955). Another failure to demonstrate displacement of aggression. *Journal of Abnormal and Social Psychology*, 51, 695–696.

Stang, D. J. (1972). Conformity, ability, and self-esteem. *Representative Research in Social Psychology*, 3, 97–103.

Stang, D. J. (1976). Group size effects on conformity. *Journal of Social Psychology*, 98, 175–181.

Stangor, C. (1988). Stereotype accessibility and information processing. *Personality and Social Psychology Bulletin*, 14, 694–708.

Stasser, G., & Davis, J. H. (1981). Group decision making and social influence: A social interaction sequence model. *Psychological Review*, 88, 523–551.

Stasser, G., & Dietz-Uhler, B. (2001). Collective choice, judgment, and problem solving. In M. A. Hogg & R. S. Tindale (Eds.), *Blackwell handbook of social psychology: Group processes* (pp. 31–55). Oxford, UK: Blackwell.

Stasser, G., Kerr, N. L., & Bray, R. M. (1982). The social psychology of jury deliberations: Structure, process, and product. In N. Kerr & R. Bray (Eds.), *The psychology of the courtroom* (pp. 221–256). New York: Academic Press.

Stasser, G., Kerr, N. L., & Davis, J. H. (1989). Influence processes and consensus models in decision-making groups. In P. B. Paulus (Ed.), *Psychology of group influence* (2nd ed., pp. 279–326). Hillsdale, NJ: Erlbaum.

Staub, E. (1974). Helping a distressed person: Social, personality and stimulus determinants. In L. Berkowitz (Ed.), *Advances in experimental social psychology* (Vol. 7, pp. 294–341). New York: Academic Press.

Staub, E. (1977). *Positive social behavior and morality: I. Social and personal influences*. New York: Academic Press.

Staub, E. (1989). *The roots of evil: The psychological and cultural origins of genocide and other forms of group violence*. New York: Cambridge University Press.

Staub, E. (1996). Cultural-societal roots of violence: The example of genocidal violence and contemporary youth violence in the United States. *American Psychologist*, 51, 117–132.

St Claire, L., & Turner, J. C. (1982). The role of demand characteristics in the social categorization paradigm. *European Journal of Social Psychology*, 12, 307–314.

Steele, C. M. (1975). Name-calling and compliance. *Journal of Personality and Social Psychology, 31*, 361–369.

Steele, C. M. (1988). The psychology of self-affirmation: Sustaining the integrity of the self. In L. Berkowitz (Ed.), *Advances in experimental social psychology* (Vol. 21, pp. 261–302). New York: Academic Press.

Steele, C. M., & Aronson, J. (1995). Stereotype vulnerability and the intellectual test performance of African-Americans. *Journal of Personality and Social Psychology, 69*, 797–811.

Steele, C. M., Spencer, S. J., & Aronson, J. (2002). Contending with group image: The psychology of stereotype and social identity threat. In M. P. Zanna (Ed.), *Advances in experimental social psychology* (Vol. 34, pp. 379–440). San Diego, CA: Academic Press.

Steele, C. M., Spencer, S. J., & Lynch, M. (1993). Self-image resilience and dissonance: The role of affirmation resources. *Journal of Personality and Social Psychology, 64*, 885–896.

Steinberg, R., & Shapiro, S. (1982). Sex differences in personality traits of female and male master of business administration students. *Journal of Applied Psychology, 67*, 306–310.

Steiner, I. D. (1972). *Group process and productivity.* New York: Academic Press.

Steiner, I. D. (1976). Task-performing groups. In J. W. Thibaut & J. T. Spence (Eds.), *Contemporary topics in social psychology* (pp. 393–422). Morristown, NJ: General Learning Press.

Steinmetz, S. K., & Straus, M. A. (1973). The family as cradle of violence. *Society, 10*, 50–56.

Steir, C. (1978). *Blue jolts: True stories from the cuckoo's nest.* Washington, DC: New Republic Books.

Stephan, W. G. (1977). Cognitive differentiation in intergroup perception. *Sociometry, 40*, 50–58.

Stephan, W. G., Berscheid, E., & Walster, E. (1971). Sexual arousal and heterosexual perception. *Journal of Personality and Social Psychology, 20*, 93–101.

Stephan, W. G., & Rosenfield, D. (1978). Effects of desegregation on racial attitudes. *Journal of Personality and Social Psychology, 36*, 795–804.

Stephan, W. G., & Stephan, C. W. (1984). The role of ignorance in intergroup relations. In N. Miller & M. B. Brewer (Eds.), *Groups in contact: The psychology of desegregation* (pp. 229–255). New York: Academic Press.

Stephan, W. G., & Stephan, C. W. (1985). Intergroup anxiety. *Journal of Social Issues, 41*, 157–175.

Stephan, W. G., & Stephan, C. W. (2000). An integrated threat theory of prejudice. In S. Oskamp (Ed.), *Reducing prejudice and discrimination* (pp. 23–46). Mahwah, NJ: Erlbaum.

Stephan, W. G., & Stephan, C. W. (2001). *Improving intergroup relations.* Thousand Oaks, CA: Sage.

Stephenson, G. M. (1992). *The psychology of criminal justice.* Oxford, UK: Blackwell.

Stephenson, G. M., Abrams, D., Wagner, W., & Wade, G. (1986). Partners in recall: Collaborative order in the recall of a police interrogation. *British Journal of Social Psychology, 25*, 341–343.

Stephenson, G. M., Clark, N. K., & Wade, G. (1986). Meetings make evidence: An experimental study of collaborative and individual recall of a simulated police interrogation. *Journal of Personality and Social Psychology, 50*, 1113–1122.

Sternberg, R. J. (1988). *The triangle of love.* New York: Basic Books.

Stevens, G., Owens, D., & Schaefer, E. C. (1990). Education and attractiveness in marriage choices. *Social Psychology Quarterly, 53*, 62–70.

Stewart, J. E. (1980). Defendant's attractiveness as a factor in the outcome of criminal trials: An observational study. *Journal of Applied Social Psychology, 10*, 348–361.

Stiglitz, J. (2002). *Globalization and its discontents.* London: Penguin.

Stith, S. M., & Farley, S. C. (1993). A predictive model of male spousal violence. *Journal of Family Violence, 8*, 183–201.

Stogdill, R. (1974). *Handbook of leadership.* New York: Free Press.

Stone, J., Wiegand, A. W., Cooper, J., & Aronson, E. (1997). When exemplification fails: Hypocrisy and the motive for self-integrity. *Journal of Personality and Social Psychology, 72*, 54–65.

Stoner, J. A. F. (1961). *A comparison of individual and group decisions including risk.* Unpublished master's thesis, Massachusetts Institute of Technology, Boston.

Storms, M. D. (1973). Videotape and the attribution process: Reversing actor's and observer's points of view. *Journal of Personality and Social Psychology, 27*, 165–175.

Storms, M. D., & Nisbett, R. E. (1970). Insomnia and the attribution process. *Journal of Personality and Social Psychology, 16*, 319–328.

Stouffer, S. A., Suchman, E. A., DeVinney, L. C., Star, S. A., & Williams, R. M. Jr. (1949). *The American soldier, I: Adjustment during Army life.* Princeton, NJ: Princeton University Press.

Strauman, T. J., Lemieux, A. M., & Coe, C. L. (1993). Self-discrepancy and natural killer cell activity: Immunological consequences of negative self-evaluation. *Journal of Personality and Social Psychology, 64*, 1042–1052.

Straus, M. A., Gelles, R. J., & Steinmetz, S. K. (1980). *Behind closed doors: Violence in the American family.* Garden City, NJ: Anchor Books.

Straus, S., & McGrath, J. E. (1994). Does the medium matter? The interaction of task type and technology on group performance and member reactions. *Journal of Applied Psychology, 79*, 87–97.

Strauss, M. A., Sugarman, D. B., & Giles-Sims, J. (1997). Spanking by parents and subsequent antisocial behaviour of children. *Archives of Pediatrics and Adolescent Medicine, 151*, 761–767.

Strickland, L. H., Aboud, F. E., & Gergen, K. J. (Eds.). (1976). *Social psychology in transition.* New York: Plenum Press.

Strodtbeck, F. L., & Lipinski, R. M. (1985). Becoming first among equals: Moral considerations in jury foreman selection. *Journal of Personality and Social Psychology, 49*, 927–936.

Strodtbeck, F. L., James, R., & Hawkins, C. (1957). Social status in jury deliberations. *American Sociological Review, 22*, 713–718.

Stroebe, W., & Diehl, M. (1994). Why groups are less effective than their members: On productivity losses in idea-generating groups. *European Review of Social Psychology, 5*, 271–303.

Stroebe, W., Diehl, M., & Abakoumkin, G. (1992). The illusion of group effectivity. *Personality and Social Psychology Bulletin, 18*, 643–650.

Stroebe, W., & Stroebe, M. S. (1995). *Social psychology and health.* Buckingham, UK: Open University Press.

Stroebe, W., Stroebe, M. S., Gergen, K. J., & Gergen, M. (1982). The effects of bereavement on mortality: A social psychological analysis. In J. R. Eiser (Ed.), *Social psychology and behavioural medicine.* New York: Wiley.

Strube, M. J., & Garcia, J. E. (1981). A meta-analytic investigation of Fiedler's contingency model of leadership effectiveness. *Psychological Bulletin, 90*, 307–321.

Strube, M. J., Turner, C. W., Cerro, D., Stevens, J., & Hinchey, F. (1984). Interpersonal aggression and the type A coronary-prone behavior pattern: A theoretical distinction and practical implications. *Journal of Personality and Social Psychology, 47*, 839–847.

Struch, N., & Schwartz, S. H. (1989). Intergroup aggression: Its predictors and distinctiveness from ingroup bias. *Journal of Personality and Social Psychology, 56*, 364–373.

Stryker, S., & Statham, A. (1986). Symbolic interaction and role theory. In G. Lindzey & E. Aronson (Eds.), *The handbook of social psychology* (3rd ed., Vol. 1, pp. 311–378). New York: Random House.

Stürmer, S., & Simon, S. (in press). Collective action: Towards a dual-pathway model. *European Review of Social Psychology.*

Suls, J. M., & Miller, R. L. (Eds.). (1977). *Social comparison processes: Theoretical and empirical perspectives.* Washington, DC: Hemisphere.

Suls, J., & Wheeler, L. (Eds.). (2000). *Handbook of social comparison: Theory and research.* New York: Kluwer/ Plenum.

Sumner, W. G. (1906). *Folkways.* Boston, MA: Ginn.

Sunafrank, M. J., & Miller, G. R. (1981). The role of initial conversations in determining attraction to similar and dissimilar strangers. *Human Communication Research, 8*, 16–25.

Sundberg, N. D. (1977). *Assessment of persons.* Englewood Cliffs, NJ: Prentice Hall.

Surgenor, L. J. (1985). Attitudes toward seeking professional help. *New Zealand Journal of Psychology, 14*, 27–33.

Swann, W. B. Jr. (1984). Quest for accuracy in person perception: A matter of pragmatics. *Psychological Review, 91*, 457–477.

Swann, W. B. Jr. (1987). Identity negotiation: Where two roads meet. *Journal of Personality and Social Psychology, 53*, 1038–1051.

Swann, W. B. Jr., Hixon, J. G., & de la Ronde, C. (1992). Embracing the bitter 'truth': Negative self-concepts and marital commitment. *Psychological Science, 3*, 118–121.

Sweeney, P. D., Anderson, K., & Bailey, S. (1986). Attribution style in depression: A meta-analytic review. *Journal of Personality and Social Psychology, 50*, 974–991.

Swim, J. K. (1994). Perceived versus meta-analytic effect sizes: An assessment of the accuracy of gender stereotypes. *Journal of Personality and Social Psychology, 66*, 21–36.

Swim, J. K., Borgida, E., Maruyama, G., & Myers, D. G. (1989). Joan McKay vs. John McKay: Do gender stereotypes bias evaluations? *Psychological Bulletin, 105*, 409–429.

Swim, J. T., & Stangor, C. (1998). *Prejudice from the target's perspective.* Santa Barbara, CA: Academic Press.

Swim, J. T., Aikin, K., Hall, W., & Hunter, B. A. (1995). Sexism and racism: Old-fashioned and modern prejudices. *Journal of Personality and Social Psychology, 68*, 199–214.

Szasz, T. (1970). *The manufacture of madness.* New York: Delta.

Szymanski, K., & Harkins, S. G. (1987). Social loafing and self-evaluation with a social standard. *Journal of Personality and Social Psychology, 53*, 891–897.

Taft, R. (1973). Migration: Problems of adjustment and assimilation in immigrants. In P. Watson (Ed.), *Psychology and race* (pp. 224–239). Harmondsworth: Penguin.

Taft, R., & Day, R. H. (1988). Psychology in Australia. *Annual Review of Psychology, 39*, 375–400.

Tajfel, H. (1957). Value and the perceptual judgement of magnitude. *Psychological Review, 64*, 192–204.

Tajfel, H. (1959). Quantitative judgement in social perception. *British Journal of Psychology, 50*, 16–29.

Tajfel, H. (1969). Social and cultural factors in perception. In G. Lindzey & E. Aronson (Eds.), *Handbook of social psychology* (Vol. 3, pp. 315–394). Reading, MA: Addison-Wesley.

Tajfel, H. (1970). Experiments in intergroup discrimination. *Scientific American, 223*, 96–102.

Tajfel, H. (1972a). Experiments in a vacuum. In J. Israel & H. Tajfel (Eds.), *The context of social psychology: A critical assessment.* London: Academic Press.

Tajfel, H. (1972b). 'La catégorisation sociale'. In S. Moscovici (Ed.), *Introduction à la Psychologie Sociale* (Vol. 1, pp. 272–302). Paris: Larousse.

Tajfel, H. (1974). Social identity and intergroup behaviour. *Social Science Information, 13*, 65–93.

Tajfel, H. (1978). Intergroup behaviour: II. Group perspectives. In H. Tajfel & C. Fraser (Eds.), *Introducing social psychology* (pp. 423–445). Harmondsworth: Penguin.

Tajfel, H. (1981a). Social stereotypes and social groups. In J. C. Turner & H. Giles (Eds.), *Intergroup behaviour* (pp. 144–167). Oxford: Blackwell.

Tajfel, H. (1981b). *Human groups and social categories: Studies in social psychology.* Cambridge: Cambridge University Press.

Tajfel, H. (1982). Social psychology of intergroup relations. *Annual Review of Social Psychology, 33*, 1–39.

Tajfel, H. (Ed.). (1984). *The social dimension: European developments in social psychology.* Cambridge: Cambridge University Press.

Tajfel, H., & Billig, M. (1974). Familiarity and categorization in intergroup behaviour. *Journal of Experimental Social Psychology, 10*, 159–170.

Tajfel, H., Billig, M., Bundy R. P., & Flament, C. (1971). Social categorization and intergroup behaviour. *European Journal of Social Psychology, 1*, 149–177.

Tajfel, H., & Turner, J. C. (1979). An integrative theory of intergroup conflict. In W. G. Austin & S. Worchel (Eds.), *The social psychology of intergroup relations* (pp. 33–47). Monterey, CA: Brooks/ Cole.

Tajfel, H., & Wilkes, A. L. (1963). Classification and quantitative judgement. *British Journal of Psychology, 54*, 101–114.

Tan, D. T. Y., & Singh, R. (1995). Attitudes and attraction: A developmental study of the similarity–attraction and dissimilarity–repulsion hypothesis. *Personality and Social Psychology Bulletin, 21*, 975–986.

Tanford, S., & Penrod, S. (1984). Social influence model: A formal integration of research on majority and minority influence processes. *Psychological Bulletin, 95*, 189–225.

Tanter, R. (1966). Dimension of conflict behavior within and between nations, 1958–1960. *Journal of Conflict Resolution, 10*, 41–64.

Tanter, R. (1969). International war and domestic turmoil: Some contemporary evidence. In H. D. Graham & T. R. Gurr (Eds.), *Violence in America* (pp. 550–569). New York: Bantam Books.

Tarde, G. (1890). *Les lois de l'imitation.* Paris: Alcan.

Tarde, G. (1898). *Etudes de psychologie sociale.* Paris: V. Giard & E. Briére.

Tarde, G. (1901). *L'opinion et la foule.* Paris: Libraire Felix Alcan.

Taylor, A. J. W. (1987). *Antarctic psychology.* Wellington: Science Information Publishing Centre.

Taylor, D. M., & Brown, R. J. (1979). Towards a more social social psychology. *British Journal of Social and Clinical Psychology, 18*, 173–179.

Taylor, D. M., & Jaggi, V. (1974). Ethnocentrism and causal attribution in a S. Indian context. *Journal of Cross-cultural Psychology, 5*, 162–171.

Taylor, D. M., & McKirnan, D. J. (1984). A five-stage model of intergroup relations. *British Journal of Social Psychology, 23*, 291–300.

Taylor, D. M., Wright, S. C., & Porter, L. E. (1994). Dimensions of perceived discrimination: The personal/group discrimination discrepancy. In M. P. Zanna & J. M. Olson (Eds.), *The psychology of prejudice: The Ontario symposium* (Vol. 7, pp. 233–255). Hillsdale, NJ: Erlbaum.

Taylor, S. E. (1981). The interface of cognitive and social psychology. In J. Harvey (Ed.), *Cognition, social behavior, and the environment* (pp. 189–211). Hillsdale, NJ: Erlbaum.

Taylor, S. E. (1982). Social cognition and health. *Personality and Social Psychology Bulletin, 8,* 549–562.

Taylor, S. E. (1983). Adjustment to threatening events: A theory of cognitive adaptation. *American Psychologist, 38,* 1161–1173.

Taylor, S. E. (1998). The social being in social psychology. In D. T. Gilbert, S. T. Fiske, & G. Lindzey (Eds.), *The handbook of social psychology* (4th ed., Vol. 1, pp. 58–95). New York: McGraw-Hill.

Taylor, S. E., & Brown, J. D. (1988). Illusion and well-being: A social psychological perspective on mental health. *Psychological Bulletin, 103,* 193–210.

Taylor, S. E., & Fiske, S. T. (1975). Point-of-view and perceptions of causality. *Journal of Personality and Social Psychology, 32,* 439–445.

Taylor, S. E., & Fiske, S. T. (1978). Salience, attention, and attribution: Top of the head phenomena. In L. Berkowitz (Ed.), *Advances in experimental social psychology* (Vol. 11, pp. 249–288). New York: Academic Press.

Taylor, S. E., Fiske, S. T., Etcoff, N. L., & Ruderman, A. J. (1978). Categorical and contextual bases of person memory and stereotyping. *Journal of Personality and Social Psychology, 36,* 778–793.

Taylor, S. E., & Koivumaki, J. H. (1976). The perception of self and others: Acquaintanceship, affect, and actor–observer differences. *Journal of Personality and Social Psychology, 33,* 403–408.

Taylor, S. E., Peplau, L. A., & Sears, D. O. (2000). *Social psychology* (10th ed.). Upper Saddle River, NJ: Prentice Hall.

Taylor, S. E., & Thompson, S. C. (1982). Stalking the elusive 'vividness' effect. *Psychological Review, 89,* 155–181.

Taylor, S. P., & Sears, J. D. (1988). The effects of alcohol and persuasive social pressure on human physical aggression. *Aggressive Behavior, 14,* 237–243.

Taynor, J., & Deaux, K. (1973). Equity and perceived sex differences: Role behavior as defined by the task, the mode, and the actor. *Journal of Personality and Social Psychology, 32,* 381–390.

Teger, A. (1970). Defining the socially responsible response. Paper presented at the 78th annual meeting of the American Psychological Association.

Teger, A. I., & Pruitt, D. G. (1967). Components of group risk taking. *Journal of Experimental Social Psychology, 3,* 189–205.

Tellis, G. J. (1987). *Advertising exposure, loyalty, and brand purchase: A two-stage model of choice* (Report no. 87–105). Cambridge, MA: Marketing Science Institute.

Tennen, H., & Affleck, G. (1993). The puzzles of self-esteem: A clinical perspective. In R. F. Baumeister (Ed.), *Self-esteem: The puzzle of low self-esteem* (pp. 241–262). New York: Plenum.

Terry, D. J., Carey, C. J., & Callan, V. J. (2001). Employee adjustment to an organizational merger: An intergroup perspective. *Personality and Social Psychology Bulletin, 27,* 267–280.

Terry, D., Gallois, C., & McCamish, M. (1993). The theory of reasoned action and health care behaviour. In D. Terry, C. Gallois, & M. McCamish (Eds.), *The theory of reasoned action: Its application to AIDS-preventive behaviour* (pp. 1–27). Oxford: Pergamon.

Terry, D. J., & Hogg, M. A. (1996). Group norms and the attitude–behavior relationship: A role for group identification. *Personality and Social Psychology Bulletin, 22,* 776–793.

Terry, D. J., & Hogg, M. A. (2001). Attitudes, behavior, and social context: The role of norms and group membership in social influence processes. In J. P. Forgas & K. D. Williams (Eds.), *Social influence: Direct and indirect processes* (pp. 253–270). Philadelphia, PA: Psychology Press.

Terry, D. J., Hogg, M. A., & Duck, J. M. (1999). Group membership, social identity, and attitudes. In D. Abrams & M. A. Hogg (Eds.), *Social identity and social cognition* (pp. 280–314). Oxford, UK: Blackwell.

Terry, D. J., Hogg, M. A., & White, K. M. (2000). Attitude-behavior relations: Social identity and group membership. In D. J. Terry & M. A. Hogg (Eds.), *Attitudes, behavior, and social context: The role of norms and group membership* (pp. 67–93). Mahwah, NJ: Erlbaum.

Tesser, A. (1988). Toward a self-evaluation maintenance model of social behavior. In L. Berkowitz (Ed.), *Advances in experimental social psychology* (Vol. 21, pp. 181–227). San Diego, CA: Academic Press.

Tesser, A. (2000). On the confluence of self-esteem maintenance mechanisms. *Personality and Social Psychology Review, 4,* 290–299.

Tesser, A., Gatewood, R., & Driver, M. (1968). Some determinants of gratitude. *Journal of Personality and Social Psychology, 9,* 233–236.

Tesser, A., Martin, L., & Mendolia, M. (1995). The impact of thought on attitude extremity and attitude–behavior consistency. In R. E. Petty & J. A. Krosnick (Eds.), *Attitude strength: antecedents and consequences* (pp. 73–92). Mahwah, NJ: Erlbaum.

Tesser, A., & Paulhus, D. L. (1976). Toward a causal model of love. *Journal of Personality and Social Psychology, 34,* 1095–1105.

Tesser, A., & Schwartz, N. (Eds.). (2001). *Blackwell handbook of social psychology: Intraindividual processes.* Oxford, UK: Blackwell.

Tesser, A., & Shaffer, D. R. (1990). Attitudes and attitude change. *Annual Review of Psychology, 41,* 479–523.

Tetlock, P. E. (1979). Identifying victims of groupthink from public statements of decision makers. *Journal of Personality and Social Psychology, 37,* 1314–1324.

Tetlock, P. E. (1983). Policymakers. Images of international conflict. *Journal of Social Issues, 39,* 67–86.

Tetlock, P. E. (1984). Cognitive style and political belief systems in the British House of Commons. *Journal of Personality and Social Psychology, 46,* 365–375.

Tetlock, P. E. (1988). Monitoring the integrative complexity of American and Soviet policy rhetoric: What can be learned? *Journal of Social Issues, 44,* 101–131.

Tetlock, P. E. (1989). The structural bases of consistency among political attitudes: Effects of political expertise and attitude importance. Structure and function in political belief systems. In A. R. Pratkanis, S. J. Breckler, & A. G. Greenwald (Eds.), *Attitude structure and function* (pp. 129–151). Hillsdale, NJ: Erlbaum.

Tetlock, P. E., & Boettger, R. (1989). Accountability: A social magnifier of the dilution effect. *Journal of Personality and Social Psychology, 57,* 388–398.

Tetlock, P. E., & Kim, J. I. (1987). Accountability and judgment processes in a personality prediction task. *Journal of Personality and Social Psychology, 52,* 700–709.

Tetlock, P.E., & Levi, A. (1982). Attribution bias: On the inconclusiveness of the cognition-motivation debate. *Journal of Experimental Social Psychology, 18,* 68–88.

Tetlock, P. E., & Manstead, A. S. R. (1985). Impression management versus intrapsychic explanations in social psychology: A useful dichotomy? *Psychological Review, 92*, 59–77.

Tetlock, P. E., Peterson, R. S., McGuire, C., Chang, S., & Feld, P. (1992). Assessing political group dynamics: A test of the group-think model. *Journal of Personality and Social Psychology, 63*, 403–425.

Thakerar, J. N., Giles, H., & Cheshire, J. (1982). Psychological and linguistic parameters of speech accommodation theory. In C. Fraser & K. K. Scherer (Eds.), *Advances in the social psychology of language* (pp. 205–255). Cambridge: Cambridge University Press.

Tham, S. W., Ford, T. J., & Wilkinson, D. G. (1995). A survey of domestic violence and other forms of abuse. *Journal of Mental Health, 4*, 317–321.

Thatcher, M. (1993). *The Downing Street years*. London: Harper-Collins.

Thibaut, J. W., & Kelley, H. H. (1959). *The social psychology of groups*. New York: Wiley.

Thomas, W. I., & Znaniecki, F. (1918). *The Polish peasant in Europe and America* (Vol. 1). Boston, MA: Badger.

Thompson, J. B. (1990). *Ideology and modern culture: Critical social theory in the era of mass communication*. Stanford, CA: Stanford University Press.

Thompson, L., & Loewenstein, J. (2003). Mental models of negotiation: Descriptive, prescriptive, and paradigmatic implications. In M. A. Hogg & J. Cooper (Eds.), *The Sage handbook of social psychology* (pp. 494–511). London: Sage.

Thompson, L., Medvex, V. H., Seiden, V., & Kopelman, S. (2001). Poker face, smiley face, and rant 'n' rave: Myths and realities about emotion in negotiation. In M. A. Hogg & R. S. Tindale (Eds.), *Blackwell handbook of social psychology: Group processes* (pp. 139–163). Oxford, UK: Blackwell.

Thompson, W. C., Fong, G. T., & Rosenhan, D. L. (1981). Inadmissible evidence and juror verdicts. *Journal of Personality and Social Psychology, 40*, 453–463.

Thompson, W. C., & Fuqua, J. (1998). 'The jury will disregard . . .': A brief guide to inadmissible evidence. In J. M. Golding & C. M. MacLeod (Eds.), *Intentional forgetting: Interdisciplinary approaches* (pp. 133–154). Mahwah, NJ: Erlbaum.

Thomson, R., & Murachver, T. (2001). Predicting gender from electronic discourse. *British Journal of Social Psychology, 40*, 193–208.

Thoreau, H. D. (1854/1997). *Walden*. Oxford: Oxford University Press.

Thorndike, E. L. (1940). *Human nature and the social order*. New York: Macmillan.

Thurstone, L. L. (1928). Attitudes can be measured. *American Journal of Sociology, 33*, 529–554.

Thurstone, L. L. (1931). The measurement of social attitudes. *Journal of Abnormal and Social Psychology, 26*, 249–269.

Tice, D. M. (1992). Self-presentation and self-concept change: The looking glass self as magnifying glass. *Journal of Personality and Social Psychology, 63*, 435–451.

Tilker, H. (1970). Socially responsible behavior as a function of observer responsibility and victim feedback. *Journal of Personality and Social Psychology, 14*, 95–100.

Tindale, R. S., Davis, J. H., Vollrath, D. A., Nagao, D. H., & Hinsz, V. B. (1990). Asymmetrical social influence in freely interacting groups: A test of three models. *Journal of Personality and Social Psychology, 58*, 438–449.

Tindale, R. S., Kameda, T., & Hinsz, V. B. (2003). Group decision making. In M. A. Hogg & J. Cooper (Eds.), *The Sage handbook of social psychology* (pp. 381–403). London: Sage.

Tindale, R. S., Meisenhelder, H. M., Dykema-Engblade, A. A., & Hogg, M. A. (2001). Shared cognition in small groups. In M. A. Hogg & R. S. Tindale (Eds.), *Blackwell handbook of social psychology: Group processes* (pp. 1–30). Oxford, UK: Blackwell.

Tindale, R. S., Nadler, J., Krebel, A., & Davis, J. H. (2001). Procedural mechanisms and jury behavior. In M. A. Hogg & R. S. Tindale (Eds.), *Blackwell handbook of social psychology: Group processes* (pp. 574–602). Oxford, UK: Blackwell.

Titus, H. E., & Hollander, E. P. (1957). The California F scale in psychological research (1950–1955). *Psychological Bulletin, 54*, 47–74.

Toch, H. (1969). *Violent men*. Chicago, IL: Aldine.

Toi, M., & Batson, C. D. (1982). More evidence that empathy is a source of altruistic motivation. *Journal of Personality and Social Psychology, 43*, 281–292.

Tolstoy, L. (1869). *War and peace*. Harmondsworth: Penguin.

Tomada, G., & Schneider, B. H. (1997). Relational aggression, gender, and peer acceptance: Invariance across culture, stability over time, and concordance among informants. *Developmental Psychology, 33*, 601–609.

Tönnies, F. (1955). *Community and association*. London: Routledge & Kegan Paul. (Originally published in German in 1887.)

Tourangeau, R., Smith, T. W., & Rasinski, K. A. (1997). Motivation to report sensitive behaviours on surveys: Evidence from a bogus pipeline experiment. *Journal of Applied Social Psychology, 27*, 209–222.

Trager, G. L. (1958). Paralanguage: A first approximation. *Studies in Linguistics, 13*, 1–12.

Triandis, H. C. (1971). *Attitude and attitude change*. New York: Wiley.

Triandis, H. C. (Ed.) (1976). *Variations in black and white perceptions of the social environment*. Champaign, IL: University of Illinois Press.

Triandis, H. C. (1977). *Interpersonal behavior*. Monterey, CA: Brooks/Cole.

Triandis, H. C. (1980). Values, attitudes and interpersonal behavior. In H. H. Howe & M. M. Page (Eds.), *Nebraska symposium on motivation* (Vol. 27). Lincoln, NE: University of Nebraska Press.

Triandis, H. C. (1989). The self and social behavior in differing cultural contexts. *Psychological Review, 96*, 506–520.

Triandis, H. C. (1994). *Culture and social behavior*. New York: McGraw-Hill.

Triandis, H. C., & Davis, E. G. (1965). Race and belief as shared determinants of behavior intentions. *Journal of Personality and Social Psychology, 2*, 715–725.

Triandis, H., Lambert, W., Berry, J., Lonner, W., Heron, A., Brislin, R., & Draguns, J. (Eds.). (1980). *Handbook of cross-cultural psychology* (Vol. 1–6). Boston, MA: Allyn & Bacon.

Triandis, H. C., & Suh, M. H. (2002). Cultural influences on personality. *Annual Review of Psychology, 53*, 133–160.

Triandis, H. C., Vassiliou, V., Vassiliou, G., Tanaka, Y., & Shanmugam, A. (Eds.). (1972). *The analysis of subjective culture*. New York: Wiley.

Tripathi, R. C., & Srivasta, R. (1981). Relative deprivation and intergroup attitudes. *European Journal of Social Psychology, 11*, 313–318.

Triplett, N. (1898). The dynamogenic factors in pacemaking and competition. *American Journal of Psychology, 9*, 507–533.

Trope, Y. (1986). Self-enhancement and self-assessment in achievement behavior. In R. Sorrentino & E. T. Higgins (Eds.), *Handbook of motivation and cognition* (Vol. 2, pp. 350–378). New York: Guilford.

Trope, Y., & Gaunt, R. (2003). Attribution and person perception. In M. A. Hogg & J. Cooper (Eds.), *The Sage handbook of social psychology* (pp. 190–208). London: Sage.

Trotter, W. (1919). *Instincts of the herd in peace and war*. London: Oxford University Press.

Tuckman, B. W. (1965). Developmental sequence in small groups. *Psychological Bulletin, 63*, 384–399.

Turkat, I. D. (1995). Divorce-related malicious mother syndrome. *Journal of Family Violence, 10*, 253–264.

Turner, J. C. (1975). Social comparison and social identity: Some prospects for intergroup behaviour. *European Journal of Social Psychology, 5*, 5–34.

Turner, J. C. (1978). Social categorization and social discrimination in the minimal group paradigm. In H. Tajfel (Ed.), *Differentiation between social groups* (pp. 101–140). London: Academic Press.

Turner, J. C. (1980). Fairness or discrimination in intergroup behaviour? A reply to Branthwaite, Doyle and Lightbown. *European Journal of Social Psychology, 10*, 131–147.

Turner, J. C. (1981a). Some considerations in generalizing experimental social psychology. In G. M. Stephenson & J. M. Davis (Eds.), *Progress in applied social psychology* (Vol. 1, pp. 3–34). Chichester, UK: Wiley.

Turner, J. C. (1981b). The experimental social psychology of intergroup behaviour. In J. C. Turner & H. Giles (Eds.), *Intergroup behaviour* (pp. 66–101). Oxford: Blackwell.

Turner, J. C. (1982). Towards a cognitive redefinition of the social group. In H. Tajfel (Ed.), *Social identity and intergroup relations* (pp. v15–40). Cambridge: Cambridge University Press.

Turner, J. C. (1983). Some comments on 'the measurement of social orientations in the minimal group paradigm'. *European Journal of Social Psychology, 13*, 351–368.

Turner, J. C. (1984). Social identification and psychological group formation. In H. Tajfel (Ed.), *The social dimension: European developments in social psychology* (Vol. 2, pp. 518–538). Cambridge: Cambridge University Press.

Turner, J. C. (1985). Social categorization and the self-concept: A social cognitive theory of group behaviour. In E. J. Lawler (Ed.), *Advances in group processes: theory and research* (Vol. 2, pp. 77–122). Greenwich, CT: JAI Press.

Turner, J. C. (1991). *Social influence*. Buckingham, UK: Open University Press.

Turner, J. C. (1999). Some current issues in research on social identity and self-categorization theories. In N. Ellemers, R. Spears, & B. Doosje (Eds.), *Social identity* (pp. 6–34). Oxford, UK: Blackwell.

Turner, J. C., & Bourhis, R. Y. (1996). Social identity, interdependence and the social group. A reply to Rabbie et al. In W. P. Robinson (Ed.), *Social groups and identities: Developing the legacy of Henri Tajfel* (pp. 25–63). Oxford, UK: Butterworth-Heinemann.

Turner, J. C., Hogg, M. A., Oakes, P. J., Reicher, S. D., & Wetherell, M. S. (1987). *Rediscovering the social group: a self-categorization theory*. Oxford: Blackwell.

Turner, J. C., & Oakes, P. J. (1986). The significance of the social identity concept for social psychology with reference to individualism, interactionism and social influence. *British Journal of Social Psychology, 25*, 237–252.

Turner, J. C., & Oakes, P. J. (1989). Self-categorization and social influence. In P. B. Paulus (Ed.), *The psychology of group influence* (2nd ed., pp. 233–275). Hillsdale, NJ: Erlbaum.

Turner, J. C., Wetherell, M. S., & Hogg, M. A. (1989). Referent informational influence and group polarization. *British Journal of Social Psychology, 28*, 135–147.

Turner, M. E., Pratkanis, A. R., Probasco, P., & Leve, C. (1992). Threat, cohesion, and group effectiveness: Testing a social identity maintenance perspective on groupthink. *Journal of Personality and Social Psychology, 63*, 781–796.

Turner, R. H. (1974). Collective behavior. In R. E. L. Faris (Ed.), *Handbook of modern sociology* (pp. 382–425). Chicago, IL: Rand-McNally.

Turner, R. H., & Killian, L. (1957). *Collective behavior*. Englewood Cliffs, NJ: Prentice Hall.

Tversky, A., & Kahneman, D. (1974). Judgment under uncertainty: Heuristics and biases. *Science, 185*, 1124–1131.

Tyerman, A., & Spencer, C. (1983). A critical test of the Sherifs' robbers cave experiments: Intergroup competition and cooperation between groups of well acquainted individuals. *Small Group Behavior, 14*, 515–531.

Tyler, T. R. (1997). The psychology of legitimacy: A relational perspective on voluntary deference to authorities. *Personality and Social Psychology Review, 1*, 323–345.

Tyler, T. R., & Lind, E. A. (1992). A relational model of authority in groups. In M. P. Zanna (Ed.), *Advances in experimental social psychology* (Vol. 25, pp. 115–191). New York: Academic Press.

Tyler, T. R., & Schuller, R. A. (1991). Aging and attitude change. *Journal of Personality and Social Psychology, 61*, 689–697.

Tyler, T., & Sears, D. O. (1977). Coming to like obnoxious people when we have to live with them. *Journal of Personality and Social Psychology, 35*, 200–211.

Tyler, T. R., & Smith, H. J. (1998). Social justice and social movements. In D. T. Gilbert, S. T. Fiske, & G. Lindzey (Eds.), *The handbook of social psychology* (4th ed., Vol. 2, pp. 595–632). New York: McGraw-Hill.

Ulman, R. B., & Abse, D. W. (1983). The group psychology of mass madness: Jonestown. *Political Psychology, 4*, 637–661.

Umadevi, L., Venkataramaiah, P., & Srinivasulu, R. (1992). A comparative study on the concept of marriage by professional and non-professional degree students. *Indian Journal of Behaviour, 16*, 27–37.

Underwood, B., & Moore, B. (1982). Perspective-taking and altruism. *Psychological Bulletin, 91*, 143–173.

US Department of Justice (2001). Bureau of Justice Statistics: *Homicide trends in the United States*. Retrieved January 2, 2002, from http://www.ojp.usdoj.gov/bjs/homicide/homtrnd.htm

Valenstein, E. S. (1975). Brain stimulation and behavior control. *Nebraska symposium on motivation, 22*, 251–292.

Valins, S. (1966). Cognitive effects of false heart-rate feedback. *Journal of Personality and Social Psychology, 4*, 400–408.

Valins, S., & Nisbett, R. E. (1972). Attribution processes in the development and treatment of emotional disorders. In E. E. Jones, D. E. Kanouse, H. H. Kelley, R. E. Nisbett, S. Valins, & B. Weiner (Eds.), *Attribution: perceiving the causes of behavior* (pp. 137–150). Morristown, NJ: General Learning Press.

van der Pligt, J. (1984). Attributional false consensus, and valence: Two field studies. *Journal of Personality and Social Psychology, 46*, 57–68.

van Dijk, T. A. (1987). *Communicating racism: ethnic prejudice in thought and talk*. Newburg Park, CA: Sage.

van Dijk, T. A. (1993). *Elite discourse and racism*. Newbury Park, CA: Sage.

van Dijk, T. A., & Wodak, R. (Eds.). (1988). *Discourse, racism and ideology* (special issues of *Text*, 8, nos 1 and 2). Amsterdam: Mouton de Gruyter.

van Goozen, S. H. M., Cohen-Kettenis, P. T., Gooren, L. J. G., Frijda, N. H., & van der Poll, N. E. (1995). Gender differences in behaviour: Activating effects of cross-sex hormones. *Psychoneuroendocrinology, 20*, 343–363.

van Gyn, G. H., Wenger, H. A., & Gaul, C. A. (1990). Imagery as a method of enhancing transfer from training to performance. *Journal of Sport and Exercise Psychology, 12*, 366–375.

van Knippenberg, D., & Hogg, M. A. (Eds.). (2004). *Leadership and power: Identity processes in groups and organizations*. London: Sage.

van Knippenberg, D., & Hogg, M. A. (in press). A social identity model of leadership in organizations. In B. M. Staw & R. M. Kramer (Eds.), *Research in organizational behavior* (Vol. 25). Greenwich, CT: JAI Press.

Vanneman, R. D., & Pettigrew, T. F. (1972). Race and relative deprivation in the urban United States. *Race, 13*, 461–486.

van Schie, E. C. M., Martijn, C., & van der Pligt, J. (1994). Evaluative language, cognitive effort and attitude change. *European Journal of Social Psychology, 2*, 707–712.

van Schie, E. G. M., & Wiegman, O. (1997). Children and videogames: Leisure activities, aggression, social integration, and school performance. *Journal of Applied Social Psychology, 27*, 1175–1194.

van Vugt, M., & de Cremer, D. (1999). Leadership in social dilemmas: The effects of group identification on collective actions to provide public goods. *Journal of Personality and Social Psychology, 76*, 587–599.

Vaughan, G. M. (1962). The social distance attitudes of New Zealand students towards Maoris and fifteen other national groups. *Journal of Social Psychology, 57*, 85–92.

Vaughan, G. M. (1964). The trans-situational aspect of conforming behavior. *Journal of Personality, 32*, 335–354.

Vaughan, G. M. (1977). Personality and small group behaviour. In R. B. Cattell & R. M. Dreger (Eds.), *Handbook of modern personality theory* (pp. 511–529). London: Academic Press.

Vaughan, G. M. (1978a). Social change and intergroup preferences in New Zealand. *European Journal of Social Psychology, 8*, 297–314.

Vaughan, G. M. (1978b). Social categorization and intergroup behaviour in children. In H. Tajfel (Ed.), *Differentiation between social groups: studies in the social psychology of intergroup relations* (pp. 339–360). London: Academic Press.

Vaughan, G. M. (1986). Social change and racial identity: Issues in the use of picture and doll measures. *Australian Journal of Psychology, 38*, 359–370.

Vaughan, G. M. (1988). The psychology of intergroup discrimination. *New Zealand Journal of Psychology, 17*, 1–14.

Vaughan, G. M., & Guerin, B. (1997). A neglected innovator in sports psychology: Norman Triplett and the early history of competitive performance. *International Journal of the History of Sport, 14*, 82–99.

Vaughan, G. M., & Hogg, M. A. (1998). *Introduction to social psychology* (2nd ed.). Sydney: Prentice Hall.

Verplanker, B., Hofstee, G., & Janssen, H. J. W. (1998). Accessibility of affective versus cognitive components of attitudes. *European Journal of Social Psychology, 28*, 23–35.

Vescio, T. K., Sechrist, G. B., & Paolucci, M. P. (2003). Perspective taking and prejudice reduction: The mediational role of empathy arousal and situational attributions. *European Journal of Social Psychology, 33*, 455–472.

Vignoles, V. L., Chryssochoou, X., & Breakwell, G. M. (2000). The distinctiveness principle: Identity, meaning, and the bounds of cultural relativity. *Personality and Social Psychology Review, 4*, 337–354.

Vine, I. (1983). Sociobiology and social psychology—rivalry or symbiosis? The explanation of altruism. *British Journal of Social Psychology, 22*, 1–11.

Viney, L., & Crooks, L. (1992). The psychological meaning. In E. Timewell, V. Minichiello, & D. Plummer (Eds.), *AIDS in Australia* (pp. 108–124). Sydney: Prentice Hall.

Vinokur, A., & Burnstein, E. (1974). The effects of partially shared persuasive arguments on group-induced shifts: A problem-solving approach. *Journal of Personality and Social Psychology, 29*, 305–315.

Vinokur-Kaplan, D. (1978). To have—or not to have—another child: Family planning attitudes, intentions, and behavior. *Journal of Applied Social Psychology, 8*, 29–46.

Visser, P. S., & Cooper, J. (2003). Attitude change. In M. A. Hogg & J. Cooper (Eds.), *The Sage handbook of social psychology* (pp. 211–231). London: Sage.

Visser, P. S., & Krosnick, J. A. (1998). Development of attitude strength over the life cycle: Surge and decline. *Journal of Personality and Social Psychology, 75*, 1389–1410.

Vittengl, J. R., & Holt, C. S. (2000). Getting acquainted: the relationship of self-disclosure and social attraction to positive affect. *Journal of Social and Personal Relationships, 17*, 53–66.

von Hippel, W., Sekaquaptewa, D., & Vargas, P. (1995). On the role of encoding processes in stereotype maintenance. *Advances in Experimental Social Psychology, 27*, 177–254.

Von Neumann, J., & Morgenstern, O. (1944). *Theory of games and economic behavior*. Princeton, NJ: Princeton University Press.

Vygotsky, L. S. (1962). *Thought and language*. New York: Wiley.

Walker, I., & Mann, L. (1987). Unemployment, relative deprivation, and social protest. *Personality and Social Psychology Bulletin, 13*, 275–283.

Walker, I., & Pettigrew, T. F. (1984). Relative deprivation theory: An overview and conceptual critique. *British Journal of Social Psychology, 23*, 301–310.

Walker, I., & Smith, H. J. (Eds.). (2002). *Relative deprivation: Specification, development, and integration*. Cambridge, UK: Cambridge University Press.

Walker, L. E. (1993). The battered woman syndrome is a psychological consequence of abuse. In R. J. Gelles & D.R. Loseke (Eds.), *Current controversies on family violence* (pp. 133–153). Newbury Park, CA: Sage.

Walkley, F. H. (1984). The relationship between interpersonal distance and violence in imprisoned offenders. *Criminal Justice and Behavior, 11*, 331–340.

Wallach, M. A., Kogan, N., & Bem, D. J. (1962). Group influence on individual risk taking. *Journal of Abnormal and Social Psychology, 65*, 75–86.

Walster, E. (1966). Assignment of responsibility for an accident. *Journal of Personality and Social Psychology, 3*, 73–79.

Walster, E., & Festinger, L. (1962). The effectiveness of 'overheard' persuasive communications. *Journal of Abnormal and Social Psychology, 65*, 395–402.

Walster, E., Walster, G. W., & Berscheid, E. (1978). *Equity theory and research*. Boston, MA: Allyn & Bacon.

Walster, E., Walster, G. W., Piliavin, J., & Schmidt, L. (1973). Playing hard-to-get: Understanding an elusive phenomenon. *Journal of Personality and Social Psychology, 26,* 113–121.

Walther, J. B. (1996). Computer-mediated communication: Impersonal, interpersonal, and hyperpersonal interaction. *Communication Research, 23,* 23–43.

Wann, D. L., Carlson, J. D., Holland, L. C., Jacob, B. E., Owens, D. A., & Wells, D. D. (1999). Beliefs in symbolic catharsis: The importance of involvement with aggressive sports. *Social Behavior and Personality, 27,* 155–164.

Ward, C., & Kennedy, A. (1992). Locus of control, mood disturbance and social difficulty during cross-cultural transitions. *International Journal of Intercultural Relations, 16,* 175–194.

Warren, P. E., & Walker, I. (1991). Empathy, effectiveness and donations to charity: Social psychology's contribution. *British Journal of Social Psychology, 30,* 325–337.

Watson, D. (1982). The actor and the observer: How are the perceptions of causality divergent? *Psychological Bulletin, 92,* 682–700.

Watson, J. B. (1913). Psychology as a behaviourist views it. *Psychological Review, 20,* 158–177.

Watson, J. B. (1930). *Behaviourism.* New York: W.W. Norton & Co.

Waxman, C. (1977). *The stigma of poverty.* New York: Pergamon Press.

Weatherall, A. (1998). Re-visioning gender and language research. *Women and Language, 21,* 1–9.

We can stop domestic violence (1994). Queensland Department of Family Services and Aboriginal and Islander Affairs.

Webb, E. J., Campbell, D. T., Schwartz, R. D., & Sechrest, L. (1969). *Unobtrusive measures: nonreactive research in the social sciences.* Chicago: Rand McNally.

Weber, M. (1930). *The Protestant ethic and the spirit of capitalism.* London: Allen & Unwin.

Weber, R., & Crocker, J. (1983). Cognitive processes in the revision of stereotypic beliefs. *Journal of Personality and Social Psychology, 45,* 961–977.

Wegener, D. T., Petty, R. E., & Smith, S. M. (1995). Positive mood can increase or decrease message scrutiny: The hedonic contingency view of mood and message processing. *Journal of Personality and Social Psychology, 69,* 5–15.

Wegner, D. M. (1987). Transactive memory: A transactive analysis of the group mind. In B. Mullen & G. R. Goethals (Eds.), *Theories of group behavior* (pp. 185–208). New York: Springer.

Wegner, D. M. (1995). A computer network model of human transactive memory. *Social Cognition, 13,* 319–339.

Wegner, D. M., Erber, R., & Raymond, P. (1991). Transactive memory in close relationships. *Journal of Personality and Social Psychology, 61,* 923–929.

Weiner, B. (1979). A theory of motivation for some classroom experiences. *Journal of Educational Psychology, 71,* 3–25.

Weiner, B. (1985). 'Spontaneous' causal thinking. *Psychological Bulletin, 97,* 74–84.

Weiner, B. (1986). *An Attributional theory of motivation and emotion.* New York: Springer-Verlag.

Weiner, B. (1995). *Judgments of responsibility.* New York: Guilford.

Weinstein, N. (1980). Unrealistic optimism about future life events. *Journal of Personality and Social Psychology, 5,* 806–820.

Weinstein, N. (1989). Why it won't happen to me: Perceptions of risk factors and illness susceptibility. *Science, 246,* 1232–1233.

Weiten, W. (1980). The attraction-leniency effect in jury research: An examination of external validity. *Journal of Applied Social Psychology, 10,* 340–347.

Weldon, E., & Weingart, L. (1993). Group goals and group performance. *British Journal of Social Psychology, 32,* 307–334.

Wells, G. L., & Turtle, J. W. (1988). What is the best way to encode faces? In M. Gruneberg, P. E. Morris, & R. N. Sykes (Eds.), *Practical aspects of memory: current research and issues* (Vol. 1, pp. 163–168). Chichester: Wiley.

West, C. (1984). *Routine complications.* Bloomington, IA: Indiana University Press.

West, S. G., & Brown, T. J. (1975). Physical attractiveness, the severity of the emergency, and helping: A field experiment and interpersonal simulation. *Journal of Experimental Social Psychology, 11,* 531–538.

West, S. G., Whitney, G., & Schnedler, R. (1975). Helping a motorist in distress: The effects of sex, race and neighbourhood. *Journal of Personality and Social Psychology, 31,* 691–698.

Westie, F. R., & DeFleur, M. L. (1959). Automatic responses and their relationship to race attitudes. *Journal of Abnormal and Social Psychology, 58,* 340–347.

Wetherell, M. S. (1986). Linguistic repertoires and literary criticism: New directions for a social psychology of gender. In S. Wilkinson (Ed.), *Feminist social psychology* (pp. 77–95). Milton Keynes: Open University Press.

Wetherell, M. S. (1987). Social identity and group polarization. In J. C. Turner, M. A. Hogg, P. J. Oakes, S. D. Reicher, & M. S. Wetherell (Eds.), *Rediscovering the social group: a self-categorization theory* (pp. 142–170). Oxford: Blackwell.

Wetherell, M. S., Taylor, S., & Yates, S. J. (2001). *Discourse as data: A guide for analysis.* London: Sage.

Wetzel, C. G., & Walton, M. D. (1985). Developing biased social judgments: The false consensus effect. *Journal of Personality and Social Psychology, 49,* 1352–1359.

Weyant, J. (1978). The effect of mood states, costs and benefits on helping. *Journal of Personality and Social Psychology, 36,* 1169–1176.

Wheeler, L. (1991). A brief history of social comparison theory. In J. Suls & T. A. Wills (Eds.), *Social comparison: Contemporary theory and research* (pp. 3–21). Hillsdale, NJ: Erlbaum.

Whitcher, S. J., & Fisher, J. D. (1979). Multidimensional reaction to therapeutic touch in a hospital setting. *Journal of Personality and Social Psychology, 37,* 87–96.

White, P. A., (1988). Causal processing: Origins and development. *Psychological Bulletin, 104,* 36–52.

White, P. A., & Younger, D. P. (1988). Differences in the ascription of transient internal states to self and other. *Journal of Experimental Social Psychology, 24,* 292–309.

Whorf, B. L. (1956). *Language, thought and reality.* Cambridge, MA: MIT Press.

Whyte, W. F. (1943). *Street corner society* (2nd ed.). Chicago, IL: University of Chicago.

Wicker, A. W. (1969). Attitudes versus actions: The relationship of verbal and overt behavioral responses to attitude objects. *Journal of Social Issues, 25,* 41–78.

Wicklund, R. A. (1975). Objective self-awareness. In L. Berkowitz (Ed.), *Advances in experimental social psychology* (Vol. 8, pp. 233–275). New York: Academic Press.

Widmeyer, W. N., Brawley, L. R., & Carron, A. V. (1985). *The measurement of cohesion in sports teams: the group environment questionnaire.* London, Ontario: Sports Dynamics.

Wiemann, J. M., & Giles H. (1988). Interpersonal communications. In M. Hewstone, W. Stroebe, J.-P. Codol, & G. M. Stephenson (Eds.), *Introduction to social psychology* (pp. 199–221). Oxford: Blackwell.

Wieselquist, J., Rusbult, C. E., Foster, C. A., & Agnew, C. R. (1999). Commitment, pro-relationship behavior, and trust in close relationships. *Journal of Personality and Social Psychology, 77,* 942–966.

Wilder, D. A. (1977). Perceptions of groups, size of opposition and social influence. *Journal of Experimental Social Psychology, 13,* 253–268.

Wilder, D. A. (1984). Predictions of belief homogeneity and similarity following social categorization. *British Journal of Social Psychology, 23,* 323–333.

Wilder, D. A. (1986). Social categorization: Implications for creation and reduction of intergroup bias. In L. Berkowitz (Ed.), *Advances in experimental social psychology* (Vol. 19, pp. 291–355). New York: Academic Press.

Wilder, D. A., & Shapiro, P. N. (1984). Role of out-group cues in determining social identity. *Journal of Personality and Social Psychology, 47,* 342–348.

Wilder, D. A., & Shapiro, P. N. (1989). Role of competition-induced anxiety in limiting the beneficial impact of positive behavior by an outgroup member. *Journal of Personality and Social Psychology, 56,* 60–69.

Wilder, D., & Simon, A. F. (1998). Categorical and dynamic groups: Implications for social perception and intergroup behavior. In C. Sedikides, J. Schopler, & C. A. Insko (Eds.), *Intergroup cognition and intergroup behavior* (pp. 27–44). Mahwah, NJ: Erlbaum.

Wilke, H., & Lanzetta, J. T. (1970). The obligation to help: The effects of amount of prior help on subsequent helping behavior. *Journal of Experimental Social Psychology, 6,* 488–493.

Williams, A. (1996). Young people's evaluations of intergenerational versus peer underaccommodation: Sometimes older is better? *Journal of Language and Social Psychology, 15,* 291–311.

Williams, A. & Nussbaum, J. F. (2001). *Intergenerational communication across the life span.* Mahwah, NJ: Erlbaum.

Williams, A. W., Ware, J. E., & Donald, C. A. (1981). A model of mental health life events and social supports applicable to general population. *Journal of Health and Social Behaviour, 22,* 324–336.

Williams, J. A. (1984). Gender and intergroup behaviour: Towards an integration. *British Journal of Social Psychology, 23,* 311–316.

Williams, J. E., & Best, D. L. (1982). *Measuring sex stereotypes: a thirty nation study.* Beverly Hills, CA: Sage.

Williams, J. G., & Solano, C. H. (1983). The social reality of feeling lonely: Friendship and reciprocation. *Personality and Social Psychology Bulletin, 9,* 237–242.

Williams, K. D. (2002). *Ostracism: The power of silence.* New York: Guilford.

Williams, K. D., Cheung, C. K. T., & Choi, W. (2000). Cyberostracism: Effects of being ignored over the internet. *Journal of Personality and Social Psychology, 79,* 748–762.

Williams, K. D., Harkins, S. G., & Karau, S. J. (2003). Social performance. In M. A. Hogg & J. Cooper (Eds.), *The Sage handbook of social psychology* (pp. 327–346). London: Sage.

Williams, K. D., Harkins, S. G., & Latané, B. (1981). Identifiability as a deterrent to social loafing: Two cheering experiments. *Journal of Personality and Social Psychology, 40,* 303–311.

Williams, K. D., & Karau, S. J. (1991). Social loafing and social compensation: The effects of expectations of co-worker performance. *Journal of Personality and Social Psychology, 61,* 570–581.

Williams, K. D., Karau, S. J., & Bourgeois, M. (1993). Working on collective tasks: Social loafing and social compensation. In M. A. Hogg & D. Abrams (Eds.), *Group motivation: social psycho-*

logical perspectives (pp. 130–148). London: Harvester Wheatsheaf.

Williams, K. D., Shore, W. J., & Grahe, J. E. (1998). The silent treatment: Perceptions of its behaviors and associated feelings. *Group Processes and Intergroup Relations, 1,* 117–141.

Williams, K. D., & Sommer, K. L. (1997). Social ostracism by coworkers: Does rejection lead to loafing and compensation? *Personality and Social Psychology Bulletin, 23,* 693–706.

Williamson, G. M., & Clark, M. S. (1989). Providing help and relationship type as determinants of changes in moods and self-evaluations. *Journal of Personality and Social Psychology, 56,* 722–734.

Wills, T. A. (1981). Downward comparison principles in social psychology. *Psychological Bulletin, 90,* 245–271.

Wilpert, B. (1995). Organizational behavior. *Annual Review of Psychology, 46,* 59–90.

Wilson, E. O. (1975). *Sociobiology: the new synthesis.* Cambridge, MA: Harvard University Press.

Wilson, E. O. (1978). *On human nature.* Cambridge, MA: Harvard University Press.

Winch, R. (1958). *Mate selection: a study of complementary needs.* New York: Harper & Row.

Wishner, J. (1960). Reanalysis of 'impressions of personality'. *Psychological Review, 67,* 96–112.

Wispé, L. G. (1972). Positive forms of social behavior: An overview. *Journal of Social Issues, 28,* 1–19.

Witkin, H. A., Mednick, S. A., Schulsinger, F., Bakkestrom, E., Christiansen, K. D., Goodenough, D. R., Philip, J., Rubin, D. B., & Stocking, M. (1976). Criminality in XYY and XXY men. *Science, 198,* 547–555.

Witte, K., Berkowitz, J. M., Cameron, K. A., & McKeon, J. K. (1998). Preventing the spread of genital warts: Using fear appeals to promote self-protective behaviours. *Health Education & Behavior, 25,* 571–585.

Wittenbrink, W., Judd, C. M., & Park, B. (1997). Evidence for racial prejudice at the implicit level and its relationship with questionnaire measures. *Journal of Personality and Social Psychology, 72,* 262–274.

Wittgenstein, L. (1953). *Philosophical investigations.* Oxford: Blackwell.

Wood, G. S. (1982). Conspiracy and the paranoid style: Causality and deceit in the eighteenth century. *William and Mary Quarterly, 39,* 401–441.

Wood, J. V. (1989). Theory and research concerning social comparisons of personal attributes. *Psychological Bulletin, 106,* 231–248.

Wood, W. (2000). Attitude change: Persuasion and social influence. *Annual Review of Psychology, 51,* 539–570.

Wood, W., Rhodes, N., & Whelan, M. (1989). Sex differences in positive well-being: A consideration of emotional style and marital status. *Psychological Bulletin, 106,* 249–264.

Wood, W., Lundgren, S., Ouellette, J. A., Busceme, S., & Blackstone, T. (1994). Minority influence: A meta-analytic review of social influence processes. *Psychological Bulletin, 115,* 323–345.

Worchel, S. (1979). Cooperation and the reduction of intergroup conflict: Some determining factors. In W. Austin & S. Worchel (Eds.), *The social psychology of intergroup relations* (pp. 262–273). Monterey, CA: Brooks/Cole.

Worchel, S. (1996). Emphasising the social nature of groups in a developmental framework. In J. L. Nye & A. M. Bower (Eds.), *What's social about social cognition: research on socially shared cognition in small groups* (pp. 261–282). Thousand Oaks, CA: Sage.

Worchel, S., Andreoli, V. A., & Folger, R. (1977). Intergroup cooperation and intergroup attraction: The effect of previous interaction and outcome of combined effort. *Journal of Experimental Social Psychology, 13,* 131–140.

Worchel, S., Cooper, J., & Goethals, G. R. (1988). *Understanding social psychology* (4th ed.). Chicago: Dorsey Press.

Worchel, S., & Novell, N. (1980). Effect of perceived environmental conditions during cooperation on intergroup attraction. *Journal of Personality and Social Psychology, 38,* 764–772.

Worchel, S., Rothgerber, H., Day, E. A., Hart, D., & Butemeyer, J. (1998). Social identity and individual productivity within groups. *British Journal of Social Psychology, 37,* 389–413.

Word, C., Zanna, M., & Cooper, J. (1974). The nonverbal mediation of self-fulfilling prophecies in interracial interaction. *Journal of Experimental Social Psychology, 10,* 109–120.

Wright, S. C., Aron, A., McLaughlin-Volpe, T., & Ropp, S. A. (1997). The extended contact effect: Knowledge of cross-group friendships and prejudice. *Journal of Personality and Social Psychology, 73,* 73–90.

Wright, S. C., Aron, A. & Tropp, L. R. (2002). Including others (and their groups) in the self: Self-expansion and intergroup relations. In J. P. Forgas & K. Williams (Eds.), *The social self: Cognitive, interpersonal and intergroup perspectives* (pp. 343–363). New York: Psychology Press.

Wright, S. C., & Taylor, D. M. (2003). The social psychology of cultural diversity: Social stereotyping, prejudice, and discrimination. In M. A. Hogg & J. Cooper (Eds.), *The Sage handbook of social psychology* (pp. 432–457). London: Sage.

Wrightsman, L. S. (1964). Measurement of philosophies of human nature. *Psychological Reports, 14,* 743–751.

Wundt, W. (1897). *Outlines of psychology.* New York: Stechert.

Wundt, W. (1916). *Elements of folk psychology: Outlines of a psychological history of the development of mankind.* London: Allen & Unwin. (German original 1912.)

Wyer, R. S. Jr. (1976). An investigation of relations among probability estimates. *Organizational Behavior and Human Performance, 15,* 1–18.

Wyer, R. S. Jr. (Ed.). (1998). *Stereotype activation and inhibition: Advances in social cognition* (Vol. 11). Hillsdale, NJ: Erlbaum.

Wyer, R. S. Jr., & Carlston, D. E. (1994). The cognitive representation of persons and events. In R. S. Wyer, Jr. & T. K. Srull, (Eds.), *Handbook of social cognition* (2nd ed., pp. 41–98). Hillsdale, NJ: Erlbaum.

Wyer, R. S. Jr., & Gordon, S. E. (1982). The recall of information about persons and groups. *Journal of Experimental Social Psychology, 18,* 128–164.

Wyer, R. S. Jr., & Gordon, S. E. (1984). The cognitive representation of social information. In R. S. Wyer, Jr. & T. K. Srull (Eds.), *Handbook of social cognition* (Vol. 2, pp. 73–150). Hillsdale, NJ: Erlbaum.

Wyer, R. S. Jr., & Gruenfeld, D. H. (1995). Information processing in social contexts: Implications for social memory and judgement. *Advances in Experimental Social Psychology, 27,* 49–91.

Wyer, R. S. Jr., & Martin, L. L. (1986). Person memory: The role of traits, group stereotypes, and specific behaviours in the cognitive representation of persons. *Journal of Personality and Social Psychology, 50,* 661–675.

Wyer, R. S. Jr., & Srull, T. K. (1981). Category accessibility: Some theoretical and empirical issues concerning the processing of social stimulus information. In E. T. Higgins, C. P. Herman, & M. P. Zanna (Eds.), *Social cognition: The Ontario symposium* (Vol. 1, pp. 161–198). Hillsdale, NJ: Erlbaum.

Wyer, R. S. Jr., & Srull, T. K. (1984). *Social cognition.* Hillsdale, NJ: Erlbaum.

Wyer, R. S. Jr., & Srull, T. K. (1986). Human cognition in its social context. *Psychological Review, 93,* 322–359.

Wyer, R. S. Jr., & Srull, T. K. (Eds.). (1994). *Handbook of social cognition* (2nd ed.). Hillsdale, NJ: Erlbaum.

Yammarino, F. J., Spangler, W. D., & Bass, B. M. (1993). Transformational leadership and performance: A longitudinal investigation. *Leadership Quarterly, 4,* 81–102.

Yancey, G., & Yancey, S. (1998). Interracial dating: Evidence from personal advertisements. *Journal of Family Issues, 19,* 334–348.

Yang, K. S., & Bond, M. H. (1990). Exploring implicit personality theories with indigenous or imported constructs: The Chinese case. *Journal of Personality and Social Psychology, 58,* 1087–1095.

Yarmouk, U. (2000). The effect of presentation modality on judgements of honesty and attractiveness. *Social Behavior and Personality, 28,* 269–278.

Yarwood, A. T., & Knowling, M. (1982). *Race relations in Australia: a history.* Sydney: Methuen.

Yates, B. T., & Mischel, W. (1979). Young children's preferred attentional strategies for delaying gratification. *Journal of Personality and Social Psychology, 37,* 286–300.

Young, J. L., & James, E. H. (2001). Token majority: The work attitudes of male flight attendants. *Sex Roles, 45,* 299–319.

Younger, J. C., Walker, L., & Arrowood, A. J. (1977). Post-decision dissonance at the fair. *Personality and Social Psychology Bulletin, 3,* 247–287.

Youngson, R. M. (1989). *Grief: rebuilding your life after bereavement.* London: David & Charles.

Yovetich, N. A., & Rusbult, C. E. (1994). Accommodative behaviour in close relationships: Exploring transformation of motivation. *Journal of Experimental Social Psychology, 30,* 138–164.

Yukl, G. (2002). *Leadership in organizations* (5th ed.). Upper Saddle River, NJ: Prentice Hall.

Zaccaro, S. J. (1984). Social loafing: The role of task attractiveness. *Personality and Social Psychology Bulletin, 10,* 99–106.

Zahn-Waxler, C., Radke-Yarrow, M., & King, R. A. (1979). Child-rearing and children's prosocial initiations toward victims of distress. *Child Development, 50,* 319–330.

Zahn-Waxler, C., Radke-Yarrow, M., Wagner, E., & Chapman, M. (1992). Development of concern for others. *Developmental Psychology, 28,* 126–136.

Zajonc, R. B. (1965). Social facilitation. *Science, 149,* 269–274.

Zajonc, R. B. (1968). Attitudinal effects of mere exposure. *Journal of Personality and Social Psychology, 9,* 1–27.

Zajonc, R. B. (1980). Cognition and social cognition: A historical perspective. In L. Festinger (Ed.), *Retrospections on social psychology* (pp. 180–204). New York: Oxford University Press.

Zajonc, R. B. (1989). Styles of explanation in social psychology. *European Journal of Social Psychology, 19,* 345–368.

Zanna, M. P. (1993). Message receptivity: A new look at the old problem of open- versus closed-mindedness. In A. A. Mitchell (Ed.), *Advertising exposure, memory and choice* (pp. 141–162). Hillsdale, NJ: Erlbaum.

Zanna, M. P., & Hamilton, D. L. (1972). Attribute dimensions and patterns of trait inferences. *Psychonomic Science, 27,* 353–354.

Zanna, M. P., Kiesler, C. A., & Pilkonis, D. A. (1970). Positive and negative affect established by classical conditioning. *Journal of Personality and Social Psychology, 14,* 321–328.

Zanna, M. P., & Rempel, J. K. (1988). Attitudes: A new look at an old concept. In D. Bar-Tal & A. W. Kruglanski (Eds.), *The social* psychology of knowledge (pp. 315–334). Cambridge: Cambridge University Press.

Zebrowitz, L. A. (1996). Physical appearance as a basis of stereotyping. In C. N. Macrae, C. Stangor, & M. Hewstone (Eds.), Stereotypes and stereotyping (pp. 79–120). New York: Guilford.

Zebrowitz, L. A., & Collins, M. A. (1997). Accurate social perception at zero acquaintance: The affordances of a Gibsonian approach. Personality and Social Psychology Review, 1, 204–223.

Zillmann, D. (1979). Hostility and aggression. Hillsdale, NJ: Erlbaum.

Zillmann, D. (1984). Connections between sex and aggression. Hillsdale, NJ: Erlbaum.

Zillmann, D. (1988). Cognition–excitation interdependencies in aggressive behavior. Aggressive Behavior, 14, 51–64.

Zillmann, D. (1996). Sequential dependencies in emotional experience and behaviour. In R. D. Kavanaugh, B. Zimmerberg, & S. Fein (Eds.), Emotion: Interdisciplinary perspectives. Mahwah, NJ: Erlbaum.

Zillmann, D., & Bryant, J. (1984). Effects of massive exposure to pornography. In N. M. Malamuth & E. Donnerstein (Eds.), Pornography and sexual aggression (pp. 115–138). New York: Academic Press.

Zimbardo, P. G. (1970). The human choice: Individuation, reason, and order versus deindividuation, impulse, and chaos. In W. J. Arnold & D. Levine (Eds.), Nebraska symposium on motivation 1969 (Vol. 17, pp. 237–307). Lincoln, NE: University of Nebraska Press.

Zimbardo, P. G. (1971). The Stanford prison experiment. Script of the slide show.

Zimbardo, P. G., Haney, C., Banks, W. C., & Jaffe, D. (1982). The psychology of imprisonment. In J. C. Brigham & L. Wrightsman (Eds.), Contemporary issues in social psychology (4th ed., pp. 230–235). Monterey, CA: Brooks/Cole.

Zimbardo, P. G., Weisenberg, M., Firestone, I., & Levy B. (1965). Communication effectiveness in producing public conformity and private attitude change. Journal of Personality, 33, 233–256.

Zimmerman, D. H., & West, C. (1975). Sex roles, interruptions, and silences in conversation. In B. Thorne & N. Henley (Eds.), Language and sex: differences and dominance (pp. 105–29). Rowley, MA: Newbury House.

Zuckerman, M. (1979). Attribution of success and failure revisited, or: The motivational bias is alive and well in attribution theory. Journal of Personality, 47, 245–287.

Zuckerman, M., DePaulo, B. M., & Rosenthal, R. (1981). Verbal and non-verbal communication of deception. In L. Berkowitz (Ed.), Advances in experimental social psychology (Vol. 4, pp. 1–59). New York: Academic Press.

Zuckerman, M., Lazzaro, M. M., & Waldgeir, D. (1979). Undermining effects of the foot-in-the-door technique with extrinsic rewards. Journal of Applied Social Psychology, 9, 292–296.

Zuckerman, M., Miserandino, M., & Bernieri, F. (1983). Civil inattention exists—in elevators. Personality and Social Psychology Bulletin, 9, 578–586.

Zukier, H. (1986). The paradigmatic and narrative modes in goal-guided inference. In R. M. Sorrentino & E. T. Higgins (Eds.), Handbook of motivation and cognition: foundations of social behavior (pp. 465–502). New York: Guilford Press.

Zuwerink, J. R., & Devine, P. G. (1996). Attitude importance and resistance to persuasion: It's not just the thought that counts. Journal of Personality and Social Psychology, 70, 931–944.

Burger, J. M. 62
Burgess, E. W. 351
Burgoon, J. K. 125, 242, 394, 401, 423–4
Burgoon, M. 156
Buriel, R. 425
Burling, J. 89
Burnham, W. H. 17
Burnstein, E. 38, 227, 253, 361
Burris, C. T. 366
Busceme, S. 174, 178
Bushman, B. J. 88, 165, 298, 305, 307, 310–11, 315
Buss, A. H. 298
Buss, D. M. 2, 13, 300, 333
Bussey, K. 363
Bustos, A. A. 395
Butemeyer, J. 192
Butler, D. 58
Butterfield, D. A. 239
Butterworth, G. 333
Buunk, B. P. 354
Byatt, G. 333
Byrd, R. E. 327
Byrne, D. 17, 186, 256, 286, 297, 336–7, 340–1, 344, 349, 379, 392
Byrne, J. L. 392

Cacioppo, J. T. 37, 98, 111, 123, 132–3, 138–41, 145, 155
Cairns, E. 205
Calder, B. J. 110
Calkin, B. 313
Callan, V. J. 204, 289, 354, 388–9, 423
Callaway, M. R. 226
Camacho, L. M. 222
Cameron, K. A. 136
Camino, L. 298
Campbell, A. 324
Campbell, B 347
Campbell, D. T. 15, 123–4, 170, 192, 199, 239, 265–6, 272, 360
Campbell, J. D. 62, 85, 88
Campbell, R. J. 192
Campbell, S. M. 340
Campbell, W. K. 345
Cannavale, F. J. 280
Canter, D. V. 66
Cantor, N. 20, 27, 32–3, 87
Caporael, L. R. 268, 394
Cappella, J. N. 385, 404
Carey, C. J. 204, 289
Carey, G. 302
Cargile, A. 385, 391
Carli, L. 138, 170, 236
Carlo, G. 359, 363
Carlsmith, J. M. 7, 19, 24, 142, 150–1, 261, 310, 396
Carlson, J. D. 307
Carlson, M. 297
Carlston, D. E. 28, 33, 40
Carlyle, T. 211
Carmichael, G. 353

Carnevale, P. J. D. 142, 289–90
Carnot, C. G. 110
Carrithers, M. 69
Carroll, J. S. 289
Carron, A. V. 194
Carter J. 244
Carter, L. F. 212
Cartwright, D. 99, 193
Carver, C. S. 76, 187, 245, 282, 305, 370, 376
Cary, M. S. 395
Casas, J. M. 246
Cash, T. F. 333
Castro, S. L. 217
Catalan, J. 144
Catalano, R. 300
Cejka, M. A. 108
Census of Prison Inmates 312
Cerro, D. 305
Cervone, J. C. 335
Chacko, T. I. 245, 247
Chaffee, S. H. 114
Chaiken, S. 43, 108, 122, 128, 132–3, 137, 139–42, 157–8, 161, 176, 434
Champion, D. S. 61
Chan, A. 398
Chance, J. E. 276
Chandra, S. 170
Chang, S. 226
Chanowitz, B. 145, 285
Chaplin, W. F. 33
Chapman, L. J. 44, 278
Chapman, M. 362
Charng, H.-W. 373
Chase, A. 359
Chassin, L. 61, 156
Chemers, M. M. 162, 210, 216
Chen, H. 60
Chen, S. 141
Cheney, S. 88
Cherek, D. R. 298
Chermack S. T. 307
Cheshire, J. 391
Chesler, P. 244
Chesner, S. P. 377
Cheung, C. K. T. 407
Chidester, T. R. 245
Child, I. L. 413
Chiles, C. 171
Chisholm, J. 389
Chiu, C. Y. 386, 409
Choi, H.-S. 195
Choi, W. 407
Chomsky, N. 26, 385
Choo, P. 329
Christensen, L. 11
Christiansen, K. D. 309
Christie, R. 254
Christy, C. A. 370
Chrvala, C. 170
Chryssochoou, X. 93
Chuang, Y. C. 110

Cialdini, R. B. 80, 138, 143–5, 155, 179, 365, 375
Cini, M. 195, 197
Claes, J. A. 319
Clark, H. H. 404
Clark, K. B. 87
Clark, L. F. 40
Clark, M. 374
Clark, M. P. 87
Clark, M. S. 23, 374, 383
Clark, N. K. 223–4
Clark, R. D. III 174, 175–6, 365, 367–8, 371–2, 376, 380
Clark, T. N. 16
Clarkson, F. E. 235–6, 244
Clary, E. G. 376
Clausen, G. T. 375
Clémence, A. 35, 66, 73–4, 116, 422
Clément, R. 392
Clore, G. L. 336–7, 340–1, 377
Close, S. 107
Clyne, M. G. 387, 389
Coates, B. 362
Coch, L. 200
Cochran, P. J. 372
Cochrane, R. 255
Cochrane, S. 173
Codol, J.-P. 228
Coe, C. L. 86
Coebergh, B. 354
Cogliser, C. C. 217
Cohen, C. 309
Cohen, D. 313, 415
Cohen, I. H. 338
Cohen-Kettenis P. T. 306
Cohn, E. G. 310–11
Cohn, N. 67
Coke, J. S. 359, 371
Collett, P. 424
Collins, B. 161–2
Collins, B. E. 57, 106
Collins, M. A. 29
Collins, N. L. 338
Collins, S. 69
Colvin, C. R. 85, 88
Commonwealth of Australia 21
Comstock, G. 316
Condie, H. 340
Condor, S. 194, 406
Condry, J. 79
Condry, J. C. 306
Congdon, C. S. 253
Conley, T. D. 106
Connell, R.W. 114
Conner, M. 107
Cook C. A. 318
Cook, S. W. 286–7, 381
Coombs, F. S. 104
Coon, H. M. 92, 416
Cooper, H. M. 137

Cooper, J. 24, 49, 71, 95, 128, 148–50, 153–4, 158, 180, 208, 228, 231, 249, 259, 288, 293, 307, 324, 356, 383, 409
Cooper, W. H. 222
Corballis, M. C. 400
Cordery, J. L. 195
Cordova, D. 235, 248
Correia, H. 116
Cose, E. 247
Costabile, A. 313
Costanzo, P. R. 12, 24, 169
Cosyns, P. 310
Cottey, T. J. 285
Cotton, S. 351
Cottrell, N. B. 184
Coupland, J. 394, 406
Coupland, N. 390, 392, 394, 406, 409
Courtright, J. A. 226
Covell, K. 114, 138
Covington, M. V. 131
Cowen, W. L. 253
Cox, C. L. 349
Cox, S. 244
Cozby, P. C. 405
Craddock, A. 405
Craig, J. 205
Craig, K. M. 407
Cramer, L. 58
Cramer, R. E. 376
Crandall, C. S. 86, 246, 361
Crandall, R. 285
Crano, W. D. 175, 178
Cravalho, M. 327
Creason, C. R. 143
Cremers, I. 162
Crisp, R. J. 204–5, 289
Crocker, J. 37–8, 44, 57, 83, 85–6, 245–8, 259, 273, 287
Crockett, W. H. 37
Crooks, L. 46
Crosby, F. 125, 235, 240, 246, 248, 263
Cross, P. 85
Cross, S. E. 338, 352
Cross, W. E. 87
Crowley, M. 377
Croyle, R. T. 153
Crum, L. 271
Crusco, A. H. 401
Crutchfield, R. A. 137, 169
Crutchfield, R. S. 19, 98
Cummings, A. 407
Cummins, R. A. 345
Cunningham, J. D. 351
Cunningham, M. R. 333, 374
Cunningham, W. A. 126, 241
Curran, N. M. 398
Currie, M. 389
Cuthbertson, G. H. 394
Cutrona, C. E. 57
Cvetkovich, G. T. 339
Czapinski, J. 271

D'Agata, P. 389–90
D'Agostino, P. R. 335
D'Emilio, J. 246
Dabbs, J. M. 306
Dabbs, J. M. Jr. 377
Dakof, G. A. 381
Dalal, A. K. 215
Danilovics, P. 37, 57
Danserau, F. Jr. 217
Darby, B. L. 144, 375
Darley, J. M. 20, 191, 229, 360–1, 367–75, 382
Darlington, R. B. 142
Darwin, C. 123, 211, 324, 357, 361, 363, 396
Davenport, P. R. 68
David, B. 178
David, T. B. 376
Davidowicz, L. C. 62
Davidson, A. R. 103–4, 107
Davidson, B. 228
Davidson, L. R. 405
Davies, J. C. 262, 311
Davis, E. G. 256
Davis, J. A. 262
Davis, J. H. 221, 229
Davis, K. E. 20, 52–3, 338
Davis, M. H. 371
Davis, T. 404
Dawes, R. 268
Dawes, R. M. 43, 267
Day, E. A. 192
Day, R. H. 21
de Cremer, D. 218, 269
de Dreu, C. K. W. 344
de Gilder, D. 202
de Groot, D. 407
de Jong, P. F. 57
de la Ronde, C. 91
De Meyer, F. 310
De Munck, V. C. 351
De Vader, C. L. 218
Dean, J. 402
Dean, L. M. 402
Deaux, K. 17, 63, 65, 182, 235–6, 238, 344
DeBrey, J. H. C. 269
Deci, E. L. 78
Decruz, P. 366
DeFleur, M. L. 123
DeJong, W. 143
Dekovic, M. 363
Delamater, J. 3, 259, 293
Dembroski, T. M. 305
Dennis, A. R. 222
Dennis, H. S. 404
DePaulo, B. M. 75, 242, 394, 403–4, 409
DePaulo, P. J. 404
Dépret, E. 43, 162, 216
Dermer, M. 335
Deschamps, J.-C. 63, 289
Desharnais, R. 107

Deuser, W. E. 315
Deutsch, M. 20, 168–9, 171–2, 267–8, 344
Devine, P. G. 101, 125, 138, 154, 235, 239–42, 427
DeVinney, L. C. 262
DeVos, G. A. 400
Devos, T. 278
Diab, L. N. 266
Diacoyanni-Tarlatzis, I. 398
Diaz-Guerrero, R. 416
Dickens, C. 15
Dickson, M. W. 192, 200
Dickson, W. 17
Diehl, M. 81, 221–3, 257, 270
Diener, E. 76, 281–2, 284–5, 309, 345
Dienstbier, R. A. 380
Dietz, T. L. 314
Dietze, C. 271
Dietz-Uhler, B. 221
DiMatteo, M. R. 395
Dindia, K. 338, 393, 405
Dion, D. 291
Dion, K. K. 29, 138, 333, 345
Dion, K. L. 138, 247, 267, 288, 345
Dipboye, R. L. 281, 333
Dittes, J. E. 335–6
Dlugolecki, D. W. 91
Dobosz, B. 350
Doherty, K. 91
Doherty, R. W. 329
Doi, L. T. 424
Doise, W. 14–5, 35, 65–6, 272, 276
Dolinski, D. 143–4
Doll, J. 102, 108, 110
Dollard, J. 252–3, 261, 300
Doms, M. 170, 177
Donald, C. A. 345
Donnerstein, E. 298, 304, 313, 316–7
Doob, L. W. 252, 261, 300
Doosje, B. 153
Doran, L. I. 165
Dorfman, D. 77
Dossett, D. L. 122
Dougherty, D. M. 298
Dovidio, J. F. 101, 234–5, 239–40, 245, 288–9, 359, 365, 367–8, 371–2, 380, 395–6
Downing, L. L. 281
Downs, D. L. 85, 90, 206
Doyle, S. 271
Dragna, M. 376
Draguns, J. 413
Driscoll, D. M. 35, 109
Driskell, J. E. 211
Druckman, D. 290
Druen, P. B. 333
Duberman, L. 405
Dubé-Simard, L. 248, 263
Dubois, N. 60
Duchan, L. 237
Duck, J. M. 111, 132–3, 139, 160, 218

Duck, S. W. 41, 353, 355–6, 437
Duckitt, J. 254–5, 259
Dudgeon, P. 87
Dugan, S. 418
Dukerich, J. M. 165
Dull, V. 242
Duncan, B. 365.371
Duncan, S. 395
Duncan, S. L. 65, 241
Dunkel-Schetter, C. 164
Dunning, D. 84–5
Dunton, B. C. 125,241
Dupuy, R. E. 320
Dupuy, T. N. 320
Durall, J. 114
Durkheim, E. 16, 20, 74, 116, 411
Durkin, K. 22, 251, 386
Durkin, K. F. 317
Dushenko, T. W. 11
Dutton, D. G. 245
Duval, S. 75, 86, 187, 281
Dworin, J. 338
Dykema-Engblade, A. A. 225
Dzindolet, M. T. 222

Eagly, A. H. 4, 35, 43, 98, 108, 122, 128,
    132, 137–9, 158, 161, 170, 176, 236–7,
    239, 306–7, 377, 395
Earle, T. C. 339
Earley, P. C. 192
Early, S. 365
Earn, B. M. 247
Easterbrook, J. A. 187
Ebbesen, E. 306
Ebbesen, E. B. 85
Ebbinghaus, H. 31
Eberly, B. W. 379
Eberly, C. C. 379
Eccles, J. 249
Eckert, P. 393
Eden, D. 238, 249
Edney, J. J. 268
Edwards, A. L. 97, 120
Edwards, C. 61
Edwards, D. 15, 223, 385, 406
Edwards, J. 389, 393
Edwards, K. 136, 139, 297
Effrein, E. A. 81
Ehrlich, H. J. 34
Eibl-Eibesfeldt, I. 398
Eichler, M. 244
Einhorn, H. J. 43
Eisen, S. V. 61
Eisenberg, N. 285, 359, 361, 363, 365,
    383
Eisenberg-Berg, N. 375
Eisenberger, R. 379
Eisenstadt, D. 240
Eiser, J. R. 35, 120, 276
Ekman, P. 396, 398–9, 404
Elder, G. H. Jr. 348
Elkin, A. P. 297

Ellemers, N. 83, 273–4
Ellen, P. S. 105, 107
Elliot, A. 239–40
Elliot, A. J. 387
Ellis, A. L. 221
Ellis, R. J. 37
Ellsworth, P. C. 7, 24, 27, 40–1, 396
Ellyson, S. L. 395–6
Elms, A. C. 11, 14, 169
Ely, P. C. 419
Emler, N. 91
Emswiller, T. 65, 238
Endicott, J. 175
English, D. 363
Enriquez, V. G. 426
Ensari, N. 204, 289
Epstein, S. 349
Erber, R. 36, 38, 223–4
Erenkrantz, B. 239
Eron, L. D. 298, 304, 315
Esser, J. K. 226, 290
Esteban, G. 134
Etcoff, N. L. 35, 277
Ethier, K. A. 182
Evans, B. K. 204
Evans, N. J. 193
Evans-Pritchard, E. E. 69
Exline, R. V. 395–6

Fabes, R. A. 359, 361, 363
Fairey, P. J. 62, 170
Fajardo, D. M. 245, 247
Falender, V. J. 81
Farber, J. 375
Faris, P. W. 136
Farley, S. C. 319
Farnham, S. D. 126, 241
Farnsworth, P.R. 19
Farr, R. M. 24, 35, 66, 74, 116, 276, 411
Faucheux, C. 174
Faust, D. 43
Fazio, R. H. 40, 81, 98, 102, 108–12,
    125, 127–8, 153–4, 241, 430
Feagin, J. 67
Feather, N. T. 21, 57, 65, 67–8, 115
Federico, C. M. 256
Feeney, J. A. 329, 350
Fehr, B. 345
Fehr, R. S. 348
Fein, S. 295
Feld, P. 226
Feldman, S. 104
Fenigstein, A. 76
Ferguson, C. K. 269
Fergusson, D. M. 318
Ferleger, N. 398
Fernandez, G. 37, 57
Fernandez-Dols, J.M. 398, 409
Fernando, K. 321
Feshbach, S. 135–6

Festinger, L. 19, 27, 79, 99, 132, 146–53,
    156–7, 160, 171, 193, 197, 202, 205,
    256, 264, 273, 280, 334, 431
Fidell, L. S. 24, 237
Fiedler, F. E. 214–6, 220, 431, 435, 437
Fiedler, K. 47, 55, 60, 128, 324
Field, N. 213
Fielding, K. S. 192, 218
Fillenbaum, S. 388, 406
Fincham, F. D. 58, 70
Firestone, I. 150–2
Fischer, C. S. 297, 306
Fischer, D. 415
Fischer, D. G. 204
Fischer, G. W. 33, 276
Fischer, W. F. 362
Fisek, M. H. 202, 229
Fish, D. 60
Fishbaugh, L. 138
Fishbein, M. 102–6, 111–5, 122, 127,
    147, 265, 439
Fisher, J. D. 401
Fisher, R. J. 266
Fisher, S. 405
Fishman, J. A. 385, 389
Fiske, A. P. 415–21, 429
Fiske, S. T. 3, 13, 22, 24, 27–8, 31, 33,
    35–43, 49–50, 59, 65, 70, 95, 128, 158,
    162, 179, 208, 216, 231, 235–6,
    239–40, 259, 277–8, 292, 324, 356,
    383, 409, 429
Fitness, J. 350, 356
Fitzpatrick, M. A. 405
Flament, C. 269
Fleishman, E. A. 213
Fleming, C. 249
Fleming, J. 11
Fletcher, G. J. O. 23, 37, 52, 57–8, 60,
    62–3, 69–70, 350, 356
Flowers, M. L. 226
Floyd, D. L. 107–8
Foa, E. B. 341
Foa, U. G. 341
Foddy, M. 268–9
Fodor, E. M. 226
Fogelson, R. M. 284
Foley, S. 349
Folger, R. 245, 288
Fong, G. T. 37, 46
Fonzi, A. 313
Ford, T. J. 318
Forgas, J. P. 34, 46–9, 68, 234, 334, 350,
    385
Forsterling, F. 52, 56
Foster, C. A. 352
Foster-Fishman, P. G. 227
Foti, R. J. 218
Foucault, M. 406
Fox, S. 145
Fox, S. A. 242, 244, 286, 394
Fox-Cardamone, L. 107, 419
Franco, F. M. 125, 252, 404

Frank, B. 239
Frank, M. G. 60
Franklin, K. 302
Fraser, C. 387
Fraser, S. C. 143, 164, 281, 309
Frazer, J. G. 412
Fredericks, A. J. 122
Freed, R. S. 239, 250
Freed, S. A. 239, 250
Freedman, J. L. 142–3, 164, 313
Freeman, S. 80, 191
Freeman, V. 333
Freiberg, S. J. 218
Freides, D. 41
French, J. R. P. 161, 169, 279
French, J. R. P. Jr. 200
Frenkel-Brunswik, E. 19, 73, 253, 322
Freud, S. 2, 73–4, 211, 280, 299, 306, 322, 404, 435
Frick, R. W. 386
Friedman, H. S. 242, 394, 409
Friedman, S. A. 45, 278
Friesen, W. V. 396, 398–9, 404
Frieze, I. 57
Frijda, N. H. 306
Frohlich, N. 190
Fromm, E. 412
Fuhrman, R. W. 33
Fuligni, A. 412
Fuller, S. R. 226
Fuqua, J. 229
Furnham, A. 67–8, 387

Gaertner, S. L. 23, 234–5, 239–41, 245, 259, 288–9, 292, 365, 367–8, 371–2, 380
Gagnon, A. 270
Galinsky, A. D. 288–9
Galizio, M. 113
Gallois, C. 106, 122, 244, 385, 388–9, 391, 394, 398, 406, 423
Gallup, G. 378, 380
Gallupe, R. B. 222
Gange, J. J. 184
Gangestad, S. 91, 333
Gao, G. 93, 423
Garcia, D. 106
Garcia, J. E. 214
Gardner, B. T. 385
Gardner, R. A. 385
Gardner, R. C. 388, 391–2, 406
Gardner, R. M. 333
Gardner, W. 80
Garfinkel, H. 198, 406, 411, 422, 43
Garrett, P. 392
Gaskell, G. 68
Gaul, C. A. 78
Gaunt, R. 71
Geen, R. G. 184, 191, 298, 300, 304, 306–7, 313, 324
Geer, J. H. 371, 374

Geertz, C. 92
Gelfand, D. M. 375, 378
Gelles, R. J. 317–9
Genta, M. L. 313
Gerard, H. B. 168–9, 171–2, 198, 271
Gergen, K. J. 14–5, 53, 80, 354–5, 376
Gergen, M. M. 354–5, 376
Gersick, C. J. 201
Gianetto, R. M. 394
Gibbons, P. 393, 405
Gifford, R. K. 44
Gigone, D. 227
Gilbert, D. T. 22, 24, 50, 54, 59–60, 95, 128, 158, 179, 208, 231, 259, 292, 324, 356, 359, 383, 409, 429
Giles H. 3, 242, 244, 286, 384–94, 406, 409, 422
Giles-Sims, J. 304
Gill, R. 406
Gilovich, T. 60, 79, 185
Ginsburg, B. 361
Girgus, J. S. 57
Gladue, B. 305–6
Glaser, J. 101, 302
Glass, C. 87
Glass, D. C. 245, 305, 375
Glenn, E. S. 424
Glick, P. 122, 237, 239–40, 324
Gliner, M. D. 227
Glunt, E. K. 243
Godfrey, S. S. 78
Godin, G. 107
Goethals, G. R. 24, 28, 133, 148, 191, 228, 231
Goffman, E. 90, 245–6, 406
Goldberg, L. R. 33, 60
Goldberg, M. E. 114
Goldberg, P. A. 239
Goldman, M. 143
Goldstein, A. P. 300, 324
Goldstein, J. H. 300
Gollwitzer, P. M. 26–7, 85
Gonzales, M. H. 7, 24
Goodenough, D. R. 309
Goodman, C. C. 34
Goodman, I. 362
Goodman, M. E. 87, 251
Goodwin, R. 339, 356
Goodwin, S. A. 162, 216
Goore, N. 185
Gooren, L. J. G. 306
Gorassini, D. R. 144
Gordon, R. A. 91
Gordon, S. E. 33, 40
Gorer, G. 312
Gorlow, L. 170
Gorn, G. J. 114, 141
Gorsuch, R. L. 107
Gosselin, C. 243
Gottlieb, J. 370
Gouldner, A. W. 364
Govender, R. 108

Graen, G. 217
Graham, S. 305
Grahe, J. E. 206
Grams, R. 239
Granberg, D. 61
Granneman, B. D. 88
Grant, G. 87
Graumann, C. F. 67, 279
Graves, J. 189–90
Graziano, W. 335
Green, D. P. 302
Green, J. 60
Green, S. K. 379
Greenberg, J. 45, 65, 89, 156, 206, 245–6
Greene, D. 61, 78
Greenfield, P. M. 412
Greenglass, E. R. 236
Greenlinger, V. 379
Greenstein, T. N. 202–3
Greenwald, A. G. 4, 42, 74, 82, 98–100, 126, 240–1
Gregg, A. P. 75, 84, 95
Gregson, R. A. M. 101, 119
Grether, J. 377
Grieve, P. 270–1, 273
Griffin, G. W. 226
Griffit, W. B. 340
Griffiths, M. 314
Griffitt, W. 372
Grise, M.-L. 222
Groff, B. D. 187
Groom, R. W. 310–1
Grosky, J. 379
Gross, A. E. 11, 38, 142, 372
Gruber-Baldini, A. L. 337
Gruder, C. L. 370
Gruenfeld, D. H. 26, 48, 162
Grune, W. E. 29
Grünert, M. 271
Grusec, J. E. 361–3
Guay, P. 340
Gubar, S. 317
Gubin, A. 162, 216
Gudykunst, W. B. 339, 392, 423
Guerin, B. 17, 184–6, 208, 412–3
Guerra, N. G. 305
Guimond, S. 248, 263
Gump, B. B. 332
Gupta, U. 351
Gurr, T. R. 262
Gustafson, R. 308
Gutek, B. A. 238
Guttman, L. A. 117, 120–1, 126–7, 434, 439
Guzzo, R. A. 192, 200

Haas, A. 393
Haas, R. G. 115
Haberkorn, G. 175
Hackman, J. R. 201
Haddock, G. 109
Haeger, G. 271

Rabbie, J. M. 220, 269, 271
Rachal, K. C. 344
Radke-Yarrow, M. 318, 362
Raiffa, H. 267
Ramirez, J. 316
Rankin, R. E. 123
Ransberger, V. M. 261
Raphael, B. 355
Rapley, M. 406
Rapoport, A. 265
Rasinski, K. A. 124
Raven, B. H. 161–2, 169
Ray, M. L. 135
Raymond, P. 223–4
Reber, R. 109
Redler, E. 363
Reeder, G. D. 37–8, 57
Regan, D. T. 110, 375
Regan, J. 142
Regan, P. C. 345
Reicher, S. D. 19, 35, 65, 68, 80, 82, 91,
    172, 194, 198, 205, 219–20, 228, 264,
    271– 2, 274, 276, 279, 282, 284, 406–7
Reid, A. 182
Reid, S. A. 162, 217, 393, 405
Reik, T. 349
Reis, H. T. 194, 341, 352, 354, 356
Reisenzein, R. 56
Reitman, J. S. 37
Rempel, J. K. 98, 339
Resnick, L. B. 48, 50
Reynolds, K. J. 81, 254, 259
Reynolds, M. A. 404
Rhoades, J. A. 407
Rhodes, G. 333
Rhodes, N. 137, 345
Rhodewalt, F. 88, 155
Rholes, W. S. 59, 329
Riccibitti, P. E. 398
Rice, M. E. 362
Rice, R. W. 215, 236
Rich, A. 362
Richards, M. J. 46
Richman, S. A. 141
Ridgeway, C. L. 202, 229
Riess, M. 62, 151
Rigoli, N. 389
Rimé, B. 394
Ringelmann, M. 189, 208, 437
Riopelle, A. J. 298
Riordan, C. A. 63
Rittle, R. H. 184
Rizzo, N. 240
Robinson, J. P. 128
Robinson, R. J. 35
Robinson, W. P. 293, 409
Roccas, S. 289
Rodgers, R. 354
Rodin, J. 66, 86, 365, 368, 370, 373
Roethlisberger, F. 17
Rogel, M. 379
Rogers, L. 338

Rogers, P. L. 395
Rogers, R. W. 107–8, 240–1, 282
Roggman, L. A. 333
Rohner, R. P. 312
Rokeach, M. 9, 115, 255–6, 417
Romeo, Y. 345
Romer, D. 370
Romero, A. A. 225
Rommetveit, R. 386
Roney, C. J. R. 37
Room, R. 112
Roper Report 296, 311
Roper, G. 228
Ropp, S. A. 287
Rosch, E. 32, 35
Rose, H. 324, 357, 361, 383
Rose, S. 324, 357, 361, 383
Rosenbaum, A. 318
Rosenbaum, D. P. 378
Rosenberg, M. 246
Rosenberg, M. J. 7, 13, 27, 98
Rosenberg, S. 27, 29
Rosenberg, S. W. 65
Rosenblatt, A. 89
Rosenblood, L. 326
Rosencrantz, P. S. 236, 244
Rosenfeld, H. M. 402
Rosenfield, D. 62, 65, 245, 254
Rosenfield, R. 62
Rosenhan, D. L. 37, 374
Rosenkoetter, L. I. 363
Rosenkrantz, P. S. 235
Rosenthal, D. 389, 425
Rosenthal, D. M. 319
Rosenthal, R. 24, 249, 254, 395, 404
Roskos-Ewoldsen, D. R. 108
Rosnow, R. L. 14, 24, 67, 165
Ross, D. 298, 303
Ross, D. F. 306
Ross, E. A. 16
Ross, L. 20, 27, 35, 37, 39, 43, 54–5,
    59–61, 69, 111, 201, 219, 289, 305
Ross, M. 52, 62, 110, 339
Ross, S. A. 298, 303
Rosselli, F. 235, 339, 394
Rosser, B. R. S. 46
Rothbart, M. 38, 276–7, 287
Rothblum, E. D. 327
Rotheram, M. J. 425
Rothgerber, H. 192
Rothman, A. J. 66, 86, 109, 137
Rothschild, G. 171
Rotter, J. B. 57, 379
Rotton, J. 310–1
Rowatt, W. C. 333
Rowley, C. D. 312
Ruback, R. B. 310
Rubenstein, A. J. 332
Rubin, A. M. 114, 249
Rubin, D. B. 309
Rubin, J. 290, 400
Rubin, M. 273

Rubin, Z. 345
Ruckmick, C. A. 17
Ruderman, A. J. 35, 277
Rudman, L. A. 237, 241
Rudolph, U. 52, 126
Rueter, H. H. 37
Ruggiero, K. M. 240
Rumelhart, D. E. 31
Runciman, W. G. 263–4, 311
Rusbult, C. E. 341, 344, 349, 352
Rushton, J. P. 359, 362–3
Russell, C. 348
Russell, D. 57
Russell, J. A. 398–9, 409
Rust, M. 288
Rutkowski, G. K. 370
Rutte, C. G. 269
Rutter, D. R. 224
Ruzzene, M. 58
Ryan, E. B. 242, 394
Ryan, M. J. 372
Ryan, M. K. 254
Ryan, R. M. 78
Ryan, T. 300
Ryen, A. H. 269, 288
Rytting, M. 401

Sabini, J. 309
Sachdev, I. 270, 389, 393
Sagarin, B. J. 365
Sagi, A. 365
Saint-Blancat, C. 389, 392
Sakhel, K. 407
Saks, M. J. 143, 229
Salas, E. 211, 221
Salovey, P. 33, 66, 86, 137, 276
Salvarani, G. 365
Salvi, D. 125, 242, 404
Sampson, E. E. 14
Samuels, C. 333
San Antonio, P. M. 392
Sanbonmatsu, D. M. 109, 125
Sanders, G. S. 61, 186, 227
Sanford, R. M. 19, 73, 253, 322
Sani, F. 205
Sanitoso, R. 85, 107
Sargant, W. 112
Saroja, K. 351
Sato, K. 268
Sattler, D. N. 269
Saucier, G. 115
Saxe, L. 125, 240
Scarr, H. A. 280
Schachter, S. 19, 52, 55, 67, 193, 205–6,
    330–4, 348, 355, 371, 437
Schadron, G. 33, 35, 45, 278
Schaefer, E. C. 337
Schaefer, R. E. 271
Schaet, D. E. 253
Schäferhoff, S. 271
Schaie, K. W. 337
Schank, R. C. 32